Lecture Notes in Computer Science 11722

More information about this series at http://www.springer.com/series/7409

Maren Scheffel · Julien Broisin ·
Viktoria Pammer-Schindler ·
Andri Ioannou · Jan Schneider (Eds.)

Transforming Learning with Meaningful Technologies

14th European Conference on Technology Enhanced Learning, EC-TEL 2019 Delft, The Netherlands, September 16–19, 2019 Proceedings

Springer

Editors
Maren Scheffel
Open University Netherlands
Heerlen, The Netherlands

Julien Broisin
Paul Sabatier University
Toulouse, France

Viktoria Pammer-Schindler
Know-Center GmbH
Graz, Austria

Andri Ioannou
Cyprus University of Technology
Limassol, Cyprus

Jan Schneider
DIPF
Frankfurt/Main, Germany

ISSN 0302-9743 ISSN 1611-3349 (electronic)
Lecture Notes in Computer Science
ISBN 978-3-030-29735-0 ISBN 978-3-030-29736-7 (eBook)
https://doi.org/10.1007/978-3-030-29736-7

LNCS Sublibrary: SL3 – Information Systems and Applications, incl. Internet/Web, and HCI

This Springer imprint is published by the registered company Springer Nature Switzerland AG
The registered company address is: Gewerbestrasse 11, 6330 Cham, Switzerland

Preface

Welcome to the proceedings of the 14th European Conference on Technology Enhanced Learning (EC-TEL), one of the flagship events of the European Association of Technology Enhanced Learning (EATEL). This year, the conference took place in Delft, the Netherlands, during September 16–19, 2019, and was hosted by the Leiden-Delft-Erasmus Centre for Education and Learning at Delft University of Technology. In addition, this year's EC-TEL was held in conjunction with the 18th World Conference on Mobile and Contextual Learning (mLearn), organized by the International Association for Mobile Learning (IAmLearn). Bringing together the two conferences, and the work of EATEL and IAmLearn, in Delft provided a unique platform for the two communities to get together and exchange ideas, and thus marked a new milestone in digital education and learning.

We currently live in a world where the use of data and technology has, for many of us, become part of our everyday life. The amount of data being produced by digital devices increases exponentially every year and it is expected that by the year 2020 there will be three times as many digital devices as there are people on earth. The United Nations have called for actions by mobilizing the data revolution for sustainable development. The buzzword of the data revolution is insight'. Once people have insight into their behavior, they can work more efficiently and more effectively. Using technology and analyzing data to detect patterns and improve processes has been a staple in business and commerce for decades and has over time also become increasingly common in the educational domain.

In an era of increased machine learning and artificial intelligence, there is a need for a shift from data-driven approaches where large amounts of data are first collected and then analyzed, to more education-oriented approaches driven by clear objectives intended to enhance the users' learning experiences, and to help in the design and implementation of technologies required to achieve these educational goals. This transformation plays a key role in the wide acceptability and adoption of future and innovative TEL solutions by the learning community. Users need more transparent and meaningful technology to understand the rationale behind it and to be convinced of its benefits for enhanced education. Thus, it is extremely important to pay attention as to why we use technology and collect data, i.e. the reason and value behind enhancing learning with technology and collecting education data needs to be clear.

EATEL and EC-TEL form a European community of researchers, practitioners, educational developers, and policy makers who discuss precisely these issues. This has also been reflected in 2019's conference theme of "Transforming Learning with Meaningful Technologies", addressing how emerging and future learning technologies can be used in a meaningful way to enhance human-machine interrelationships and to contribute to efficient and effective education. The conference called for papers, posters, demonstrations, workshops, and doctoral thesis outlines that focus on bringing research and practice in the field forward. Participants were especially encouraged to extend the debate around the role of and challenges for cutting-edge 21st century meaningful technologies and advances, such as artificial intelligence and robots, augmented reality, and ubiquitous computing technologies, while at the same time connecting them to different pedagogical approaches, types of learning settings, and application domains that can benefit from such technologies.

Of the 149 research papers submitted to EC-TEL this year, 41 were accepted (27.52% acceptance rate). In addition, 34 poster and 16 demo papers were accepted. These are published within the present proceedings. We have also accepted 6 practitioner papers, which are published in Companion Proceedings via CEUR, and 12 workshops. This year, EC-TEL for the first time did not distinguish between long and short papers but instead included only one category of high-quality research papers regardless of their length where all submissions were expected to be mature research contributions to the field of technology enhanced learning. We have further continued the format of practitioner papers to foster the dialogue between research and practice. We believe this to be vital to disseminate research results into practice and in turn inform research with experiences and results from practical problems and solutions. This year, we introduced two different tracks for EC-TEL's well-established Doctoral Consortium: an early-stage track where PhD candidates received guidance about their project and an advanced track where PhD students further along in their trajectory received in-depth feedback from senior researchers during the conference. Thereby, EATEL and EC-TEL as community and conference aim to strengthen doctoral education and the level of future researchers in the field.

Lessons learned from the past and directions for the future in technology-enhanced learning have also been discussed by EC-TEL 2019's keynoters. These were, in alphabetical order: Rose Luckin, Professor of Learner Centred Design at University College London, UK; Danielle McNamara, Professor of Psychology at Arizona State University, USA; and Geoff Stead, Chief Product Officer (CPO) at Babbel, a successful commercial e-learning system for language learning.

We wish to highlight that a community and a conference such as EATEL and EC-TEL respectively live via the contributions of many people: first, of course, via the contributions from the authors, and second and equally important, via the contributions from all Programme Committee members who sincerely and with all their expertise at hand gave feedback to authors and supported decision making on paper acceptance, thereby creating part of the scientific discourse within a community. Finally, deep thanks go to Sylvia Walsarie Wolff and Marcus Specht for hosting this year's conference and for heading the local organization team to perfection.

July 2019

Viktoria Pammer-Schindler
Maren Scheffel
Julien Broisin
Andri Ioannou
Jan Schneider

Organization

Program Committee

Marie-Helene Abel	Université de Technologie de Compiègne, HEUDIASYC, France
Andrea Adamoli	Università della Svizzera italiana, Switzerland
Carlos Alario-Hoyos	Universidad Carlos III de Madrid, Spain
Patricia Albacete	University of Pittsburgh, USA
Laia Albó	Universitat Pompeu Fabra, Spain
Vincent Aleven	Carnegie Mellon University, USA
Liaqat Ali	Simon Fraser University, Canada
Luis Anido Rifon	Universidade de Vigo, Spain
Alessandra Antonaci	Open Universiteit, The Netherlands
Inmaculada Arnedillo-Sánchez	Trinity College Dublin, Ireland
Juan I. Asensio-Pérez	Universidad de Valladolid, Spain
Mohammed Bahja	University of Birmingham, UK
Antonio Balderas	University of Cádiz, Spain
Anthony Basiel	University of London, UK
Merja Bauters	University of Helsinki, Finland and AALTO University, Finland
Jason Bernard	University of Saskatchewan, Canada
Anis Bey	University of Paul Sabatier, IRIT, France
Miguel L. Bote-Lorenzo	Universidad de Valladolid, Spain
François Bouchet	Sorbonne Université, LIP6, France
Yolaine Bourda	LRI, CentraleSupélec, France
Bert Bredeweg	University of Amsterdam, The Netherlands
Andreas Breiter	Universität Bremen, Germany
Gert Breitfuss	evolaris next level GmbH, Germany
Julien Broisin	Université Toulouse 3 Paul Sabatier, IRIT, France
Ilona Buchem	Beuth University, Germany
Daniela Caballero	Universidad de Chile, Chile
Manuel Caeiro Rodríguez	Universidade de Vigo, Spain
Manuel Castro	UNED, Spain
Teresa Cerratto-Pargman	Stockholm University, Sweden
Sven Charleer	Katholieke Universiteit Leuven, Belgium
Irene-Angelica Chounta	University of Tartu, Estonia
Miguel Ángel Conde	University of León, Spain
John Cook	University of West of England, UK
Audrey Cooke	Curtin University, Australia
Raquel M. Crespo García	Universidad Carlos III de Madrid, Spain

Mutlu Cukurova	University College London, UK
Mathieu D'Aquin	National University of Ireland Galway, Ireland
Mihai Dascalu	University Politehnica of Bucharest, Romania
Peter de Lange	RWTH Aachen University, Germany
Maria De Marsico	Sapienza University of Rome, Italy
Carlos Delgado Kloos	Universidad Carlos III de Madrid, Spain
Stavros Demetriadis	Aristotle University of Thessaloniki, Greece
Sebastian Dennerlein	Graz University of Technology, Austria
Michael Derntl	University of Tübingen, Germany
Philippe Dessus	Université Grenoble Alpes, LaRAC, France
Daniele Di Mitri	Open Universiteit, The Netherlands
Stefan Dietze	GESIS, Leibniz Institute for the Social Sciences, Germany
Yannis Dimitriadis	University of Valladolid, Spain
Vania Dimitrova	University of Leeds, UK
Monica Divitini	Norwegian University of Science and Technology, Norway
Juan Manuel Dodero	Universidad de Cádiz, Spain
Hendrik Drachsler	Open Universiteit, The Netherlands and Leibniz Institute for Research and Information in Education, DIPF, Germany
Benedict du Boulay	University of Sussex, UK
Erkan Er	GSIC-EMIC, Universidad de Valladolid, Spain
Maka Eradze	Tallinn University, Estonia
Iria Estévez-Ayres	Universidad Carlos III de Madrid, Spain
Baltasar Fernandez-Manjon	Universidad Complutense de Madrid, Spain
Alejandro Fernández	Universidad Nacional de La Plata, Argentina
Carmen Fernández-Panadero	Universidad Carlos III de Madrid, Spain
Rafael Ferreira	Federal Rural University of Pernambuco, Brazil
Angela Fessl	Know-Center GmbH, Austria
Olga Firssova	Open Universiteit, The Netherlands
Mikhail Fominykh	Norwegian University of Science and Technology, Norway
Rolf Fricke	Condat AG, Germany
Fernando Gamboa Rodríguez	CCADET, UNAM, México
Jesús Miguel García-Gorrostieta	INAOE, México
Serge Garlatti	IMT Atlantique, France
Dragan Gašević	Monash University, Australia
Sébastien George	LIUM, Le Mans Université, France
Michail Giannakos	Norwegian University of Science and Technology, Norway
Denis Gillet	Ecole Polytechnique Fédérale de Lausanne, Switzerland

Carlo Giovannella	University of Tor Vergata, Italy
Christian Glahn	Leiden-Delft-Erasmus Centre for Education and Learning, The Netherlands
Samuel González-López	Technological University of Nogales, México
Sabine Graf	Athabasca University, Canada
Monique Grandbastien	LORIA, Université de Lorraine, France
Andrina Granić	University of Split, Croatia
Wolfgang Greller	Vienna University of Education, Austria
David Griffiths	University of Bolton, UK
Nathalie Guin	Université de Lyon, LIRIS, France
Gabriel Gutu-Robu	University Politehnica of Bucharest, Romania
Franziska Günther	TU Dresden, Germany
Christian Gütl	Graz University of Technology, Austria
Thanasis Hadzilacos	Open University of Cyprus and The Cyprus Institute, Cyprus
Carolin Hahnel	Leibniz Institute for Research and Information in Education, DIPF, Germany
Rawad Hammad	King's College London, UK
Cecilie Johanne Hansen	uniRes, Norway
Mohammed Hassouna	Greenwich University, UK
Matthias Hauswirth	University of Lugano, Switzerland
Eelco Herder	Radboud University, The Netherlands
Josefina Hernandez	Pontificia Universidad Católica de Chile, Chile
Davinia Hernandez-Leo	Universitat Pompeu Fabra, Spain
Ángel Hernández-García	Universidad Politécnica de Madrid, Spain
Tore Hoel	Høgskolen i Oslo og Akershus, Norway
Adrian Holzer	University of Neuchâtel, Switzerland
Ulrich Hoppe	University Duisburg-Essen, Germany
Tasos Hovardas	University of Cyprus, Cyprus
Sharon Hsiao	Arizona State University, USA
Petri Ihantola	University of Helsinki, Finland
Andri Ioannou	Cyprus University of Technology, Cyprus
Seiji Isotani	University of São Paulo, Brazil
Patrick Jermann	Ecole Polytechnique Fédérale de Lausanne, Switzerland
Ioana Jivet	Open Universiteit, The Netherlands
Srecko Joksimovic	University of South Australia, Australia
Ken Kahn	University of Oxford, UK
Marco Kalz	Heidelberg University of Education, Germany
Anastasios Karakostas	Aristotle University of Thessaloniki, Greece
Julia Kasch	Open Universiteit, The Netherlands
Michael Kickmeier-Rust	Graz University of Technology, Austria
Andrea Kienle	University of Applied Sciences Dortmund, Germany
Ralf Klamma	RWTH Aachen University, Germany

Styliani Kleanthous	Open University of Cyprus and Research Centre on Interactive Media, Smart Systems and Emerging Technologies, Cyprus
Roland Klemke	Open Universiteit, The Netherlands
Tomaž Klobučar	Jozef Stefan Institute, Slovenia
Carolien Knoop-Van Campen	Radboud University, The Netherlands
Ola Knutsson	Stockholm University, Sweden
Thomas Koehler	TU Dresden, Germany
Simone Kopeinik	TUGraz, Austria
Panagiotis Kosmas	Cyprus University of Technology, Cyprus
Vitomir Kovanovic	The University of South Australia, Australia
Milos Kravcik	DFKI GmbH, Germany
Birgit Krogstie	Norwegian University of Science and Technology, Norway
Michael Kvas	bit schulungscenter GmbH, Austria
Mart Laanpere	Tallinn University, Estonia
Elise Lavoué	Université Jean Moulin Lyon 3, LIRIS, France
Effie Lai-Chong Law	University of Leicester, UK
Marie Lefevre	Université Lyon 1, LIRIS, France
Dominique Lenne	Heudiasyc, Université de Technologie de Compiègne, France
Marina Lepp	University of Tartu, Estonia
Leo Leppänen	University of Helsinki, Finland
Elisabeth Lex	Graz University of Technology, Austria
Tobias Ley	Tallinn University, Estonia
Paul Libbrecht	German Institute for International Educational Research, DIPF, Germany
Andreas Lingnau	Ruhr West University of Applied Science, Germany
Martin Llamas-Nistal	University of Vigo, Spain
Christoph Lofi	Delft University of Technology, The Netherlands
Aurelio Lopez-Lopez	INAOE, México
Domitile Lourdeaux	CNRS, France
Ulrike Lucke	University of Potsdam, Germany
Vanda Luengo	Sorbonne Université, LIP6, France
Piret Luik	University of Tartu, Estonia
Kathryn MacCallum	Eastern Institute of Technology, New Zealand
Katherine Maillet	Institut Mines-Télécom, Télécom Ecole de Management, France
Jorge Maldonado-Mahauad	Universidad de Cuenca, Spain and Pontificia Universidad Católica de Chile, Chile
Nils Malzahn	Rhine-Ruhr Institute for Applied System Innovation e.V., Germany
Katerina Mangaroska	Norwegian University of Science and Technology, Norway
Estefania Martin	Universidad Rey Juan Carlos, Spain

Roberto Martinez-Maldonado	University of Technology Sydney, Australia
Jean-Charles Marty	LIRIS, equipe SICAL, France
Carlos Martínez Gaitero	Escola Universitària d'Infermeria Gimbernat, Spain
M. Antonia Martínez-Carreras	University of Murcia, Spain
Alejandra Martínez-Monés	Universidad de Valladolid, Spain
Agathe Merceron	Beuth University of Applied Sciences Berlin, Germany
Vasileios Mezaris	Information Technologies Institute, Centre for Research and Technology Hellas, Greece
Christine Michel	Université de Lyon, LIRIS, France
Konstantinos Michos	Universtitat Pompeu Fabra, Spain
Alexander Mikroyannidis	The Open University, UK
Riichiro Mizoguchi	Japan Advanced Institute of Science and Technology, Japan
Inge Molenaar	Radboud University, The Netherlands
Yishay Mor	Levinsky College of Education, Israel
Kamran Munir	UWE, UK
Mathieu Muratet	LIP6, France
Pedro J. Muñoz-Merino	Universidad Carlos III de Madrid, Spain
Rob Nadolski	Open Universiteit, The Netherlands
Petru Nicolaescu	RWTH Aachen University, Germany
Lyndon Nixon	MODUL Technology GmbH, Austria
Jalal Nouri	Stockholm University, Sweden
Alexander Nussbaumer	Graz University of Technology, Austria
Xavier Ochoa	NYU, USA
Jennifer Olsen	Ecole Polytechnique Fédérale de Lausanne, Switzerland
Alejandro Ortega-Arranz	Universidad de Valladolid, Spain
Viktoria Pammer-Schindler	Know-Center GmbH and Graz University of Technology, Austria
Abelardo Pardo	University of South Australia, Australia
Cesare Pautasso	University of Lugano, Switzerland
Mar Perez-Sanagustin	Pontificia Universidad Católica de Chile, Chile
Donatella Persico	ITD-CNR, Italy
Niels Pinkwart	Humboldt-Universität zu Berlin, Germany
Gerti Pishtari	Tallinn University, Estonia
Elvira Popescu	University of Craiova, Romania
Francesca Pozzi	Istituto Tecnologie Didattiche, CNR, Italy
Luis P. Prieto	Tallinn University, Estonia
Michael Prilla	TU Clausthal, Germany
Ronald Pérez Álvarez	Pontificia Universidad Católica de Chile, Chile
Hans Põldoja	Tallinn University, Estonia
Juliana Elisa Raffaghelli	University of Florence, Italy
Christoph Rensing	TU Darmstadt, Germany

Marc Rittberger	Leibniz Institute for Research and Information in Education, DIPF, Germany
Maria Jesus Rodriguez Triana	Tallinn University, Estonia
Elisabeth Rolf	Stockholm University, Sweden
Adolfo Ruiz Calleja	Universidad de Valladolid, Spain
Demetrios Sampson	Curtin University, Australia
Eric Sanchez	Université Fribourg, Switzerland
Olga C. Santos	aDeNu Research Group (UNED), Spain
Patricia Santos	UPF-GTI, Spain
Maren Scheffel	Open Universiteit, The Netherlands
Daniel Schiffner	Leibniz Institute for Research and Information in Education, DIPF, Germany
Andreas Schmidt	Karlsruhe University of Applied Sciences, Germany
Marcel Schmitz	Zuyd Hogeschool, The Netherlands
Jan Schneider	Leibniz Institute for Research and Information in Education, DIPF, Germany
Ulrik Schroeder	RWTH Aachen University, Germany
Karim Sehaba	Université Lumière Lyon 2, LIRIS, France
Paul Seitlinger	Tallinn University, Estonia
Stylianos Sergis	University of Piraeus, Greece
Kshitij Sharma	Norwegian University of Science and Technology, Norway
Puneet Sharma	University of Tromsø, Norway
Mike Sharples	The Open University, UK
Leo A. Siiman	University of Tartu, Estonia
Bernd Simon	Knowledge Markets Consulting, Austria
Tanmay Sinha	ETH Zurich, Switzerland
Andrzej M. J. Skulimowski	AGH University of Science and Technology, Poland
Alan Smeaton	Dublin City University, Ireland
Sergey Sosnovsky	Utrecht University, The Netherlands
Daniel Spikol	Malmö University, Sweden
Slavi Stoyanov	Open Universiteit, The Netherlands
Alexander Streicher	Fraunhofer IOSB, Germany
Bernardo Tabuenca	Universidad Politécnica de Madrid, Spain
Kairit Tammets	Tallinna Ülikool, Estonia
Esther Tan	Delft University of Technology, The Netherlands
Stefano Tardini	USI Università della Svizzera italiana, Switzerland
Ali Tarhini	Sultan Qaboos University, Oman
Deborah Tatar	Virginia Tech, USA
Stefaan Ternier	Open Universiteit, The Netherlands
Stefan Thalmann	University of Graz, Austria
Vladimir Tomberg	Tallinn University, Estonia
Tamsin Treasure-Jones	University of Leeds, UK
Yi-Shan Tsai	The University of Edinburgh, UK
Chrysanthi Tseloudi	University of Bristol, UK

Katrien Verbert	Katholieke Universiteit Leuven, Belgium
Markel Vigo	The University of Manchester, UK
Massimo Vitiello	Graz University of Technology, Austria
Jo Wake	NORCE, Norway
Denise Whitelock	The Open University, UK
Fridolin Wild	Oxford Brookes University, UK
Jane Yin-Kim Yau	University of Mannheim, Germany
Amel Yessad	Sorbonne Université, LIP6, France
Tanja Zdolsek	Jožef Stefan Institute, Slovenia
Yue Zhao	Delft University of Technology, The Netherlands
Olga Zlatkin-Troitschanskaia	University of Mainz, Germany

Additional Reviewers

Ahmad, Atezaz
Belghis-Zadeh, Mohammad
Bernard, Jason
Biedermann, Daniel
Broos, Tom
Chaabi, Hasnâa
Chen, Guanliang
Ciordas-Hertel, George-Petru
El Emrani, Soumaya
Gómez-Sánchez, Eduardo
Htun, Nyi Nyi
Krieter, Philipp
Liaqat, Salaar
López Valencia, Gabriel
Maitz, Katharina
Michos, Kostas
Millecamp, Martijn
Moreno-Marcos, Pedro Manuel
Orlic, Davor
Praharaj, Sambit
Rodriguez Espinoza, Indelfonso
Schneider, Oliver
Schophuizen, Martine
Schulz, Sandra
Venant, Rémi
Wollny, Sebastian

Contents

Research Papers

Research Papers

Facilitating Students' Digital Competence: Did They Do It?

Margarida Lucas([✉])

CIDTFF, University of Aveiro, 3810-193 Aveiro, Portugal
mlucas@ua.pt

Abstract. The ability to facilitate the development of students' digital competence has become an integral part of teachers' professional demands. The focus on this area is relatively recent and therefore research available is limited. This paper aims at presenting students' perceptions regarding teachers' use of tablets to facilitate the development of their digital competence, when performing information and communication related tasks. Data were collected using a questionnaire and four focus groups. Findings suggest the lack of didactical and pedagogical elements in guidelines provided to perform such tasks and a poor mediation role played in facilitating students' digital competence.

Keywords: DigComp · DigCompEdu · Digital competence · Teaching practices · Communication · Collaboration · Information literacy

1 Introduction

Digital competence is a priority in the agendas of different international organizations, who understand it as essential for social inclusion, for active and conscious civic participation in society, and for competitive, intelligent and sustainable growth of today's society [1, 2]. It can be broadly defined as the set of skills, knowledge and attitudes that make citizens able to use digital technologies in a creative, critical, meaningful and responsible manner for work, leisure, participation, learning and socializing, independently and with others [3, 4]. As citizens, teachers need to be equipped with this competence to participate in different spheres of society; as professionals dedicated to teaching they need to be able to use digital technologies to enhance students' learning experiences and facilitate the development of their digital competence [5, 6]. Nevertheless, the rapid digitization of education over the past years has brought different challenges to teachers attempting to integrate technology in the classroom. Apart from the technical aspects related to the management of different hardware and software, teachers must make decisions about how they should be pedagogically used, why and what for.

Digitizing education often takes place in the form of mobile technology-driven projects implemented in schools. Tablet devices have attracted the interests of policy-makers and school leaders, who understand them as drivers of innovation and modernization [7]. They have also attracted the interest of researchers who wish to examine different aspects stemming from their use in educational settings [8]. Recent research

M. Scheffel et al. (Eds.): EC-TEL 2019, LNCS 11722, pp. 3–14, 2019.
https://doi.org/10.1007/978-3-030-29736-7_1

focus on positive outcomes, such as the use of tablets to enhance self-assessment and reflection [9]. Others report neutral ones, such as the lack of difference between students' reading performance with tablets and printed books [10], while still others report negative outcomes, such as the disadvantage of using tablets to support collaborative tasks as compared to nontechnology based ones [11]. However, little is known about tablet use to facilitate students' digital competence in classroom.

This paper puts forward students' perceptions regarding teachers' practices mediated by tablets to facilitate the development of their digital competence, specifically in the areas of Information and data literacy and Communication and collaboration [12]. The context of the study corresponds to a tablet initiative implemented in two Portuguese lower secondary schools involving 19 teachers and 80 students. The initiative was promoted by a business consortium with the support of the Portuguese government to create a technological ecosystem that could (i) challenge teachers to transform teaching practices and (ii) help students develop their digital skills. The ecosystem included (i) the distribution of tablets to teachers and students to be used at school and at home; (ii) a classroom with an interactive whiteboard and access points to the network and the school server and (iii) a storage/charging cabinet for tablets and mobile workstations. The IT companies comprising the consortium provided the equipment and the two major Portuguese educational publishers provided the digital textbooks and free access to their learning platforms. As part of the ecosystem, teachers received training covering the technological aspects of handling the tablet and the exploration of different pedagogical strategies. Typically, 15 h were assigned to technology and 50 h to pedagogy, including practical sessions in classroom with students.

The findings presented in this paper are part of a larger study, which evaluated the implementation of the tablet initiative [13] and its impact on the development of students' digital competence [14]. As digital competence is driven by several contextual factors, the study also looks into teaching practices, as narrated by students, with a view to achieve a deeper understanding of the little evidence of impact observed.

2 Background

In recent years, digital competence has become a key concept in the discussion of what individuals should be able to do and achieve when using digital technologies. It is a broad, multidimensional and complex concept that covers different areas of study [3, 15] and a dynamic one, as it tends to follow the rapid evolution of technologies and their uses in society [16]. It is also a concept with political nuances [17], since it reflects the political objectives and the expectations of future needs, driven by the economic competition of the knowledge society, in which technologies are seen as a solution and an opportunity [1, 2].

Different studies focus on students' digital competence. Some suggest students develop it spontaneously, by simply using technology [18, 19], while others demonstrate that this is not always the case: the development of digital competence has to be closely linked with well-founded pedagogy and didactics [20, 21]. Therefore, teachers play a key role in helping students become digitally competent and take advantage of digital technologies to update knowledge and personalize lifelong learning. This, however, requires them to develop their own digital competence.

There are several frameworks aimed at teachers' digital competence [5, 22–24]. In general, they provide a set of descriptors to enable the development of concrete instruments for self-reflection and evaluation or to support the incorporation of technology into training processes. A recent one is the European Framework for the Digital Competence of Educators: DigCompEdu [5]. DigCompEdu aims to capture and describe the specifics of teachers' digital competence by proposing 22 elementary competences organized in 6 areas: Professional engagement, Digital resources, Teaching and Learning, Assessment, Empowering learners and Facilitating learners' digital competence.

The last area – Facilitating learners' digital competence and the focus of our study – is captured by the European Digital Competence Framework for Citizens (DigComp) [12], which describes the competences needed to creatively and responsibly use digital technologies for Information, Communication, Content creation, Safety and Problem-solving. With regards to Information and Communication related areas, DigComp specifies nine competences, detailed in Table 1 and corresponding to the ones covered by our study.

Table 1. Overview of the competences outlined for the competence areas Information and data literacy and Communication and collaboration

Competence areas	Competences
1. Information and data literacy	1.1 Browsing, searching and filtering data, information and digital content 1.2 Evaluating data, information and digital content 1.3 Storing and retrieving data, information and digital content
2. Communication and collaboration	2.1 Interacting through digital technologies 2.2 Sharing through digital technologies 2.3 Engaging in online citizenship through digital technologies 2.4 Collaborating through digital channels 2.5 Netiquette 2.6 Managing digital identity

Literature concerning the abilities of teachers to develop students' digital competence is limited. Most of the existing studies focus on teacher's pedagogical beliefs, technology integration practices or perceived usefulness [25, 26]. In a study seeking to measure Chilean teachers' ability to teach students how to solve information and communication tasks in a digital environment, results showed that very few of them mastered all the tasks and knowledge tested and that more than one-fourth of them did not master any of them at all [27]. In another study, future teachers perceived they had a low level of digital competence. They scored highest in information (search, filtering, evaluation, storage, and retrieval of information), but showed unawareness of behavioral norms in digital communication and preservation of digital identity [28].

Teachers' abilities to facilitate the development of students' digital competences may be understood through the analysis of their practices, as they convey a qualitative rather than a quantitative facet of digital technologies use [25]. How teachers implement learning activities requiring students to find information in digital environments, to organize and manage it and to critically evaluate its credibility and reliability may be indicative of their emphasis on digital competence. The same can be said for learning activities, which require students to effectively and responsibly use digital technologies for communication and collaboration. As such, the research question guiding this article is: "What are students' perceptions regarding teachers' practices to facilitate the development of their digital competence?"

3 Methodology

The study used a multiple case research design involving two lower secondary schools in central Portugal, more specifically, four classes (two per school). Data were collected from students who completed their second year of participation in the tablet initiative through an online questionnaire filled in by students during class hours. All students, 80 students (35 boys and 45 girls, M_{age} = 14.19; SD_{age} = 0.82) answered the questionnaire. The perceptions of their digital competence development, regarding Information and data literacy and Communication and collaboration were measured using 14 statements (Table 2), inspired by DigComp, against which students had to position themselves using a five-point Likert scale (Totally agree - Totally disagree). It being a five-point ordinal scale allows us to assume statistical continuity and therefore use measures of central tendency. As such, the scores between points 1 and 2 were grouped in the "Totally disagree" band, the scores between points 2 and 2.9 in the "Disagree" band, the scores between 3.1 and 4 in the "Agree" band and the scores between 4 and 5 in the "Totally agree" band. The midpoint (3) was removed from the analysis of the classification bands.

The quantitative measure was complemented by four focus groups (one per class) involving a total of 26 students (11 boys and 15 girls, M_{age} = 13.89; SD_{age} = 0.81). In this particular case, adopting a qualitative approach allowed us to capture students' experiences and thoughts about a specific phenomenon, to a greater extent than mere quantitative research approaches [29], namely their perceptions regarding teachers' practices regarding the use of the tablet to facilitate the development of their digital competence.

The interview protocol was also inspired by DigComp and included two questions, one focusing on the competence areas Information and data literacy and the other on Communication and collaboration (Table 3). For every focus group, a semi-structured interview of approximately 60 min was conducted. All focus group interviews were videotaped and transcribed. Content analysis was used to analyze the transcripts of the interviews. The data were coded according to categories and subcategories identified in Table 3. Partial data were coded independently and later compared. An agreement of $\kappa = 0.81$ was achieved and the remaining data were analyzed and triangulated across in order to increase credibility. Each student received a code (S1 - S26) that is used in Table 4 to identify their individual voices. Although the focus group interview did not include questions directly related to competences 2.5 "Netiquette" and 2.6 "Managing digital identity" (Table 1) examples of these competences emerged due to the semi-structured nature of the focus groups. The same did not occur for competence 2.3 "Engaging in citizenship through digital technologies" (Table 1), which is therefore left out of the findings section.

Table 2. Statements presented to students, prompted by the initial statement 'After participating in the tablet initiative, I started to …'

Label	Statements	Ca[a]
A	Filter information more carefully	Information and data literacy
B	Search for information more effectively	
C	Evaluate the credibility and reliability of websites better	
D	Select information more critically	
E	Be more organized in storing and managing the information that interests me	
F	Backup all my files using the cloud	
G	Communicate with teachers and colleagues more often	Communication and collaboration
H	Be more confident communicating online	
I	Share the assignments I do with my class	
J	Check the property right of content	
K	Better understand the potential of technologies for civic participation	
L	Work at a distance with colleagues using online collaborative tools	
M	Be more aware of netiquette rules	
N	Be more aware of the risks and benefits related to my digital identity	

[a]Ca = Competence areas

Table 3. Questions included in the focus groups and coding applied

Category	Question	Sub-categories
1. Information and data literacy	Describe the guidelines your teachers give you when they request an activity that requires you to browse and search the web for a specific topic, evaluate and organize information found	Searching
		Evaluating
		Managing
2. Communication and collaboration	Comment the following statement: We interact more with each other outside school now, because all our group assignments are done at a distance using collaborative digital tools, such as Google Docs or Slides, and shared in a common digital place"	Interacting
		Collaborating
		Sharing
	–	Netiquette
	–	Identity

4 Findings

In what the perceptions of students regarding the development of their digital competence is concerned, we decided to use graphs to present the mean scores obtained for each area of competence. The average scores obtained by the sample regarding the statements that compose the area of Information and data literacy are presented in Fig. 1.

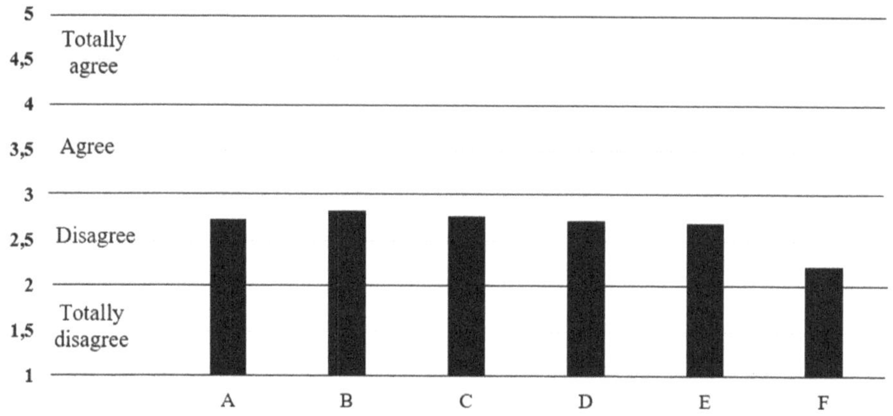

Fig. 1. Mean scores obtained by the participants regarding statements pertaining to the competence area Information and data literacy

When analyzing it, we can verify that the students' positioning regarding the statements presented fell into the "Disagree" classification band, i.e., on average, students do not agree that they have improved their digital competences after starting using the tablet within the scope of the tablet initiative. The means obtained by the sample regarding the statements that compose the area of digital competence Communication and collaboration are presented in Fig. 2.

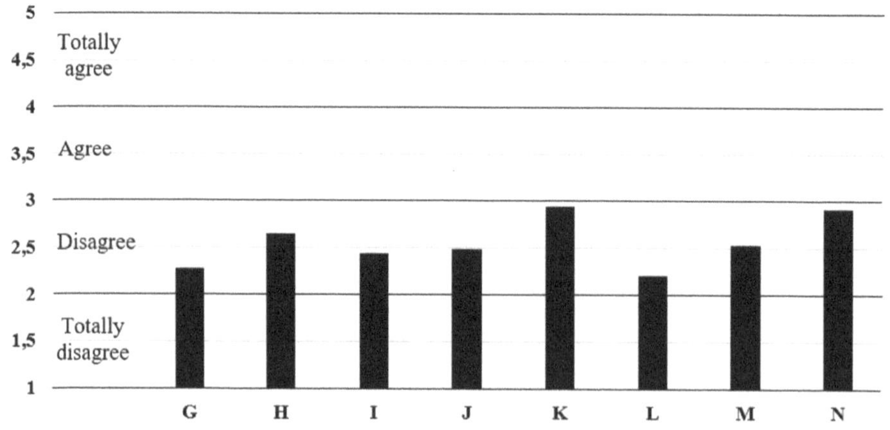

Fig. 2. Mean scores obtained by the participants regarding statements pertaining to the competence area "Communication and collaboration"

Just as for the competence area Information and data literacy, the average of answers provided by the participants also fell into the "Disagree" classification band regarding the competence area Communication and communication, i.e., on average, participants do not agree that they have developed digital competences after having participated in the initiative under study.

Given the (somehow) unexpected results reported above, we decided to look at teachers' practices, as narrated by students, with a view to find a deeper understanding of the lack of impact found. The examples below illustrate practices associated with competences from the competence areas Information and data literacy and Communication and collaboration, with the exception of the competence 2.3 Engaging in citizenship through digital technologies. They follow the categorization described in Table 3.

Table 4. Examples of students' perceptions

Sub-categories	Examples
Searching	Usually we are told to access the Internet and search for information using Google. That's it. (S3) Our English teacher gives us some websites that we can look into and we just have to select the information that is relevant for the task we are doing. (S6) I normally use keywords to refine my search, but that is something I always do and not because teachers tell me to. (S15) But learning how to search for information is something we should do in ICT. (S23)
Evaluating	To check for language issues… for instance if it is written in European or Brazilian Portuguese. (S7) We have to learn to evaluate if something is fake by ourselves. (S13) For example, in Geography, we had to write an assignment about natural disasters. I searched for information on the National Civil Protection website, because the teacher told me that the information on that website would be reliable. (S11) If I think the information suits the topic, I copy and paste it. (S14)
Managing	He (History teacher) also used Google Drive for the assignments, but other teachers didn't. They say they weren't born in the digital era and are not used to working with these tools and therefore have more difficulties. (S3) The Geography teacher created a Dropbox for the class, to share presentations. I don't use it a lot, but I know the presentations are there and I can access them. (S6) I'm actually not a big fan (of Google Drive). I'm afraid to use it. (S9) What happens (after copying and pasting) is that very often I don't know where I took the information from. (S14)

(continued)

Table 4. (*continued*)

Sub-categories	Examples
Interacting	We don't interact with teachers very often. We can email them, but there isn't much need. (S1) There was a Hangouts account for the class, but not for teachers. And we didn't use it much to talk about school things. (S3) We are constantly interacting with each other! Sometimes we talk about school… like if there is any homework or what is it we need to study. But usually is just for fun. (S18) At first we used Moodle, but not for long. The English teacher used it a lot at the beginning, but for posting assignments, not to interact. (S20)
Collaborating	I don't know what Google Docs is. But we all work at the same time. I mean… not quite at the same time. We divide the work and then someone puts all parts together and sends them to the teacher. (S2) For example, if we are not together, one does the introduction and sends it by email, then the other writes another section and sends it, and then at the end we put everything together and create a presentation. (S8) Does that [Google Docs and Slides] mean we could have stayed at home working on the same thing? (S18) I know what it (Google Docs) is, but maybe they (teachers) don't know. It doesn't surprise me. (S23)
Sharing	They said they would create a forum so that we could share ideas and questions, but that never happened. (S7) I prefer to share my documents or presentations by email. That's what we usually do. Or we simply send things on Messenger or WhatsApp. (S9) We use Padlet for some subjects… to share assignments and presentations. But it's almost like Dropbox. We don't comment assignments or make revisions. (S10)
Netiquette	They're immature. The teacher had to close the forum, because some students were writing bad words and insulting each other. (S19) X even uploaded movies for others to download. (S21)
Identity	We had some sessions on the risks of sharing our lives and identity online. And also on how to protect ourselves from some online dangers. (S5) I have multiple profiles and accounts. Whoever uses these services must be aware of the risks and can't hide. I use them to meet new people. (S25)

5 Discussion and Conclusions

Results suggest that the implementation of activities requiring students to use the tablet to search and gather information was not always accompanied by explicit guidelines provided by the teachers. Although there are examples indicating this type of approach (e.g. S6 in "Searching" or S11 in "Evaluating"), there are also examples indicating the lack of specific guidelines or structured orientation (e.g. S3 or S15 in "Searching"). Interestingly, students' opinions suggest that learning how to browse and search for information is not necessarily a transversal competence to be worked in different subjects, but a specific competence of the ICT curricular subject (e.g. S3 in "Searching"). The same may be understood regarding the critical evaluation of the credibility and reliability of the information found (e.g. S13 in "Evaluating"). These notions can be reversed by giving students the ability to discuss and learn to discern reliable and credible information or sources from unreliable and non-credible ones in the context of any subject. Students' difficulty in doing so is reported in different studies [30, 31].

Regarding the competence "Managing" and looking at the average obtained for statement F in Fig. 1 – the lowest in the set of six statements – examples provided seem to indicate that activities to organize and store information or content in a structured online environment are not generally promoted by the teachers. In fact, examples point at notions of resistance and difficulty in the use of these services by the teachers (e.g. S3) and those of fear and insecurity by the students (e.g. S9). In the case of students, it may be possible that without the example and encouragement of their teachers, they do not have a positive attitude towards exploring possible risks and limits of using online storage services and trusting they are able to deal with them.

As to a possible increase regarding online interaction among students and teachers, which was not verified, as one can see in Fig. 2, statement G, examples demonstrate that it barely exists for learning purposes. Although students recognize they interact with each other, (e.g. S3 or S18), the low level of online interaction between teacher-students and vice versa can be justified by i) the absence of need, when students and teachers meet face-to-face (e.g. S1) or (ii) the lack of activities promoted by teachers encouraging and requiring such interaction (e.g. S20). Similar reasons may justify the results found for "Sharing" (Fig. 2). Nevertheless, there is evidence of the use of digital spaces to share assignments and presentations (e.g. S10), but not as a suggestion coming from teachers (e.g. S9).

In relation to the competence area Communication and collaboration, online collaboration is the competence students feel to have developed the least (Fig. 2, statement L). Looking at Table 4, examples reveal some unfamiliarity with what collaborative tools are (e.g. S2 and S18) and what their purpose is (e.g. S2, S8 and S18). Examples also reveal that although concrete collaborative activities such as group work are implemented, strategies to develop them do not include the integration of collaborative tools or the possibility of addressing the main principles of online collaboration. This may be related with teachers' unfamiliarity with these tools and principles as well (e.g. S23).

Regarding online etiquette or "Netiquette", there seems to be some lack of knowledge of the behavioral norms of online interaction. In fact, there are examples referring the non-compliance with communication strategies to the specific audience and context (e.g. S19) and even with ethical principles in the use and publication of content (e.g. S21). In such cases, examples illustrate actions taken by one teacher to stop those behaviors (e.g. S19). To be aware of behavioral norms and knowhow while using digital technologies and interacting in digital environments is tied to the question of "Identity". How students build their online identity, the way they present themselves and behave online is an aspect that can be discussed in class, across subjects. This can contribute to the awareness of the risks and benefits related to online behavior and what it entails for individual reputation. Similar practices are put forward by studies which acknowledge students' need to adequate their online behavior with a view to protect their online identity and safety [31, 32].

While examples of practices facilitating the development of students' digital competence exist, findings suggest that overall teachers did not do it. Findings suggest a lack of both didactical and pedagogical elements in guidelines provided by teachers to perform activities related to the competence areas of Information and data literacy and Communication and collaboration areas. In general, teachers did not provide orientations for the developing of such activities nor played a mediation role in facilitating students' digital competence. One of the reasons may be related to teachers' level of digital proficiency, whose measurement was not covered by our study. Nevertheless, findings are in line with the assumption made by some authors regarding the need to address digital competence in schools in a way that digital technologies are used with a view to increase acquisition in a gradual and progressive manner [20, 21]. They may also be in line with findings from other studies, which point at teachers' low level of digital competence [27, 28]. This is an aspect to be considered in future studies.

Apart from this limitation, others can be pointed to the present study. First, the participants correspond to four classes from two schools and, therefore, results cannot be generalized. Second, results should be read and related to other findings from the larger study, including, for example, the context and strategies for the implementation of the 1:1 initiative, the school leadership, the existing support (technical and professional), the conditions and access to the equipment and technological infrastructure, the frequency of tablet use, among others [13]. Third, it reflects students' perceptions of their teachers' teaching practices, which may differ from the actual classroom practice. Four, it lacks a look at teachers' beliefs and attitudes toward technology, and tablets in particular, as well as more detailed information on the pedagogical approaches implemented.

Despite these, this paper contributes to the existing body of knowledge in several aspects, such as students' perceptions regarding teachers' ability to facilitate their digital competence, which is an under-researched topic, the discussion about the use of tablets in teaching and learning, or the opportunity to further investigate other emerging aspects that can contribute to more positive impacts.

Acknowledgement. This work was supported by the Portuguese Foundation for Science and Technology (FCT) under grant number SFRH/BPD/100367/2014 and project UID/CED/00194/2013.

References

1. European Commission: A new skills agenda for Europe - Working together to strengthen human capital, employability and competitiveness (2016)
2. OECD: Ministerial Declaration on the Digital Economy ('Cancún Declaration') (2016)
3. Ferrari, A.: Digital Competence in Practice: An Analysis of Frameworks. Publications Office of the European Union, Luxembourg (2012)
4. Hatlevik, O.E., Guðmundsdóttir, G.B., Loi, M.: Digital diversity among upper secondary students: a multilevel analysis of the relationship between cultural capital, self-efficacy, strategic use of information and digital competence. Comput. Educ. **81**, 345–353 (2015)

5. Redecker, C.: European Framework for the Digital Competence of Educators: DigCompEdu. Publications Office of the European Union, Luxembourg (2017)
6. Krumsvik, R.J.: Teacher educators' digital competence. Scand. J. Educ. Res. **1**(12), 269–280 (2012)
7. Tamim, R., Borokhovski, E., Pickup, D., Bernard, R.: Large-Scale, Government-Supported Educational Tablet Initiatives. Commonwealth of Learning, Montreal (2015)
8. Haßler, B., Major, L., Hennessy, S.: Tablet use in schools: a critical review of the evidence for learning outcomes. J. Comput. Assist. Learn. **36**(2), 139–156 (2016)
9. Tasker, T., Herrenkohl, L.: Using peer feedback to improve students' scientific inquiry. J. Sci. Teacher Educ. **27**(1), 25–39 (2016)
10. Dundar, H., Akcayir, M.: Tablet vs. paper: the effect on learners' reading performance. Int. Electron. J. Elementary Educ. **4**(3), 441–450 (2012)
11. Culén, A., Gasparini, A.: Tweens with the iPad classroom—cool but not really helpful? In: Proceedings of the International Conference on e-Learning and e-Technologies in Education (ICEEE), pp. 1–6. IEEE Press, Lodz (2012)
12. Carretero, S., Vuorikari, R., Punie, Y.: DigComp 2.1: The Digital Competence Framework for Citizens with Eight Proficiency Levels and Examples of Use. Publications Office of the European Union, Luxembourg (2017)
13. Lucas, M.: External barriers affecting the successful implementation of mobile educational interventions. Comput. Hum. Behav. (2018). https://doi.org/10.1016/j.chb.2018.05.001
14. Lucas, M., Bem-Haja, P., Moreira, A., Costa, N.: Is it all about frequency: students' digital competence and tablet use. In: Adeli, A.R.H., Reis, L.P., Constanzo, S. (eds.) Advances in Intelligent Systems and Computing, WorldCist 2019, vol. 932, pp. 234–243. Springer, Cham (2019). https://doi.org/10.1007/978-3-030-16187-3_23
15. Calvani, A., Fini, A., Ranieri, M.: Digital competence in K-12: theoretical models, assessment tools and empirical research. Anàlisi **40**, 157–171 (2010)
16. Ala-Mutka, K.: Mapping Digital Competence: Towards a Conceptual Understanding. Publications Office of the European Union, Luxembourg (2011)
17. Ilomäki, L., Paavola, S., Lakkala, M., Kantosalo, A.: Digital competence – an emergent boundary concept for policy and educational research. Educ. Inf. Technol. **21**(3), 655–679 (2016)
18. Holmström, T., Siljebo, J.: Developing digital competence or exploring teaching with digital technologies? Master Thesis (2013)
19. Escueta, M., Quan, V., Joshua, A., Oreopoulos, N.P.: Education Technology: an evidence-based review. In: NBER Working Paper Series. National Bureau of Economic Research. Working Paper 2374 (2017)
20. Sung, Y.T., Chang, K.E., Liu, T.C.: The effects of integrating mobile devices with teaching and learning on students' learning performance: a meta-analysis and research synthesis". Comput. Educ. **94**, 252–275 (2016)
21. Tamim, R., Bernard, R., Borokhovski, E., Abrami, P., Schmid, R.: What forty years of research says about the impact of technology on learning: a second-order meta-analysis and validation study. Rev. Educ. Res. **81**, 4–28 (2011)
22. Mishra, P., Koehler, M.J.: Technological pedagogical content knowledge: a framework for teacher knowledge. Teachers Coll. Rec. **108**(6), 1017–1054 (2006)
23. Almerich, G., Orellana, N., Suárez-Rodríguez, J., Díaz-García, I.: Teachers' information and communication technology competences: a structural approach. Comput. Educ. **100**, 110–125 (2016)
24. Tondeur, J., Aesaert, K., Pynoo, B., Braak, J., Fraeyman, N., Erstad, O.: ICT competencies for preservice teachers. Br. J. Educ. Technol. **48**, 462–472 (2017)

25. Tondeur, J., van Braak, J., Ertmer, P.A., Ottenbreit-Leftwich, A.: Understanding the relationship between teachers' pedagogical beliefs and technology use in education: a systematic review of qualitative evidence. Educ. Tech. Res. Dev. **65**(3), 555–575 (2017)
26. Scherer, R., Siddiq, F., Teo, T.: Becoming more specific: measuring and modeling teachers' perceived usefulness of ICT in the context of teaching and learning. Comput. Educ. **88**, 202–214 (2015)
27. Claro, M., et al.: Teaching in a Digital Environment (TIDE): defining and measuring teachers' capacity to develop students' digital information and communication skills. Comput. Educ. **121**, 162–174 (2018)
28. Fraile, M.N., Peñalva-Vélez, A., Lacambra, A.M.: Development of digital competence in secondary education teachers' training. Educ. Sci. **8**(104), 1–12 (2018)
29. Krueger, R.A., Casey, M.A.: Focus Groups: A Practical Guide for Applied Research. SAGE, Thousand Oaks (2009)
30. Van Deursen, A., Van Diepen, S.: Information and strategic Internet skills of secondary students: a performance test. Comput. Educ. **63**, 218–226 (2013)
31. Calvani, A., Fini, A., Ranieri, M., Picci, P.: Are young generations in secondary school digitally competent? A study on Italian teenagers. Comput. Educ. **58**(2), 797–807 (2012)
32. Livingstone, S., Mascheroni, G., Staksrud, E.: European research on children's internet use: assessing the past and anticipating the future. New Media Soc. **20**(3), 1103–1122 (2018)

Enjoyed or Bored? A Study into Achievement Emotions and the Association with Barriers to Learning in MOOCs

Maartje Henderikx[1(✉)], Ansje Lohr[1], and Marco Kalz[2]

[1] Welten Institute, Open University of the Netherlands, Heerlen, The Netherlands
{maartje.henderikx, ansje.lohr}@ou.nl
[2] Heidelberg University of Education, Heidelberg, Germany
kalz@ph-heidelberg.de

Abstract. MOOCs are accessible online personal development opportunities in which learners can expand their knowledge on many topics. Yet, the experience of barriers to learning often hinders learners from achieving their personal learning goals. Therefore, it is important to have insight into determinants that may influence the experience of (certain) barriers. This study investigated whether the emotional determinants enjoyment and boredom, which are known to impact learner achievement and motivation, affect the experience of (specific) barriers while learning in MOOCs. The results show that boredom did affect the experience of barriers related to technical and online related skills, social context and time, support and motivation, yet it did not affect the experience of barriers related to the design of the MOOC. Enjoyment was not correlated to any of the barriers. Furthermore, the same analysis comparing men to women again revealed that boredom did not significantly affect the experience of barriers related to the design of the MOOC, yet did significantly affect the experience of the other barriers. No, significant differences were found between males and females These findings may serve as input for supporting learners in achieving their individual learning goals.

Keywords: MOOCs · Barriers · Achievement emotions · Online learning · Open education

1 Introduction

MOOCs offer learners easy accessible personal development opportunities online, in which they can expand their knowledge on many topics at their own time and pace [1]. These learners each have their individual goals they intent to achieve, which can range from finishing a certain number of modules, following the whole course without doing assignments to completing the course and getting a certificate [2]. However, Henderikx, Kreijns and Kalz [3] found that learners do not always succeed in reaching their individual goals because they encounter barriers to learning. These barriers can be either directly related to the MOOC (e.g. lack of instructor presence, bad course content, lack of instant feedback) or not directly related to the MOOC (e.g. lack of

M. Scheffel et al. (Eds.): EC-TEL 2019, LNCS 11722, pp. 15–27, 2019.
https://doi.org/10.1007/978-3-030-29736-7_2

motivation, family issues, technical problems with the pc or internet) and hinder or prevent learners from pursuing their individual learning goals [3, 4]. As barriers seem to have a substantial impact on academic achievement [5, 6], knowledge about factors that affect the encounter of these barriers would be valuable. A recent study by Henderikx, Kreijns and Kalz [7] examined possible factors affecting the encounter of barriers to learning in MOOCs. They found that age (specifically the group between 20–50 years), gender, educational level and previous online learning experience increased the encounter of (certain) barriers in MOOCs.

These factors like age, gender, educational level and previous online learning experience, which have been often studied in various learning contexts (traditional face-2-face contexts, online contexts) specifically in relation to academic achievement, could be classified as "hard" factors as they are visible or quantifiable. "Soft" factors however, which are less tangible and harder to quantify, like achievement emotions also play a part in the encounter of barriers to learning in MOOCs.

Achievement emotions, which can be defined as "emotions tied directly to achievement activities or achievement outcomes" [8], have been identified as very important as they can affect learner engagement, motivation and subsequently academic achievement [9–11]. Especially the emotions 'enjoyment' and 'boredom', which are related to the activity of learning, can be activating (enjoyment) or deactivating (boredom) emotions with regard to learning motivation [11]. Most studies, regarding achievement emotions, were set in traditional face to face settings, but an increasing number of studies investigated the influence of learner emotions in online learning environments [12–14]. However, research using Pekrun et al.'s [10] enjoyment and boredom scales in MOOC settings is sparse. With this paper, we provide two contributions to the field of learning in open online environments: (1) We examine the enjoyment and boredom scales in a MOOC context and (2) we investigate whether there is an association between enjoyment or boredom and the extent to which learners experience barriers in MOOCs.

2 Theoretical Background and Related Work

2.1 Barriers to Learning in MOOCs

Learning and succeeding in open non-formal learning environments like MOOCs can be challenging [15]. A reason why learners do not always reach their personal learning goals is that they encounter barriers to learning, which prevent or hinder them in their learning progress. These barriers can be either MOOC-related or non-MOOC related [3, 4]. Typical MOOC-related barriers often mentioned by learners are lack of interaction [5, 16, 17], lack of instructor presence [17] and course content [5, 18]. Non-MOOC related barriers experienced by learners are insufficient academic knowledge [6, 19, 20], lack of time [5, 6, 19, 21]. A principal component analysis study by Henderikx et al. [4], distinguished four different barrier components and interestingly found that most barriers could be classified as non-MOOC related (see Table 1).

Table 1. Classification of barrier components [4]

Component	Type	Barrier examples	Coping level
1-Technical and online related skills	Non-MOOC related	• Lack of software skills • Lack of typing skills	Can be dealt with on a personal level
2-Social context	Partly MOOC and non-MOOC related	• Feeling of isolation • Lack of student collaboration	Can be dealt with on both personal and MOOC-level
3-Course design	MOOC-related	• Low quality materials • Lack of timely feedback	Can be dealt with on MOOC-level
4-Time, support and motivation	Non-MOOC related	• Family issues • Lack of time • Lack of motivation	Can be dealt with on personal level

Furthermore, the participants in this study indicated that own responsibility for learning, lack of time, bad course content, lack of motivation, low quality of instruction and/or materials and family issues were most often considered as barriers.

2.2 Achievement Emotions

Achievement emotions or academic emotions are essential to understand as they can affect a learner's effort, motivation to persist and strategies for learning [11]. According to Pekrun and Linnenbrink-Garcia [11] achievement emotions can be either related to the activity of learning i.e. activity-related emotions such as enjoyment or boredom or related to the outcome i.e. outcome-related emotions such as hope and pride. These emotions can occur in class-related, learning-related and test-related environments and can be divided into positive and negative, activating and deactivating emotions with respect to their impact on student performance and motivation (see Table 2; [22]).

For example, enjoyment is regarded as an activity-related positive activating emotion as it is found to enhance effort and motivation [23]. Boredom, on the other hand, is considered an activity-related negative deactivating emotion while it undermines effort and motivation [23]. For the purpose of this study we solely focus on enjoyment and boredom as emotions during learning. As mentioned in the introduction, the majority of the studies about achievement emotions are set in traditional face to face (offline) contexts.

Table 2. Overview achievement emotions adapted from Pekrun [23]

	Positive activating	Positive deactivating	Negative activating	Negative deactivating
Activity related	*Enjoyment*	Relaxation	Anger	*Boredom*
Outcome related	Hope	Relief	Anxiety	Hopelessness
	Pride	Contentment	Shame	Despair

One of the major differences between offline and online learning environments is the lack of interaction between the learner and the instructor when it comes to identifying and responding to the emotional state of the learner [24]. Emotions are a reaction to the environment and thus in the case of limited interaction with an instructor, these emotions are mainly fuelled by the online learning environment [24]. Dillon et al. [13] explored self-reported emotions learners experience while learning in MOOCs. During the runtime of a MOOC, learners were asked, at seven different occasions, to indicate their feelings about the content (i.e. video's, assessments) by picking 2 emotions. These emotions were in part selected from Pekrun et al. [10]. The results of their study indicated that emotions are content sensitive, meaning that different content evoked different emotions. Furthermore, positive emotions, more specifically enjoyment, were the most often experienced emotions with regard to the various contents and negative emotions affected dropout and thus learner achievement. A study by Tze, Daniels, Buhr and Le [35] has analysed the connection between achievement in MOOCs and emotions. Results show that learners with low levels of boredom and low levels of guilt are more likely to deal with the course material and the instructional logic of the course design.

A recent study by Beirne, Mac Lochlainn and Mhichíl [25], examined self-reported learner emotions in a MOOC. During the 3-week runtime of the MOOC, learners were prompted 6 times per week at various points in the MOOC to indicate their emotions they experienced at that moment in time. Similar to Dillon et al. [13], they found that positive emotions were predominant during the course and that certain content evoked negative emotions which may affect achievement. In addition, a meta-analysis on achievement emotions in technology based learning environments implies that levels of emotions differ across learning environments but that the effect of emotions generally supported the hypotheses that positive emotions like enjoyment are positively related to achievement and that negative emotions like boredom are negatively related to achievement [26]. Furthermore, their meta-analysis also indicated that there is no exclusive effect between gender and positive or negative emotions. These findings indicate that the interaction with the content in MOOCs as opposed to the interaction with an instructor in offline learning environments, recalls positive as well as negative emotions and affects learner achievement regardless of gender.

Nevertheless, our aim was to explore a possible relationship between emotions (enjoyment and boredom) and barriers experienced by learners in MOOCs, as opposed to individual achievement. As online learning in a MOOC is very different from offline classroom learning, regarding time, pace, location and intellectual support [27] boredom might affect the experience of barriers, as this activity-related deactivating emotion was found to activate avoidance motivation [28] and "…triggers impulses to escape the situation" [23, p. 533]. In other words, learners who experience higher levels of boredom may feel the impulse to escape the situation and may therefore be more susceptible to experiencing barriers to learning. Therefore, we expected that boredom is positively associated with the experience of barriers. Learners who experience more boredom also experience barriers to learning in MOOCs as more severe. For enjoyment we expect to find the opposite direction, learners who experience higher levels of enjoyment will experience barriers while learning in MOOCs as less severe. In addition, while enjoyment and boredom are known to affect learner motivation [10, 11], we again predict a negative association between enjoyment and a positive association between boredom and motivation related barriers i.e. 'procrastination', 'motivation' and 'responsibility for one's own learning' specifically.

3 Method

3.1 Participants

Sample 1. The participants were individuals who took part in the MOOC on Marine Litter developed by UN environment and the Open University. The MOOC aimed at stimulating leadership and offered opportunities for actionable and change-oriented learning, related to marine litter [29]. It ran from May until July 2017, covering eight blocks for eight weeks by providing not only in-depth knowledge, but also useful tools and instruments in addressing marine litter problems. In total 39 participants completed the survey (26 women, 13 men, M_{age} = 42,15 years, age range: 25–68 years).

Sample 2. The participants were individuals who took part in one or more MOOCs in the Spanish language from different MOOC providers and on different topics in the last 2 years and who indicated that we could contact them for further research, regardless of whether or not they successfully achieved their personal goals in these MOOCs. 1618 Potential respondents received an invitation to participate in the survey of whom 299 actually completed the survey (146 women, 153 men, M_{age} = 47,02 years, age range: 20–83 years). The samples were added together for the purpose of analysis.

3.2 Materials

Achievement Emotions. The achievement emotions were measured using the respective scales of the Achievement Emotions Questionnaire developed by Pekrun et al. [10]. Participants were asked to refer to the most recent MOOC they participated in when answering these questions related to enjoyment and boredom. As achievement emotions are context specific, it is important to differentiate between academic settings [10]. In addition, achievement emotions may refer to before, during or after learning or to the outcome [11]. For this reason, we focused on the learning related emotions enjoyment and boredom and more specifically only used the items referring to enjoyment (6 items, e.g. 'I enjoy acquiring new knowledge') and boredom (9 items, e.g. 'The material bores me to death') during learning (the items referring to before and after learning were thus excluded). The items were slightly adjusted to fit the learning context of MOOCs and scored on a five-point Likert scale, 1 = totally disagree and 5 = totally agree.

These scales have been validated in multiple studies in traditional face to face contexts [10], however as the online learning context fundamentally differs from the traditional learning context, the construct validity of both scales was tested using principal axis factoring with direct oblimin rotation. The factorability of the data was supported by the Kaiser-Meyer-Olkin measure that showed a value of .93 [the recommended minimum value is .6; 30, 31] and the Bartlett's Test of Sphericity which was statistically significant ($p < .05$). The number of factors was determined by combining the results of the scree-plot which indicated a break after the 2nd factor, the eigenvalues exceeding 1 and the parallel analysis, which produced 2 random eigenvalues smaller than the first 2 eigenvalues of the principal axis factoring analysis. These two factors explain 79,6% of the variance. Furthermore, all items had primary loadings well exceeding the cut-off point of .4 on one single factor. In addition, the standardized factor loadings were mainly between .8 and 1, which can be regarded as excellent quality loadings [32] and showed a very high internal consistency per factor (see Table 3). These indices all point towards a good construct validity.

Table 3. Factor analysis and scale reliability of enjoyment and boredom

	Factor 1	Factor 2	α
Enjoyment			.91
I enjoy the challenge of learning in this MOOC	.824		
I enjoy acquiring new knowledge in this MOOC	.813		
I enjoy dealing with the course material of this MOOC	.881		
I study more than required in this MOOC because I enjoy it so much	.753		
When studying in this MOOC is going well, it gives me a rush	.818		
I get physically excited when studying this MOOC is going well	.635		
Boredom			.98
The MOOC material bores me to death		.884	
Studying this MOOC bores me		.936	
Studying this MOOC is dull and monotonous		.937	
While studying this boring MOOC material, I spend my time thinking of how time stands still		.958	
The MOOC material is so boring that I find myself daydreaming		.965	
I find my mind wandering while studying this MOOC		.927	
Because I'm bored I get tired sitting at my desk		.902	
The MOOC material bores me so much that I feel depleted		.990	
While studying in this MOOC, I seem to drift off because it's so boring		.997	

Barriers. A 'Barriers to MOOC-learning' survey was developed, which contained items drawn from general online learning, distance education and MOOC-specific context literature on barriers and enablers to learning, as discussed in previous section. After answering several general questions about gender, age, educational background, employment status, MOOC-learning experience and preferred learning context, respondents were asked to indicate to what extent they considered the 44 listed items as barriers to learning in a MOOC on a 5-point Likert scale ranging from 1 = to a very large extent' to 'not at all'. Examples of items are 'lack of decent feedback', 'family issues', 'technical problems with the computer' and 'lack of instructor presence'.

3.3 Procedures

Sample 1. In week 5 of the MOOC on Marine Litter, participants were invited to complete a survey, via a link in the MOOC, about barriers to learning in the MOOC which also included questions about the experience of enjoyment or boredom during learning. Participation was voluntary and filling out the questionnaire took 5–10 min.

Sample 2. Over the course of several weeks potential respondents were invited via email batches using the open source online survey tool Limesurvey (visit http://www.limesurvey.org) to complete a survey about barriers to learning in MOOCs which also included questions about the experience of enjoyment or boredom during learning. Participation was voluntary and filling out the questionnaire took 5–10 min. After four and six weeks, a reminder was sent to those who did not yet completed the survey.

3.4 Data Screening

The Mahalanobis distance was calculated to identify possible outliers. Based on these calculations, 34 outliers were determined and removed. Due to the high number of outliers we ran the analyses twice, with and without outliers, to verify whether it would influence the analyses. Yet no difference in outcomes was detected. The final sample of included 304 cases, which exceeds the generally accepted item ratio to conduct a factor analysis of 5 to10 respondents per item [33].

4 Results

The relationships between the four different barrier components as determined by Henderikx et al. [4], the motivation specific barriers and the achievement emotions enjoyment and boredom [10] were investigated using Pearson product-moment correlation coefficient. Table 4 shows the associations between the 4 barrier components and enjoyment and boredom. A small statistically significant correlation was found between boredom and the barrier components 1, 2 and 4, indicating that learners who experience higher levels of boredom experience barriers related to 'technical and online learning related skills', 'social context' and 'time, support and motivation' more severe. Enjoyment was not statistically significantly correlated to any of the barrier components.

Table 4. Correlations between achievement emotions and barrier components (N = 304)

	Component 1 tech and online learning related skills	Component 2 social context	Component 3 course design	Component 4 time, support and motivation
Boredom	−.152**	−.192**	−.111	−.254**
Enjoyment	.054	.100	.033	.083

Note: **p <. 01

Table 5 displays the correlation results of the analysis between the motivation related barriers 'procrastination', 'motivation' and 'responsibility for one's own learning' and enjoyment and boredom. The results indicate a small statistically significant correlation between boredom and each of the motivation related barriers and a small significant correlation between enjoyment and the barrier 'own responsibility for learning'. Learners with higher levels of boredom experience each of the motivation related barriers more severe and learners with higher levels of enjoyment experience the barrier 'own responsibility for learning' less severe.

Table 5. Correlations between achievement emotions and motivation related barriers (N = 304)

	Procrastinate	Lack of motivation	Own responsibility for learning
Boredom	−.205**	−.178**	−.201**
Enjoyment	.090	.108	.123*

Note: *p <. 05, **p <. 01

While the findings of Loderer, Pekrun and Lester [26] did not find an exclusive effect between gender and positive or negative emotions, we were interested in whether a difference in association between the variables could be detected for male and female learners. Table 6 shows that, for males, a small statistically significant correlation was found between boredom and the barrier components 1, 2 and 4 and a small statistically significant correlation between enjoyment and the barrier component 4. Men who experience higher levels of boredom experience barriers related to 'technical and online learning related skills', 'social context' and 'time, support and motivation' more severe. In addition, men with higher levels of enjoyment experience the barriers related to 'time, support and motivation' less severe. For females, a small statistically significant correlation was detected between boredom and the barrier components 2 and 4, indicating that females who are more bored experience barriers related to 'social context' and 'time, support and motivation' more severe. No statistically significant correlation was found between female enjoyment and any of the barrier components.

Table 6. Correlations between achievement emotions and barrier components by gender

	Component 1 tech and online learning related skills	Component 2 social context	Component 3 Course design	Component 4 time, support and motivation
Male (N = 147)				
Boredom	−.181*	−.217**	−.074	−.286**
Enjoyment	.046	.084	.032	.168*
Female (N = 157)				
Boredom	−.121	−.175*	−.142	−.220**
Enjoyment	.056	.115	.024	−.001

Note: *p <. 05, **p <. 01

The results in Table 6 showed that for both men and women a small statistically significant correlation was found between boredom and the barrier components 2 and 4. To test whether the difference between these correlations is statistically significant the observed value of z (z_{obs}) was calculated. The z_{obs} for the established correlations between boredom and barrier component 2 and 4 are respectively 0.362313 and 0.646987. These values are both within the range of $-1.96 < Z_{obs} < 1.96$, which indicates that there is no statistical difference in the strength of the correlation between boredom and barrier components 2 and 4 for males and females.

Furthermore, examining the results of the analysis by gender of the motivation related barriers and enjoyment and boredom in Table 7, it can be inferred that for both males and females a small statistically significant correlation between boredom and each of the motivation related barriers was found. Men as well as women with higher levels of boredom experience each of the motivation related barriers more severe. For neither men nor women an association between enjoyment and the motivation related barriers was found.

Table 7. Correlations between achievement emotions and motivation related barriers by gender

	Procrastinate	Lack of motivation	Own responsibility for learning
Male (N = 147)			
Boredom	−.246**	−.164*	−.230**
Enjoyment	.042	.097	.151
Female (N = 157)			
Boredom	−.180*	−.187*	−.237**
Enjoyment	.138	.112	.101

Note: *p <. 05, **p <. 01

Again, the z_{obs} was calculated to establish whether the difference between the found correlations for men and women was statistically significant. The z_{obs} for the correlations between boredom and the motivation related barriers 'procrastination', 'motivation' and 'responsibility for one's own learning' were respectively 0.629734, −0.26742 and −0.094891. Similar to previous found scores, these values are all within the range of $-1.96 < z_{obs} < 1.96$, and thus indicate that there is no statistical difference in the strength of the correlation between boredom and each of the motivation related barriers for males and females.

5 Discussion

This study analysed the association between the emotional states "boredom" and "enjoyment" and the severity of the experience of barriers in Massive Open Online Courses. Based on earlier research we expected that boredom is positively associated with the experience of barriers while enjoyment is negatively associated with the experience of barriers. More specifically we expected a negative association between enjoyment and motivation-related barriers like 'procrastination', 'lack of motivation' and 'responsibility for one's own learning' while assuming a positive association with boredom and these barriers.

Our findings confirm a small statistically significant correlation between boredom and the barrier components 'Tech and online learning related skills', 'social context' and 'time, support and motivation'. A lack of skills related to handling the online learning environment can be without question a source of boredom during the activity of learning. By facing this type of barriers the emotional state could potentially decrease the likeliness of overcoming these barriers and finally lead to a stop of learning activities. For the social context component, boredom can arise depending on the expectation of the learners. Some learners might enter the MOOC with the expectation to find an open course with a vibrant learning community while being confronted with mainly content-related interactions that do not require a lot of social activity. Last but not least the correlation to the barrier component 'time, support and motivation' can be explained from the perspective of self-regulated learning. Research conducted by Pekrun and others [8] has confirmed that boredom relates negatively to self-regulated learning. Surprisingly, the barrier component 'course design' was not significantly associated with boredom. An explanation for this may be that we did not collect data in one specific MOOC, but rather targeted MOOC-learners in general who at some point in the near past participated in a MOOC and were asked to refer to that MOOC when answering the survey questions. As emotions are known to be a reaction to the environment [24], MOOC-specific future research should aim to analyze the association between course designs of MOOCs or specific learning activities embedded into a MOOC environment and achievement emotions.

Our expectations regarding enjoyment and the encounter of barriers could not be confirmed. No significant correlation between any barrier component and the emotional state of enjoyment could be identified. Only when analyzing the motivation-related barriers more fine-grained, we could see that learners with higher levels of enjoyment experience the barrier 'own responsibility for learning' as less severe. It is a question for future research how the process of resolving the encountered barriers is influenced by different emotional states. In addition, research by Artino and Jones [27] has shown the complexity and association between self-regulated learning behavior, positive emotional states and metacognitive activities. Future research on barriers in MOOCs needs to further untangle the different background variables of learners, their emotional states during learning, the encounter and solving of different barriers and last but not least the influence of this whole system on individual achievement.

The study has resulted in some interesting findings related to gender differences between emotional states and barriers. Men with higher levels of boredom experience barriers related to 'technical and online learning related skills', 'social context' and 'time, support and motivation' more severe while men with higher levels of enjoyment experience the barriers related to 'time, support and motivation' less severe. Female learners who are more bored, on the other hand, experience barriers related to 'social context' and 'time, support and motivation' more severe. Although the difference between men and women was not found statistically significant, the results provide interesting starting points for further research into gender, emotional states and the experience of barriers. Similar results could be confirmed for motivation related barriers and gender differences.

6 Conclusions

Since most correlations were statistically significant but small, it is an open question how influential emotions are for the experience of barriers. Current findings can be interpreted in two directions: On the one hand, emotions can contribute to the experience of barriers, on the other hand, barriers can also be a source of these emotions. Future research needs to differentiate between these different types of emotions and the direction of their relation to the experienced barriers. Furthermore, future studies should take into consideration that additional variables may influence this relation and the direction of the relationship.

With a focus on enjoyment and boredom, this study has compared an extreme pair of learning-related emotions. Research by D'Mello, Blair, Lehman and Person [34] on affective states during problem solving has shown the importance of analysing the fluctuations between emotional states. The authors recommend to go beyond a basic valence-arousal framework. This recommendation is highly related to the research study at hand. In the current study, we have only focused on a limited set of emotional states. Future work should untangle the flow of emotions during the occurrence of barriers and examine potential problem-solving approaches related to these barriers.

This research has contributed to the emerging field of the role of emotions in open online learning environments. The novelty of the study comes from the theoretical approach used in the study and the new research direction of investigating the connection between emotions and barriers. It would be especially promising if future research were to expand the research focus not only into different types of barriers, but also towards the intrapersonal process that allows learners to cope with the experience of barriers and the control of connected emotions.

Acknowledgement. This work is financed via a grant by the Dutch National Initiative for Education Research (NRO)/The Netherlands Organisation for Scientific Research (NWO) and the Dutch Ministry of Education, Culture and Science under the grant nr. 405-15-705 (SOONER/ http://sooner.nu).

References

1. Hew, K.F.: Promoting engagement in online courses: what strategies can we learn from three highly rated MOOCS. Br. J. Educ. Technol. **47**(2), 320–341 (2016)
2. Henderikx, M.A., Kreijns, K., Kalz, M.: Refining success and dropout in massive open online courses based on the intention–behavior gap. Distance Educ. **38**(3), 353–368 (2017). https://doi.org/10.1080/01587919.2017.1369006
3. Henderikx, M., Kreijns, K., Kalz, M.: Intention-behaviour dynamics in MOOCs learning; what happens to good intentions along the way? In: 2018 Learning With MOOCS (LWMOOCS), pp. 110–112. IEEE, September 2018. https://doi.org/10.1109/lwmoocs.2018.8534595
4. Henderikx, M., Kreijns, K., Kalz, M.: A classification of barriers that influence intention achievement in MOOCs. In: Pammer-Schindler, V., Pérez-Sanagustín, M., Drachsler, H., Elferink, R., Scheffel, M. (eds.) EC-TEL 2018. LNCS, vol. 11082, pp. 3–15. Springer, Cham (2018). https://doi.org/10.1007/978-3-319-98572-5_1

5. Hone, K.S., El Said, G.R.: Exploring the factors affecting MOOC retention: a survey study. Comput. Educ. **98**, 157–168 (2016). https://doi.org/10.1016/j.compedu.2016.03.016
6. Shapiro, H.B., Lee, C.H., Roth, N.E.W., Li, K., Çetinkaya-Rundel, M., Canelas, D.A.: Understanding the massive open online course (MOOC) student experience: an examination of attitudes, motivations, and barriers. Comput. Educ. **110**, 35–50 (2017). https://doi.org/10.1016/j.compedu.2017.03.003
7. Henderikx, M., Kreijns, K., Castaño Muñoz, J., Kalz, M.: What hinders learners in pursuing goals in MOOCs? An empirical study on factors influencing barriers to learning. Distance Educ. **40**(2) (2019). https://doi.org/10.1080/01587919.2019.1600364
8. Pekrun, R., Frenzel, A.C., Goetz, T., Perry, R.P.: The control-value theory of achievement emotions: an integrative approach to emotions in education. Bibliothek der Universität Konstanz (2007)
9. Lüftenegger, M., Klug, J., Harrer, K., Langer, M., Spiel, C., Schober, B.: Students' achievement goals, learning-related emotions and academic achievement. Front. Psychol. **7** (2016)
10. Pekrun, R., Goetz, T., Frenzel, A.C., Barchfeld, P., Perry, R.P.: Measuring emotions in students' learning and performance: the achievement emotions questionnaire (AEQ). Contemp. Educ. Psychol. **36**(1), 36–48 (2011)
11. Pekrun, R., Linnenbrink-Garcia, L.: Academic emotions and student engagement. In: Christenson, S., Reschly, A., Wylie, C. (eds.) Handbook of Research on Student Engagement, pp. 259–282. Springer, Boston (2012). https://doi.org/10.1007/978-1-4614-2018-7_12
12. Baker, R.S., D'Mello, S.K., Rodrigo, M.M.T., Graesser, A.C.: Better to be frustrated than bored: the incidence, persistence, and impact of learners' cognitive–affective states during interactions with three different computer-based learning environments. Int. J. Hum Comput Stud. **68**(4), 223–241 (2010)
13. Dillon, J., et al.: Student emotion, co-occurrence, and dropout in a MOOC context. In: EDM, pp. 353–357 (2016)
14. Leony, D., Merino, P.J.M., Valiente, J.A.R., Pardo, A., Kloos, C.D.: Detection and evaluation of emotions in massive open online courses. J. UCS **21**(5), 638–655 (2015)
15. Misopoulos, F., Argyropoulou, M., Tzavara, D.: Exploring the factors affecting student academic performance in online programs: a literature review. In: Khare, A., Hurst, D. (eds.) On the Line, pp. 235–250. Springer, Cham (2018). https://doi.org/10.1007/978-3-319-62776-2_18
16. Khalil, H., Ebner, M.: Interaction possibilities in MOOCs – how do they actually happen? In: International Conference on Higher Education Development, pp. 1–24. Mansoura University, Egypt (2013)
17. Onah, D.F., Sinclair, J., Boyatt, R.: Dropout rates of massive open online courses: behavioural patterns. In: International Conference on Education and New Learning Technologies, EDULEARN14 Proceedings, Barcelona, vol. 1, pp. 5825–5834 (2014)
18. Adamopoulos, P.: What makes a great MOOC? An interdisciplinary analysis of student retention in online courses. In: Proceedings of the Thirty Fourth International Conference on Information Systems, Milan, Italy (2013)
19. Belanger, Y., Thornton, J.: Bioelectricity: a quantitative approach Duke University's First MOOC (2013)
20. Kizilcec, R.F., Saltarelli, A.J., Reich, J., Cohen, G.L.: Closing global achievement gaps in MOOCs. Science **355**(6322), 251–252 (2017)
21. Khalil, H., Ebner, M.: MOOCs completion rates and possible methods to improve retention - a literature review. In: World Conference on Educational Multimedia, Hypermedia and Telecommunications, pp. 1236–1244. AACE, Chesapeak (2014)

22. Pekrun, R.: The impact of emotions on learning and achievement: towards a theory of cognitive/motivational mediators. Appl. Psychol. **41**(4), 359–376 (1992)
23. Pekrun, R., Goetz, T., Daniels, L.M., Stupnisky, R.H., Perry, R.P.: Boredom in achievement settings: exploring control–value antecedents and performance outcomes of a neglected emotion. J. Educ. Psychol. **102**(3), 531–549 (2010)
24. Swerdloff, M.: Online learning, multimedia, and emotions. In: Emotions, Technology, and Learning, pp. 155–175 (2016)
25. Beirne, E., Mac Lochlainn, C., Mhichíl, M.N.G.: Moody MOOCS: an exploration of emotion in an LMOOC. In: Towards Personalized Guidance and Support for Learning, vol. 22 (2018)
26. Loderer, K., Pekrun, R., Lester, J.C.: Beyond cold technology: a systematic review and meta-analysis on emotions in technology-based learning environments. Learning and Instruction (in press)
27. Artino Jr., A.R., Jones II, K.D.: Exploring the complex relations between achievement emotions and self-regulated learning behaviors in online learning. Internet High. Educ. **15**(3), 170–175 (2012)
28. Pekrun, R.: Facets of adolescents' academic motivation: a longitudinal expectancy-value approach. Adv. Motiv. Achievement **8**, 139–189 (1993)
29. Löhr, A.J., Savelli, H., Beunen, R., Kalz, M., Ragas, A., Van Belleghem, F.: Solutions for global marine litter pollution. Curr. Opin. Environ. Sustain. **28**, 90–99 (2017)
30. Kaiser, H.F.: A second-generation little jiffy. Psychometrika **35**(4), 401–415 (1970)
31. Kaiser, H.F.: An index of factorial simplicity. Psychometrika **39**(1), 31–36 (1974)
32. McNeish, D., An, J., Hancock, G.R.: The thorny relation between measurement quality and fit index cutoffs in latent variable models. J. Pers. Assess. **100**(1), 43–52 (2018)
33. Comrey, A.L., Lee, H.B.: A First Course in Factor Analysis, 2nd edn. Lawrence Erlbaum, Hillsdale (1992)
34. D'Mello, S.K., Lehman, B., Person, N.: Monitoring affect states during effortful problem solving activities. Int. J. Artif. Intell. Educ. **20**(4), 361–389 (2010)
35. Tze, V., Daniels, L.M., Buhr, E., Le, L.: Affective profiles in a massive open online course and their relationship with engagement. Front. Educ. **2**. (2017)

Identifying Factors for Master Thesis Completion and Non-completion Through Learning Analytics and Machine Learning

Jalal Nouri[1(✉)], Ken Larsson[1], and Mohammed Saqr[2]

[1] Stockholm University, Stockholm, Sweden
{jalal, kenlars}@dsv.su.se
[2] University of Eastern Finland, Joensuu, Finland
mohammed.saqr@uef.fi

Abstract. The master thesis is the last formal step in most universities around the world. However, all students do not finish their master thesis. Thus, it is reasonable to assume that the non-completion of the master thesis should be viewed as a substantial problem that requires serious attention and proactive planning. This learning analytics study aims to understand better factors that influence completion and non-completion of master thesis projects. More specifically, we ask: which student and supervisor factors influence completion and non-completion of master thesis? Can we predict completion and non-completion of master thesis using such variables in order to optimise the matching of supervisors and students? To answer the research questions, we extracted data about supervisors and students from two thesis management systems which record large amounts of data related to the thesis process. The sample used was 755 master thesis projects supervised by 109 teachers. By applying traditional statistical methods (descriptive statistics, correlation tests and independent sample t-tests), as well as machine learning algorithms, we identify five central factors that can accurately predict master thesis completion and non-completion. Besides the identified predictors that explain master thesis completion and non-completion, this study contributes to demonstrating how educational data and learning analytics can produce actionable data-driven insights. In this case, insights that can be utilised to inform and optimise how supervisors and students are matched and to stimulate targeted training and capacity building of supervisors.

Keywords: Thesis · Master · Learning analytics · Completion · Dropout · Retention · Machine learning

1 Introduction

The master thesis is the last formal step in most universities around the world. However, all students do not finish their master thesis. A considerable number of students struggle with the thesis process, resulting in delays, disruptions, and non-completion of their degrees [1–3]. Such outcomes are devastating for individual students and academic institutions that waste time, money and energy, and for societies that are not

M. Scheffel et al. (Eds.): EC-TEL 2019, LNCS 11722, pp. 28–39, 2019.
https://doi.org/10.1007/978-3-030-29736-7_3

strengthened with high-skilled workers [2, 4, 5]. Therefore, ensuring that students enrolled in graduate programs obtain their degrees in a timely fashion is in the best interest of students, higher education institutions and societies [4, 6].

However, the thesis is a challenging endeavour that requires skills, aptitude, and determination for successful, timely completion [5, 7–10]. Thus, it is reasonable to assume that non-completion of higher education degrees should be viewed as a substantial problem that requires serious attention and proactive planning [2, 4, 5, 11–13].

Previous research related to thesis projects has identified some variables that influence the performance of students undertaking thesis projects; variables that, in particular, point out the relation between the student candidate and the supervisor [2, 5, 14]. The specific student variables that have been indicated as influencing thesis completion are students' attitudes and motivation [10], the students' average entry grade [12], and the students' communication and language skills [13]. Among the supervisor variables, it has been shown that the supervisor's experience, research output and workload constitute factors of thesis success [13, 15]. However, the review of the literature leads to the conclusion that there are few studies explicitly focusing on master thesis projects. Studies on completion of thesis projects mostly concern the doctorate thesis [16, 17] while studies on master thesis completion tend to focus on the whole program, not the thesis specifically [18–20]. Furthermore, most studies have used a qualitative approach to investigate factors for thesis completion; single factors have been looked at in an isolated way with a primary focus on student variables and on completion factors (and not on non-completion and supervisor variables) [21–23]. Furthermore, there are few contemporary studies that look at factors for success and failure related to thesis work.

Today, the introduction of thesis management systems, such as SciPro from Stockholm University [24] and Thesis Writer (TW) from Zurich University of Applied Sciences [25], generate a lot of data concerning many aspects of the thesis process. This paves the ground for using learning analytics techniques in order to gain data-driven insights about thesis management and the factors that affect thesis retention [26]. Learning analytics have been used successfully to early map the indicators of successful course completion, inform course design, provide insights and feedback to teachers and students, as well as improve education outcome [27].

This study takes as a departure point to better understand factors that influence completion – and in particular – non-completion of master thesis projects. More specifically, we ask: which student and supervisor variables influence completion and non-completion of master thesis? Can we predict completion and non-completion of master thesis using such variables in order to optimize the matching of supervisors and students?

To answer these research questions, we extracted data about supervisors and students from two thesis management systems, Daisy and SciPro from the Department of Computer and Systems Sciences, Stockholm University, which record large amounts of data related to the thesis process. The sample used was 755 master thesis projects supervised by 109 teachers. By applying traditional statistical methods (descriptive statistics, correlation tests and independent sample t-tests), as well as machine learning algorithms, we identify five central factors that can accurately predict master thesis completion and non-completion. Besides the identified factors and predictors that explain master thesis completion and non-completion, this study contributes to demonstrating how educational data and learning analytics can produce actionable data-driven insights. In this case, insights that can be utilised to, on the one hand, inform and optimise how supervisors and students are matched, and on the other hand, stimulate targeted training and capacity building of supervisors.

2 Identified Factors in the Literature Explaining Thesis Completion and Non-completion

Our literature review has led to the identification of two groups of factors that influence thesis outcomes: related to the student candidate and the supervisor. Below we give an account of what is known about these two groups of factors.

Rennie and Brewer [10] using a grounded theory approach to investigate the problem of thesis delay proposed the term ‘thesis-blocking’. They propose that thesis blocking factors are more numerous than factors leading to completing it in a timely fashion. Successful thesis completion is dependent on the candidate’s conformity and acceptance of the process. Failure of the supervisor to handle a candidate’s negative feelings is the reason why many candidates to be stuck in the middle of the path [10]. House and Johnson’s findings point to the applicants’ average entry grade as a decisive predictive factor of successful, timely completion [12], a finding that was corroborated by Jiranek [13] and Wright and Cochrane [28].

On the other hand, studies have shown that entry grade is not a significant predictor of completion [28, 29]. In a study by Pascarella and Terenzini [30], it was shown that the background characteristics, including entry grades, only explain a small part of retention, while academic and social integration explain more.

Other student factors affecting the completion or non-completion include communication skills and language proficiency skills [13], self-reliance and independence [31]. However, a right balance and proactive planning along with institutional support could mitigate the impact and assist the candidates [2, 5, 13, 15, 31, 32]. Contrary to what is a common belief, part-time older candidates appear to be better than their counterparts in their approach to research, other duties and being independent [28].

It has also been shown that supervisors behaviours are crucial in every stage of the thesis work, in supporting the thesis writing process, rectifying errors, suggesting directions and being responsible for arranging the defence [33]. Rennie and Brewer compare the supervisor’s role in these cases to the writer’s block phenomenon [10]. They suggested that both share essential features, the main problem being the writer’s internalisation of the critical feedback by the supervisor and poor management of duties and time constraints.

A healthy relationship between student and supervisor is helpful for the success of the thesis. The thesis is an embedded social exercise more than most of the other educational projects, therefore collaborating with the supervisor, regular productive meetings and the ability to reach a shared understanding are central to the success of the project [2, 5, 14, 34, 35]. A relationship where the supervisor exerts a moderate control of the process and more significant affiliation was found to influence the successful outcome in terms of time to completion and completion rates [36]. Supervisor experience and research production is a factor that might affect positively [13].

In general, the supervisors support through all the stages of the thesis process is an indispensable factor [5, 13, 32, 34, 37]. On the contrary, supervisors that are overwhelmed by research work, teaching or multiple students have less time for students who have negative results on the thesis work [2, 15]. Furthermore, students report that its central that supervisors provide constructive, on-time feedback, as well as encouragement [38].

3 Method

3.1 Sample and Context

The sample for this study consisted of master students' thesis projects (n = 755) during the period between 2010 and 2017 at the Department of Computer and Systems Sciences, Stockholm University, Sweden. Since it takes approximately 350 days for students to complete a thesis project (from course registration to grade registration), data from the year, 2018 were excluded as they contained many projects likely to be completed after the data extraction. The dropout rate for the thesis project at the department is approximately 43% for the period studied. We have included all master thesis projects that adhere to the present curriculum for thesis projects.

3.2 Data Collection

A challenge in data collection for learning analytics is to avoid amplifying errors from different standards in data sources, especially if some sources are external and out of control. In this study, to minimise this risk for all data sources, we used data that are under the control of the university.

Data collection was performed in several iterative steps. Using SQL (structured query language) queries, we extracted data from two different data systems used by the department to record data about the thesis projects. From these systems, we collected thesis project data concerning both students and supervisors. Informed by factors identified by previous research [12, 13], and taking into account additional variables that were available in the systems that record thesis data. We focused in general on three groups of factors that influence the academic thesis process, namely: (1) student's previous performance in the master program; (2) supervisor's thesis project performance and experience; and (3) supervisor's research output.

More specifically, we extracted the following variables:

- Thesis project: start and completion date. From this, the number of days to completion was calculated.
- The students (n = 755): the grade of the thesis, the average grade in the study before the master thesis, and the number of course credits received within the educational program.

- The supervisors (n = 105): number of scientific publications, the average number of scientific publications per year, number of complete/incomplete thesis projects, the average grade of thesis projects, number of started thesis projects, and average days of supervisors to complete thesis projects were calculated from the projects.

All data was anonymised by converting personal identifiers to fictive IDs. The researchers who did the analysis did not know the identity of the subjects. The data was subsequently prepared for statistical and predictive analytics by removal of extreme- and null values and through the computation of relevant variables.

Ethical approval for this study was obtained through the Regional Board of Ethical Vetting in Stockholm. Consent for participating in this research was also obtained from the selected supervisors in the sample. Six supervisors and their associated thesis projects were excluded due to no consent for using their data were received.

3.3 Data Analysis

The analysis was performed using SPSS, and R. Spearman correlation test was conducted to investigate the correlation between incomplete thesis projects (dropouts) and student and supervisor variables. Multiple independent sample t-tests were performed in order to explore differences between completers and non-completers with regards to student and supervisor variables. The Shapiro–Wilk test of normality was employed and confirmed that the assumptions for the t-tests were satisfied.

For the predictive analytics, seven supervised machine learning classifiers were applied: Naive Bayes, Logistic Regression, Gradient Boosted Trees, Neural Network, Deep Learning, Decision Tree, and Random Forest in order to predict completers and non-completers of thesis projects. These classifiers were chosen because they are frequently used for predicting dropout, and each has demonstrated good and comparable performance in predicting at-risk students and dropout [39, 40]. The data set was split into a training and testing set. The training set consisted of 70% of the total data set, and the testing set the remaining 30%. After the implementation of the predictive models, features were ranked using the information gain ratio. To prevent overfitting and increase robustness, 10-fold cross-validation was performed, where performances were measured from multiple iterations of cross-validation and averaged over iterations. To measure the prediction performance of the different models, the area under the receiver operating characteristic curve (AUC) was obtained, along with measures for precision and recall.

4 Results

In Table 1 the full descriptive statistics are presented. Among the 755 thesis projects studied, 57% were completed, and 43 remained non-completed (see Fig. 1).

After performing the descriptive analysis presented in Table 1, a correlations tests (Spearman's) was performed in order to study the correlation between completion of thesis projects and all student and supervisor variables presented in the above table. This analysis revealed that completion is significantly correlated with the ratio of

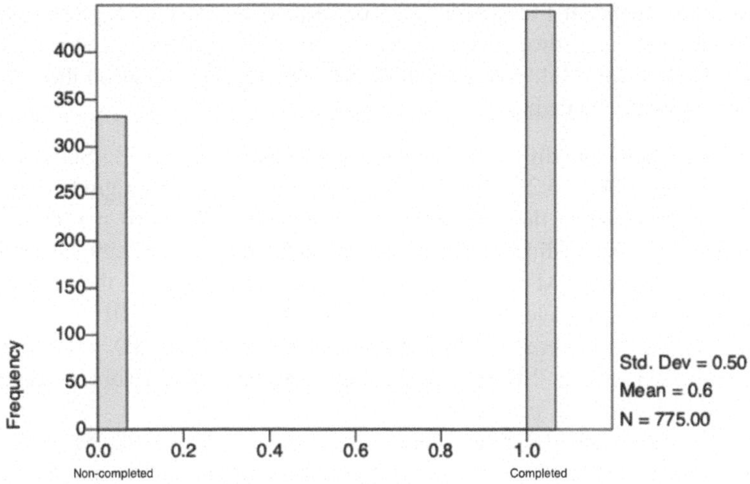

Fig. 1. Histogram over completed and non-completed thesis projects

Table 1. Descriptive statistics

Variable	N	M	SD	Range	Min	Max
Student average study grade	775	3.53	.83	4.00	1.00	5.00
Student average thesis grade	775	2.16	2.04	5.00	.00	5.00
Supervisor average days to complete	772	417.44	183.85	1415.00	157.00	1572.00
Supervisor average thesis grade	772	3.72	.51	3.50	1.50	5.00
Supervisor no. of scientific publications	760	59.82	48.69	271.00	1.00	272.00
Supervisor no. of incomplete thesis projects	774	11.11	7.80	33.00	.00	33.00
Supervisor no. of started thesis projects	774	29.27	16.14	77.00	1.00	78.00
Supervisor ratio incomplete thesis projects	774	38.25	17.65	83.33	.00	83.33
Supervisor average no. of publication per year	774	4.84	3.67	13.25	.00	13.25
Student no. of course credits within program	769	62.65	45.25	206.00	.00	206.00
Completed vs non-completed thesis projects	775	.57	.50	1.00	.00	1.00

All grade-related variables on a 6-item scale ranging from F = 0 to A = 5

incomplete thesis projects of supervisors ($r = -0.36$, $p < 0.01$), students' average grade in their study program at the university ($r = 0.28$, $p < 0.01$), supervisors total number of incomplete thesis projects ($r = -0.17$, $p < 0.01$), the average time it takes for supervisors to complete thesis projects ($r = -0.14$, $p < 0.01$), the ratio of supervisor thesis ideas ($r = 0.10$, $p < 0.05$), and supervisors average thesis grade ($r = 0.09$, $p < 0.04$). As can be noted, the ratio and total amount of unfinished thesis projects by supervisors presented the strongest correlations with thesis dropout, together with students' average grade during the educational program.

Multiple independent t-tests were also performed in order to explore differences between completers and dropouts with regards to many student and supervisor variables. See Table 3 for a full presentation of the t-test results. Based on these tests, the following can be concluded:

- there is a significant difference between completers (M = 3.73, SD = 0.85) and non-completers (M = 3.26, SD = 0.74) regarding their average grade during their studies in the program they are seeking to graduate in, $t(-8.26) = 1.07$, $p < 0.01$;
- there is a significant difference between completers (M = 399.99, SD = 166.02) and non-completers (M = 440.92, SD = 203.33) in terms of their supervisors' average days to complete thesis projects, $t(3.08) = 5.57$, $p < 0.01$;
- there is significant difference between completers (M = 3.76, SD = 0.49) and non-completers (M = 3.66, SD = 0.53) in terms of their supervisors average thesis grade, $t(-2.51) = 0.32$, $p < 0.05$;
- there is a significant difference between completers (M = 9.98, SD = 7.45) and non-completers (M = 12.63, SD = 8.01) in terms of their supervisors' total number of incomplete thesis projects $t(4.75) = 2.28$, $p < 0.01$;
- there is a significant difference between completers (M = 32.71, SD = 15.90) and non-completers (M = 45.65, SD = 17.17) in terms of their supervisors' ratio of incomplete thesis projects, $t(4.75) = 2.28$, $p < 0.01$, and

Significant differences were, however, not revealed concerning the total number of scientific publications published by supervisors, the total number of thesis projects supervised by the supervisors, or the total course credits received by students within the educational program prior the master thesis (Table 2).

Table 2. Significant differences between completed and non-completed thesis projects (t-test)

Variable		M	SD	F	t	p
Student average study grade	Complete	3.73	0.85	1.07	−8.26	<0.01
	Incomplete	3.26	0.74			
Supervisor average days to complete	Complete	399.99	166.02	5.57	3.08	<0.01
	Incomplete	440.92	203.33			
Supervisor average thesis grade	Complete	3.76	0.49	0.32	−2.51	<0.05
	Incomplete	3.66	0.53			
Supervisor no. of incomplete thesis projects	Complete	9.98	7.45	2.28	4.75	<0.01
	Incomplete	12.63	8.01			
Supervisor ratio incomplete thesis projects	Complete	32.71	15.90	2.28	4.75	<0.01
	Incomplete	45.65	17.17			

4.1 Predicting Completion and Non-completion

Then predictive analytics was performed using several machine learning models (Naive Bayes, Logistic Regression, Deep Learning, Decision Tree, Random Forest and Gradient Boosted Trees) in order to predict the completion/non-completion variable using the features described in Table 1. The performance across the models showed AUC values between 0.74 and 0.83 (see Table 3).

Table 3. Prediction accuracy and ROC

Model	AUC	Accuracy	F-measure	Recall
Gradient Boosted Trees	0.83	71.6%	0.66	67.0%
Logistic Regression	0.82	73.5%	0.65	58.9%
Naive Bayes	0.80	70.7%	0.58	49.7%
Deep Learning	0.76	70.3%	0.63	64.2%
Random Forest	0.74	63.5%	0.21	12.4%
Decision Tree	0.50	59.0%	na	4.2%

The Gradient Boosted Trees model proved to perform best concerning accuracy and AUC, with almost 72% accuracy in predicting completers and non-completers. The actual non-completers could be predicted with a 66% precision and 67% class recall; while the completers could be predicted with 76% precision and 75% class recall (see Table 4).

As can be seen from Table 5, the features with most weight were the ratio of unfinished thesis projects of supervisors, students' average grade during university studies, supervisors' total number of incomplete projects and the average time it takes for supervisors to complete a thesis project.

Table 4. Prediction of completers and non-completers using Gradient Boosted Trees

	True completer	True non-completer	Class precision
Predicted Completer	96	31	76%
Predicted Non-completer	32	63	66%
Class Recall	75%	67%	

Table 5. Weights of selected features

Features	Weight
Supervisor ratio incomplete thesis projects	1.0
Student average study grade	0.78
Supervisor no. of incomplete thesis projects	0.45
Supervisor average days to complete	0.31
Supervisor average thesis grade	0.23
Supervisor average no. of publications per year	0.17

5 Discussion

Not finishing a master thesis is a devastating personal experience for students that costs precious time, loss of money and energy. Non-completion also results in a vast waste of faculty time and institutional resources, and a societal loss of high skilled workers [2, 4, 5]. This study took as a departure point to address this problem by using large amounts of thesis-related data generated in thesis management systems in order to create data-driven insights about the factors that influence completion and non-completion of master thesis projects. Such a learning analytics approach led us to identify factors that have not been reported on in the research literature.

The analysis of the data resulted in the identification of five central factors that influence students' completion and non-completion of master thesis projects. The strongest factor and predictor for non-completion, not reported on before, showed to be supervisors' history of incomplete thesis projects. This factor correlated *more* with incomplete thesis projects *than* student's academic performance before starting the thesis (which was the second strongest predictor) and was the factor/feature that had most information gain (weight) in the predictive models produced by the employed machine learning algorithms. Three additional factors/predictors were identified related to the supervisor, namely: (1) the average days it takes for supervisors to complete thesis projects; (2) the average grade of thesis works supervised, and (3) the average number of scientific publications produced by the supervisor per year.

Thus, the supervisor's historical thesis supervision performance and their performance as researchers, together with students' academic performance prior to the thesis, to a high extent determine success and failure of master thesis projects. While previous research mainly through qualitative studies has demonstrated that supervisors indeed play a significant role in the thesis process, by in particular pointing out *how* successful teachers supervise, this quantitative study identify actual predictors related to the supervisor and demonstrate the significant effect of supervisor historical performance on master thesis completion and non-completion, which constitute a central contribution of this study. However, the finding that students' academic performance prior to the thesis is a significant predictor has been reported on before and corroborate previous research [12, 13, 28].

Besides the identified factors and predictors that explain master thesis completion and non-completion, this study contributes to demonstrating how educational data and learning analytics can produce actionable data-driven insights. In this case, gained insights can be utilized to, on the one hand, inform and optimize how supervisors and students are matched, and on the other hand, stimulate targeted training and capacity building of supervisors.

Future research work can build upon this study and bridge its limitations by adding more contextual factors to the analysis, such as students' internal conditions and dispositions [41–43]. By dispositions, we mean behavioral and cognitive factors such as motivation (to write a master thesis, for instance), engagement, self-regulation skills, strategies and attitudes [43, 44]. Such an approach would most likely increase the probability of finding additional factors that influence the master thesis process and increase accuracy, replicability and transferability of prediction models [27, 45, 46].

References

1. Kamler, B., Thomson, P.: The failure of dissertation advice books: toward alternative pedagogies for doctoral writing. Educ. Res. **37**(8), 507–514 (2008)
2. Rauf, F.A.: Challenges of thesis work: towards minimizing the non-completion rate in the postgraduate degree program. Eur. J. Bus. Manag. **8**(7), 113–124 (2016)

3. Wong, P.T.P.: Meaning making and the positive psychology of death acceptance. Int. J. Existential Psychol. Psychother. **3**(2), 73–82 (2010)
4. Baum, S., Ma, J., Payea, K.: Education pays. The Benefits of Higher Education for Individuals and Society (2013)
5. Ho, J.C., Wong, P.T., Wong, L.C.: What helps and what hinders thesis completion: a critical incident study. Int. J. Existential Psychol. Psychother. **3**(2) (2010)
6. Bourke, S., et al.: Attrition, completion and completion times of PhD candidates. In: AARE Annual Conference, Melbourne (2004)
7. Agu, N., Oluwatayo, G.K.: Variables attributed to delay in thesis completion by postgraduate students. J. Emerg. Trends Educ. Res. Policy Stud. **5**(4), 435–443 (2014)
8. Ferrer, F.P.: Determinants of performance in thesis: evidence from selected filipino graduate students. Int. J. Educ. Res. **2**(10), 189–202 (2014)
9. Morton, K.R., Worthley, J.S.: Psychology graduate program retention, completion and employment outcomes. J. Instr. Psychol. (1995)
10. Rennie, D.L., Brewer, L.: A grounded theory of thesis blocking. Teach. Psychol. **14**(1), 10–16 (1987)
11. Chin, W.Y., et al.: Analyzing the factors that influencing the success of post graduates in achieving graduate on time (GOT) using analytic hierarchy process (AHP). In: AIP Conference Proceedings. AIP Publishing (2017)
12. House, J.D., Johnson, J.J.: Predictive validity of Graduate Record Examination scores and undergraduate grades for length of time to completion of degree. Psychol. Rep. **71**(3), 1019–1022 (1992)
13. Jiranek, V.: Potential predictors of timely completion among dissertation research students at an Australian faculty of sciences. Int. J. Doctoral Stud. **5**(1), 1–13 (2010)
14. Pitchforth, J., et al.: Factors affecting timely completion of a PhD: a complex systems approach. J. Scholarsh. Teach. Learn. **12**(4), 124–135 (2012)
15. van de Schoot, R., et al.: What took them so long? Explaining PhD delays among doctoral candidates. PLoS ONE **8**(7), e68839 (2013)
16. Can, E., et al.: Supervisors' perspective on medical thesis projects and dropout rates: survey among thesis supervisors at a large German university hospital. BMJ Open **6**(10), e012726 (2016)
17. Van Ours, J.C., Ridder, G.: Fast track or failure: a study of the graduation and dropout rates of Ph D students in economics. Econ. Educ. Rev. **22**(2), 157–166 (2003)
18. DesJardins, S.L., Kim, D.-O., Rzonca, C.S.: A nested analysis of factors affecting bachelor's degree completion. J. Coll. Student Retention Res. Theor. Pract. **4**(4), 407–435 (2003)
19. Graham, L.D.: Predicting academic success of students in a master of business administration program. Educ. Psychol. Measur. **51**(3), 721–727 (1991)
20. Herzog, S.: Estimating student retention and degree-completion time: decision trees and neural networks vis-à-vis regression. In: New Directions for Institutional Research, vol. 131, pp. 17–33 (2006)
21. Ishitani, T.T.: Studying attrition and degree completion behavior among first-generation college students in the United States. J. High. Educ. **77**(5), 861–885 (2006)
22. Kovacic, Z.: Early prediction of student success: mining students' enrolment data. In: Informing Science + Information Technology Education Joint Conference, Cassino, Italy (2010)
23. Zwick, R., Sklar, J.C.: Predicting college grades and degree completion using high school grades and SAT scores: the role of student ethnicity and first language. Am. Educ. Res. J. **42**(3), 439–464 (2005)
24. Hansen, P., Hansson, H.: Optimizing student and supervisor interaction during the SciPro thesis process – concepts and design. In: Li, F.W.B., Klamma, R., Laanpere, M., Zhang, J.,

Manjón, B.F., Lau, R.W.H. (eds.) ICWL 2015. LNCS, vol. 9412, pp. 245–250. Springer, Cham (2015). https://doi.org/10.1007/978-3-319-25515-6_23
25. Rapp, C., Ott, J.: Learning analytics in academic writing instruction–opportunities provided by Thesis Writer (TW). In: Igel, C., Ullrich, C., Martin, W. (eds.) Bildungsräume 2017, pp. 391–392. Gesellschaft für Informatik, Bonn (2017)
26. Rapp, C., Kauf, P.: Scaling academic writing instruction: evaluation of a scaffolding tool (Thesis Writer). Int. J. Artif. Intell. Educ. **28**, 1–26 (2018)
27. Ifenthaler, D., Mah, D.-K., Yau, J.Y.-K.: Utilizing Learning Analytics to Support Study Success. Springer, Cham (2018)
28. Wright, T., Cochrane, R.: Factors influencing successful submission of PhD theses. Stud. High. Educ. **25**(2), 181–195 (2000)
29. Siegel, L.: A study of Ph. D. Completion at Duke University. CGS Communicator, XXXVIII **1**(1), p. 2 (2005)
30. Pascarella, E.T., Terenzini, P.T.: Predicting voluntary freshman year persistence/withdrawal behavior in a residential university: a path analytic validation of Tinto's model. J. Educ. Psychol. **75**(2), 215 (1983)
31. Castro, V., et al.: The road to doctoral success and beyond. Int. J. Doctoral Stud. **6**, 51–78 (2011)
32. Manathunga, C.: Early warning signs in postgraduate research education: a different approach to ensuring timely completions. Teach. High. Educ. **10**(2), 219–233 (2005)
33. Retalis, S., et al.: Towards networked learning analytics–a concept and a tool. In: Banks, S., Vivien, H., Jones, C., Kemp, B., McConnell, D., Smith, C. (eds.) Fifth International Conference on Networked Learning, pp. 1–8. Lancaster University (2006)
34. Koskenoja, M.: Factors supporting and preventing master thesis progress in mathematics and statistics. Int. Electron. J. Math. Educ. (2019)
35. Styles, I., Radloff, A.: The synergistic thesis: student and supervisor perspectives. J. Further High. Educ. **25**(1), 97–106 (2001)
36. de Kleijn, R.A., et al.: Master's thesis supervision: relations between perceptions of the supervisor–student relationship, final grade, perceived supervisor contribution to learning and student satisfaction. Stud. High. Educ. **37**(8), 925–939 (2012)
37. Lindsay, S.: What works for doctoral students in completing their thesis? Teach. High. Educ. **20**(2), 183–196 (2015)
38. de Kleijn, R.A., et al.: Master's thesis projects: student perceptions of supervisor feedback. Assess. Eval. High. Educ. **38**(8), 1012–1026 (2013)
39. Jayaprakash, S.M., et al.: Early alert of academically at-risk students: an open source analytics initiative. J. Learn. Anal. **1**(1), 6–47 (2014)
40. Kashyap, A., Nayak, A.: Different machine learning models to predict dropouts in MOOCs. In: 2018 International Conference on Advances in Computing, Communications and Informatics (ICACCI). IEEE (2018)
41. Gašević, D., Dawson, S., Siemens, G.: Let's not forget: learning analytics are about learning. TechTrends **59**(1), 64–71 (2015)
42. Schumacher, C., Ifenthaler, D.: The importance of students' motivational dispositions for designing learning analytics. J. Comput. High. Educ. **30**(3), 599–619 (2018)
43. Tempelaar, D., et al.: Student profiling in a dispositional learning analytics application using formative assessment. Comput. Hum. Behav. **78**, 408–420 (2018)
44. Papamitsiou, Z., Economides, A.A.: Learning analytics and educational data mining in practice: a systematic literature review of empirical evidence. J. Educ. Technol. Soc. **17**(4), 49–64 (2014)

45. Sedrakyan, G., et al.: Linking learning behavior analytics and learning science concepts: designing a learning analytics dashboard for feedback to support learning regulation. Comput. Hum. Behav. (2018)
46. Nouri, J., Larsson, K., Saqr, M.: Bachelor thesis analytics: using machine learning to predict dropout and identify performance factors. Int. J. Learn. Anal. Artif. Intell. Educ. **1**(1) (2019)

Analyzing Learners' Behavior Beyond the MOOC: An Exploratory Study

Mar Pérez-Sanagustín[1,3(✉)], Kshitij Sharma[2], Ronald Pérez-Álvarez[3,4], Jorge Maldonado-Mahauad[3,5], and Julien Broisin[1]

[1] Institut de Recherche en Informatique de Toulouse (IRIT), Université Paul Sabatier Toulouse III, Toulouse, France
{mar.perez-sanagustin,julien.broisin}@irit.fr
[2] Norwegian University of Science and Technology, Department of Computer Science, Trondheim, Norway
kshitij.sharma@ntnu.no
[3] Pontificia Universidad Católica de Chile, Santiago, Chile
{raperez13,jjmaldonado}@uc.cl
[4] Universidad de Costa Rica, Puntarenas, Costa Rica
[5] Universidad de Cuenca, Department of Computer Science, Cuenca, Ecuador

Abstract. Most of literature on massive open online courses (MOOCs) have focused on describing and predicting learner's behavior with course trace data. However, little is known on the external resources beyond the MOOC they use to shape their learning experience, and how these interactions relate with their success in the course. This paper presents the results of an exploratory study that analyzes data from 572 learners in 4 MOOCs to understand (1) what the learners' activities beyond the MOOC are, and (2) how they relate with their course performance. We analyzed frequencies of the students' individual activities in and beyond the MOOC, and the transitions between these activities. Then, we analyzed the time spent on outside the MOOC content as well as the nature of this content. Finally, we predict which transitions better predict final learners' grades. The results show that we can predict accurately students' grades of the course using only internal-course fine-grained data of student's interactions with video-lectures and exams combined with trace data of interactions with content outside the MOOCs. Also, data shows that learners spent 75% of their time on the MOOC, but go frequently to other content, mainly social networking sites, mail boxes and search engines.

Keywords: MOOCs · Massive Open Online Courses · Learning Analytics · Exploratory study

1 Introduction

In the past years, lot of research in Learning Analytics (LA) have focused on studying learners' behavior through the analysis of student's activity trace data

M. Scheffel et al. (Eds.): EC-TEL 2019, LNCS 11722, pp. 40–54, 2019.
https://doi.org/10.1007/978-3-030-29736-7_4

collected from Massive Open Online Courses (MOOCs) platforms. Using computational methods, researchers have seen in this vast amount of data an opportunity to unveil students' behavior and extract activity patterns to understand their learning strategies in digital environments [8].

Some studies have focused on analyzing fine-grained data from learners' interaction with the course content for predicting students' performance and dropout rates [4,15,23]. Other studies proposed combining trace data with students' self-reported information for identifying the traits and behaviors influencing success [10] or self-regulated learning strategies [9,11,12]. But other researchers went even further by combining both, course trace data and data from external third-party tools or social networks associated with the course content [2,5,21,22]. This latest pool of research works showed that students' learning in MOOCs is not restricted only to interactions with the course content but complemented by social interactions taking place beyond. This points out the need of extending our datasets for expanding our current vision of students' learning in MOOCs.

However, the literature on how learners nurture and complement their learning experience beyond the MOOC is still scarce. The limited amount of work in this line is due in part to the lack of tools and mechanisms for researchers to capture the actions of students beyond the content and structure of the course. Moreover, in case of counting with the appropriate tools, the data usually comes from social networks (i.e., Facebook, Twitter) or explicit content provided to students as part of the course design [2,6]. Therefore, understanding what type of activities and contents learners seek beyond the MOOC, and how these activities relate with their performance are still open challenges.

As a first approach to overcome these challenges, in this paper we present an exploratory study that analyzes learners' behavior beyond the MOOC by combining, not only MOOC trace data, but also clickstream data from students' interactions with an external third-party tool called NoteMyProgress [17,18]. This tool was designed to support students' learning strategies in online environments, but it also collects the digital resources students interact with during their study sessions. This dataset represents an important research opportunity to investigate how MOOC learners enrich their learning experience beyond the course content.

Two research questions drive this exploratory study: (RQ1) What are the learners' activities beyond the MOOC?, and (RQ2) How these activities relate with their course performance? Firstly, we examine the outside-the-MOOC resources most consulted by students during their study sessions. Results show that three-fourths of the interactions during their study sessions is outside the MOOC content, mainly in social networks such as Facebook, Mail Boxes and Google searches, but this interactions are short, since they spend three-fourths of their time with the MOOC content. Secondly, using predictive models, we analyze what transitions between the MOOC content and other external resources better predict students' course grades. The results indicate that considering single few fine-grained events (video watching and exams' interactions) combined with transitions towards external resources allows to predict students' performance accurately. The rest of the paper presents the prior work that we take as a reference (Sect. 2), the details of the exploratory study (Sect. 3), and the results of categorizing and of the final grade predictions (Sect. 4). Finally, we discuss future research avenues and implications of this work (Sect. 5).

2 Related Work

In MOOCs, learners' behavior has been extensively studied, and every research work differs from each other not only on the final objective or analytics methods employed, but also on the dataset they consider for the analysis. In terms of the dataset, we identify two different tendencies: (1) works that use only fine-grained events from records of learners' interaction with the course content; and (2) works which combine this fine-grained data with external data sources. Within the first group, there is a large group of scientific papers that use different techniques for identifying students' activity patterns, and computational models for predicting patterns related with good performance or dropouts [15]. These studies obtain accurate predictive results using variables such as students' interaction with videos clickstreams [4], or with the platform functionalities [23]. Within the second group, some researchers propose studying the factors influencing students' success by combining both, trace data and students' characteristics obtained from self-reported questionnaires [9,12]. Examples of these works are those that extract learning strategies from trace data and relate them with personal students' traits such as intrinsic motivation [10], or self-regulated learning profile and skills [9,12] to predict learning attainment [11].

So far, these studies show that using trace data of students' interaction with the course content, combined or not with other external information about learners' profile, serves for predicting students' performance in the course and identify what the most predictive variables are [11]. However, when studying in digital environments, the frontiers of the learning space are not limited only to the MOOC contents, but to other resources available on the internet (i.e., outside the platform) to complement and enrich their learning experience.

Some prior work has contributed on providing insights on how learning happens beyond the MOOC by combining trace data with data from external third-party tools associated to the course. For example, in [6], authors propose an architecture for extending the MOOC ecosystem and connecting it to social network tools such as Twitter for analyzing good and bad social interactions. Authors in [2] used data from external social tools combined with students' activity within the course forum, and observed that the preferred communication channel was the forum. Authors in [21] studied the use of Twitter in two MOOCs, concluding that this is a valuable complementary social tool to address questions and answers related to the course topics. Authors in [14] studied the use of Facebook group and Twitter feeds associated with the MOOC content. The authors conclude that additional social spaces can enhance the learning experience outside the MOOC and provide an environment for resource sharing and communication with others. The result of these studies reinforces other studies that stressed the importance of the digital connections between participants taking place in external social environments beyond the course [22].

Although these works provide some insights about students' learning experience in and beyond the MOOC, only few studies in the literature address this, and have some limitations. First, when using data from social tools external to the MOOC platform architecture it is difficult to identify MOOC participants accurately; authors in [5] collected learners' traces across 18 MOOCs and 5 popular social web platforms. They indicated as part of their study limitations that they were able of matching only 5% of learners of the course with their activity in social networks. Second, studies usually analyze participants' activity within external tools or content included by the practitioners as a complementary resource from the course design [2,22]. That is, they do not consider interactions with other resources chosen by the learners themselves during their study sessions. And finally, studies providing evidence about the learning experience outside the MOOC are based only on students' perceptions from self-reported data [16].

In this work, we contribute to expand current knowledge about study learners' behavior in MOOCs. We build upon prior work in predicting learners' course attainment but combining both, trace data from students' interaction with the course content with data from an external third-party tool capturing the resources they seek and use beyond the MOOC.

3 Exploratory Study

3.1 Context: Tools and Sample

In 2016, the Pontificia Universidad Católica de Chile developed the web application NoteMyProgress (NMP) [17,18], a tool designed to support students' strategies in MOOCs. Within its functionalities, NMP supports note-taking, strategic planning and goal-setting; and provides learners with a set of interactive visualisations showing information about their performance in the course (i.e., the time spent in the course content versus the time outside the course, or the time invested in each of the activities of the course). Currently, there is an available version that works with Coursera[1]. NMP is composed by a Google Chrome plugin that is activated when a registered learner initiates a session in Coursera, and a Web-based application that is always available through the plugin. The plugin offers an overview of the time invested in the course and the note-taking functionality, whereas the website provides learners with more detailed information about their study behavior through interactive visualisations. One of the key characteristics of NMP is that it captures not only the information about what learners are doing with the course content, but also the URL's websites that learners visit during their study sessions. This information is only recorded

[1] NMP Source Code: https://git.cti.espol.edu.ec/LALA-Project/PUC.

while the plugin detects that the user is interacting with the course content. Otherwise, the tool logs out automatically and stops recording trace data.

For this exploratory experiment, NoteMyProgress was launched for 4 months, from March to June 2018, in different editions of 4 MOOCs: one on learning programming (Course 1), and three on organisations management (Course 2, Course 3 and Course 4). Data was gathered from the four months in which NoteMyProgress was available.

The installation and use of the application were voluntary. Also, for ethical and privacy issues, installing the tool requires users to accept the terms and conditions about privacy data, and a consent form indicating the type of data collected and the purpose of the study. Both, the terms and conditions, as well as the consent form was validated and approved by the Ethical Committee of the institution.

The study sample are the 572 students that downloaded NoteMyProgress during the exploratory study period and used it at least once. Table 1 shows the number of learners who used NoteMyProgress per course, the course duration, and the number of students that finished the course.

Table 1. The number of learners who used NoteMyProgress

Course	Course duration	Number of students	Students passing the course
Introduction to Programming in Python (Course 1)	6 weeks	149	70
Organizational management (Course 2)	6 weeks	59	28
Project Management (Course 3)	5 weeks	193	79
Management for small and medium enterprises (Course 4)	4 weeks	171	71

3.2 Data Categorization and Features

Two data sources were used for categorizing outside-the-MOOC content and for extracting the features for the predictive analysis: (1) the logfiles collected by NMP, from which we only used the URLs accessed by learners during their study sessions; (2) the Coursera logfiles of those learners using NMP, with trace data about learners' interaction with the course content; and (3) the Coursera booknotes indicating the score of students at the end of the course.

For categorizing outside-the-MOOC content, we examined the type of URLs logged in NoteMyProgress and organized them by type in the following categories:

1. Coursera – All the URLs captured from resources and functionalities accessed by students within the Coursera platform.
2. Social – The URLs recorded from platforms like, Facebook, Twitter, Whatsapp, Youtube.

3. Mail – E-mail related URLs such as, gmail, yahoo, outlook.
4. Google Search – URLs recorded while the students were searching for something on Google. For this analysis we do not distinguish between those searches that were related to course content.
5. Google services – URLs from the other google services such as, photos, books, maps, drive, webstore, calendar, translate.
6. Group 2-10 – URLs that occur between 2 and 10 times in the NoteMyProgress logs and do not belong to any category from 1 to 4.
7. Group 10-20 – URLs that occur between 10 and 20 times in the NoteMyProgress logs and do not belong to any category from 1 to 4.
8. Group 20-40 – URLs that occur between 20 and 40 times in the NoteMyProgress logs and do not belong to any category from 1 to 4.
9. Other – URLs that do not appear more than once in the logs.

We categorised the URLs into three groups in terms of individual frequencies of appearance because we observed that these groups were a common pattern in all courses. As features, we used the frequencies of the individual activities and the transitions between the different activities. The various activities considered were: lecture, exam, supplement, outside-the-MOOC-activity, help (on Coursera), information (on Coursera). Our target variable for this contribution is the grade at the end of the course. In order to show that the information collected from NoteMyProgress is indeed important, we used simplistic and basic features from the logs.

3.3 Methods

For addressing RQ1 about students' activity beyond the MOOC, we conducted several analysis based on the categorisation of the URLs logged by NMP (see Sect. 3.2). First, we analysed the URLs recorded by NMP in terms of their frequency of occurrence. Second, we calculated the time students' spent in each outside-the-MOOC resources and compared it with the time spent in the course content. Finally, we visually represented the proportion of time spent in each outside-the-MOOC resource to have an overview of the type of content visited by the learners. Notice that, for this study, we treated all the URLs equally, without distinguishing those that might be explicitly mentioned within the MOOC.

For addressing the RQ2 about how students' activities relate with performance we conducted predictive analysis of students' course overall course grade. Using different models, we first calculated the frequencies of the individual activities that each learner conducted with the video-lectures and the assessment (lecture, exam, other documents, outside-the-MOOC-activity, help on Coursera, information on Coursera). Then, we computed the frequency in the transitions between the different activities. We used these numbers as the features to predict the final grade in the different courses. For these predictions, we use four different algorithms: Random Forest, Neural Network, Support Vector Machines (SVM) with a polynomial kernel and a simple linear model. For the prediction setting, we divided the dataset into 80% training and 20% testing subsets on the training we used a 5-fold cross-validation for all the algorithms. Afterwards, we used the same features for predicting the final grade of the course per week: week 1, weeks 1 and 2 and so on.

4 Results

4.1 Outside the MOOC Behavioral Patterns

When analyzing the type of content learners' interact with during their study sessions outside the MOOC, we observe that, in terms of **number of interactions (frequency)** only 33.29% corresponds to interactions with in-course content. The remaining 66.71% of the interactions are of content outside the MOOC. However, when analysing the **time spent** in the different resources, we observe that students spent close to 75% of their time on the MOOC content. That is, during their study sessions, learners interact more with outside-MOOC content than with content within the MOOC, although they spend around three fourths of their study time with the MOOC content. Figure 1 shows the proportion of the time spent and the frequency of occurrence of the different websites visited **outside the MOOC platform**. In Table 2, showing the percentages of all the websites recorded, we observe that the most frequent individual (not counting groups or others) content visited outside the MOOC are: mails, facebook, google searches and youtube. These are, also the most time consuming outside-MOOC URLS (not counting groups or others).

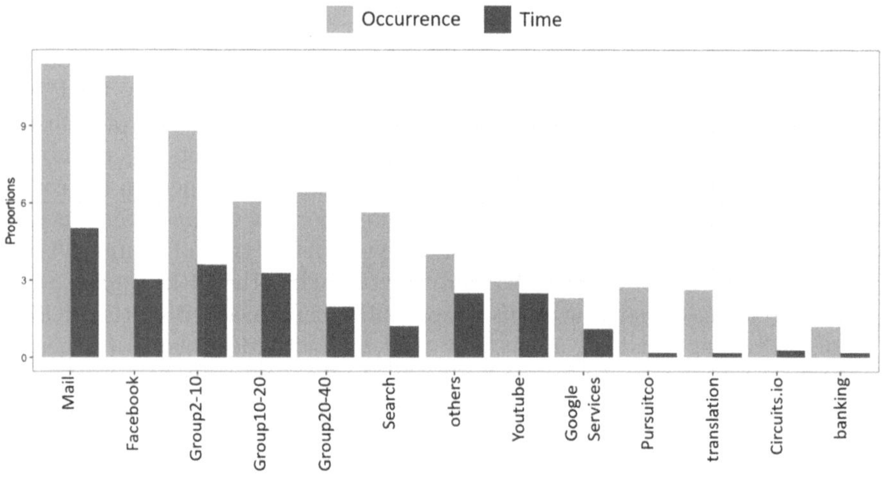

Fig. 1. Distribution of the websites visited outside Coursera platform during learners' study sessions considering data from all 4 courses.

Contrary to the overall distribution of the websites, when looking in the time invested by learners in individual courses, the results are different (Fig. 2).

Table 2. Percentages of different "outside-the-MOOC" websites visited by the students during their study sessions, in terms of frequency and time.

	Course 1		Course 2		Course 3		Course 4	
Website	Freq.	Time	Freq.	Time	Freq.	Time	Freq.	Time
Coursera	37.51	74.34	41.41	76.49	33.02	72.02	28.73	77.34
Social	9.07	3.33	21.96	12.86	25.79	13.57	4.74	3.65
Mail	9.35	4.60	5.55	2.00	18.19	7.33	11.07	4.25
Search	6.26	1.42	7.82	1.13	4.13	1.00	6.23	1.00
Google services	7.20	1.00	1.01	1.00	4.33	1.17	2.72	1.00
group2-10	9.72	5.63	5.80	2.98	5.10	2.09	5.01	2.79
group10-20	13.37	6.38	3.03	2.19	6.44	1.00	3.86	1.00
group20-40	3.74	1.29	6.06	1.14	0.00	0.00	28.64	7.33
Others	4.49	2.01	8.33	0.21	4.52	1.82	10.19	1.46

In Fig. 2, we observe that, in the cases of *Course 2* and *Course 3*, the sites in which learners invested more time (outside MOOCs) are the social networks. On the other hand, for *Course 1* and *Course 4*, the students spent time on various course related websites such as "notebook.azure", "pythonforbeginners" and "python.org". But, Fig. 2 also shows that the time spent in search engines is also significant. This can bias our results, since we consider using search engines as another resource.

The least frequent groups of websites (Group2-10, Group10-20, Group20-40) are represented together in the Fig. 3. The first and the smallest group is formed by the websites that were visited between 20 and 40 times; they contribute 6.41% to the number of outside-the-MOOC URLs but only contribute 1.95% of the outside-the-MOOC time. The second group is formed by the websites that were visited between 10 and 20 times; they contribute 6.07% to the number of outside-the-MOOC URLs but only contribute 3.25% to the outside-the-MOOC time. The third group and the largest is formed by the websites that were visited between 2 and 10 times; they contribute 8.80% to the number of outside-the-MOOC URLs but only contribute 3.60% to the outside-the-MOOC time. Finally, the websites categorized as **Others** are those visited only once, they contribute 4.00% to the number of outside-the-MOOC URLs but only contribute 2.50% to the outside-the-MOOC time. The reason of websites from Group2-10 contributing more (in terms of numbers) than Group10-20 and Group20-40 is that the sheer numbers of the websites visited between 2 and 10 times is more than the websites visited in the other two groups. Figure 3 shows the distribution of the percentage time spent on the websites.

4.2 General and Weekly Grade Prediction

First, we present the overall grade prediction based on the data collected from NoteMyprogress. Table 3 shows the comparison between different prediction

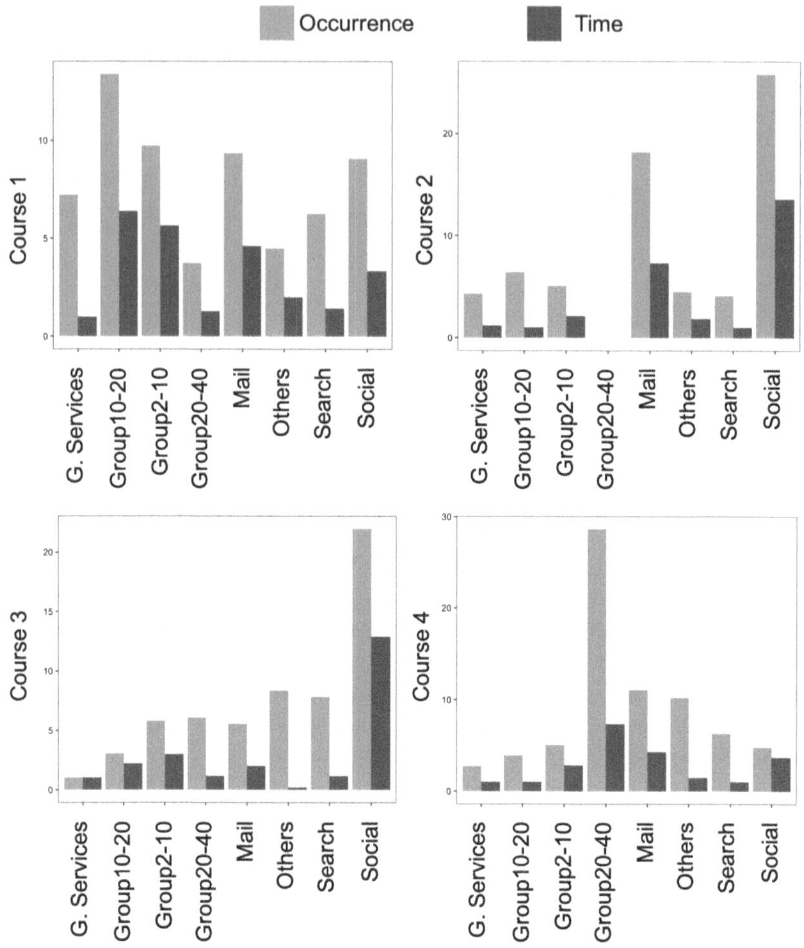

Fig. 2. Distribution of the websites visited outside Coursera platform during learners' study sessions considering data for individual courses.

methods used. We can observe that random forest gives the best accuracy (least error) for predicting the grades of the students. Notice that, for this analysis, we are using data from students' MOOC activity beyond the MOOC in a very semantic-less manner. That is, we are looking only at the interactions students' do with outside the MOOC content, without analyzing what type of content this is. In spite of this fact, the prediction accuracy achieved is significant. Further, we also computed the variable importance and the top few features contributing to the low error rate. These variables are:

1. Transitions from outside-MOOC to lecture – how many times the students go from outside-MOOC to lectures

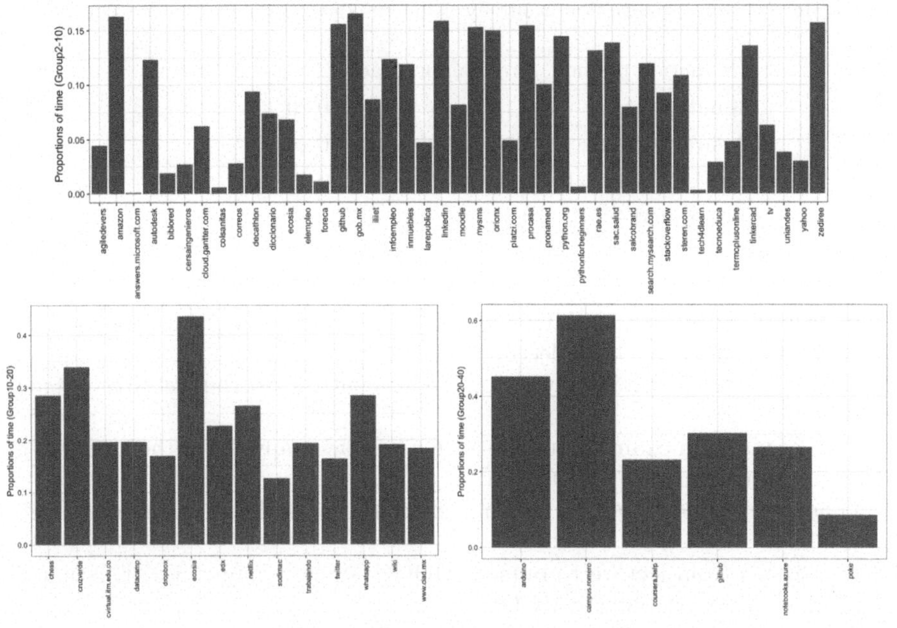

Fig. 3. Websites in Group2-10, Group10-20 and Group20-40 visited outside Coursera platform.

2. Outside-MOOC – how many times the students go to the websites outside-MOOC
3. Transitions from exam to outside-MOOC – how many times the students go from exam to outside-MOOC
4. Time on outside-MOOC – how much time the students spent on outside-MOOC.
5. Transitions from lecture to outside-MOOC – how many times the students go from lecture to outside-MOOC
6. Transitions from outside-MOOC to exam – how many times the students go from outside-MOOC to exams
7. Transitions from other documents to outside-MOOC – how many times the students go from supplements to outside-MOOC

Next, we present the results from weekly predictions. Each row in Table 4 shows the random forest prediction results using the data upto the different weeks of the course. Each row shows the results of applying the prediction with more data than the row before. We observe that, by using the data upto the 4th week of the course we achieve similar prediction results as the ones obtained when using the whole dataset. When analyzing the most important features, we observe that some of them are similar to those identified when predicting using all data, but there are also notable differences. In this case, the features are, organized by importance:

Table 3. Overall prediction accuracy using the data from all the four courses

Prediction method	Training accuracy	Testing accuracy
Random forest	0.18	0.20
Neural network	0.23	0.24
SVM Polynomial	0.21	0.23
linear model	0.24	0.25

1. Transitions from outside-MOOC to lecture – how many times the students go from outside-MOOC to lectures
2. outside-MOOC – how many times the students go to the websites outside-MOOC
3. Transitions from exam to outside-MOOC – how many times the students go from exam to outside-MOOC
4. Time on outside-MOOC – how much time the students spent on outside-MOOC.
5. Transitions from lecture to outside-MOOC – how many times the students go from lecture to outside-MOOC
6. Transitions from outside-MOOC to exam – how many times the students go from outside-MOOC to exams
7. Transitions from lecture to exam – how many times the students go from lectures to exams
8. Transitions from exam to lecture – how many times the students go from exams to lectures

Table 4. Prediction results using data from different lengths of the course – the prediction method used is the best model from the Table 3, i.e., random forest.

Data used upto	Training accuracy	Testing accuracy
Week 1	0.21	0.23
Week 2	0.20	0.23
Week 3	0.20	0.23
Week 4	0.18	0.20

5 Conclusions and Future Work

This paper presented an exploratory study in which we analyzed trace-data of 572 students participating in 4 different MOOCs. MOOC data was complemented with records of the URLs consulted by students during their study sessions collected with the third-party NoteMyProgress (NMP). We first described the outside-the-MOOC resources resources visited by the learners in terms of frequency and time spent, and then, we used predictive methods for identifying those behavioral patterns that better relate with students' success.

Firstly, the results of the descriptive analysis of students' behavior beyond the MOOC show that, in general, students spend around 25% of their study time interacting with other materials than the course content, even if they knew that their study session activities were recorded. Mail boxes, social networks and google searches are the most frequent sites (in terms of frequency they contribute upto 66% of the total URLs). However, when looking at each course individually, we observe some variations in the percentages of time dedicated to each site type. Further research would require a semantic exploration of the sites accessed by the learners in order to see whether they relate somehow with the MOOC content. Also, comparisons on the predictions of grades only using MOOC traces, only NMP data and a combination of both data sources will be conducted in order to further understand the predictive power of using outside-MOOC data.

Secondly, our results show that using data from interactions with video-lectures and exams of the course, combined with semantic-less data from their activity beyond the MOOC, predicts learners' grades accurately. From this analysis, we also observed that transitions from outside-MOOC to video-lectures, as well as activities outside the MOOC and from the exams to external content are the three most predictive variables when considering the overall data. However, time spent mainly in social networks is one of the most predictive values when analyzing weekly behavioral data. We qualify this behaviour as procrastination as defined by [20]; that is, to intentionally deferring or delaying work that must me completed. However, we cannot assure with the data available whether the activity students perform in social networks are related or not to the course. Future work will require further analysis of these procrastination behaviour and see if, as in prior work, this influences students' success [13]. Further, analyzing whether there is a relationship between the frequency of the transitions that better predict learners' success with their performance on the course is also a future research line.

In terms of the prediction results we would like to emphasise on the fact that neither the features nor the prediction methods were very sophisticated. Despite this fact, we observe a prediction quality that is comparable to the contemporary results. Most of the RMSE reporting studies have reported similar prediction qualities (to the best of our knowledge). For example, an RMSE of 0.20 was reported in a study with about ten thousand students [7], other studies report RMSE values of 0.17 [1,19] and 0.18 [3] with two to three courses each. The most notable difference between the previous studies and the present study relies in the nature of the features used. Previous studies used the data completely from within the MOOC platforms [1,3,7,19], while we used the minimal subset of information from the MOOC platform. This result suggests that the Coursera and NoteMyProgress datasets have similar prediction power, since they produce similar errors (comparing our results with the ones reported in literature), thus they have similar "amount" of information; but we know by design that the "nature" of information from Coursera is different from the information from NoteMyProgress. Therefore, we can conclude from these results that NoteMyProgress provides complementary information to understand student behavioral and successful patterns. Further studies analysing the semantics of the visited websites captured by NMP would potentially improve the predictive power.

In conclusion, this paper contributes with empirical data on students' learning in MOOCs and opens new research avenues. Although results are preliminary and could be extended, we believe that this first overview does already expand our knowledge on the type of activities and content students' use for enriching their learning experience. Further, the results of this work may have implications on MOOC design and tools implemented for supporting students' learning. For example, analysis of the most frequent consulted sites could be facilitated to the teacher, so as to engage students in critical discussions about its content. Also, the results of the predictive models could serve for identifying when students' are struggling and suggest them resources where they could seek for help.

Yet, this study has its limitations that should be also addressed in future work. First, we are only considering as "outside-activity" the URLs captured by NMP. However, there might be other applications used in the study time that we are not capturing. Other research protocols, including observations or other qualitative approaches, would allow a more profound analysis of these other activities.

Acknowledgments. This work was supported by FONDECYT (11150231), University of Costa Rica (UCR), CONICYT Doctorado Nacional 2017/21170467, and CONICYT Doctorado Nacional 2016/21160081, the project "Analítica del aprendizaje para el estudio de estrategias de aprendizaje autorregulado en un contexto de aprendizaje híbrido - DIUC_XVIII_2019_54" financiado por la Dirección de Investigación de la Universidad de Cuenca (DIUC), Cuenca-Ecuador, and the LALA project (grant no. 586120-EPP-1-2017-1-ES-EPPKA2-CBHE-JP). This project has been funded with support from the European Commission. This publication reflects the views only of the author, and the Commission and the Agency cannot be held responsible for any use which may be made of the information contained therein.

References

1. Agapito, J.B., Sosnovsky, S., Ortigosa, A.: Detecting symptoms of low performance using production rules. In: Educational Data Mining, July 2009
2. Alario-Hoyos, C., Pérez-Sanagustín, M., Delgado-Kloos, C., Munoz-Organero, M.: Delving into participants' profiles and use of social tools in MOOCs. IEEE Trans. Learn. Technol. **7**(3), 260–266 (2014)
3. Ashenafi, M.M., Riccardi, G., Ronchetti, M.: Predicting students' final exam scores from their course activities. In: 2015 IEEE Frontiers in Education Conference (FIE), pp. 1–9. IEEE, October 2015
4. Brinton, C.G., Chiang, M.: MOOC performance prediction via clickstream data and social learning networks. In: 2015 IEEE Conference on Computer Communications (INFOCOM), pp. 2299–2307 (2015)
5. Chen, G., Davis, D., Lin, J., Hauff, C., Houben, G.J.: Beyond the MOOC platform: gaining insights about learners from the social web. In: Proceedings of the 8th ACM Conference on Web Science, pp. 15–24. ACM, Hannover, May 2016

6. Cruz-Benito, J., Borrás-Genè, O., García-Peñalvo, F.J., Blanco, Á.F., Therón, R.: Extending MOOC ecosystems using web services and software architectures. In: Proceedings of the XVI ACM International Conference on Human Computer Interaction, pp. 52–57, September 2015
7. Elbadrway, A., Studham, R.S., Karypis, G.: Collaborative multi-regression models for predicting students' performance in course activities. In: Proceedings of the Fifth International Conference on Learning Analytics and Knowledge, pp. 103–107. ACMl, March 2015
8. Kizilcec, R.F., Brooks, C.: Diverse big data and randomized field experiments in MOOCs. In: Lang, C., Siemens, G., Wise, A., Gašević, D. (eds.) Handbook of Learning Analytics, pp. 211–222. Society for Learning Analytics Research (2017)
9. Kizilcec, R.F., Pérez-Sanagustín, M., Maldonado, J.J.: Self-regulated learning strategies predict learner behavior and goal attainment in Massive Open Online Courses. Comput. Educ. **104**, 18–33 (2017)
10. Littlejohn, A., Hood, N., Milligan, C., Mustain, P.: Learning in MOOCs: motivations and self-regulated learning in MOOCs. Internet High. Educ. **29**, 40–48 (2016)
11. Maldonado-Mahauad, J., Pérez-Sanagustín, M., Moreno-Marcos, P.M., Alario-Hoyos, C., Muñoz-Merino, P.J., Delgado-Kloos, C.: Predicting learners' success in a self-paced MOOC through sequence patterns of self-regulated learning. In: Pammer-Schindler, V., Pérez-Sanagustín, M., Drachsler, H., Elferink, R., Scheffel, M. (eds.) EC-TEL 2018. LNCS, vol. 11082, pp. 355–369. Springer, Cham (2018). https://doi.org/10.1007/978-3-319-98572-5_27
12. Maldonado-Mahauad, J., Pérez-Sanagustín, M., Kizilcec, R.F., Morales, N., Munoz-Gama, J.: Mining theory-based patterns from big data: identifying self-regulated learning strategies in Massive Open Online Courses. Comput. Hum. Behav. **80**, 179–196 (2018)
13. Michinov, N., Brunot, S., Le Bohec, O., Juhel, J., Delaval, M.: Procrastination, participation, and performance in online learning environments. Comput. Educ. **56**(1), 243–252 (2011)
14. Liu, M., McKelroy, E., Kang, J., Harron, J., Liu, S.: Examining the use of Facebook and Twitter as an additional social space in a MOOC. Am. J. Distance Educ. **30**(1), 14–26 (2016). https://doi.org/10.1080/08923647.2016.1120584
15. Moreno-Marcos, P.M., Alario-Hoyos, C., Muñoz-Merino, P.J., Kloos, C.D.: Prediction in MOOCs: a review and future research directions. IEEE Trans. Learn. Technol. (2018)
16. Oura, H., Anzai, Y., Fushikida, W., Yamauchi, Y.: What would experts say about this?: An analysis of student interactions outside MOOC platform. In: Proceedings of the 11th International Conference on Computer Supported Collaborative Learning (CSCL 2015), Gothenburg, Sweden, vol. 2, pp. 711–712 (2015)
17. Pérez-Álvarez, R., Pérez-Sanagustín, M., Maldonado-Mahauad, J.J.: NoteMyProgress: supporting learners' self-regulated strategies in MOOCs. In: Lavoué, É., Drachsler, H., Verbert, K., Broisin, J., Pérez-Sanagustín, M. (eds.) EC-TEL 2017. LNCS, vol. 10474, pp. 517–520. Springer, Cham (2017). https://doi.org/10.1007/978-3-319-66610-5_53
18. Pérez-Álvarez, R., Maldonado-Mahauad, J., Pérez-Sanagustín, M.: Design of a tool to support self-regulated learning strategies in MOOCs. J. Univ. Comput. Sci. (JUCS) **24**(8), 1090–1109 (2018)
19. Ren, Z., Rangwala, H., Johri, A.: Predicting performance on MOOC assessments using multi-regression models. arXiv preprint arXiv:1605.02269 (2016)

20. Schraw, G., Wadkins, T., Olafson, L.: Doing the things we do: a grounded theory of academic procrastination. J. Educ. Psychol. **99**(1), 12 (2007)
21. Veletsianos, G., Collier, A., Schneider, E.: Digging deeper into learners' experiences in MOOCs: participation in social networks outside of MOOCs, notetaking and contexts surrounding content consumption. Br. J. Educ. Technol. **46**(3), 570–587 (2015)
22. Van Treeck, T., Ebner, M.: How useful is twitter for learning in massive communities? An analysis of two MOOCs. In: Twitter & Society, pp. 411–424 (2013)
23. Xing, W., Du, D.: Dropout prediction in MOOCs: using deep learning for personalized intervention. J. Educ. Comput. Res. (2018). https://doi.org/10.1177/0735633118757015

Building a Learner Model for a Smartphone-Based Clinical Training Intervention in a Low-Income Context: A Pilot Study

Timothy Tuti[1,3](✉), Chris Paton[2], Mike English[2,3], and Niall Winters[1]

[1] Department of Education, University of Oxford, 15 Norham Gardens, Oxford OX2 6PY, UK
timothy.tuti@kellogg.ox.ac.uk
[2] Centre for Tropical Medicine and Global Health, University of Oxford, Oxford OX1 3SY, UK
[3] KEMRI-Wellcome Trust Research Programme, Nairobi 00100, Kenya

Abstract. Research is lacking on developing adaptive learning applications for training health workers in low-resource settings making student modelling approaches supporting individualised learning to remain largely unexplored. This study targeted a clinical training intervention using smartphones in a low-resource context to explore if clinicians' performance patterns can be differentiated into distinctive groups based on an inferred proficiency level using cluster analysis. We also explored the applicability of Knowledge-Component (KC) cognitive learning models-Additive and Performance Factor Models (AFMs, PFMs) - in describing these patterns and their accuracy in predicting performance. The intervention provides simulation training on contextualised management of new-born resuscitation through a series of learning interactions that elicit responses through multiple-choice answers and interactive tasks. AFMs and PFMs were used to explore the impact of previous exposure to KCs within the learning intervention on learner performance. We demonstrate that effectiveness of low-dose-high-frequency training might be linked to successful attempts in previous learning sessions. Additionally, there exists intermediate and expert cadres of health workers who would benefit more from cascading-challenge scenarios. From these results, we propose a preliminary cognitive learning model as a basis for adaptive instructional support on smartphones for clinical training in low-resource settings.

Keywords: Serious gaming · Predictive accuracy · Clinical training · Smartphones · Neonatal care · Emergency care · Sub-Saharan Africa · Performance Factor Models · Additive Factor Models

1 Background

Sub-Saharan Africa (SSA) produces over 24% of the global disease burden but only has 3% of the global health workforce [1, 2]. This severe workforce shortage, coupled with health workforce skill imbalance and maldistribution, and lack of training opportunities

M. Scheffel et al. (Eds.): EC-TEL 2019, LNCS 11722, pp. 55–68, 2019.
https://doi.org/10.1007/978-3-030-29736-7_5

are major contributors to the poor quality of neonatal care outcomes in the region [3]. Mobile technologies (smartphones and tablet computers) have shown potential to address this learning challenge in SSA, given their uptake rate (around 30–50% of adult populations) and pattern of usage (around 30–35% use it to access internet for information sourcing) [4, 5]. A typical health worker in this setting works very long hours, would find it hard to pay personally for face-to-face training, is likely unable to spend much time or money on learning online, and the institution they work for would usually also be constrained financially from funding further training [6, 7]. Consequently, their learning must be flexibly integrated into very busy working lives and mechanisms for reinforcing learning must be strengthened. There is little evidence from low-resource contexts such as Africa of learning interventions that are cognisant of this context, that take into account individual health workers' initial and continuing clinical training needs, and that deliver tailored learning content, feedback and resources in light of skill mastery and performance as they continue to develop knowledge through it (i.e. adaptive learning) [4, 8, 9].

Such learning adaptations are common in the Intelligent Tutoring Systems (ITSs) literature, where while not necessarily cognisant of contexts like SSA, learner interactions within the digital learning platform tend to be tracked as a sequence of student-driven steps [10]. That is, when a student attempts a learning task (step), the ITS records whether it was successful, whether any system-initiated assistance was provided, and may provide instructional support based on the learner's performance. These kinds of data points are what are used for student learning needs' modelling and subsequently adapting content [11]. The learning tasks that produce these data points represent unique Knowledge Components (KC) which reflect learning "…concepts, principle, fact, skill, schema, production rule, misconception…" [12]. The most common student modelling approaches for KCs are Additive Factor Models (AFMs) [13], and Performance Factor Models (PFMs) [14], and detailed explanations of these are provided in the next section. Appreciating that reinforcement of KCs is useful, interventions in emergency care training in low resource settings have tended towards face-to-face group training and, more recently, have used low-dose high-frequency (LDHF) in-person training in group settings (but did not utilise technology) [15, 16]. Evidence of the successful implementation of student-modelling approaches on digital platforms in clinical training in order to facilitate adaptive learning and improve learning outcomes is scarce [17], and virtually non-existent for emergency care training in low income settings [18]. In high income settings, despite the important role of smartphones in facilitating personalised learning, there is still a lack of research investigating mobile-based ITSs [19]. These are the gaps that ITS are yet to systematically address. Additionally, differences between learners' achievement goal orientations (such as skill mastery-intrinsic, mastery-extrinsic, performance-approach, performance-avoidance etc.) [20] and how that is reflected in the uptake of smartphones-based learning approaches in low-income settings is largely unexplored. Inclusion of such metrics in reporting the rate of progress in gaining experience or new skills (i.e. learning curves) and learning outcomes in digital-based clinical training interventions is rather sparse [21]. Such metrics would arguably help inform the successful implementation of digital training platforms to bridge the skills gap in clinical care provided in low-income settings where low-cost highly accessible training opportunities are hard to come by.

1.1 Additive Factor Models (AFMs) and Performance Factor Models (PFMs)

Student-step data are important in breaking down the level of skill mastery in dealing with any emergency care rapid response and specifically what constitutes skill mastery. Skill-mastery has commonly been conceptualised as the odds of learners completing a task correctly as a linear function of the prior opportunities they had for the learning task, conditioned on skill difficulty (i.e. AFMs). It has also been commonly conceptualised as the odds of learners completing a task correctly after taking the correctness of learners' responses into account based upon previous performance features such as the number of previous successful and unsuccessful practices (i.e. PFM). Additive Factor Models (AFM) are used to evaluate conjunctive skills in learning data. Its ***additive*** nature is due to a linear combination of skill parameters determining p_{ij} described in the equation below:

$$ln \frac{p_{ij}}{1 - p_{ij}} = \theta_i + \sum_k \beta_k Q_{kj} + \sum_k Q_{kj}(\gamma_k N_{ik}) \tag{1}$$

Where: i represents student i, j represents step j, k represents knowledge component/ skill k, p_{ij} is the probability that student i would be correct on step j, θ_i is the coefficient for proficiency of student i, β_k is coefficient for difficulty of the knowledge component or skill k, Q_{kj} is the Q-matrix cell for step j using skill k, γ_k is the coefficient for the learning rate of skill k, N_{ik} is the number of practice opportunities student i has had on the skill k. Q-matrices are used to represent the relationship between individual steps and knowledge components, typically encoded as a binary 2-dimensional matrix with rows representing knowledge components and columns representing steps [11]. AFM posits that the probability of a learner getting a step correct is proportional to the amount of required knowledge they already know, together with skill difficulty and amount of learning opportunity they have been already exposed to [13]. On the other hand, Performance Factor Models (PFMs) given by the equation below, seek to predict performance on the current item using the entire history of success and failures on previous items addressing the same student step [22]. It estimates the different effects of practicing learning opportunities.

$$logit(p_{ijt}) = \theta_i + \beta_j + \alpha_j S_{ijt} + \rho_j F_{ijt} \tag{2}$$

Where: i represents student i, j represents step j, θ_i is the coefficient for proficiency of student i, β_j is coefficient for difficulty of the step j, X_{ijt} is binary correct/incorrect outcome for student i at step j on trial t, S_{ijt} is the count of previous success up to trial t, F_{ijt} is count of previous failures, up to trial t, p_{ijt} is $\Pr(X_{ijt} = 1)$. Due to PFA's linear structure, it may still yield implausible parameters e.g. estimating that practice on a skill is associated with a decrease in the probability that the learner will correctly answer a problem on that skill: To address this challenge, parameters are artificially restricted [23].

1.2 The Intervention

The Life-Saving Instruction for Emergencies (LIFE) project [24] -which is the platform this research uses- is a serious games platform intended for use with low-cost smartphones to provide training in the care of very sick neonates, particularly in low resource settings with the hope of expanding it to include other clinical care scenarios. It evolves scenario-based teaching where the components being assessed emphasise the tenets of paediatric critical care with early recognition of children who need immediate care. This is achieved by using game-like training techniques to reinforce the key steps that need to be performed by a healthcare worker to manage an emergency, an approach commonly referred to as serious gaming [25, 26]. Consequently, it follows a specific ordering of clinical care-giving algorithms with each learning task being timed. The learner starts a scenario which provides some background information to the learning task, and on each learning task, must provide input either through multiple choice questions, selection of items necessary for the learning task, or performing on-screen interactive tasks (e.g. navigating to equipment, switching on machines etc.) (Fig. 1).

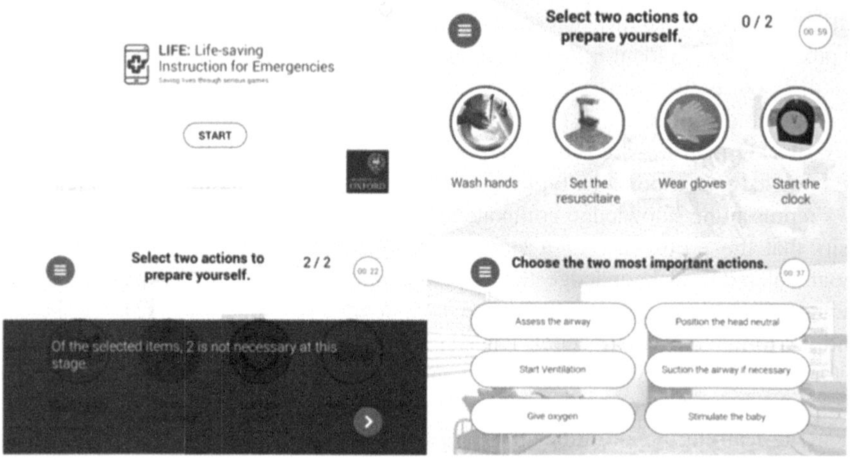

Fig. 1. Selected screenshots of LIFE application

On each incorrect attempt by the learner, standardised feedback is provided with the option of more information and the learner must repeat until they successfully respond to the question before being allowed by the smartphone application to proceed. The end of the scenario is signalled by a crying baby indicating that the baby is now breathing, with a breakdown of scores by quiz provided. The scenario model that is used is one that replicates Emergency Triage, Assessment and Treatment plus admission care i.e. ETAT+ face-to-face training approach training that is validated [27, 28]. The ETAT+ content it adapts has already been used to train over 5,000 healthcare workers and 2,000 medical students across Eastern and Southern Africa, and now East Asia [27, 28]. LIFE is meant to be accessible at scale by healthcare providers and able to function off-line on low-end smartphone devices and provide self-regulated training opportunities akin to continuous professional development at almost no cost. We don't know have much evidence about adaptive learning in this context and using these types of interventions.

The aim of this study was to analyse data from a mixed cohort of LIFE users to: (1) Explore existence of learning patterns indicative of individual differences between players; (2) Compare AFM and PFM directly on a learning dataset derived from clinical training on smartphone devices to evaluate their predictive accuracy of learners' performance in a low-income context; (3) Propose a preliminary cognitive model of learning as a basis for adaptive student-step instructional support on smartphone devices for a low-income setting based on the observed behaviours in (1) and (2). This was done to generate a working model for how adaptive learning might work as a basis of an ITSs model.

2 Methods

2.1 Study Design, Setting and Participants

This study was a retrospective observational study [29] of healthcare providers from both public and private hospitals in Kenya, in clinical cadres such as nurses, clinical officers and medical doctors, with experience levels varying from students to consultants. Participants were enrolled into the study through a combination of snowballing and convenience sampling strategy. Recruitment occurred through use of peer referrals among clinicians, private professional social network accounts, regional clinical meetings, medical conferences, medical training institutions and local hospitals. In total, 187 participants were recruited. The eligibility criteria for inclusion were that the participants had to be either in training for, or active in, clinical care. Therefore, the participants included those with experience in offering clinical care.

2.2 Study Variables, and Data Management

The LIFE version used in this study provides simulation training on the contextualised management of new-born resuscitation through a series of sixteen learning interactions that elicit responses from learners in the form of multiple-choice answers or performing interactive tasks. At the end of a successful completion of simulation tasks, the platform provides performance score feedback based on the learner's first attempt at each learning interaction. Data collection was through Android-based LIFE smartphone application, which would securely transmit a copy of anonymised data to a Google Firebase distributed database. For the purposes of the proposed analysis, the outcome of interest was specified as getting each answer correct on the first try. The variables of interest were time spent on learning task, number of previous tries (i.e. opportunities) per learning task, and whether hints had been provided for each unique try per learning task.

2.3 Statistical Methods, Missing Data, and Sensitivity Analyses

Data manipulation and statistical analyses were performed using R software's *glmer and TraMineR* packages [30–32]. Variables of interest are reported using their mean value and standard deviation. Longest Common Subsequence (LCS) cluster analysis [31] was used to explore whether there existed differentiable student learning trajectories from the sequence of their performance on LIFE content on first try. LCS was used to ensure that the conjunctive nature of LIFE content (steps to resuscitate a neonate in distress) was factored into how learning trajectories are derived. Time on task, hint usage and previous opportunities on the learning task were used as illustrative variables to explore how the derived clusters vary by these features. In the second phase of analyses, Additive Factor Model (AFM) and Performance Factor Model (PFM) were used to construct a cognitive model based upon the learning behaviours and performance data observed from LIFE, and to explore the ability of these models to make predictions on the patterns of learning by adult students using LIFE platform in low-income context and for clinical training. Finally, from the analyses we propose a model for implementation of adaptive personalised learning on smartphone devices for clinical training in low-resource settings. For the purposes of analysis, users with missing data (i.e. incomplete learning session on LIFE) were omitted. However, to evaluate whether excluding observations with missing data would bias the results, analysis of the difference in means for the features of interest between the complete and missing data group was conducted. The sensitivity of the prediction accuracy for AFM and PFM is reported as both the average classification accuracy from 10-fold cross-validation [33] of the dataset, and the area under curve (AUC) computed from training the models on 70% of the data and testing their performance on remaining 30% (test dataset). This was done to assess how well these models can distinguish between unseen learner performances on the seen ETAT+ content delivered through LIFE and evaluate if these models were overfitting the learning data.

3 Results

The data reported were observed between 23rd April 2018 and 13th October 2018. Of the 187 users recorded as having downloaded and started playing the LIFE game in this period, 77 learners (41.17%) completed a full learning session. Table 1 describes all learners who attempted to use LIFE, divided into those who had a complete learning session and those who did not complete a learning session. Due to inability to collect demographic data within the LIFE application at the time of data collection, a detailed breakdown of participants' backgrounds is not possible. LIFE training session data from non-completers of the game was not included in subsequent analyses as we are confident of minimal bias due to only using the complete dataset in the subsequent analysis given that we demonstrated non-significant differences in indicators of interest between completers and non-completers (Table 1). Only data from learners who completed a session were used in subsequent analyses. The use of the dataset with complete learning sessions was to ensure that analysis was reflective of the sequentially conjunctive nature of LIFE content (ordered steps to resuscitate a neonate in distress) and learner's actual performance across all quiz items.

Table 1. Summary statistics of pilot data from LIFE game play

Indicator	Complete*		Incomplete**		P-Value[ǂ]
	Mean	*SD*	*Mean*	*SD*	
Time spent on each question (in seconds)	12.78	9.19	14.57	10.96	0.228
Number of feedback messages provided for failed attempts per question i.e. feedback	0.26	0.44	0.32	0.46	0.369
Cumulative tries on a question across sessions i.e. Opportunities	2.18	2.72	2.62	3.4	0.328
Average performance (%)***	55.66	28.08	49.02	31.42	0.132

Note:
**Learners who completed at least one session: N = 77.*
***Learners who did not complete at least on learning session: N = 110.*
****Average performance based on number of quizzes attempted.*
[ǂ]*From evaluating if there is a difference in the mean of the values between 'Complete' and 'Incomplete' groups*

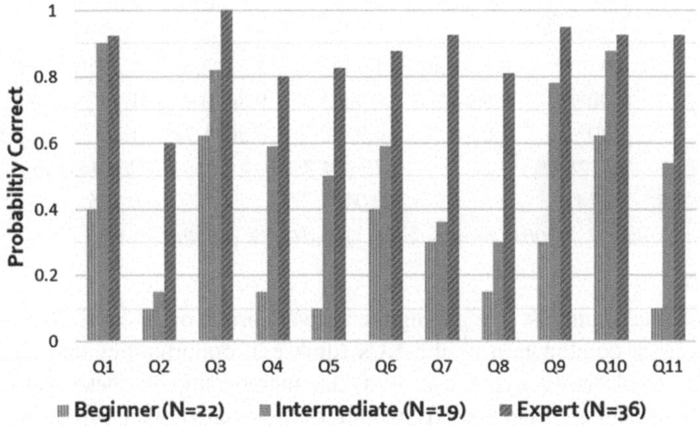

Fig. 2. Distinctive clusters of learning trajectories as defined by performance. Y axis represents proportion of answers that are correct.

From the cluster analysis, learner performance could be categorised into three distinctive groups based on inferred proficiency level to reflect individual differences (Fig. 2). The identification of the three clusters was guided by the Point Biserial Correlation, Average Silhouette Width, and Calinski-Harabasz indices [34]. From Fig. 2, quiz two -which was about the selection of equipment necessary for resuscitation- appeared problematic for all learners, with beginners performing poorly across all quizzes, while learners in the intermediate cluster struggled in quizzes between five and eight. Learners in expert category had exemplary performance that improved with subsequent quizzes. This also suggests the need to classify the 'difficulty' of the questions as well as the learners. From the variables in Table 1, there was no substantive difference in the odds of the time taken to complete a learning task between the 'beginner' and 'expert' proficiency cluster (Table 2). A possible explanation for this might be that beginners might be guessing a lot and experts know so both appear to be quick. However, the relevance of time spent on learning task for the 'intermediate' proficiency cluster was almost twice the odds of the other two. As expected, provision of feedback on incorrect attempts significantly predicted membership to the 'beginner' group unlike the other proficiency categories, with learners in this category having almost twice the odds of being provided with this type of feedback compared to the other groups (Table 2).

The effect of previous opportunities at attempting the quiz was significant across all proficiency groups, with 'expert' proficiency group associated with a better use of these opportunities than the other proficiency groups. Based upon the observed behaviours reported in Table 2, we sought to apply common cognitive models (AFM and PFM) and evaluate their ability to explain student performance in this setting.

Table 2. How learner proficiency clusters vary by learning metrics

	Beginner		Intermediate		Expert	
Predictors	*Odds Ratios*	*95% CI*	*Odds Ratios*	*95% CI*	*Odds Ratios*	*95% CI*
Task time	0.67***	0.53–0.85	1.94***	1.53–2.46	0.69**	0.52–0.90
Opportunity	0.90**	0.83–0.97	0.90**	0.84–0.97	1.17***	1.10–1.25
Feedback	1.89*	1.02–3.50	0.95	0.50–1.78	1.16	0.53–2.51
Learners, N (%)	*22 (28.6%)*		*19 (24.7%)*		*36 (46.8%)*	
Nagelkerke's R^2	*0.214*		*0.065*		*0.226*	

*Note: *** = p-value ≤ 0.001, ** = p-value ≤ 0.01, * = p-value ≤ 0.05*

The outcome of interest was getting the answer correct on first try. The independent variables were a combination of the KCs (quizzes), opportunities and cluster membership. The exploratory hypothesis was that membership in these learner clusters (beginner, intermediate, and expert) would be associated with progressively better learning rates and behaviours for utilisation of time on task, feedback and when skill difficulty and opportunities at knowledge components are considered. From the results of the AFM and PFM student modelling analyses, in general, as expected, (1) the odds of a learner completing a learning task correctly increased based on the proficiency clusters, from 'beginner' to 'expert' clusters, and (2) the time on learning task had a significant positive effect on the odds a learner in 'intermediate' cluster completing a learning task correctly given prior opportunities they had at the learning task and conditioned on skill difficulty. However, the use of feedback on incorrect attempts had a significant positive effect for increasing the odds of completing the learning task in the 'intermediate' group when the number of prior opportunities at the learning task were considered.

It is also shown to have a positive effect on the odds of learning outcome in the 'expert' group, when previous opportunities were broken down into successful and unsuccessful attempts on learning task (Table 3). Overall, across all proficiency groups, previous successes were associated with a better rate of a progress in gaining

Table 3. Results from student modelling based on learning opportunity modes

	AFM prediction		PFM prediction	
Predictors	*Estimates*	*95% CI*	*Estimates*	*95% CI*
Task Time	−0.04***	−0.06–−0.03	−0.05***	−0.07–−0.03
Feedback (Ref: No Feedback)	−0.04**	−0.07–−0.02	−0.04	−0.07–0.00
Ref: Beginner				
Intermediate	0.14***	0.11–0.17	0.16***	0.12–0.20
Expert	0.35***	0.32–0.37	0.39***	0.35–0.43
Task Time (Ref: Beginner)				
Task Time (Intermediate)	0.03 **	0.01–0.05	0.04**	0.01–0.07
Task Time (Expert)	−0.01	−0.03–0.01	0.01	−0.02–0.04
Feedback (Ref: Beginner)				
Feedback (Intermediate)	0.05*	0.01–0.09	0.04	−0.02–0.10
Feedback (Expert)	0.02	−0.02–0.06	0.06*	0.01–0.11
AIC/BIC	*2023.6/2159*		*1844.3/2044.7*	
Nagelkerke's R^2	*0.467*		*0.384*	

Note: *** = *p-value* $\leq$ *0.001,* ** = *p-value* $\leq$ *0.01,* * = *p-value* $\leq$ *0.05, N = 1663*

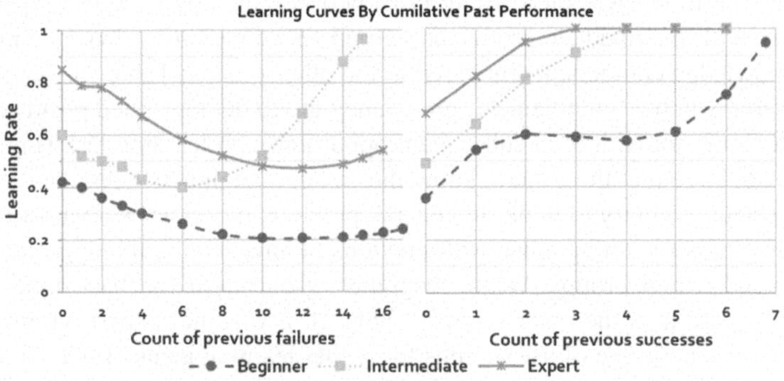

Fig. 3. LIFE learning curves from performance factor model

experience or new skills i.e. learning curves. However, there was an unexpected activation of a significant positive association from previous failures in the intermediate proficiency group, who continued to attempt learning tasks despite initial decline in learning rate, which in the long run – was associated with increasingly better learning outcomes (Fig. 3).

The evaluation of how accurate these cognitive models are in constructing and predicting the learning behaviours and performance data observed from LIFE was tested on 30% of the data with 70% being used as training set. From a 10-fold cross-validated model evaluation on the training set, AFM had an accuracy of 68% while PFM had an accuracy of 71%. When the models were tested on the 30% of the data set not used in training them, AFM had and AUC score of 77% while PFM had a score 81%. In both instances, PFM outperformed AFM in accurately predicting and distinguishing the performance from 'unseen' students on LIFE knowledge components. While the R-squared values reported paint AFM to be better than PFM for modelling LIFE learning data, the accuracy and AUC scores indicate that the AFMs might be overfitting the data more than PFM, given relatively weaker performance in prediction of learning data from 'unseen' students on 'seen' steps. Overall, it would appear that PFM model has best model performance (Table 3), minimises bias of overfitting compared to AFM, and explains learner behaviour relatively well.

4 Discussion

4.1 Summary of Findings

The aim of this study was to explore users' learning patterns from a smartphone based clinical training intervention in low-income settings and explore which student modelling approaches are best representative of the learning performance and intervention use behaviour. This was done to provide a basis for proposing a cognitive model of adaptive learning on smartphone devices for a low-income setting based on the observed learning behaviours. From analyses, based on patterns of performance on LIFE content, three proficiency learner groups were uncovered: beginner, intermediate and expert. The time spent on learning tasks between the beginner and expert groups was similar, with intermediate proficiency group spending almost twice as much time on each knowledge component compared to the other groups (Table 2). Despite initial failures, learners in the 'intermediate' proficiency group demonstrated positive learning gains in the long run with each subsequent opportunity on learning task (Fig. 2). This might be indicative that the experts know the content, beginners guess and learners in the intermediate group try to think. In general, previous successes were most influential in producing higher learning gains with previous failures having the opposite effect on 'beginner' and expert groups. While 'beginner' group used feedback hints approximately 50% more than the other groups (Table 2), it was the 'expert' group that was able to capitalise on usage of use of hints for higher learning gains (Table 3). For LIFE content delivered through smartphone, the predictive accuracy of 80% for performance factor models was moderately good [35] and is comparatively better than use of additive factor models. This would make it more appropriate in constructing cognitive model of learners who use LIFE for clinical training.

4.2 Relation to Other Studies

The emphasis of emergency care training in low resource settings to use low-dose high-frequency (LDHF) training is not new but has been recently introduced in SSA [36]. Our findings support this approach by demonstrating how learning gains are most improved where the opportunity to learn is high. This is commonly done to facilitate gains in knowledge and skills within health workers [16]. However, this study goes further by demonstrating that in general, gains in the effectiveness of high-frequency low-dose training might be linked to successful attempts in previous training sessions. Additionally, we found within health workers, a cluster of learners (intermediate and experts) who would arguably benefit more from challenging scenarios which require more time in reflection. How different clinical training intervention use metacognitive scaffolds to improve knowledge gains is not new [37–39], but hardly present in research from low resource settings [18]. Moreover, while using adaptive learning demonstrates significantly better knowledge gains than alternatives [37–39], the current LDHF training models –which are not adaptive to individual learner needs- are still the most commonly implemented models of learning, usually face-to-face, and at a very high cost [15, 16, 36]. This study further explores how the use of smartphone devices to deliver clinical training using short simulation-based learning activities, can begin to accommodate self-regulated learning over time, which have been show to optimise learning in similar settings [40].

4.3 Implications of Findings

From our findings, in low resource settings, LDHF scenario-based clinical training conditioned on skill difficulty and learner proficiency, might produce higher cumulative learning gains where previous opportunities at the learning task are successful. Additionally, such education interventions might need to accommodate learners who prefer to struggle, who take their time in making attempts, who purposefully underutilise feedback, preferring repeated unguided attempts. While this might not be true for all learners, using smartphone devices to offer LDHF clinical training is yet to adopt ways to pin-point differentiated learning preferences that might guide better instructional design. Given the limited data used for these analyses, additional qualitative work will be conducted to validate the findings. For interventions such as LIFE, where the content (neonatal resuscitation) is implicitly time-sensitive, time spent on learning task might not necessarily reflect learners' adoption of that assumption. Rather, it might be more indicative some of the learners individualised achievement goals which are arguably not linked to getting high performance in the shortest time possible but rather, taking time to reflect on the learning concept(s). This however, might not be true for all learners. From our smartphone intervention, a cognitive model for clinical training in low-resource settings using smartphone devices might be better served if it encourages repeated practice, while allowing learners to take control of how long they prefer to struggle on knowledge components, with feedback as a way out. From our findings, this would allow for learners who are activated to learn in presence of both past failures and successes respectively, while offering more support to those in most need, such as beginners.

4.4 Limitations

While AFMs and PFMs models had reasonably moderate performance on LIFE data, the relatively low accuracy of cross-validation values on figure is disconcerting. This might be due to the low numbers of observations analysed in the whole study in general, making it challenging to provide more accurate estimates. However, given that the data collected is from a pilot -arguably unique- study looking at the utility of digital learning metrics in prediction of skill-mastery for clinical training in low-income settings, it sheds light into a previously underexplored topic. This limitation can be addressed at a later stage as we continue to generate data to support the evidence base of these kinds of interventions. Further qualitative studies will be conducted to support interpretation of findings. While this study's sample is hardly generalisable, its inclusive constitution (from students to consultants, in all clinical cadres) makes it highly informative as a realistic data source on developing cognitive models for adaptive emergency care training on smartphone platforms delivered to health workers in low income settings. We are yet to find a comparable student-step data source (and studies) for this subject in this context.

5 Conclusions

In this study, we analyse the smartphone-based learning patterns for a clinical training intervention in low-income settings and explore which cognitive approaches are best representative of the learning performance and intervention use behaviour. Overall, this research found that in scenario-based learning approaches can extend low-dose high-frequency training approaches offered through smartphone devices, by targeting differentiated learner groups whose learning rates significantly vary. While in general, they all share positive learning gains from previous successes at learning tasks, among them, are those whose use of time on learning tasks in combination of presence of past failures, produced positive learning gains. Additionally, hints through feedback are utilised more by those with 'low' proficiency but produce significantly higher learning gains in those with higher proficiency. Future work will explore the comparative effectiveness on learning outcomes, of differentiated feedback conditioned on proficiency level in low-dose high-frequency training approaches delivered through smartphone devices.

Acknowledgements. Funds from Economic and Social Research Council (ESRC) awarded to TT through Oxford University, with additional funds from GCRF's Intelligent Support Project and Saving Lives at Birth supporting this work. The funders had no role in drafting or submitting this manuscript.

References

1. Anyangwe, S., Mtonga, C.: Inequities in the global health workforce: the greatest impediment to health in Sub-Saharan Africa. Int. J. Environ. Res. Public Health **4**(2), 93 (2007)
2. Sousa, A., Flores, G.L.: Transforming and scaling up health professional education and training, in policy brief on financing education of health professionals. WHO, Geneva, Switzerland (2013)
3. UNICEF, Levels and Trends in Child Mortality. Report 2013, New York, USA (2013)
4. Edgcombe, H., Paton, C., English, M.: Enhancing emergency care in low-income countries using mobile technology-based training tools. Arch Dis Child (2016)
5. Silver, L., Johnson, C.: Internet connectivity seen as having positive impact on life in Sub-Saharan Africa. Pew Research Center - Global Attitudes and Trends (2018). http://www.pewglobal.org/2018/10/09/majorities-in-sub-saharan-africa-own-mobile-phones-but-smartphone-adoption-is-modest/. Accessed 18 Dec 2018

6. Couper, I., et al.: Curriculum and training needs of mid-level health workers in Africa: a situational review from Kenya, Nigeria, South Africa and Uganda. BMC Health Serv. Res. **18**(1), 553 (2018)
7. Barteit, S., et al.: E-learning for medical education in Sub-Saharan Africa and low-resource settings. J. Med. Internet Res. **21**(1) (2019)
8. Bollinger, R., et al.: Leveraging information technology to bridge the health workforce gap. Bull. World Health Organ. **91**, 890–892 (2013)
9. Greenhalgh, T.: Computer assisted learning in undergraduate medical education. BMJ **322** (7277), 40–44 (2001)
10. Vanlehn, K.: The behavior of tutoring systems. Int. J. Artif. Intell. Educ. **16**(3), 227–265 (2006)
11. Chi, M., et al.: Instructional factors analysis: a cognitive model for multiple instructional interventions (2011)
12. VanLehn, K., Jordan, P., Litman, D.: Developing pedagogically effective tutorial dialogue tactics: experiments and a testbed. In: Workshop on Speech and Language Technology in Education (2007)
13. Cen, H., Koedinger, K., Junker, B.: Comparing two IRT models for conjunctive skills. In: Woolf, B.P., Aïmeur, E., Nkambou, R., Lajoie, S. (eds.) ITS 2008. LNCS, vol. 5091, pp. 796–798. Springer, Heidelberg (2008). https://doi.org/10.1007/978-3-540-69132-7_111
14. Pavlik Jr., P.I., Cen, H., Koedinger, K.R.: Performance Factors Analysis–A New Alternative to Knowledge Tracing. Online Submission (2009)
15. Chaudhury, S., et al.: Cost analysis of large-scale implementation of the 'Helping Babies Breathe' newborn resuscitation-training program in Tanzania. BMC Health Serv. Res. **16**(1), 681 (2016)
16. Willcox, M., et al.: Incremental cost and cost-effectiveness of low-dose, high-frequency training in basic emergency obstetric and newborn care as compared to status quo: part of a cluster-randomized training intervention evaluation in Ghana. Globalization Health **13**(1), 88 (2017)
17. Fontaine, G., et al.: Effectiveness of adaptive e-learning environments on knowledge, competence, and behavior in health professionals and students: protocol for a systematic review and meta-analysis. JMIR Res. Protoc. **6**(7) (2017)
18. Opiyo, N., English, M.: In-service training for health professionals to improve care of seriously ill newborns and children in low-income countries. Cochrane Database Syst. Rev. **5**, 1 (2015)
19. Mousavinasab, E., et al.: Intelligent tutoring systems: a systematic review of characteristics, applications, and evaluation methods. Interact. Learn. Environ., 1–22 (2018)
20. Rawlings, A.M., Tapola, A., Niemivirta, M.: Predictive effects of temperament on motivation. Int. J. Educ. Psychol. IJEP **6**(2), 148–182 (2017)
21. Vandewaetere, M., et al.: Adaptivity in educational games: including player and gameplay characteristics. Int. J. High. Educ. **2**(2), 106–114 (2013)
22. Galyardt, A., Goldin, I.: Recent-performance factors analysis. In: Educational Data Mining 2014 (2014)
23. Gong, Y., Beck, J.E., Heffernan, N.T.: How to construct more accurate student models: comparing and optimizing knowledge tracing and performance factor analysis. Int. J. Artif. Intell. Educ. **21**(1–2), 27–46 (2011)
24. University of Oxford: Life-Saving Instructions for Emergency (LIFE) (2016)
25. Bergeron, B.: Developing Serious Games. Game Development Series. Charles River Media. Inc., Massachucetts (2006)
26. Wang, R., et al.: A systematic review of serious games in training health care professionals. Simul. Healthc. **11**(1), 41–51 (2016)

27. Ayieko, P., et al.: A multifaceted intervention to implement guidelines and improve admission paediatric care in Kenyan District Hospitals: a cluster randomised trial. PLOS Med. **8**(4), e1001018 (2011)
28. Irimu, G., et al.: Developing and introducing evidence based clinical practice guidelines for serious illness in Kenya. Arch. Dis. Child. **93**(9), 799–804 (2008)
29. Mann, C.: Observational research methods. Research design II: cohort, cross sectional, and case-control studies. Emerg. Med. J. **20**(1), 54–60 (2003)
30. R Core Team: A Language and Environment for Statistical Computing. R Foundation for Statistical Computing, Vienna, Austria (2013)
31. Gabadinho, A., et al.: Analyzing and visualizing state sequences in R with TraMineR. J. Stat. Softw. **40**(4), 1–37 (2011)
32. Bates, D., et al.: Fitting linear mixed-effects models using lme4. arXiv preprint arXiv:1406. 5823 (2014)
33. Kohavi, R.: A study of cross-validation and bootstrap for accuracy estimation and model selection. In: IJCAI, Montreal, Canada (1995)
34. Desgraupes, B.: Clustering indices. University of Paris Ouest-Lab Modal'X, vol. 1, p. 34 (2013)
35. Khajah, M., Lindsey, R.V., Mozer, M.C.: How deep is knowledge tracing? arXiv preprint arXiv:1604.02416 (2016)
36. Atukunda, I.T., Conecker, G.A.: Effect of a low-dose, high-frequency training approach on stillbirths and early neonatal deaths: a before-and-after study in 12 districts of Uganda. Lancet Glob. Health **5**, S12 (2017)
37. Feyzi-Behnagh, R., et al.: Metacognitive scaffolds improve self-judgments of accuracy in a medical intelligent tutoring system. Instr. Sci. **42**(2), 159–181 (2014)
38. Veredas, F.J., et al.: A web-based e-learning application for wound diagnosis and treatment. Comput. Methods Programs Biomed. **116**(3), 236–248 (2014)
39. Wong, V., et al.: Adaptive tutorials versus web-based resources in radiology: a mixed methods comparison of efficacy and student engagement. Acad. Radiol. **22**(10), 1299–1307 (2015)
40. van Houten-Schat, M.A., et al.: Self-regulated learning in the clinical context: a systematic review. Med. Educ. **52**(10), 1008–1015 (2018)

Unsupervised Automatic Detection of Learners' Programming Behavior

Anis Bey[1(✉)], Mar Pérez-Sanagustín[1,2], and Julien Broisin[1]

[1] Institut de Recherche en Informatique de Toulouse, IRIT, Université Paul Sabatier Toulouse III, Toulouse, France
{anis.bey,mar.perez-sanagustin,julien.broisin}@irit.fr
[2] Pontificia Universidad Católica de Chile, Santiago, Chili

Abstract. Programming became one of the most demanded professional skills. This reality is driving practitioners to search out better approaches for figuring out how to code and how to support learning programming processes. Prior works have focused on discovering, identifying, and characterizing learning programming patterns that better relate to success. Researchers propose qualitative and supervised analytic methods based on trace data from coding tasks. However, these methods are limited for automatically identifying students in difficulties without human-intervention support. The main goal of this paper is to introduce a three-phase process and a case study in which unsupervised clustering techniques are used for automatically identifying learners' programming behavior. The case study takes place in a Shell programming course in which we analyzed data from 100 students to extract learners' behavioral trajectories that positively correlate with success. As a result, we identified: (1) a list of features that improve the quality of the automatic learners' profiles identification process, and (2) some students' behavioral trajectories correlated with their performance at the final exam.

Keywords: Learning programming · Educational data mining · Unsupervised analysis methods · Learners' behavior · Learning analytics

1 Introduction

The demand for programmers over the last decade has led to a significant increase of programming learning initiatives. These efforts have resulted in, for example, policies to integrate programming as part of high school curriculum (e.g., in France [1]), or national training courses to update programming skills of professionals (e.g., in Finland [2–4]). But widening the training sector also means supporting practitioners regarding the variety of problems and situations they have to deal with when teaching and learning programming. So, in the recent years,

M. Scheffel et al. (Eds.): EC-TEL 2019, LNCS 11722, pp. 69–82, 2019.
https://doi.org/10.1007/978-3-030-29736-7_6

there has been a growing interest in the research community to better understand how learning programming occurs and when to (automatically) intervene for supporting the various stakeholders in this process.

Reiser et al. claim that automatic systems to help teachers better understand student's programming behavior could have profound educational implications [12]. Based on this idea, and thanks to the vast amount of data collected through programming learning environments, research on learning programming have moved from subjectively anecdotally-oriented, to empirically-based and data-driven methods [22]. These methods use data collected as students work on coding problems to study their behavior and inform teaching interventions. Some researchers have focused on learners' trace data to automatically analyze their coding behavior and to propose a qualitative categorization of their programming profiles [8]. Recent prior works go further, and use educational data mining for proposing models that predict successful coding strategies [9], programming problem-solving time [20], or students' performance [21].

In all these works, researchers propose indicators and models derived from the analysis of students' trace data while coding open-ended programming exercises, such as compilation errors or time between compilations. However, the solutions proposed to characterize students' programming behavior so far entail some limitations when used with datasets from other learning scenarios with large groups of students or extended periods of time. First, current approaches proposing automatic methods for categorizing learners' programming behavior require human intervention at some steps. In some cases, they use supervised machine learning algorithms that require a human to discriminate good or bad learners' classification [20,21]. In other cases, they assume qualitative learners' categorization in prior steps [9]. And second, current solutions relating programming behavior to performance use unit tests [9]. These approaches only apply to learning scenarios in which teachers provide unit tests, which is far from being always the case. Thus, new unsupervised approaches are required to categorize and classify learners' coding behavior in order to provide teachers and students with actionable information to support them in their tasks.

In this paper, we introduce a three-phase process and a case study in which unsupervised clustering methods are used to automatically identify learners' programming behavior. The case study takes place in a Shell programming course with data from 100 students, and has been conducted to answer the three following research questions: (1) What behavioral-based features are needed for a reliable unsupervised and automatic identification of students' programming profiles? (2) Do students change their behavior over the learning process and, if they do, what are the behavioral trajectories they follow? (3) What representative behavioral trajectories can be identified, and how they relate to students' performance?

The next section reviews prior initiatives investigating learners' programming behaviors, and focuses on methods and features used for identification of programming profiles, but also on limitations introduced by existing qualitative and supervised approaches. Section 3 introduces the three phases of the analytical process based on clustering algorithms to discover sequences of behaviors that are representative of learners' behavioral trajectories. The learning context of our case study is presented in Sect. 4 before results are discussed. The impact of our proposed process on new intelligent capabilities that can be integrated into existing programming environments represent the concluding remarks of the paper.

2 State of the Art

This research expands upon previous attempts to understand students' behavior using trace data recorded while coding exercises. In recent literature, some researchers have started to explore mechanisms for automatic trace data analysis in order to analyze student programs and characterize their behavior accordingly. For example, Perkins et al. [11] analyzed data from several students' programs to classify novice programmers as *stoppers* and *movers* based on the strategy they choose when facing a problem. By mining snapshots from code repositories, Berland and Martin [14] found that novice students developed successful program code by following one of two progressions *planner* and *tinkerer*. Planners found success by carefully structuring programs over time, and tinkerers found success by accreting programs over time. Also, Blikstein [8,13,15,16] used thousands of time-stamped snapshots of students' code and found markedly diverse strategies between experienced and novice programmers. These authors propose an automatic approach for analyzing students' behavior and classify them into: *intellects*, students that run tests less frequently, as they are skilled and confident; *thinkers* run tests more frequently to receive early feedback regarding progress; and *probers* are students that run tests most frequently, as they experience difficulty. However, their classification is based on a qualitative categorization to split students based only on the total number of unit tests run by each student and, therefore, limited when an unsupervised analysis of the data is desired.

These studies rely on different clustering methods that facilitate grouping data into homogeneous clusters that can be further interpreted. Hierarchical and partitioning methods such as k-means are the ones typically employed. However, these methods are heuristic, and not based on formal models, so usually they are randomly initialized. As a consequence, different runs of the same algorithm will often yield different results for the same dataset, which makes heuristic classification approaches unreliable for unsupervised classification methods.

Other researchers build upon these previous studies to define features for describing students' behavioral patterns and, in some cases, identify how certain behaviors correlate to success so that appropriate interventions can be applied. Table 1 shows a summary of the features used in prior works organized into five categories: (1) Time, (2) Execution, (3) Compilation, (4) Unit tests and (5) Code edition. As we can observe, there are lots of features that are common in different works to identify students' programming behaviors. Depending on the context of application and the dataset available, researchers choose and combine different features to describe students' behavior. For example, Jadud [10] used compilation features to better understand how students progress through a programming task. Kato et al. [20] used features from different categories including time, execution and compilation to analyze programming behaviors. The purpose of this study was to present some features of students' behavior to teaching assistants to improve the effectiveness of their support. In another work, Wang et al. [21] represented students' programming knowledge using deep learning methods. Their code edition-based approach uses indicators about abstract syntax trees to learn nuanced representations of students' knowledge, and predicts future student performance. Sharma et al. [9] discovered the programming strategies used by students for coding exercises with different difficulty levels, and searched for any relation between these strategies and the success in solving the coding tasks. These authors used indicators from students' testing behavior reflecting the time and effort differences between two successive unit test runs to predict success in the coding exercises.

Table 1. Description of the main features used in the literature for detection of learners' programming behavior.

Categories	Extracted features
Time	Time between two compilations (Avg.) [8,20]; Time between two executions (Avg.) [9,20]; Time difference edit (Avg.) [9]
Execution	Number of submissions [18]; Number of executions [20]
Compilation	Number of compilation errors [8,10,19]; Compilation success [8,10]; Percentage of compilation errors [19]; Number of compilations [10,20]; Number of errors [10,20]; Number of same errors [10,20]
Unit tests	Number of test runs [9]; Improvement in unit test success [9]; Improvement in errors [9]; Number of passed unit tests [9]; First test run [9]
Code edition	Size edit [8,9]; Number of lines [18]; Number of nodes per AST (Abstract Syntax Tree) [18,21]
Others	Errors times and same errors times [20]

Current state of the art on analysis of students' trace data provides insights on what features and methods are considered to detect behavioral patterns. However, current proposals are limited when looking for mechanisms to automatically detect and classify learners' behavior. First, most of the features and methods used in prior works to characterize learners' behavior can be typically obtained from trace data records of any programming platform. However, data and methods for features extraction are hard-bounded with the learning context, and are not directly applicable to datasets characterized by different properties and extracted from other learning scenarios. Second, most of these studies rely on features of code correctness based on unit tests. But units tests are not always available, as their production requires significant efforts from instructors.

And third, most of studies use methods that explain students' strategies based on qualitative approaches that require human intervention.

Therefore, in order to propose approaches based on unsupervised models able to identify and classify learners' behavior automatically, more research on behavioral features and classification methods is needed. This study contributes with an analytical process and a case study that characterize and classify students' programming behaviors and relate them to success. Our aim is to propose a solution based on behavioral features as semantic-less as possible in order to facilitate its application in other contexts and promote replication studies.

3 Unsupervised Automatic Detection of Learners' Programming Behavior

In this section we present the unsupervised process proposed for automatically characterizing learners' programming behavior. This process consists of three phases of analysis. The objective of phase 1 is to classify students into categories according to their most meaningful behavioral profile. Phase 2 identifies learners' behavioral trajectory all along the course according to the behavioral profiles identified in the first phase. Finally, phase 3 serves for identifying the trajectories that are the most representative of students' behavior. This section describes the analytic procedures in each phase and shows how they are applied to a dataset collected from a course in Shell programming.

It is important to notice that the process we propose stands on the assumption that human behaviors form clusters naturally. Despite students' differences in personalities and learning habits, our approach assumes that their behaviors are not completely heterogeneous and can be organized in groups of similar patterns. This assumption restricts our proposal to datasets characterized by a high clustering tendency, i.e., to datasets containing meaningful clusters.

3.1 Application Dataset

The dataset was obtained from a three-week course on the essential of Shell programming with 100 students registered. Students in this course do not have prior knowledge of Shell programming, but they master basic operations to use a computer system. The course includes theoretical sessions and two hands-on sessions of 90 min per week. In these hands-on sessions, students are asked to submit between 6 and 8 exercises on the generation of Shell scripts of different difficulty levels using a Debian distribution as operating system. At the end of the course, students pass a practical exam to evaluate their skills in Shell scripting. Teachers evaluate each exam manually and assign a score in a scale between 0 and 10, where 0 is the lowest mark and 10 the maximum.

The dataset selected for this study includes the students' scripts produced during the six hands-on sessions of the course. Each time students save the modifications of their Shell script, a copy of the script together with its timestamp and a student identification is stored. At the end, we obtain a dataset including, for each students' submission: (1) the source code that has been submitted, (2) the timestamp of the submission, and (3) the identifier of the student.

Our final dataset comprises 13148 scripts produced by 100 students. Descriptive statistics about the number of submissions per week are illustrated in Table 2. In addition to the dataset of submissions, we also assign students to three different categories according to their performance score at the practical exam: Low ($score < 5$; n = 39), Medium ($5 \leq score < 7$; n = 33) and High ($score \geq 7$; n = 28). As we show later on, this performance score is used for validation purposes only (see Sect. 4.3).

Table 2. Statistics about the number of submissions per week extracted from analyzing the activity of the 100 students that we considered for the analysis.

Weeks	#Submissions	Max.	Min.	Mean	Standard deviation
1	2909	93	4	29	17.5
2	5731	212	6	57.3	33.4
3	4508	223	7	45	34

3.2 Phase 1: Identification of Programming Profiles

This phase results in the characterization of students' profiles according to their programming behavior. The first step for this categorization relies on evaluating whether the dataset follows a high clustering tendency. In this study, we used the Hopkins statistic (see Sect. 4.1).

The second step consists in analyzing the dataset to extract the features that characterize students' programming activity. These features will later be used for defining a learner model and apply clustering methods in order to identify students' programming behavioral profiles. For defining these features, we took as a basis some features defined in prior works (i.e., number of submissions, average time between two submissions, average number of changes, and percentage of syntactical errors). However, prior work shows that these features are not always enough to produce significant results, as clusters often overlap. In particular, we observed that the average time between two submissions, as well as the average number of changes, do not reflect a reliable distribution of our dataset. Thus, we carried out a deeper analysis to add new features that would enhanced our clustering methods. Two new features were obtained from this process: the standard deviation of the average time between two submissions, and the standard deviation of the average number of changes in the code. The standard deviation measures the amount of variation, or dispersion, of a set of data values from the mean of these values. In our case, this information is useful to separate two distributions having the same mean but different dispersion of data, and to add a new dimension into the behavioral features.

As a result, we defined the following list of features describing students' programming activity:

- **Number of Submissions** represents the number of submissions made by a student.
- **Average time between two submissions** represents the average time (in seconds) spent by a student between two submissions.
- **Average number of changes** represents the average number of changes within the source code between two submissions; it is expressed in terms of tokens added or deleted.
- **Percentage of syntactical errors** represents the percentage of submissions that have syntactical errors (i.e., that cannot be executed).
- **Time standard deviation** represents the standard deviation of the average time between two submissions.
- **Code standard deviation** represents the standard deviation of the average number of changes.

Once the features are defined, we used them to characterize the students' behavior for each week. Prior works investigating learners' programming behavior often model learners as a single vector composed of various features (see Sect. 2), and compute the values of these features from the whole set of data [9,20]. The originality of our approach relies on considering not only the features along the whole course, but also on investigating how these features change each week. In other words, since our objective is to identify not only the programming profiles of students, but also their behavioral trajectory all along the course, we model learners' behavior as a set of vectors according to the course duration: the number of vectors matches with the number of weeks of the course. Here we make the assumption, supported by the divergent statistics of Table 2, that a period of several weeks is sufficient for learners to develop their programming skills and abilities, and thus to change their programming behavior. Therefore, in our case study, learners are modeled by three vectors describing students during the first, second and third week of the course respectively.

Finally, as a third step of this first phase, we applied a model-based clustering algorithm that allows to identify some students' programming behaviors. Model-based clustering algorithms consider the data as coming from a distribution which is a mixture of two or more clusters [5,6], and use soft assignment where each data point has a probability of belonging to each cluster. Groups are determined by the expectation-maximization (EM) algorithm for maximum likelihood, with initial values resulting from k-means clustering. Models are compared using an approximation to the Bayes factor based on the Bayesian information criterion (BIC). The number of clusters and the clustering method are solved simultaneously by choosing the best model.

3.3 Phase 2: Identification of Students' Behavioral Trajectories

The second phase of the process aims to extract a learner model according to the meaningful behaviors identified in phase 1. In this model, students are represented as a vector whose length matches with the number of weeks of the course, and where each element describes student in terms of behaviors identified in phase 1. In this way, we extract the learner's behavioral trajectory all along the course and express how learners change their programming behavior over time. That is, our learner model express the behavioral trajectories (or sequences of behaviors) through the whole course. In our case study, learners are modeled as a 3-dimensional vector where the three elements describe the behavior of the student during the first, second and third week of the course respectively.

This process does not require any specific mining methods. It is completed by exploring the clusters resulting from the first phase to retrieve, for a given student, the location of the various vectors of features built in phase 1.

3.4 Phase 3: Identification of Significant Behavioral Trajectories

Starting from the learner model emerged in phase 2 expressing students' programming trajectories, the objective of the last phase is twofold: to identify whether some trajectories are correlated to the performance score, and to identify the most representative sequences of low and high performers.

This phase implements a hierarchical clustering method where each trajectory is initially considered as a single-element cluster. At each step of the algorithm, the two most similar clusters are combined into a new bigger cluster, and this procedure is iterated until all points are members of one single big cluster. Hierarchical and partitional algorithms rely on a similarity measure to judge whether two objects (or trajectories) should be clustered together. The result of the clustering process is thus strongly related to this metric. We chose the Optimal Matching metric [7], as it aims to assess the dissimilarity of time-ordered arrays of tokens; in our approach, arrays of tokens are implemented by learners' behavioral trajectories over time built in phase 2.

4 Applying the Process with a Real Dataset

This section presents the results of applying the proposed process to the dataset described in Sect. 3.1.

4.1 Phase1: Identification of Programming Profiles

Firstly, we evaluated the clustering tendency of our dataset in order to see whether the process is applicable. For that, we used the Hopkins (H) statistic methods [17], which measures the probability that a given dataset is generated by a uniform data distribution. Results revealed that it is highly clusterable, as $H = 0.10$ is far below the threshold 0.5. Secondly, we created the files representing the features characterizing the students' programming activity (see Sect. 3.2). And thirdly, we applied the mixture Gaussian Clustering algorithm.

From this process, three significant clusters of programming behaviors were identified. Let us note that we do not affect explicit labels to each behavior in order to avoid semantic biases. Indeed, works from the literature are used to give explicit labels to clusters they identify, but this qualitative labelling introduces misinterpretations and confusions.

The values of the features for each cluster are exposed in Table 3. Cluster 1 reflects students who submit frequently a large number of submissions with short time intervals between submissions, and who make irregular changes in their source code characterized by the most important number of syntactical errors. Cluster 2 represents students who do not submit an important number of submissions, as they spend more time to make significant changes in their source code. Students of this cluster make however a significant number of syntactical errors as well. Finally, Cluster 3 reveals students who submit the lowest number of submissions even if they need a short period of time between two submissions. This behavior can be explained by students who spend a significant period of time to think about the design of their program before submitting the first production. Students of this cluster make minor changes in their source code, which is also characterized by a significant number of syntactical errors.

Table 3. Mean and standard deviation of the features for the three clusters.

Clust.	Size	Nb. sub.	Avg. time	Avg. chg.	%Errors	Time SD	Code SD
1	113	63.8 ± 38.5	62.4 ± 23.0	6.6 ± 2.4	52.3 ± 16.6	84.8 ± 36.0	12.4 ± 5.2
2	24	38.0 ± 29.1	114.2 ± 62.1	16.5 ± 16.3	48.9 ± 18.2	208.5 ± 114.3	31.8 ± 43.4
3	163	30.9 ± 15.0	70.3 ± 28.2	2.7 ± 1.1	48.5 ± 21.5	98.5 ± 48.1	4.9 ± 2.3

To validate the clustering results we run ANOVA test using clusters as the independent variable, and the features as dependent variables once ANOVA assumptions were verified with Levene's test for homogeneity of variance and the Shapiro-Wilk. Results of these tests are reported as follows:

- Significant difference on the number of submissions ($F[2, 297] = 48.66, p < .001$): post-hoc pairwise comparisons (PhPC) show that Cluster 1 has a higher number of submissions than Cluster 2 and Cluster 3, while there is no significant difference between Cluster 2 and Cluster 3.
- Significant difference on the average time spent between two submissions ($F[2, 297] = 28.5, p < .001$): post-hoc pairwise comparisons show that Cluster 2 spends regularly more time before submitting compared to Cluster 1 and Cluster 3, while Cluster 3 spends a little more time than Cluster 1. These differences are confirmed by PhPC computed on time standard deviation ($F[2, 297] = 55.6, p < .001$).
- Significant difference on the average number of changes between two submissions ($F[2, 297] = 92.56, p < .001$): post-hoc pairwise comparisons show clearly that Cluster 2 makes important changes compared to Cluster 1 and Cluster 3, while Cluster 1 makes little more changes than Cluster 3. Here also, these results are aligned with the PhPC computed on code standard deviation ($F[2, 297] = 51.4, p < .001$).

- No significant difference on the percentage of syntactical errors ($F[2, 297] = 1.27, p = 0.28$): post-hoc pairwise comparisons show that Cluster 1 commit more syntactical errors than Cluster 2.

4.2 Phase 2: Identification of Students' Behavioral Trajectories

The objective of this phase is to understand how learners move from one behavioral cluster to another over time. The three clusters of behaviors identified above offer the opportunity to model each student through their behavioral trajectory over the three weeks of the course. In addition, using the categories of the academic performance score, we are able to build the different behavioral trajectories of high, mid and low performing students illustrated in Fig. 1.

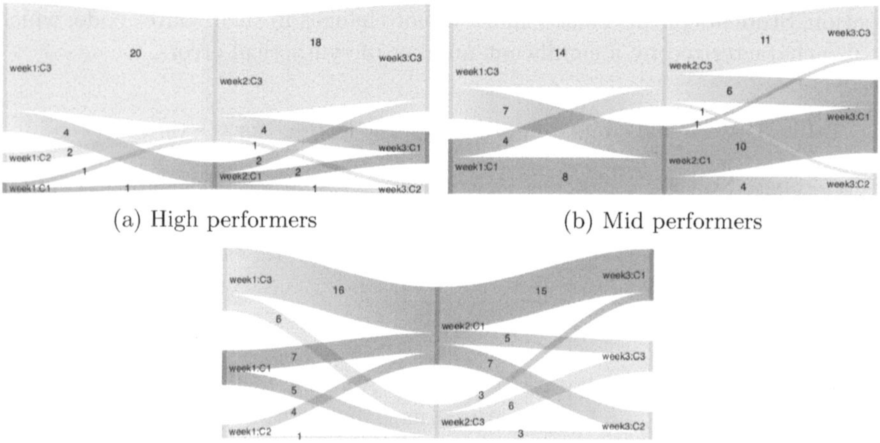

(a) High performers

(b) Mid performers

(c) Low performers

Fig. 1. Students' behavioral trajectories during the course.

Figure 1 shows that learners are used to change their programming behavior over the duration of the course, and confirms the hypothesis we considered in Sect. 3.2. Behavioral trajectories are heterogeneous within a group of students, and especially chaotic regarding the low performers. The last phase thus investigates whether typical trajectories of high, mid and low performers can be discovered so as to better characterize and identify these groups of students.

4.3 Phase 3: Identification of Significant Behavioral Trajectories

The objective here is to identify patterns of behavioral sequences that are representative of learners' behavior. To this aim, the clustering algorithms described in Sect. 3.4 are applied to the set of sequences of Fig. 1. According to the inertia and interpretability of the results, two significant clusters emerge. To avoid confusion with the behavioral clusters identified in the first phase, the clusters of sequences are called *seq-clusters* in the remaining of the paper.

The seq-clusters have been validated with the performance score. Table 4 exposes the descriptive statistics of both seq-clusters according to this variable, and reports significant differences. Results show that Seq-cluster 1 tends to represent low performing students ($M = 4.2, SD = 2.2$). Seq-cluster 2 tends to represent high performers ($M = 6.5, SD = 2.6$).

Table 4. Statistics of the seq-clusters regarding the academic performance score.

Seq-cluster	Min.	1st Qu.	Median	Mean	3rd Qu.	Max.
1	0.0	2.5	4.0	4.2	6.0	10.0
2	0.0	5.2	7.0	6.5	8.5	10.0

To strengthen the seq-clustering results, we built the contingency table between the two clusters of sequences and the categories of performance score. Table 5 shows that both seq-clusters are well discriminated: 82% of low performers are classified in Seq-cluster 1, whereas 78.5% of high performers are classified in Seq-cluster 2. However, since there are two seq-clusters only, 45.4% and 54.6% of mid performers are classified in Seq-cluster 1 and Seq-cluster 2 respectively. This might be due to the fact that mid performers sometimes behave as high performing students, and sometimes as low performers.

Table 5. Contingency table.

Seq-cluster	Size	Ground truth		
		High	Medium	Low
1	53	6	15	**32**
2	47	**22**	18	7

The two seq-clusters then allow to retrieve the behavioral trajectories of students classified in each seq-cluster; these sequences, together with their frequency and representativeness, are reported in Table 6.

4.4 Discussion of the Results

We can notice that the most significant trajectory of Seq-cluster 2, which represents the behavior of 68% of the students included into this seq-cluster, is the sequence *Cluster* 3 $\rightarrow$ *Cluster* 3 $\rightarrow$ *Cluster* 3. This suggests that successful students may spend time to think about the solution of a problem before submitting the first version of their program, and then make regularly minor changes

Table 6. Frequency of trajectories for each seq-cluster.

	Seq-cluster 1			Seq-cluster 2		
	Sequence	Frequency	%	Sequence	Frequency	%
	$\mathbf{C3 \rightarrow C1 \rightarrow C1}$	**16**	**30.19**	$\mathbf{C3 \rightarrow C3 \rightarrow C3}$	**32**	**68.09**
	$\mathbf{C1 \rightarrow C1 \rightarrow C1}$	**9**	**16.98**	$\mathbf{C3 \rightarrow C3 \rightarrow C1}$	**5**	**10.64**
	$\mathbf{C1 \rightarrow C3 \rightarrow C1}$	**7**	**13.21**	$C3 \rightarrow C3 \rightarrow C2$	3	6.38
	$\mathbf{C3 \rightarrow C1 \rightarrow C3}$	**6**	**11.32**	$C2 \rightarrow C3 \rightarrow C3$	2	4.26
	$C3 \rightarrow C1 \rightarrow C2$	5	9.43	$C2 \rightarrow C1 \rightarrow C2$	2	4.26
	$C1 \rightarrow C1 \rightarrow C2$	5	9.43	$C2 \rightarrow C1 \rightarrow C1$	2	4.26
	$C1 \rightarrow C1 \rightarrow C3$	2	3.77	$C2 \rightarrow C3 \rightarrow C1$	1	2.13
	$C1 \rightarrow C3 \rightarrow C2$	2	3.77			
	$C1 \rightarrow C3 \rightarrow C3$	1	1.89			
Total		53	100.00		47	100.00

in their source code. Moreover, these students adopt this behavior for the whole duration of the course, which aligns with prior studies showing that high performers spend more time on their programs [19]. On the other hand, students of Seq-cluster 1 often adopt the behavior of Cluster 1. According to the characteristics of this cluster, those students regularly execute a lot of submissions without spending a lot of time between submissions.

From a more general perspective, our results show that the four first sequences of Seq-cluster 1 already represent the behavior of 71.70% of the students in this cluster. Also, 78.73% of the students in Seq-cluster 2 follow two particular trajectories.

5 Conclusion and Future Works

The process introduced in this paper uses unsupervised methods for automatically identifying students' programming behavior. The process comprises three phases, none of them requiring human intervention or a priori qualitative classification of data. Learner models used in the clustering algorithms extend those of the literature with new behavioral features. Also, learners are represented as a multi-dimensional data structure that describes their behavior over time in the form of trajectories. We showed how this process can be successfully applied to a dataset gathered from an authentic learning context. Results are encouraging, as the proposed process is able to automatically identify behavioral trajectories which tend to lead to high or low performance. Therefore, our findings have important implications for understanding how students behave when they learn programming.

This outcome opens up new opportunities to enrich programming systems with new analytics, providing insights about learners' behavior to both teachers and students. As an example, an intelligent tutoring system could suggest to a student following the behavior of Cluster 1 (i.e., a behavior not adopted by high performers when they start programming) at the end of the first week to think deeper about the solution of the problem instead of executing numerous submissions. Also, visualizations for instructors could provide them with awareness about the individual and/or collective behavioral trajectories of learners so as to support pedagogical decision-making. Learning programming tools such as Algo+ [23] or Lab4CE [24] could implement this approach to enhance users' educational support.

Some limitations of our approach will be investigated in further studies. The first limitation is the missclassification of mid performers. This limitation is inherent to this type of students, who have a *fuzzy* behavior. Second, in order to evaluate the context-agnostic characteristic of the process as well as its genericity, additional analysis with datasets from other learning contexts have to be carried out. A study with C and C++ MOOC courses are planed for next fall to this aim. Other analysis with larger datasets, and deeper exploration of the results to find out additional behavioral features are future research avenues of this work.

References

1. https://www.onisep.fr/Choisir-mes-etudes/Au-lycee-au-CFA/Au-lycee-general-et-technologique/L-informatique-au-lycee-cap-sur-plusieurs-specialites. Accessed 25 June 2019
2. www.elementsofai.com. Accessed 25 June 2019
3. https://www.helsinki.fi/en/news/data-science-news/finland-is-challenging-the-entire-world-to-understand-ai-by-offering-a-completely-free-online-course-initiative-got-1-of-the-finnish-population-to. Accessed 25 June 2019
4. https://www.politico.eu/article/finland-one-percent-ai-artificial-intelligence-courses-learning-training/. Accessed 25 June 2019
5. Fraley, C., Raftery, A.E.: Model-based clustering, discriminant analysis, and density estimation. J. Am. Stat. Assoc. **97**(458), 611–631 (2002)
6. Fraley, C., Raftery, A.E., Murphy, T.B., Scrucca, L.: mclust Version 4 for R: Normal Mixture Modeling for Model-Based Clustering, Classification, and Density Estimation. Technical Report (2012)
7. Abbott, A., Tsay, A.: Sequence analysis and optimal matching methods in sociology: review and prospect. Sociol. Methods Res. **29**(1), 3–33 (2000)
8. Blikstein, P.: Using learning analytics to assess students' behavior in open-ended programming tasks. In: Proceedings of the 1st International Conference on Learning Analytics and Knowledge, pp. 110–116. ACM (2011)
9. Sharma, K., Mangaroska, K., Trætteberg, H., Lee-Cultura, S., Giannakos, M.: Evidence for programming strategies in university coding exercises. In: Pammer-Schindler, V., Pérez-Sanagustín, M., Drachsler, H., Elferink, R., Scheffel, M. (eds.) EC-TEL 2018. LNCS, vol. 11082, pp. 326–339. Springer, Cham (2018). https://doi.org/10.1007/978-3-319-98572-5_25
10. Jadud, M.C.: Methods and tools for exploring novice compilation behaviour. In: Proceedings of the Second International Workshop on Computing Education Research, pp. 73–84. ACM (2006)
11. Perkins, D.N., Hancock, C., Hobbs, R., Martin, F., Simmons, R.: Conditions of learning in novice programmers. J. Educ. Comput. Res. **2**(1), 37–55 (1986)

12. Reiser, B., Anderson, J., Farrell, R.: Dynamic student modelling in an intelligent tutor for LISP programming. In: Proceedings of the 9th International Joint Conferences on Artificial Intelligence, pp. 8–14 (1985)
13. Blikstein, P., Worsley, M., Piech, C., Sahami, M., Cooper, S., Koller, D.: Proramming pluralism: using learning analytics to detect patterns in the learning of computer programming. J. Learn. Sci. **23**(4), 561–599 (2014)
14. Berland, M., Martin, T.: Clusters and patterns of novice programmers. In: The Meeting of the American Educational Research Association (2011)
15. Blikstein, P., Worsley, M.: Learning analytics: assessing constructionist learning using machine learning. In: American Educational Research Association Annual Meeting (2011)
16. Blikstein, P.: An Atom is known by the company it keeps. Unpublished Ph.D. dissertation, Northwestern University, Evanston (2008)
17. Lawson, R.G., Jurs, P.C.: New index for clustering tendency and its application to chemical problems. J. Chem. Inf. Comput. Sci. **30**(1), 36–41 (1990)
18. Nguyen, A., Piech, C., Huang, J., Guibas, L.: Codewebs: scalable homework search for massive open online programming courses. In: Proceedings of the 23rd International Conference on World Wide Web, pp. 491–502. ACM (2014)
19. Tabanao, E.S., Rodrigo, M.M.T., Jadud, M.C.: Predicting at-risk novice Java programmers through the analysis of online protocols. In: Proceedings of the 7th International Workshop on Computing Education Research, pp. 85–92. ACM (2011)
20. Kato, T., Kambayashi, Y., Terawaki, Y., Kodama, Y.: Analysis of students' behaviors in programming exercises using deep learning. In: Uskov, V.L., Howlett, R.J., Jain, L.C. (eds.) SEEL 2017. SIST, vol. 75, pp. 38–47. Springer, Cham (2018). https://doi.org/10.1007/978-3-319-59451-4_4
21. Wang, L., Sy, A., Liu, L., Piech, C.: Learning to represent student knowledge on programming exercises using deep learning. In: Proceedings of the 10th International Conference on Educational Data Mining, pp. 324–329 (2017)
22. Ihantola, P., et al.: Educational data mining and learning analytics in programming: literature review and case studies. In: Proceedings of the 2015 ITiCSE on Working Group Reports, pp. 41–63. ACM (2015)
23. Bey, A., Jermann, P., Dillenbourg, P.: A comparison between two automatic assessment approaches for programming: an empirical study on MOOCs. Educ. Technol. Soc. **21**(2), 259–272 (2018)
24. Broisin, J., Venant, R., Vidal, P.: Lab4CE: a remote laboratory for computer education. Int. J. Artif. Intell. Educ. **27**(1), 154–180 (2017)

"Mirror, mirror on my search...": Data-Driven Reflection and Experimentation with Search Behaviour

Angela Fessl[1(✉)], Aitor Apaolaza[2], Ann Gledson[2], Viktoria Pammer-Schindler[1,3], and Markel Vigo[2]

[1] Know-Center GmbH, Inffeldgasse 13, 8010 Graz, Austria
{afessl,vpammer}@know-center.at
[2] School of Computer Science, University of Manchester, Manchester, UK
{aitor.apaolaza,ann.gledson,markel.vigo}@manchester.ac.uk
[3] Institute for Interactive Systems and Data Science, Graz University of Technology, Graz, Austria

Abstract. Searching on the web is a key activity for working and learning purposes. In this work, we aimed to motivate users to reflect on their search behaviour, and to experiment with different search functionalities. We implemented a widget that logs user interactions within a search platform, mirrors back search behaviours to users, and prompts users to reflect about it. We carried out two studies to evaluate the impact of such widget on search behaviour: in Study 1 (N = 76), participants received screenshots of the widget including reflection prompts while in Study 2 (N = 15), a maximum of 10 search tasks were conducted by participants over a period of two weeks on a search platform that contained the widget. Study 1 shows that reflection prompts induce meaningful insights about search behaviour. Study 2 suggests that, when using a novel search platform for the first time, those participants who had the widget prioritised search behaviours over time. The incorporation of the widget into the search platform after users had become familiar with it, however, was not observed to impact search behaviour. While the potential to support un-learning of routines could not be shown, the two studies suggest the widget's usability, perceived usefulness, potential to induce reflection and potential to impact search behaviour.

Keywords: Search behaviour · Reflective learning · Activity log data analysis

1 Introduction

Searching the Web has become a routine behaviour for workers and learners. However, users still experience problems in finding the information they are looking for [4]. Explanations put forward for this are that people typically use simple search strategies like using only a couple of query terms, or do not spend

M. Scheffel et al. (Eds.): EC-TEL 2019, LNCS 11722, pp. 83–97, 2019.
https://doi.org/10.1007/978-3-030-29736-7_7

much time on the search or only check the first result page [3]. In addition, people are creatures of habit to the extent that their usual search behaviour is independent of the information they are looking for, or how successful they are in finding it [4]. Users tend not to use other or new functionalities, even where these might be more efficient [6].

From the perspective of technology enhanced learning, we focus in this work on reflective learning as a learning mechanism that serves to learn from experience. The experience is in our case the past search behaviour that should be improved by users (who are seen at the same time as learners). Therefore, in this paper we present research that aimed to motivate users to reflect on their search behaviour, and to experiment with different types of search functionality. To this purpose, we developed a widget for data-driven reflective learning. The widget uses low-level activity log data to mirror back past search behaviour in terms of the used search functionalities to users. In combination with reflection prompts, this is expected to trigger reflection [18]. In this work we ask the following research questions with respect to the widget:

- RQ1. Users' reaction to the widget: How do participants use the widget in the search environment and engage with it? Is the widget perceived as useful?
- RQ2. Reflection: Do users generate meaningful insights about their own search behaviour in response to reflection prompts?
- RQ3. Search behaviour: Does the widget induce users to experiment with further search functionalities?

2 Related Work

The goal of a search on the web is to satisfy users' information needs and search behaviour indicates how these needs might be fulfilled. Search behaviour is influenced by a number of factors including the users' search expertise, the information needs, the search engine used and the search task itself. Although searching the web is a routinised behaviour [3], people often struggle to find what they are looking for [4]. This costs people significant time as they spend on average more than 10 min before they give up their search task [8]. And, when their information needs are not satisfied, people are not sure about how to change their search behaviour, or whether and how to use other search features [4].

A plethora of works explore how search behaviour is exhibited on the Web. However, it is not clear yet, if classifying users into novices or experts [20,23], or using the task completion speed [3] to model the search success are meaningful approaches to understand what is good, to-be-imitated search behaviour. Therefore, we are looking at reflective learning as means for every searcher to individually develop own search competence. Reflecting on one's search behaviour could be a mechanism by which users can become better researchers in that reflection enables individuals to critically question their own behaviour, with the goal to learn from it to improve relevant aspects [5]. When it comes to online search, Edwards and Bruce [7] showed that students who are search novices do not reflect when looking for information. In contrast, experienced students not only reflect but are also aware of their own changes in their search strategy. Activity log data can be an important basis for reflective learning: Bateman et al. [4] developed a search dashboard to mirror back search history including the clicks per query, the time to click a result, or the search terms used, also in comparison to others. They showed that reflecting on search behaviour can lead to change with respect to behaviour and attitudes about search. In line with this, Malacria et al. [16] showed that a reflective widget was helpful to incite reflection on learning to use shortcuts in software. Pammer et al. [17] have shown that reflection on time log data incited users to generate insights about time management, and experiment with different time management strategies. Prior research has also shown that automatic reflection prompts can support reflective learning based on data: Fessl et al. [9] implemented and evaluated reflection prompts that were embedded both directly within action, and with a larger temporal separation from action in informal and workplace learning contexts. The authors' reflection prompts reminded users to reflect, and pointed out salient data to users. Kocielnik et al. discussed reflection prompts in private life settings (i.e. physical health [13]) as well as in a workplace setting (i.e. time management [12]). These authors' prompts were based on users' self-set goals for behaviour change.

Literature therefore suggests that online search can get difficult. One of the salient features that distinguishes experienced searchers from novice searchers is their capacity to reflect on their search behaviour and strategies. In parallel, we can build on past known successful designs for data-driven reflective learning and reflection guidance technologies based on data collected within informal learning settings. Both the design of our widget for reflective search (description below) and research question as stated above, are based on this understanding.

3 A Widget for Reflective Search

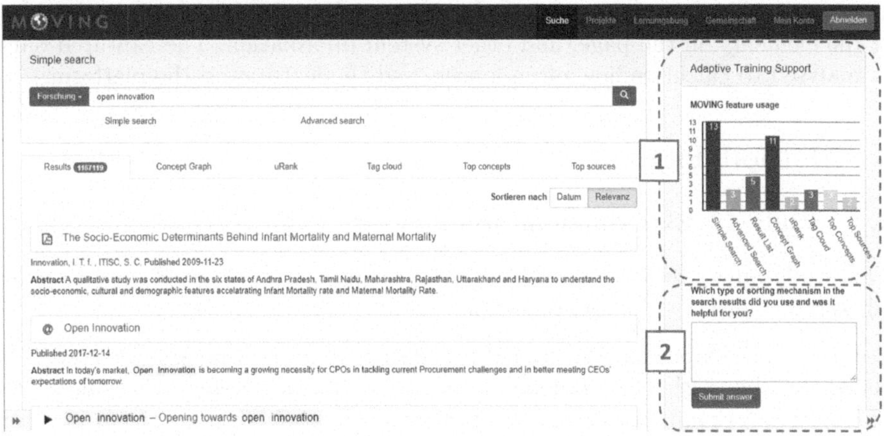

Fig. 1. Widget for behaviour change embedded in the search platform.

The widget for reflective search that we have developed is embedded into a newly developed search platform [24] that offers multiple search interfaces, such as the typical text search, a graph visualisations of search lists, an interactively ranked visualisation of search results based on keywords according to di Sciascio et al. [22], a tag cloud visualisation based on keywords' frequency, and a bar chart visualisation presenting properties of the retrieved documents. While using this custom search platform constrained the available content for searching, it enabled us to track user interaction with the widget in a fine-granular manner.

The widget consists of two parts: First, it visualises search behaviour in terms of which functionalities are used, inspired by Malacria et al. [16]. Second, the widget prompts users to reflect on whether and in what sense the used search functionalities were used, and on overall search behaviour. These prompts constitute generic reflection prompts [10] in the sense of not directing users towards particular solutions. While directed prompts in principle have advantages especially for novices (ibid), as it is unknown what exactly constitutes good search behaviour, it is known that reflecting and adapting search behaviour to the search task is a characteristic of experienced searchers, generic reflection prompts were assumed to be the best approach in this work. The search behaviour visualisation (see Fig. 1, component 1) shows how often a user used a search feature.

The reflective prompts (see Fig. 1, component 2) are phrased as questions. Many of them refer directly to the user's way of using search functionalities, such that used features, and the number of times a feature has been used are variables that are inserted into template sentences. Examples are *"You have not tried the 'Tag Cloud'. Why haven't you tried it out before?"* or *"What did you learn by using the 'Concept Graph' feature?"*. Some reflective prompts overarch wider issues, like *"Which of the features listed above do you find the most useful, and why?"*[1].

On the server-side, we have implemented an activity tracking tool that collects all events a user is performing on the platform. The captured events include all mouse and keyboard interactions, browser window events, changes to the state of the elements on the page, and other system information. The captured data is analysed to calculate how often a user used the features on the platform.

4 Methodology

4.1 Study 1 - Experimental Study

This study aimed to answer RQ1 on users' reaction to the widget, and RQ2 on whether the prompts incited reflection.

Setting: The experimental study was designed as a comparative study. It lasted for about 2 h. Two different user groups participated in the study: the "Researcher" group, consisting of master students of "Computer Science" or "Software Engineering and Management" of Graz University of Technology

[1] All reflective prompts are listed in an online appendix published on Zenodo: https://tinyurl.com/y5wlgeyx.

(TUG), who were recruited during a lecture. The "Auditor" group consisting of auditors from a big auditing company in Germany and students of Software Engineering and Managmement (TUG) with a strong background in economy. Additionally, each group was divided in two subgroups, resulting in four groups: group 1S and group 1V for the researchers and group 2S and group 2V for the auditors. While the groups with "S" had to deal with search input interfaces, the groups with "V" were asked about search result visualisations.

Group 1S (researchers) and group 2S (auditors): the participants of these groups were asked to perform a search task on the search platform and to use either a typical one-line input field (simple search) or another search input page offering several input fields including domain, title, abstract, full text and person (advanced search). The screenshots of the widget were adapted to this task. For group 1S, the reflection widget screenshot showed simple search to be used more frequently than advanced search. The reflective question posed was: *"You are mostly using the 'Simple Search'. What could help to motivate you to use some other search features like the 'Advanced Search'?"*. For group 2S the screenshot showed the advanced search as the most often feature used. The reflective question was *"You are mostly using the 'Advanced Search'. What could help to motivate you to use some other search features like the 'Simple Search'?"*.

Group 1V (researchers) and group 2V (auditors): the participants of these two groups were asked to use the ranked result visualisation based on keywords in the first search task, and to use the graph visualisation of search results in the second search task. We then prepared for group 1V a screenshot of the reflection widget showing the interactively ranked visualisation as most frequently used search functionality, and the following reflective question: *"Do you think that using the 'interactively ranked result visualisation' can improve your search performance/search skills...? And if yes how?"*. Group 2V was presented with a reflection widget screenshot that showed the graph visualisation as the most frequently used search functionality, and presented the following reflective question: *"Do you think that using the 'Graph Visualisation' can improve your search performance/search skills...? And if yes how?"*.

Metrics and Tools: We used Google Forms to administrate the workflow of the experiment. We created a sequence/condition for each group, which provided step-by-step instructions of the tasks to perform as well as all questionnaires that needed to be filled in. While each condition followed the same structure, it differed on the search tasks, the corresponding screenshots of the widget and the reflective questions. First, all participants gave their consent to participate and were asked to provide demographic information. Then they were introduced to the search platform, and were asked to familiarise themselves with the platform and the widget. Afterwards, each of the four groups was asked to look at a screenshot of the widget and to answer a reflective question about the screenshot as well as further open questions. The questionnaire also measured constructs from the Technology Acceptance Model [19] such as perceived ease of use, perceived usefulness, attitude towards the widget, widget specific questions, learning outcome, behaviour intention, technological self-efficacy, subjective norm and system accessibility. All the questions were defined using a 7-point Likert scale where 1 indicated 'strongly disagree' and 7 'strongly agree'. Additionally, qualitative data was collected through open-ended questions.

Participants: 76 participants (61 male, 15 female) took part in the study. 42 were assigned to the research group (35 male, 7 female) and 34 participants were assigned to the auditor group (27 male, 8 female). 80% of the participants were aged between 18–27, 18.5% between 28–37 and 1.5% was aged between 48–57.

4.2 Study 2 - Field Study

This study aimed to answer RQ1 on users' reaction to the widget, and RQ3 whether the widget influenced the search behaviour.

Setting: The field study was split into two periods of one week. For each period, all participants were asked to carry out one search task per working day. The tasks followed a strict order, so if a participant missed one, they would have to carry it out the following day before they were given the next one. Hence, up to five tasks could be realised per one-week period. We kept the tasks from both periods analogous by using the same instructions, but changing the search topic. The participants were split into two groups: in group A the widget was available on the search platform during both weeks. In group B the widget was introduced at the beginning of the second week. The order of the assigned topics "Big data" and "Global warming" was randomised to counterbalance the effect of a particular topic on participants' behaviour. Henceforth we use the notation A1, A2, B1 and B2 to indicate group membership and period of the study.

Metrics and Tools: We used three questionnaires: A pre-questionnaire was distributed to the participants at the beginning of the study. It included a consent form, a demographic questionnaire and questions about the participants' computer and Web experience as informed by [3]. The in-between weeks questionnaire, was sent out after the first study period (i.e. after a week). It captured the first impressions about the platform and the widget. The post-questionnaire was sent on completion of the study. It measured constructs of the Technology Acceptance Model [19] such as ease of use, perceived usefulness, attitude to the widget, widget specific questions, learning outcomes, search behaviour, technological self-efficacy. All questions were defined on a 5-point Likert scale, where 1 indicated 'strongly disagree' and 5 'strongly agree'.

We computed *engagement metrics* and *interactive patterns of use* from usage data logged on the search platform [14,15]. The engagement metrics were:

- Active time: the time elapsed carrying out the task where periods that were longer than 50 s were not accounted for.
- Number of searches: the number of searches carried out.
- Number of selected results: the number of times a user clicks on a search result can be an indicator of search engine efficiency, but also of engagement.
- Number of episodes per task: a timeout of 40 min is used to split interaction into different episodes.

- Amount of scroll: measuring the scroll interaction from users is a common metric to measure engagement with a site.

The interactive patterns of use were based on pattern mining and n-gram analysis. N-grams are typically used in computational linguistics [25] and in computational biology (e.g. protein sequencing [2]). They are a useful method for capturing low-level sequences, whilst avoiding the need for full parsing. We define a user interaction event n-gram as consisting of a time ordered sequence of n consecutive events by a single user that is fully contained within a single user *episode*. We computed n-grams of size 4 as we empirically found them to be large enough to allow patterns to be extracted for a large number of frequent n-grams in this dataset, across all users who were fully engaged in the study [1]. We visually compared the emerging patterns to look for differences between groups.

Participants: Fifteen participants (10 male, 5 female) aged between 17–46 ($M = 28.8$) took part in the study. On average, they had 15 years of experience with computers ($SD = 7.2$) and 14 with the Web ($SD = 4.4$). 73% use search engines and the Web on a daily basis, and 66.6% of them use a computer dailySelf-reported search skills suggest that 20% of the participants considered themselves to be very skilled, 60% skilled and only 20% reported to be neutral.

5 Results

5.1 RQ1: Users' Reaction to the Widget

Table 1 shows average values of users' active time, the number of selected search results, the number of episodes and searches conducted per task and the amount of scrolling. We compared whether the availability of the widget in Study 2 led to significant differences across groups. A Wilcoxon test on the metrics extracted for engagement suggest that there are no statistically significant differences: When comparing A1 and B1 (between subjects) the range of the Wilcoxon coefficient was $W = 2203–2384$ (all $p > 0.33$). When comparing B1 and B2 (within subjects), the range of the Wilcoxon coefficient was $W = 2859–3095$ (all $p > 0.09$).

Table 1. Average engagement metric per group

Metric	A1	A2	B1	B2
Active time in minutes	7.24	5.58	5.52	5.52
Number of searches	10.08	7.69	9.62	7.57
Number of selected results	2.35	2	1.61	1.62
Number of episodes per task	1.14	1.14	1.26	1.08
Amount of scroll	253.32	175.63	264.13	147.89

Questionnaires: In Study 1 and Study 2, we conducted t-tests per study to compare the reaction on the ease of use and the usefulness of the widget of the different user groups. Yet, we found no statistical significant differences, neither in Study 1 between those who performed tasks using the search input interfaces and those who performed tasks using the graphical search result visualisations, nor in Study 2 between those who had the widget during the whole study and those who had the widget only after the first week.

We therefore, for this RQ, treat all participants for each study as one group. Firstly, participants tended to perceive the widget to be easy to use (Study 1 (7-point Likert scale): $M = 4,82$, $SD = 1.08$; Study 2 (5-point Likert scale): $M = 3.68$, $SD = 0.58$ and useful (Study 1: $M = 4.26$, $SD = 1.42$; Study 2: $M = 3.13$, $SD = 0.92$). In Study 2, this is supported by comments we received when asking an open question about the ease of use and the usefulness of the widget: *"The widget is quite useful. I like the design and that it helps me to use the search engine more efficiently"* and some other neutral *"For me using the widget didn't make much of a difference. The system's bunch of functions is easy enough to overlook, so you rather quickly find what helps you search best and what not with or without the widget"*.

In both studies, we also asked the participants if they thought the widget would raise their engagement with the different platform functionalities. Participants' answers were varied, with no clear tendency overall (Study 1: $M = 4.04$, $SD = 1.81$; Study 2: $M = 3.27$, $SD = 1.03$). Furthermore, we asked all participants if they thought the widget would be useful to explore different search functionalities (Study 1: $M = 4.26$ $SD = 2.06$; Study 2: $M = 3.57$, $SD = 1.10$), which participants were again hesitant about, with a large variance in answers. One participant of Study 2 highlighted that whether the widget would, or wouldn't, encourage exploration of different search functionalities was highly dependent on whether their information needs were met in any given search task: *"It depends on how satisfied I am with the results I got with the usual methods. For some searches it could be useful to use other tools and the widget suggests them. As for which one: I would try them all to see which one could be useful."*.

5.2 RQ2: Reflection

In order to investigate if learning occurred when answering the reflective questions in Study 1, we textually analysed all answers given by study participants in response to reflection questions. We coded answers according to a coding schema for reflective content [21] with which reflective expressions can be characterised according to three levels of depth of reflection, namely low, medium and high. For example, answers that describe an experience without interpretation count as low depth of reflection; answers that contain an interpretation or justification count as medium depth; and answers that describe gained insights count as high depth. One rater coded all 58 answers (given by participants in Study 1 to the four reflective questions). In case of doubt, the coding was discussed with a second coder. Agreement could be reached for all quotes. 48 answers were identified as reflective. 10 answers didn't contain any reflective content like for example *"No"* or *"I don't think so"*. Altogether 81% of the answers were

Table 2. Number of answers per coding category.

Categories of coding schema	Number of codes
Low-level reflection	
1. Description of an experience	41
Medium-level reflection	
3. Interpreting or explaining behaviour in the experience	24
4. Linking an experience explicitly to other experiences	5
5. Linking an experience to knowledge	7
6b. Responding to the explanation of an experience by challenging or supporting assumptions	2
Non-reflective answers	10

assigned to the lowest level and 66% to the medium level of reflection. Some of the answers given belong to more than one category. Table 2 presents the number of answers per category. Categories, to which no answers could be assigned to, were omitted from Table 2 (hence, e.g., the missing category number 2 in the table). Table 3 presents coded examples of answers by participants from group 1V to the question *"Do you think that using 'interactively ranked result visualisation' can improve your search performance/search skills...? And if yes how?"*.

Table 3. Examples of analysed answers given

Categories	Example
1: experience	I think it can, using key words makes a huge difference
1, 3: interpretation	If I know for what keywords I'm looking for, I'm quite sure to find relevant papers very quickly
1, 5: linking experiences to experience	I think it can help me with searching because it simplifies finding the right results for some more complicated queries
1, 3, 6b: supporting assumptions	Yes, because i have an overview of documents that are related to my keywords. Searching for a specific document is far easier than searching for a keyword to find an appropriate document

Besides asking the participants a reflective question about the widget, we also asked them if such a question would motivate them to reflect about the own search behaviour. The answers given were ambivalent. Many confirmed to think about the own search behaviour, but others did not. For example, participants were stating that *"Yes, I would try different methods for optimised search results."*, *"A bit yes, I never thought how I can improve my searching skills and it is a valuable asset."*, *"Yes, It helps but in real life I might not have time to try out other visualisations and just use the one I am most comfortable with."*, and *"A little bit, maybe. But I still prefer text based searches due to my habit."*. On the other hand, some said just *"No"* or *"Not really"*, *"No, because I'm happy with my current way of searching."* or *"Not really, because normally when I search I get the results that I'm looking for in a fast way, changing my behaviour therefore would cost time for doing something that is already efficient for me."*.

5.3 RQ3: Search Behaviour

Based on the activity log data captured in Study 2, an n-gram analysis was performed to compare the effect of the widget on the interactive behaviour exhibited on the search platform between those users who:

- Used the platform for the first time with (A1) and without the widget (B1);
- Used the widget for the first time but had already been exposed to the platform (B2) and used the platform and the widget for the first time (A1);
- Used the platform without the widget (B1) and had the widget introduced later on (B2);
- Used the platform with the widget from the beginning (A1) and continued using it in the second period (A2);
- On the second week, were already familiar with the widget (A2) and had it just introduced (B2).

We conducted a correlation analysis between the frequencies of the top-100 n-grams on the above users groups. Next we provide a guide to interpret Table 4, where coefficients around 0.4 and above are considered to be moderate correlations, and those above 0.6 are strong correlations for the following statistical tests: a high Kendall τ and Spearman ρ correlation indicates that the rankings of two vectors of n-grams are similar. The former is considered more strict and will typically produce a lower correlation coefficient. When in doubt, the p-value of Kendall's test is known to be more reliable. A high Pearson r suggests that the frequencies of the n-grams are associated (despite their ranking in their respective vectors). The results on Table 4 and an observational analysis of the top-10 n-grams suggests that:

- **A1 vs B1:** a high Pearson correlation and low Spearman suggest that behaviours are exhibited a proportionately similar number of times but their rankings are not the same (i.e. the frequency based order changes). Using the search functionality, exploring the results after searching and interacting with visualisations are within the top-5 behaviours exhibited by those who had the widget, while they are ranked in positions 6–8 for those who did not.
- **A1 vs B2:** low correlations tending toward moderate correlations indicate slightly different behaviours on first exposure to the widget, which suggests that having the widget from the outset may make a difference in that we do not observe search activity patterns on the top-10 n-grams of B2 users.

- **B1 vs B2:** high correlations that are consistent across rankings and frequencies suggest that there was no behaviour change when the widget was introduced. On the first week the participants without the widget (B1) carried out simple search activities, while in the second week (B2), we observe more interaction with visualisations and exploratory search behaviours through the use of the scroll.
- **A2 vs B2:** low correlations suggest different behaviours between those who have been exposed equally to the platform but get the widget later. While both groups show exploratory search activity patterns and interaction with visualisations, the group using the widget for a second week (A2) shows interactions with advance search features (i.e. use of filters).
- **A1 vs A2:** low correlations across the tests we run indicate that behaviours changed over time probably due to the learning effect, and exposure to the platform and the widget. As we say above, we observe the emergence of sophisticated search functionalities on the second week.

The conclusion derived from these findings suggests that the widget does not make users exhibit *new* behaviours, but *makes users prioritise other behaviours that are already in their repertoire* (A1 vs B1). The effect of the widget is particularly noticeable for those who interact with the search platform for the first time as once users get familiar with the platform (B1 vs B2), *the posterior incorporation of the widget does not lead to using further search functionalities.* This indicates that support for training is more effective when the learning gap is perceived to be large, i.e. the first time one is exposed to such system (A1 vs B2). We do not know how long it would take to make the two groups similar as one week does not seem to be enough time (A2 vs B2).

Table 4. Widget user group vs period: correlations of top-100 n-grams, where N = 4.

	Kendall τ	p value	Pearson r	p value	Spearman ρ	p value
A1 vs B1	0.16	0.02	0.62	0.00	0.27	0.007
A1 vs A2	0.08	0.28	0.23	0.02	0.11	0.27
A1 vs B2	0.21	0.005	0.38	0.00	0.27	0.006
B1 vs A2[a]	0.11	0.15	0.17	0.08	0.14	0.17
B1 vs B2	0.39	0.00	0.58	0.00	0.50	0.00
A2 vs B2	0.15	0.06	0.10	0.32	0.12	0.07

[a]B1 vs. A2 is added for completeness reasons but the comparison is not meaningful.

Questionnaires: In Study 2, we asked participants about their search behaviour and a possible change of it. Most of the participants (especially group A) supported the idea that the widget encouraged reflection about their search behaviour (Group A: $M = 3.71$, $SD = 1.11$; Group B: $M = 3.38$, $SD = 1.06$). Whether the widget enabled search behaviour change was less clear as participants leaned toward being neutral (Group A: $M = 3.29$, $SD = 0.76$; Group B: $M = 3.25$, $SD = 0.89$), and event the intention to change it (Group A:

$M = 3.14$, $SD = 0.69$; Group B: $M = 3$, $SD = 1.07$). This was supported by a participant: *"I didn't learn from using the widget – it just made me more aware of how I'm usually doing my search without wanting to change that behaviour"*.

6 Discussion

RQ1: Users' Reaction to the Widget. The widget was perceived to be easy to use and useful by participants in both studies, and via both questionnaires and engagement metrics. We understand this to be a necessary prerequisite for supporting learning and behaviour change (cp. Kirkpatrick's [11] hierarchical model of evaluating learning interventions).

RQ2: Reflection. From the analysis of the answers given to the reflective questions we can show that reflection took place mostly on the lowest level (81%) and the medium level (66%) of reflection (dual coding, hence the sum is larger than 100%). This could be explained by the following two facts. First, it is easier to describe (low-level reflection) or interpret an experience (medium level reflection) than to derive insights from reflection and put them in writing (high level reflection) [9]. Second, the experimental study (about 2 h) may have been too far outside participant's real search practice for them to be able to derive deeper insights search behaviour. Additionally, we received further thoughts from participants when asking them if the reflective question motivated them to reflect on their search behaviour. The thoughts of some study participants include on the one hand that they would like to improve their search skills to receive optimised search results. On the other hand, others mentioned after becoming aware of how they search, that they are happy with the way they currently search. They still prefer using the one-input line they are used to and do not want to un-learn or change their search behaviour due to time reasons. As a consequence this shows that people are creatures of habit, thus, changing internally operationalised behaviour is difficult as it requires a significant investment of time, effort and motivation on the user's side [4,16]. This is explained by the *active user paradox* in that users tend not to use other or new functionalities, even where these might be more efficient [6].

RQ3: Search Behaviour. The n-gram analysis suggests that the widget influenced the activity patterns of those participants who were introduced to the new search platform and widget together (group A). This group of users were more active searchers than those who did not have the widget (group B). Interestingly, on the second week of use, they (group A) exhibited activity patterns that signaled search behaviours that were beyond the traditional search box. However, we observed that users did not exhibit those search behaviours when the widget was incorporated on the second week (group B). This may indicate that having the widget from the beginning might have facilitated the initial prioritisation of search behaviours upon which, more sophisticated behaviours were exhibited in the second week.

7 Conclusions

In this work, we focused on reflective learning as a learning mechanism that serves to learn from experience to drive future search behaviour. We have presented two studies that investigate if a widget that mirrors back users' current search behaviour in terms of search features used is able to stimulate reflective learning and experimentation with different search behaviours. In Study 1, we could show that reflective learning took place, and that the improvement of own search skills was thought of. However, a search behaviour change is still refused due to being a creature of habit. In Study 2, we could show that there was an effect on the search behaviour in the second week on those participants (group A) that had been exposed both to the novel search platform and the widget from the study outset. We didn't see an effect on those users (group B), however, that used the novel search platform without the widget in week 1 and with the widget in week 2 of the study. We suspect that there are two reasons: First, unlearning behaviour is harder than exploring a novel technology, especially in the presence of technology that aims to incite reflection and exploration. Second, learning the widget, reflecting on search behaviour, and experimenting with novel search behaviours may take longer than a week; which was all the time that study participants had with the widget in group B.

While the two studies therefore show the widget's usability, perceived usefulness, potential to induce reflection, and potential to impact search behaviour; the potential to support unlearning of routines could not be shown. The immediate outlook to future work is a longer-term experimental field study. Beyond this, this work shows that there are knowledge gaps in existing research with respect to evidence for best search practices; and with respect to designing for reflective search practice.

Acknowledgements. The project "MOVING - TraininG towards a society of datasaVvy inforMation prOfessionals to enable open leadership iNnovation" is funded under the Horizon 2020 of the European Commission (project number 693092). The Know-Center is funded within the Austrian COMET Program - Competence Centers for Excellent Technologies - under the auspices of the Austrian Federal Ministry of Transport, Innovation and Technology, the Austrian Federal Ministry of Economy, Family and Youth and by the State of Styria. COMET is managed by the Austrian Research Promotion Agency FFG.

References

1. Apaolaza, A., et al.: MOVING Project, Deliverable 1.4: Final implementation of user studies and evaluation (2019)
2. Asgari, E., Mofrad, M.R.: Continuous distributed representation of biological sequences for deep proteomics and genomics. PLoS ONE **10**(11), e0141287 (2015)
3. Aula, A., Nordhausen, K.: Modeling successful performance in web searching. J. Am. Soc. Inf. Sci. Technol. **57**(12), 1678–1693 (2006)

4. Bateman, S., Teevan, J., White, R.W.: The search dashboard: how reflection and comparison impact search behavior. In: Proceedings of the SIGCHI Conference on Human Factors in Computing Systems, pp. 1785–1794. ACM (2012)
5. Boud, D., Keogh, R., Walker, D.: Promoting reflection in learning: a model. In: Reflection: Turning Experience into Learning, pp. 18–40. Routledge Falmer, New York (1985)
6. Carroll, J.M., Rosson, M.B.: Paradox of the active user. In: Interfacing Thought: Cognitive Aspects of Human-computer Interaction, pp. 80–111. MIT Press, Cambridge (1987)
7. Edwards, S.L., Bruce, C.S.: Panning for gold: Understanding students' information searching experiences. In: Transforming IT Education: Promoting a Culture of Excellence, pp. 351–369 (2006)
8. Evans, B.M., Chi, E.H.: An elaborated model of social search. Inf. Process. Manage. **46**(6), 656–678 (2010)
9. Fessl, A., Wesiak, G., Rivera-Pelayo, V., Feyertag, S., Pammer, V.: In-app reflection guidance: lessons learned across four field trials at the workplace. IEEE Trans. Learn. Technol. **10**(4), 488–501 (2017)
10. Ifenthaler, D.: Determining the effectiveness of prompts for self-regulated learning in problem-solving scenarios. Ed. Technol. Soc. **15**(1), 38–52 (2012)
11. Kirkpatrick, D.L., Kirkpatrick, J.D.: Evaluating Training Programs: The Four Levels, 3rd edn. Berrett-Koehler Publishers, San Francisco (2006)
12. Kocielnik, R., Avrahami, D., Marlow, J., Lu, D., Hsieh, G.: Designing for workplace reflection: a chat and voice-based conversational agent. In: Proceedings of the 2018 Designing Interactive Systems Conference, pp. 881–894. ACM (2018)
13. Kocielnik, R., Xiao, L., Avrahami, D., Hsieh, G.: Reflection companion: a conversational system for engaging users in reflection on physical activity. Proc. ACM Interact. Mob. Wearable Ubiquitous Technol. **2**(2), 70:1–70:26 (2018)
14. Lagun, D., Lalmas, M.: Understanding user attention and engagement in online news reading. In: Proceedings of the Ninth ACM International Conference on Web Search and Data Mining, pp. 113–122. ACM (2016)
15. Lalmas, M., O'Brien, H., Yom-Tov, E.: Measuring user engagement. Synth. Lect. Inf. Concepts Retrieval Serv. **6**(4), 1–132 (2014)
16. Malacria, S., Scarr, J., Cockburn, A., Gutwin, C., Grossman, T.: Skillometers: reflective widgets that motivate and help users to improve performance. In: Proceedings of the 26th ACM Symposium on User Interface Software and Technology, pp. 321–330. ACM (2013)
17. Pammer, V., Bratic, M., Feyertag, S., Faltin, N.: The value of self-tracking and the added value of coaching in the case of improving time management. In: Conole, G., Klobučar, T., Rensing, C., Konert, J., Lavoué, É. (eds.) EC-TEL 2015. LNCS, vol. 9307, pp. 467–472. Springer, Cham (2015). https://doi.org/10.1007/978-3-319-24258-3_41
18. Pammer, V., Krogstie, B., Prilla, M.: Let's talk about reflection at work. Int. J. Technol. Enhanced Learn. (IJTEL) **9**(2/3), 151–168 (2017)
19. Park, S.Y., et al.: An analysis of the technology acceptance model in understanding university students' behavioral intention to use e-learning. Educ. Technol. Soc. **12**(3), 150–162 (2009)
20. Perrone, V.: Librarians and the nature of expertise. In: Proceedings LIANZA Conference 2004, LIANZA (2004)
21. Prilla, M., Renner, B.: Supporting collaborative reflection at work: a comparative case analysis. In: Proceedings of the 18th International Conference on Supporting Group Work, pp. 182–193. ACM (2014)

22. Sciascio, C.D., Sabol, V., Veas, E.: Supporting exploratory search with a visual user-driven approach. ACM Trans. Interact. Intell. Syst. **7**(4), 18 (2017)
23. Tucker, V.M.: The expert searcher's experience of information. In: Information experience: Approaches to Theory and Practice, pp. 239–255. Emerald Group Publishing Limited (2014)
24. Vagliano, I., et al.: Open innovation in the big data era with the moving platform. IEEE MultiMedia **25**(3), 8–21 (2018)
25. Xia, Y., Cambria, E., Hussain, A., Zhao, H.: Word polarity disambiguation using bayesian model and opinion-level features. Cogn. Comput. **7**(3), 369–380 (2015)

Evaluating Teachers' Perceptions of Learning Design Recommender Systems

Soultana Karga(✉) and Maya Satratzemi

Department of Applied Informatics, University of Macedonia, 156 Egnatia Street, 54636 Thessaloniki, Greece
tania.karga@gmail.com

Abstract. Nowadays, researchers in the field of Learning Design are investigating ways to assist teachers in realizing their role as Learning Designers in the context of online and blended learning. This is a major quest for the field researchers due to the fact that it can affect the broader adoption of the Learning Design practices by teachers, with resulting improvements on the quality of teaching and learning outcomes. In this context, this paper investigates teacher-perceived experience and acceptance of a Recommender System (RS) that supports teachers in the designing process, by providing them with Learning Design recommendations. To this end, we conducted a user-centric evaluation experiment, which involved 50 teachers and was based on the ResQue model. According to the results, an RS which proposes existing Learning Designs is a highly accepted technology by teachers. Additionally, teachers believe that the use of the proposed RS can make the designing process easier and faster while it would also favor the sharing of good teaching practices and provide teachers with a valuable source of inspiration. The implications of this study suggest that developers in the Learning Design field should incorporate RSs into existing Learning Design environments in order to facilitate the designing process.

Keywords: Learning design · Recommender systems · Teachers · Reuse of learning designs

1 Introduction

Nowadays, the use of online and blended learning in all levels of education, from primary to higher, and even to non-formal education like lifelong learning, is growing rapidly worldwide [1, 2]. In this new reality, the teacher is identified not as a means of knowledge transfer, a perception that prevailed in the past, but as the Learning Designer who creates pedagogically informed learning experiences that enable students to build their knowledge [3]. The fact that the new teacher's role as the Learning Designer is becoming more widely accepted these days can be confirmed by the ever growing trend to research the field of Learning Design [4–6]. Conole [7] describes the Learning Design process as "a methodology for enabling teachers/designers to make more informed decisions in how they go about designing learning activities and interventions, which is pedagogically informed and makes effective use of appropriate resources and technologies". Simultaneously, the Learning Design term is used to refer to the design process outcome [8].

M. Scheffel et al. (Eds.): EC-TEL 2019, LNCS 11722, pp. 98–111, 2019.
https://doi.org/10.1007/978-3-030-29736-7_8

In order for the concept of Learning Design to be implemented in the context of online and blended learning, field researchers have developed specifications for digital representation of Learning Designs and tools that allow teachers to create, manage and even enact their Learning Designs [9–11]. The bulk of the work done so far in the field concerns the development of the above technologies. Recently, the first studies on the results of using Learning Design in the context of online and blended learning have been conducted. These studies have linked the adoption of Learning Design to improving the quality of the learning process and learning outcomes [4, 12–14]. Despite the important findings, teachers' wide adoption of Learning Design practices remains a challenge mainly for the following reasons: the Learning Design requires teachers to have specialized knowledge and time, the tools that teachers are asked to use are quite complex, and no support is given to them in their new role as Learning Designers [15, 16].

Taking into consideration the need for supporting teachers in their new role as Learning Designers, we have proposed in a previous paper the integration of a Recommender System (RS) into the Learning Activity Management System (LAMS) [17]. LAMS is one of the most popular environments which allow teachers to create, manage and enact Learning Designs [18]. The proposed RS provides teachers with Learning Design recommendations based on existing designs, created by other teachers. It is important to highlight that sharing and reusing ideas and teaching practices among teachers is a common practice in traditional education.

This paper investigates the teacher-perceived experience and acceptance of the proposed RS and so addresses the following research questions:

(RQ1): What is the teacher-perceived experience of an RS which proposes existing Learning Designs?

(RQ2): What is the teacher acceptance of an RS which proposes existing Learning Designs?

In order to answer these questions, we conducted a survey involving 50 teachers from all levels of education. The most important contribution of the research presented is that it proposes a way of supporting teachers in their new role as Learning Designers, which, based on the results of the research conducted, is acceptable to the teachers themselves. This is a major contribution in the quest of technologies that has the potential to favor teachers' adoption of Learning Design practices in the context of online and blended learning, with implications on the quality of teaching and learning outcomes.

The rest of this paper is structured as follows: Sect. 2 reviews the literature regarding both the reuse of Learning Designs and RSs. Section 3 outlines the implemented RS and Sect. 4 describes the methodology of the research conducted. Section 5 presents the results, while Sect. 6 discusses the results, the implications and the limitations of the study. Section 7 concludes this paper.

2 Related Work

2.1 Reuse of Learning Designs

Over the past two decades, many projects have been carried out in the reuse of Learning Designs. The "information and communication technologies and their role in flexible learning" project, which was funded by Australian Universities Teaching Committee (AUTC) in 2000, is one of the first attempts to cultivate the culture of reusing Learning Designs among teachers in the higher education context. The outcome of the project was a repository of high quality Learning Designs in the form of texts and graphical representations that could be shared and reused among teachers. Regarding the project's resulting benefits, researchers have reported that the project's Learning Designs proved to be a valuable source of inspiration and reference for teachers in their effort to design their own Learning Designs [19]. Other significant benefits of reusing Learning Designs have also been documented in the bibliography and include [20, 21]: the decrease of the cost in terms of the time and effort needed on behalf of the teachers to create Learning Designs, the improvement in the quality of Learning Designs due to peer review processes and the dissemination of best teaching practices. As the reuse of Learning Designs facilitates teachers in their new role as Learning Designers, it is sensible that it also favors the adoption of Learning Design practices by them.

The traditional context for sharing and reusing Learning Designs is the repositories, like Open Discovery Space Repository (https://portal.opendiscoveryspace.eu) and MERLOT (https://www.merlot.org/) [22, 23]. However, sharing and reusing through repositories have not been adopted by teachers widely [24]. In fact, relevant surveys show that the rates of teachers contributing to them are not high [25]. Research by Reed [26] and Rolfe [27] revealed that teachers are more willing to share at a local level with colleagues they are close to. Thus, it seems more likely for teachers to be involved in the sharing and reusing of Learning Objects through an Institutional Learning Management System (LMS), which can be a local course-based repository instead of an international online repository. This view is further supported by the research of Ochoa and Duval [28] in the field of contexts for sharing and reusing Learning Objects, which concludes that the best context for sharing and reusing Learning Objects is LMSs instead of global repositories and other contexts. The community developing around LMSs seems to play an important and positive role in the following benefits: the number of LMSs' users increase over time, the number of those who decide to contribute increase, the productivity of contributors does not stop as long as their courses last.

Another trend context for sharing and reusing Learning Designs is the integrated environments that enable teachers not only to share and reuse Learning Designs but also to create, manage or even enact them with students. For instance, the Integrated Learning Design Environment (ILDE) is an online platform which integrates various tools to support teachers in creating, sharing and reusing Learning Designs [29]. Teachers can use tags in order to browse the community's designs and find the ones to adopt and reuse but no recommendations are provided to teachers in order to help them find the most suitable Learning Designs for their needs and preferences. A second example is a microworld, named "Learning Designer", which allows teachers to create, share and reuse Learning Designs, while also providing them with recommendations on learning activities that can be re-used in a particular application context [30]. Laurillard et al. [12] evaluated teachers' satisfaction with the use of "Learning Designer" and found that the majority of the participants said they found the tool useful and are willing to use it. However, a major drawback of "Learning Designer" is that it does not allow teachers to enact their designs with students. Thus, teachers are burdened with the extra effort to deploy their Learning Designs in an LMS (e.g. Moodle).

From the above, it is clear that supporting teachers in their new role as Learning Designers through the reuse of existing designs is a promising prospect of the benefits they can offer and that is why it has already garnered the interest of the researchers. The review of the relevant bibliography reveals the small amount of work that has been done on the research conducted so far to capture the teachers' view of the technologies they offer to facilitate their role as Learning Designers through the reuse of existing designs. Our work is a contribution to this particular research area as we provide evidence that the recommendation technology is a teacher-accepted technology that supports them as Learning Designers when it is incorporated in the context of existing Learning Design environments like LAMS. LAMS is an advantageous context for share and reuse due to the following reasons: (a) LAMS is an innovative type of LMS which provides an integrated environment to support teachers to design, manage and even enact their Learning Designs with students. (b) LAMS is an open source software that can be adopted by any institution and installed on its own servers, which means that a local course-based repository can be achieved. The proposal of a teacher-accepted technology that supports teachers in creating Learning Designs by redesigning existing ones is important, due to its potential to enhance the adoption of Learning Design practices by teachers which can effect positively the quality in online and blended learning.

2.2 Recommender Systems

RSs aim to generate recommendations for their users tailored to ones personal needs and preferences [31]. The selection of the Recommendation technology as a means of supporting teachers was made taking into account that there are many studies proved that the recommendation technology is a highly user-accepted technology in various application fields (e.g. entertainment, tourism, e-commerse); such as the review study of Xiao and Benbasat [32] which reveals a lot of highly accepted RSs in the field of e-commerce. Moreover, in the field of Technology Enhanced Learning (TEL) many paradigms of implemented RSs included in the review studies of Drachsler et al. [33] and Manouselis et al. [34]. Recent work has documented positive results on the teacher-perceived acceptance of RSs in areas related to Learning Design. For example, the Torre and Torsani survey [35] records the positive attitude of teachers towards using an RS as a support tool for language teachers who want to develop technology-enhanced activities for given conditions regarding learning goals, the special features of learners, etc. Moreover, the preliminary results of the study of Mota et al. [36] reveal that teachers accept with enthusiasm the proposed RS which help them decide which teaching method best suits to a specific learning activity.

3 The Implemented Recommender System

The proposed RS aims to help a teacher create Learning Designs by suggesting existing ones that have high community ratings and are matched to an application context which is defined by the teacher regarding the following aspects: (a) teacher's preferred pedagogical strategy: refers to the preferred teaching methods influenced by learning theories, (b) subject domain: refers to the subject area that will be covered by the Learning Design, (c) level: refers to learners' educational level regarding the subject domain (introductory or intermediate etc.), (d) evaluation model: refers to teacher's preferred evaluation technique e.g. diagnostic or formative etc., (e) delivery model: refers to whether the design will be delivered in a synchronous or asynchronous manner, and (f) time: refers to the time needed by learners in order to execute the Learning Design. Thus, the teacher is relieved of the exhaustive work of creating a Learning Design from scratch. After the teacher chooses a suggested Learning Design then he can edit it in order to create his own design. It is important to highlight that each suggested LD is a ready to execute contextualized example. However, each suggested LD needs to be refined by the teacher to whom it is addressed, in order to cater better to each particular application context. The proposed RS was integrated into LAMS. The proposed RS has been thoroughly presented in our previous work [17]. For the purposes of the current paper only a brief description of the operation of the proposed RS is given in the following paragraph.

The operation of the proposed RS consists of the following steps: (a) the teacher completes a preference form regarding the aforementioned aspects of the intended application context, (b) the RS searches the item-database for Learning Designs that implement the preferred pedagogical strategy, (c) the RS groups the found Learning Designs based on similarities in the sequence of learning activities, (d) the RS sorts the Learning Designs' groups in a list, according to the number of items they contain, (e) in each of the two top groups of the list, the RS finds the most suitable Learning Designs according to the specified application context and also Learning Designs with the highest community ratings, (f) the RS presents Learning Design recommendations, which are accompanied by explanations and also by a 5-star rating system, to teachers.

4 Method

4.1 Participants

Teachers from three different sources were invited to participate in the research: (a) users of the "Learning Activities Management" service, which is provided by the Greek School Network, is hosted at http://lams.sch.gr/ and is available to teachers of Greek public education, (b) members of the Greek Educators LAMS community (https://blogs.sch.gr/groups/lams/) and (c) users of the "Electronical courses" service which is provided by the Aristotle university of Thessaloniki and is hosted at https://elearning.auth.gr/.

Having a minimum experience with LAMS was a prerequisite for participating in the research so as to avoid training participants in the use of LAMS. Finally, 50 teachers accepted to participate voluntarily in the survey and completed valid questionnaires. The majority of participants were female (58%) and most of them were between aged 31 to 40 years (54%). Regarding the participants' academic discipline, 70% have studied formal sciences (e.g. informatics). 12% of the participants were elementary teachers, 28% were secondary teachers, 32% teach in higher education, 14% in lifelong learning context and 14% in other forms of education.

4.2 Materials

An online questionnaire was used for this study. The questionnaire consisted of four subscales, each of which matched one of the four layers of the ResQue model. The ResQue model is a well-known evaluation framework for RSs that assesses user's experience and acceptance of them [37]. The four subscales of the questionnaire were the following: (a) Perceived Quality Layer: includes questions that assess users' perception of RS's characteristics across different dimensions such as the system's interface and interaction adequacy. (b) Beliefs Layer: includes questions that assess user's perceived effectiveness and efficiency of RS to help him/her to accomplish tasks. It is focused on dimensions like perceived usefulness of the system and perceived ease of use. (c) Attitudes Layer: includes questions that assess users' overall feeling toward the RS. (d) Behavioral Intentions Layer: includes questions that assess the RS's capability to engage users to use it regularly. The questions which are included in the first three subscales measure the teacher-perceived experience of the proposed RS in order to answer the RQ1, while the questions included in the last subscale focus on the teacher acceptance of the proposed RS and so answer the RQ2. All the questionnaire items were Likert scale (from 1 = strongly disagree to 5 = strongly agree) and were adopted from the ResQue model (see Table 1). The only exception is question 11, which was designed by the authors in order to further explore the teacher's perceived usefulness of RS. Q11 is an open-ended question which asks participants to record their opinion upon the most important advantage of using the proposed RS.

Table 1. List of questionnaire items.

Layer/Dimension/Questionnaire item	Cronbach alpha	Factor loading	Mean	SD
Perceived quality layer	.744		4.56	.394
Dimension of Recommendation quality				
(Q1) "The recommended Learning Designs corresponded satisfactorily to my preferences"		.400	4.40	.535
Dimension of Interface adequacy				
(Q2) "I liked the RS's interface"		.812	4.58	.642
Dimension of Interaction adequacy				
(Q3) "The interaction mechanism (use of stars) to inform the system how satisfied I was with the RS's recommendations was adequate"		.774	4.52	.646
Dimension of information sufficiency				
(Q4) "The information provided for the recommended items was sufficient for me to make a decision"		.816	4.80	.404

(continued)

Table 1. (*continued*)

Layer/Dimension/Questionnaire item	Cronbach alpha	Factor loading	Mean	SD
Dimension of explicability				
(Q5) "The RS explained satisfactorily the reasons for recommending a Learning Design"		.720	4.48	.544
Beliefs layer	.749		4.62	.379
Dimension of Perceived ease of use				
(Q6) "I became familiar with the RS very quickly"		.535	4.88	.328
Dimension of Control				
(Q7) "The RS allowed me to set a satisfying number of preferences based on which it provided recommendations to me"		.828	4.54	.542
Dimension of Transparency				
(Q8) "I understood why the Learning Designs were recommended to me"		.642	4.68	.513
Dimension of Perceived usefulness				
(Q9) "The proposed RS helped me find a good Learning Design to rely upon for creating my own"		.737	4.38	.530
(Q10)"By using the RS I managed to create a Learning Design in less time than in the default LAMS environment"		.778	4.60	.700
(Q11) "What is the most important advantage of using the RS"				
Attitudes layer	.695		4.43	.631
Dimension of Overall satisfaction				
(Q12) "Overall, I am satisfied with the RS"		.903	4.62	.490
Dimension of Confidence				
(Q13) "The RS made me more confident about the Learning Design finally created"		.903	4.24	.894
Behavioural intentions layer	.879		4.76	.407
Dimension of use intention				
(Q14) "I would use the RS again"		.945	4.78	4.18
(Q15) "I would recommend the RS to colleagues"		.945	4.74	4.43

Finally, with the purpose of collecting the participants' demographic data a background questionnaire was also used.

4.3 Design and Procedure

Communication with the participants was via email. Initially, the participants were informed about the purposes of the survey and the terms and conditions they would have to accept. They, then, acquired personal login accounts for a demo installation of the integrated environment of LAMS and the proposed RS. The next steps for each participant were as follows: (a) Login to the demo installation, (b) Interact freely with the system without a task scenario or any time limit, (c) Create a Learning Design about the Internet Safety with the support of the proposed RS, (d) Complete the online questionnaire. While using the demo installation, users had access to a video tutorial which explained the use of the proposed RS.

The demo installation was populated with Learning Designs retrieved from "https://lamscommunity.org/lamscentral/?language=el" under the "CC BY-NC-SA 2.0" license.

4.4 Data Analysis

Each subscale of the questionnaire was assessed for reliability by using Cronbach's alpha analysis. A Principal Component Analysis was also run in order to further test whether the individual questions correspond sufficiently to each subscale.

In order to examine whether the findings of this study confirm and validate the basic assumption of the ResQue model that each layer effects on the next one, the correlations between the adjacent layers were investigated by using the Spearman's rank correlation coefficient. The Spearman's rank correlation was chosen due to its advantages of being suitable to analyze ordinal variables and being robust to outliers.

The SPSS version 25 was used in order to analyze the data from the questionnaire.

5 Results

Regarding the subscales' reliability results the Cronbach's alpha values indicated that all the subscales had an adequate level of inter-item reliability (see Table 1). Moreover, the principal component analysis results indicated high factor loadings for each question which means that the relation between each question and the corresponding subscale was strong (see Table 1).

Regarding the correlations between the adjacent layers, Tables 2, 3 and 4 present the correlations which were found. In particular: (a) Table 2 show significant correlations between teachers' beliefs layer and all of the questions of the perceived quality layer (i.e. Q1, Q2, Q3, Q4 and Q5), (b) Table 3 show significant correlations between teachers' attitudes layer and all of the questions of the beliefs layer (i.e. Q6, Q7, Q8, Q9 and Q10), and (c) Table 4 show significant correlations between behavioural intentions layer and all the questions of attitudes layer (i.e. Q12 and Q13).

Table 2. Correlations between teachers' beliefs and teachers' perception of the objective characteristics of the proposed RS.

	Spearman's rho	Q1	Q2	Q3	Q4	Q5
Beliefs layer	Correlation coefficient	.386	.515	.499	.617	.517
	Sig. (2-tailed)	.006	.000	.000	.000	.000

Table 3. Correlations between teachers' attitudes and teachers' perception on how effectively the proposed RS helped them both accomplish tasks and interact with the system.

	Spearman's rho	Q6	Q7	Q8	Q9	Q10
Attitudes layer	Correlation coefficient	.325	.627	.484	.678	.597
	Sig. (2-tailed)	.021	.000	.000	.000	.000

Table 4. Correlations between teachers' behavioural intentions and teachers' feelings from their experience with the proposed RS.

	Spearman's rho	Q12	Q13
Behavioural intentions layer	Correlation Coefficient	.617	.505
	Sig. (2-tailed)	.006	.000

The following two sections report the findings of the current study in regard with the research questions.

5.1 The Teacher-Perceived Experience of the Proposed Recommender System (RQ1)

Table 1 presents descriptive statistics regarding all questions concerned the teacher-perceived experience of the proposed RS. The mean value for all questions was above 4 while the standard deviation value for all the questions was below 1 point, which indicates that teachers' responses were consistent.

The answers to questions 1 to 5 revealed that teachers have a positive experience regarding the recommendation quality (mean value for Q1 = 4.40, SD = .535), the interface adequacy (mean value for Q2 = 4.58, SD = .642), the interaction adequacy (mean value for Q3 = 4.52, SD = .646), the explicability of the system (mean value for Q4 = 4.80, SD = .404) and the information sufficiency (mean value for Q5 = 4.48, SD = .544). In order to calculate a score for teachers' perceived quality of RS, we summed up all the mean values of the questionnaire items within the perceived quality subscale and we divided the sum by the number of these items. The mean value for the subscale was found to be 4.56 with an SD of .394, which indicates that teachers' perceived quality of the RS was high.

The high teachers' perceived quality of the proposed RS would have a positive impact on teachers' beliefs subscale, according to the ResQue model. Indeed, the mean value for the Beliefs subscale was also high (Mean = 4.62, SD = .379). In particular, teachers believe that: (a) it was easy to use the RS (mean value for Q6 = 4.88, SD = .328), (b) the RS allowed them to feel in control while interacting with it (mean value for Q7 = 4.54, SD = .542), (c) the RS revealed its inner logic (mean value for Q8 = 4.68, SD = .513), (d) the RS was useful as it helped teachers to find a good Learning Design to rely upon for creating their own (mean value for Q9 = 4.38, SD = .530) and they managed to create their Learning Designs in less time (mean value for Q10 = 4.60, SD = .700).

Regarding the subscale of attitudes, one would expect that the users' overall satisfaction would be high, if s/he considers that according to the ResQue model the perceived ease of use, the perceived usefulness and the control feeling have a strong impact on the overall satisfaction. Indeed, teachers' overall satisfaction was high (mean value for Q12 = 4.64, SD = .490). Moreover, according to the ResQue model the perceived usefulness significantly impacts on confidence so the high score on Q13 was also expected (mean value for Q13 = 4.24, SD = .894).

Some of the most representative responses to Q11 are presented below and reveal teachers' perceptions on the most important advantage of using the proposed RS:

> "Designing for learning is a time-consuming process. Re-designing could be a good solution regarding the time needed to create a Learning Design."

> "I found it easier to create a Learning Design when based on an existing one."

> "As a novice teacher I found it extremely useful to be inspired by colleagues' Learning Designs."

> "Some of the activities of the suggested Learning Designs confirmed my views about what I should include in the requested Learning Design."

> "Reusing Learning Designs could result in more qualitatively designs if you consider that I invested my time to make improvements on the suggested one."

> "The recycling of existing Learning Designs could be used as a mechanism able to widespread good teaching paradigms."

5.2 The Teacher Acceptance of the Proposed Recommender System (RQ2)

According to the ResQue model, the users' behavioural intentions towards an RS is most significantly influenced by: overall satisfaction, perceived usefulness and perceived ease of use. Therefore, the high scores on Q6, Q9, Q10 and Q11 would reasonable result in a high teachers' acceptance score. Indeed, the behavioural intentions subscale has a mean value of 4.76 with an SD of .407. In particular, teachers mostly agreed that they would use the proposed RS again (mean value for Q13 = 4.78, SD = .418) and that they would recommend it to their colleagues (mean value for Q14 = 4.74, SD = .443).

6 Discussion

According to the findings of this study: (a) the teacher-perceived experience of an RS, which proposes existing Learning Designs is positive (RQ1) (b) the proposed RS, which suggests existing Learning Designs, is a highly accepted technology by teachers (RQ2). These findings are in consistence with the findings of other studies, which have already shown that the recommendation technology is a highly user-accepted technology in various application fields [32, 38, 39]. Specifically for the TEL field, our findings are in agreement with relative studies, which have already reported the teachers' positive attitudes towards the RSs [35, 36]. By focusing exclusively on the Learning Design settings, only one relative study was found. In particular, Laurillard et al. [12] have also noted the positive attitude of teachers towards the use of the "Learning Designer" tool, which allows the creation, management, sharing and reuse of Learning Designs. A disadvantage, of course, in the case of the Learning Designer is the fact that teachers, after identifying the Learning Design they want to reuse, should deploy it into an LMS. In the case of our proposal, teachers have a unified environment that allows them to create, manage, share and reuse Learning Designs, but also performs Learning Designs by students without burdening teachers with the extra effort of transporting the Learning Design to another system. Moreover, the comparative advantage of the proposed system is that it is based on an already widely-used open-source software.

In addition to the above findings, according to teachers' responses to Q11, some teachers believe that the use of an RS which suggests Learning Designs can make the designing process easier and faster for them. Furthermore, some teachers believe that the use of the proposed RS would favor the sharing of good teaching practices and provide them with a valuable source of inspiration. These findings are in consistence with the studies of Philip and Cameron [20] and Wills and Pegler [21], who also report that reusing Learning Designs can decrease the cost in time and effort needed by teachers to create Learning Designs and also disseminate best teaching practices among teachers. What is more, the aforementioned findings of our study pave the way for further investigation towards the teachers' perceived usefulness of using RSs which propose Learning Designs. For example, it would be interesting to know whether there are any effects of teaching subject on the teachers' perceptions on those RSs. Disentangling these effects would require different research methods than those applied in this study.

The implications of this study suggest that the researchers and developers in the Learning Design settings should focus on RSs as a teacher-accepted technology which can be incorporated into existing environments so as to create integrated environments that can support teachers in all Learning Designs' tasks (from designing, managing, sharing and reusing even to enacting them). Providing teachers with a teacher-accepted technology that allows them to reuse Learning Designs is an important step across the broader adoption of reusing Learning Designs, which can result in significant benefits (presented in the section related work). At the same time, since the proposed technology makes it easier to create Learning Designs by teachers, it makes sense to encourage a wider adoption of the Learning Design by teachers, which can have a positive impact on the quality of teaching and learning outcomes.

Finally, it is important to acknowledge the main limitation of this study, which is the small sample size. We attribute this fact mainly to the effort a participant should exert in order to create a Learning Design, which was a prerequisite for participating in the study. It must be mentioned that the small sample size is a common limitation between user studies that measure user satisfaction and acceptance of RSs. Beel, Gipp, Langer, and Breitinger [40] reviewed 26 studies on user satisfaction and acceptance of RSs and found that the 74% of the reviewed studies had less than 50 participants. Additionally, Erdt, Fernandez and Rensing [41] reviewed 65 user studies that evaluate RSs in the domain of TEL and found that the median of participants in these studies was 25.

7 Conclusion

Teachers' new role as Learning Designers requires researchers in the field of Learning Design to investigate ways to support teachers on realizing their new role in the context of online and blended learning. To this end, this paper examined the Recommendation technology as a possible support mechanism for Learning Designers. The proposed RS provides teachers with Learning Design recommendations, based on existing Learning Designs, which have been created by other teachers. The main contribution of this paper is that it provides evidence that the Learning Design RSs is a teacher-accepted technology that can be integrated into existing Learning Design environments, like LAMS. As the proposed system facilitates teachers in their role as Learning Designers it is sensible to assume that the proposed system favors the adoption of the Learning Design by teachers. This has significant implications, since according to the literature the Learning Design can potentially advance the quality of both teaching and learning outcomes.

Future work could be focused on the effects of using RSs which propose existing Learning Designs on the quality of the Learning Designs which are created based on Learning Design recommendations. Moreover, it would be quite interesting to know if there are any effects of Learning Designs which are created based on Learning Design recommendations on the learning outcomes achieved by learners. These studies would require long-term authentic usage of the proposed RS.

References

1. Al-Samarraie, H., Teng, B.K., Alzahrani, A.I., Alalwan, N.: E-learning continuance satisfaction in higher education: a unified perspective from instructors and students. Stud. High. Educ. **43**, 2003–2019 (2018). https://doi.org/10.1080/03075079.2017.1298088
2. Ferdig, R.E., Kennedy, K. (eds.): Handbook of Research on K-12 Online and Blended Learning. ETC Press, Pittsburgh (2014)
3. Mor, Y., Craft, B., Hernández-Leo, D.: Editorial: the art and science of learning design (2013)
4. Beetham, H., Sharpe, R.: Rethinking pedagogy for a digital age: designing and delivering e-learning (2007). https://doi.org/10.4324/9780203961681
5. Dalziel, J., et al.: The larnaca declaration on learning design. J. Interact. Media Educ. **1**(7), 1–24 (2016). https://doi.org/10.5334/jime.407
6. Lockyer, L., Bennett, S., Agostinho, S., Harper, B.: Handbook of Research on Learning Design and Learning Objects. IGI Global, Hershey (2009)
7. Conole, G.: Designing for Learning in an Open World. Springer, New York (2013)
8. Koper, R., Bennett, S.: Learning design concepts. In: Adelsberger, H.H., Kinshuk, P.J.M., Sampson, D.G. (eds.) Handbook on Information Technologies for Education and Training, pp. 135–154. Springer, Heidelberg (2008). https://doi.org/10.1007/978-3-540-74155-8_8
9. Celik, D., Magoulas, George D.: A review, timeline, and categorization of learning design tools. In: Chiu, Dickson K.W., Marenzi, I., Nanni, U., Spaniol, M., Temperini, M. (eds.) ICWL 2016. LNCS, vol. 10013, pp. 3–13. Springer, Cham (2016). https://doi.org/10.1007/978-3-319-47440-3_1

10. Griffiths, D., Blat, J., García, R., Vogten, H., Kwong, K.L.: Learning design tools. In: Learning Design, pp. 109–135 (2005). https://doi.org/10.1007/3-540-27360-3_7
11. IMS Global Learning Consortium: IMS Learning Design Best Practice and Implementation Guide (2003)
12. Laurillard, D., Kennedy, E., Charlton, P., Wild, J., Dimakopoulos, D.: Using technology to develop teachers as designers of TEL: evaluating the learning designer. Br. J. Educ. Technol. **49**, 1044–1058 (2018). https://doi.org/10.1111/bjet.12697
13. Rienties, B., Toetenel, L.: The impact of learning design on student behaviour, satisfaction and performance: a cross-institutional comparison across 151 modules. Comput. Human Behav. **60**, 333–341 (2016)
14. Maina, M., Craft, B., Mor, Y.: The Art & Science of Learning Design. Sense Publishers, Rotterdam (2015)
15. Dagnino, F.M., Dimitriadis, Y.A., Pozzi, F., Asensio-Pérez, J.I., Rubia-Avi, B.: Exploring teachers' needs and the existing barriers to the adoption of learning design methods and tools: a literature survey. Br. J. Educ. Technol. **49**, 998–1013 (2018). https://doi.org/10.1111/bjet.12695
16. Masterman, E., Manton, M.: Teachers' perspectives on digital tools for pedagogic planning and design. Technol. Pedagog. Educ. **20**, 227–246 (2011). https://doi.org/10.1080/1475939X.2011.588414
17. Karga, S., Satratzemi, M.: A hybrid recommender system integrated into LAMS for learning designers. Educ. Inf. Technol. **23**, 1297–1329 (2018). https://doi.org/10.1007/s10639-017-9668-0
18. Dalziel, J.: Implementing learning design: the learning activity management system (LAMS). In: 20th Annual Conference of the Australasian Society for Computers in Learning in Tertiary Education (ASCILITE), 7–10 December 2003, Adelaide, pp. 7–10 (2003). https://doi.org/10.1016/j.actao.2004.05.005
19. Agostinho, S., Bennett, S., Lockyer, L., Jones, J., Harper, B.: Learning designs as a stimulus and support for teachers' design practices. In: Rethinking Pedagogy for a Digital Age: Designing for 21st Century Learning, pp. 119–132 (2013)
20. Philip, R., Cameron, L.: Sharing and reusing learning designs: contextualising enablers and barriers. In: Luca, J., Weippl, E. (eds.) ED-MEDIA 2008: World Conference on Educational Multimedia, Hypermedia and Telecommunications, pp. 453–462. Association for the Advancement of Computing in Education (AACE), Vienna, Austria (2008)
21. Wills, S., Pegler, C.: A deeper understanding of reuse: learning designs, activities, resources and their contexts. J. Interact. Media Educ. **2016**, 1–11 (2016). https://doi.org/10.5334/jime.405
22. Rodés-Paragarino, V., Gewerc-Barujel, A., Llamas-Nistal, M.: Use of repositories of digital educational resources: state-of-the-art review. IEEE Rev. Iberoam. Tecnol. del Aprendiz. **11**, 73–78 (2016). https://doi.org/10.1109/RITA.2016.2554000
23. Clements, K., Pawlowski, J., Manouselis, N.: Open educational resources repositories literature review - towards a comprehensive quality approaches framework (2015)
24. Casali, A., Cechinel, C., Ochoa, X.: Special issue on strategies to improve the usability of learning object repositories. IEEE Rev. Iberoam. Tecnol. del Aprendiz. **11**, 71–72 (2016). https://doi.org/10.1109/RITA.2016.2553999
25. Bates, M., Loddington, S., Manuel, S., Oppenheim, C.: Attitudes to the rights and rewards for author contributions to repositories for teaching and learning. ALT-J. **15**, 67–82 (2007). https://doi.org/10.1080/09687760600837066
26. Reed, P.: Awareness, attitudes and participation of teaching staff towards the open content movement in one university. Res. Learn. Technol. **20** (2012). https://doi.org/10.3402/rlt.v20i0.18520

27. Rolfe, V.: Open educational resources: staff attitudes and awareness. Res. Learn. Technol. **20** (2012). https://doi.org/10.3402/rlt.v20i0.14395
28. Ochoa, X., Duval, E.: Quantitative analysis of learning object repositories. IEEE Trans. Learn. Technol. **2**, 226–238 (2009)
29. Hernández-Leo, D., et al.: An integrated environment for learning design. Front. ICT. **5**, 1–19 (2018). https://doi.org/10.3389/fict.2018.00009
30. Laurillard, D., et al.: A constructionist learning environment for teachers to model learning designs. J. Comput. Assist. Learn. **29**, 15–30 (2013). https://doi.org/10.1111/j.1365-2729.2011.00458.x
31. Aggarwal, Charu C.: An Introduction to Recommender Systems. Recommender Systems, pp. 1–28. Springer, Cham (2016). https://doi.org/10.1007/978-3-319-29659-3_1
32. Xiao, B., Benbasat, I.: Research on the use, characteristics, and impact of e-commerce product recommendation agents: a review and update for 2007–2012. In: Martínez-López, Francisco J. (ed.) Handbook of Strategic e-Business Management. PI, pp. 403–431. Springer, Heidelberg (2014). https://doi.org/10.1007/978-3-642-39747-9_18
33. Drachsler, H., Verbert, K., Santos, Olga C., Manouselis, N.: Panorama of recommender systems to support learning. In: Ricci, F., Rokach, L., Shapira, B. (eds.) Recommender Systems Handbook, pp. 421–451. Springer, Boston, MA (2015). https://doi.org/10.1007/978-1-4899-7637-6_12
34. Manouselis, N., Drachsler, H., Verbert, K., Santos, Olga C. (eds.): Recommender Systems for Technology Enhanced Learning. Springer, New York (2014). https://doi.org/10.1007/978-1-4939-0530-0
35. Torre, I., Torsani, S.: A recommender system as a support and training tool. In: 2016 12th International Conference on Signal-Image Technology Internet-Based Systems (SITIS), pp. 773–780 (2016). https://doi.org/10.1109/SITIS.2016.127
36. Mota, D., Reis, L.P., de Carvalho, C.V.: A recommender model of teaching-learning techniques. In: Oliveira, E., Gama, J., Vale, Z., Lopes Cardoso, H. (eds.) EPIA 2017. LNCS (LNAI), vol. 10423, pp. 435–446. Springer, Cham (2017). https://doi.org/10.1007/978-3-319-65340-2_36
37. Pu, P., Chen, L.: A user - centric evaluation framework for recommender systems. In: Proceedings 5th ACM Conference Recommender Systems - RecSys 2011, pp. 157–164 (2011). https://doi.org/10.1145/2043932.2043962
38. De Pessemier, T., Courtois, C., Vanhecke, K., Van Damme, K., Martens, L., De Marez, L.: A user-centric evaluation of context-aware recommendations for a mobile news service. Multimed. Tools Appl. **75**, 3323–3351 (2016)
39. Braunhofer, M., Elahi, M., Ge, M., Ricci, F., Schievenin, T.: STS: design of weather-aware mobile recommender systems in tourism. In: Proceedings 1st Work. AI* HCI Intelligent User Interfaces (AI* HCI 2013), p. 1125 (2013)
40. Beel, J., Gipp, B., Langer, S., Breitinger, C.: Research-paper recommender systems: a literature survey. Int. J. Digit. Libr. **17**, 305–338 (2016). https://doi.org/10.1007/s00799-015-0156-0
41. Erdt, M., Fernandez, A., Rensing, C.: Evaluating recommender systems for technology enhanced learning: a quantitative survey. IEEE Trans. Learn. Technol. **1382**, 1 (2015). https://doi.org/10.1109/TLT.2015.2438867

The Diagnosing Behaviour of Intelligent Tutoring Systems

Renate van der Bent[1], Johan Jeuring[1,2(✉)], and Bastiaan Heeren[2]

[1] Department of Information and Computing Sciences, Universiteit Utrecht, Utrecht, The Netherlands
J.T.Jeuring@uu.nl
[2] Faculty of Management, Science & Technology, Open University of the Netherlands, Heerlen, The Netherlands
Bastiaan.Heeren@ou.nl

Abstract. Intelligent Tutoring Systems (ITSs) determine the quality of student responses by means of a diagnostic process, and use this information for providing feedback and determining a student's progress. This paper studies how ITSs diagnose student responses. In a systematic literature review we compare the diagnostic processes of 40 ITSs in various domains. We investigate what kinds of diagnoses are performed and how they are obtained, and how the processes compare across domains. The analysis identifies eight aspects that ITSs diagnose: correctness, difference, redundancy, type of error, common error, order, preference, and time. All ITSs diagnose correctness of a step. Mathematics tutors diagnose common errors more often than programming tutors, and programming tutors diagnose type of error more often than mathematics tutors. We discuss a general model for representing diagnostic processes.

Keywords: Intelligent Tutoring Systems · Diagnosis · Feedback

1 Introduction

More than a decade ago, VanLehn published his paper on the behaviour of Intelligent Tutoring Systems (ITSs) [60]. An ITS consists of an outer loop, which serves tasks to a student matching her progress, and an inner loop, which gives a student feedback and hints about steps she takes towards solving a task. Completing a task in an ITS often requires multiple steps, where "a step is a user interface action that the student takes in order to achieve a task" [60]. An important responsibility of the inner loop is what VanLehn calls step analysis.

Diagnosing student steps is essential for determining progress, and for giving feedback and hints. Feedback and hints are important factors supporting learning [28]. How do different ITSs diagnose a student step? We perform a systematic literature review of available step-based ITSs to classify the diagnostic processes of these systems. We determine the various components that play a role in diagnosing student steps, and study how these components are combined

M. Scheffel et al. (Eds.): EC-TEL 2019, LNCS 11722, pp. 112–126, 2019.
https://doi.org/10.1007/978-3-030-29736-7_9

to perform a full diagnosis. Furthermore, we compare the diagnoses of ITSs from different domains (such as mathematics, programming, and physics), and ITSs using different approaches (such as constraint-based tutoring [50], model tracing [5], example tracing [43], and intention-based tutoring [39]). The results of our study inform the design of ITSs, and might in the future be combined with results from effectiveness studies [61] to get a better understanding of what kind of diagnostic processes are likely to be more effective.

The research question we address in this paper is: How do ITSs determine the quality of student responses? To answer this question, we will look at the aspects that can be distinguished in the diagnosis of a student response, how these aspects are combined in various ITSs, and if there are patterns or perhaps even a general scheme that can be identified in the diagnostic processes of the different ITSs. The contributions of this paper are:

- we distinguish eight aspects that are used in various tutors in diagnosing a student step;
- we describe patterns in combining these aspects;
- we compare how diagnosing differs between domains and tutoring approaches.

This paper is organised as follows. Section 2 discusses related work. Section 3 describes the research method, and the resulting diagnostic aspects and processes are presented in Sect. 4. Section 5 concludes.

2 Related Work

We are not aware of research on comparing diagnostic processes of ITSs across various domains and using different tutoring approaches. In the 1970 s and later, research focused on diagnosing a particular aspect of students' work, namely misconceptions [14]. Diagnosing misconceptions requires collecting and checking for buggy rules, which sometimes leads to overwhelming and impractical numbers of buggy rules, even for simple domains such as fractions [31]. Modern approaches, such as algorithmic debugging [68], automatically distinguish buggy rules. Heeren and Jeuring present an advanced diagnose service, which is used in ITSs for mathematics, logic, and programming [29].

Diagnosis of student steps has been studied extensively in ITSs and assessment systems for mathematics, such as Stack [54] and ActiveMath [24]. El-Kechaï et al. [21] evaluate the diagnosing behaviour of PépiMep, a diagnosis system for algebra that is part of a web-based mathematics platform. This system can distinguish 13 different patterns in student responses. Chanier et al. [16] review how errors are analysed in several ITSs for second-language learning. More related work on diagnosing student steps is described later in this paper.

3 Research Method

For our review we selected papers describing an ITS that is capable of providing feedback at the level of individual steps and that has been used in classrooms, or tested on data from real students. These inclusion criteria ensure that the ITS has an inner loop with a step analysis, and ensure ecological validity, i.e. that the ITS makes realistic diagnoses.

We searched for relevant papers in two ways. First, we considered systems discussed in three relevant reviews. Keuning et al. [41] classify the types of feedback given in programming tutors. Specifically, we included papers describing systems that are labelled as providing feedback on task-processing steps, because these papers are assumed to meet the first two criteria. VanLehn's review on the effectiveness of tutoring systems [61] classifies systems as answer-based, step-based, or substep-based. The step-based and substep-based systems satisfy our inclusion criteria. Finally, Cheung and Slavin's review [17] discusses the effectiveness of educational software in mathematics. From these reviews, we included 14, 17, and 0 papers, respectively (i.e. 31 papers in total). The papers in Cheung and Slavin's review [17] did not meet the inclusion criteria, or lacked a description of the system's working.

Second, we searched for papers using a literature search. A preliminary search in several search engines (Google Scholar, Scopus, and ERIC) revealed that Scopus produces the most relevant search results. See Van der Bent's thesis [12] for different search terms and the resulting number of papers. We judged relevance of papers by reading the abstract and, when necessary, by skimming through the article. The search term that produced the most relevant results was

```
intelligent AND (tutoring OR tutor) AND systems
  AND ((step AND based) OR stepwise)
```

in Scopus, giving 195 papers. Using the same terms in ERIC resulted in fewer papers, largely a subset of documents found in Scopus. Searching in Google Scholar resulted in many more, but less relevant, papers. The papers found in Scopus were also found in Google Scholar. Hence, we used the 195 documents found in Scopus. Note that using the search term `(step AND based) OR stepwise` may have resulted in finding fewer papers from less-structured domains.

Next, we checked this initial selection of papers for the inclusion criteria. The first author read the abstracts. If the information in the abstract was insufficient to determine whether a system meets all criteria, she read the full paper. If this did not result in a decision, the second author read the paper, and discussed the paper's relevance with the first author. The literature search resulted in 16 more papers that meet the inclusion criteria.

We categorized the ITSs described in the selected papers by their tutoring approach (model tracing, example tracing, constraint-based, or intention-based: Aleven et al. [2] explain the differences between the first three of these paradigms) and by domain. Then, starting with a small subset of papers (around 10), we iteratively designed a system for labelling the diagnostic processes and diagnosed aspects. With this labelling system we categorized the rest of the selected ITSs.

After labelling the diagnostic processes, we checked whether there are any noticeable differences between approaches or domains, by comparing the frequency at which aspects are diagnosed per approach and per domain. We also described the diagnostic processes in diagrams and tried to abstract a general model from the labelling system.

4 Diagnostic Aspects and Processes

We found 47 papers on 40 ITSs that satisfy our inclusion criteria. Table 1 gives an overview of the ITSs, including references, domain, and tutoring approach. We found 26 model tracing tutors, 8 example tracing tutors, 11 constraint-based tutors, and 1 intention-based tutor. An ITS can make use of multiple approaches, for example, Andes [63] and Mathtutor [1] use constraints in combination with the example tracing approach. We could not determine the approach used by the Technical Troubleshooting tutor [38].

Subsection 4.1 describes the diagnostic aspects we found based on a small sample of papers, which we used to label the rest of the ITSs. Subsection 4.2 describes the frequency of aspects per approach and domain. Subsection 4.3 discusses models representing the diagnostic processes of some tutoring systems, followed by a general model for diagnostic processes in Subsect. 4.4.

4.1 Diagnostic Aspects

We found that ITSs use the following aspects to diagnose a student step: correctness, difference, redundancy, type of error, common error, order, preference, and time. We explain and illustrate these aspects below. Whenever relevant, the running example will be the following algebra problem: "Solve for x: $5x+6 = 7x$".

Correctness (C) determines whether or not a student step matches an expected step, or does not violate any constraint. Possible outcomes are *correct* and *incorrect*. For instance, if a student submits $2x + 6 = 0$, this step is diagnosed as incorrect because it does not match the expected next step $5x - 7x + 6 = 0$. The equation $5x + 6 - 7x = 0$ is considered correct because it is semantically equivalent to the expected answer.

Difference (D) is similar to correctness, in that it determines whether or not a step matches an expected step. The result is a measure such as a number or percentage that indicates the edit distance between the student step and an expected step. When the difference is zero, the step is correct. For example, if we use the edit distance, the above incorrect response results in a difference value of 1, since it requires one edit operation (replace "+" by "−") to change the incorrect step into the expected step.

Redundancy (R) refers to a superfluous step: this includes steps that are too small to be recognized as a meaningful step. Possible outcomes are *redundant*, *not redundant*, and *unknown*. For example, the rewrite step from $5x-7x+6 = 0$ into $-7x + 5x + 6 = 0$ can be considered redundant.

Type of Error (ToE) refers to a classification of errors. Possible outcomes differ per problem domain or ITS. For example, $5x - (7x + 6 = 0$ can be classified as a syntax error.

Common Errors (CE) or buggy rules are misconceptions that a student may have. Possible outcomes differ per problem domain or ITS. An example of a buggy rule is forgetting to change the sign when moving an expression from one side of the equation to the other side, for instance, rewriting an expression of the form $5x + 6 = 7x$ into $5x + 6 + 7x = 0$.

Table 1. Overview of the 40 systems with their domain, tutoring approach (mt: model tracing, ex: example tracing, cb: constraint-based, ib: intention-based), and diagnosed aspects; the eight aspects are correctness (C), difference (D), redundancy (R), type of error (ToE), common errors (CE), order (O), preference (P), and time (T)

ITS	Domain and approach		C	D	R	ToE	CE	O	P	T
(Why2-)Atlas [62]	Qualitative physics	mt	•			•	•			
(Why2-)Autotutor [26, 25]	Physics & Computer literacy	mt	•	•			•			
ACT Programming Tutor [18]	Programming	mt	•				•			
AITS [27]	Search algorithms	ex	•	•	•	•				
Andes [63]	Physics	mt,cb	•		•	•			•	
ANGLE [44]	Geometry	mt	•				•			
APROPOS2 [49]	Prolog programming	ex	•	•	•	•	•	•	•	
Ask-Elle [34]	Haskell programming	mt,cb	•			•	•		•	
Assistment [51]	Mathematics	mt	•				•			
AzAR 3.0 [20]	Foreign language pronunciation	ex	•	•		•	•			
CIMEL ITS [13]	OO design and programming	mt	•			•				
CIRCSIM-TUTOR [42, 23]	Circulatory physiology	mt	•			•		•		
C-Tutor [57]	C programming	ib	•			•				
Design-A-Plant [46, 47]	Botany	cb	•							
Dragoon [66]	Dynamic systems	ex	•		•	•				
ELM-ART [64]	LISP programming	mt	•			•				
Geometry Explanation [4, 3]	Geometry	mt	•			•	•			
Geomtery Tutor [6]	Geometry	mt	•				•			
HBPS [9, 10]	Algebra word problems	mt	•			•	•			
Hong04 [32]	Prolog programming	mt	•			•				
iList [22]	Computer Science	cb	•			•	•			
ITAP [52]	Python programming	ex	•			•				
Jin12 [35]	Programming	ex	•			•				
Jin14 [36]	Programming	ex	•			•				
JITS [59]	Java programming	mt	•			•				
KERMIT [58]	Database design	cb	•			•				
Keuning14 [40]	Imperative programming	mt	•		•	•			•	
Mathesis [55, 56]	Algebra	mt	•			•	•	•		
Mathtutor [1]	Mathematics	ex,cb	•				•	•		
Ms. Lindquist [30]	Algebra word problems	mt	•			•	•			
Newton's Pen [45]	Statics	mt,cb	•			•				
PAT2Math [33]	Algebra	mt	•				•			
PHP ITS [65]	PHP programming	cb	•		•	•				
PLATO [15]	Arithmetic	cb	•			•	•		•	
Quantum Accounting [37]	Accounting	mt	•			•				
RMT [11]	Psychology research methods	mt	•	•						
Technical Troubleshooting [38]	Aircraft engineering	mt,cb?	•							
The Invention Lab [53]	Scientific inquiry	mt,cb	•			•	•			
The LISP Tutor [19, 7]	LISP programming	mt	•				•			
Zatarain-Cabada13 [67]	Arithmetic	mt	•							•

Order (O) refers to the order in which a student takes steps. Possible outcomes are *correct order*, *incorrect order*, and *unknown*. Note that this is a diagnosis over multiple steps.

Preference (P): some solutions may be preferable over others. Possible outcomes are *preferred*, *not preferred*, and *unknown*. For instance, in a programming tutor, a particular algorithm may produce the correct result, but be less efficient than the preferred algorithm. A teacher can express a preference for pedagogical reasons, if she wants students to use a particular approach rather than another.

Time (T) refers to the time a student takes to submit a step or solve a problem, measured in (milli)seconds. This aspect was only labelled when time was used for diagnostic purposes. While many systems measure time, only few use it for diagnostic purposes.

Table 1 gives an overview of the diagnosed aspects per ITS.

Of the eight aspects that ITSs diagnose, correctness is the most common aspect, and is used in all systems. Most other aspects depend on its outcome. For example, type of error relies on correctness, because errors can only be found in steps that are known to be incorrect. Likewise, preference also depends on correctness, because it can only determine preference between correct steps. Aside from correctness, the most commonly diagnosed aspects are the type of error and common errors.

Only one ITS [67] diagnoses time with the assumption that the time it takes to answer a question reflects the difficulty of the question. Why are other ITSs not diagnosing time? Most ITSs can be accessed at home, without supervision. This makes it difficult to monitor how much time is actually spent on answering a question. For example, a student might take a long time to answer because she is taking a break or doing something else. Perhaps this is why most ITSs do not use time for diagnosis.

4.2 Diagnostic Aspects per Approach and Domain

We distinguish four ITS approaches: model tracing (mt), example tracing (ex), constraint-based (cb), and intention-based (ib). There is some overlap between these categories: five ITSs combine model tracing and the constraint-based approach, and one ITS (Mathtutor) uses example tracing and the constraint-based approach. Only one ITS uses the intention-based approach. Table 2 (left-hand side) shows the frequency of the occurrence of aspects in the various ITS approaches. The results do not show very different patterns for the approaches.

The ITSs we study deal with tasks in a large variety of problem domains. At an abstract level, we can group them into four domains: mathematics, programming, physics, and other domains. Mathematics includes topics such as algebra, arithmetic, and geometry. Programming includes programming in specific languages, and more general topics such as object-oriented design and data structures. Physics includes qualitative physics and statics. The remaining ITSs involve topics such as botany, foreign language pronunciation, database design,

Table 2. Frequency of diagnostic aspects per tutoring approach and problem domain, both in absolute numbers and their relative frequency of occurrence (as bars)

	approach				domain			
Aspect	mt	ex	cb	ib	math	progr	physics	other
Correctness	26	8	11	1	11	15	4	12
Type of Error	16	7	8	1	5	13	3	8
Common Errors	14	3	5		10	5	2	4
Preference	3	1	3		1	3	1	
Difference	2	3	1			1	1	4
Order	2	2	1		2	1		1
Redundancy	1	3	1			3		2
Time	1				1			

and aircraft engineering. The domains partially overlap. (Why2-)Autotutor is in both the physics and 'other domains' category, because it teaches both physics and computer literacy. iList is in both the programming and 'other domains' category, because it teaches students about lists, which is an important data structure in programming, but not programming per se. Table 2 (right-hand side) also shows the frequency of the occurrence of aspects in the various ITS domains.

Table 2 shows that ITSs in the domain of mathematics more often diagnose common errors than ITSs in the other domains: 91% of the math tutors diagnose common errors, compared to only 33% of programming tutors, 50% of physics tutors, and 33% of the tutors in other domains. In mathematics, problems typically have a single correct solution, and there are only a few ways to reach that solution. Many errors in student steps can be explained by buggy rules, also because the solution space is relatively small. This partially explains why common errors are relatively often diagnosed in ITSs for mathematics.

In the domain of programming, ITSs diagnose the type of error more often than in other domains: 87% of the programming tutors diagnose the type of error, compared to 46% of the mathematics tutors, 75% of the physics tutors, and 67% of the tutors in other domains. This is perhaps due to the solution space in the domains. In programming tutors, the solution space is usually very large, which makes diagnosing common errors infeasible. Programs may have errors on different levels: syntax, dependency, typing, semantics, and more. This makes type of error a more informative diagnosis than in situations where only syntax and semantics play a role, as is usual in mathematics.

Redundancy is diagnosed in three programming tutors and two other domain tutors, but not in any mathematics or physics tutor. Because of the small sample size, we did not perform a statistical test to determine the significance of these results. The rest of the aspects seem to be diagnosed at a lower frequency across domains.

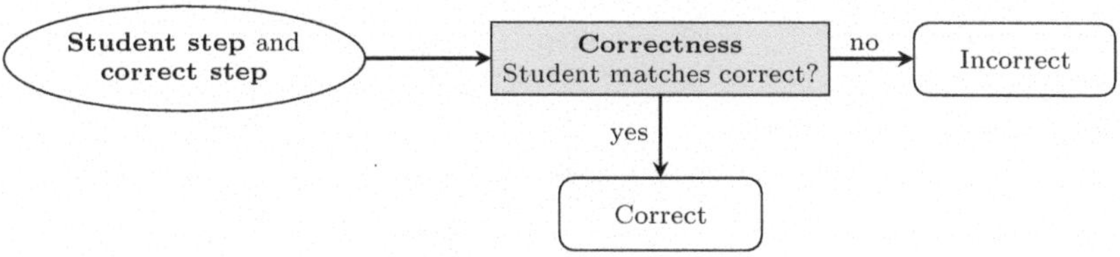

Fig. 1. Diagnostic process of Assistment, Design-a-Plant, and Quantum Accounting

4.3 Diagnostic Processes

Most ITSs use multiple aspects for diagnosing student responses. How are these aspects combined in a diagnosis? We discuss how the different aspects are combined by the different ITSs to arrive at a diagnosis, and what the commonalities are between these systems. Not all ITSs are covered here, because some papers do not provide enough detail to extract the precise diagnosing process.

Figure 1 shows the most basic diagnostic process. Ovals represent input, grey nodes represent diagnostic ITS components, and rounded rectangles represent a diagnosis. This diagram represents the diagnostic processes in Assistment, Design-a-Plant, and Quantum Accounting. A student step is checked against a single good step. If it matches, the response is correct; if not, the response is incorrect. Although Assistment and Quantum Accounting have an additional diagnostic aspect, namely type of error, this is not shown in the diagram, because it is unclear where the type of error is determined. RMT's diagnostic process is very similar, except that it uses cosine similarity to check whether a step matches an expected step.

The basic diagram in Fig. 1 can be extended in several ways. The diagnostic processes of the ACT Programming Tutor, LISP Tutor, Geometry Tutor, and PAT2Math add a second diagnostic component (i.e. a grey block) after correctness has determined that the student step does not match a good step. In this second component, common errors are searched for by using a set of buggy rules. Dragoon, on the other hand, extends the diagram with a diagnostic component that determines redundancy before checking correctness.

We give a single example of a more involved diagnostic process, and refer the reader to Van der Bent's thesis [12] for many more diagrammatic representations of diagnostic processes that were found in ITSs.

The diagnostic process of AITS is illustrated in Fig. 2. AITS calculates the difference using edit distance. This information is used to infer correctness. If the edit distance is zero, the node sequence is correct. Otherwise, AITS checks the number of nodes and the content of the nodes in the submitted answer, and uses this to determine redundancy and type of error: AITS treats redundancy as one type of error. The *complete* and *accurate* diagnoses are labelled as types of errors. In AITS, a type of error is a combination of completeness and accuracy, so a step can be *complete but inaccurate*, *incomplete but accurate*, or *incomplete and inaccurate*. The diagnosis *complete and accurate* never occurs since then the edit distance would be zero, and the step would have been diagnosed as correct.

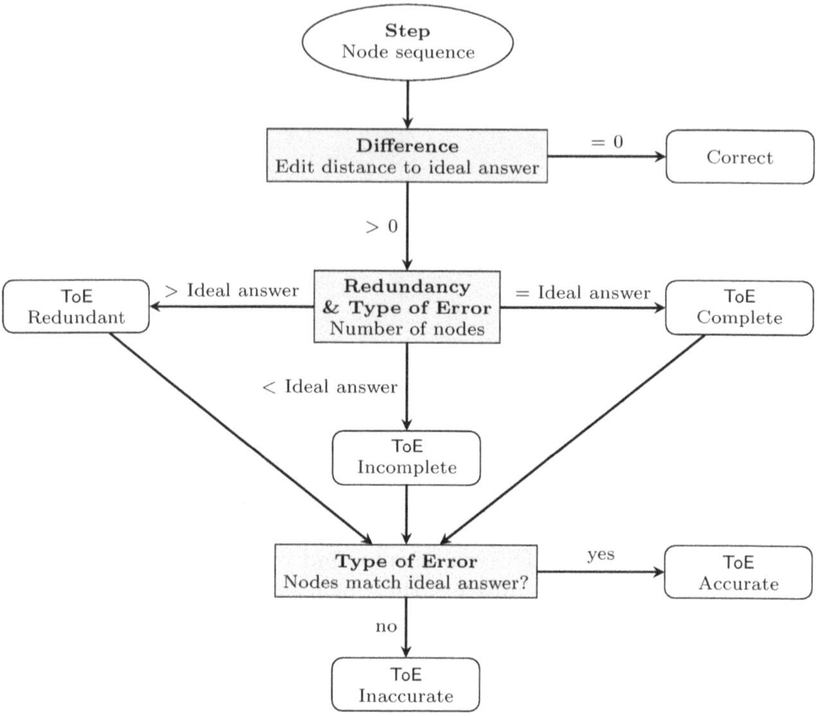

Fig. 2. Diagnostic process of AITS

4.4 Patterns in Diagnostic Processes

Figure 3 illustrates the general diagnostic process. A dashed border indicates that the components are optional. All tutors check whether a step is correct using correctness or difference. Before this is done, however, some tutors check the order of steps or how much time was taken to submit a step. After it has been determined that a step is correct, some tutors check whether the correct step is also a preferred step. Some tutors also check whether a correct step is redundant. For incorrect steps, some tutors check whether the step contains common errors, and what type of error was made. Lastly, some tutors check whether an incorrect step is redundant. Note that, as was mentioned before, some tutors consider redundancy as an error, while others treat it as correct.

Some ITSs make more fine-grained diagnoses than the ones discussed in this study [8,48]. For example, in Arends' ITS [8] expressions can be semantically equivalent after an incorrect step. To signal such a step, the system can diagnose expressions that are semantically equivalent while also following a buggy rule, or expressions that are expected by a strategy despite not being semantically equivalent. Since these types of diagnoses only appear in this particular ITS, and seem to be very particular to the domain, we did not include them in our research.

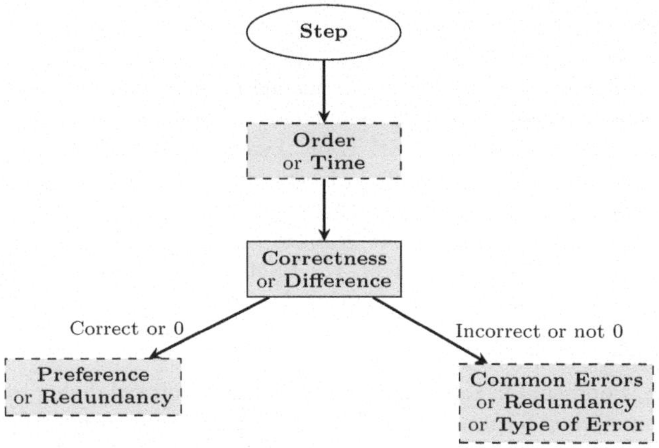

Fig. 3. General diagnostic process

5 Conclusion

As an answer to our research question, we found eight diagnostic aspects of student responses in Intelligent Tutoring Systems: correctness, difference, redundancy, type of error, common error, order, preference, and time. The diagnostic aspects are combined in various ways in the full diagnoses of the ITSs. Although these processes vary widely between systems, we distilled a general, abstract process that is used in all ITSs. All ITSs diagnose correctness, and although there are differences between domains, common errors and the type of error are also often diagnosed. The main difference between domains is that common errors is the second most frequently diagnosed aspect in mathematics tutors, whereas type of error is the second most frequently diagnosed aspect in programming tutors. Our analysis found no difference between four common tutoring approaches.

A limitation of our work is that the analysis of diagnostic processes is based on the information given in the papers written about the ITSs, rather than on the source code of the ITSs. Not all papers provide an in-depth description of how student steps are diagnosed, which made it impossible to describe the diagnostic processes of some systems. Sometimes we had to interpret the text to determine the diagnostic process.

Our analysis of diagnostic processes in ITSs contributes to a better understanding of the diagnosing behaviour of ITSs. For future research, the results of this study could be combined with results from evaluations of the effectiveness of tutoring systems [61]. This would give insight into which diagnostic processes are most effective at improving learning. This insight could then inform the design and development of tutoring systems in the future.

Acknowledgements. The authors would like to thank the anonymous reviewers and the members of the Utrecht reading club on educational technology for their helpful suggestions.

References

1. Aleven, V., McLaren, B.M., Sewall, J.: Scaling up programming by demonstration for intelligent tutoring systems development: an open-access web site for middle school mathematics learning. IEEE Trans. Learn. Technol. **2**(2), 64–78 (2009)
2. Aleven, V., Mclaren, B.M., Sewall, J., Koedinger, K.R.: A new paradigm for intelligent tutoring systems: example-tracing tutors. Int. J. Artif. Intell. Educ. **19**(2), 105–154 (2009)
3. Aleven, V., Popescu, O., Koedinger, K.: Pilot-testing a tutorial dialogue system that supports self-explanation. In: Cerri, S.A., Gouardères, G., Paraguaçu, F. (eds.) ITS 2002. LNCS, vol. 2363, pp. 344–354. Springer, Heidelberg (2002). https://doi.org/10.1007/3-540-47987-2_38
4. Aleven, V., Popescu, O., Koedinger, K.R.: Towards tutorial dialog to support self-explanation: adding natural language understanding to a cognitive tutor. In: Proceedings of Artificial Intelligence in Education, pp. 246–255. Citeseer (2001)
5. Anderson, J.R., Boyle, C.F., Reiser, B.J.: Intelligent tutoring systems. Science **228**(4698), 456–462 (1985)
6. Anderson, J.R., Boyle, C.F., Yost, G.: The geometry tutor. In: IJCAI, pp. 1–7 (1985)
7. Anderson, J.R., Reiser, B.J.: The LISP tutor. Byte **10**, 159–175 (1985)
8. Arends, H., Keuning, H., Heeren, B., Jeuring, J.: An intelligent tutor to learn the evaluation of microcontroller I/O programming expressions. In: Proceedings of the 17th Koli Calling Conference on Computing Education Research, pp. 2–9. ACM (2017)
9. Arevalillo-Herráez, M., Arnau, D., Marco-Giménez, L.: Domain-specific knowledge representation and inference engine for an intelligent tutoring system. Knowl.-Based Syst. **49**, 97–105 (2013)
10. Arnau, D., Arevalillo-Herráez, M., Puig, L., González-Calero, J.A.: Fundamentals of the design and the operation of an intelligent tutoring system for the learning of the arithmetical and algebraic way of solving word problems. Comput. Educ. **63**, 119–130 (2013)
11. Arnott, E., Hastings, P., Allbritton, D.: Research methods tutor: evaluation of a dialogue-based tutoring system in the classroom. Behav. Res. Methods **40**(3), 694–698 (2008)
12. van der Bent, R.: The diagnosing behaviour of intelligent tutoring systems. Master's thesis, Universiteit Utrecht (2018)
13. Blank, G., Parvez, S., Wei, F., Moritz, S.: A web-based ITS for OO design. In: Proceedings of Workshop on Adaptive Systems for Web-based Education at 12th International Conference on Artificial Intelligence in Education (AIED 2005), Amsterdam, the Netherlands, pp. 59–64 (2005)
14. Brown, J.S., Burton, R.R.: Diagnostic models for procedural bugs in basic mathematical skills. Cogn. Sci. **2**(2), 155–192 (1978)
15. Burton, R.R., Brown, J.S.: A tutoring and student modelling paradigm for gaming environments. ACM SIGCUE Outlook **10**(SI), 236–246 (1976)
16. Chanier, T., Pengelly, M., Twidale, M., Self, J.: Conceptual modelling in error analysis in computer-assisted language learning systems. In: Swartz, M.L., Yazdani, M. (eds.) Intelligent Tutoring Systems for Foreign Language Learning. NATO ASI Series, pp. 125–150. Springer, Heidelberg (1992). https://doi.org/10.1007/978-3-642-77202-3_9

17. Cheung, A.C., Slavin, R.E.: The effectiveness of educational technology applications for enhancing mathematics achievement in k-12 classrooms: a meta-analysis. Educ. Res. Rev. **9**, 88–113 (2013)
18. Corbett, A.T., Anderson, J.R.: Locus of feedback control in computer-based tutoring: impact on learning rate, achievement and attitudes. In: Proceedings of the SIGCHI conference on Human factors in computing systems, pp. 245–252. ACM (2001)
19. Corbett, A.T., Anderson, J.R., Patterson, E.G.: Student modeling and tutoring flexibility in the Lisp intelligent tutoring system. In: Gauthier, G., Frasson, C. (eds.) Intelligent Tutoring Systems: at the crossroads of artificial intelligence and education, pp. 83–106. Intellect Ltd. (1990)
20. Demenko, G., Wagner, A., Cylwik, N.: The use of speech technology in foreign language pronunciation training. Arch. Acoust. **35**(3), 309–329 (2010)
21. El-Kechaï, N., Delozanne, É., Prévit, D., Grugeon, B., Chenevotot, F.: Evaluating the performance of a diagnosis system in school algebra. In: Leung, H., Popescu, E., Cao, Y., Lau, R.W.H., Nejdl, W. (eds.) ICWL 2011. LNCS, vol. 7048, pp. 263–272. Springer, Heidelberg (2011). https://doi.org/10.1007/978-3-642-25813-8_28
22. Fossati, D., Di Eugenio, B., Ohlsson, S., Brown, C., Chen, L.: Data driven automatic feedback generation in the ilist intelligent tutoring system. Technol. Instr. Cogn. Learn. **10**(1), 5–26 (2015)
23. Glass, M.: Some phenomena handled by the circsim-tutor version 3 input understander. In: Proceedings of the Tenth Florida Artificial Intelligence Research Symposium, Daytona Beach, pp. 21–25 (1997)
24. Goguadze, G., Melis, E.: Combining evaluative and generative diagnosis in activemath. In: Proceedings of the 2009 Conference on Artificial Intelligence in Education: Building Learning Systems That Care: From Knowledge Representation to Affective Modelling, pp. 668–670 (2009)
25. Graesser, A.C., et al.: Autotutor: a tutor with dialogue in natural language. Behav. Res. Methods Instrum. Comput. **36**(2), 180–192 (2004)
26. Graesser, A.C., Wiemer-Hastings, P., Wiemer-Hastings, K., Harter, D., Tutoring Research Group, T.R.G., Person, N.: Using latent semantic analysis to evaluate the contributions of students in autotutor. Interact. Learn. Environ. **8**(2), 129–147 (2000)
27. Grivokostopoulou, F., Perikos, I., Hatzilygeroudis, I.: An educational system for learning search algorithms and automatically assessing student performance. Int. J. Artif. Intell. Educ. **27**(1), 207–240 (2017)
28. Hattie, J., Timperley, H.: The power of feedback. Rev. Educ. Res. **77**(1), 81–112 (2007)
29. Heeren, B., Jeuring, J.: Feedback services for stepwise exercises. Sci. Comput. Program. **88**, 110–129 (2014)
30. Heffernan, N.T., Koedinger, K.R.: An intelligent tutoring system incorporating a model of an experienced human tutor. In: Cerri, S.A., Gouardères, G., Paraguaçu, F. (eds.) ITS 2002. LNCS, vol. 2363, pp. 596–608. Springer, Heidelberg (2002). https://doi.org/10.1007/3-540-47987-2_61
31. Hennecke, M.: Online Diagnose in intelligenten mathematischen Lehr-Lern-Systemen. Ph.D. thesis, Hildesheim University (1999). in German
32. Hong, J.: Guided programming and automated error analysis in an intelligent prolog tutor. Int. J. Hum Comput Stud. **61**(4), 505–534 (2004)
33. Jaques, P.A., et al.: Rule-based expert systems to support step-by-step guidance in algebraic problem solving: the case of the tutor pat2math. Expert Syst. Appl. **40**(14), 5456–5465 (2013)

34. Jeuring, J., Gerdes, A., Heeren, B.: A programming tutor for haskell. In: Zsók, V., Horváth, Z., Plasmeijer, R. (eds.) CEFP 2011. LNCS, vol. 7241, pp. 1–45. Springer, Heidelberg (2012). https://doi.org/10.1007/978-3-642-32096-5_1
35. Jin, W., Barnes, T., Stamper, J., Eagle, M.J., Johnson, M.W., Lehmann, L.: Program representation for automatic hint generation for a data-driven novice programming tutor. In: Cerri, S.A., Clancey, W.J., Papadourakis, G., Panourgia, K. (eds.) ITS 2012. LNCS, vol. 7315, pp. 304–309. Springer, Heidelberg (2012). https://doi.org/10.1007/978-3-642-30950-2_40
36. Jin, W., Corbett, A., Lloyd, W., Baumstark, L., Rolka, C.: Evaluation of guided-planning and assisted-coding with task relevant dynamic hinting. In: Trausan-Matu, S., Boyer, K.E., Crosby, M., Panourgia, K. (eds.) ITS 2014. LNCS, vol. 8474, pp. 318–328. Springer, Cham (2014). https://doi.org/10.1007/978-3-319-07221-0_40
37. Johnson, B.G., Phillips, F., Chase, L.G.: An intelligent tutoring system for the accounting cycle: enhancing textbook homework with artificial intelligence. J. Account. Educ. **27**(1), 30–39 (2009)
38. Johnson, S.D., et al.: Application of cognitive theory to the design, development, and implementation of a computer-based troubleshooting tutor (1992)
39. Johnson, W.L.: Intention-Based Diagnosis of Novice Programming Errors. MorganKaufmann, Los Altos (1986)
40. Keuning, H., Heeren, B., Jeuring, J.: Strategy-based feedback in a programming tutor. In: Proceedings of the Computer Science Education Research Conference, pp. 43–54. ACM (2014)
41. Keuning, H., Jeuring, J., Heeren, B.: A systematic literature review of automated feedback generation for programming exercises. ACM Trans. Comput. Educ. **19**(1), 3:1–3:43 (2018)
42. Kim, N., Evens, M., Michael, J.A., Rovick, A.A.: Circsim-tutor: an intelligent tutoring system for circulatory physiology. In: Maurer, H. (ed.) ICCAL 1989. LNCS, vol. 360, pp. 254–266. Springer, Heidelberg (1989). https://doi.org/10.1007/3-540-51142-3_64
43. Koedinger, K.R., Aleven, V., Heffernan, N., McLaren, B., Hockenberry, M.: Opening the door to non-programmers: authoring intelligent tutor behavior by demonstration. In: Lester, J.C., Vicari, R.M., Paraguaçu, F. (eds.) ITS 2004. LNCS, vol. 3220, pp. 162–174. Springer, Heidelberg (2004). https://doi.org/10.1007/978-3-540-30139-4_16
44. Koedinger, K.R., Anderson, J.R.: Reifying implicit planning in geometry guidelines for model-based intelligent. In: Lajoie, S., Derry, S. (eds.) Computers as Cognitive Tools. Erlbaum, Hillsdale (2013)
45. Lee, W., de Silva, R., Peterson, E.J., Calfee, R.C., Stahovich, T.F.: Newton's pen: a pen-based tutoring system for statics. Comput. Graph. **32**(5), 511–524 (2008)
46. Lester, J.C., Stone, B.A., O'Leary, M.A., Stevenson, R.B.: Focusing problem solving in design-centered learning environments. In: Frasson, C., Gauthier, G., Lesgold, A. (eds.) ITS 1996. LNCS, vol. 1086, pp. 475–483. Springer, Heidelberg (1996). https://doi.org/10.1007/3-540-61327-7_146
47. Lester, J.C., Stone, B.A., Stelling, G.D.: Lifelike pedagogical agents for mixed-initiative problem solving in constructivist learning environments. User Model. User-Adap. Inter. **9**(1–2), 1–44 (1999)
48. Lodder, J., Heeren, B., Jeuring, J.: A domain reasoner for propositional logic. J. Univ. Comput. Sci. **22**(8), 1097–1122 (2016)
49. Looi, C.K.: Automatic debugging of prolog programs in a prolog intelligent tutoring system. Instr. Sci. **20**(2–3), 215–263 (1991)

50. Mitrovic, A., Suraweera, P., Martin, B.: Intelligent tutors for all: the constraint-based approach. IEEE Intell. Syst. **22**(4), 38–45 (2007)
51. Razzaq, L.M., et al.: Blending assessment and instructional assisting. In: AIED, pp. 555–562 (2005)
52. Rivers, K., Koedinger, K.R.: Data-driven hint generation in vast solution spaces: a self-improving python programming tutor. Int. J. Artif. Intell. Educ. **27**(1), 37–64 (2017)
53. Roll, I., Aleven, V., Koedinger, K.R.: The invention lab: using a hybrid of model tracing and constraint-based modeling to offer intelligent support in inquiry environments. In: Aleven, V., Kay, J., Mostow, J. (eds.) ITS 2010. LNCS, vol. 6094, pp. 115–124. Springer, Heidelberg (2010). https://doi.org/10.1007/978-3-642-13388-6_16
54. Sangwin, C.: Computer Aided Assessment of Mathematics. Oxford University Press, Oxford (2013)
55. Sklavakis, D., Refanidis, I.: An individualized web-based algebra tutor based on dynamic deep model tracing. In: Darzentas, J., Vouros, G.A., Vosinakis, S., Arnellos, A. (eds.) SETN 2008. LNCS (LNAI), vol. 5138, pp. 389–394. Springer, Heidelberg (2008). https://doi.org/10.1007/978-3-540-87881-0_38
56. Sklavakis, D., Refanidis, I.: Mathesis: an intelligent web-based algebra tutoring school. Int. J. Artif. Intell. Educ. **22**(4), 191–218 (2013)
57. Song, J., Hahn, S., Tak, K., Kim, J.: An intelligent tutoring system for introductory C language course. Comput. Educ. **28**(2), 93–102 (1997)
58. Suraweera, P., Mitrovic, A.: KERMIT: a constraint-based tutor for database modeling. In: Cerri, S.A., Gouardères, G., Paraguaçu, F. (eds.) ITS 2002. LNCS, vol. 2363, pp. 377–387. Springer, Heidelberg (2002). https://doi.org/10.1007/3-540-47987-2_41
59. Sykes, E.R.: Design, development and evaluation of the Java intelligent tutoring system. Technol. Instr. Cogn. Learn. **8**(1), 25–65 (2010)
60. VanLehn, K.: The behavior of tutoring systems. Int. J. Artif. Intell. Educ. **16**(3), 227–265 (2006)
61. VanLehn, K.: The relative effectiveness of human tutoring, intelligent tutoring systems, and other tutoring systems. Educ. Psychol. **46**(4), 197–221 (2011)
62. VanLehn, K., et al.: The Architecture of Why2-Atlas: A Coach for Qualitative Physics Essay Writing. In: Cerri, S.A., Gouardères, G., Paraguaçu, F. (eds.) ITS 2002. LNCS, vol. 2363, pp. 158–167. Springer, Heidelberg (2002). https://doi.org/10.1007/3-540-47987-2_20
63. VanLehn, K.: The andes physics tutoring system: lessons learned. Int. J. Artifi. Intell. Educ. **15**(3), 147–204 (2005)
64. Weber, G., Brusilovsky, P.: Elm-art: an adaptive versatile system for web-based instruction. Int. J. Artif. Intell. Educ. (IJAIED) **12**, 351–384 (2001)
65. Weragama, D., Reye, J.: Analysing student programs in the php intelligent tutoring system. Int. J. Artif. Intell. Educ. **24**(2), 162–188 (2014)
66. Wetzel, J., et al.: The design and development of the dragoon intelligent tutoring system for model construction: lessons learned. Interact. Learn. Environ. **25**(3), 361–381 (2017)

67. Zatarain-Cabada, R., Barrón-Estrada, M.L., Pérez, Y.H., Reyes-García, C.A.: Designing and implementing affective and intelligent tutoring systems in a learning social network. In: Batyrshin, I., Mendoza, M.G. (eds.) MICAI 2012. LNCS (LNAI), vol. 7630, pp. 444–455. Springer, Heidelberg (2013). https://doi.org/10.1007/978-3-642-37798-3_39
68. Zinn, C.: Algorithmic debugging to support cognitive diagnosis in tutoring systems. In: Bach, J., Edelkamp, S. (eds.) KI 2011. LNCS (LNAI), vol. 7006, pp. 357–368. Springer, Heidelberg (2011). https://doi.org/10.1007/978-3-642-24455-1_35

Learners Self-directing Learning in FutureLearn MOOCs: A Learner-Centered Study

Inge de Waard(✉) and Agnes Kukulska-Hulme

The Open University, Walton Hall, MK7 6AA Milton Keynes, UK
ingedewaard@gmail.com,
Agnes.Kukulska-Hulme@open.ac.uk

Abstract. This qualitative research study focuses on how experienced online learners self-direct their learning while engaging in a MOOC delivered on the FutureLearn platform. Self-directed learning is an important concept within informal learning and online learning. This study distinguishes itself from previous MOOC learner studies, by reporting the self-directed learning using a bottom-up approach. By looking at self-reported learning logs and interview transcripts an in-depth analysis of the self-directed learning is achieved. The data analysis used constructed grounded theory [1], which aligns with the bottom-up approach where the learner data is coded and investigated in an open, yet evidence-based way, leaving room for insights to emerge from the learner data. The data corpus is based on 56 participants following three FutureLearn MOOCs, providing 147 learning logs and 19 semi-structured one-on-one interviews with a selection of participants. The results show five specific areas in which learners react with either the material or other learners to self-direct their learning: context, individual or social learning, technology and media provided in the MOOCs, learner characteristics and organising learning. This study also indicates how intrinsic motivation and personal learning goals are the main inhibitors or enablers of self-directed learning.

Keywords: Self-Directed learning · MOOC · Informal learning · FutureLearn

1 Literature

1.1 The Need for Bottom-up Self-Directed Learning Studies in MOOCs

Research focusing on self-directed learning (SDL) is important if we want to understand how learners set out their path in online courses such as MOOCs [2, 3]. When looking at who engages in MOOCs, most learners are already employed, well educated, from developed countries and have higher levels of formal education [4, 5]. This means that learning within MOOCs is done by adults, and concepts from adult learning are of interest in MOOC research. Knowles [6] promoted the concept of andragogy for adult learning and he defined SDL as: the process in which individuals take the initiative, with or without the help of others, in diagnosing their learning needs, formulating

M. Scheffel et al. (Eds.): EC-TEL 2019, LNCS 11722, pp. 127–141, 2019.
https://doi.org/10.1007/978-3-030-29736-7_10

learning goals, identifying human and material resources for learning, choosing and implementing learning strategies, and evaluating learning outcomes.

When looking at MOOC research a gap can be situated regarding its topics. Investigating research topics, Zhu, Sari, and Bonk [7] systematically reviewed MOOC research methods and topics based on 197 studies published from October 2014 to July 2017 (in two phases). They found that 52% were student-focused, but the topics were related to learner motivation, retention and completion, assessment, and instruction design using a more top down approach based on indicators coming from formal education. This aligns with earlier research where Veletsianos and Shepherdson [4] made a systematic analysis of 183 empirical MOOC papers published between 2013 – 2015. They [4] identified student-focused studies as the most common research strand within empirical MOOC research, accounting for 84% of the literature in their study. Their analysis also reveals that these student-centered studies were mainly looking at completion and retention rates, as well as learner subpopulations, but not the full MOOC learning experience. Veletsianos and Shepherdson [4] add that even though their results suggest that research on MOOCs focuses on student-related topics, learners' voices were largely absent in the literature, with learner voices referring to data coming straight from the learners' stories. The study we report in this paper provides a better understanding of how adult learners self-direct their learning within FutureLearn courses, to shed light on the overall learning experience and enabling the learners' voices to emerge from the data, using a bottom-up approach.

1.2 Learners Engaging in MOOCs

Kizilcec and Schneiders [8] concluded that there has not been a systematic approach to identifying learners' motivations or how these motivations relate to subsequent learning. But understanding motivational factors is not enough. As Terras and Ramsay [9] pointed out, researchers also need to understand learners' expectations and how they cope with the specific challenges that are associated with MOOCs. Wong et al. [3] emphasized that highly diverse groups of learners enrolled in MOOCs are required to make decisions related to their own learning activities to achieve academic success. Wong et al. [3] saw that many studies find positive self-regulated learning and learning outcomes among undergraduates, but there is no evidence or indication that such findings would transfer to a different population or setting. Guo and Renicke [10] investigated how learners navigate through MOOCs and they found that most learners engage in non-linear learning trajectories that do not follow a pre-established, sequential progression. Guo and Renicke also concluded that older learners follow non-linear, self-defined learning paths, indicative of a field-independent learning style. However, 'older' might not be a valid term when it comes to online learning, as age is much more relevant in formal learning than in online learning or lifelong learning. Due to the limited interaction between MOOC facilitators and learners, the onus is placed on individual learners to create and navigate their own learning journey [11]. This also puts greater responsibility on the learner. Reich [12] stated that a collective research effort is required to fully understand the impact of MOOCs, and added that we have terabytes of data about what students clicked and very little understanding of what changed in their heads.

1.3 Self-regulated Versus Self-directed Learning

Self-directed and self-regulated learning have similarities with respect to active engagement, goal-directed behaviour, metacognitive skills, and intrinsic motivation [13] adding that SDL sees learners as having more control over the learning environment, which provides the learner with the potential of initiating a learning task. Loyens, Magda & Rikers [13] look at SDL in problem-based learning and its relationship to self-regulated learning. The paper established conceptual clarity between SDL and self-regulated learning. They conclude that the concept of SDL is broader than self-regulated learning. SDL as a design feature of the learning environment stresses students' freedom in the pursuit of their learning [13]. This fits the content reality of MOOCs, where learners are supposed to choose what to learn, when and why.

2 Research Questions

The following c**entral research question** and consecutive sub-questions emerged after several iterations of research questions based on the learner experiences shared by the participants. The central research question is: What characterises the informal self-directed learning of experienced, adult online learners engaging in individual and/or social learning using any device to follow a FutureLearn MOOC?

The central research question is divided into **four sub-questions**:

- Which individual characteristics influence the learning experience?
- What are the technical & media elements influencing a learning experience?
- How does individual and social learning affect the participants' learning?
- Which actions (if any) did the learners undertake to organise their learning?

3 Research Methodology

Literature showed that little was known about the actual learning experience of adult learners in FutureLearn courses, which embedded the study in the empirical world. It also needed an inductive direction: beginning with observing the empirical world, and then reflecting on what is taking place while moving towards theoretical concepts. There were two potential qualitative research approaches: a phenomenological approach or using Grounded Theory. Both strategies of inquiry provided guidance on investigating human beings in a specific setting. Both methods provided options for consciously integrating the researchers' point of view into the actual experiences. This was important to monitor possible personal assumptions on the subject, allowing a more reflective stance towards data emerging from the data analysis phase. Creswell [14] mentioned that using a Grounded Theory approach evokes the need to select a purposeful, homogeneous sample of participants to build a sound theoretical framework. In GT, the individuals may not be located at a single site; in fact, if they are dispersed, they can provide important contextual research. This openness of GT towards the dispersed location of participants fits the reality of global online learners.

3.1 Target Population

A selection of 56 participants was made to investigate their self-directed learning. All the participants signed the informed consent after they were voluntarily attracted from three FutureLearn courses: "The Science of Medicines" organised by Monash University in Australia, "Basic science: Understanding Experiments" organised by The Open University in the United Kingdom, and "Decision Making in an Increasingly Complex and Uncertain World" organised by the University of Groningen in the Netherlands. These three publicly available courses were all rolled out for the first time during the last months of 2014. All the participants had at least 2 years experience in online learning.

3.2 Data Collection

The data for this study were collected at three different stages: an online survey (at the start of the course consisting of 3 multiple choice questions and 1 open question), learning logs (during the course consisting of 18 open and closed questions), and semi-structured one-on-one interviews with participants (post-course, 12 questions) carried out remotely. The online survey was sent to the participants at the beginning of the course, to be able to gather background information on prior online learning experience and the use of different devices (tablets, smartphones, laptops, etc.). Based on the information shared through the online survey the target group of experienced online learners with at least two years of prior online learning was chosen. This was important to ensure that the self-directed learning would not be blurred by having to learn how to learn in an online environment such as a MOOC platform.

The learners self-reported on their FutureLearn course learning experiences by filling in learning logs provided to them via mail by the principal researcher. The learning logs [15] consisted of open and closed questions, inviting the participants to describe their learning episodes. A learning episode consists of a sustained, deliberate effort from the learner to learn [16]. A learning episode can consist of one or multiple learning actions undertaken during the same learning episode. The information provided in their learning logs were where possible cross-checked with the data log files in the platform (not all learner actions can be cross-checked, as the platform data logs are limited). The semi-structured one-on-one interviews took place post-course to gain a more in-depth understanding of the actual learning experience of the learners based on their reflections on the experience. The questions for those interviews were derived from the sub-questions related to this study, as well as from emerging themes when going through the data from the learning logs.

3.3 Data Analysis

The qualitative data from the online surveys, the learning logs and the one-on-one interviews were analysed using Charmaz's [1] method for constructing a Grounded Theory (GT). 3 different coding cycles were used based on Charmaz constructivist GT, the coding cycles consisted of several iterations until saturation was reached.

- Initial coding: quickly screening all the data to get a feel of possible big subjects mentioned by the data
- Line-by-line coding, a strategy which prompts the researcher to study the data closely and begin conceptualization of the ideas (Charmaz, 2006)
- Focused coding, which permits the researcher to separate, sort and synthesize large amounts of data (Charmaz, 2006)

GT provides a flexible way of conducting research that prioritizes exploration of the given phenomenon in a predominantly inductive theory development paradigm [16]. Using an approach that covered the pre-course, during course and post-course data coming from the learners' voices, offered a view into the learner experience from the beginning which is an important factor of Constructed GT as suggested by Charmaz [1]. The participant data was coded as described in Table 1.

Table 1. Learner data coding description

Participant identifier: #DMCW/I/222	Description of each element of the participant's identifier
#DMCW	#Course, i.e. Science of Medicines (SOM), Basic Science – Understanding Experiments (BSE), Decision Making in an Increasingly Complex World (DMCW)
/LL	/Learning log (LL) or Interview (I)
/222	/participant ID

Participants were asked to submit a learning log every two weeks. Although not all participants sent their learning logs as requested, the learning log frequency per two weeks (see Table 2) shows participant persistency through their course.

Table 2. Learning Logs (LL) received per 2 weeks from n participants per course

	Number of LL weeks 1 and 2 (n=participants having submitted at least 1 learning log)	Number of Learning Logs weeks 3 and 4	Number of Learning Logs weeks 5 and 6	Total Learning Logs (total number of participants)
SOM	4 (n=3)	6 (n=3)	5 (n=2)	15 (n=4)
BSE	19 (n=13)	22 (n=14)	N/A (BSE lasted only 4 weeks)	41 (n=15)
DMCW	31 (n=22)	28 (n=22)	32 (n=24)	91 (n=37)

This persistency is consistent with Charmaz's [1] emphasis on the importance on retrieving data from participants at different points in time. This adds to the validity and rigor of this study in terms of consistently having collected participant data throughout the duration of the study.

4 Research Findings

4.1 Individual Characteristics

The term 'individual characteristic' identifies the character traits of the learner. The character traits were self-identified by the learner. Two main categories emerged: motivation and personal traits including emotions influencing the learning process.

Motivation. Motivation can influence what, when, and how people learn. Motivation is stimulated or limited within MOOCs by: choosing the course, professional versus personal motivation, and leisure learning. In motivation a distinction is made between intrinsic and extrinsic motivation based on the different reasons or goals that give rise to an action. Intrinsic motivation, which refers to doing something because it is inherently interesting or enjoyable, and extrinsic motivation, which refers to doing something because it leads to a separable outcome [17].

Choosing a Course. The learners chose and registered for specific MOOCs following their own preferences. This choice was based on a personal decision.

Motivation as Mentioned Pre-course. In the pre-course online survey, one question investigated the learners' reason for registering for that course. Motivation overall, as well as the percentages for motivation per course are provided in Table 3.

Table 3. Looking at personal or professional interest for joining the FutureLearn courses (n=115, multiple answers possible)

Motivation	All courses	SOM	BSE	DMCW
Professional interest	38%	38%	15%	42%
Personal interest	61%	61%	85%	57%
Other	1%	1%	–	1%

61% of the participants indicated they had a specific personal interest in the course. The personal interest for the BSE course is significantly higher than the other two courses. The learning logs and the interviews showed that the BSE learners were primarily interested in enhancing the family's knowledge of scientific experiments, e.g. learning about experiments with their children. Among all the participants 38% had a professional interest.

Motivation as Mentioned in Learning Logs and Interviews. When coding the learning logs and post-course interviews, they revealed that the professional or personal motivation varies per course (see Table 4).

Table 4. Percentage of motivational excerpts from learning logs referring to either personal or professional motivation per course

FutureLearn course	Percentage of motivational excerpts from the learning log data referring to personal motivation	Percentage of motivational excerpts from the learning log data referring to professional motivation
DMCW	40%	65%
BSE	29%	15%
SOM	31%	20%

The biggest difference in motivation was in the DMCW and BSE courses. The DMCW course is mentioned more frequently in relation to the participants' professional motivation, and the BSE course had more learners referring to it based on their personal interest. Comparing the content, the DMCW participants refer to the immediate integration of the course content into their professional work and/or the work of colleagues. The BSE learners refer to family and learning within the family unit.

Personal and Professional Motivation for Completing a Learning Episode. The log data on completing a learning episode (see Table 5) revealed that learning episodes were more frequently finished within their course weeks by the professionally motivated learners (74%) especially if the content was immediately of interest, while the personally motivated learners intended to pick up the learning activities later on (62%).

Table 5. Motivation in relation to completing a learning episode

Learning episode completion or not compared to motivation	Personal motivation	Professional motivation
I completed this learning episode	38%	74%
I have not completed this learning episode, but I will complete it later	62%	26%

In the self-reported learning logs the participants indicated that 79% of their learning episodes were successful. Success is task-related, and a personal feeling of success made explicit by an emotional remark or indicated as successful by the participant.

The results show that self-directed learning within MOOCs is driven or held back by intrinsic motivation, depending on the course content and personal interpretation of the usefulness of the course for the learner's benefit. This makes intrinsic motivation an inhibitor or enabler of self-directed learning in MOOCs.

Personal Traits and Emotions Influencing the Learning Process. Two personal traits emerged most frequently during the line-by-line data analysis: perseverance and self-confidence.

Perseverance. Perseverance was mentioned by 16 participants. Some learners referred to it in relation to 'learning to perfection', where learners indicated that they had to reflect on whether or not to learn all the details of a course: "I only deem it fit to quit after I have learned all there is to learn on the subject matter. I hate failure, especially, in achieving a learning objective." (#DMCW/I/220). Perseverance was also linked to a general view of learning and how learning should be undertaken, e.g. "first I need to understand before moving on" (#DMCW/LL/152).

The act of persevering can be linked to a specific personal learning interest, e.g. "I persevered to understand what was important for me to know and left the rest. So nobody motivated me and I am not motivated to understand what is irrelevant to my health and wellbeing." #SOM/LL/113.

Self-confidence. Self-confidence was mentioned explicitly by 15 participants. The data related to self-confidence ranged from the learner's views on their own learning: "I've found that my brain wasn't so stiff and still opened for some new knowledge" (#DMCW/I/167), to learning within the course itself: "First I felt stupid but then I reminded myself that that is why we do experiments, to test our hypothesis and not just make assumptions" (#BSE/LL/132). Self-confidence was most frequently referred to in terms of daring or doubting to engage in social learning.

Self-confidence impacting social learning: Self-confidence plays a role in triggering social learning action. Hovering between individual and social learning are those learners that seem to be willing to interact with others, yet do not always feel certain enough. Sometimes this is due to a practical element: "Connecting with others was a bit more difficult this time, because it was in English and I'm not a native speaker in English" (#DMCW/I/222), at other times it is related to a personal sense of esteem or pride or emotion: "I wouldn't dream of asking anyone to help me. This is not life or death and does not involve money so I just get on with it myself" (#SOM/LL/113). Or has a positive effect: "I found it helped to discuss what I had learned with someone…. This is something I have avoided doing until now, it really helps" (#SOM/LL/101).

Emotional language and learning: In both learning logs and interviews the participants used emotional language to support their self-reported learning experience. The emerging data suggested that content and facilitators can inspire the learner, e.g. "I enjoyed learning, especially the content of the first few weeks and both the content that Jennifer presented and her enthusiasm in the second half of the MOOC were great." (#DMCW/I/222). Emotional language was also used when learners decided to stop learning at that moment in time: "so I reckoned that I was not in the mood for learning and so I gave up" (#DMCW/LL/140).

Personal traits and emotions play a role in the MOOC learning experience. Specific personal traits such as self-confidence and perseverance let the learners self-direct their learning towards specific learning actions. While emotions color the learning experience, they can deter or stimulate learners from learning.

4.2 Technical and Media Elements Influencing SDL

Technology is a necessary component of online learning, as learners need technology to access the learning material. Two categories emerged: devices used and learning new tools suggested in the courses.

Devices Used. MOOCs are only accessible online, but some resources (e.g. videos, transcripts, and texts) could be downloaded for offline use. Table 6 gives an overview of which devices were used to access the course.

Table 6. Devices used by the learners to access the course (n=147)

Devices	Smartphone	Tablet	Laptop	Desktop	Other
Percentages	13%	12%	45%	26%	4%

The other devices comprised smart-TVs and a hybrid device. Depending on the demand of the course resources (e.g. processor demanding tools, or visually complex tools) different devices were chosen. Learners indicated that they worked with a preferred device, e.g. "We used the tablet when we were performing the experiments in the kitchen" (#BSE/I/111). Depending on the context learners switched to other devices: "I used mainly my laptop. Tablet in bed and smartphone outside." (#DMCW/I/148).

Learning New Tools Suggested in Courses. Learners shared remarks on specific tools that were part of a MOOC. In the case of the Decision Making in a Complex World course, the facilitators referred to tools that are used to demystify complexity in networks. One tool was called Lightbeam (for Firefox browser). This tool was highlighted in the learning logs by 11% of the DMCW learners, although it was not a mandatory tool to explore. The tool triggered interest due to its personal and professional potential. Lightbeam is a tool to visualize who is following your own writing or any electronic actions on the web: "I learned how to detect who was monitoring my online activities" (#DMCW/LL/126). Another tool was mentioned by 34% of the participants: NetLogo. This tool had a professional use and was suggested as part of the course exercises. While Lightbeam provoked a higher personal interest, NetLogo aroused an immediate professional implementation interest. In both cases the participants were eager to learn these new tools, even though it required extra effort.

4.3 Individual Versus Social Learning

The main categories that emerged were: individual learning actions, social learning in relation to connecting and sharing, and social learning actions.

Individual Learning Actions. 63% of the learners completed the learning episodes by themselves, learning individually and subsequently addressed as 'individual learners' in this section. Individual learners use a variety of learning actions, such as: viewing and reading course media, reflecting on content, looking for answers on the internet, linking to prior knowledge. Although lurking, the individual learners did testify that they looked at particular MOOC spaces to find answers to their course related questions: e.g. "I did the whole course individually although I did read other student's inputs which in many cases answered any questions I might have posed" (#BSE/I/109). Lurking seemed to be a deliberate action, following unresolved questions, "I really only look to see what others have written if I don't know the answer" (#SOM/LL/104).

Individual learners find learning solutions by looking at online and offline options to increase what they perceive as learning success in the MOOCs.

Social Learning: Connecting and Sharing. Social learning is a natural learning phenomenon, as people use dialogue to increase their understanding.

Looking for Answers Versus Experience Sharing. When investigating who learners turned to while learning, this study made a distinction between who participants turn to while looking for answers (i.e. asking questions on subject), and who they share their course experiences with (i.e. sharing the experience), see Table 7. In this section only the quantitative data from BSE and the DMCW course were considered, as there were only 4 SOM participants engaging in social learning activities.

Table 7. Who people turned to in order to find answers and who people connected to in order to share their MOOC experiences

	Mostly inside course (%)			Mostly outside course (%)				
Cross tabulation (n = 147)	Course	Facilitators	Peers	Professional colleagues	Friends	Family	Partner	Other (%)
Looking for answers	BSE	12	37	11	4	19	11	6
	DMCW	17	45	10	8	5	8	7
Sharing experiences	BSE	2	35	13	13	30	7	0
	DMCW	1	32	17	16	19	15	0

Learners consider who would be able to help them, indicating an overlap of interests or contexts within their personal relationships: with friends "I will contact people that I know, my friends, who are experts in a certain field. Sometimes I would write an email to an expert that I do not know personal" (#DMCW/LL/132), and partners: "The [theoretical] principals are very useful in a number of ways. For my partner it answers a number of questions of what is happening in her work too" (#DMCW/LL/131). Learners also shared their own knowledge. Learners considered where their additions would be helpful: "I picked up the course where I had left off yesterday, and started by looking at the comments left on my posts (mostly comments on other people's posts to start with), and responded to those where I felt that I had something to say" (#DMCW/LL/149).

Social Learning Actions. Social learning involves learners interacting with each other, either online or in real life.

Choosing Who to Interact With. In a MOOC, learners need to decide who they want to connect to within a short timeframe (duration of the MOOC). FutureLearn offers the option to 'follow' other learners or indicate which comments you 'like', both options being used by learners to facilitate their learning, but because of the size of the learner group this selection procedure does not always feel exactly right as the following learner testifies: "The comments in a MOOC of this size are really difficult to keep track of … even selecting accurately whom I would like to 'follow' ". (#DMCW/LL/124). The learners who engage in social learning are actively searching for ways to optimise their social learning experience.

Reflective Actions and Cohort Learning. Reflecting on the content was a recurring action in the learning logs, ranging from individual reflecting to social reflecting.

FutureLearn MOOCs have a clear starting point, thus offering the opportunity to move forward in a cohort of learners. Cohort learning can provide a group feeling for learners: "I found posting on the comments sections on pages and reading replies helped my understanding. I decided to do this when I read the first 30 or so comments and found useful information in them that made sense to me" (#DMCW/I/107). Although not everyone learns in the designated timeframe as set out by the course organiser, cohort learning adds to a group feeling, as well as to the participants' learning experience.

4.4 Structuring Learning

The MOOC participants self-directed their learning based on: scheduling, taking notes, and personal goal setting.

Scheduling. The option to learn the MOOC modules or elements in a way that feels logical for the participant (not necessarily to the prescribed learning path), leaves room to the participant for self-directing and organizing their learning based on their own agenda and needs.

Available Time. Learners mediate the time they are willing and able to put into the course throughout the duration of the course and will re-evaluate that time investment depending on new factors (e.g. workload increase, relevance of content): "work has been very busy and so the course has taken a bit of a back seat. Previously, if learning episodes have been difficult I will sometimes just move on and accept I may not understand or complete that particular challenge" (#DMCW/LL/125).

Time Investment in Social Learning. Learners referred to the time investment of social learning or time they were willing to dedicate to discussions: "The discussions are sometimes so long as to be unreadable (200+ comments). One thing I have learnt is that reading everything is impossible." (#DMCW/LL/124). Social learning depends on the learner's willingness to invest time, e.g. "Time management has enabled me to prioritise my learning into depth of meaningfulness" (#BSE/I/134). The renegotiation of time stands in relation to the usefulness of the content as perceived by the learner.

Keeping Notes. Keeping notes was a frequent action to organise learning, and it occurred in all three courses. 70% of the participants indicated that they kept a personal learning record, either digitally or on paper or a mixture of both. What changed was the sorts of notes they were kept: some skipped between tools, others used different types of note taking: "For the important information from the course I either create mind maps for quick reference or write brief notes. This enables me to go back through the information to firm up my understanding" (#DMCW/LL/125). 48% of the participants indicated that they used some sort of personal notebook. Learners used tools for taking notes as described in Table 8.

Table 8. Keeping a personal notebook

Results (n = 147)	(in %)
The activity booklet provided by the course (Basic Science: Understanding Experiments)	10
A paper notebook	38
A blog	1
An e-portfolio	4
I do not keep a record of what I learn	30
Other	17

The 'other' options for keeping a personal notebook comprised specific online tools: Evernote, OneNote, audio recordings, digital notes (Word), and Notepad. Keeping notes emerged as a common way to self-direct and organise learning. The way learners keep notes is related to their previous familiarity with certain note-keeping tools.

Personal Goal Setting. The informal character of MOOCs allows learners to look set out personal learning goals when registering for courses, as learners can access the content and interact based on their own preferences or needs. The personal goals can be related to personal and professional interests. Some learners saw the MOOCs as a form of continued professional development, e.g. "[I want to] understand what entrepreneurship is and reflect on how it might apply to my work (director in a local authority)" (#DMCW/LL/111), or a way to further their personal goals, e.g. "The main impact is that I'm now putting together my PhD proposal on Network models, thanks to the course" (#DMCW/I/220).

Range of Personal Learning Goals. The learning goals set by the participants vary from specific, personal goals ("prepare for my Bsc which starts in 2015", #BSE/LL/126), to a more general interest ("start thinking like a scientist", #BSE/LL/136), and include specific time related content actions ("I wanted to finish this week's work, videos, quiz etc. before going away", #SOM/LL/105). Twelve learners indicated not having specific learning goals.

Selecting Content. The way learners select content is part of their personal learning goals (based on learning needs they self-define), but also based on prior online learning experiences. Learners selecting specific weeks or sections of a MOOC has an effect on the way they use all the media in those sections. One learner selected quiz questions: "I completed only those quizzes that involved the material I had already covered." (#BSE/LL/106). Another learner solved a quiz question by first discussing it with peers: "One of the quiz questions was difficult and I felt I could not find the response in the course. So I asked the question in the discussion forum, and the professor answered, as did also a bunch of students" (#DMCW/LL/124). MOOC facilitators sometimes include assignments which the learner can embed into their own context or learning goals: "it is definitely a great learning strategy to construct an essay in response to a question based on my professional reality. It is very functional." (#DMCW/I/148).

Building (on) Personal Learning Action. Organising learning as well as selecting content and tasks provided, seems to be part of a bigger SDL action. Experienced adult learners have constructed these self-directed actions while building on prior learning experiences. The learning actions often relate to familiar learning practices and were perceived as useful: "This is the sixth FutureLearn course that I have undertaken. In two I was learning new skills and I had to work very hard, practice repeatedly and ask for help for educators and other learners. This learning is still with me" (#DMCW/LL/128).

Personal learning actions can refer to prior knowledge of the learner. They can refer to pedagogically related learning actions such as reflection. Personal learning actions are built upon prior learning experiences but adjusted depending on the learning goals of the learner, as well as the content provided in the course platform.

4.5 Context

Context was a reoccurring category which emerged during the data analysis but was not present in the research sub-questions. Context is interpreted here as defined by Downes [18] from the perspective of the learner and related to three personal environments: the learner's external environment (workplace, learning space, social relations, etc.), internal environment (prior knowledge, philosophical views, learning goals, etc.) and digital environment (prior technological experiences, online tools, etc.).

Contextualizing Content. Content which is applicable to the learner's own profession or interest, works as an extra motivation. This could be content with a direct link to the learner's profession: "the history of medicines was interesting and so was the pharmacology as I felt that I could relate it to my work as a nurse and trainer" (#SOM/I/500), or related to a parallel process: "as a teacher and developer I apply the concept of emergence in curriculum development and in my lessons social sciences at the University of Applied Sciences" (DMCW/I/222).

Proximity of Context as Motivator. Context emerged while learners referred to their working or personal environment and the impact of circumstances on their learning. For example: "I just find the course and info very helpful as I am studying similar topics" (#DMCW/LL/114). The content related data revealed that a learner's context, whether personal and/or professional, influences their motivation. If part of the content did not seem to be of interest to their own context, learners indicated that they skipped that part, "Did not find the technical section on networks relevant to my work, so I skipped it" (#DMCW/I/196). This indicates there is a relation between the context of the learner and the resulting motivation to learn.

5 Conclusion

Recapturing SDL by Knowles [6], we can align the findings of this study to SDL for adults. Individuals take the initiative for learning, we can see that it is with or without the help of others (individual versus social learning), they diagnose their learning needs (context, structuring learning), they formulate learning goals (structuring learning), identify human and material resources for learning (technological and media elements), choose and implementing learning strategies (according to their individual characteristics), and evaluate learning outcomes (context and aligning learning with their learning goals). SDL in MOOCs results in a heightened ownership of learning. MOOC learning is guided by the learner. Reich [12] stated that a collective research effort is required to fully understand the impact of MOOCs and added that we have terabytes of data about what students clicked and very little understanding of what changed in their heads. This qualitative, learner-centered, bottom-up study shows that learners make conscious decisions when learning in MOOCs. It is the learner who establishes what they will learn, when, and how, which puts the pre-described MOOC structure as envisioned by the MOOC organizer in question. Future work implies taking another look at the SDL and investigating whether this can be set up in a framework that embraces all the elements influencing SDL in MOOCs.

References

1. Charmaz, K.: Constructing Grounded Theory. Sage, Thousand Oaks (2014)
2. de Waard, I., Kukulska-Hulme, A.: A conceptual framework for learners self-directing their learning in MOOCs. In: Emerging Technologies and Pedagogies in the Curriculum, Eds. Ally, M., Prof. Shengquan Yu. Springer publishing (2019)
3. Wong, J., Baars, M., Davis, D., Van Der Zee, T., Houben, G.J., Paas, F.: Supporting self-regulated learning in online learning environments and MOOCs: a systematic review. Int. J. Human-Comput. Interact. **35**, 1–18 (2018)
4. Veletsianos, G., Shepherdson, P.: A systematic analysis and synthesis of the empirical MOOC literature published in 2013–2015. Int. Rev. Res. Open Distrib. Learn. **17**(2), 198–221 (2016)
5. Liyanagunawardena, T.R., Lundqvist, K.O., Williams, S.A.: Massive open online courses and economic sustainability. Eur. J. Open Distance. E-Learn. **18**(2), 95–111 (2015)
6. Knowles, M.S.: The modern practice of adult education. Association Press, New York (1970)
7. Zhu, M., Sari, A., Bonk, C.: A systematic review of MOOC research methods and topics: comparing 2014–2016 and 2016–2017. In: Proceedings of EdMedia: World conference on Educational Media and Technology. 25 June 2018. EdMedia Innovate Learning 2018, Amsterdam, The Netherlands (2018)
8. Kizilcec, R.F., Schneider, E.: Motivation as a lens to understand online learners: Toward data-driven design with the OLEI scale. ACM Trans. Comput.-Hum. Interact. (TOCHI) **22** (2), 6 (2015)
9. Terras, M.M., Ramsay, J.: Massive open online courses (MOOCs): Insights and challenges from a psychological perspective. Br. J. Educ. Technol. **46**(3), 472–487 (2015)
10. Guo, P.J., Reinecke, K.: Demographic differences in how students navigate through MOOCs. In: Proceedings of the First ACM Conference on Learning@ Scale Conference, pp. 21–30. ACM (2014)
11. Littlejohn, A., Hood, N., Milligan, C., Mustain, P.: Learning in MOOCs: motivations and self-regulated learning in MOOCs. Internet High. Educ. **29**, 40–48 (2016)
12. Reich, J.: Rebooting MOOC research. Science **347**(6217), 34–35 (2015)

13. Loyens, S.M.M., Joshua, M., Rikers, R.M.J.P.: Self-directed learning in problem-based learning and its relationships with self-regulated learning. Educ. Psychol. Rev. **20**(4), 411–427 (2008)
14. Cresswell, J.W.: Research Design: Qualitative, Quantitative, and Mixed Methods Approaches. Sage Publications, Inc., Thousand Oaks (2009)
15. Learning logs and all research instruments have been made available here. https://www.academia.edu/9703990/Research_instruments_Learning_logs_questions_for_researching_Self-Directed_Learning_in_experienced_online_learners_engaged_in_FutureLearn_courses
16. Vavoula, G., O'Malley, C., Taylor, J.: A study of mobile learning as part of everyday learning. In: Attewell, J., Savill-Smith, C. (eds.) Mobile Learning Anytime Everywhere: a Book of Papers from MLEARN 2004, pp. 211–212. Learning and Skills Development Agency, London (2005)
17. Ryan, R.M., Deci, E.L.: Self-determination theory and the facilitation of intrinsic motivation, social development, and well-being. Am. Psychol. **55**(1), 68 (2000)
18. Downes, S.: What is learning context? (blogpost 11 November 2004) (2004). https://www.downes.ca/cgi-bin/page.cgi?post=18

Challenging the Alignment of Learning Design Tools with HE Lecturers' Learning Design Practice

Dilek Celik(✉) and George D. Magoulas

Knowledge Lab, Birkbeck College, University of London, London, UK
{dilek,gmagoulas}@dcs.bbk.ac.uk

Abstract. Extensive research has been carried out for the development of learning design tools; nevertheless, their adoption by HE lecturers remains low. Sharing, guidance, and various forms of representation are the main pillars of learning design tools. However, these features do not seem to be sufficient reasons to convince lecturers to adopt these tools in daily learning design practices in HE. This is attached to the gap between learning design tools and actual learning design practice of university lecturers. Sociomateriality provides an analytical lens for unpacking complex practices for identifying the design space of digital tools for learning design without predetermined boundaries. This paper is a first step in exploring how we can follow sociomaterialty in unpacking complex learning design practices in HE to inform the development of software for learning design. It conducts a survey with one hundred ten university lecturers on their learning design practices. It analyses data through sociomaterial theory and derives a sociomaterial evaluation framework. This is used as an instrument for the analysis of seven available learning design tools. A misalignment between tools and HE lecturers' learning design practice is revealed. Points of misalignment extend the space for what it means to design digital tools that support-learning design practices in HE, and they could be used to highlight areas for improvement to inform and strengthen further the way we design support tools for learning design.

Keywords: Learning design tools · Learning design · Sociomateriality

1 Introduction

The past decade has seen an expanding body of literature that seeks to develop Learning Design (LD) tools. LD tools have been conceived to enable teachers to define or portray efficient teaching ideas so that they can be shared with, and adopted by, other teachers. To our knowledge, there are twenty-nine LD tools in the LD [1], which is quite a lot when considering the maturity of the LD [2].

Despite the richness of LD tools, their adoption by HE lecturers remained low [3]. This is attributed to the development of LD tools based on suppositions about Learning Design Practice (LD-P) rather than empirical evidence [4]. Despite previous work investigating how HE lecturers actually design for learning, such as [2, 4–9], the issue of matching/mismatching of LD tools and HE lecturers' LD-P has not been studied in the LD field.

M. Scheffel et al. (Eds.): EC-TEL 2019, LNCS 11722, pp. 142–157, 2019.
https://doi.org/10.1007/978-3-030-29736-7_11

The notion of sociomateriality has been introduced in [10]. It has been established on the agential realist philosophy [11] and offers an analytic lens for unpacking complex practices for identifying the design space of technology [12]. The use of socio-materiality as a theoretical and emergent concept in educational studies has been brought to the agenda and it is used in technology-enhanced related studies resulted with valuable findings [13].

The present study aims to explore the alignment of LD tools and HE lecturers' LD-P using sociomaterial theory as an analytical lens in un-packing complex practices and inform further development in software tools for LD. To this end, a survey with one hundred ten HE lecturers about their LD-P is conducted. The data are analysed through the sociomaterial theory to derive a sociomaterial evaluation framework. This is used to analyse seven LD tools in terms of their matching/mismatching with LD-P.

The present study is significant as it extends existing studies focusing on an aspect, which has not been studied adequately in the LD, i.e. how LD tools align with HE lecturers' LD-P. The findings potentially take the LD studies beyond the current stage by providing misalignment points of LD tools with HE lecturers' LD-P using socio-materiality, therefore, informing the software design for LD.

The remainder of this paper is as follows. Section 2 discusses the related work. Section 3 discusses the methodology. Section 4 presents the evaluation framework and Sect. 5 analysis seven LD tools and presents the misalignment points of these tools with LD-P of HE lecturers. Section 6 presents the discussion, Sect. 7 presents the conclusions, and future works.

2 Related Work

There have been limited studies into the HE lecturers' LD-P regarding how they design for learning, what influences their decisions, and what supports they use [4, 9]. The study described in [5] was the first step in understanding LD-P of HE lecturers. [5] focused on North American college teachers' LD-P and concluded, however, that further in-depth research is needed about the actual decisions teachers make about the form of instruction. The other studies point out the importance of contextual factors in LD-P such as discipline, class size, year level, or teaching space [6, 7]. Later, [8] and [4] focused on the factors that shape HE teachers' design decisions, with the work described in [8] focusing on the specific context of Australian HE teachers. The most recent study by [9] focused on how novice teachers go about technology-enhanced learning design processes.

An evaluation framework for LD tools was proposed in [14]. Later, this framework was reconceptualised in [1]. However, both of these attempts did not exploit empirical evidence about HE lecturers' LD-P.

Further work on design principles for LD tools was conducted in [15]. However, these principles were derived from conceptualisation and ongoing development of a single LD tool rather than from an analysis of HE lecturers' LD-P.

Lastly, the main theoretical underpinnings of LD studies so far have been, understandably, educational theory and pedagogy. This paper is an attempt to complement these studies, extending the design space of LD tools, by looking LD and software tools' design from a sociomaterial perspective. Sociomateriality has been proven to be useful in studying information system phenomenon that integrates entanglement of social entities and technological artefacts (e.g. [17–20]).

3 Methodology

The alignment of LD tools with LD-P in HE was investigated through a process of analysis, design, evaluation, and revision of design-based research (DBR) project which integrates three iteration cycles [20]. The cyclic structure of the whole development process is illustrated in Fig. 1. This study employs the Design Cycle 3 from Fig. 1 highlighted with a red rectangle.

In the analysis phase, the study conducts surveys on HE lecturers' LD-P and need analysis on LD tools with one hundred ten HE lecturers and analysis the data using qualitative data analysis method. In the design phase, the data is investigated using sociomateriality and the evaluation framework is developed based on that. In the evaluation phase, seven LD tools are evaluated using the evaluation framework. In the reflection phase, misalignment points are revealed.

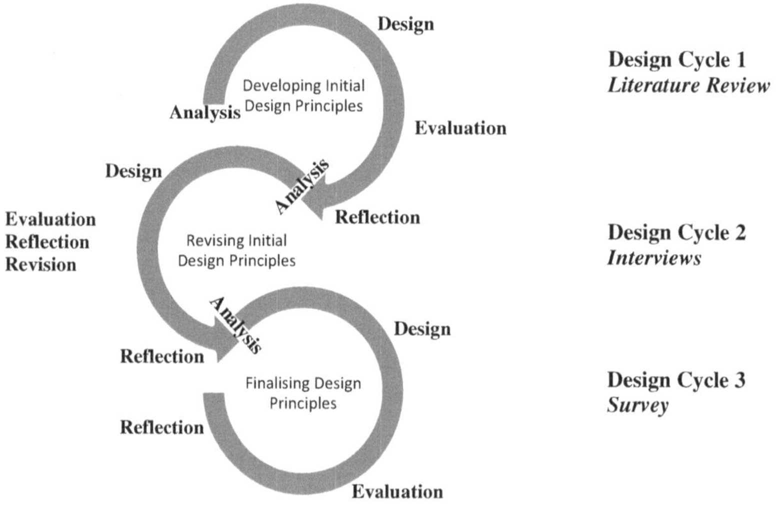

Fig. 1. The methodological framework of the study

The target population of the online survey was HE lecturers from a variety of countries, disciplines, and levels of teaching. The random sampling method was adopted [21]. The participants were randomly selected, and the online survey was sent to them via his/her institutional email address using an online survey tool, Survey

Monkey (https://www.surveymonkey.com/). The survey was conducted individually, where participants filled the online survey in their appropriate time [21].

The survey was completed by 61 males and 49 female HE lecturers. The participants were from 27 different countries. The participants had taught courses at various levels in HE institutions: Bachelor's (66), Master's (75), Doctorate (63). Most of the participants had more than 15 years of teaching experiences. 21 of them had 1–5 years, 20 of them had 6–10 years and 22 of them had 11–15 years of teaching experiences.

A survey is developed based on the key elements revealed in the LD [24]. The content validity of the survey instrument was confirmed by three pilot studies. The survey comprised of three sections: the first section, "Demographics", contained three multiple choice questions about sex, teaching experience of participants, and country, one open-ended question on lecturing domains and one checkbox question about levels of teaching. The second section, "LD tools", contained one checkbox question, one multiple-choice question, four open-ended questions, and a matrix/rating scale question. The participants could refer to up to three LD tools that they had experienced and they were asked to specific questions about these tools. The third section, "LD-P of HE lecturers", contained five open-ended questions, five checkbox questions, and one matrix/rating scale question to examine how HE lecturers design for learning, what factors influence their design decisions, and what tools they use. Therefore, the resulting survey comprised of thirty-five questions. Figure 2 shows some of the questions and the HE lecturers' responses.

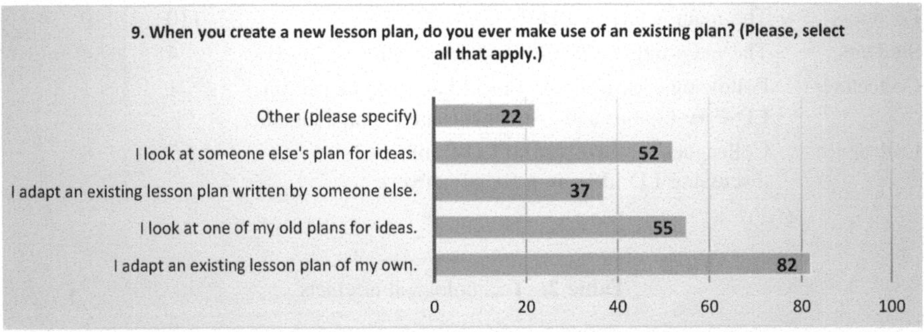

Fig. 2. Selected questions from the online survey

The qualitative data analysis steps were followed using the QSR NVivo software (www.qsrinternational.com) for the analysis [21]. These involve preparing the data for analysis, reading all the data, start coding, using coding to generate description, advancing how the themes will be presented, and interpretation.

After having analysed data in Nvivo, socio-materiality was used as an analytical lens to explore the data using the following sociomaterial questions (Q1) What are the actors - human and non-human- involved in the LD-P? (Q2) What are the entangled relations of these actors? In the sociomaterial literature, human actors are people; non-human actors refer to technological artefacts; abstract concepts refer to any other actors that might have an influence in the domain under investigation. Q1 is answered identifying the actors involved in the HE lecturers' LD-P and creating them as nodes in Nvivo by scrutinising the survey data. The Q2 is answered identifying the relations between actors by looking at the entwined relations of the actors in the LD-P of HE lecturers.

The seven LD tools are chosen among the most cited LD tools in the LD to be used in the sociomaterial analysis.

The research adhered to our college's ethics framework and code of practice on research integrity (College's Ethics Link will be provided after the review process).

4 Sociomaterial Evaluation Framework

Investigation of the analysed data using the sociomateriality led to the identification of sixty-one actors involved in the HE lecturers' LD-P: four of them are identified as human actors; fourteen are technological artefacts; forty-three are abstract concepts.

Names, descriptions, number of files (number of respondents who mentioned to the actor) coded, number of references (number of times respondents referred to the actor) of human actors and digital artefacts are presented in Tables 1 and 2 respectively.

Table 1. Human actors

Human actors	Description	Files	References
Lecturers	The main actors of LD-P	110	110
Students	The main target audience and a key actor of LD-P	4	4
Co-lecturer	Following a co-teaching model has an influence on LD-P as sessions and assessments are planned together	1	1
Colleagues	Colleagues are involved in LD-P informally discussing LD ideas in a social network	7	8

Table 2. Technological artefacts

Technological artefacts	Description	Files	References
Virtual Learning Environment (VLE)	LDs need to be deployed into VLEs at the end	28	28
Website	Lecturers create websites to share course design	3	3
Whiteboard	Whiteboards are used to draw the overall LD structure	7	7
Wiki	Wiki is used to share learning designs	1	1
Google docs	They are to develop the LDs together with colleagues	1	1
Mind map tools	Lecturers create a mind map of LDs using the tools	6	6
Note-taking tool	Note-taking tools are used to outline the LDs	1	1

(continued)

Table 2. (*continued*)

Technological artefacts	Description	Files	References
Paper-based tools	Paper-based tools are used to draft a plan of LDs	39	40
Post-it	It is used to brainstorm LD ideas and organise them	1	1
Video tools	Video tools are used to create videos for the class	2	2
Slide tools	Slides are used to bring LD ideas together and to present	68	67
LD tools	LD tools are used to design LDs	3	3
Word processors	Word processors are used to designing LDs	2	2
Learning technologies	Technologies that can be used to enhance the learning experience	3	3

Abstract concepts are grouped into four themes: human-related, course-related, institutional, and feedback related - these are presented in Tables 3, 4, 5 and Table 6 respectively.

Table 3. Human-related abstract concepts

Abstract concepts related to human actors	Description	Files	References
Lecturers' values	Lecturers' values influence LD-P	1	1
Students' prior knowledge	Students' prior learning is important in LD-P	4	4
Students' needs	Lecturers think of students' needs in LD-P	2	2
Students' access to resources	Availability of institutional or remotely accessible resources is important	1	1
Students' motivation	Students' motivation influences LD-P	1	1
Time	Lecturers and students' time affect LD-P	1	1

Table 4. Course related abstract concepts

Abstract concepts related to course	Description	Files	References
Course	LD is driven by overall course requirements	17	17
Course aims	Course aim represents what lecturers want students to achieve in terms of the learning experience	10	10
Educational level	LDs are designed according to the level of the course	1	1
Learning objectives	The learning objective is a starting point of LD-P	5	5
Learning outcomes	The learning outcome represents what students should be able to do at the end of a unit	71	71
Activities	Lecturers need to think about and design activities	32	38

(*continued*)

Table 4. (*continued*)

Abstract concepts related to course	Description	Files	References
Assessment	Assessment serves also as a starting point for LD-P	18	19
Teaching-learning approach	The type of learning influences LD-P	1	1
Course sequence	Sequencing the topics and activities is part of LD-P	4	4
Course timing	Timing of the LD and activities is part of LD-P	2	2
Existing slides	Lecturers reuse existing slides and refine them	5	5
Online research	Search online for materials relevant to the LDs	2	2
Existing LDs	Lecturers adopt and refine previous LDs	6	6

Table 5. Institutional abstract concepts

Abstract concepts related to institutions	Description	Files	References
National standards	LDs need to align with national standards	1	1
Cultural norms	Workplace culture shapes LD-P	1	1
Institutional standards	LDs need to align with institutional standards	3	3
Resources	Availability of learning resources influences LD-P	1	1
Syllabus	The syllabus influences LD-P	4	4
Course book	Some lecturers follow book chapters in their course	4	4
Availability of technology	Availability of technology in the classroom affects LD-P	1	1
Curriculum	The curriculum influences LD-P	3	4
Delivery method	How the course is delivered influences LD-P	15	15

Table 6. Feedback-related abstract concepts

Abstract concepts related to feedback	Description	Files	References
Feedback	Feedback is about how well the lesson went in relation to the LD	3	3
Personal notes	Lecturers note the things that need improvement during class time	1	1
Observation	Lecturers observe the way students react in class to indirectly get feedback	10	10
Review at the end	Lecturers review LDs at the end of a course	1	1

(*continued*)

Table 6. (*continued*)

Abstract concepts related to feedback	Description	Files	References
Success criteria	Lecturers measure LDs according to whether the student has reached the success criteria	1	1
Self-reflection	Lecturers reflect on LDs at the end of a course	10	10
Learning Analytics (LA)	LA can be exploited as a feedback mechanism	1	1
Formal students' evaluation	This is a standard formal evaluation method	21	22
Examination	Exam results are also used as feedback	3	3
Feedback form	The institutional feedback forms are used	10	10
Survey	A survey is a way of getting feedback	22	22
Informal students' evaluation	Feedback is received via informal methods	38	38
Written students' evaluation	Students write anonymous comments to the lecturers about the course	6	6
Discuss with students	Lecturers discuss the lesson with students	38	38
Word of mouth	Word of mouth is a way of getting students' feedback on the course	1	1

From the above-shared tables shared, it can be seen that some of the actors are mentioned by several participants while others are highlighted by few HE lecturers. From the sociomaterial perspective, anything that has an influence on the practice matters and should not be neglected. Therefore, all the actors mentioned have equal value in LD-P.

The sociomaterial perspective allowed us to analyse the various ways technology is enacted into LD endeavours to achieve teaching-learning tasks in HE institutions. To design tools that follow sociomaterial design principles we need to investigate current LD artefacts, e.g. tools and approaches, analysing actors involved and their boundaries practices. To this end, an evaluation framework for the analysis and evaluation of LD tools is developed next. Its utility is further demonstrated by evaluating the alignment of seven LD tools with LD-P from the sociomaterial perspective in the next section.

Based on the definition given to each actor by HE lecturers and the information presented in the tables above, the dimensions of the sociomaterial framework are presented in Table 7. It comprised of six dimensions: lecturers/designers, students, institution, course, technology, and feedback. Even though HE lecturers mentioned sixty-one actors, we combined some of the related actors and associated those actors with thirty-five questions which can be used to explore the various aspects or features of LD tools. The formed dimensions are defined as follows.

- "Designers/Lecturers" dimension considers LD-P from the HE lecturers' perspective. According to the results given in the above-presented tables, lecturers' time and values are two important actors that need attention, and HE lecturers practice

LD in collaboration with a design co-lecturer and colleagues. Therefore, it would be useful to explore the role of these actors in LD tools using questions like the three questions shown in Table 7.

- The "Students" dimension deals with whether the artefact (e.g. LD tool) offers features that enable designers to meet students' requirements. Students' prior knowledge, needs, access to resources, motivation, and time are the factors for consideration when taking up LD-P.
- The "Institution" dimension is about considering the organisational and national requirements when a designer practises LD. According to HE lecturers' view, national standards, cultural norms, institutional standards, resources, syllabus, course book, availability of technology, curriculum, and delivery method all have an influence on LD-P in organisational contexts.
- The "Course" dimension considers the actors related to aspects of a course. Course, course aims, learning objectives, learning outcomes, activities, assessment, educational level, teaching-learning approach, course sequence, course timing, existing slides, online research, existing LDs are the main components of LD at the course level and they need to be defined.
- "Technology" dimension is concerned with the requirements or impact of technology in LD-P, such as desirable features of LD tools (exporting/importing LDs in different file formats, communication and interoperability tools, advice, guidance and recommendation capabilities), and other technological artefacts relevant to LD-P.
- "Feedback" dimension considers if LD tools integrate any kind of feedback mechanism. Personal feedback, formal students' evaluation, informal students' evaluation, and LA are the kind of feedback used by HE lecturers.

Table 7. Sociomaterial Evaluation Framework for LD tools

Dimensions	Actors	Exploratory question
Designers/lecturers	Lecturers' time	Is time spent on learning design reduced?
	Lecturers' values	How are lecturers' values considered?
	Co-lecturer	Is the nature of the lecturers' collaborative practice, e.g. when discussing ideas or co-designing, accommodated?
	Colleagues	
Students	Prior knowledge	How are students' prior knowledge, needs, access to resources, and motivation presented and accommodated?
	Needs	
	Access to resources	
	Motivation	
	Time	How is students' study time organised?
Institution	National standards	How are national standards of LD-P considered?
	Cultural norms	How are the cultural norms of LD-P considered?

(*continued*)

Table 7. (*continued*)

Dimensions	Actors	Exploratory question
	Institutional standards	How are institutional standards of LD-P considered?
	Resources	Is information about learning resources available at the institution provided?
	Syllabus	How is the syllabus of LD-P considered?
	Course book	Are LDs based on the core reading text provided or can they be easily created?
	Availability of technology	How is information about available learning technologies at the institutions considered?
	Curriculum	How is the curriculum of LD-P considered?
	Delivery method	Is the delivery method of the course considered?
Course	Course	Is it possible to define and align course aims, learning objectives, learning outcomes, assessment, and activities?
	Course aims	
	Learning objectives	
	Learning outcomes	
	Activities	
	Assessment	
	Educational level	Is it possible to design based on educational level?
	Teaching-learning approach	What features/functions are provided to enable defining learning-teaching approaches?
	Course sequence	Are the course and activities sequencing considered?
	Course timing	Is the arrangement of course timing considered?
	Existing slides	What tools/functions are available to import and edit existing slides?
	Online research	What tools/functions are available to online research?
	Existing LDs	What functions are available to edit past LDs?
Technology	VLE	Are functionalities to import/export LDs and exchange data with VLEs provided?
	Website	Is it possible to publish LDs as a webpage?
	Wiki	Is it possible to publish LDs as a Wiki?
	Whiteboard	Whiteboard, mind-map tools, post-it, note-taking tools, and paper-based tools are used in the conceptualization of LD. Is it possible to draft the ideas in the LD tool?
	Mind map tools	
	Post-it	

(*continued*)

Table 7. (*continued*)

Dimensions	Actors	Exploratory question
	Note-taking tool	
	Paper-based tools	
	Google docs	Are facilities to export LDs in various file formats available?
	Word Processors	
	Slides making tools	
	Video tools	What feature to enable video integration is provided?
	LD tools	What features for communication, interoperability and data exchange with other LD tools are available?
	Learning technology	What feature to suggest learning technology is provided?
Feedback	Personal feedback	Is it possible to put notes regarding LDs in the LD tool?
	Formal Students' evaluation	Is it possible to integrate the results of formal evaluations within the tool to inform the designers?
	Informal students' evaluation	Is it possible to integrate the results of informal evaluations within the tool to inform the designers?
	Learning analytics	Is it possible to integrate LA into LD tools?

5 Analysis of LD Tools

This section employs the sociomaterial evaluation framework developed in the previous section to evaluate well-known seven LD tools. The LD tools analysed are: ILDE [22], OpenGLM [23], WebCollege [24], exeLearning [25], CADMOS [26], the Learning Designer [27] and the ScenEdit [28] - the version presented in the cited paper was considered for the analysis of each tool.

Table 8 provides an overview of the alignment/misalignment identified: the alignment points are indicated with "+" and misalignment points are indicated with "–" and highlighted with a grey background colour.

From Table 8, we see that even though there are various human and non-human actors engaged in the LD-P of HE lecturers and they all, have explanatory value when trying to understand the various ways technology is enacted into LD in HE, we see barely overlap of these actors with existing LD tools.

Table 8. Evaluation Framework for LD tools

		ILDE Tool						
Dimensions	Actors	OpenGLM	WebCollege	xeLearning	CADMOS	ILDE	The Learning Designer	ScenEdit
Designers/ Lecturers	Lecturers' Time	-	-	-	-	-	+	-
	Lecturers' Values	-	-	-	-	-	-	-
	Co-lecturer	-	-	-	-	-	-	-
	Colleagues	-	-	-	-	-	-	-
Students	Prior Knowledge	-	-	+	-	-	-	-
	Needs	-	-	-	-	-	-	-
	Access to Resources	-	-	-	-	-	-	-
	Motivation	-	-	-	-	-	-	-
	Time	-	-	-	-	-	+	-
Institution	National Standards	-	-	-	-	-	-	-
	Cultural Norms	-	-	-	-	-	-	-
	Institutional Standards	-	-	-	-	-	-	-
	Resources	-	-	-	-	-	-	-
	Syllabus	-	-	-	-	-	-	-
	Course Book	-	-	-	-	-	-	-
	Availability of Technology	-	-	-	-	-	-	-
	Curriculum	-	-	-	-	-	-	-
	Delivery Method	+	+	+	+	+		-
Course	Course	+	+	+	+	+	+	+
	Course Aims	+	+	+	+	+	+	+
	Learning Objectives	+	+	+	+	+	+	+
	Learning Outcomes	+	+	+	+	+	+	+
	Activities	+	+	+	+	+	+	+
	Assessment	+	+	+	+	+	+	+
	Educational Level	+	+	+	+	+	+	+
	Teaching-learning Approach	+	+	+	+	+	+	+
	Course Sequence	+	+	+	+	+	+	+
	Course Timing	-	-	-	-	-	+	-
	Existing Slides	+	+	+	+	+	+	-
	Online Research	+	+	+	+	+	+	-
	Existing LDs	+	+	+	+	+	+	-
Technology	VLEs	+	+	+	+	+	+	-
	Website	-	-	-	-	-	-	-
	Wiki	-	-	-	-	-	-	-
	Whiteboard	-	-	-	-	-	-	-
	Mind Map Tools	-	-	-	-	-	-	-
	Post-it	-	-	-	-	-	-	-
	Note-taking tool	-	-	-	-	-	-	-
	Paper-based tools	-	-	-	-	-	-	-
	Google Docs	+	+	-	-	+	+	-
	Word Processors	+	+	-	-	+	+	-
	Slides Making Tools	-	-	-	-	-	-	-
	Video Tools	-	-	-	-	-	-	-
	LD Tools	-	-	-	-	-	+	-
	Learning Technology	-	-	-	-	-	-	-
Feedback	Personal Feedback	-	-	-	-	-	-	-
	Formal Students' Evaluation	-	-	-	-	-	-	-
	Informal Students' Evaluation	-	-	-	-	-	-	-
	Learning Analytics	-	-	-	-	+	+	-

The "designers" dimension is slightly covered by the Learning Designer. The other tools did not take into account the designers-related actors.

The "students" related actors are barely covered by exeLEarning and ILDE tools. The other tools did not consider the students-related actors that influence LD at all.

The "course" dimension with its relevant actors are the actors covered mostly by the LD tools. Among the course related actors, course timing is not taken into account by any LD tools except the Learning Designer. Another point to highlight is here is that ScenEdit partially covered course related actors: course timing, existing slides, online research, and existing LDs are not adequately represented.

Among "technology" related actors, VLE is the actor covered by all the LD tools except ScenEdit. LD tools that consider VLE offer features to deploy LDs created within the tool to VLE. OpenGLM, webCollege, ILDE and the Learning Designer also covered Google Docs and Word Processor dimensions meaning that these tools can export LDs in various file formats. The other "technology" related actors are not taken into account by the LD tools.

These seven LD tools do not offer any functionalities to gather direct feedback about the course. Only ILDE tool recently announced edCrumble [15] that considers integrating LA into LD tools. In addition, the Learning Designer provided analytical pie chart to inform the lecturers in terms of the proportion of the pedagogy chosen for LD.

6 Discussion

Analysing the LD-P of HE lecturers from sociomaterial perspective extends our understanding of LD-P by revealing the actors' complex interrelations and the boundaries that come into existence in LD-P. In the literature, there have been studies that investigated LD-P of the HE lecturers, such as work by [2, 4–9]. However, these studies did not consider the complex sociomaterial environment and all the actors. Unlike these studies, where the main emphasis was on human-centric factors, this study contributes by considering all the human and non-human actors as a matter in LD-P. Furthermore, to the best of our knowledge, this study is the first one challenging the alignment of LD tools with LD-P in HE identifying misalignment points, as summarised below.

M1: None of the LD tools analysed in this study cover all the actors involved in the LD-P of HE lecturers. ILDE is the most recent tool developed in the LD field and it is dedicated to bringing various LD tools together. Nevertheless, according to the proposed sociomaterial framework, ILDE still requires enhancements to accommodate the actors highlighted by the HE lecturers that participated in this study.

M2: Another point highly valued by HE lecturers, which is not unfortunately widely supported by LD tools is the designing for learning collaboratively. ILDE, OpenGLM, WebCollege, exeLearning, CADMOS and the Learning Designer provide a function for only adapting and sharing LDs from others and editing them. However, HE lecturers collaborate with colleagues or co-teachers in the design of the LDs.

M3: HE lecturers' time is an important factor that influences LD-P. Most LD tools do not adequately consider this issue, apart from the Learning Designer.

M4: The information regarding students' prior knowledge, needs, access to resources, motivation, and time are influencers of LD-P. Although these actors are widely acknowledged, they are not adequately accommodated in the LD tools.

M5: HE lecturers' LD-P is shaped by the national and institutional standards and they deploy the LDs into the VLE that is chosen by the institutions. The LD tools evaluated in this study do not consider national and institutional standards. The LDs developed within ILDE, OpenGLM, WebCollege, exeLearning, and CADMOS can be deployed into VLEs. However, they still do not support all kind of VLEs.

M6: Course timing is an important component of LD. However, it rarely is taken into account by LD tools - see the Learning Designer.

M7: At the end of the designing for the learning process, HE lecturers deploy their LDs into the VLE, but LD tools encounter with several challenges in terms of data exchange and interoperability and offer limited functionality. The LD tools are not adequately equipped to support all kind of VLE to easily deploy LDs developed with the tools.

M8: Supporting export of LDs into well-known file formats. The HE lecturers LDs are usually in the form of slides or word processor file. Even though, some of the tools export LDs in word processor format, they do not support any other formats.

M9: HE lecturers use various ways to get feedback regarding how well the lesson went in relation to the LD. Personal notes, observation of the students during the class time, review at the end of the class, self-reflection, and student criteria are the forms of getting personal feedback used by HE lecturers. However, LD tools are not sufficiently equipped to provide relevant functionalities.

M10: HE lecturers use several ways to get feedback from students regarding how well the lesson went in relation to LD formally and informally. Examination, feedback forms, and survey are the kinds of receiving formal feedback from students used by HE lecturers. The informal ways of getting feedback from students are written students' evaluation, discussing with students, and word of mouth.

M11: HE lecturers care about LA. HE lecturers see LA as an additional feedback mechanism to get valuable information about their students' performance and learning experience. However, even though there is an effort such as [15], more research is needed to link LA with LD.

6.1 Limitations

The findings of this study are subject to some limitations due to the nature of data, and methodological choices. It is essential to bear in mind the possible bias in the responses and analysis process. In order to avoid bias, increase objectivity, explore the credibility and therefore to improve transferability of the results of the study, the number of the participants to the survey is kept high. The sample size of this study was sufficiently large compared to the existing studies in the LD (32 was the largest sample size identified in the recent LD literature [8]).

7 Conclusions and Future Works

In this paper, we have explored the alignment of LD tools with LD-P of HE lecturers from sociomaterial perspective. A survey designed and conducted with one hundred ten HE lecturers on their LD-P helped to identify relevant actors and led to the design of a sociomaterial evaluation framework for LD tools. Guided by the framework's thirty-five exploratory questions, we analysed the alignment of seven LD tools to identify points of misalignment with LD-P. The identified misalignment points are summarised in eleven bullet points and discussed.

This study contributes to LD by augmenting the current picture of HE lecturers' LD-P from a sociomaterial perspective, identifying areas of mismatching between LD tools and HE lecturers' LD-P. This can be useful to inform the design of future LD tools. In future work, we would like to extend our analysis to other LD tools using the sociomaterial evaluation framework and finally propose sociomaterial design guidelines to inform the development of future LD tools. A holistic view of the LD-P through socio-materiality can potentially help LD practitioners and researchers, in general, as well as decision-makers, develop an enhanced conceptual understanding of factors influencing LD tools' adoption and embedding in educational organisations, and of the requirements for these tools.

References

1. Celik, D., Magoulas, G.D.: A review, timeline, and categorization of learning design tools. In: Chiu, D.K.W., Marenzi, I., Nanni, U., Spaniol, M., Temperini, M. (eds.) ICWL 2016. LNCS, vol. 10013, pp. 3–13. Springer, Cham (2016). https://doi.org/10.1007/978-3-319-47440-3_1
2. Prieto, L.P., Tchounikine, P., Asensio-Pérez, J.I., Sobreira, P., Dimitriadis, Y.: Exploring teachers' perceptions on different CSCL script editing tools. Comput. Educ. **78**, 383–396 (2014)
3. Dagnino, F.M., Dimitriadis, Y.A., Pozzi, F., Asensio-Pérez, J.I., Rubia-Avi, B.: Exploring teachers' needs and the existing barriers to the adoption of learning design methods and tools: a literature survey. Br. J. Educ. Technol. **49**, 998–1013 (2018)
4. Bennett, S., Agostinho, S., Lockyer, L.: Technology tools to support learning design: implications derived from an investigation of university teachers' design practices. Comput. Educ. **81**, 211–220 (2014)
5. Stark, J.S.: Planning introductory college courses: content, context and form. Instr. Sci. **28**, 413–438 (2000)
6. Norton, L., et al.: Teachers' beliefs and intentions concerning teaching in higher education. High. Educ. **50**, 537–571 (2005)
7. Bennett, S.S., Agostinho, S., Lockyer, L., Kosta, L., Jones, J., Harper, B.: Understanding university teachers' approaches to design. In: ED-MEDIA World Conference on Educational Multimedia, Hypermedia and Telecommunications, Chesapeake, Virginia, pp. 3631–3637 (2008)
8. Bennett, S., Thomas, L., Agostinho, S., Lockyer, L., Jones, J., Harper, B.: Understanding the design context for Australian university teachers: implications for the future of learning design. Learn. Media Technol. **36**, 151–167 (2011)

9. Nguyen, G.N.H., Bower, M.: Novice teacher technology-enhanced learning design practices: the case of the silent pedagogy. Br. J. Educ. Technol. **49**, 1027–1043 (2018)
10. Orlikowski, W.J.: Sociomaterial practices: exploring technology at work. Organ. Stud. **28**, 1435–1448 (2007)
11. Barad, K.: Getting real: technoscientific practices and the materialization of reality. Differ. A J. Fem. Cult. Stud. **10**, 87–128 (1998)
12. Orlikowski, W.J., Scott, S.V.: Sociomateriality: challenging the Separation of technology, work and organization. Acad. Manag. Ann. **2**, 433–474 (2008)
13. Fenwick, T.: Sociomateriality and Learning: A Critical Approach. Sage, London, UK (2015)
14. Britain, S.: Learning design systems: current and future developments. In: Rethinking Pedagogy for a Digital Age: Designing and Delivering E-Learning, pp. 103–104. Routledge, Oxford (2007)
15. Albó, L., Hernández-Leo, D.: Identifying design principles for learning design tools: the case of edCrumble. In: Pammer-Schindler, V., Pérez-Sanagustín, M., Drachsler, H., Elferink, R., Scheffel, M. (eds.) EC-TEL 2018. LNCS, vol. 11082, pp. 406–411. Springer, Cham (2018). https://doi.org/10.1007/978-3-319-98572-5_31
16. Owusu-Oware, E., Effah, J., Boateng, R.: Biometric technology for fighting fraud in national health insurance: Ghana's experience. In: Americas Conference on Information Systems, New Orleans, USA, pp. 1–10 (2018)
17. Sesay, A., Ramirez, R., Oh, O.-O.: Digital transformation in police work: a sociomaterial perspective on police body worn cameras (BWC). In: Proceedings of 50th Hawaii International Conference on System Sciences, pp. 4266–4275 (2017)
18. Jones, M.: A matter of life and death: exploring conceptualizations of sociomateriality in the context of critical care. MIS Q. **38**, 895–925 (2017)
19. Doolin, B., McLeod, L.: Sociomateriality and boundary objects in information systems development. Eur. J. Inf. Syst. **21**, 570–586 (2012)
20. Amiel, T., Reeves, T.C.T.: Design-based research and educational technology: rethinking technology and the research agenda. Educ. Technol. Soc. **11**, 29–40 (2008)
21. Creswell, J.W.: Research Design. SAGE Publications, Thousand Oaks (2014)
22. Hernández-Leo, D., Chacón, J., Prieto, L.P., Asensio-Pérez, J.I., Derntl, M.: Towards an integrated learning design environment. In: Hernández-Leo, D., Ley, T., Klamma, R., Harrer, A. (eds.) EC-TEL 2013. LNCS, vol. 8095, pp. 448–453. Springer, Heidelberg (2013). https://doi.org/10.1007/978-3-642-40814-4_37
23. Derntl, M.: OpenGLM : Integrating open educational resources in IMS learning design authoring. In: The Art and Science of Learning Design, pp. 157–168. Sense Publishers, Rotterdam (2015)
24. Villasclaras-Fernández, E., Hernández-Leo, D., Asensio-Pérez, J.I., Dimitriadis, Y.: Web collage: an implementation of support for assessment design in CSCL macro-scripts. Comput. Educ. **67**, 79–97 (2013)
25. Britain, S.: A review of learning design: concept, specifications and tools (2004)
26. Boloudakis, M., Katsamani, M., Retalis, S., Georgiakakis, P.: CADMOS: a learning design tool for Moodle courses. In: Moodle Research Conference, Heraklion, Crete-Greece, pp. 25–32 (2012)
27. Laurillard, D., et al.: A constructionist learning environment for teachers to model learning designs. J. Comput. Assist. Learn. **29**, 15–30 (2013)
28. Emin, V., Pernin, J.-P., Aguirre, J.L.: ScenEdit: an intention-oriented authoring environment to design learning scenarios. In: Wolpers, M., Kirschner, Paul A., Scheffel, M., Lindstaedt, S., Dimitrova, V. (eds.) EC-TEL 2010. LNCS, vol. 6383, pp. 626–631. Springer, Heidelberg (2010). https://doi.org/10.1007/978-3-642-16020-2_65

WEKIT.One: A Sensor-Based Augmented Reality System for Experience Capture and Re-enactment

Bibeg Limbu[1](✉), Alla Vovk[2], Halszka Jarodzka[1], Roland Klemke[1,3], Fridolin Wild[2], and Marcus Specht[1,4]

[1] Open University of Netherlands, Heerlen, The Netherlands
bibeg.limbu@ou.nl
[2] Oxford Brookes University, Oxford, UK
[3] Cologne Game Lab, Cologne, Germany
[4] LDE Centre for education and learning, Delft, The Netherlands

Abstract. Body-worn sensors can be used to capture, analyze, and replay human performance for training purposes. The key challenge to any such approach is to establish validity that the captured expert experience is actually suitable for training. In this paper, to evaluate this, we apply a questionnaire-based expert assessment and a complementary trainee knowledge assessment to study the approach adopted and the models generated with the WEKIT solution, a hardware and software application that complements Augmented Reality glasses with wearable sensor-actuator experience. This solution was developed using the ID4AR framework which as also developed within the WEKIT project. ID4AR framework is a domain agnostic framework which can be used to design augmented reality and sensor based applications for training. The study presented triangulates validity across three independent test-beds in the professional domains of aircraft maintenance, medical imaging, and astronaut training, with 61 experts completing the expert survey and 337 students completing the trainee knowledge test. Results show that the captured expert models were positively received in all three domains and the identified level of acceptance suggests that the solution is capable of capturing models for training purposes at large.

Keywords: Augmented Reality · Sensors · Expert model · Training

1 Introduction

Augmented reality (AR) and sensors are becoming mainstream, also in professional technology enhanced learning and performance augmentation. Deploying AR for training, however, currently requires significant investment with regards to time and other resources, as most task-practice requires bespoke AR solutions. Arguably, the lack of standards and content to this day are one, if not *the* obstacle in the way of a widespread adoption, see [5], despite apparent benefits.

M. Scheffel et al. (Eds.): EC-TEL 2019, LNCS 11722, pp. 158–171, 2019.
https://doi.org/10.1007/978-3-030-29736-7_12

To mitigate this situation, we developed an abstract, domain-independent Instructional Design for AR (ID4AR) framework [7] in the WEKIT project, so as to foster adoption across different training domains. The model is designed to help reduce associated entry costs by providing the theoretical foundation and practical instructional design building blocks, so-called instructional design methods (IDMs), required to design and deploy AR and senor-based training applications. ID4AR includes a systematic collection of domain independent instructional design methods (IDMs) as its unit component. IDMs are based on the study of affordances of AR and wearable sensors and are also independent of hardware (and sensor) choice. Each IDM relies on recorded expert performance and performance-relevant data in order to support training with AR and a wearable sensors. The framework, which is rooted in the 4CID model for learning complex tasks [6,7], also supports instructional designers in the selection of required IDMs to meet the requirements of the intended solution. In addition, the framework defines, systematically, all procedures needed to record and replay such expert data. By satisfying the framework‘s requirements, instructional designers can more easily design complex AR and wearable sensor solutions for training. This paper provides the validation of this theoretical framework as domain independent tool for supporting instructional designers. To do so, WEKIT solution was developed using ID4AR framework which was used in all three professional domains of aircraft maintenance, medical imaging,and astronaut training.

The WEKIT solution (also called WEKIT.One) supports recording experts performance for efficient and in-situ authoring of learning materials. The solution, to cater to all three domains mention above, implements common IDMs found across all three domains, which were selected after extensive task analysis with the experts from the three domains. This was done to meet the time and resource constraints, instead of creating three different applications for each domain. While, [8] used domain experts to review the solution's compliance to the framework, this study investigates whether the solution can in fact be used to record expert models across the different domains. By deploying the solution in three different domains and evaluating the expert model created, we can draw back conclusions on the validity of the framework and its utility to design AR and sensor based solutions regardless of their application domain. Thus, in this paper we aim to examine: Are recorded expert performances from ID4AR based solutions fit to be used as expert models for training in all three domains?

To do so, we asked expert peers to evaluate the expert model according to their fitness for training. In addition, we also conducted a knowledge assessment study with students to validate that the model captured with the solution does not impact negatively on their learning, or, ideally, even improves in areas. In this paper, we present results of this expert-peer evaluation and the students knowledge assessment study which assessed the expert model recorded by the WEKIT solution built with the ID4AR framework.

Table 1. List of IDMs in WEKIT application.

IDM	Description	Visuals
Directed focus	Visual pointer for relevant objects outside the visual area of the trainee.	
Point of view video	Provides expert point-of-view video which may provide perspectives not available in a third person.	
Annotations	Allow a physical object to be annotated by the expert during task execution (similar to sticky notes but with more modalities).	
Ghost track	Allows visualization of the whole-body movement of the expert or the earlier recording of the trainees themselves for imitation and reflection.	
Highlight objects of interest	Highlight physical objects in the visual area indicating to the trainee that the expert marked it as an object of interest.	
Object enrichment	Virtually amplify the effect of the process to enable trainees to understand the consequences of certain events or actions in the process which may be too subtle to notice.	

(*continued*)

Table 1. (*continued*)

IDM	Description	Visuals
Contextual information	Provide information about the process that is frequently changing but is important for performance.	
3D models and animation	3d models and animations assist in easy interpretation of Complex models and phenomena which require high spatial processing ability.	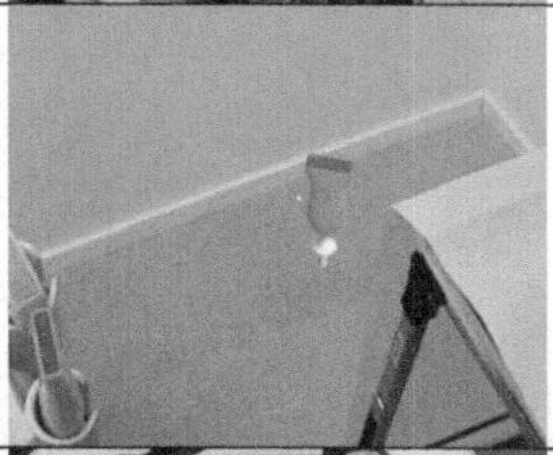
Interactive virtual objects	Interactable virtual objects to practice with physical interactions relying on the 3d models and animation.	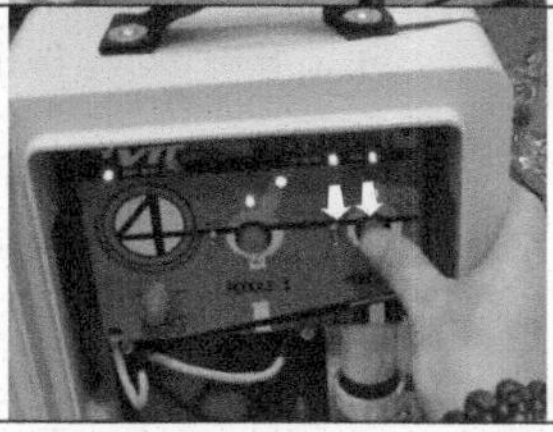
Cues and clues	Cues and clues are pivots that trigger solution search. They can be in any form of media but should represent the solution search with a single annotation.	
Haptic feedback	Lightweight force feedback for perception and manipulation of authentic objects by means of haptic sensor, to provide feedback and guidance.	

2 Method

To capture and evaluate the expert models, 61 experts and 337 students used the WEKIT solution during WEKIT trials held at Lufttransport in Norway for the aircraft maintenance, Ebit in Italy for medical imaging and Altec in Italy for astronaut training. These trails were conducted in a time span of more three months independently by the above mentioned use case organizations with out any intervention by other researchers and technical partners.

2.1 Participants

61 experts participated in the study from three different domains. The expert participants were defined as those who had experience in the domain they took part in. There were 47 male and 14 female expert participants, with the majority of them falling in the age range of 25–44. Among these participants, there were 8 supervisor, 8 trainers, 31 engineers and 19 from several other roles. 32 expert participants had more than 10 years of experience, 20 had less than 5 years and 9 between 5–10 years. Demographics for individual domains are detailed in Table 2

Table 2. Demographics for individual domains.

Domain	N	Gender		Age range	Experience			Trainers
		M	F		<5	5–10	>10	N
Astronaut	13	11	2	25–34	2	4	7	2
Medical	26	18	8	25–54	13	0	13	2
Aeronautics	22	18	4	35–44	5	5	12	4
Total	61	47	14		20	9	32	8

2.2 Apparatus

The WEKIT solution is built for the Microsoft Hololens, an AR platform. It is developed with Unity3D, Vuforia (marker-based image recognition toolkit for AR), and the Microsoft MixedReality Toolkit. The application consists of two main interfaces: the Recorder interface and the Player interface (see Fig. 1).

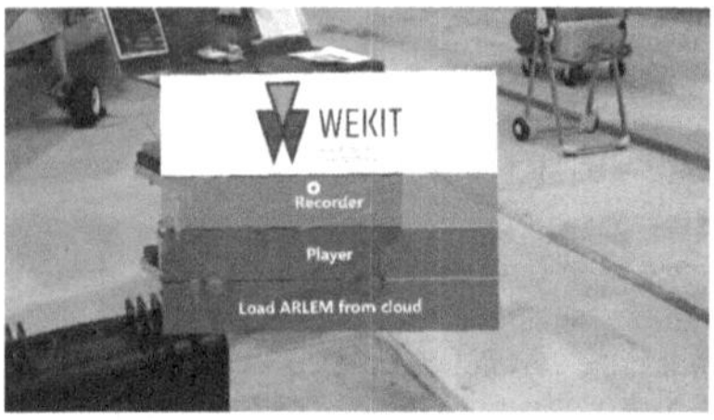

Fig. 1. Recorder and player interface.

Fig. 2. Creating task stations.

Recorder Interface. The recorder interface supports experts in creating learning content with two main functionalities: annotation of objects and locations in the physical space (using text, image, video, audio, 3D object annotations) and more implicit, observation-based, multi-modal capture of the expert performance, using sensor data. It provides two different methods of connecting virtual annotations to the physical space: marker-based and anchor-based. The marker-based approach relies on prepared image targets (using Vuforia for tracking), which binds augmented content to the physical environment to place the attached annotations relative to the marker image. The anchor-based approach uses the infrared scanner of the smart glasses to generate a spatial map of the environment to then attach all augmented content relative to physical anchor-points. Experts create so-called 'task stations' to record the learning activity in a systematic manner. Task stations can be placed by pointing the gaze cursor to the desired location and then performing a double-tap gesture, or by sticking the pretrained image target marker onto an object or location (see Fig. 2). Task stations and their attached annotations are then subsequently translated to a linear or branched sequence of action steps in the player interface. Recorded units typically contain a longer sequence of such task stations (see Fig. 5), each typically with a combination of annotations attached. Experts can enrich the physical space with virtual images, point-of-view videos, voice recordings, place 3D models, mark the physical location as a point of interest, and record sensor data (see Fig. 3). The annotations working with sensor data currently make use of hand position, relative orientation (relative to the device), and the head position and orientation (relative to physical environment). Captured learning activities can be saved in the ARLEM format and can be uploaded to a cloud repository, when complete. ARLEM standard specifies how to represent activities for training knowledge, skills, and other abilities in a standardized interchange format for AR applications.

Fig. 3. List of annotations.

Fig. 4. Sequence of task stations.

Player Interface. The player interface allows trainees to learn from the experts created learning contents. Students can download a learning activity from the cloud. Once downloaded, the player interface generates the user interface as a task list and task cards for step-wise guidance (see Fig. 5. The player interface projects the augmentations at the right location and in the right sequence (see Fig. 6). Students can navigate between the steps using voice commands or gestures.

2.3 Materials and Measures

We aimed to evaluate the expert model's validity based on the recorded performances. Experts were considered to be experienced or working in the domain of the test-bed. For the actual evaluation, first, an expert performance was recorded in all three domains, producing three different models. These models were not

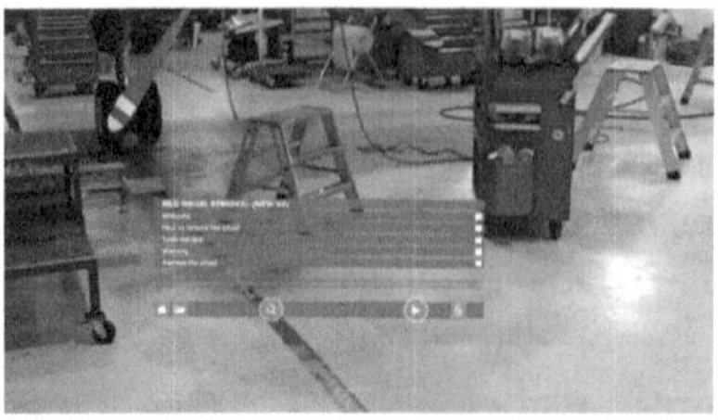

Fig. 5. Steps in a recording.

Fig. 6. Content of a step.

post-processed. Second, the model was loaded and used by the peer experts according to their respective domains. Third, the peer experts evaluated the model using a specific questionnaire, i.e., the expert model evaluation questionnaire (EMEQ) which was the same for all three domains. Aim of the questionnaire, which is based on [4], was to assess the characteristics of the expert model by judging its fitness for training. Participants responded by scoring questionnaire items on a Likert scale from 1 (=strongly disagree) to 7 (=strongly agree). The responses were collected through LimeSurvey, an online survey tool.

2.4 Design and Procedure

The expert who captured the model was introduced to the WEKIT solution's user manual first to ensure he/she was familiar with the solution (e.g., using a generic gesture training). Prior to the recording, the expert was asked to plan the action steps and accordingly, the task stations with the affordances of the solution in mind. These included considerations such as how many task stations need to be created and what type of content would be presented in each of the task stations. During the subsequent recording of the activity, the expert was free to ask support questions. The expert was allowed to repeat the capturing process until satisfied. The peers who evaluated the model used both recorder and player. They used the recorder to understand how the model was created. In the player, the model that was initially created was loaded, and the peers followed through all the steps. The peers were also given as much time as they requested for the whole procedure. In the end, all the expert peers filled the questionnaire for evaluating the expert model.

3 Results

At the end of the three months duration of the WEKIT trials, the data was downloaded from LimeSurvey. In the following, we present the overall results and the results per domain. The mean response for the items across all three domains is presented in Table 3.

The average mean and the median response of experts across all trials for all the items were above average (see Fig. 7). Experts strongly agreed on EMEQ 1 (Mdn = 6.07), on the importance for the students to understand what each key

Table 3. Descriptive statistics for all three domains.

Descriptive statistics for EMEQ				
Items		N	M	SD
EMEQ 1	It is important that the student knows what each key concept means	61	6.066	.834
EMEQ 2	For this student, all key concepts are defined just in time	61	5.574	.884
EMEQ 3	For this student, the procedure is explained in comprehensible enough terms	61	5.198	.781
EMEQ 4	For this student, the procedure is explained in enough detail	61	5.705	.882
EMEQ 5	All the information that the student needs to follow the procedure is contained	61	5.852	.813
EMEQ 6	All the information that the student needs to follow the procedure is provided just in time	61	5.574	.991
EMEQ 7	All the contained information is important to the student	61	5.787	.951
EMEQ 8	All the information provided is non-obtrusive for the student	61	5.639	.967
EMEQ 9	All the objects/items required by the student in the procedure is easily located/identified	61	5.577	1.203
EMEQ 10	It is clear for the student which physical area to move next	61	5.459	.993
EMEQ 11	All relevant information that is frequently updated, such as temperature, is made aware to the student	61	4.787	1.171

concept meant. Similarly, there is an agreement between expert participants for EMEQ 2 (Mdn = 5.57), EMEQ 4 (Mdn = 5.70) and EMEQ 6 (Mdn = 5.57) which verifies that the expert model explained the procedure in comprehensible terms and included all important information required for the procedure. Most expert participants had high degree of agreement in EMEQ 3 (Mdn = 5.92), EMEQ 5 (Mdn = 5.85) and EMEQ 7 (Mdn = 5.79). The procedure was found to have been explained in enough details, just in time and in an unobtrusive manner by the expert participants. The expert participants also found that the model guided students to the correct location and items in the physical space which was shown by EMEQ 9 (Mdn = 5.57) & EMEQ 10 (Mdn = 5.46). The SD of EMEQ 9 and EMEQ 11 was higher than acceptable. EMEQ 11 was rated between 1–7 with lower quartile rating the item between 1–4. Experts opinion vary hugely in terms of how well and often critical dynamic information were updated. Results of the study for individual domains are presented below.

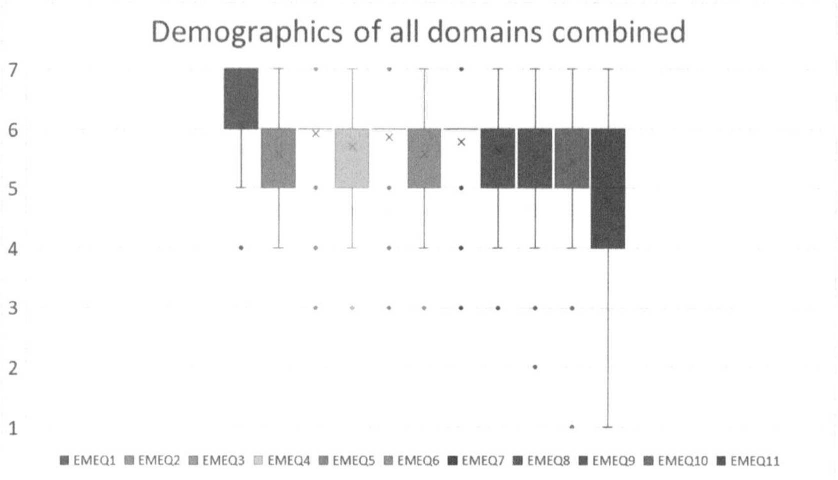

Fig. 7. Demographics of all domain together

3.1 Astronaut Domain

The expert participants mostly responded positively to the model with the median of all items above 4 (see Fig. 7). Most expert participants responded positively on EMEQ 1 (Mdn = 5.692) with only 1 participant rating it 4. For EMEQ 2 (Mdn = 5.538), with the upper quartile between 6–7 and lower quartile between 4–5. This supported that most concepts were defined just in time in the expert model. Expert participants had a high level of agreement on EMEQ 3 (Mdn = 5.769) with only 1 expert participant rating it 4. Item EMEQ 4 (Mdn = 5.307), show that the expert model explained the procedure in comprehensible terms and details. Results of item EMEQ 5 (Mdn = 5.692) show that the contained information in the expert model is complete. EMEQ 6 (Mdn = 5.230) showed larger variation in expert participants agreement in terms of if the information was provided in the right time. EMEQ 7 (Mdn = 5.615) and EMEQ 8 (Mdn = 5.461) validates that the expert model contains all the important information, which are presented in an unobtrusive manner. Only 1 participant rating EMEQ 8 below 4. Item EMEQ 9 (Mdn = 5.307) verified that the participants were fairly able to locate the objects required for the procedure most of the time. The participants were also able to identify the place where the next step of the procedure was to be done. This is shown by the strong agreement between the expert participants in item EMEQ 10 (Mdn = 5.538). EMEQ 11 (Mdn = 4.692) showed loose agreement between expert participants with 75% rating it between 4–6 and the rest 25% voting it between 2–4.

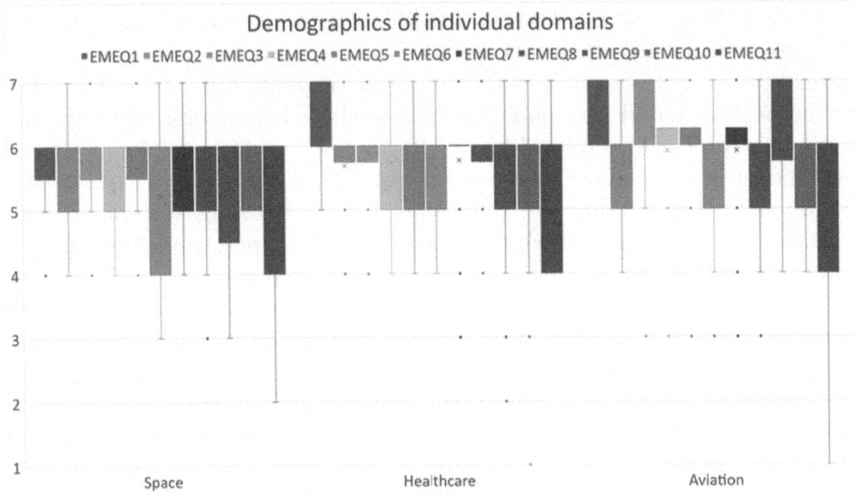

Fig. 8. Demographics of study in individual domains

3.2 Medical Domain

The median response of experts for each item is above 4 (see Fig. 7). There is consistent agreement among the expert participants for EMEQ 1 (Mdn = 6.12), emphasizing that the students need to know the key concepts. While the majority of the expert participants think that most terms have been defined and in comprehensive manner, EMEQ 2 (Mdn = 5.69) & EMEQ 3 (Mdn = 5.75), 5 expert participants rated EMEQ 2 and 1 participant rated EMEQ 3 as 4. EMEQ 4 (Mdn = 5.73), EMEQ 5 (Mdn = 5.81) and EMEQ 6 (5.65) validate that the expert model was contained complete information which was provided just in time for the students. For all these three tiems, the middle quartile fell between 5–6. With only one expert participant rating EMEQ 7 (Mdn = 5.77) and EMEQ 8 (Mdn = 5.75) below 4, it can be argued that all information contained in the expert model were important for the procedure and were not presented obtrusively. The students were able to find the objects in the work space and were able to pinpoint the location for the next step in the procedure as shown by EMEQ 9 (Mdn = 5.42) and EMEQ 10 (Mdn = 5.31), with only 2 expert participants each rating them below 4. EMEQ 11 (Mdn = 4.96) shows that the relevant types of information were updated. However, 11 of the expert peers rated it at 4.

3.3 Aeronautics Domain

The median response of the expert participants in this domain for each item are above 4. As with other domains expert in Aeronautics domain experts strongly agree that students should know what each key concept means, which is shown by EMEQ 1 (Mdn = 6.23). EMEQ 2 (Mdn = 5.45) shows that most key concepts were well defined in the model. 75% participants rated the item EMEQ 3 (Mdn = 6.05) between 6–7, with only 1 participant rating it 3. This shows that the experts found the model was comprehensible enough. Only 2 expert participants rated EMEQ 4 (Mdn = 5.91) below 4, which validated that the expert model was explained in enough detail. Similarly only one expert participant rated EMEQ 5 (Mdn = 6.00) below 4, with a strong agreement among the other expert participants which showed that the expert model contained all the information that the student needed to follow the procedure. EMEQ 6 (Mdn = 5.68) shows that the expert participants found that the information needed were provided in just in time fashion. All contained information was found to be important to the student in EMEQ 7 (Mdn = 5.91), with only one expert disagreeing with a score of 3. EMEQ 8 (Mdn = 5.59) validates that the expert model was fairly unobtrusive for the students. The recorded model was also able to direct the participants to the location of the object required during the procedure most of the time as shown by EMEQ 9 (Mdn = 5.75). Similarly, EMEQ 10 (Mdn = 5.59) showed agreement among the participants that the students were provided guidance to move from one place to another during the procedure. Expert participants were divided for EMEQ 11 (Mdn = 4.64) which was rated 4 by 11 people, with distribution varying wildly from 1–7. The central quartile falls between 4–6.

One-way ANCOVA was conducted to determine any statistically significant difference between the three test-beds on EMEQ items. There is no significant effect of the application domain on EMEQ 1 [$F(1, 59) = 3.126$, $P = .082$], EMEQ 2 [$F(1, 59) = .175$, $P = .667$], EMEQ 3 [$F(1, 59) = 1.905$, $P = .300$], EMEQ 4 [$F(1, 59) = 3.720$, $P = .059$], EMEQ 5 [$F(1, 59) = 1.281$, $P = .262$], EMEQ 6 [$F(1, 59) = 1.423$, $P = .238$], EMEQ 7 [$F(1, 59) = .792$, $P = .377$], EMEQ 8 [$F(1, 59) = .049$, $P = .826$], EMEQ 9 [$F(1, 59) = 2.466$, $P = .122$], EMEQ 10 [$F(1, 59) = .104$, $P = .746$], EMEQ 11 [$F(1, 59) = .093$, $P = .762$], which shows that the mean for each item across all three application areas are similar. This supports the hypothesis that the WEKIT solution can be used to create expert models independent of the domain.

The results of the study show similar pattern across all three domains. For example, the median of EMEQ 11 was between 4–5 with large disagreement, while participants in all application domains seemed to strongly agree for EMEQ 1. The variance for EMEQ 11 can be explained with the complexity of the sensor framework built into the application. It is up to the expert author of the learning activity to decide where and when to stream sensor data. It is well possible that the chosen task may not have required data updates. Moreover, the automated adaptation of the activity based on sensor values may also hide that this happens from sensor data. We deem it therefore likely not all participants paid attention to the 'data updating' possibility.

Average results show, however, that the expert participants found the expert model created by the WEKIT application to be usable for training students.

3.4 Knowledge Assessment

The aim of the Knowledge Assessment test was to evaluate the student participants performance after the training. The test was designed by the experts at the domain and almost each knowledge test question is testing knowledge acquired during consequent procedure step. In total there were nine procedure steps and 14 knowledge test questions in Medical domain and 15 procedure steps and 15 knowledge test questions in Aeronautics and Space training domain.

In the Aeronautics domain, there were 59 students in the experimental group, which used the player and 16 people in the control group which used paper based instructions. The group which used the application completed 66% of the questions correctly while the control group completed 63% of the questions correctly. The results (Z-score = 0.37 and p-value = 0.7) show there is no statistically significant difference between the two groups in Aeronautics domain.

In the medical domain, 73 students in experimental group used the player and 12 students were part of the Control group who used paper based instructions. The experimental group completed 66% of the questions correctly while the control group completed 92% of the questions correctly. The results show there is no statistically significant difference between the two groups(Z-score = -1.7 and p-value = 0.08).

In the Astronaut domain, 147 students in the experimental group used the player and 30 students were part of the Control group who used paper-based instructions. The experimental group completed 66% of the questions correctly while the control group completed 63% of the questions correctly. The results show that there is no statistically significant difference between the two groups (Z-score = 0.3 and p-value = 0.76).

4 Conclusion

This study evaluated the validity and utility of expert models captured using the WEKIT solution in three independent test-beds. Results show that the WEKIT solution was rated positively in all three application domains with no statistically significant difference between test-beds. Experts agree that the model captured with the solution (and its affordances) are fit to be used for training in all three domains. The WEKIT solution implements the ID4AR framework [7] and all three models were captured using it. Therefore, the results of this study suggest the framework can be used more broadly across different domains for designing AR and sensor-based solutions for training. Moreover, the results of the knowledge assessment show that the AR and senor-based training is equally effective as the learning of the control group and there are positive effects with regards to acceptance (see [2]) and user experience [3]. The use of the solution did not impede learning in comparison to the traditional methods and both group scored similarly in these knowledge assessment tests.

The WEKIT solution is a reference implementation of the ID4AR framework, an abstract framework for building sensor-based and AR based training applications. The presented evaluation results hold across the independent test-beds and thus support the claim that the framework can be used independent of application domain. The implementation and its evaluation underline that sensor-based AR systems are high-potential training tools. Moreover, they suggest that the adoption of the framework for designing AR training applications potentially can help mitigate risk, cost, and facilitate overcoming the complexity associated with their design and development.

4.1 Limitations and Future Work

Expert participants who peer evaluated the WEKIT solution based model did not have any pre/post sessions to help them prepare for the evaluation. The experts needed to recall their sessions to respond to the EMEQ questionnaire which may have affected the quality of the response. While the model was peer-evaluated by the other experts, there was no review of the model from the studentś perspective. The knowledge assessment results in individual domains show none to very little significant difference in the learning performance of students who used the application than those who didn't. However, the assessment didn't take pre-knowledge and other factors into account. In addition, more work needs to be done to reap the benefits of the affordances of modern technologies such as AR to enhance the learning outcomes from the students. The WEKIT solution was a single solution to all three domains which was essential to meet the time and resource constraint. Using the ID4AR framework to design specific solutions for individual domain can increase the affordances making it a more effective modeling tool.

Eventually, the work done so far has presented potentials and many opportunities for further development and research. Even though several milestones have been met in the development of the ID4AR framework, limitations exist. The framework itself is designed to be a support for training where experts are limited. The solutions designed with the framework are not for substituting the expert but for complementing them. While implementing the framework, the need to perform an extensive task analysis to select the proper set of IDMs on the domain still exists and is resource-intensive. In addition, with the evolving technology, the framework's pool of IDMs must expand to support the affordances of new technologies. The framework also does not claim explicating expertise and any tacit knowledge from the expert. While explicating the tacit knowledge is possible by rigorous manual means, by nature it cannot be done unobtrusively. Instead, the framework leverages on the performance metrics of the expert and visible attributes of expert performance to support training efficiently. While feedbacks are integral part of the framework in order to support training, the WEKIT solution has only focused on didactic methods and guidelines. No summative/formative feedback was provided based on expert data. Providing such feedback, especially formative, requires further research on both technology and methodology to be able to compare streaming data and experts recorded data in the physical time and space. [9] and [1] has been making significant efforts for achieving this feat. Their work so far has involved synchronized multi-modal data collection and annotation of such data which are crucial steps for being able to provide realtime feedback with sensor data.

Acknowledgements. This study is partially funded by the WEKIT project, the Safepat project, and the TCBL project. The WEKIT project received funding from the European Union's Horizon 2020 research and innovation programme under grant agreement No 687669. The Safepat project is co-funded by the European Union under the Interreg EMR Programme. The TCBL project received funding from the European Union's Horizon 2020 research and innovation programme under grant agreement No 646133.

References

1. Di Mitri, D., Schneider, J., Klemke, R., Specht, M., Drachsler, H.: Read between the lines: an annotation tool for multimodal data for learning. In: Proceedings of the 9th International Conference on Learning Analytics and Knowledge, LAK 2019, pp. 51–60. ACM, New York (2019)
2. Guest, W., et al.: A technology acceptance model for augmented reality and wearable technologies. J. Univ. Comput. Sci. **24**(2), 192–219 (2018)
3. Xue, H., Sharma, P., Wild, F.: User satisfaction in augmented reality-based training using microsoft HoloLens. Computers **8**(1), 9 (2019)
4. Jucks, R., Schulte-Löbbert, P., Bromme, R.: Supporting experts' written knowledge communication through reflective prompts on the use of specialist concepts. Zeitschrift für Psychol./J. Psychol. **215**(4), 237–247 (2007). https://doi.org/10.1027/0044-3409.215.4.237
5. Langlotz, T., Grubert, J., Grasset, R.: Augmented reality browsers: essential products or only gadgets? CACM **56**(11), 34–36 (2013). https://doi.org/10.1145/2527190
6. Limbu, B., Fominykh, M., Klemke, R., Specht, M., Wild, F.: Supporting training of expertise with wearable technologies: the WEKIT reference framework. In: Yu, S., Ally, M., Tsinakos, A. (eds.) Mobile and Ubiquitous Learning. PRRE, pp. 157–175. Springer, Singapore (2018). https://doi.org/10.1007/978-981-10-6144-8_10
7. Limbu, B.H., Jarodzka, H., Klemke, R., Specht, M.: Using sensors and augmented reality to train apprentices using recorded expert performance: a systematic literature review. Educ. Res. Rev. **25**, 1–22 (2018). https://doi.org/10.1016/J.EDUREV.2018.07.001
8. Limbu, B.H., Jarodzka, H., Klemke, R., Wild, F., Specht, M.: From AR to expertise: a user study of an augmented reality training to support expertise development. J. Univ. Comput. Sci. **24**(2), 108–128 (2018)
9. Schneider, J., Di Mitri, D., Limbu, B., Drachsler, H.: Multimodal learning hub: a tool for capturing customizable multimodal learning experiences. In: Pammer-Schindler, V., Pérez-Sanagustín, M., Drachsler, H., Elferink, R., Scheffel, M. (eds.) EC-TEL 2018. LNCS, vol. 11082, pp. 45–58. Springer, Cham (2018). https://doi.org/10.1007/978-3-319-98572-5_4

Gamification of MOOCs Adopting Social Presence and Sense of Community to Increase User's Engagement: An Experimental Study

Alessandra Antonaci[1(✉)], Roland Klemke[1], Johan Lataster[2], Karel Kreijns[1], and Marcus Specht[1]

[1] Welten Institute - Research Center for Learning, Teaching and Technology, Open University of the Netherlands, Heerlen, The Netherlands
Alessandra.antonaci@ou.nl

[2] Faculty of Psychology and Educational Sciences, Open University of the Netherlands, Heerlen, The Netherlands

Abstract. Over the past few years, massive online open courses (MOOCs) have been increasingly identified as technologies that could transform education, by providing free and high-quality content to anyone with an Internet connection. However, despite these potentials, MOOCs generally fail to keep their participants on board. One of the reasons for this phenomenon can lie in a lack of participants' engagement. Social presence and sense of community (SoC) theories claim that a user in an online shared environment may feel more engaged if s/he perceives the others as 'real persons' and feels part of a community. Therefore, we developed our game elements with the purpose of developing social presence and SoC among MOOC users. The results of our experiment, from one side, show that our gamification design did positively impact users' development of social presence and SoC, as well as their learning performance. From the other, data did not confirm that higher levels of social presence and SoC corresponded to higher engagement of MOOC users. These results have important implications for the field by enriching it with a more technologically enhanced approach towards implementing gamification, and by augmenting the social potentials of MOOCs.

Keywords: Gamification · Social presence · Sense of community · Engagement · MOOCs · Experimental study

1 Introduction

In 2012, when the use of Massive Online Open Courses (MOOCs) exploded, many academics were looking at them as a new avenue with great potential for transforming and improving education. The use of advanced technology made it possible to scale up and reach massive amounts of users, potentially bringing (free) education within arm's reach for anyone with an Internet connection. However, almost seven years later, MOOCs have only partially fulfilled their potential, as they manage to draw in large numbers of users, but also see the majority of them dropping out [1]. Based on an analysis of "565 course iterations from 261 different courses, with a combined 12.67

M. Scheffel et al. (Eds.): EC-TEL 2019, LNCS 11722, pp. 172–186, 2019.
https://doi.org/10.1007/978-3-030-29736-7_13

million course registrations from 5.63 million learners" [1, p. 130], it appears that the majority of people who enrol in a MOOC never enter the course (52% of the study sample), and those who do join, are mainly active during the first two weeks, after which their level of activities drops sharply [1]. We argue that a drop in activity levels may be partly due to a lack of user engagement, and MOOCs may benefit from a gamified intervention targeted at increasing engagement.

Inspired by social presence theory, we propose to stimulate engagement by making MOOC users aware of the presence of fellow students, thus, emphasizing the 'social factor' in MOOCs, in contrast with the rather individual-oriented approach typically followed so far. Our assumption is that by enabling users to perceive the (social) presence of their fellow students, a sense of community (SoC) can be generated, which may positively impact levels of engagement and learning performance. According to social presence theory [2], engagement can be enhanced in online learning environments by creating a sense of community and belonging among users [3]. However, as this theory postulates, to develop a SoC it is important that users perceive others as 'real persons' in the shared online learning environment (i.e., the MOOC). Perceiving the presence of others online is not an inherent characteristic of MOOC platforms, where usually the only 'social' feature, the only 'social affordance[1]', available is the discussion forum [4]. Several studies have investigated how forums should be designed to foster user engagement [4, 5], but only few have considered to include and design solutions, for generating a SoC among MOOC users in order to raise engagement levels [6].

Taking inspiration from games and social presence theory, we have designed, developed, and implemented several game elements (which are described in Sect. 3 - experimental design) to address the issue of user engagement in MOOCs. In designing gamification, we have taken into consideration the characteristics of the scenario of application, the problem found in this scenario that we aim to address, and the target audience (in accordance with our previous work [7]).

- *Scenario of application*: The MOOC platform for the current study, Open edX, lacks features that enable users to perceive their fellow students. The only space where people can interact within this platform is the discussion forum, and the perception of which and how many people are online is not immediate. Most participants are not aware of how many other users are following the same course. *Implication for the gamification design*: to facilitate a SoC, the shared online learning environment should facilitate sociability, which is the degree in which the online environment supports social affordances[8, p. 284]. In the shared social space, it is important to perceive the other as real, close. *Proximity* has been shown to play an important role in the development of a SoC [9]. One way to create "virtual proximity" in online learning scenarios, is to provide awareness information about group members, in our case MOOC fellow students. Furthermore as [10] reports, different types of interactions (student-instructor and student- student) are important, because together these "strengthen students' sense of membership"

[1] [8] pointed out that such social features (affordances) may add to what they call the 'sociability' of the online learning environment. They purport that sociability affects the degree of social presence and social interaction among learners and, thus, their engagement.

[7, p. 153]. Therefore MOOC users will not only need to be aware of the other members, but also to interact with them.

- *Target audience*: MOOC learners can be as heterogeneous as the general public. Interactive technology has to consider user characteristics, and more specifically their perceptions and predispositions. While some people easily perceive others as being present, others may require more explicit input to perceive the same level of presence.
  Implication for the gamification design: considering the heterogeneity of our target audience, the game elements need to be developed in such a way that each user determines her/his own level of social involvement, respecting and taking into account the individual needs and characteristics.
  - *Problem to solve*: we aim to address the lack of engagement and retention of users within an online open course.
    Implication for the gamification design is to address the lack of social features (affordances) in the Open edX platform, with the purpose of enhancing its sociability. By doing so, we aim to generate a feeling of others (social presence, in term of awareness and proximity) among MOOC users, which will lead to the generation of a SoC. In turn, this is expected to increase levels of participant engagement in the gamified (experimental) condition compared to the non-gamified (control) condition.

To present our gamification design and its effects, we have organised the remainder of this paper as follows: section two introduces our theoretical framework, based on social presence theory and SoC. The third section presents related works, mainly with respect to how engagement has so far been investigated in MOOCs. Section four details our research questions and hypothesis, then the experimental procedure is described, followed by the results, discussion and conclusions.

2 Theoretical Background

The term and theory of *social presence* has evolved over the recent years. It has been coined in the field of telecommunications by [2]. Initially *social presence* was defined as the "degree of salience of the other person in the interaction" [2, p. 65], using a communication medium. [2] conceptualised *social presence* as "a quality of a communication medium that can determine the way people interact and communicate" [8, p. 117]. According to [2] the degree of *social presence* can vary in relation to the medium used (i.e. videos have a higher level of social presence than audio). [12] shifted the attention from the medium to the person, defining social presence as "the degree to which a person is perceived as a real person in mediated communication" [9, p. 151]. Lastly with the Community of Inquiry (CoI) framework [13] the focus has passed from the person to the community.

To understand how *social presence*, *sense of community* (SoC) and *engagement* are linked, we can refer to the study of [3]. Results from this study suggest that social presence correlated with SoC and students with a stronger perception of SoC also felt more engaged [3]. Furthermore, "Online researchers emphasise social presence as a key factor in student engagement" [11, p. 3] and relate it positively to "students learning [...] and student satisfaction" [11, p. 3]. Engagement in general is an abstract and multidimensional concept [14], and students' engagement in particular, has been investigated and conceptualised in many ways across several disciplines [15–17]. From a technology enhanced learning perspective, the type of engagement we aim to study and foster is generated in online environments and for which social presence and SoC is needed. The latter is seen as an element of the social space that exists among participants and described in previous work [8, 18]. Therefore, in the framework of this study, engagement is studied as the degree in which the learners are involved in online activities and interact, communicate, with others (mediators and peers). Engagement, as such, is generated and influenced by the experienced presence of the others and social presence. In other words: "Engagement is composed of individual attitudes, thoughts, and behaviours as well as communication with others. Student engagement is about students putting time, energy, thought, effort, and, to some extent, feelings into their learning" [11, p. 147].

3 Related Work: Engagement in MOOCs

Engagement is a popular topic in the literature on MOOCs. Authors have described the construct via literature review [19], through theoretical frameworks, such as self-determination theory [20], learning analytics [21], and machine learning algorithms [22]. The studies conducted have identified, among other results, the type of users that engage in MOOCs [4]. Furthermore, it has been shown that teacher/instructor styles play an important role in engaging students [23], as well as videos [24], formative assessment, feedback practices [25], and time management solutions that support learners [26].

Gamification has been suggested as a potential strategy to stimulate user engagement in MOOCs [27, 28]. For designing a gamified solution we have investigated the 'games' literature, with the aim of understanding which factors retain millions of players within their online communities. Based on [29], the two factors that seem to retain players in a specific group or guild are: (1) *SoC* (membership, sense of belonging, group identity), which positively impacts retention and 'relation switching cost.' Such a cost in online games can be described as "the losses accompanied with the breaking of the bonds that have been formed with other gamers" [29]. A high *SoC* is accompanied by high relation switching costs, yielding players more likely to stay in the same group (or guild). (2) The second factor that retains players in a specific group is *interdependence*. "Interdependence is the degree to which members in a community rely on each other to make decisions and take actions [30]" [29]. In order to create a SoC and interdependence within MOOCs, it is vital to make the users aware of the others and generate social presence.

Although the importance of social presence in online learning settings has been well documented [7, 31–33], most research in the area of social presence is situated within the formal education context [6]. Only a few studies examine learner perceptions of social presence in MOOCs [6]. What we propose in this study, is not only a conceptual elaboration but also a technological solution that embraces the concept of social presence and SoC to enhance engagement of users within a MOOC learning environment. Lastly, in our previous work [33], we also theorize on the correlation between social presence and SoC, hypothesizing their impact on engagement and learning performance. This work is also an attempt to empirical verify this connection.

4 Research Question and Hypotheses

The main research question underlying our study is: *Can a gamified solution help to increase MOOC user engagement and learning performance through mechanisms of social presence and SoC?* We hypothesize that *by enabling users to perceive the (social) presence of their fellow students through gamified solutions, a SoC can be generated, which positively impacts levels of engagement and learning performance,* see Fig. 1. From this assumption, the following research hypotheses (H) are derived with regard to our experiment (detailed below):

H1: Our gamification design contributes to the feeling of social presence among MOOC users: perceived social presence will be higher for users in the experimental (gamified) vs. control (non-gamified) condition;

H2: Our gamification design contributes to the SoC among MOOC users: SoC will be higher for users in the experimental (gamified) vs. control (non-gamified) condition;

H3: Social presence and SoC are positively associated, i.e., higher levels of social presence are associated with higher levels of SoC;

H4: Our gamification design contributes to MOOC user engagement: engagement will be higher for users in the experimental (gamified) vs. control (non-gamified) condition;

H5: SoC is positively associated with user engagement, i.e., higher levels of SoC are associated with higher levels of engagement.

H6: Our gamification design contributes to MOOC user learning performance: test performance will be better for users in the experimental (gamified) vs. control (non-gamified) condition;

H7: Our gamification design contributes to MOOC user retention: retention will be higher, c.q. dropout will be lower and later for users in the experimental (gamified) vs. control (non-gamified) condition;

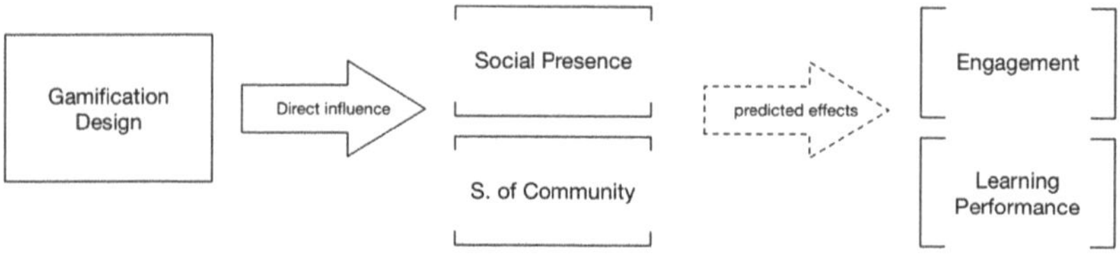

Fig. 1. Representation of the connection among variables

5 Method

Participants and Procedure[2]

A total of 255 people enrolled in the MOOC, of which 154 were active. Participation in the MOOC as well as in the experiment was voluntary, and information about it was provided in the introductory video and via additional information. At the beginning of the course, participants' background information and the consent to use their data were collected. 155 participants provided background data and informed consent. The average age of the participants was 43.4 (SD = 13.89), n = 53 had a master's degree; n = 47 a bachelor's degree, and n = 25 a high school diploma (the rest declared 'other'). The majority (n = 108) of the participants were from NL, but also BE, IN, ES, PK, GB, FR and AU were represented.

Log data (H4, H6–7) were registered during the MOOC for 154 online users. In addition, one week after the MOOC had started, participants were asked to fill in a survey containing the social presence scale (SPS) and the SoC measure (H1–3, H5). The SPS was filled in by 45 (of 98, 45.9%) users in the experimental condition and by 19 (of 56, 33.9%) in the control, whereas for SoC, data were complete for 47 (48.0%) users in the experimental condition, and 23 (41.1%) in the control condition.

The Study Site

The MOOC under investigation was titled "How Cryptography keeps the Internet Secure", at its first edition. It ran between January 2019 and February 2019, spanning four weeks in total. Each week had dedicated content and included a knowledge test. Video lectures, video scripts and lecture notes were available for all participants, and were released weekly. The MOOC was provided by the Open University of The Netherlands on Open edX platform.

Experimental Design

To test the above mentioned hypotheses, MOOC users were randomly assigned to an experimental (gamified) or control (non-gamified) study condition. The gamification design consisted of the game elements listed below (see Table 1), manipulated between groups with the purpose of targeting MOOC users' feelings of social presence and SoC, which were expected to positively affect levels of engagement. Within the experimental group, users were further assigned randomly to one of two clans (Fig. 5).

[2] The ethical conformity in the procedure carried in this study, data collection, and storage has been evaluated and approved by cETO, the Ethical Committee of the Open University of The Netherlands, which assessed also their compliance with the GDPR (General Data Protection Regulation).

Table 1. Overview of included game elements and experimental manipulations thereof.

Experimental group (gamified condition)	**Control group (non-gamified condition)**
Avatar "Abstract representations of the person" [35].	
Provided with set of images (see Fig. 1), including a gender neutral icon, from which users could select their favourite.	Only a default icon was provided, no avatar selection available.
Clans / Guilds are groups of people, that work together to define their own identity and common goal.	
Users were randomly assigned to one of two clans, with the task of choosing their own name, logo and rules (see Fig. 2). The aim was to a 'feeling of belonging' from each other.	No reference to or participation in clans, participants in this condition had the "solo mode" only.
Challenges	
The two clans faced four different challenges during the course, described below	No challenges, no collaboration or group voting.
Cooperation "allows players [in games] to divide goals between them and rely upon each other's abilities and resources" [35].	
During all challenges, clans were asked to act as a group, and each answer and choice was based on a group voting (see Fig. 2).	No reference to or participation in clans, "solo mode" only.
Competition	
Set up between clans with regard to the challenges.	No inter-user competitive elements.
Communication channels	
Provided with chat function, enabling cooperation among clan' members (see Fig. 4).	Provided with chat function, without reference to clans and avatar visualization.
Online status (proximity) of other users	
On each MOOC page, users could visualize the colour coded online status (online, recently online and offline) of the members of their clan and have an overview about the online clans' activities (see Fig. 3). The order of the users on the bar was regulated by virtual *proximity*, meaning that those that were online and on the same page, were visualized first	On each page of the MOOC, users could visualize the colour coded online status (online, recently online and offline) of other users in control group, without any reference to or participation in clans. All users were represented with the same icon (no avatars), the order of the users on the bar was regulated by virtual *proximity*.

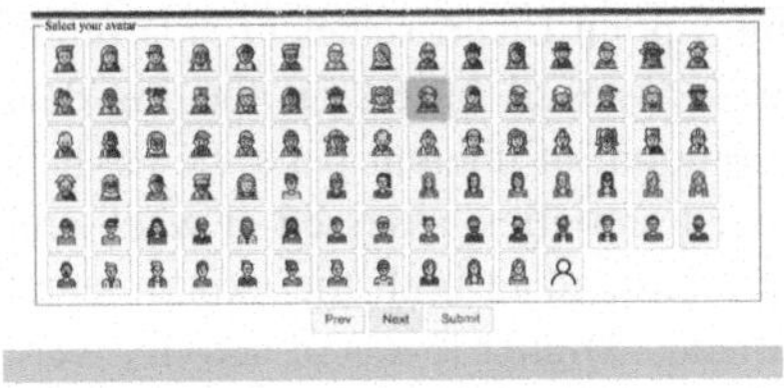

Fig. 2. Avatar selection interface (Exp view)

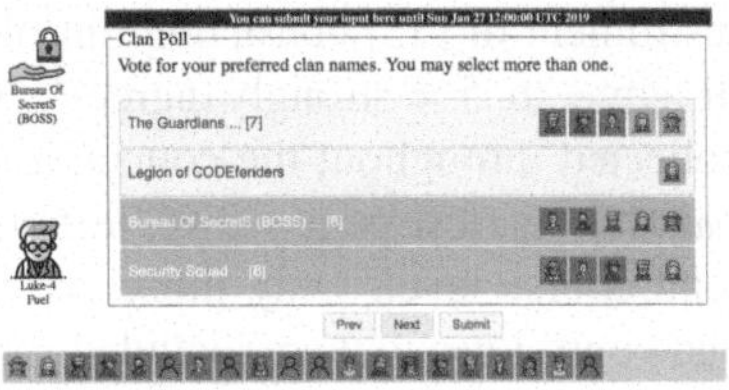

Fig. 3. Clan name definition (Exp view)

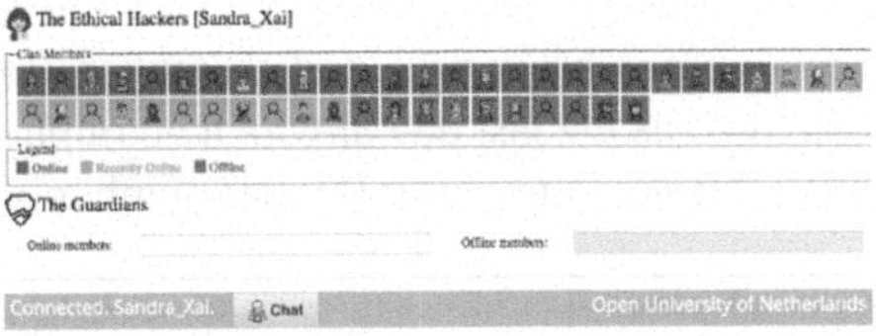

Fig. 4. Online Status (Exp view)

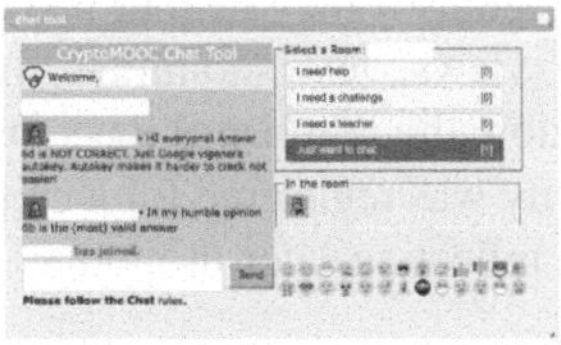

Fig. 5. Chat tool (Exp view)

As mentioned in Table 1, the experimental group was asked to perform a number of challenges:

- first week: (1) group identity challenge, participants used the group voting system needed to agree on their clan name, aim, logo, rules, and roles, (see Fig. 2, representing the group voting system used to define the clan name); (2) knowledge challenge (test), (in competition with the other clan);
- second week: the (1) crypto-challenge, which consisted of sending an encrypted message to the other clan and decrypt the response back, and the (2) knowledge challenge (test);
- third week: was a very information heavy week and we asked only for the knowledge challenge (test);
- fourth week: (1) discussion challenge, where all groups (clans and control) were asked to challenge a peer or the teacher in a discussion and (2) the knowledge challenge (test).

Measures

Social presence was measured using a shorter version of [35]'s scale. The scale assesses social presence across the two dimensions of 'awareness of the others' and 'proximity to the others', with 4 and 12 items respectively, all rated on a 5-point Likert scale (1 = strongly disagree to 5 = strongly agree)[3] *SoC* was measured using the

[3] The longer social presence measure used 15 and 12 items respectively. Considering the novelty of the measure, Rasch analyses [36, 37] were performed and the psychometric quality of the measures found were appropriate for the awareness dimension (Cronbach's $\alpha = .92$) and for the proximity dimension (Cronbach's $\alpha = .94$) as well. The analyses also delivered the Rasch person measures as alternatives to the total scores of each person.

instrument of [32] consisting out of 10 items using 5-point Likert scales (1 = strongly disagree to 5 = strongly agree)[4]. *Engagement* was assessed based on the log-data collected throughout the course, and included the amount of content page views, info page views, test page views, test submittals, and chat activities, assessed at week and total course level. Only those activities that were measured in both the experimental and control group were included for group comparisons. Higher levels of activity were assumed to reflect higher levels of engagement. *Learning performance* was operationalized as the percentage of correct answers on the weekly knowledge tests. A higher proportion of correct answers reflected better performance. *Retention*, cumulative dropout was assessed at week level in both groups, with users being defined as dropouts if they neither had any registered content page views, info page views, test page views, test submittals, or chat activities within that week, nor thereafter. In addition, the number of days to dropout were defined as the last day at which an online activity was registered for a certain user, calculated from course start (higher number of days reflecting later dropout).

Analyses

In order to test hypothesis H1 (social presence), and H2 (SoC) independent samples t-tests were performed. To test H3 (association between SoC and social presence), a regression analysis was performed with social presence as independent (predictor) variable, and SoC as dependent (outcome), as well as a Pearson correlation. Regression was also performed to test H5 (association between SoC and engagement).

H4 (engagement) was assessed by using independent samples t-tests to test whether the amount of content page views, info page views, test page views, test submittals, and total amount of online activities were significantly higher in the experimental versus control group, and χ^2 to test whether the proportion of participants using chat functionalities was significantly higher in the experimental vs. control condition. H6 (learning performance) was assessed using χ^2 to test whether the proportion of correct answers on the knowledge tests was significantly higher in the experimental vs. control condition. Lastly, χ^2 and independent samples t-tests were performed to test, respectively, whether the proportion of participants dropping out was lower in the experimental vs. control condition, and whether the average number of days to dropout were higher in the experimental vs. control condition (H7; retention/dropout).

6 Results

H1: Perceived social presence will be higher for users in the experimental (gamified) vs. control (non-gamified) condition;

[4] Rasch analyses were performed to confirm the uni-dimensionality of the SoC measure. Furthermore, the psychometric quality of the measure was excellent (Cronbach's $\alpha = .96$). The analyses also delivered the Rasch person measures as alternatives to the total scores of each person.

Table 2. Comparison social presence and sense of community between control and experimental groups on the base of questionnaire data.

	Control Group (n=23)	Experimental Group (n=47)	t[a]	p-value
Social Presence, M(SD)	2.04 (.82)	2.51 (.73)	t(62)[b] = -2.235	**.029**
Proximity	1.93 (.82)	2.44 (.74)	t(62)[b] = -2.400	**.019**
Awareness	2.37 (.93)	2.72 (.85)	t(62)[b] = -1.456	.150
Sense of Community	3.10 (1.01)	3.88 (1.13)	t(68)[b] = -2.787	**.007**

[a]. Independent samples t-test.
[b]. SPS missing for 4 subjects in ctrl condition and 2 subjects in EXP condition

As Table 2 reports, the levels of social presence were significantly higher for users in the experimental group, compared to those in the control group thus *confirming the hypothesis*. Furthermore, the dimension of social presence in which the two groups differ significantly is 'proximity with others', which is higher in the experimental group compared to the control one.

H2: Perceived SoC will be higher for users in the experimental (gamified) vs. control (non-gamified) condition, as Table 2 shows, the level of SoC were significantly higher for users in the experimental group, compared to those in the control group, thus *confirming H2.*

H3: Higher levels of social presence are associated with higher levels of SoC: a regression analysis has been performed with SPS as independent (predictor) variable, and SoC as dependent (outcome) variable, the association is significant ($F_{(2,61)} = 44.79$; $\beta = .707$, $p < .001$; $R^2 = .595$), regardless of treatment or control conditions, thus social presence and SoC are significantly associated in both groups, *H3 is confirmed.* Furthermore the Pearson correlation performed with Rasch measures,

Table 3. Correlation sense of community and social presence- experimental and control groups (Rasch measures)

	Sense of Community	Proximity	Awareness
Number of participants in the **EXP** Group = 39- Pearson Correlation (Sig. 2-tailed)			
Sense of Community	1	. 528** (.001)	.644** (.000)
Proximity	**.528**** (.001)	1	.757** (.000)
Awareness	**.644**** (.000)	.757** (.000)	1
Number of participants in the **Control** Group = 18- Pearson Correlation (Sig. 2-tailed)			
Sense of Community	1	.315 (.203)	.430 (.075)
Proximity	.315 (.203)	1	.806**(.000)
Awareness	.430 (.075)	.806** (.000)	1

*. Correlation is significant at the 0.05 level (2-tailed).
**. Correlation is significant at the 0.01 level (2-tailed).

reported in Table 3, shows a positive correlation between social presence and SoC only in the experimental group, see the first column of Table 3, *supporting therefore H3.*

H4: Engagement will be higher for users in the experimental (gamified) vs. control (non-gamified) condition: see Table 4. Users in the experimental and control group did not significantly differ with regard to the total amount of registered content page views, test page views, test submittals, and total number of online activities at course level.

However, more info page views were registered for users in the experimental group, and a significantly larger proportion of users in the experimental condition used chat functionalities compared to the control condition. Also, the data suggest that activity for users in the control group dropped more steeply after course start, compared to that of users in the experimental group, with a trend-significant difference in the last week of the course ($t_{(152)} = -1.573$, $p = .069$). The two clans in the experimental group did not significantly differ on any of the engagement measures. Taken together, *H4 was only partially confirmed.*

Table 4. Comparison control and experimental groups on the base of log-data

	Control Group (n=56)	Experimental Group (n=98)	t^a / χ^2	p-value
No. of online activities [b], M (SD)	138.46 (114.85)	148.53 (179.67)	t(152) = -.377	.707
Week1	49.02 (34.32)	46.84 (48.22)	t(152) = .298	.766
Week 2	47.71 (49.12)	46.06 (52.60)	t(152) = .192	.848
Week 3	27.63 (41.40)	30.15 (54.47)	t(152) = -.301	.764
Week 4	14.11 (26.77)	25.48 (50.13)	t(152) = -1.573	*.069*
Cumulative proportion dropout[c], % Week1	0.00	0.00	-	-
Week 2	26.8	26.5	χ^2(1)= .001	.558
Week 3	57.1	50.0	χ^2(1)=. 729	.247
Week 4	67.9	61.2	χ^2(1)= .677	.259
No. of days to dropout[d], M (SD)	14.36 (9.14)	15.47 (9.10)	χ^2(1)= -.728	.467
No. of content page views, M (SD)	81.93 (72.31)	91.93 (102.33)	t(152) = -.645	.520
No. of info page views, M (SD)	7.82 (6.31)	12.69 (16.60)	t(152) = -2.109	**.010**
Proportion of participants using chat functionalities, %	10.7	28.6	χ^2(1)= 6.605	**.007**
No. of test page views, M (SD)	34.14 (31.23)	28.60 (43.85)	t(152) = .832	.407
No. of tests submitted, M (SD)	13.75 (12.39)	10.24 (14.10)	t(152) = 1.549	.123
Proportion correct answers on knowledge test, %	65.6	78.0	χ^2(1)= 27.411	**< .001**

[a] Independent samples t-test;
[b] Including: content page, info page, test page views, test submittals, and chat activities
[c] Defined as: neither having any registered content, info, and test pages views, test submittals, or chat activities within that week, nor thereafter
[d] Defined as: last day at which an online activity was registered, calculated from course start

H5: Higher levels of SoC are associated with higher levels of engagement: no association was found between SoC scores and online activities ($F_{(1,68)} = .382$; $\beta = .075$, $p = .539$; $R^2 = .006$; adjusted for treatment condition: $F_{(2,67)} = .749$; $\beta = .032$, $p = .805$; $R^2 = .022$). *H5 was not confirmed.*

H6: Test performance will be better for users in the experimental (gamified) vs. control (non-gamified) condition: as Table 4 reports, the proportion of correct answers on the knowledge tests was significantly higher in the experimental group compared to the control group, *thus confirming H6*. The two clans in the experimental group performed equally well on the knowledge tests (clan 1: 77.3% correct answers; clan 2: 78.7% correct answers; $\chi^2_{(1)} = .237$, $p = .627$).

H7: Dropout will be lower and later for users in the experimental (gamified) vs. control (non-gamified) condition: see Table 4. Although the data suggested differences in rate and speed of dropout in favour of the experimental condition, these differences were not statistically significant, *thus not supporting H7.*

7 Discussion and Conclusion

This study investigated the effects of a gamified intervention targeting user engagement in MOOCs through mechanisms of social presence and SoC. To this end, seven game elements were designed and implemented in the MOOC embedded in the platform Open edX. Using an experimental design, users were randomly assigned to a gamified or non-gamified condition (experimental vs. control group).

The data showed that the game elements did trigger social presence and SoC among MOOC users, however, the expected association between these measures and user engagement was not confirmed. More specifically, seven hypotheses were tested, of which four were confirmed (H1-3, and H6), one was only partially confirmed (H4), and the remaining two (H5 and H7) were not supported by our data. From this we conclude that our gamification intervention had an effect on (i) users' learning performance (H6): MOOC participants accomplished significantly better results compared to participants in the control condition; (ii) the development of feelings of social presence (H1), in particular for the proximity dimension; and (iii) development of a SoC (H2). Furthermore, social presence and SoC were associated (H3), particularly in the experimental group, however, we did not observe a direct association between these feelings and user engagement (H5). As far as engagement is concerned, users in the experimental condition showed to be significantly more engaged compared to the control group in the usage of the chat tool and in the view of the info pages. This enables us to only partially confirm H4. Moreover, users in the experimental group seemed to have a higher level of retention compared to their colleagues in the control group, showing a less pronounced decline in activities as a function of course duration compared to what was typically reported in previous work [1]. However, possibly due to the scarce number of participants involved, this apparent difference was not statistically significant, therefore H7 was not confirmed. Results from this study should be viewed in the light of several limitations. First of all, the sample size was limited, thus the possibility of null findings representing 'false negatives' cannot be excluded. Secondly, although log-data were collected for the complete sample, only a selection of users provided questionnaire data, thereby potentially biasing results. Lastly, we cannot ascertain that the implementation of our game elements in the online environment was without technical problems for all users. Further studies are therefore warranted, in which these issues are addressed.

Despite these limitations, this study represents a step forward for the field of gamification of MOOCs. It enriches the gamification field by introducing a technological solution that embraces theories known in the field but never applied to gamification before. Furthermore, it shows a more technologically advanced way towards designing and implementing gamification within MOOCs, taking into consideration the application scenario, the target audience and what is actually done in the game world. Also, this study enhances MOOCs: MOOC platforms, in general, do not allow to seize upon this potential, the "social" aspect seems totally left aside. In Open edX, in particular, it is hard to understand that there are other users online in that same course: if a user is keen to be involved in some kind of social interaction, s/he has to hunt for the discussion forum. Our solution instead enables MOOC users to be aware of the others without the need of taking any action, by simply being online.

In conclusion our data show that the game elements designed to produce social presence and SoC among MOOC users were proven to successfully fulfill their purpose.

References

1. Reich, J., Ruipérez-Valiente, J.A.: The MOOC pivot. Science **363**(80), 130–131 (2019)
2. Short, J., Williams, E., Christie, B.: The Social Psychology of Telecommunications. Wiley, London (1976)
3. Liu, X., Magjuka, R.J., Seung-hee, L.: An empirical examination of sense of community. Instr. Technol. Distance Learn. **3**, 1–12 (2006)
4. Crues, R.W., Bosch, N., Perry, M., Angrave, L., Shaik, N., Bhat, S.: Refocusing the lens on engagement in MOOCs. In: Proceedings of the Fifth Annual ACM Conference on Learning at Scale - L@S 2018, pp. 1–10 (2018)
5. Reischer, M., Khalil, M., Ebner, M.: Does gamification in MOOC discussion forums work? In: Delgado Kloos, C., Jermann, P., Pérez-Sanagustín, M., Seaton, D.T., White, S. (eds.) EMOOCs 2017. LNCS, vol. 10254, pp. 95–101. Springer, Cham (2017). https://doi.org/10.1007/978-3-319-59044-8_11
6. Poquet, O., et al.: Social presence in massive open online courses. Int. Rev. Res. Open Distrib. Learn. **19**, 43–68 (2018)
7. Antonaci, A., Klemke, R., Kreijns, K., Specht, M.: Get gamification of MOOC right! Int. J. Serious Games **5**, 61–78 (2018)
8. Kreijns, K., Kirschner, P.A., Vermeulen, M.: Social aspects of CSCL environments: a research framework. Educ. Psychol. **48**, 229–242 (2013)
9. Festinger, L., Schachter, S., Back, K.W.: Social Pressures in Informal Groups: A Study of Human Factors in Housing. Stanford University Press, Palo Alto (1963)
10. Luo, N., Zhang, M., Qi, D.: Effects of different interactions on students' sense of community in e-learning environment. Comput. Educ. **115**, 153–160 (2017)
11. Lowenthal, P.R.: The evolution and influence of social presence theory on online learning. In: Dasgupta, S. (ed.) Social Computing: Concepts, Methodologies, Tools, and Applications, pp. 113–128. Hershey, IGI Global (2009)

12. Gunawardena, C.N., Zittle, F.J.: Social presence as a predictor of satisfaction within a computer-mediated conferencing environment. Am. J. Distance Educ. **11**, 8–26 (1997)
13. Garrison, D.R.: Communities of inquiry in online learning. In: Rogers, P.L. (ed.) Encyclopedia of Distance Learning, 2nd edn, pp. 352–355. Hershey, IGI Global (2018)
14. Anderson, A.R., Christenson, S.L., Sinclair, M.F., Lehr, C.A.: Check & connect: the importance of relationships for promoting engagement with school. J. Sch. Psychol. **42**, 95–113 (2004)
15. Hu, M., Li, H.: Student engagement in online learning: a review. In: Proceedings of the 2017 International Symposium on Educational Technology, ISET 2017, pp. 39–43 (2017)
16. Dewan, M.A.A., Murshed, M., Lin, F.: Engagement detection in online learning: a review. Smart Learn. Environ. **6**, 1 (2019)
17. Azevedo, R.: Defining and measuring engagement and learning in science: conceptual, theoretical, methodological, and analytical issues. Educ. Psychol. **50**, 84–94 (2015)
18. Kreijns, K., Kirschner, P.A.: Extending the SIPS-model: a research framework for online collaborative learning. In: Pammer-Schindler, V., Pérez-Sanagustín, M., Drachsler, H., Elferink, R., Scheffel, M. (eds.) EC-TEL 2018. LNCS, vol. 11082, pp. 277–290. Springer, Cham (2018). https://doi.org/10.1007/978-3-319-98572-5_21
19. Anderson, A., Huttenlocher, D., Kleinberg, J., Leskovec, J.: Engaging with massive online courses. In: Proceedings of the 23rd International Conference on World Wide Web - WWW 2014, pp. 687–698 (2014)
20. Sun, Y., Ni, L., Zhao, Y., Shen, X.L., Wang, N.: Understanding students' engagement in MOOCs: an integration of self-determination theory and theory of relationship quality. Br. J. Educ. Technol. **0**, 1–19 (2018)
21. Khalil, M., Ebner, M.: Clustering patterns of engagement in Massive Open Online Courses (MOOCs): the use of learning analytics to reveal student categories. J. Comput. High. Educ. **29**, 114–132 (2017)
22. Hew, K.F., Qiao, C., Tang, Y.: Understanding student engagement in large-scale open online courses: a machine learning facilitated analysis of student's reflections in 18 highly rated MOOCs. Int. Rev. Res. Open Distance Learn. **19**, 69–93 (2018)
23. Watolla, A.-K.: Distributed teaching: engaging learners in MOOCs. In: Khalil, M., Ebner, M., Kopp, M., Lorenz, A., Kalz, M. (eds.) Proceedings of the European Stakeholder Summit on experiences and best practices in and around MOOCs (EMOOCS), pp. 305–318. Books on Demand GmbH, Norderstedt (2016)
24. Guo, P.J., Kim, J., Rubin, R.: How video production affects student engagement: an empirical study of MOOC Videos. In: Proceedings of L@S, pp. 41–50. ACM (2014)
25. Floratos, N., Guasch, T., Espasa, A.: Recommendations on formative assessment and feedback practices for stronger engagement in MOOCs. Open Prax. **7**, 141–152 (2015)
26. Nawrot, I., Doucet, A.: Building engagement for MOOC students. In: International World Wide Web Conference Committee (IW3C2), pp. 1077–1082. ACM (2016)
27. Vaibhav, A., Gupta, P.: Gamification of MOOCs for increasing user engagement. In: Proceedings of the 2014 IEEE International Conference on MOOCs, Innovation and Technology in Education, MITE 2014, pp. 290–295. IEEE (2014)
28. Khalil, M., Ebner, M., Admiraal, W.: How can gamification improve MOOC studentengagement? In: Proceedings of the 11th European Conference on Games Based Learning, ECGBL 2017, pp. 819–828. Curran Associates, Inc. (2017)
29. Tseng, F.C., Huang, H.C., Teng, C.I.: How do online game communities retain gamers? Social presence and social capital perspectives. J. Comput. Commun. **20**, 601–614 (2015)
30. Parks, M.R., Floyd, K.: Making friends in cyberspace. J. Comput. Commun. **1**, JCMC144 (1996)

31. Joksimović, S., Gašević, D., Kovanović, V., Riecke, B.E., Hatala, M.: Social presence in online discussions as a process predictor of academic performance. J. Comput. Assist. Learn. **31**, 638–654 (2015)
32. Picciano, A.G.: Beyond student perceptions: issues of interaction; presence; and performance in an online course. J. Asynchronous Learn. **6**, 21–40 (2002)
33. Rovai, A.: Building sense of community at a distance. Int. Rev. Res. Open Distance Learn. **3**, 1–16 (2002)
34. Björk, S., Holopainen, J.: Patterns in Game Design. Charles River Media, Needham (2005)
35. Kreijns, K., Weidlich, J., Rajagopal, K.: The psychometric properties of a preliminary social presence measure using Rasch analysis. In: Pammer-Schindler, V., Pérez-Sanagustín, M., Drachsler, H., Elferink, R., Scheffel, M. (eds.) EC-TEL 2018. LNCS, vol. 11082, pp. 31–44. Springer, Cham (2018). https://doi.org/10.1007/978-3-319-98572-5_3
36. Bond, T.G., Fox, C.: Applying the Rasch Model: Fundamental Measurement in the Human Sciences. Lawrence Erlbaum Associates, New Jersey (2007)
37. Boone, W.J., Yale, M.S., Staver, J.R.: Rasch analysis in the human sciences. Springer, Dordrecht (2014). https://doi.org/10.1007/978-94-007-6857-4

Exploring Social Learning Analytics to Support Teaching and Learning Decisions in Online Learning Environments

Rogers Kaliisa(✉), Anders I. Mørch, and Anders Kluge

Department of Education, University of Oslo, Oslo, Norway
{rogers.kaliisa, anders.morch, anders.kluge}@iped.uio.no

Abstract. Most teachers to date have adopted summative assessment items as a benchmark to measure students' learning and for making pedagogical decisions. However, these may not necessarily provide comprehensive evidence for the actual learning process, particularly in online learning environments due to their failure to monitor students' online learning patterns over time. In this paper, we explore how social learning analytics (SLA) can be used as a proxy by teachers to understand students' learning processes and to support them in making informed pedagogical decisions during the run of a course. This study was conducted in a semester-long undergraduate course, at a large public university in Norway, and made use of data from 4 weekly online discussions delivered through the university learning management system Canvas. First, we used NodeXL a social network analysis tool to analyze and visualize students' online learning processes, and then we used Coh-Metrix, a theoretically grounded, computational linguistic tool to analyze the discourse features of students' discussion posts. Our findings revealed that SLA provides insight and an overview of the students' cognitive and social learning processes in online learning environments. This exploratory study contributes to an improved conceptual understanding of SLA and details some of the methodological implications of an SLA approach to enhance teaching and learning in online learning environments.

Keywords: Social Learning Analytics · Teaching and learning · Online learning environments · NodeXL · Coh-Metrix

1 Introduction

Most teachers rely on summative assessments (coarse-grained analysis) such as the end of term examinations, as a benchmark to measure students' learning and to retrospectively make decisions regarding how best to teach their subjects to the next cohort of students [20, 25]. However, such methods are prone to challenges such as personal bias, and the failure to monitor students' online learning patterns (i.e., course logins, discussions attended, student-student, and student-course artefact interactions) during the run of the course [23], yet this could enable teachers to provide adaptive feedback and to adjust teaching strategies. At the same time, teaching and learning are gradually

M. Scheffel et al. (Eds.): EC-TEL 2019, LNCS 11722, pp. 187–198, 2019.
https://doi.org/10.1007/978-3-030-29736-7_14

transferred to online environments (LMS, MOOCs, etc.). One way to deal with this challenge is by using more objective and automated methods to evaluate students' online learning in real time and to enable teachers to make timely informed (formative) educational decisions. Drawing on this, this paper suggests social learning analytics (SLA) as a possible approach to explore students' online learning patterns. Specifically, we are interested in exploring students' online interactions/networks and their digital artefacts (i.e. discussion posts) to produce insights into students' participation, and meaningful discourse patterns that could support teaching and learning decisions. As a methodological contribution, we use NodeXL [24] a social network analysis tool to analyze and visualize students' online learning combined with Coh-Metrix, a theoretically grounded, computational linguistic tool [4] to analyze the discourse features of students' discussion posts. Consequently, we gained insight and a richer understanding of the students' social and cognitive learning processes. In the following sections, we provide a brief overview of SLA situated within the context of the social learning perspective, highlight the research questions, describe the research methodology, present findings, and discuss research, limitations and suggestions for future research.

2 Background

2.1 Social Perspectives of Learning

Theoretical and empirical evidence in the learning sciences view learning as a social process that cannot be only accounted for by cognition and behaviors of the individual [7]. This is arguably, why teachers and researchers have increasingly applied pedagogical approaches such as interactive representations associated with socio-constructivist principles [16]. According to the socio-cultural perspectives, learning is an aspect of self-organization of both the human organism and the ecosocial system in which individual functions as a human being [17, 22]. This implies that learning is defined through interaction with others and mediated by artefacts, technology and semiotic tools such as language [13, 17]. Indeed, the joint interaction between individuals forms a basis for mastery of useful strategies, skills, concepts and knowledge [13]. Online learning environments where students and teacher interactions are usually mediated by technological tools [11], offer a new context in which to explore key aspects of learning from a sociocultural perspective. For example, more recently, the increase in computer-mediated learning has created new conditions for teaching and learning [22], through tools such as wikis, and online discussion forums. These produce a gold mine of data that social learning analytics techniques can utilize to explore and identify pedagogically valuable social, cognitive and affective features related to students' social learning processes [4].

2.2 Social Learning Analytics (SLA)

SLA is a subset of learning analytics, which is concerned with the collection, measurement and analysis of students' digital artefacts and online interactions in order to understand their activities, social behaviours, and knowledge creation in a social learning setting [7, 15]. SLA draws on the significant educational research work evidencing that new skills and ideas are developed and passed on through interactions and collaboration, and that learning cannot be understood without reference to context [13]. Ferguson and Shum (2012) identified five categories of SLA under the umbrella of inherent social analytics and socialized analytics. The inherent ones include; social network analytics (SNA) and discourse analytics (DA), while the socialized ones include; content analytics (CA); disposition analytics (DA), and context analytics (CA). In this current study, we explore how the analysis of students' online interactions and discourse can provide insights into the students' learning processes. Therefore, social network analytics and discourse analytics which are regarded as inherently social are the focus of this study. In this paper, we use SLA as an umbrella concept combining social network analytics (SNA) and discourse analytics (DA).

2.3 Social Network Analytics (SNA)

Social network analytics (SNA) is derived from the concept of social network analysis which studies and analyses social ties, relations, roles and network formations [3]. The principles of social network analysis derive from graph theory, which looks at patterns of relational connections between nodes in a graph. The nodes in a social network graph are the actors, who can be individuals or collective units such as teams or organizations [11]. In learning and education settings, the actors may be students connected to each other within a class or learning activity; or teachers and students in a class. Based on the principles of social network analysis, social network analytics aims at interpreting the individual and group interactions and how these support learning. An example is Hernández-García and colleagues [12] who applied social network analytics to examine the relation between social network analysis parameters and student outcomes. The study showed that social network analytics can highlight the visible and invisible interactions occurring in online environments, thus helping to improve the learning process based on the information about the actors and their activity in the online learning environment.

2.4 Discourse Analytics (DA)

The social ties and relations occurring in social learning environments are strengthened through dialogue between students and teachers [8]. DA involves the analysis of the large amounts of text generated during the online interactions [7]. Previous research has reported that educational success is related to the quality of learners' educational dialogue [9], which can be measured through discourse analysis. This implies that DA can be used to analyze large amounts of educational text, and potentially provide insights into the quality of students' text and speech posted in online environments. For example, Dowell and colleagues (2015) combined language and discourse as a tool to explore the association between students' traditional academic performance and social centrality in a MOOC environment. The findings revealed that students who engaged in a more expository style of discourse performed better while those that used a more narrative style of discourse gained a more central position in their social network. More recently, Joksimović et al. [14] used discourse analysis to examine the association between social capital, linguistic and discourse patterns. The findings showed that learners with more connections had a linguistic profile that is more narrative with lower referential cohesion and more complex syntax.

3 Identified Gaps and Research Questions

The application of social network analysis to educational contexts in this study is not novel, but our preliminary literature review shows that there is no sufficient empirical evidence for the use of SLA to identify and generate insights to teachers, in order to support informed learning and teaching decisions. More importantly, most of the previous studies are limited to the description of social networks, without analysis of the discourse dimensions of these interactions. However, the combination of social network and discourse analysis of students' artefacts could allow for a more nuanced description of student engagement and learning [1, 21], and necessary to reach an overall interpretation of such complex dynamics generated among students [10]. From this background, this study aims to explore the potential of SLA (i.e. social network analytics and discourse analytics), as a way to understand the underlying learning processes within online learning environments. Towards this goal, we address the following research question: What are the opportunities of SLA in terms of generating relevant insights about students' online learning processes which teachers can use to make timely and informed pedagogical decisions?

4 Methodology

4.1 Context and Participants

This study employed a mixed methods approach, by combining social network and discourse analysis to analyze and visualize students' online learning processes [8]. We extracted and analyzed data from the discussion forum contributions posted on Canvas, a learning management system, within a blended bachelors course (*i.e. involving face to face and online activities*) at a public university in Norway. This course is taught as a part of the university's bachelor in pedagogy. The main course objective was to introduce selected learning technologies and applications and to familiarize students with the central theoretical perspectives and studies of learning technologies. The course had a total number of 34 students and four teachers. To ensure active use of the online discussions, in parallel to the face to face classroom; all students had to participate in a weekly online discussion forum that ran for 7 weeks in the period of January 2019 to April 2019. The discussions were conducted asynchronously, and all subsequent messages in the thread were text-only. Participation in the discussion was compulsory with each student expected to make two contributions and respond to at least one other student every week. For each week, teachers created a new discussion thread based on the topic of the next lecture. Thereafter, students posted their contributions in response to the main discussion question or responding to posts by other students.

4.2 Data Preparation and Analyses

Prior to the analysis, the students' network and linguistic/discourse data were extracted, cleaned and categorized by week, to provide a benchmark for further analysis and identification of relevant patterns. In order to generate initial insights and relevant hypotheses, this study focuses on interaction and discourse on discussion posts published during the first four weeks of the course. Students' network and discourse data was extracted and analyzed using two methods. First, social network analysis to identify significant interaction patterns among students, and secondly, discourse analysis to identify significant linguistic/discourse features connected to the students' contributions. Individual students were the unit of analysis.

4.3 Social Network Analysis

To perform social network analysis, we re-constructed social network relationships based on student-student, student-teacher, and teacher-student interactions. Although the Canvas LMS has in-built Canvas analytics, there is currently no plug-in that supports the automatic mining of discussion forum data directly from the platform. Thus, the first author manually extracted students' interaction data from Canvas into NodeXL (version 1.0.1.410) a third-party social network tool [24]. Specifically, the coding process in NodeXL included all students and teachers who posted in the discussion forum. For example, if student S4 posted a message in response to the main discussion question (DQ), we coded this as (S4 > DQ), then if student S10 posted a message in response to S4's initial thread message, we coded this as (S10 > S4). Thus, the analyzed ties represent unweighted and undirected graphs which were constructed to represent the students' interactions on the Canvas platform. After the coding, we used the social network analysis measures suggested in previous studies [1] (i.e. degrees, closeness, and betweenness) to assess and determine the level of importance, strength, and influence each node/student had on the broader social network [2]. The degree centrality measure is used to determine the number of ties an individual student has with other actors in the network [2]. Closeness centrality indicates the degree of relationships an actor has formed with the entire network, while betweenness centrality refers to the extent to which an actor occurs within the shortest path between other nodes, thus facilitating the spread of information within the network [3].

4.4 Discourse Analysis

In this study, we analyzed the content of students' contributions in order to extract significant discourse patterns. This analysis was performed using Coh-Metrix (version 3.0), which is an automated textual assessment tool [4, 19], and used in previous studies [19]. Coh-Metrix is a computational linguistics facility that analyzes higher-level features of language and discourse [19]. In this study, the following five principal components of Coh-Metrix were calculated. (1) *Narrativity.* That is the extent to which the text is in the narrative genre, which conveys a story, a procedure, or a sequence of episodes of actions and events with animate beings (2) *Deep cohesion*. The extent to which the ideas in the text are cohesively connected at a deeper conceptual level that signifies causality or intentionality, (3) *Referential cohesion.* The extent to which explicit words and ideas in the text are connected with each other as the text unfolds, (4) *Syntactic simplicity.* Which reflects the degree to which the sentences in the text contain fewer words and use simpler, familiar syntactic structures, and (5) *Word concreteness.* The extent to which content words are concrete, meaningful, and evoke mental images as opposed to abstract words [19].

5 Findings and Discussion

5.1 Social Network Findings

First, we analyzed students' interactions in the online discussion forum as illustrated in socio-grams Figs. 1, 2, 3 and 4, with each figure representing a weekly discussion forum.

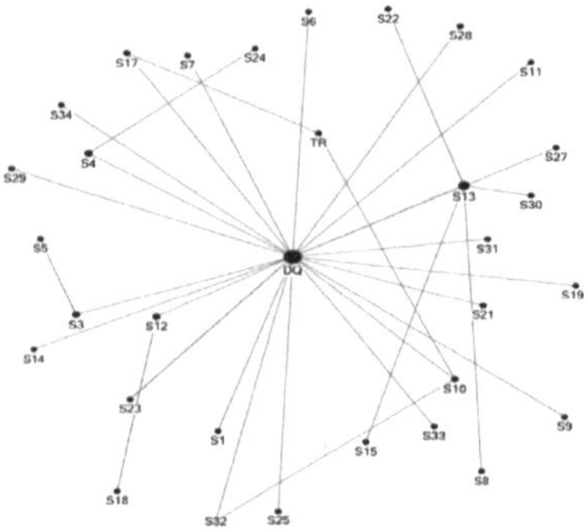

Fig. 1. Sociogram of week one discussions.

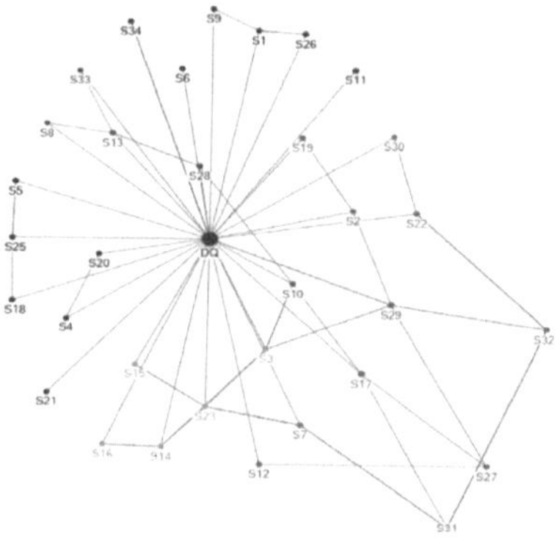

Fig. 2. Sociogram of week two discussions.

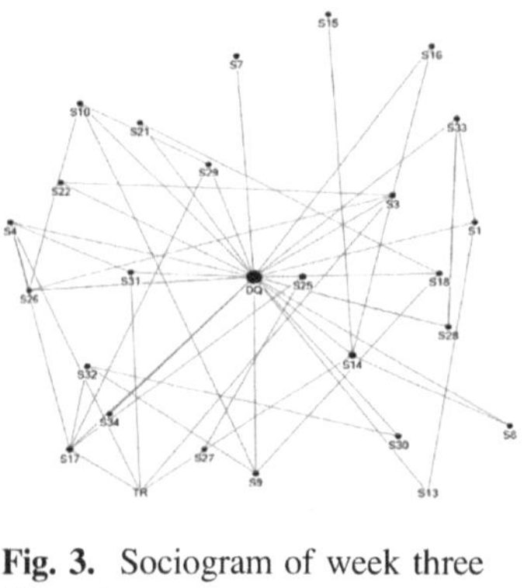

Fig. 3. Sociogram of week three discussions.

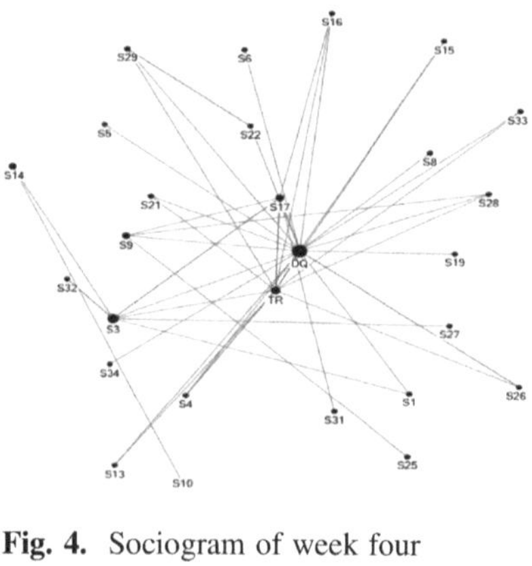

Fig. 4. Sociogram of week four discussions

The social network visualizations (Figs. 1, 2, 3 and 4) provide an aggregate visual representation of the social structure connecting 34 students and 4 teachers during the 4 weeks of online discussion activities. Despite the fact that student names have been removed for confidentiality purposes, the labels demonstrate the position of each student within the network in a given week. Consequently, in these figures, the size and location of the nodes correspond to their degree centrality or the number of edges in the network. This means that the bigger a node is, the more messages the student/teacher represented by that node sent and received. Similarly, the more central a node is to the center or main discussion question (DQ) the more powerful it is. Thus, these networks can be used to identify students and teachers that were highly/less engaged in the discussion network. For example, Fig. 1 clearly illustrates a less engagement and interaction among students, with most of the communication directed to the original discussion question here coded as (DQ). However, improved interactions are observed in Figs. 2, 3 and 4 with students and teachers interacting more than in week one. For example in Fig. 4, the average degree centrality increased, which is seen by enlarged node sizes (e.g. S3, S17, and S9).

In addition, detailed analysis detected interesting patterns with some students having more activity and standing out across the 4 weeks. For example, in week 1, S13 was the most active with a betweenness centrality of 114. In week 2, S29 had a betweenness centrality of 27.4, and in week 3, S14 scored a high betweenness centrality of 29.7. In week 4, S3 had the highest betweenness centrality of 94.7. Similarly, the figures also indicate some disconnected/less-active students. For example, S18 in week 1 and 2 with a betweenness centrality of 0.0, while S34 and S25 both have a betweenness value of 0.0 in week 3 and 4 respectively. More importantly, the active involvement of teachers in week 3 and 4 as illustrated in Figs. 3 and 4 had an impact on the frequency of some students' posting. For example, a deeper analysis showed that S3 and S17, who were associated with the strongest brokerage role across the 4 weeks, recorded the highest degree centrality in week 3 and 4. This is partly attributed to the teachers' involvement as witnessed in the number of interactions these two students had with the teachers in both weeks.

5.2 Discourse Findings

Next, we performed automated discourse analysis for the 4 weeks discussion content using Coh-Metrix. We used social network analysis data presented in the previous section to "zoom in" on the most active and less active students for subsequent discourse analysis. Tables 1 and 2 illustrate social network analysis and discourse analysis values for the 10 selected students in week 1 and 2.

Tables 1 and 2 present an analysis of the discourse features of students' discussion contributions for students with high centrality measures and those with low centrality/peripherally located in the network. In week one (see Table 1), the results suggest that the students who had high centrality measures exhibit different discourse/linguistic features than the students with low centrality measures. For example, S13 who had the biggest degree, betweenness and closeness centrality values was associated with high narrativity (73), deep cohesion (69) and referential cohesion (67). Conversely, S18 who had the lowest SNA scores was associated with higher

Table 1. Week 1 discourse and SNA metrics results

	Active students					Less active students				
SNA	S13	S3	S4	S12	S10	S5	S18	S24	S8	S11
Degree	5	2	2	2	3	1	1	1	1	1
Betweenness	114	30	30	30	15	0.0	0.0	0.0	0.0	0.0
Closeness	0.016	0.015	0.015	0.015	0.015	0.010	0.010	0.010	0.011	0.014
Discourse analysis results										
No of words	264	212	1006	133	373	100	204	114	121	206
Narrativity	73	73	47	68	53	94	37	64	74	64
Deep Cohesion	69	48	37	94	99	10	55	32	23	62
Referential Cohesion	67	43	62	35	46	83	15	31	70	25
Syntax Simplicity	41	19	62	49	25	6	68	17	19	50
Word Concreteness	4	41	18	5	13	13	10	10	17	42

Table 2. Week 2 discourse and SNA metrics results

	Active students					Less active students				
SNA	S29	S17	S7	S22	S3	S6	S11	S21	S34	S18
Degree	5	4	3	3	5	1	1	1	1	2
Betweenness	27.4	23.6	13.3	12.3	4.4	0.0	0.0	0.0	0.0	0.0
Closeness	0.016	0.016	0.016	0.016	0.016	0.015	0.015	0.015	0.015	0.015
Discourse analysis results										
No of words	522	505	337	1273	402	158	110	225	457	820
Narrativity	57	85	29	61	75	82	95	79	41	40
Deep Cohesion	97	96	98	64	93	11	30	44	85	45
Referential Cohesion	7	51	24	64	77	40	28	45	80	24
Syntax Simplicity	71	73	89	57	9	20	35	17	23	57
Word Concreteness	1.8	6	43	9	58	50	5	40	28	65

syntactic simplicity and word concreteness. Similarly, in week 2 (see Table 2), S29 who was better positioned within the network of learners, had a narrativity score of (57), deep cohesion (97), referential cohesion (7), syntax simplicity of (71) and word concreteness of (1.8). On the other hand, S34 with low SNA values had a high referential cohesion (80), and word concreteness of (28). This finding means that the text for less active students contained words and ideas that overlap across sentences and the entire text, while the higher word concreteness means the text was less abstract and meaningful [4].

In addition, an interesting observation from a combined analysis of students' network and discourse patterns revealed an overall change in the linguistic profile of all students (those with high and low centrality values), towards week 3 and 4, which was identified by a higher deep cohesion. This finding suggests that students moved from less narrative/informal discourse styles to a more formal discourse. In practice, the identification of such discourse patterns may help teachers to monitor and detect the quality of the discussions in line with course/task expectations, and to provide personalized support based on students' discourse features.

6 General Discussion and Conclusion

This paper explored the possibility of using social learning analytics (SLA) as a proxy by teachers to understand students' online learning processes and to support them in making informed pedagogical decisions. First, we adopted a social network analysis approach to identify the interactions between students and teachers across the 4 weeks of online discussion. The analysis showed that some students (i.e., S13, S3, S29, and S14) were very active across the 4 weeks hence being regarded as information brokers or bridge builders [1, 8]. Moreover, some weeks recorded more interactions than others (i.e., week 2, 3 and 4). While a deeper analysis of the nature of the content discussed in each week was not done, the differences in students' interactions and networks across the 4 weeks could be attributed to some elements of course structure in the different weeks [9] as well as the involvement of the teachers in week 3 and 4. This finding confirms previous research that teachers' role and level of participation could affect the level of online discussions [8]. In practice, as noted by Macfadyen and Dawson (2010), these findings reveal that social network analytics can afford insight into students' social learning processes, which teachers can use to identify deviations between the observed and intended interactions [18]. Moreover, in blended learning environments like the one presented in this study, teachers can be alerted about the students to keep an eye on during the face-to-face interactions, and at the same time learn about the direction in which they need to moderate online discussions [8]. This study affirms that the analysis of online social networks can support the collection of pedagogically meaningful information such as, how a student has engaged in a task. This provides teachers with a richer understanding of students' social learning processes in online learning environments, thus providing them with a basis to make informed pedagogical decisions and the creation of more effective learning environments.

Further, discourse analysis results demonstrated that the deep exploration of students' online text can reveal the quality and type of contributions made by students. In other words, even though social networks do not necessarily show evidence of knowledge construction among students, this process can be monitored through discourse analysis, thus gaining a richer understanding of students' cognitive learning processes. For example, a detailed discourse analysis of students' texts across the 4 weeks revealed that students with higher centrality values were associated with higher deep cohesion and syntax simplicity. This suggests that their texts use a more formal style of discourse, put in more effort and engage in increased elaboration [19]. This finding is consistent with previous research, which reported that high performing learners are characterized by a formal discourse [5].

In contrast, students with low centrality values had a more narrative style, which implies a more informal, and story-like style of discourse [19]. Moreover, some students' linguistic profiles changed over time (i.e. from a narrative style to more deep cohesion). Such a finding means that teachers could monitor the progress of students' learning overtime based on the linguistic profile and level of cognitive presence in each post [6] since these are important dimensions for students' learning. By doing so, the teacher can evaluate the effectiveness of the learning design, and suggest appropriate strategies to adapt the teaching and learning process. In other words, the linguistic profiles of students' posts could indicate that the discussion forum is not being used according to pedagogical intent, thus, suggesting the teacher to intervene to keep the learning process on track. More importantly, these discourse features have strong implications for understanding students' learning, since constructivist theories imply that comprehension is an important feature to measure students' learning [13, 16].

Overall, the analysis of students' contributions and online interactions reveal that combining social network analytics and discourse analytics can provide quick and useful insights for understanding both the cognitive and social characteristics of students' learning processes which in turn can be used to support teachers in making informed and timely decisions to improve the teaching and students' learning processes (e.g., encouraging less central but involved students to extend their network). This finding supports the claims of many in the technology enhanced learning community that it is important to understand what students are doing and talking about, how they are interacting with the course material, and where comprehension problems arise [26] besides examining who is talking to whom, in order to evaluate the quality of collaborative online learning activities [8]. However, we argue that if teachers and researchers are to benefit from the results coming out of social network and discourse analytics, they should have a clear understanding of the course context and be provided with simple analytics tools/training for meaningful interpretations.

In summary, this exploratory study makes methodological and conceptual contributions to SLA and technology-enhanced learning research. The study demonstrates how teachers and researchers can utilize students' data from online collaborative learning activities, to identify the cognitive and social characteristics of students' learning, using an innovative methodology of combining analysis of social networks and discourse using automated tools like Coh-Metrix. If teachers and researchers identify cognitive/learning features that are directly reflected in students' online activities, there is a great potential to intervene while a course is being taught, an approach to assessment which is difficult to achieve through the more typical surveys and end of term assessments.

7 Limitations and Suggestions for Future Research

There are a number of limitations that affect the generalizability and interpretation of the findings of this exploratory study. First, the conclusions of the study are limited by its focus on data collected from a single course, and with a sample size of only 34 students. We also recognize that the analyzed data is based on students' activity of only 4 weeks which could limit a comprehensive view of the students' learning process during this course. Moreover, the discourse analysis we conducted is of exploratory nature aiming at generating theoretical linkages/hypotheses rather than testing hypotheses. These limitations necessitate the need for further studies with well-developed hypotheses, analyzing longer durations of students' learning, and with larger samples to validate these initial findings. Nonetheless, despite these limitations, this exploratory paper contributes to methodological and conceptual implications for the use of SLA in blended learning environments, and provides a strong foundation for future rigorous research on the sub-field of SLA.

Acknowledgements. We wish to thank the members of the LiDA Research Group at the Department of Education, the University of Oslo for the constructive feedback on the primary data that informed this article. Special thanks go to Emily Oswald (University of Oslo) for useful comments on a previous version of the article. We thank the anonymous reviewers for their valuable comments on our manuscript. The first author received financial support by a PhD fellowship from the Faculty of Educational Sciences, University of Oslo.

References

1. Andersen, R., Mørch, A.I.: Mutual development in mass collaboration: Identifying interaction patterns in customer-initiated software product development. Comput. Hum. Behav. **65**, 77–91 (2016)
2. Dawson, S., Bakharia, A., Heathcote, E.: SNAPP: Realising the affordances of real-time SNA within networked learning environments (2010)
3. De Nooy, W., Mrvar, A., Batagelj, V.: Exploratory Social Network Analysis with Pajek: Revised and Expanded Edition for Updated Software, vol. 46. Cambridge University Press, Cambridge (2018)
4. Dowell, N.M., Graesser, A.C., Cai, Z.: Language and discourse analysis with Coh-Metrix: applications from educational material to learning environments at scale. J. Learn. Anal. **3**(3), 72–95 (2016)
5. Dowell, N.M., et al.: Modeling learners' social centrality and performance through language and discourse. In: Proceedings of the 8th International Conference on Educational Data Mining (2015)
6. Farrow, E., Moore, J., Gašević, D.: Analysing discussion forum data: a replication study avoiding data contamination. In: Proceedings of the 9th International Conference on Learning Analytics & Knowledge (2019)
7. Ferguson, R., Shum, S.B.: Social learning analytics: five approaches. In: Proceedings of the 2nd international conference on learning analytics and knowledge (2012)
8. Gasevic, D., Joksimovic, S., Eagan, B.R., Shaffer, D.W.: SENS: network analytics to combine social and cognitive perspectives of collaborative learning. Comput. Hum. Behav. **92**, 562–577 (2019). https://doi.org/10.1016/j.chb.2018.07.003
9. Gilbert, P.K., Dabbagh, N.: How to structure online discussions for meaningful discourse: a case study. Br. J. Educ. Technol. **36**(1), 5–18 (2005)
10. Haya, P.A., Daems, O., Malzahn, N., Castellanos, J., Hoppe, H.U.: Analysing content and patterns of interaction for improving the learning design of networked learning environments. Br. J. Edu. Technol. **46**(2), 300–316 (2015). https://doi.org/10.1111/bjet.12264
11. Haythornthwaite, C., De Laat, M.: Social network informed design for learning with educational technology. In: Olofsson, A.D., Lindberg, J.O. (eds.) Informed Design of Educational Technologies in Higher Education: Enhanced Learning and Teaching, pp. 352–374. IGI Global, Hershey (2012)
12. Hernández-García, Á., González-González, I., Jiménez-Zarco, A.I., Chaparro-Peláez, J.: Applying social learning analytics to message boards in online distance learning: a case study. Comput. Hum. Behav. **47**, 68–80 (2015)

13. John-Steiner, V., Mahn, H.: Sociocultural approaches to learning and development: a Vygotskian framework. Educ. Psychol. **31**(3–4), 191–206 (1996)
14. Joksimović, S., et al.: Exploring development of social capital in a CMOOC through language and discourse. Internet High. Educ. **36**, 54–64 (2018)
15. Kent, C., Rechavi, A.: Deconstructing online social learning: network analysis of the creation, consumption and organization types of interactions. Int. J. Res. Method Educ., 1–22 (2018). https://doi.org/10.1080/1743727X.2018.1524867
16. Kluge, A.: Learning science with an interactive simulator: negotiating the practice-theory barrier. Int. J. Sci. Educ. **41**, 1–25 (2019)
17. Lemke, J.L.: Cognition, context, and learning: a social semiotic perspective, pp. 37–56 (1997)
18. Macfadyen, L.P., Dawson, S.: Mining LMS data to develop an "early warning system" for educators: a proof of concept. Comput. Educ. **54**(2), 588–599 (2010)
19. McNamara, D.S., Graesser, A.C., McCarthy, P.M., Cai, Z.: Automated Evaluation of Text and Discourse with Coh-Metrix. Cambridge University Press, Cambridge (2014)
20. Persico, D., Pozzi, F.: Informing learning design with learning analytics to improve teacher inquiry. Br. J. Educ. Technol. **46**(2), 230–248 (2015)
21. Rabbany, R., Elatia, S., Takaffoli, M., Zaïane, O.R.: Collaborative learning of students in online discussion forums: a social network analysis perspective. In: Peña-Ayala, A. (ed.) Educational Data Mining. SCI, vol. 524, pp. 441–466. Springer, Cham (2014). https://doi.org/10.1007/978-3-319-02738-8_16
22. Rasmussen, I., Ludvigsen, S.: Learning with computer tools and environments: a sociocultural perspective. In: Littleton, K., Wood, C., Staarman, J.K. (eds.) International Handbook of Psychology in Education, pp. 399–433. Emerald Group Publishing, Bingley (2010)
23. Rienties, B., Cross, S., Zdrahal, Z.: Implementing a learning analytics intervention and evaluation framework: what works? In: Kei Daniel, B. (ed.) Big Data and Learning Analytics in Higher Education, pp. 147–166. Springer, Cham (2017). https://doi.org/10.1007/978-3-319-06520-5_10
24. Smith, M.A., et al.: Analyzing (social media) networks with NodeXL. In: Proceedings of the Fourth International Conference on Communities and Technologies (2009)
25. Schmitz, M., van Limbeek, E., Greller, W., Sloep, P., Drachsler, H.: Opportunities and challenges in using learning analytics in learning design. In: Lavoué, É., Drachsler, H., Verbert, K., Broisin, J., Pérez-Sanagustín, M. (eds.) EC-TEL 2017. LNCS, vol. 10474, pp. 209–223. Springer, Cham (2017). https://doi.org/10.1007/978-3-319-66610-5_16
26. Scheffel, M., et al.: Key action extraction for learning analytics. In: Ravenscroft, A., Lindstaedt, S., Kloos, C.D., Hernández-Leo, D. (eds.) EC-TEL 2012. LNCS, vol. 7563, pp. 320–333. Springer, Heidelberg (2012). https://doi.org/10.1007/978-3-642-33263-0_25

Systematic Literature Review of Automated Writing Evaluation as a Formative Learning Tool

Ana Isabel Hibert(✉)

University of Edinburgh, Edinburgh EH8 8AJ, UK
ana.hibert@ed.ac.uk

Abstract. Automated Writing Evaluation (AWE) has been increasingly used to provide writing feedback in ESL and EFL classrooms. However, research into the use of these technologies is not only scarce, but theoretically and methodologically fragmented, making it hard to draw any conclusions about their effectiveness as tools for formative evaluation. This paper reviews 29 studies into the use of AWE in ESL/EFL classrooms conducted between 2007 and 2018, analysing their theoretical and methodological underpinnings. There were two main findings. First, current AWE research ignores theoretical constructs informing other research into the use of technologies in the classroom. Second, AWE research copies the methodology used for general written corrective feedback research without using the extra tools afforded by the technology. Future AWE research should take advantage of the wealth of available theory regarding the use and implementation of technology into classrooms, as well as the new methodological possibilities offered by the technology itself.

Keywords: Self-regulated learning · Automated writing evaluation · Technology-enhanced learning · Formative evaluation

1 Introduction

Automated Writing Evaluation (AWE) programs were originally designed to provide summative evaluation on writing, and most of the research done into the topic has focused on comparing AWE grading against human raters [1], but the growing use of AWE programs in universities has spurred research on its effects as a formative evaluation tool in classrooms [2, 3]. In its present state, however, research into the use of AWE in the classroom is not only sparse [4], but "paucity of research, heterogeneity of existing research, the mixed nature of research findings, and methodological issues" [8; p. 62] make it difficult to draw any clear conclusions on its effectiveness as a learning tool. Beyond that, there is little comprehensive research on "the theoretical dimensions that can inform both knowledge of AWE and its implementation" [9; p. 420] and how AWE technology can be integrated into the classroom to provide written corrective feedback (WCF) for formative purposes [7]. Even then, most of the research has focused on the effects of AWE in L1 classrooms, but little has been done on its use in English as a second language (ESL) or English as a foreign language

M. Scheffel et al. (Eds.): EC-TEL 2019, LNCS 11722, pp. 199–212, 2019.
https://doi.org/10.1007/978-3-030-29736-7_15

(EFL) classrooms. This is important because, although programs like Criterion and MyAccess were designed for L1 English speakers, they have been increasingly used in ESL and EFL classrooms [5, 12–17]. Few programs, like Pigai, are specifically designed to provide WCF to ESL/EFL learners, in this case in China [14–17]. Furthermore, it has long been understood that L1 and L2 writing are different [18], so it makes sense to inquire separately into the use of AWE in ESL/EFL contexts specifically.

To address this issue, this paper analyses the theoretical foundations that underpin research done into AWE and its application within the classroom. Another issue with WCF is that, not only do applications of feedback vary between studies [25], it is hard to draw conclusions from existing research because of the differing methodologies [6, 26]. Therefore, it is important to examine the methodological approaches used to study the effectiveness of AWE interventions in university classrooms. This review, therefore, focuses on current research into the use of AWE in ESL and EFL classrooms, focusing on the following questions to identify the most salient issues that need to be addressed in future AWE research:

(1) What theoretical foundations have been used to justify the use of AWE to help ESL/EFL university students improve their writing?
(2) What are the most common methodological approaches to studying the effects of AWE in ESL/EFL university students?

2 Literature Review

AWE software usually allows students to submit a piece of writing, either original or following a built-in prompt to offer immediate feedback and scoring. Although each program is different, most use statistical models and algorithms, natural language processing, or latent semantic analysis to analyse lexical, syntactic, semantic and discourse features [5]. Another common feature is that they allow the submission of multiple drafts, which, some argue, encourages students to practice their writing skills [1, 7, 24].

While WCF has been criticised because it is time-consuming for teachers and prevents them from focusing on other important aspects of writing and language instruction [19, 27], AWE circumvents that issue by providing the feedback automatically. Some authors have explored ways in which teachers can take advantage of that feature to focus their efforts on other aspects of the writing process [1, 28, 29], while others have also successfully used the scoring functions of some AWE programs to incentivize revision [1, 4, 7, 8, 13, 17, 28, 30].

The immediacy of feedback has also been promoted as one advantage of AWE [24, 31], and students seem to appreciate receiving feedback immediately after submitting their work [8, 9, 13], something that allows them to revise quickly so they can receive more feedback [28]. Furthermore, some authors have argued that AWE allows for the development of student autonomy, by giving them the tools to self-learn and improve their own grammar [2, 16, 29, 32].

However, implementing AWE into the ESL/EFL classroom is not without issues. AWE-provided feedback has been criticised as formulaic and repetitive, and can sometimes be confusing to students [1, 10, 32], who get frustrated because they cannot ask the computer program for clarification [30]. This lack of communication is another drawback of AWE, as writing is considered a social process based on the negotiation of meaning [1]. Some authors, however, argue that intrapersonal negotiation of meaning could be as important for the writing process as interpersonal negotiation [6]. Some of these criticisms have been addressed by combining AWE feedback with teacher or peer feedback so students can still work with an audience [24, 28, 30, 33]. Others have pointed out that, even with its flaws, allowing AWE programs to focus on mechanics gives teachers more time to focus on content and organisation [2, 29]. Still, not all authors as optimistic due to the limitations inherent in AWE programs and the lack of well thought-out pedagogical implementations of these tools in the classroom [1].

Despite criticisms, and due to the promising characteristics of the technology and the fact that it is already being implemented in many universities, there has been an increase in research into the use of AWE technologies in ESL/EFL classrooms, but the amount of research remains small [14]. Moreover, the research is far from conclusive: different researchers use different methodologies and implementations of AWE, sample sizes are usually small, and many studies do not include control groups. Even though there have been several meta-analysis and literature reviews involving WCF in recent years [20, 22, 23, 25, 28], to my knowledge only Stevenson and Phakiti [5] have examined AWE in particular and they did not focus exclusively on ESL/EFL.

3 Methodology

3.1 Literature Search and Inclusion Criteria

A systematic literature review was conducted to address the research questions. With AWE research being so sparse and methodologically inconsistent [5], and with the increased use of AWE technologies in ESL and EFL classrooms, it seems important to analyse the gaps and limitations of current research to help guide future research in a more productive direction.

The first stage of the literature search included performing a database search for articles published in the last 10 years using the following databases: JSTOR, ScienceDirect, EBSCOhost, ProQuest, Taylor & Francis, Web of Science, and Wiley. A second search was carried out using the Google Scholar search engine to find additional studies. Both searches were carried out applying the following criteria:

- Title, abstract or keywords must contain the following (either in full or using the commonly accepted abbreviations in parentheses): English as a Second Language (ESL) OR English as a Foreign Language (EFL) OR L2 OR English for Specific Purposes (ESP) AND
- Title, abstract or keywords must contain the following (either in full or using the commonly accepted abbreviations in parentheses): Automated Writing Evaluation (AWE) OR Computer Assisted Language Learning (CALL) OR intelligent Computer Assisted Language Learning (iCALL) AND

- Title, abstract or keywords must contain: "writ* feedback" OR "writ* corrective feedback"

The initial search resulted in 45 studies. To ensure comprehensiveness, a manual search was conducted on the following journals: Computers & Education, British Journal of Educational Technology, Journal of Educational Technology & Society, The Internet and Higher Education, The International Review of Research in Open and Distributed Learning, Journal of Computer Assisted Learning, Educational Technology Research and Development, International Conference on Learning Analytics And Knowledge, Australasian Journal of Educational Technology, Distance Education, TechTrends, Language Learning & Technology, Journal of Online Learning and Teaching, Learning, Media and Technology, International Journal of Computer-Supported Collaborative Learning, Research in Learning Technology, IEEE Transactions on Learning Technologies, Journal of Educational Computing Research, and Education and Information Technologies. These journals were chosen because they had the highest h5-index according to Google Scholar metrics within the Educational Technology category. This search yielded an additional 47 articles. Finally, the reference sections of the articles found in the initial search were scoured to find any studies that might have been missed, yielding 36 more studies for a total of 128 studies.

The next step was to apply an inclusion criterion to screen the studies. This was done by reading the title and abstract from the articles and, when the information contained in them was insufficient to reach a decision, by reading more in-depth into the article, especially the methodology and conclusion sections. The inclusion criteria comprised the following items:

(1) Presents an original (primary) research analysing the application of AWE in a classroom setting
(2) Analyses the use of AWE in providing feedback to ESL/EFL students
(3) Focuses on higher education
(4) Studies the application of AWE and not its validity or reliability
(5) Focuses on the use of automated feedback and not the use of computer programs to enhance or enable peer/teacher feedback
(6) Is published in a peer reviewed journal or conference proceedings
(7) Is less than 10 years old, therefore was published between 2007 and 2018

Two of the papers obtained by looking at reference sections were written in Chinese, but were considered relevant because they study the effects of an AWE program specifically designed for EFL students, Pigai, and complied with all the inclusion criteria. The application of the inclusion criteria left us with 29 systematically selected studies.

3.2 Analysis

In order to understand the theoretical constructs and bases used in current AWE research and answer the first research question, the chosen papers were analysed using an inductive coding method. Each paper was read in its entirety and all named mentions of theories or constructs were coded. These include theories used to explain or frame the usage of AWE technologies in a broader sense, how the AWE program was introduced into the classroom, and the interpretation of the results from the study.

Once all the different theories were coded, broad themes were found among them, and theories were classified as belonging to each of those themes. Three broad themes emerged from this preliminary analysis: theories related to second language acquisition, theories related to the writing process itself and theories related to student autonomy and self-regulation (see supplementary electronic materials for a breakdown of the coding process. Supplementary materials can be found at https://bit.ly/2X3pVbx).

Regarding the second research question, close attention was also paid to several aspects of the methodology used in the sample, especially the size of the samples, whether they used a control group, how long the intervention lasted, whether they had pre-tests and/or post-tests and how they measured the success of the intervention. A summary of all these different aspects can be found in the supplementary electronic materials.

3.3 Limitations

Methodologically, it is difficult to draw generalisations because studies defined the "success" of their interventions differently. Some studies measure the effectiveness of the AWE intervention through student perceptions of its effectiveness, others measure how successfully the students have revised a piece of work after being given AWE feedback, and others yet measure the ratio of mistakes produced in a new piece of writing. Studies also differ in whether the feedback students receive is limited to the AWE software, or if its paired with teacher and/or peer feedback.

This wide range of methodologies and terminologies used in these studies makes it hard to evaluate the effectiveness of AWE interventions in the classroom, but the focus of this review is precisely on the methodological issues that have plagued current research on AWE. Therefore, although it is difficult to reach any conclusions regarding the effectiveness of AWE, this is not the focus of this study. Instead, this paper focuses on the features of current research that make these conclusions difficult to reach.

4 Results and Discussion

4.1 Theoretical Foundations of AWE Research (RQ1)

Of the broad themes found through the initial coding, writing theory was the most present, being included in 18 different studies. Of these, a salient theory was the socio-cognitive model of writing (N = 8), which emphasises the social and communicative dimensions of writing as a meaning-making activity [1]. Another theory (N = 8) was that of process-oriented approaches to writing, based on multiple drafts and scaffolded feedback to allow students to iterate through their text [34]. AWE programs are thought to help process-oriented approaches because the immediacy and permanent availability of the feedback allows students more opportunities for revision and drafting [7].

As for studies that used Second Language Acquisition (SLA) theory as a theoretical underpinning (N = 12), most of them focused on different aspects of SLA to study the effects of AWE feedback in the classroom. Many studies, however, mentioned scaffolding (N = 8), especially in relation to process writing approaches, as some believed that the constant, immediate feedback provided by AWE programs could be used as a scaffolding mechanism for process oriented approaches to writing [11, 13, 29, 31, 33].

Several studies also mentioned either self-regulated learning or the role of AWE technologies in the fostering of student autonomy (N = 11). In part, this may be due to the nature of the research on WCF in general brought about by L2 writing approaches, whose main goal seems to be the creation of self-sufficient writers [35], but also because of AWE technologies themselves, as research has noted that "learning technologies can engage learners in self-regulated cycles of learning" [35; p, 238]. It is surprising that so few studies focus on self-regulation or student autonomy, given that AWE technologies are meant to be used by the students in their own time and the adoption of new technologies can be aided by good self-regulatory strategies from learners [37].

Writing Theory. The role of writing feedback as a tool for SLA has been hotly contested in the literature [21]. Current research on AWE programs suggests that they help students more when used as part of a process approach to writing that encourages multiple drafts and revisions. Process approaches to writing consider evaluation of the written text to be part of the writing process itself [21], and AWE programs are considered useful because their immediate feedback allows for a multiple drafts, something that is encouraged as it empowers learners to move toward self-expression [26]. Several authors in the sample [10, 13, 16, 24, 31] analysed the impact AWE software can have on a process writing approach that emphasises multiple drafts as a way to develop writing proficiency. Many of the studies in the selected sample found that the use of AWE programs seems to encourage students to write multiple drafts [1, 6–9, 13, 28, 29, 31, 33], either because of the ease of doing so compared to traditional methods of receiving feedback and revising [32], or because the AWE interface could feel like a game for some students, encouraging them to revise and resubmit in order to get a higher score [4]. In Koh's [24] study, constant and immediate feedback was not found to overload students and correlated to better performance in grammar and content when compared with students who only received feedback right before submission as dictated by traditional process writing approaches.

The use of AWE as a tool for process-based approaches to writing is not without its downsides, however. As they are now, AWE tools focus mostly on surface features and mechanical aspects of writing [7], but a complete process approach to teaching writing in the classroom should focus mostly on meaning and the communicative qualities of writing [27]. However, it is not clear whether this also applies to L2 writers, as accuracy still plays a role in conveying meaning [24]. Some researchers have attempted to address this shortcoming by making the use of AWE one part of the process, with the other being supplemented either by peer review or teacher feedback that allows students to engage with the socio-communicative aspects of writing [1, 7, 10, 16, 28–31, 38]. Liao [33], for example, designed her writing program using a multiple-draft cycle in which the AWE program gave feedback on form, and on subsequent iterations teachers gave feedback on meaning and composition, addressing more global concerns in students' texts [1, 16, 29] and responding to Zamel's [27] criticism that teachers became so distracted by local language-related problems they completely missed bigger meaning-related problems. In this way, AWE feedback can help learners scaffold [11].

Second Language Acquisition. Sociocultural theory considers scaffolding to be an important part of SLA, as research shows learners are ready to focus on different linguistic and surface features at different times, so when and how they are exposed to said features is important for their acquisition of the target language [34]. Some authors have argued that the immediacy of AWE feedback can be useful in scaffolding [11, 31] and that this role could be "manifested in the dynamic, formative assessment of the writing process" that encouraged students to interact with the AWE program through a process-oriented approach as described in the previous section [34; p. 133].

However, there are some issues inherent in using AWE programs to construct scaffolding mechanisms for students to improve their writing, the main one being the formulaic nature of the feedback provided. Liao [13] found that the feedback was often too confusing to be useful for low-performance learners, whereas high-performance learners seemed to benefit the most from the scaffolding provided by the AWE program. Interestingly, Chen and Cheng [1] came to the opposite conclusion, as higher-level students felt constrained by the writing rules imposed on them by the machine and lower-level students felt more supported by the feedback received. Li et al. [28] seemed to take a more middle ground; although they pointed out the AWE feedback might be more useful for lower-proficiency students, they also noted that the instructor's pedagogical approach to integrating AWE into the classroom and their attitudes towards the use of the software influenced how students interacted with it. In general, it seems important to complement AWE feedback with teacher-provided scaffolding to understand said feedback, as well as content, organisation, meaning and other features of written discourse that cannot be adequately tackled by the program [17, 33].

Research on SLA, especially into usage-based approaches, also emphasises the importance of immediateness on feedback in language learning. Oral teaching of second languages make a lot of emphasis on the effectiveness of recasts because their immediateness helps students notice their usage of target forms [39], although this has usually been considered impracticable in written feedback because of the time it takes teachers to read through essays, provide feedback, and then return them to the students for revision [19]. An advantage of AWE is that it can provide immediate feedback on pieces of writing. Many of the authors in the sample found that students reacted positively to the immediateness, noting that it motivated them to practice their writing more often [1, 28, 32], allowed them to keep track of their errors [8, 13], helped them notice linguistic forms [2, 6, 40], and provided constant timely feedback whenever the student needed it and without limitations [28, 30, 32].

Regarding skill acquisition theory and how it informs the use of WCF in the classroom, it established that explicit knowledge is important and "must be proceduralized through practice" [48; p. 381], and that feedback should be meaningful, timely, constant and manageable [41]. The timeliness of the feedback provided by AWE is practically immediate, and it has also been mentioned that some students appreciate that the AWE program is always available, providing them with constant feedback [30]. The question of meaningfulness, however, is still contested in research. Students found that AWE feedback could be generic and not very informative [1, 10, 15, 17, 28, 30], although some of the studies noted that the personalised nature of the feedback provided by the AWE programs seemed to help students in their revision and learning processes [11, 31, 32]. As with other aspects of the implementation of AWE software as a learning tool in the L2 classroom, it seems that the way in which teachers introduce the program, its capabilities and limitations, and the additional support and feedback given to the students determines whether the intervention will be useful to the students [1, 28, 29].

Self-regulated Learning. Another consideration when implementing AWE programs in the classroom is the fact that they will be used in the student's own time. One of the argued benefits of AWE is that it may promote student autonomy and self-regulated learning because of its immediate provision of scores, diagnostic tools and writing resources beyond mere feedback. However, "whether students can develop more autonomy in revising their writing through computer-generated feedback and making use of the self-help writing and editing tools available to them is uncertain" [5; p. 97].

Although some authors have feared that students will just passively accept the feedback given by the program [7], the research sample shows that students actively engaged with the feedback, critically analysing it and adopting only the feedback they found useful [13, 16, 17], as well as engaging with their own writing [8, 13, 15, 29, 31–33, 38, 42]. In fact, some of the studies found that students who actively engaged with the materials and resources offered by the AWE software demonstrated higher levels of grammatical accuracy [7, 13, 16, 17].

Furthermore, some AWE programs offer extra resources such as dictionaries, thesauri, editing tools, web resources and portfolios [1, 16, 32], with the AWE programs specifically designed for EFL speakers also offering collocation information [16]. It is, however, not entirely clear whether these tools were taken up by the students or were even useful, as the collocation tools in Pigai, for example, have been criticised as inaccurate [7, 15] and other tools, such as thesaurus, have been used by students for vocabulary-building rather than revision [7, 14].

It is therefore important to focus research the role that AWE programs might play in fostering student autonomy and letting them be in control of their own learning. As Bai and Hu [7] pointed out, "students were active and autonomous agents" when using the AWE programs, adjusting "their perceptions of the AWE system through repeated use and developed mature understandings of its functions and drawbacks" [p. 78]. This indicates students used monitoring activities to self-regulate their use of these programs for revising their work and improving their English writing skills.

AWE also seems to help with goal-setting, an important feature of effective learning that enhances achievement as long as it is appropriate, specific and challenging [43]. Liao [13] found that students who engaged with the AWE program by using the information it provided to set learning goals and self-monitoring their progress showed the most gains in writing accuracy by the end of the treatment. Tang [29] and Li [12] also explored how the use of AWE allowed teachers to set clear goals for the students, either by adapting the assessment criteria provided by the program or by asking students to achieve a certain score before submitting it for teacher feedback. More research needs to be carried out exploring whether feedback provided by the AWE programs could help enhance the standards learners use for their metacognitive monitoring.

Research should therefore focus on how teachers can help students understand the task, set clear goals, and provide them with study tactics and strategies related to the use of AWE, that is, how teachers can scaffold students into self-regulating their use of these programs [14]. Teacher scaffolding helps students develop self-regulation strategies for second language learning [21] and, more generally, to successfully apply tools to help with their learning tasks [44], both of which are important when integrating any technology into a classroom environment.

However, at least in the sample reviewed, self-regulated learning theory seems to be used as an explanation mechanism and not necessarily as a framework for implementing AWE into the classroom, ignoring the wealth of research into the relationship between self-regulated learning and the use of technology to enhance one's own learning process or support classroom activities [36, 45, 46]. Although none of this research has focused specifically on AWE, many of its core concepts are useful in understanding the role these programs could have in an ESL/EFL classroom, which makes it surprising that they seem to be all but absent in the sample.

4.2 Methodological Approaches to AWE (RQ2)

One of the methodological aspects analysed focused on how the studies measured the success of the intervention, either through scores (N = 6), student perceptions (N = 7), both (N = 11) or other methods (N = 5), and whether they measured success through producing a new piece of writing as opposed to revising an existing piece. This last consideration is very important, as learning necessitates the application of knowledge to new contexts [47], and studies that focus on revision offer "no measure of changes in students' ability to write accurately, i.e. their learning" [23; p. 257]. Even though those studies might be useful to gauge the utility of AWE software as a revision tool in the classroom, it is difficult to draw any conclusions on its usefulness as a learning tool.

Sample sizes ranged from 1 to 1,275 students, but except for three outliers (N = 1275, N = 463 and N = 460), most studies did not reach 200 students. Only 6 of the studies analysed used a control group in their experimental design. The duration of the intervention also varied, from a one-time revision activity to an entire year, although most studies (N = 15) applied the intervention throughout a semester (see the supplementary electronic materials for a breakdown of the studies and their methodology).

When Truscott [19] famously challenged the use of WCF in second language classrooms, his objections to the practice were both theoretical and methodological. The theoretical issues, and their applications to AWE, were explored in the previous section. Among the methodological concerns Truscott [19, 20] raised were lack of control groups in existing research, lack of longitudinal studies, and lack of post-tests to determine whether the students retained any of the new information.

Regarding the first point, only 8 out of the 29 selected studies employed control groups within their experimental design. The issue here is twofold. Without control groups, it is hard to ascertain whether the effects observed are due to the inclusion of AWE feedback in the classroom, or other factors [20, 25]. On the other hand, it has been pointed out that deliberately withholding feedback from a group of students in order to configure a control group may be considered ethically dubious [48]. This argument in particular did not seem to apply to most of the research, as most of the sample

[16, 29, 32, 42] simply used a control group where feedback was provided in the traditional way, with teachers annotating the work and giving it back to students, therefore comparing the effectiveness between AWE and traditional feedback rather than comparing feedback to no feedback conditions. The distinction is important because, as has been pointed out, there were two exceptions to this: Grami and Alkazemi [49] did not provide any guidance or feedback to their control group, and Chodorow et al. used two control groups: one which used AWE feedback but the students were told it was teacher generated, and another where they received no feedback at all. Other papers in the sample specifically identified the lack of a control group as a limitation in their experimental results [6, 9, 13, 28, 38].

With regards to the second point raised by Truscott, most of the studies in the sample lasted from 4 weeks to a whole year. There are two notable exceptions, however, that rely solely on a one-shot revision exercise: the study done by Chodorow et al. and the study done by Grami and Alkazemi. In both cases, the students produced a piece of writing which they subsequently revised, either using teacher feedback, AWE feedback, or no feedback, depending on experimental conditions. As Truscott argued, revision-based studies do not allow to understand how, or if, "correction affects learners' ability to use the language in realistic ways" [23; p. 270], putting into question the ecological validity of the research [48, 50]. This issue is especially salient in Grami and Alkazemi, which concluded, perhaps unsurprisingly, that students made better revisions when they were given tools to carry them out.

A similar issue stems from the lack of post-tests to determine whether long-term learning has occurred as a result of the intervention. Of the studies in the sample, only 11 used both pre-tests and post-tests to compare the writing competence of the students before and after the treatment and one used only a post-test. Pre-test and post-test designs have long been used in educational research to determine whether a particular treatment has had an effect on a specific population [51]. Pre-tests are also useful because they allow us to determine the starting levels of grammar proficiency in experimental groups [38]; this is important because even using natural groups for the treatment may result in wildly varying levels of writing proficiency among the students participating in the study [50], and it has been noted that AWE feedback has different effects on different levels of proficiency [1, 13]. The lack of pre-test and post-test data makes it hard to reach conclusions on whether AWE feedback had a measurable impact on student writing [25], and is tied to the way in which the studies in the sample measure the success (or lack thereof) of the intervention.

Six of the studies in the selected sample look at scoring on the writing produced by students to determine whether the intervention was successful, seven look at student perceptions to determine success, and 11 use a combination of both. Of the remaining studies, two focus on how the students use the feedback and the last three look at error rates before/after the treatment.

The sample studies mainly use two types of scores to determine whether the intervention was successful: holistic scores and error counts, with only one study [6] administering a test to see whether the students could identify the target form. Both holistic scores and error counts have their merits as tools intended to see whether the students have improved their writing skills, and both have their issues. One issue with the holistic approach to determining the success of the intervention is that most of the studies in the sample rely on the scores given by the AWE programs, which research has proven to be problematic at times for being perceived as unfair [9], inconsistent with teacher grading [28] and biased toward certain formulaic structures [1]. Error counts, on the other hand, focus on the mechanical aspects of writing feedback in which AWE excels, but do not tell us enough about the overall gain in writing proficiency by the students (complexity of ideas, lexical variety, structure, composition, etc.).

When it comes to data collection, however, it is interesting to note that beyond using the scores provided by the program or using the program to collect several samples of data, few studies in the sample took advantage of the data-collection capabilities of the software itself (a notable exception being Bai). Research into the use of AWE seems to be heavily modelled by traditional WCF research, ignoring the fact that AWE differs fundamentally in that the tool itself gathers usage data, unlike traditional paper settings. In its most basic form, AWE programs can track how many submissions a user has made and what the score of each submission has been, their editing behaviours, etc. [7]. Learning analytics has been a growing field that measures digital traces produced by students in their interactions with learning software in order to study learners and their contexts and has even been used to study self-regulation in students [37], which makes it especially relevant for the study of AWE programs in ESL classrooms.

5 Conclusions

Research into the use of AWE is still in its infancy. It is fragmented, both theoretically and methodologically, which results in two main issues: first, implementations of these programs lack a proper framework to justify and inform their use in the classroom and second, the methodology of the research itself suffers from a lack of direction. This makes it difficult, at this point, to use the existing research to make any claims about best practices or evidence-informed guidelines.

There are three main conclusions that can be reached from the way theory has been handled in current AWE research. First, AWE programs are meant to be used individually and in the students' own time, making self-regulated strategies important for their successful uptake of the tool. There is a wealth of research into how self-regulation helps the adoption of new technologies into learning [36, 37, 45] that should not be ignored when studying the use of AWE technologies. Second, the role of teachers is essential in scaffolding the use of AWE in the classroom, not only because the social component is important in the adoption of any new technology [52], but because teachers have an important role in motivating students to engage with their own learning and develop self-regulated study strategies [21]. Third, it is important to rethink what success means in AWE research and what is the goal in implementing these programs into the classroom. AWE programs have been shown to help in process approaches to writing [6, 26], and therefore it warrants looking deeper into how these programs can help students engage with their own texts.

Methodologically, AWE research not only needs to address the issues that are already present in WCF research, it needs to recognise that the very nature of the programs allows for new modes of data collection that can give us a better insight into how students develop as writers, how they use these programs and how they engage with their own texts. This includes using existing tools for natural language processing, several of which are already in use to study the development of language skills in ESL students like Coh-Metrix or L2SCA [53–55].

If research into the use of AWE is help us understand the role of these technologies in the ESL/EFL classroom, it needs to move beyond copying the methods of traditional WCF research and embrace its technological aspect in order to achieve its full potential. It also needs to move away from merely trying to prove quantitative gains in arbitrary measures of writing proficiency and focus on how these tools help develop autonomous writers [21]. The wealth of available theory regarding the use and implementation of technology into the classrooms, as well as the new methodological possibilities offered by learning analytics and natural language processing, cannot be ignored if the research of AWE is to grow into a field in its own right.

References

1. Chen, C.-F., Cheng, W.-Y.E.: Beyond the design of automated writing evaluation: pedagogical practices and perceived learning effectiveness in EFL writing classes. Lang. Learn. Technol. **12**(2), 94–112 (2008)
2. Ranalli, J., Link, S., Chukharev-Hudilainen, E.: Automated writing evaluation for formative assessment of second language writing: investigating the accuracy and usefulness of feedback as part of argument-based validation. Educ. Psychol. **37**(1), 8–25 (2017)
3. Stevenson, M.: A critical interpretative synthesis: the integration of automated writing evaluation into classroom writing instruction. Comput. Compos. **42**, 1–16 (2016)
4. Wang, P.: Can automated writing evaluation programs help students improve their English writing? Int. J. Appl. Linguist. Engl. Lit. **2**(1), 6–12 (2013)
5. Stevenson, M., Phakiti, A.: The effects of computer-generated feedback on the quality of writing. Assessing Writ. **19**, 51–65 (2014)
6. Cotos, E.: Potential of automated writing evaluation feedback. CALICO J. **28**(2), 420–459 (2011)
7. Bai, L., Hu, G.: In the face of fallible AWE feedback: how do students respond? Educ. Psychol. **37**(1), 67–81 (2017)
8. El Ebyary, K., Windeatt, S.: The impact of computer based feedback on students' written work. Int. J. Engl. Stud. **10**(2), 121–142 (2010)
9. Fang, Y.: Perceptions of the computer-assisted writing program among EFL college learners. Educ. Technol. Soc. **13**(3), 246–256 (2010)
10. Lai, Y.H.: Which do students prefer to evaluate their essays: peers or computer program. Brit. J. Educ. Technol. **41**(3), 432–454 (2010)
11. Lavolette, E., Polio, C., Kahng, J.: The accuracy of computer-assisted feedback and students' responses to it. Lang. Learn. Technol. **19**(2), 50–68 (2015)
12. Li, S.: The effectiveness of corrective feedback in SLA: a meta-analysis. Lang. Learn. **60**(2), 309–365 (2010)
13. Liao, H.C.: Using automated writing evaluation to reduce grammar errors in writing. ELT J. **70**(3), 308–319 (2016)
14. Huang, S., Renandya, W.A.: Exploring the integration of automated feedback among lower-proficiency EFL learners. Innov. Lang. Learn. Teach. 1–12 (2018). https://www.tandfonline.com/action/showCitFormats?doi=10.1080%2F17501229.2018.1471083

15. Xia, L., Zhong, L.: 作文自动评价系统在大学英语写作教学中的实证研究. Res. Teach. **40**(1), 57–61 (2017)
16. Yang, X., Dai, Y.: 基于批改网的大学英语自主写作教学模式实践研究. Comput. Assist. Foreign Lang. Educ. **162**, 17–23 (2015)
17. Zhang, Z.V.: Student engagement with computer-generated feedback: a case study. ELT J. **71**(3), 317–328 (2017)
18. Silva, T.: Toward an understanding of the distinct nature of L2 writing: the ESL research and its implications. TESOL Q. **27**(4), 657–677 (1993)
19. Truscott, J.: The case against grammar correction in L2 writing classes. Lang. Learn. **46**(2), 327–369 (1996)
20. Truscott, J.: The effect of error correction on learners' ability to write accurately. J. Second Lang. Writ. **16**, 255–272 (2007)
21. Andrade, M., Evans, N.: Principles and Practices for Response in Second Language Writing: Developing Self-Regulated Learners. Routledge, New York (2013)
22. Ferris, D.R.: Written corrective feedback in second language acquisition and writing studies. Lang. Teach. **45**(4), 446–459 (2012)
23. Kang, E., Han, Z.: The efficacy of written corrective feedback in improving L2 written accuracy: a meta-analysis. Mod. Lang. J. **99**(1), 1–18 (2015)
24. Koh, W.: Effective applications of automated writing feedback in process-based writing instruction. Engl. Teach. **72**(3), 91–118 (2017)
25. Biber, D., Nekrasova, T., Horn, B.: The effectiveness of feedback for L1-English and L2-Writing Development: A meta-analysis (2011)
26. Ferris, D.R.: Does error feedback help student writers? New evidence on the short-and long-term effects of written error correction. In: Hyland, K., Hyland, F. (eds.) Feedback in Second Language Writing: Contexts and Issues, pp 81–104. Cambridge University Press, Cambridge (2006)
27. Zamel, V.: Responding to student writing. TESOL Q. **19**(1), 79–101 (1985)
28. Li, J., Link, S., Hegelheimer, V.: Rethinking the role of automated writing evaluation (AWE) feedback in ESL writing instruction. J. Second Lang. Writ. **27**, 1–18 (2015)
29. Tang, J., Rich, C.S.: Automated writing evaluation in an EFL setting: lessons from China. JALT CALL J. **13**(2), 117–146 (2017)
30. Wang, M., Goodman, D.: Automated writing evaluation: students' perceptions and emotional involvement. Engl. Teach. Learn. **36**(3), 1–37 (2012)
31. Cotos, E., Huffman, S.: Learner fit in scaling up automated writing evaluation. Int. J. Comput. Assist. Lang. Learn. Teach. **3**(3), 77–98 (2013)
32. Wang, Y.-J., Shang, H.-F., Briody, P.: Exploring the impact of using automated writing evaluation in English as a foreign language university students' writing. Comput. Assist. Lang. Learn. **26**(3), 234–257 (2013)
33. Liao, H.C.: Enhancing the grammatical accuracy of EFL writing by using an AWE-assisted process approach. System **62**, 77–92 (2016)
34. Hyland, K.: Second Language Writing. Cambridge University Press, Cambridge (2003)
35. Van Beuningen, C.: Corrective feedback in L2 writing: theoretical perspectives, empirical insights and future directions. Int. J. Engl. Stud. **10**(2), 1–27 (2010)
36. Bartolome, A., Steffens, K.: Technologies for self-regulated learning. In: Carneiro, R. (ed.) Self-Regulated Learning in Technology Enhanced Learning Environments, pp. 21–31. Sense, Rotterdam (2011)
37. Winne, P.H.: How software technologies can improve research on learning and Bolster School Reform. Educ. Psychol. **41**(1), 5–17 (2006)
38. Saadi, Z.K., Saadat, M.: EFL learners' writing accuracy: effects of direct and metalinguistic electronic feedback. Theory Pract. Lang. Stud. **5**(10), 2053–2063 (2015)

39. Polio, C.: The relevance of second language acquisition theory to the written error correction debate. J. Second Lang. Writ. **21**, 375–389 (2012)
40. Li, Z., Feng, H., Saricaoglu, A.: The short-term and long-term effects of AWE feedback on ESL students' development of grammatical accuracy. CALICO J. **34**(3), 355–375 (2017)
41. Hartshorn, K.J., Evans, N.W., Merril, P.F., et al.: Effects of dynamic corrective feedback on ESL writing accuracy. TESOL Q. **44**(1), 84–109 (2010)
42. Zaini, A., Mazdayasna, G.: The impact of computer-based instruction on the development of EFL learners' writing skills. J. Comput. Assist. Learn. **31**, 516–528 (2015)
43. Hattie, J.: Influences on student learning. In: Inaugural Lecture: University of Auckland, pp 1–25 (1999)
44. Gašević, D., Mirriahi, N., Dawson, S., Joksimović, S.: Effects of instructional conditions and experience on the adoption of a learning tool. Comput. Hum. Behav. **67**, 207–220 (2017)
45. Kitsantas, A.: Fostering college students' self-regulated learning with learning technologies. Hellenic J. Psychol. **10**, 235–252 (2013)
46. Lust, G., Juarez Collazo, N.A., Elen, J., Clarebout, G.: Content management systems: enriched learning opportunities for all? Comput. Hum. Behav. **28**(3), 795–808 (2012)
47. Hattie, J., Timperley, H.: The power of feedback. Rev. Educ. Res. **77**(1), 81–112 (2007)
48. Liu, Q., Brown, D.: Methodological synthesis of research on the effectiveness of corrective feedback in L2 writing. J. Second Lang. Writ. **30**, 66–81 (2015)
49. Grami, G.M.A., Alkazemi, B.Y.: Improving ESL writing using an online formulaic sequence word-combination checker. J. Comput. Assist. Learn. **32**, 95–104 (2016)
50. Guénette, D.: Is feedback pedagogically correct? Research design issues in studies of feedback on writing. J. Second Lang. Writ. **16**, 40–53 (2007)
51. Dugard, P., Todman, J.: Analysis of pre-test-post-test control group designs in educational research. Educ. Psychol. **15**(2), 181–198 (1995)
52. Venkatesh, V., Davis, F.D.: A theoretical extension of the technology acceptance model: four longitudinal field studies. Manag. Sci. **46**(2), 186–204 (2000)
53. Ortega, L.: Syntactic complexity measures and their relationship to L2 proficiency: a research synthesis of college-level L2 writing. Appl. Linguist. **24**(4), 492–518 (2003)
54. Graesser, A.C., McNamara, D., Louwerse, M.M., Cai, Z.: Coh-metrix: analysis of text on cohesion and language. Behav. Res. Methods Instrum. Comput. **36**(2), 193–202 (2004)
55. Lu, X.: Automatic analysis of syntactic complexity in second language writing. Int. J. Corpus Linguist. **15**(4), 474–496 (2010)

Elo, I Love You Won't You Tell Me Your K

Michael Yudelson(✉)

ACT, Inc., Iowa City, IA 52243, USA
michael.yudelson@act.org

Abstract. Elo is a rating schema used for tracking player level in individual and, sometimes, team sports, most notably – in chess. Also, it has found use in the area of tracking learner proficiency. Similar to the 1PL IRT (Rasch), Elo rating schema could be extended to serve the most demanding needs of learner skill tracking. Elo's advantage is that it has fewer parameters. However, the computational efficiency side of the search for the best-fitting values of these parameters is rarely discussed. In this paper, we are focusing on questions of implementing Elo and a gradient-based approach to find optimal values of its parameters. Also, we compare several variants of Elo to learning modeling approaches like Bayesian Knowledge Tracing. Our results show that the use of analytical gradients results in computational and, sometimes, statistical fit improvements on small and large datasets alike.

Keywords: Modeling Student Learning · Model Comparison · Elo rating schema

1 Introduction

Computer-assisted testing and computer-guided learning rely on computational models of student knowledge and learning to produce personalized value for test-takers and learners. Models like 1PL IRT [11] and Log-Linear Test Model (LLTM) [21] were used and elaborated upon by the measurement community to compile test forms and compute student test scores. The field of computer-guided learning, most notably, intelligent tutoring systems, long relied on Bayesian Knowledge Tracing (BKT) [2] model for operational student-modeling or an approach in ASSISTments where three corrects in a row earn the student skill mastery [4]. Among the analytical models of learning that were used extensively, we could mention the Additive Factors Model (AFM) [1].

Elo recently rediscovered by learning analytics and educational data mining communities and several research investigations were published. While Elo is different from statistical models traditionally used in assessment and learning (often referred to as rating schema, not a model), it has highly desirable properties for these fields. First, Elo is designed to completely sidestep cold start problem and doesn't require substantial tuning (fitting) – known Elo variants all have under a

M. Scheffel et al. (Eds.): EC-TEL 2019, LNCS 11722, pp. 213–223, 2019.
https://doi.org/10.1007/978-3-030-29736-7_16

dozen parameters. Second, Elo relies on local, often, asynchronous updates and that resonates well with computational issues assessment and learning models often have to combat with. Third, Elo is intuitively explainable – wrong answer results in a decrement of student's ability ratings and vice versa, plus, the more unexpected the outcome, the more the update to the rating value is.

One of the shortcomings of Elo is that parameter fitting is largely done by hand-picking or grid search [13]. Our attempts to find traces of attempts to address Elo's parameter optimization resulted in no reference from the fields of assessment or learning. The only publication we found was from the field of biology where Elo was used for explaining behaviors of primates [5]. In this paper, we attempt to address the fitting of Elo parameters when applied to educational data and to work out analytical gradients for two forms of Elo rating schema. We then fit Elo on several sets of publicly available learning data and show that the use of analytical gradients follows the results when gradients are computationally approximated. Also, often, a computational improvement is observed.

2 Prior Work and Uses of Elo

Elo rating schema has long been used to rate chess players. In addition, Elo is also used for rating players in multiplayer competition in several video games [22], association football, American football, basketball [15], Major League Baseball, tennis [6], Scrabble, and other games. A Bayesian approach, based on Elo called TrueSkill™ was developed by Herbrich and colleagues [7] to address performance in team sports. In biology, Elo has found use to explain the formation of dominance hierarchies of primates [5].

In education, there are several cases of successful use of Elo both as a theoretical and operational model. For example, members of Pelánek's research group published several works where variants of Elo rating schema were used in connection to learning Geography, specifically to track student recall of the shapes of maps of the Northern European countries [13]. One of the most at-scale operational uses of Elo rating schema in education is in the system Math Garden [8] that is widely used in a K-12 setting in the Netherlands. An Elo-based system of student ratings was used by Ivanovo State Power University, Russia to track student progress as they complete the courses overall, as well as the intermediate and partial exams within the courses [9,24]. This approach called Developing Individual Creating Thinking (RITM in Russian transliteration) was implemented in 1992 and is still in use today.

3 Elo Rating Schema

Elo is a rating schema named after its inventor Arpad Elo [3]. In chess, where Elo found initial use, the modeled events are chess matches and the variables are opponent 1 ability and opponent 2 ability. After each match, the ratings of opponents' abilities are updated based on the outcome (a win of either opponent or a draw). In the fields of measurement and learning, an event is the student's opportunity to answer a question item correctly. The student is opponent 1, and the item is opponent 2. Sometimes, a set of skills relevant to the question item are used to collectively represent opponent 2. When applied to tracking learner proficiency a standard version of Elo is often compared to a Rasch model that used in psychometrics. We will start by describing the Rasch model first and then focus on Elo.

3.1 Rasch Model

Rasch model [11], also known as 1PL IRT, captures test-taker performance with the help of two classes of variables: unidimensional abilities of test-takers, and unidimensional difficulties of test items. Both abilities and difficulties are thought of as stationary values that do not change over the time of assessment. Refer to Eqs. 1 and 2 for the formulation of the Rasch model. Here, θ_i – is the ability of student i, β_j – is the difficulty of item j, X_{ij} – is i^{th} student's response to item j, p_{ij} – is the estimate of the probability of student answering the item correctly, and m_{ij} – is the log-odds value of that probability.

$$p_{ij} = Pr(X_{ij} = 1) = \sigma(m_{ij}) = \frac{1}{1 + e^{-m_{ij}}} \quad (1)$$

$$m_{ij} = \theta_i - \beta_j \quad (2)$$

3.2 Student-Item Elo

A simple formulation of Elo capturing students and items is given in Eq. 3. It is related to the Rasch model's formulation in Eq. 1. In Elo, s_i – is the current logit rating of student's unidimensional ability and b_j – is the current logit rating of item's unidimensional difficulty. We are only defining Elo's m_{ij}, since the probabilistic form is the same as shown in Eq. 1.

$$m_{ij} = s_i - b_j \quad (3)$$

If we are to draw comparisons between Rasch's θ_i and β_j and Elo's s_i and b_j, the former would be stationary values and the latter would be functions of time since, in Elo, s_i and b_j are incrementally updated as new data arrives. One may hypothesize that say, s_i could be asymptotically approaching θ_i. However, unlike θ_i, the distribution of s_i has not been theoretically described and s_i constantly changes which complicates such theoretical description. The same is true for b_j. Additionally, in the Rasch model, θ_i and β_j are parameters, while s_i and b_j in Elo are not. In some literature, for example [14], Elo-tracked student abilities and item difficulties are written as θ_i and β_j. However, in order to separate the meanings, we would use different notation.

As mentioned before, tracked Elo values are updated as new data points are observed. Refer to Eqs. 4, 5 for the updating rules. Here, K is a sensitivity parameter controlling the magnitude of the update. Thus, the Elo variant as in Eq. 3 has one parameter K. We will refer to this Elo version as **E1**.

$$s_i = \begin{cases} 0, \text{ if this is the first time we see data of student } i \\ s_i + K \cdot (X_{ij} - p_{ij}), \text{ otherwise} \end{cases} \tag{4}$$

$$b_j = \begin{cases} 0, \text{ if this is the first time we see data of item } j \\ b_j - K \cdot (X_{ij} - p_{ij}), \text{ otherwise} \end{cases} \tag{5}$$

We could modify the previously defined Student-Item Elo model by defining two sensitivity parameters: ${}_iK$ for updating student abilities, and ${}_jK$ for updating item difficulties. Here, the $_i$ nd $_j$ mean that the corresponding K values belong to student updates and item updates respectively. The corresponding changes are shown in Eqs. 6 and 7. This version of Elo we will call **E2**.

$$s_i = s_i + {}_iK \cdot (X_{ij} - p_{ij}) \tag{6}$$

$$b_j = b_j - {}_jK \cdot (X_{ij} - p_{ij}) \tag{7}$$

4 Gradients of Elo Parameters

4.1 Preliminary Definitions

We use $O = \{o_t\}$, to denote observations, where $o_t \in \{0, 1\}$ is the student's response to an item at some time t. Here, $t \in [1, T]$ is the time slice and it indexes the data of all students answering all items sorted by time. 0 and 1 denote incorrect and correct student responses respectively. Vector of Elo parameters is denoted as λ. An element of the vector is λ_m, where $m \in [1, M]$ and $\lambda_m \in (-\infty, +\infty)$.

We will be using maximum-likelihood estimation in our further work. For optimization, we are going to rely on negative total log-likelihood of data given parameters and will try to minimize that value. Total negative log-likelihood denoted as J is defined in Eq. 8. In simple terms, the total likelihood of the data is the product of the probabilities of the actual observations given the parameters of Elo. Negative log-likelihood is the negative sum of the logarithms of the probabilities of actual observations. Here, p_t – is the probability (expected value) of the observation being the correct response at time t and is equivalent to p_{ij} in Eq. 1. Also, m_t – a logit form of the expected performance – would be equivalent to m_{ij} from Eq. 3.

$$J = -ln(L_{tot}) = -\sum_{t=1}^{T} (o_t ln(p_t) + (1 - o_t) ln(1 - p_t)) \tag{8}$$

4.2 General Partial Derivative

Partial derivative of J with respect to λ_m assumes the form shown in Eq. 9. Depending on how m_t is defined in a particular variant of Elo, the $\partial m_t / \partial \lambda_m$ would change. As a simplification, we would write $o_t - \sigma(m_t)$ or $o_t - p_t$ as δ_t – the prediction error at time t and rewrite Eq. 9 as shown in Eq. 10.

$$\frac{\partial J}{\partial \lambda_m} = -\sum_{t=1}^{T}\left(\frac{o_t}{p_t}\frac{\partial p_t}{\partial \lambda_m} - \frac{1-o_t}{1-p_t}\frac{\partial p_t}{\partial \lambda_m}\right)$$
$$= -\sum_{t=1}^{T}\left(\left[\frac{o_t}{p_t} - \frac{1-o_t}{1-p_t}\right]\frac{\partial p_t}{\partial \lambda_m}\right)$$
$$= -\sum_{t=1}^{T}\left(\frac{o_t - p_t}{p_t(1-p_t)}\frac{\partial p_t}{\partial \lambda_m}\right)$$
$$using \frac{\partial p_t}{\partial \lambda_m} = \frac{\partial \sigma(m_t)}{\partial \lambda_m} = \sigma(m_t)\left(1-\sigma(m_t)\right)\frac{\partial m_t}{\partial \lambda_m}$$
$$= -\sum_{t=1}^{T}\left(\frac{o_t - \sigma(m_t)}{\sigma(m_t)(1-\sigma(m_t))}\sigma(m_t)\left(1-\sigma(m_t)\right)\frac{\partial m_t}{\partial \lambda_m}\right)$$
$$= -\sum_{t=1}^{T}\left(o_t - \sigma(m_t)\right)\frac{\partial m_t}{\partial \lambda_m} \tag{9}$$
$$\frac{\partial J}{\partial \lambda_m} = -\sum_{t=1}^{T}\delta_t\frac{\partial m_t}{\partial \lambda_m} \tag{10}$$

4.3 Detailed Partial Derivatives

The Elo variant **E1** accounts for unidimensional student ability s_i and unidimensional item difficulty b_j. In order to bridge the notation defining Elo in Eqs. 4–7 to indexing data by time slice t, we define functions $g_i(t)$ and $g_j(t)$ that, for a given data point t produce the respective student and item indexes i and j.

Let's now define how the data points of the same student or item are counted. Function $c_i(t)$ and function $c_j(t)$ produce the count of data points before time t belonging to, respectively, student i and item j. Let's also define indexing functions $r_i(t)$ and $r_j(t)$ that, for a data point t, gives the time slice of the data point when a student or an item were seen last. Thus, for example, $r_i(t) < t$ is the prior data point corresponding to student $g_i(t)$. Refer to the first eight columns of Table 1 for an example that covers all of the indexes we talked about thus far. There, t, $g_i(t)$, and $g_j(t)$ – are given; the rest – follow from the definitions.

Given the above definitions, for Elo variant **E1** (simplest student-item Elo) the expected logit-scale value of student's performance is given in Eq. 11a. Note that the expected value is defined by using prior estimates of student ability s_i and item difficulty b_j. The initial values of student ability and item difficulty are given in Eqs. 11c and 11d for the top cases when the respective opportunity counts are 0's.

The rules of updating s_i and b_j upon processing data point t in the bottom cases of Eqs. 11c and 11d, where the respective $c_\bullet$ counts are non-zero. Computation of the the gradient of the negative log-likelihood of the data given sensitivity K is in Eq. 11e. An example of updating rating and gradient values for Student-Item Single Sensitivity Elo based on is in Table 1 in columns 9

$$
\begin{aligned}
i &= g_i(t), \text{ index of student for row } t \\
j &= g_j(t), \text{ index of item for row } t \\
r_i(l) &= r_i(g_i(l)), \text{ time student } i \text{ was seen prior to time } l \\
r_j(l) &= r_j(g_j(l)), \text{ time item } j \text{ was seenprior to time } l \\
c_i &= c_i(g_i(l)), \text{ count of times student } i \text{ seen prior to time } l \\
c_j &= c_j(g_j(l)), \text{ count of times item } j \text{ seen prior to time } l \\
m_t &= s_i - b_j && \text{(11a)} \\
\delta_t &= o_t - \sigma(m_t) && \text{(11b)} \\
s_i &= \begin{cases} 0 & \text{if } c_i = 0 \\ s_i + K \cdot \delta_t & \text{if } c_i > 0 \end{cases} && \text{(11c)} \\
b_j &= \begin{cases} 0 & \text{if } c_j = 0 \\ b_j - K \cdot \delta_t & \text{if } c_j > 0 \end{cases} && \text{(11d)} \\
\frac{\partial J}{\partial K} &= -\sum_{t=1}^{T} \delta_t \cdot \sum_{l=1}^{t} \left[(c_i > 0) \cdot \delta_{r_i(l)} + (c_j > 0) \cdot \delta_{r_j(l)} \right] && \text{(11e)}
\end{aligned}
$$

through 19. If we are using Elo variant E2, and, instead of a single sensitivity K for updating tracking values for both students and items, we were to use separate sensitivities – ${}_iK$ for students and ${}_jK$ for items, the gradients would be as shown in Eqs. 12a–12d.

$$
\begin{aligned}
s_i &= \begin{cases} 0 & \text{if } c_i = 0 \\ s_i + {}_iK \cdot \delta_t & \text{if } c_i > 0 \end{cases} && \text{(12a)} \\
b_j &= \begin{cases} 0 & \text{if } c_j = 0 \\ b_j - {}_jK \cdot \delta_t & \text{if } c_j > 0 \end{cases} && \text{(12b)} \\
\frac{\partial J}{\partial_i K} &= -\sum_{t=1}^{T} \delta_t \cdot \sum_{l=1}^{t} \left[(c_i > 0) \cdot \delta_{r_i(l)} \right] && \text{(12c)} \\
\frac{\partial J}{\partial_j K} &= -\sum_{t=1}^{T} \delta_t \cdot \sum_{l=1}^{t} \left[(c_j > 0) \cdot \delta_{r_j(l)} \right] && \text{(12d)}
\end{aligned}
$$

5 Computational Validation

In order to give the analytical gradients of the described versions of the Elo rating schema approach, we have made comparative runs of Elo schema fitting procedures. We relied on `R` statistical package and its base function `optim` that

Table 1. An example of updating ratings and computing gradient of Student-Item-Single Sensitivity Elo where $K = 0.4$. The total log-likelihood (the sum of J_t's) $J = 5.768$, and the gradient of the K is 0.777.

t	o_t	$s = g_i(t)$	$i = g_j(t)$	$c_i(t)$	$c_j(t)$	$r_i(t)$	$r_j(t)$	s_1	s_2	s_3	b_1	b_2	b_3	p_t	J_t	$\frac{\partial J_t}{\partial K}$
0								0.000	0.000	0.000	0.000	0.000	0.000			
1	0	1	1	0	0	0	0	−0.200			0.200			0.500	0.693	0.000
2	0	1	2	1	0	1	0	−0.380				0.180		0.450	0.598	−0.225
3	1	2	1	0	1	0	1		0.220		−0.020			0.450	0.798	0.275
4	0	2	2	1	1	3	2		0.016			0.384		0.510	0.713	0.051
5	0	1	3	2	0	2	0	−0.543					0.162	0.406	0.521	−0.386
6	1	1	3	3	1	5	5	−0.275					−0.105	0.331	1.106	1.180
7	0	3	1	0	2	0	3			−0.202	0.182			0.505	0.703	0.025
8	1	2	3	2	2	4	6		0.204				−0.293	0.530	0.634	−0.142

implements the BFGS algorithm [12]. Instead of the BFGS algorithm, we could have chosen gradient descent or conjugate gradient descent or any other method that would rely on log-likelihood and gradient. Instead of focusing on *the* algorithm, we picked *an* algorithm and controlled for that choice.

For all versions of the Elo, we implemented objective functions computing negative log-likelihood from the data given the parameter(s) and the gradient of the parameters. Since `optim` function relies on natively compiled code written in `C/C++`, we implemented the objective function (negative log-likelihood) and gradient computations in `C/C++` as well. Thus, the relative speeds of the core BFGS algorithm and the functions are comparable.

BFGS algorithm implemented in `optim` function could run with approximated gradients relying on the objective function alone or with the supplied gradient function. For each test case to be discussed below, we recorded the resulting negative log-likelihood, fit metrics, time, and the number of iterations it took the parameter fitting to complete. In all runs, the sensitivity parameter(s) K were seeded to 0.4.

To better position the results within the relevant literature, we compared the performance of the Elo models in question to Bayesian Knowledge Tracing (BKT) model. Since all of the data we will use comes from the Carnegie Learning Cognitive Tutor that relies on BKT, the choice is natural. To fit BKT models we used a package `hmm-scalable` [23] written in `C/C++` that is known to be efficient in dealing with large datasets of learning data.

6 Data

We used four datasets. Two are made available by LearnLab's LearnSphere repository [10] and two available as part of KDD Cup 2010 [19]. The first LearnSphere dataset **D1** – Geometry Area (1996-97) – consists of 5,104 records belonging to 59 students working through a Geometry Area unit of Carnegie Learning Cognitive Tutor. Students there were interacting with 139 distinct items (problem steps).

The second LearnSphere dataset **D2** [18] has 128,493 rows belonging to 123 students working with a Geometry Area unit of Carnegie Learning Cognitive Tutor. Here, students were interacting with 16,485 distinct items (problem steps). The third dataset **D3** [16] has Carnegie Learning's Cognitive Tutor data collected in the 2008–2009 school year in Algebra I classrooms. This dataset had 8,918,055 transactions of 3,310 students working with 206,596 items (problems). Finally, the fourth dataset **D4** [17] has Carnegie Learning's Cognitive Tutor data collected in the 2008–2009 school year in Bridge to Algebra classrooms. This dataset had 20,012,499 transactions of 6,043 students working with 61,848 items (problems).

One could see that we used problem steps as items in datasets **D1** and **D2**, but problems as items in datasets **D3** and **D4**. There is a much larger ratio of unique problem steps to data points in the latter case and that is why we resorted to using problems. Even after the adjustment, the resulting item per datapoint ratios are rather different – 36.72, 7.79, 43.17, and 323.58 for datasets **D1**, **D2**, **D3**, and **D4** respectively. A different problem step to datapoint ratio is due to a greater variety of content units in datasets **D3** and **D4** that cover the whole year, while datasets **D1** and **D2** only cover one section of content.

7 Results

Table 2 is a summary of the comparative runs of fitting the two versions of the Elo rating schema and one regular BKT model to each dataset. The table is ordered by the dataset (**D1**, **D2**, **D3**, and **D4**), the Elo version (**E1** and **E2**), and BKT model comes after Elo models for every dataset.

The first thing to note is that both the negative log-likelihood and the reached parameter values are quite close across all 8 pairwise comparisons. The same is especially true for statistical fitness metrics – accuracy and RMSE – the difference is always in the third or fourth decimal digit. The second thing we can note is that the use of the analytical gradient results in longer run time for datasets **D1** and **D2**, but shorter time run for the datasets **D3** and **D4**. This could be due to the effect of the size – larger datasets do not incur as much relative computational overhead. When dividing the overall run time by the number of iterations[1] the relative speed of the analytical gradients is consistently higher.

If we look at single vs. double sensitivity Elo, we notice that, in terms of the negative log-likelihood, a 2-sensitivity model has a slight edge. However, in terms of fit metrics – accuracy and RMSE – the differences aren't so pronounced. In terms of time, not surprisingly, the 2-sensitivity Elo takes longer to fit.

[1] Since `optim` function does not output iterations explicitly, we have substituted iterations count with the sum of the number of times objective function and gradient were executed – both required a pass over the dataset.

Table 2. Comprative performace of approximated and analytical gradients when fitting the two Elo variants and BKT.

Model	Data	Grad.-s	Neg. LL	RMSE	Acc.	Param.(s)	Iter.	Tm., s	Tm./It.
E1	D1	Approx.	2639	0.4139	0.7453	0.3583	19	0.022	0.0011
E1	D1	Analyt.	2640	0.4140	0.7467	0.3701	60	0.035	0.0006
E2	D1	Approx.	2634	0.4137	0.7443	0.2619, 0.4427	25	0.029	0.0012
E2	D1	Analyt.	2634	0.4138	0.7437	0.2603, 0.4717	76	0.047	0.0006
BKT	D1	Yes	2537	0.4034	0.7663	-	-	0.099	-
E1	D2	Approx.	27930	0.2417	0.9299	1.0431	38	0.423	0.0111
E1	D2	Analyt.	27957	0.2420	0.9298	0.9381	63	0.687	0.0109
E2	D2	Approx.	27269	0.2412	0.9283	0.4128, 1.5169	50	0.738	0.0148
E2	D2	Analyt.	27270	0.2411	0.9283	0.4188, 1.5333	137	1.339	0.0098
BKT	D2	Yes	29921	0.2500	0.9291	-	-	0.504	-
E1	D3	Approx.	3447761	0.3422	0.8538	0.1282	45	22.780	0.5062
E1	D3	Analyt.	3450255	0.3422	0.8538	0.0986	49	17.404	0.3552
E2	D3	Approx.	3437226	0.3417	0.8539	0.1965, 0.0340	72	40.827	0.5670
E2	D3	Analyt.	3440697	0.3421	0.8540	0.1601, 0.0789	152	60.354	0.3971
BKT	D3	Yes	3412619	0.3389	0.8572	-	-	46.237	-
E1	D4	Approx.	7108867	0.3263	0.8653	0.1212	62	53.871	0.8689
E1	D4	Analyt.	7108948	0.3263	0.8653	0.1171	47	38.136	0.8114
E2	D4	Approx.	7101767	0.3261	0.8654	0.1697, 0.0734	77	98.708	1.2819
E2	D4	Analyt.	7111965	0.3264	0.8652	0.1071, 0.1267	68	65.542	0.9638
BKT	D4	Yes	6906909	0.3178	0.8722	-	-	110.052	-

Together with Elo performance, for every dataset, we included the performance of a fit BKT model. Across the four datasets, it is not possible to determine a clear winner. In some cases, BKT has the edge in terms of shorter running time but loses slightly on the accuracy. We were especially happy that Elo *holds its ground* well on the large datasets **D3** and **D4**.

8 Conclusions

In this paper, we have discussed an approach to finding optimal parameters for Elo rating schema using analytically derived gradients. To the best of our knowledge, this is the first attempt to derive analytical gradients for Elo and fit it as a machine learning model. We were primarily interested in the [relative] speed of the search for the best-fitting parameter and how close are the achieved log-likelihoods of the analytical and approximated gradient approaches. When comparing approximated and analytical gradients, it is expected to see differences in convergence and even statistical fit, the latter being of slightly elevated importance. The result we obtained should not be taken as a hard conclusion. In order to draw inferences, one should run series of cross-validations instead of a single fit of the modal to the whole dataset.

While we were fitting Elo parameters, we controlled for the kernel search algorithm – BFGS. Admittedly, different search algorithms (conjugate gradient descent, Brent, L-BFGS, to name a few) could result in slightly better or worse performance. Although our brief experimentation with conjugate gradient descent did not show any difference in terms of run time and performance.

When it comes to a particular variant of Elo rating schema, we only considered student-item Elo with one or two constant sensitivity of the update (K). There exist far more complex and expressive variants of Elo (see, for example, [20] and [14]) where student tracked values are hierarchical and skill ratings are tracked instead of item ratings. Also, instead of the single sensitivity, authors sometimes use a form of an uncertainty function that diminishes the magnitude of the update to the rating as more data is used to re-compute it. Starting with the derivations in this paper, the analytical gradient approach we presented could be used to formalize those Elo variants as well.

A worked-out analytical gradient for a variant of Elo could be useful in several ways. One might think of an extension where each student receives an individualized weight (say, a multiplier) to go with the sensitivity parameter. Having worked out an analytical gradient, one might regularise these individual weights treating them as a random factor. Of course, individualized weights would have to change as a function of time just as student abilities and item difficulties do in Elo.

Also, Elo functionality could be employed for infusing the self-adjusting nature of tracked ratings onto other models. For example, an iBKT model [23] is not operationalizable to this day since student-level parameters need to be re-fit frequently using a lot of data. Treating student-level features as ratings updated using Elo-like procedure could make such Elo-infused iBKT operationalizable by definition.

References

1. Cen, H., Koedinger, K., Junker, B.: Comparing two IRT models for conjunctive skills. In: Woolf, B.P., Aïmeur, E., Nkambou, R., Lajoie, S. (eds.) ITS 2008. LNCS, vol. 5091, pp. 796–798. Springer, Heidelberg (2008). https://doi.org/10.1007/978-3-540-69132-7_111
2. Corbett, A.T., Anderson, J.R.: Knowledge tracing: modeling the acquisition of procedural knowledge. User Model. User-Adap. Inter. **4**(4), 253–278 (1994)
3. Elo, A.E.: The Rating of Chessplayers. Past and Present. Arco Publishers, New York (1978)
4. Feng, M., Heffernan, N., Koedinger, K.: Addressing the assessment challenge with an online system that tutors as it assesses. User Model. User-Adap. Inter. **19**(3), 243–266 (2009)
5. Franz, M., McLean, E., Tung, J., Altmann, J., Alberts, S.: Self-organizing dominance hierarchies in a wild primate population. Proc. R. Soc. B: Biol. Sci. **282**(1814), 20151512 (2015)
6. Glickman, M.E.: Parameter estimation in large dynamic paired comparison experiments. J. Roy. Stat. Soc.: Ser. C (Appl. Stat.) **48**(3), 377–394 (1999)

7. Herbrich, R., Minka, T., Graepel, T.: Trueskill^{TM}: a bayesian skill rating system. In: Advances in Neural Information Processing Systems, pp. 569–576 (2007)
8. Hofman, A., Jansen, B., de Mooij, S., Stevenson, C., van der Maas, H.: A solution to the measurement problem in the idiographic approach using computer adaptive practicing. J. Intell. **6**(1), 14 (2018)
9. Ivanovo State Power University: Ritm-rating. a system of tracking student ratings. http://ritm.ispu.ru/old/help
10. Koedinger, K., Baker, R., Cunningham, K., Skogsholm, A., Leber, B., Stamper, J.: A Data Repository for the EDM Community: The PSLC DataShop. CRC Press, Boca Raton (2010)
11. Van der Linden, W., Hambleton, R.: Handbook of Modern Item Response Theory. Springer, New York (1997). https://doi.org/10.1007/978-1-4757-2691-6
12. Nash, J.C.: Compact Numerical Methods for Computers: Linear Algebra and Function Minimisation. CRC press, Boca Raton (1990)
13. Nižnan, J., Pelánek, R., Rihák, J.: Student models for prior knowledge estimation. In: Proceedings of the 8th International Conference on Educational Data Mining, pp. 109–116. ACM, New York (2015)
14. Pelánek, R.: Applications of the Elo rating system in adaptive educational systems. Comput. Educ. **98**, 169–179 (2016)
15. Silver, N., Fischer-Baum, R.: How we calculate NBA Elo ratings, 21 May 2015
16. Stamper, J., Niculescu-Mizil, A., Ritter, S., Gordon, G., Koedinger, K.: Algebra i 2008–2009. challenge data set from KDD cup 2010 educational data mining challenge (2010). http://pslcdatashop.web.cmu.edu/KDDCup/downloads.jsp
17. Stamper, J., Niculescu-Mizil, A., Ritter, S., Gordon, G., Koedinger, K.: Bridge to algebra 2008–2009. challenge data set from KDD cup 2010 educational data mining challenge. http://pslcdatashop.web.cmu.edu/KDDCup/downloads.jsp (2010)
18. Stamper, J.C., Koedinger, K.R.: Human-machine student model discovery and improvement using datashop. In: Biswas, G., Bull, S., Kay, J., Mitrovic, A. (eds.) AIED 2011. LNCS (LNAI), vol. 6738, pp. 353–360. Springer, Heidelberg (2011). https://doi.org/10.1007/978-3-642-21869-9_46
19. Stamper, J., Pardos, Z.A.: The 2010 KDD cup competition dataset: engaging the machine learning community in predictive learning analytics. J. Learn. Analytics **3**(2), 312–316 (2016)
20. Von Davier, A., Deonovic, B., Polyak, S., Woo, A.: Applications of the Elo rating system in adaptive educational systems. Front. Psychol. (2019, in press)
21. Wilson, M., De Boeck, P.: Descriptive and explanatory item response models. In: De Boeck, P., Wilson, M. (eds) Explanatory Item Response Models. Statistics for Social Science and Public Policy. Springer, New York (2004). https://doi.org/10.1007/978-1-4757-3990-9_2
22. Wood, B.: Enemydown uses Elo in its counterstrike: source multilplayer ladders, 12 June 2009
23. Yudelson, M.V., Koedinger, K.R., Gordon, G.J.: Individualized bayesian knowledge tracing models. In: Lane, H.C., Yacef, K., Mostow, J., Pavlik, P. (eds.) AIED 2013. LNCS (LNAI), vol. 7926, pp. 171–180. Springer, Heidelberg (2013). https://doi.org/10.1007/978-3-642-39112-5_18
24. Нуждин, В. Н., Шишкин, В. П.: РИТМ в вопросах и ответах. Министерство науки, высшей школы и технической политики Российской Федерации, Комитет по высшей школе, Ивановский энергетический институт, Иваново. (1992)

Identifying Learning Activity Sequences that Are Associated with High Intention-Fulfillment in MOOCs

Eyal Rabin[1,2](✉), Vered Silber-Varod[1], Yoram M. Kalman[1], and Marco Kalz[2,3]

[1] The Open University of Israel, 1 University Road, Ra'anana, Israel
{eyalra, vereds, yoramka}@openu.ac.il
[2] UNESCO Chair of Open Education, Faculty Management, Science and Technologies, Open University of the Netherlands, Valkenburgerweg 177, 6419 AT Heerlen, The Netherlands
kalz@ph-heidelberg.de
[3] Heidelberg University of Education, Im Neuenheimer Feld 561, 69120 Heidelberg, Germany

Abstract. Learners join MOOCs (Massive Open Online Courses) with a variety of intentions. The fulfillment of these initial intentions is an important success criterion in self-paced and open courses. Using post course self-reported data enabled us to divide the participants to those who fulfilled the initial intentions (high-IF) and those who did not fulfill their initial intentions (low-IF). We used methods adapted from natural language processing (NLP) to analyze the learning paths of 462 MOOC participants and to identify activities and activity sequences of participants in the two groups. Specifically, we used n-gram analysis to identify learning activity sequences and keyness analysis to identify prominent learning activities. These measures enable us to identify the differences between the two groups. Differences can be seen at the level of single activities, but major differences were found when longer n-grams were used. The high-IF group showed more consistency and less divergent learning behavior. High-IF was associated, among other things, with study patterns of sequentially watching video lectures. Theoretical and practical suggestions are introduced in order to help MOOC developers and participants to fulfill the participants' learning intentions.

Keywords: Massive Open Online Courses · Intention-fulfilment · Keyness · N-gram · Learning activity sequences

1 Introduction

1.1 Participants Retention and Completion in MOOCs

Massive Open Online Courses (MOOCs) demonstrate the potential of scaling higher education by means of digital media and the Internet. More than 100 million participants signed up to 11,400 courses from 900 universities around the globe [27]. MOOCs

M. Scheffel et al. (Eds.): EC-TEL 2019, LNCS 11722, pp. 224–235, 2019.
https://doi.org/10.1007/978-3-030-29736-7_17

enable participants of different academic backgrounds to study at any time and in any place, to enhance their learning experience and to gain important 21st-century skills free or at significantly lower costs. The high potential of MOOCs has been criticized due to low retention and completion rates [10, 22] that often drop below 10% of the participants who registered to the course [5, 13, 18].

1.2 Intention-Fulfillment

Some researchers have questioned whether completion rates and completion certificates are the appropriate measures for evaluating the success of this new form of lifelong learning [12, 21]. Their basic claim was that the success of lifelong learning in MOOCs should be evaluated not through traditional instructor-focused measures such as dropout rates and earning of completion certificates, but rather through learner-centered measures that take into account the informal nature of MOOC learning. One such measure is intention-fulfillment (IF) which measures the extent to which the learners fulfilled the initial intentions they had when accessing the course. This measure takes into account the personal objectives that the learners intend to achieve, rather than external success criteria [12]. In MOOCs and in other forms of open education, students may enroll with different intentions that effect their learning behavior [17, 19, 30]. From that point of view, a successful learning experience can take a variety of forms ranging from viewing a single lecture, attaining a specific skill, or studying a topic of interest, to studying a whole course and fulfilling all of its formal requirements. Thus, the participants′ intentions and their fulfillment should take center stage when evaluating the participants′ success in the course.

1.3 Learning Activity Sequences

Learning behavior in MOOCs is mostly visible through logs, which record access and usage patterns of the different course resources (e.g. video lecture, quiz, etc.). Many MOOC studies are based on simple access logs, counting each time the learner accessed or used a course resource, but ignored the order of the activities and their sequential nature [16]. Taking into consideration only the number of activities that the participants performed and ignoring the sequence of activities, provides only a partial picture. For example, as demonstrated by Li et al. [16], if we consider three imaginary participants who watched videos (V) and answered quiz questions (Q), one of them can watch all the videos and then answer the quizzes (V-V-V-Q-Q-Q) while another participant might first try to answer the quiz questions and only then watch the video lectures (Q-Q-Q-V-V-V). A third participant might follow each video by a quiz (V-Q-V-Q-V-Q). Although all three fictional participants watched three videos and answered three quizzes, their learning paths, or sequences, are fundamentally different.

Several researchers attempted to understand differences between the learning paths of MOOC participants who passed or failed a course. It was found that learners who passed the course followed a path that had different characteristics than those who did not pass the course [7, 11]. For example, replaying videos more than once, and watching a relatively high percentage of the course videos, were positively correlated with finishing the MOOC [28]. On the other hand, Van den Beemt, Buijs and Van der

Aalst [29] found that successful students exhibit a more steady learning behavior and that this behavior is highly related to regularly watching course successive videos in batches.

Several studies used natural language processing (NLP) features in order to study MOOC participants dropout and retention mainly by studying the language students use [6, 14, 23]. However, we found only few studies that applied NLP methods such as n-gram analysis, to study learner activity sequences [16]. None of those studies had used NLP methods in order to predict subjective success outcomes in MOOCs such as intention-fulfilment. In this study, we apply methods that originate from the NLP realm, to analyze learning activities and learning activity sequences and to compare those activities and activities sequences between participants who report high-IF and participants who report low-IF.

2 Method

2.1 Sample

In the current study, we used clickstream data gathered from log files of 462 participants in a MOOC teaching the subject English as a Second Language (ESL) to identify the learning process of the participants. The data collection for the current study was carried out between July 2016 to February 2018. During this period, the participants were able to join and leave the offered MOOC whenever they liked to.

2.2 Course Activities and Their Annotations

MOOCs usually comprise of modules such as video lectures, quizzes and other resources [15]. The manner in which students interact with these course resources are considered conceptualizations of their higher-order thinking, which lead to knowledge construction [4]. In this ESL-MOOC, the participants were able to choose ten different types of activities in any order, place and time. The course was arranged by units. Each unit contained an introductory page (I). This page pointed participants to several additional resources: a list of learning strategy videos (S), a PDF reading comparison text that is used throughout the unit (P), a recommended learning track (T), several lessons (L) quizzes (Q) and a final exam (E). Each of the lessons comprises of a single video (V) and links to specific learning strategy videos (S). Participants who watched videos could click the video play/pause button according to their personal progress during the video lecture. Although the course does not provide academic credit, the participants could get a participation badge (B) if they answered all the questions in the quizzes and achieved a predefined minimum score. The participants were also able to watch the list of rights (R) (credits) of the course materials. In total, we harvested 61,713 activities. It is important to note that the logs only recorded the clicks, and did not record other activities (e.g. reading text, feedback on quizzes). Table 1 summarized the courses' activities, their codes, and a short description of each.

Table 1. Course activities – codes and description.

Activity	Code	Description
Badge	B	A page that enables the participant to see their achievements during the course
Exam	E	Self-administered final exam that summarizes the entire course
Introductory page	I	The participant accessed an introductory page of the course
Lesson	L	The participant entered a page that includes a video lecture, a list of skills that will be taught in the unit and relevant learning strategies (S)
Pdf text	P	The participant accessed a reading comprehension PDF text that was used in the lesson
Quiz	Q	Closed questions with immediate feedback. The participant had been able to answer the same quiz more than one time
Rights	R	A page that includes the credits and rights to course materials
Learning strategy	S	The participant watched short and focused videos dealing with learning strategies
Track	T	The participant accessed the page that provides the recommended learning track of a lesson
Video play/pause	V	Each time a participant pressed the play/pause button in a video lecture

2.3 Computational Tool Kit for Sequence Analysis

Preprocessing: In order to use the NLP tools to analyze learning sequences, each participant's sequence of learning activities was coded as mentioned above in Table 1.

For the sequence analysis, we used Antconc 3.5.7, a multiplatform toolkit developed for carrying out corpus linguistics research and data-driven learning [1, 2]. Specifically, we used two NLP methods: n-gram tool, and keyness tool.

The n-gram tool allows us to find common "expressions", i.e., common sequences of activities, and their transitional probabilities. In the current study, the n-gram analysis consisted of uni- bi-, tri-, and four-grams calculations by Antconc. For each group separately (high-IF or low-IF), we sorted the n_i-gram lists according to their probability values. We then excluded activities with probability below 0.1, and calculated two measures:

1. The *relative frequency* of each n_i-gram sequence was calculated by dividing the absolute frequency of that n_i-gram sequence of activities by the total number of n_i-grams in that group. For example, the bi-gram sequence V-V occurred 6,767 times in the low-IF group, which was divided by 25,742 (total number of bi-grams in that group), resulting in a relative frequency of 26%.
2. *Participation range* was calculated by dividing the number of participants that performed each n_i-gram sequence of activities by the total number of participants in that group. Thus, the participation range is the relative distribution (entropy) of each n_i-gram sequence. For example, 186 participants out of the 231 participants in the low-IF group performed the V-V sequence. Therefore, the relative distribution of this sequence is 81%.

The keyness analysis was carried out in order to identify the activities that are unusually frequent (or infrequent) in one group in comparison with the activities in the other group. The keyness analysis provides an indication of a keyword's importance as a content descriptor in a given corpus relative to a reference corpus [3]. "A word is said to be "key" if [...] its frequency in the text when compared with its frequency in a reference corpus is such that the statistical probability as computed by an appropriate procedure is smaller than or equal to a p-value specified by the user" [25]. The statistical significance of keyness is calculated by using the value of log likelihood [2, 26] and the size of the differences is calculated by effect size [9].

2.4 Dependent Variable

The fulfilment of the initial intention (IF) was measured by 4 items on 7-point Likert scale ranging from 1 'totally don't agree' to 7 'strongly agree' (e.g. 'I achieved my personal learning goals by participating in this MOOC', 'the MOOC met my expectations'; Cronbach's alpha = .89). The participants were split into two groups according to their post-course IF level divided by the sample median (med = 4.75). Two hundred and twenty participants had been identified as high-IF and 242 participants had been identified as a low-IF. Participants that carried out less than four activities were not included in the sample, leaving a total of 445 participants – 214 with high-IF and 231 with low-IF. Due to the anonymization process, no demographic information was available about the participants.

3 Results

In the following section, we first present the differences between the two groups in total activities per participant – high and low IF. We then present the learning sequences findings using the n-gram and keyness measurements.

Table 2 shows the descriptive statistics of the number of activities per participant in each group. In total, 61,713 activities were analyzed (high-IF = 35,790; low-IF = 25,973). The non-parametric Mann-Whitney U test indicated that the number of activities per participant was significantly higher for the high-IF group compare to the low-IF group ($U = 17223.5$, $p < .001$). In order to check if there are differences between the two groups in their level of heterogeneity, we checked whether the standard deviations in the number of activities are significantly different between the low and the high IF groups. Levene's test of the homogeneity of group variances showed significant difference ($F_{(1,443)} = 1.46$, $p < .05$). Although on average the number of activities in the high-IF is higher compared to the low-IF group, the standard deviation of the number of activities and the maximum activities per participant are both higher in the low-IF group compared to the high-IF group (see Table 2).

3.1 N-gram Analysis

In order to identify the learning sequences of the two groups, we used n-gram analysis to compare sequences of activities (activities' relative frequency analysis) and their distribution among the participants (range analysis). The two analyses are complementary to each other. While the activities' relative frequency analysis answers the question of what is the relative prevalence of an activity or sequence of activities in a specific group of participants, the range analysis answers the question, what is the percentage of participants that participated in an activity or sequence of activities?

The number of the unique tokens in the unigram analysis is 10 (representing the 10 codes of activities), the bigrams – 95, the trigrams – 682 and the four-grams – 3,134.

Figures 1a–d present the results of the activities' relative frequency n-gram analysis and Figs. 1e–h present the results of the range n-gram analysis. In both cases, only activities with probability above 0.1 were included.

Table 2. Descriptive statistics of the number of activities per participant and the activity frequencies in the high and low IF groups.

	Low-IF group	High-IF group
Num. of participants	231	214
Mean num. of activities	112.44	167.24
Mean rank of activities	190.56	258.02
Median num. of activities	50.00	122.50
S.D. of activities	192.35	159.16
Maximum activities	1776	857
V	12,426 (47.84%)	19,344 (54.05%)
T	4,255 (16.38%)	5,127 (14.33%)
Q	3,170 (12.20%)	3,535 (9.88%)
P	2,222 (8.56%)	2,795 (7.81%)
I	1,687 (6.50%)	1,911 (5.34%)
L	1,276 (4.91%)	1,640 (4.58%)
E	567 (2.18%)	857 (2.39%)
S	305 (1.17%)	493 (1.38%)
R	53 (0.02%)	70 (0.20%)
B	12 (0.05%)	18 (0.05%)

Figure 1a presents the comparison of the unique unigrams in both groups (the figure represents the information in Table 2). The video activity (V) is more salient in the high-IF group compared to the low-IF one. On the other hand, the track (T), lessons (L), quiz (Q) and exam (E) activities have higher occurrences in the low-IF group compared to the high-IF group.

Figure 1b presents a difference in the V-V bigram between the low-IF and high-IF groups that is larger than the differences in the other bigrams. The participants in the high-IF group sequentially press the video play/pause button more than the participants in the low-IF group. Interestingly, five of the bigrams (Q-Q, P-Q, S-L, V-L, and T-Q) are unique to the low-IF group.

Figure 1c presents the trigrams activities that show a similar pattern to the bigrams, with more participants in the high-IF group that sequentially press the play/pause button video (V-V-V). While looking at the sequences that are unique to one of the groups, it can be seen that in the low-IF group, there is a unique sequence of practicing the final exam (E-E-E), a sequence that does not exist in the high-IF group.

The four-gram figure (Fig. 1d) presents a prominent presence of the high-IF group compared to a minor presence of the low-IF group. The participants in the high-IF group made more four-gram sequences of video watching (V-V-V-V), and sequences of video watching after watching the recommended learning track (T-V-V-V), accessing the lessons (L-V-V-V), answering a quiz (Q-V-V-V) accessing the reading comprehension text (P-V-V-V), self-practicing the final exam (E-V-V-V), etc.

The results of the range n-gram analysis show similar trends. The range shows the percentage of participants who actually did each activity (or sequence of activities) out of the overall activities (or sequence of activities) in each group. The calculation of the range enables us to calculate the relative distribution (entropy) of each activity. Figure 1a shows that, in the high-IF group, four activities have been performed by above 80% of participants, while in the low-IF group only two activities were carried out by 80% or more of participants. Two activities in the high-IF group were performed by 50% to 79% of the participants compared to five activities in this range of participation in the low-IF group. In both groups, the three activities - S, R, and B - were carried out by less than 40%. A higher percentage of participants in the high-IF group pressed the play/pause video button (V), accessed the quizzes (Q), accessed the reading comprehension PDF text (P), accessed the introductory page of the course (I), and accessed to the video lessons dealing with learning strategies (S). No differences were found between the two groups in the range of participants who accessed the recommended learning track (T), the self-practice exam (E), the right of use (R), and the achievements page (B).

The differences in the range parameters between the two groups increase when we look at the bi-, tri- and four-grams (Fig. 1f–h). This is evident by the fact that the longer the n-gram, the higher the participation range in the high-IF group compared to the low-IF group. The low-IF participants, on the other hand, performed five unique bigram sequences, one unique tri-gram sequence, and no unique four-gram sequence of activities. The decrease in unique sequences and the fact that we only analyzed n-grams with relatively high probability (>0.1), means that the low-IF participants use more varied sequences by less and less participants. This also means that in the range parameter, the high-IF group behaves more consistently and that more participants behave similarly (lower entropy).

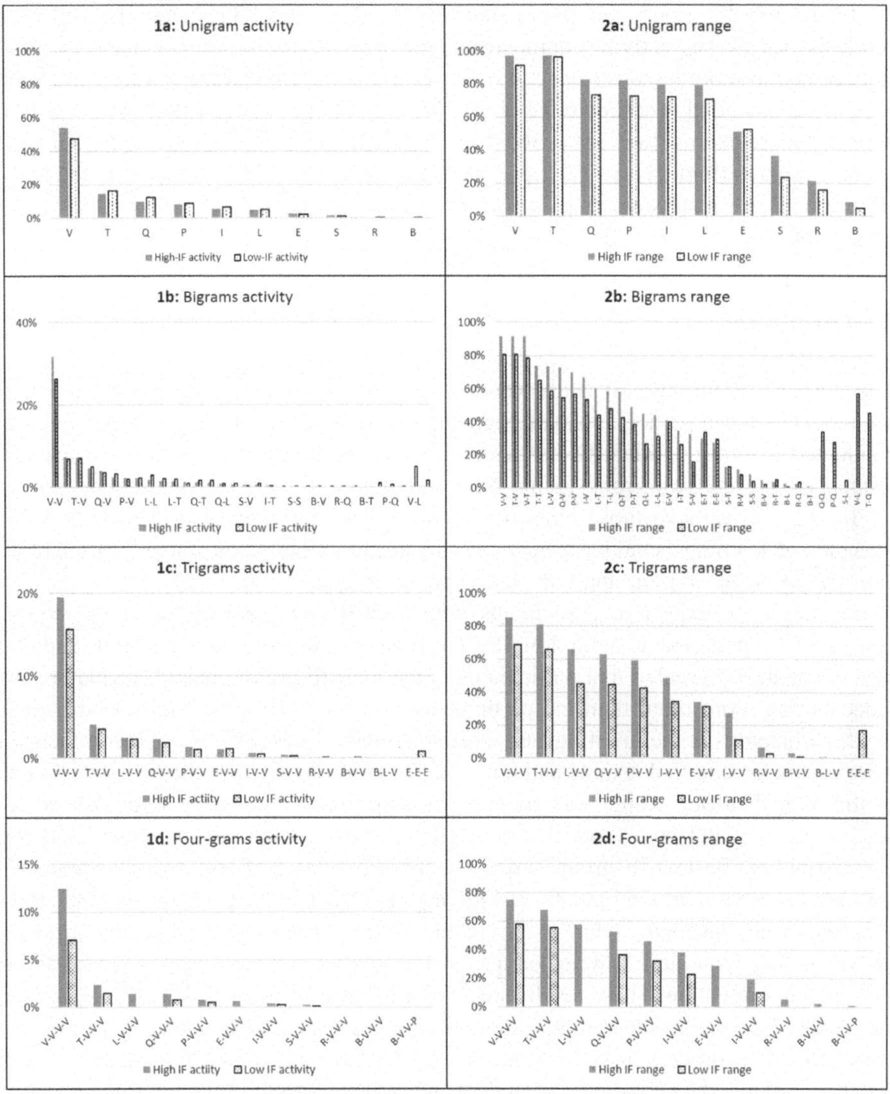

Fig. 1. (a–h) Relative frequency of activities (a–d) and relative range distribution (e–h) among the two groups in uni- bi- tri- and four- grams.

3.2 Keyness Results

Video play/pause activity (V) was identified as a key activity in the high-IF group compared to the low-IF group. Participants in the high-IF group pressed the play/pause video (V) button 1.28 more than the participants in the low-IF group (log(.25) = 232.11, $p < .001$, Effect Size = 1.28).

In the low-IF group, we found that lessons (L), track (T), exam (E) and quiz (Q) activities are key activities compared to the high-IF group. Participants at the low-IF accessed to more lessons (log(.25) = 84.28, $p < .001$, Effect Size = 1.27), followed more recommended learning track (log(.25) = 49.44, $p < .001$, Effect Size = 1.71), accessed more exams (log(.25) = 36.64, $p < .001$, Effect Size = 1.23) and participated in more quizzes (log(.25) = 11.21, $p < .001$, Effect Size = 1.10) compared to the high-IF group. These results are reflected in the relative frequency unigram analysis mentioned above.

4 Discussion

The purpose of the current study was to compare behavioral patterns and learning sequences between participants with high and low IF in a MOOC. The comparison was conducted in order to identify behavioral differences between activities and activity sequences of these two groups using NLP techniques, namely n-gram and keyness.

In order to achieve those aims, we compared the differences in the relative frequencies of learning behavior sequences and in the participation range (participation entropy) by using n-gram analyses and keyness analysis.

As might be expected, participants with high-IF are more active in the course compared to participants with low-IF. Furthermore, the unigram analysis and the keyness analysis revealed that participants in the high-IF group pressed the play/pause video button more often than the participants in the low-IF group did. On the other hand, participants in the low-IF group more frequently accessed lessons, recommended learning tracks, and took exams and quizzes. These results suggest that the participants in the high-IF group were more focused on acquiring knowledge, as evidenced by watching the video lectures, which contained the course content. On the other hand, the participants in the low-IF group showed a more diverse and less orderly ("messy") learning behavior. Our interpretation of these patterns is that the participants in the low-IF group were less sure what to do in the course. They spent more attention on understanding what and how to learn, and on quizzes and final exams, and less on knowledge acquisition. These results are similar to the results by Mukala, Buijs, & Van Der Aalst (2015), who showed that students who passed a Coursera MOOC followed a more structured process in submitting their weekly quizzes until the final quiz and in watching video, when compared to students who did not pass the course. It is important to note that our conceptual replication of the results uses a broader perspective about success and failure in MOOCs. We see that the activities of the participants in the current MOOC can predict more subjective success outcomes, namely intention-fulfilment.

The n-gram analysis enabled us to compare the most probable sequences of activities and their distribution among the participants. Although Li et al. [16], showed that the most effective n-gram for predicting students' activity in MOOCs is the tri-gram, our analysis suggests that we can differentiate between the groups even with a shorter string of annotation, meaning a bi-gram. The bigram analysis reveals that the high-IF group was characterized mostly by a two step sequence of the knowledge acquisition activity of watching video lectures sequentially (V-V), while the low-IF group was characterized by diverse bigram activities such as repeating the assessment tasks (Q-Q), moving from the reading comprehension to the quizzes without watching the video lecture (P-Q), moving from the short and focused videos dealing with learning strategies to the lesson (S-L), moving from the video lecture to the lesson (V-L), and moving from the recommended learning track to the quizzes (T-Q). These results are similar to the findings of Van den Beemt et al. [29] who used other success criteria such as passing rates. The researchers showed that regularly watching successive videos in batches leads to high passing rates.

Nevertheless, for the two parameters – activity frequency and participation range – we found that looking at longer n-gram sequences is beneficial in predicting the level of IF. The longer the n-gram, the higher the divergence between the two groups. Moreover, the longer the n-gram, the more prominent are the participants from high-IF group. The results showed that the activities of the high-IF group are more predictable, suggesting that this group behaves more consistently and similarly. When we analyze longer sequences, it is clearer that the participants in the high-IF group are following the designed path, i.e. the learning path suggested by the course designers in this particular MOOC.

Several limitations should be considered. First, we used median splits in order to distinguish between participants with high and low IF. This technique helped us to simplify our analyses and discussion. Recording continuous variables into categorical variables is often criticized due to the rough segmentation of the continuous variable [8], but this simplification was useful in our case. The results showed that we could easily differentiate between, and predict the learning sequences of the different participants. Future work could use a more sensitive segmentation and a larger amount of clusters. Another simplification that was used in this research is the use of only one learner-centered success measure, namely IF. Future research should use additional subjective success measures such as learner satisfaction [21] and perceived achievement [20, 24, 31].

Future research could also look at additional kinds of knowledge acquisition with video lectures. The MOOC studied here offered two kinds of video lectures – content-based lectures (V) and learning strategy lectures (S). As shown in Fig. 1e and f, in the high-IF group, a wider range of participants accessed the learning strategy videos (S) and learning strategy videos following by video lectures watching (S-V) compared to the low-IF group. Further investigation of the effect of using those learning strategy lectures on the level of IF is outside the scope of this study, but could be productive.

5 Conclusions

To conclude, the purpose of the current research was to distinguish between the low and the high IF groups based on their learning behavior. The results suggest that the single activity and sequential behavior of the participants enable us to identify their affiliation group. As has been shown by the keyness analysis, the two groups are different in the pattern of single activities, and bigger differences become apparent in the longer n-grams, both in terms of the relative prevalence of the activity and in terms of the number of participants who performed it. The high-IF group showed more homogeneous behavior. One of the contributions of our study is the feasibility of developing automatic intervention systems, which will analyze learning sequences in real time and identify inconsistent participant behavior, to support the participants in real time. For example, such system could propose a different learning track for learners, depending on their behavioural pattern. Alternatively, learning strategies could be proposed for specific sub-groups supporting their self-regulated learning.

References

1. Anthony, L.: AntConc Help (manual) (2018)
2. Anthony, L.: AntConc (2018). http://www.laurenceanthony.net/software
3. Biber, D., Connor, U., Upton, T.: Discourse on the Move: Using Corpus Analysis to Describe Discourse Structure. John Benjamin, Amsterdam (2007)
4. Chi, M.T.: Self-explaining expository texts: the dual processes of generating inferences and repairing mental models. Adv. Instr. Psychol. **5**, 161–238 (2000)
5. Chuang, I., Ho, A.D.: HarvardX and MITx: Four Years of Open Online Courses - Fall 2012-Summer 2016. SSRN Electron. J. (2016)
6. Crossley, S., Paquette, L., Dascalu, M., McNamara, D.S., Baker, R.S.: Combining click-stream data with NLP tools to better understand MOOC completion. In: Proceedings of the Sixth International Conference on Learning Analytics and Knowledge - LAK 2016, pp. 6–14. ACM Press, New York (2016)
7. Davis, D., Chen, G., Hauff, C., Houben, G.: Gauging MOOC learners' adherence to the designed learning path. In: 9th International Conference on Educational Data Mining, EDM 2016 (2016)
8. DeCoster, J., Gallucci, M., Iselin, A.-M.R.: Best practices for using median splits, artificial categorization, and their continuous alternatives. J. Exp. Psychopathol. **2** (2011). https://doi.org/10.5127/jep.008310
9. Gabrielatos, C., Marchi, A.: Keyness: appropriate metrics and practical issues. In: CADS International Conference, Bologna, Italy (2012)
10. Gardner, J., Brooks, C.: Student success prediction in MOOCs. User Model. User-adapt. Interact. **28**, 127–203 (2018)
11. Guo, P., Reinecke, K.: Demographic differences in how students navigate through MOOCs. In: Proceedings of the First ACM Conference on Learning @ Scale Conference,. pp. 21–30. ACM, New York (2014)
12. Henderikx, M.A., Kreijns, K., Kalz, M.: Refining success and dropout in massive open online courses based on the intention–behavior gap. Distance Educ. **38**, 353–368 (2017)
13. Jordan, K.: Initial trends in enrolment and completion of massive open online courses. Int. Rev. Res. Open Distrib. Learn. **15**, 133–160 (2014)
14. Kim, J., Singh Chaplot, D., Rhim, E.: Predicting student attrition in MOOCs using sentiment analysis and neural networks. In: AIED 2015 Workshop Proceedings (2015)
15. Lackner, E., Kopp, M., Ebner, M.: How to MOOC?–a pedagogical guideline for practitioners. In: Proceedings of the 10th International Scientific Conference on eLearning and Software for Education, Bucharest (2014)
16. Li, X., Wang, T., Wang, H.: Exploring N-gram features in clickstream data for MOOC learning achievement prediction. In: Bao, Z., Trajcevski, G., Chang, L., Hua, W. (eds.) DASFAA 2017. LNCS, vol. 10179, pp. 328–339. Springer, Cham (2017). https://doi.org/10.1007/978-3-319-55705-2_26

17. Littlejohn, A., Hood, N., Milligan, C., Mustain, P.: Learning in MOOCs: motivations and self-regulated learning in MOOCs. Internet High. Educ. **29**, 40–48 (2016)
18. Margaryan, A., Bianco, M., Littlejohn, A.: Instructional quality of Massive Open Online Courses (MOOCs). Comput. Educ. **80**, 77–83 (2015)
19. Onah, D., Sinclair, J., Boyatt, R.: Dropout rates of massive open online courses: behavioural patterns. In: 6th International conference on Education and New Learning, Barcelona, Spain, pp. 5825–5834 (2014)
20. Rabin, E., Silber-Varod, V., Kalman, Y.M.: Using natural language processing techniques to predict perceived achievements in Massive Online Open Courses. In: KM Conference, Warsaw, Poland (2019)
21. Rabin, E., Kalman, Y.M., Kalz, M.: Predicting learner-centered MOOC outcomes: satisfaction and intention-fulfillment. Int. J. Educ. Technol. High. Educ. 16 (2019)
22. Reich, J., Ruipérez-Valiente, J.A.: The MOOC pivot. Science **363**, 130–131 (2019)
23. Robinson, C., Yeomans, M., Reich, J., Hulleman, C., Gehlbach, H.: Forecasting student achievement in MOOCs with natural language processing. In: Proceedings of the Sixth International Conference on Learning Analytics and Knowledge - LAK 2016, pp. 383–387. ACM Press, New York (2016)
24. Ross, J.A.: The reliability, validity, and utility of self-assessment. Pract. Assessment Res. Eval. **11**, 1–13 (2006)
25. Scott, M.: WordSmith Tools Manual (2011)
26. Scott, M., Tribble, C.: Textual Patterns: Key Words and Corpus Analysis in Language Education. Benjamins, Amsterdam (2006)
27. Shah, D.: By The Numbers: MOOCs in 2018 — Class Central. https://www.class-central.com/report/mooc-stats-2018/
28. Sinha, T., Jermann, P., Li, N., Dillenbourg, P.: Your click decides your fate: inferring information processing and attrition behavior from MOOC video clickstream interactions (2014)
29. Van den Beemt, A., Buijs, J., Van der Aalst, W.: Analysing structured learning behaviour in Massive Open Online Courses (MOOCs): an approach based on process mining and clustering. Int. Rev. Res. Open Distrib. Learn. **19** (2018)
30. Wang, Y., Baker, R.: Grit and intention: why do learners complete MOOCs? Int. Rev. Res. Open Distrib. Learn. 19 (2018)
31. Yoon, S., Kim, S., Kang, M.: Predictive power of grit, professor support for autonomy and learning engagement on perceived achievement within the context of a flipped classroom. Act. Learn. High. Educ. (2018)

Teaching Assistants in MOOCs Forums: Omnipresent Interlocutors or Knowledge Facilitators

Anastasios Ntourmas[1(✉)], Nikolaos Avouris[1], Sophia Daskalaki[1], and Yannis Dimitriadis[2]

[1] University of Patras, Patras, Greece
a.ntourmas@upnet.gr, {avouris, sdask}@upatras.gr
[2] Universidad de Valladolid, Valladolid, Spain
yannis@tel.uva.es

Abstract. A major issue that concerns course instructors of massive open online courses (MOOCs) is the low retention ratio of learners. One of the key factors of this problem is the lack of support and interactivity in MOOC discussion forums. The support provided to learners in MOOC forums is critical to retain their motivation. Teaching assistants (TAs) play a crucial role in providing support to learners within the discussion forums, so an interesting research subject is to study the approaches they follow. In this study, we investigate the TAs' instructional approaches through a mixed-methods approach. This has been performed on two MOOCs delivered through the OpenEdX platform. The goal was to assess the main characteristics of their interventions by using an evaluation framework derived from social constructivism theory and to capture the main issues of their approaches. The results of this study reveal that TAs did not promote problem-centered learning and collaboration, and they acted more as 'omniscient interlocutors' rather than as facilitators. Thus, these issues should be addressed, through either a guided learning design process by the instructors, and support to the TAs, regarding their intervention strategy in forums.

Keywords: MOOC · Discussion forum · Learners support · Instructional design · Social constructivism

1 Introduction

Massive Open Online Courses (MOOCs) attract great numbers of learners due to the wide range of opportunities they offer for online learning. Despite their growing popularity and their large enrollment, a critical issue they face is the high learner dropout rate, which puts the efficacy of MOOCs into question [1]. In their survey, Hone and El Said [2] investigated the main factors that affect learner retention in MOOCs. It was found that effective interaction with the instructional staff may affect learner retention directly, while the quality of course content seems to affect learners through its perceived effectiveness. Several other studies also address the problem of learner

M. Scheffel et al. (Eds.): EC-TEL 2019, LNCS 11722, pp. 236–250, 2019.
https://doi.org/10.1007/978-3-030-29736-7_18

retention and reveal that a key factor to this issue is the lack of adequate support and interactivity in the discussion forum [3, 4].

The discussion forum is a crucial part of a MOOC platform. Through asynchronous communication and active participation in the forum [5], learners can receive support through discussions with their peers or with the course instructional staff. It has been suggested that a well-run discussion forum provides a sense of community that promotes engagement across learners and may have a positive impact on their motivation [6]. On the other hand, the main actors that provide support to learners within the discussion forum are the instructors and the teaching assistants [7]. Teaching assistants (TAs) have a crucial role in keeping learners motivated and engaged with the course [8]. Their role is to keep track of the forum discussions and make prompt interventions to help learners with their problems related to the course.

A key requirement of the MOOC discussion forum is to promote the main principles of social constructivism [9], which posits that "each learner constructs means by which new knowledge is both created and integrated with existing knowledge" [10]. According to this theoretical framework, the TAs step aside to a new role as facilitators in the learning process by connecting learners with peers and learning processes, while the students create their own knowledge and open up new learning pathways [11]. Moreover, it is understood that the way TAs handle discussions within the forum and the pedagogical strategies they follow, can play an important role in motivating learners enhancing their learning experience [12].

The pedagogical approaches that are promoted within a MOOC, determine the course's instructional design [13]. Several studies have been performed to assess the instructional design of MOOCs [14, 15]. In their research, Guàrdia et al. [16] revealed that a deep pedagogical approach is still missing from the instructional design of MOOCs. In another study, Margaryan et al. [17] investigated the quality of the instructional design in 76 MOOCs by using an evaluation framework that they proposed. This framework includes the First Principles of Instruction, known as Merril's criteria [18], and has its roots on the theory of social constructivism. The results of their high-impact study revealed that the majority of the MOOCs performed poorly judged by most instructional design principles. On the other hand, in terms of quality and presentation of the course material, most MOOCs were described as 'well-packaged'. The evaluation process focused more on the activities that were designed by the MOOC instructors but did not address the issues that are related to the discussion forum. TAs have an important role in facilitating learners and in promoting learning within the forum, but this aspect was not considered during the evaluation process.

Being motivated by the work of Margaryan and colleagues [17], in this paper we extend their analysis on the activity that takes place within the discussion forum of a MOOC. We present a mixed-methods study, which aims to investigate the main intervention strategies that TAs followed in the discussion forums of two MOOCs and assess their instructional approaches by using the framework proposed by Margaryan and colleagues [17]. These MOOCs were delivered through the OpenEdX platform, one of the major MOOC platforms [19]. This study reveals some important issues related to the TAs' instructional approaches that may be related to the instructional design of the courses. These issues should be considered by MOOC instructors and designers in order for them to focus, not only on their courses' material quality and activities, but also on the instructional approaches that the TAs follow within the forum. This way, learners may be motivated and effective learning promoted.

2 Literature Overview

Despite the growing interest in the assessment of MOOCs' instructional design, little research exists that focuses specifically on the facilitation strategies and pedagogies of the MOOC instructors [20]. In their study, Watson et al. [21] applied the 'Community of Inquiry' framework to examine a team of MOOC instructors' use of social presence and teaching presence by examining course announcements and the team's participation in the discussion forums. Results of this study highlight the need for further research in the field of MOOC instruction and facilitation and their importance for an effective instructional design. Evans and Myrick [22] performed a mixed-methods survey on 162 professors with the goal to understand how MOOCs are perceived by them, in the role of instructors. It was found that most MOOC professors were experienced faculty members with relatively little prior experience in teaching online. This issue led to insufficient instructional approaches regarding the MOOCs they created. In another research, Haavid and Sistek-Chandler [8] revealed that the main issue that the instructors faced was the massive audience they had to satisfy and the fact that they had to adapt their pedagogies to them. From these studies, it is evident that, even instructors who are experienced teachers, face difficulties in following adequate instructional approaches in the MOOCs that they create.

For the instructors, one of their main challenges is the massiveness of MOOCs. Wiley and Edwards have called this challenge as the teacher 'bandwidth problem' [23], which is especially an issue in MOOCs if teaching is understood as more than lecturing. To overcome this problem, instructors hire relatively inexpensive teaching assistants into their courses [24]. TAs have a supportive role in MOOCs, usually within the discussion forum, and their goal is to reduce the workload of the instructor during the MOOC's time schedule and facilitate learners with their problems. The number of TAs required to provide sufficient learning assistance to all students of a MOOC with thousands of registrants is prohibitively high. To resolve this issue, several studies have attempted to build forum posts classification models that will assist TAs in the discussion forum of a MOOC [24, 25]. The results of these studies suggest that post classifiers may contribute in resolving the issue of massiveness in MOOCs, as they support TAs in identifying posts that require their intervention.

Most of the studies, in the field of MOOC instructional design evaluation, focus on instructors' pedagogical approaches, and on the quality of the course material and the activities that they provide to learners. Limited research has been performed on the pedagogies that TAs follow during their supportive role in the forum. It seems that the instructional approaches followed by the TAs are mostly considered as 'black-box' during the design of the courses. This is an important issue that should be considered by MOOC evaluators due to the importance of TAs' role in promoting social construction of knowledge [9]. The evaluation framework proposed by Margaryan et al. [17] is based on social constructivism, and can be used to effectively assess the quality of support that is provided within the MOOC discussion forum. It is important to include the TA supporting activity during the MOOC evaluation process due to the fact that it reflects an important part of the course's instructional design.

In the next section, we discuss the method we used in our study, which was inspired by this background research and was based on this theoretical framework.

3 Methodology

3.1 Research Design

As discussed in the previous section, the main purpose of this study was to investigate the instructional approaches that TAs followed in the discussion forum of two MOOCs and assess them according to the evaluation framework proposed by Margaryan et al. [17]. To achieve this goal, we followed a mixed-methods approach, and more specifically a *Convergent Parallel Mixed-Methods Design* [26] (Fig. 1). According to this design, we triangulated different qualitative and quantitative data col-lection techniques in order to capture the TAs' instructional approaches. This method allowed us to increase the quality, reliability, and rigor of our results [27]. Next we performed the evaluation of the TAs' instructional approaches through the selected framework (Table 1).

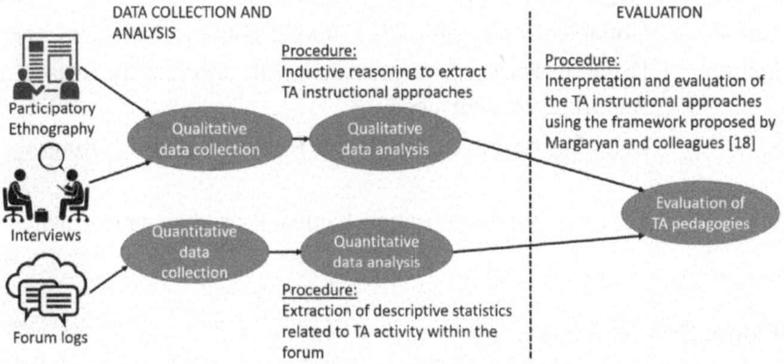

Fig. 1. Convergent Parallel Mixed-Methods Design of this research

3.2 Context of Study

The study was performed on two MOOCs offered in the mathesis.cup.gr, a major Greek MOOC platform based on OpenEdX technology. The first course, 'Introduction to Python' (PY course), aimed to introduce learners to computer programming through Python. The second one, 'Differential Equations 1' (DE course), aimed to introduce learners to the mathematical theory of differential equations and their practical use. The duration of both courses was 6 weeks, and the enrolled learners were 5569 for PY and 2153 for DE. Within each course discussion forum support was pro-vided by TAs. The TAs were mostly learners that had attended former MOOCs of the same instructor with high engagement and performance. They were subsequently contacted by the instructors, assigned the role of TAs and were asked to contribute to subsequent editions of the courses. For the courses in our study, the active TAs were 5 for the PY course and 2 for the DE one.

Using the data derived from the two courses we focused on gaining insight on the main instructional approaches that the TAs followed during their interventions within each discussion forum. Then, during the evaluation process, we assessed which of the principles listed in Table 1, were promoted and which were violated or neglected judging from the nature of their interventions. Thus, the main issues of the instructional design, which are related to the way the support is provided within the discussion forum, will be revealed.

Table 1. Evaluation framework of the TA instructional approaches.

Principle	Description
[p1] Problem-centered	Learners acquire skill in the context of real-world problems
[p2] Activation	Learners activate existing knowledge and skill as a foundation for new skill
[p3] Demonstration	Learners observe a demonstration of the skill to be learned
[p4] Application	Learners apply their newly acquired skill to solve problems
[p5] Integration	Learners reflect on, discuss, and defend their newly acquired skill
[p6] Collective knowledge	Learners contribute to the collective knowledge
[p7] Collaboration	Collaboration is promoted among learners with their peers
[p8] Differentiation	Different learners are provided with different avenues of learning, according to their need
[p9] Authentic resources	Learning resources are drawn from real-world settings
[p10] Feedback	Learners are given expert feedback on their performance

3.3 Data Collection Sources

To reveal and record the instructional approaches the TAs used for their interventions, we employed different data collection methods, both qualitative and quantitative (Table 2).

Table 2. Data collection methods.

Method	Description	Purpose
Participatory Ethnography (ETH method)	Participated in the course forums as regular users and performed observations regarding the type of TA interventions into learner discussions. Interventions were characterized based on Formality, Directness and Promptness	Gain a phenomenological account [28] of the TAs' behavior and of their instructional approaches. Record TA interactions with learners and register the problems that they faced

(continued)

Table 2. (*continued*)

Method	Description	Purpose
Interviews with TAs (INT method)	Qualitative, semi-structured, face-to-face interviews with two TAs of each course. The interviews were guided by the questionnaire shown in Table 3	Capture the TAs' personal opinions and experiences; understand their motivation and reasoning for acting the way we observed during the ETH method. Provide the opportunity to view and understand the topic at hand [29]
Discussion forum log analysis	Log data from both discussion forums were retrieved and analyzed. The results of the analysis are related to the TA activities within the forum discussions	Provide quantitative data to validate, triangulate our observations from the participatory ethnographic approach and the interviews with the TAs

Table 3 gives the questionnaire that guided the semi-structured interviews with the TAs of the two courses. In the next section the obtained results are presented.

Table 3. Guide of the semi-structured interviews with the TAs.

Code	Question
[Q1]	What is your educational background?
[Q2]	What were the main instructions that you received from the course instructor related to the ways that you should provide support to learners within the discussion forum?
[Q3]	How often were you tracking the forum discussions? Did you have a specific timetable? Explain your discussion tracking methods
[Q4]	Under what criteria did you consider that a discussion required your intervention?
[Q5]	What is the best way to structure a reply to a learner's question, according to your opinion?
[Q6]	Are you satisfied with your contribution to the course's discussion forum?

4 Results

In this section the collected results are presented. Due to the Convergent Parallel Design that was followed, we present the results from the qualitative and quantitative methods separately.

4.1 Discussion Forum Log Analysis

The log files from the two MOOCs in our study provided information on all activities that were taking place in the discussion forums.

Table 4 presents the descriptive statistics for a number of important variables, such as the 'Total number of discussions in a forum' and the 'Number of discussions with or without TA participation', as measured from the discussion forum of each course. Comparing the two courses, the discussions that took place in the PY forum were almost double the discussions in the DE course. This reflects the fact that PY had more than double the number of enrolled learners, compared to DE.

Table 4. Descriptive statistics of the discussion forum in each course.

	PY course	DE course
Total number of discussions in the forum	1216	548
Discussions with TA participation	493	285
Discussions where the 1st reply was provided by a TA	360	244
Discussions that received zero replies	265	87
Average number of replies in discussions with TA participation	4.0 (std = 3.9)	3.8 (std = 3.4)
Average number of replies in discussions without TA participation	1.4 (std = 1.8)	1.78 (std = 1.9)

It is further observed that the PY TAs intervened in 40.54% (493 out of 1216) of all discussions while in the DE TAs in 52.01% (285 out of 548) of all discussions, while 21.79% and 15.87% of the courses' discussions respectively received zero replies. The fact that the TAs in both courses did not participate in about half of the discussions of the corresponding forum in conjunction with the number of discussions that didn't receive any replies, could be the effect of teacher's bandwidth problem [23] discussed in Sect. 2. Another important observation for both courses, is the large percentage of discussions where a TA provided the first reply to a starting post of a discussion. For the PY course this was 73.02% (360 out of 493) and for the DE course 85.61% (244 out of 285). Lastly, the mean length of discussions with TA participation was found significantly higher than those without TA participation ($p \ll 0.01$) for both courses. It seems that learners mostly chose to participate in discussions with TAs instead of their peers.

4.2 Participatory Ethnography

During this part of the study, the TA interventions were studied by the researcher who participated in the forum and recorded several observations. The observations referred to three possible characteristics of the interventions, formality, directness and promptness, while at the same time they were judged for posting any problems. These observations are briefly discussed next.

Formality of the Interventions. All TAs in both courses were very supportive throughout the entire duration of each course. In addition, their behavior was very polite and formal towards all learners. They did not attempt to develop any personal relationship with the learners, by extending discussions onto non content-related topics or by changing their attitude towards a more informal communication. Apparently that was an indication and this may imply that they took their role very seriously (Table 5, Formality-A, B).

Directness of the Interventions. In the PY course, most learner questions were related to the code they had to write, and in many of their interventions, TAs responded by giving the correct answer directly (Table 5, Directness-A). By adopting such an approach, in a way they were putting an end to the discussion and were not promoting any initiatives from the learners' side. Moreover, in some occasions they even provided alternative solutions and examples related to their problems (Table 5, Direct-ness-B). For the DE course, learner questions were mostly related to mathematical problems and theories. The TAs of this course were also providing very analytical replies with many theoretical explanations (Table 5, Directness-C), even though often the required content of the answers could easily be found in the video lectures of that same week.

Promptness of the Interventions. The participator in the discussion forums observed that the way TAs were intervening in discussions was quite similar in both courses according to promptness. In many occasions the TAs were the first to reply to a post that was starting a new discussion. This is verified by the results of the discussion forum log analysis presented in Table 4. A possible reason may be that they were keeping track of the forum discussions quite frequently. This can be confirmed by the fact that many interventions were performed only a few minutes after the original learner's post (Table 5, Promptness-A).

Registered Problems. A problem that was observed quite often was the repetition of certain questions, posted by learners in different discussions (Table 5, Registered Problems-A, B). This was an issue for both courses and TAs expressed frustration. Another issue that was recorded, mostly at the PY course, refers to learner's questions that were related to more advanced courses. These questions were still answered by the TAs (Table 5, Registered Problems-C). Learners seemed to take advantage of the willingness TAs exhibited in intervening in the forum and didn't seem to comply with their prompts. The fact that TAs still provided full-fledged answers probably encouraged learners to keep acting likewise.

Table 5. Selected extracts of evidence from TA interventions within the discussion forum.

Topic	Extract [COURSE-TA#]
Formality	**A.** *Mr. [USERNAME] you are absolutely right. I just originally thought that the point x = 0 which is a singular point...[ANSWER]...* [ETH-DE-TA1] **B.** *Dear [USERNAME], the resulting value of the «while» statement you are using is always TRUE. This is the reason why you need the «break» command.* [PY-TA1]
Directness	**A.** *Add a check for the case where the first character is '-'. Rather than x.isdigit (), insert the following code: [python code]* [PY-TA2] **B.** *You should add a check for the case where the first character is '-'. Rather than x.isdigit (), you should insert the following code: [PYTHON CODE]. You can see that in this case [explanation]* [PY-TA2] **C.** *The solutions of this equation are also t = 2k. The period here has to do with the time of repetition of both position and ... [THEORY]...* [DE-TA2]

(*continued*)

Table 5. (*continued*)

Topic	Extract [COURSE-TA#]
Promptness	**A. [Learner]** - *Good evening. Why my code is still returning this error? [CODE] [ERROR-MESSAGE]* || Posted 16:34 **[PY-TA2]** – Dear [USERNAME], it is obvious that your code [ANSWER] || Posted 16:47
Registered problems	**A.** *Before creating a new discussion, please check the older ones first. The answer that you are seeking is here [LINK].* [PY-TA2] **B.** *But why do you put me in this unpleasant position Mr. [USERNAME]? Your question has been answered here [LINK].* [DE-TA2] **C.** *In this situation you should use an extra «while» statement... [ANSWER]...however, I would like to let you know that your question may confuse other learners because it does not belong to the course's curriculum. Please visit the advanced Python course for this type of questions.* [PY-TA2]

4.3 TA Interviews

The main findings of the interviews are provided here per question (Table 3).

Q1 (TA's Education). Each one of the TAs had a different educational background. In the DE course, TA1 was a military person (Table 6, [Q1]-A) that had built a mathematical background through participation in related online courses, while TA2 had pre and post graduate degree in physics. In the PY course, both TAs had a degree in computer science. It is evident that all TAs had an adequate educational back-ground in order to provide support to learners within the discussion forum.

Q2 (Instructions to TAs). All four TAs gave the same answer, that there were no specific instructions related to the way that they should provide support within the discussion forum (Table 6, [Q2]-A, B). They were also not prompted to have a strict timetable in terms of their forum participation. The only instruction they received was to chasten learners that do not behave according to the forum's policies, thus acting more as forum moderators.

Q3 (Forum Tracking). The TAs discussed the methods that they used to keep track of forum discussions. PY-TA1 reported that he used to enter into the discussion forum during late hours or morning hours before he went to his work. PY-TA2 was entering in the forum every two hours during the day. He followed this strict schedule so as not to leave lots of unmanaged workload for PY-TA1 (Table 6, [Q3]-A). Apparently they cooperated quite smoothly. For the DE course DE-TA1 stated that the fact that he works in an office allowed him to be in the Internet during the day and keep track of the forum discussions. Lastly, DE-TA2 was spending mostly midnight hours in the forum, and that was the reason that he rarely participated in dialogues with learners.

Q4 (Intervention Criteria). The criteria that TAs followed in considering which discussions needed their intervention seemed to have been affected by the available time for forum participation. PY-TA1 and DE-TA2 said that they did not have enough

Table 6. Selected extracts of evidence from the interviews.

Question	Extract [COURSE-TA#]
[Q1]	**A.** *I work as an air force officer. I do not have a degree in mathematics. I have watched, though, all of the MOOCs of Mr[instructor] and I managed to build a proper mathematical background so as to become a TA.* [DE-TA1]
[Q2]	**A.** *No, there were not any instructions given to me by Mr.[instructor]. He prompted me to act like I did in his previous courses as an active user in the forum.* [DE-TA1] **B.** *There were no specific instructions for my role as a TA. I had previous experience from Mr[instructor]'s previous courses.* [PY-TA2]
[Q3]	**A.** *I set a personal goal at the start of the course's schedule, to enter the forum every two hours, even from my mobile phone. There was so much participation that I wanted to facilitate [TA1_name] and reduce his workload.* [PY-TA2]
[Q4]	**A.** *I didn't have the luxury of time to choose in which discussions to intervene. My goal was to not let any questions unanswered so as to please every possible learner.* [DE-TA2] **B.** *My prior experience helps me to understand who really needs my support. There were learners who it was obvious that they needed my support and they were my first priority. There were other learners that were totally unaware of the forum and kept posting duplicate or advanced questions. That was unacceptable.* [PY-TA2] **C.** *When I enter the discussion forum I try to find all recent unanswered questions. When I spot them I see the time duration that each question remained unanswered. If it is more than an hour or two then I intervene, else I wait till other learners intervene first.* [DE-TA1]
[Q5]	**A.** *I consider that providing the correct answer to the learner directly is a wrong approach. I usually try to help learners reach the solution themselves by guiding them with proper questions.* [PY-TA1] **B.** *I want to provide learners with comprehensive answers to their problems. My reply should be accompanied with extra examples of code in order for the learners to fully understand the solution.* [PY-TA2] **C.** *It is important for learners to comprehend each week's theory in order to keep up with the video lectures. I put a lot of effort in providing full-fledged answers. Thankfully Mr[TA2 name] usually complements my replies because he knows that I do not have an academic background in mathematics.* [DE-TA1] **D.** *I want learners to fully understand the mathematical theory and practice behind their problems. This is the reason why I explain in depth the solution that I provide.* [DE-TA2]
[Q6]	**A.** *I couldn't be more satisfied. I spent more time supporting learners in the forum than helping my own child in his homework [humorously].* [INT-DE-TA1] **B.** *I am very satisfied by my effort. I love Python and I do my best to make other learners love it too.* [PY-TA1]

time to assess every new discussion (Table 6, [Q4]-A). They just intervened in random unanswered questions they found. On the other hand, PY-TA2 reported that selected questions to answer, according to their nature. Some learners needed support, as they were inexperienced in programming. There were also learners who used the provided support on trivial or more advanced questions (Table 6, [Q3]-B). This led to TA's frustration and there were times that he refused to answer. Finally, DE-TA1 had also constructed his own intervention criteria. He stated that he put a time threshold of 1 to 2 h in each discussion and if no one responded, he intervened (Table 6, [Q3]-C). This strategy tallies with the available time he had within the day, according to his replies in question Q3.

Q5 (Reply Structure). In the PY course there was a contrast between the approaches that TAs followed in structuring their replies during their forum interventions. The main goal of PY-TA1 was to help the learners reach the solution by themselves. By providing extra questions, PY-TA1 was prompting learners to make an effort and figure out the solution (Table 6, [Q5]-A). He considered this approach as a more constructive way to learn. On the other hand, PY-TA2 considered that more comprehensive answers followed by examples are more appropriate for learners (Table 6, [Q5]-B). In the DE course, both TAs seem to have almost the same approach on the way they form their forum interventions. They considered important to provide learners with the proper theory related to the problem's solution.

Q6 (Own Evaluation). The last interview question was related to their satisfaction according to their effort as TAs. All TAs were pleased with their contribution (Table 6, [Q6]-A, B). This is due to the fact that they are highly motivated, they participate in a voluntary basis and yet they choose to spend a lot of time in the forum.

4.4 Evaluation of TA Instructional Approaches

During the interviews, all TAs stated that no specific instructions were given to them by the course instructor. This was one of the reasons that the TAs followed different instructional approaches. According to their educational background, they were able to provide adequate support to learners. The fact that there were signs of cooperation between the TAs of each course implies that they were well-organized and felt responsible for their role.

The study findings, revealed that the instructional approaches of the TAs were not promoting *Collaboration* (p7) and *Collective Knowledge* (p8), see Table 1 for instruction principles. The fact that TAs provided the first reply in many discussions did not promote further discussions between learners. This observation was verified during interviews where most TAs said that there were no criteria in terms of when to intervene. According to social constructivism, participating in group discussions allows learners to generalize and transfer knowledge and thus evolve in their communication skills [9]. In addition, building the sense of a community within the discussion forum is of great importance [6] and TAs should be directed to follow approaches that pro-mote interactions among learners.

A serious problem that TAs faced was the large number of duplicate and advanced questions. Specifically, PY-TA2 reported that there was a specific group of learners that were causing this issue and they were exploiting the TAs' support. This issue may be related to the instructional approach of the TAs. The fact that TAs were so responsive in the forum may have encouraged some learners to post continually assuming that TAs will promptly reply, thus monopolizing their attention.

Despite these problems, the TAs were flexible enough and promoted *differentiation* (p8). In MOOCs there are learners from different educational backgrounds, prior experience and motivation, so it is very important to treat them differently according to their needs, hoping that this may prevent dropout due to disappointment [3]. The TAs were aware of this issue and they appeared to have implemented different instructional strategies for specific categories of learners. Specifically, PY-TA2 mentioned that discussions created by inexperienced learners were the first in priority that he responded to. On the other hand, *feedback* principle (p10) seemed to be absent from the TAs' strategies. This is reasonable because TAs did not have the time to remember each learner's progress so as to provide a proper feedback to each one of them. The main reasons were the limited available time of TAs and the large number of active learners in the course.

A major problem of TAs' instructional approaches was that they were not promoting *problem-centered* (p1) learning. In both courses TAs were providing the correct solution to learners directly. The only exception was PY-TA1 who stated that he didn't follow such approach. His approach was to lead learners to the correct solution through intermediate questions so as learners could divide the main problem into sub-problems. The TAs' goal was to provide full-fledged answers to learners by adding complementary theory (DE course) or Python code (PY course), but this approach affects the *activation* (p2), *application* (p4) and *integration* (p5) principles in a negative way. From one perspective, learners receive high quality support but on the other they do not explore the problem and construct new knowledge. This may be another reason why learners kept exploiting the TAs' support due to the fact that TAs encouraged them to do so with their willingness to intervene frequently and provide comprehensive replies.

Finally, as discussed, in the PY course, the instructional approaches of TAs promoted *demonstration* (p3) and *authentic resources* (p9) principles by providing alternative solutions and examples in their replies. This way learners were provided with a variety of approaches to tackle their problems. On the other hand, TAs of the DE course did not seem to promote this kind of learning. This may be related to the subject matter of mathematics. Comparing the subject matter of the two courses, in computer programming there is a flexibility of different approaches that learners could follow to solve a problem, while in mathematics alternative solutions are limited in many cases.

5 Discussion and Conclusion

In this study, we attempted a contribution to the study of the instructional approaches of TAs in MOOC forums. By using a mixed-methods approach we investigated the instructional approaches used in the forums of two MOOCs and evaluated them using the framework proposed by Margaryan et al. [17]. The main findings are: The key observation was that TAs acted more as "*omniscient interlocutors*" rather than as "*knowledge facilitators*" according to our results from both the participatory ethnography and the TA interviews. The fact that they were so active in the forum in conjunction with the instant and comprehensive answers that they provided resulted in their exploitation by many learners. TAs' frustration was conspicuous on this issue. The '*direct reply*' approaches that TAs followed did not seem to promote interactions among learners and moreover this violates a key principle of social constructivism, i.e. *collaboration* [9]. In the discussion forum learners should be the main actors of communication so as *collective knowledge* is endorsed. TA should facilitate them [10] in resolving their issues and not provide them with the direct answers. Learners should make an effort to construct their knowledge, and by implementing a *problem-centered* approach towards learning they can also improve their critical thinking skills [30]. Thus, *activation* (p2) of their gained knowledge is achieved and can be applied in future problems [18]. On the other hand, TAs were promoting *demonstration* (p3), which is also an important principle for skill-oriented courses. It is important for learners to observe examples of the knowledge that they will acquire and this principle was the most common characteristic of the TAs' instructional approaches. Finally, the fact that the *feedback* (p10) principle was absent, raises the need for the development of new run-time tools that will assist TAs not only to keep track of the forum discussions, but also to track learners' progress. By using such tools, even if TAs spend limited time in the forum, they will have the chance to provide feedback to learners, according to their progress in their future interventions.

The factors that led to the observed instructional approaches of TAs are multiple and highly inter-related. Firstly, the fact that no instructions were given to them by the course instructor means that each TA had to follow a personal approach according to her intuition. They often have domain knowledge capacity to support learners but they do not necessarily have the instructional skills. As a result they adopted different strategies in the forum. Another factor that seems to have affected their instructional approaches is the available time that they had, as they participated in voluntary basis [24]. From the interviews, it was revealed that they spent limited time in the forum and this may have led to their '*direct reply*' behavior. By having time restrictions caused them the need to fulfill every learner's needs, in the fastest way.

The results of this study highlight some important issues related to the instructional approaches that TAs followed and this may be related to the lack of explicit instructional design of the course forum. Course instructors and designers should consider these issues and not limit their instructional design on the quality of the course con-tent, but also focus on the quality of the support that should be provided in the forum, in order to promote effective learning. In future research we will focus on further investigating TAs instructional approaches on courses of different subject matters in order to study the effect of different domains. Previous studies [31] has shown that intervention characteristics of the TAs may depend on the subject matter of the course. The exploration of such issues may lead to the development of guides that can assist course instructors and designers in order to better structure their future instructional design of their courses. We will also perform experimental research on the development of machine learning run-time tools that will provide automatic intelligent support to TAs and assist them to properly design and orchestrate their interventions.

Acknowledgements. This research is performed in the frame of collaboration of the University of Patras with online platform mathesis.cup.gr. Supply of MOOCs data, by Mathesis is gratefully acknowledged. Doctoral scholarship "Strengthening Human Resources Research Potential via Doctorate Research – 2nd Cycle" (MIS-5000432), implemented by the State Scholarships Foundation (IKY) is also gratefully acknowledged. This research has also been partially funded by the Spanish State Research Agency (AEI) under project grants TIN2014-53199-C3-2-R and TIN2017-85179-C3-2-R, the Regional Government of Castilla y León grant VA082U16, the EC grant 588438-EPP-1-2017-1-EL-EPPKA2-KA.

References

1. Clow, D.: MOOCs and the funnel of participation. In: Proceedings of the Third International Conference on Learning Analytics and Knowledge, pp. 185–189 (2013)
2. Hone, K.S., El Said, G.R.: Exploring the factors affecting MOOC retention: a survey study. Comput. Educ. **98**, 157–168 (2016)
3. Kizilcec, R.F., Halawa, S.: Attrition and achievement gaps in online learning. In: Proceedings of the Second ACM Conference on Learning at Scale (2015)
4. Daniel, J.: Making sense of MOOCs: musings in a maze of myth, paradox and possibility. Presented at the Journal of Interactive Media in Education (2012)
5. Kumar, M., Kan, M.-Y., Tan, B.C., Ragupathi, K.: Learning instructor intervention from MOOC forums: early results and issues. Int. Educ. Data Min. Soc. 218–225 (2015)
6. Xiong, Y., Li, H., Kornhaber, M.L., Suen, H.K., Pursel, B., Goins, D.D.: Examining the relations among student motivation, engagement, and retention in a MOOC: a structural equation modeling approach. Global Educ. Rev. **2**, 23–33 (2015)
7. Brouns, F., Mota, J., Morgado, L.: A networked learning framework for effective MOOC design: the ECO project approach. In: 8th EDEN Research Workshop Challenges for Research into Open & Distance Learning: Doing Things Better: Doing Better Things, pp. 161–171 (2014)
8. Haavind, S., Sistek-Chandler, C.: The emergent role of the MOOC instructor: a qualitative study of trends toward improving future practice. Int. J. E-learning **14**, 331–350 (2015)
9. Fischer, G.: Beyond hype and underestimation: identifying research challenges for the future of MOOCs. Distance Educ. **35**, 149–158 (2014)
10. Anderson, T., Dron, J.: Three generations of distance education pedagogy. Int. Rev. Res. Open Distrib. Learn. **12**, 80–97 (2011)
11. Reese, S.A.: Online learning environments in higher education: connectivism vs. dissociation. Educ. Inf. Technol. **20**, 579–588 (2015)
12. Shapiro, H.B., et al.: Understanding the massive open online course (MOOC) student experience: an examination of attitudes, motivations, and barriers. Comput. Educ. **110**, 35–50 (2017)
13. Yousef, A.M.F., Chatti, M.A., Schroeder, U., Wosnitza, M.: What drives a successful MOOC? An empirical examination of criteria to assure design quality of MOOCs. In: International Conference on Advanced Learning Technologies, pp. 44–48 (2014)
14. Lowenthal, P., Hodges, C.: In search of quality: using quality matters to analyze the quality of massive, open, online courses (MOOCs). Int. Rev. Res. Open Distrib. Learn. **16**, 83–101 (2015)
15. Jansen, D., Rosewell, J., Kear, K.: Quality frameworks for MOOCs. In: Jemni, M., Kinshuk, K.M. (eds.) Open Education: From OERs to MOOCs, pp. 261–281. Springer, Heidelberg (2017). https://doi.org/10.1007/978-3-662-52925-6_14
16. Guàrdia, L., Maina, M., Sangrà, A.: MOOC design principles: a pedagogical approach from the learner's perspective. eLearning Papers 33 (2013). ISSN: 1887-1542
17. Margaryan, A., Bianco, M., Littlejohn, A.: Instructional quality of massive open online courses (MOOCs). Comput. Educ. **80**, 77–83 (2015)
18. Merrill, M.D.: First principles of instruction. Educ. Technol. Res. Dev. **50**, 43–59 (2002)
19. Sandeen, C.: Integrating MOOCs into traditional higher education: the emerging "MOOC 3.0" era. Change Mag. High. Learn. **45**, 34–39 (2013)

20. Liyanagunawardena, T.R., Adams, A.A., Williams, S.A.: MOOCs: A systematic study of the published literature 2008-2012. Int. Rev. Res. Open Distrib. Learn. **14**, 202–227 (2013)
21. Watson, S.L., Watson, W.R., Janakiraman, S., Richardson, J.: A team of instructors' use of social presence, teaching presence, and attitudinal dissonance strategies: an animal behavior and welfare MOOC. Int. Rev. Res. Open Distrib. Learn. **18**, 69–91 (2017)
22. Evans, S., Myrick, J.G.: How MOOC instructors view the pedagogy and purposes of massive open online courses. Distance Educ. **36**, 295–311 (2015)
23. Wiley, D.A., Edwards, E.K.: Online self-organizing social systems: the decentralized future of online learning. Q. Rev. Distance Educ. **3**, 33–46 (2002)
24. Drachsler, H., Kalz, M.: The MOOC and learning analytics innovation cycle (MOLAC): a reflective summary of ongoing research and its challenges. J. Comput. Assist. Learn. **32**, 281–290 (2016)
25. Chaturvedi, S., Goldwasser, D., Daumé III, H.: Predicting instructor's intervention in MOOC forums. In: Proceedings of the 52nd Annual Meeting of the Association for Computational Linguistics, pp. 1501–1511 (2014)
26. Creswell, J.W.: Research Design Qualitative Quantitative and Mixed Methods Approaches (2003)
27. Greene, J.C., Caracelli, V.J., Graham, W.F.: Toward a conceptual framework for mixedmethod evaluation designs. Educ. Eval. Policy Anal. **11**, 255–274 (1989)
28. Blomberg, J., Giacomi, J., Mosher, A., Swenton-Wall, P.: Ethnographic field methods and their relation to design. In: Participatory Design, pp. 123–155. CRC Press (2017)
29. McIntosh, M.J., Morse, J.M.: Situating and constructing diversity in semi-structured interviews. Global Qual. Nurs. Res. **2**, 1–12 (2015)
30. Bali, M.: MOOC pedagogy: gleaning good practice from existing MOOCs. J. Online Learn. Teach. **10**(1), 44–55 (2014)
31. Ntourmas, A., Avouris N., Daskalaki S., Dimitriadis Y.: Teaching assistants' interventions in online courses: a comparative study of two massive open online courses. In: Pan-Hellenic Conference on Informatics, pp. 288–293 (2018)

Design and Operationalization of Connectivist Activities: An Approach Through Business Process Management

Aïcha Bakki[1,2](✉), Lahcen Oubahssi[1], and Sébastien George[1]

[1] Le Mans Université, LIUM, EA 4023, Laboratoire d'Informatique de l'Université de Mans, Avenue Messiaen, 72085 Le Mans Cedex 9, France
aicha.bakki@univ-lemans.fr
[2] IRF-SIC Laboratory, Ibn Zohr University, Agadir, Morocco

Abstract. The work presented in this paper focuses on massive open online course (MOOC) environments, and more specifically on the activity of designing and implementing pedagogical scenarios for a connectivist MOOC (cMOOC). This paper presents a research work, which aims to propose a model and tool to support the design of connectivist MOOC scenarios. The major contribution of this work is a visual authoring tool that is intended for the design and deployment of cMOOC-oriented scenarios. The tool is based on the BPMN notation that we have extended to suit our objectives. The tool was evaluated primarily from the point of view of utility and usability. The findings confirm that the tool can be used to design connectivist pedagogical scenarios and can provide all the necessary elements to operationalize such courses.

Keywords: TEL · MOOC · cMOOC · Authoring tool · BPMN · Connectivism

1 Introduction: Motivation and Aims

The research work presented in this paper is part of a general issue of TEL. It deals, more specifically, with pedagogical scenario design of connectivist MOOCs. Nowadays, MOOCs correspond to an effective learning method, which offers a free, distributed, and open access to education and training. They have increased remarkably by adopting collaborative mechanisms and offering new features promoting communication and exchange between learners. Between new trends and innovative pedagogical concepts, MOOCs have stood out and have received acclaims, as well as criticisms on several levels. This research work has explored some of the multiple facets of MOOC as a research object through pedagogical design support and assistance to teachers. The intended purpose is to conceive models and implement tools to assist teachers in the cMOOC design process by taking into account complementary and plural aspects of e-learning, through individual, collaborative, social and massive dimensions. With the advent of MOOCs in higher education, the stakeholders intended to transcribe the aspects of transmissive pedagogy into MOOCs: xMOOCs then appeared. Although this categorization is considered minimalist, we have relied on the distinction between xMOOC and cMOOC in our proposal. By comparing these types of MOOCs, some

M. Scheffel et al. (Eds.): EC-TEL 2019, LNCS 11722, pp. 251–265, 2019.
https://doi.org/10.1007/978-3-030-29736-7_19

differences were observed, particularly in regards to: the roles played by the teacher and the learner, the pedagogical aspects targeted and the openness and freedom granted to learners [5]. Despite the potential benefits of cMOOCs, the literature review has shown that the most widely deployed types of MOOCs are xMOOCs. Based on an analysis of a panorama of 76 MOOCs, [33] revealed that only 10% of these courses can be categorized as cMOOCs. This observation was addressed by [24] who explained this by pointing out that the majority of teachers do not feel confident and are lacking the technical skills to deal with connectivist environments that are mainly focused on the use of technology. We share this point of view, and believe that a limitation for the emergence of cMOOCs is the lack of methodologies, models and tools to support pedagogical scenario development [3] as the current literature provides a description of pedagogical practices in cMOOCs in a purely descriptive manner. Based on this observation, we have hypothesized that modeling a cMOOC scenario and reifying it in an information system that is easy to use by teachers with no computer expertise will help them to move toward this type of MOOC. Our objective is to assist the teacher-designer who desires to create a cMOOC to produce a pedagogical scenario that respects the specificity of this kind of learning environment. From a conceptual point of view, the major difficulties faced by teachers are, firstly, how to put in place a scenario that emphasizes the new roles played by the learner, and secondly, the lack of adequate tools and/or models for designing cMOOC scenarios without prior knowledge of the underlying pedagogical model. Indeed, in order to meet teachers' expectations, an idea is therefore to use the benefits of Business Process Model and Notation (BPMN). More especially as the latter has been able to stand out in the TEL field by its graphic notation easily understandable by different actors as it provides a set of generic business process elements, independently from a specific domain; its compliance with the standard and as it is intended for different audiences and especially for computer novice users [14].

The remainder of the paper is structured as follow: in Sect. 2, the cMOOC pedagogical scenario domain specifications are summarized. In Sect. 3, we present overview of the BPMN and its benefits for connectivist context. In Sect. 4, we present a brief description of the deployed extension design and method. Since the objective represents an artifact including extended notation and its technical implementation, Sect. 5 present the proposed authoring tool. The Sect. 6 highlights our proposal for the operationalization and deployment phase. The Sect. 7 presents an evaluation of the proposed tool. The paper ends with a conclusion and an outlook on obtained results.

2 Characteristic of a cMOOC Pedagogical Scenario

cMOOCs designate connectivist MOOCs driven by the principles of pedagogical innovation in a widely interconnected social learning mode. They are based on "*a sophisticated and innovative design*" of learning practices [12], and involves the promotion of learning through collaboration, production, sharing and connections between peers in quasi-total openness. The openness of cMOOCs might suggest that pedagogical scenario building is not essential, and that this would be contrary to the underlying principles of a connectivist course. However, we believe that connectivist course design can be enhanced by the implementation of scenario-building practices.

Indeed, despite this openness, it is essential to create suitable conditions for the emergence of connectivist activities. In this sense, several solutions have been suggested to facilitate the implementation of such courses [2, 28]. These studies focus on cMOOCs from a theoretical point of view, and aim to demonstrate the value of a methodology for the scenario development and implementation of connectivist courses. They also offer frameworks that describe the main axes of the design process and the implementation of a cMOOC course, but define the administrative aspects rather than the elements that should be contained by a cMOOC scenario [18, 26, 28]. These studies confirm that cMOOCs rely on a specific conceptual model to help teachers to conceive such courses, but they didn't provide neither a model to describe a cMOOC pedagogical scenario nor concrete and simple software tools to design and deploy connectivist MOOCs.

One of the major difficulties faced by teachers wanting to design such courses is to determine how to model educational activities within this connectivist context. The issue lies in creating pedagogical and monitoring scenarios to support learners so that they do not feel overwhelmed. Designing such scenarios is challenging, since it requires an effective collaboration between the teacher and learners throughout the course. Another difficulty involves setting up cMOOCs in order to respects the freedom of learners to define their own educational objectives. In this perspective, teachers should not establish a specific linear course plan, but should suggest resources and activities that can guide learners toward the main objective of the cMOOC and then encourage them to create, produce and collaborate. These complexities require some mechanisms and methods that can guide and support teachers in the design of the cMOOC.

Pedagogical questions have been raised and constitute one of the major criteria to characterize cMOOCs. In this sense, a study of the pedagogical practices of a connectivist course is essential to define the elements that regulate a cMOOC scenario and model them. That being said, we had to conduct a literature review on the pedagogical aspects of cMOOCs. In accordance with the theoretical grounding of the connectivist approach, we found that cMOOCs are structured into four essential activities [16, 21]: *Aggregating* activities aim to encourage learners to read and consult the content and resources that are most relevant to their learning objectives. The learners are encouraged to read, choose and filter what is most relevant and appropriate to achieve their personal learning objectives. *Remixing* activities can be defined as interpreting the information collected during the aggregation phase and searching for relevant additional resources. *Repurposing* activities aim to support learners through an individual or group production process. *Feed forwarding* activities aim to encourage learners to share their products over the web. These are essentially transmission activities. We assume that a cMOOC scenario should contain all four groups of activities presented above. In the remainder of this paper, we will explain how we purposed to conceptualize this theoretical fundament through a technology-aware framework.

3 BPMN as Pedagogical Language in cMOOC Context

Before the advent of Learning Design (LD) tools, teachers used to create their scenarios using a narrative textual format. Such scenarios do not use a standardized template, meaning that it is difficult to disseminate and reuse them [20], and thus the IMS-LD specification emerged [13]. IMS-LD is essentially a *description language* that allows to model the lesson plan and describes roles and activities without handling the implementation processes [14]. Since IMS-LD *is not an easy-to-understand process for the teachers* [2, 24], the first generation of LD authoring tools was proposed.

A significant number of research works has proposed tools and languages to help with the visualization of learning designs, and these works can be divided into two main groups. The first concerns solutions that provide specific notations for the creation of a pedagogical scenario, but that are not implemented in a tool. The second group concerns visual modeling tools that offer teachers more abstract languages; these are visual or graphical tools, and their use is more intuitive [7]. Thus far, none of these tools have allowed teachers to design cMOOC and to automatically deploy them on a platform. In addition, some of these LD tools are directed toward a particular pedagogical approach, are specific to a particular platform, or meets the requirement of the IMS-LD standard which does not correspond to our needs because although it is a so-called pedagogically neutral standard, it has shown its limits for designing collaborative and constructivist situations [10, 17]. Other works were inspired by business modeling, and specifically by the workflow approach. In this sense, BPMN is offered as an alternative to LD languages. Several studies have been conducted [2, 14] to illustrate and support the use of this workflow language within the LD process. BPMN has stood out in the educational field due to its advantages and in particular its expressiveness, its simplicity of use and the graphical representation of pedagogical scenarios.

The LD tools have advantages and disadvantages that influence their use and execution. Several studies have been carried out to specify the requirements and/or needs for LD tools and languages [8, 25]. According to these works, from a techno-descriptive point of view, BPMN has several advantages that offer a teacher an intuitive tool, through its visual notation, its formal character and its level of stratification in layers that offers a different representation for each modeling element. From a pedagogical point of view, BPMN allows the representation of learning modalities by specifying the different activities, their dependencies and especially by offering the possibility to define a non-linear pedagogical scenario with several connections.

According to [17], when a learning environment model is confronted with significant variations in its initial conditions, the adaptation of the model that supposedly represents it becomes very difficult: this is the case of connectivism approach. Hence, to successfully cope with the complexity of the cMOOC learning process and its dynamics the targeted LD systems have to facilitate the cMOOC scenario design process in its entirety. Such support must include tools that provide a support for all components of the process, as well as possibilities to simply manage changes in that process. Based on all the points above, one possible approach to provide such a support might be a reuse of the experiences, and practices from business processes. Reusing the BPM notation and extending it with domain-specific concepts are expected to be less expensive than deploying a domain specific modeling language from scratch. However, in order to meet our objective to offer the teacher support in the design of cMOOC-oriented pedagogical scenarios, the use of BPMN is not directly conceivable. Since BPM notations are meta-modeling notations, a pedagogy-specific vocabulary based on these abstract elements should be constructed [19]. In this sense, there are research developments that need to be realized for a successful application of BPMN in our context. Those developments aim to support the whole cycle of a cMOOC pedagogical scenario, i.e., *first*, facilities for conceiving cMOOC scenarios are addressed; and *second*, mechanisms for automatic mapping, deploying, and executing of pedagogical scenario within the available Learning Management Systems (LMS) are taken into account. To do so, we have to first propose an extension of the BPMN concept to take into account the specificities of a cMOOC-oriented pedagogical scenario (Sect. 4). Then, we embed the extended meta-model and notation in an authoring tool (Sects. 5 and 6). Finally, we develop a mapping and automatic-deployment service to existing LMS (Sect. 7).

4 BPM Notation and Meta-Model Extension

In 2011, OMG introduced the latest version of BPMN: BPMN 2.0. The BPMN 2.0 specifications define the different graphical notations that form the basic set of BPMN elements. It is one of very few modeling languages that provides generic extension elements within the meta-model that enables the definition of domain-specific language extensions [27]. Nevertheless, BPMN does not provide any methodological guidance or support to comply with domain-specific extension issues. In this sense, [31] proposed a Method for the Development of BPMN Extensions that consists of the steps listed below: (**1**) Definition of a Conceptual Domain Model of the Extension (CDME) describing the concepts of the domain to be represented in extended BPMN models and their relationships with the concepts of the BPMN meta-model. (**2**) Definition of a BPMN plus Extensions model (BPMN+X) describing an extension based on the specification of the BPMN extension mechanism. (**3**) Transformation of the BPMN+X model into an XML Schema Extension Definition Model. (**4**) Transformation of the XML Schema Extension Model into an XML Schema Extension Definition Document.

[9] proposed an extension of [31] method by integrating the analysis of the domain and its conceptualization. The authors proclaim that for a domain-specific extension, a domain requirement analysis is important in order to explicit all the necessary concepts of the domain and its semantics, and to consider whether the domain-specific concept is semantically equivalent to an existing BPMN element or not. As our aim is to propose a cMOOC pedagogical scenario specific extension, we consider as necessary to integrate the equivalence check procedure proposed by the authors. For this purpose, we are illustrating essentially how the first two steps of the [31] procedure model will be applied. We also add an Equivalence Mapping according to Equivalence check procedure proposed by [9]. Referring to the presented process model (Fig. 1.) the design of the proposed extension is briefly presented below.

Domain Analysis. In order to conceptualize the targeted educational domain, we have analyzed the pedagogical concepts related to the connectivist approach, and we propose a model, named cORPS [4], that allows expressing the structural properties specific to a connectivist environment as well as the temporal properties.

Equivalence Mapping. The BPMN extension is based on specific domain concepts of our proposed Model. Each of these concepts are semantically compared to the BPMN concepts in order to define the needed extension in form of a new element or properties. As result of equivalence mapping a classification of the connectivist element as BPMN element or as an extension concept is made. The first one refers to the elements of our model that has an equivalent BMPN concept and second one corresponds to the elements who have no equivalent or who had no obvious semantic matching with standard elements, but rather situational discussion is necessary in order to provide arguments for a possible mapping.

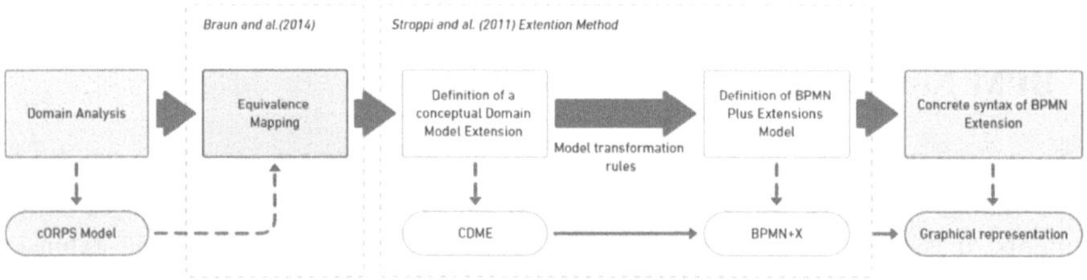

Fig. 1. Process for the development of domain specific BPMN extension

BPMN Metamodeling Extension. Based on the model transformation rules proposed by [31] we define an extension model (BPMN+X) by applying a set of transformation rules. The semantics and the abstract syntax of the extension model are based on BPMN extension mechanism. Depending on several rules in this phase [31], we had defined for each element, according to the domain specification, if we will use an existing BPMN element, define a new one or extend the attributes of the original BPMN elements; and how this changes will occur on BPMN meta-model. With the respect of the limited space of the paper, the entire transformation rules cannot be presented.

Proposed Graphical Notation. We proposed an advanced concrete syntax that defines the specific new graphical representation. As defined by the [27], the following extension can be made by: adding new markers or indicators, coloring graphical elements or changing the line style of a graphical element. According to these rules, *Task* elements are specified by colored borders and new markers that vary depending on the activity type. A pedagogical resource is represented as *Data Object* with a marker that reflects the selected *Resource Type* of the element. Subprocess line shape was also changed in order to differentiate it from generic *Activity* Element. The concrete graphical notation of the extension is presented in Sect. 5.2.

5 MOOC Authoring Tool: Elements and Architecture

As described in Sect. 3, BPMN represent a good alternative to conceive and deploy pedagogical scenarios, nevertheless it need of several adjustments to fulfill our conceptual needs. These adjustments can occur at three levels, namely: (**1**) the definition of pedagogical components based on cMOOC pedagogical principles. (**2**) The proposition of an authoring component for the creation of cMOOC learning procedures. (**3**) The development an automatic or semi-automatic mechanism for mapping learning procedures onto the online learning infrastructure (existing LMS). The first level corresponds to the domain analysis phase mentioned in the Sect. 3. As a result, we had proposed a cMOOC Pedagogical Scenario Model, named cORPS [4]. It allows expressing the structural properties specific to a connectivist environment, as well as the temporal properties. To describe a cMOOC, the pedagogical scenario is based on a semantic description of the course. It consists of a description of the activities and resources it contains, but also of the properties of these entities, as well as their organization. The role of the pedagogical scenario as we perceive it is not merely to describe the actions that the learner must perform to complete a task. The teachers express the organization of pedagogical activities and their sequencing, bearing in mind that participants will participate in these learning activities in a non-linear context, in a conditional way [22, 30]. When the teachers create a pedagogical scenario, they have explicit access to these concepts, by creating a pedagogical workflow and then defining a temporal sequence of the proposed activities. They can also define different execution paths within the pedagogical scenario. In fact, activities are not necessarily organized in a sequential way. We have defined the root element by the *scenario* class, which is the entity that aggregates the different components of the pedagogical scenario. It is composed of one or several *Learning Unit* often with a fixed duration, usually equal to a week and can be composed of one or multiple lessons, which structure learning and assessment activities. A given activity can be assigned to one of the four categories: Aggregation (consultation and cognition), Remixing (communication, sharing and metacognition), Repurposing (production and collaboration) and Feed Forwarding (production sharing). We propose to add a category to the four categories corresponding to Evaluation activities (referring to evaluation activities: e-evaluation, peer evaluation or self-evaluation). Once the model scenario was defined, the aim was to embed it in a tool to design cMOOC-oriented scenarios. It is the main objective of the steps 2 and 3 cited above and described in the remainder of this section.

5.1 cMOOC Authoring Tool Architecture

In Sect. 3, we discussed the advantages of BPMN as a pedagogical modeling language. We should point out that this language has also been used to design various pedagogical situations in several contexts (face-to-face, hybrid, collaborative, etc.) [10, 27]. However, as explained in Sect. 3, in order to meet our requirements to provide the teacher with support for designing cMOOC-oriented pedagogical scenarios, the use of BPMN is not considered as it stands. The objective is not to rebuild a new platform, but to start from an existing tool and extend it. We therefore selected the BPMN.io tool, which is an open source web application that uses BPMN 2.0. The architecture of the

BPMN.io application is composed of three main modules, as follows: ***Bpmn-js*** is the principal module of the tool, and controls the simple and visual human-computer interface used for creating, visualizing and validating BPMN schemas. This module displays and operates the toolbox elements, the modeling rules specific to BPMN 2.0, and the main modeling interface. It provides a viewer element for visualizing BPMN diagrams, and a modeler module to create, to edit and validate BPMN workflows. In this module, we have incorporated changes relating to the extension of the BPM notation and redefined the behavior of each element toolbox elements via the embedded business model expressed as a set of rules that regulates the behavior of each element. ***Bpmn-moddle*** embeds the metamodel defined by the BPMN 2.0 standard, and allows for mapping between the graphical notation and the elements of the BPMN metamodel. This module provides the appropriate modeling rules to validate BPMN workflows, and also allows reading and writing of XML files according to BPMN 2.0. In this module, we have added the elements of the our model through an extension of the BPMN metamodel. We have also modified the moddle-XML file to allow the identification of objects added to the toolbox (new elements specific to the building of cMOOC scenarios) and to indicate how these will be represented in the BPMN workflow. Finally, ***Diagram-js*** provides features that display and memorize changes in BPMN workflows during the conception process. In this module, we define the graphical aspect of the new notation. We add the *MOOCAT ElementFactory* module, which describes the visual appearance of each new element added to the toolbox and allows a mapping between the graphical representation and bpmn-moddle (Fig. 2).

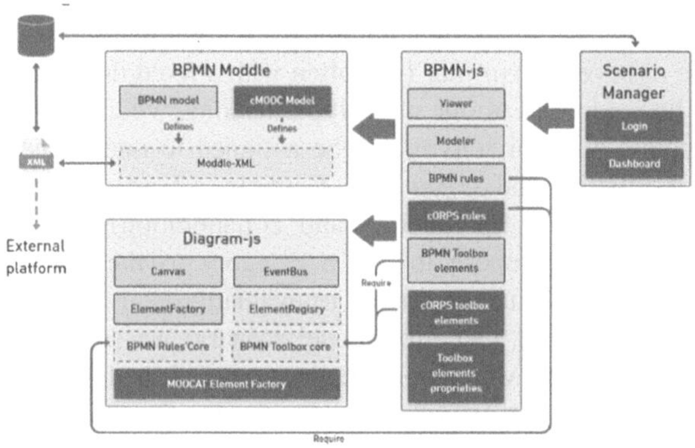

Fig. 2. Authoring tool architecture

5.2 MOOCAT: Features and Interfaces

MOOCAT is a web application accessible via a web browser that not requires any prior installation. Once the teachers are connected to MOOCAT, they can either create a new scenario or modify an existing one (Fig. 3B). In the following, we consider that the teacher choose to create a new scenario (Fig. 3B). After specifying the name of their scenario and choosing the blank model, the teacher is redirected to the conception page (Fig. 3C). When starting a scenario conception with MOOCAT, the teachers start by creating a learning session. They had access to it via the toolbox (Fig. 3F) on the left under the "*Learning session*" block. In order to support the teachers, we propose to ensure that the modeling space (Fig. 3D) is not empty when creating a new scenario. A first learning session is thus created by default. Commonly in MOOCs, one session represents one week. The teachers are then provided with an interface containing a pool, which can be renamed or deleted. They can then use the "Properties" section (Fig. 3E) to specify the duration of this session (start date and end date). After creating there first session and specifying roles, the teachers can start creating there different lessons. We assume that a lesson is an entity that encompasses a number of activities. The teachers can thus continue his modeling by dragging from the toolbox the activities they want to model. In order to facilitate the identification of activities according to the four principles of a connectivist course, we have classified them into four blocks with different color codes. The different types of activities in the toolbox have been explicated in Sect. 2. Each of the activities has its own properties. For example, for a consultation activity, the teachers specify whether it is a resource or an HTML page describing the activities to be carried out or presenting a description of the activity's progress. If it is a resource, they specify its type and the link to access it. Once the scenario modeling is complete, the teachers can possibly save the scenario in different formats (Fig. 3D) or deploy it on an online platform ("Export to…" button). This action activates the transformation of the BPMN file into a file that can be imported by the learning platform.

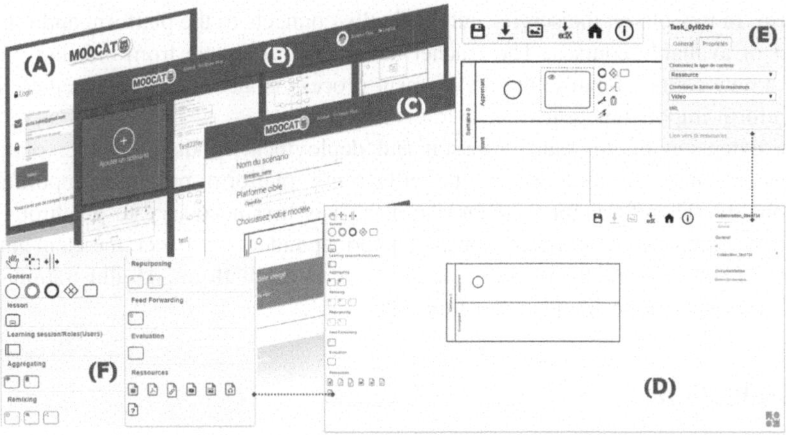

Fig. 3. Interfaces and features of proposed tool

6 MOOCAT Scenario Operationalization Service

In order to support the teacher, a service allowing the deployment of pedagogical scenarios carried out by MOOCAT has emerged. Operationalization represents an intermediate phase between learning and scenario design. It aims essentially to ensure that the scenario described by the teacher can be used and manipulated on a learning device while preserving the described pedagogical semantics [1]. In the literature, there are two types of approaches to operationalize pedagogical scenarios: a manual approach and an automated approach. [1] has classified these operationalization approaches into four categories: (1) Approaches based on the use of standards such as IMS-LD; (2) Approaches based on teachers' needs and practices [17, 32]; (3) Proprietary approaches proposed by platforms such as LAMS [15]; (4) Hybrid approaches based on processes and tools inspired and/or applied by model-driven engineering [11]. Our contribution is based on the last one. Consequently, we have implemented an operationalization service that allows teachers to automatically deploy their pedagogical scenarios on a specific target platform. In line with our work, we have provided a solution that allows transforming the pedagogical workflow into a deployable scenario. In order to demonstrate the technical feasibility of our proposal, we have chosen to develop importation modules for OpenEDX and moodle platforms. We thus proposed the approach that goes through two phases: (1) **Transformation - Pretreatment**. The aim is to propose a confrontation between the two models, in order to resolve all ambiguities and to match each concept in the MOOCAT scenario with a concept in the chosen platforms. It is a surjective transformation, i.e. each MOOCAT element has at least one correspondence on the platform. The general idea of the transformation algorithm is to: (i) Generate the BPMN pedagogical workflow. (ii) Create the tree structure of files from the information specified in the BPMN file. (iii) Transform the scenario into the format required by OpenEDX or Moodle. (2) **Deployment.** The operationalization module acts as a communication gateway from our tool to a learning platform. In this phase, the service automatically connects to the platform and retrieves the list of available courses. The teacher can choose a course from existing ones or create a new course. Finally, the deployment process is automatically executed, using the platform import function.

An extension of the transformation and deployment module to other platforms remains possible, as long as the target-learning platform provides import/export functionality. Therefore, for a given platform, it is first necessary to go through the confrontation phase; the purpose is to find a correspondence between the elements of a MOOCAT scenario and the scenario model of the target platform. An illustration of the overall process can be found at the following link[1].

7 Evaluation

Objective and Description. In this research, the contributions were evaluated and tested as they were specified through simulations and user tests, in order to confront them with the real needs of the target users. The final evaluation was established as part of an experimentation with 40 participants to evaluate the benefits of the extended notation and tool. Our objective is to evaluate the usability of MOOCAT as a cMOOC-oriented pedagogical authoring tool and the expressivity of the proposed notation. In other words, we wanted to verify the ability of the proposed extension to express a

[1] https://youtu.be/JwRSyFxATUc.

cMOOC oriented pedagogical scenario. In order to reach the most diversified participants, a call for participation was broadcast to the TEL community through different mailing lists. We have also experimented our tool during a pedagogical scenario-building workshop with Master degree students that have previously designed pedagogical situations and manipulated different instructional design tools.

Experimental Protocol. The evaluation protocol we have adopted consists of three steps, namely: (1) *Preparation*. We provided participants with a MOOCAT user guide that explains the MOOCAT philosophy and describes the functionalities of the tool and an experimentation guide that describes the different steps to be performed during this evaluation as well as the scenario to be deployed. (2) *Conception*. This step aims to design a pedagogical scenario for a cMOOC course according to the instructions provided during the preparation phase. (3) Results. For this step, we provided participants with a questionnaire that they could complete at the end of the evaluation in order to validate the utility and usability of some aspects of MOOCAT and to obtain more information on the participants' experience.

Data Collection. The methodology used to collect the data from this experimentation is based on two data sources, namely: (1) data derived directly from the work on MOOCAT, including produced scenarios; and (2) participant opinion data collected through questionnaires. The scenarios produced by the participants were analyzed using a *rubric evaluation* grid to assess, on a scale from one to three (1: low - 3: high). We examined all the scenarios and assigned a score for each criterion, then calculated the average scores, which were then compared to the median of two. At the end of the experimentation, participants were asked to complete an online questionnaire contained 25 closed-ended questions, evaluated using a 6-point Likert scale (from Strongly Disagree to Strongly Agree). The first part of the questionnaire focused mainly on the expressivity of the notation. The second part concerns the measurement of the usability of the tool, for this part we used the SUS questionnaire *System Usability Scale* [6].

Experimental Results. All the scenarios created by the participants were collected and analyzed according to an evaluation grid that we defined. Table 1 presents the measured criteria and the average score for each criterion for all submitted scenarios. The criteria we have defined can be divided into two groups, qualifiable indicators that we have evaluated by observation (C2, C4 and C5), and quantifiable indicators that can be automatically calculated from the collected traces (C1 and C3). Criteria C2 and C4 shows that participants were able to create structured and organized pedagogical scenarios. This shows that teachers can easily create pedagogical workflows, proving the advantages of using BPMN as a pedagogical scenario language. The averages obtained for criteria C1 and C2 show that the majority of participants were able to create a well-structured cMOOC scenario that contained all the essential connectivist elements.

The analysis of the first part of the questionnaire aimed to determine whether the tool allowed for the simple design of a connectivist course. This section also assessed whether participants were satisfied with the tool and whether the tool's notation was easy to understand. Finally, it aimed to evaluate the potential of MOOCAT for designing a cMOOC course. In the first part of the questionnaire, 31 participants stated that the organization of the toolbox allowed them to identify the elements. In addition, 33 of the

Table 1. Average scores per evaluation criterion for all submitted pedagogical scenarios

n °	Criterion	Score/3
C1	Number of designed weeks	2,7
C2	Expressiveness of the scenario representation	2,7
C3	Use of all connectivist scenario concepts	2,5
C4	Relevance of the proposed learning resources and activities related to the course topic	2,5
C5	Visual representation and organization of the scenario	2,7

participants stated that the four connectivist activity blocks helped them to identify the activities and their usefulness. A total of 37 participants indicated that MOOCAT offered all the concepts required designing a cMOOC course, whereas only 3 of them did not agree with this statement. In addition, 34 indicated that the visual representation of a scenario was expressive and facilitated the course design. In the second part, the SUS questionnaire was used to measure the usability of MOOCAT. SUS is a popular and effective tool for assessing the usability of various systems [6]. It uses closed-ended questions with a Likert scale, which provides a 5-point gradation for each question ranging from *"(1) totally disagree" to "(5) totally agree"*. Before calculating the SUS score, we pre-processed the participants' responses to remove any errors. In order to detect these errors, we used the grid presented by [23], which consists in considering all responses where the participant provided a score greater than 3 for all negative statements as incorrect. Of the 40 responses received, 6 were withdrawn. Overall, the average SUS score of all participants was 69.25 with a SD of 14.96. This score corresponds to the 55th percentile according to the standardization of [29] (Fig. 4).

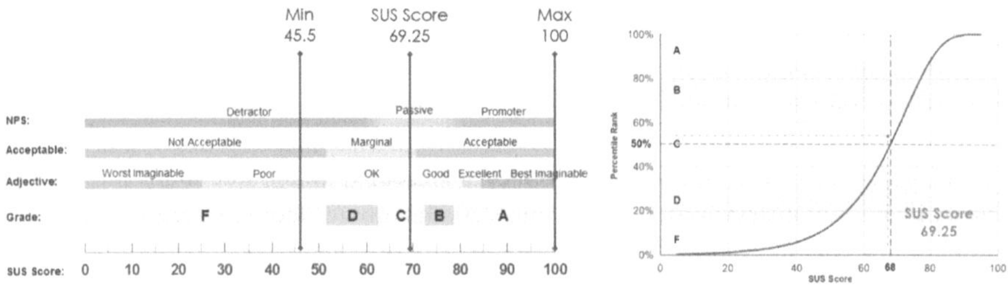

Fig. 4. SUS Score

In accordance with the empirical rule of interpretation of SUS scores [6], systems with scores under 50 are considered unacceptable, products with a score between 50 and 70 are marginally acceptable and those with a score above 70 are acceptable. By positioning the score obtained on the acceptability scale and the rating proposed by [6], the average SUS score of 69.25 indicates that MOOCAT is generally perceived as being close to the boundary between "*marginally acceptable*" and "*acceptable*" and between "*OK*" and "*Good*" for the notation.

8 Conclusion

The main objective of this research work is to support teachers in designing connectivist activities. We identify two steps leading from the design to the operationalization of a cMOOC-oriented scenario. The first consists of modeling the pedagogical scenario using a visual authoring tool; this editor is based on the BPMN graphical notation, and is aimed at teachers without specific technical knowledge or knowledge of the embedded model. We chose to adapt an existing open source BPMN modeling tool (BPMN. io) to embed our cMOOC scenario model. The second step consists of the automatic deployment of a scenario designed using MOOCAT on a MOOC platform. For this deployment phase, a web service solution was developed for the OpenEDX platforms. Our tool ensures that the mappings between the elements of its own scenario and those of the LMS (OpenEDX) are correct and comprehensible from both a semantic and a functionality point of view. These proposals were evaluated from utility and usability point of view. The findings confirm that MOOCAT can be used to design connectivist pedagogical scenarios and can provide all the necessary elements for the design of such courses. In our approach, the cMOOC is initially designed by the teacher, and learners are then encouraged to adapt the scenario according to their learning objectives. As a perspective of our work, we therefore consider that a methodology based on the co-design of a scenario that is currently in use would be a possible solution to this challenge, by giving access to the learners to MOOCAT with special and restricted roles and privileges. However, several scientific issues arise regarding the articulation of adaptation needs, the capitalization of these proposals, and the negotiation and validation of any changes carried out, especially in a massive environment.

References

1. Abedmouleh, A., Laforcade, P., Oubahssi, L., Choquet, C.: Operationalization of learning scenarios on existent learning management systems the moodle case-study. In: Proceedings 6th International Conference Software Database Technology, ICSOFT 2011, vol. 2, pp. 143–148 (2011). https://doi.org/10.5220/0003486001430148
2. Adesina, A., Molloy, D.: Capturing and monitoring of learning process through a business process management (BPM) framework. In: Proceedings of 3rd International Symposium for Engineering Education (2010)
3. Alario-Hoyos, C., Pérez-Sanagustín, M., Cormier, D., Delgado-Kloos, C.: Proposal for a conceptual framework for educators to describe and design MOOCs. J. Univers. Comput. Sci. **20**, 6–23 (2014). https://doi.org/10.3217/jucs-020-01-0006
4. Bakki, A., Oubahssi, L., George, S., Cherkaoui, C.: A model to assist pedagogical scenario building process in cMOOCs. In: 2017 IEEE 17th International Conference on Advanced Learning Technologies (ICALT), pp. 5–7 (2017)
5. Bakki, A., Oubahssi, L., George, S., Cherkaoui, C.: MOOCAT: a visual authoring tool in the cMOOC context. Educ. Inf. Technol. **24**, 1185–1209 (2019). https://doi.org/10.1007/s10639-018-9807-2
6. Bangor, A., Kortum, P., Miller, J.: Determining what individual SUS scores mean: adding an adjective rating scale. J. Usability Stud. **4**, 114–123 (2009). http://doi.org/66.39.39.113

7. Barchino, R., et al.: Interoperability between visual UML design applications and authoring tools for learning design. Inf. Control Int. J. Innov. Comput. **8**, 845–865 (2012)
8. Botturi, L., Derntl, M., Boot, E., Figl, K.: A classification framework for educational modeling languages in instructional design. In: 6th IEEE International Conference on Advanced Learning Technologies (ICALT 2006) (2006)
9. Braun, R., Schlieter, H., Burwitz, M., Esswein, W.: BPMN4CP: design and implementation of a BPMN extension for clinical pathways. In: 2014 IEEE International Conference on Bioinformatics and Biomedicine (BIBM), pp. 9–16 (2014)
10. Britain, S.: A review of learning design: concept, specifications and tools. A Rep JISC E-learning Pedagog Program 2006 (2004)
11. Caron, P.-A.: Bricoles: une approche dispositive des applications Web 2.0 utilisables pour enseigner. In: Actes de la conférence EIAH 2007, pp. 137–142 (2007)
12. Clow, D.: MOOCs and the funnel of participation. In: Proceedings of the Third International Conference on Learning Analytics and Knowledge, pp. 185–189 (2013)
13. Consortium IMSGL, et al.: IMS learning design specification (2003). Accessed 7 Feb 2009
14. Da Costa, J.: BPMN 2.0 pour la modélisation et l'implémentation de dispositifs pédagogiques orientés processus. University of Geneva (2014)
15. Dalziel, J.: Visualising learning design in LAMS: a historical view. Teach. English Technol. **11**, 19–34 (2011)
16. Downes, S.: Places to go: connectivism & connective knowledge. Innov. J. Online Educ. **5**, 6 (2008)
17. Ferraris, C., Martel, C., Vignollet, L.: LDL for collaborative activities. In: Handbook of Visual Languages for Instructional Design: Theories and Practices, pp. 224–251. IGI Global (2008)
18. Glance, D.G., Forsey, M., Riley, M.: The pedagogical foundations of massive open online courses. First Monday **18** (2013)
19. Helic, D.: Technology-supported management of collaborative learning processes. Int. J. Learn. Chang. **1**, 285–298 (2006)
20. Katsamani, M., Retalis, S.: Orchestrating learning activities using the CADMOS learning design tool. Res. Learn. Technol. **21**, 1–12 (2013)
21. Kop, R.: The challenges to connectivist learning on open online networks: learning experiences during a massive open online course. Int. Rev. Res. Open Distance Learn. **12**, 19–37 (2011). https://doi.org/10.19173/IRRODL.V12I3.882
22. Kopp, M., Lackner, E.: Do MOOCs need a special instructional design? In: EDULEARN14 Proceedings, pp. 7138–7147 (2014)
23. Mclellan, S., Muddimer, A., Peres, S.C.: The effect of experience on system usability scale ratings. J. Usability Stud. **7**, 56–67 (2012)
24. Morrison, D.: The ultimate student guide to xMOOCs and CMOOCs. MOOC News Rev. (2013)
25. Nodenot, T.: Scénarisation pédagogique et modèles conceptuels d'un EIAH: Que peuvent apporter les langages visuels? Rev Int des Technol en Pédagogie Univ (RITPU). Int. J. Technol. High Educ. **4**, 85–102 (2007)
26. O'Brien, K.L., Forte, M., Mackey, T.P., Jacobson, T.E.: Metaliteracy as Pedagogical Framework for Learner-Centered Design in Three MOOC Platforms: Connectivist, Coursera and Canvas. Open Prax **9**, 267 (2017). https://doi.org/10.5944/openpraxis.9.3.553
27. OMG: Business Process Model and Notation **95,** 206–242 (2011). https://doi.org/10.1007/978-3-642-25160-3
28. Pettenati, M.C., Cigognini, M.E.: Social networking theories and tools to support connectivist learning activities. Int. J. Web-Based Learn. Teach. Technol. **2**, 42–60 (2007). https://doi.org/10.4018/jwltt.2007070103

29. Sauro, J., Lewis, J.R.: When designing usability questionnaires, does it hurt to be positive? In: Proceedings of the SIGCHI Conference on Human Factors in Computing Systems, pp. 2215–2224 (2011)
30. Sergis, S., Sampson, D.G., Pelliccione, L.: Educational design for MOOCs: design considerations for technology-supported learning at large scale. In: Jemni, M., Kinshuk, K.M. (eds.) Open Education: From OERs to MOOCs. Lecture Notes in Educational Technology, pp. 39–71. Springer, Heidelberg (2017). https://doi.org/10.1007/978-3-662-52925-6_3
31. Stroppi, L.J.R., Chiotti, O., Villarreal, P.D.: Extending BPMN 2.0: method and tool support. In: Dijkman, R., Hofstetter, J., Koehler, J. (eds.) BPMN 2011. LNBIP, vol. 95, pp. 59–73. Springer, Heidelberg (2011). https://doi.org/10.1007/978-3-642-25160-3_5
32. Stylianakis, G., Moumoutzis, N., Arapi, P., Mylonakis, M., Christodoulakis, S.: COLearn and open discovery space portal alignment: a case of enriching open learning infrastructures with collaborative learning capabilities. In: Proceedings 2014 International Conference Interactive Mobile Communication Technologies and Learning, IMCL 2014, pp. 252–256 (2015). https://doi.org/10.1109/imctl.2014.7011142
33. Toven-Lindsey, B., Rhoads, R.A., Lozano, J.B.: Virtually unlimited classrooms: pedagogical practices in massive open online courses. Internet High Educ. **24**, 1–12 (2015)

Mature ELLs' Perceptions Towards Automated and Peer Writing Feedback

Amna Liaqat[1(✉)], Gokce Akcayir[2], Carrie Demmans Epp[2], and Cosmin Munteanu[3]

[1] Department of Computer Science, University of Toronto, Toronto, Canada
a.liaqat@mail.utoronto.ca

[2] EdTeKLA Research Group, Department of Computing Science, University of Alberta, Edmonton, Canada
{akcayir,demmanse}@ualberta.ca

[3] Institute for Communication, Culture, Information, and Technology, University of Toronto Mississauga, Toronto, Canada
cosmin.munteanu@utoronto.ca

Abstract. Mature English Language Learners (ELLs) learning to write in informal environments have little access to instructor feedback and must rely on other sources to support their writing development. While it is known that mature ELLs trust instructor feedback, their perceptions towards feedback from non-expert sources may be mixed. We report on mature ELLs' perceptions and interpretations of peer and automated feedback when using dashboard visualizations of their writing skills derived from several metrics and sources of feedback. These perceptions and interpretations were collected through a short-term deployment of the dashboard within a writing app with 16 mature ELLs, followed by interviews with the learners. From analyses of these interviews, we suggest three design guidelines (DG) related to learning analytics dashboard design for mature ELLs in informal learning contexts. First, analytics-based feedback should contextualize ELLs' learning progress by providing temporal information about learner performance. Second, justifications should accompany feedback to avoid criticism arising from ELLs' prior beliefs. Third, learner autonomy should be fostered by offering explicit mechanisms for reflecting on feedback that is inconsistent with learner beliefs since learners are willing to question automated feedback. We discuss how these three guidelines can be used to benefit learners when an instructor is not present.

Keywords: Learning analytics · Writing · Adult learners · Migrants · Dashboards

1 Introduction

Receiving timely and meaningful feedback is crucial for writing skills development [13]. However, those studying in informal settings may not have access to instructors who can provide such feedback. One such population is mature immigrant English Language Learners (ELLs). Many of these learners are not able to receive formal education to improve their English writing skills even though they need to excel at

M. Scheffel et al. (Eds.): EC-TEL 2019, LNCS 11722, pp. 266–279, 2019.
https://doi.org/10.1007/978-3-030-29736-7_20

writing English to achieve professional and social success. Without consistent and timely feedback from instructors, mature ELLs struggle to identify errors and how to prevent them in their writing. Most of these ELLs face barriers in achieving their learning goals because of their inability to access individualized feedback tailored to them. A way to tackle this issue is to provide automated and peer feedback. However, ELLs' perceptions towards these kinds of feedback need to be explored to see the extent to which this approach can compensate for a lack of instructor feedback, as perceived expertise of the feedback source affects acceptance [22]. For this reason, this study asks "How do mature ELLs perceive and respond to automated and peer feedback on their writing?".

2 Writing Support Tools

Several tools aim to support ELL learning in informal environments. However, many tools were not designed to provide support in settings when an instructor is not present [26]. Mobile apps for vocabulary acquisition or pronunciation consist of short, spaced activities, but provide summative rather than formative feedback through gamification elements [16] or simple error counts [17]. In a study of technology use by new migrants in informal contexts, ELLs expressed that they want tools that help them plan and rehearse [12]. As well, these tools should guide them in closing knowledge gaps, especially when they are unsure of how to do so [12]. To provide such formative guidance, tools with greater socio-collaborative components are needed. Additionally, existing tools primarily focus on language skills related to vocabulary acquisition, pronunciation, and listening, rather than emphasizing writing skill development.

Several tools have been designed targeting members of other populations. These tools use peer-review processes to provide feedback for writing support: ARISE [36], Peerceptiv [32], and Peer Portal [1] are among this class of tools. Having learners assess each other's writing in this way promotes the development of evaluation and judgement skills through reflection on the peer's work, which also encourages learners to reflect on their own writing [10]. Most of these existing tools require an instructor to facilitate the peer-review activities to some degree. However, many ELLs may not be taking writing classes and therefore have no access to an instructor to manage this process. This requirement makes these systems impracticable for immigrant ELLs who need to develop their skills outside of formal learning environments. In contexts where an instructor presence is minimal, other system designs are needed for providing sustainable and meaningful feedback.

3 Learning Analytics Dashboards and Open Learner Models

Open Learner Models (OLMs) and Learning Analytics Dashboards (LADs) are feedback approaches that could be used to support this need since these student-facing-analytics can provide feedback to learners in a timely fashion without requiring instructor involvement [3]. OLMs and LADs, hereafter jointly referred to as LADs, are representations of information that a system has about a learner or group of learners [5, 7].

Traditionally, learners have been given LADs because these tools can support learner reflection and monitoring; they can even foster collaboration among peers [7].

According to the SMILI☺ framework [6, 7], several factors should be considered when designing LADs. Among these factors, is the evaluation of the tool. Ideally, field evaluations with the target users are performed to determine if the feedback is understandable. Evaluations should focus on how learners engage with the LAD, including what information they access and the accuracy of their interpretations [7]. Though many such LADs have been evaluated, they often fail to motivate design decisions and fail to analyze evaluation results with learning science concepts [29]. Few evaluations have focused on learner acceptance of the analytics, even though trust and confidence is a major barrier to learning analytics adoption [3, 19, 24]. Learner comprehension and preferences should be evaluated [38] as a first step to understanding feedback effectiveness because the objective of these tools is to motivate change. As a result, the perceived usefulness and ease-of-use should be included as part of evaluations of the potential benefits associated with LAD use [24].

The mounting body of work evaluating LADs provides evidence of their potential usefulness. However, LADs are often used within formal learning contexts, with most implementations focusing on STEM subjects [3]. These LADs may not help mature ELLs learning to write in informal environments. We, therefore, study the perceptions of this feedback mechanism by an understudied and underserved population: mature ELLs who are trying to improve their writing skills without teacher support.

4 Method

This case study was conducted to examine mature ELLs' perceptions and interpretations of automated and peer feedback delivered via an LAD from a user-centered design perspective [31]. The LAD implements visualizations of learners' writing skills, derived from several automated metrics and sources of feedback (expert and peer). We collected writing samples from immigrant ELLs through a short-term deployment of an app that provides both automated and peer feedback. We then conducted post-deployment focus groups where participants were presented with dashboards to gauge their perceptions of automated and peer feedback.

4.1 Participants

The study was approved by the university's research ethics board. The first author visited classes in the Language Instruction for Newcomers to Canada (LINC) program in a large, predominantly English-speaking metropolitan area to invite students to participate. LINC is a government-funded program offering free English-language classes to recent migrants: 16 mature ELLs (Female = 13) consented and received an honorarium of $50 and reimbursement for travel expenses to the study site.

The gender split in this study is representative of that found in LINC classes (72% of students are female [18]), where students are assessed using the Canadian Language Benchmarks (CLB) standard before placing them in classes. The CLB is a scale describing language proficiency that has three stages. At the time of the study, all participants were CLB stage 2. Individuals in the second stage can participate in a variety of contexts and independently engage in routine and familiar situations [20].

The average age of participants was 38.56 (SD = 6.48). Seven participants spoke Farsi, five spoke Mandarin/Cantonese, and each of the remaining participants spoke one of French, Italian, Spanish, Ukrainian, Russian, Korean, Portuguese, or Azari. Excluding English, four of the participants spoke more than one language. All participants held at least a college diploma or a bachelor's degree. Additionally, some had a master's degree (six) or a PhD (two).

This sample reflects the Canadian immigration system, which favours highly-educated immigrants selected using a competitive point-based system. Most participants (11) were unemployed at the time of the study. Three worked part time and two had full-time work. For eight participants, improving English for daily life was an important motivator for taking English-language classes, followed by getting a job (three), preparing to study (two), passing a test to get certified in a trade or profession (two) and preparing for a citizenship test (one).

4.2 Dashboard Data Sources

In this section, we introduce each measurement used to create the dashboard that provides automated and peer feedback. These measurements include feedback from an instructor using a rubric and an automatically generated score.

CELPIP Derived Rubric. An independent instructor who specializes in adult ELL instruction derived an assignment grading rubric based on the Canadian English Language Proficiency Index Program (CELPIP) [37]. CELPIP is a standardized exam that measures the test-taker's communication abilities in informal, routine contexts, such as interacting with coworkers and friends. The CELPIP was selected for this study as it is a standardized rubric for ELL informal writing, which was the focus of this study. The rubric consists of four dimensions: Task completion and coherence, format and tone, mechanical convention, and lexical resource. These dimensions are scored on a scale of 1 (some proficiency) to 5 (advanced proficiency).

Instructor Feedback. The same instructor who created the rubric used it to grade all the assignments submitted during the deployment. The instructor provided scores for each of the four dimensions. The instructor also wrote a brief (three to six sentences) profile for each learner based on all the assignments (up to three) submitted by that learner. The instructor was asked to base the content of the profiles on the rubric and to include observations of the learners' writing strengths and weaknesses, to provide direction for improvement, and to comment on any general trends across assignments. This profile was the instructor feedback that we compared learner reflections against.

Automated Scoring. In the dashboard, learners were presented with automated scores for each of their assignments. Assignment scores were predicted by running simple linear regression on the first assignment (n = 14), which had been graded by the instructor to generate equations for predicting instructor scores. Feature selection was done with SiNLP (Simple Natural Language Processing Tool). SiNLP is a linguistic analysis tool that evaluates 17 features of writing (e.g., number of pronouns and number of future words). SiNLP was used for feature analysis because it is a simple tool that has been shown to provide similar levels of accuracy to more complex discourse analysis tools, such as Coh-Metrix, when predicting essay scores [11].

From the feature set produced by SiNLP, a subset was selected using WEKA's CfsSubsetEval method with best first search to identify the features that most accurately predicted instructor scores. WEKA is a software package that provides tools for data analysis and predictive modelling. The CfsSubsetEval method evaluates the subset of features with the highest predictive power while minimizing inter-correlation [21]. Feature selection was done for the overall score, as well as for each of the four dimensions. Next, simple linear regression was run on each of the five scores. The resulting equations were used to calculate the predicted scores for the three assignments (Eqs. 1–5). Definitions for the features are taken from [11] and provided below:

- TTR (Type Token Ratio): A measure of lexical diversity computed by dividing the number of types (categories of words) in the text by the number of tokens (total words) in the text, with a higher value indicating more diverse vocabulary use.
- F (Future): A measure of text temporality. Tense use can indicate the rhetorical stance and cohesion of a text.
- NW (Number words): The total word count of the text. Text length is related to discourse sophistication and structure.
- SPP (Second person pronouns): This count can be used as a measure of anaphor use (referencing earlier parts of the text) and can indicate text coherence.
- N (Negations): A count of a type of connective that indicates a contradiction (e.g., "however", "but"), and it is a measure of text coherence.
- D (Demonstratives): A count of words such as "this", "that", and "these". Demonstratives indicate references to information present elsewhere in the text, and they serve as a measure of cohesion.

$$\text{Task Completion and Coherence} = 11.9\,\text{TTR} + 25.2\text{F} + -5.0 \tag{1}$$

$$\text{Format and Tone} = -0.0073\text{NW} + 13.8\text{SPP} + 107.6\text{N} + 34.3\text{F} + 3.2 \tag{2}$$

$$\text{Mechanical Conventions} = -19.3014\text{D} + 3.6 \tag{3}$$

$$\text{Vocabulary} = 5.1\text{TTR} + 23.8\text{F} + -0.5 \tag{4}$$

$$\text{Total} = 5.5\text{TTR} + -15.8\text{D} + 21.7\text{F} + -0.4 \tag{5}$$

The predicted scores resulting from the equations were compared with the instructor graded scores. The predicted scores from our equations were fairly accurate. Across all four dimensions and three assignments, there was an average difference of 0.62 points (SD = 0.50) on a 5-point scale between the predicted and instructor-assigned score.

4.3 The Dashboard Visualization

The visualization (Fig. 1) was designed to display a line graph of a user's automated score for each of the three assignments in blue. The red line displays the average score across all participants. This provides learners with a temporal view of their performance, as was suggested by [15, 25]. Scores were rounded to nearest the .25 point. This accounts for a portion of the uncertainty associated with automated scoring, as suggested by [14]. If an assignment was not submitted, the score was displayed as zero.

Each user receives five graphs: one for each of the four dimensions and one for the overall score. Below each graph, general feedback is provided via text. This feedback is drawn from the rubric feedback corresponding to the average score across the three assignments. This general feedback uses text to provide further context to the graph above, as suggested by [2]. The general feedback is intended to provide users with a holistic impression of their performance. Below the general feedback, users can view the peer-feedback they have received for each assignment. This was intended to provide detail and clarity to the general, automated feedback. Per the framework proposed by [6], the analytics were designed to allow learners access to different levels of detail. Learners could view a general overview or explore a single dimension. Within each dimension, learners were provided with a temporal view of how they performed across the three assignments and could access peer-feedback for each assignment.

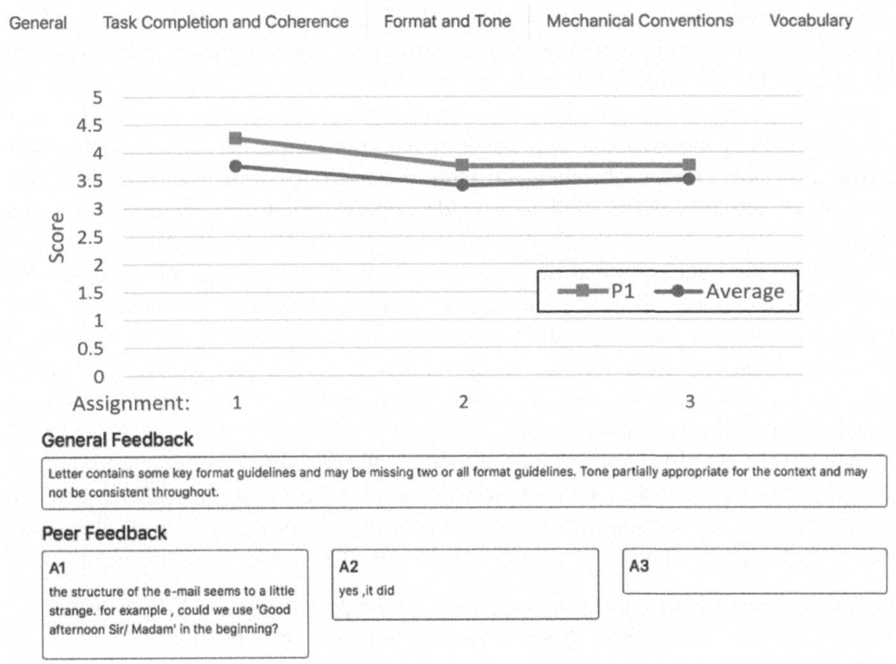

Fig. 1. The visualization of the dashboard combines automated and peer feedback to present data on performance over time, across dimensions, and on each activity. (Color figure online)

4.4 Study Procedures and Learning Tasks

Participants completed three informal writing assignments and used the app to provide peer-feedback over nine days, with an assignment due every three days. To submit assignments as well as provide and receive feedback, participants used a web-app that runs in any browser but is more suitable for larger screens (e.g., laptops). In the app, participants receive writing prompts and can submit a response. Users are also assigned a partner. After the participant submits a writing assignment, the partner can provide peer-feedback and vice versa. During peer-review, reviewers are asked four general questions to guide their feedback. Each question corresponds to a dimension on the CELPIP rubric and is listed below:

1. Did the letter address all the main points required to complete the task? Which parts of the task are missing? (Task completion and coherence)
2. Was the letter organized well so that it was easy to understand? What can be done to ensure good flow and organization? (format and tone)
3. Did the ideas of the writer connect well? How can this be improved? (mechanical convention)
4. Did the writer use a wide range of vocabulary for the task? How can this be improved? (lexical resource)

After the activities were complete, all participants were invited to the lab for a focus group session where they were presented with the dashboard. Twelve of the 16 participants attended the group session phase. The four participants who were unable to attend a group session (due to scheduling constraints) met with the researcher one-on-one online. The 12 participants attending the focus group sessions each joined one group, for a total of three groups, consisting of three, four, and five mature ELLs. As almost all participants attended ELL classes at the same centre, participants in the focus groups generally knew each other. All three focus groups were audio recorded and transcribed, and they were used to provide context when answering our research question.

Author 1 first demonstrated the visualization. Participants were informed that the information they received was not produced by an expert and may be inaccurate. They were given time to interact with their visualizations and reflect on the following questions: "Based on what you see, what would you say are your writing challenges? What are you good at? How do you think you can improve? Please write a few lines reflecting on your observations."

After everyone had submitted their responses, the researcher led the group through several questions about their interaction with and perceptions of the dashboard. As all participants were at an intermediate to advanced English proficiency level, they were able to understand and participate in the discussion. The below questions were asked:

1. Did you find the automated scores accurate? The peer feedback? Why or why not?
2. Do you think the feedback (scores, general, and peer) was helpful?
3. Did seeing the average scores of all the learners help you understand anything about your own performance?
4. Did you feel surprised or anxious about any of the information your received?

4.5 Data Analysis

Data gathered from students' written reflections and the focus-group transcriptions were analyzed using inductive data analysis [28]. In this approach, there are no pre-developed schemes or templates: codes emerge from the data. This coding procedure was part of an overarching analysis approach where the flow model of content analysis was used [30]. This model employs three steps in sequence: (1) data reduction, (2) data displays, and (3) conclusion drawing and verification. In Step 1, data was reviewed to determine patterns and codes, independent of the type of code displayed. Step 2 included reorganizing data to make the patterns and codes more explicit and easily accessible. In Step 3, themes were grounded in the data and clearly appeared from those suggested in Step 1 and Step 2. Finally, verification was performed by repeating all of the steps three times.

The peer-feedback data was not appropriate for content analysis because it is limited both in number and content (e.g., "Yes", "yes, it did"). While we could not reliably analyze the feedback provided by peers as a result of these limitations, we report participants' opinions about peer feedback. These data came from the focus groups.

For data analysis, each participant's reflection was compared against the information presented in the LAD. Through this process, it was determined how accurate learner reflections on their writing skills and learning process were (i.e., how closely their perceptions aligned with the dashboard). Next, the strengths and weaknesses identified in participants' reflections were compared with those contained in the instructor's feedback.

Analyses were handled by a researcher (Author 2) who is experienced in qualitative data analysis. Additionally, another expert in the field (Author 3) reviewed all of the steps of this analysis and confirmed the output.

5 Findings

We report our findings in accordance with the themes that emerged during data analysis. These themes consist of learners' focus on challenges over strengths, evaluation of performance over time, incorrect interpretations possibly tied to past beliefs, and a tendency to question automated and peer feedback.

5.1 Focus on Challenges Over Strengths

Participants stated 11 strengths and 26 weaknesses. Almost half the students (n = 7) only specified their weaknesses without discussing any of their strengths. These findings suggest learners were focused on identifying weaknesses rather than strengths in their writing. This tendency towards understanding weaknesses to improve their writing skills also can be seen in nearly all participants' (n = 15, 93.8%) expressed desire to improve further. Learner identified methods for improving their writing skills usually centered on practicing more (n = 9). Other approaches included finding sources of additional feedback and guidance, as stated by P5, "the key is to have some professors to review and to give advice", and investing more time, as was stated by P9: "I need really do more practice and more time to improve my level". These expressions may also be evidence of participants' high motivation, which would be consistent with prior work showing that mature ELLs have high intrinsic motivation for learning to write [32].

5.2 Evaluation of Performance Over Time

Almost half of the ELLs (n = 7, 46.7%) reviewed their performance by looking at their improvements throughout the app deployment, as can be seen through P13's comment that "My general feedback about mechanical convention was near to average and was progressive in my third assignment", and P9's comments that "In first practice in task completion and coherence I was lower than average but after I understood my weak points so I arrived near the average point and the same thing happens for format and tone parts."

This behaviour is consistent with that of other adult language learners who have used this class of feedback tools [13, 15]. However, this type of comparison goal is not typically supported within the visualizations we provide to learners [14] as temporal analytics are a relatively new area of exploration [25].

5.3 Incorrect Interpretations Possibly Tied to Past Beliefs

Participant interpretations of their feedback contain incorrect or sub-optimal interpretations of both their strengths (n = 5, 45.5%) and weaknesses (n = 8, 30.8%). While the percentage of potential misinterpretation of weaknesses is almost double that of their strengths, this rate is consistent with the rate at which they identified strengths and weaknesses. An example of an incorrect interpretation from P14 (Fig. 2) demonstrates how participants interpreted the visualizations. P14 stated "My challenges are the mechanism [mechanical conventions] and vocabulary". However, Fig. 2 shows the participant's performance with respect to mechanical conventions was above average for the two assignments he had submitted; the third assignment measure is missing because it was not submitted. The visualizations for the task completion and coherence dimension (Fig. 2) indicate P14 has an area where he is weaker, which this learner failed to see. This makes P14's identification of the mechanical conventions dimension as his primary weakness an incorrect interpretation of the provided feedback.

Participants' suboptimal or incorrect interpretations may come from their past experiences and the prior beliefs that stem from these experiences [33]. These prior beliefs likely play a role in mature ELLs' interpretation of these charts since we know that members of this population can possess strong epistemic writing beliefs [27].

5.4 Tendency to Question Automated and Peer Feedback

Average scores shown in the visualization were perceived as helpful but providing more details would have improved perceived usefulness: "I see the line and it makes sense but [inaudible] the structure it's very weak for my writing I need to improve more and more, I don't know. Just from the scores, it's maybe not enough" (P5). P5 added there is "not so much context" and suggested model assignments for different scores:

> In my opinion not just the score. It shows that you have some gaps from others, so I need to improve to make scores improve. It just shows the scores. If possible, it could show some model assignments to show us how others write. (P5)

The request for more detail was agreed to by P2 ("yeah") and P4 ("Yeah, I agree").

Participants think that all feedback (scores, general, and peer) was useful, in general. However, the peer feedback was perceived as unreliable because it was not always available: "my partner didn't respond to me for the second assignment. So, I think that affected my feedback and my graph is strange" (P13). These perceptions carried over to the writing platform with most participant opinions focusing on how helpful or "very useful" (P16) it was for them. Comments included:

> I can see others people's writings, and it helps me a lot. But maybe it should provide more partners at the same time. Because one partner's writing skills are not enough, sometimes she couldn't give me the correct advice. After all, I like this program (P7)

> Using the App has helped me to have a better understanding of what I was asked for. In short, I could say it's been a good practice. (P16)

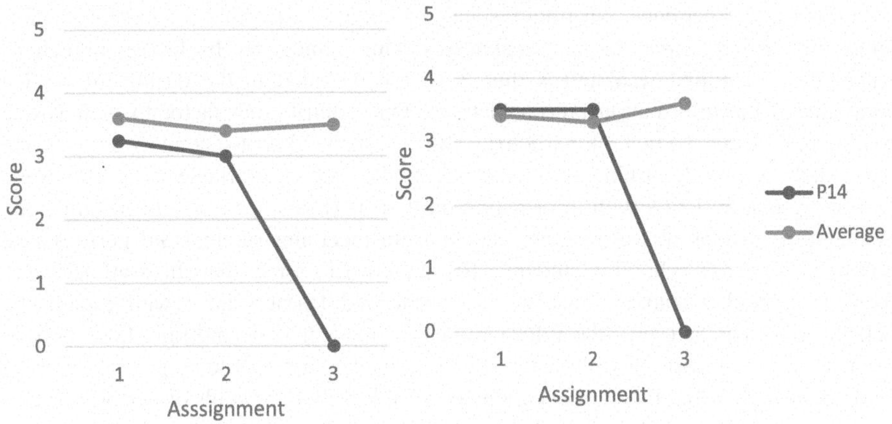

Fig. 2. P14 performed below average in the task completion and coherence dimension (left). However, P14 identified mechanical conventions as a weakness despite better performance, which was above average, in this dimension (right). (Color figure online)

5.5 Design Guidelines for Feedback in Informal Learning

In light of the above findings, we suggest three design guidelines (DG) to consider when creating feedback tools for mature ELLs in informal learning contexts.

DG1: Feedback should contextualize performance by showing how learners are progressing over time, while allowing learners to compare their performance against a reference point.

DG1 is based on our finding that when presented with two dimensions of comparison (temporal versus peers) mature ELLs chose to evaluate progress by looking at their performance over time. Temporal analyses that present learners with historic data on past performance can prompt reflection on performance over time [15]. While these participants did not strongly emphasize comparison with peers, it is a common reference point used to contextualize analytics of student performance [23, 35], suggesting it could be used in this context. Moreover, some participants compared the average score to their own when identifying gaps in their performance and through that their need to seek strategies for improvement. Participants also requested access to sample assignments to make sense of expectations. If peer work is used to provide these exemplars, it would give learners the opportunity to learn from stronger peers [8]. Therefore, it may be beneficial to allow mature ELLs the choice to view peer scores and samples.

DG2: Feedback should be presented with clear and detailed justification to prevent possible bias arising from mature ELLs' prior beliefs.

Our mature ELLs already have substantial educational experience and possess a strong skillset for achieving learning success, suggesting that we need to design learning activities and tools that recognize and support this learner characteristic. Along with this prior experience, our findings suggest mature ELLs hold pre-existing beliefs about their writing strengths and weaknesses. This is indicated by learner reflections where they identified weaknesses that were not included in the dashboard or that contradicted the information presented there. One contributing factor to their strong writing beliefs may be that our participants have completed post-secondary degrees and have likely acquired learning skills and beliefs they are comfortable with. Therefore, presenting mature ELLs with information on their performance may not be sufficient. While some groups of learners can benefit from receiving summarized performance reports (e.g., lower achieving students) [6], mature ELLs may benefit from access to their full, detailed student models. As experienced learners have well established beliefs, they may interpret the information in a manner that confirms those beliefs. Thus, in informal learning with mature ELLs, consideration should be given to helping learners identify when their beliefs are incompatible with their skills or performance so that the system can scaffold belief revision.

DG3: Foster learner critical thinking and autonomy using mechanisms that support learners' tendency to question automated feedback.

We found that mature ELLs were comfortable questioning scores they disagreed with. This may be because learners do not perceive automated feedback as having the same authority as that provided by an instructor. Perceiving automated feedback as having less authority may benefit learners because those who view the teacher's role as one of authority take less responsibility for their learning [9]. Additionally, online platforms in blended language-learning classes have been shown to increase learner awareness of feedback importance, improve confidence, and trigger a shift in learner perceptions of the instructors' role from that of director to that of facilitator [34].

Thus, we find automated feedback could play an important role in scaffolding learners towards critical assessment of their writing by offering explicit mechanisms for users to challenge the feedback or to reflect on why they may disagree with it, as is commonly done in negotiated and persuadable open learner models [4].

6 Limitations

Our participants consisted of a specific subset of ELLs (highly educated), thus our findings may not be representative of other immigrant contexts. In our analysis, we were unable to include peer-feedback as it lacked detail or was not provided. So, the role of peer-feedback in prompting learner reflections has not been assessed. In future studies, mechanisms should be designed to elicit more detailed, meaningful peer feedback.

7 Conclusion

In this paper, we explored mature ELLs' perceptions of writing skills visualizations, derived from several automated metrics and sources of feedback (expert and peer). The importance of providing such types of feedback comes from the lack of available instructor feedback for our target population, immigrants. This population usually does not have access to formal language education, even though their language proficiency is one of the biggest factors affecting socio-economic status in their new country. In this sense, a dashboard that provides customized feedback for the writing activities they perform on their own contributes not only to the success of individuals but also the development of community. Based on our findings, we presented three design guidelines that can be used to help others create similar types of systems within their contexts.

Future studies should employ long-term deployments and explore ways to facilitate high quality peer feedback. A study exploring the effectiveness of peer and automated feedback compared to instructor feedback could show whether these practices influence language learning. Alternatively, a similar type of technology could be built to support the development of recent migrants' speaking skills with automated and peer feedback of learner speech being used to advance their fluency and pronunciation accuracy.

Acknowledgements. This work was supported by AGE-WELL NCE Inc., a member of the Government of Canada's Networks of Centres of Excellence.

References

1. Aghaee, N., Hansson, H.: Peer portal: quality enhancement in thesis writing using self-managed peer review on a mass scale. Int. Rev. Res. Open Distrib. Learn. **14**(1), 186 (2013)
2. Ali, L., Hatala, M., Gašević, D., Jovanović, J.: A qualitative evaluation of evolution of a learning analytics tool. Comput. Educ. 58(1), 470–489 (2012)

3. Bodily, R., et al.: Open learner models and learning analytics dashboards: a systematic review. In: Proceedings of the 8th International Conference on Learning Analytics and Knowledge, pp. 41–50 (2018)
4. Bull, S., Ginon, B., Boscolo, C., Johnson, M.: Introduction of learning visualisations and metacognitive support in a persuadable open learner model, pp. 30–39, April (2016)
5. Bull, S., Kay, J.: Open learner models. In: Nkambou, R., Bourdeau, J., Mizoguchi, R. (eds.) Advances in Intelligent Tutoring Systems, pp. 301–322. Springer, Heidelberg (2010). https://doi.org/10.1007/978-3-642-14363-2_15
6. Bull, S., Kay, J.: SMILI☺: a framework for interfaces to learning data in open learner models, learning analytics and related fields. Int. J. Artif. Intell. Educ. **26**(1), 293–331 (2016)
7. Bull, S., Kay, J.: Student models that invite the learner in: the SMILI:() open learner modelling framework. Int. J. Artif. Intell. Ed. **17**(2), 89–120 (2007)
8. Bull, S., Nghiem, T.: Helping learners to understand themselves with a learner model open to students, peers and instructors, April 2003
9. Ceylan, N.O.: Fostering learner autonomy. Procedia Soc. Behav. Sci. **199**, 85–93 (2015). https://doi.org/10.1016/j.sbspro.2015.07.491
10. Cho, Y.H., Cho, K.: Peer reviewers learn from giving comments. Instr. Sci. **39**(5), 629–643 (2011). https://doi.org/10.1007/s11251-010-9146-1
11. Crossley, S.A., Allen, L.K., Kyle, K., McNamara, D.S.: Analyzing discourse processing using a simple natural language processing tool. Discourse Process. **51**(5–6), 511–534 (2014). https://doi.org/10.1080/0163853X.2014.910723
12. Demmans Epp, C.: Migrants and mobile technology use: gaps in the support provided by current tools. J. Interact. Media Educ. **2017**(1), 2 (2017)
13. Demmans Epp, C.: Protutor : a pronunciation tutor that uses historic open learner models. University of Saskatchewan (2010)
14. Demmans Epp, C., Bull, S.: Uncertainty representation in visualizations of learning analytics for learners: current approaches and opportunities. IEEE Trans. Learn. Technol. **8**(3), 242–260 (2015). https://doi.org/10.1109/TLT.2015.2411604
15. Demmans Epp, C., McCalla, G.: ProTutor: historic open learner models for pronunciation tutoring. Artif. Intell. Educ. **2011**, 441–443 (2011)
16. Edge, D., Cheng, K.-Y., Whitney, M., Qian, Y., Yan, Z., Soong, F.: Tip tap tones: mobile microtraining of mandarin sounds, pp. 427–430, September 2012
17. Edge, D., Searle, E., Chiu, K., Zhao, J., Landay, J.A.: MicroMandarin: mobile language learning in context. In: Proceedings of the 2011 Annual Conference on Human Factors in Computing Systems - CHI 2011, Vancouver, BC, Canada, 2011, p. 3169 (2011)
18. Evaluation of the Language Instruction for Newcomers to Canada (LINC) Program (2011). https://www.canada.ca/en/immigration-refugees-citizenship/corporate/reports-statistics/evaluations/language-instruction-newcomers-canada-2010/intro.html#a2
19. Greller, W., Drachsler, H.: Translating learning into numbers: a generic framework for learning analytics. J. Educ. Technol. Soc. Palmerston North **15**(3), 42–57 (2012)
20. Hajer, A., Kaskens, A.-M.: Canadian Language Benchmarks: English as a Second Language for Adults. Citizenship and Immigration Canada (2012)
21. Hall, M.A.: Correlation-based feature selection of discrete and numeric class machine learning. University of Waikato, Department of Computer Science (2000)
22. Ilgen, D.R., Fisher, C.D., Taylor, M.S.: Consequences of individual feedback on behavior in organizations. J. Appl. Psychol. **64**(4), 349–371 (1979)
23. Jivet, I., Scheffel, M., Drachsler, H., Specht, M.: Awareness is not enough: pitfalls of learning analytics dashboards in the educational practice. Data Driven Approaches Digital Educ. **2017**, 82–96 (2017)

24. Jivet, I., Scheffel, M., Specht, M., Drachsler, H.: License to evaluate: preparing learning analytics dashboards for educational practice. In: Proceedings of the 8th International Conference on Learning Analytics and Knowledge, pp. 31–40 (2018)
25. Knight, S., Wise, A.F., Chen, B.: Time for change: why learning analytics needs temporal analysis. J. Learn. Anal. 4(3), 7–17 (2017)
26. Kukulska-Hulme, A., Shield, L.: An overview of mobile assisted language learning: from content delivery to supported collaboration and interaction. ReCALL **20**(3), 271–289 (2008). https://doi.org/10.1017/S0958344008000335
27. Liaqat, A., Munteanu, C.: Towards a writing analytics framework for adult english language learners. In: Proceedings of the Seventh International Learning Analytics & Knowledge Conference (LAK 2017), Sydney, Australia (2018)
28. Mackey, A., Gass, S.: Second Language Research, Methodology and Design. Lawrence Erlbaum Associates (2005)
29. Marzouk, Z., et al.: What if learning analytics were based on learning science? Australas. J. Educ. Technol. **32**(6), 1–18 (2016)
30. Miles, M.B., Huberman, A.M.: Qualitative Data Analysis: An Expanded Sourcebook, 2nd edn. Sage Publications Inc., Thousand Oaks (1994)
31. Norman, D.A.: User Centered System Design: New Perspectives on Human-Computer Interaction. CRC Press, Boca Raton (1986)
32. Peerceptiv - Data Driven Peer Assessment. http://www.peerceptiv.com/wordpress/
33. Ross, S.: Self-assessment in second language testing: a meta-analysis and analysis of experiential factors. Lang. Test. **15**(1), 1–20 (1998)
34. Snodin, N.S.: The effects of blended learning with a CMS on the development of autonomous learning: a case study of different degrees of autonomy achieved by individual learners. Comput. Educ. **61**, 209–216 (2013)
35. Verbert, K., Duval, E., Klerkx, J., Govaerts, S., Santos, J.: Learning analytics dashboard applications. Am. Behav. Sci. **57**(10), 1500–1509 (2013)
36. Vista, A., Care, E., Griffin, P.: A new approach towards marking large-scale complex assessments: developing a distributed marking system that uses an automatically scaffolding and rubric-targeted interface for guided peer-review. Assessing Writ. **24**, 1–15 (2015). https://doi.org/10.1016/j.asw.2014.11.001
37. What is CELPIP? https://www.celpip.ca/what-is-celpip/. Accessed 10 Jan 2018
38. Zapata-Rivera, D., et al.: Designing and evaluating reporting systems in the context of new assessments. Augmented Cogn. Users Contexts **2018**, 143–153 (2018)

Patterns and Loops: Early Computational Thinking

Marielle Léonard[1], Yvan Peter[2(✉)], and Yann Secq[2]

[1] France-IOI, Villeneuve-d'Ascq, France
marielleleonard59@gmail.com

[2] Univ. Lille, CNRS, Centrale Lille, UMR 9189 - CRIStAL - Centre de Recherche en Informatique Signal et Automatique de Lille, 59000 Lille, France
{yvan.peter,yann.secq}@univ-lille.fr

Abstract. This article presents a large scale quasi-experiment to introduce primary school pupils to Computational Thinking. The aim is to enhance their capability to spot repetitive patterns and to express them as loops. Unplugged and plugged-in activities are used to train the pupils. Trace analysis and pre and post questionnaires were used to measure the impact of the intervention. This article deals with the 2018 session involving 20 classes. The results show a positive impact of the activities and give information about the skills acquired.

Keywords: Computational thinking · Computer science education · Elementary school · Repetitive patterns and loops · Pedagogical sequence

1 Introduction

Computational thinking (CT) brings abstraction and problem solving skills that can be exploited in many contexts and subject matters at school and in broader contexts. While not being equal to computer science and programming, computational thinking skills definitively lays the ground to explore more computer science related topics such as algorithms. In her seminal article about Computational Thinking, J. Wing advocates for the introduction of CT to non-majors in Computer Science and pre-college students [12]. Since then CT has been considered in many domains like mathematics and experimental sciences [11], arts [6] and even language learning [8].

In this article, we present our work to bring CT skills to pupils in elementary school (8–10 years old) in France. Within this project, we have mainly considered the ability of pupils to abstract data, to recognize redundant patterns in data and to express them as a loop structure. This opens the way to systematic and repetitive treatment of data. Towards this end, we have devised a pedagogical sequence including unplugged and plugged-in activities. We will focus in this article on the result from year 2018 which involved 20 classes from 16 schools and 447 pupils. For this quasi-experiment, we have set up pre and post tests to

M. Scheffel et al. (Eds.): EC-TEL 2019, LNCS 11722, pp. 280–293, 2019.
https://doi.org/10.1007/978-3-030-29736-7_21

assess the capability to identify patterns and we have collected traces from their on line programming activities.

This article seeks to answer the following questions:

RQ1 Does the pedagogical sequence presented in this article (Sect. 3) bring an improvement of the pupils cognitive skill of recognizing and expressing repetitive patterns as loop structure ?

RQ2 To what extent do the pupils manage to transfer their skills from one kind of language to the other while solving similar puzzles ?

In the next section, we review existing works about CT, its introduction in pre-college classes and the assessment of CT skills. Section 3 presents the pedagogical sequence we have devised and the experimental setting described in Sect. 4. In Sect. 5 we discuss the analysis of the experimental data before drawing conclusion and perspectives.

2 Related Works

In this section, we review general definitions about Computational Thinking before considering how it is introduced in schools. We then review existing frameworks to assess CT skills.

2.1 Introducing Computational Thinking Concepts

The first concepts of Computational Thinking date back to the work of Seymour Papert with Logo [7]. More recently, the article by Jeannette Wing advocating CT as a primary skill along reading, writing and arithmetic raised a great interest in the education and research community [12]. Wing stresses that CT is not equal to programming but rather the capability to manipulate abstractions and to solve problems that can be applied to many fields. She called for the introduction of CT to pre-college audience.

Since then, the research community has explored ways and means to introduce CT at school: what are the fundamental concepts to teach ? Which technology can support that learning? Etc. These questions are even more important since many countries have started to update their curricula to introduce these topics at different school levels.

Different works try to organize CT concepts around taxonomies. Gouws *et al.* propose a CT framework that describe skills related to computational thinking [4]. The framework proposes different kind of CT skills learned through programming out of their literature review: *Processes and Transformations*, *Models and Abstractions*, *Patterns and Algorithms*, *Tools and Resources*, *Inference and Logic*, *Evaluations and Improvements*. They combine these skills with a level of mastery inspired by Bloom's taxonomy of learning: *Recognize*, *Understand*, *Apply*, *Assimilate*. The framework can be used as an analysis or design framework. Weintrop *et al.* consider the introduction of CT practices in maths and science providing the ground for a definition of CT activities away from computer science [11]. The authors define a taxonomy of 22 CT practices grouped into the following categories: *Data and Information*, *Modeling and Simulation*, *Computation*, *Problem Solving* and *Systems Thinking*.

Ching *et al.* rather take a technological entry to the introduction of CT concepts [3]. They provide an analysis of existing readily available technologies for teaching computational thinking. They have identified *robot toys*, *robot kits*, *board games*, *augmented reality tools*, *(visual) programming applications/websites* and *animation/game development tools*. These categories vary by whether it uses physical manipulation or screen interaction and concrete (i.e., robot) or visual feedback. Concepts learned through these technologies range from sequence and loop to more advanced concepts and may imply creativity and problem solving for some of them.

These taxonomies do not necessarily provide insights about the order in which CT concepts should be introduced. Based on a literature survey, Rich *et al.* have started to work on *Learning Trajectories* to define the concepts that can be addressed depending on the grade level and at which level of details. A *Learning Trajectory* is formalized as a set of learning goals, an associated learning path to achieve these goals and illustrative activities. Their literature study shows that many research results focus on a single or independent learning goals. They observe that the same goals have been introduced at multiple grade levels since they usually address inexperienced learners. For this reason, they have relied on maths pedagogical approaches and curricula to propose an ordering of the concepts introduced (learning path). Their article illustrates their approach on three CT concepts: *Sequence*, *Repetition*, and *Conditionals*.

The notion of repetition is one of the fundamental concepts present in all these works. We also believe that pattern recognition and redundant patterns reduction constitute one of the atomic skill in computational thinking, which is why we have focused specifically on this aspect in this study.

2.2 Assessment of CT Skills

The assessment of students' skills is an additional dimension of the introduction of CT at school. One can find different approaches in the literature. Brennan & Resnick articulate CT around three dimensions: computational concepts (programming level: loops, parallelism...), computational practices (iterative development, debugging...), and computational perspectives (expressing oneself, connecting to others...) [1]. They propose to assess these dimensions through portfolio analysis, artifact-based interviews and design scenario (projects).

The SRI report by Snow *et al.* considers the means to assess CT skills (problem solving, abstraction...) in the context of the year long high school course "Exploring Computer Science" (ECS) [10]. Towards this end, they propose design patterns to create sound assessments to measure knowledge and practices. The report covers the assessment of the following ECS units: HCI, Problem Solving, Web Design and Introduction to Programming. The assessments include quizzes, problems and code reading and tracing.

Grover *et al.* used formative and summative assessment in the context of a 6 weeks middle school module involving computational concepts [5]. The assessments relied on multiple choice quizzes many of them including Scratch code snippets. Some exercises involved reordering code blocks or code tracing/ debugging activities.

Seiter *et al.* propose a framework to assess CT skills in primary grades (1 to 6) called Progression of Early Computational Thinking (PECT) [9]. The framework provides measures based on Scratch programs (use of specific instructions) in the scope of common design patterns (e.g., animation, collision management...). These patterns are then related to CT concepts. The framework has been evaluated against programs found on the Scratch web site.

This later work as well as the approach by Brennan & Resnick are rather time consuming since they involve the study of students' productions potentially in the context of open-ended activities. The other approaches are more tractable since they rely on different kinds of quizzes.

3 Pedagogical Sequence

The sequence we have designed is based on two main inspirations. The first one is the pioneering work of Seymour Papert with his work on Logo [7] and the importance of thinking about the way we think by describing procedures that have to be interpreted by a computer. The second inspiration comes from work done by Bruner [2] on stages of representation: enactive (action-based), iconic (image-based) and symbolic (language-based). The pedagogical sequence was designed along these stages to support knowledge construction by the pupils.

The pedagogical sequence is presented Fig. 1. This progression includes unplugged and plugged-in activities to support the identification and synthesis of repetitive patterns and their expression in the form of sequence of actions and loops. There are three different phases. The first two ones last one hour and half, the last one takes two hours. The pupils came to university for a whole day. They have the first two phases in the morning and the last one in the afternoon. The different phases are described hereafter.

3.1 Absolute Orientation

In this phase pupils have to move a character on a grid to a given square using absolute directions (North, South, East, West). They start with a board game (see Fig. 2). Pupils work by groups of four to six and take turn at different roles: defining a solution, *program counter* (telling the instruction to perform), and *processor* (executing the instruction). The activity evolves from simple paths to more complex ones with the addition of obstacles and bonuses. When the sequence of instructions starts to get longer, pupils usually start to express frustration. This is the right time to introduce the loop notion (*repeat n times*).

When main concepts of instruction, sequence, loop, execution (and bugs...) are (dis)covered, the pupils switch to a similar activity on tablets by groups of

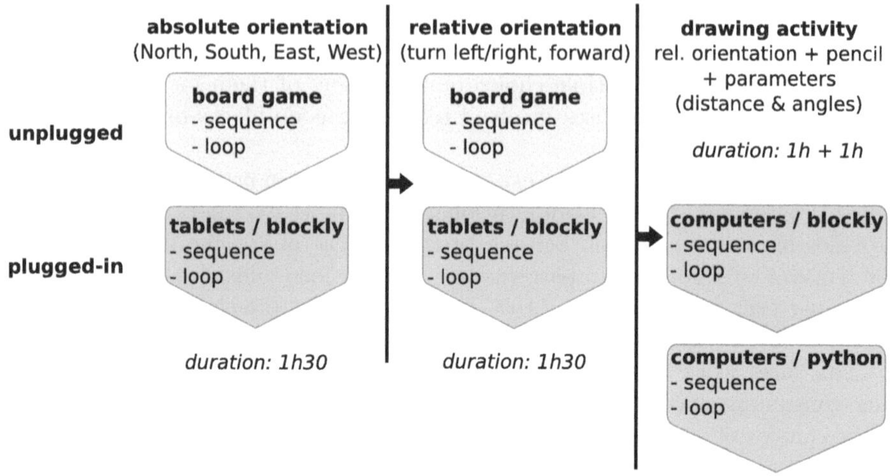

Fig. 1. Pedagogical sequence to train loop recognition and expression

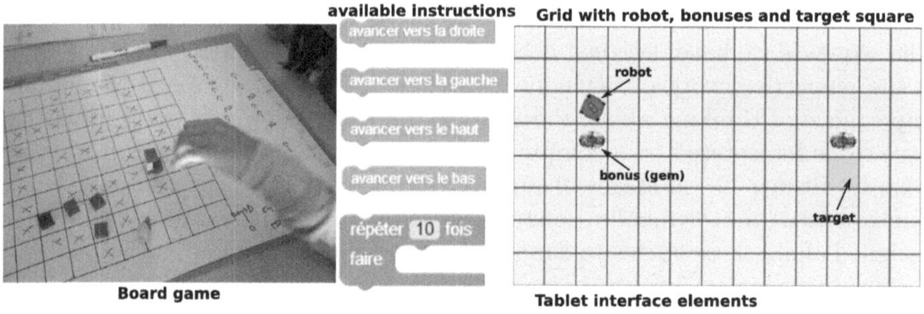

Fig. 2. Board game and tablet interface.

two. They use a visual block-based programming language (*Blockly*). Figure 2 shows one of the puzzles presented on tablets. For each puzzle, there is a specific instruction set provided (Fig. 2). The activities and instructions set evolve again from sequence to loop. The goal of this sequence on tablet is to reinforce learnings done through the unplugged activity and to lead slowly pupils towards autonomy by working by two instead of 4 to 6 in the first phase.

3.2 Relative Orientation

This phase follows a similar organization to the previous one. The main change is that by using an oriented character, the pupils have to handle a different instructions set (*turn left*, *turn right*, *forward*). This also implies remembering the character orientation when planning the moves. Turning is only by 90° and is not parameterized. It prepares the last phase where orientation is necessary for the drawing activity.

3.3 Drawing Activity: Back to Papert's Turtle

The last phase is done in a computer laboratory where each pupil is alone with a computer. The activities are oriented towards drawing with a turtle (in the spirit of Logo). The instructions set is similar to the previous one with addition of the pencil management (putting it up or down to draw) and parameterized functions (e.g. `forward(`*distance*`)` or `turn right(`*angle*`)`). The pupils use the same platform as on the tablets. In the first part, they continue to use the *blockly* block-based programming language. In the second part, we introduce some Python programming making them switch from a graphical to a textual notation within the same context (Fig. 3). To make it easier for the pupils, they use functions translated in French (e.g. `forward(10)` becomes `avancer(10)`), as it is their primary language. Nonetheless, they are introduced to the regular Python loop notation. This last part enables us to observe the transfer of competencies from block-based to textual programming.

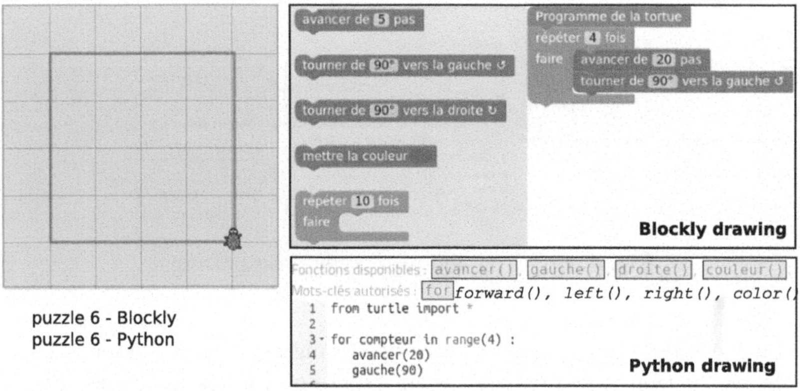

Fig. 3. From block-based to textual programming

4 Experimental Setting

4.1 Participants and Organization

The 2018 experiment involved pupils from 16 elementary schools around the university. Twenty classes participated for a total of 447 pupils. The age of the pupils is 8–10 years old and we had a balanced gender representation (49% girls). The experiment lasted for one week with 5 classes per day (excluding Wednesday). The classes came to the university for a whole day. To cope with the large number of pupils, they where supervised by second year computer science students with the support of their teachers. The students were presented with the pedagogical progression and learning activities beforehand so as to be able to manage the pupils and help them during activities.

4.2 Data Collection: Questionnaires and Online Activities Logging

Pre and Post Tests. The pupils passed a test at the beginning and the end of the day to measure if there was a progress in their ability to spot repetitive patterns and to express them in a condensed notation opening the way to loop treatment. These tests are not intended to be a full assessment of the pupils' skills as presented in Sect. 2.2 but rather to answer our first research question (*RQ1*).

The tests involved the coding of patterns as letters. The pupils were instructed they could use any notation they would see fit including shorthand notation. The pre test was presented as coding a graphical notation for music (Fig. 4, left - each color corresponding to a music note) while the post test involved coding pasta necklace crafting instructions (Fig. 4, right). We have chosen two different contexts to avoid pupils just remembering the patterns from the pre test. But it should be noted that patterns to be recognized and synthesized are strictly the same in the pre and post test.

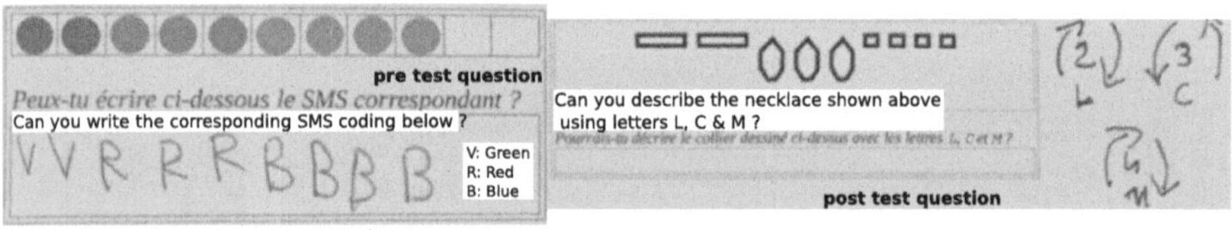

Fig. 4. Pre (left) and post (right) test patterns.

Table 1 presents patterns that were used ranging from a sequence based on a single instruction and up to three instructions for the most complex. The notation shown here corresponds to the pre test, but as stated before patterns are exactly the same in pre and post tests. The *Pattern* corresponds to what the pupils are given and the *loop notation* shows the kind of coding expected. Table 1 also presents the pattern types and correspondence. To answer RQ1, we look at the answers from the pupils. For instance for pattern type `1i` a pupils that has the notion of repetition would write something corresponding to `11R` (11 times R(ed)). In the other case, s.he would write all the letters.

Table 1. Patterns used in pre and post questionnaires

Type	Correspondence	Pattern	Loop notation
1i	1 instruction pattern	RRRRRRRRRRR	11R
Nx1i	N × 1 instruction pattern	VVRRRBBBB	2V 3R 4B
2i	2 instructions pattern	BRBRBRBRBR	5x(BR)
3i+2i	2 instructions + 1 instruction patterns	VRRVRRBBBBB	2(VRR) 4B/2(V 2R) 4B

Programming Activities. The plugged-in activities were realized on a France-IOI platform[1]. The four sequences include a set of puzzles of growing difficulty and build on each other. The study of the results from these activities will provide insights for our second research question about the transfer of skills from one language to the other (*RQ2*). As a whole, they include successively puzzles that can be solved by a sequence of instructions, a loop with one instruction, mixed sequence and loop, loop with multiple instructions and up to nested loops. The first sequence includes 24 puzzles and is very progressive so the pupils can build their skills. The next sequences provide between 15 and 18 puzzles. They all go through the easier puzzles (e.g. sequence) so that the pupils can transfer their skills to a new set of instructions. Then difficulty grows. Figure 5 presents some of the puzzles that are further analyzed in the next section.

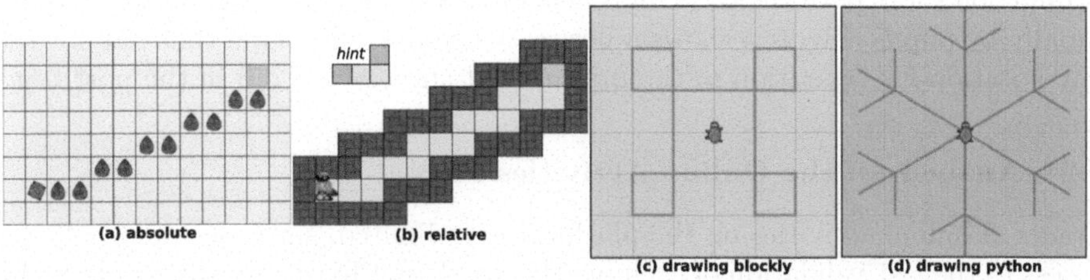

Fig. 5. Examples of tricky puzzles in each phase.

The platform progresses from one puzzle to the other upon success but it also allows to select a specific puzzle in a list. Each phase of the plugged-in activities lasted between 30 and 45 min depending on the groups. For this reason the pupils did not do the same number of puzzles depending on how quick they were and if they were stuck on some puzzles. When introducing new concepts or patterns, we have a tutorial puzzle with instructions or hints for resolution.

5 Results

5.1 Analysis of Pre and Post Questionnaires

The pre and post activity questionnaires (Fig. 4) have been coded to reflect whether the pupils have correctly coded patterns. This gave us a value between 0 and 1. For the 447 pupils, we have a mean $m = 0.147$, with a standard deviation $sd = 0.07$ for the pre test and $m = 0.241$, $sd = 0.12$ for the post test. A paired t-test gives us a value $t(446) = -6.76$ ($p < .0001$) which shows that the pedagogical sequence had a significant impact on pupils' capability to spot and code repetitive patterns.

[1] Association that organizes the Bebras computer science challenge in France (http://www.castor-informatique.fr).

Table 2. Successful coding of repetitive patterns

	1i	Nx1i	2i	3i+2i
Pre test	118 (27%)	102 (23%)	29 (8%)	14 (4%)
Post test	166 (38%)	140 (32%)	70 (17%)	56 (14%)

Table 2 presents the number (and percentage) of pupils that have used a shorthand notation (i.e. recognized the repetitive patterns) in the pre and post tests. It is interesting to first note that the awareness of 1 instruction patterns has significantly raised as well as sequences of several 1 instruction loop (+40% for both). But, the most interesting aspect is probably that more complex patterns (2 and 3 instructions) have increased even more. This could mean that after some training on short patterns the skill is generalized to more complex patterns quite rapidly by pupils. Figure 4 shows a best case example of a pupil that did not use any notation for repetition in the pre test but successfully did in the post test.

5.2 Analysis of the Online Activities Logs

Traces of online activities on the platform were limited, since we could only get access to the last validation of each puzzle. We do not have an history of the trial and errors of pupils. This means that for this experiment we can only compute the number of successful vs. unsuccessful validation for the last trial.

For each sequence of puzzles we present a graph showing the success rate (number of successful validation/total number of trials) and the total number of trials for each puzzle. We also show the transitions between the levels of difficulty (e.g., from sequence to loop) which enables to spot at which point the pupils are in trouble. For the first two phases pairs of pupils share a tablet and take turn at resolving the puzzles. In practice, they would usually collaborate in the resolution even if they were not instructed to. This explains why we have a maximum number of trials around 200. For the last phase, pupils are alone in front of a computer giving a maximum of 447 trials (number of pupils). We have lost some trials on the first and the last sequence due to some technical problems which explains lower numbers of trials reported.

Absolute Orientation. Figure 6 presents results from the first phase. We have a very smooth progression in the puzzle difficulty giving a success rate above 90%. We observe a decrease in the number of trials when we enter the loop puzzles showing that some of the pupils start to get stuck. However, the real gap in success rate shows when we have loops with more than one instruction (i.e. longer patterns to identify) with the success rate going down to 66% for puzzle 19 (Fig. 5(a)) (puzzle 18 being a tutorial).

Relative Orientation. Figure 7 corresponds to the second phase. The success rate around or above 90% indicates that the pupils successfully managed to cope

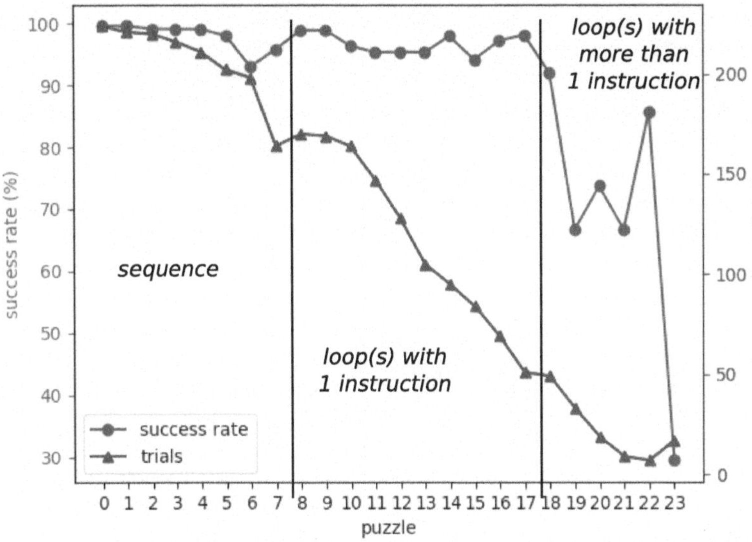

Fig. 6. Absolute orientation: success rate and trials.

with a different set of instructions. There was also an improvement in their ability to handle loops with one instructions since we still have 139 trials for puzzle 7 (comparing to the 51 trials on puzzle 17 from previous phase) still with a good success rate. Again, moving to puzzles with more than one instruction is a major difficulty with puzzle 8 reaching a 56% success rate while having a significant number of trials. Figure 5(b) shows the corresponding puzzle. It should be noted that being the first puzzle of this kind in the sequence there was a hint about the pattern to manage.

Drawing: Visual Syntax (Blockly). Entering the drawing phase introduces new challenges. First instructions are parameterized, second we start to use different kind of angles (i.e. other than 90°) that the pupils have not studied yet. Again, the number of trials and success rates for the first puzzles (including loops) indicate that the change of language is not a problem for pupils and they are still able to manage sequence and loop concepts (Fig. 8).

Mixing sequence and loops with more than one instructions seems to be quite difficult (puzzle 9–11, 9 providing hints) has we see the number of trials dropping. Figure 5(c) shows puzzle 11 which still had 129 trials but a success rate of 58%. Few pupils did the nested loops puzzles but with more than 60% of success. This result could sustain the hypothesis that once patterns of length 2 are acquired, they are quickly generalized to more complex patterns.

Drawing: Textual Syntax (Python). As one can see on Fig. 3, pupils can use buttons corresponding to the instructions to avoid too much typing. Nonetheless,

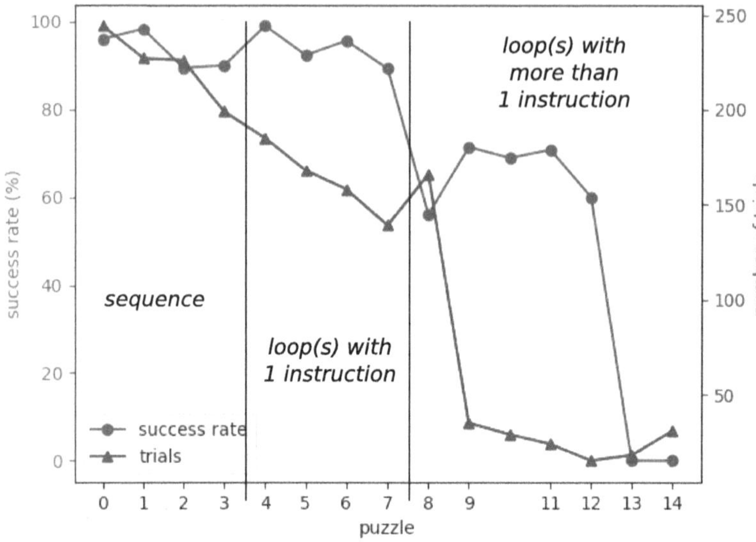

Fig. 7. Relative orientation: success rate and trials.

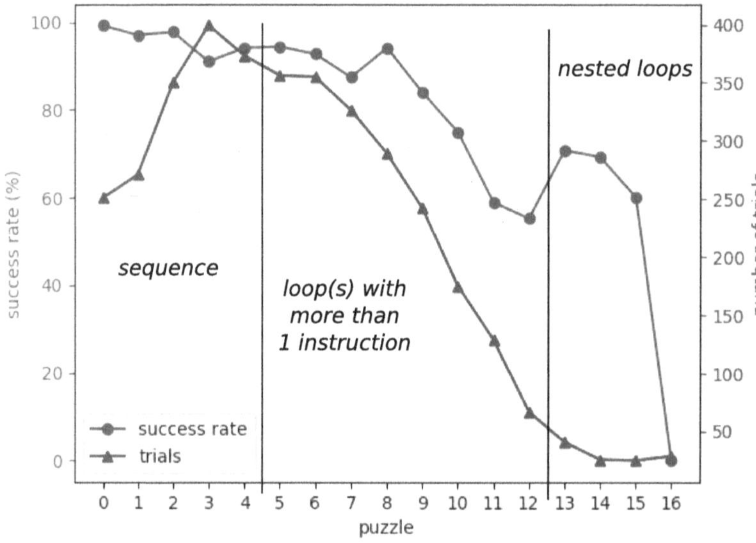

Fig. 8. Blockly drawing: success rate and trials.

they still have to adapt the parameters to their needs. As can be seen on Fig. 9, the first sequence puzzles still achieve good results above 82% with a good participation[2]. This is an interesting result that shows that the pupils transferred

[2] we have lost some logs due to a technical problem.

well their skills from visual to textual language. Again mixed sequence and loops seem quite difficult (puzzles 8 and 9) with success rate barely above 50%. Nested loops are also a hard point. Puzzle 10 is a tutorial puzzle. Puzzle 11 shown Fig. 5(d) has only 18% success with very few trials. The last puzzle corresponds to a free activity where the pupils could draw what they want with no validation condition. The graph shows that a good number of pupils enjoyed it.

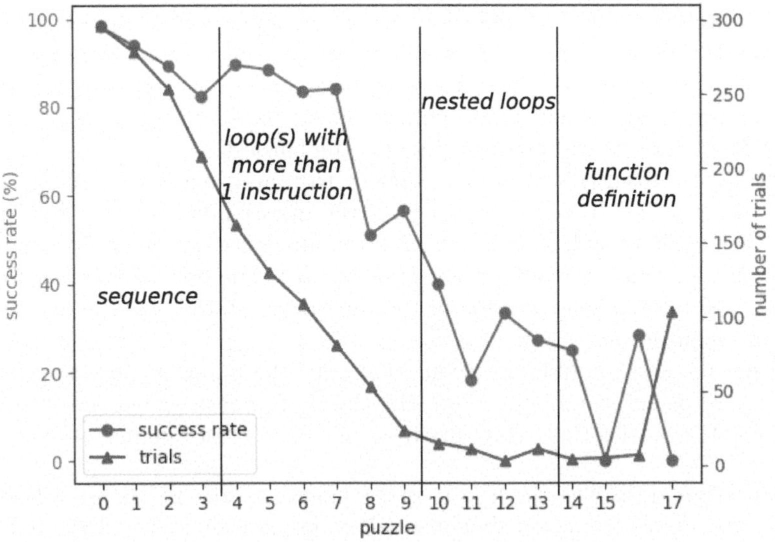

Fig. 9. Python drawing: success rate and trials.

6 Conclusion and Perspectives

This paper is focused on the learning of some fundamental Computational Thinking concepts and abilities by 8–10 years old pupils. We have designed a pedagogical sequence to initiate pupils to notions of instruction, sequence and loops, and to practice these concepts with several languages (free form (unplugged), block-based and textual language).

The quasi-experiment reported in this article considered two research questions: whether the pedagogical sequence improves pupils' ability to recognize and express repetitive patterns as loops (RQ1) and to which extent they can transfer these skills to different languages (RQ2)

The statistical analysis of the questionnaires shows a significant impact of the sequence and we have a clear increase of pupils that identify repetitive patterns and are able to synthesize their description by using some notation to express a loop (RQ1). More interestingly it seems that when pupils acquire a pattern of length 2 (2 instructions) they quickly generalize it to longer patterns.

The results form the analysis of activities should be handled with more care since, being a learning session for the pupils, they, of course, get help from the students and even their professors and accompanying parents. However, having a student for 4 to 6 pupils, we hopefully get the results from their own thinking. The analysis shows that the pupils transfer quite easily their skills from one language to the other (RQ2). They manage well sequences and loops with one instruction then we have a gradual degradation of the results (number of trials) for loops with more than one instruction. Nested loops is a real hard point with very few trials and low success rate.

The pupils get a diploma which provides the address of the platform as well as their identifying code. This allowed us to see that around 300 of them did get back to the platform in the following days and up to two months later (by which we retrieved the data). All sequences were used by the pupils and we had 271 trials for the Python one which seems the hardest.

The results from this study can benefit to practitioners who could use the proposed activities. In terms of research, the questionnaires are a first step to assess the cognitive skill with a non-programming activity which, to our knowledge, is not so much explored as seen in Sect. 2.2. There is still further work to quantify the relative contribution of the unplugged and plugged-in activities to the skills acquisition.

Future research should explore at what time the pupils acquire the concepts of repetitive patterns and loops and what level of practice is necessary for them to be able to transfer these concepts from one context or language to the other.

Acknowledgments. This work is partially funded by the EU Interreg Dig-e-Lab project. We thank the France-IOI association for providing the platform for the experiment.

References

1. Brennan, K., Resnick, M.: New frameworks for studying and assessing the development of computational thinking. In: Annual American Educational Research Association meeting, Vancouver, BC, Canada, pp. 1–25 (2012)
2. Bruner, J.: Towards a Theory of Instruction. Harvard University Press, Cambridge (1974)
3. Ching, Y.H., Hsu, Y.C., Baldwin, S.: Developing computational thinking with educational technologies for young learners. TechTrends **62**(6), 563–573 (2018). https://doi.org/10.1007/s11528-018-0292-7
4. Gouws, L., Bradshaw, K., Wentworth, P.: Computational thinking in educational activities. In: Proceedings of the 18th ACM Conference on Innovation and Technology in Computer Science Education - ITiCSE 2013, p. 10 (2013). https://doi.org/10.1145/2462476.2466518
5. Grover, S., Cooper, S., Pea, R.: Assessing computational learning in K-12. In: Proceedings of the 2014 Conference on Innovation and Technology in Computer Science Education - ITiCSE 2014, pp. 57–62 (2014). https://doi.org/10.1145/2591708.2591713. http://dl.acm.org/citation.cfm?doid=2591708.2591713
6. Knochel, A.D., Patton, R.M.: If art education then critical digital making: computational thinking and creative code. Stud. Art Educ.: J. Issues Res. **57**(1), 21–38 (2015)

7. Papert, S.: Mindstorms: Children, Computers, and Powerful Ideas. Basic Books, Inc., New York (1980)
8. Sabitzer, B., Jarnig, M.: Computational thinking through modeling in language lessons. In: IEEE Global Engineering Education Conference (EDUCON), pp. 1913–1919 (2018)
9. Seiter, L., Foreman, B.: Modeling the learning progressions of computational thinking of primary grade students. In: Proceedings of the Ninth Annual International ACM Conference on International Computing Education Research, pp. 59–66 (2013). https://doi.org/10.1145/2493394.2493403
10. Snow, E., Tate, C., Rutstein, D., Bienkowski, M.: Assessment design patterns for computational thinking practices in secondary computer science. Techniical report December, SRI International (2017)
11. Weintrop, D., et al.: Defining computational thinking for mathematics and science class-rooms. J. Sci. Educ. Technol. **25**(1), 127–147 (2016). https://doi.org/10.1007/s10956-015-9581-5
12. Wing, J.M.: Computational thinking. Commun. ACM **49**(3), 33–35 (2006). https://doi.org/10.1145/1118178.1118215

Adaptive Gamification in Education: A Literature Review of Current Trends and Developments

Stuart Hallifax[1(✉)], Audrey Serna[2], Jean-Charles Marty[3], and Élise Lavoué[1]

[1] University of Lyon, University Jean Moulin Lyon 3, iaelyon school of Management, CNRS, LIRIS UMR5205, 69621 Lyon, France
{stuart.hallifax,elise.lavoue}@liris.cnrs.fr
[2] INSA de Lyon - CNRS, LIRIS UMR5205, 69621 Villeurbanne, France
audrey.serna@liris.cnrs.fr
[3] Université de Savoie Mont Blanc - CNRS, LIRIS UMR5205, 69621 Chambéry, France
jean-charles.marty@liris.cnrs.fr

Abstract. Gamification, the use of game elements in non-game settings, is more and more used in education to increase learner motivation, engagement, and performance. Recent research in the gamification field suggests that to be effective, the game elements should be tailored to learners. In this paper, we perform an in-depth literature review on adaptive gamification in education in order to provide a synthesis of current trends and developments in this field. Our literature review addresses 3 research questions: (1) What are the current kinds of contributions to the field? (2) What do the current contributions base their adaptation on, and what is the effect of this adaptation on the gamified system? (3) What is the impact of the adaptive gamification, and how is this impact measured? We also provide future research guidelines in the form of three needs that should be fulfilled for exploring this field.

Keywords: Gamification · Education · Adaptation

1 Introduction

Gamification, defined as the use of game elements in non-game contexts [12], has been used for close to ten years in educational settings to increase learner performance, motivation, or engagement [1,24,27]. Recent studies conducted in other contexts such as health [33] and sport [26] on the effects of gamification show that to be effective, gamification should be tailored to users. In education, research on adaptation has mainly concerned educational content and its adaptation to learners and context. It is a well explored research topic [8] that has been shown to be effective. Adaptive gamification in education attempts to leverage both of these concepts in order to provide a better learner experience.

M. Scheffel et al. (Eds.): EC-TEL 2019, LNCS 11722, pp. 294–307, 2019.
https://doi.org/10.1007/978-3-030-29736-7_22

It is therefore important to take a step back and analyse how game elements can be adapted to learners in educational contexts. In this paper, we review the research on adaptive gamification in education and present the results of our analysis. In order to examine the current state of research in this field, and to understand how adaptive gamification is applied in education, we performed a literature review based on twenty papers. Through our review, we highlight the advances in the field and limitations that need to be addressed. Our review aims to answer the following questions:

- What are the current kinds of contributions to the field of adaptive gamification in education? We distinguish three kinds of contributions: (1) preliminary research on recommendations for game elements adapted to learner profiles, (2) technical contributions on architectures that have not been tested yet and (3) studies that look at the impact of adaptive gamification that make use of such architectures, and that provide valuable results into this research approach. The analysis of these three contribution types show the maturity of this field.
- What do the current contributions base their adaptation on, and what is the effect of this adaptation on the gamified system? We clearly distinguish static (i.e. initial) adaptation and dynamic adaptation, that rely on different kinds of information, such as player types or interaction traces.
- What is the impact of the adaptive gamification and how is this impact measured? We identify studies conducted on short and on long terms, as results obtained may depend on the duration. We also distinguish studies according to the adaptation mechanism used (static or dynamic).

In this paper we first present our literature review process in Sect. 2. Then, in Sect. 3 we present three parts, each part being dedicated to a research question. We finally provide future directions for research in this field in Sect. 4, by pointing out three needs that future research in this field should aim to resolve: the need for richer learner models, the need to explore different adaptation methods, and the need for more structured studies.

2 Literature Review Process

Our structured literature review process was based on the guidelines and processes described in [38,39]. First, we defined our review scope, by specifying our research questions and therefore explicating our search query (we explain this more in detail in Sect. 2.1). Then, we ran our search query and filtered the papers that did not fit our review scope (see Sect. 2.2).

2.1 Defining Our Review Scope

We are interested in the current state of adaptive gamification in education research. We studied what exactly is adapted, and what characteristics or variables are used to tailor learner experience. This lead us to define our three research questions. We then clearly defined our search terms, as to cover the topic of adaptive gamification in education. More specifically we used the search query:

(gamif) AND (learning OR education OR teaching) AND (adapt* OR tailor* OR personali*)*

The first part of our query (i.e. gamif*) was used to capture all terms that start with "gamif" (i.e. gamification, gamified etc.). Note that the queries "gamif*" and "gamif" were used depending on the capabilities of the search engines used as some allowed for wildcard characters and others not. After testing different permutations of "teaching words" we settled on "Learning" "Education" and "Teaching" (when we added alternatives such as "learn" or "learner" the result count did not change, so we stuck with a more focused approach). Finally for the adaptive part, we had a similar reasoning as with "gamif". The three base words ("adapt", "tailor" and "personali") allowed us to capture the different keywords used to describe these works (and also allow for regional variants such as the British "personalised" versus the American "personalized").

2.2 Paper Search and Filter

We ran our search query on the major scientific digital libraries (ACM, IEEE, Science Direct, Springer) and Google Scholar. Due to the fairly large nature of our search query, we received a large number of initial hits (370 papers, see Table 1), which lead to a rigorous filtration process in order to remove false hits.

Table 1. Number of papers before and after content filtering. The number of papers excluded is given for each filtration step.

Filtration step	Source				
	ACM	IEEE	Science direct	Springer	Google Scholar
Keyword query	64	94	17	35	160
Removed - format	18	8	1	2	49
Removed - scope	41	79	13	26	74
Removed - duplicate	2	1	1	1	34
Final count	3	6	2	6	3

Papers were first reviewed by scanning the keywords and title, then the abstract, and finally the full text if the paper was not excluded from the previous two steps. Papers were then excluded for the following reasons:

- Format: Results that were either abstracts, preview content, posters or workshop papers were removed. We made this decision so that we only studied mature works. Finally, we also removed papers that were not in English (many of the results from Google Scholar had English abstracts or titles, but the rest of the paper is in another language).

- Scope: Here we analysed the content discussed in the papers. Papers were excluded due to scope because they did not specifically deal with adaptive gamification in learning. For example papers that discussed adaptive gamification for health or sport were removed.
- Duplicates: A few references were found in multiple databases, as some of the databases contain references to papers that are cited by papers that they publish. Furthermore some of the papers found were extended versions of previous papers. The non extended versions were therefore excluded.

After this filtering, we were left with a final total of twenty papers that we included in our final analysis.

3 Literature Analysis

We analysed the papers through the lenses of each of our three research questions. We first identify the type of the contribution (Sect. 3.1) to identify the degree of maturity of the research field. We then present the different adaptation systems by identifying what they are based on, and what they adapt (Sect. 3.2). We more particularly distinguish static and dynamic adaptation as they rely on different mechanisms and different kinds of information. Finally we review the results of studies on the impact of the adaptation of game elements on learners' motivation and performances (Sect. 3.3).

3.1 Contributions: Recommendations, Architectures and Studies

We examined the degree of maturity of the research field in light of two criteria. First, we identified the contribution type of each reviewed paper (Table 2). Second, we reviewed the vocabulary used to describe the adapted content in each contribution.

Table 2. Type of each contribution: Recommendations, Architecture, or Study. These types are described below.

Contribution type	Recommendations	8	[2,4,6,9–11,21,23]
	Architecture	2	[22,29]
	Study	10	[18–20,25,28,30,31,34–36]

Regarding the first criterion, we classify the papers into three types of contributions that emerged from the review:

- Recommendations: identification of game elements that would be adapted to different categories or classes of learners, based on literature review, or general surveys (8 papers). These recommendations correspond to preliminary research and they have not been implemented in a system yet.

- Architectures: adaptation engines based on existing theoretical works, that have not yet been tested in real world situations (2 papers).
- Adaptation studies: an adaptation engine, based on recommendations to adapt game elements to learners, tested with learners through a real world study (the combination of an adaptation architecture, theoretical recommendations, and a real world study) (10 papers).

Recommendations: We found two major categories of papers: papers that base their recommendations on literature surveys, and those that base their recommendations on user surveys, or feedback. In the first category, Borges et al. [4] review literature on "player types" (archetypal reasons why users seek out game experiences) and link these to learner roles and different game elements based on the motivational aspects they provide. Challco et al. [6] also link motivational aspects with player types and game elements. Škuta et al. [23] also use player types, but link them to higher level game principles. They then propose a matrix that associates game elements to player types based on how well each game element implements the linked game principles. In the second category, Denden et al. present three user studies, two based on a feedback after using a non adapted gamified tool [9,11], and one based on a user survey [10] where participants rated statements based on game elements in order to determine their preference. Knutas et al. [21] analysed videos and interviews with learners in a software engineering project to create clusters of learners based on their interactions. These clusters were then linked to Bartle player types and relevant game elements. Barata et al. [2] used a similar approach, creating four types of learners based on their strategies during an online course. They then propose different goals that could be provided to each of the learner types. These studies serve to provide valuable information about what game elements learners might prefer, but still need to be implemented and tested in a real adaptation system.

Architectures: We found only two papers that describe adaptation engine architectures without any associated study. They present what the engine takes into account, what it adapts, and how it adapts it. Kuntas et al. [22] describe their process for designing an algorithm based personalised gamification system. They detail learner characteristics on which they base the adaptation of some game elements and the algorithm used to link the two. Monterrat et al. [29] describe an architecture that presents game elements as "epiphytes", completely separate from the learning content. They can therefore swap out game elements as needed. They also propose a module that tracks learner interactions in order to more finely adapt the game elements. They use a learner model that contains data on learner (gender, age, player type), usage data, and environment data.

Studies: Half of the reviewed papers present studies that rely on an adaptive gamification system in an educational setting [18–20,25,28,30,31,34–36]. These papers provide valuable results about the impact of adaptive gamification on learner motivation and performance. We present them in Sect. 3.3.

Vocabulary: Regarding the second criterion, we observed that the papers reviewed have a general consensus about the vocabulary used to describe the gamification elements. Twelve of the papers reviewed [2,4,6,9–11,18–20,23,34,35] used the term "game element" to describe the low level implementations they use, such as points, levels, leaderboards, progress. Four papers from the same authors [25,28–30] use the term "game features" to present the same level of implementation. Knutas et al. [21,22] use the terms "game like elements". Mora et al. [31] present different gamification "situations" (that combine different game elements). We can therefore observe that the papers reviewed generally agree on the term "game element" to designate what is adapted.

In summary, we find the field of adaptive gamification in education to be emergent, as there is a relatively low number of papers, that cover a wide variety of contribution types. Regarding the kind of contributions, twelve papers (two architectures and ten studies) take advantage of the ground work that the eight recommendations papers lay out. Furthermore, we found the vocabulary used to describe what is adapted to be quite stable, pointing towards a general consensus among authors.

3.2 Information Used for Adaptation and Its Effect on Game Elements

In this section we analyse both (1) what information is considered for adaptation (learner profile or activity) and (2) what the effect of the adaptation is (a change of the game element, or a modification of how the game element works). Our review analysis also allowed us to identify two major types of systems: static systems, and dynamic systems (see Table 3). In a static system, the adaptation occurs once, usually before the learners start using the learning environment. In a dynamic system, the adaptation happens multiple times during the learning activity. We present our analysis according to these two categories as information considered for adaptation and its effect clearly depends on them.

Table 3. Classification of the papers according to the kind of information used for adaptation (user profile and/or activity), its effect (game element **change** or **modification** of its functioning) and the kind of adaptation (static or dynamic). The learner activity concerns either context based **performance**, or general **behaviours**. Some papers use multiple types of information, and are present on multiple rows.

		Static				Dynamic			
		Change		Modification		Change		Modification	
Profile	Player Type	8	[4,6,23,25,28,30,31,36]	0		2	[21,29]	0	
	Personality	4	[9,11,18,35]	0		0		0	
	Expertise	1	[4]	0		0		0	
	Other	2	[4,10]	0		1	[29]	1	[22]
Activity	Performance	0		0		0		2	[19,20]
	Behaviours	0		0		2	[21,29]	4	[2,22,34]

Static Adaptation. Systems that use static adaptation all work in a similar manner. They base their adaptation on a learner profile, and adapt by changing game elements. Learners' profiles are identified, learners are sorted into different categories based on these profiles, and different game elements are given to each of the different categories of learners.

For learner profiles, the static adaptation systems generally use player types and more rarely learner personality. Player types are archetypal reasons or motivations that explain why players play games. The papers reviewed used either the Bartle Player types [3] (used in two papers [6,23]), the Brainhex player satisfaction model [32] (used in three papers [25,28,36]), the Hexad player types [37] (used in one paper [31]), or the categories of players described by Ferro et al. [14] (used in one paper [4]). These different categorisations of players types describe the reasons why players prefer different games. For example the Hexad player classification describes "Achievers" as people who "like to prove themselves by tackling difficult challenges" [37]. The papers that use these player types typically use the definitions of the different categories as a basis for their adaptation rules, for example the Hexad classification suggests using badges and levels (amongst others) for Achievers. Brainhex and Hexad provide a questionnaire to determine a player profile, i.e a set of values that define how well the player fits each type. Generally studies adapt using the dominant player type, i.e. the type that scores the highest for a given learner. However, Mora et al. [31] question the precision of only using the dominant type and propose to consider several dimensions of the profile to tailor gamification.

For the personality traits, two of the five papers [9,11] used the Big Five Factors personality traits [15]. Two papers used a user motivation questionnaire: Roosta et al. [35] used the framework presented by Elliot et al. [13]; Hassan et al. [18] used the questionnaire developed by Chen et al. [7]. Only a few static systems used other kinds of user characteristics, such as gender and gaming frequency [10], or learner role (tutor or tutee) [4].

Dynamic Adaptation. In dynamic adaptation, systems use learner activity to adapt game elements, either alone or in combination with a learner profile.

Systems that only use learner activity make adaptation by modifying the functioning of the game element. Two papers adapt the goals presented to learners. Paiva et al. [34] categorise all learner actions as either collaborative, gamification, individual or social interactions; the system adapts the kind of goals the learner receives according to the kind of actions they perform. Barata et al. [2] propose a system that varies the goals and rewards given to learners based on their behaviours, by distinguishing four types of learners: achievers, disheartened, underachievers, and late bloomers (a learner is not fixed into a specific category, as their behaviour may vary over time). Jagušt et al. [19] present two dynamic adaptation situations, both of them using learner activity. In the first situation, learners are timed in a maths quiz. Each time the learner gets a question right, they are given less time for the next question, essentially increasing the difficulty based on the learner's performance. In the second situation, the learners are shown a target score that changes depending on how they respond to questions: the more correct answers they give, the more the target score increases. Kickmeier-rust et al. [20] change the types of badges presented to, and feedback received by the learner based on the mistakes they make.

Two systems use both learner activity and profile. Monterrat et al. [29,30] aim to modify the learners' profile based on their activity. The system then uses previously established static adaptation rules. When the learners' profile changes significantly, a different game element is given to the learner. The learner profile is based on the Ferro player types in earlier versions of their work [29], and in more recent work [30] they propose to use the Brainhex model (in [29] they also use gender and age for adaptation). This is a straight forward way of implementing dynamic adaptive gamification using static adaptation rules. The systems proposed by Knutas et al. [21,22] use an algorithm that also uses learners' profile and interactions. In both systems, they use the Hexad player profile, and in the more recent one [22] they also use learner skills. In [21] they analysed videos of students during project meetings and classified their interactions and propose different game elements based on a combination of profile and interaction types. They lay the ground rules for a dynamic adaptation based on learner activity, but do not offer a method to detect these actions in real time. In [22] they use learner chat activity and profile to provide personalised goals.

In summary, adaptation of game elements is made using two major categories of information: static adaptation mainly relies on learners' profile (mainly their preferences and motivations), dynamic adaptation is based on how learners perform with regards to the learning content, or how the learners interact with the system in general. The majority of systems then use this information to select which game elements would be the most appropriate for learners. Only a few (five) adapt by modifying how the game elements function.

3.3 Impact of Adapted Gamification on Learners

We examined the impact of adaptive systems reported in the "study" papers identified in Sect. 3.1. We found that the results could be split into two categories (see Table 4) those that show a general positive impact on learner's motivation or performance, and (2) those that show more mitigated results. We also split the studies based on (1) whether they used a static or dynamic adaptation, and (2) the duration to investigate whether these factors influence the impact of adaptive gamification on learners. We identified short studies as those lasting less than two weeks, and long studies as lasting more than two weeks (with an experimental process that is closer to real world learning practices).

Short Studies. We found two studies that lasted less than two weeks [19,20], with both of these studies using a dynamic adaptation. All of these studies reported positive results on learners. In [20], learners used the adaptive system over two sessions, for a total possible time of thirty minutes. According to the authors the personalised system reduced the amount of errors that learners made.

Table 4. Impact of the reviewed studies. The numbers show how many studies are present in each category.

Duration	Static				Dynamic			
	Positive		Mitigated		Positive		Mitigated	
Short	0		0		2	[19,20]	0	
Long	4	[18,28,31,35]	2	[25,30]	0		1	[34]

Learners with the adaptive situation showed a larger decrease in errors made in the second session when compared to learners that used the non adaptive situation. In [19] Jagust et al. test two adaptive situations that learners used for 15 min each. In the first situation, the time learners had to answer questions changed depending on how quickly they answered the previous question. In the second situation, a target score changed depending on group performance. In both situations the authors report an increase in learner performance (learners completed more tasks than compared to a non gamified situation), although the first situation caused a larger increase than the second one.

Long Studies. Seven of the reviewed studies lasted more than three weeks [18, 25,28,30,31,34,35]. Four studies showed generally positive results [18,28,31,35]. Roosta et al. [35] presented learners with a different game element based on their motivation type. Learners used an online tool for one month. The authors find that learners who had game elements that were suited to their motivation type showed significant differences in motivation, engagement, and quiz results when compared to learners who had randomly assigned game elements. They used learner participation rates in the online activities as a metric to gauge motivation and engagement. Monterrat et al. [28] split learners into three different groups: one group received game elements adapted to their Brainhex player type, one group received counter-adapted game elements, and the third group received random game elements. Learners were then free to use the learning environment as they wanted over a three week period. The authors found that learners with the adapted game elements spent more time using the learning tool that those with the counter adapted elements. Hassan et al. [18] also showed a widely positive result in their study: learners who used game elements adapted to their learning style showed a higher course completion rate than those who used random game elements. This impact was also observed with learners' self-reported motivation using a questionnaire. Finally Mora et al. [31] also report a general positive impact from their adaptation, with an increase in behavioural and emotional engagement in learners, reported using a questionnaire that was given to learners after using the tool. In this study, university learners were sorted into different groups based on their Hexad profile (the groups contained users that had similar Hexad profiles) and used a learning tool over a period of 14 weeks, with each of the different Hexad groups receiving different game elements. However, the authors themselves point out that these results are not significant due to the small sample size.

The other three studies showed more mitigated results [25,30,34]. In Monterrat et al. [30] learners used the learning environment during 3 structured learning sessions, each lasting 45 min set over a three week period. The learners were middle school students, and used the learning environment as normal part of their lessons. The results show that learners with counter-adapted game elements found their game elements to be more fun and useful than learners with adapted or random elements. The authors performed a similar study reported in [25], with adults who used the learning tool voluntarily. Learners were free to use the learning tool over three weeks. They found little to no difference for the majority of learners. They found that adaptation had an influence only on the more invested learners: learners with adapted game elements showed less amotivation (calculated using a questionnaire [16]). They did not find any difference in learner enjoyment for those particular learners. Paiva et al. [34] analysed the usage data during the month after the introduction of tailored goals in their learning tool. Learners received personalised goals to encourage them to increase the number of specific learning actions they performed (for example learners who performed a low number of individual learning actions were shown goals designed to increase their number of individual learning actions). The authors found that the social and collaborative goals were effective in increasing the number of related actions. However this effect was not observed with individual learning goals (they do not observe an increase in the number of individual learning actions).

In summary we can see that shorter studies tend to show positive results from adaptive gamification, where as the longer ones show more mitigated results. The two short studies compared the impact of the adaptive gamified situation to a non adaptive gamified situation, this does not allow us to understand if the impact on learners is due to the adaptive nature of the gamified system, or due to the introduction of a novel gamified system itself. With the longer studies, we can assume that the novelty effect wears off, thus leading to more mitigated results, as the static adaptation tested in the longer studies may not be precise enough to take learner variations into. This novelty effect was also identified by Hamari et al. in [17]. Furthermore, we can see that there is some contradictory results from the different papers. [28] and [18] both report an increase in learner motivation for all learners in their studies, whereas [25] only show an increase in the more invested learners. This could be due to the nature of the metrics used to gauge learner motivation. In [18] they use a questionnaire to establish this, but [25,28] both use the time learners spent using the tool.

4 Future Research Agenda

Adaptive gamification in education is a novel and cutting edge research field, that has been gaining in popularity in the past few years. In order to better understand the current state of research in this field we performed an in-depth literature review that included twenty papers. Our analysis highlights a strong theoretical base, with eight papers that present recommendations for game elements, two that propose architectures that use these recommendations, and ten papers that test various adaptation engines in real world learning settings. We observed a variety of information used as a basis for adaptation, with both static and dynamic approaches to adaptation. This shows that this is a wide and diverse research field. In order to guide future research, we present three needs that emerge from our literature analysis that should be addressed in the future.

4.1 The Need for Richer Learner Models

As pointed out in Sect. 3.2, half of the reviewed papers use learner player types to adapt game elements. Generally they use the dominant player type identified to classify the learners. Mora et al. [31] question this in their study and show promising results when adapting to more than the dominant player type (although as the authors state, their results are not significant). Furthermore very few systems (only two) take learning characteristics into account, such as learner expertise [4] or learning styles [18]. We believe that the mitigated results identified in Sect. 3.3 could be partly due to the complex nature of learner preferences that are not represented in these simplified learner classifications. We therefore firstly advise taking into account more complex learner profiles, that include more specific learning data, such as learner expertise, learner skills as well as learner player types. Furthermore, learner activity should also be better explored as a means for adapting game elements.

4.2 The Need to Explore Different Adaptation Methods

We identified in Sect. 3.2 how adaptation of gamification may affect the gamified learning environment by changing the game element itself, or by modifying its functioning. In their current state, most adaptation systems work in a static way. We highly believe that there is more to be explored in the domain of dynamic adaptation. For example the question of how and when a dynamic adaptation presents itself to a learner still has to be addressed. If the change brought on by the adaptation is not explained or presented to the learner in a clear and understandable manner this could confuse and could distract the learner from his/her learning activity. In the field of user interface adaptation Bouzit et al. [5] show that change needs to be observable, intelligible, predictable and controllable for the user. We believe therefore that research needs to be done into how these concepts can be applied to educational settings.

4.3 The Need for Longer and More Structured Studies

As identified in Sect. 3.3, we advise that future adaptive gamification studies should aim for longer durations, as the results from short studies may be affected by the novelty effect of introducing gamification and not the adaptive nature of the gamified system. Furthermore, studies should compare the effectiveness of the adaptive system to that of a non adaptive system, which would also help with identifying if the impact on learners is due to gamification in general or to the adaptive nature. We also observed two ways for studies to quantify the effectiveness of the tested systems: either as an impact on learner performance or learner motivation. For learner performance it is fairly straightforward, using metrics such as course completion rate [18], or test results [20]. However, for learner motivation, the process was some-what more complex, as studies used ad-hoc metrics to infer learner motivation (for example [25] used time spent on the learning tool, [30,34] used learner feedback). This makes the comparison of the results from different studies difficult to make. We therefore advise that more research be performed into a more structured manner to estimate learner motivation levels.

5 Conclusion

In this paper we presented an in depth literature review in order to better understand the field of adaptive gamification in education. We identified that the field is emergent, with a theoretical base that several studies in real world learning settings build upon, and a general consensus on the language used. There is still room for this field to grow and develop, especially regarding dynamic adaptation that has been studied only once on a long term. We listed three needs that should be fulfilled in future research, based on the shortcomings we have identified. First, we highlighted the need for richer learner models that adaptation systems can use for adaptation. Second, dynamic adaptation methods should be deepened to better adapt to learner behaviour. Third, there is a need for longer and more structured studies in order to better understand and be able to compare the impact of adaptive systems on learners.

Acknowledgements. This work is a part of the LudiMoodle project financed by the e-FRAN Programme d'investissement d'avenir, operated by the Caisse des Dépots.

References

1. Attali, Y., Arieli-Attali, M.: Gamification in assessment: do points affect test performance? Comput. Educ. **83**, 57–63 (2015)
2. Barata, G., Gama, S., Jorge, J., Gonçalves, D.: Gamification for smarter learning: tales from the trenches. Smart Learning Environments, p. 10 (2015)
3. Bartle, R.: Hearts, clubs, diamonds, spades: players who suit MUDs. J. MUD Res. **1**(1), 19 (1996)
4. Borges, S.S., Mizoguchi, R., Durelli, V.H.S., Bittencourt, I.I., Isotani, S.: A link between worlds: towards a conceptual framework for bridging player and learner roles in gamified collaborative learning contexts. In: Koch, F., Koster, A., Primo, T., Guttmann, C. (eds.) CARE/SOCIALEDU -2016. CCIS, vol. 677, pp. 19–34. Springer, Cham (2016). https://doi.org/10.1007/978-3-319-52039-1_2
5. Bouzit, S., Calvary, G., Coutaz, J., Chêne, D., Petit, E., Vanderdonckt, J.: The PDA-LPA design space for user interface adaptation. In: 2017 11th International Conference on Research Challenges in Information Science (RCIS), pp. 353–364 (2017)

6. Challco, G.C., Moreira, D.A., Mizoguchi, R., Isotani, S.: An ontology engineering approach to gamify collaborative learning scenarios. In: Baloian, N., Burstein, F., Ogata, H., Santoro, F., Zurita, G. (eds.) CRIWG 2014. LNCS, vol. 8658, pp. 185–198. Springer, Cham (2014). https://doi.org/10.1007/978-3-319-10166-8_17
7. Chen, K.C., Jang, S.J.: Motivation in online learning: testing a model of self-determination theory. Comput. Hum. Behav. **26**(4), 741–752 (2010)
8. De Bra, P., et al.: AHA! The adaptive hypermedia architecture. In: Proceedings of the Fourteenth ACM Conference on Hypertext and Hypermedia, pp. 81–84. ACM (2003)
9. Denden, M., Tlili, A., Essalmi, F., Jemni, M.: Educational gamification based on personality. In: 2017 IEEE/ACS 14th International Conference on Computer Systems and Applications (AICCSA), pp. 1399–1405 (2017)
10. Denden, M., Tlili, A., Essalmi, F., Jemni, M.: An investigation of the factors affecting the perception of gamification and game elements. In: 2017 6th International Conference on Information and Communication Technology and Accessibility (ICTA), pp. 1–6 (2017)
11. Denden, M., Tlili, A., Essalmi, F., Jemni, M.: Does personality affect students' perceived preferences for game elements in gamified learning environments? In: 18th International Conference on Advanced Learning Technologies (ICALT), pp. 111–115. IEEE (2018)
12. Deterding, S., Dixon, D., Khaled, R., Nacke, L.: From game design elements to gamefulness: defining gamification. In: Proceedings of the 15th International Academic MindTrek Conference: Envisioning Future Media Environments, pp. 9–15. ACM (2011)
13. Elliot, A.J., Murayama, K.: On the measurement of achievement goals: critique, illustration, and application. J. Educ. Psychol. **100**(3), 613 (2008)
14. Ferro, L.S., Walz, S.P., Greuter, S.: Towards personalised, gamified systems: an investigation into game design, personality and player typologies. In: Proceedings of The 9th Australasian Conference on Interactive Entertainment: Matters of Life and Death, pp. 7:1–7:6. ACM (2013)
15. Goldberg, L.R.: An alternative "description of personality": the big-five factor structure. J. Pers. Soc. Psychol. **59**(6), 1216 (1990)
16. Guay, F., Vallerand, R.J., Blanchard, C.: On the assessment of situational intrinsic and extrinsic motivation: the situational motivation scale (SIMS). Motiv. Emot. **24**(3), 175–213 (2000)
17. Hamari, J., Koivisto, J., Sarsa, H.: Does gamification work? - a literature review of empirical studies on gamification. In: 47th Hawaii International Conference on System Sciences, pp. 3025–3034 (2014)
18. Hassan, M.A., Habiba, U., Majeed, F., Shoaib, M.: Adaptive gamification in e-learning based on students' learning styles. Interactive Learning Environments, pp. 1–21 (2019)
19. Jagušt, T., Botički, I., So, H.J.: Examining competitive, collaborative and adaptive gamification in young learners' math learning. Comput. Educ. **125**, 444–457 (2018)
20. Kickmeier-Rust, M.D., Hillemann, E.C., Albert, D.: Gamification and smart feedback: experiences with a primary school level math app. Int. J. Game-Based Learn. **4**(3), 35–46 (2014)
21. Knutas, A., Ikonen, J., Maggiorini, D., Ripamonti, L., Porras, J.: Creating student interaction profiles for adaptive collaboration gamification design. Int. J. Hum. Cap. Inf. Technol. Prof. **7**(3), 47–62 (2016)

22. Knutas, A., van Roy, R., Hynninen, T., Granato, M., Kasurinen, J., Ikonen, J.: A process for designing algorithm-based personalized gamification. Multimed. Tools Appl. **78**, 13593–13612 (2018)
23. Škuta, P., Kostolányová, K.: Adaptive approach to the gamification in education. In: DIVAI 2018 (2018)
24. Landers, R.N., Armstrong, M.B.: Enhancing instructional outcomes with gamification: an empirical test of the Technology-Enhanced Training Effectiveness Model. Comput. Hum. Behav. **71**, 499–507 (2015)
25. Lavoué, E., Monterrat, B., Desmarais, M., George, S.: Adaptive gamification for learning environments. IEEE Trans. Learn. Technol. **12**(1), 16–28 (2018)
26. Lopez, C., Tucker, C.: Towards personalized adaptive gamification: a machine learning model for predicting performance. IEEE Trans. Games (2018)
27. de Marcos, L., Garcia-Lopez, E., Garcia-Cabot, A.: On the effectiveness of game-like and social approaches in learning: comparing educational gaming, gamification & social networking. Comput. Educ. **95**, 99–113 (2016)
28. Monterrat, B., Desmarais, M., Lavoué, É., George, S.: A player model for adaptive gamification in learning environments. In: Conati, C., Heffernan, N., Mitrovic, A., Verdejo, M.F. (eds.) AIED 2015. LNCS (LNAI), vol. 9112, pp. 297–306. Springer, Cham (2015). https://doi.org/10.1007/978-3-319-19773-9_30
29. Monterrat, B., Lavoué, É., George, S.: Toward an adaptive gamification system for learning environments. In: Zvacek, S., Restivo, M.T., Uhomoibhi, J., Helfert, M. (eds.) CSEDU 2014. CCIS, vol. 510, pp. 115–129. Springer, Cham (2015). https://doi.org/10.1007/978-3-319-25768-6_8
30. Monterrat, B., Lavoué, E., George, S.: Adaptation of gaming features for motivating learners. Simul. Gaming **48**(5), 625–656 (2017)
31. Mora, A., Tondello, G.F., Nacke, L.E., Arnedo-Moreno, J.: Effect of personalized gameful design on student engagement. In: IEEE Global Engineering Education Conference (EDUCON), pp. 1925–1933 (2018)
32. Nacke, L.E., Bateman, C., Mandryk, R.L.: BrainHex: a neurobiological gamer typology survey. Entertainment Comput. **5**(1), 55–62 (2014)
33. Orji, R., Nacke, L.E., DiMarco, C.: Towards personality-driven persuasive health games and gamified systems. In: Proceedings of SIGCHI Conference on Human Factors in Computing Systems (2017)
34. Paiva, R., Bittencourt, I.I., Tenório, T., Jaques, P., Isotani, S.: What do students do on-line? modeling students' interactions to improve their learning experience. Comput. Hum. Behav. **64**, 769–781 (2016)
35. Roosta, F., Taghiyareh, F., Mosharraf, M.: Personalization of gamification-elements in an e-learning environment based on learners' motivation. In: 8th International Symposium on Telecommunications (IST), pp. 637–642 (2016)
36. dos Santos, W.O., Bittencourt, I.I., Vassileva, J.: Gamification design to tailor gamified educational systems based on gamer types. In: SBGames 2018 (2018)
37. Tondello, G.F., Wehbe, R.R., Diamond, L., Busch, M., Marczewski, A., Nacke, L.E.: The gamification user types hexad scale. In: Symposium on Computer-Human Interaction in Play, pp. 229–243. ACM (2016)
38. Vom Brocke, J., Simons, A., Niehaves, B., Riemer, K., Plattfaut, R., Cleven, A.: Reconstructing the giant: on the importance of rigour in documenting the literature search process. In: ECIS Proceedings 161, vol. 9, pp. 2206–2217 (2009)
39. Webster, J., Watson, R.T.: Analyzing the past to prepare for the future: writing a literature review. MIS Q. **26**, xiii–xxiii (2002)

A Supervised Learning Model for the Automatic Assessment of Language Levels Based on Learner Errors

Nicolas Ballier[1(✉)], Thomas Gaillat[2], Andrew Simpkin[3], Bernardo Stearns[3], Manon Bouyé[2], and Manel Zarrouk[3]

[1] Université de Paris-Diderot, CLILLAC-ARP, 75013 Paris, France
nicolas.ballier@univ-paris-diderot.fr
[2] University of Rennes LIDILE, Rennes, France
thomas.gaillat@univ-rennes1.fr, mbouye@eila.univ-paris-diderot.fr
[3] Insight Centre for Data analytics, NUI Galway, Galway, Ireland
{andrew.simpkin,bernardo.stearns,manel.zarrouk}@insight-centre.org

Abstract. This paper focuses on the use of technology in language learning. Language training requires the need to group learners homogeneously and to provide them with instant feedback on their productions such as errors [8,15,17] or proficiency levels. A possible approach is to assess writings from students and assign them with a level. This paper analyses the possibility of automatically predicting Common European Framework of Reference (CEFR) language levels on the basis of manually annotated errors in a written learner corpus [9,11]. The research question is to evaluate the predictive power of errors in terms of levels and to identify which error types appear to be criterial features in determining interlanguage stages. Results show that specific errors such as punctuation, spelling and verb tense are significant at specific CEFR levels.

Keywords: CEFR level prediction · Error tagset · Regression · Unsupervised clustering · Proficiency levels

1 Introduction

This paper focuses on the use of technology in language learning. For individuals, learning a language requires regular assessments for both learners and teachers to focus on specific areas to train upon. For institutions, there is a growing demand to group learners homogeneously in order to set adequate teaching objectives and methods. These two requirements rely on language assessment tests whose design and organization are labour-intensive and thus costly. Currently, language learning centres rely on instructors to design and manually correct tests.

This paper benefited from the support of the Partenariat Hubert Currien Ulysse 2019 funding for the project "Investigating criterial features of learner English and AI-driven automatic language level assessment" (ref 43121RJ).

M. Scheffel et al. (Eds.): EC-TEL 2019, LNCS 11722, pp. 308–320, 2019.
https://doi.org/10.1007/978-3-030-29736-7_23

Alternatively, they use specifically designed short-context and rule-based online exercises in which a set of specific language errors are used as a paradigm for scoring. Both approaches retain certain error types over others, which may introduce a bias regarding the importance given to these errors. Even though it may be argued that the linguistic complexity of a student's essay and its quality rely on more than some errors, errors as a whole play a role in language assessment by experts. This raises the question of their importance in the overall process.

The literature on Automatic Scoring Systems applied to learner language shows that a comprehensive set of criterial features is necessary to obtain accuracy [7]. Many studies have focused on the use of various types of linguistic features such as syntactic and lexical complexity as well as word frequencies and lexicons [12]. In parallel, much effort has been invested in error-detection systems which also rely on linguistic features [15]. However, little work has been done to understand the role of errors in the assessment of levels by expert readers. Yet, such understanding could inform their potential use as features. Combining criterial features to CEFR levels could also inform on specific errors related to specific levels, hence unraveling aspects of Interlanguage [20].

Our research question is to investigate the predictive power of errors in terms of levels and to identify which error types appear to be criterial features in determining proficiency levels. To do so, a possible approach is to use error annotated corpora [9,11] in which student writings are annotated in terms of proficiency level. By applying mathematical methods, it is possible to isolate significant error types in selecting proficiency levels. This paper analyses the possibility of automatically predicting Common European Framework of Reference (CEFR) language levels [5] on the basis of manually annotated errors in the EFCAMDAT [10] written learner corpus.

The paper is organised as follows: In Sect. 2, the literature related to automatic level assessment and language scoring is briefly discussed. In Sect. 3, we describe the data and the error tagset adopted for the EFCAMDAT corpus[1]. Section 4 reports on the prediction of the CEFR levels using regression analysis and clustering based on errors found for each level. In Sect. 5, we conclude on the possibility of automatically detecting errors that could be used as criterial features for a given CEFR level.

2 Automatic Essay Scoring Systems and Second Language Learning

Automatic Scoring Systems (ASS), and more specifically Automatic Essay Scoring (AES) systems for open-ended questions, have been developed to automate student essay assessments. Early on, ASS focused on native English and applied probabilistic methods in which specific textual features were used in regression

[1] The EFCAMDATA is hosted by the University of Cambridge and data is accessible for academic and non-commercial purposes. Our scripts will be available on our github. Data was selected and manipulated independently of the participation of the Cambridge and Education First research teams.

models. Page's PEG-IA system [18] included 30 features in a multiple-regression approach. With the recent advent of supervised learning methods, probabilistic models have become more complex in terms of features and thus more powerful. They also provide the benefit of consistency compared with human scorers.

More recently, AES systems have focused on learner language data [2,21,26], which has raised the need to use learner corpora to train models [3,13]. Two shared-tasks organised in conferences have made use of learner corpora for the purpose of scoring. The two editions of the Spoken CALL shared Task [4] focused on the distinction between linguistically correct and incorrect short open-ended constructs in Swiss German learners' speech. Language level assessment, which can be seen as a sub-part of research on scoring, was the focus of the CAP18 conference. The conference included a shared task [1] on predicting CEFR levels. The distributed dataset was sourced from texts written by French L1 English learners and classified according to CEFR levels. Features were provided in the form of lexical and syntactic complexity and readability metrics. Specific studies have been conducted on automatic level assessment in learner English [2,28] but also in other languages such as Estonian [24] and Swedish [25]. All papers report on different methods that use n-grams, errors, syntactic and lexical features to rank learner texts. They may focus on scoring specific language aspects such as text coherence or global proficiency levels of learners. Some of these approaches are deployed in commercial products[2].

Errors have been used as features in some learner-language AES. Nevertheless, their impact on proficiency levels has not received much attention. [28] reports on the classification of English as a Second or Other Language (ESOL) texts. Error rates are used as one type of features. Rates are computed automatically on the basis of syntactic patterns. The metric was found to improve correlation measures between predicted and annotated scores. [16] used spelling errors in a simple regression model but the feature significance was not evaluated. [23] implemented error features in a classification model. The set of error features included spelling and grammar errors which were automatically detected using the spelling and grammar check LanguageTool[3]. Results showed that the error features did not perform well (51% classification) when taken independently of the other features. [6] reports on an regression analysis linking various linguistic features to TOEFL-essay scores. They approached the issue of errors by comparing essays which were scored high by an AES and low by human raters, and vice versa. They observed that the AES misinterpreted spelling and syntactic complexity errors as positive features for predictions. Conversely, syntactic accuracy was not taken into account by the system, revealing the need to operationalise such features. Their study highlights the need to investigate the use of error features on a larger dataset including more error types.

---

[2] For instance, see the Intelligent-Essay-Assessor™developed at Pearson Knowledge Technologies; the IntelliMetric™-Essay-Scoring-System developed by Vantage Learning.

[3] http://languagetool.org.

Our contribution is to extend on [6] by using a larger dataset made up of 24 different error types extracted from Cambridge's EFCAMDAT corpus [10]. It also uses categorical levels of the CEFR as the outcome variable in learner English. The classification task allows to quantify the effect and the significance of each error-type in the model. It also gives an insight in the error tagset used to annotate the essays.

3 Data and Error Sets

In this section, we present the EFCAMDAT corpus and the error codes used to annotate it.

3.1 Corpus Description

The data used in this study are the French and Spanish L1 subsets of the EFCAMDAT corpus, an 83 million word learner corpus collected by Cambridge University [10]. The two subsets include writing essays of different Englishtown[4] levels ranging from 1 to 16, which were then mapped onto the six CEFR levels using the equivalence grid provided in [10]. A total of 49,813 annotated texts from 8,851 French and Spanish learners were downloaded from the EFCAMDAT database. Close analysis revealed that only 34,308 texts actually included errors, and there were 15,505 texts without error annotation. Those without errors were removed prior to modelling.

The EFCAMDAT corpus was processed and is freely available as an XML-format dataset containing text IDs, speakers' L1s and levels. It was also manually annotated for errors by [27], using an ad-hoc tagset which we describe in the following subsection.

3.2 The Cambridge Tagset of Errors

The Cambridge tagset consists of 24 types of errors, detailed in Table 1. As to September 2017, 66% of the whole EFCAMDAT corpus had been tagged by teachers using these codes [27].

Five tags in the tagset are linked to mechanic errors: they include punctuation, inappropriate or missing spaces, capitalization issues and spelling. Characteristic examples of spelling and typographic errors are illustrated in the examples below (respectively extracted from A1, B2 and C1 productions).

Example 1. I'm cleaning the living room and the <u>kitcheen</u>.

Example 2. Moreover that, they suscribe for you a full accident insurance and every year, you <u>benefites</u> of one month holiday every year.

[4] See https://englishlive.ef.com.

Table 1. EFCAMDAT error tagset

Code	Meaning	Code	Meaning
XC	change from x to y	NSW	no such word
AG	agreement	PH	phraseology
AR	article	PL	plural
AS	add space	PO	possessive
CO	combine sentences	PR	preposition
C	capitalization	PS	part of speech
D	delete	RS	remove space
EX	expression of idiom	SI	singular
HL	highlight	SP	spelling
IS	insert	VT	verb tense
MW	missing word	WC	word choice
NS	new sentence	WO	word order

Of particular interest are the tags used to label morphosyntactic errors, in particular Verb Tense (VT, see Example 3 below) or Plural (PL) and Singular (SI).

Example 3. She was recently catch by paparazzis drinking and smoking.

Other tags include error categories which pertain to syntax (Missing word, Word order), information packaging (Combine sentences) and lexical or collocation errors (e.g. Expression of idiom and Phraseology). As stated by the authors, "the purpose of these corrections was to provide feedback to learners and as such it cannot be viewed as error annotation based on a specific annotation scheme developed specifically for annotating learner corpora" [27]. This raises a number of issues concerning the error codes used on the EFCAMDAT corpus. First, as inter-rater agreement was not a concern, errors were only hand-coded once by different annotators, which may explain why similar error types are sometimes coded differently, as illustrated in the following examples:

Example 4. This movement prepare the ways to the Abstract Art.

Example 5. The other have to hide. (...) When the person stopped counting, he try to find the others.

If *prepare* is coded as a subject-verb Agreement error in Example 4, *have* is coded as a Word Choice error in Example 5, while *try* has no annotation at all. Similarly, some errors which are coded as morphosyntactic violations in some essays are tagged as spelling mistakes or collocation errors in others. This is related to the second main problem arising from the tagset: the ambiguity and possible overlap between categories. While some tags are precise in their scope, like Preposition, Article, Plural, Singular and Spelling, which bear on specific part of speech or individual words, other broader categories seem to overlap with others. As no theoretical discussion backs up the different tag labels, the difference between some of them seems tenuous, as illustrated by the example below.

Example 6. I hope to see you again soon, maybe can we lunch together the next week?

The annotation file shows that the verb *lunch* is tagged as a *Word choice* error. Several codes from the tagset could have been equally appropriate here: Expression of idiom, or Phraseology (two categories which themselves appear to be very similar), since the error seems to stem from a lack of awareness of the collocation *have lunch*, which is expressed by a verb-noun collocation in English but by a single verb in both French and Spanish. The category *Insert* could thus also have been used. This example reveals that several types of categories can fit one type of error, and vice versa. The tag *Word Choice* (WC), in particular, is such a versatile, overarching category that it can either be substituted by more precise categories, as we have just seen, when in relation to collocational errors, or by morphosyntactic categories, as shown below.

Example 7. The other have to hide.

Here the subject-verb agreement error, which is a morphosyntactic violation, is tagged as Word choice and not Agreement, which demonstrates a difference in scope across the same tag (WC). This is also the case for the Spelling category, as we will now see.

Example 8. Timotie, the next door neighbor to Serena and Dave, he told us that Dave was an inestable man.

Example 9. If there are moving, he losed.

It could be argued here that *inestable* and losed could both be tagged as No such word (NSW), the first being so distorted that it hardly resembles its correct version *unstable* and the second constituting an unacceptable and ungrammatical preterit form of lose. They are, however, both tagged as spelling mistakes (SP), although they do not encompass exactly the same type of error. This is again due to the overarching scope of some error categories.

The ambiguities and inconsistencies of the error feedback, which was not, strictly speaking, designed as an annotation tagset, have to be kept in mind when processing the results further. These are, however, isolated examples which are by no means the result of a systematic assessment of the error tags. Our next section investigates the possibility to use these annotated errors as predictors for the CEFR levels.

4 Using the EFCAMDAT Annotated Errors as Predictors for CEFR Levels

4.1 Experimental Design and Model Building

The aim of this study was to construct a classification model of learner levels (A1, A2, B1, B2, C1, C2), based on a corpus submitted by the learners.

In order to test the efficacy of the error variables, we built a classification model using 24 error types. We report on the precision, recall, accuracy and F1-score of each model. To find the optimal classifier, we compared multinomial logistic regression, random forests, linear discriminant analysis, k-nearest neighbours, Gaussian naive Bayes, support vector machine and decision tree classifier.

A second analysis used logistic regression to investigate the relative importance of the 24 error types across learner level. We split the data based on learner levels (A, B and C) and ran separate logistic regressions on these data using only the error variables. We report on the strongest positive and negative associated errors in terms of their Wald test statistic or z-score for each level, i.e. A2 v A1, B2 v B1 and C2 v C1. A positive association suggests that the error is more common in advanced learners, whereas a negative association suggests that the error is less common in advanced learners. A z-score comprised in the $[-2; 2]$ interval indicates non significant variables (p-value > 0.05). We report on the odds ratios of the errors to explore how much the occurrence of an error increases the odds of being an advanced learner.

We split the data into 75% training and 25% test data, resulting in 17,154 learners in the testing data. Among the seven model types tested here, the optimal classification performance in the testing dataset was found using a random forest model.

4.2 Results and Discussion

Using the error variables, the classifier achieved 70% accuracy with results in full given in Tables 2 and 3. Classification performance using error variables shows that errors are a good predictor of CEFR levels given by human raters as they seem to account for 70% of the variance in their judgments. Results show that accuracy drops with higher levels of proficiency (C1 & C2). Nevertheless, precision shows that predictions are consistent as few essays classified as C2 are actually of another level.

Table 2. Confusion matrix from the testing dataset using error variables

Real	Predicted					
	A1	A2	B1	B2	C1	C2
A1	5486	1227	878	467	111	11
A2	572	2918	383	211	33	4
B1	317	324	2398	177	46	3
B2	106	102	110	988	12	3
C1	10	13	15	8	196	0
C2	3	0	0	0	2	20

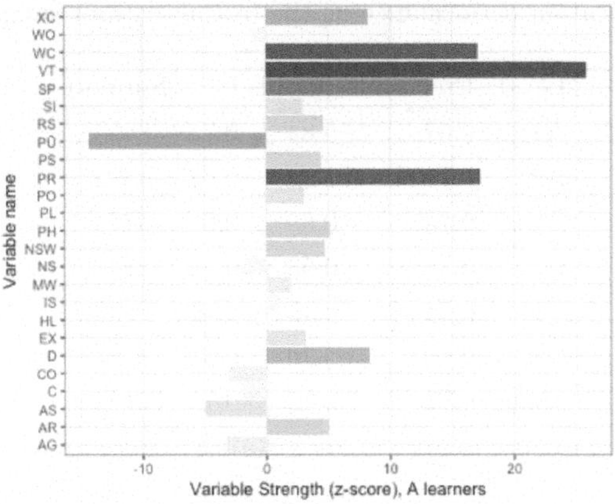

(a) Variable Importance for Level-A Learners

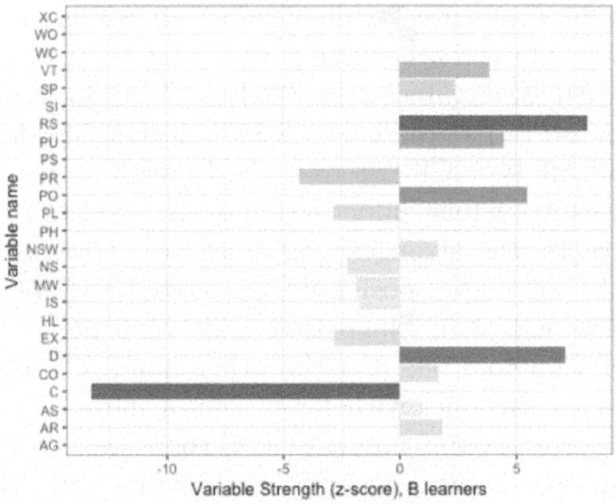

(b) Variable Importance for Level-B Learners

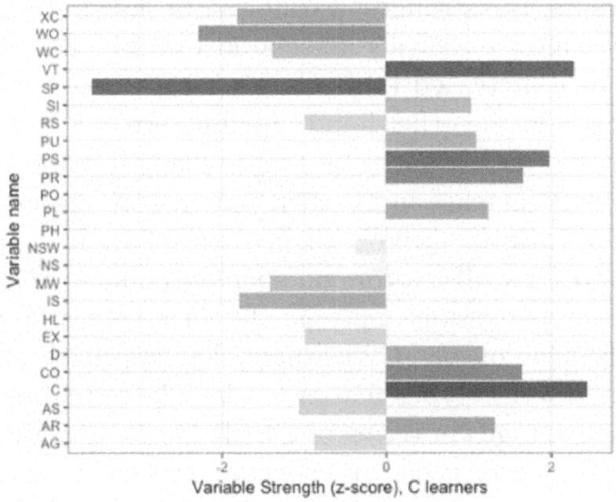

(c) Variable Importance for Level-C Learners

Fig. 1. Variable importance per CEFR level

Table 3. Classification performance on the testing dataset using error variables

Level	Precision	Recall	F1	Support
A1	0.67	0.84	0.75	6494
A2	0.71	0.64	0.67	4584
B1	0.73	0.63	0.68	3784
B2	0.75	0.53	0.62	1851
C1	0.81	0.49	0.61	400
C2	0.80	0.49	0.61	41
Mean	0.71	0.70	0.70	17154

For level-A learners, the strongest variables are shown in Fig. 1a. Verb Tense (VT) was the strongest positively associated variable. For every unit increase in VT there was a 80% increased odds of being an A2 learner (odds ratio 1.8, 95% CI 1.72 to 1.88). On the other hand, Punctuation (PU) was the strongest negative variable, with lower values more likely in A2 than A1 leaner on average. For every unit increase in PU there was a 11% decreased odds of being an A2 learner (odds ratio 0.89, 95% CI 0.88 to 0.91). In other terms, verb tense errors tend to predict A2 essays whilst punctuation errors tend to predict A1 essays.

For level-B learners, the strongest variables are shown in Fig. 1b. Remove Space (RS) was the strongest positively associated variable. For every unit increase in RS there was a 6% increased odds of being a B2 learner (odds ratio 1.06, 95% CI 1.05 to 1.08). On the other hand, Capitalization (C) was the strongest negative variable, with lower values more likely in B2 than B1 essays on average. For every unit increase in C there was a 13% decreased odds of being a B2 learner (odds ratio 0.87, 95% CI 0.85 to 0.89). In short, errors on spaces between words seem to point towards B2 whilst errors on capitalization tend to suggest B1 writings.

For level-C learners, the strongest variables are shown in Fig. 1c. Capitalization (C) was the strongest positively associated variable. For every unit increase in C there was a 13% increased odds of being a C2 learner (odds ratio 1.13, 95% CI 1.02 to 1.24). On the other hand, Spelling errors (SP) was the strongest negative error variable, with lower values more likely in C2 than C1 learners on average. For every unit increase in SP there was a 14% decreased odds of being an C2 learner (odds ratio 0.86, 95% CI 0.79 to 0.93). In a nutshell errors on capitalization lead to C1 whilst errors on spelling point to C2.

To summarize our regression analysis, the 24 error variables achieved 70% accuracy for classification of A1 - C2 learners. The approach also focused on the relative importance of error types across levels. The experimental setup operionalises Interlanguage stages in terms of CEFR levels. It allows the exploration of correlations between error types and specific levels. The analysis reveals that mechanic errors (see Sect. 3.2) are significant across all levels. Only sub-types correlate with specific levels. The results also show that some syntax-error types only correlate with the A level (Word Choice and Word Order). Conversely, the syntax error linked to Verb Tense is significant in the three models. This indicates that learners of all levels experience difficulties on this issue but the category does not distinguish tenses. It may be that learners face problems with different tense choices or constructions. In short, fine-grained tags appear to tie closely with levels while coarser grained categories do not.

Classifying C2 learners was difficult since very few C2 learners were available in the dataset. If data from more advanced learners were available, model accuracy would be improved, especially where features are calculated. We then tried another method to assess the possibility of predicting a CEFR level on the basis of clusters of error tags, in other words to predict CEFR levels on the basis of error clusters.

4.3 Using Unsupervised Clustering of Errors

To analyse the similarities in errors across texts, we used multivariate clustering to find an optimal number of groups of texts. We used model-based clustering through the mclust package in R v3.4 [19]. This clustering is unsupervised, i.e. learner level is unknown to the model. To investigate how well the errors cluster by level, we present the confusion matrix of learner level against group membership according to the model.

Table 4. Confusion matrix of cluster membership against learner level

	A1	A2	B1	B2	C1	C2
1	744	512	662	344	70	10
2	842	1020	1038	610	120	12
3	2998	2690	1868	882	138	12
4	17660	11262	8196	3798	788	66
5	1772	1280	1334	630	134	10
6	1332	1306	1302	644	146	10
7	492	526	790	364	190	12

The model is computed with the error-annotated texts (see Sect. 3.1). The optimal model found seven clusters in these data. Table 4 shows that these clusters do not match the identified learner level, with no clear cross classification apparent. Table 5 shows a breakdown of the proportion of learners in the whole data compared to those who had any errors. Surprisingly, the main discrepancy is in A1 learners who make up 41% of the overall cohort, but are less well represented in those who made an error. This suggests they are less likely to make errors in their text. This may be explained by the fact that learners of level A were given prompts and examples prior to writing, hence facilitating their endeavours so much so that few errors, if any, were identified.

Table 5. Proportion of learner levels in the entire data compared with those in which errors were found

Level	All data	With errors
A1	0.41	0.38
A2	0.27	0.27
B2	0.20	0.22
B1	0.09	0.11
C1	0.02	0.02
C2	0.00	0.00

The 24 error variables achieve 70% accuracy for classification of A1 - C2 learners. Classifying C2 learners was difficult since very few C2 learners were available in the dataset. If data from more advanced learners were available, model accuracy would be improved. Unsupervised clustering of the multivariate error data does not map well to the learner levels, which bodes badly on the relevance of using error annotation for level prediction. Caution should be exerted, though, as some specific error types have been found to be associated with specific levels. This may be explained by the fact that the error tagset was not employed for level assignment by human raters but rather to provide feedback to the learners.

5 Conclusion and Future Research

In this paper, we have presented a predictive model for the prediction of CEFR levels in learner-English essays. The purpose was to test the predictive power of error types as features in a supervised learning approach. Even though errors appear to predict levels with significant accuracy, the clustering approach showed that not all errors help in the predictions. In other terms, only some error types defined in the tagset contribute to level assignment.

The experiment also shows that the tagset employed in error annotation must be carefully defined in terms of categories to avoid overlaps and to include error types which belong to the same dimension. For instance the capitalisation variable is significant but it is not comparable in nature with *Missing Word* errors. Some errors are indicative of Interlanguage stages whereas other reveal typos or spelling issues. This method could be applied on other error annotated corpora such as the NUCLE used in [17]. Other such tagsets may yield more consistency in terms of tags, which would support better classification. Another strategy might rely on making tagsets interoperable in order to apply a new tagset to an already annotated corpus prior to classification of the same texts.

Our next step is to build a fully automated prediction system for new texts. Hence the challenge is to have a workflow based on automatic detection of features, including errors. The present study highlights some error types which could be detected automatically. For instance Spelling errors appear to be an error type to consider for the implementation of an automatic detection heuristic. Lexicons could be used to exclude non-English words. Similarly, morphosyntactic error types may be identified by using POS patterns. [14] reports the robustness of parsers when analysing learner data, and that dependency parsing is more sensitive to errors than PoS-tagging. Conversely, error types such as verb tense remain challenging in terms of implementation due to the semantic value of contexts.

Transforming learning with meaningful technologies addresses how emerging and future learning technologies can be used in a meaningful way to enhance human-machine interrelations, to contribute to efficient and effective education, and to assess the added value of such technologies. AES applied to learner data can be a part of ICALL (Intelligent Computer-Assisted Language Learning) systems characterized by rich formative feedback [22]. Indicating level along with specific and goal-oriented feedback to learners would provide a strong incentive to motivation and learning performance.

References

1. Arnold, T., Ballier, N., Gaillat, T., Lissón, P.: Predicting CEFRL levels in learner English on the basis of metrics and full texts. arXiv:1806.11099 [cs] (2018)
2. Attali, Y., Burstein, J.: Automated essay scoring With e-rater V.2. J. Technol. Learn. Assess. **4**(3), 3–30 (2006)
3. Barker, F., Salamoura, A., Saville, N.: Learner corpora and language testing. In: Granger, S., Gilquin, G., Meunier, F. (eds.) The Cambridge Handbook of Learner Corpus Research, pp. 511–534. Cambridge Handbooks in Language and Linguistics, Cambridge University Press (2015)
4. Baur, C., et al.: Overview of the 2018 Spoken CALL Shared Task. In: Interspeech 2018, pp. 2354–2358. ISCA (2018)
5. Council of Europe, Council for Cultural Co-operation. Education Committee. Modern Languages Division: Common European Framework of Reference for Languages: learning, teaching, assessment. Cambridge University Press, Cambridge (2001)
6. Crossley, S.A., Kyle, K., Allen, L.K., Guo, L., McNamara, D.S.: Linguistic Microfeatures to Predict L2 Writing Proficiency: A Case Study in Automated Writing Evaluation (2014)
7. Crossley, S.A., Salsbury, T., McNamara, D.S., Jarvis, S.: Predicting lexical proficiency in language learner texts using computational indices. Lang. Test. **28**(4), 561–580 (2011)
8. Dale, R., Anisimoff, I., Narroway, G.: HOO 2012: a report on the preposition and determiner error correction shared task. In: Proceedings of the Seventh Workshop on Building Educational Applications Using NLP, NAACL HLT 2012, pp. 54–62. Association for Computational Linguistics, Stroudsburg (2012). event-place: Montreal, Canada
9. Díaz-Negrillo, A., Fernandez-Domingez, J.: Error tagging systems for learner corpora. Spanish J. Appl. Linguist. (RESLA) **19**, 83–102 (2006)
10. Geertzen, J., Alexopoulou, T., Korhonen, A.: Automatic linguistic annotation of large scale L2 databases: the EF-Cambridge Open Language Database (EFCamDat). In: Miller, R.T., et al. (eds.) Proceeedings of the 31st Second Language Research Forum. Cascadilla Press, Carnegie Mellon (2013)

11. Granger, S., Gilquin, G., Meunier, F. (eds.): The Cambridge Handbook of Learner Corpus Research. Cambridge University Press, Cambridge (2015)
12. Hawkins, J.A., Buttery, P.: Criterial features in learner corpora: theory and illustrations. English Profile J. **1**(01), 1–23 (2010)
13. Higgins, D., Xi, X., Zechner, K., Williamson, D.: A three-stage approach to the automated scoring of spontaneous spoken responses. Comput. Speech Lang. **25**(2), 282–306 (2011)
14. Huang, Y., Murakami, A., Alexopoulou, T., Korhonen, A.L.: Dependency parsing of learner English (2018)
15. Leacock, C.: Automated Grammatical Error Detection for Language Learners. Morgan & Claypool Publishers, California (2010)
16. Nedungadi, P., Raj, H.: Unsupervised word sense disambiguation for automatic essay scoring. In: Kumar Kundu, M., Mohapatra, D.P., Konar, A., Chakraborty, A. (eds.) Advanced Computing, Networking and Informatics- Volume 1. SIST, vol. 27, pp. 437–443. Springer, Cham (2014). https://doi.org/10.1007/978-3-319-07353-8_51
17. Ng, H.T., Wu, S.M., Briscoe, T., Hadiwinoto, C., Susanto, R.H., Bryant, C.: The CoNLL-2014 shared task on grammatical error correction. In: Proceedings of the Eighteenth Conference on Computational Natural Language Learning: Shared Task, pp. 1–14. Association for Computational Linguistics (2014), event-place: Baltimore, Maryland
18. Page, E.B.: The use of the computer in analyzing student essays. Int. Rev. Educ. **14**(2), 210–225 (1968)
19. Scrucca, L., Fop, M., Murphy, T.B., Raftery, A.E.: mclust 5: clustering, classification and density estimation using Gaussian finite mixture models. R J. **8**(1), 205–233 (2016)
20. Selinker, L.: Interlanguage. Int. Rev. Appl. Linguist. Lang. Teach. **10**(3), 209 (1972)
21. Shermis, M.D., Burstein, J., Higgins, D., Zechner, K.: Automated essay scoring: writing assessment and instruction. Int. Encycl. Educ. **4**(1), 20–26 (2010)
22. Shute, V.J.: Focus on formative feedback. Rev. Educ. Res. **78**(1), 153–189 (2008)
23. Vajjala, S.: Automated assessment of non-native learner essays: investigating the role of linguistic features. Int. J. Artif. Intell. Educ. (2017). arXiv: 1612.00729
24. Vajjala, S., Loo, K.: Automatic CEFR level prediction for estonian learner text. NEALT Proc. Ser. **22**, 113–128 (2014)
25. Volodina, E., Pilán, I., Alfter, D.: CALL communities and culture - short papers from EUROCALL 2016. In: Papadima-Sophocleous, S., Bradley, L., Thouësny, S. (eds.) Classification of Swedish Learner Essays by CEFR Levels, pp. 456–461. Research-publishing.net (2016)
26. Weigle, S.C.: English language learners and automated scoring of essays: critical considerations. Assessing Writ. **18**(1), 85–99 (2013)
27. Yan, H., Jeroen, G., Rachel, B., Anna, K., Theodora, A.: The EF Cambridge Open Language Database (EFCAMDAT) information for users (2017)
28. Yannakoudakis, H., Briscoe, T., Medlock, B.: A new dataset and method for automatically grading ESOL texts. In: Proceedings of the 49th Annual Meeting of the Association for Computational Linguistics: Human Language Technologies, HLT 2011, vol. 1, pp. 180–189. Association for Computational Linguistics, Stroudsburg (2011)

Automatic Generation of Coherent Learning Pathways for Open Educational Resources

Chaitali Diwan[1(✉)], Srinath Srinivasa[1], and Prasad Ram[2]

[1] IIIT Bangalore, 26/C, Electronics City, Bengaluru 560100, India
chaitali.diwan@iiitb.org, sri@iiitb.ac.in
[2] Gooru Inc., 350, Twin Dolphin Dr, Redwood City, CA 94065, USA
pram@gooru.org

Abstract. Learners and educators all over the world have been increasingly relying on the internet for education, thus generating and consuming vast amounts of online learning resources. Selecting appropriate learning resources among them and structuring them in a way that maximises comprehension and skill building is a challenging task. In this work, we propose a model to automatically generate learning pathways from available open learning resources, such that the generated pathways are semantically coherent and pedagogically progressive. The proposed model has two components– a Greedy Generator and a Validator based on Support Vector Machine (SVM) and Long Short-Term Memory (LSTM) models respectively. The Greedy Generator chooses the next resource in the learning pathway based on local considerations and the Validator validates the learning pathway as a whole. They work in tandem with each other connected by a feedback loop. Since we work with open educational resources that lack standard meta-data, we also propose methods to generate metrics that compare a pair of learning resources. The learning pathways generated by our model from a corpus of open learning resources show promising results.

Keywords: Learning pathway generation · Deep Learning · Natural language processing · Technology enhanced learning

1 Introduction

There are a large number of open learning resources available today and the number is increasing everyday. An interested learner could easily obtain the information or the learning materials he needs to learn a topic, mostly as a set of learning resources presented by a search engine. However, selecting and organising adequate learning resources could pose challenges to the learner. As discussed by Tsai and Tsai [19] and Heish et al. [8], learners may lack the ability to meaningfully integrate unstructured information. Without sufficient prior knowledge, learners may not comprehend the concepts that they need to learn and could spend a lot of time in browsing and sorting through the information they find, leading to disorientation and anxiety.

M. Scheffel et al. (Eds.): EC-TEL 2019, LNCS 11722, pp. 321–334, 2019.
https://doi.org/10.1007/978-3-030-29736-7_24

An effective way of organising learning resources into a sequenced learning content would be a great help for the learners. Such meaningful and effective sequences of learning resources that aid in learning are called as "learning pathways".

Creating learning pathways automatically require that the learning resources are annotated with semantically rich, standardised, widely used and recognised meta-data. This is usually seen in MOOCs (Massive Open Online Courses) or ITS/AEHS (Intelligent Tutoring System and Adaptive Educational Hypermedia Systems) where the learning resources are in closed settings and are most likely created and curated by a single source. However, generating learning pathways automatically from open educational resources is a challenging task [3]. This is due to the following facts: Open learning resources are created independently by different platforms and people. They are of different media types, have different presentations and teaching methodologies. There is no general consensus among education stakeholders for standardisation and development of meta-data, since it requires large amount of time and effort, and is expensive.

We address this problem of lack of standardisation and meta-data in open learning resources, by proposing methods to compute various metrics (called pathway metrics) for comparing learning resources and embedding all the learning resources of the given corpus in a logical learning space. These help in automatically building the learning pathways. The learning pathways generated by our model are coherent and have a smooth learning experience such that it maximises comprehension and skill building. Coherence in this context means the topical dissonance between the consecutive learning resources is minimal but not zero and the overall pathway itself is pedagogically progressive. By progressive pathways, we mean that there is a learning progression in the pathway and a user learns something novel as he progresses through the pathway. To create effective learning experiences, the learning pathway should have the right balance between coherence and novelty.

Automatic generation of learning pathways has two components – a Greedy Generator and a Validator. Ideally a learning pathway validated by a teacher or an educator would have been the best option, but this being a tedious and expensive process, we create a Validator based on Long Short-Term Memory (LSTM) network that is trained by the learning pathways created by the teachers and educators. This Validator provides feedback to the Greedy Generator and improves the pathway produced by it. Generator adopts a greedy method where it picks the next learning resource by comparing it with the current learning resource, but the Validator has a global outlook – it validates if the pathway is coherent as a whole.

The paper is organised as follows. Section 2 discusses the literature survey of various works on learning pathway generation. Section 3 describes methods to compute metrics that compare learning resources. Section 4 describes the model of automatically generating the learning pathways. Section 5 discusses the experiments and results. Lastly, Sect. 6 summarises this work and discusses possible directions for future study.

2 Literature Survey

Computing learning pathways has been pursued by researchers in various forms that include: rules based approaches, data mining techniques, swarm optimisation and recommender systems.

Methods studied in [10,20,21] and in some recommender systems [16,22] generate and personalise learning pathways based on the paths taken by other learners. Knauf el al. [10] propose a storyboard approach where a nested hierarchy of directed graphs of learning activities forms a storyboard and successful storyboard patterns are learnt. Wong and Looi [20] propose rule-based prescriptive planning and ant colony optimisation methods for recommending learning paths, by stochastically observing past learner's travelled paths and their performances. Model proposed by Shen and Shen [16] is a recommendation mechanism based on sequencing rules formed from the knowledge base, ontology and competency gap analysis. Yueh-Min et al. [22] propose a recommender system that analyses group learning experiences to predict and provide a personal learning list for each learner. In all the above methods, a path taken by a successful student is recommended to another one with similar characteristics. Also, these methods are in closed settings and have standardised format of learning resources, whereas our model generates learning pathways from open educational resources with no particular format.

Fung et al. [7] model learning path generation based on existing learning pathway using concept clustering. The concept clusters are sent to a rule-based genetic algorithm to find the best learning path using correlation. Manrique [13] proposes a model to build learning concept graph to represent prerequisite relationships between concepts using linked open data like Yago and DBPedia. Perez et al. [15] discuss Wikipedia based learning path generation based on sorting articles in descending order of their semantic relatedness with the learning resource considered. Siehndel et al. [17] discuss a model based on clustering techniques and association rule mining. They propose a method to find the complexity of a learning object based on its distance from the root in a dataset and use this to sequence the learning objects. Yu et al. [21] present a recommender system that uses semantic relatedness calculated using ontology to generate learning pathways. Above solutions are based on using ontologies, linked open data or large corpus like Wikipedia. Building these usually results in high cost and/or requires a very high collaborative effort. However, our model is based solely on the provided dataset, and does not require training on larger, generic corpora. For educational resources in a niche area of study, or for a field that is emerging, our model would be a natural choice.

Chen [5] proposes constructing customised learning paths by identifying concept gaps from the results of the pre-tests. Learning resources are picked for the concept gaps and are sequenced by difficulty level. This approach requires manual labelling of educational resources with difficulty level. Changuel et al. [4] discuss resource sequencing using automatic prerequisites and outcome annotations which is used to produce an automatic sequencing. Labutov and Lipson [11] propose curating learning paths from heterogeneous learning resources by performing a shallow term-level classification of what concepts are explained and assumed in any given text.

The solutions proposed in above methods [4,5,11] and in [13,15,17,21] address the issue of generating meta-data for open learning resources and use it for generating the learning pathways. But these solutions consider and generate only a particular meta-data and use that for sequencing, whereas our model generates many different features and considers different aspects for sequencing learning resources. It not only considers the explicit features as mentioned in the pathway metrics but also the latent features of learning pathways discovered by the deep learning network of LSTM. The combination and feedback loop between the Generator using explicit features and the Validator based on implicit features, creates a powerful model for generating learning pathways.

3 Pathway Metrics

The proposed model is presented in a setting comprising of a corpus of open learning resources for a given subject of study, created by several authors independently. In order to sequence the open learning resources that lack standardisation and meta-data, we propose methods that compute various metrics to compare a pair of learning resources. Further part of the section discusses about the pre-processing of the learning resources and methods to compute each of these metrics.

A learning resource is any kind of digital resource, that provides a tutorial introduction to a given topic. A learning resource could be in the form of a text document, a video, a set of slides, a podcast, etc. These disparate kinds of learning resources are converted into a canonical, text-based model. First the transcript generators are used to obtain transcripts from various resources. We use pdfminer[1], pytube[2] and pydub[3] to extract text from the PDFs, videos and audios respectively. The transcripts are then summarised to a few sentences using an extractive graph-based text summarisation library sumy[4] based on graph-based centrality scoring of sentences. Different tokens are identified and lemmatized from the summaries of the learning resources.

3.1 Semantic Coherence

Word Embedding: Domain-specific word embedding model based on the popular skip gram word embedding method introduced by Mikolov et al. [14] is trained on our corpora of open educational resources. Each keyword is represented as a word vector v_i and a learning resource is represented as a word vector set $V = \{v_1, v_2, ..., v_n\}$, where $v_i \in R_d$, d is the dimension of the word embedding model and n is the number of keywords in the learning resource. Embedding for a learning resource $l_{i_{we}}$ is obtained by summing the word vectors for all the keywords in V of a learning resource: $l_{i_{we}} = \sum_{i=1}^{n} v_i$.

[1] https://pypi.org/project/pdfminer/.
[2] https://github.com/topics/pytube.
[3] https://github.com/topics/pydub.
[4] https://github.com/miso-belica/sumy.

Semantic coherence score $sc_1(l_1, l_2)$ for a pair of resources l_1 and l_2 is the cosine similarity between their word embeddings $l_{1_{we}}$ and $l_{2_{we}}$ and is given by:

$$sc_1(l_1, l_2) = \frac{l_{1_{we}} l_{2_{we}}}{\|l_{1_{we}}\| \|l_{2_{we}}\|} = \frac{l_{1_{we}} l_{2_{we}}}{\frac{\sum_{i=1}^{n} l_{1_{we\,i}} l_{2_{we\,i}}}{\sqrt{\sum_{i=1}^{n} (l_{1_{we\,i}})^2} \sqrt{\sum_{i=1}^{n} (l_{2_{we\,i}})^2}}} \quad (1)$$

Learning Resource Embedding: are created using the TF-IDF (Term Frequency/Inverse Document Frequency) weighted sum of embedding vectors as mentioned in the work by Lilleberg [12]. TF-IDF score reflects how important a word is to a document but is offset by the frequency of the word in the corpus [18]. Suppose there are l number of learning resources and t number of words in the vocabulary, then for each learning resource, bag-of-words representation for all the words present in it are computed along with TF-IDF scores resulting in a $l * t$ matrix $lrTFIDF$. Next, for each word in the vocabulary, a d dimensional word embedding is calculated resulting in a $t * d$ matrix $EmbVecs$. The *Learning resource embedding* $l_{i_{re}}$ for each learning resource l_i is obtained from the matrix formed by multiplying $lrTFIDF$ and $EmbVecs$. Word embeddings and TF-IDF are trained on our open learning resources corpus.

Semantic coherence score $sc_2(l_1, l_2)$ for a pair of resources l_1 and l_2 is the cosine similarity between their learning resource embeddings $l_{1_{re}}$ and $l_{2_{re}}$ and is given by:

$$sc_2(l_1, l_2) = \frac{l_{1_{re}} l_{2_{re}}}{\|l_{1_{re}}\| \|l_{2_{re}}\|} = \frac{l_{1_{re}} l_{2_{re}}}{\frac{\sum_{i=1}^{n} l_{1_{re_i}} l_{2_{re_i}}}{\sqrt{\sum_{i=1}^{n} (l_{1_{re_i}})^2} \sqrt{\sum_{i=1}^{n} (l_{2_{re_i}})^2}}} \quad (2)$$

3.2 Exposition Coherence

A new measure for computing coherence metrics for learning resources was proposed by Diwan et al. [6] where exposition coherence between a pair of learning resources was computed by defining a graph kernel function. The *Exposition coherence* is defined as a function that measures consistency in exposition between any two learning resources. Exposition refers to a way in which a particular narrative is presented and can be thought of as *unfolding sequence of topics* which is computationally modelled as a random walk.

A corpus-wide term co-occurrence graph is first built from all the learning resources in the corpus. Given a pair of learning resources, semantic context graphs are created for each of the learning resources. Semantic context graph is an induced sub-graph containing the nodes formed by the keywords and their neighbourhoods, together with the edges. The edge weights are the same as in the term co-occurrence graph. The kernel function first merges the two semantic context graphs and makes the merged graph as an irreducible Markov chain. On this merged graph, several sequences of random walks are executed.

Given a pair of learning resources (l_1, l_2), the seed or initial node for the random walk is selected from the first resource of the pair. The question addressed by the random walk is that, if we start from any keyword in the first learning resource, how likely are we to encounter common keywords between a pair of learning resources? To calculate this, the trace comprising a sequence of terms that characterises the random walk r_i is recorded. For each such trace, an *intersection score* is calculated, which is the ratio of number of common nodes $n_{\psi(l_1)\cap\psi(l_2)}$ between the semantic context graphs $\psi(l_1)$ and $\psi(l_2)$ divided by the total number of nodes n_n in the trace. It is formally represented as:

$$is(r_i) = \frac{n_{\psi(l_1)\cap\psi(l_2)}}{n_n}$$

Exposition coherence $ec(l_1 \rightarrow l_2)$ between the two learning resources is an average of the *intersection scores* taken for all the n random walk sequences generated till stabilisation, and is given by the following equation:

$$ec(l_1 \rightarrow l_2) = \frac{\sum_{i=1}^{n} is(r_i)}{n} \tag{3}$$

3.3 Novelty

Novelty measures the extent of new or novel concepts in the learning resource as compared to the previous learning resource in a pathway. It also represents the progression in the learning pathway. We propose a method to compute *novelty* based on a random walk based graph kernel.

A corpus-wide term co-occurrence graph is created from all the learning resources in the corpus. When comparing a learning resource pair (l_1, l_2), semantic context graphs $\psi(l_1)$ and $\psi(l_2)$ are generated for both the learning resources in the pair as described in the above sub-section. A random walk r_i is started with a seed node from the keywords of the first learning resource l_1. The trace for this random walk is recorded which comprises of a sequence of terms encountered during the walk. For each such random walk, number of novel nodes $n_{\psi(l_2)-\psi(l_1)}$ is calculated which is the number of nodes present in the semantic context graph of the second learning resource $\psi(l_2)$ and not present in the semantic context graph of the first learning resource $\psi(l_1)$. The ratio of the number of novel nodes divided by the total number of nodes n_n in the trace gives the novelty score for the random walk r_i and is given by:

$$ns(r_i) = \frac{n_{\psi(l_2)-\psi(l_1)}}{n_n}$$

Several such random walks are generated on the merged graph until stabilisation. Then, an average of novelty scores taken over all the random walks n until stabilisation gives the *Novelty* score $ns(l_1 \rightarrow l_2)$ for a learning resource l_1 followed by a learning resource l_2 and is given by the following equation:

$$ns(l_1 \rightarrow l_2) = \frac{\sum_{i=1}^{n} ns(r_i)}{n} \tag{4}$$

3.4 Characteristic Anchor Divergence

Characteristic anchor for a learning resource is represented as a probability density function over a set of topics. Let T_k be a set of representative topics that the corpus represents and k be the number of topics. If l_{j_i} is the probability of the ith topic t_i for a learning resource l_j, then characteristic anchor $l_j(k)$ is given by

$$l_j(k) = \sum_{\forall t_i \in T_k} l_{j_i} t_i = 1.$$

Topic modelling as described in [2] is used to generate characteristic anchors where latent topics are generated. We say that the topical distribution between two consecutive learning resources in the learning pathway should be minimal but not zero. Hence *characteristic anchor divergence* $ca(l_1 \rightarrow l_2)$ is calculated using KL-divergence method and is defined as follows:

$$ca(l_1 \rightarrow l_2) = \sum_{t_i \in T_k} l_{1_i}(t_i) log \frac{l_{1_i}(t_i)}{l_{2_i}(t_i)} \tag{5}$$

4 Learning Pathway Generator

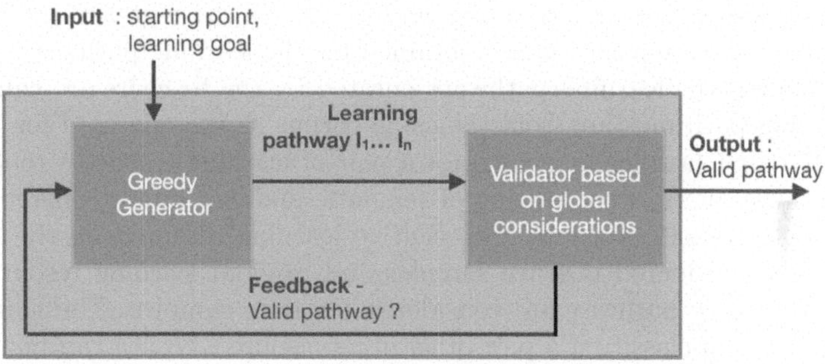

Fig. 1. Block diagram of learning pathway generation

Our model to generate learning pathways comprises of two components– a Greedy Generator and a Validator. Figure 1 shows the *Learning Pathway Generator* block diagram. All the learning resources in the corpus of open learning resources for a subject are embedded in a logical learning space. The learning resource embedding is obtained as mentioned in Sect. 3.1. As we can see in the figure, a learning pathway is calculated from any starting resource till a learning goal is reached or there are no other learning resources in the neighbourhood that are coherent to the current pathway. For a learning resource in a pathway, the next resource is chosen by the Greedy Generator using a LR Pair Classifier which suggests a potential next learning resource in the pathway based on coherence and learning progression computed in terms of pathway metrics. When the pathway length reaches the window size of the Validator, the Validator is called which validates if that segment of the pathway is coherent as a whole. It also provides feedback to the Generator which adapts itself based on it.

Validator model validates a learning pathway and is built as a Long Short-Term Memory (LSTM) model. LSTM network is a type of recurrent neural network designed to handle sequence dependence. Without any features specified beforehand, the network attempts to learn the underlying structure of the input sequences. Sliding window approach of LSTM is considered in our model which slides one learning resource at a time in a pathway. Choosing an optimal window size is crucial, since having a larger window size would mean that the farther learning resources may not be topically coherent with the earlier learning resources and a smaller window size would mean that the Validator would end up making local considerations. For training, learning pathways hand curated by the teachers are considered as positive data samples and the negative data samples are generated by randomly picking the learning resources in the corpus.

LR Pair Classifier model classifies if a pair of learning resources can be consecutive in terms of coherence and progression. LR Pair Classifier is built using Support Vector Machine (SVM) which is a discriminative classifier. Learning resource pairs are considered as input to the LR Pair Classifier. The goal of pairwise framework is to learn a preference function over the learning resource pairs, where the output of the learned function indicates the degree to which one learning resource is preferred over another. Since these preference functions are transitive, the sequence can be obtained for the learning pathways.

For training, the learning pathways curated by the teachers are considered, these learning pathways are from the same corpus as the one used for the Validator. LR Pair Classifier is trained for a pair of learning resources represented by the pathway metrics comprising of semantic and exposition coherence, novelty and characteristic anchors. Consecutive learning resources in the learning pathways are considered positive samples and random learning resource pairs not from the same pathway are considered negative samples. The trained LR Pair Classifier can classify if a pair of learning resources (l_1, l_2) can be consecutive, i.e., if l_2 can follow l_1 in the learning pathway. The confidence score of the classification is also considered while choosing the next learning resource.

Learning Pathway Generator model is outlined in Algorithm 1. Given an initial learning resource l_i, all the learning resources in the neighbourhood of l_i in the embedding space are selected based on cosine distance of around θ from it. Let $C = \{c_1, c_2, c_3 .... c_n\}$ be a set of such candidate learning resources in the neighbourhood of l_i with approximate cosine similarity of θ. The initial value of θ is computed by finding out mode of cosine similarity for all pairs of consecutive learning resource pairs in the corpus. One of the candidate resources say c_j, is picked randomly from the set of candidate resources and paired with initial learning resource l_i. For this pair of learning resource (l_i, c_j), all the pathway metrics are obtained. The functions *getSemanticCoherenceWordEmbedding*, *getSemanticCoherenceLREmbedding*, *getExpositionCoherence*, *getNovelty*, *getCharacteristicAnchorDivergence* are called to obtain pathway metrics - semantic coherence sc_1 and sc_2, exposition coherence ec, novelty ns and characteristic anchor divergence ca respectively, as described in Sect. 3.

These pathway metric scores (sc_1, sc_2, ec, ns, ca) are passed as input to the LR Pair Classifier model, which classifies the learning resource pair as consecutive or nonconsecutive. It also gives the confidence score. If the confidence of choosing preferred next resource is above a threshold α, then that candidate is included in the pathway and the next learning resource is picked in the same way. α is initially chosen empirically.

Algorithm 1: Learning Pathway Generator

```
Input: Initial learning resource l_1
Output: Learning pathway L = {l_1, l_2 ..., l_n}
L ← l_1
Set cosine distance value θ to choose neighbouring learning resources
Set confidence value α to choose next preferred learning resource
Set w to validator window size
Assign l_1 to initial learning resource variable, l_i = l_1
while true do
    C ← getNearestNeighbours(l_i, θ)
    foreach c_j ∈ C do
        sc_1 = getSemanticCoherenceWordEmbedding(l_i, c_j)
        sc_2 = getSemanticCoherenceLREmbedding(l_i, c_j)
        ec = getExpositionCoherence(l_i, c_j)
        ns = getNovelty(l_i, c_j)
        ca = getCharacteristicAnchorDivergence(l_i, c_j)
        consecutive, confidence ← LRPairClassifier(sc_1, sc_2, ec, ns, ca)
        if consecutive and confidence > α then
            L ← c_j
            l_i = c_i
            break
    if |L| > w then
    while true do
        valid ← Validator(l_i − w, l_i − w + 1, ..., l_i)
        if valid = true then
            break
        else
            remove c_i from L, choose other c_i ∈ C and assign it to l_i
            send feedback to tune hyper-parameters
    if c_i is learning goal or there are no more coherent resources in the
    neighbourhood of c_i then
        stop
return L
```

If the pair (l_i, c_j) is nonconsecutive, then next candidate resource c_{j+1} is picked from set C. This continues till a learning resource pair ordering is consecutive as certified by LR Pair Classifier. When the learning pathway segment is greater than or equal to the Validator window size w, then the Validator is called. Depending on the output from the Validator, either the pathway picks the next learning resource (if the output is valid) or it goes back and picks another learning resource for l_i (if the output is invalid). In either case, the feedback is sent to the Generator. If all candidate learning resources for l_i are picked and the pathway is not coherent, then the Generator decides if it has to go back to l_{i-1} and re-pick another candidate learning resource or stop the generator, this is decided by the feedback function. The algorithm stops when the learning goal is reached or there are no more learning resources that are coherent to the learning pathway. The feedback from the Validator is sent to the Generator and the hyper parameters – θ, α and w are tuned accordingly.

5 Experiment and Results

To evaluate our proposed models, we use a dataset of open learning resources aggregated by an educational platform *Gooru.org*[5]. The dataset comprises of about 4.2 million learning resources in total that are independently created by several authors, mostly obtained from the open educational resources.

The learning pathways in the platform are hand curated by the teachers and contain a variety of resource formats. These pathways have been successfully implemented in classrooms supporting innovative practices and are maintained and updated by the educators [1]. These learning pathways thus represent coherent and pedagogically progressive sequences of learning resources that the students could use to achieve a learning goal. We used the subset of these hand curated learning pathways for subject Mathematics as the gold standard for training and testing.

In this section, we present the results of the LR Pair Classifier and Validator models. We also discuss the results of the learning pathways that are generated by our model. For LR Pair Classifier and Validator, we report the evaluation results based on Accuracy, PPV-Positive Predictive Value, TPR - True Positive Rate and F1 score. From the confusion matrix entries, the performance metrics are calculated as follows:

$$\text{Accuracy} = \frac{\sum TruePostives + \sum FalsePositves}{\sum TotalPopulation}$$

$$\text{Positive Predictive Value (PPV)} = \frac{\sum TruePostives}{\sum TruePostives + \sum FalsePositves}$$

$$\text{True Positive Rate (TPR)} = \frac{\sum TruePostives}{\sum TruePostives + \sum FalseNegatives}$$

$$\text{F1 score} = \frac{2 * PPV * TPR}{PPV + TPR}$$

LR Pair Classifier Results. A Support Vector Machine (SVM) classifier is trained as described in the previous section using the machine learning library scikit-learn[6]. To choose the input features for the LR Pair Classifier, we trained

[5] https://gooru.org.
[6] https://scikit-learn.org.

the classifier with many features individually and in various combinations. We recorded their performances on the above performance metrics and chose the features that had very high performance metrics. The chosen features are as described in the pathway metrics (Sect. 3), specifications of which are given as follows: semantic coherence word embedding and learning resource embedding of 100 dimensions each, exposition coherence and novelty scores between 0–1 and characteristic anchor divergence of 20 dimensions.

The classifier is trained on the balanced dataset of 5000 learning resource pairs, divided with a standard 80% training and 20% testing data. The consecutive learning resource pairs of learning pathways are the positive data samples and the randomly chosen learning resource pairs are the negative data samples.

Table 1 shows the results for the LR Pair Classifier based on the performance metrics listed above. We see that the LR Pair Classifier has high values for all the metrics considered and hence it is reliable to find the next preferred learning resource.

Validator Results. Validator is implemented using one LSTM (Long Short Term Memory networks) layer with 220 inputs and one hidden to output softmax layer. Each learning resource is represented as 220 dimensions comprising of learning resource embedding of 100 dimensions, concatenated word embedding of 100 dimensions and characteristic anchor of 20 dimensions (Sects. 3.1 and 3.4). We use python Deep Learning library keras[7] for our implementation. We used the dataset of 4800 learning pathways hand curated by the teachers and an equal number of randomly generated learning pathways. We divided this combined dataset into 80% training data and 20% testing data. Table 2 shows the results for the Validator on this dataset. We see that all the performance metrics of the Validator are very high.

Table 1. LR Pair Classifier performance

Metric	Value
Accuracy	90.53%
Positive Predictive Value (PPV)	89.23%
True Positive Rate (TPR)	90.98%
F1-score	90.09%

Table 2. Validator performance

Metric	Value
Accuracy	98.55%
Positive Predictive Value (PPV)	94.08%
True Positive Rate (TPR)	98.75%
F1-score	96.34%

We investigated the contribution of the window size by varying the window sizes from 1 to 5 learning resources. We observed that, for our corpora, window sizes of 3 to 5 gave significantly good results. Smaller window size and very large window sizes reported low accuracy. Also, window size above 5 significantly increased the pathway generation time. The results reported in Table 2 are for a window size of 4.

[7] https://keras.io.

Learning Pathway Generator Results. We validate our model by comparing the learning pathways generated by our model to the learning pathways hand curated by the teachers. This approach of comparing learning resource sequence is effective in determining if the generated learning pathways are valid [9]. We compare the main topic or the title of the learning resources in the pathways and not the exact learning resource. This is due to two reasons: First, there are many learning resources for a single topic since we have a very large corpus of open educational resources for the subject we considered. Second, the gold standard learning pathway is not an exhaustive list.

Equivalent fractions - Equivalent fractions are different fractions that name the same number. The numerator and the denominator of a fraction must be multiplied by the same nonzero whole number in order to have equivalent fractions.

Compare fractions - To compare fractions, or tell if one fraction is bigger than another, check if the fractions have the same denominator. If they do, just see which numerator is bigger. If not, you can make both denominators the same by multiplying them together—this is called finding a common denominator.

Add or Subtract fractions - Before you can add or subtract fractions with different denominators, you must first find equivalent fractions with the same denominator, like this: 1. Find the smallest multiple (LCM) of both numbers. 2. Rewrite the fractions as equivalent fractions with the LCM as the denominator.

Decompose fraction - The most basic way to decompose a fraction is to break into unit fractions, which is when the numerator (top number) is 1. Suppose we have 5/8, we can see that 5/8 is the same as the unit fraction 1/8 five times. Let's try it with an improper fractions, which consists of a whole number and a fractions. For example, 2 1/6 is same as 6/6 two times and 1/6

Decompose fraction Tape diagram - Smaller unit fraction using tape diagram - The total length of each tape diagram represents 1 whole. Decompose fractions as the sum of smaller unit fractions in at least two different ways.

Rename fractions - Rename fractions as mixed numbers using decomposition step by step procedure. Modelling the decomposition with a number line and a number bond.

Fig. 2. Example of a Learning Pathway generated by our model

We use Kendall's tau to calculate the correlation between the generated pathways and the hand curated pathways. Kendall's tau coefficient is between -1 to $+1$, with correlation of $+1$ if the ordering of two pathways are equal and -1 if the ordering of two pathways are exactly reverse of each other. The Kendall's tau τ coefficient is defined as:

$$\tau = \frac{(\text{number of concordant pairs}) - (\text{number of discordant pairs})}{n(n-1)/2}$$

where, for two pathways X and Y, a pair of topics a and b are concordant if the ranks for both the topics agree: that is, if both $x_a > x_b$ and $y_a > y_b$ or if both $x_a < x_b$ and $y_a < y_b$. They are said to be discordant, if $x_a > x_b$ and $y_a < y_b$; or if $x_a < x_b$ and $y_a > y_b$. n is the number of learning resources in the pathway.

For evaluation, we generate the learning pathways with the same starting learning resource and length as the hand curated pathway, thus enabling the comparison with them. We obtain Kendall's tau for each such pair of generated learning pathway and its corresponding hand curated learning pathway and report the average of Kendall's tau for all such pairs. If there are minor mismatches in the pathways such that they contain one or two additional or missing learning resources or topics, then instead of ignoring the mismatches, we append them to the bottom of the other list. This helps us get more accurate results for the comparisons.

Figure 2 shows one of the learning pathways generated by our *Learning Pathway Generator* model. The example shows the titles and short summaries of the learning resources in the pathway. This pathway has a very good Kendall's tau coefficient of 0.733 when compared to its corresponding hand curated learning pathway. The average Kendall's tau for all the generated learning pathways when compared to their corresponding gold standard learning pathways is 0.57.

6 Conclusions and Future Work

We proposed a model to automatically generate coherent and pedagogically progressive learning pathways for open educational resources. Our method relies solely on the content of the learning resources for generating sequences. This is possible because of the proposed pathway metrics that compare a pair of learning resources. Our model considers both– explicit features defined by the pathway metrics and latent or implicit features discovered in a LSTM based Validator, resulting in coherent and progressive learning pathways. Evaluation of the learning pathways generated by our model showed promising results.

In future, we plan to personalise the learning pathways generated by our model by creating learning pathway network of generic or reference learning pathways. This is done by generating learning pathways between different starting points and learning goals in an embedded learning space. When a learner wants to learn a topic, one of these reference learning pathways would be chosen and modified according to the learner's learning goal, current knowledge, preferences and characteristics.

Acknowledgements. The authors would like to thank the project associates Abhiramon Rajasekharan, Nikhil Sai Bukka, and Vibhav Agarwal for their contribution.

References

1. Arnett, T.: Connecting Ed & Tech: Partnering to Drive Student Outcomes. Clayton Christensen Institute for Disruptive Innovation (2016)
2. Blei, D.M., Ng, A.Y., Jordan, M.I.: Latent dirichlet allocation. J. Mach. Learn. Res. **3**, 993–1022 (2003)
3. Brusilovsky, P., Henze, N.: Open corpus adaptive educational hypermedia. In: Brusilovsky, P., Kobsa, A., Nejdl, W. (eds.) The Adaptive Web. LNCS, vol. 4321, pp. 671–696. Springer, Heidelberg (2007). https://doi.org/10.1007/978-3-540-72079-9_22
4. Changuel, S., Labroche, N., Bouchon-Meunier, B.: Resources sequencing using automatic prerequisite-outcome annotation. ACM Trans. Intell. Syst. Technol. (TIST) **6**(1), 6 (2015)
5. Chen, C.M.: Intelligent web-based learning system with personalized learning path guidance. Comput. Educ. **51**(2), 787–814 (2008)

6. Diwan, C., Srinivasa, S., Ram, P.: Computing exposition coherence across learning resources. In: Panetto, H., Debruyne, C., Proper, H., Ardagna, C., Roman, D., Meersman, R. (eds.) On the Move to Meaningful Internet Systems. Lecture Notes in Computer Science, vol. 11230, pp. 423–440. Springer, Cham (2018). https://doi.org/10.1007/978-3-030-02671-4_26
7. Fung, S., Tam, V., Lam, E.Y.: Enhancing learning paths with concept clustering and rule-based optimization. In: 2011 11th IEEE International Conference on Advanced Learning Technologies (ICALT), pp. 249–253. IEEE (2011)
8. Hsieh, T.C., Lee, M.C., Su, C.Y.: Designing and implementing a personalized remedial learning system for enhancing the programming learning. J. Educ. Technol. Soc. **16**(4), 32–46 (2013)
9. Karampiperis, P., Sampson, D.: Adaptive learning resources sequencing in educational hypermedia systems. J. Educ. Technol. Soc. **8**(4), 128–147 (2005)
10. Knauf, R., Sakurai, Y., Takada, K., Tsuruta, S.: Personalizing learning processes by data mining. In: 2010 IEEE 10th International Conference on Advanced Learning Technologies (ICALT), pp. 488–492. IEEE (2010)
11. Labutov, I., Lipson, H.: Web as a textbook: curating targeted learning paths through the heterogeneous learning resources on the web. In: EDM, pp. 110–118 (2016)
12. Lilleberg, J., Zhu, Y., Zhang, Y.: Support vector machines and word2vec for text classification with semantic features. In: 2015 IEEE 14th International Conference on Cognitive Informatics & Cognitive Computing (ICCI* CC), pp. 136–140. IEEE (2015)
13. Manrique, R.: Towards automatic learning content sequence via linked open data. In: Proceedings of the International Conference on Web Intelligence, pp. 1230–1233. ACM (2017)
14. Mikolov, T., Sutskever, I., Chen, K., Corrado, G.S., Dean, J.: Distributed representations of words and phrases and their compositionality. In: Advances in Neural Information Processing Systems, pp. 3111–3119 (2013)
15. Pérez Martínez, C., López Morteo, G., Martínez Reyes, M., Gelbukh, A.: Wikipedia-based learning path generation. Computación y Sistemas **19**(3), 589–600 (2015)
16. Shen, L., Shen, R.: Learning content recommendation service based-on simple sequencing specification. In: Liu, W., Shi, Y., Li, Q. (eds.) ICWL 2004. LNCS, vol. 3143, pp. 363–370. Springer, Heidelberg (2004). https://doi.org/10.1007/978-3-540-27859-7_47
17. Siehndel, P., Kawase, R., Nunes, B.P., Herder, E.: Towards automatic building of learning pathways. In: WEBIST, vol. 2, pp. 270–277 (2014)
18. Sparck Jones, K.: A statistical interpretation of term specificity and its application in retrieval. J. Documentation **28**(1), 11–21 (1972)
19. Tsai, M.J., Tsai, C.C.: Information searching strategies in web-based science learning: the role of internet self-efficacy. Innov. Educ. Teach. Int. **40**(1), 43–50 (2003)
20. Wong, L.H., Looi, C.K.: Adaptable learning pathway generation with ant colony optimization. J. Educ. Technol. Soc. **12**(3), 309 (2009)
21. Yu, Z., Nakamura, Y., Jang, S., Kajita, S., Mase, K.: Ontology-based semantic recommendation for context-aware e-learning. In: Indulska, J., Ma, J., Yang, L.T., Ungerer, T., Cao, J. (eds.) UIC 2007. LNCS, vol. 4611, pp. 898–907. Springer, Heidelberg (2007). https://doi.org/10.1007/978-3-540-73549-6_88
22. Yueh-Min, H., Tien-Chi, H., Wang, K.T., Hwang, W.Y.: A markov-based recommendation model for exploring the transfer of learning on the web. J. Educ. Technol. Soc. **12**(2), 144 (2009)

Automatic Text Difficulty Estimation Using Embeddings and Neural Networks

Anna Filighera(✉), Tim Steuer, and Christoph Rensing

Multimedia Communications Lab, Technische Universität Darmstadt, Rundeturmstr. 10, 64283 Darmstadt, Germany
{anna.filighera,tim.steuer,christoph.rensing}@kom.tu-darmstadt.de

Abstract. Text difficulty, also called reading difficulty, refers to the complexity of texts on a language level. For many educational applications, such as learning resource recommendation systems, the text difficulty of text is highly relevant information. However, manual annotation of text difficulty is very expensive and not feasible for large collections of texts. For this reason, many approaches to automatic text difficulty estimation have been proposed in the past. All text difficulty estimation models published thus far have one thing in common: they rely on manually engineered feature sets. This is problematic as features are tailored to a specific type of text and do not generalize well to other types and languages. To alleviate this problem we propose a novel approach using neural networks and embeddings to the task of text difficulty classification. Our approach distinguishes between 5 reading levels which correspond to non-overlapping age groups ranging from ages 7 to 16. It performs comparably to existing state-of-the-art approaches in terms of accuracy and Pearson correlation coefficient while being easier and cheaper to adapt to new types of text.

Keywords: Text difficulty · Deep learning · Embeddings

1 Introduction

Text difficulty captures linguistic aspects which determine how difficulty a text is to read. The used vocabulary, grammatical and discourse structure are all examples for such linguistic aspects. Having text difficulty information about a text helps estimate if the text conveys information in a suitable way for the reader. Search engines, such as those in repositories of open educational resources, or didactic recommendation systems profit greatly from having text difficulty metadata of their textual items. Especially systems selecting relevant reading material for language acquisition require text difficulty information to challenge learners without overwhelming them. However, manual annotation of text difficulty metadata is expensive to the point where it is not feasible for large collections of text. Therefore, automatic text difficulty estimation methods are needed.

M. Scheffel et al. (Eds.): EC-TEL 2019, LNCS 11722, pp. 335–348, 2019.
https://doi.org/10.1007/978-3-030-29736-7_25

In the past, multiple approaches using manually engineered feature sets have been proposed. The main disadvantage of such approaches lies in fact that feature engineering is expensive and the resulting feature sets do not generalize well to other types of texts [6,7,10,23]. With the recent success of approaches using neural networks and embeddings in various natural language processing fields, a transfer of deep learning methods to the task of text difficulty estimation is promising. Especially, since the usage of embeddings makes in-depth feature engineering obsolete. For this reason, we conducted 8 types of multiclass classification experiments using varying embedding models and neural network architectures on the modified WeeBit corpus introduced by Xia et al. [23]. The corpus contains educational news articles separated into 5 distinct reading levels targeted at non-overlapping age groups ranging from ages 7 to 16. For each of the 8 combinations of embeddings and architectures we report the performance of the best model in terms of macro-averaged F1 score on the development set found in the experiments. Finally, we formed an ensemble of the 6 best performing models found in the experiments and compare the ensemble's performance to the state-of-the-art model proposed by Xia et al. [23]. We use accuracy and Pearson correlation coefficient as metrics for the comparison. However, we also report the macro F1 score of the ensemble.

2 Related Work

The earliest approaches to automatic text difficulty/readability assessment consisted of calculating readability scores with manually crafted formulae. One of the most famous being the Flesch-Kincaid score [13]. It takes the average number of words per sentence, as well as the average number of syllables per word and returns a linear combination of both averages. However, readability formulae were outperformed by machine learning approaches in the early 21st century [20]. Si and Callan used a linear combination of an unigram language model and a sentence length model to capture content-based as well as surface linguistic features of the document. Since then many works have experimented with more complex features and classifiers.

Schwarm and Ostendorf chose a Support Vector Machine (SVM) classifier instead of simply combining their features linearly [19]. Their feature set utilized multiple language models and basic parse tree features, including the average number of noun or verb phrases. They also added traditional readability measures, such as the Flesch-Kincaid score. Heilman et al. experimented with a linear regression model to estimate grade level instead of predicting predefined readability classes [9]. They also included grammatical features, namely relative frequencies of parse subtrees. Discourse-based features proved to further improve readability estimation [5,18]. Examples for discourse-based features are the percentage of named entities per document and the average length of text spanned by semantic relations between entities.

Vajjala and Meurers compared the performance of multiple lexical features, syntactic features and classifiers [21]. For this purpose, they introduced the

WeeBit corpus. It combines documents downloaded from the WeeklyReader and BBC-Bitesize websites. The documents are labeled with one of five grade levels, corresponding to age groups of the intended audience between 7 and 16 years. Their best performing model was a Multilayer Perceptron and achieved an accuracy of 93.3%. However, the original WeeBit corpus was shown to be problematic, as it contained broken sentences and extraneous content form the websites [23]. For example, each document included a copyright declaration from its respective source. For this reason, Xia et al. re-extracted the text documents form the raw HTML of the crawl. They achieved an accuracy of 80.3% using a SVM and a combination of traditional, lexico-semantic, syntactic parse tree, language modeling and discourse-based features.

All of the work described so far only contemplated English texts. However, there are also approaches dealing with other languages, such as French [6], German [8], Swedish [17], Japanese [22] or Chinese [11].

Another interesting approach was proposed by González-Garduño and Søgaard [7]. They applied multi-task Multilayer Perceptrons and Logistic Regression models to manually crafted feature representations of two different readability corpora, as well as the Dundee eye-tracking corpus. The Dundee eye-tracking corpus is a collection of eye-tracking recordings of native English speakers reading news articles [12]. All parameters in the hidden layers were shared between the tasks of predicting readability and various gaze statistics, such as predicting how long the eyes of the reader fixate on a region of text from the moment he first enters it until he leaves it. They report a small but significant increase in readability prediction accuracy when using the multi-task setup instead of a single task setup of the same architecture.

Jiang et al. experimented with tailoring word embeddings to the task of readability assessment by utilizing domain knowledge on English and Chinese datasets [10]. They use information about the acquisition, usage and structure difficulty of words to construct a knowledge graph. The acquisition difficulty of a word refers to the age children typically learn the meaning of it. Usage difficulty is estimated by differentiating between frequently and rarely used words. The number of syllables and characters contained in the word make up its structure difficulty. Their constructed knowledge graph captures how similar pairs of words are on a difficulty level. The final embeddings are trained by predicting the difficulty context derived from the knowledge graph as well as the typical context words surrounding the target word in a corpus. Their best model combines their embeddings with a manually crafted feature set and is evaluated on four different datasets. Jiang et al. report the following accuracies on their datasets: 95.87% (English), 70.05% (English), 60.23% (Chinese) and 35.52% (Chinese).

3 Implementation

To avoid the expense and lack of generalizability connected to manually crafting features, an approach utilizing embeddings and neural networks was chosen. A schematic representation of the text difficulty prediction architecture can be seen in Fig. 1. The first step of the prediction process involves tokenizing and padding/trimming all texts to a common length. This is described in more detail in the Preprocessing Section. Next, the resulting tokens are embedded. The following pre-trained embedding models were used in our experiments: the word2vec [14], the uncased Common Crawl GloVe [15], the original ELMo [16], the uncased small BERT and the uncased large BERT [4] model. The word2vec and GloVe models both produce context independent 300 dimensional word embeddings and were selected for their simplicity and speed. The original ELMo model produces 1024 dimensional deep contextualized word embeddings and mean-pooled sentence embeddings. In contrast to all of the other models used in this work, this model uses a character level representation of input words and is therefore able to generate meaningful embeddings for out-of-vocabulary tokens. The small and large BERT models produce deep contextualized word embeddings with 768 and 1024 dimensions, respectively. The ELMo and BERT models were selected for their high performance on multiple natural language processing tasks.

The embedded input sequence is then passed to a series of neural network layers, which are detailed in the Neural Network Layers Section. Finally, the output layer returns the probabilities of the input sequence belonging to the classes predefined in the modified WeeBit corpus, which is outlined in Sect. 4.1. The document is assigned the class with the highest probability.

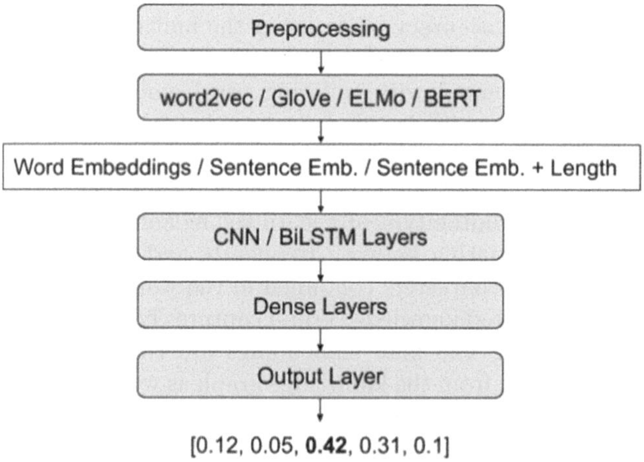

Fig. 1. Schematic depiction of the text difficulty prediction architecture.

3.1 Preprocessing

Before the neural network is able to deal with the input documents, raw text has to be transformed into a mathematical representation. The first step of preprocessing consists of separating the raw text into sentences. Then each sentence is tokenized. For the simple GloVe and word2vec embeddings, this is done by the Keras [3] built-in Tokenizer. The Keras Tokenizer has the benefit of automatically constructing a mapping of words to unique indices, while tokenizing the text. This mapping can later be used to build the embedding matrix. The Tokenizer also converts all words to lower case.

For the ELMo and BERT embeddings, the Natural Language Toolkit (NLTK) 3.3 [2] functions *sent_tokenize* and *word_tokenize* were used. The main reason for the different tokenizers lies in the fact that the ELMo and BERT models produce contextualized embeddings. This means that the same word has a different vector representation depending on the context it is in. Therefore, there is no need for an index mapping.

After tokenizing, the documents are brought to a common length. Deciding on a length is a trade-off between retaining as many words of a document as possible while staying computationally feasible. This decision must be made on the basis of the documents to be analysed. The longest document contained in the modified WeeBit dataset described in Sect. 4.1 is 5229 tokens long. However, on average documents only contain 390.54 tokens. Thus, padding all documents to the maximum document length would introduce a significant number of computations performed solely on padding. An analysis of the distribution of document lengths depicted in Fig. 2 showed a maximum number of tokens of 700 to be well suited for this task. This way 85.41% of the documents remain untrimmed while keeping the computation overhead reasonable.

Since the ELMo model takes batches of whole sentences as input, the trimming process had to be adapted slightly for this embedding. Sentences of a batch must have the same length. For this reason, each sentence in a document is padded to the length of the longest sentence of the document. Additionally, cutting each document off after 700 tokens would lead to incomplete sentences. To avoid this, the last incomplete sentence is fully discarded.

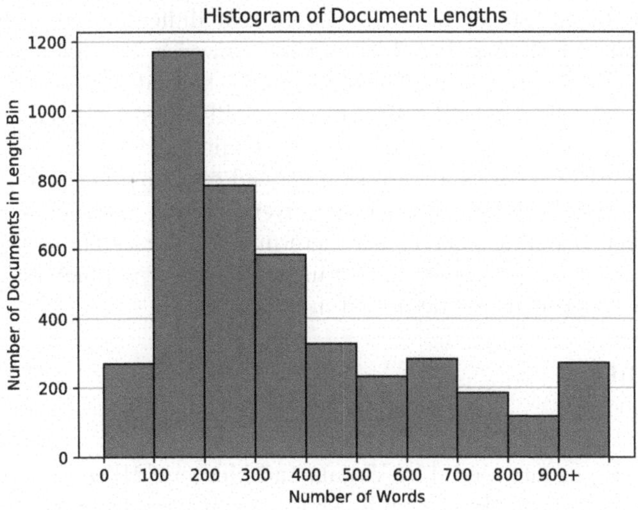

Fig. 2. Distribution of document lengths in the modified WeeBit corpus.

No trimming and padding was done in the preprocessing for the BERT model. It takes a file containing one sentence in each line and brings it into the appropriate shape on its own.

3.2 Neural Network Layers

The neural network models were implemented and trained using Keras 2.1.6 with the Tensorflow backend. Using Keras instead of only Tensorflow is advantageous, due to the fact that the additional abstraction layer allows for easier and faster implementation.

The first layer of the neural network accepts a dense vector representation of the text. The goal of the first layers is to efficiently handle the high dimensional input and to reduce the dimensionality for the following dense layers. We conducted experiments using either convolutional or bidirectional LSTM layer for this purpose. The first layer is followed by an optional series of further dimensionality reducing layers of the same kind. Although convolutional layers are typically used in combination with pooling layers, this was deliberately avoided in this work. The studies experimenting with manually crafted features described in Sect. 2 showed that syntactic, discourse and other features dependent on word order are very important for the task of text difficulty prediction. Pooling layers discard information about word order. Therefore, they are likely not well suited for this task.

Following the dimensionality reducing layers are a series of variable sized dense layers. The final dense layer has 5 nodes, one for each possible class. It uses softmax as activation function. The loss is categorical cross entropy. The combination of cross entropy loss and the softmax activation function in the final layer was chosen for its property to return and evaluate a probability distribution over a set of classes. This is well suited for multiclass classification tasks with distinct classes. A result of this decision is that the ordering of the classes is not taken into account. In reality, text difficulty estimation is closer to a regression task than a classification task. However, the differently sized age groups corresponding to reading levels and the lack of differentiation of difficulty within reading levels makes the WeeBit corpus ill-suited for training regression models. With a more differentiated dataset it might be beneficial to formulate text difficulty estimation as a regression instead of a classification problem.

The activation functions of the other layers, as well as dropout rates, batch size and other hyperparameters are determined by random hyperparameter searches in various experiments. The ranges the hyperparameters are sampled from in each experiment are described in Sect. 4.2.

4 Evaluation

4.1 Data

The WeeBit corpus introduced by Vajjala and Meurers [21] contains educational newspaper articles from the WeeklyReader magazine and the BBC-Bitesize website. They are labeled with a reading level, corresponding to non-overlapping age groups. The target audience are native speakers. The class distribution of the original WeeBit corpus can be seen in Table 1. Articles of the classes Key Stage 3 (*KS3*) and General Certificate of Secondary Education (*GCSE*) were crawled from the BBC-Bitesize site. The others stem from the WeeklyReader magazine. As discussed in Sect. 2 the original corpus articles contain extraneous content which clearly indicates the website the article was downloaded from. This is likely to distort results obtained on this corpus.

Table 1. Class distribution of the original WeeBit corpus.

Grade level	Age group	Number of articles	Avg. number of sentences/article
Level 2	7–8	629	23.41
Level 3	8–9	801	23.28
Level 4	9–10	814	28.12
KS3	11–14	644	22.71
GCSE	14–16	3500	27.85

For this reason, this work uses the modified WeeBit corpus introduced by Xia et al. [23]. They re-extracted the articles so that only the actual text of the articles remained. The class distribution of the modified corpus can be seen in Table 2. The number of articles on the KS3 level differ because Vajjala and Meurers omitted a group of articles in their original experiments. The modified corpus contains less articles because many documents of the original corpus only contained extraneous content, such as navigational links. In this work, the corpus is further reduced by 9 articles as they were duplicates to other articles in the corpus. This results in the corpus containing 4221 articles in total instead of 4230.

4.2 Experiment Setup

Several experiments were conducted. They can be grouped into 8 types of experiments depending on the embedding and dimensionality reducing layer used. Each experiment consists of random sampling 20 different configurations from a range of possible hyperparameters. Random search was preferred over grid search, because some hyperparameters typically have little impact on the performance of the model. A grid search would unnecessarily sample along those axis just as often as the relevant ones. Since the set of important hyperparameters could be different for each task, it is not possible to systematically exclude hyperparameters from the search. For this reason, random searches are more efficient [1].

The sampled hyperparameter configurations were then trained on a portion of the modified WeeBit corpus. 10% of the dataset were held back from the experiments and only used for testing the final model, so as to avoid overestimating the performance of this approach. This corresponds to 422 documents.

Table 2. Comparison of the class distributions of the original and modified WeeBit corpora.

Grade level (old)	Age group	Original corpus	Modified corpus
Level 1 (level 2)	7–8	629	529
Level 2 (level 3)	8–9	801	767
Level 3 (level 4)	9–10	814	801
Level 4 (KS3)	10–14	1969	1288
Level 5 (GCSE)	14–16	3500	845

The remaining documents were split into a development set (20%/759) and a training set (80%/3040). The modified WeeBit corpus was shuffled before splitting to ensure that the assignment of a an article to one of the three sets was random. This is done to have an identical class distribution in every data split and to exclude confounding factors due to the ordering of the corpus.

The number of epochs was limited to 500. Early stopping was applied. This means that the models were trained only as long as the performance on the development set improved. This prevents the model from overfitting on the training set. The monitored performance metric was the loss on the development set. The patience, meaning the number of epochs the early stopping waits for an improvement, varied between 1 and 5 in the experiments.

In the context of hyperparameter sampling in this work, drawing from an exponential distribution with scale β implies the underlying density function shown in 1.

$$f(x; \frac{1}{\beta}) = \frac{1}{\beta} e^{-x/\beta} \tag{1}$$

The following experiments were run:

1. An experiment using convolutional layers for dimensionality reduction. The type of embedding was either GloVe or word2vec with equal chance. The number of convolutional layers was uniformly sampled between 1 and 5, with each layer having 10 to 200 different filters. The window size was uniformly sampled between 3 and 9 for each layer. The stride was fixed to 1. The number of dense layers was drawn from an exponential distribution with scale $\beta = 2$. A list with layer sizes for each layer was sampled from an exponential distribution with scale $\beta = 200$. The list was then ordered in a descending order. This was done, because networks that go from wide to narrow layers seem to perform better. Regularization rates for L1 and L2 regularization were uniformly picked between 0 and 0.001. The optimizer was randomly selected from the options: RMSprop, Adagrad, Adadelta, Adam, Adamax and Nadam. Each optimizer was used with the Keras default parameters. The activation functions for the dense and convolutional layers were separately chosen, but remained the same for all layers of the respective type. The possible activation functions were *tanh*, *sigmoid*, *hard_sigmoid*, *elu* and *relu*. Finally, the dropout rate was uniformly sampled between 0 and 0.55.

2. Another experiment exchanged the convolutional layers with bidirectional LSTM (biLSTM) layers. GloVe or word2vec were used as embeddings as above. The optimizer, dropout rates, regularizer rates and the activation function for the dense layers were selected in the same way as well. Furthermore, at least 1 and at most 4 dense layers were sized as described above. However, *elu* and *relu* were exuded from the selection process for the activation function of the LSTM layers. The size of the hidden state was uniformly sampled between 50 and 600, just as the number of LSTM layers between 1 and 4. The batch size was either 32, 64, 128 or 256. This experiment as well as experiment 1 function as a baseline to evaluate if the more complex embeddings, with their additional computation time and memory requirements, prove beneficial. Additionally, these fast experiments are used to determine the best performing dimensionality reducing layer which is to be used in the following experiments.
3. The next experiment used only the ELMo sentence embeddings and biLSTM layers. The other hyperparameters were similarly selected as in the biLSTM experiment before, with only some ranges adapted to the different embedding. Models of this experiment are expected to outperform the simple embedding baselines.
4. A series of experiments was conducted using biLSTM layers and the ELMo sentence embeddings with the normalized sentence length appended. Appending the sentence length to the sentence embedding is expected to increase the performance of the model as this information is lost when mean-pooling and was found to be one of the most important features in multiple studies [21,23]. The series included broad hyperparameter searches as well as fine-tuning by searching locally around hyperparameter configurations which worked well in the broad searches. One major difference to the experiments before lies in the fact that the number of biLSTM layers was fixed to one. This was done because the training times for models with more than one biLSTM layer had been long in earlier experiments while resulting in models that performed worse than their one layered counterparts.
5. A series of experiments involving the ELMo word embeddings and biLSTM layers. This experiment setup is expected to perform better than the sentence embedding experiments because there is no information loss caused by mean-pooling. To reduce computation time and RAM demand on the graphics card the input text were further shortened to 500 words and the possible batch sizes were reduced to 16, 20 and 32. Since early models in this series tended to only predict the majority class, later experiments in this series included class weighting the input samples so that every class has the same impact on the loss function. The specific weights were 2.44 for Level1, 1.67 for Level2, 1.61 for Level3, 1 for Level4 and 1.52 for Level5.
6. An experiment using the small BERT sentence embeddings and biLSTM layers. BERT sentence embeddings were obtained by mean pooling the final hidden layer representation of each word in the sentence. This experiment was used as a pilot to determine if the BERT architecture produces results

comparable to ELMo to decide if the additional computation time for the large BERT model should be spent.
7. Two experiments using the large BERT sentence embeddings and biLSTM layers. As Devlin et al. report the large BERT model to outperform the ELMo model on multiple natural language processing tasks, this experiment setup is expected to outperform all models of the previous experiments.
8. A series of experiments employing the large BERT sentence embeddings with the normalized sentence lengths appended and biLSTM layers.

4.3 Results

All experiments were run on a machine with a NVIDIA Geforce GTX 1060 6 GB graphics card, an AMD Ryzen 5 1600X Six-Core Processor and 24 GB RAM. Approximately, training a model to its early stopping point took between a few minutes and three hours of time. Only the experiments with the ELMo word embeddings took significantly longer with training times up to 14 h per model. Since the input texts were embedded once and stored on disk beforehand, these time estimates do not include the time needed by the embedding model.

The results of the best models of each experiment type described in Sect. 4.2 can be seen in Table 3. A model was determined to be the best of an experiment type if it had the highest macro-averaged F1 score on the development set of all the models using the same dimensionality reducing layer type (CNN vs. BiLSTM) and the same embedding selection. As depicted, all models but the model using ELMo word embeddings outperform the majority baseline on every metric. The model using the ELMo sentence embeddings with the normalized sentence lengths appended generalizes best to unseen data. This is demonstrated by its performance on the development set. The ELMo sentence embedding model without the sentence lengths achieved the best performance on the training set. However, this model does not generalize as well to new data.

The BiLSTM architecture seems to outperform the CNN approach on this task, which is also the reason why the BiLSTM architecture was chosen for all following experiments. Also interesting to note is the fact that the GloVe embeddings seem to be better suited for this dataset than the word2vec embeddings. While the embeddings were not directly compared, the best models of the first two experiments always used the GloVe embeddings. The ELMo sentence embeddings outperform the BERT sentence embeddings on all metrics. Additionally, appending the normalized sentence length to the sentence embedding seems to improve the performance of models. Interestingly, the ELMo word embedding model hardly beats a majority baseline on unseen data, while still approximating the training data comparably to the other models.

The selection of the best models for the ensemble was conducted in the following way. First, all models were sorted by their accuracy on the development set. Then the first 5 models were combined to an ensemble and the ensemble was evaluated on the development set. Successively, the next worse model was added to the ensemble until the performance on the development set declined. This resulted in an ensemble with the 6 models which performed best in terms of accuracy on the development set. All of these models used the ELMo sentence embeddings with the sentence lengths appended. The specific hyperparameters of each model are listed in Table 4 for reproducibility purposes.

The performances of the best models and the ensemble are depicted in Table 5. Even though Model 5 achieves the best scores on the training set, its lower scores on the development set indicate that the model is overfitted on the training samples. The majority voting ensemble containing all 6 models performs better than each individual model on the development set. It achieved an accuracy of 81.3% and a macro F1 score of 80.6% on the development set. Therefore, the ensemble is the best classification model found for this task in this work.

Optimally, the ensemble and the model proposed by Xia et al. would now be compared on a test set using multiple metrics. However, Xia et al. do not report results on a test set which was held back from the model selection process or metrics other than accuracy and Pearson correlation coefficient. For this reason, the ensemble's performance on the development set in terms of accuracy and Pearson correlation coefficient are compared to Xia et al.'s reported results. Xia et al.'s best model achieved an accuracy of 80.3% and a Pearson correlation coefficient of 0.900 in their five-fold cross-validation experiments on the modified WeeBit corpus. Our ensemble achieves an accuracy of 81.3% and a Pearson correlation coefficient of 0.914 on the development set. However, this comparison is not entirely valid due to the different experiment setups.

On the test set, the ensemble achieved a macro-averaged F1 score of 72.2% and had 74.4% accuracy.

Table 3. Comparison of the best models (in terms of macro-averaged F1 score on the development set) of each experiment type specified in Sect. 4.2. The best result of each metric is emphasized.

	Metric		
Experiments	Accuracy train	Accuracy Dev	Macro F1 Dev
1. CNN GloVe/word2vec	88.5%	52.3%	57.8%
2. BiLSTM GloVe/word2vec	80.6%	69.0%	66.2%
3. BiLSTM ELMo Sent	***97.3%***	75.4%	74.6%
4. BiLSTM ELMo Sent + Len	93.2%	***79.2%***	***78.4%***
5. BiLSTM ELMo Word	86.1%	24.2%	23.1%
6. BiLSTM S BERT Sent	84.0%	74.2%	73.3%
7. BiLSTM L BERT Sent	96.4%	69.6%	69.6%
8. BiLSTM L BERT Sent + Len	87.8%	76.0%	74.1%
9. Majority baseline	30.4%	31.4%	9.5%

Table 4. Hyperparameters of the 6 best models which were selected for the ensemble. All values are rounded to 4 decimal places.

	Model					
Parameter	1	2	3	4	5	6
Dropout	0.088	0.0508	0.0336	0.0059	0.0302	0.0063
Dense Drop.	0.0894	0.0777	0.0725	0.0659	0.0806	0.1003
Rec. Drop.	0.3037	0.4096	0.3706	0.0739	0.4718	0.3199
Activation	tanh	tanh	tanh	tanh	tanh	tanh
Dense Act.	tanh	sigmoid	sigmoid	sigmoid	tanh	sigmoid
Rec. Act.	sigmoid	sigmoid	sigmoid	sigmoid	sigmoid	sigmoid
Optimizer	adamax	adamax	adamax	adamax	adamax	adamax
Hidden Dim.	420	480	237	348	364	591
Dense1 Dim.	137	691	443	178	41	161
Dense2 Dim.	129	-	-	-	-	-
Dense3 Dim.	22	-	-	-	-	-
Batch size	64	64	32	64	128	32
Bias Reg. L1	0.0003	0.0004	0.0003	0.0005	0.0006	0.0002
Bias Reg. L2	0.0002	0.0005	0.0003	0.0005	0.0000	0.0003
Activity Reg. L1	0.0000	0.0003	0.0000	0.0002	0.0003	0.0006
Activity Reg. L2	0.0003	0.0004	0.0007	0.0001	0.0001	0.0002
Kernel Reg. L1	0.0001	0.0007	0.0002	0.0007	0.0001	0.0003
Kernel Reg. L2	0.0006	0.0002	0.0008	0.0002	0.0000	0.0002

Table 5. Results in terms of accuracy and macro-averaged F1 score of models composing the ensemble and the ensemble. In comparison, the approach of Xia et al. [23] achieved 80.3% accuracy in their cross-validation experiments. The best result of each metric is emphasized. On the test set, the ensemble achieved a macro-averaged F1 score of 72.2% and had 74.4% accuracy.

Experiments	Accuracy train	Macro F1 train	Accuracy Dev	Macro F1 Dev
Model 1	93.2%	93.3%	79.2%	78.4%
Model 2	87.7%	87.9%	78.4%	78.0%
Model 3	90.4%	90.4%	78.7%	77.6%
Model 4	87.6%	88.5%	77.3%	77.2%
Model 5	***98.1%***	***98.2%***	77.9%	77.6%
Model 6	91.6%	91.6%	77.9%	76.7%
Ensemble	94.6%	94.8%	***81.3%***	***80.6%***

5 Conclusion and Discussion

In conclusion, we have contributed a deep learning approach to text difficulty classification which performs comparably to the state-of-the-art approach in terms of accuracy and Pearson correlation coefficient while being easier and cheaper to adapt to new types of text. This enables a larger range of educational applications, such as didactic recommendation systems, to profit from text difficulty metadata of their textual items. We have investigated the effect of various embedding models and neural network architectures on the performance of text difficulty models in terms of accuracy and F1 score. Surprisingly, the BERT model and ELMo word embedding model performed worse than expected. One possible reason for this could be the fact that both embedding models were not utilized to their full potential due to hardware constraints.

In future work, the surprising results could be investigated further on better hardware. Additionally, the generalizability of this approach to new datasets should be empirically examined. For this heterogeneous texts have to be annotated and collected into new datasets.

References

1. Bergstra, J., Bengio, Y.: Random search for hyper-parameter optimization. J. Mach. Learn. Res. **13**, 281–305 (2012)
2. Bird, S., Klein, E., Loper, E.: Natural Language Processing with Python: Analyzing Text with the Natural Language Toolkit. O'Reilly Media Inc., Sebastopol (2009)
3. Chollet, F., et al.: Keras. https://keras.io. Accessed 13 Apr 2019
4. Devlin, J., Chang, M.W., Lee, K., Toutanova, K.: BERT: pre-training of deep bidirectional transformers for language understanding. arXiv preprint arXiv:1810.04805 (2018)
5. Feng, L., Jansche, M., Huenerfauth, M., Elhadad, N.: A comparison of features for automatic readability assessment. In: Proceedings of the 23rd International Conference on Computational Linguistics: Posters. Association for Computational Linguistics (2010)
6. François, T., Fairon, C.: An AI readability formula for French as a foreign language. In: Proceedings of the 2012 Joint Conference on Empirical Methods in Natural Language Processing and Computational Natural Language Learning. Association for Computational Linguistics (2012)
7. Gonzalez-Garduno, A.V., Søgaard, A.: Using gaze to predict text readability. In: Proceedings of the 12th Workshop on Innovative Use of NLP for Building Educational Applications (2017)
8. Hancke, J., Vajjala, S., Meurers, D.: Readability classification for German using lexical, syntactic, and morphological features. Proc. COLING **2012**, 1063–1080 (2012)
9. Heilman, M., Collins-Thompson, K., Eskenazi, M.: An analysis of statistical models and features for reading difficulty prediction. In: Proceedings of the Third Workshop on Innovative Use of NLP for Building Educational Applications. Association for Computational Linguistics (2008)

10. Jiang, Z., Gu, Q., Yin, Y., Chen, D.: Enriching word embeddings with domain knowledge for readability assessment. In: Proceedings of the 27th International Conference on Computational Linguistics (2018)
11. Jiang, Z., Sun, G., Gu, Q., Chen, D.: An ordinal multi-class classification method for readability assessment of Chinese documents. In: Buchmann, R., Kifor, C.V., Yu, J. (eds.) KSEM 2014. LNCS (LNAI), vol. 8793, pp. 61–72. Springer, Cham (2014). https://doi.org/10.1007/978-3-319-12096-6_6
12. Kennedy, A., Hill, R., Pynte, J.: The Dundee corpus. In: Proceedings of the 12th European Conference on Eye Movement (2003)
13. Kincaid, J.P., Fishburne Jr., R.P., Rogers, R.L., Chissom, B.S.: Derivation of new readability formulas (automated readability index, fog count and flesch reading ease formula) for navy enlisted personnel (1975). https://stars.library.ucf.edu/istlibrary/56/. Accessed 13 Apr 2019
14. Mikolov, T., Sutskever, I., Chen, K., Corrado, G.S., Dean, J.: Distributed representations of words and phrases and their compositionality. In: Advances in Neural Information Processing Systems (2013)
15. Pennington, J., Socher, R., Manning, C.: Glove: global vectors for word representation. In: Proceedings of the 2014 Conference on Empirical Methods in Natural Language Processing (EMNLP) (2014)
16. Peters, M.E., et al.: Deep contextualized word representations. arXiv preprint arXiv:1802.05365 (2018)
17. Pilán, I., Vajjala, S., Volodina, E.: A readable read: automatic assessment of language learning materials based on linguistic complexity. arXiv preprint arXiv:1603.08868 (2016)
18. Pitler, E., Nenkova, A.: Revisiting readability: a unified framework for predicting text quality. In: Proceedings of the Conference on Empirical Methods in Natural Language Processing. Association for Computational Linguistics (2008)
19. Schwarm, S.E., Ostendorf, M.: Reading level assessment using support vector machines and statistical language models. In: Proceedings of the 43rd Annual Meeting on Association for Computational Linguistics. Association for Computational Linguistics (2005)
20. Si, L., Callan, J.: A statistical model for scientific readability. In: Proceedings of the Tenth International Conference on Information and Knowledge Management. ACM (2001)
21. Vajjala, S., Meurers, D.: On improving the accuracy of readability classification using insights from second language acquisition. In: Proceedings of the Seventh Workshop on Building Educational Applications Using NLP. Association for Computational Linguistics (2012)
22. Wang, S., Andersen, E.: Grammatical templates: improving text difficulty evaluation for language learners. arXiv preprint arXiv:1609.05180 (2016)
23. Xia, M., Kochmar, E., Briscoe, T.: Text readability assessment for second language learners. In: Proceedings of the 11th Workshop on Innovative Use of NLP for Building Educational Applications (2016)

Automatic Detection of Peer Interactions in Multi-player Learning Games

Mathieu Guinebert[1(✉)], Amel Yessad[1], Mathieu Muratet[1,2], and Vanda Luengo[1]

[1] Laboratoire d'Informatique de Paris 6, LIP6, Sorbonne Université, CNRS, 75005 Paris, France
mathieu.guinebert@lip6.fr
[2] INS HEA, 58-60 Avenue des Landes, 92150 Suresnes, France

Abstract. In Multi-player learning games (MPLG), learners interact with each other through game activities. This paper aims to establish the basis of automatic detection of peer interactions that could emerge from MPLG scenarios. The information provided by this detection could help learning game designers to construct scenarios fostering the interactions they need/desire. We present an algorithm extracting interaction features from MPLG scenarios. Because of the high number of possible sequences of activities in a scenario, we work only on a subset of the sequences which must preserve the information on the interactions emerging from the scenario. We evaluated this algorithm by comparing the calculated subset to the traced game paths obtained from 114 students. The results of this evaluation show that (1) the subset cover well the learners' traced paths and that (2) the calculated features from the subset have the same types and are distributed similarly to the ones extracted from the traced paths.

Keywords: Peer interactions · Multi-player learning games · Scenario analysis

1 Introduction

Learning Games are learning environments that can, if well designed, increase learners' involvement and motivation in learning [1, 2]. In particular, Multi-Player Learning Games (MPLG) foster a growing interest by teachers in creating scenarios in which learners interact with each other [3, 4]. Several papers have already shown a correlation between peer interactions within MPLG and the learners' motivation and involvement [5, 6]. In this paper, we will use the term interaction to refer to peer interactions.

In this context, it seems interesting to assist teachers and/or game designers to detect (semi)-automatically peer interactions that could emerge from their scenarios. Our approach is based on the analysis of the scenario's description. Research like those presented in [7] allow us to understand partly the problem related to the analysis of interactions. That research established three possible sources of information for manual analysis: video recording, systems' traces and screencasts. Unlike that research, our research is focused on the automatic detection of interactions relying on the scenario's description of MPLG without using the learners' traces. The latter point signifies that the analysis we propose is performed before the execution of the scenario by learners.

M. Scheffel et al. (Eds.): EC-TEL 2019, LNCS 11722, pp. 349–361, 2019.
https://doi.org/10.1007/978-3-030-29736-7_26

Interactions are particularly complex social phenomenon composed of verbal, non-verbal and social elements [8] making them hard to detect automatically. They are often ill-defined, ambiguous [9] and not consensual. The frequent confusion between collaboration and cooperation is a perfect example of this [10–12]. For these reasons, we focus our research to define and detect low-level features extracted from the descriptions of the MPLG activities. Those features could be used by users to specify what they mean by a more abstract interaction such as cooperation or competition. Those features are logical expressions that are true if some conditions are met inside a game activity. An example of a feature could be to verify if one game resource is critical or not. It means that the acquisition of this resource by a player would prevent another from acquiring it. This low-level feature could then be a strong indicator in favor of more abstract phenomena like the competition between learners. Thus, our first research question is the following: How to formally describe peer interactions' features? (RQ1)

Furthermore, MPLG are environments that can foster a great variety of interactions depending on the freedom degree granted to the learner. Many sequences of activities allow the learners to reach the end of the game. Each one of those sequences could potentially foster new interactions. Thus, in order to detect all the interactions, the learners would encounter in a scenario, it is mandatory to calculate every sequence they could use to reach the end of the game. However, the computational complexity of such calculation on complex scenarios shows that this approach is costly and time-consuming (probably reaching months or years for the more complex games). To answer this issue, we decided to look for a subset of sequences of activities called SA, that should carry most of the information on the interactions emerging from the scenario. Therefore, our second research question is the following: Is it possible to calculate a subset of scenario's sequences that well sums up the interactions of the scenario? (RQ2)

To evaluate the algorithm that calculate the subset SA and answer the RQ2, we carried out an experiment with students enrolled in second year at university. The experiment consisted in comparing the calculated SA to the players' traced paths. A traced path corresponds to the logs generated by the players in a MPLG session and transformed to an ordered sequence of activities. We note the traced path TP. The objective of this experiment is to verify that the subset SA is at least as good as the traced paths TP obtained from the learners' logs, for representing the scenario sequences. Thus, two criteria were defined to evaluate the algorithm:

1. The SA cover ratio: Are each TP generated by the players included in SA?
2. Are the interaction features calculated a priori from SA identical and similar distributed as the ones calculated from TP?

In Sect. 2, we present a detailed description of our Framework: the used activity model, the feature detection system and finally the SA building algorithm. The Sect. 3 details the experimental study we carried out with 114 students to evaluate the algorithm that compute the SA, as well as the obtained results.

2 Detecting Peer Interactions in MPLG Scenarios

2.1 Scenario and Activity Model

To detect automatically interactions in a MPLG scenario, it is important to formalize both the activities and the scenarios. A complete description of the model can be found in [13]. The model is inspired from concurrent systems [14]. A lot of concurrent systems are considered as consumer-producer problems in which the system dynamic is modelled with functions consuming and producing resources [14, 15]. We transpose this system's representation onto MPLG and consider that the actions of learners inside game activities, as well as game events, change the system state through producing and consuming resources. Our research hypothesis is that the interactions emerge from the dynamic of the scenario related to the resources' production and consumption, similarly to concurrent systems. Thus, the activity model representing this dynamic could allow the detection of peer interactions in MPLG automatically.

We model an activity as a set of roles. Those roles describe how the players behave in the MPLG activity. In the game, players consume and produce game objects, they also work on competencies. These indicate how the player manages his/her resources, similarly to concurrent systems that evolve thanks to their processes' production and consumption.

Given an activity composed of several roles, there is a possibility for players from various teams (opposite or not) to take roles in the same activity. Some roles may need players to be from different (or similar) teams, it is thus described in the role itself.

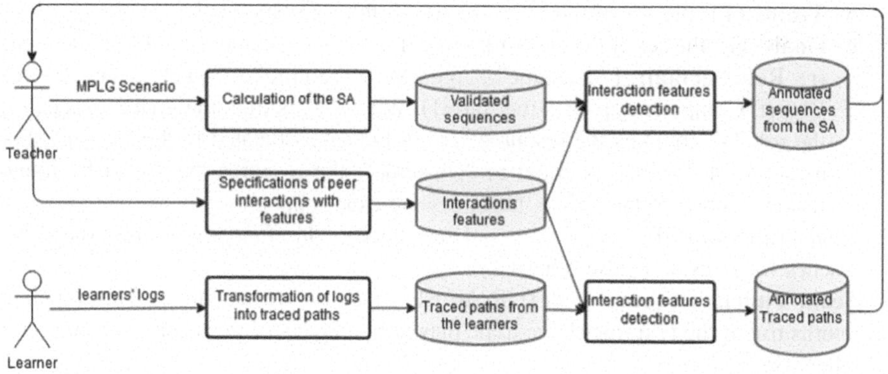

Fig. 1. Framework for peer interactions automatic detection in scenarios and traces

As presented in the introduction, we formalize a MPLG scenario as set of activity sequences. To verify our research hypothesis, we defined a framework (Fig. 1.) composed of three processes: (1) the calculation of a subset SA, (2) the transformation of learners' logs into TP, and (3) the automatic detection of interaction features from both SA and TP. The framework has two use cases.

Our first use case consists in extracting the interactions thanks to an automatic analysis of a MPLG scenario. This analysis is based on the description of the scenario. The first phase of this analysis consists in establishing a SA of admissible sequences from the scenario and then to validate them (cf. Sect. 2.2). Afterwards, the interactions features are extracted from each sequence (cf. Sect. 2.3).

The second use case consists in extracting the interaction features from learners' logs. Our system for peer interactions detection bases itself on our model for activities. The actions reported in the learners' logs do not use this model and it is, therefore, necessary to transform them. The Sect. 2.4 presents how we apply our model to the learner's logs in order for them to be analyzed by our system for peer interaction detection.

A MPLG scenario is a set of activity sequences. In the scope of this paper, we examine an activity with the following interactions' analysis framework:

1. **Roles (R):** the set of the roles that the learners can assume in the activity. A role is defined by resources, goals and teams.
   a. **Resources:** defined by four sets of game objects and competencies managed by the role.
      (1) **Consumed game objects (Cons):** the set of the game objects consumed by the role.
      (2) **Produced game objects (Prod):** the set of the game objects produces by the role.
      (3) **Competencies required (Cr):** the set of the knowledge and competencies required by the role.
      (4) **Competencies targeted (Ct):** the set of the knowledge and competencies targeted by the role.
   b. **Teams (T):** the set of the teams to which the role belongs.
   c. **Goals (G):** the set of the goals of a role. Each goal is composed of four elements (**r:** Role, **action:** {"consume", "produce", "require", "target"}, **re:** {Game Object, Competency}, **b:** {true, false}). When "b" is true, the goal is reached if the role "r" contains the resource "re" in the set associated to the "action". For example, if "action" is equal to "consume", the resource "re" must be found inside "Cons". When "b" is false, it's the exact opposite.
2. **Goal Function (GF): <r:** Role> → {true, false}. This function returns true if "r" reaches its goals and false otherwise.
3. **Team Function (TeamF): <r1:** Role, **r2:** Role> → {true, false}. This function returns true if the two roles have to be played by players of the same team and false otherwise.

2.2 Calculation of a Subset of Activity Sequences

As previously described, a MPLG scenario is a set of activity sequences. Extracting interactions emerging from a scenario needs the calculation of all the sequences of the scenario. However, the computational complexity of such calculation on complex scenarios shows that this approach is costly and time-consuming. For this reason, we decided to look for a subset, noted SA, of activity sequences that should carry the essential information about the interactions emerging from the scenario. The risk of such approach is to lose information. Indeed, there is a risk of not selecting meaningful sequences in terms of interactions. Therefore, we carried out a study to evaluate the proposed algorithm (see Sect. 3).

The algorithm we proposed is based on the precedence graph of the MPLG activities and is decomposed into two steps. The first one consists in calculating a set of activity sequences respecting the precedence constraints between the activities. The second one is to verify the feasibility of each calculated sequence by finding an execution of the sequence (eventually by repeating activities of the sequence) allowing the player to reach the end of the game from an initial state. The sequences respecting the precedence constraints are called admissible sequences and those that are feasible are called validated sequences.

The consumption and production of resources in MPLG activities create an implicit order between the activities. We consider that an activity A precedes an activity B if A produces resources consumed by B. The more precedence links there are, the less admissible sequences we calculate (if A_1 precedes A_2, the sequence $\langle A_1, A_2 \rangle$ is admissible but the sequence $\langle A_2, A_1 \rangle$ is impossible). To represent those precedence links, we build a precedence graph where the nodes represent MPLG activities and the arcs the precedence links between the activities. The Fig. 2 is an example of such a graph where the activities ‘c’, and ‘d’ precede ‘e’ and are both mandatory (link AND). On the contrary, only one activity between ‘a’ and ‘b’ must be executed before executing ‘c’ (link OR).

Based on the precedence graph, the algorithm we developed, analyzes the structure of the scenario and establishes the set of sequences that are consistent with the precedence links. For example, with the graph in Fig. 2 and by considering ‘e’ as the final activity of the scenario, we obtain 14 possible sequences: <a, b, c, d, e>, <a, b, d, c, e>, <a, d, b, c, e>, <d, a, b, c, e>, <b, a, c, d, e>, <b, a, d, c, e>, <b, d, a, c, e>, <d, b, a, c, e>, <a, c, d, e>, <a, d, c, e>, <d, a, c, e>, <b, c, d, e>, <b, d, c, e>, <d, b, c, e>.

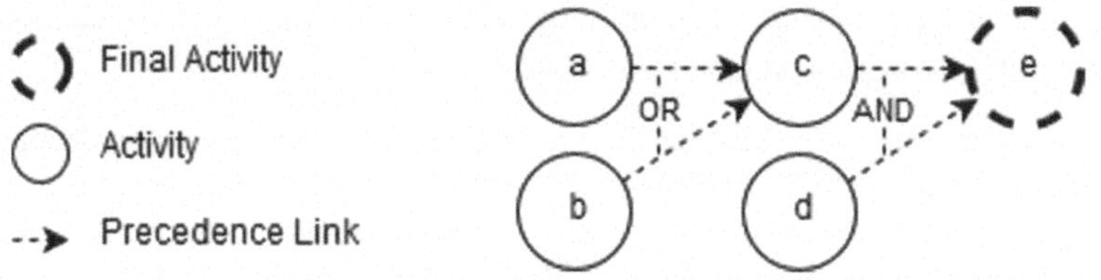

Fig. 2. Precedence graph AND/OR

All those sequences are consistent with the precedence links, but it is not sure that all these sequences allow the player to reach the end of the game from its initial state. Thus, it is necessary to verify their feasibility. To verify the feasibility of a sequence, the algorithm searches for an execution of the sequence that would allow the player to reach the end of the game by using only activities from the sequence in the given order and by repeating the activities as much as needed. To do so, the feasibility process start from the final activity and tries to reach a subset of the initial state.

In our approach, we consider that the interaction features emerging from an activity are independent from the position of the activity in the scenario and we are interested only on their distribution in the scenario. Thus, the order of the activities in a sequence has no influence on the number and type of the detected interaction features. If two sequences use the same activities but ordered differently, then the same type and number of interactions will be detected. Consequently, we can filter the sequences obtained in the first step by eliminating the redundant sequences (the sequences that contain the same activities). The number of admissible sequences from the example in Fig. 2 can then be reduced to only 3 sequences (instead of 14): <a, c, d, e>, <b, c, d, e> et <a, b, c, d, e>. Consequently, we reduce the number of admissible sequences before the feasibility step.

2.3 Detections of Peer Interaction Features

The literature review showed that there are no consensual definitions for peer interactions. In our research, we consider peer interactions as complex phenomena and propose to define low-level features to formalize them. These features are based on the activity model and are less hard to define in comparison with interactions. Each interaction could be defined as a logical combination of low-level features. This approach is flexible because users could define interactions differently, in function of their perceptions. For example, the collaboration can be defined as (1) having two players or more belonging to the same team, (2) working on the same competences in the activity (i.e. having the same "targeted" attribute) and (3) not being in conflict with one another (the acquisition of a resource by a player does not prevent the other from reaching his goals).

In a MPLG scenario, several features can appear. The detection of those features based on the activity model, is a bottom-up process. The first step consists in detecting the features related to each activity and then to count their number of occurrences for each sequence of the SA and finally in the whole subset. The feature formalization (R, GF and TeamF) is based on the analysis framework (cf. Sect. 2.1). In this paper we present 5 different features defined as follows:

1. Individualist (Ind): We consider the interactions in an activity to be dependent of the players' goals. Thus, to represent the lack of interaction, if no goal is associated to a role, the role is considered "passive", otherwise, it is "active". A learner that takes a role in an activity is Individualist if s/he is the only active player in the activity, i.e., the players involved in the other roles in this activity have no goals. The feature "Individualist" is extracted if:
   $\exists R_1 \in R \; \forall R_2 \in R$ such as $(R_2 \neq R_1) \wedge (R_1.G \neq ø) \wedge (R_2.G = ø)$
2. External Conflict (EC): this feature is verified if, in an activity, players from a team reach their goals while players from another team don't. The feature "External Conflict" is extracted if:
   $\exists R_1, R_2 \in R$ such as $\neg TeamF\,(R_1, R_2) \wedge \neg GF(R_1) \wedge GF\,(R_2)$
3. Internal Conflict (IC): this feature is verified if, in an activity, players from one team reach goals of players from the same team that don't reach them themselves. To extract the feature "Internal Conflict" we need to define a new function that verify if

a role would reach its goals with others resources. Indeed, in this case we want to check if a player would reach its goals if s/he manages resources of another player. Thus, we have the following function:

Goal function with replacing resources (GFRR): <**r**: R, **res**: Resources> $\rightarrow$ {true, false}. This function affects “res” to “r.resources” and returns the call of GF on this new “r”.

The feature “Internal Conflict” is extracted if:

$\exists R_1, R_2 \in R$ such as TeamF $(R_1, R_2) \wedge \neg$GF $(R_2) \wedge$ GFRR $(R_2, R_1.\text{Resources})$

4. Common Agreement (CA): this feature is verified if learners from the same team are active and have no internal conflicts. The feature “Common Agreement” is extracted if:

   $\forall R_1, R_2$ such as TeamF $(R_1, R_2) \wedge$ (GF (R_1) = GF (R_2)) $\wedge R_1.G \neq \emptyset) \wedge \neg\exists R_3$(TeamF $(R_1, R_3) \wedge$ (GF $(R_3) \neq$ GF (R_1)))
5. Shared Construction of Knowledge (SCK): this feature is verified if the learners are active, have no internal conflict (Common Agreement CA) and use all the same competencies in the activity. The feature “Shared Construction of Knowledge” is extracted if:

   $\forall R_1, R_2$ such as CA $(R_1, R_2) \wedge (R_1.\text{Resources.Ct} = R_2.\ \text{Resources.Ct})$

If we use those features on one of the described sequenced of the 2.2 example, that is to say <a, c, d, e>, we would apply the previously described formulas on the description of each activity. Let’s take the activity ‘a’, if this one answer the conditions for the features External Conflict (EC) and Common Agreement (CA), we would add 1 to the value of External Conflict and Common Agreement of the sequence. We will then repeat the process on each of its activities. The features used by the sequences would thus be summed with every activities of the SA sequence.

2.4 Transformation of Logs into Traced Paths

A Traced path (TP) is an ordered sequence of activities modelled similarly to the sequences of SA presented in Sect. 2.2. The difference between a TP and a SA sequence, is that a TP is obtained from the players’ logs, whereas a sequence of SA is calculated from the analysis of the scenario model. The transformation of logs into a TP is divided into two steps. Firstly, the individual logs of the players involved in the same game session are merged together into a unique log composed of ordered actions. Those latter are then grouped into activities thanks to the activity model of the MPLG (cf. Sect. 2.1). Finally, we obtain an activity sequence similar to the sequences of SA and becomes possible to apply the features detection Framework (cf. Sect. 2.3) on TP (Fig. 3).

To illustrate how the logs are transformed into a TP, let’s take an example of two players P_1 and P_2 playing a MPLG scenario. The latter contains 5 individual possible actions a_1, a_2, a_3, a_4 and a_5. The scenario is modelled with two activities A_1 and A_2 that are described as following:

- A_1 <Role 1: $a_1 \rightarrow a_2 \rightarrow a_3$; Role 2: $a_1 \rightarrow a_2 \rightarrow a_4$>
- A_2 <Role 1: a_5; Role 2: $a_5 \rightarrow a_1$>

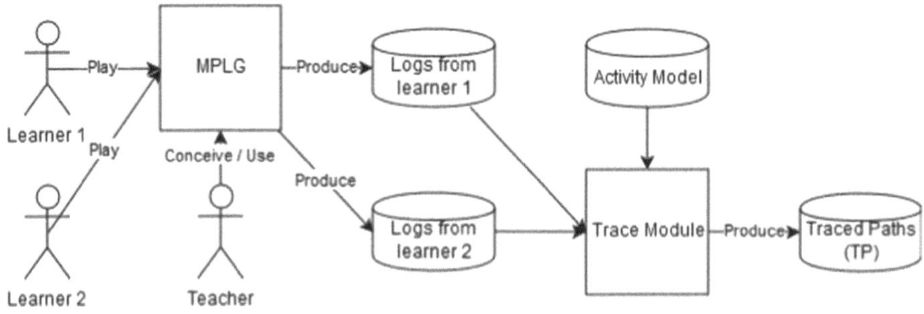

Fig. 3. Transformation process of logs into traced paths

The two players produce the following actions' sequence: $P_1a_1 \rightarrow P_1a_2 \rightarrow P_1a_5 \rightarrow P_2a_1 \rightarrow P_2a_2 \rightarrow P_1a_3 \rightarrow P_2a_4 \rightarrow P_2a_5 \rightarrow P_2a_1$. P_ka_i depicts that the player P_k does the action a_i. This sequence is the merge of two action sequences associated to each player:

- P_1: $P_1a_1 \rightarrow P_1a_2 \rightarrow P_1a_5 \rightarrow P_1a_3$
- P_2: $P_2a_1 \rightarrow P_2a_2 \rightarrow P_2a_4 \rightarrow P_2a_5 \rightarrow P_2a_1$

The transformation process of the logs into a traced path infers that the two player performed the traced path $A_1 \rightarrow A_2$.

3 Experimental Study

We carried out an experimental study related to the research question 2 (RQ2). The goal of the study was to evaluate the calculated subset SA of scenario sequences. To do so, we made comparisons between the subset SA and the TPs of two MPLG scenarios. The objective of these comparisons is to verify that the subset SA is at least as good as the traced paths TP obtained from the learners' logs, for representing the scenario sequences. If this is the case, the interactions extracted from the sequences of SA are probably representative of the interactions that could emerge from the scenario. Thus, the goal of this experiment was to answer the following questions:

1. Does the SA cover all the TP extracted from the players' logs?
2. Which peer interactions features are detected in the subset SA?
3. Are those features extracted from the SA similar to those extracted from the set of the TP? Are the features extracted from the set of the TP and those from the SA similarly distributed?

3.1 MPLG Scenarios

We developed a Multi-Player LOgic Game (MP-LOG), which allows students to experiment various kinds of interactions. MP-LOG targets students enrolled in the university's course of mathematical logic. MP-LOG uses a gameplay inspired from Tower Defense games (TD) in which the player has to defend his life points from incoming attackers by placing defense elements on their path. In MP-LOG, the defense elements are given to the learner solving quizzes on mathematical logic. MP-LOG is composed of two different scenarios.

In the first scenario, Tower Defense 4 (TD4), two teams of two players compete with each other. Each team has three lives and must give correct interpretations to logical formula in order to gather tokens. Those tokens can then be spent to create either defenders or attackers. If an attacker reaches the end line of a team, it destroys one life of opponent. If it is intercepted by a defender, both the attacker and the defender are destroyed. The first team with no live loses. The learners of a same team can decide to solve the enigma together or alone (the gathered number of tokens depends on this decision).

In the second scenario, Tower Defense 2 (TD2), two players face enemy waves controlled by the computer. Once again, the students can solve logical enigmas together or alone. A good answer grants them defenders to battle the computer and thus hold longer. A bad answer speeds the arrival of the next enemy wave. The game finishes when the players' lives are destroyed.

Each game session is quite short, the students were then asked to replay as much as possible the scenarios. The idea is that the players try different strategies and try to reach different goals. We note that the enigmas changed randomly between each game sessions.

3.2 Experimental Design and Data

Six university classes took part in the study (114 students in total). The students were enrolled in second year of computer science studies. The male/female ratio was 2:1. The game was presented to the students for 15–20 min without suggesting any strategy. The students' team were formed randomly. We gathered 264 individual logs for the TD2 and 248 for TD4. Once merged, we obtained 132 game sessions for TD2 and 62 for TD4. We then transformed those logs into traced paths accordingly to Sect. 2.3.

3.3 Results

We consider a TP as non-covered if no valid SA sequences correspond to it. Moreover, we consider a SA sequence as played, if at least one TP corresponds to it. The Table 1 summarizes the results after the analysis of the scenario and the logs. The results of the analysis show that the proposed algorithm is able to cover most of the TP played by the learners. Only two TP of the 62 (TD4) are not covered, or 3%. This result is encouraging but invite us to learn why those two TP aren't covered. In the proposed scenario model [13], a MPLG scenario can allow players to achieve several learners' objectives. After manually analyzing those two TP, we gathered that those two game sessions correspond to an equality between the players. This final state not having been anticipated during the TD4 scenario modeling, the sequences allowing to realize this "objective" were not generated by the algorithm. This result allowed us to reiterate on the scenario modeling to add this new final state. Those two TP are now covered by the new calculated SA.

Table 1. Number of SA sequences played by learners, number of non-covered TP (TD2 and TD4)

	Number of valid SA sequences	Number of TP	Number of SA sequences played	Number of TP non-covered by SA
Scenario TD2	256	132	35	0
Scenario TD4	510	62	38	2

A second result shows that many sequences were not used by the learners whereas some were used several times (for TD4 for example, 8 TP correspond to only one sequence). This last point explains why the number of TP is superior to the number of played SA sequences. The players followed similar strategies despite the freedom that were granted to them (same finding for TD2).

In some of the sequences found in the SA, the executed activities are quite diverse and highly improbable to find in a consistent play from players. Indeed, the fact that a particular combination of activities is possible in the game does not mean it is consistent for players to execute (useless activities, far too complex strategies, conflicting interactions, …). With this in mind, a lot of sequences established by the SA will probably never be used by the learners.

This is interesting in two aspects. First of all, it means the number of sequences in the SA could be further reduced by applying semantics verifying the consistence of the sequences regarding learners' strategies. Secondly, it means that our system (without semantics) is able to detect sequences rarely found in traces, thus giving complementary information to an approach based on traces.

Once the static analysis carried out on TD2 and TD4, we applied the detection process of interaction features, both on the sequences of SA and the set of TP. Table 2 synthesizes our results. We can observe, in both scenarios TD2 and TD4, that the learners' TP features and the SA features are differently distributed. This shows that the students favored some interactions. For example, for TD4, the features Ind (Individualistic) and IC (Internal Conflict) have the exact same proportion in the SA sequences (10.53%) whereas in TP, the learners were more in internal conflict (10.96%) than individualistic (4.24%).

Table 2. The distribution percentage of features in SA sequences, in played SA sequences and in the players' TP

Features (%)	TD2			TD4		
	SA sequences	Played sequences	TP	SA sequences	Played sequences	TP
EC	0	0	0	47.33	48.4	48.01
IC	20	17.34	15.14	10.53	10.56	10.96
Ind	20	16	22.69	10.53	6.15	4.24
CA	40	41.33	36.08	21.08	21.11	21.26
SCK	20	25.33	26.09	10.53	13.78	15.51

We applied the khi2 test to verify the independence of the features' distribution of SA and TP. The test shows a clear dependency between the features' distribution of SA and that of TPs and thus for both TD2 and TD4. This means, in the case of this study, that the interaction features extracted from SA sequences are similar (in type and distribution) to the one extracted from the players' TP. The analysis, a priori, of a MPLG scenario can thus provide meaningful information on the interactions. This result is important, because it allows the users to detect peer interactions in their scenario, before any playing of the students. Thus, they can modify/adapt when interactions do not meet their needs. However, those results are proper to the context of the study presented here, other studies should be carried on to validate them.

4 Conclusion

In this paper, we worked on the issues of the automatic detection of peer interactions in MPLG. We proposed a framework allowing the a priori analysis of a MPLG scenario. In this work, we chose to define an interaction, such as collaboration or competition, as a logical combination of low-level features based on the activities modeling. Our first research question concerns the nature of those features and their formalization. Those features will allow the users to have a greater flexibility in the definition of peer interactions. The Framework allows thus to define and extract interactions features that could emerge from a MPLG scenario.

Depending on the amount of freedom granted to players inside a MPLG, a great number of activity sequences can be played to achieve the end of the game. The importance of this number can lead to a combinatorial explosion of the scenario sequences' calculation. To answer this issue, we worked on an algorithm that calculates a subset of the activity sequences (SA). The latter should carry the essential information about the interactions emerging from the scenario. Our second research question concerns the existence of such subset.

We carried out an experimentation with 114 students in second year at university to evaluate the algorithm with two criteria: the covering of the SA and the features' distribution in the SA. To do so, we realized comparisons between the sequences of SA and the traced paths (TP) gathered from game sessions.

The results provide two answers to the second research question. In case of an exhaustive scenario modeling with the proposed model, our algorithm is able to calculate a SA that covers every path undertaken by the students. Furthermore, the interaction features' distribution between the set of TP and SA seems to indicate that the SA sequences can be qualified with the same features (in both type and distribution) as those extracted from players' TP.

This work provides interesting bases for the automatic detection of peer interaction in MPLG. Despite those bases needing more studies to allow the generalization of those results to other contexts, this work still open the way to several possibilities for future works. The framework is technical and is not yet adapted to users like teachers. We have to develop an authoring system to allow teachers to use it. The idea behind such authoring system would be to help teachers and users define their own features.

Users with a more technical background could also define and add to it new functionalities for the analysis of peer interactions in activities.

It would be interesting to reflect upon indicators (analytics) calculated on the basis of interaction features for teachers/designers of MPLG. The teachers could use them to modify the scenario to meet their needs and goals.

Acknowledgements. We would like to thank the EIAH Chair of Sorbonne-Universités for financing this work.

References

1. Paraskeva, F., Mysirlaki, S., Papagianni, A.: Multiplayer online games as educational tools: facing new challenges in learning. Comput. Educ. **54**(2), 498–505 (2010)
2. Wouters, P., Van Nimwegen, C., Van Oostendorp, H., Van Der Spek, E.D.: A meta-analysis of the cognitive and motivational effects of serious games. J. Educ. Psychol. **105**(2), 249 (2013)
3. Sourmelis, T., Ioannou, A., Zaphiris, P.: Massively multiplayer online role playing games (MMORPGs) and the 21st century skills: a comprehensive research review from 2010 to 2016. Comput. Hum. Behav. **67**(2017), 41–48 (2017)
4. Turkay, S., et al.: Toward understanding the potential of games for learning: learning theory, game design characteristics, and situating video games in classrooms. Comput. Schools **31** (1–2), 2–22 (2014)
5. Eseryel, D., Law, V., Ifenthaler, D., Ge, X., Miller, R.: An investigation of the interrelationships between motivation, engagement, and complex problem solving in game-based learning. Educ. Technol. Soc. **17**(1), 42–53 (2014)
6. Wendel, V., Gutjahr, M., Göbel, S., Steinmetz, R.: Designing collaborative multiplayer serious games. Educ. Inform. Technol. **18**(2), 287–308 (2013)
7. Dyke, G., Girardot, J.J., Lund, K., Corbel, A.: Analysing face to face computer-mediated interactions. In: 12th Biennial International Conference on EARLI (European Association for Research, Learning and Instruction), August 2017
8. Kumpulainen, K., Mutanen, M.: The situated dynamics of peer group interaction: an introduction to an analytic framework. Learn. Instr. **9**(5), 449–473 (1999)
9. Kreijns, K., Kirschner, P.A., Jochems, W.: Identifying the pitfalls for social interaction in computer-supported collaborative learning environments: a review of the research. Comput. Hum. Behav. **19**(3), 335–353 (2003)
10. Dillenbourg, P.: Introduction; What do you mean by "collaborative learning"? In: Dillenbourg, P. (ed.) Collaborative Learning: Cognitive and Computational Approaches, pp. 1–19 (1999)
11. Roschelle, J., Teasley, S.D.: The construction of shared knowledge in collaborative problem solving. In: O'Malley, C. (ed.) Computer Supported Collaborative Learning, vol. 128, pp. 69–97. Springer, Berlin (1995). https://doi.org/10.1007/978-3-642-85098-1_5
12. Kozar, O.: Towards better group work: seeing the difference between cooperation and collaboration. In: English Teaching Forum, vol. 48, no. 2, pp. 16–23 (2010)

13. Guinebert, M., Yessad, A., Muratet, M., Luengo, V.: An ontology for describing scenarios of multi-players learning games: toward an automatic detection of group interactions. In: Lavoué, É., Drachsler, H., Verbert, K., Broisin, J., Pérez-Sanagustín, M. (eds.) EC-TEL 2017. LNCS, vol. 10474, pp. 410–415. Springer, Cham (2017). https://doi.org/10.1007/978-3-319-66610-5_35
14. Manna, Z., Pnueli, A.: The Temporal Logic of Reactive and Concurrent Systems: Specification. Springer, Heidelberg (2012)
15. Magee, J., Kramer, J.: State Models and Java Programs. Wiley, Hoboken (1999)

Characterizing Comment Types and Levels of Engagement in Video-Based Learning as a Basis for Adaptive Nudging

Yassin Taskin[1(✉)], Tobias Hecking[1], H. Ulrich Hoppe[1], Vania Dimitrova[2], and Antonija Mitrovic[3]

[1] University of Duisburg-Essen, Duisburg, Germany
taskin@collide.info
[2] University of Leeds, Leeds, UK
[3] University of Canterbury, Christchurch, New Zealand

Abstract. Video is frequently used as a learning medium in a variety of educational settings, including large online courses as well as informal learning scenarios. To foster learner engagement around instructional videos, our learning scenario facilitates interactive note taking and commenting similar to popular social video-sharing platforms. This approach has recently been enriched by introducing nudging mechanisms, which raises questions about ensuing learning effects. To better understand the nature of these effects, we take a closer look at the content of the comments. Our study is based on an ex post analysis of a larger data set from a recent study. As a first step of analysis, video comments are clustered based on a feature set that captures the temporal and semantic alignment of comments with the videos. Based on the ensuing typology of comments, learners are characterized through the types of comments that they have contributed. The results will allow for a better targeting of nudges to improve video-based learning.

Keywords: Learning analytics · Video-based learning · Learner engagement · Adaptive nudging

1 Introduction

Being an integral part of digital learning, videos are utilized to enhance the educational experience and increase student satisfaction [17] in a broad range of educational settings, e.g. MOOCs, flipped classroom, informal learning. Social video-sharing platforms, such as YouTube, are becoming the first source for learners when they want to learn something new. However, watching videos is a passive activity, often resulting in a low level of engagement which hinders the effectiveness of video-based learning [2,18]. Automatic engagement detection can inform personalized interventions, e.g. motivational messages, questions, reminders, to prevent disengagement and to enhance the learning experience.

M. Scheffel et al. (Eds.): EC-TEL 2019, LNCS 11722, pp. 362–376, 2019.
https://doi.org/10.1007/978-3-030-29736-7_27

In previous work, we developed AVW-Space, a controlled platform for informal video-based learning through note-taking where students watch and comment on videos [21]. Several studies using AVW-Space with undergraduate and postgraduate university students in the context of presentation skills have shown that students who write comments instead of passively watching improve their understanding of presentation skills.

Gathering requirements for the effectiveness of AVW-Space in an earlier study indicated the need to encourage student commenting, which was positively correlated with conceptual learning, while at the same time preserving students' freedom to interact with videos in a way they prefer [21]. This informed the extending of AVW-Space by adding nudges [11] - interventions that influence people's behavior to make beneficial choices (paternalism) in a non-compulsory manner (libertarian). Two forms of nudges have been implemented [22]: signposting (interactive visualizations showing video intervals where past students have commented) and personalized prompts (noting student's commenting behavior or showing example past comments). A user study with the extended AVW-Space [22] indicated a significant increase in comment-writing in the nudging condition, thus providing evidence that the nudges encouraged student commenting. However, this did not lead to significant improvement of the students' conceptual knowledge.

Therefore, there is a need to gain a deeper understanding of the students' cognitive engagement while interacting with videos in order to better assess the impact of nudges in AVW-Space. This is the prime goal of the research presented here. It lays the grounds for more adaptive and selective nudging by addressing the following research questions:

RQ1: How can student comments be characterized with regard to cognitive engagement?

RQ2: Are there any notable individual differences with regard to commenting and cognitive engagement?

To answer these questions, we first differentiate levels of engagement in learner produced comments. By analyzing the content of the comments, we classify comments by distinguishing "shallow" types of engagement, such as echoing or affirmation, from deeper elaborations that draw associations, summarize, compare or transform the given material. In the second step, we project the comment classification back to the learners, i.e. we characterize learners through their specific set of comment types. This allows us to explore the dependencies between commenting behavior and individual learning characteristics and personal traits.

The paper is structured as follows: We start by providing an overview of related work on engagement detection specially for learning with videos, followed by a brief description of the experimental setting in which the data were collected. The data analysis reported in Sect. 4 includes the initial classification of comments through clustering, as well as the ensuing characterization of learners and their engagement levels. Finally, we reflect the findings in relation to background theories and potential applications.

2 Background

The work presented here falls in the broad area of analyzing engagement in digital learning. Generally, engagement analytics approaches utilize the vast amount of data collected while students interact with the system. There is an established research stream on predicting behavior that can have adverse effect on learning, such as quitting in systems that embed free learning tasks (e.g. reading [20] and solving problems [16]), disengagement in MOOC courses [2,6,18], and 'gaming the system' (i.e. taking advantage of system's properties to superficially complete the task) [4]. Another stream of work looks at detecting engagement aspects that can be linked to cognition, such as zoning out and mind wandering [5,12], and information seeking/giving [14]. Thirdly, the affective response to instructions (e.g. frustration [26] and confusion [1]) was also studied. These engagement behaviors, e.g. quitting, mind-wandering, zoning out, capture a rather 'shallow level' of engagement which does not show how the learner engages with the educational material. In contrast, our work investigates deeper cognitive levels of engagement by characterizing content (comments) produced by learners.

The prime focus of our work is engagement analytics for improving video-based learning. Existing research analyzes data about the learners' interaction with and navigation of videos by analyzing play, pause, and seeking actions and which parts of the video are most important [7,13,19]. Other works focus on students' reflections on videos, using their comments to determine students' conceptual understanding of the specific topics [10,15]. While the actual content of the video provides valuable information that can be analyzed using text mining methods on the video transcripts [3], the relation of both - student generated content and video content - has not been investigated. We call this relationship "semantic alignment", and provide computational means for its measurement. This helps us to better understand to what extent knowledge conveyed in the video is taken up by students. Moreover, this enables automatic differentiation (without manual knowledge engineering) between deeper engagement with the course material and shallower student contributions noting points in the videos.

Hence, our work contributes to research on engagement in video-based learning, e.g. [1,18], with a specific focus on cognitive engagement. We build on the ICAP framework [8] to link cognitive engagement activities to observable behaviors. While ICAP has been used to categorize information seeking in MOOC forums [14,27], its adoption for analyzing video engagement is novel. In our adoption, we have shifted the focus from behavioral aspects derived from interaction log files (e.g. [9]) to characterizing engagement based on learner-generated content. In our scenario (see next section), the primary unit of study are video comments. In turn, we use the classification of comments (i.e. comment types) as a means to characterize learners and their level of cognitive engagements, which leads to a specific adaptation of the ICAP framework.

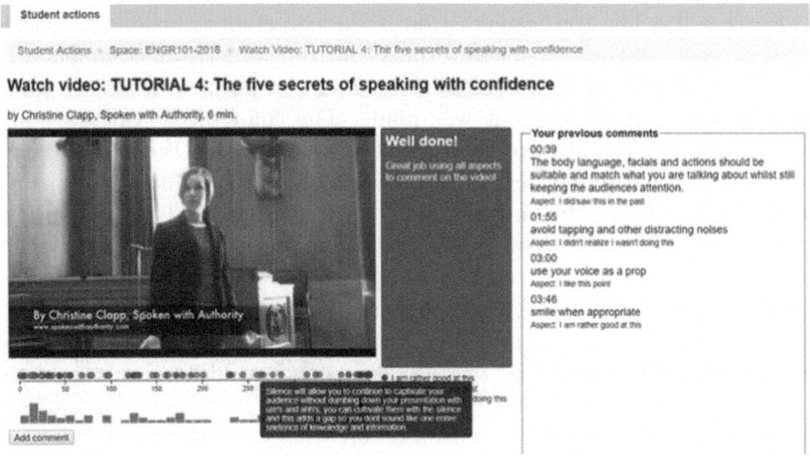

Fig. 1. Screenshot of AVW-Space, showing a *Diverse Aspects* nudge.

3 Experimental Setting

Educational Context. Our data was collected in the context of a large (1039 students) first-year course on fundamental engineering skills at the University of Canterbury. In this course, students work on a group project, and present their results in the last week of the course. Presentations are marked by two human tutors, who provide two group scores (one for the content of the presentation, the other for visual aids, both with the maximum of 5 marks), as well as an individual mark for each student (with the maximum of 5 marks). Due to an already full curriculum, there was no time in the course to teach students how to give presentations. Instead, the students were directed to AVW-Space as an online resource for presentation skills. The AVW-Space instantiation included eight short videos [22]: four tutorials on how to give presentations, and four videos showing example presentations. We limit analysis in this paper to tutorial videos only, as this is a common form of video content widely used for informal learning in a variety of educational contexts. The learning consisted of students watching and commenting on the videos individually.

Platform. The study involved two versions of AVW-Space. The **control condition** included watching and commenting on videos without any intervention from the system. The only support was the offering of reflective micro-scaffolds (aspects) - in addition to entering the text for a comment, students needed to select an aspect indicating the intention of the comment. For the tutorials, aspects (i.e. micro-scaffolds that encourage reflection) were: *I did not realize I was not doing this*, *I am rather good at this*, *I like this point* and *I did/saw this in the past*. The **experimental condition** included an enhanced version of AVW-Space, which additionally provided interactive nudges to enhance engagement, including visualizations and personalized prompts. Interactive visualizations, aimed to support social learning (i.e. learning from peers), are shown below the video (Fig. 1). The top visualization is the comment timeline; its goal is to provide signposts to the student in terms of previously written comments. Each comment is represented as a colored dot along the horizontal axis, representing the time when the comment was made. The color of the dot depends on the aspect used by the student who wrote that comment. When the mouse is positioned over a particular dot, the student can see the comment (as in Fig. 1). Clicking on a dot begins playing the video from that point. The bottom visualization is the comment histogram visualization; it shows a bar chart representing the number of comments written for various segments of the video. This visualization allows the student to quickly identify important parts of a video, where other students made many comments. These visualizations meet two identified needs: (1) providing social reference points so that students can observe others' comments, and (2) indicating important parts of a video and what kind of content can be expected in those parts, differentiated by aspect colors.

Personalized prompts, which appear next to the video (as in Fig. 1), are designed to encourage students to write comments [22]. For example, reminding the student to make comments when they tend to watch without commenting, encouraging the student to use diverse aspects, or showing examples from past comments to promote attention and stimulate engagement. AVW-Space maintains a profile for each student, used to decide which prompts are appropriate for the learner at a particular time during interaction.

Procedure. All students enrolled in the course were invited to take part in the study. Participants' profile was collected with a *pre-test survey*, including demographic information, background experiences and the Motivated Strategies for Learning Questionnaire (MSLQ) [23]. The survey also contained questions on the participants' knowledge of presentations (conceptual knowledge questions). students were asked to list as many concepts related to Structure, Delivery and Speech, and Visual Aids as they could. For each of those three questions, students had one minute to write responses. These answers were judged to what extent they covered concepts from an expert-generated domain taxonomy [11]. After a period in which the students interacted with AVW-Space, a *post-test survey* was issued. It included the same questions on knowledge about presentations (to measure change in conceptual knowledge), as well as some usability questions.

Participants. 347 participants have used AVW-Space writing at least one comment, of whom 180 were from the control group (124 males, 55 females, 1 other) and 167 from the experimental group (118 males, 49 females). The majority of participants (79.83%) were native English speakers; most participants (95.39%) were aged 18–23. There were no significant differences between the two groups on their experiences in giving presentations and using YouTube for learning, as well as on MSLQ scales.

Data. The data used for the analysis presented below includes:

- *user-generated data*: for each comment, AVW-Space records the text, selected aspect, the timestamp as well as the cue (i.e. the time in the video when the comment was entered).

- *learner MSLQ profile*: items that are relevant for this study are *intrinsic motivation* (degree of participation in academic activities for reasons of challenge, curiosity, and mastery), *extrinsic motivation* (academic activities mainly for grades and rewards), and *elaboration* (ability to integrate and connect new information with prior knowledge).
- *learning scores*: this includes the presentation scores obtained in the course and the conceptual knowledge (number of concepts named in post- and pre-test surveys)

4 Data Analysis

The first step of the data analysis was to identify different types of student comments. For this purpose, we clustered the comments using a feature set based on the comment content and the time at which a comment was made. This analysis will be presented in more detail in Sect. 4.1. The categorized comments can then be mapped back to the students to characterize these in terms of their commenting profiles. The relation between these profiles and other student variables are investigated in Sect. 4.2.

The data set consists of 1831 student comments. The domain knowledge used in this analysis originated from two sources: (1) a domain taxonomy that was manually created by experts containing key concepts about giving presentations in general, and (2) a set of concepts (per video) based on terms extracted from the videos in a processing chain that involved a speech-to-text transformation followed by term extraction. Using (1), we can determine the number of general domain concepts used in each comment. The video-specific terms (2) allow for a further differentiation: counting the overlap of terms between a comment and the terms extracted from the whole video we get a "global alignment" between the comment and this video. This reflects whether the comment takes up the general theme of the video. Since we know in which parts of the video (on a timeline) the specific terms are used, we can also compute a "local alignment" that only looks at the content of the video around the time the comment was made. This is useful to identify whether the content of a comment reflects the specific focus of the corresponding video section. For this analysis, we used a time window of -30 and $+10$ s around the time of entering the comment.

Our study only relies on the tutorial videos. We had to exclude the example videos, since the presentations in those videos covered various areas (such as medicine or chemistry), and therefore cannot be matched to our general knowledge domain (related to presentation skills). The tutorial videos deal with presentation techniques and do not show this discrepancy. This corpus comprises 1144 comments overall.

4.1 Classification of Comments

We used the K-Means algorithm to cluster the tutorial comments. The features used for the clustering were global and local video alignment, number of domain specific concepts and the relative time at which a comment was made. All features were normalized to values between 0 and 1. Different cluster counts were explored to spot meaningful differences in clusters which would allow differentiating between comment types. The chosen number of clusters was 7, which identified more distinct cluster types, compared to lower number of clusters. Clustering quality was also assessed based on silhouette analysis [24], which compares the distance of a sample to its own cluster to the distance of the sample to the nearest other cluster, to calculate whether clusters are well separated. Clustering quality improved as we increased the number of clusters to seven clusters. Higher numbers of clusters did not reveal any additional significant differences or increase silhouette scores. The results of the clustering can be seen in Fig. 2. For the first four clusters, comments mention on average a little more than two domain concepts. The local video alignment is low, especially close to the beginning of a video. This is to be expected, since there is not yet much content from the video to compare them to. Global video alignment tracks domain concepts. For the comments in these clusters, both domain concepts and global video alignment generally extract the same concepts with the global video alignment having some false positives. Each of these clusters has around 200 comments, which means these types of comments are made very frequently.

	0	1	2	3	4	5	6
domain concepts	2.09	2.17	2.18	2.21	3.66	4.17	11.81
local video alignment	1.07	0.49	0.95	1.58	4.17	4.99	1.19
global video alignment	2.69	2.73	3.19	3.00	5.92	7.41	14.73
relative_time	0.39	0.08	0.93	0.65	0.23	0.76	0.11
comment count	217	254	182	225	131	109	26

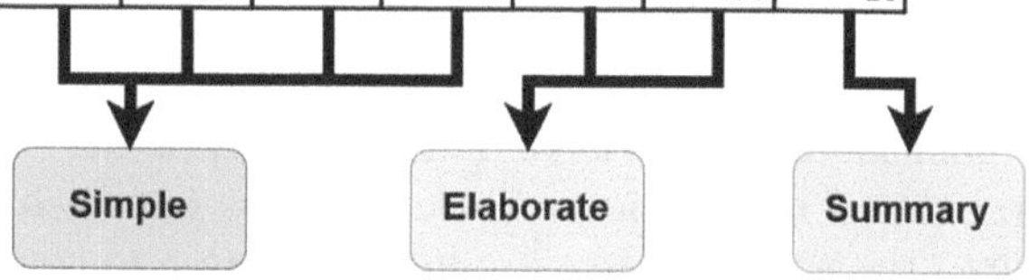

Fig. 2. Comment clusters and mapping to comment types.

Clusters 4 and 5 are different from clusters 0–3 in that they have a higher number of domain concepts. They also have a high local video alignment, showing that students who made these comments strongly engaged with the video content at that particular time. Cluster 5 has somewhat more domain concepts and higher local video alignment than cluster 4. Comments from this cluster are made at about 3/4 of the video time. Around that time, generally the last major point of the video is made, and students have already received a substantial amount of information on the topic. This might make students more confident to talk about the video content and relate it to previous information. This is also indicated by the high global video alignment. In contrast, the comments from cluster 4 are made earlier in the video, roughly at 1/4 of the video time, where students cannot relate the content as much to previously seen information.

Comments from cluster 6 have the highest number of domain concepts and the highest global video alignment. However, their local video alignment is very low, and they are made close to the start of the video. These comments seem to be summaries of the video content. We analyzed the text of comments in different clusters and identified three types of comments.

Simple Comments take up a single point made in the video and generally contain two domain concepts. Example:

> "each slide to one idea//people cant read slides and listen."

Elaborate Comments take up multiple points and elaborate on them, rather than simply repeating the content of the video. They contain a high number of domain concepts and have a high local video alignment. Example:

> "I always try to stand up straight, with good posture and little movement as it gives the impression of confidence. I think that by keeping the hands by your side and using them for hand gestures when needed it creates the feeling that the presenter is at ease in the situation."

Summary Comments are made at the start of the video and summarize the points made in the video. They therefore have a high amount of domain concepts and low local video alignment. Example:

> "confident speaker - stance - hip width, stand tall, neutral position, gestures -sound - projection, lower the shoulders, slow understandable pace, tones, loud and quiet, dynamics . . . -sight - eye contact, establish with all parts"

For each cluster, we looked at a sample of the comments and labelled them according to which comment type best fit the pattern of the comments in the sample. This process resulted in clusters 0–3 being labelled as simple comments, clusters 4 and 5 as elaborate comments, and cluster 6 as summary comments.

To analyze the quality of this mapping and compute decision rules which further solidify the differences between the comment types, we trained a decision tree to predict the comment type based on the same features used in the clustering. The resulting decision tree can be seen in Fig. 3. To create the decision tree, we used the CART algorithm [25] with the Gini Impurity as a criterion for deciding how to split samples at each node. The Gini Impurity is 1 for an equal distribution of the classes and 0 if there is only one class represented in a sample. The class distribution of the sample at each node is given in the form [simple, elaborate, summary]. The first split is made on the local video alignment being lower than 3.5. If that is the case, the sample is further split on the number of domain concepts. All comments with less than 8.5 domain concepts are classified as simple comments and comments with a value higher than that are summary comments. The classification works well for simple and elaborate comments, but

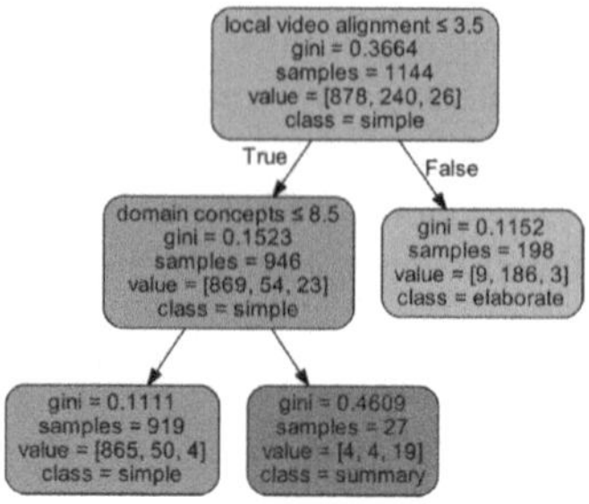

Fig. 3. Decision tree for classifying comments.

has problems separating out the summary comments. This indicates that the decision boundaries between summary and other types of comments are not that clear. Using 10-fold cross validation, the model has an average accuracy of 0.93 which supports that the mapping of the clusters works well.

4.2 Characterizing Learners and Learner Engagement

To characterize learners and their engagement, we count the number of comments of each type that a student made to create student profiles. These profiles are then related to the data collected about students in the form of MSLQ scores, conceptual knowledge pre- and post-tests (c.f. Section 3) and scores for a group presentation the students gave after the learning activity. For the experimental group, we also included the number of nudges a student received. Statistical measures were reported as significant for $p <= .05$. The number of different comments in the different categories and the number of learners who posted such comments are summarized in Table 1.

Table 1. Statistics of comments in different classes.

Comment type	Comments	Students	Comments/student
Simple	878	179	4.90
Elaborate	240	80	3.00
Summary	26	18	1.44

The majority of comments were of the simple type. There were 193 students in total, of which 179 wrote at least one simple comment. The number of elaborate comments were about 1/4 of simple comments and only 80 users made at least one. Summary comments were made by only 18 students. Thus, this type of comment indicates divergent behavior of a small subset of students. System logs showed that these students fully watched a video then restarted it at which point they made the summary comment, explaining this phenomenon.

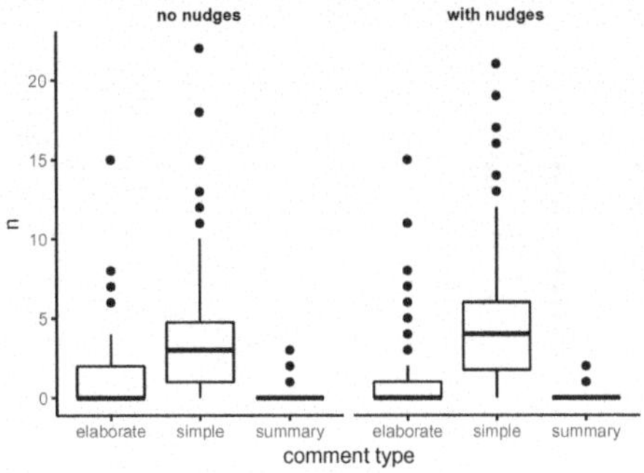

Fig. 4. Distribution of different comment types in both conditions.

Figure 4 shows the distribution of comments for the two groups. The average number of simple and elaborate comments between the two groups is very similar. However, the experimental group has a higher number of simple comments.

Relation Between Nudging and Commenting Behavior. A linear regression for the students in the experimental condition shows that the number of nudges is a significant predictor for the amount of simple comments, ($b = .12, t(106) = 4.67, p < .01$). The predicted number of simple comments is equal to ($3.30 + 0.12 * n_{nudges}$). The regression also significantly explained a portion of the variance ($F(1, 106) = 21.86, p < .01, R^2 = .17$). However, statistically significant relationships between the number of nudges and elaborate or summary comments could not be observed. These results suggest that the implemented nudges animate students to post comments, but often do not trigger deeper reflection on the video content.

Relation Between Commenting Behavior and Student Variables. After the learning activity with AVW-Space, students gave group presentations in the last week of the course. We found a statistically significant correlation between the presentation score and the number of elaborate comments, ($r(191) = .3, p < .01$). Correlations between the presentation score and simple or summary comments were not significant. Extrinsic motivation was negatively correlated with number of elaborate comments, ($r(192) = -.18, p < .01$). In particular, students who are just compliant to meet the external requirements do not tend to invest high effort in commenting. Conversely, if students are motivated less by grades or rewards, they tend to write more elaborate comments. Surprisingly, there was no significant correlation between writing elaborate comments and the MSLQ score for elaboration (as a learning strategy). This suggests that motivational state during the learning activities is a more decisive factor for higher engagement in the commenting task than the personality trait.

With respect to the gain in conceptual knowledge measured as the difference in scores between the post- and the pre-test, it cannot be said that those who

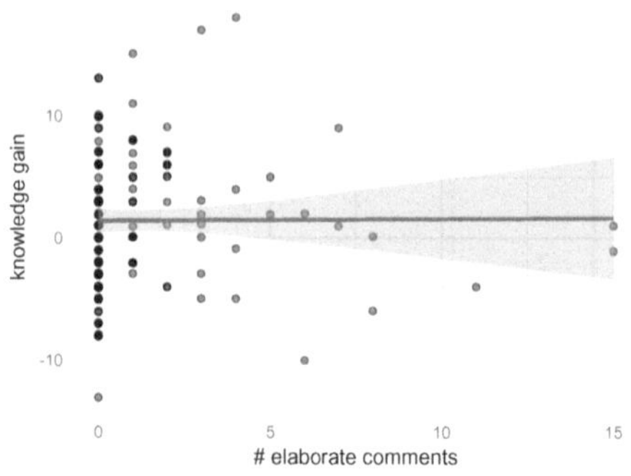

Fig. 5. The total number of elaborate comments of a user does not indicate an increase in conceptual knowledge.

post more elaborate comments have higher gain, as it can be seen from Fig. 5. Only the post-test score correlates significantly with the number of elaborate comments, ($r(144) = .19, p = .05$). However, the figure shows that among the learners who do not write any elaborate comments there is a tendency towards no or a lower increase in conceptual knowledge. This is also depicted more explicitly in Fig. 6. On average, learners who wrote at least one elaborate comment had a higher gain in conceptual knowledge ($M = 2.95, SD = 5.52$) compared to other learners ($M = 0.49, SD = 5.19$). A t-test reports that this difference is significant, $t(144) = -2.71$, $p = .007$.

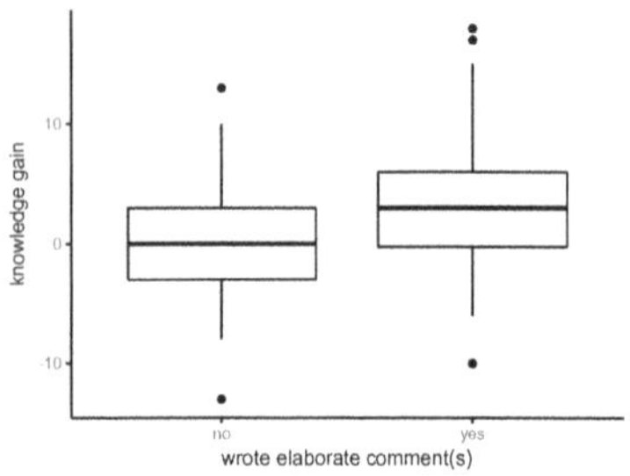

Fig. 6. Comparison of the conceptual knowledge gain of learners with and without elaborated comments.

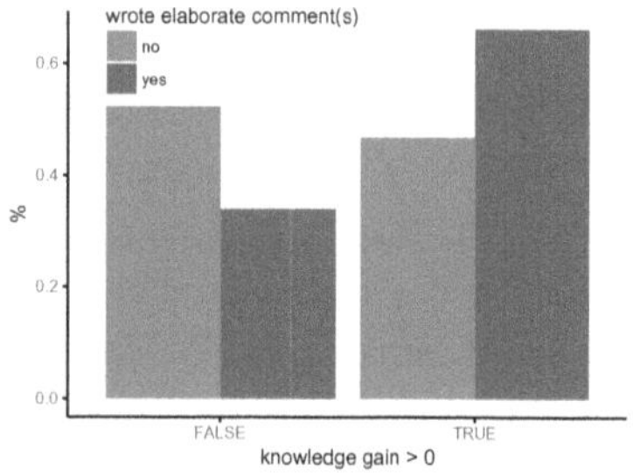

Fig. 7. Learner writing elaborate comments are more likely to increase their conceptual knowledge.

A limitation of these result is that some students did not perform as well in the post-test as in the pre-test, which unreasonably leads to negative values in knowledge gain. This was the case for 52 of the 146 participants who completed the post-test. Reasons can be a ceiling effect (already high pre-knowledge) or a lack of motivation to participate in another test. For these reasons, we have compared the commenting behavior of learners with positive or no gain separately from the one of learners with the negative knowledge gain. Figure 7 shows the fraction of participants who had increased conceptual knowledge after active video watching among the 56 participants who wrote elaborate comments and among the 90 remaining participants respectively.

Evidently, there is a significant difference in the number of students with an increase in conceptual knowledge in the two groups of participants with and without elaborate comments ($\chi^2(1) = 4.48$, $p = .034$). The majority (66%) of the 56 students who posted elaborate comments showed increased conceptual knowledge reflecting on concrete issues mentioned in the video while this is only the case for 47% of the participants without such comments. There are two possible explanations for the observation that the learners with elaborate comments did better in the post test than others. Either these findings can be attributed to the overall higher level of engagement of these students during and after video watching, or a deeper reflection of the video content enables them to be also more elaborate in their answers in the post-test.

5 Discussion and Conclusion

Following ICAP [8] as a theoretical framework, we would identify simple commenting with "active learning" (A) and elaborate and summary type of commenting with "constructive learning" (C). The learning activities facilitated and analyzed in our study did indeed not foresee co-construction, so there was no "interactive learning" (I) in terms of ICAP. Different from the original activity-based specification of engagement levels, our analysis is based on artifacts in the form of textual comments. This content-analytic approach is particularly well-suited for dealing learner-generated content and can possibly be extended to other learning scenarios beyond video-based learning.

Distinguishing between learners who have written at least one elaborate comment ($E > 1$) and those who have not ($E = 0$), we have seen that $E > 1$ goes along with higher average knowledge gain, although we could not back the assumption that "more is better". We have also seen from this and previous analyses that nudging increases the number of comments written, yet not particularly in the "elaborate" category. The finding that extrinsic motivation is negatively correlated with elaborate commenting corroborates the assumption that mere "compliance", also in response to nudges, does not lead to the desired types of higher-level contributions. Elaborate commenting as a higher form a cognitive engagement appears to be very much driven by motivational state during learning activities rather than by more stable personality traits.

Although our findings indicate that the students' writing of elaborate comments (interpreted as higher cognitive engagement) goes along with better learning results, we should refrain from interpreting this empirical coincidence as a causality. Yet, the we can refer to the ICAP framework as a theoretical underpinning for the assumption that increasing the degree of elaboration in the students' commenting behavior would be beneficial for learning. Certainly, this would be beneficial for the richness and the ensuing affordances of the learning environment. Accordingly, the introduction of nudges should not just stimulate activity but should also support elaboration. The semantic features used to classify comments (including the "alignment" relationship) can serve as conditions for "adaptive nudging" that takes into consideration the learner's engagement with the video.

The immediate future challenge is to validate the findings, i.e. the comment types and prediction model, and to investigate their generalizability in similar learning contexts. We will apply the analytics approach on another AVW-Space dataset (from another course). The prospect is to enhance the nudges by improving the student modeling mechanism to take into account not just the fact that a student is commenting but also the student's cognitive engagement as evidenced in the comments.

The work presented here has potentially broader application in digital learning contexts with learner-generated content. Measures of semantic alignment with lecture materials applied to learner-created artifacts (such as notes, comments, forum posts, summaries) can indicate different levels of cognitive engagement and elaboration and thus offer insights to better inform interventions to promote deeper learning. Evidently, this can also be applied to other types of learning materials beyond videos (e.g., textbooks or slide presentations). Our approach can also be extended towards using content analysis to indicate the quality of reflections or critical discussions, thus increasing the system awareness of the students' learning achievements and needs as a basis for adaptive scaffolding.

References

1. Agrawal, A., Venkatraman, J., Leonard, S., Paepcke, A.: YouEDU: addressing confusion in MOOC discussion forums by recommending instructional video clips (2015)
2. Anderson, A., Huttenlocher, D., Kleinberg, J., Leskovec, J.: Engaging with massive online courses. In: Proceedings of the 23rd International Conference on World Wide Web, pp. 687–698. ACM (2014)
3. Atapattu, T., Falkner, K.: Impact of lecturer's discourse for student video interactions: video learning analytics case study of MOOCs. J. Learn. Anal. **5**(3), 182–197 (2018)
4. Baker, R.S.J., Mitrović, A., Mathews, M.: Detecting gaming the system in constraint-based tutors. In: De Bra, P., Kobsa, A., Chin, D. (eds.) UMAP 2010. LNCS, vol. 6075, pp. 267–278. Springer, Heidelberg (2010). https://doi.org/10.1007/978-3-642-13470-8_25
5. Bixler, R., D'Mello, S.: Automatic gaze-based user-independent detection of mind wandering during computerized reading. User Model. User-Adap. Inter. **26**(1), 33–68 (2016)
6. Brooks, C., Thompson, C., Teasley, S.: A time series interaction analysis method for building predictive models of learners using log data. In: Proceedings of 5th Conference on Learning Analytics and Knowledge, pp. 126–135. ACM (2015)

7. Chatti, M.A., et al.: Video annotation and analytics in coursemapper. Smart Learn. Environ. **3**(1), 10 (2016)
8. Chi, M.T., Wylie, R.: The ICAP framework: linking cognitive engagement to active learning outcomes. Educ. Psychol. **49**(4), 219–243 (2014)
9. Cocea, M., Weibelzahl, S.: Disengagement detection in online learning: validation studies and perspectives. IEEE Trans. Learn. Technol. **4**(2), 114–124 (2011)
10. Daems, O., Erkens, M., Malzahn, N., Hoppe, H.U.: Using content analysis and domain ontologies to check learners' understanding of science concepts. J. Comput. Educ. **1**(2), 113–131 (2014)
11. Dimitrova, V., Mitrovic, A., Piotrkowicz, A., Lau, L., Weerasinghe, A.: Using learning analytics to devise interactive personalised nudges for active video watching. In: Proceedings of the 25th Conference on User Modeling, Adaptation and Personalization, pp. 22–31. ACM (2017)
12. Drummond, J., Litman, D.: In the zone: towards detecting student zoning out using supervised machine learning. In: Aleven, V., Kay, J., Mostow, J. (eds.) ITS 2010. LNCS, vol. 6095, pp. 306–308. Springer, Heidelberg (2010). https://doi.org/10.1007/978-3-642-13437-1_53
13. Giannakos, M.N., Chorianopoulos, K., Chrisochoides, N.: Making sense of video analytics: lessons learned from clickstream interactions, attitudes, and learning outcome in a video-assisted course. Int. Rev. Res. Open Distrib. Learn. **16**(1), 260–283 (2015)
14. Hecking, T., Chounta, I.A., Hoppe, H.U.: Role modelling in MOOC discussion forums. J. Learn. Anal. **4**(1), 85–116 (2017)
15. Hecking, T., Dimitrova, V., Mitrovic, A., Ulrich Hoppe, U.: Using network-text analysis to characterise learner engagement in active video watching. In: ICCE 2017 Main Conference Proceedings, pp. 326–335. Asia-Pacific Society for Computers in Education (2017)
16. Hong, J.K., Mitrovic, A., Neshatian, K.: Predicting quitting behaviour in SQL-tutor. In: Proceedings of the 23th International Conference on Computers in Education, pp. 37–45. APSCE (2015)
17. Kaltura Inc.: The state of video in education (2017)
18. Koedinger, K.R., Kim, J., Jia, J.Z., McLaughlin, E.A., Bier, N.L.: Learning is not a spectator sport: doing is better than watching for learning from a MOOC. In: Proceedings of 2nd ACM Conference on Learning@Scale, pp. 111–120 (2015)
19. Kovacs, G.: Effects of in-video quizzes on MOOC lecture viewing. In: Proceedings of the 3rd ACM Conference on Learning@ Scale, pp. 31–40. ACM (2016)
20. Mills, C., Bosch, N., Graesser, A., D'Mello, S.: To quit or not to quit: predicting future behavioral disengagement from reading patterns. In: Trausan-Matu, S., Boyer, K.E., Crosby, M., Panourgia, K. (eds.) ITS 2014. LNCS, vol. 8474, pp. 19–28. Springer, Cham (2014). https://doi.org/10.1007/978-3-319-07221-0_3
21. Mitrovic, A., Dimitrova, V., Lau, L., Weerasinghe, A., Mathews, M.: Supporting constructive video-based learning: requirements elicitation from exploratory studies. In: André, E., Baker, R., Hu, X., Rodrigo, M.M.T., du Boulay, B. (eds.) AIED 2017. LNCS (LNAI), vol. 10331, pp. 224–237. Springer, Cham (2017). https://doi.org/10.1007/978-3-319-61425-0_19
22. Mitrovic, A., Gordon, M., Piotrkowicz, A., Dimitrova, V.: Investigating the effect of adding nudges to increase engagement in active video watching. In: Isotani, S., Millán, E., Ogan, A., Hastings, P., McLaren, B., Luckin, R. (eds.) Artificial Intelligence in Education. LNCS, pp. 320–332. Springer, Cham (2019). https://doi.org/10.1007/978-3-030-23204-7_27

23. Pintrich, P.R., et al.: A manual for the use of the motivated strategies for learning questionnaire (MSLQ). (1991)
24. Rousseeuw, P.J.: Silhouettes: a graphical aid to the interpretation and validation of cluster analysis. J. Comput. Appl. Math. **20**, 53–65 (1987)
25. Steinberg, D., Colla, P.: CART: classification and regression trees. Top Ten Algorithms Data Min. **9**, 179 (2009)
26. Vail, A.K., Wiggins, J.B., Grafsgaard, J.F., Boyer, K.E., Wiebe, E.N., Lester, J.C.: The affective impact of tutor questions: predicting frustration and engagement. In: International Educational Data Mining Society (2016)
27. Wang, X., Wen, M., Rosé, C.P.: Towards triggering higher-order thinking behaviors in MOOCs. In: Proceedings of the 6th International Conference on Learning Analytics & Knowledge, pp. 398–407. ACM (2016)

How Students Fail to Self-regulate Their Online Learning Experience

Maxime Pedrotti[1(✉)] and Nicolae Nistor[2,3]

[1] Leibniz Supercomputing Centre of the Bavarian Academy of Sciences and Humanities, Garching n. Munich, Germany
maxime.pedrotti@lrz.de
[2] Faculty of Psychology and Educational Sciences, Ludwig-Maximilians-Universität München, Munich, Germany
[3] Richard W. Riley College of Education and Leadership, Walden University, Minneapolis, MN, USA

Abstract. Given the rising popularity of online-based learning scenarios such as MOOCs, flipped classrooms and regular lecture recordings, students face new challenges compared to traditional classroom settings. This paper explores the role of self-regulated learning (SRL) strategies in online learning environments – specifically when working with online lecture recordings – and how university students apply SRL strategies to reach their learning goals. To this end, a series of thirteen problem-centered interviews was conducted with undergraduate students of the learning sciences at a major German university. The findings reveal a dramatically suboptimal use of SRL strategies, leading us to the conclusion that interventions such as basic time management and general planning strategy training may have to be implemented more firmly in undergraduate education, in order to enhance university students' future learning experience.

Keywords: Learning strategies · Self-regulated learning · Online learning · Problem-centered interviews · Higher education

1 Introduction

Given the rising popularity of online-based learning scenarios such as MOOCs, flipped classrooms and regular lecture recordings, students face new challenges compared to traditional classroom settings. While higher education in general is marked by a higher level of self-regulation – most lectures do not require or register attendance by students, online-based classroom settings take this to a whole new level.

Traditional face-to-face classes have fixed, mostly regularly recurring session times, during which attendance is required at least for learners to be able to receive the contents taught in class. In blended or purely online-based learning scenarios, however, learning materials are usually placed somewhere accessible online, ready to be used on demand with limited time constraints (the only fixed dates being final or intermediate exams or exercise returns). The "when" and "where" of students' accessing and working on the contents is left up to the students themselves, which significantly raises

M. Scheffel et al. (Eds.): EC-TEL 2019, LNCS 11722, pp. 377–385, 2019.
https://doi.org/10.1007/978-3-030-29736-7_28

the level of self-regulation required to successfully reach the learning goals set by instructors (and students, albeit to themselves) for the respective course program [1].

As recent research has shown [2], learning strategies can have positive impact on students' academic achievement, however, there are individual differences, and some strategies (e.g. help-seeking, elaboration) may rely on the learner's prior knowledge and experience, as well as their prior application of strategies known to them. This paper explores the role of self-regulation learning (SRL) strategies [3] employed by students in higher education while using an online learning environment providing online lecture recordings. The aim of this work is to gain insight into how students actually regulate their online learning experience, in order to derivate possible pedagogic interventions to enhance students' learning experience and to assist them in a more strategic application of useful learning strategies.

The remainder of this paper is divided into three main sections: First, a brief overview of the theoretical background and existing work on SRL strategies in online learning environment is given. Second, the interview study's design and methodology are presented, together with main findings from the data analysis. Finally, the results are discussed, providing an outlook on future research opportunities.

2 SRL Strategies in Online Learning Environments

Self-regulated learning is understood as "an individual's deliberate and strategic planning, enactment, reflection, and adaptation when engaged in any task in which learning occurs" [3]. Thus, it encompasses active processes students undertake to advance their learning [4]. SRL theory has a strong foundation in self-determination theory [5] and social cognitive theory [6, 7].

A recent investigation of SRL strategies and their influence on goal achievement in MOOCs observed goal-setting and strategic planning to have a particularly positive influence on course goal achievement, while the other four strategies analyzed (self-evaluation, task strategy, elaboration, and help-seeking) appeared to provide limited to no support for learners [8]. Surprisingly, help-seeking appeared to have a negative impact on course goal achievement, on closer look, however, this effect proved to be particularly pronounced in learners with less SRL skills, particularly students, while learners with higher educational degrees and more developed SRL skills could profit from relying on others for assistance.

In contrast, in a meta-analysis of recent studies on SRL strategies and their influence on academic achievement in online learning environments [2] peer learning was found to have the strongest positive effect on academic achievement, followed by time management and effort regulation. However, the 95% confidence interval for peer learning was extremely wide with a range from high effect down to slight negative effect on learners' achievement, which suggests additional factors may moderate the positive influence peer assistance can have on learners' success. The other eight SRL strategies included in this meta-analysis (metacognition, time management, effort regulation, peer learning, elaboration, rehearsal, help seeking, and critical thinking) were less effective, with elaboration being nearly completely ineffective, and rehearsal showing a slight negative effect.

These findings were at least partially reproduced in a recent comparison of online and blended learning environments concerning use and effects of SRL strategies on academic achievement [9]: The findings show time management and effort regulation strategies to be the only significant positive influences on academic success of online learners, while blended learners appear to profit from more strategies such as elaboration and metacognition techniques, as well as critical thinking.

To summarize, recent research shows a positive influence of SRL strategies on students' academic achievement. Especially organizational strategies such as goal setting, time management, effort regulation and strategic planning appear to influence the learning experience in a positive way. The positive effect of peer-assisted learning appears to be quite volatile and likely depends on external moderating factors.

For researchers and university instructors, one of the main open questions is how they can adapt their curricula and create a learning environment encouraging and scaffolding students' effective use of SRL strategies in order for them to achieve academic success. The following study aims to provide insight into the current state of university students' SRL behavior by investigating how they apply which strategies in their online learning.

3 Interview Study

3.1 Design and Methodology

To gain a more detailed and qualitative view of students' motivational backgrounds and use of SRL strategies in the context of online lecture videos, a series of guided, problem-centered interviews [10, 11] was conducted with thirteen undergraduate students at Ludwig-Maximilians-Universität Munich, Germany (LMU Munich). This particular method of data gathering has the advantage of being open enough to allow for possibly new revelations from interview subjects' responses, while still following a thematic guideline which focuses the contents of the interview on a certain subject, in this case the interviewee's learning strategies while using online lecture videos from a web site provided by their university.

The central tool for problem-centered interviews is the interview guide, which is supposed to guide the interview conversation, presenting the interviewer with a fall-back mechanism in case the open conversation becomes stalled or runs the risk of going off-topic. The guide for this study was prepared by participants of an advanced seminar in the learning sciences as part of their course assignment.

The contents of the interviews were to be focused on students' learning strategies in the context of their use of online lecture videos. The main structuring points were thus: personal learning goals (long and short term), overall planning strategy, task-related planning and regulation strategy, time management, elaboration techniques, self-evaluation strategies, and peer learning and academic help-seeking. These strategies are combined derivates of SRL strategies found to be present in higher education contexts according to previous research [8, 9].

Interview subjects ($N = 13$) were enrolled in undergraduate study programs in the learning sciences or teacher education and had to be at least in their second year of studies, to ensure at least basic experience in self-regulated learning in general and the online learning environment mentioned below. Subjects were recruited and interviewed by the same aforementioned seminar participants in advanced learning sciences.

Each interview session lasted between 30 and 60 min. The interviews were recorded digitally using personal recording devices and subsequently transcribed and anonymized. These transcripts were then analyzed using MAXQDA 2018 for Mac for coding and result aggregation.

3.2 The Learning Environment

At LMU Munich, several undergraduate lectures in the educational sciences and in teacher education programs are regularly recorded and made available online for students to work with – either as a replacement for classroom attendance during lecture times, or as supplementary material, e.g. to review certain subjects during exam preparations [12]. Apart from providing a general service to students, in some cases instructors make a full lecture course available exclusively online, e.g. when they are on sabbatical and still want to or are required to offer the course, and sometimes instructors use pre-recorded video sessions to experiment with modern teaching concepts such as flipped classrooms.

These online video lectures are made available via a public web site of the university, with some lectures being openly accessible, some restricted to students of the university or certain departments, according to instructors' wishes. Online lecture recordings usually include audio and video from the instructor and synchronized presentation slides. Students who log into the site with their university credentials have access to some more functionality, namely a personalized viewing history and bookmarks for their recently accessed lectures, as well as a more interactive user interface with an enhanced video player, allowing them to add time- and location-sensitive annotations to the online presentation slides, either for their private use, or as means of interaction amongst themselves and with instructors.

3.3 Main Findings

This section presents the key results found by analyzing the anonymized interview transcripts.

Goal Setting. In terms of goal-setting and overall motivation, most subjects speak about wanting to graduate successfully overall, only two students state they aim for high marks as well. Having a bachelor's degree is understood as a requirement for later success on the job market, and high marks are perceived as enhancing factor for job success, guaranteeing higher job positions and/or higher wages. Aside from the longer-term goals, passing the exams and graduating within the prescribed time seems to be a prevailing sentiment – the latter most pronounced in those interview subjects with previous educational experience, be it from an earlier apprenticeship or an earlier university degree.

Strategic Planning. About half of the interview subjects do not strategically plan and distribute their learning activities during the course of a semester, focusing their main effort on immediate exam preparations, usually near the end of the semester. Those students who do apply strategic planning to their learning experience create study plans – mostly weekly, some per semester – and try to stick to them. Only one student reports regularly working with study groups.

Task Strategy & Effort Regulation. With respect to short term planning, only very few students report actually planning their learning task and setting up their learning environments. Actions are usually limited to choosing a place to work – the choice apparently being only between the university library and home – making sure the environment is relatively quiet and putting the phone out of immediate reach. For two students, this last point does not appear to be strong either, as one states they watch lectures while doing housework, and another admits playing video games on their phone while having the lecture video running on their laptop.

Time Management. Two students report watching the online lectures in (self-)predefined blocks of 30–45 min, two students usually watch the full 90 min of a regular lecture session, with breaks between sessions. The other students either do not reserve explicit time frames for watching the online videos, or they have no fixed schedule, watching the recordings when it suits them or when the exam date sets limits to procrastination.

Elaboration & Rehearsal. Almost all interview subjects rely on personal notes, which are usually consulted at a later time, e.g. before the next lecture session, but more frequently during immediate exam preparation. The actual implementation of this strategy varies between individuals, as some take initial notes with the presentation slides as base material before viewing the online video, adding more context to these notes during video playback, while others take notes during their watching the lecture recording, either with and/or on printed or digital presentation slides or on a separate notepad. One student reported not taking notes at all, relying solely on the video recording.

Self-evaluation. Self-evaluation strategies are only mentioned in few interview subjects' responses, and usually they consist of testing their knowledge against exam questions from earlier years.

Peer Learning & Help Seeking. Only four interview subjects talk about relying on peers to assist their learning experience. One student participates in regular study group sessions at the university library (mentioned above), the other three falling back to peer support mainly on specific topics or to check if they missed important parts during their solitary study sessions. Academic help seeking (i.e. turning to instructors or mentors at university) was not mentioned during any of the interviews and did not appear to be a viable option for the students.

4 Conclusion

4.1 Discussion

The findings presented in the previous section paint a mixed picture of university students' knowledge and use of SRL strategies to achieve academic success.

The strategies employed most fall into the rehearsal and elaboration category, as well as time management. The latter might seem positive at first glance, since previous research shows time management to be a key supporting strategy for academic success in online learning contexts [2, 9]. However, more than half of the subjects focus most of their time and effort on reviewing video recordings and their notes during their acute exam preparation. Focusing cognitive energy on elaboration and rehearsal may seem like an appropriate strategy to reach the goal of passing the next exam, however, these strategies have been shown to have no significant influence on academic success [2, 8]. Considering a regular semester at LMU Munich consists of 13–15 weeks of regular classes, followed by what is commonly called the "exam phase" of 2–4 weeks where most lecture exams take place, and the lecture-free time, which is usually reserved for writing term papers, internships to gain job experience, and vacation time, the usually allocated period of time of 2–6 weeks of immediate exam preparation seems rather short for long-term academic success. In contrast, students' stated goals in general appear to be mostly long-term, i.e. looking to graduate or at least pass all the exams in a timely fashion. While these long-term goals may help keep the overall focus on their studies, the lack of smaller, more short-term learning goals may explain the pattern described by most of the interviewed students, i.e. focusing time and energy on the time frame shortly before the exam at the end of semester.

Another striking observation is the very limited or non-existent level of task-related strategy combined with little effort regulation regarding students' personal learning space and environment. Though effort regulation is a key effective SRL strategy with respect to academic success [2, 9], little effort is put into actually using this strategy for a more effective learning experience. It is highly doubtful that the behavioral manifestation displayed in this study's interviews can yield long-term positive results, especially in cases such as the two students deciding not only to not exclude possible distractions from their work space, but rather decide to undertake additional, external activities, e.g. doing housework or playing games on their phones – most notably since off-task multi-tasking has been shown to be detrimental to learners' success [13].

The lack of reliance on peer support or academic help via instructors or mentors at university may be surprising, but is actually in line with cited research, e.g. Broadbent's study comparing blended and online learners' SRL strategies [9]. As posited by Broadbent, students may not necessarily know all possible forms of peer learning, which may lead to the underrepresentation observed here as well. If students do not view non-obvious forms of peer assistance as such, they will not readily report this type of SRL strategy in an open question interview. Other factors at play may be individual differences such as previous learning experience, and low-barrier support for help seeking – be it from peers or instructors. Kizilcec et al. [8] note course participants with higher educational background are less likely to seek help and attribute this to their higher degree of self-regulation and stronger confidence in their own capabilities, while students were more likely to seek help, but often did not act on this, at least not observably in course forums or chat rooms.

4.2 Implications for Research and Educational Practice

Despite the obvious limitations of a qualitative interview analysis with respect to reliability and external validity, this study provides additional insight into university students' use of and experience in SRL strategies. The limited and suboptimal use of SRL strategies even by students of the learning sciences who are not new to higher educational contexts (both in theory through their course programs as well as in practice by being in their second or higher year of studies at university) leads to questions about the underlying reasons for students' problems in dealing with online learning requiring high SRL skills, and how instructors can provide a scaffolding environment for students to acquire and use the necessary skills to successfully reach the goals set by curricula and themselves.

From a research perspective, more in-depth analyses are needed in order to present instructors with detailed teaching interventions they can implement to enhance their students' learning experience. Broadbent [9] suggests the use of measuring tools more specialized to online learning environments such as the Online Self-regulated Learning Questionnaire (OSLQ) [14] or the Online Help Seeking Questionnaire (OHSQ) [15] for quantitative analysis, which might deliver more accurate data on help seeking and peer learning behavior in online learning contexts. One major implication for future research is the need to pursue a mixed-method approach, combining self-reported with objective data from more than one source, e.g. by adding the online learning system's log, artifacts from user forums in online learning environments, etc. [2, 3, 16].

Following the results of this study alone, a few recommendations can be made for instructors to start from. To counter the lack of effective time management and effort regulation strategies, specific training courses may be needed. These should probably be implemented and offered at an early stage in study programs, preferably during the first two semesters, in order to lay the foundation for successful transference into advanced studies. Such courses might be led by advanced students of the same subject, providing peer support, coaching younger students on how to effectively integrate SRL strategies when working with online lecture videos. Ideally, such an arrangement could also be leveraged to create a sense of community [17], leading to the building and integration of online communities of practice [18].

University students today seem to fail at effectively self-regulating their online learning experience. They may pass exams and graduate with bachelor's and higher degrees, but questions may be raised as to whether they are actually gaining the knowledge they should be able to reach, and how instructors can improve this situation by providing more scaffolds in learning environments in general.

References

1. Hartley, K., Bendixen, L.D.: Educational research in the internet age: examining the role of individual characteristics. Educ. Res. **30**, 22–26 (2001)
2. Broadbent, J., Poon, W.L.: Self-regulated learning strategies & academic achievement in online higher education learning environments: a systematic review. Internet High. Educ. **27**, 1–13 (2015)
3. Järvelä, S., Hadwin, A., Malmberg, J., Miller, M.: Contemporary perspectives of regulated learning in collaboration. In: Fischer, F., Hmelo-Silver, C.E., Goldman, S.R., Reimann, P. (eds.) International Handbook of the Learning Sciences, pp. 127–136. Routledge, New York (2018)
4. Zimmerman, B.J.: Investigating self-regulation and motivation: historical background, methodological developments, and future prospects. Am. Educ. Res. J. **45**, 166–183 (2008)
5. Deci, E.L., Ryan, R.M.: Self-determination theory. In: van Lange, P.A.M., Kruglanski, A.W., Higgins, E.T. (eds.) Handbook of Theories of Social Psychology, vol. 1, pp. 416–437. SAGE Publications Ltd., London (2012)
6. Bandura, A.: Self-efficacy: toward a unifying theory of behavioral change. Psychol. Rev. **84**, 191–215 (1977)
7. Bandura, A.: Social cognitive theory. In: van Lange, P.A.M., Kruglanski, A.W., Higgins, E.T. (eds.) Handbook of Theories of Social Psychology, vol. 1, pp. 349–374. SAGE Publishing Ltd., London (2012)
8. Kizilcec, R.F., Pérez-Sanagustín, M., Maldonado, J.J.: Self-regulated learning strategies predict learner behavior and goal attainment in Massive Open Online Courses. Comput. Educ. **104**, 18–33 (2017)
9. Broadbent, J.: Comparing online and blended learner's self-regulated learning strategies and academic performance. Internet High. Educ. **33**, 24–32 (2017)
10. Witzel, A.: The Problem-centered Interview. Forum Qualitative Sozialforschung/Forum: Qualitative Social Research, vol 1, No 1 (2000): Qualitative Research: National, Disciplinary, Methodical and Empirical Examples (2000)
11. Witzel, A., Reiter, H.: The Problem-Centred Interview: Principles and Practice. Sage Publications, London (2012)
12. Pedrotti, M., Aulinger, J., Nistor, N.: Vorlesungsaufzeichnungen zur Unterstützung der Lehramtsausbildung an der LMU München. Zeitschrift für Hochschulentwicklung **9**, 74–84 (2014)
13. Wood, E., Zivcakova, L., Gentile, P., Archer, K., De Pasquale, D., Nosko, A.: Examining the impact of off-task multi-tasking with technology on real-time classroom learning. Comput. Educ. **58**, 365–374 (2012)
14. Barnard, L., Lan, W.Y., To, Y.M., Paton, V.O., Lai, S.-L.: Measuring self-regulation in online and blended learning environments. Internet High. Educ. **12**, 1–6 (2009)
15. Cheng, K.-H., Tsai, C.-C.: An investigation of Taiwan University students' perceptions of online academic help seeking, and their web-based learning self-efficacy. Internet High. Educ. **14**, 150–157 (2011)
16. Panadero, E.: A review of self-regulated learning: six models and four directions for research. Front. Psychol. **8**, 422 (2017)

17. Nistor, N., Daxecker, I., Stanciu, D., Diekamp, O.: Sense of community in academic communities of practice: predictors and effects. High. Educ. Int. J. High. Educ. Educ. Plann. **69**, 257–273 (2015)
18. Nistor, N., Schworm, S., Werner, M.: Online help-seeking in communities of practice: modeling the acceptance of conceptual artifacts. Comput. Educ. **59**, 774–784 (2012)

On the Use of Gaze as a Measure for Performance in a Visual Exploration Task

Catharine Oertel[1(✉)], Alessia Coppi[2], Jennifer K. Olsen[1], Alberto Cattaneo[2], and Pierre Dillenbourg[1]

[1] EPFL, Lausanne, Switzerland
{catharine.oertel,jennifer.olsen,pierre.dillenbourg}@epfl.ch
[2] SFIVET, Lugano, Switzerland
{alessia.coppi,alberto.cattaneo}@iuffp.ch

Abstract. Visual exploration skill acquisition is important for many vocational professions, yet many apprentices struggle to acquire these skills, impacting both their grades and practical work. Traditionally, the learning of visual skills is facilitated through exercises where it can be difficult to identify struggling apprentices early. We propose the use of gaze patterns to identify apprentices who may need additional support. In this paper, we investigated differences in gaze patterns between teachers and apprentices and the relationship between gaze patterns and student performance. In a study with 18 fashion design apprentices and 16 fashion design teacher, we found teachers have a higher gaze coverage of an image than apprentices and there is a correlation between the verbalisation score of apprentices and their similarity of gaze patterns to the teacher average. Using these results, we may be able to adapt exercises to apprentices' particular needs early in the learning process.

Keywords: Eye tracking · Vocational education · Visual skill acquisition

1 Introduction

Across most domains, apprentices must learn the important skill of how to read and interpret different visualizations. Within some domains, like statistics, the visualizations are an important tool for communicating information. In other domains, such as those within vocational education, the visualizations are a core aspect to the everyday tasks in which domain professionals engage. For example, gardeners must be able to read landscaping plans, carpenters construction plans, and fashion designers fashion sketches. However, as apprentices are learning, they often struggle to explore these visualizations, and it can be difficult for the teacher to understand how to provide support given the limited amount of information that they have regarding what the apprentices are doing during the task. Currently, teachers may ask the apprentices to verbalise what they are seeing, but this limits the teachers to only being able to help a few apprentices at

M. Scheffel et al. (Eds.): EC-TEL 2019, LNCS 11722, pp. 386–395, 2019.
https://doi.org/10.1007/978-3-030-29736-7_29

a time and they may have trouble identifying who needs support. In this paper, we propose using gaze patterns to identify apprentices who are struggling and identify when support is needed.

Vocational education is an important pillar in the Swiss-educational system. About 70% of all high-school apprentices choose vocational training over a university education. Vocational professions encompass many different professions (e.g., bakers, carpenter, florists and fashion designers). Across every profession, understanding visual information is an important skill that is used on a daily basis within their professional careers. However, it can be difficult for apprentices to identify and describe the relevant areas of an image even after they spend time looking at them during a task.

In the current paper, we focus on visual skill acquisition in fashion designers. A task that is typical for fashion design apprentices is to explore a photograph of a piece of clothing, for example a shirt, and to encode and identify the important details of that clothing item. Because the task involves the exploration of images, there is not a prescribed method that is correct for engaging in the task. Therefore, to identify apprentices that may be struggling, we propose to analyze their gaze patterns and how they may relate to those of experts. Specifically, we ask the following questions: First, what are the differences, if any, between apprentices and experts in a visual exploration task essential for the training of fashion designers? Second, are apprentices with a higher verbalisation score more similar to the experts in terms of gaze patterns than apprentices with lower scores?

2 Background

Within educational research, eye-tracking data has become an important source of process data. It has been used across a range of contexts to understand the learning processes that apprentices engage in [9,11,12]. Additionally, it has been used to provide apprentices with real-time interventions that can adapt to the apprentices' needs [2,13]. However, much of this work has focused on providing support to problem-solving tasks and less focus has been given to image assessment, as is more common in professional domains.

On the other hand, within professional domains, eye-tracking has also been extensively used to understand how apprentices process different visual stimuli and how this may differ from experts [4,6,7,20]. Across studies and domains, it was found that experts tend to have a longer fixation on the areas of importance in the images [7,10,19,20] while novices spent more time looking at irrelevant areas of the images [5]. Additionally, experts compared to novices are faster at detecting the areas of interest in the images [5,20]. Despite the longer time spent on the areas of interest, studies have also shown that experts spend more time exploring the image before focusing on an area [4,6] and that the timing of a behavior may matter [7]. In other words, experts are able to identify the important areas of the image and spend more time observing the relevant features and less time on irrelevant ones. These differences can even be found between individuals with small differences in expertise [18] and seen within the same individual as they gain expertise over time [3].

However, these differences may be mitigated by the task. For example, professionals exposed to a non-professional task (e.g., search task) will not necessarily differ from non-experts [8] and tasks that are simple have not shown a discrimination between novices and experts [17]. Many of the above findings have been done with identification tasks in which the goal of the task is to find a mistake in the image. For example, in radiology, the novices need to detect if there is a fracture visible in the image [20]. In these cases, the task is a search task rather than an exploration task, as is the case for fashion designers.

Additionally, much of the work with gaze on images has focused on areas of interest (AOIs), which treats all other areas as irrelevant. More recent work in education has incorporated a grid rather than AOIs as to treat all areas of the screen as equally important [9,15]. Using a grid, we are able to discover places that may be of interest on the image that were not identified ahead of time.

2.1 Contributions

In the current paper, we contribute to the literature on gaze analysis by providing further insights into the relationship between novice and expert gaze patterns and their relationship to performance. Additionally, we contribute to learning on visual exploration tasks by furthering our understanding of how apprentices engage with the image in a specific context, namely with fashion designers. In contrast to previous research, we focus on apprentices engaged in a visual exploration task, which is very typical in vocational education, rather than identifying mistakes [7] or problematic areas [6,20]. Similar to [5], we focus on apprentices identifying characteristics of the visualization. However, unlike [5], we focus on static images rather than dynamic stimuli. Additionally, we use a methodology that allows for calculating the amount of similarity between teachers and apprentices without the need to predefine AOIs, which are typically used in learning with visualisations.

3 Methods

The data presented in this paper is based on the data gathered within the context a larger study described in [1]. To investigate gaze patterns between apprentices and teachers in a visual exploration task we focused on a typical task for second year apprentices in a three-year program. The task consisted of the visual exploration of shirts described in more detail below.

3.1 Participants

A total of 34 participants from two vocational fashion design schools in Switzerland participated in our study. There were 18 fashion design apprentices and 16 fashion design teachers. The apprentices were all in their second year of a three-year certificate program. They had little or no experience with sewing shirts. On the other hand, all the teachers were regarded as experts. They completed fashion design training, had 10–20 years of working experience and taught at the fashion design school.

3.2 Procedure

For the study, we used a pull-out design that took place at the apprentices' schools but where the participants were asked to enter a separate room from their normal classroom. In this room, a computer with an external screen and an eye-tracker was set up. Specifically, we used a Tobii Pro X2-60 eyetracker and a 15 in. PC screen.

At the beginning of each session, the participants were provided with basic information about the experiment and the functioning of the eyetracker. The participants were asked to avoid movements such as tilting or turning the head, looking away from the screen or at the researcher and obstructing the eyetracker in any way. After the instructions, the eyetracker was calibrated for each participant.

For primary task, the participants were asked to observe a set of five images, which were presented to participants on a screen. Each of the images showed a model wearing a shirt. Each of the shirts was of a different cut and featured specific details such as for example embroidery or special buttons. The images are described in further detail in the following section. Apprentices were told to observe the details of the image and to verbally describe them. Each of the images was presented to participants for 40 s. Between each image there was a black screen for 20 s.

3.3 Stimuli

The images used in the study were identified with the help of the teachers. They were chosen to resemble as closely as possible the types of images used typically during fashion design training. Specifically, the teachers proposed the use of photographs representing models wearing different kind of shirts with a range of peculiarities related to shape, style, details and parts. Different parts in a shirt comprise the middle part, the shoulders, sleeves, opening and hem. Teachers who were not participating in this study, provided detailed descriptions of the images. These descriptions included information on the details of the shirt such as the opening (an open section at the top of a garment for the neck of the wearer), shoulders, stitching, pockets, sleeves, cuffs, hem and buttons. All of these parts are essential for apprentices to pay attention to and to visually explore. An example of an image used can be seen in Fig. 1.

3.4 Variables

To quantify gaze patterns without the need to manually assign areas of interests and find a more global measures applicable to any picture, we defined and calculated a similarity measure between gaze distributions as well as calculated the gaze coverage of the image and the fixations on the image. As a ground truth for apprentices' performance, we used their verbalisation score.

Fig. 1. Example stimuli focusing on a shirt design.

Similarity Calculation. The gaze similarity is a measure of how much an individual is looking at the same region of the image as an other individual during an interval of time. To quantify the attention towards regions, we computed the main region of interest of an image by finding the smallest rectangular area containing all the fixations of all participants for the given image. Given the size of the remaining region of interest is then divided into a regular grid of size 16 × 10. Afterwards for a given participant and time window, we counted the amount of gaze hits towards each cell of the grid. This process led to a vector representation of 160 dimensions containing the per-region gaze counts, which we will refer as the *gaze count vector*. This gaze count vector was used to compute both our similarity and gaze coverage measures.

To compute the similarity between two individual gaze count vectors, we normalized the vectors to be unitary and computed their scalar product as in [14]. Specifically, to compute the similarity between an apprentice and the average of all teachers, we computed gaze count vectors over time windows of 5 s for the entire 40 s for the apprentice and each teacher. We then created a prototypical teacher by averaging the gaze count vectors over all teachers within the same time windows. Using the prototypical teacher, we computed the similarity with the apprentice for every time window and computed an average.

Gaze Coverage Calculation. We define gaze coverage as the proportion of the image which is observed by the individual at least once. To compute the coverage, we first retrieved the heatmap for the given main region of interest, estimated over the duration of the stimuli. Using this heatmap, we computed the gaze coverage as the ratio of pixels which were above a threshold based on a fixed value over the total amount of pixels in the image. In our experiments, the threshold was set to 0.005, given that the heatmap values were normalized such that the maximum value was 1.

Verbalisation Score. The verbalisation score is calculated for each image and for each apprentices. Specifically that means that teachers would listen to an audio recording of apprentices' verbalisations. They would count the number of uniquely correctly identified and named details and devide this by the number of actual items to be identified times 100.

4 Research Questions

In order to answer the research questions defined in the introduction section of this paper we define the following sub-questions. Both R1 and R2 are designed to further define the question of whether there are quantifiable differences between the gaze patterns of apprentices and teachers. R3 clarifies the question whether apprentices with a higher verbalisation score are more similar to the teachers in terms of gaze patterns.

R1: Are there significant differences in terms of gaze exploration between apprentices and teachers ? In previous studies it has been found that experts and apprentices differ in the amount to which they explore the image/video [4,6]. In order to answer this question we calculated the amount of "gaze coverage" for all images and compare the groups of apprentices and teachers.

R2: Are there significant differences between apprentices and teacher in terms of fixation on area of interests? As discussed in the background section, differences in terms of fixations on areas of interests have been found in studies carried out on related by different tasks [7,10,19,20]. Therefore, in the current study, we investigate whether we can also find signification differences in fixation for this visual exploration task.

R3: Are apprentices with a higher verbalisation score more similar to the teachers in terms of gaze patterns? In order to answer this research question, we calculated the similarity of gaze distribution patterns between the average teacher (the average of gaze distribution patterns of all teachers) and each participant. We then correlated each apprentices' verbalisation score with their similarity score.

5 Results

R1: To test if there were differences in gaze exploration between apprentices and teachers, we ran an ANOVA comparing the two groups in terms of their gaze coverage of the image. A boxplot illustrating the proportionate amount of gaze coverage of the image between the groups of teachers and the group of apprentices can be seen in Fig. 2. The ANOVA tests revealed that the group category had an effect on the gaze coverage $F(1{,}163) = 11.42$, ($p < .01$) with the teachers having more gaze coverage than the apprentices.

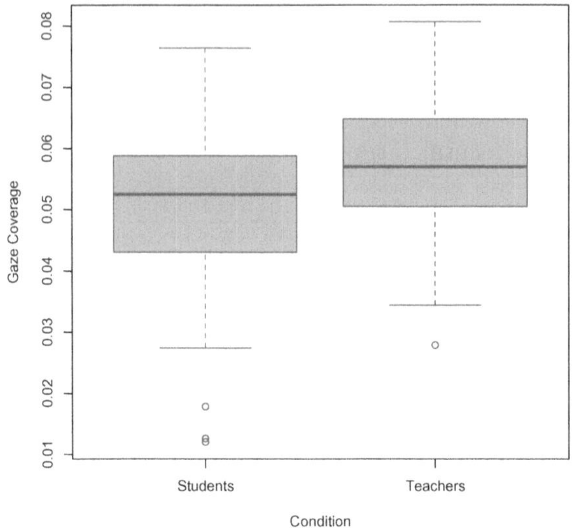

Fig. 2. Gaze Coverage contrasting teachers and apprentices.

R2: To test if there were differences in the time spent on the predefined important area of interests in each picture, we conducted a MANOVA since there is dependence between the time spent in each area. The MANOVA examined the average fixation per participant in the areas of interest as dependent variables with the teacher and apprentice classification as the independent variable. No significant multivariate effect could be found, $F(10{,}240) = 1.38$ ($p = .25$).

R3: Finally, a Pearson correlation was computed to assess the relationship between apprentices' verbalisation score and their gaze similarity to the average teacher. One participant was removed before analysis due to missing data. There was a positive correlation between the two variables, $r(15) = .87$ ($p < .01$), with the higher the verbalisation score the more similar the gaze pattern.

6 Discussion

In this paper we investigated gaze patterns between apprentices and teachers in an image exploration task that is relevant to vocational education training for fashion designers. We found differences of gaze patterns distinguishing teachers and apprentices. Specifically, we found that teachers have a higher gaze coverage of the image than apprentices. This result is in line with previous research where it was found that experts spend more time exploring the image [4,6]. Specifically in our study, this result may have been due to the nature of our task in which the goal was to explore (i.e. spend time looking at more of the image) where this may have been an acquired skill by the teachers Fig.3.

Further, in this study, we did not find any significant differences between the teachers and apprentices with the amount of time spent on the important areas

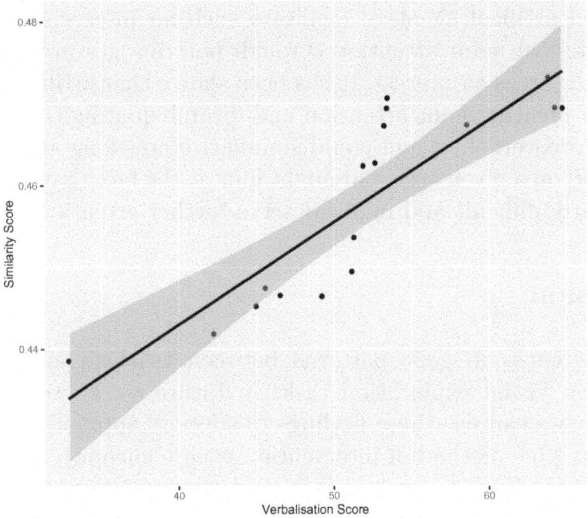

Fig. 3. Scatter plot illustrating the relation between verbalisation and similarity score.

of interest. A factor that might have contributed to this finding is that in the case of this experiment, the images the clothing design teachers recommended as stimuli, displayed several areas that were of relevance. These were also the same areas that were the most visually prominent ones and would attract the visual attention of complete novices. This prominence might have contributed to there not being any clear differences in proportionate amount of fixations between experts and apprentices.

We also found a correlation between apprentices' verbalisation score and similarity of gaze patterns to the average teacher. The higher the verbalisation score the more similar the gaze pattern. This finding is in line with previous research indicating that there are also differences in gaze patterns where the expertise level is small between novices and experts [18]. For future work, it might be interesting to compare apprentices' gaze patterns not to the average teacher but to the teacher who achieves the highest verbalisation score. While using an average teacher has the advantage that not everything is modeled based on the gaze behaviour of one expert alone and takes into account different ways of exploring the images, it also bears the danger that differences are being averaged out.

One limitation of the study is the duration to which apprentices were exposed to the stimuli. Forty seconds is in hindsight a rather long time for exploring the stimulus and differences might have been more pronounced if a shorter period of time was chosen.

Finally, the aim of this study was also to work towards building a system that is able to detect if apprentices are diverging from teachers gaze patterns. Both "Gaze Coverage" and "Similarity Score" appear to be useful measures to identify such divergences. In future work, we are planning to explore the use of an embodied artifical agent to facilitate such an intervention. An artificial agent could establish joint attention through pointing gestures or also verbally indicate different areas of interest. It has been shown that artificial agents can be quite useful for creating joint attention and disambiguating confusing attention targets [16]. Moreover, the agent could summarize how long an expert/or group of experts spend on a given area and might hint at the fact that this area appears to be particularly difficult and might deserve further attention.

7 Conclusion

We found differences in gaze patterns between teachers and fashion design apprentices in a visual exploration task. In future work, we are planning to investigate how we can use these findings to support apprentices in their visual skill acquisition. One method of intervention we are currently considering is the use of cueing. By using cues, such as fashion design specific annotations, apprentices' attention could be guided towards all relevant details of the garment.

References

1. Coppi, A., Cattaneo, A., Dillenbourg, P.: Observing like an expert: effects of using annotations on apprentices' gaze patterns and verbalizations. In: 6th congress on Research in Vocational Education and Training of the Swiss Federal Institute for Vocational Education and Training (SFIVET) (2019)
2. D'Angelo, S., Begel, A.: Improving communication between pair programmers using shared gaze awareness. In: Proceedings of the 2017 CHI Conference on Human Factors in Computing Systems, pp. 6245–6290. ACM (2017)
3. Haider, H., Frensch, P.A.: Eye movement during skill acquisition: more evidence for the information-reduction hypothesis. J. Exp. Psychol. Learn. Mem. Cogn. **25**(1), 172 (1999)
4. Jaarsma, T., Jarodzka, H., Nap, M., van Merrienboer, J.J., Boshuizen, H.P.: Expertise under the microscope: processing histopathological slides. Med. Educ. **48**(3), 292–300 (2014)
5. Jarodzka, H., Scheiter, K., Gerjets, P., Van Gog, T.: In the eyes of the beholder: how experts and novices interpret dynamic stimuli. Learn. Instr. **20**(2), 146–154 (2010)
6. Krupinski, E.A., et al.: Eye-movement study and human performance using telepathology virtual slides. Implications for medical education and differences with experience. Hum. Pathol. **37**(12), 1543–1556 (2006)
7. Moreno, F., Reina, R., Luis, V., Sabido, R.: Visual search strategies in experienced and inexperienced gymnastic coaches. Percept. Mot. Skills **95**(3), 901–902 (2002)
8. Nodine, C.F., Krupinski, E.A.: Perceptual skill, radiology expertise, and visual test performance with NINA and WALDO. Acad. Radiol. **5**(9), 603–612 (1998)
9. Olsen, J., Sharma, K., Aleven, V., Rummel, N.: Combining Gaze, Dialogue, and Action from a Collaborative Intelligent Tutoring System to Inform Student Learning Processes. International Society of the Learning Sciences, Inc.[ISLS] (2018)
10. Pappas, I., Sharma, K., Mikalef, P., Giannakos, M.: A comparison of gaze behavior of experts and novices to explain website visual appeal (2018)

11. Prieto, L.P., Sharma, K., Dillenbourg, P.: Studying teacher orchestration load in technology-enhanced classrooms. In: Conole, G., Klobučar, T., Rensing, C., Konert, J., Lavoué, É. (eds.) EC-TEL 2015. LNCS, vol. 9307, pp. 268–281. Springer, Cham (2015). https://doi.org/10.1007/978-3-319-24258-3_20
12. Raca, M., Dillenbourg, P.: System for assessing classroom attention. In: Proceedings of the Third International Conference on Learning Analytics and Knowledge, pp. 265–269. ACM (2013)
13. Sharma, K., Alavi, H.S., Jermann, P., Dillenbourg, P.: A gaze-based learning analytics model: in-video visual feedback to improve learner's attention in MOOCs. In: Proceedings of the Sixth International Conference on Learning Analytics & Knowledge, pp. 417–421. ACM (2016)
14. Sharma, K., Caballero, D., Verma, H., Jermann, P., Dillenbourg, P.: Looking AT versus looking THROUGH: A Dual Eye-Tracking Study in MOOc Context. International Society of the Learning Sciences, Inc. [ISLS] (2015)
15. Sharma, K., Olsen, J.K., Aleven, V., Rummel, N.: Exploring causality within collaborative problem solving using eye-tracking. In: Pammer-Schindler, V., Pérez-Sanagustín, M., Drachsler, H., Elferink, R., Scheffel, M. (eds.) EC-TEL 2018. LNCS, vol. 11082, pp. 412–426. Springer, Cham (2018). https://doi.org/10.1007/978-3-319-98572-5_32
16. Skantze, G., Hjalmarsson, A., Oertel, C.: Turn-taking, feedback and joint attention in situated human-robot interaction. Speech Commun. **65**, 50–66 (2014)
17. Tsuchiya, R., et al.: The characteristic of nurses' eye movements during observation of patients with disturbed consciousness. Open J. Nurs. **7**(12), 1502 (2017)
18. Van Gog, T., Paas, F., Van Merriënboer, J.J.: Uncovering expertise-related differences in troubleshooting performance: combining eye movement and concurrent verbal protocol data. Appl. Cogn. Psychol. **19**(2), 205–221 (2005)
19. Wolff, C.E., Jarodzka, H., van den Bogert, N., Boshuizen, H.P.: Teacher vision: expert and novice teachers' perception of problematic classroom management scenes. Instr. Sci. **44**(3), 243–265 (2016)
20. Wood, G., Knapp, K.M., Rock, B., Cousens, C., Roobottom, C., Wilson, M.R.: Visual expertise in detecting and diagnosing skeletal fractures. Skeletal Radiol. **42**(2), 165–172 (2013)

Identifying Critical Features for Formative Essay Feedback with Artificial Neural Networks and Backward Elimination

Mohsin Abbas[1,4(✉)], Peter van Rosmalen[2(✉)], and Marco Kalz[1,3(✉)]

[1] UNESCO Chair of Open Education, Faculty Management, Science and Technologies, Open University of the Netherlands, Heerlen, The Netherlands
{mohsin.abbas,marco.kalz}@ou.nl
[2] Faculty of Health, Medicine and Life Sciences, Maastricht University, Maastricht, The Netherlands
p.vanrosmalen@maastrichtuniversity.nl
[3] Heidelberg University of Education, Heidelberg, Germany
kalz@ph-heidelberg.de
[4] Faculty of Information Technology, University of Central Punjab, Lahore, Pakistan
mohsin.a@ucp.edu.pk

Abstract. For predicting and improving the quality of essays, text analytic metrics (surface, syntactic, morphological and semantic features) can be used to provide formative feedback to the students. In this study, the intent was to find a small number of features that exhibit a fair proxy of the scores given by the human raters. Using an existing corpus and a text analysis tool for the Dutch language, a large number of features were extracted. Artificial neural networks, Levenberg Marquardt algorithm and backward elimination were used to reduce the number of extracted features automatically. Irrelevant features were eliminated based on the inter-rater agreement between predicted and human scores calculated using Cohen's Kappa (κ). By using our algorithm, the number of features in this study was reduced from 457 to 23. The selected features were grouped into six different categories. Of these categories, we believe that the features present in the groups "Word Difficulty" and "Lexical Diversity" are most useful for providing automated formative feedback to the students. The approach presented in this research paper is the first step towards our ultimate goal of providing meaningful formative feedback to the students for enhancing their writing skills and capabilities.

Keywords: Formative feedback · Natural Language Processing · Neural Networks · Backward Elimination · Dimensionality reduction · Feature selection

M. Scheffel et al. (Eds.): EC-TEL 2019, LNCS 11722, pp. 396–408, 2019.
https://doi.org/10.1007/978-3-030-29736-7_30

1 Introduction

Providing meaningful formative feedback to students about the quality of their written assignments and texts is a time-consuming task [1,2]. Giving it immediately is sometimes not possible for teachers due to the large number of students [3] and the time required to grade an individual written assignment. Providing it automatically is possible using Natural Language Processing and Machine learning techniques [4–7]. Several systems have been implemented to provide feedback on essays.

Ellis Page, an English teacher proposed in the 1960s to use computers for assessments tasks [8]. PEG (Project Essay Grade) was his system that automatically graded essays. The scores given by PEG were comparable with the scores given by human judges with a correlation scores varying between 0.65 to 0.71. The focus of using PEG was to reduce the workload of the teachers which is one of the motivations of our work. The current version of PEG [9] provides automated essay scoring along with immediate feedback on texts through recommendations on how to improve the scores. IntelliMetric [10], another early AES system used artificial intelligence to score essays. IntelliMetric calculated more than 300 discourse, semantic and syntactic features to give a final score based on coherence, organization, elaboration, sentence structure and overall mechanics of the essay [11]. Educational Testing Services (ETS) uses E-rater [12] to automatically score GMAT essays. In order to provide scores, E-rater uses a huge corpus of graded responses to train its system. The first version of E-rater used approximately 50 features and with an agreement of 0.87 to 0.94 between the system and expert readers' scores on GMAT essay prompts [13]. In the newer version of E-rater (version 2.0), 12 more features were added with a kappa (κ) value of 0.58 [12]. Despite the existence of these systems, there is still a need to develop these types of feedback systems for languages other than English.

For the development of these questions, one of the critical questions is, which textual features are most important for automated feedback and how these features can be identified. The textual features (surface, syntactic, morphological and semantic features) that contribute the most in predicting the quality of students' texts can be extracted using machine learning techniques to provide formative feedback to the students. These metrics may be used to provide formative feedback to the students to improve their learning with an intent to calculate a small number of features that are required to provide meaningful feedback.

Several approaches for feature selection exist. In a study [14], an automatic linguistic and textual feature extraction tool Coh-Metrix [15] was used to select the features required to predict the essay quality; this selection was based on the highest values of Pearson correlation of features compared to scores given by human raters. Statistical techniques (discriminant analysis and stepwise regression) were used in a similar study [16] to select Coh-Metrix features significant in predicting the quality of high and low scoring essays. The feature classes related to lexical diversity, word frequency and syntactic complexity were reported to be the most predictive ones in determining the essay proficiency. Writing-Pal [17], an Intelligent Tutoring System, also uses features selected from Coh-Metrix using statistical procedures [18]. Features were selected in another study [19] using Principal Component Analysis and the effectiveness of chosen features was analyzed for providing formative feedback to the writers. 211 features used in the study were extracted from 3 different tools: Coh-Metrix, Linguistic Inquiry and Word Count [20], and the Writing Assessment Tool [18]. Feature Selection techniques in text mining using deep learning have been reviewed in [21].

Several existing text analysis tools can calculate a huge number of textual features against input texts. ReaderBench [22] is an open source multilingual framework that makes use of natural language processing techniques to provide text analysis tools. The framework is multilingual [23] – text analysis tools are available in Dutch, French, Romanian and English. Readerbench provides more than 200 textual complexity indices related to linguistic features of the text including surface, syntactic, morphological, semantic, and discourse features. Using ReaderBench, a research to choose features that contribute the most towards the scores given by human raters has already been conducted for the French language [24]. That research uses a different approach, namely Discriminant Function Analysis. T-scan [25,26] is a Dutch language analysis tool that calculates more than 400 text features which can be used for lexical and syntactic analysis. Experiments in this research have been conducted using T-scan that heavily relies on the Alpino parser [27] while calculating its features.

The current study explores a data-driven approach to identify textual features and metrics for an essay feedback system for the Dutch language. Machine learning algorithms such as Neural Networks can be used to create models using a corpus of scored texts. In this study it was investigated whether features that may be used to provide formative feedback on essays written in Dutch can be identified using artificial neural networks and backward elimination. The analysis was done by calculating more than 400 features against a scored corpus of Dutch texts extracted using T-Scan. To understand and comprehend the meaning behind all these features is time-consuming task. These features are meant for technical experts, therefore, not all the features are useful in providing meaningful formative feedback to the students. In this study, as a first step, we reduce the number of features using machine learning techniques. This paper is divided into four sections - the algorithm used in the research is described in the following section. Next we present the outcomes and the findings of our experiment. Finally we discuss the significance of our findings and discuss limitations of the research and conclude implications for future research that can be conducted using our algorithm.

2 Methods

We regard Automatic Essay Scoring as a subfield of Natural Language Processing where the prediction of scores against input texts is done automatically. The input of these models are features that are calculated from the corpus. The features are used as an input and the scores given by the human raters are used as output of machine learning algorithms to create the learned models. These can then be used to predict the scores against unknown texts. The performance of applications involving machine predicted scores is done by finding the inter-rater reliability between the predicted score and the scores given by human raters. For this purpose, a value of Cohen's Kappa (κ) [28] is calculated. This value lies between -1 to 1. A value less than zero means that there is no agreement between the predicted and the human scores. For the values of Cohen' Kappa (κ), the interpretation of inter-rater agreement is presented in Table 1.

Table 1. Inter-rater agreement for different values of Cohen's Kappa (κ).

Sr.no.	Kappa value (κ)	Inter-rater agreement
1	$\kappa \leq 0$	None
2	$0 < \kappa \leq 0.20$	Slight
3	$0.20 < \kappa \leq 0.40$	Fair
4	$0.40 < \kappa \leq 0.60$	Moderate
5	$0.60 < \kappa \leq 0.80$	Substantial
6	$0.80 < \kappa \leq 1$	Perfect

Existing research [9–13] focused on increasing the value of Kappa (κ) so that agreement between human raters and machine predicted scores is impeccable. In our research, the goal was to reduce the number of input features until the value of Kappa (κ) remains greater than zero. We used a corpus of scored Dutch texts and extracted different features from them using T-Scan. For our experiment, features extracted from Readerbench could have been used, however, we went for T-Scan since the number of features calculated by T-Scan is greater than the ones calculated by Readerbench. The input text features were used to train a machine learning model and an agreement between the scores given by the human raters and the predicted scores was found by calculating the value of Cohen's Kappa (κ). Then, the number of input features was reduced using Neural Networks Backward Elimination Technique [29,30]. This process (involving the training of the machine learning models and applying the Neural Networks Backward elimination technique) was repeated while the value of Kappa (κ) at the end of each feature elimination remained greater than zero.

2.1 Instruments

A corpus of scored texts was used to train a machine learning model to predict scores against texts. In this research, quality of Dutch texts is correlated with the scores obtained in these texts using the CLiPS Stylometry Investigation (CSI) [31]. This Dutch language corpus of scored texts was used to train models using a Neural Networks algorithm after extracting features from T-Scan. The corpus provides 517 essays of which 436 essays are graded. For each of the 436 scored Dutch essays, there exists a single score that lies between 0 to 20. The minimum score given of a text in this corpus is 5 and the maximum score is 18. A histogram of scores present in the corpus is shown in Fig. 1.

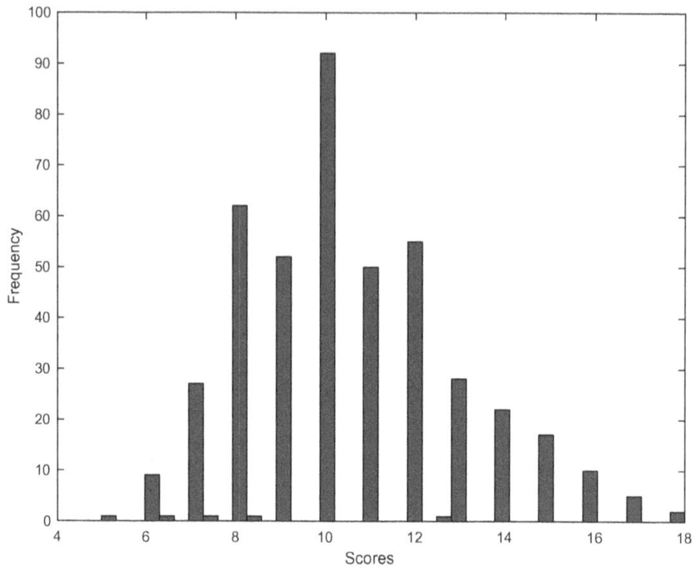

Fig. 1. Histogram of scores in the CLiPS corpus

T-Scan is an analysis tool for Dutch texts that provides text complexity features for input texts. This analysis tool was used to extract features from the texts present in the CLiPS corpus. For the texts, the number of features calculated by T-Scan is 457. However, not all these features can be shown to the students to provide formative feedback, therefore, the number of features was reduced. Textual features against each of the 436 texts were extracted using the T-scan online tool [32]. These extracted features were then used to train a neural networks prediction model to predict scores against unknown texts.

The neural networks algorithm used in our experiments was Levenberg-Marquardt algorithm [33–35]. The texts in the corpus were divided into two parts - one part for training and another one for testing the Neural Networks prediction model. MATLAB was used to create these models using the Levenberg Marquardt algorithm. For dimensionality reduction, the technique that was used was backward elimination. The Backward Elimination technique is a greedy algorithm that starts with n input features with a target to eliminate one out of these n features. In our research, for eliminating a single input feature, using backward elimination, n machine learning models were trained leaving each of the *n-1* features at a time. The models were created using Levenberg Marquardt algorithm and the value of kappa (κ) was calculated after leaving out each of the feature. After n models were trained, that feature was eliminated without which the value of kappa (κ) remained the maximum. The fact that the value of kappa (κ) stayed maximum was an indication that the inter-rater reliability between the human and predicted scores was still the best without the eliminated feature.

2.2 Procedure

For all of the 457 features extracted using T-Scan, one feature was eliminated at a time using Backward Elimination until the value of Kappa (κ) remained greater than zero. The procedure followed to achieve our goal is shown in Fig. 2 and is described below:

1. Extract features from Dutch texts using T-Scan
2. Start the experiment with all the 457 extracted features
3. Train the model using Neural Networks with chosen features
4. Test the model trained in Step 3 and calculate the value of kappa (κ)
5. If kappa (κ) is greater than zero, go to step 6, otherwise, go to step 7
6. Use the backward elimination technique to eliminate one feature and then repeat steps 3 to 5
7. Stop the experiment

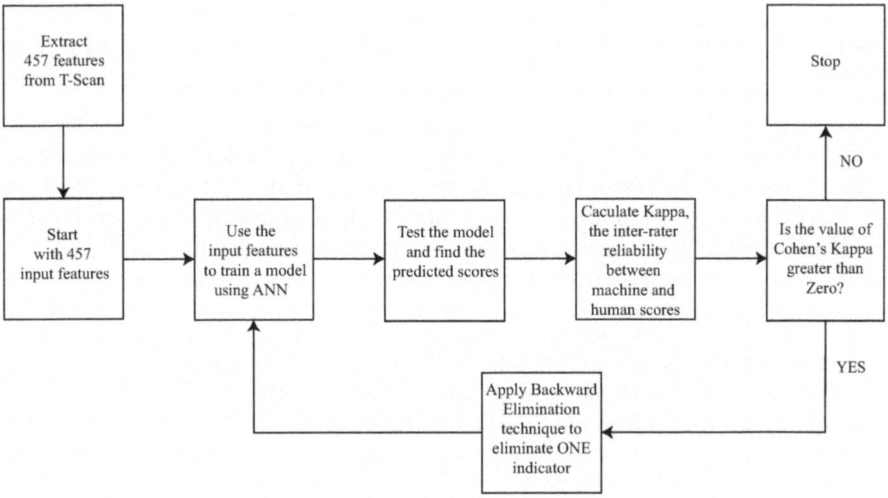

Fig. 2. The procedure followed to reduce the number of features

3 Results

The experiment was run on MATLAB R2017b on an iMac with MacOS version 10.14.4 having an Intel core i7, 4 GHz processor with 32 GB of RAM. The experiment ran for 13 days after which the stopping criteria was reached. The total neural network learning models trained during the experiment were 104,440. The value of Cohen's Kappa (κ) varied between 0.05 to 0.52. The variation in the value of Cohen's Kappa (κ) against different number of features is shown in Fig. 3. At the end of the experiment, we were left with 23 features; these features are given in Table 2. A brief description of each of the feature category is given below:

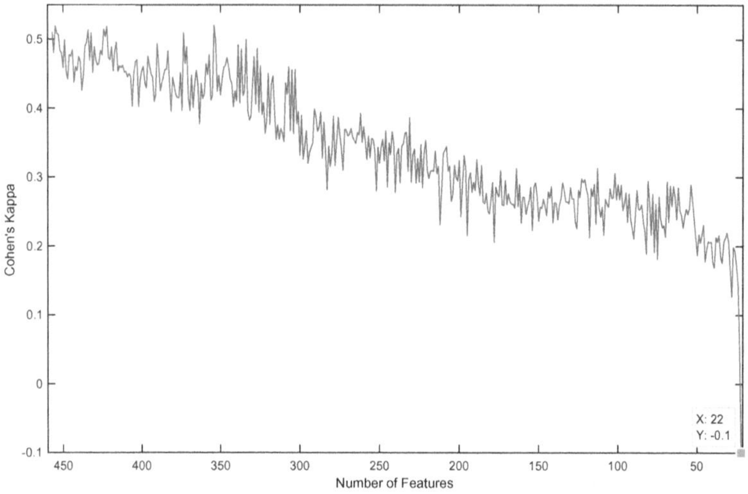

Fig. 3. The variation in the value of Cohen's Kappa (κ) against different number of features

Word Difficulty: The first seven features in Table 2 are related to the difficulty of words used in the texts. One of the features calculates the number of words per morpheme where a morpheme is a unit of the language that cannot be subdivided. Remaining features of this category compute the frequency of the words used in the texts. Four of these features quantify the proportion of:

1. the words that belong to most frequent 2000 words,
2. content words associated with the most frequent 1000 words,
3. nouns associated with the most frequent 20000 words,
4. words pertaining to the most frequent 1000 words.

The remaining two features related to word difficulty are the logarithm of frequency of words and the logarithm of frequency of nominal compositions. Nominal composition is the process of forming words that include lexemes that have more than one stem.

Sentence Complexity: There is only one feature in Table 2 associated with the sentence complexity. This feature provides the average of the number of words present in each sentence.

Lexical Diversity: Six features in the list of are related to lexical diversity and can be used to determine the richness of vocabulary used in a text. One of the features measures the lexical diversity of words and represent the uniqueness of words used in a text. Features such as the type token ratio (TTR) for words, density of content words and the number of arguments that occur in the previous sentence per sentence are also present in this category. TTR is defined as a ratio

Table 2. A description of the 23 reduced features after completion of the experiment.

Sr.no.	Feature name	Explanation	Category
1	Wrd_per_morf_zn	Words per morpheme, without names	Word Difficulty
2	Wrd_freq_log_sam_nw	Logarithm of word frequency of the nominal compositions	Word Difficulty
3	Wrd_freq_zn_log	Logarithm of word frequency without names	Word Difficulty
4	Freq2000	The word that belongs to the most frequent 2000 words	Word Difficulty
5	Freq1000_inhwrd	The proportion of content words associated with the most frequent 1000 words	Word Difficulty
6	Freq20000_nw	Proportion nouns associated with the most frequent 20000 words	Word Difficulty
7	Freq1000_corr	Corrected proportion of words pertaining to the most frequent 1000 words	Word Difficulty
8	Wrd_per_zin	Words per sentences	Sentence Complexity
9	MTLD_wrd	Measure of Lexical Diversity for words	Lexical Diversity
10	TTR_wrd	Type token ratio for words	Lexical Diversity
11	Inhwrd_d	Density of content words	Lexical Diversity
12	Arg_over_vzin_dz	Number of arguments that occur in the previous sentence per part sentence	Lexical Diversity
13	Tijd_d	Density of time words	Lexical Diversity
14	Tijd_MTLD	Measure of Lexical Diversity in text for time words	Lexical Diversity
15	Concr_ov_nw_p	Proportion of other specific nouns	Semantic Classes
16	Gedekte_nw_p	Proportion of nouns and names in the list	Semantic Classes
17	Alg_nw_p	Proportion of general nomina to all nomina	Semantic Classes
18	Ep_ev_bvnw_p	Proportion of nouns that evaluate epistemically	Semantic Classes
19	Conc_ww_p	Proportion of concrete verbs	Semantic Classes
20	Alg_ww_rel_sit_p	Proportion of general verbs around relationships between situations on all verbs	Semantic Classes
21	Spec_bijw_p	Proportion of specific adverbs to adverbs	Semantic Classes
22	Proceswww_p	Proportion of process verbs to verbs	Verb Characteristics
23	Perplexiteit_bwd	Perplexity, backwards	Probability Measures

between the total number of unique words (type) to the total number of words (token) in a text [36]. Content words are the words in the texts that carry meaning. The remaining two features in this class are the density of time words and the measure of lexical diversity in text for time words.

Semantic Classes: Semantic features represent the meaning of lexical components in the text. There are seven features in this class of features. These features measure the proportion of:

1. specific nouns - these nouns specify a particular thing
2. nouns and names in the list (provided by T-Scan)
3. general nomina to all nomina
4. nouns that evaluate epistemically
5. concrete verbs - in the verbs of motion, these represent unidirectional aspect of the verb
6. general verbs around relationships between situations on all verbs
7. specific adverbs to adverbs

Verb Characteristics: One feature is related to the verb characteristics in the text. This feature delineates the proportion of process verbs to all the verbs used in the text.

Probability Measures: Lastly, a feature calculates the logarithm of the backward perplexity. In Natural Language Processing, "perplexity" is a way to evaluate the language model [37] and has an inverse relation with the probability. A lower value of perplexity refers to a higher value of probability.

4 Discussion and Conclusions

In this research, the goal was to reduce the number of features calculated against input texts written in Dutch language via a data-driven approach. The results of our research present the features for which there remained a slight agreement between machine predicted scores and human ratings by the end of our experiment. The number of features in this research was reduced from 457 to 23 by using a combination of machine learning and feature reduction technique. These 23 features were grouped into different categories based on their description given in the T-Scan documentation [25]. Of these features, we believe that the features present in the categories "Word Difficulty" and "Lexical Diversity" are most useful for providing automated formative feedback to the students. Informing the students immediately about the richness in the vocabulary, the fraction of words that carry meaning, the type token ratio, the proportion of words that belong to a specific set of words (such as words or content words associated with the most frequent 1000 words) or the frequency of certain words used in their text may help them in improving the quality of their writing.

The features present in the categories "Sentence Complexity", "Semantic Classes" and "Verb Characteristics" need to be explored further. The results obtained from these categories serve as a starting point for our future research where the experts of Dutch language will analyze if these features can be used to provide meaningful formative feedback. The only feature present in the category "Probability measures" that calculates the logarithm of the backward perplexity is too technical and may not be helpful in providing meaningful feedback to the students.

The results in our study are restrained by the corpus used in the experiments - there are a lot of texts in the corpus having an average score, however, the texts having a high score, or the ones having a low score are not sufficient. The machine learning algorithms therefore sometimes tend to overfit on those texts that have an average score. This problem can be solved by using such a corpus that includes texts having scores that are uniformly distributed. In these experiments, the corpus that was used had a normal distribution of scores given by the human raters. Secondly, the corpus used in this work does not have texts that belong to the same subject or topic. There could be certain features that correspond to higher values for certain domains and lower values for others - using a domain specific corpus may improve the results further. Lastly, the texts in the corpus used in our experiments have been written by people having different backgrounds, age groups and levels of education. The type of writing may have different features that distinguish the type of writer (such as their age, gender etc...). Conducting the experiment with texts written by people having same age group, same level of education and similar background also needs to be investigated.

In future, the same experiment can be repeated using machine learning algorithms other than neural networks, or, by using different neural network algorithms such as gradient descent [38] or quasi-Newton [39] methods to explore whether there is an improvement in results by using a different algorithm. Finally, applying the algorithm on features extracted from texts using a different tool such as ReaderBench may add to the existing set of our chosen features. The approach presented is in this research paper is the first step of the three-step approach. In the first step, dimensionality of the input features was reduced automatically - as presented in this paper. The future work will include feedback on the usefulness of these features by humans (teachers/experts) and then by students. The ultimate goal is to provide meaningful formative feedback to the learners for improving the quality of their texts.

References

1. Irons, A.: An Investigation into the Impact of Formative Feedback on the Student Learning Experience (2010)
2. Shute, V.J.: Focus on formative feedback. Rev. Educ. Res. **78**(1), 153–189 (2008). https://doi.org/10.3102/0034654307313795

3. Irons, A.: Enhancing Learning through Formative Assessment and Feedback. Routledge, Taylor and Francis, London (2007)
4. Mehmood, A., On, B.W., Lee, I., Choi, G.S.: Prognosis essay scoring and article relevancy using multi-text features and machine learning. Symmetry **9**(1), 1–16 (2017). https://doi.org/10.3390/sym9010011
5. Nguyen, H., Xiong, W., Litman, D.: Iterative design and classroom evaluation of automated formative feedback for improving peer feedback localization. Int. J. Artif. Intell. Educ. **27**(3), 582–622 (2017). https://doi.org/10.1007/s40593-016-0136-6
6. Ramachandran, L., Gehringer, E.F., Yadav, R.K.: Automated assessment of the quality of peer reviews using natural language processing techniques. Int. J. Artif. Intell. Educ. **27**(3), 534–581 (2017). https://doi.org/10.1007/s40593-016-0132-x
7. Taghipour, K., Ng, H.T.: A neural approach to automated essay scoring. In: Proceedings of the 2016 Conference on Empirical Methods in Natural Language Processing, Austin, Texas, pp. 1882–1891 (2016). https://doi.org/10.18653/v1/d16-1193
8. Page, E.B.: The imminence of... grading essays by computer. Phi Delta Kappa Int. **47**(5), 238–243 (1966)
9. PEG Writing. https://pegwriting.com. Accessed 4 Dec 2018
10. Rudner, L.M., Garcia, V., Welch, C.: An evaluation of the IntelliMetric essay scoring system. J. Technol. Learn. Assess. **4**(4), 1–22 (2006)
11. Shermis, M., Burstein, J.: Automated Essay Scoring: A Cross-Disciplinary Perspective (2003)
12. Attali, Y., Burstein, J.: Automated essay scoring with E-Rater®V.2.0. J. Technol. Learn. Assess. **4**(3), 1–21 (2006)
13. Burstein, J., Kukich, K., Wolff, S., Lu, C., Chodorow, M.: Computer analysis of essays. In: Proceedings of the NCME Symposium on Automated Scoring, pp. 1–13 (1998)
14. Crossley, S.A., Roscoe, R., McNamara, D.S.: Predicting human scores of essay quality using computational indices of linguistic and textual features. In: International Conference on Artificial Intelligence in Education (AIED 2011), pp. 438–440 (2011). https://doi.org/10.1007/978-3-642-21869-9_62
15. Graesser, A.C., McNamara, D.S., Louwerse, M.M., Cai, Z.: Coh-Metrix: analysis of text on cohesion and language. Behav. Res. Methods Instrum. Comput. **36**(2), 193–202 (2004). https://doi.org/10.3758/BF03195564
16. McNamara, D.S., Crossley, S.A., McCarthy, P.M.: Linguistic features of writing quality. Written Commun. **27**(1), 57–86 (2010). https://doi.org/10.1177/0741088309351547
17. Roscoe, R.D., Allen, L.K., Weston, J.L., Crossley, S.A., McNamara, D.S.: The writing pal intelligent tutoring system: usability testing and development. Comput. Compos. **34**, 39–59 (2014). https://doi.org/10.1016/j.compcom.2014.09.002
18. McNamara, D.S., Crossley, S.A., Roscoe, R.: Natural language processing in an intelligent writing strategy tutoring system. Behav. Res. Methods **45**(2), 499–515 (2013). https://doi.org/10.3758/s13428-012-0258-1
19. Crossley, S.A., Kyle, K., Mcnamara, D.S.: To aggregate or not? linguistic features in automatic essay scoring and feedback systems. J. Writ. Assess. **8**(1), 1–16 (2015)
20. LIWC - Linguistic Inquiry and Word Count. https://liwc.wpengine.com. Accessed 23 Mar 2019

21. Liang, H., Sun, X., Sun, Y., Gao, Y.: Text feature extraction based on deep learning: a review. EURASIP J. Wirel. Commun. Networking **2017**(1), 1–12 (2017). https://doi.org/10.1186/s13638-017-0993-1
22. Dascalu, M., Westera, W., Ruseti, S., Trausan-Matu, S., Kurvers, H.: *ReaderBench* learns dutch: building a comprehensive automated essay scoring system for Dutch language. In: André, E., Baker, R., Hu, X., Rodrigo, M.M.T., du Boulay, B. (eds.) AIED 2017. LNCS (LNAI), vol. 10331, pp. 52–63. Springer, Cham (2017). https://doi.org/10.1007/978-3-319-61425-0_5
23. Dascalu, M., et al.: *ReaderBench*: a multi-lingual framework for analyzing text complexity. In: Lavoué, É., Drachsler, H., Verbert, K., Broisin, J., Pérez-Sanagustín, M. (eds.) EC-TEL 2017. LNCS, vol. 10474, pp. 495–499. Springer, Cham (2017). https://doi.org/10.1007/978-3-319-66610-5_48
24. Dascalu, M., Dessus, P., Thuez, L., Trausan-Matu, S.: How well do student nurses write case studies? a cohesion-centered textual complexity analysis. In: Lavoué, É., Drachsler, H., Verbert, K., Broisin, J., Pérez-Sanagustín, M. (eds.) EC-TEL 2017. LNCS, vol. 10474, pp. 43–53. Springer, Cham (2017). https://doi.org/10.1007/978-3-319-66610-5_4
25. Kraf, R., Pander Maat, H.: Leesbaarheidsonderzoek: oude problemen, nieuwe kansen. Tijdschrift Voor Taalbeheersing **31**(2), 97–123 (2014). https://doi.org/10.5117/tvt2009.2.lees356
26. Maat, H.P., et al.: T-Scan: a new tool for analyzing Dutch text. Comput. Linguist. Netherlands J. **4**, 53–74 (2014)
27. Bouma, G., van Noord, G., Malouf, R., Noord, G.V.: Alpino: wide-coverage computational analysis of Dutch. Lang. Comput. **37**, 45–59 (2000)
28. Viera, A.J., Garrett, J.M.: Understanding interobserver agreement: the kappa statistic. Fam. Med. **37**(5), 360–363 (2005)
29. Leray, P., Gallinari, P.: Feature selection with neural networks. Behaviormetrika **26**(1), 145–166 (1999)
30. Koller, D., Sahami, M.: Toward optimal feature selection. In: ICML 1996 Proceedings of the Thirteenth International Conference on International Conference on Machine Learning, Bari, pp. 284–292 (1996)
31. Verhoeven, B., Daelemans, W.: CLiPS Stylometry Investigation (CSI) corpus: a Dutch corpus for the detection of age, gender, personality, sentiment and deception in text. In: The 9th International Conference on Language Resources and Evaluation (LREC) (2014)
32. T-Scan Online Tool. https://webservices-lst.science.ru.nl/tscan/. Accessed 18 Nov 2018
33. Levenberg, K.: A method for the solution of certain non-linear problems in least squares. Q. Appl. Math. **2**, 164–168 (1944). https://doi.org/10.1090/qam/10666
34. Marquardt, D.W.: An algorithm for least-squares estimation of nonlinear parameters. J. Soc. Ind. Appl. Math. **11**(2), 431–441 (1963)
35. Hagan, M.T., Menhaj, M.B.: Training feedforward networks with the marquardt algorithm. IEEE Trans. Neural Networks **5**(6), 989–993 (1994)
36. Kettunen, K.: Can type-token ratio be used to show morphological complexity of languages? J. Quant. Linguist. **21**(3), 223–245 (2014). https://doi.org/10.1080/09296174.2014.911506
37. Chen, S.F., Beeferman, D., Rosenfeld, R.: Evaluation metrics for language models. In: Proceedings of the DARPA Broadcast News Transcription and Understanding Workshop (1998)

38. Baldi, P.: Gradient descent learning algorithm overview: a general dynamical systems perspective. IEEE Trans. Neural Networks **6**(1), 182–195 (1995). https://doi.org/10.1109/72.363438
39. Robitaille, B., Marcos, B., Veillette, M., Payre, G.: Modified quasi-newton methods for training neural networks. Comput. Chem. Eng. **20**(9), 1133–1140 (1993). https://doi.org/10.1016/0098-1354(95)00228-6

A Real-Life School Study of Confirmation Bias and Polarisation in Information Behaviour

Simone Kopeinik[1(✉)], Elisabeth Lex[1,2], Dominik Kowald[1], Dietrich Albert[2,3], and Paul Seitlinger[3,4]

[1] Know-Center GmbH, Graz, Austria
{skopeinik,dkowald}@know-center.at
[2] ISDS, Graz University of Technology, Graz, Austria
{elisabeth.lex,dietrich.albert,}@tugraz.at
[3] Institute of Psychology, University of Graz, Graz, Austria
[4] School of Educational Sciences, Tallinn University, Tallinn, Estonia
pseiti@tlu.ee

Abstract. When people engage in Social Networking Sites, they influence one another through their contributions. Prior research suggests that the interplay between individual differences and environmental variables, such as a person's openness to conflicting information, can give rise to either public spheres or echo chambers. In this work, we aim to unravel critical processes of this interplay in the context of learning. In particular, we observe high school students' information behavior (search and evaluation of Web resources) to better understand a potential coupling between confirmatory search and polarization and, in further consequence, improve learning analytics and information services for individual and collective search in learning scenarios. In an empirical study, we had 91 high school students performing an information search in a social bookmarking environment. Gathered log data was used to compute indices of confirmatory search and polarisation as well as to analyze the impact of social stimulation. We find confirmatory search and polarization to correlate positively and social stimulation to mitigate, i.e., reduce the two variables' relationship. From these findings, we derive practical implications for future work that aims to refine our formalism to compute confirmatory search and polarisation indices and to apply it for depolarizing information services.

Keywords: Learning analytics · Real-life school study · Information behaviour · Polarisation · Confirmatory search

1 Introduction

When people engage in online discussions in Social Networking Sites (SNSs) or different online forums, they interact with content shared by others, get

M. Scheffel et al. (Eds.): EC-TEL 2019, LNCS 11722, pp. 409–422, 2019.
https://doi.org/10.1007/978-3-030-29736-7_31

influenced by this content, and then, influence others through their interactions [6]. Particular dynamics between user dispositions (e.g., open- vs. closed-mindedness) and content of interaction (e.g., controversial vs. consensual topics) can create a *public sphere* [14], i.e., a place where people gather, share information and participate in critical debates about public affairs [5]. In principle, SNSs can support processes of a public sphere as they connect people and expose users to political differences online [4]. This confrontation with different viewpoints can encourage decision-making that draws on alternative information sources [7]. However, as discussed in related work (e.g., [1,26]), users of SNSs show a propensity to engage with like-minded others and tend to be closed-minded about alternative information [23]. One reason for the reinforcement of such processes is personalized filtering [27], which helps us find information related to what we prefer or already know. This caters to people's tendency to seeking information that corresponds to their existing beliefs (i.e., confirmatory search). As a consequence, people move towards extreme positions and attitudes [16,33] (i.e., polarization). Messages in the daily press about hateful Facebook postings make us aware that such dynamics quite often result in emotionalized and derogative stances to alternative viewpoints. Thus, it becomes of public interest to strengthen peoples' education in digital literacy. The motivation of this work is two-fold. On the one hand, our long-term goal is to help increase students' awareness and competences to consume information online critically, a skill many students lack to this date [25]. On the other hand, we aim to contribute to the development of learning analytics services for teaching and improving teaching strategies of digital competences in schools. We believe the progress towards these goals should be built upon a thorough understanding of underlying mental processes.

In this work, we propose means to study confirmatory search (search for consensual resources) and polarisation (drifting towards extreme positions) dynamics in an educational context. Our main aim is to better understand socio-cognitive dynamics leading to either deliberate, open-minded or biased, polarised information behavior [35]. To this end, we present a study that observes and interprets students' information behavior in a semi-controlled online environment. In particular, we investigate the impact of shared artifacts (i.e., social tags and bookmarks) on a collective search process and expect two artifact-mediated benefits: (i) the introduction of potentially new ideas (i.e., concepts labeled by freely chosen tags) will help a student activate new associations to a given topic and thereby, mitigate a tendency towards monotonous thoughts regarding a given problem [32], and (ii) the revealing of tags other students have previously chosen to index underlying concepts (e.g., by recommending social tags) will support the collective of students to mitigate the vocabulary problem, i.e., to agree on a common terminology of concepts more quickly [34].

We, therefore, raise the following two research questions:

RQ1: What is the impact of shared artifacts (social tags and bookmarks) on confirmatory search and polarisation in collective search processes?

RQ2: Can shared artifacts (social tags and bookmarks) be applied to reduce the vocabulary problem in collective search processes?

To examine these questions under natural conditions, we have conducted a study with 91 high-school students performing an information search task in an adapted version of the open-source social bookmarking system *SemanticScuttle*, This system can be used as a platform to collect and share information online and, from a research perspective, allows for recording user data related to information selection and opinion formation processes. Furthermore, to examine the impact of shared artifacts on these processes, three different conditions have been varied experimentally: As a baseline for comparisons, we had one group of students receiving no recommendations at all. In the following, this baseline is denoted 'None'. By contrast, the other two groups have been supported by tag recommendations, which we derived either inclusively from the entire group's tagging activities ('social' condition) or exclusively only from the student's personal tagging history ('individual' condition).

The present work contributes to current research on technology-enhanced learning by demonstrating how students' search and sharing behavior on the Web can be observed under natural conditions and how this behavior can be analyzed automatically in cognitive terms. Beyond that, it highlights a depolarizing impact of shared artifacts and can thus guide future design processes aiming towards more effective recommender systems in computer-supported learning scenarios. We, therefore, believe that the study helps to further learning analytics services for the teaching and training of critical and nuanced search behavior.

2 Related Work

The productive use of online information tools demands teaching strategies that address relevant competences [22]. To date, students' competencies and awareness to critically consume information are still widely lacking [25]. There is no evidence of digital skills that exceed the level of using technologies frequently [13]. Quite to the contrary, existing research reports on students' superficial understanding of new technologies and their lack of information seeking and analytical skills necessary to assess and learn from online resources (e.g., [3]).

2.1 Supporting Collective Search

A central motive to engage in SNSs is to acquire information, in private, societal-political, or vocational contexts. Therefore, this engagement can be framed as participation in a collective search, where the term collective means that different individuals act in a common environment and influence each other through shared artifacts, such as links to external news sites. Prior work has shown that even simple features, such as shared keywords (i.e., social tags) can become sources of mutual influences and can alter mental states (e.g., information goals) through the process of semantic priming (e.g., [11,31]). The term priming refers to an increased availability of traces in long-term memory evoked by an environmental stimulus (e.g., the tag "polarisation"), which is mentally connected to these traces (e.g., the associations of "echo_chamber" or "confirmatory_search") as well as to the subsequent behavioral consequences that follow from such priming, like performing a keyword-based search or accepting/declining recommended pieces of information.

When it comes to designing effective learning analytics services, which observe and support students' search behavior, the question should be raised, in which manner shared artifacts need to be (re)presented to facilitate a collective and open information search. In the context of the present study, we ask for the extent to which the prominence of other members' ideas and contributions should be increased or decreased to reduce the coupling between confirmatory search and polarisation eventually. Technology-enhanced group creativity provides some answers to these questions (e.g., [28]), which, e.g., explores the effects of shared artifacts on individuals' divergent thinking abilities during a collective information search (e.g., [32]). Among others, this research demonstrates that the recommendation of social tags (i.e., tags that are semantically related to a user's search but are generated by someone else) are on average more conducive to each group member's ideational fluency (i.e., the rate at which new ideas come to one's mind) than the recommendation of individual tags (i.e., semantically related tags drawn from a user's own tag vocabulary).

From a cognitive-psychological perspective, neurophysiological processes are stimulated by environmental influences and help trains of thoughts diverge. These processes should function antagonistically to mental processes that would otherwise actuate the convergence of contents of consciousness [15], such as the convergence of a current belief or opinion and an ongoing information goal. Put differently, cognitive processes during a search that support divergent thinking should simultaneously counteract confirmatory tendencies (e.g., the conversion of beliefs into search goals) and in further consequence, mitigate forces driving polarisation. Therefore, we assume and predict that providing social recommendations in the form of shared artifacts (e.g., social tags and social bookmarks) will result in a relatively weaker coupling between confirmatory search and polarisation than providing individual or even no recommendations.

2.2 Tagging and Semantic Stabilisation

Tagging is a mechanism to annotate resources individually or socially [36]. In TEL, it has demonstrated its potential to facilitate search, to foster reflection upon retrieved learning contents [19] and to promote the development of a metacognitive level of knowledge [2]. Throughout the learning process, structures of users in a social tagging environment assimilate [12]. Such implicit agreement on a common vocabulary over time and in meaning is called semantic stability [34]. The term semantic stabilization describes the evolution of convergence in vocabulary choices of different groups [18]. Research has described a mutual influence between learners' internal knowledge representation and the tagging vocabulary that emerges in the social information system, in which they interact [10]. Ley and Seitlinger [20] investigate these dynamics and prove a positive influence of semantic stabilization on individual learning. Consequently, it can be argued that a high level of semantic stability provides a structure that supports individual learning activities and therefore, can be conducive to individual learning gains [20]. Because students' typically struggle with the achievement of a semantically stable vocabulary in their usage and amongst their learning peers [20] recommendation mechanisms that introduce shared artifacts (e.g., tags) have been proposed [9]. Thus, expending prior research in inquiry-based learning [18], we explore the impact of shared artifacts (recommended tags) on semantic stabilization in an information search task.

3 Experimental Setup

For this study, we monitored and explored students' information search behavior in a real-life classroom setting. The study took place at Graz University of Technology, Institute of Interactive Systems and Data Science, as part of a top citizen science funding program, in which citizens are encouraged to participate in research endeavors actively. Three teachers and four high-school classes from two schools were recruited to participate in different project stages during the school terms of 2017 and 2018. In this time, 91 students (60 female and 31 male), aged between 14 and 18, took part in workshops that included completing worksheets, questionnaires, interviews, focus groups, and information search tasks. Here, we report on data insights extracted from the students' information search task.

3.1 Study Procedure and Design

Before the study, each participating student was provided with a brief description of the study setup and its main research goals. They were informed about the tasks they had to complete, the data that was gathered and potential privacy concerns. To ensure data protection and anonymity, students were identified by a pseudonym they created for themselves. After obtaining guardians' informed consent, students attended an introductory workshop to familiarize with the problems of echo chambers, filter bubbles, and fake news. Also, they were informed about the means to evaluate the quality of information. Before the search task, teachers selected a topic and associated topic aspects that fit the curriculum of the age group. This topic was depicted in the environment.

Within the information search task, students were instructed to explore the topic "global nutrition" by collecting information to the four defined aspects "genetic engineering", "conservation", "sustainable consumption" and "development aid". They had to upload their articles as bookmarks to the study environment. Students used the annotation tool shown in Fig. 1 to reflect on their Web resources. They had to select at least one predefined topic aspect, indicate their attitude and an estimation of the author's attitude towards the chosen aspects. The requested set of information provides insights on different facets of the opinion formation process, such as confirmatory search or polarisation.

To simulate a search environment with social, individual or no stimulation on appearing information dynamics, students were split into three groups. Depending on the group, the environment provided for the social and individual stimulation tag clouds and tag recommendations based on social or individual data. Students of the third group were neither presented with a tag cloud nor tag recommendations. This leads to the independent variable "search condition" with the three levels "Social", "Individual" and "None". As dependent variables, we observed semantic stabilization, recommender accuracy, confirmatory search, and polarisation.

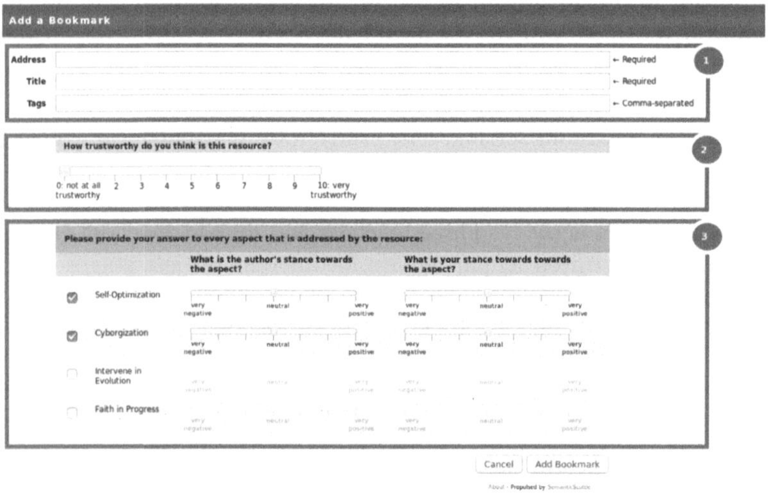

Fig. 1. Study environment: annotation interface.

3.2 Evaluation Measures

Semantic Stabilisation. While there is a multitude of metrics to evaluate semantic stability [34], few methods can deal with narrow folksonomies, where items are tagged only by the uploading user (as it is in our case). Lin et al. [21] present the Macro Tag Growth Method (MaTGM) that measures social vocabulary growth at a systemic level, looking at the social tagging system as a whole. In this study, experimental groups (i.e., "Social", "Individual" and "None") are observed as separate environments. The MaTGM is applied to compare the tag growth within these systems. For each group, the collected bookmarks (tag assignments) are sorted according to their timestamps. The tag growth after each bookmark, is calculated as a value pair $(tg_i, f(tg_i))$, where tg_i is the cumulative number of tags, and $f(tg_i)$ is the cumulative number of unique tags occurring in i bookmarks.

Recommender Accuracy. To evaluate the efficacy of the tag recommendation algorithms that operate either on social or individual tagging data, the performance metrics recall and precision [24] were applied. To calculate recall and precision, we determined for each bookmark the relation of tags recommended to a user for a Web resource to the tags that the user assigned to a resource.

Recall (R) indicates how well the recommendation supported the user, giving the relation between correctly recommended tags (i.e., the subset of recommended tags that the user assigned to the Web resource) and the set of tags the user needed to describe the Web resource.

$$R(T_{u,r}, \hat{T}_{u,r}) = \frac{|T_{u,r} \cap \hat{T}_{u,r}|}{|T_{u,r}|} \tag{1}$$

Precision (P) is the number of tags that have been recommended correctly divided by the number of recommended tags.

$$P(T_{u,r}, \hat{T}_{u,r}) = \frac{|T_{u,r} \cap \hat{T}_{u,r}|}{|\hat{T}_{u,r}|} \tag{2}$$

3.3 Behavioral Indicators

Confirmatory Search. Confirmatory search is described as the process of seeking information that is biased towards existing believes [29]. Prior research deduces confirmatory search in laboratory studies, by numerical comparisons of experimental and control groups' document selections, which confirm current beliefs or not [30]. With the environments' Annotation Interface (see Fig. 1) such data is tracked with every resource upload. In Eq. 3, we present one option to calculate confirmatory search (CS) with such data:

$$CS_{i,t} = (1 - \frac{\mid ASt_{i,t} - USt_{i,t} \mid}{diff_{max}}) * (1 - e^{-|ASt_{i,t}|}) \tag{3}$$

Here, CS with respect to a Web resource i and a topic t is defined as the difference of a user's stance USt towards t and the author's stance ASt towards t with respect to i. The second term includes an exponential function to increase the impact of strongly polarised Web resources on the one hand, and to subtract out resources with a balanced author stance (i.e., $ASti, t == 0$) on the other hand. CS of a user u is calculated as the mean value over all observed topic events of u, as formalized in Eq. 4:

$$CS_{u,t} = \sum_{i=0}^{n} \frac{CS_i, t}{n} \tag{4}$$

Polarisation. Equation 5 gives a value for a user's polarisation. In line with [8], we understand polarisation as a twofold construct that is characterized by a state and a process. Polarisation as a state is defined by the distance of an attitude position to a theoretical maximum of that attitude. The polarisation process $\Delta Pol_{u,t}$ describes the development of the attitude position in relation to this theoretical maximum over time. This is represented by the normalized difference of the user's stance towards t captured at the first topic event to the nth one.

$$\Delta Pol_{u,t} = \frac{\mid USt_{n,t} - USt_{0,t} \mid}{diff_{max}} \tag{5}$$

Equation 6 calculates a users' polarisation as a combination of polarisation change and the extremes of the final user stance USt_n.

$$Pol_u = \frac{w_1 * \Delta Pol_u + w_2 * \frac{|USt_n|}{o_n}}{2} \tag{6}$$

where o_n is the number of possible absolute values (except zero) the user or author stance can capture.

3.4 Study Environment

The study environment is based on the open-source social bookmarking system *SemanticScuttle*[1], which is a collaborative platform to collect and share information online. To fit the requirements of the experimental setting, it was adapted in its annotation and browsing interfaces and expanded by matching log data services. This has been realized with adaptations in the platform's range of functionality, in its database, user interfaces and the deployment of data logging services. To support users' reflection on their collected Web resources, the Annotation Interface was adapted as illustrated in Fig. 1. It is designed to enable the observation of students' ability in assessing the credibility of information, their tendency of polarisation during information search and information consumption as well as their ability to embed new concepts into their knowledge representation. Figure 1 illustrates the interface that takes basic information about the resource in input fields labeled with "one". It consists of the URL, a name and freely chosen keywords (i.e., tags). Tags assigned by a user can be used to observe particular semantics of the opinion formation process. Marked with "two" is a slider that asks for the user's perception of trustworthiness towards the selected resource. The slider ranges from 0 ("not at all trustworthy") to 10 ("very trustworthy"). In combination with the resource's URL, this information can be used to better understand users' ability to evaluate the quality of information and information sources. In the last block marked with "three", a set of topic aspects is presented to the user. These aspects vary with the search topic and therefore, can be configured by the site administrator. A bipolar rating scale is given by two sliders, ranging from −3 ("very negative"), over 0 ("neutral") to 3 ("very positive"). The sliders ask for the author and user stance towards single aspects and allow for inferring confirmatory search behavior and polarisation. Further details on the study environment and its technical adaptations are given in Kopeinik et al. [17].

[1] http://semanticscuttle.sourceforge.net/.

3.5 Data Characteristics

Table 1 shows the data characteristics separated according to the three experimental conditions: "Social", "Individual" and "None".

Table 1. Illustration of the data characteristics, given by the number of users (#users), bookmarks (#bmks) and tags (#tags), the average number of topics covered by a user ($\overline{T_{user}}$) and the captured events of topic attitudes (#E_{TA}).

	#users	#bmks	#tags	$\overline{T_{user}}$	#E_{TA}
Social	35	407	1078	3.86	603
Individual	35	362	753	3.83	527
None	21	276	895	3.76	297

The final dataset combines collected data from students of four participating school classes. Students of each class were randomly assigned to one experimental condition.

4 Results and Discussion

This section presents the result of our study that examines the impact of shared artifacts on aspects of information selection and opinion formation processes.

4.1 RQ1: What Is the Impact of Shared Artifacts (Social Tags and Bookmarks) on a Coupling Between Confirmatory Search and Polarisation in a Collective Search?

Based on prior empirical work, we expected a coupling, i.e., systematic relationship between participants' tendency towards confirmatory search (CS) (Eqs. 3 and 4) and polarisation (Eqs. 5 and 6). According to our theoretical assumptions (see Sect. 2.1), we predicted this coupling to be smaller under the "Social" condition, when users are supported by social tag recommendations and shared bookmarks, than under the "Individual" and "None" search condition. To test both of these predictions, we performed a linear regression of CS (criterion) on the continuous predictor "polarisation" and the categorical predictor "search condition", and included an interaction term to quantify potential differences in the slope (as an index of the CS-polarisation coupling) across the three search conditions. 91 data points have entered the regression (N_{None} = 20, $N_{Individual}$ = 35, N_{Social} = 36 participants) explaining about 50% of variance in polarisation (adjusted R^2 = .467, p <.001). This effect is represented well by the scatter plot of Fig. 2, which draws polarisation against CS and whose best fitting regression lines indicate a positive and moderate slope for each of the three conditions. The outcome for the "None" condition is represented by the steep red line, for which we have found a standardized beta coefficient of $\beta = 1.07$ ($t = 5.86, p < .001$). The other two lines appear to be flatter ($\beta_{Individual} = 0.65$; $\beta_{Social} = 0.46$), suggesting an interaction between the two predictors of CS and search condition. In line with our expectation, however, this decrease in the CS-polarisation relationship is significant only under the social condition ($t = -2.59, p < .05$) but not under the individual ($t = -1.98$, n.s.). We can therefore conclude that (i) similar to [33], the present study provides evidence of a CS-polarisation coupling too, which (ii) gets mitigated through the influence of shared artifacts (under the "Social" condition).

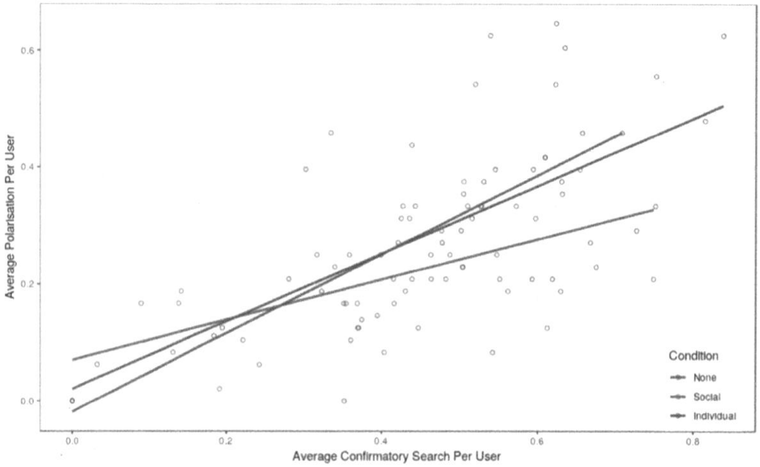

Fig. 2. Correlation between confirmatory search and polarisation illustrated in the three experimental conditions.

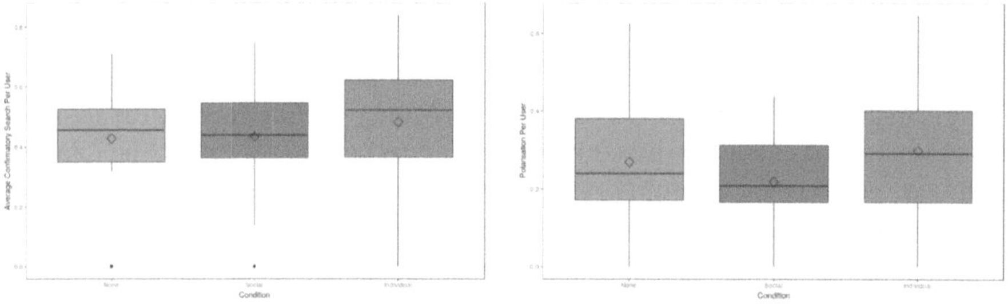

(a) Confirmatory Search (CS)

(b) Polarisation

Fig. 3. Box plots depicting medians and quartiles of the CS and polarisation scores separately for the three groups "None", "Social", and "Individual".

As we now gained clear evidence that the CS-polarisation coupling is looser under the "Social" than the other two conditions, we further examined whether these group differences are also reflected by differences in the overall range of values in the two variables. Given that the two variables fuel each other in this coupling, the main group effect for both polarisation and CS should come about, with relatively smaller levels under the "Social" condition.

We find a strong effect in the case of polarisation and a weak effect in the case of CF. First, the descriptive results, as represented by the plots in Figs. 3a and b, point towards a pattern that is in line with both expectations, i.e., the median is relatively lower in the social than in the other two groups. However, the test of significance, for which we have run a non-parametric, i.e., the Kruskal-Wallis test, to take into account the apparent violation of the equal variance assumption (see the box plots' interquartile ranges), has underlined this pattern only in case of polarisation ($\chi^2(2) = 7.20, p < .05$) but not of CS ($\chi^2(2) = 4.55$, n.s.).

We conclude that a relatively stronger CS-polarisation coupling indeed manifests in a higher CS value range and that prospectively, the same can be anticipated for polarisation as well, given a sufficiently long period of observation and a relatively more extensive sample of participants. Of course, the latter anticipation needs to be validated in future work.

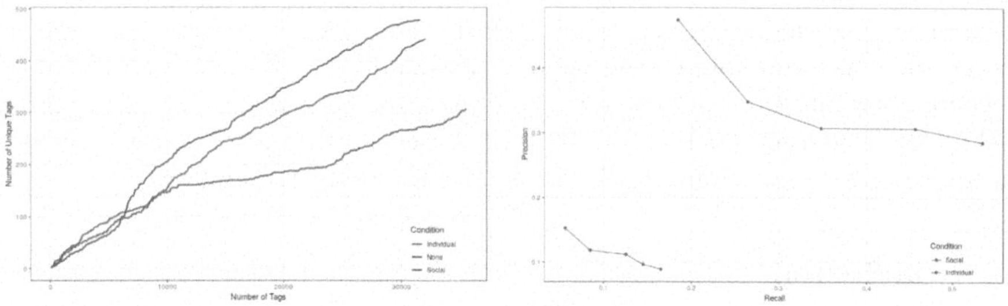

(a) Macro Tag Growth Method shows the semantic stabilization on a system level. The graphs plot the search conditions: "None", "Social" and "Individual".

(b) Recall/Precision plots showing the accuracy of recommendation algorithms in the "Social" and the "Individual" experimental condition.

Fig. 4. The impact of shared artifacts on vocabulary development in the individual and collective search task.

4.2 RQ2: Can Shared Artifacts (Social Tags and Bookmarks) Be Applied to Reduce the Vocabulary Problem in Collective Search Processes?

We address this research question considering two angles. First, we look at the semantic stabilization itself. Second, we investigate which recommendation approach can best support the process of semantic stabilization in the context of online information. Figure 4a illustrates the tag growth in the three experimental conditions represented as Macro Tag Growth Function. Comparing the vocabulary development of the groups, we find that while initially, the graphs overlap in all three groups, students in the two groups that receive tag recommendations (i.e., "Social" and "Individual"), start to introduce less new vocabulary in relation to tags than the group with no recommendations. This effect is even stronger for the group in the "Social" condition. In other words, we can observe two phenomena: (i) students in the "Individual" condition reuse their own words more frequently and thus, apply a more consistent terminology in their personal resource annotation; (ii) students in the "Social" condition start to reuse and pick up the vocabulary of their peers faster. This demonstrates the positive effect of social tag recommendations on semantic stabilization. In summary, results show the benefit of tag recommendations on semantic stabilization, even when applied in the context of individual information scenarios, which implies that previous findings [18] can be generalized to a collective information setting.

Results presented in Fig. 4b pay attention to the efficiency of provided tag recommendations. The recall/precision plot highlights the strong performance of tag recommendations based on the collaborative vocabulary of a group ("Social" condition) in comparison to recommendations based on individual tag traces. To the best of our knowledge, such an effect has not been reported in any other TEL recommender study. We explain the effect with the open and dynamic nature of the information search task itself. Students were asked to research a given topic and related aspects throughout four school lessons. This constitutes an explorative learning endeavor, where information takes place within a specific scope, while also developing over time. Consequently, we observe that social tag recommendations can support the explorative process within the information task, while tag recommendations that are based on the historic word traces of an individual are not suited to depict such continuous development.

5 Conclusion

In this paper, we presented an approach to study opinion dynamics in a collaborative search task. In a two-week real-life classroom study, we collected data on students' information behavior, their ability to evaluate information, and their tendencies towards confirmatory search and polarization. Based on the data that we gathered in the presented semi-controlled study environment, we proposed a formalism to calculate confirmatory search and polarisation in information behavior and found a strong correlation between the two constructs. This is in line with prior research and constitutes a proof of concept of the platform's field application. We understand the presented platform with its functionality and the formalism of behavioral indicators as a starting point for further discussion and exploration towards understanding and supporting critical information behavior in formal and informal learning. Gained insights will contribute to the prospective design and development of depolarising discourse services, learning analytics services, and visualizations.

Moreover, we found a positive impact of shared artifacts on polarisation and semantic stabilization. This highlights the benefit of social influence on the early ideation process. In the future, we plan to corroborate our findings in long term studies.

Acknowledgements. This work is supported by the Austrian Science Fund (FWF) TCS-034 Project, the European Union's Horizon 2020 research and innovation programme under grant agreement No. 669074 and by the Know-Center. The Know-Center is funded within the Austrian COMET Program - Competence Centers for Excellent Technologies. We are grateful for the help of Helena Flemming, Kevin Harkim and Marcel Jud in the realization of the school workshops, and the Projects Miles and HELI-D funded the Gesundheitsfond Steiermark.

References

1. Bakshy, E., Rosenn, I., Marlow, C., Adamic, L.: The role of social networks in information diffusion. In: Proceedings of WWW 2012, pp. 519–528. ACM (2012)
2. Bateman, S., Brooks, C., Mccalla, G., Brusilovsky, P.: Applying collaborative tagging to e-learning. In: Proceedings of WWW (2007)
3. Brown, C., Czerniewicz, L.: Debunking the 'digital native': beyond digital apartheid, towards digital democracy. J. Comput. Assist. Learn. **26**(5), 357–369 (2010)
4. Brundidge, J.: Encountering "difference" in the contemporary public sphere: the contribution of the internet to the heterogeneity of political discussion networks. J. Commun. **60**(4), 680–700 (2010)
5. Dahlgren, P.: The internet, public spheres, and political communication: dispersion and deliberation. Polit. Commun. **22**(2), 147–162 (2005)
6. Danescu-Niculescu-Mizil, C., West, R., Jurafsky, D., Leskovec, J., Potts, C.: No country for old members: user lifecycle and linguistic change in online communities. In: Proceedings of WWW 2013, pp. 307–318. ACM (2013)
7. De Liddo, A., Buckingham Shum, S.: The evidence hub: harnessing the collective intelligence of communities to build evidence-based knowledge (2013)
8. DiMaggio, P., Evans, J., Bryson, B.: Have American's social attitudes become more polarized? Am. J. Sociol. **102**(3), 690–755 (1996)
9. Font, F., Serrà, J., Serra, X.: Analysis of the impact of a tag recommendation system in a real-world folksonomy. ACM Trans. Intell. Syst. Technol. **7**(1), 6:1–6:27 (2015)
10. Fu, W.T.: The microstructures of social tagging: a rational model. In: Proceedings of CSCW 2008, pp. 229–238. ACM (2008)
11. Fu, W.T., Dong, W.: Collaborative indexing and knowledge exploration: a social learning model. IEEE Intell. Syst. **27**(1), 39–46 (2012)
12. Fu, W.T., Kannampallil, T.G., Kang, R.: A semantic imitation model of social tag choices. In: Proceedings of CSE 2009, vol. 4, pp. 66–73. IEEE (2009)
13. Gallardo-Echenique, E.E., Marqués-Molías, L., Bullen, M., Strijbos, J.W.: Let's talk about digital learners in the digital era. Int. Rev. Res. Open Distrib. Learn. **16**(3), 156–187 (2015)
14. Habermas, J., Habermas, J., Mccarthy, T.: The Structural Transformation of the Public Sphere: An Inquiry Into a Category of Bourgeois Society. MIT Press, Cambridge (1991)
15. Hommel, B.: Convergent and divergent operations in cognitive search. Cogn. Search: Evol. Algorithms Brain **9**, 221–235 (2012)
16. Huckfeldt, R., Mendez, J.M., Osborn, T.: Disagreement, ambivalence, and engagement: the political consequences of heterogeneous networks. Polit. Psychol. **25**(1), 65–95 (2004)

17. Kopeinik, S., Eskandar, A., Ley, T., Albert, D., Seitlinger, P.C.: Adapting an open source social bookmarking system to observe critical information behaviour. In: Proceedings of LILE (2018)
18. Kopeinik, S., Lex, E., Seitlinger, P., Albert, D., Ley, T.: Supporting collaborative learning with tag recommendations: a real-world study in an inquiry-based classroom project. In: Proc. of LAK 2017, pp. 409–418. ACM (2017)
19. Kuhn, A., Cahill, C., Quintana, C., Schmoll, S.: Using tags to encourage reflection and annotation on data during nomadic inquiry. In: Proceedings of CHI 2011, pp. 667–670. ACM (2011)
20. Ley, T., Seitlinger, P.: Dynamics of human categorization in a collaborative tagging system: how social processes of semantic stabilization shape individual sensemaking. Comput. Hum. Behav. **51**, 140–151 (2015)
21. Lin, N., et al.: The dynamic features of delicious, Flickr, and YouTube. J. Am. Soc. Inform. Sci. Technol. **63**(1), 139–162 (2012)
22. Livingstone, S.: Critical reflections on the benefits of ICT in education. Oxford Rev. Educ. **38**(1), 9–24 (2012)
23. MacKuen, M., Wolak, J., Keele, L., Marcus, G.E.: Civic engagements: resolute partisanship or reflective deliberation. Am. J. Polit. Sci. **54**(2), 440–458 (2010)
24. Marinho, L.B., et al.: Recommender Systems for Social Tagging Systems. Springer, Heidelberg (2012). https://doi.org/10.1007/978-1-4614-1894-8
25. McGrew, S., Breakstone, J., Ortega, T., Smith, M., Wineburg, S.: Can students evaluate online sources? Learning from assessments of civic online reasoning. Theory Res. Soc. Educ. **46**(2), 165–193 (2018)
26. Nikolov, D., Oliveira, D.F., Flammini, A., Menczer, F.: Measuring online social bubbles. PeerJ Comput. Sci. **1**, e38 (2015)
27. Pariser, E.: The Filter Bubble: What the Internet is Hiding From You. Penguin, London (2011)
28. Sarmiento, J.W., Stahl, G.: Group creativity in interaction: collaborative referencing, remembering, and bridging. Intl. J. Hum.-Comput. Interact. **24**(5), 492–504 (2008)
29. Schulz-Hardt, S., Frey, D., Lüthgens, C., Moscovici, S.: Biased information search in group decision making. J. Pers. Soc. Psychol. **78**(4), 655 (2000)
30. Schwind, C., Buder, J.: Reducing confirmation bias and evaluation bias: when are preference-inconsistent recommendations effective-and when not? Comput. Hum. Behav. **28**(6), 2280–2290 (2012)
31. Seitlinger, P., Ley, T., Albert, D.: Verbatim and semantic imitation in indexing resources on the web: a fuzzy-trace account of social tagging. Appl. Cogn. Psychol. **29**(1), 32–48 (2015)
32. Seitlinger, P., et al.: Balancing the fluency-consistency tradeoff in collaborative information search with a recommender approach. Int. J. Hum.-Comput. Interact. **34**(6), 557–575 (2018)
33. Stroud, N.J.: Polarization and partisan selective exposure. J. Commun. **60**(3), 556–576 (2010)
34. Wagner, C., Singer, P., Strohmaier, M., Huberman, B.: Semantic stability and implicit consensus in social tagging streams. IEEE Trans. Comput. Soc. Syst. **1**(1), 108–120 (2014)
35. Wang, Y., Luo, J., Niemi, R., Li, Y.: To follow or not to follow: analyzing the growth patterns of the trumpists on Twitter. In: Proceedings of ICWSM (2016)
36. Xu, Z., Fu, Y., Mao, J., Su, D.: Towards the semantic web: collaborative tag suggestions. In: Proceedings of WWW (2006)

Fostering Learners' Performance with On-demand Metacognitive Feedback

Zacharoula Papamitsiou[1,2(✉)], Anastasios A. Economides[2], and Michail N. Giannakos[1]

[1] Norwegian Universtiy of Science and Technology, 7034 Trondheim, Norway
{zacharoula.papamitsiou,michailg}@ntnu.no
[2] University of Macedonia, 54636 Thessaloniki, Greece
economid@uom.gr

Abstract. Activating learners' deeper thinking mechanisms and reflective judgement (i.e., metacognition) improves learning performance. This study exploits visual analytics to promote metacognition and delivers task-related visualizations to provide on-demand feedback. The goal is to broaden current knowledge on the patterns of on-demand metacognitive feedback usage, with respect to learners' performance. The results from a between-group and within-group study (N = 174) revealed statistically significant differences on the feedback usage patterns between the performance-based learner clusters. Foremost, the findings shown that learners who consistently request task-related metacognitive feedback and allocate considerable amounts of time on processing it, are more likely to handle task-complexity and cope with conflicting tasks, as well as to achieve high scores. These findings contribute to considering task-related visual analytics as a metacognitive feedback format that facilitates learners' on-task engagement and data-driven sense-making and increases their awareness of the tasks' requirements. Implications of the approach are also discussed.

Keywords: Feedback usage patterns · Learning analytics · Metacognitive feedback · Performance · Visual analytics

1 Introduction

Assisting learner during her learning is an important part of the cognitive process [36]. Contemporary learning theories highlight the significant role of feedback on the learner' personal development [8,17]. Feedback can be provided in different forms (e.g., oral, written) of (physical/digital, teacher/peer) tutor's response to learner's needs, actions, emotions, intentions, etc. It is assistive to the learner, either to motivate and reward her, or to help her deal with stressful/ conflicting learning conditions [14,17]; it is a key tool for guiding and sustaining learner's involvement in the self-regulated learning process and goal attainment [34,48].

The most common formats of feedback delivered to the learner are prompts, cues and/or questions, to help her to reason, think, understand and reflect about

M. Scheffel et al. (Eds.): EC-TEL 2019, LNCS 11722, pp. 423–435, 2019.
https://doi.org/10.1007/978-3-030-29736-7_32

success or failure concerning the task at hand, and allowing her to engage in self-regulatory learning mechanisms [8,29]. However, feedback on its own might not impact learning as expected, unless the learner is willing to use it [17]. To enable learner to use feedback efficiently, she needs to possess sufficient knowledge about how to use it [43], and feedback should be provided regularly during the learning tasks [48] so as the learner can practice with it [45]. Therefore, the challenge is to design learner-centered feedback, aiming at motivating learner to request for it at the moment she actually needs it, as well as at efficiently supporting her self-regulation [11,37]. In other words, the goal is to deliver meaningful information to the learner, and promote her metacognition. This increases learner's awareness and sense-making, and finally, her evidence-based decision and actions [39].

The importance of metacognition has been acknowledged in studies that attempt to improve learning in digital learning environments [4,12,13,21,22,26, 37]. Metacognition is related to the ability to monitor and control one's own knowing, and comprises the executive processes of reflective judgment and regulation of one's own deeper thinking; in simple terms, it is "thinking about thinking" [15]. Through those processes, the learner acquires her metacognitive knowledge from metacognitive monitoring, and controls her learning using the metacognitive knowledge [30]. Activating learner's metacognition with appropriate feedback is expected to improve learning performance [21,23,26,38].

However, previous studies demonstrated that engaging the learner in metacognitive processes is not a straightforward task, unless she is explicitly encouraged to do so through specialized instructional activities [16,25].

The rapid developments of different forms of visual analytics have opened new perspectives and opportunities on the design of metacognitive feedback [13]. Specifically, learning analytics dashboards are instruments intended to increase awareness of learning goals [10,40], to foster self-regulation [4,12], and to improve decision-making [6,47] by capitalizing on human perceptual capabilities.

This paper examines the potential of providing task-related visual analytics as task-specific metacognitive knowledge extracted from all learners' interaction trace data (i.e., learner-centered), that would reinforce the learner to complete a task. Thus, this study investigates visual analytics as a metacognitive feedback mechanism, and associates its usage patterns with learners' performance.

2 Related Work

Visual analytics, such as dashboards, pose novel feedback opportunities that enhance learning [10,12,20,40]. Previous works explore the effects of visual analytics on student performance outcomes through self-reflection, awareness, and self-assessment [5,10,20]. In fact, the process of providing students with "self-knowledge" has been outlined as key to developing metacognitive skills for self-regulated learning [13,44]. Information visualization is an effective sense-making tool due to its ability to synthesize complex data in a way for viewers to quickly understand, compare, reflect and ultimately decide [18].

However, most current visual analytics (e.g., dashboards) are based only on learner performance-oriented indicators (e.g., where a learner is doing well/poor, how much time was spent, how learners' progress compares to teacher specified and/or peer scores) that do not seem to contribute to learners" motivation and engagement [44]. Being performance-oriented, those implementations decrease learner mastery orientation [27]. Seminal research [40] demonstrates that effective feedback needs to be grounded in the regulatory mechanisms underlying the learning processes. This is particularly important when the learner is the main end-user of visual analytics, with a central goal to reinforce self-reflection and self-regulation [20]. Contemporary visual analytics, like dashboards, appear to promote antagonism between learners rather than chasing knowledge mastery [20], and there is always a concern that the learners might not know how to make-sense of this information [28]. Nonetheless, feeding this information to the learner encounters the danger that she may focus too much on her own self (ego), with unwanted effects on the learning (e.g., might lose motivation if the performance indices are low, or stop trying if the indices are high, just to preserve her reputation and avoid failure).

This raises the question of how to provide meaningful metacognitive feedback to the learner, to encourage efficient feedback usage, to shift her focus on the learning task (rather than feeding the self), as well as to help her master the skill/knowledge. To address this issue, this study suggests and explores the use of task-related visual analytics.

3 The Task-Related Visual Analytics

During the design of task-related visual analytics as on-demand metacognitive feedback, two design models were considered: (a) the metacognitive computational model of help-seeking [2] for guiding the desired feedback seeking behavior (i.e., the learner should ask for feedback only when she really needs it, and receives meaningful information), and (b) the Contextualized Attention Metadata schema [46] for providing coordinated views over the data. Based on these principles, the content and the format of the on-demand feedback were decided.

Regarding the content, what task-related information should be provided to the learner was determined so as this knowledge to activate learner's monitoring, reflection and judgment (i.e., metacognition) about the tasks, with an ultimate goal to help the learner to meet the requirements of each task, i.e., the actual difficulty, the actual effort needed to deal with each task, and the time required to allocate on each task. Providing this information *per se* could easily be perceived as the typical performance-oriented indicators (see previous section). Indeed, although those indexes have similarities with typical performance-oriented indexes computed per learner, however, they facilitate different goals: (a) since they are calculated from all learners' data when dealing with a specific task, the aggregated information describes the task and not the learner, (b) the accumulative information about the tasks is more action-oriented and aim to trigger deeper evaluation of the actual requirements of the tasks and guide learner's judgment and metacognitive inference, than the abstractly deduced "user-model" values, commonly delivered to learners. In a sense, those indexes do not intent to inform the learner (who requested this information) about how well all other students are performing, but rather about what one can infer about the real requirements of the task, and to engage with it in a "solution-behavior" manner.

Next, concerning the presentation of this information, it was decided to be delivered in three simple (easy-to-read) bar/column charts, including: (a) the number of correct vs. the number of wrong solutions submitted for this task (for inferring its difficulty), (b) the average students' effort expenditure vs. their average performance (i.e., correctness of solutions) for this task, and (c) the average time spent to solve this task correctly vs. the average time spent to solve the task wrongly vs. the average time spent to solve the task. Figure 1 illustrates the task-related visual analytics delivered as metacognitive feedback.

Every time the learner needs (or believes she needs) additional information about a task, i.e., beyond cognitive clarifications, she has the option to ask for the above analytics. Using properly this information is expected to support the learner to efficiently regulate herself, i.e., to improve her effort allocation, time-management and help-seeking skills, and metacognitive inference-making [27]. Previous research has shown that visualization of aggregated temporal indexes increases the teachers' awareness on students' progress and helps them revise their considerations about the actual requirements of the assessment tasks [31].

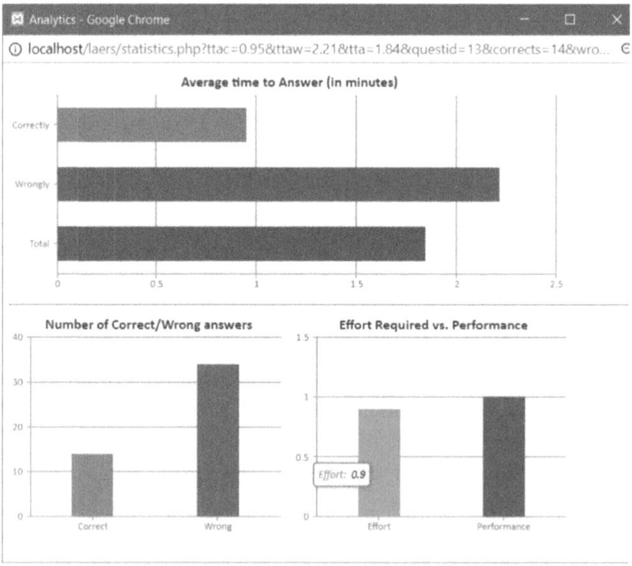

Fig. 1. The task-related visual analytics.

The visual analytics tool obtains the necessary temporal and performance indicators from the learning environment, and instantly generates the charts on-demand, by analyzing all learners' logged interactions (i.e., actual usage) with that task. For resolving "cold-start" issues, (i.e., absence of data the first time a task is being viewed by the students) the analytics from former learning procedures are employed. Those analytics are produced during the calibration of the task pool and are updated upon request with the arriving observations.

3.1 Methods

3.2 Participants and Study Design

Overall, 174 undergraduate students (93 females [53.4%] and 81 males [46.6%], 19–26 years-old [M = 20.582, SD = 1.519]) at a European University were enrolled in a self-assessment activity for the Management Information Systems II course (related to databases, e-commerce) at the University computers lab, for 60 mins.

The study reported in this paper followed an experimental design [9]. All students had previously used the self-assessment environment [33], and they were randomly assigned into two groups: 88 students (50.6%) were assigned to the "feedback" group (i.e., the experimental group), and 86 students (49.4%) were assigned to the "no-feedback" group (i.e., the control group). Prior to the self-assessment, the students in the experimental group had a brief introductory presentation of the task-related visual analytics, to explain them what information would be available to them, and how to use it [25]. Those instructions were also available to that group throughout the procedure.

During the self-assessment activity, all students had to answer 15 multiple-choice questions (from now on referred to as "tasks"); each task had four possible answers, but only one was the correct. The tasks were delivered to the participants in predetermined order. The students could temporarily save their answers on the tasks, review them, alter their initial choices, and save new answers; they could also skip a task and answer it later. Moreover, the experimental group could ask for task-related visual analytics for each task.

Prior to the self-assessment, the difficulty of the tasks (easy, medium, hard) was determined using prior assessment results, according to the number of correct answers. Each task's participation in the score was according to its difficulty, varying from 0.5 points (easy) to 0.75 points (medium) to 1 point (hard), and only the correct answers were considered (i.e., no penalizing wrong answers).

The participation in the activity was optional. All participants signed an informed consent form prior to their participation, explaining them the procedure and giving the right to researchers to use the data collected for research purposes. Students were aware that their interactions were anonymized prior to being analyzed, and that the collected data would be stored for 3 years.

3.3 Data Collection

Data were collected with an online self-assessment environment [33]. For both groups, students' performance (i.e., scores) was computed as: $\sum_{i=1}^{k} d_i z_i$ where

$z_i \in \{0, 1\}$ is the correctness of the student's answer on task i, and d_i is the difficulty of the task. In addition, for the experimental group, other measurements commonly used in the field of learning analytics, acknowledged to satisfactorily explain students' engagement (e.g., response-times, frequencies) [1,19,32], and quantifying how students use the feedback, were computed, as well. Table 1 illustrates the measurements captured and coded for each group.

Table 1. Measurements considered in this study

Variable	Name	Description	Experimental group	Control group
TTAV	Time-spent on viewing visual analytics	The average time students spend on viewing the visual analytics	X	
FVAR	Frequency of visual analytics request	How many times the students ask for visual analytics	X	
LP	Learning Performance	The score the student achieves	X	X

In this table, Time-spent on Viewing Visual Analytics (TVVA) is the average time all students spend on viewing the visualizations (per task) and engage on reflection, judgment and sense-making (i.e., metacognition). Frequency of Visual Analytics Request (FVAR) is the average value of a counter (per task) that increases every time that the students make the respective request (metacognitive monitoring of tasks) [1].

3.4 Data Analysis

To investigate the effect of task-related visual analytics on learning performance, independent samples t-test was applied between the control and the experimental groups. The minimum required total sample size and per-group sample size, given the probability level ($p < 0.05$), the anticipated effect size (Cohen's $d > 0.5$), and the desired statistical power level ($\geq$0.8), is 128 and 64 respectively. In our study, the sample size is 174, and the subgroup sizes are 88 and 86 respectively. Since, not every significant result refers to an effect of high impact, we calculated the effect size in order to evaluate the strength of the effect. Hedge's g effect size was considered, because the sample size of each sub-group is considered small. Ranges for Hedge's g effect size are small > 0.2, medium > 0.5 and large > 0.8.

In order to explore potential differences between low, medium and high performers, students of the experimental group were grouped into three clusters according to their performance: High-performers: final grade > 7, Medium-performers: final grade ≥ 5, and Low-performers: final grade < 5. Then, an Analysis of Variance (ANOVA) test was performed to investigate differences in each one of the feedback usage measurements (i.e., TVVA, FVAR) between the different performance-based student clusters. The impact of these parameters was explored as well, and the η^2 effect size was computed for evaluating the strength of each one of these parameters. Ranges for η^2 effect size are small > 0.01, medium > 0.06 and large > 0.14. The decision to use ANOVA test instead of multiple t-tests was because ANOVA controls the Type I error so as it remains at 5%, when the number of groups is higher than two. The analyses were performed with SPSS 25.0 for Windows.

4 Results

Table 2 demonstrates the descriptive statistics for the two groups with respect to the learning performance.

Table 2. Descriptive statistics for performance

Group	N	Mean	Std. Dev (SD)
Experimental	88	6.534	1.735
Control	86	4.372	1.681

Table 3 depicts the independent samples t-test results regarding students' learning outcomes between the experimental and the control groups. In this table, the last column illustrates the Hedge's g effect size. As seen from this table, there were significant differences in performance between the experimental and control groups, and the effect of task-related visual analytics on performance was relatively large (g = 0.68).

Table 3. Independent samples t-test results for learning performance (*p < 0.05)

				95% CI		
Groups	F	df	t	Lower	Upper	Hedges' g
Experimental vs. Control	0.009	172	5.486*	0.6507	1.6733	0.68

Table 4 presents the results for ANOVA tests for each one of the parameters of visual analytics usage (i.e., FVAR, TVVA). The η^2 effect size was calculated, as well. The Levene's test for homogeneity of variances could not reject the hypothesis of equal variances (sig. > 0.05).

Since the statistical analysis revealed significant differences in the parameters of visual analytics usage with respect to the performance-based learner clusters, next we looked for specific usage patterns per cluster: we visualized the parameters of on-demand metacognitive feedback-seeking per task, per cluster.

Table 4. ANOVA results for the learning analytics factors on the performance-based clusters (*p < 0.05)

	F	p-value	η^2
Frequency of visual analytics requests	23.002	0.00001	0.351*
Time-spent on viewing visual analytics	19.073	0.00001	0.310*

Figures 2 and 3 illustrate the analytics parameters of feedback usage per task, for each one of the performance-based learner clusters (in different shaped lines). In both Figures, on the x-axis are the task, ordered according to their increasing difficulty from easy to hard (as it was initially defined – see Sect. 3.2 – i.e., tasks 1–8 are easy, tasks 9–12 are medium, and tasks 13–15 are hard).

In Fig. 2, the y-axis corresponds to the average time-spent on viewing the visualizations (in seconds), and in Fig. 3, the y-axis corresponds to the respective average requests for task-related visual analytics.

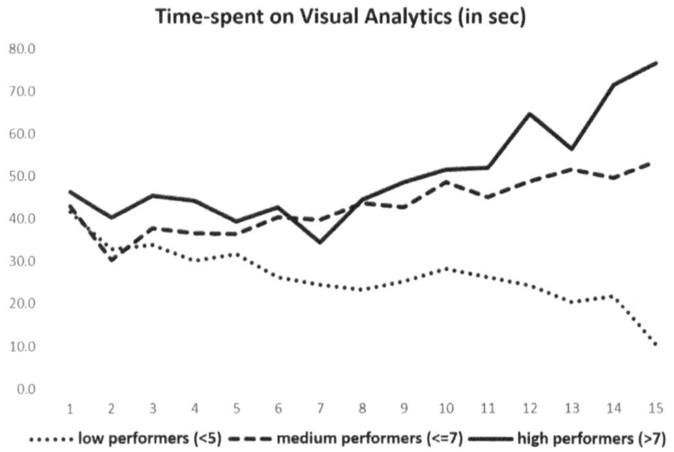

Fig. 2. Average time-spent on viewing task-related visual analytics per task.

As seen from these figures, there are significant differences in the patterns of usage of visual analytics between high, medium and low performers. For example, as the difficulty of the tasks increases, low-performers tend to gradually use less the metacognitive feedback, both in terms of the average requests for on-demand metacognitive information and of the average time allocated to view and study this information. It is interesting to note, though, that those learners put a lot of effort (in time and requests) to understand the visual information in the beginning of the process, on the easy tasks. Further exploring those patterns of the feedback usage across the performance-based learners' profiles, is expected to provide useful insights regarding the learners' metacognitive skills.

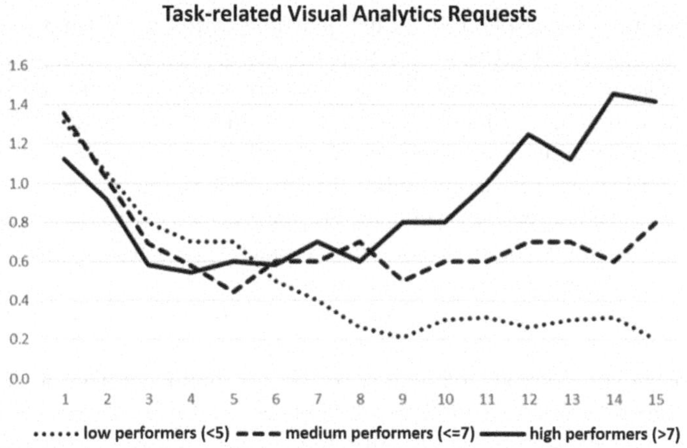

Fig. 3. Average requests for task-related visual analytics per task.

5 Discussion and Conclusions

Despite the concern that learners might not know how to make-sense of learning analytics [28], previous studies argued that learners can interpret their own performance indices, yet they reserve a skepticism on how to practically convert this information into actionable insights [10]. The innovation of this work derives from exploiting easy-to-read task-related visual analytics to provide learners with meaningful information about the tasks, and investigates how they use it and how they adjust their answering behavior. The overall results of this study demonstrate a coherent relationship between the actual use of on-demand metacognitive feedback and learning performance. Additional consistent patterns of feedback usage behavior were identified, as well.

Specifically, the t-test shown a large effect size (Hedge's $g = 0.68$) of the usage of on-demand feedback on learners' performance, between the experimental and the control group. The one-way ANOVA revealed statistically significant differences between the high, medium and low performers with respect to the frequency they requested for visual analytics ($F(2, 85) = 23.002$, $p = 0.000$), and to the time-spent on viewing the metacognitive information ($F(2, 85) = 19.073$, $p = 0.000$). The effect sizes of both measurements about the actual usage of feedback were strong ($\eta^2 = 0.351$ for FVAR; $\eta^2 = 0.310$ for TVVA), as well.

Combined with the results from the graphical representation of help-seeking behavior with respect to the performance-based learner clusters (Figs. 3 and 2), this finding can be interpreted as follows: high performing students use visual analytics more often and allocate considerable time to think and reflect about the received information and infer its implications. On the contrary, low-performers rarely request for analytics about the tasks (probably because they don't know how to use it or feel uncomfortable with this type of information or simply they don't care). This finding provides additional empirical evidence to previously reported results that associated higher learning gains with time allocated on hint reasoning [3,41]. Furthermore, this finding is in line with prior research works that claim that students in need usually don't ask for feedback, while students who can achieve higher - even without additional support - tend to ask for complementary hints and resources [7,35,42].

Beyond confirming previous results, this study is the first one - to the best of our knowledge - that dives into the learners' interactions with the metacognitive support and associates the usage of this feedback type with performance-based learner clusters. From the exploratory analysis Figs. 2 and 3, it becomes apparent that most students ask for visual analytics on the first task. From that point on, high-performers seek for additional information mostly on hard tasks, low-performers successively avoid requesting for metacognitive feedback, and medium-performers follow a more stable pattern and ask for analytics on most of the tasks, regardless of their difficulty, but do not allocate significant amounts of time on processing the information. This implies that these students are aware that they need support, they seek for it, but they are uncertain regarding the actions they should take afterwards.

In accordance with the literature [24], this study argues that learner data have the potential to support decision-making and enhance learning (e.g., via quantified-self technologies). Such a support can be transformative for students, especially the ones who are already familiar with such technologies and motivated [24]. Future work needs to collect data from other learning settings (e.g., MOOCs, problem solving), at larger scale and use different and repeated survey data collections. Cross-validating and extending our findings will allow us to generalize them and even identify activities were on-demand metacognitive feedback might be more important (i.e., higher effect). This will allow us to identify why and how on-demand metacognitive feedback can be used to optimize its potential.

References

1. Ada, M.B., Stansfield, M.: The potential of learning analytics in understanding students' engagement with their assessment feedback. In: 2017 IEEE 17th International Conference on Advanced Learning Technologies (ICALT), pp. 227–229, July 2017. https://doi.org/10.1109/ICALT.2017.40
2. Aleven, V., Mclaren, B., Roll, I., Koedinger, K.: Toward meta-cognitive tutoring: a model of help seeking with a cognitive tutor. Int. J. Artif. Intell. Ed. **16**(2), 101–128 (2006)
3. Arroyo, I., Woolf, B.P.: Inferring learning and attitudes from a bayesian network of log file data. In: Proceedings of the 2005 Conference on Artificial Intelligence in Education: Supporting Learning Through Intelligent and Socially Informed Technology, pp. 33–40. IOS Press, Amsterdam (2005)
4. Azevedo, R., Taub, M., Mudrick, N.V., Millar, G.C., Bradbury, A.E., Price, M.J.: Using data visualizations to foster emotion regulation during self-regulated learning with advanced learning technologies. In: Buder, J., Hesse, F.W. (eds.) Inf. Environ., pp. 225–247. Springer, Cham (2017). https://doi.org/10.1007/978-3-319-64274-1_10

5. Bodily, R., Verbert, K.: Review of research on student-facing learning analytics dashboards and educational recommender systems. IEEE Trans. Learn. Technol. **10**(4), 405–418 (2017). https://doi.org/10.1109/TLT.2017.2740172
6. Bodily, R., et al.: Open learner models and learning analytics dashboards: a systematic review. In: Proceedings of the 8th International Conference on Learning Analytics and Knowledge, LAK 2018, ACM, New York, NY, USA, pp. 41–50 (2018). https://doi.org/10.1145/3170358.3170409
7. Broadbent, J., Poon, W.L.: Self-regulated learning strategies & academic achievement in online higher education learning environments: a systematic review. Internet High. Educ. **27**, 1–13 (2015)
8. Butler, D.L., Winne, P.H.: Feedback and self-regulated learning: a theoretical synthesis. Rev. Educ. Res. **65**(3), 245–281 (1995). https://doi.org/10.3102/00346543065003245
9. Cobb, P., Confrey, J., DiSessa, A., Lehrer, R., Schauble, L.: Design experiments in educational research. Educ. Researcher **32**(1), 9–13 (2003). https://doi.org/10.3102/0013189X032001009
10. Corrin, L., de Barba, P.: How do students interpret feedback delivered via dashboards? In: Proceedings of the Fifth International Conference on Learning Analytics and Knowledge, LAK 2015, ACM, New York, NY, USA, pp. 430–431 (2015). https://doi.org/10.1145/2723576.2723662
11. Daley, S.G., Hillaire, G., Sutherland, L.M.: Beyond performance data: improving student help seeking by collecting and displaying influential data in an online middle-school science curriculum. Br. J. Educ. Technol. **47**(1), 121–134 (2016). https://doi.org/10.1111/bjet.12221
12. Davis, D., Chen, G., Jivet, I., Hauff, C., Houben, G.J.: Encouraging metacognition & self-regulation in MOOCs through increased learner feedback. In: Bull, S., Ginon, B.M., Kay, J., Kickmeier-Rust, M.D., Johnson, M.D. (eds.) LAL 2016 - Learning Analytics for Learners, CEUR Workshop Proceedings, CEUR, pp. 17–22 (2016)
13. Durall, E., Gros, B.: Learning analytics as a metacognitive tool. In: Proceedings of the 6th International Conference on Computer Supported Education, pp. 380–384 (2014). https://doi.org/10.5220/0004933203800384
14. Economides, A.A.: Conative feedback in computer-based assessment. Comput. Schools **26**(3), 207–223 (2009). https://doi.org/10.1080/07380560903095188
15. Flavell, J.H.: Metacognition and cognitive monitoring: a new area of cognitive-developmental inquiry. Am. Psychol. **34**(10), 906–911 (1979). https://doi.org/10.1037/0003-066X.34.10.906
16. Gama, C.: Metacognition in interactive learning environments: the reflection assistant model. In: Lester, J.C., Vicari, R.M., Paraguaçu, F. (eds.) ITS 2004. LNCS, vol. 3220, pp. 668–677. Springer, Heidelberg (2004). https://doi.org/10.1007/978-3-540-30139-4_63
17. Hattie, J., Timperley, H.: The power of feedback. Rev. Educ. Res. **77**(1), 81–112 (2007). https://doi.org/10.3102/003465430298487
18. Heer, J., Agrawala, M.: Design considerations for collaborative visual analytics. Inf. Vis. **7**(1), 49–62 (2008). https://doi.org/10.1145/1391107.1391112
19. Henrie, C.R., Halverson, L.R., Graham, C.R.: Measuring student engagement in technology-mediated learning: a review. Comput. Educ. **90**, 36–53 (2015)
20. Jivet, I., Scheffel, M., Drachsler, H., Specht, M.: Awareness is not enough: pitfalls of learning analytics dashboards in the educational practice. In: Lavoué, É., Drachsler, H., Verbert, K., Broisin, J., Pérez-Sanagustín, M. (eds.) EC-TEL 2017. LNCS, vol. 10474, pp. 82–96. Springer, Cham (2017). https://doi.org/10.1007/978-3-319-66610-5_7

21. Kautzmann, T.R., Jaques, P.A.: Effects of adaptive training on metacognitive knowledge monitoring ability in computer-based learning. Comput. Educ. **129**, 92–105 (2019). https://doi.org/10.1016/j.compedu.2018.10.017
22. Kim, J.H.: The effect of metacognitive monitoring feedback on performance in a computer-based training simulation. Appl. Ergon. **67**, 193–202 (2018). https://doi.org/10.1016/j.apergo.2017.10.006
23. Labuhn, A.S., Zimmerman, B.J., Hasselhorn, M.: Enhancing students' self-regulation and mathematics performance: the influence of feedback and self-evaluative standards. Metacognition Learn. **5**(2), 173–194 (2010). https://doi.org/10.1007/s11409-010-9056-2
24. Lee, V.R., Drake, J.R., Thayne, J.L.: Appropriating quantified self technologies to support elementary statistical teaching and learning. IEEE Trans. Learn. Technol. **9**(4), 354–365 (2016). https://doi.org/10.1109/TLT.2016.2597142
25. Lin, X.: Designing metacognitive activities. Educ. Technol. Res. Dev. **49**(2), 23–40 (2001). https://doi.org/10.1007/BF02504926
26. Long, Y., Aleven, V.: Enhancing learning outcomes through self-regulatedlearning support with an open learner model. User Model. User-Adap. Inter. **27**(1), 55–88 (2017). https://doi.org/10.1007/s11257-016-9186-6
27. Lonn, S., Aguilar, S.J., Teasley, S.D.: Investigating student motivation in the context of a learning analytics intervention during a summer bridge program. Comput. Hum. Behav. **47**, 90–97 (2015)
28. MacNeill, S., Campbell, L.M., Hawksey, M.: Analytics for education. J. Interact. Media Educ. 1–12 (2014)
29. van Merriënboer, J., Kirschner, P.: Ten Steps to Complex Learning: A Systematic Approach to Four-Component Instructional Design. Routledge, New York (2017)
30. Nelson, T., Nahrens, L.: Metamemory: a theoretical framework and new findings. In: Bower, G.H. (ed.) The Psychology of Learning and Motivation, pp. 125–173. Academic Press, New York (1990)
31. Papamitsiou, Z., Economides, A.A.: Temporal learning analytics visualizations for increasing awareness during assessment. Int. J. Educ. Technol. High. Educ. **12**(3), 129–147 (2015)
32. Papamitsiou, Z., Pappas, I.O., Sharma, K., Giannakos, M.N.: Utilizing multimodal data through an fsQCA approach to explain engagement in adaptive learning. IEEE Trans. Learn. Technol. (2019)
33. Papamitsiou, Z., Economides, A.: Towards the alignment of computer-based assessment outcome with learning goals: the LAERS architecture. In: 2013 IEEE Conference on e-Learning, e-Management and e-Services, IC3e 2013 (2013). https://doi.org/10.1109/IC3e.2013.6735958
34. Pintrich, P.R.: A conceptual framework for assessing motivation and self-regulated learning in college students. Educ. Psychol. Rev. **16**(4), 385–407 (2004). https://doi.org/10.1007/s10648-004-0006-x
35. Puustinen, M., Rouet, J.F.: Learning with new technologies: help seeking and information searching revisited. Comput. Educ. **53**(4), 1014–1019 (2009). https://doi.org/10.1016/j.compedu.2008.07.002
36. Richardson, M., Abraham, C., Bond, R.: Psychological correlates of university students' academic performance: a systematic review and meta-analysis (2012). https://doi.org/10.1037/a0026838
37. Roll, I., Aleven, V., McLaren, B.M., Koedinger, K.R.: Improving students' help-seeking skills using metacognitive feedback in an intelligent tutoring system. Learn. Instruct. **21**(2), 267–280 (2011)

38. Roll, I., Aleven, V., McLaren, B.M., Ryu, E., Baker, R.S.J., Koedinger, K.R.: The help tutor: does metacognitive feedback improve students' help-seeking actions, skills and learning? In: Ikeda, M., Ashley, K.D., Chan, T.-W. (eds.) ITS 2006. LNCS, vol. 4053, pp. 360–369. Springer, Heidelberg (2006). https://doi.org/10.1007/11774303_36
39. Schwendimann, B.A., et al.: Perceiving learning at a glance: a systematic literature review of learning dashboard research (2017). https://doi.org/10.1109/TLT.2016.2599522
40. Sedrakyan, G., Malmberg, J., Verbert, K., Järvelä, S., Kirschner, P.A.: Linking learning behavior analytics and learning science concepts: designing a learning analytics dashboard for feedback to support learning regulation. Comput. Hum. Behav. (2018)
41. Shih, B., Koedinger, K.R., Scheines, R.: A response time model for bottom-out hints as worked examples. In: de Baker, R., Barnes, T., Beck, J. (eds.) Proceedings of the 1st International Conference on Educational Data Mining, pp. 117–126 (2008)
42. Stahl, E., Bromme, R.: Not everybody needs help to seek help: surprising effects of metacognitive instructions to foster help-seeking in an online-learning environment. Comput. Educ. **53**(4), 1020–1028 (2009). https://doi.org/10.1016/J.COMPEDU.2008.10.004
43. Stone, N.J.: Exploring the relationship between calibration and self-regulated learning. Educ. Psychol. Rev. **12**(4), 437–475 (2000). https://doi.org/10.1023/A:1009084430926
44. Verbert, K., et al.: Learning dashboards: an overview and future research opportunities. Pers. Ubiquit. Comput. **18**(6), 1499–1514 (2014). https://doi.org/10.1007/s00779-013-0751-2
45. Winne, P.H.: Experimenting to bootstrap self-regulated learning. J. Educ. Psychol. **89**(3), 397–410 (1997). https://doi.org/10.1037/0022-0663.89.3.397
46. Wolpers, M., Najjar, J., Verbert, K., Duval, E.: Tracking actual usage: the attention metadata approach. J. Educ. Technol. Soc. **10**(3), 106–121 (2007)
47. Yigitbasioglu, O.M., Velcu, O.: A review of dashboards in performance management: implications for design and research. Int. J. Account. Inf. Syst. **13**(1), 41–59 (2012)
48. Zimmerman, B.J.: Self-regulated learning and academic achievement: an overview. Educ. Psychol. **25**(1), 3–17 (1990). https://doi.org/10.1207/s15326985ep2501_2

Training Customer Complaint Management in a Virtual Role-Playing Game: A User Study

Julia Othlinghaus-Wulhorst(✉), Anne Mainz, and H. Ulrich Hoppe

University of Duisburg-Essen, Duisburg, Germany
{othlinghaus, hoppe}@collide.info,
anne.mainz@stud.uni-due.de

Abstract. Handling customer complaints properly, especially through chat or phone-based interaction, has become an increasingly important social skill and is the subject of professional training in companies, markets, and multinational corporations. In order to develop such skills, training methods can involve videos and role plays. Virtual role play scenarios can provide a fairly authentic experience of realistic conflict situations with customers and allow for trying out different problem-solving strategies without consequences in the real world. This paper presents an attempt to train customer complaint handling through an educational role-playing game based on theories of consumer psychology and complaint management using a chatbot system with intelligent support. The playability, game experience, and perception of the virtual role play environment, as well as the interaction with the chatbot, have been evaluated in a mixed method study. The results indicate that the idea and approach of the game, in general, are assessed positively and the scenarios are perceived as useful and realistic. Furthermore, the study confirms that the chatbot's conversation style is influencing the game experience and the perception of the chatbot significantly.

Keywords: Virtual role play · Intelligent support · Customer complaint management

1 Introduction

Especially in the e-business sector, customers can choose between a variety of different products and providers, which makes customer loyalty a core challenge. Excellent online customer service is one of the most important factors for ensuring customer satisfaction [1]. Accordingly, handling customer complaints has been identified as an important social skill and is the subject of professional training in companies, markets, and multinational corporations [2]. Video-based learning and role plays can be utilized in this context to consolidate the proper concepts and to develop professional behavior when handling customer complaints [3]. Especially virtual role plays help people experience conflict situations with customers and learn how to handle complaints. They provide a safe environment for trying different problem-solving strategies, and although their actions have no consequences in the real world, this training can prepare them to react adequately in similar situations.

M. Scheffel et al. (Eds.): EC-TEL 2019, LNCS 11722, pp. 436–449, 2019.
https://doi.org/10.1007/978-3-030-29736-7_33

This paper presents an attempt to train customer complaint handling through an educational role-playing game based on theories of customer psychology and complaint management using chatbots and intelligent support. At this point, the main evaluation questions address playability, usability, and perceived authenticity of the environment. A user study has been conducted to investigate these aspects. In the rest of this paper, we first elaborate on the background before presenting the study and its results.

2 Background and Related Work

The following subsections provide an overview of the two main fields of interest that constitute the basis for the application design: educational games for the training of soft skills and customer complaint management as the field of application.

2.1 Educational Games for Soft Skills Training

Digital role-playing and simulation-based training systems have been increasingly adopted for the training and development of soft skills [4]. The so-called technology enhanced educational role-playing games (EduTechRPGs) are digital environments that support the training of soft skills through the application of psycho-pedagogical methodology. The term soft skills describes personal attributes or traits that express how people know and manage themselves and their relationships with others [4]. It is a broad concept that includes many dimensions of the personal sphere development involving emotional, behavioral, and cognitive components [4]. The goal of EduTechRPGs is to combine education and fun, thereby increasing the (intrinsic) motivation of the players. One major advantage of EduTechRPGs is their ability to promote learning by doing. Players are supposed to undergo an active learning process of experience and reflection, which imparts soft skills in the best possible way.

There is a number of EduTechRPGs addressing different social skills. ENACT (*Enhancing Negotiation skills through online Assessment of Competencies and interactive mobile Training*) [4] is a 3D single-player game to assess and train a user's negotiation and communication skills. In the game, two on-stage agents represented by 3D avatars simulate a dialog between two people. One is controlled by the player and the other by a AI-controlled bot. The simulation includes three dimensions of communication: verbal (the words used in a sentence), para-verbal (tone, pitch, and volume of the voice), and non-verbal (body language), and has eight different scenarios. An important aspect of the game is the assessment element, which allows the measuring of soft skills based on a psychometric approach.

Virtual Leader [5] is a role-playing based simulation program, which is supposed to help students practice different leadership styles and approaches in a 3D environment. In the game, players participate in virtual business meetings with animated computer-controlled characters. The game includes five scenarios with increasing complexity. It was designed to provide an immersive environment to practice leadership skills like negotiation, collaboration, influencing, and conflict resolution, and provides immediate feedback in the form of a leadership score that is based on their effectiveness in achieving specific scenario goals.

ColCoMa [6] is a collaborative game for training workplace-oriented conflict management in a role-playing scenario. It employs two human actors in the role of the conflicting parties and an AI-controlled chatbot in the role of a mediator, who is moderating a mediation talk. The main goal of the players is to resolve the conflict by showing appropriate and constructive behavior during the conversation. The learning process is supported by adaptive feedback based on an individual performance analysis. The idea behind this is that players experience enhanced self-understanding and immersion through collaborative play, which is expected to effectively foster their conflict resolution skills.

Ziebarth et al. [7] developed a web-based game for medical students to support the training of patient-centered medical interviews. Here, players assume the role of a locum doctor for family medicine, and their goal is to find out as many of the patient's symptoms as possible within a given time frame. To identify a symptom, the player has to communicate with the patient via text input and non-verbal actions. The behavior of the patient depends on the level of trust and empathy the players have established during the conversation. Post-role-play reflection is supported by a recording of the role play session, which is further enhanced by the results of an automated analysis of the communication behavior based on models of doctor-patient communication (and general communication) used to describe general rules and strategies for medical interviews.

While all of the above games address the training of specific social skills, there is no existing approach explicitly targeting the training of customer complaint management strategies. Also, most of the studies do not come with thorough empirical evaluation. Our work aims to create a meaningful and structured approach for training customer complaint management using role play based on best practices of complaint management.

2.2 Customer Complaint Management

Complaint management can be understood as the complete system provided by the company that affords the opportunity to resolve complaints [8]. Original complaint channels, such as telephone, mail, or even personal conversations, have been more and more replaced by electronic channels (for example, email, social media, or specially created complaint platforms) [1]. The resolution of a complaint is always associated with costs: employees have to be hired, compensations for customers have to be made (e.g., refunds, repair service), and much more. Nevertheless, the mathematical model of Fornell and Wernerfelt [8] suggests that companies should encourage customers to complain and compensate them generously because complaint management serves as an effective tool for customer retention by increasing the expected benefits of the purchase for the customer. Even if the complaints are objectively not justified, it can make economic sense to react fairly, as in most cases complaints are considered to be justified from the customers' perspective [9].

There are three groups of measures available as basic solution possibilities to customer problems [9]: financial, tangible, and intangible. *Financial* solutions include money return, price reduction, and compensation for damages. *Tangible* solutions are payments in kind like exchange, repair, another product or gift. *Intangible* reactions include all customer-oriented forms of communication that aim to reduce the customer's dissatisfaction, such as information, explanation, and apology. The choice of the appropriate compensation is confined by product-specific factors and cost considerations. According to Chase and Dasu [10], financial or tangible solutions are appropriate in case of production mistakes, whereas intangible solutions are advisable in case of corporate malpractice.

Stauss [11] differentiates between two dimensions of complaint satisfaction: outcome complaint satisfaction and process complaint satisfaction. *Outcome complaint satisfaction* encompasses the evaluation of what the customer actually gets from the company as a compensation, while *process complaint satisfaction* refers to the evaluation of how the complaint is handled. Factors creating process complaint satisfaction are access, friendliness, empathy, individual handling, effort, active feedback, reliability, and speed of response [11].

3 Virtual Role Play Environment: CuCoMaG

Based on the idea to implement a virtual customer complaint management training embedded in a role-playing scenario, we designed the EduTechRPG *CuCoMaG (Customer Complaint Management Group reflection)*. In this game, the player assumes the role of a customer service employee in *LittleOnes*, a fictitious company producing and selling personalized clothing for children via an online shop. Complaint management is particularly important for such a company because it sells sensory products, has a large number of competitors, and high quality elasticity is possible [8]. However, children's clothing does not require complex warranty regulations. In addition, clothing and accessories are the product categories most commonly associated with complaints [1].

3.1 Game Design

Players find themselves in a conversation with a chatbot in the role of a complaining customer, who has a specific problem. The player communicates with the customer through a simple chat interface (Fig. 1). In order to create a chat message, the player has to select a sentence opener from a predefined set and supplement it with free text. The sentence openers (a) provide support to the player and (b) help the chatbot to understand the intention and general gist of each message. The free text supplementation enables players to express themselves more naturally and also allows a more detailed evaluation of a player's communicative behavior. The offered set of sentence openers depends on the phase of the conversation. The player can also access the company's database to search for additional information on a customer and their order, which is necessary in order to receive all information required to resolve the situation. In summary, the user choices are: (1) selection of a predefined sentence opener, (2) input of free text to complete the user message, (3) information retrieval using the database.

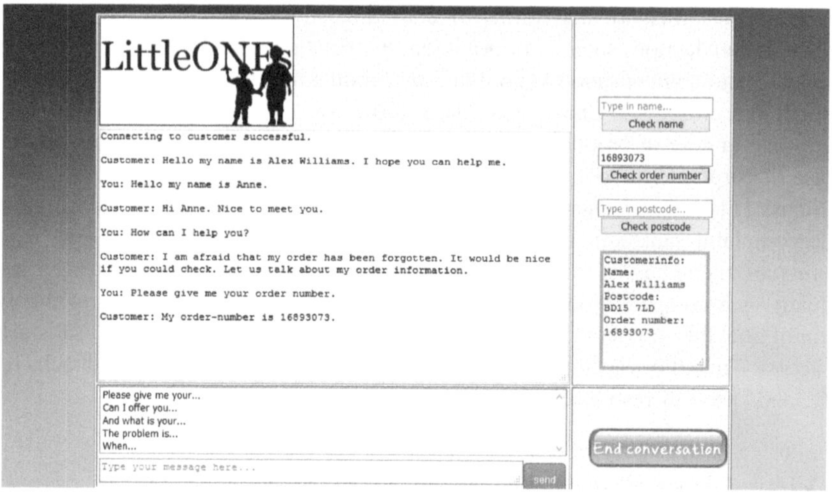

Fig. 1. Chat interface of CuCoMaG

The game includes three different scenarios. The scenarios differ based on the type of customer used, especially in terms of (a) conversation style based on the model of Rahim and Bonoma [12], who differentiated between five different styles of handling interpersonal conflicts, and (b) the problem situation of the customer based on the findings of a study conducted by Cho et al. [1], who investigated current sources and causes of online complaints, and thus (c) in the level of difficulty. Each scenario consists of five conversational phases following the typical structure of a complaint conversation according to Stauss and Seidel [9]: (1) greeting phase, (2) aggression-reduction phase, (3) conflict-settlement phase, (4) problem-solution phase, and (5) conclusive phase.

The first scenario serves as an introductory level including a tutorial. The customer in this scenario can be classified as an *integrating* customer, who is open to reach a solution acceptable for both parties and exhibits problem-solving behavior. The customer's problem in this scenario is the third most common cause of non-public online customer complaints [1]: delivery problems. The aim of this scenario is to help the player becoming acquainted with the user interface and experience the basic milestones of the complaint conversation.

In the second scenario, the level of difficulty increases. The customer is emotional about the problem and must be calmed down. According to the classification of Rahim and Bonoma [12], this customer is considered a *compromising* customer. The customer's problem is the most common problem within non-public online complaints [1]: he has, among other things, problems with the customer service. This also makes the customer a *follow-up complainant*, as it is the second time that he has contacted the customer service about the same problem [9]. The goal of the scenario is to pass through all five phases of a complaint process successfully.

The third scenario is the one with the highest level of difficulty. The customer in this scenario can be classified as a *dominating* customer [12] and a grouser [9].This type of customer tries to force a solution that is optimal for them and is looking for a continuation of the conflict, while showing little or no understanding for the other side. The customer has problems with the business terms and conditions, which is the second most common problem with non-public online complaints according to Cho et al. [1]. The costumer is not reasonable and reacts abusive. The player's best result may be not responding to the customer's provocations and eventually ending the conversation. This is called *active farewell* [9]. The goal of this scenario is to deal with extreme situations and to prove the player's ability to deal with provocations and difficult customers.

Each scenario has three possible outcomes: (1) The player reaches a predefined end state of the conversation, (2) the player leaves the conversation, (3) the player does not reply for a certain amount of time and fails to react to repeated requests of the customer to answer so the customer terminates the conversation and leaves the chat.

To increase the learning effect of this virtual role play, it is followed by a group reflection phase based on an automated analysis of player performances. Reflection, and group reflection in particular, is a successful tool to improve learning processes [13]. A tool designed for supporting the group reflection phase visualizes the analysis of data generated from the individual player's behaviors in a dashboard design. It is assumed that the separation into the actual role-playing game (immersive phase) and the group reflection session (reflective phase) supports the learning process [6, 7]. It is important to note that the group reflection phase has not been part of our study.

3.2 Implementation

The conversational logic of the customer chatbot has been implemented using the *Artificial Intelligence Markup language* (AIML). AIML is an XML-based solution for intelligent chatbots [14]. The flow of the dialog was first specified in UML activity diagrams and later transcribed into AIML scripts using the *GaitoBot*[1] AIML editor. The limited capabilities and the passive nature of AIML required several creative workarounds: (1) improve the appropriateness of the chatbot's responses to player input by preprocessing and using sentence openers, (2) use external triggers to enable the bot to become active when needed, (3) use atomic patterns [15] to reduce possible text inputs to their semantic content in order to create maximally efficient scripts, and (4) use variables to control the flow of the conversation and to enable the chatbot to "remember" past in- and outputs despite the simple stimulus response structure of the AIML scripts.

The logic and interface of the game client have been designed as a web-based application using common web technologies such as HTML, CSS, and JavaScript to ensure easy access and platform independency. The backend of the game has been implemented as a multi-agent blackboard system and consists of twelve program modules (agents) that are running independently from each other. The information exchange between the agents and the client is established by the use of an implementation of the TupleSpace concept called *SQLSpaces* [16]. According to the blackboard paradigm, the client and all agents only communicate with the central blackboard (and not one-to-one), writing and reading tuples in order to exchange information. As a result, agents can

[1] www.gaitobot.de.

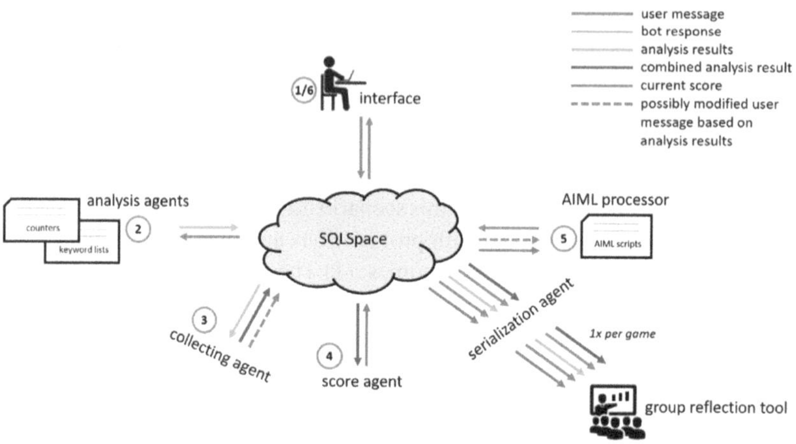

Fig. 2. Architecture and message flow of the multi-agent system

easily be added, amended, or replaced if necessary, which characterizes this loosely coupled and adaptive system. All agents are implemented in Java.

The overall process is displayed in Fig. 2. The *user interface* sends each user message to the tuple space where it is processed in parallel by several *analysis agents*. Each of them is responsible for one certain aspect of input analysis. Their main task is to check the input against predefined lists of keywords, expressions, or phrases (e.g. to find inappropriate, rude, aggressive or especially polite behavior), or to measure certain quantitative aspects, such as the number of inputs until a scenario has been completed or the time needed to send an input. The *collecting agent* collects the results of the single agents and merges them. The results of the analysis influence the answering behavior of the chatbot as well as the player's individual score, which is calculated by the *score agent*. If the collecting agent finds something that requires an immediate reaction of the chatbot (e.g. aggressive or rude behavior), it modifies the user messages by replacing it by a keyword that triggers an appropriate reaction of the chatbot. Based on the combination of the selected sentence opener, the free text input, and the analysis results, the chatbot (*AIML processor*) creates the customer's response to the user message. SQLSpaces enables the logging of the whole conversation and all important game data, which is needed to provide the replays and statistics embedded in the group reflection tool. The *serialization agent* is responsible for this task.

4 Evaluation

Our goal for the evaluation was to investigate if the developed scenarios and the chatbots qualify for a real training situation. In a mixed-method study, qualitative and quantitative methods have been used to gain insights regarding the playability and perception of the chatbots.

4.1 Experimental Design

Population. 20 participants (average 26.05, SD = 7.99, 15 females, 5 males) participated in the study. 80% of the participants had a university-entrance diploma, 5% a vocational diploma, and 15% already had a university degree. 4 out of 20 participants indicated that they have experience in customer complaint management. The participants were recruited from the University of Duisburg-Essen campus, as well as through announcements and social media.

Procedure and Data Collection. After the briefing, the participants were asked to fill in a descriptive questionnaire. They were introduced to the game and started playing the first scenario, which was design to allow the participants to familiarize with the user interface. After completing it, they played either the second or the third scenario. The distribution was randomized. Every participant received a checklist presenting some basic rules in regard to complaint handling based on the complaint management checklist from Stauss and Seidel [17]. The gaming session was followed by answering several post-experiment questionnaires to collect the experiences and perceptions during the gaming session. Afterwards, a short interview gave the participants the opportunity to describe their experience with the game in their own words before the debriefing commenced. The whole experiment took roughly one hour per participant.

4.2 Goals and Hypotheses

Our main goal for this study was to investigate whether the developed scenarios are perceived as realistic and can be used in real training situations. In addition, we wanted to examine if the developed chatbots behave as desired and whether their conversation style is influencing the users' perception of the chatbots. We assumed that people with prior knowledge in customer complaint management would perform better than people without prior knowledge. To answer these questions and examine the validity of our assumptions, three main hypotheses were established:

1. Participants who play the second scenario ("compromising") achieve different results in the *game experience questionnaire* (GEQ) dimensions *tension*, *negative affect*, and *challenge* than participants who play the third scenario ("dominating").
2. Participants who play the second scenario ("compromising") achieve different results in the Holtgraves questionnaire dimensions *comfortable*, *thoughtful*, *polite*, *responsive*, and *engaging* than participants who play the third scenario ("dominating").
3. Participants with prior experience/knowledge in complaint management achieve better results than participants without prior experience/knowledge.

4.3 Method of Analysis

Subjective Measures. The questionnaire was composed of four different parts. The first part included the collection of demographic data and prior experience in complaint management. For the assessment of game experience, the GEQ [18] was used in the second part. It covers the seven dimensions of game experience*: immersion, tension,* *competence, flow, positive affect, negative affect*, and *challenge*. A total of 42 items have been rated on a five-point scale. In the third part, the playability and perceived usefulness of the scenarios were measured with the questionnaire developed in the context of the evaluation of the game ENACT (hereinafter referred to as the *Edu-TechRPG questionnaire)*. Because CuCoMaG is a text-based role-playing game without avatars, only nine of the initial thirteen items were used. The items have been rated on a five-point scale. To measure the perception of the chatbot, a questionnaire concerning the human-like qualities of the chatbots was used (developed by Holtgraves, Ross, Weywadt and Lin [19]). The conversation with the chatbot was to be rated with seven bipolar adjective pairs. Each pair has been rated on a nine point scale with the positive adjective corresponding to the value nine and the negative to the value one. To gain qualitative data from the participants, the following questions were asked in a short qualitative interview: (1) How did you experience the conversation with the chatbot? (2) How did you act during the dialog? (3) How did you behave when problems occurred during the ongoing conversation?

Objective Measures. To complement the results from the questionnaires and the interview, the dialog scripts were evaluated in regard to the answer quality of the chatbot. The answers were assigned to one of three categories: *constructive*, *comprehensible,* and *nonsensical*. The categorization relied on human coding based on a clear operational classification inspired by Shawar and Atwell [20]. For each scenario, we determined the mean number for each category. In addition, the frequency of uses for each sentence opener was counted to estimate which were used frequently, rarely, or not at all. With regard to hypothesis 3, the success in the game is operationalized in two different ways. First, the relative score is determined by dividing the total score as calculated by the internal scoring system of the game by the number of text inputs. Rude, aggressive, or inappropriate behavior as well as long pauses reduce the score while polite behavior and fast response times increase it. The second indicator is the number of inputs because it is assumed that a rapid completion of the scenarios indicates an effective complaint management. The result from the two scenarios a participant completed has been added up to an overall value.

4.4 Results

GEQ. In order to assess the overall game experience, the arithmetic mean of the values from all participants are considered. As can be seen in Table 1, all dimensions with the exception of *negative affect* are above average, with the dimensions *flow*, *positive affect*, and *immersion* achieving the highest values. In order to provide a more differentiated view on the different scenarios, the mean values of the two data sets (second scenario and third scenario) are compared by applying a t-test. Levene's test only becomes significant for the dimension *tension* ($p = -0.37$), so we used the corrected values for this, whereas variance homogeneity can be assumed in the other cases. Overall, only the difference regarding the dimension *negative affect* is significant according to the t-test ($t(18) = -3.10$, $p = .006$).

Table 1. Results of the GEQ (0 to 4 scale)

	M (scenario 1 + 2)	M (scenario 1 + 3)	M (total)	SD	Min	Max
Immersion	3.18	2.97	3.08	0.74	1.50	4.17
Tension	1.85	2.45	2.15	0.88	1.00	3.83
Competence	3.22	2.62	2.92	0.92	1.00	4.50
Flow	3.35	3.08	3.22	0.64	1.83	4.50
Positive affect	3.43	3.10	3.27	0.81	1.17	4.33
Negative affect	1.45	2.35	1.90	0.78	1.00	3.67
Challenge	2.75	2.78	2.77	0.48	1.83	3.67

EduTechRPG Questionnaire. The arithmetic mean values for all items of the EduTechRPG questionnaire are above average, while the items "The scenarios deal about real-life situations" (M = 4.30 of 5), "The information given are useful and clear" (4.15 of 5), "The agents are behaving differently in each scenario" (4.10 of 5), and "I found it easier to negotiate with some agents than others" (4.00 of 5) achieve the highest values (Table 2). 85% of the participants stated that they would be willing to play the game again with different scenarios and characters. All participants who declared that they would not play the game again had played the third scenario ("dominating").

Table 2. Results of the EduTechRPG questionnaire (1 to 5 score)

	M	SD
The conversation with the agents is realistic	3.35	1.18
The user interface is intuitive and good-looking	3.50	0.83
The information given are useful and clear	4.15	0.67
The scenarios deal about real-life situations	4.30	0.66
The agents are behaving differently in each scenario	4.10	0.72
I found it easier to negotiate with some agents than others	4.00	0.65
I am motivated to negotiate even with the toughest agent	3.85	1.14
I find the overall experience with the CoCoMaG game positive	3.90	1.07
Would you play this game again with different scenarios and characters?	85% Yes 15% No	–

Perception of the Chatbots. The results regarding the perception of the chatbots of scenarios 1 and 2 show that they are perceived as especially *responsive* (M = 6.50), *comfortable* (M = 6.20 of 9), *polite* (M = 6.20 of 9), and *skilled* (M = 6.10 of 9). The mean values of the items *human* (M = 5.90 of 9), *thoughtful* (M = 5.90 of 9), and *engaging* (M = 5.70 of 9) are above average, too. In comparison, the chatbots of the scenarios 1 and 3 reach a value slightly above average on the item *skilled* (M = 5.10 of 9), whereas the values of the items *engaging* (M = 3.90 of 9), *responsive* (M = 3.80 of 9), *thoughtful* (M = 3.70 of 9), and polite are far below average. Again, a t-test was done in order to compare the mean values of the two groups. Since Levene's test does not show any significant results, variance homogeneity can be assumed. The t-est shows significant differences for the items *thoughtful* ($t(18) = 3.75$, $p = .001$), *polite* ($t(18) = 3.95$, $p = .001$), *responsive* ($t(18) = 4.26$, $p < .001$), and *engaging* ($t(18) = 2.22$, $p = .039$).

Evaluation of Chat Protocols. Concerning the answer quality derived from the analysis of the chat protocols, the results show that the number of *constructive* bot responses is the highest for all scenarios. The number of *comprehensible* bot responses is lower than the number of *constructive* bot responses but higher than *nonsensical* bot responses (Table 3). The biggest number of the *comprehensible* (but not *constructive*) bot responses are default outputs, which were implemented for each sentence opener in case no input match could be found for the free text part of a chat message. These default outputs are supposed to show the players that the chatbot did not fully understand the message while still being aware of the context, and to encourage them to rephrase the message. The smallest part of the three answer categories in each scenario form the *nonsensical* answers. This category includes answers that either did not fit the player's input or were semantically correct but did not make sense in the context of the scenario.

Table 3. Mean values of the answer categories in the three different scenarios

	Scenario 1	Scenario 2	Scenario 3
M (constructive)	9.60 (SD = 4.39)	17.50 (SD = 4.74)	16.10 (SD = 6.26)
M (comprehensible)	3.65 (SD = 4.28)	5.40 (SD = 5.82)	5.70 (SD = 5.42)
M (nonsensical)	0.85 (SD = 0.99)	1.90 (SD = 2.03)	0.40 (SD = 0.52)

Differences in Success Depending on Prior Experience. For both indicators of the variable *success in game* (relative score and number of inputs) a t-test for independent samples was conducted. The two test groups are "participants with prior experience in complaint management" ($n = 4$) and "participants without prior experience in complaint management" ($n = 16$). The t-tests do not show significant results.

Frequency of Sentence Openers. Sentence openers that could be used to obtain information from the customers were the ones used most frequently. Those included "Tell me …" ($M = 3.50$) or "Please describe…" ($M = 3.90$). The sentence opener "I am sorry…" was the one used most frequently both in the third scenario ($M = 4.80$) as well as overall in the game ($M = 3.75$). Sentence openers that were not or barely used are "I cannot do that…" ($M = 0.00$) and "What do you think about…" ($M = 0.05$). Overall, the frequency of all sentence opener increases from the first to the second scenario that was played.

Qualitative Interviews. The results of the qualitative interviews on conversation perception vary greatly. Five participants stated that they attribute a *high degree of difficulty* to the scenarios. All of them played the third scenario and had no experience in complaint management. Three other participants found the scenarios *pleasant* and *uncomplicated*. Seven participants found the use of the sentence openers to be *inhibitory* and *restrictive*. All participants described their own behavior in the chat conversations as *polite*, while ten of them stated that they behaved in a *problem-oriented* or *solution-oriented* manner. The problem-solving approaches of the participants are distinguished by four main approaches: Ten participants stated that they had rephrased their input in case a chatbot did not understand or did not provide meaningful answers. Eight participants tried to phrase their input with other sentence openers. Five participants reported having phrased completely new messages, and four that they were trying to repeat the same message. Some participants reported several of these solutions.

4.5 Discussion

Hypothesis 1 could be partially confirmed. There were significant differences in the GEQ dimension *negative affect* but not in the dimensions *tension* and *challenge* between the participants that completed the second or third scenario. The lack of significant results could be caused by methodical conditions like the small number of participants or the experimental design, as the participants were asked to evaluate the perception of both played scenarios combined.

Hypothesis 2 could be partially confirmed as well. Participants who played the second scenario showed significant differences in the dimensions *thoughtful*, *polite*, *responsive,* and *engaging*. This result supports the successful character design of the chatbots. As predicted, there were no significant differences in the dimensions of *human* and *skilled*, which suggests that there is only a difference in the chatbots' conversation style but not in the quality of their implementation. The dimension *comfortable* was not significant between the scenarios. This could also be caused by methodical conditions.

Hypothesis 3 could not be confirmed. We expected to find differences in the performance between participants with and without prior experience in complaint management, but statistical tests were not possible because of the small sample size ($n = 4$).

In general, the results of the GEQ and the EduTechRPG questionnaire indicate that the scenarios are perceived as realistic and that the game experience is quite positive. Especially good results have been achieved in the items "The scenarios deal about real-life situations", "The information given are useful and clear", "The agents are behaving differently in each scenario", and "I found it easier to negotiate with some agents than others" of the EduTechRPG questionnaire, which could be the result of the sophisticated design based on psychologically supported models underlying the developed scenarios [1, 8, 10, 11]. Only 15% of the participants stated that they would not want to play the game again with other characters and scenarios. All of these participants played the third scenario, which had significantly higher values in *negative affect*.

The participants' response behavior is consistent with the results of the chat feedback. All of the participants reported having been polite, which corresponds to the results of the analysis agents. Rephrasing was most commonly used as a solution to comprehension problems, which may have been supported by the tailored default responses of the bots.

The high frequencies of the sentence openers for the collection of information can be explained by their very variable possibilities of supplementation. The frequent use of the sentence opener "I am sorry" is not surprising, since apologies are phrases that are almost always suitable as a reaction and are very clearly associated with polite behavior [10]. Some of the participants claimed that they had problems expressing themselves and creating sentences based on the predefined sentence openers. This feedback should be used to improve and expand the offered set of sentence openers in order to support the players and provide more and better opportunities to express themselves. One other important result of the evaluation is that the dialog scripts have potential for improvement and that they need to be expanded, e.g., by covering more synonyms and unexpected inputs.

A major limitation of this preliminary study is the sample size (especially for participants with experience in customer complaint management), which may be the reason, why hypotheses 1 and 2 could only be partially confirmed and hypothesis 3 could not be statistically tested. The experiment needs to be repeated with a considerably larger sample in order to allow for generalization.

5 Conclusion and Future Work

Although there are a number of educational games and simulations addressing the training of specific social skills, no approach exists explicitly targeting the training of customer complaint management strategies. In this paper, we have presented a novel and innovative approach towards providing a 2D role-playing environment for the training of customer complaint management in the form of an educational game that adequately fits and supports the training of complaint conversations. There is no existing approach explicitly targeting the training of customer complaint management strategies. Our system environment can be naturally extended with new customer cases representing challenges that focus on a specific subset of skills each and thus allows for organizing the learning process as a sequence of cases. The evaluation of the game showed on the one hand that the idea and approach of the game in general were assessed positively and most of the participants considered it worthwhile to play the game several times. On the other hand, the evaluation revealed problems, especially with the application of the predefined sentence openers, which will be adapted to further improve the game flow.

Although the hypotheses have been only partially confirmed, it could be validated that the discussion style of the chatbots is influencing the players' perception of the dialog partner and the game experience, which underlines the successful design of the chatbots. Due to the small number of participants, a generalization cannot be made, but the results are promising and should be expanded in larger studies after a revision and extension of the prototype. More scenarios could be added to increase the variety and to offer more levels of difficulty. To evaluate the chatbot in its intended field of application, it would be reasonable to test the training scenarios directly in companies that might use this kind of training software for the professional training of their employees.

References

1. Cho, Y., Im, I., Hiltz, R., Fjermestad, J.: An analysis of online customer complaints: implications for web complaint management. In: Proceedings of the 35th Annual Hawaii International Conference on System Sciences, pp. 2308–2317. IEEE (2002)

2. Liljander, V., Strandvik, T.: Emotions in service satsifaction. Int. J. Serv. Ind. Manag. **8**(2), 148–169 (1997)
3. Heung, V.C.S., Lam, T.: Customer complaint behaviour towards hotel restaurant services. Int. J. Contem. Hospitality Manag. **15**(5), 283–289 (2003)
4. Dell'Aquila, E., Marocco, D., Ponticorvo, M., Di Ferdinando, A., Schembri, M., Miglino, O.: Educational Games for Soft-Skills Training in Digital Environments. Springer, Switzerland (2017)
5. Knode, S., Knode, J.-D.: Using a simulation program to teach leadership. In: Proceedings of the 2011 ASCUE Summer Conference, pp. 86–92 (2011)
6. Emmerich, K., Neuwald, K., Othlinghaus, J., Ziebarth, S., Hoppe, H.U.: Training conflict management in a collaborative virtual environment. In: Herskovic, V., Hoppe, H.Ulrich, Jansen, M., Ziegler, J. (eds.) CRIWG 2012. LNCS, vol. 7493, pp. 17–32. Springer, Heidelberg (2012). https://doi.org/10.1007/978-3-642-33284-5_2
7. Ziebarth, S., Kizina, A., Hoppe, H.U., Dini, L.: A serious game for training patient-centered medical interviews. In: 14th International Conference on Advanced Learning Technologies, pp. 213–217. IEEE (2014)
8. Fornell, C., Wernerfelt, B.: A model for customer complaint management. Mark. Sci. **7**(3), 287–298 (1988)
9. Stauss, B., Seidel, W.: Beschwerdemanagement: Unzufriedene Kunden als profitable Zielgruppe. Carl Hanser Verlag, Munich (2014)
10. Chase, R.B., Dasu, S.: Want to perfect your company's service? use behavioral science. Harvard Bus. Rev. **79**, 78–84 (2001)
11. Stauss, B.: The dimensions of complaint satisfaction: process and outcome complaint satisfaction versus cold fact and warm act complaint satisfaction. Managing Serv. Qual. Int. J. **12**(3), 173–183 (2002)
12. Rahim, A., Bonoma, T.V.: Managing organizational conflict: a model for diagnosis and intervention. Psychol. Rep. **44**(3), 1323–1344 (1979)
13. Jonassen, D., Mayes, T., McAleese, R.: A manifesto for a constructivist approach to uses of technology in higher education. In: Duffy, T.M., Lowyck, J., Jonassen, D.H., Welsh, T.M. (eds.) Designing Environments for Constructive Learning, pp. 231–247. Springer, Heidelberg (1993). https://doi.org/10.1007/978-3-642-78069-1_12
14. Wallace, R.: The elements if AIML Style. ALICE AI Foundation (2004)
15. Ghose, S., Barua, J.J.: Toward the implementation of a topic specific dialogue based natural language chatbot as an undergraduate advisor. In: 2013 International Conference on Informatics, Electronics & Vision (ICIEV), pp. 1–5. IEEE (2013)
16. Weinbrenner, S., Giemza, A., Hoppe, H.U.: Engineering heterogenous distributed learning environments using TupleSpaces as an architectural platform. In: Proceedings of the 7th IEEE International Conference on Advanced Learning Technologies (ICALT 2007), pp. 434–436. IEEE (2007)
17. Stauss B., Seidel, W.: Complaint management. In: Introduction to Service Engineering, pp. 414–432. Wiley, New Jersey (2010)
18. Ijsselsteijn, W.A., De Kort, Y.A.W., Poels, K.: The game experience questionnaire. Technische Universität Eindhoven (2013)
19. Holtgraves, T.M., Ross, S.J., Weywadt, C.R., Lin, H.T.: Perceiving artificial social agents. Comput. Hum. Behav. **23**(5), 2163–2174 (2007)
20. Shawar, B.A., Atwell, E.: Chatbots: are they really useful? LDV Forum **22**(1), 29–49 (2007)

Modelling Learners' Behaviour: A Novel Approach Using GARCH with Multimodal Data

Kshitij Sharma(✉), Zacharoula Papamitsiou, and Michail N. Giannakos

Department of Computer Science, Norwegian University of Science and Technology, Trondheim, Norway
{kshitij.sharma,zacharoula.papamitsiou,michalig}@ntnu.no

Abstract. Most of the contemporary approaches in learner behaviour modelling either quantize continuous data into discrete states/events (e.g., HMM), or assume that the patterns in the data are distributed homogeneously in time (e.g., auto-regression). This paper proposes a novel approach that overcomes the above mentioned issues and models learner behaviour using Generalized Auto-Regressive Conditional Heteroskedasticity (GARCH). GARCH uses continuous time-series data, without the need for information quantization, and it considers the heterogeneity of event distribution in the time-series. A study was conducted to demonstrate how GARCH can be configured in an adaptive assessment setting. Specifically, GARCH was applied on six different constructs from eye-tracking and electroencephalogram (EEG) data, and compared with existing methods of modelling time-series data, such as Markov Models and models having auto-regressive components. The comparison shows that the models having a GARCH component outperform other models for most of the students, for all the variables considered. The results are encouraging towards building accurate learner behaviour models, adequate to drive the design and development of adaptive feedback tools (e.g., an early alert system), but further investigation is required.

Keywords: Adaptive assessment · Multi-modal learning analytics · MMLA · GARCH · User modelling

1 Introduction

Learner modelling can be defined as the process of information extraction from different data sources and its compilation into profile representations of learners' behaviour, knowledge mastery (on a specific domain or topic), affective states, cognitive and meta-cognitive skills [36]. Essentially, learner models are *estimations* of learners' current states, based on the available observational data from their activity and behaviour within a learning environment.

A big body of relevant literature focuses on modelling learner knowledge [18,19,44]. However, it is incomplete to model student's knowledge alone, without considering other behavioural or affective aspects [19]. For example, if the

M. Scheffel et al. (Eds.): EC-TEL 2019, LNCS 11722, pp. 450–465, 2019.
https://doi.org/10.1007/978-3-030-29736-7_34

student is fundamentally unmotivated (e.g., not paying attention), or experiencing a stressful situation, or even not taking the learning seriously in general, then it is likely that in terms of knowledge, unwanted results might raise. Disengaged and unmotivated students experience much lower learning gains (cf. [8]).

Therefore, modelling learner behaviour is not only necessary and important, but it is also challenging, because the behavioural constructs - when are not coming from the potentially biased questionnaires [25] - are not easy to capture, and usually are coded using proxies from physiological data. For example, attention – a behavioural construct closely related to learning gains – is often measured using eye-tracking as a proxy [29]. Similarly, cognitive load – typically measured using EEG data – needs to be efficiently managed to maintain engagement [42].

Most of the contemporary approaches in learner behaviour modelling either quantize continuous data into discrete states/events (e.g., HMM), or assume that the patterns in the data are distributed homogeneously in time (e.g., autoregression). Quantizing the data into states/events is sensitive to information loss due to discretization and quantization-error. Moreover, the temporal pattern distribution might be heterogeneous in some cases.

To overcomes these limitations, this paper adapts a method from finance and enterprise risk assessment, namely Generalized Auto-Regressive Conditional Heteroskedasticity (GARCH) [1,23,31,35]. GARCH has been used with time-series data for forecasting purposes, such as stock prices and rates [24,46], and models the financial time-series data to detect the clusters of prices or losses in a short time-span. Once the temporal clusters are detected, the model can be used to forecast a "value-at-risk" that should be avoided (ideally) by the enterprises.

This paper applies GARCH with learners' physiological time-series data to model their behaviour, and make suggestions about how the models can be further utilized to provide proactive feedback to learners. Ultimately, this paper aims to detect the "risk" of unwanted behavioural patterns occurring close to each other in time (clusters in time) and to forecast any possible behavioural "value-at-risk" to inform the design a proactive feedback tool.

2 Different Approaches in Learner Behaviour Time-Series Modelling

Among the most popular methods used to model time-series data are Hidden Markov Models (HMM) or Markov Chains (MC), Sequential Analysis (SA), Statistical Discourse Analysis (SDA) and Recurrence Analysis (RA) or Recurrent Quantification Approach (RQA). This section presents a brief overview of how those techniques have been used to model time-series data in different learning settings in the fields of Learning Analytics and Technology Enhanced Learning.

Hidden Markov Models (HMM) or Markov Chains (MC): HMMs and/or MCs have been used to predict students' performance [9,49], to understand attention and engagement patterns [4,5], to optimise the delivery of upcoming question (in adaptive setting) [50] and to give feedback [30]. For example, to predict the grades in coding exercises, HMM was used to model the code snippets [9]. Moreover, the correctness of students' responses was modelled using MC to understand students' memorisation behaviour [49] and to optimise the sequence of the questions to be asked next [50]. Yet, HMMs with students' motion clusters have been used to understand students' reasoning patterns [4], whereas, when used with multimodal data (speech, posture, gaze) HMMs detected students' engagement with the content [5].

Sequential Analysis (SA): SA has been commonly used to understand student behaviour in collaborative knowledge construction communities using their discussions in terms of reasoning [41], or key collaborative moments [34], and to differentiate "opinion-giving" and "transitioning between the questions, answers and theories" [13]. SA has been also used to detect the effect of self-regulatory feedback on students' behaviour and the changes in behaviour when feedback was provided [56]. The method was also employed to model the log data from students' interactions with a digital book, to understand the interactions and improve the system and the content, accordingly [56]. Moreover, SA has been used to understand the relation between diverse behavioural patterns and later to predict the correctness of an answer and performance [14].

Statistical Discourse Analysis (SDA): SDA has been used mostly with dialogues in online and/or collocated collaborative settings to examine the effect of cognitive [16] and socio-metacognitive [15] cues on the new information/ explanations provided in knowledge forums, and to study the key moments during collaboration [17]. SDA has been also used to predict cognitive [52] and learning [38] outcomes in online discussion forums, and to model relation between the improvable quality of ideas and the community's level of interest in sharing and discussing them [32]. Furthermore, SDA has been used to understand the relation between "opinion-giving" and "questions", "answers" and "theorising" dialogues during collaborative knowledge construction process [12].

Recurrence Analysis (RA) or Recurrent Quantification Approach (RQA): RA (RQA) has been used in online learning conditions to model students' discourse for predicting their performance [2], and for automatic essay assessment [3]. In collaborative learning settings, a bivariate version of RA, i.e., cross-recurrence analysis (CRA), has been used to detect misunderstandings [6] and mutual regulation among peers [20]. CRA has been also used to understand the relation between expertise and performance of pair-programmers [53,54] and predict group satisfaction and performance in project-based learning setting [47].

3 Methodology

3.1 The Proposed Modelling Method

In this study, the GARCH method is suggested and evaluated for learner behaviour modelling, using multimodal physiological data. GARCH models are similar to AutoRegressive Moving Average (ARMA) models but they are applied to the variance of the data instead of being applied to the mean. GARCH processes $X(t)_{t\in\mathbb{Z}}$ take the general form

$$X_t = \sigma_t Z_t, t \in \mathbb{Z} \tag{1}$$

where σ_t, the conditional deviance (so-called volatility in finance), is a function of the history up to time $t-1$ represented by H_{t-1} and $(Z_t)_{t\in\mathbb{Z}}$ a strict white noise process with mean zero and variance one. We assume that Z_t is independent of H_{t-1}. Mathematically, σ_t is H_{t-1} measurable, where H_{t-1} is a filtration generated by $(X_s)_{s\leq t-1}$, and therefore

$$X_t|H_{t-1} = \sigma_t^2 \tag{2}$$

The series (X_t) follows a $GARCH(p,q)$ process if for all t

$$\sigma_t^2 = \alpha_0 + \sum_{j=1}^{p} \alpha_j X_{t-j}^2 + \sum_{k=1}^{q} \eta_k \sigma_{t-j}^2, \alpha_j, \eta_k > 0 \tag{3}$$

The condition on the parameters, $\alpha_j = 1 \dots p$ and, $\eta_k = 1 \dots q$ for the GARCH equations to define a covariance stationary process with finite variance is that

$$\sum_{j=1}^{p} \alpha_j + \sum_{k=1}^{q} \eta_k < 1 \tag{4}$$

The intuition behind Eq. (3) is that, first, opposite to AutoRegressive Moving Average (ARMA) models, which are models for the conditional mean, the GARCH is a model for the conditional standard deviation. By "conditional" we mean "given the history up to time t", that is given H_{t-1}. Second, the model shows that more persistence is built into the variability. In other words, GARCH models the variance at time t in the time-series as the linear combination of the history of variances up to time $t-1$. For more details see [51]. The coefficients $\alpha_0 \dots \alpha_p$ and $\eta_1 \dots \eta_p$ can be estimated by maximizing a likelihood function. The most popular GARCH model is $GARCH(1,1)$, that is, $p = q = 1$ in (3) meaning that the current action variability is explained by the latest action and the latest action number only (lag time of one). This model often suffices to explain the variability clustering of measurements of the students and is useful to predict student performance. Prediction is done by using any standard machine learning algorithm on the estimated coefficients $\hat{\alpha}$ and $\hat{\eta}$. For example, one can use Support Vector Machines (SVM) with the estimated coefficients to predict students' performance.

If there is some evidence of a serial correlation at small lags (using a Ljung-Box test, [33]), one can use a hybrid ARMA-GARCH process in which

$$\begin{aligned} X_t &= \mu_t + \epsilon_t \\ \epsilon_t &= \sigma_t Z_t \end{aligned} \tag{5}$$

where μ_t follows an ARMA process specification, σ_t follows a GARCH specification (3), and (Z_t) is $(0,1)$ strict white noise. μ_t and σ_t are respectively the conditional mean and standard deviation of X_t given history up to time $t-1$; they satisfy

$$\begin{aligned} E(H_t|H_{t-1}) &= \mu_t \\ H_t|H_{t-1} &= \sigma_t^2 \end{aligned} \tag{6}$$

An ARMA process combines the Auto-regressive and the moving average features. More precisely, $X(t)_{t\in\mathbb{Z}}$ follows an ARMA process if for every t the random variable X_t satisfies

$$X_t = \sum_{j=1}^{p} \phi_j X_{t-j} + \sum_{i=1}^{q} \theta_i \epsilon_{t-i} + \epsilon_t \tag{7}$$

In order for these equations to define a covariance stationary causal process (depending only on the past innovations) the coefficients ϕ_j and θ_i must obey certain conditions.

3.2 The Evaluation Study – Participants and Experimental Procedure

An adaptive self-assessment activity was offered at a European University for the Web Technologies course (related to front-end development), using an online adaptive assessment platform [43]. Thirty-two (32) undergraduate students (15 females [46.9%] and 17 males [53.1%], aged 18–21 years-old [M = 19.24, SD = 0.831]) were enrolled and undertook the self-assessment activity individually, at an especially equipped and organized University lab, for approximately 45 min each student, on October 2018. Prior to their participation, all students signed an informed consent form that explained to them the data collection and the adaptive assessment procedure, and was giving the right to researchers to use the data collected for research purposes. After granting consent, the participants had to wear an EEG cap and be connected to the eye-tracker. Then, the actual adaptive self-assessment activity started and the students had to answer to the tasks delivered to them one-by-one (for the details see [42]). The participation to the procedure was optional. The adaptive self-assessment activity was offered to facilitate the students' self-preparation before the final exams, to help them track their progress, and self-reflect. The scores on the self-assessment had no participation to the students' final grade in the course.

3.3 Data Collection

During the study, the following sensor data were collected from students:

Eye-Tracking: Students' gaze was recorded using the Tobii X3-120 eye-tracking device at 120 Hz sampling rate and using 5-point calibration. The device is non-invasive and mounted at the bottom of the screen. The screen resolution was 1920 × 1080 and the participants were 50–70 cm away from screen. Tobii's default algorithm was used to identify fixations and saccades (for details please see [40]).

EEG: EEG data was recorded with a standard 20 channel actiCAP layout using international 10–20 system, as shown in Fig. 3. We built upon previous studies that utilize EEG headsets in detecting cognitive engagement during learning [26,27]. The raw EEG data was recorded at a 500 Hz using a head-mounted portable EEG cap by ENOBIO (ENOBIO 20 EEG device), 2 channels were used for EOG correction, 1 channel for reference and 3 Channel Accelerometer sampling rate at 100 Hz. We also applied a filter to remove noise from blinks.

3.4 Features

For EEG based features, first we compute the features for each individual channel and then we compute the average for all the 17 channels. Table 1 summarises the features used in this paper.

Table 1. The measurements used and their definitions.

Measurement	Definition	Data source
Attention	Average fixation duration [22,29]	Eye-tracking
Anticipation	Saccade velocity skewness [11,48]	Eye-tracking
Fatigue	Blink rate per second [39,55]	Eye-tracking
Cognitive load	Decreasing alpha and increasing theta band power [7,21]	EEG
Mental workload	Alpha magnitude [10,45]	EEG
Load on memory	theta band power [28,37]	EEG

3.5 Comparing Methods

For the purpose of comparing the different time-series modelling approaches, the following models were chosen. The main reason for selecting these modelling approaches is the one common theme, i.e., all the models estimate the current value of a time-series as a function of its past values and they all apply to continuous data streams. For the Markov Chains, the data was simply quantized into ten levels using the 10th to 90th percentiles with equal step size.

Markov Chains: Markov Models estimate the probability of a state at time t as a condition probability of the joint probability distribution of previous state.

$$\begin{aligned} &Pr(X_n = x_n|X_{n-1} = x_{n-1}, X_{n-2} = x_{n-2}, ..., X_1 = x_1) \\ &= Pr(X_n = x_n|X_{n-1} = x_{n-1}, X_{n-2} = x_{n-2}, ..., X_{n-m} = x_{n-m}) \end{aligned} \quad (8)$$

AR: Auto-regressive models compute the value of a time-series at time t as a weighted sum of the previous values of the time-series. An AR model is given by

$$X_t = \alpha_0 + \sum_{i=1}^{p} \alpha_i X_{t-i} + \epsilon_t \tag{9}$$

ARMA: ARMA models are combinations of the auto-regressive model and a moving average feature. The mathematical formulation of an ARMA model is given in (7).

GARCH: see Sect. 3.1 for the details on the GARCH models.

ARMA-GARCH: it is a combination of ARMA and GARCH models, the mathematical details are given in the Sect. 3.1. The basic in tuition behind ARMA-GARCH models is the fact that the predictive information might include both the average and the variance of the time-series.

Comparison Metric: Adjusted R-Squared Adj. R^2 is the metric selected to compare the models presented in the previous subsection. The Adj. R^2 is derived from the normal R-squared as:

$$Adj.R^2 = 1 - (1 - R^2)\left[\frac{n-1}{n-(k+1)}\right] \tag{10}$$

where, n is the sample size; and k is the number of parameters estimated using a given time-series modelling approach. Since the four modelling approaches compared in this paper have different number of parameters estimated by them, the adjusted R^2 value is most suitable for this purpose as it normalises for the number of estimated parameters. In the case of two models having equal adjusted R^2 values, the model with less parameters will be chosen.

4 Results

4.1 Parameter Estimation for Individual Students

For parameter estimation for each of the methods, this section reports the distribution of participants with different number of lags for the four methods. The Figs. 1, 2, 3 and 4 show the number of parameters estimated for all students, using different physiological measures (attention, cognitive load, fatigue and load on memory). The number of parameters estimated for each individual model was based on AIC. In each of the Figs. (1, 2, 3 and 4) the x-axis has the different lags in the models and the y-axis has the number of students for which those lags yielded the best model.

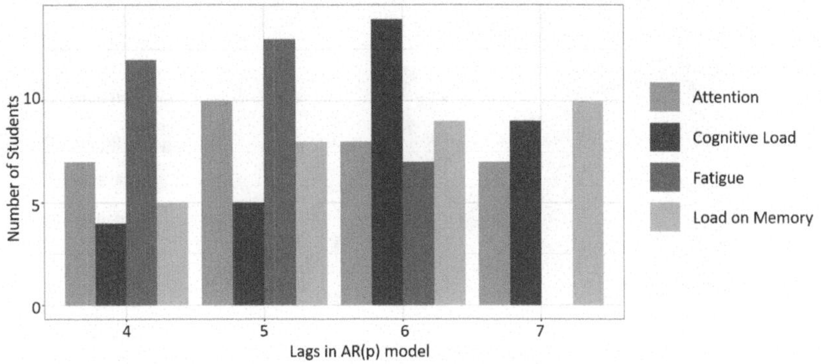

Fig. 1. Distribution of students based on the number of lags computed for the AR models.

Fitting each model incurs estimation of different number of lags for each component; the number of lags determine the number of parameters to be estimated which is the sum of all the lags in the model. An AR model has only one lag to be estimated, which is shown on the x-axis in the Fig. 1. An ARMA model has two lags one for the AR component and the other for the size of the moving window, they are shown as a pair on the x-axis in the Fig. 2.

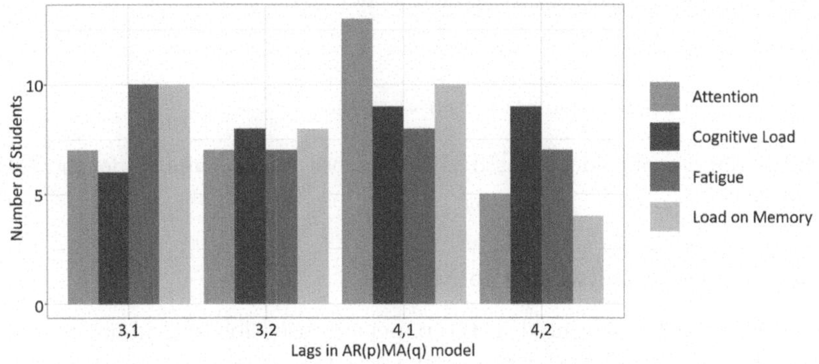

Fig. 2. Distribution of students based on the number of lags computed for the ARMA models.

A GARCH model also has two lags one for the history and the other for the variance, they are shown as a pair on the x-axis in Fig. 3. Finally, the ARMA-GARCH models have 4 lags according to the AR, MA and GARCH components, they are shown as a 4-tupple on the x-axis in Fig. 4.

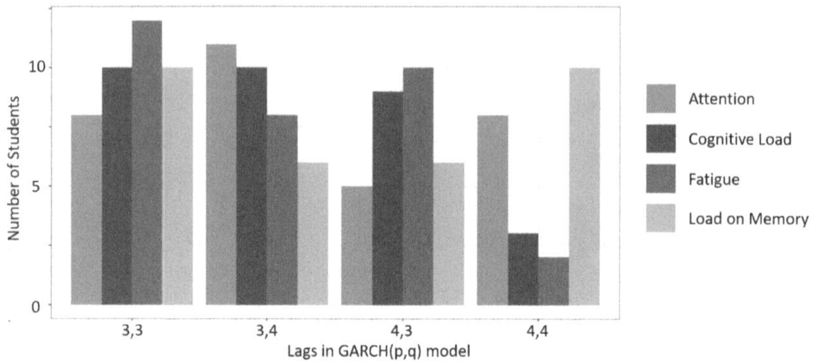

Fig. 3. Distribution of students based on the number of lags computed for the GARCH models.

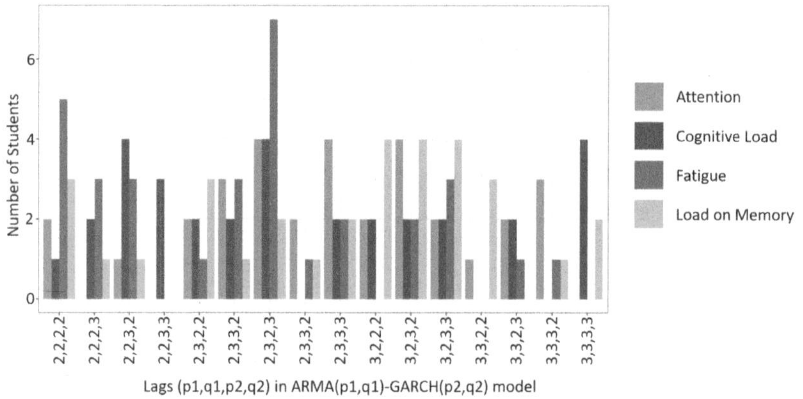

Fig. 4. Distribution of students based on the number of lags computed for the ARMA-GARCH models.

4.2 Comparison Between the Models

Since all the models presented in the paper are used for individual time-series, this section first demonstrates the model selection process for one student and then generalizes the process to the whole sample.

Let us consider the case of one student for explaining the results. Table 2 shows the five models using the six measurements for one example student. For each measurement five models were fitted on the temporal data and the adjusted R^2 values were compared. The highest adjusted R^2 values are shown in bold in Table 2. One can observe that for the example student, the highest adj. R^2 values are from the model having a GARCH component. For Load on memory, attention, fatigue and anticipation the best model is the GARCH model, while for cognitive load and mental workload the best model is the ARMA-GARCH. In case of a tie, the model with the less number of estimated parameters will be selected as the best model.

Table 2. Example comparison for one student based on adjusted R^2 values.

Model	EEG measurements			Eye-tracking measurements		
	Cognitive load	Load on memory	Mental workload	Attention	Fatigue	Anticipation
Markov chain	0.59	0.44	0.46	0.54	0.62	0.42
AR	0.49	0.50	0.52	0.42	0.48	0.45
ARMA	0.53	0.54	0.52	0.47	0.54	0.46
GARCH	0.78	**0.75**	0.70	**0.77**	**0.77**	**0.74**
ARMA GARCH	**0.79**	0.74	**0.76**	0.74	0.72	0.72

As shown in the example with one student's data in Table 2, the same procedure was carried out in the case of all students. Table 3 shows the percentage of the total sample for which a specific model yielded the highest adj. R^2 value for a given measurement. The results show that for all the measurements the best model has one GARCH component, for a vast majority of the students. Five out of the six measurements considered are best modelled using GARCH approach, while the "load on memory" is best modelled using the ARMA-GARCH approach. This shows that the variance and heterogeneity in the time-series are important when it comes to modelling the physiological measurements.

Table 3. Comparison of the different methods based on adjusted R^2 values

Model	EEG measurements			Eye-tracking measurements		
	Cognitive load	Load on memory	Mental workload	Attention	Fatigue	Anticipation
Markov chain	0	0	0	0	0	0
AR	0	0	0	0	0	0
ARMA	0	0	0	0	0	0
GARCH	**86.66**	16.66	**90.00**	**96.66**	**93.33**	**90.00**
ARMA GARCH	13.33	**83.33**	10.00	3.33	6.66	10.00

5 Discussion

5.1 Implication of the Results from the Example Study

This paper presents a novel approach to model learner behaviour using time-series data. The approach exploits the GARCH method to overcome two basic issues with the common time-series modelling methods used in the fields of Learning Analytics and Technology Enhanced Learning. The two limitations of those methods are the dependency on information quantization and the assumption of homogeneous pattern distribution in time. The results from an evaluation study show that the proposed method, i.e., GARCH, outperforms the other methods used in this study, such as Markov Chains and Auto-Regressive models.

The fact that for all students the best model turned out to contain a GARCH component (Table 3), indicates a strong presence of temporal clusters in the behavioural data. The results also indicate that there is a higher amount of heterogeneity in the physiological learner data (than there is homogeneity), since the variance for most of the measurements was better explained by GARCH than by ARMA-GARCH. Combining these two findings, it becomes apparent that there exist recurrent, unevenly distributed in time behavioural patterns.

The above findings prompt for a shift in the design and delivery of proactive feedback, taking advantage of the information-rich GARCH models. To provide feedback based on forecasting a continuous measurement (all methods listed in Sect. 3.3 can be used for forecasting), one must take the uneven distribution of recurrent patterns into account. The GARCH (or, ARMA-GARCH) models can be used to estimate a "value-at-risk" in the near future and then, this value can be used to determine the nature and type of feedback given to the learner.

5.2 Methodological and Theoretical Differences

In this sub-section, the inherent differences between GARCH and the other methods presented in related work (Sect. 2), are discussed here to point-out how those differences affect the models' estimation.

In specific, HMMs or MCs were designed to analyse time-series of *discrete* events/states. In contemporary implementations of HMMs or MCs, data need to be quantized into several a-priori categories, so as to fit the requirements of HMM/MC. The quantization process "cancels-out" a lot of variance in the data, which might be important for modelling purposes (lower adj. R^2 in Table 2). In HMM/MC, many different continuous values are quantized as one labelled category, which also means that their difference in no longer modelled, probably resulting in poor estimations. GARCH on other hand, requires no such prior quantization, since this is an approach designed for continuous time-series data.

Furthermore, Sequential Analysis typically uses a transition matrix up to 3–4 discrete state changes, and the features are the contingency counts of the different states co-occurring in the time-series. This is similar to N-grams methods (or a Markov Chain of order "N"), where "N" needs to be decided a-priori and does not take any longer (than N) history into account; on the other hand, the length of history using GARCH can be empirically decided using a likelihood estimation and there is no need for the contingency counts, as explained in Sect. 3.1.

Regarding SDA (Statistical Discourse Analysis), there are two primary differences between this method and GARCH. First, SDA requires the semantics of the discourse to be included in the analysis, while GARCH models have no such requirements. Second, in mathematical terms, SDA models the "creativity" at time "t" as a linear combination of "creativity" at time "t − 1" and a certain number of check points (similar to a Covariate Analysis); thus, SDA models the conditional mean of the time-series (similar to AR models). On the contrary, GARCH models the conditional variance in the time-series with an option of being used with a model that uses the conditional mean (as shown in Table 3).

Finally, Recurrence Analysis of time-series data, is one class of algorithms, in which there is no aggregation, no deep semantics are required and the historical information is considered in the analysis. However, Recurrence Analysis requires the time-series to be stationary in nature, i.e., there is an inherent assumption of homogeneity of the event/value distribution, similar to the Auto-Regressive models. GARCH improves on this aspect of RA by modelling the heterogeneity of event/value distribution in the time-series. One could model the heterogeneity in the time-series using GARCH and then apply the AR models on the residuals of the time-series to conduct an RA. Thus, GARCH also provides a complementary way of analysing time-series data.

5.3 Conclusions and Future Work

The results from the empirical evaluation show that GARCH models outperform the commonly used methods (e.g, Markov and AR). However, the limitation to the method proposed is that GARCH assumes that all "positive" and "negative" (recommended or avoidable behaviour) behaviour have the same effects on the model, which might or might not be true. To verify the nature of the behaviour (recommended or avoidable) one has to estimate the "value-at-risk". There are extensions of the method to incorporate such information in GARCH models, which will be the source of future endeavours for this research.

Further, GARCH can also be used with the data-fusion for conducting multimodal analysis. This can be accomplished using a "multivariate" version of the present method, which is another direction led by the current results, since we know that all the measurements considered are better modelled using GARCH.

Finally, another direction for future exploration is to add the contextual information from learner and the learning settings, and to the model parameters in order to provide not only proactive, but also a personalized feedback to the learners.

Acknowledgements. This work is supported from the Norwegian Research Council under the projects FUTURE LEARNING (number: 255129/H20) and Xdesign (290994/F20). This work was carried out during the tenure of an ERCIM "Alain Bensoussan" Fellowship Programme.

References

1. Alexander, C.: Market Models: A Guide to Financial Data Analysis. Wiley, Hoboken (2001)
2. Allen, L.K., Perret, C., Likens, A., McNamara, D.S.: What'd you say again?: Recurrence quantification analysis as a method for analyzing the dynamics of discourse in a reading strategy tutor. In: Proceedings of the Seventh International Learning Analytics and Knowledge Conference, pp. 373–382. ACM (2017)
3. Allen, L.K., Likens, A.D., McNamara, D.S.: Recurrence quantification analysis: a technique for the dynamical analysis of student writing. In: The Thirtieth International Flairs Conference (2017)

4. Andrade, A.: Understanding student learning trajectories using multimodal learning analytics within an embodied-interaction learning environment. In: Proceedings of the Seventh International Learning Analytics and Knowledge Conference, pp. 70–79. ACM (2017)
5. Andrade, A., Delandshere, G., Danish, J.A.: Using multimodal learning analytics to model student behavior: a systematic analysis of epistemological framing. J. Learn. Anal. **3**(2), 282–306 (2016)
6. Andrist, S., Ruis, A., Shaffer, D.W.: A network analytic approach to gaze coordination during a collaborative task. Comput. Hum. Behav. **89**, 339–348 (2018)
7. Antonenko, P., Paas, F., Grabner, R., Van Gog, T.: Using electroencephalography to measure cognitive load. Educ. Psychol. Rev. **22**(4), 425–438 (2010)
8. Baker, R.S.: Modeling and understanding students' off-task behavior in intelligent tutoring systems. In: Proceedings of the SIGCHI Conference on Human Factors in Computing Systems, CHI 2007, pp. 1059–1068. ACM, New York (2007)
9. Blikstein, P., Worsley, M., Piech, C., Sahami, M., Cooper, S., Koller, D.: Programming pluralism: using learning analytics to detect patterns in the learning of computer programming. J. Learn. Sci. **23**(4), 561–599 (2014)
10. Borghini, G., Astolfi, L., Vecchiato, G., Mattia, D., Babiloni, F.: Measuring neurophysiological signals in aircraft pilots and car drivers for the assessment of mental workload, fatigue and drowsiness. Neurosci. Biobehav. Rev. **44**, 58–75 (2014)
11. Bronstein, A., Kennard, C.: Predictive eye saccades are different from visually triggered saccades. Vis. Res. **27**(4), 517–520 (1987)
12. Chen, B., Resendes, M.: Uncovering what matters: analyzing transitional relations among contribution types in knowledge-building discourse. In: Proceedings of the Fourth International Conference on Learning Analytics And Knowledge, pp. 226–230. ACM (2014)
13. Chen, B., Resendes, M., Chai, C.S., Hong, H.Y.: Two tales of time: uncovering the significance of sequential patterns among contribution types in knowledge-building discourse. Interact. Learn. Environ. **25**(2), 162–175 (2017)
14. Chen, S.Y., Yeh, C.C.: The effects of cognitive styles on the use of hints in academic English: a learning analytics approach. J. Educ. Technol. Soc. **20**(2), 251–264 (2017)
15. Chiu, M.M., Fujita, N.: Statistical discourse analysis: a method for modeling online discussion processes. J. Learn. Anal. **1**(3), 61–83 (2014)
16. Chiu, M.M., Fujita, N.: Statistical discourse analysis of online discussions: Informal cognition, social metacognition and knowledge creation. In: Proceedings of the Fourth International Conference on Learning Analytics And Knowledge, pp. 217–225. ACM (2014)
17. Chiu, M.M., Lehmann-Willenbrock, N.: Statistical discourse analysis: modeling sequences of individual actions during group interactions across time. Group Dyn.: Theory Res. Pract. **20**(3), 242 (2016)
18. Chrysafiadi, K., Virvou, M.: Review: student modeling approaches: a literature review for the last decade. Expert Syst. Appl. **40**(11), 4715–4729 (2013)
19. Desmarais, M.C., Baker, R.S.: A review of recent advances in learner and skill modeling in intelligent learning environments. User Model. User-Adap. Interact. **22**(1–2), 9–38 (2012)
20. Dindar, M., Alikhani, I., Malmberg, J., Järvelä, S., Seppänen, T.: Examining shared monitoring in collaborative learning: a case of a recurrence quantification analysis approach. Comput. Hum. Behav. (2019)

21. Doppelmayr, M., Klimesch, W., Schwaiger, J., Auinger, P., Winkler, T.: Theta synchronization in the human eeg and episodic retrieval. Neurosci. Lett. **257**(1), 41–44 (1998)
22. Engbert, R., Nuthmann, A., Richter, E.M., Kliegl, R.: SWIFT: a dynamical model of saccade generation during reading. Psychol. Rev. **112**(4), 777 (2005)
23. Engle, R.: GARCH 101: The use of ARCH/GARCH models in applied econometrics. J. Econ. Perspect. **15**(4), 157–168 (2001)
24. Franses, P.H., Van Dijk, D.: Forecasting stock market volatility using (non-linear) garch models. J. Forecast. **15**(3), 229–235 (1996)
25. Gollwitzer, P.M., Sheeran, P., Michalski, V., Seifert, A.E.: When intentions go public: does social reality widen the intention-behavior gap? Psychol. Sci. **20**(5), 612–618 (2009)
26. Hassib, M., Khamis, M., Schneegass, S., Shirazi, A.S., Alt, F.: Investigating user needs for bio-sensing and affective wearables. In: Proceedings of the 2016 CHI Conference Extended Abstracts on Human Factors in Computing Systems, pp. 1415–1422. ACM (2016)
27. Huang, J., et al.: FOCUS: enhancing children's engagement in reading by using contextual BCI training sessions. In: Proceedings of the 32nd Annual ACM Conference on Human Factors in Computing Systems, pp. 1905–1908. ACM (2014)
28. Jensen, O., Tesche, C.D.: Frontal theta activity in humans increases with memory load in a working memory task. Eur. J. Neurosci. **15**(8), 1395–1399 (2002)
29. Just, M.A., Carpenter, P.A.: A theory of reading: from eye fixations to comprehension. Psychol. Rev. **87**(4), 329 (1980)
30. Kennedy, G., Ioannou, I., Zhou, Y., Bailey, J., O'Leary, S.: Mining interactions in immersive learning environments for real-time student feedback. Aust. J. Educ. Technol. **29**(2) (2013)
31. Kerkhof, J., Melenberg, B., Schumacher, H.: Model risk and capital reserves. J. Bank. Financ. **34**(1), 267–279 (2010)
32. Lee, A.V.Y., Tan, S.C.: Temporal analytics with discourse analysis: tracing ideas and impact on communal discourse. In: Proceedings of the Seventh International Learning Analytics and Knowledge Conference, pp. 120–127. ACM (2017)
33. Ljung, G.M., Box, G.E.: On a measure of lack of fit in time series models. Biometrika **65**(2), 297–303 (1978)
34. Malmberg, J., Järvelä, S., Järvenoja, H.: Capturing temporal and sequential patterns of self-, co-, and socially shared regulation in the context of collaborative learning. Contemp. Educ. Psychol. **49**, 160–174 (2017)
35. Matei, M.: Assessing volatility forecasting models: why garch models take the lead. Rom. J. Econ. Forecast. **12**(4), 42–65 (2009)
36. McCalla, G.I.: The central importance of student modelling to intelligent tutoring. In: Costa, E. (ed.) New Directions for Intelligent Tutoring Systems, pp. 107–131. Springer, Berlin (1992). https://doi.org/10.1007/978-3-642-77681-6_8
37. Missonnier, P., et al.: Frontal theta event-related synchronization: comparison of directed attention and working memory load effects. J. Neural Transm. **113**(10), 1477–1486 (2006)
38. Molenaar, I., Chiu, M.M.: Effects of sequences of socially regulated learning on group performance. In: Proceedings of the Fifth International Conference on Learning Analytics and Knowledge, pp. 236–240. ACM (2015)
39. Morris, T., Miller, J.C.: Electrooculographic and performance indices of fatigue during simulated flight. Biol. Psychol. **42**(3), 343–360 (1996)

40. Olsen, A.: The Tobii I-VT fixation filter: algorithm description [white paper]. Tobii Technology (2012). http://www.tobiipro.com/siteassets/tobiipro/learn-and-support/analyze/how-do-we-classify-eye-movements/tobii-pro-i-vtfixation-filter.pdf
41. Ozturk, H.T., Deryakulu, D., Ozcinar, H., Atal, D.: Advancing learning analytics in online learning environments through the method of sequential analysis. In: 2014 International Conference on Multimedia Computing and Systems (ICMCS), pp. 512–516. IEEE (2014)
42. Papamitsiou, Z., Pappas, I.O., Sharma, K., Giannakos, M.N.: Utilizing multimodal data through an fsQCA approach to explain engagement in adaptive learning. IEEE Trans. Learn. Technol. (2019)
43. Papamitsiou, Z., Economides, A.: Towards the alignment of computer-based assessment outcome with learning goals: the LAERS architecture. In: 2013 IEEE Conference on e-Learning, e-Management and e-Services, IC3e 2013 (2013)
44. Pelánek, R.: Bayesian knowledge tracing, logistic models, and beyond: an overview of learner modeling techniques. User Model. User-Adap. Interact. **27**(3), 313–350 (2017)
45. Ryu, K., Myung, R.: Evaluation of mental workload with a combined measure based on physiological indices during a dual task of tracking and mental arithmetic. Int. J. Industr. Ergon. **35**(11), 991–1009 (2005)
46. Sadorsky, P.: Modeling and forecasting petroleum futures volatility. Energy Econ. **28**(4), 467–488 (2006)
47. Sharma, K., Pappas, I., Papavlasopoulou, S., Giannakos, M.: Towards automatic and pervasive physiological sensing of collaborative learning (2019)
48. Smit, A., Van Gisbergen, J.: A short-latency transition in saccade dynamics during square-wave tracking and its significance for the differentiation of visually-guided and predictive saccades. Exp. Brain Res. **76**(1), 64–74 (1989)
49. Taraghi, B., Ebner, M., Saranti, A., Schön, M.: On using Markov chain to evidence the learning structures and difficulty levels of one digit multiplication. In: Proceedings of the Fourth International Conference on Learning Analytics And Knowledge, pp. 68–72. ACM (2014)
50. Taraghi, B., Saranti, A., Ebner, M., Schön, M.: Markov chain and classification of difficulty levels enhances the learning path in one digit multiplication. In: Zaphiris, P., Ioannou, A. (eds.) LCT 2014. LNCS, vol. 8523, pp. 322–333. Springer, Cham (2014). https://doi.org/10.1007/978-3-319-07482-5_31
51. Teräsvirta, T.: An introduction to univariate GARCH models. In: Mikosch, T., Kreiß, J.P., Davis, R., Andersen, T. (eds.) Handbook of Financial Time Series, pp. 17–42. Springer, Heidelberg (2009). https://doi.org/10.1007/978-3-540-71297-8_1
52. Thomas, M.J.: Learning within incoherent structures: the space of online discussion forums. J. Comput. Assist. Learn. **18**(3), 351–366 (2002)
53. Villamor, M., Rodrigo, M.: Characterizing collaboration based on prior knowledge: a pair program tracing and debugging eye-tracking experiment. In: 15th National Conference in Information Technology Education (2017)
54. Villamor, M., Rodrigo, M.M.T.: Characterizing collaboration in the pair program tracing and debugging eye-tracking experiment: a preliminary analysis. In: EDM (2017)

55. Wolkoff, P., Nøjgaard, J., Troiano, P., Piccoli, B.: Eye complaints in the office environment: precorneal tear film integrity influenced by eye blinking efficiency. Occup. Environ. Med. **62**(1), 4–12 (2005)
56. Yin, C., et al.: Learning behavioral pattern analysis based on students' logs in reading digital books. In: Proceedings of the 25th International Conference on Computers in Education, pp. 549–557 (2017)

A Learning Analytics Study of the Effect of Group Size on Social Dynamics and Performance in Online Collaborative Learning

Mohammed Saqr[1,2(✉)], Jalal Nouri[2], and Ilkka Jormanainen[1]

[1] University of Eastern Finland, Joensuu, Finland
{mohammed.saqr, ilkka.jormanainen}@uef.fi
[2] Stockholm University, Stockholm, Sweden
jalal@dsv.su.se

Abstract. Effective collaborative learning is rarely a spontaneous phenomenon. In fact, it requires that a set of conditions are met. Among these central conditions are group formation, size and interaction dynamics. While previous research has demonstrated that size might have detrimental effects on collaborative learning, few have examined how social dynamics develop depending on group size. This learning analytics paper reports on a study that asks: How is group size affecting social dynamics and performance of collaborating students? In contrast to previous research that was mainly qualitative and assessed a limited sample size, our study included 23,979 interactions from 20 courses, 114 groups and 974 students and the group size ranged from 7 to 15 in the context of online problem-based learning. To capture the social dynamics, we applied social network analysis for the study of how group size affects collaborative learning. In general, we conclude that larger groups are associated with decreased performance of individual students, poorer and less diverse social interactions. A high group size led to a less cohesive group, with less efficient communication and less information exchange among members. Large groups may facilitate isolation and inactivity of some students, which is contrary to what collaborative learning is about.

Keywords: Collaborative learning · Learning analytics · Group size · Social network analysis · Complexity · Interaction analysis · Problem based learning · Medical education

1 Introduction

Over the past decades, a large number of studies have demonstrated that collaboration can benefit learning from various theoretical and methodological perspectives. In fact, findings from over 1,200 research studies have consolidated and refined theories of collaborative learning [1]. Against this background, a strong consensus is asserting the higher achievement effects of collaborative learning on individual cognitive development as compared to individualistic learning and traditional instructional methods [2, 3]. Along with previous and ongoing research, collaborative learning has also

M. Scheffel et al. (Eds.): EC-TEL 2019, LNCS 11722, pp. 466–479, 2019.
https://doi.org/10.1007/978-3-030-29736-7_35

increasingly gained momentum in educational systems [1]. Since the foundation of the field of Computer supported collaborative learning (CSCL), a substantial body of research has also provided evidence on the positive effects of introducing technology into collaborative learning tasks. Several large meta-analyses indicate that participants who collaborate making use of information technology show greater increases in motivation, elaboration, dialogue and debate, higher-order thinking, self-regulation, meta- cognitive processes, and divergent thinking [4, 5].

However, effective collaboration is rarely a spontaneous phenomenon, and not always the result of putting students together for collaborative work, but rather the result of orchestration and scaffolding of productive interactions [6]. That is, successful collaborative learning requires that necessary conditions are met. As one of the goals of collaborative learning is to maximize the learning performance of all participating students, group composition and size become a central aspect [7].

2 Related Work

So far research has shed light on several factors that needs to be considered when forming collaborative groups, such as students learning achievement, engagement, and interpersonal relationships [7–9]. However, there is little quantitative research that have investigated how group size affect the nature of collaboration and the social dynamics in groups. Furthermore, most of the research conducted have investigated smaller groups, such as dyads and triples with relatively small sample size (comparing 8–12 groups of students) [10], or as in the study of Cen et al. (2016), groups of 3 to 6 students with an analytical focus on how group size affect performance [11]. Akyol et al. used the concept community of inquiry (CoI) to find out that there was more effective communication in an online course than in a blended learning course. Furthermore, their results indicate that group cohesion in an online course developed throughout the course. Students' use of inclusive pronouns was low at the beginning but increased towards the end of the course. The students in the online course indicated that the class size was too big for effective development of social presence, whereas students in the other blended learning setting group with approximately same size were pleased with the class size [12].

In a meta-study by Lou et al. (2001), it was concluded that small group size is a significant indicator towards individual's achievement when learning with computing technologies: the students learn better in small groups [13]. This finding is also verified in the context of problem-based learning (PBL) by Lohman and Finkelstein [14]. Their results show that small and medium sized PBL groups (3–6 students) rated the value of the small group discussions higher than those in larger groups [14]. Tu and McIsaac in turn, suggest that especially in real-time online collaboration settings the group size should be limited to three participants. Otherwise, a strategy providing equal turn-taking need to be applied to ensure equal opportunities for all participants. Obviously, this issue is not equally relevant in asynchronous communication, for example in discussion forums in a learning management system [15].

While indications have been put forward that larger group sizes might decrease participation in collaborative learning and for instance magnify the "free rider" effect (the most able members make most effort) and the "sucker effect" (the most able members expend less mental effort because of a perceived free rider situation)[16], few are the studies that in detail have investigated how social dynamics and social networks develop depending on group size. That is, that have scrutinized how the nature of intra-group collaboration changes with group size.

In this paper, we report a study that asks: How is group size affecting social dynamics, social networks, and performance of collaborating students? In contrast to previous research, in this learning analytics study, we examine group sizes of 7 to 15 students in the context of problem-based learning in online environments in medical education. The sample studied consist of 20 courses, 114 groups of students, and a total of 974 students. To capture the social dynamics and the social networks, we applied social network analysis, which we argue is a novel approach for the study of how group size affects collaborative learning.

2.1 Social Network Analysis

Social network analysis (SNA) is a group of analytical methods and tools that are used to examine the social structures. A social structure is a collection of entities that are networked through a relationship; examples include a group of people, employees in an organization, animals in a forest, or a group of websites etc. The entities are always referred to as actors, nodes or vertices and the relationships are always referred to as links or edges [17]. SNA methods enable the study of the interactions and the relationships among the members of the structure through an established set of visual and mathematical methods. SNA visualization is a powerful graphical method of conveying the complexity of the relations among participants in an intuitive and easy to interpret way [17–19]. The structural properties of the actors and the structure may be more accurately captured through SNA quantitate analysis. Quantitative analysis may be performed on the structure level by computing metrics that describe the properties of the structure, such as size, interactivity or connectedness; or on the individual level by calculating the actor importance or influence in the social structure or what is known as centrality. Since importance varies in different contexts, a group of centrality measures were developed that quantify different importance concepts. Examples include popularity (degree centrality), connectedness to powerful actors (Eigen centrality), or eccentricity (isolation) [18, 20–22].

SNA has been used to study interactivity of online collaborative and face-to-face learning. The most common topic was the mapping the interactivity among collaborators in online computer supported collaborative learning (CSCL) [23, 24]. Researchers were able to map the interactions among students and identify the active, the inactive and the isolated students [25]. The role of teachers or moderating tutors have also been examined and how their interactions might help or otherwise hinder collaboration. SNA has also been used to diagnose and improve gaps in collaborative learning by examining the structure of networks and creating an appropriate intervention [26]. Researchers have used SNA centrality measures to identify roles such as leaders, collaborators, and influential students in online forums. In the same vein, centrality measures have also been used as a proxy for students' online activity to predict performance using learning analytics methods [10, 27, 28]. SNA has been used to study semantic and epistemic networks, by examining the content of interactions and finding insights in how knowledge is constructed and exchanged among collaborators [29, 30].

Although the breadth of applications of SNA in collaborative learning are quite extensive, the small group dynamics have received little attention. The previous examples have studies diverse types of social structures however, limited in size. In other words, most of the research so far have examined whole course networks, or few groups in a course. The small group as a unit have also garnered a considerable attention in the realm of qualitative research. However, the dynamic complex and unique structure of small group have not received the due attention with a reasonable sample size. The small group as a unit could be considered as a complex adaptive system, in which independent participants interact, self-organize and contribute to a shared understanding of a common learning objectives [30–32]. We therefore, set our research to study the group dynamics using network analysis technique as a main method for studying interactions in collaborative learning, and complex systems as well. Our study offers a window into the dynamics of interactions in the group, how number of students affects it and how that affects enrolled students.

3 Methodology

3.1 The Context

Students in the University of Qassim study a problem based medical curriculum. The guiding philosophy of the curriculum is a constructivist collaborative small group teaching and learning. In each course, students are divided randomly into small groups and each group is assigned a weekly patient problem as a stimulant for discussions. Students are expected to follow the seven jump PBL approach where they start with clarifying the terms, identify the problem, brainstorm using their previous knowledge, and then formulate their learning objectives. Throughout the week, they share information online, discuss the learning issues, and by the end of the week they are supposed to reach a shared understanding of the assigned problem and the learning objectives. The PBL process is mostly online where each group discusses the assigned problem with the help of a tutor. The online discussions are based on Moodle learning management system fora. The fora are organized one thread per each weekly problem discussion, and each group is separate and can't see the other group work until the end of the week. The seven jump approach is detailed in references like [33].

3.2 Methods

Interactions of the PBL groups were extracted from Moodle learning management system using a custom script that extracted the time stamp of each post, the subject of the post, the author, the group ID, the course ID, and the content of the post, the replies to the post and the target of each interaction. Users' metadata were also extracted such as username, email, grade, course enrollment, and completion. Data were compiled and analyzed using R programming language version 3.52. The libraries Igraph and Centiserve were used to compute the centrality measures and network parameters [34–37].

Statistical analysis was also performed with R, correlations were calculated using spearman correlation coefficient since most of the parameters violated the normality assumption [37]. SNA visualization was done using Gephi version 9.2, using a force directed layout [18, 38]. The layout algorithm is a simulation of a physical system in which "Nodes repulse each other like charged particles, while edges attract their nodes, like springs. These forces create a movement that converges to a balanced state". The final visualization places each node according to relationships with other nodes, so well connected nodes will be central and isolated nodes will be peripheral [38].

SNA Analysis. Mathematical SNA analysis was performed to calculate two levels of parameters: a group level and individual students' level. Since each group was separate and users were not allowed to enroll in other group discussions, all the centrality and SNA parameters reported here were done per group basis. In other words, the 114 student groups were separately analyzed as individual networks, all then all results were combined.

Network Level Parameters. For each network, we calculated the following parameters: Group size (number of participants in the group); edge count (number of interactions in the group); and average distance (average shortest path among participants in the group), which corresponds to the average reachability of all nodes in the network and indicate the efficiency of the network to transfer information; network density (the number of interactions in the group as a ratio to the maximum possible), which reflects the relative interactivity, cohesion and inclusion of every group member in the interactions. Other cohesion parameters calculated were the cluster coefficient which measures the tendency of the group members to cluster together; reciprocity which measures how many of the interactions were reciprocated among the same users (replied to each other's post); efficiency which reflect the efficiency of the network to act as an information exchange medium and is calculated as the inverse path length among all nodes; we also calculated group cohesion which is the minimum number of nodes to be removed that makes the graph disconnected and as such inefficient. Centralization parameters were also calculated to reflect how interactions are dominated around a central participants who acts as a hub (a dominant actor). A score of 1 means that all interactions are targeting a single person and it decreases when the interactions are distributed among participants. We also calculated the average centralities of group members (indegree, outdegree, degree, betweenness, closeness centrality and Eigen centralities) [20–22, 39, 40]. A description of these terms will follow in the next section.

Individual Level Parameters. For each individual participant, we calculated the centrality measures most relevant to a collaborative learning context and commonly used for educational contexts. There are: the *indegree* (number of received interactions by a participant), which represent number of replies to the content posted by a student, and signifies that the user has posted a content that is relevant or worth to argue, add or compliment it; the *outdegree* (outdegree is the number of interactions posted by the student) to reflect activity and effort; *degree* is the sum of indegree and outdegree. We also calculated the *closeness centrality* which is a measure of how close is a participant to all other participants in the group and is calculated as the reciprocal average shortest path to all others. *Betweenness centrality* reflects how many times a person connected unconnected others (lied between them) and reflects the bridging role of a collaborator. *Eigen* and *page rank* centralities both reflect not just the number of connections but how strong their connections are and how the nodes a user connected to are important, a reflection of the worth of connections. *Efficiency* and *clustering* have been reflected upon above. While we have tried to give an account on all used indices and parameters, an elaborated discussion about these parameters is beyond the scope of this paper [20–22, 40]. Rich description of the concepts and their mathematical background is presented in other papers [20–22].

4 Results

The study included 20 courses, 974 students, 114 tutors. Forty-one students in all courses were assigned to groups but did not attend the course and their data were removed. The number of students per course ranged from 45 to 54, the mean number of interactions per course was 1,198.95 (range 420 to 3,134) totaling 23,979 interactions. Twelve courses had 5 groups, six courses had 7 groups and two courses had six groups with a total of 114 groups. The number of students per group ranged from 7 to 15 with 11 being the mode (the most frequent). Since the courses were organized into small groups and each group was separate, we report the properties of the groups in details in Table 1. The mean density of interactions was 0.42, a fairly high density indicating the high reactivity of most groups. The mean degree per course was 33.44 which is also relatively high, indicating that the groups were mostly active. The average mean distance was 1.57, which indicates that students were reasonably connected. The average Eigen centrality was 0.46, an indication of high connectedness. In summary, the general properties of the groups are of dense interactive groups with participation of most students. Of course, some groups were not active as others as shown in Fig. 1. Eight groups had a mean degree less than 4, and seven groups had a density of interactions below 0.1. A visual plot of all groups is shown in Fig. 1. A closer visualization of two groups presented in Fig. 2 shows an example of the difference between a small group and a large group. In Fig. 2, the larger group is almost divided into two almost isolated subgroups. An efficient group would have all members engaged in a mutual discussion, inclusive of all members and not divided.

4.1 Correlation with Grade

There was a statistically significant negative correlation between the size of the group and the performance of the group members ($r = 0.22$, $p < 0.001$). To have a deeper look into the group dynamics and how interactions influence participants, we investigate four groups of parameters worth studying in relation to group size, namely: group effort and productivity, group connectivity and cohesion, efficiency of interactions as well as centralization.

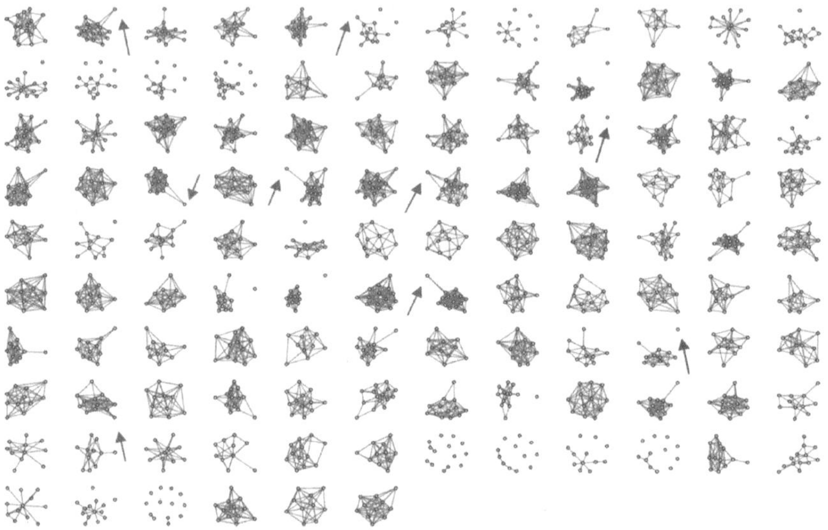

Fig. 1. A visualization of 114 groups' interactions plotted in graphs. The figure shows that small groups seem to be cohesive and dense, while large groups tend to have isolated students as pointed with the blue arrows. It also shows some isolated nodes, which represent course organizers who visited the groups to announce or comment (examples are pointed at with green arrows). (Color figure online)

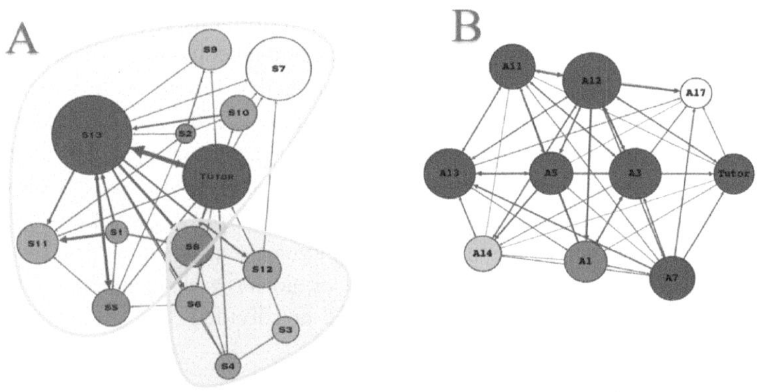

Fig. 2. A visualization of two groups, a large group (left) and small group (right): the figure presents two groups, Group "A" on the left, which is a large group of 14 students, where there are two interacting subgroups, a small of subgroup of five, and a larger subgroup of 9 students. The overall interactions in group A were low, density of interactions (density = 0.34), with less cohesive structure, and the collaborators were distanced by longer path (Average path = 2.1). Furthermore, the group A shows lower clustering (0.46) and lower efficiency of information exchange (efficiency = 0.69). On the right, group B shows with more interactions and cohesion (Density = 0.89, Average path = 1.1, Clustering 0.96, efficiency = 0.98). Legend: each circle represents a node, arrows represents direction of interactions, the size of the nodes correspond to number of interactions (degree), color represents closeness centrality. (Color figure online)

4.2 Group and Size Dynamics

Regarding group effort and interactivity, there was a positive correlation between the number of interactions and group size ($r = 0.225^*$, $p = 0.016$), however, using the mean degree and its variants (in and outdegree), which control for the group size showed that they were not significantly positively correlated ($r = 0.028$, $p < 0.764$), which means that the average number of interactions per a member is comparable in small and large groups. Groups with larger sizes did not motivate members to participate more than in small groups. Similarly, the mean reciprocity was not correlated with size of the group ($r = -0.032$, $p = 0.736$). As such, members of all groups would receive comparable number of replies. These findings indicate that larger groups did not result in more productive members or more replies. Regarding connectivity, expectedly, the larger was the group size, the more it was associated with higher levels of mean betweenness centralities ($r = 0.405$, $p < 0.001$), as more participants play the bridging role among group members.

With larger group members there was more chances of connecting and bridging the distant others. The mean closeness centrality was negatively and strongly correlated with group size ($r = -0.725$, $p < 0.001$). This is an indication of how large group size would facilitate the isolation of some students and may also create isolated subgroups as shown in Fig. 2. Furthermore, isolated students may go unnoticed by the moderators or rely on others who do the work. In the mean vein, the average distance was positively correlated with group size ($r = 0.268$, $p < 0.001$), confirming the closeness and reachability difficulties in larger groups. The mean Eigen centrality were also negatively correlated with group size ($r = -0.343$, $p < 0.001$). This is an interesting result, as one would expect the opposite, that is, with a larger group it would be easier to make connections to influential people.

Table 1. Descriptive statistics

Statistic	Minimum	Maximum	Mean	Std. Deviation
Number of students	7	15	8.54	1.89
Number of interactions	39	835	210.34	149.7
Network density	0.02	0.89	0.42	0.21
Mean distance	1.00	2.50	1.57	0.29
Mean degree	5.57	104.38	33.44	21.20
Mean betweenness centrality	0.00	16.38	5.07	3.04
Mean closeness centrality	0.01	0.11	0.06	0.02
Mean Eigen centrality	0.08	0.81	0.46	0.17

Regarding the cohesion parameters, we measured four parameters. Density of interactions was negatively correlated with the group size ($r = -0.294$, $p < 0.001$). This is an indication that an increasing group size negatively impacts the cohesion of the group. Efficiency – a measure of communicability – was also negatively correlated with group size ($r = -0.34$, $p < 0.001$), as well as vertex cohesion ($r = -0.236$, $p < 0.001$), and clustering coefficient ($r = -0.209$, $p < 0.001$), indicating that a larger group tends to be less cohesive, and members tend not to cluster together. These results confirm the previous ones that larger groups tend to have less reachability, therefore act as a good medium for isolated and inactive students, which is contrary to what collaborative learning is about. The last group of parameters that we examined, was the emergence of hubs or leader participants who would drive or motivate the interactions in larger groups. However, the results showed that group size is not correlated with the likelihood of having such leaders (Table 2).

Table 2. Correlation between group parameters and size

Node count	r	p
Edge count	.225	0.016
Reciprocity	−0.032	0.736
Mean degree	0.028	0.764
Mean in degree/outdegree	0.028	0.764
Mean distance	0.268	0.004
Mean betweenness centrality	0.405	<0.001
Mean closeness centrality	−0.725	<0.001
Mean Eigen centrality	−0.343	<0.001
Vertex cohesion	−0.236	0.012
Network Density	−0.294	0.001
Efficiency	−0.340	<0.001
Transitivity	−0.209	0.026
Hubs	0.091	0.337
Centralization indegree	−0.022	0.819
Centralization outdegree	0.041	0.662

4.3 Individuals Students' Level

On the individual students' level, there were some interesting results. Being in a small or larger group did not affect the average level of interactions (as measured by the quantity of indegree or outdegree centralities). Larger groups however had, as mentioned before, a longer path distance and less closeness centrality, which was manifested as a negative correlation coefficient between group size and student performance. That was also demonstrated through a positive correlation between eccentricity and performance. Students in larger groups tended to have fewer valuable connections to connected students (lower Eigen centrality and page rank). Also, it's worth noting that the efficiency (role in exchange of information) was negatively correlated with the group size. In summary, the results of individual students corroborate those of the groups; that larger groups tend to have negative influence on interacting students. Full details are shown in Table 3.

Table 3. Correlation of individual centrality measures with group size

Centrality measure	r	p
Indegree	−.003	0.931
Outdegree	−.016	0.608
Degree	−.010	0.755
Closeness	−.317	<0.001
Betweenness	.023	.480
Clustering	−.086	0.007
Eccentricity	.105	0.001
Efficiency	−.130	<0.001
Eigen c.	−.093	.004
Page rank	−0.233	<0.001

5 Discussion

Today collaborative learning is a quite common pedagogical method in higher education and we see that many educational institutions enact this method in online environments. However, from previous research we have learned that effective collaborative learning rarely is a spontaneous phenomenon and that several factors needs to be considered for achieving successful collaboration [6]. One such factor relates to group size. While previous research has demonstrated that larger group sizes might have detrimental effects on collaborative learning (for example [14, 15, 28]), few are the studies that in detail have examined how social dynamics develop depending on group size, especially when the group size is in the range of 7–15 students which is common in for instance medical education where students work in teams in problem-solving scenarios. Thus, in this learning analytics study, we used social network analysis to understand the effect of group size on performance and in particular on the social dynamics in the collaborative groups. The analysis conducted resulted in the following conclusions:

In general, we conclude that larger groups are negatively correlated with individual students' performance. While this result might be expected also in the light of the previous research [12–14], the social network analysis shed light on the "why" by describing how specific aspects of collaboration, and how the nature of the social dynamics, changes with increasing group size. Firstly, the findings demonstrated that there was a positive correlation between the number of interactions and group size, however, the mean degree and its variants (in and out degree) were not significant. This means that a group size increases the total number of interactions but does not motivate members to participate more or less than in small groups. In our study, the closeness centrality, the average distance, and the mean Eigen centrality measures rendered negative correlations with group size. Based on this, we conclude that students in larger groups have more difficulties to make connections to influential peers. Looking at these results from a theoretical perspective, one could make the interpretation that larger groups create less opportunities for students to work in their proximal development zones with more competent peers [41], as the distance to the competent peers is larger (captured by the average distance, closeness and Eigen centrality measures).

Furthermore, the findings also showed that density of interactions was negatively correlated with group size, an indication that an increasing group size, negatively impacts the cohesion of the group. Group efficiency and communicability were also negatively correlated with group size, as well as cohesion and clustering coefficient, indicating that a larger group tends to be less cohesive, and members tend not to socially cluster together. These findings are in line with the results by Akyol et al. [12], where it was concluded that development of social presence in a big group was more difficult in an online course than it was in a blended learning setting. Thus, we can conclude that a larger group does not lead to more interactions, but to a less cohesive group, with less efficient communication and information exchange among members. That is, as the group size increases it likely becomes more difficult to achieve the fundamental characteristics of productive collaborative learning, namely: "*a coordinated, synchronous activity that is the result of a continued attempt to construct and maintain a shared conception of a problem*" [42].

Generally speaking, this quantitative social network analysis of group size corroborates and extend Lohman & Finkelstein's who provided a student perspective on group size, showing that students in small and medium sized PBL groups (3–6 students) rated the value of the small group discussions higher than those in larger groups [14]. This study corroborates and extends Lohman & Finkelstein's in the sense that we quantitatively have shown that the nature of social dynamics in larger groups indeed are different from small group dynamics, and at the same time, we extend their work by providing detailed quantitative and visual descriptions for *how* social dynamics change as group size increases, using the lens of social network analysis. As far as we are aware, this is the first study that have used social network analysis to study group size effects on social dynamics in the context of collaborative learning, which is one of the novel contributions of this paper [14].

Overall, the results of this study encourage us to rethink the group sizes that are used in collaborative learning scenarios in education. Although it might be practical because of limited teacher resources and economy, larger groups seem to perform less well and we risk that students that need learning with more competent peers but don't have the conditions to do so, risk to underachieve and dropout, which has severe consequences for individuals, institutions and societies. For future work, we recommend the use of social network analysis to study how social dynamics are shaped in smaller groups than the ones focused on in this paper.

References

1. Johnson, D.W., Johnson, R.T.: An educational psychology success story: social interdependence theory and cooperative learning. Educ. Res. **38**, 365–379 (2009). https://doi.org/10.1037/pspa0000044
2. Johnson, D.W., Johnson, R.T.: The internal dynamics of cooperative learning groups. In: Slavin, R., Sharan, S., Kagan, S., Hertz-Lazarowitz, R., Webb, C., Schmuck, R. (eds.) Learning to Cooperate, Cooperating to Learn, pp. 103–124. Springer, Boston (1985). https://doi.org/10.1007/978-1-4899-3650-9_4

3. Slavin, R.E.: Research on cooperative learning and achievement: what we know, what we need to know. Contemp. Educ. Psychol. **21**, 43–69 (1996)
4. Tutty, J.I., Klein, J.D.: Computer-mediated instruction: a comparison of online and face-to-face collaboration. Educ. Technol. Res. Dev. **56**, 101–124 (2008)
5. Dillenbourg, P., Järvelä, S., Fischer, F.: The evolution of research on computer-supported collaborative learning. In: Balacheff, N., Ludvigsen, S., de Jong, T., Lazonder, A., Barnes, S. (eds.) Technology-Enhanced Learning, pp. 3–19. Springer, Dordrecht (2009). https://doi.org/10.1007/978-1-4020-9827-7_1
6. Dillenbourg, P., Schneider, D.: Mediating the mechanisms which make collaborative learning sometimes effective. Int. J. Educ. Telecommun. **1**, 131–146 (1995)
7. Lin, Y.-T., Huang, Y.-M., Cheng, S.-C.: An automatic group composition system for composing collaborative learning groups using enhanced particle swarm optimization. Comput. Educ. **55**, 1483–1493 (2010)
8. Wilkinson, I.A.G., Fung, I.Y.Y.: Small-group composition and peer effects. Int. J. Educ. Res. **37**, 425–447 (2002)
9. Meyer, D.: OptAssign—a web-based tool for assigning students to groups. Comput. Educ. **53**, 1104–1119 (2009)
10. Veerman, A., Veldhuis-Diermanse, E.: Collaborative learning through computer-mediated communication in academic education. In: Euro CSCL, pp. 625–632 (2001)
11. Cen, L., Ruta, D., Powell, L., Hirsch, B., Ng, J.: Quantitative approach to collaborative learning: performance prediction, individual assessment, and group composition. Int. J. Comput. Collab. Learn. **11**, 187–225 (2016)
12. Akyol, Z., Garrison, D.R., Ozden, M.Y.: Online and blended communities of inquiry: exploring the developmental and perceptional differences. Int. Rev. Res. Open Distrib. Learn. **10**, 65 (2009). https://doi.org/10.19173/irrodl.v10i6.765
13. Lou, Y., Abrami, P.C., D'Apollonia, S.: Small group and individual learning with technology: a meta-analysis. Rev. Educ. Res. **71**, 449–521 (2001). https://doi.org/10.3102/00346543071003449
14. Lohman, M.C., Finkelstein, M.: Designing groups in problem-based learning to promote problem-solving skill and self-directedness. Instr. Sci. **28**, 291–307 (2000). https://doi.org/10.1023/A:1003927228005
15. Tu, C.-H., McIsaac, M.: The relationship of social presence and interaction in online classes. Am. J. Distance Educ. **16**, 131–150 (2002). https://doi.org/10.1207/S15389286AJDE1603_2
16. Salomon, G., Globerson, T.: When teams do not function the way they ought to. Int. J. Educ. Res. **13**, 89–99 (1989)
17. Borgatti, S.P., Mahra, A., Brass, D.J., Labianca, G.: Network analysis in the social sciences. Science **323**, 892–895 (2009). (80), https://doi.org/10.1126/science.1165821
18. Le Grand, B., Heymann, S.: Visual analysis of complex networks for business intelligence with Gephi. In: 1st International Symposium on Visualisation and Business Intelligence, in conjunction with the 17th International Conference Information Visualisation. (2013)
19. Saqr, M., Fors, U., Tedre, M.: How the study of online collaborative learning can guide teachers and predict students' performance in a medical course. BMC Med. Educ. **18** (2018). https://doi.org/10.1186/s12909-018-1126-1
20. Freeman, L.C.: Centrality in social networks conceptual clarification. Soc. Netw. **1**, 215–239 (1978). https://doi.org/10.1016/0378-8733(78)90021-7
21. Lü, L., et al.: Vital nodes identification in complex networks. Phys. Rep. **650**, 1–63 (2016). https://doi.org/10.1016/j.physrep.2016.06.007
22. Liao, H., Mariani, M.S., Medo, M., Zhang, Y.C., Zhou, M.Y.: Ranking in evolving complex networks. Phys. Rep. **689**, 1–54 (2017). https://doi.org/10.1016/j.physrep.2017.05.001

23. Cela, K.L., Sicilia, M.Á., Sánchez, S.: Social network analysis in E-Learning environments: a preliminary systematic review. Educ. Psychol. Rev. **27**, 219–246 (2014). https://doi.org/10.1007/s10648-014-9276-0
24. Dado, M., Bodemer, D.: A review of methodological applications of social network analysis in computer-supported collaborative learning. Educ. Res. Rev. **22**, 159–180 (2017). https://doi.org/10.1016/j.edurev.2017.08.005
25. Rabbany, R., Elatia, S., Takaffoli, M., Zaïane, O.R.: Collaborative learning of students in online discussion forums: a social network analysis perspective. In: Peña-Ayala, A. (ed.) Educational Data Mining. SCI, vol. 524, pp. 441–466. Springer, Cham (2014). https://doi.org/10.1007/978-3-319-02738-8_16
26. Saqr, M., Fors, U., Tedre, M., Nouri, J.: How social network analysis can be used to monitor online collaborative learning and guide an informed intervention. PLoS One **13**, 1–22 (2018)
27. Kovanovic, V., Joksimovic, S., Gašević, D., Hatala, M.: What is the source of social capital? the association between social network position and social presence in communities of inquiry. In: Proceedings of the Workshop Graph-Based Educational Data Mining Conference (G-EDM 2014), vol. 1183, pp. 1–8 (2014)
28. Saqr, M., Fors, U., Nouri, J.: Using social network analysis to understand online Problem-Based Learning and predict performance. PLoS One. **13**, e0203590 (2018)
29. Shaffer, D.W., et al.: Epistemic network analysis: a prototype for 21st-century assessment of learning. Int. J. Learn. Media. **1**, 33–53 (2009). https://doi.org/10.1162/ijlm.2009.0013
30. Mennin, S.: Small-group problem-based learning as a complex adaptive system. Teach. Teach. Educ. **23**, 303–313 (2007). https://doi.org/10.1016/j.tate.2006.12.016
31. Cristancho, S., Field, E., Lingard, L.: What is the state of complexity science in medical education research? Med. Educ. **53**, 95–104 (2019). https://doi.org/10.1111/medu.13651
32. Decuyper, S., Dochy, F., Van den Bossche, P.: Grasping the dynamic complexity of team learning: an integrative model for effective team learning in organisations. Educ. Res. Rev. **5**, 111–133 (2010). https://doi.org/10.1016/j.edurev.2010.02.002
33. Morrison, J.: ABC of learning and teaching in medicine: evaluation. BMJ. **326**, 385–387 (2003). https://doi.org/10.1136/bmj.326.7385.385
34. Fruchterman, T.M.J., Reingold, E.M.: Graph drawing by force-directed placement. Softw. Pract. Exp. **21**, 1129–1164 (1991)
35. Csardi, G., Nepusz, T.: The igraph software package for complex network research. Int. J. Complex Syst. **1695**, 1–9 (2006)
36. Jalili, M., et al.: CentiServer: a comprehensive resource, web-based application and R package for centrality analysis. PLoS One **10**, e0143111 (2015). https://doi.org/10.1371/journal.pone.0143111
37. R Core Team: R: A Language and Environment for Statistical Computing (2018). https://www.r-project.org
38. Jacomy, M., Venturini, T., Heymann, S., Bastian, M.: ForceAtlas2, a continuous graph layout algorithm for handy network visualization designed for the Gephi software. PLoS One **9**, 1–12 (2014). https://doi.org/10.1371/journal.pone.0098679
39. Latora, V., Marchiori, M.: Efficient behavior of small-world networks, pp. 3–6 (2001). https://doi.org/10.1103/PhysRevLett.87.198701
40. Salter-Townshend, M., White, A., Gollini, I., Murphy, T.B.: Review of statistical network analysis: Models, algorithms, and software. Stat. Anal. Data Min. **5**, 243–264 (2012). https://doi.org/10.1002/sam.11146

41. Vygotsky, L.S.: Mind in Society: The Development of Higher Psychological Processes. Harvard University Press, Cambridge (1980)
42. Roschelle, J., Teasley, S.D.: The construction of shared knowledge in collaborative problem solving. In: O'Malley, C. (ed.) Computer Supported Collaborative Learning, pp. 69–97. Springer, Heidelberg (1995). https://doi.org/10.1007/978-3-642-85098-1_5

Design and Deployment of a Better Course Search Tool: Inferring Latent Keywords from Enrollment Networks

Matthew Dong[1], Run Yu[2], and Zachary A. Pardos[1](✉)

[1] University of California, Berkeley, CA 94720, USA
{mdong,zp}@berkeley.edu
[2] Wuhan University, Wuhan 430072, Hubei, China
run.yu@whu.edu.cn

Abstract. Liberal arts universities possess a vast catalog of courses from which students can choose. The common approach to surfacing these courses has been through traditional keyword matching information retrieval. The course catalog descriptions used to match on may, however, be overly brief and omit important topics covered in the course. Furthermore, even if the description is verbose, novice students may use search terms that do not match relevant courses, due to their catalog descriptions being written in the specialized language of a discipline outside of their own. In this work, we design and user test an approach intended to help mitigate these issues by augmenting course catalog descriptions with topic keywords inferred to be relevant to the course by analyzing the information conveyed by student co-enrollment networks. We tune a neural course embedding model based on enrollment sequences, then regress the embedding to a bag-of-words representation of course descriptions. Using this technique, we are able to infer keywords, in a system deployed for a user study, that students (N = 75) rated as more relevant than a word drawn at random from a course's description.

Keywords: Course search · Inferred keywords · Latent topics · Course2vec · Skip-gram · Higher education · Recommender systems

1 Introduction

The course catalog is often the first resource consulted by current and prospective students when wanting to familiarize themselves with the topical offerings of a university. With many universities offerings thousands of distinct courses over the span of several years, browsing through the description of each is untenable. Instead, classical information retrieval (i.e., search) using keyword matching is now offered at many, but not all, institutions. A keyword matching approach; however, is only as good as the words the description contains and the users' ability to craft a query using those words. Many course descriptions can be

M. Scheffel et al. (Eds.): EC-TEL 2019, LNCS 11722, pp. 480–494, 2019.
https://doi.org/10.1007/978-3-030-29736-7_36

overly brief, omitting topical terms from the description that are nevertheless contained in the course. Furthermore, for novice students, it can be difficult to gauge the similarity of courses in different departments because of the superficial differences in how different disciplines describe the same material.

In this paper, we seek to mitigate the shortcomings of topic omission and non-standardized keywords across disciplines in catalog descriptions by leveraging the regularizing power of machine learned embeddings. We apply neural embedding models to historic sequences of student course enrollments in order to embed courses into a space regularized by abstract features, or concepts, associated with courses. We then regress from this space to the space of course descriptions in order to add semantics to the course vectors. These semantics become the keywords which can be added to an enhanced university course search.

Showing the utility of a data mining, or technology enhanced learning approach in the real-world, sometimes called "closing the loop," is an objective of growing emphasis in the community. To integrate this modeling process into a larger design scheme that includes the deployment of this enhanced course search feature in a production level course recommender system, we first conduct a user study (N = 75) to measure the degree to which our model's inferred keywords correlate with student perceptions of relevance. Choosing six courses they have completed, students rated the relevance of keywords for each course generated from several sources, including random keyword selection baselines. Using these data, we were able to identify a probability threshold for which generated keywords were statistically significantly more relevant than words chosen randomly from the course's description. We use this threshold to dynamically determine the number of inferred keywords to display per course in the deployed search feature. The overall structure of the paper follows the process we followed for designing the enhanced search, outlined in Fig. 1.

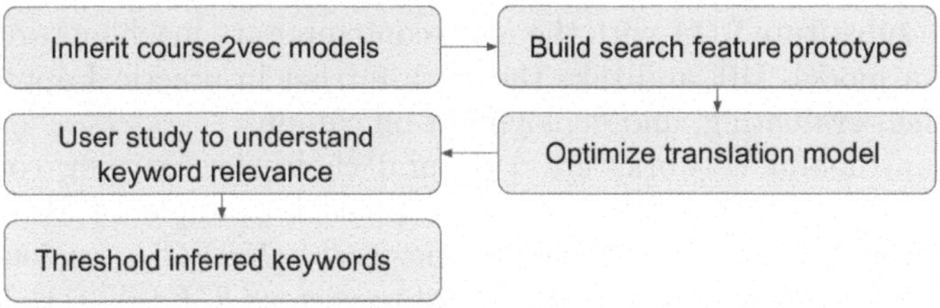

Fig. 1. Design process for the enhanced search feature

2 Related Work

Recommendation of courses and course grade prediction in formal higher education contexts has become an active area of research in data mining applied to education [1,4,15], with neural network based approaches to recommendation manifesting in deployed systems [13]. The degree of adaptivity is a significant element in deciding the type of recommendation experience a student will receive. Collaborative-based approaches, for example, have high adaptivity, whereby a student's course history is evaluated as input and suggestions are generated based on what courses the student is predicted to most likely take next. Similar approaches to social activity recommendation [5] or within-course resource recommendation have also been proposed [17]. Some shortcomings with a collaborative-based course recommendation approach are that the predicted courses may likely be courses the student already knows about, and furthermore they may be biased towards courses already popular at the university. Search is a different kind of approach, one in which a user's query represents an object (or topic) on the boundary of what the user is familiar with. In this case there is minimal adaptation, other than to the query provided. Systems taking this more knowledge-based or simple information systems approach have also seen emergence in the real-world, with one providing course evaluation and grade distributions for queried courses [3].

However, users may still experience problems in finding the information they are looking for with the classical search experience [16]. The typical approach can be improved through augmenting the search interface itself using assistive widgets [6] or by adding inferred keywords to course description, and allowing them to be matched on by the user's query. This adding of keywords to an object can be thought of as a form of classical semantic annotation [7], but with big data and modern machine learning used to generate the semantics. Mesbah et al. [8] also leverage the tagging of educational resources, such as MOOCs, using more classical natural language processing to provide the end user a synopsis of the course content. This tagging could alternatively be framed as a form of topic modeling. Motz et al. [12] provide an approach in this vein most relevant to ours in which they use students' course enrollments as a signature with which to learn themes of studying using Latent Dirichlet Allocation (LDA) [2]. Our approach is closer to the user experience of an information system but using machine learning techniques more commonly seen in collaborative-based models. We substitute LDA with the more contemporary machine regularization of skip-gram models [10] and take the work further in practical application by implementing, evaluating, and deploying it on campus.

Skip-gram neural networks are a natural choice for learning concepts, or regularities in sequential data. In the canonical example of their application to natural language, vector arithmetic, $vector[KING] - vector[MAN] + vector[WOMAN]$, results in a vector closest to $vector[QUEEN]$ [11]. In essence, the embedding has learned the concept of gender and royalty, albeit abstractly as a geometric regularity. By applying this approach to course enrollment sequences (e.g., CS101 MATH88 ECON141), we expect the skip-gram to learn similar types of concepts about courses, which we will then associate with words used to augment a course's searchable description. Prior work has found success in embedding courses in this manner, validating the model by its agreement with campus sources of course similarity [13]. We extend this application into course search and contribute a novel tuning of the semantic association process.

3 Models

Our approach to generating inferred course keywords comprises of three fundamental modeling elements: (1) a vector representation of courses learned from enrollment histories (2) a bag-of-words representation of course catalog descriptions (3) a model that translates from the enrollment-based representation to the catalog-based representation. This is essentially a machine translation, not between languages [9], but between a course representation space formed from student enrollment patterns and a semantic space constructed from instructors' descriptions of the knowledge imparted in each course.

3.1 Course2Vec

The course2vec model involves learning distributed representations of courses from students' enrollment records throughout semesters by using a notion of a enrollment sequence as a "sentence" and courses within the sequence as "words", borrowing terminology from the linguistic domain. For each student s, a chronological course enrollment sequence is produced by first sorting by semester then randomly serializing within-semester course order. Then, each course enrollment sequence is trained on like a sentence in a skip-gram model. In language models, two word vectors will be cosine similar if they share similar sentence contexts. Likewise, in the university domain, courses that share similar co-enrollments, and similar previous and next semester enrollments, will likely be close to one another in the vector space. Course2vec learns course representations using a skip-gram model by maximizing the objective function of context prediction over all the students' course enrollment sequences.

It is important to stress that our method of producing a course vector from enrollments (i.e., course2vec) does **not** use any course description information. It is based only on sequences of course IDs, with no natural language used. The generalizing principal is that patterns of student collective course taking can produce representations of courses containing abstract concepts [14] of relevance to student course search. The trick to exploiting this is to associate these abstract concepts with concrete keywords, accomplished by the translation model, explained in the section after the next.

3.2 Bag-of-Words Representation

We represent course catalog descriptions using the simple but indelible approach of bag-of-words and its variants. To create a course description vector, the length of the number of unique words across all items serves as the dimension of the vector, with a non-zero value if the word in that vocabulary appears in the description. We experiment with the description vector as binary or as one of two weighting schemes described here:

- binary: value of 1 indicating that the term occurred in the document, and 0 indicating that it did not.

- tf-idf scheme [16], the product of term frequency and inverse document frequency, which increases proportionally to the number of times a word appears in the document and is offset by the frequency of the word in the corpus and helps to adjust for the fact that some words appear more frequently in general.
- custom weighting scheme such as tf-bias:

$$tf - bias = \left(\frac{number\ of\ occurences\ of\ words}{total\ word\ count}\right)^{-bias} \quad (1)$$

Empirically, lower bias has been found to produce more general words whereas higher bias produced more specific terms [14], which may be useful in surfacing course semantics at different levels of granularity.

We evaluate all three variants in our model selection phase.

3.3 Translation Model

Our premise is that there are useful concepts learned in the embedding of course2vec, but these concepts left in number form are not associated with any semantics. To associate the patterns learned in course2vec with semantics, we apply a translation from the course2vec vector to its respective natural language course description vector.

We use a multinomial logistic regression to conduct this semantic mapping, where the skip-gram based course vectors are used as input and the corresponding descriptions of every course as bag-of-word encodings are the multi-hot labels being predicted. After this model is trained, the probabilities of each word in the vocabulary belonging to a skip-gram course vector can be computed by consulting the softmax probability distribution over the entire vocabulary. Using this probability distribution, it is now possible to find the high probability words predicted based on course2vec which are NOT in the course description. These words can subsequently serve as inferred keywords in our enhanced course search.

Logistic regression is used to represent translation between languages because the spaces being translated to and from are linear vector spaces (skip-grams have no non-linear activations). However, in case the relationship between spaces in the course domain is non-linear, we evaluate a single hidden layer neural network with non-linear activation as an additional candidate translation model in our optimization experiments.

4 Experimental Environments

4.1 Off-Line Dataset

Course descriptions were sourced from the official campus course catalog API and the data was pre-processed in the following steps: (1) concatenate each description with its respective title (2) remove stop words (3) remove punctuation (4) tokenize and collect unigram and bigram phrases to constitute our vocab (5) finally compile the binary value vector, tf-idf vector, and tf-bias vector representation for each course. In addition, we filter out certain types of courses including freshman seminars and special topics courses that shared identical generic departmental descriptions and titles. A total of 6,582 courses remained in our final course dataset.

The course embeddings used in this experiment were trained and optimized to a source of validation from a previous study [13]. We inherit this course embedding from that work, where a vector size of 229 was used.

While the above are data artifacts used for the experiments reported in this paper, the data are automatically refreshed at the university, and models retrained as part of the regular maintaining of the search feature in the production system, described more in the next section.

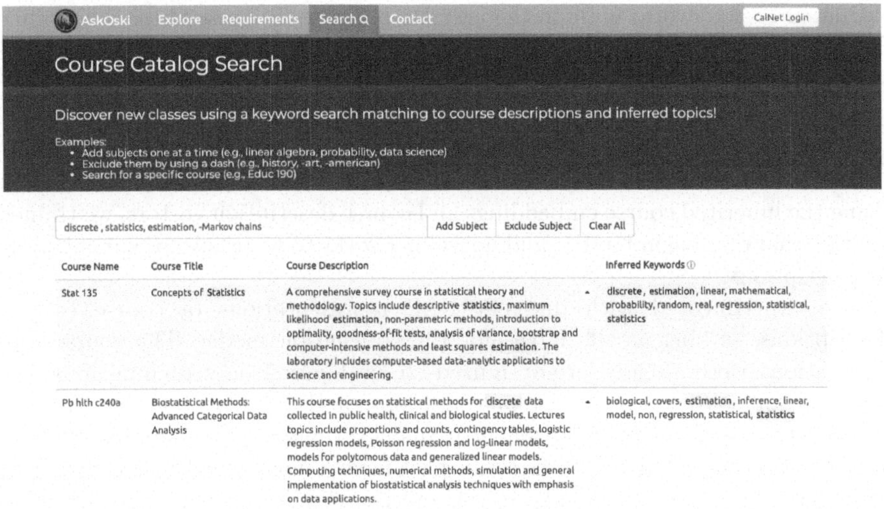

Fig. 2. A prototype of the course search feature before model tuning and user testing

4.2 Online Environment

Our first step, after inheriting a course embedding, was to apply a machine translation to the bag-of-words binary space without any optimization and design a search interface to surface the predicted words not in the course description. Figure 2 shows this prototype of the intelligent search feature as part of the campus course recommender system. Users may enter queries into the search box, which are string matched to terms in the course title, description, and inferred keywords and returns courses where any matches exist, prioritizing results that match to multiple fields. The inferred keywords serve as an additional source of semantics to match on that is intended to improve the relevancy and accessibility of the returned results. As seen in Fig. 2, the courses returned from the queries are based on keywords that do not necessarily belong to the course description, but are still relevant to the user through the inferred keywords. The keywords in this demo were produced by a model trained under default settings and validated by inspection. We simply select the top 10 predictions from the model to display in the "inferred keywords" column. This prototype exists on a beta testing server. Before deploying it to the production server, we sought to first refine the translation model and perform a user study to insure that the inferred keywords were of real relevance to students at the University.

5 Offline Model Optimization

In this section, we conduct offline predictive model experiments intended to optimize for heuristics pertinent to online user relevancy ratings. The goal was to select a single model after this optimization, that would serve as the model evaluated by real-world users in the user study phase. Because there is no offline data on student's perceptions of keyword relevancy, we came up with heuristics to optimize to as substitutes.

5.1 Tuning Parameters

Using the inherited course embeddings and course description vectors, we trained multinomial regression models and neural networks to translate from embedding to descriptions.

We experimented with different NLP representations of course catalog descriptions, serving as the labels for the translation model. The course representations were already pre-optimized so we focused on searching hyperparameters for the bag-of-words representations of their respective descriptions. We sweep a range of max document-frequency (max-df) for building the collective vocabulary, which ignores terms that have a document frequency strictly higher than the given threshold, filtering out common, often generic words found across all catalog descriptions such as "student", "semester", and "course" that are not useful as search keywords. Bag-of-words vectors are also characterized using a range of tf-bias weights and also tf-idf and binary values. We explored using a multinomial logistic versus a single hidden layer neural network to serve as the translation model. Hyperparameters in the grid search included max-df, BOW representations (binary, tf-idf, tf-bias), and translation models (multinomial logistic, 1 hidden layer neural net), totalling 144 experiment runs.

5.2 Model Selection Heuristics

In order to select which model to use in our user study, we produced the following heuristic metrics for each (all ranging from 0 to 1) and then selected the model with the highest sum of all metrics. The metrics were *recall@max_length*, *precision@10*, *department frequency*, and *distribution similarity*. The rationale for their use was as follows:

Precision and Recall. Precision and recall are meant to capture the most direct evidence of relevancy of the inferred keywords to its respective course. Precision@10, where 10 is the likely number of keywords to be shown in the search interface, is the proportion of keywords in the top 10 model predictions that also appear in the course description. Recall@max_len, where max_len is the maximum length of any description (182 words), represents the proportion of keywords found in the description if the model were to predict the entire description.

Using precision and recall alone is not sufficient in our case. A high, or perfect score for either would indicate that our model has simply learned the description of a course without capturing any additional signal surfaced from behavioral patterns. To measure the generalizability of our model in uncovering hidden semantics, we utilized two other quantifiable metrics of success, department frequency and distribution similarity, described next.

Department Frequency. Department frequency is the standard measure of document frequency in text mining, replacing document with course department. The department frequency of word w_i is:

$$dept\_freq(w_i) = \frac{number\ of\ departments\ with\ w_i}{number\ of\ total\ departments} \tag{2}$$

A department frequency of 1 indicates that a particular keyword appeared across every department. For every model trained, the average department frequency was calculated across all the words predicted. This metric is intended to measure the ability of the model to identify words from related disciplines and therefore extrapolate from the original course itself. This is intended to help overcome the lack of standardization found in the language used to describe similar courses in different departments.

Distribution Similarity. Distribution similarity is the cosine similarity between the vector of keyword frequencies from the model's predictions and the vector of uniform frequencies where each entry is the total number of possible keywords to be predicted, divided by the number of unique keywords actually predicted. This metric is intended to help us select a model that offers a more equal spread of keywords and does not overly favor a limited vocabulary, which was observed to occur during early development training phases.

Since we want to maximize each one of these metrics, our single value used for model selection is the sum across all four. Simply taking the sum has the convenient property that the combined distribution looks similar when training the regression model and the neural net, but the two are distinguishable when stratifying by each of the metrics.

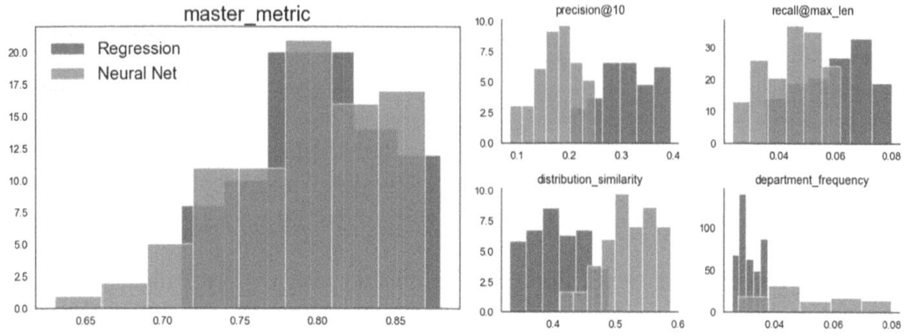

Fig. 3. Distribution of keyword evaluation metrics colored by translation model (Color figure online)

Model Evaluation. The experiment proceeds with the algorithmic optimization of our model via a grid search over the selected hyperparameters and the calculation of the described metrics for every hyperparameter set. For testing, we elected to test the model both with and without cross-validation. Because the use case of the search feature involves predicting course keywords only for existing courses rather than new courses, the model is trained on the entire dataset to allow it to learn all possible words across the collective descriptions. For thoroughness, we repeated the same grid search with 5-fold cross-validation but there was insufficient variance across each of the metrics to perform model selection.

Results of the hyperparameter search is shown in Fig. 3, where we find that a logistic regression model outperforms the neural network in terms of our relevancy heuristics (recall and precision) but the neural net outperforms the regression model by our heuristics of generalizability (department frequency and distribution similarity). We opt to use the regression model to err on the side of relevance so users are not off-put by seemingly unrelated results returned to their queries. Our optimal model and corresponding hyperparameters received the highest score sum, but was not the max precision nor recall model.

6 User Study

Following the offline experiment model selection, we follow up with a human judgment evaluation to better gauge how the model results are aligned with students' perception of relevance. A user study was conducted during which students were asked to rate keywords belonging to five different groups:

1. *Model Sorted (All)*: Top five overall keywords as predicted by the model.
2. *Model Sorted (Description)*: Top five words in the description in order of likelihood as predicted by the model.
3. *Model Sorted (Non-Description)*: Top five words not in the description in order of likelihood as predicted by the model.

4. *Random (Description)*: Five random words from within the description.
5. *Random (All)*: Five random words across all collective descriptions.

An example of these keyword groups for a select course are shown in Table 1.

Table 1. Keywords drawn from each of our five groups for STAT 135

Course: STAT 135 - Concepts of Statistics
Course Description: A comprehensive survey course in statistical theory and methodology. Topics include descriptive statistics, maximum likelihood estimation, non-parametric methods, introduction to optimality, goodness-of-fit tests, analysis of variance, bootstrap and computer-intensive methods and least squares estimation. The laboratory includes computer-based data-analytic applications to science and engineering
Model Sorted (All): regression, statistics, random, statistical, estimation
Model Sorted (Description): statistics, statistical, estimation, variance, tests
Model Sorted (Non-Description): regression, random, real, linear, discrete
Random (Description): course, engineering, includes, methods, computer-based
Random (All): diverse collection, topics problems, year credit, planning research, user interfaces

The random (all) words represent a baseline relevancy score. We expect the description groups to perform much better than this baseline and desire that the model predicted non-description words are also better than randomly selected words. The random (description) group provides the second benchmark to compare our model sorted non-description group to, quantifying how much value our enhanced search may add on top of the catalog description. These groups are not necessarily disjoint; the unique of all 5 groups were taken and randomized before showing them to the student, with an average of 18.5 unique keywords per course.

6.1 Study Design

Undergraduates were recruited from popular student Facebook groups to participate remotely in our keyword rating study in exchange for a $10 Amazon gift certificate. Study participants logged into the main *AskOski* recommender site using their University credentials in order to access the survey. The survey system looked-up the courses the student had taken and then asked them to choose six to rate the keywords of. Figure 4 shows the course selection interface for the study. Student were asked to rate solely on their experience with the class to prevent bias in keyword ratings whereby a student may be tempted to simply rate a word as relevant only if it appeared in the description.

For every keyword, students were asked for their five point Likert scale agreement with the following statement: *This keyword is relevant to the course*, where

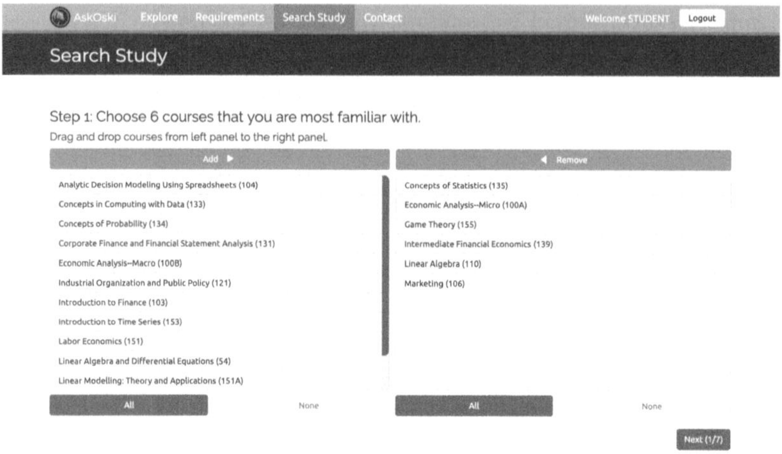

Fig. 4. Personalized survey interface after user authentication

a score of 1 corresponded with *Not Relevant At All* and a score of 5 corresponded with *Very Relevant*. A total of 75 students participated in our study, rating a total of 8,355 keywords.

6.2 Results

The average student relevancy ratings of keywords from each of the five groups is shown in Fig. 5. All three Model Sorted groups, and the Random (Description) group, scored between a 3 (neutral) and 4 (relevant) in keyword relevance. Selecting keywords at random from the entire vocabulary, Random (All), scored a 1.836 (below "Not Very Relevant"), representing students' lower bound for perception of relevance. All pairwise differences between keyword groups were statistically significantly reliable at $p < 0.05$, after applying a Bonferroni correction for multiple (10) Wilcoxon rank sum tests, except between Model Sorted (All) and Random (Description) groups, which was not statistically separable ($p = 0.019$).

The benefit of the model-based approach in terms of improving relevance of chosen keywords can be quantified by the difference in ratings between the random within-description selection group, Random (Description), 3.612, and the model-based within-description selection group, Model Sorted (Description), 3.916. A breakdown of the proportion of each rating level by group can be seen in Fig. 5. The majority (51%) of Model Sorted (Description) keywords received a 5 rating (Very Relevant), compared to Random (Description), for which 42.1% were Very Relevant. Model Sorted (Non-Description) has a much lower proportion of Very Relevant ratings (31.5%), but still considerably higher than the Random (All) baseline, with 7.3%, and with 62.3% of keywords in its group receiving the lowest relevancy rating as compared with Model Sorted (Description), that received 20.6% Not Relevant ratings.

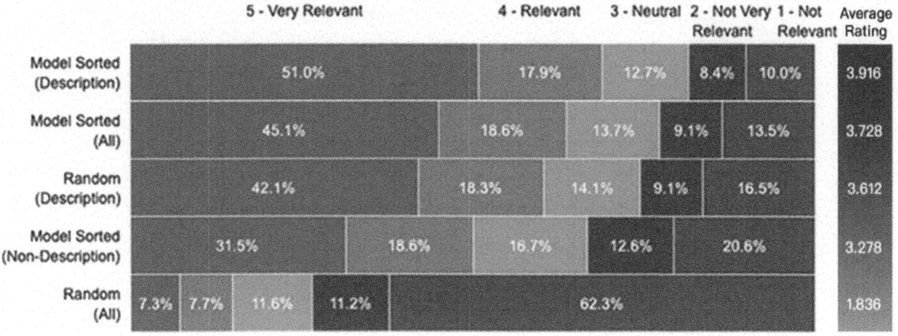

Fig. 5. User study relevancy ratings by keyword group

The way in which student relevancy ratings played out with respect to the within-group ranking of the keyword, based on model probability, is shown in Fig. 6. The average relevancy rating (y-axis) by rank (x-axis) is plotted for each of the three model-based approaches. Since the two random models do not involve any model probabilities, they also are not associated with a rank. Therefore, they are represented in the plot as horizontal lines corresponding to their averages (Fig. 5). The Model Sorted (All) trend shows the highest average ratings at rank 1, followed by an apparent asymptote down to just above the average random within-description level. Differences in ratings between these two at each rank level are statistically significantly reliable except at ranks 3 and 4. The Model Sorted (Non-Descrip) trend is initially above Random (Description) at rank 1, but then dips down and asymptotes to a Neutral average rating of 3.

A premised benefit of the predictive model was to surface relevant keywords that are not in a course's description (Non-Descrip). If we were to highlight inferred keywords, we would like to show only keywords that are "better" than words chosen randomly from the description, or at least not show words statistically significantly worse. The Model Sorted (All) ratings are statistically reliably higher than Random (Description) at ranks 1 and 2. We use this information to tailor our strategy for when and how many inferred keywords to display in the production version of our enhanced course search feature.

6.3 Selecting Inferred Keywords to Display in Search

With an improved understanding of the model predicted keywords' relevancy, we discuss how to leverage this information towards improving the search feature by updating our inferred keyword selection criteria. In the prototype, the criterion was to always display the top 10 model keywords, which did not exclude words in the description. We continue to not exclude keywords from the description, as showing them could serve the added benefit of a topic category source for reference. Thus, we choose Model Sorted (All) for this analysis.

We leverage the observation that Model Sorted ratings correlate with rank to investigate how well the underlying model probabilities of those words correlate

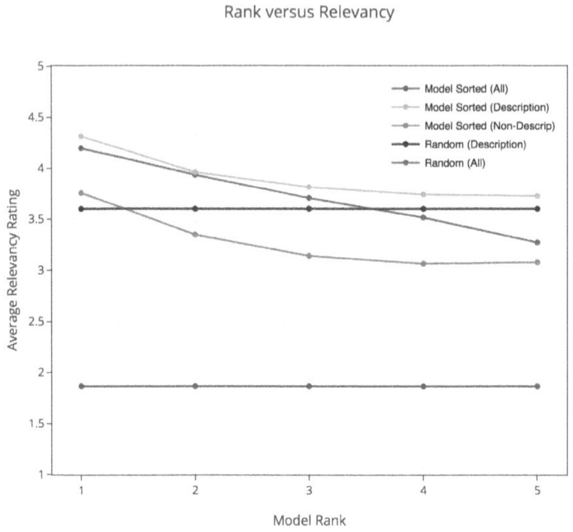

Fig. 6. Keyword group rank vs relevancy

with student relevancy ratings. If there is a correlation, then the probabilities, along with a threshold, could be used to dynamically determine which words should be included as inferred keywords on a per course basis. To conduct an analysis comparing model probabilities to user ratings, we normalize these two sets of ratings using Z-scores and then average them by Model Sorted rank. We find a substantive correlation between probability and rank and would like to choose a threshold of probability from Model Sorted (All), such that all keywords with that probability or above can generally be expected to produce keywords perceived by students to be more relevant, on average, than a word chosen at random from the description. The analysis in the previous section (Fig. 6) found that user relevancy ratings for Model Sorted (All) were significantly higher than Random (Description) at ranks 1 and 2. Therefore, we use the probability at rank 2 as the cut-off. Using this probability cut-off, we find 4.32 total words on average expected to be displayed for each course, with 2.33 within-description words and 2.00 non-description words surfaced on average within these semantics.

7 Conclusion

We explored surfacing novel, searchable semantics of a course using an embedding of courses informed by course selection histories, and supported our methodology through a user study to evaluate the relevancy of these keywords. Our experiment contributes both methodologically to the use of embeddings to surface latent semantic tags and to the design of data-driven information systems in educational settings. Our process of interface prototyping, followed by offline model optimization, user testing, and incorporation of study findings into the production software system can also serve as a design model and guide for other technologies to tune data and technology enhanced analyses towards better student learning and exploration experiences.

References

1. Backenköhler, M., Scherzinger, F., Singla, A., Wolf, V.: Data-driven approach towards a personalized curriculum. In: Proceedings of the 11th EDM Conference (2018)
2. Blei, D.M., Ng, A.Y., Jordan, M.I.: Latent Dirichlet allocation. J. Mach. Learn. Res. **3**, 993–1022 (2003)
3. Chaturapruek, S., Dee, T., Johari, R., Kizilcec, R., Stevens, M.: How a data-driven course planning tool affects college students' GPA: evidence from two field experiments. In: Proceedings of the 5th Learning @ Scale Conference (2018)
4. Chen, W., Lan, A.S., Cao, D., Brinton, C., Chiang, M.: Behavioral analysis at scale: learning course prerequisite structures from learner clickstreams. In: Proceedings of the 11th EDM Conference (2018)
5. Farzan, R., Brusilovsky, P.: Social navigation support in a course recommendation system. In: Wade, V.P., Ashman, H., Smyth, B. (eds.) AH 2006. LNCS, vol. 4018, pp. 91–100. Springer, Heidelberg (2006). https://doi.org/10.1007/11768012_11
6. Fessl, A., Wertner, A., Pammer-Schindler, V.: Digging for gold: motivating users to explore alternative search interfaces. In: Pammer-Schindler, V., Pérez-Sanagustín, M., Drachsler, H., Elferink, R., Scheffel, M. (eds.) EC-TEL 2018. LNCS, vol. 11082, pp. 636–639. Springer, Cham (2018). https://doi.org/10.1007/978-3-319-98572-5_62
7. Kiryakov, A., Popov, B., Ognyanoff, D., Manov, D., Kirilov, A., Goranov, M.: Semantic annotation, indexing, and retrieval. In: Fensel, D., Sycara, K., Mylopoulos, J. (eds.) ISWC 2003. LNCS, vol. 2870, pp. 484–499. Springer, Heidelberg (2003). https://doi.org/10.1007/978-3-540-39718-2_31
8. Mesbah, S., Chen, G., Valle Torre, M., Bozzon, A., Lofi, C., Houben, G.-J.: Concept focus: semantic meta-data for describing MOOC content. In: Pammer-Schindler, V., Pérez-Sanagustín, M., Drachsler, H., Elferink, R., Scheffel, M. (eds.) EC-TEL 2018. LNCS, vol. 11082, pp. 467–481. Springer, Cham (2018). https://doi.org/10.1007/978-3-319-98572-5_36
9. Mikolov, T., Le, Q.V., Sutskever, I.: Exploiting similarities among languages for machine translation. CoRR (2013). http://arxiv.org/abs/1309.4168
10. Mikolov, T., Sutskever, I., Chen, K., Corrado, G.S., Dean, J.: Distributed representations of words and phrases and their compositionality. In: Advances in Neural Information Processing Systems, pp. 3111–3119 (2013)
11. Mikolov, T., Yih, W.t., Zweig, G.: Linguistic regularities in continuous space word representations. In: Proceedings of the 2013 Conference of the North American Chapter of the Association for Computational Linguistics: Human Language Technologies, pp. 746–751 (2013)
12. Motz, B., Busey, T., Rickert, M., Landy, D.: Finding topics in enrollment data. In: Proceedings of the 11th EDM Conference (2018)
13. Pardos, Z.A., Fan, Z., Jiang, W.: Connectionist recommendation in the wild: on the utility and scrutability of neural networks for personalized course guidance. User Model. User-Adap. Inter. **29**(2), 487–525 (2019). https://doi.org/10.1007/s11257-019-09218-7

14. Pardos, Z.A., Nam, A.J.H.: A map of knowledge. CoRR preprint, abs/1811.07974 (2018). https://arxiv.org/abs/1811.07974
15. Polyzou, A., Karypis, G.: Feature extraction for classifying students based on their academic performance. In: Proceedings of the 11th EDM Conference (2018)
16. Salton, G., McGill, M.J.: Introduction to Modern Information Retrieval. McGraw-Hill Inc., New York (1986)
17. Shani, G., Shapira, B.: Edurank: a collaborative filtering approach to personalization in e-learning. In: Proceedings of the 7th EDM Conference (2014)

EmAP-ML: A Protocol of Emotions and Behaviors Annotation for Machine Learning Labels

Felipe de Morais[1(✉)], Tiago R. Kautzmann[1], Ig I. Bittencourt[2], and Patricia A. Jaques[1]

[1] Universidade do Vale do Rio dos Sinos (UNISINOS), São Leopoldo, RS, Brazil
{felipmorais,tkautzmann}@edu.unisinos.br, pjaques@unisinos.br
[2] Universidade Federal de Alagoas (UFAL), Maceió, AL, Brazil
ig.ibert@ic.ufal.br

Abstract. The detection of students' emotions in computer-based learning environments is a complex task. Although emotions can be detected from sensors, a less intrusive method is to train supervised machine learning algorithms for the emotions prediction based on the log of students' actions on the system. For these algorithms to work as expected, they need to be trained with a large amount of reliable ground truth labels. Generally, labels are generated by students themselves or by coders monitoring students, watching videos from the students, or reviewing logs of students' actions. Younger learners (i.e., children) are unable to label their emotions properly. Still, it is difficult for a coder to identify students' emotions only from their face since the emotional facial expression is generally subtle in a learning setting. This article describes EmAP-ML (Emotions Annotation Protocol for Machine Learning), a protocol for coders to annotate students' learning emotions and behaviors based on video records, which contains facial expressions, ambient audio, and computer screen. The screen and ambient audio records allow coders to infer students' appraisal (an evaluation that elicits an emotion) to identify emotions even when the facial expression is subtle. This protocol was evaluated by two coders who annotated videos obtained from 55 students while using a tutoring system, having achieved an agreement coefficient of 0.62, measured through Cohen's Kappa statistics.

Keywords: Annotation Protocol · Learning emotions and behaviors · Affective computing · Machine learning · Educational Data Mining

1 Introduction

Researchers in Educational Data Mining (EDM) use data mining and machine learning algorithms to identify patterns of students' actions, in educational software, that correlate with field observations related to learning, metacognitive skills, behaviors, and affective states [1,2,14,21,23]. Thus, supervised machine

M. Scheffel et al. (Eds.): EC-TEL 2019, LNCS 11722, pp. 495–509, 2019.
https://doi.org/10.1007/978-3-030-29736-7_37

learning algorithms that use these patterns can be applied to educational software for automatic detection of personal information about the student, i.e., behaviors, mental and affective states, knowledge, etc.

In the area of affective computing, machine learning algorithms can be used for automatic detection of learning emotions and behaviors during the use of computer-based learning environments while students interact with these systems. The online detection of these emotions and behaviors enables educational software to make instructional decisions based on the information detected, such as reducing the difficulty of tasks when students are confused or making changes in the graphical interface to make it more exciting when the students are bored.

For machine learning algorithms to be efficient and work as expected in the detection of learning emotions and behaviors, it is necessary to create ground truth labels for the training samples of these algorithms. The quality of machine-learned models for detecting emotions and behaviors of the students depends on the quality of the ground-truth labels used in the training stage of these models. Detection models that use data bound to labels generated from misconceptions of emotions may even yield good results when false conceptions are present in both training and validation labels. However, these problematic models are fitted over incorrect predictive data of learning emotions and behaviors, leading to inaccurate predictions and leading affective-sensitive learning computing environments to make wrong decisions. These wrong decisions taken by the system could make the students get annoyed, leading them to stop using the learning environment, impairing learning.

Students emotion detectors, integrated into computational learning environments, have used the following methods to obtain ground-truth labels for predictive models of learning emotions and behaviors: (*a*) methods based on students observation by coders in the learning environment [17,27] or through videos [2,7,16]; (*b*) students self-report methods [2,3,7,27], and (*c*) methods based on the annotation of log files [13].

Students self-report methods (*b*) found in the studies are methods of concurrent [7] or retrospective annotation [2,3]. In the concurrent methods, students report their emotions during learning activities, such as the emote-aloud method, in which students verbally tell their emotions [20]. These reports may be through free-response when students are free to tell their emotions while they are experimenting it [9] or through forced reporting, such as when the system shows pop-up forms in predefined periods [6]. However, these pop-ups keep forcing the students to tell their emotions, even if they do not feel comfortable with it. Thus, when it happens, the students can negligence the pop-ups, just closing them, they can answer it incorrectly, to get rid of it, or, even worst, they can get annoyed with the pop-ups and stop using the system. Self-reports can also be retrospective, when students perform learning activities first and only after report their experiences, as in the studies in which students watched their learning videos and reported their affective experiences [15].

The quality of labels in self-report methods depends on participants' age [6,24], cultural aspects [11], and their ability to report their emotions through meta-affective skills [20]. Some disadvantages of students' concurrent self-reports are the following [20]: increases student's cognitive load; interferes the primary task; learner may feel uncomfortable in demonstrating it weakness (frustration, boredom); it could influence the emotions experienced by the students; requires extra engagement for both task and self-report; the subjectivity of data. Students' retrospective self-reports also have some disadvantages [20]: the distance between the task and the self-report; requires extra time per students (time in task + time for self-reports); requires meta-cognitive skills; subjective data.

Due to restrictions of the self-report methods, other protocols suggest using coders (*a*). Coders can annotate emotions during learners activities (*in loco* observation) or recording users' face and actions for later analysis. Although the annotation by coders during learners activities can make students feel monitored, they usually end up forgetting they are being recorded or observed after a certain period. To annotate emotions by observing only students' face record is a challenging task for coders since the facial expression of some emotions can be subtle (e.g., engagement and boredom) and due to negative social connotations associated with some emotions, leading the student to control its emotions [10].

A third method found in the literature to make annotations of students emotions is the annotation of log files (*c*) [13]. In this method, the coders retrospectively label samples of student compilation logs in the system. A limitation of this method is the single modality of data logs for the making-decision of coders. Thus, multi modals might be needed for a coder to observe different expressions associated with given emotions for making its annotations judgments [10].

The main objective of this paper is to present EmAP-ML, Emotions Annotation Protocol for Machine Learning, a protocol for the task of annotation of students learning emotions and behaviors in computer-based learning environments, conducted by trained coders, using multi modals of affect expressions associated with emotions. Our protocol aims to improve the accuracy of emotions annotation by allowing coders to infer students' appraisal from records of the students' actions on learning system interface (screen recording) and ambient audio, besides considering students' facial expression. Emotions are elicited by a cognitive process of evaluation of the good or bad aspects of an event (or person's action or object appeal) according to one's goals [25], which is called appraisal. For example, a person feels frustration when a future event with positive outcomes do not materialize [18], for instance, to succeed in a task. Thus, the screen record allows the coder to infer that a student is frustrated with failure (an expected success in a task that did not happen). The videos of the screen can also help coders to identify prototypical situations, such as the student is blocked on a task, which usually is an indication of confusion.

The protocol presented in this work has phases of training and testing of coders. In our protocol, coders are also trained on the appraisals of the emotions to be annotated and on emotions common expressions. Once trained, the coders become able to make annotations of learning emotions and behaviors observed in videos. The coders can watch the same videos as many times as necessary to make decisions about their annotations. Besides, as the protocol aims the annotation of a sequence of labels from the same student, it allows the registration of transitions of emotions and behaviors. This kind of data enables the inference of relevant information such as which emotions are more frequent after a specific emotion occurs. A tool for the annotation of learning emotions and behaviors was also developed and make part of this protocol.

For the quality evaluation of EmAP-ML, two coders were trained to annotate four learning emotions (engagement, confusion, frustration, and boredom) and five behaviors (on-task, on-task-conversation, on-task-out, on-system, and off-task). For both learning emotions and behaviors, coders could also write down "?" whenever they identify some other type of affective state or behavior unintended by the study, or when they had doubts about which learning emotion or behavior to annotate. The coders participated from the training and test phases. The results are presented and discussed.

2 Definitions

This section presents the definitions of terms and nomenclatures used in the description of this protocol. In our protocol, an **annotation** consists of identifying one or more learning emotions and one or more behaviors, called **labels**, in a clip during a session. A **clip** is a segment of a session to be annotated by an **annotator or coder**. In this work, we use the terms annotator and coder as synonyms. The size of the clips could vary depending on the research interest.

A **session** represents a part of the full video that was chosen to be annotated by coders. It has a start time (the starting point of the video to be analyzed), duration (the size of the session) and a set of clips. The **full video** contains the student's face and ambient audio in one side and the computer screen on other. A set of sessions is called a **study**, for example, the video sessions for the training phase.

Two types of data are annotated by the coders in each session: learning emotions and behaviors. EmAP-ML is not restricted to any specific emotion or behavior, however, it is important that researchers clearly define the constructs used to the coders. It is also important to consider the appraisals of the emotions and the common expressions of emotions in the student's behavior in the learning environment for the annotation of the learning emotions and behaviors.

3 Suggestion of Values for the Protocol Parameters

In this section, we describe some values chosen for EmAP-ML's parameters. One first important parameter to define is the duration of the clips. Although it can be defined by researchers according their needs, we recommend clips with a duration of five seconds. This duration was chosen for two reasons. First, emotions have a short duration [25]. Second, we empirically observed, after more than 20 annotations' tasks, that when the clip duration was longer than 5 s, the students experienced more than one or two emotions per clip. Thus, the coders were forced to choose the most representative ones. However, this strategy of choosing an emotion causes data not to represent reality, resulting in inconsistent labels.

In relation to the number of coders, we recommend two or more annotators during the training phase, which helps in leveling the understanding of each of the affective states and behaviors. It is also important to highlight that at least one of the coders should have strong knowledge of the constructs employed in the protocol. This "expert" will be the one to "train" the others coders (more detail in Sect. 4). This person should be already trained in the protocol or should have a good understanding about the constructs (learning emotions and behaviors) considered in the research. Assuming this strategy, it guarantees that the untrained coders will understand the protocol and will achieve a common understanding based on the considerations of an expert.

Concerning sessions, our suggestion is five minutes of duration, independently of the duration of the video record. For example, the videos that we used for our evaluation (see Sect. 6) had an average duration of 40 min, since they were recorded in a school and this was the duration of a math class. A duration of five minutes give enough time for the coder to be aware of the student's context without leaving him/her bored or tired with a lengthy annotation task. Therefore, if the session duration is equal to five minutes and the clip size is five seconds, for each session, each coder generates 60 annotations. We also suggest to start the session 10 min after the beginning of the video, to discard the initial part when students are logging in and are more aware of the camera.

About the selection of the students' videos to be annotated, we suggest to select them at random and to apply the following criteria: (*a*) avoid to have more than one video with the same student; (*b*) avoid to have more than one video collected on the same class; if it is not possible, choose the videos uniformly based on the number of collection days. These criteria let the videos samples to have a better representation of different students' characteristics and different domain contents and levels of difficulty in the tasks assigned to students.

4 Protocol

The execution of EmAP-ML is divided into four phases, being (*i*) collection and development of the materials, (*ii*) the training phase of the coders, (*iii*) the test phase of the coders, and (*iv*) the annotation phase. The phases and their flow change are illustrated in Fig. 1.

The initial phase is about the collection of materials (videos) and the definitions of the parameters for the annotation tool configuration by the researchers. After, the coders are able to start the initial discussion about the constructs (learning emotions and behaviors) of the protocol, the process of annotation, and the tool functioning. Next, the coders can start the video annotation followed by a discussion about the results for each video (training phase). We suggest at least three iterations (individual annotation followed by group discussion) of this phase (3 sessions), but researchers can opt for more iterations if they find too much divergence yet. We also suggest, in the training phase, during the annotations discussion, for the coders to compare the annotation one-by-one between

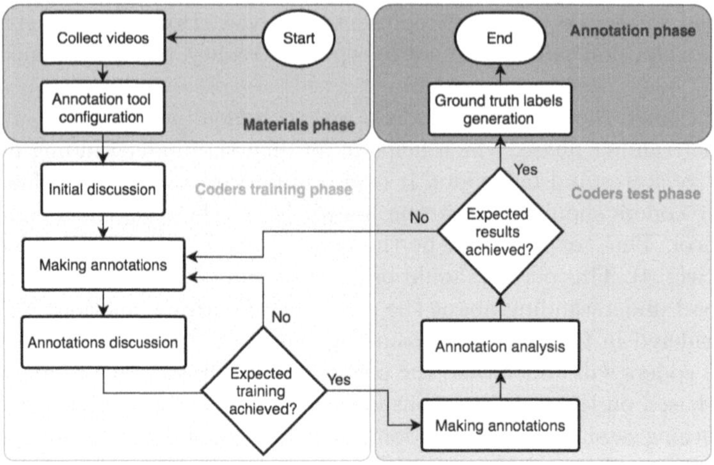

Fig. 1. The phases of the protocol and their flow change.

each of the coders. Thus, the coders can identify some misunderstanding of the concepts and solve them before starting the test phase.

Once the divergence of results is minimal, the coders can test themselves in the test phase. This phase is pretty similar to the training phase, with the difference that there is no discussion after the annotations. Instead, in the end, researchers analyze the convergence of the annotations with agreement statistical measurements. We suggest not to include statistical analysis during the training phase to avoid having the coders thinking that the training phase consists of achieving a threshold. The most used agreement measure for this kind of task is Cohen's Kappa coefficient K. Thus, if the coders get a good result in the test phase, i.e., a kappa equals to or greater than 0.6 (described in Sect. 4.3), then they are considered able to generate the ground truth labels by themselves alone, that is, the annotation phase. Otherwise, they are suggested to go back to the training phase and reinforce their agreement about the concepts. We also suggest at least three iterations in the test phase or 180 annotations.

4.1 Materials Phase

The materials phase comprises the collection of the videos to be analyzed and also the configuration or development of the annotation tool, if it is needed (more details in Sect. 5). To record the videos (screen and face) simultaneously, we recommend researchers to use a software that allows recording both students' face and screen besides registering ambient audio. We usually use the online software Wistia Soapbox (https://soapbox.wistia.com), which works as a plugin for Google Chrome browser and records both videos (computer screen and student's face through a webcam). However, researchers can opt for other similar tools. One useful feature of this plugin is that it does not show on the computer screen that the student is being recorded. Thus, students can not see their face while they are being recorded, what makes them less aware of the recording.

We also recommend some precautions for the videos to be recorded. Each student should use a single computer. Thus, the data collected is unique for each student. Also, before beginning the recording of the videos, the students should be instructed to remain in a comfortable posture, so that the webcams could be appropriately adjusted according to each student.

4.2 Coders Training Phase

The coders training phase consists of the training of coders in the detection of learning emotions and behaviors. This phase has three tasks, called (*i*) initial discussion, (*ii*) making annotations and (*iii*) annotations discussion. The **initial discussion** involves an initial conversation between the coders of the study, aiming at reaching a mutual understanding of each of the constructs (learning emotions and behaviors) to be annotated. In this phase, theories already known as state of the art are presented to the coders, so that the understanding, even mutual, is correct and according to literature. Specifically for EmAP-ML, it is imperative to explain for the coders the appraisal theory and discuss possible events and associated students' appraisals and common expressions of emotions in the learning environment. In this phase, researchers should also instruct the coders about the annotation tool working and the process of annotation (for instance, what to do when more than one emotion is seen in a clip).

After the discussion, the coders perform separately the process of annotation in the annotation tool, called **making annotations**. The **annotations discussion** task consists of collecting all the annotations made by each coder in a session, analyze and compare between annotations of different annotators within the same session. The three tasks occur in sequence, but the training phase as a whole represents several cycles of repetition of making annotation and annotation analysis and discussion, until the desired training result is achieved. We suggest at least three cycles of the training phase and the presence of researchers for a better understanding of the emotions and behaviors definitions and the mediation of the discussions. We consider as desired results the fact that the coders are achieving a good level of understanding and agreement. However, the judgment of an expert at that time is essential. Once the desired training result is achieved, the researchers have to decide the number and which videos are going to be used for the test phase.

4.3 Coders Test Phase

The difference between the testing phase and the training phase is that in the test phase, there are no discussions for understanding and clarifying doubts about the constructs or annotation. Once the session attributes have been settled, at the end of the training phase, the coders will perform the task of making annotations for the test phase, just as they did before, in the training phase. At the end of the annotations of all the sessions, the data will be collected, and instead of being manually compared one by one (like in the annotations discussion task), researchers should measure the agreement between the annotators for learning emotions and behaviors separately. This is a concordance study between different annotators for the same set of data, where the data assume nominal categorical values, these being the categories of learning emotions and behaviors.

Currently, the works that perform this type of comparison use the calculation of Kappa value, proposed by Cohen's [5]. The Kappa coefficient K is a statistical measure of inter-rater agreement for nominal categorical values. It is considered to be more robust than a simple calculation of agreement percentage since K takes into account the agreement that occurs by chance. According to the BROMP protocol [17], a Kappa value considered adequate for this type of analysis is greater than 0.6, where the K value varies from -1 to 1, being 1 representing a perfect agreement. This agreement measure is applied to test the agreement between two individuals. Thus, the Kappa value should be tested pair by pair of coders.

4.4 Annotation Phase

After completing the training and test phases, the coders can perform the annotation process independently of each other; each coder can annotate different sessions, without making some comparison between them, once they have already been adequately trained and evaluated. This strategy is also assumed by other protocols, such as BROMP [17]. The annotation phase is the phase responsible for generating a set of ground truth labels to be used in supervised machine learning algorithms.

5 The Annotation Tool

For the annotation of the learning emotions and behaviors, we have developed a web tool, which receives both videos, face with audio and screen, that should be captured simultaneously. The tool displays both videos synchronously, i.e., for the annotation, the coder sees the student and what s/he is doing on the system at the same time, side-by-side. The annotation tool is shown in Fig. 2.

After login, the coder must select the study and the session to write down. Sessions have a full video, start time, and session duration size, as described in the definitions section (Sect. 2). When accessing a session, these predefined information are loaded and configured automatically. So, when the coders play the video, they will automatically see the first clip to insert their annotation.

The system plays the video for the clip size and automatically stops when that time runs out. Thus, the annotators can quietly reflect on their annotation and insert it into the system screen. If necessary, the coders may review the clip as many times as they want to have higher accuracy in their judgment. After performing the clip annotation, the coder presses the next button to see the next clip and to clear the data from the last annotation on the system screen. The coder can review previous annotations and modify them, if necessary. Knowing

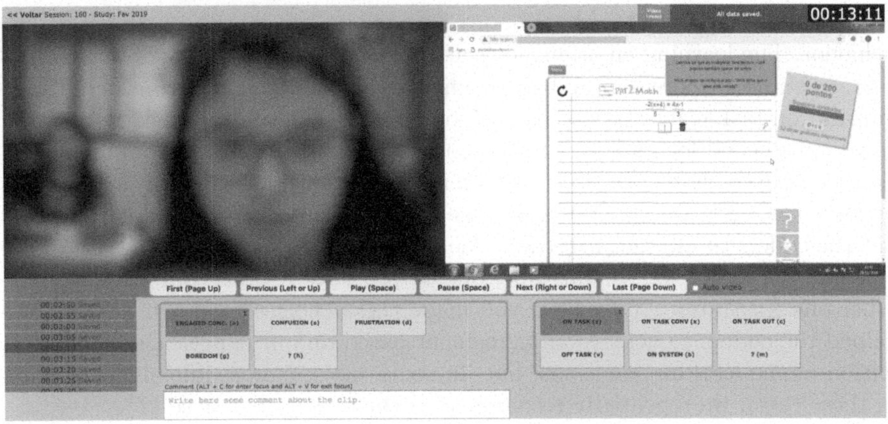

Fig. 2. The annotation tool.

that the coder can select more than one learning emotion or behavior per clip, the tool displays a number indicating the order of the annotation, so that the coder is sure about the annotations' sequence.

6 Evaluation of the Protocol

To evaluate the reliability of EmAP-ML, we have invited two persons to participate in an experiment. The coders were volunteers, graduated students in Computer Science. Although we first hesitated in inviting people without background in the area, e.g., students from Psychology, we opted for students of our lab because we wanted to verify if our annotation protocol would generate reliable results even for non-professionals in emotions. Coders annotated videos obtained from 55 seventh-grade students while using the algebraic Intelligent Tutoring System PAT2Math [12]. We believe this data to be suitable for representing the emotions and behaviors considered in this protocol because it came from a real case scenario where the students used a computer-based educational environment during the regular class period in their school's lab.

The evaluation comprised three phases of EmAP-ML (materials, training, and test phases). As the primary goal of this evaluation was only to test our protocol, there was no annotation phase at this point. First, in the materials phase, the authors collected the videos that would be used in the study. Seven sessions of five minutes were selected, from 55 different students and 21 different collection days, as suggested in Sect. 3: three sessions for the training phase and three sessions for the test phase. Besides, one extra video has been used to illustrate to the coders how the annotation tool works and also to show some examples of manifestations of learning emotions and behaviors from the student.

In the training phase, during the initial discussion, the authors explained to the coders about the concepts of the learning emotions and behaviors chosen, as well as the appraisal and commons expressions of emotion in the student's behavior. The learning emotions for the application of this protocol were confusion, frustration, boredom and engagement, and the behaviors considered were on-task, on-task-conversation, on-task-out, on-system, and off-task. Afterward, coders proceeded for making annotations of the first session (five minutes duration) separately. Each one used a different computer. At the end of each making annotations task, we generated a table of comparison of the annotations and put the coders to interact together. The discussion was conducted by one of the authors. For example, "in this line, one of you have chosen confusion, but the other one frustration. Why have you made these choices?". When possible, we helped the coders to achieve an agreement based on our experience on the definition of the learning emotions, but, in some cases, it was difficult to be sure. In these cases, we repeatedly recommended the coders to choose "?".

Thus, the training phase occurred three times, as suggested. It means, for three sessions, the coders have separately annotated the videos and discussed the results of the annotations. This process lasted four hours. Afterward, the coders had 24 h to annotate the last three videos. For this phase (test phase), the coders have not interacted among them. They annotated three more sessions of five minutes each in this phase.

6.1 Emotions Considered

EmAP-ML was developed to consider the annotation of confusion, frustration, boredom, and engagement. However, it is important to highlight that it could be expanded and generalized for different learning emotions or affective states and for different applications. This demand varies based on the study's objectives. In our case, these four learning emotions were chosen because they have been seen more frequently in computer-based learning environments [4].

During the training phase, some concepts about the learning emotions were given to the coders. These conceptions are related to the appraisals that elicit the emotions. **Confusion** happens when the students seem to be having difficulty to understand the lesson materials or the task they are trying to solve. It was already reported evidences that confusion arises from a cognitive appraisal of a mismatch between the knowledge needed to solve the current task and the student's prior knowledge [8]. **Frustration** arises because an expected desirable consequence for a given event (situation) did not happen [18], according to appraisal theory models. **Boredom** is caused by the subjective lack of value in a given situation or activity [19]. Finally, in the state of **engagement** students are focused on and paying attention to the current task or they are performing multiple tasks while they continue focused on and paying attention to all of these tasks. Also, we have presented to the coders some "common expressions" (student's behaviors) seen in the students and what they mean. These student's behaviors are emotion indicators and were taken from [22,26]. The appraisals of emotions and student's behaviors presented to coders are described in Table 1.

Based on the examples from Table 1, it was possible to illustrate to the coders some of the "common expressions" normally seen in the students, and

Table 1. Descriptions of appraisal of emotions and student's behaviors.

State	Appraisals of emotions	Student's behaviors
Engagement	The student is actively involved in the task. There is some cognitive effort	Mouthing solutions to him/herself; Making mental calculations; Typing at a fast pace; Reflecting with attention; Looking towards the screen with interest;
Confusion	Student shows s/he does not know how to proceed. S/he is having difficulty in identifying his/her next action should be (there is a gap between his/her knowledge and the knowledge necessary to solve the step) or cannot understand the system feedback	Move around the mouse in the screen without objective; Staring the screen with no action; Ask colleagues/teacher for help; Pouts/Lip biting; Frown; Statements such as "Why didn't it work?"
Frustration	The student is unpleasant with his progress on the task solving or with his/ her performance (on problem-solving or gamification score), possibly because it is different from what he/she expects from himself/herself	Statements such as "What's going on?!"; Deep breath; Pulling at his/her hair; Cursing;
Boring	The student is not interested in the task. The task is monotonous or boring for the student	The student looks around to observe what colleagues are doing; The student initiates an off-topic conversation with a colleague; Rest head in hands;

also describe what they represent as learning emotions. Thus, the coders could take their annotations more wisely. However, if the coders were not sure about which state to annotate, we always recommend annotating "?", meaning a lack of information to take the right decision.

6.2 Behaviors Considered

In this protocol, we have considered the annotation of on-task, on-task-conversation, on task-out, on-system, and off-task behaviors of students, while using a computer-based learning environment. However, this could, again, be expanded and generalized for different studies and applications.

The concepts of each behavior considered were given to the coders during the training phase. Students are **on-task** when they are focusing on solving the current task. They are **on-task-conversation** when they are working on a task while talking to the teacher or another student specifically about the task they are doing. The students are **on-task-out** when they are working on their task, but they are using an external resource, e.g., notes or notebooks, and not using the learning environment. The students are considered **on-system** when they are using the learning environment, but they are not focused on solving their task (equation), for example when the student is looking at the system logo or choosing a task to solve. Finally, when the students are not working on the task assigned by the system, they are considered *off-task*. Again, if the coders were unsure about which behavior to choose, we advised them to code "?".

6.3 Evaluation Results

After the coders have finished the annotations, in the testing phase, we have then calculated the Cohen's kappa to evaluate the agreement among the coders for the sessions. The coders have reached, for the three making annotations tasks, a Kappa value of 0.62 for learning emotions and a Kappa value of 0.89 for behaviors. Thus, the participants achieved the minimal threshold we expected of Cohen's Kappa equals to or greater than 0.6. It is important to highlight that we have not discarded the annotations where one of the coders have chosen "?' for learning emotion or behavior. It means that, in our study, we wanted to verify if coders agree that a clip does not have enough information to annotate. Other protocols discard these annotations with a "?" [17].

7 Conclusion

In this paper, we have presented EmAP-ML, a protocol for annotation of learning emotions and behaviors based on recorded videos of students' screen and face with ambient audio in computer-based learning environments. Our protocol has four phases to be accomplished altogether by at least two coders: (1) materials, where researchers collect videos and define parameters for the annotation tool; (2) training phase, in which coders intercalate sessions of annotations with discussions to achieve a mutual understanding; (3) test phase, in which coders only annotate videos for the calculation of their agreement rate (Cohen's Kappa) at the end; and (4) annotation phase, in which, once trained, the coders can annotate videos for ground truth labels for machine learning algorithms. We recommend each phase to be composed of at least three sessions with full videos of five minutes each, clips of five seconds each and 180 annotations. We evaluated EmAP-ML with two participants and we were able to train them as coders with no prior experience in the annotation of emotions and behaviors; they have reached a Cohen's Kappa of 0.62 for learning emotions and 0.89 for behaviors.

The method of annotation proposed in this paper is suitable for the annotation of students' learning emotions and behaviors in computer-based learning environments for the generation of labels to compose training samples for machine learning algorithms; for example, sensor-free algorithms for detection of emotions. This method is useful when researchers are not able to take online notes in the classroom environment. Besides, it uses information from students' actions in the system interface to highlight their emotion appraisals to improve the quality of the annotations. Also, EmAP-ML allows the identification of learning emotions and behaviors transitions, once the coders can annotate multiple emotions and behaviors for the same student in sequence, thus gathering all the occurrences in the order that they occur.

The present method can be used for generating a high volume of labels, once there is at least one label for every five seconds of observation. Also, as the trained coders do not need to be in the data collection session, the data could be collected from different students, from different schools in the world, acquiring samples much more representative, which could produce more generalizable results. This work also presented a model for an annotation tool that can be implemented by interested research groups. We suggest synchronizing this tool with the log data obtained in the computer-based learning environment to facilitate the sampling for algorithms. Also, it is interesting to highlight one usability benefit of EmAP-ML, where the coder can have a break when s/he feels some fatigue. It happens when the coder spends a long time making the annotations. To solve this, the coders can pause the videos and return later to finish it. On the other hand, in online protocols, the coders cannot have a break because there will be a loss of data. Thus, the coder could start to generate inconsistent labels.

This protocol also has some limitations. Although this method let us get a high number of labels, it can require a significant amount of time to make the annotations. It occurs mainly because the coders can re-watch the clips whenever they want to better their judgments. Also, the concepts of the learning emotions and behaviors should be very clear for all coders, and accordingly to the literature. To mediate this problem, an expert in the area should be present during the training and test phases of the protocol. Thus, the labels generated by the coders represent reality, leading to a real detection of the learning emotions and behaviors. Another limitation is regarding the number of labels per each emotion. The emotion engagement occurred much more often than negative emotions. This is because of the gamification features of the tutor system used as a case study. Thus, we had less amount of data to training negative learning emotions. For future work, we plan to conduct an experiment to investigate the correlation between non-verbal behaviors and emotions. The findings in this new experiment could lead us to a better understanding, presenting more reliable examples to coders, which could lead to a better inter-rater agreement.

Acknowledgments. This study was financed in part by the Coordenação de Aperfeiçoamento de Pessoal de Nível Superior - Brasil (CAPES) - Finance Code 001, STICAMSUD 18-STIC-03, FAPERGS (granting 17/2551-0001203-8) and CNPq from Brazil.

References

1. Ahadi, A., et al.: Exploring machine learning methods to automatically identify students in need of assistance. In: ICER, pp. 121–130. ACM (2015)

2. Bixler, R., D'Mello, S.: Detecting boredom and engagement during writing with keystroke analysis, task appraisals, and stable traits. In: IUI. ACM (2013)
3. Bosch, N., D'Mello, S., Mills, C.: What emotions do novices experience during their first computer programming learning session? In: Lane, H.C., Yacef, K., Mostow, J., Pavlik, P. (eds.) AIED 2013. LNCS (LNAI), vol. 7926, pp. 11–20. Springer, Heidelberg (2013). https://doi.org/10.1007/978-3-642-39112-5_2
4. Calvo, R.A., D'Mello, S.: Affect detection: an interdisciplinary review of models, methods, and their applications. IEEE Trans. Affect. Comput. **1**(1), 18–37 (2010)
5. Cohen, J.: A coefficient of agreement for nominal scales. Educ. Psychol. Measure. **20**(1), 37–46 (1960)
6. Conati, C., Maclaren, H.: Empirically building and evaluating a probabilistic model of user affect. User Model. User-Adap. Interact. **19**(3), 267–303 (2009)
7. Craig, S.D., D'Mello, S., Witherspoon, A., Graesser, A.: Emote aloud during learning with autotutor: applying the facial action coding system to cognitive-affective states during learning. Cogn. Emot. **22**(5), 777–788 (2008)
8. D'Mello, S., Lehman, B., Pekrun, R., Graesser, A.: Confusion can be beneficial for learning. Learn. Instr. **29**, 153–170 (2014)
9. D'Mello, S.K., Craig, S.D., Sullins, J., Graesser, A.C.: Predicting affective states expressed through an emote-aloud procedure from autotutor's mixed-initiative dialogue. Int. J. Artif. Intell. Educ. **16**, 3–28 (2006)
10. D'Mello, S.K., Graesser, A.: Multimodal semi-automated affect detection from conversational cues, gross body language, and facial features. User Model. User-Adap. Interact. **20**(2), 147–187 (2010)
11. Elfenbein, H.A., Ambady, N.: Universals and cultural differences in recognizing emotions. Curr. Direct. Psychol. Sci. **12**(5), 159–164 (2003)
12. Jaques, P.A., et al.: Rule-based expert systems to support step-by-step guidance in algebraic problem solving: the case of the tutor PAT2Math. Expert Syst. Appl. **40**(14), 5456–5465 (2013)
13. Lee, D.M.C., Rodrigo, M.M.T., Baker, R.S.J., Sugay, J.O., Coronel, A.: Exploring the relationship between novice programmer confusion and achievement. In: D'Mello, S., Graesser, A., Schuller, B., Martin, J.-C. (eds.) ACII 2011. LNCS, vol. 6974, pp. 175–184. Springer, Heidelberg (2011). https://doi.org/10.1007/978-3-642-24600-5_21
14. Leinonen, J., Longi, K., Klami, A., Vihavainen, A.: Automatic inference of programming performance and experience from typing patterns. In: ACM Technical Symposium on Computing Science Education, pp. 132–137. ACM (2016)
15. Mills, C., D'Mello, S.: Emotions during writing on topics that align or misalign with personal beliefs. In: Cerri, S.A., Clancey, W.J., Papadourakis, G., Panourgia, K. (eds.) ITS 2012. LNCS, vol. 7315, pp. 638–639. Springer, Heidelberg (2012). https://doi.org/10.1007/978-3-642-30950-2_99
16. Mota, S., Picard, R.W.: Automated posture analysis for detecting learner's interest level. In: CVPRW 2003, vol. 5, pp. 49–49. IEEE (2003)
17. Ocumpaugh, J., Baker, R.: Baker Rodrigo Ocumpaugh monitoring protocol (BROMP) 2.0 technical and training manual (2015)
18. Ortony, A., Clore, G.L., Collins, A.: The Cognitive Structure of Emotions. Cambridge University Press, Cambridge (1990)
19. Pekrun, R., Goetz, T., Daniels, L.M., Stupnisky, R.H., Perry, R.P.: Boredom in achievement settings: exploring control-value antecedents and performance outcomes of a neglected emotion. J. Educ. Psychol. **102**, 531 (2010)
20. Porayska-Pomsta, K., Mavrikis, M., D'Mello, S., et al.: Knowledge elicitation methods for affect modelling in education. IJAIED **22**(3), 107–140 (2013)

21. Reis, H., Alvares, D., Jaques, P., Isotani, S.: Analysis of permanence time in emotional states: a case study using educational software. In: Nkambou, R., Azevedo, R., Vassileva, J. (eds.) ITS 2018. LNCS, vol. 10858, pp. 180–190. Springer, Cham (2018). https://doi.org/10.1007/978-3-319-91464-0_18
22. Rodrigo, M.M.T., et al.: Affective and behavioral predictors of novice programmer achievement, vol. 41, no. 3, pp. 156–160 (2009)
23. Sabourin, J., Shores, L.R., Mott, B.W., Lester, J.C.: Predicting student self-regulation strategies in game-based learning environments. In: Cerri, S.A., Clancey, W.J., Papadourakis, G., Panourgia, K. (eds.) ITS 2012. LNCS, vol. 7315, pp. 141–150. Springer, Heidelberg (2012). https://doi.org/10.1007/978-3-642-30950-2_19
24. Sayfan, L., Lagattuta, K.H.: Grownups are not afraid of scary stuff, but kids are: young children's and adults' reasoning about children's, infants', and adults' fears. Child Dev. **79**(4), 821–835 (2008)
25. Scherer, K.R.: What are emotions? And how can they be measured? Soc. Sci. Inform. **44**(4), 695–729 (2005)
26. Vea, L., Rodrigo, M.M.: Modeling negative affect detector of novice programming students using keyboard dynamics and mouse behavior. In: Numao, M., Theeramunkong, T., Supnithi, T., Ketcham, M., Hnoohom, N., Pramkeaw, P. (eds.) PRICAI 2016. LNCS (LNAI), vol. 10004, pp. 127–138. Springer, Cham (2017). https://doi.org/10.1007/978-3-319-60675-0_11
27. Woolf, B., et al.: Affect-aware tutors: recognising and responding to student affect. Int. J. Learn. Technol. **4**(3–4), 129–164 (2009)

Policy Matters: Expert Recommendations for Learning Analytics Policy

Maren Scheffel[1(✉)], Yi-Shan Tsai[2], Dragan Gašević[2,3], and Hendrik Drachsler[1,4,5]

[1] Open Universiteit, Valkenburgerweg 177, 6419AT Heerlen, The Netherlands
{maren.scheffel,hendrik.drachsler}@ou.nl
[2] The University of Edinburgh, 10 Crichton Street, Edinburgh EH8 9AB, UK
yi-shan.tsai@ed.ac.uk
[3] Monash University, 25 Exhibition Walk, Clayton, VIC 3800, Australia
dragan.gasevic@monash.edu
[4] DIPF, Schloßstr. 29, 60486 Frankfurt am Main, Germany
[5] Goethe Universität, Robert-Mayer-Str. 11-15, 60629 Frankfurt am Main, Germany

Abstract. Interest in learning analytics (LA) has grown rapidly among higher education institutions (HEIs). However, the maturity levels of HEIs in terms of being 'student data-informed' are only at early stages. There often are barriers that prevent data from being used systematically and effectively. To assist higher education institutions to become more mature users and custodians of digital data collected from students during their online learning activities, the SHEILA framework, a policy development framework that supports systematic, sustainable and responsible adoption of LA at an institutional level, was recently built. This paper presents a mix-method study using a group concept mapping (GCM) approach that was conducted with LA experts to explore essential features of LA policy in HEI in contribution the development of the framework. The study identified six clusters of features that an LA policy should include, provided ratings based on ease of implementation and importance for each of the six themes, and offered suggestions to HEIs how they can proceed with the development of LA policies.

Keywords: Learning analytics · Policy · Group concept mapping

1 Introduction

Learning analytics (LA) has attracted much attention by its promise to offer insights into some of the key challenges faced by higher education institutions (HEIs) [17,45]. Examples of the challenges that LA can address include student retention, adaptive learning, personalised feedback at scale, and quality enhancement. In spite of many reports indicating the positive results with the use of LA addressing these challenges, there have been few examples of systemic adoption

M. Scheffel et al. (Eds.): EC-TEL 2019, LNCS 11722, pp. 510–524, 2019.
https://doi.org/10.1007/978-3-030-29736-7_38

of LA in HEIs [8]. One of the key reasons for the limited adoption is the shortage of LA policies that would guide the way how HEIs address some of they key legal, ethical, privacy, and security issues vis-à-vis LA [42].

This paper contributes to the broader body of the literature in LA by reporting the findings of a study that solicited expert input on the directions of what LA policy in HEIs should include. Specifically, the contributions of the paper include: (1) a methodologically collected list of features that a LA policy in HEIs should include, (2) empirically systematised and rated themes that encompass the features that a LA policy in HEIs should include, and (3) suggestions for HEIs how to proceed with the development of LA policy.

2 Literature

2.1 Issues in the Adoption of Learning Analytics

LA aims to close feedback loops with real-time data about learners and learning contexts based on learner engagement and performance, e.g. log data collected from virtual learning environments, academic and demographic data held in student information systems, and the social interactions of learners in online forums or social media. Clow [5] illustrates the feedback loop with four elements that form an iterative cycle: learners, data, metrics, and interventions. LA analyses data about learners and produces feedback based on pre-identified metrics, for the purpose of supporting learners with interventions such as feedback dashboards, personal messages, face-to-face meetings, and curriculum adjustment [4,20,30]. However, closing a LA feedback loop can be challenging due to various issues associated with each of the four elements.

The learner is the main subject of data in a LA cycle. The large scope and velocity of data being collected from them could induce a sense of surveillance and intrusion into spaces considered private or personal [31]. There is a prevailing conflict in the LA field where anonymity policy that guides institutional data practices runs against the requirement of LA in retaining certain degrees of individual linkages to deliver customised interventions [36]. The dilemma that HEIs face here is the duty of care in terms of protecting students from being datafied or having their privacy violated, and the opportunity to improve educational quality through a more personalised approach. This has led to a call for more transparency and control of data for students [32,33].

However, the operation of LA based on individual consent could be problematic in that not only the quality and integrity of data are threatened, but also the received consent is hardly ever fully informed. Prominent issues with informed consent are the lack of interest or information that can help students understand the implications of agreeing to share data about themselves [32,36]. This has also led to a question of timing as to when consent should be sought [32]. In light of this issue and in response to the consent requirements in the General Data Protection Regulation 2016/679, the UK non-profit educational consultancy Jisc suggests that institutions should seek 'downstream consent' (consent for personalised intervention), as there is usually clearer information about consequences on individuals at this stage than in the phase of finding patterns in data [7].

LA relies on data and metrics to provide so-called 'evidence-based' insights. However, a number of issues have been raised in relation to the two elements. In terms of data, common issues include the challenges of integrating information systems and different types of data [2], breaking down silos of data [3,38], and embedding data technologies into existing learning environments [13]. In addition to technical issues associated with data, there is a concern that the choice of data sources and metrics for LA narrows learning to activities that happen in the digital domain, ignoring activities that are not 'capturable' or 'perceivable' but are an integral part of learning processes [28]. This concern has led to criticisms on LA being driven by behaviourism that tends to focus on describing rather than explaining actions [35]. It has also resulted in the problem of metrics being disconnected from the educational contexts and the broader social and cultural conditions in which learning takes place [25]. As a result, several scholars contend that the design and implementation of LA need to consider educational theories and practice [14,15,21,22,24]. In particular, the interpretation of analytics results about learners needs to consider learning design choices [27]. In light of the issues related to data and metrics, Gašević and colleagues [17] argue that approaches to LA should be question-driven rather than data-driven, and that institutions need to explore creative data sourcing to tackle learning issues, while acknowledging the inherent limitations of data.

A common issue with LA-based interventions is the limited availability of time and skills from key users [43]. The perception of LA being a burden on workload has been observed especially among teaching staff [19,26]. This has often resulted in resistance to the adoption of new technology, including LA. Moreover, to close the feedback loop effectively, key users are expected to have a certain degree of data literacy that allows them to interpret data and make critical decisions as to whether and how to act on the feedback [2,31,42,46] but insufficient data literacy among students could lead to misinterpretation of LA dashboards and negative emotions as a consequence [16]. Both the constraints of time and skills can stagnate the development of a data-informed culture in decision making, which is arguably a key step to enable institutional transformation with LA [17].

Another common issue to consider when designing interventions is the impact on student well-being and the equity of treatment, e.g. the mechanism of nudging students when being identified as at risk of failing or underperforming could potentially demotivate learners and cause undue anxiety or damage to self-esteem [19]. Similarly, the peer-comparison function of learning dashboards has often attracted polarised views from students [16,21,34]. Although LA has been recognised for its potential to enhance learning by personalising educational support, this strength has also been perceived as an issues when it comes to equity of treatment, i.e., educational resources being directed to some learners but not the others [34,44]. On the other hand, the highly personalised approach also raises concerns about spoon-feeding students and impeding independent skill development as a result [19]. The above-mentioned issues are crucial to the closure of a LA feedback loop and systemic adoption of LA at an institutional level. In the next section, we discuss approaches that have been suggested in the literature to tackle these prominent challenges.

2.2 LA Adoption Frameworks and Policy

Issues that hamper institutional adoption of LA tend to derive from the interactions of technical, social and cultural factors in a complex educational system. A LA sophistication model [41] paints five stages of deployment maturity, starting from awareness and moving on to experimentation, implementation, organisational transformation and finally sector transformation. The current deployment of LA in the higher education landscape is mostly at the first three stages, with no large-scale systemic adoption being reported yet. Recent studies have echoed the observation of the field as thriving but yet to mature [8,42], e.g. studies by Ferguson et al. [12] and Viberg et al. [45] show that the potential of LA in improving learning and teaching is yet to be verified with more empirical evidence. Moreover, in their review of 252 papers on the adoption of LA in higher education, Viberg et al. found that only a small number of the studies are deemed scalable (6%). Similarly, Dawson et al. [8] examined 522 papers and found that the majority of LA studies focus on small-scale projects or independent courses.

In view of the tangled interactions between technology and the myriads of human and social elements in a complex educational system, scholars have proposed strategic frameworks and approaches to guide LA adoption. For example, Greller and Drachsler [18] proposed a framework of critical dimensions of LA processes to highlight technical requirements, key stakeholders, and social constraints that require attention when formulating LA design. Similarly, the Learning Analytics Readiness Instrument (LARI) [2] assesses five readiness components: governance/infrastructure, ability, data, culture, and process. The beta analysis of this framework revealed that culture particularly plays a key role in institutional readiness for LA [29]. In light of the resistant culture to change in higher education, Ferguson and others [13] proposed the Rapid Outcome Mapping Approach (ROMA), originally developed to inform policy process in international development [47], to promote strategic planning that is responsive to the constantly changing environment of higher education. In addition to the elements of objectives, stakeholders and capacity considered by the two frameworks mentioned above, this framework highlights a context-specific approach to identifying drivers for LA and desired changes.

LA adoption frameworks need to work along with a sound policy that speaks to different stakeholders and takes into consideration issues that derive from the interactions of social, cultural, technological, and educational dimensions. Jisc for example developed a code of practice for LA and carried out a series of expert consultation activities and identify six types of stakeholders and their responsibility in LA processes [39,40]. The purpose of the code is to ensure that LA benefits students and is carried out transparently. A similar approach is seen in the wider European context where an EU-funded project, Learning Analytics Community Exchange (LACE), drove the development of the DELICATE checklist to demystify pervasive uncertainty about legal boundaries and ethical limits when it comes to LA [10]. The list's eight action points are meant to help institutional leaders to develop a trust relationship with key stakeholders in their deployment of LA.

Existing LA policies do not address all the dimensions deemed as important factors in LA processes. This is revealed in a study by Tsai and Gašević [42]. In their review of eight policies, including Jisc's code of practice and the DELICATE checklist [10,39,40], they noted the lack of two-way communication channels among stakeholders in a stratified institutional structure and indications of required skills or training for LA, despite the fact that stakeholder involvement and data literacy has been highlighted as key elements of capacity building [1,18,29,41]. They also found that while all the reviewed policies clearly state that enhancing learning and teaching were the ultimate goals for LA, there was no indication about any pedagogy-based approach that teaching staff, technology developers, or decision makers should consider when developing LA metrics or interventions. Similarly, Dawson et al. [8] point out that attention paid to evaluating LA-based interventions has been insufficient to date. The discrepancies mentioned above show that existing policies and guidelines tend to focus on ensuring ethical and legally compliant conducts, while giving relatively little attention to other dimensions that are equally important to LA deployment, as identified in the LA adoption frameworks discussed above.

In light of this, we conducted a group concept mapping (GCM) study intended to explore disparities between what is considered important and what is easy to implement in a LA policy context. Other aspects within the domain of LA have already been explored making use of GCM, e.g. quality indicators of LA [37], specific changes that learning analytics will trigger in Dutch education [11], and continued impact of learning analytics on learning and teaching [6]. These studies have shown that GCM is an effective method to collect and cluster grounded data based on the opinions of participants. However, none of these previous studies specifically uses GCM to analyse key stakeholder's views towards policy in the context of learning analytics. An essential part of policy formation is the consultation of experts who have research and practical experience in implementing LA. Hence, we carried out an expert consultation using a GCM approach to identify essential elements of LA policy and directions for policy development in the field.

3 Methods

Group Concept Mapping (GCM) is a common methodology to identify a group's understanding of any given issue. Making use of quantitative as well as qualitative measures and providing specific analysis and data interpretation methods, GCM is a very structured approach that creates maps of the involved stakeholders' ideas of the chosen topic [23]. Our study was conducted using a GCM online tool[1] and consisted of three steps: (1) brainstorming, i.e. collection of ideas about a topic, (2) sorting of the collected ideas into clusters, and (3) rating of the ideas according to their importance and their ease of implementation. The data collected with the GCM tool were with statistical techniques such as multidimensional scaling and hierarchical clustering to reveal shared patterns. The

[1] http://conceptsystemsglobal.com.

GCM tool also provides visualisations of the analyses to help grasp the emerging structures and to interpret them. The appeal of using a GCM is its bottom-up approach: experts are given ideas to sort and rate that were generated by the community itself.

Our study was divided in two phases: the community phase and the experts phase. The community phase consisted of the brainstorming step where participation was accessible via a link and was conducted openly, i.e. people did not have to register with the GCM tool in order to participate. Calls for participation were circulated among the academic research community via several channels, e.g. Twitter, project websites, Google groups, personal contact, email etc., specifically trying to reach those interested in LA policies. Participants were asked to generate ideas by completing the statement "*An essential feature of a higher education institution's learning analytics policy should be ...*". The brainstorming phase was open for ten days from October 1, 2016 to October 10, 2016. Sixty-five people participated in the brainstorming phase and generated a total of 136 ideas. Before the ideas were released into the second phase, identical statements were unified while those statements containing more than one idea were split so that each statement contained one possible LA policy feature. After this cleaning process, the 99 ideas[2] that were left were randomised and pushed into phase Two.

The second phase of the study consisted of the sorting and the rating steps. Seventy-five experts from the field of LA (including members of the project consortium) were selected for this part of the study based on their specific experience and expertise (i.e. they had been involved in the domain for several years, had published about LA-related topics, were from the higher education sector and preferably had a PhD degree) and personally invited by email to participate. In order to participate, they had to register with the GCM tool. The sorting and rating module of the tool was open for participation for three weeks from October 27, 2016 to November 18, 2016. Participants first sorted the features according to their view of the features' similarity in meaning or theme and were asked to also name the clusters. Dissimilar features were not to be put into a 'miscellaneous' cluster but rather into their own one-feature-cluster in order to ensure feature similarity within the clusters. Then, the participants rated all features on a scale of 1 to 7 according to their *importance* and *ease of implementation* in an institution's LA policy, with 1 being of lowest and 7 being of highest *importance*/*ease*. In the end, the sortings of 30 participants were included in the study, while the *importance* ratings of 29 participants and the *ease* ratings of 25 participants were included (the difference in numbers stems from partial responses being excluded from the analysis).

4 Results

For the sorted features, the GCM tool offers multidimensional scaling and hierarchical clustering, while means, standard deviation and correlation analyses were

[2] Available at https://sheilaproject.eu/2019/07/01/gcm-study/99statements/.

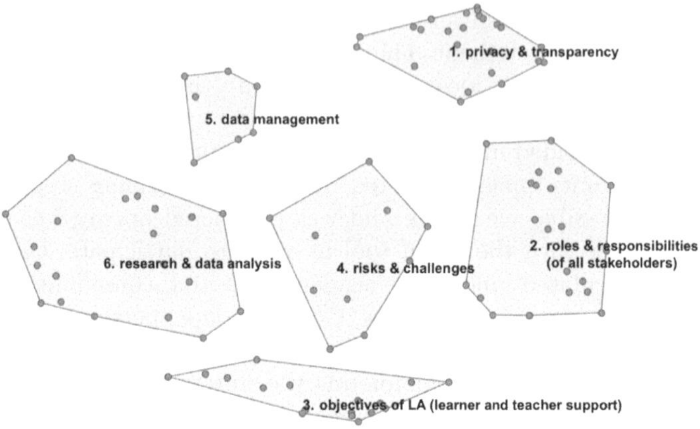

Fig. 1. Cluster map with labels

done for the ratings. The outcome of the multidimensional scaling analysis is a so-called point map that can be read like a geographic map of a landscape with having semantically similar feature points in the North, South, West or East. Feature points that are clustered for instance in the North are semantically highly different from statements clustered in other parts of the map (see the points visible in the cluster map in Fig. 1). In the multidimensional scaling analysis, each feature is assigned a bridging value between 0 and 1. Features with low bridging values were grouped with other similar features around them. In cases where the bridging values were higher, features could still be grouped together but the distance to the surrounding points on the map was then bigger.

In order to determine boundaries between the groups of features, i.e. to determine clusters, the GCM tool's hierarchical clustering analysis was used. Making use of cluster replay maps (i.e. the tool's different cluster solutions to a given point map) and starting with a larger number (e.g., 12 clusters) and working down to a lower number (e.g., two) for each cluster-merging step, we looked at the features of clusters that were to be combined and checked whether that merge made sense. In our case, the solution with six clusters best represented the collected data and the purpose of our study. Once the number of clusters was settled, the clusters needed to be labelled meaningfully. Using the suggestions made by the GCM tool is one way of finding these labels. Alternatively, one could look for an overarching theme for all features in a cluster or for those with low bridging values only. Combining all three methods we labelled our clusters in the following way (see Fig. 1): (1) *privacy & transparency*, (2) *roles & responsibilities (of all stakeholders)*, (3) *objectives of learning analytics (learner and teacher support)*, (4) *risks & challenges*, (5) *data management*, and (6) *research & data analysis*. The GCM tool also assigned a bridging value to each cluster. The lower the bridging value was, the more coherent a cluster was. Cluster 1, *privacy & transparency*, was the most coherent one (0.12), followed by Cluster 3,

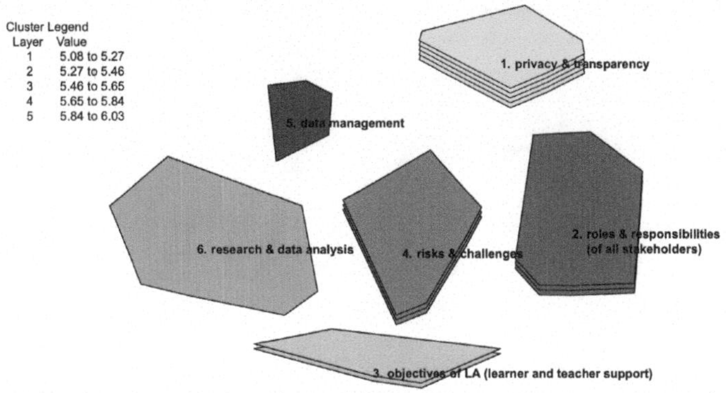

Fig. 2. Rating map on *importance* (legend shows average ratings of layers)

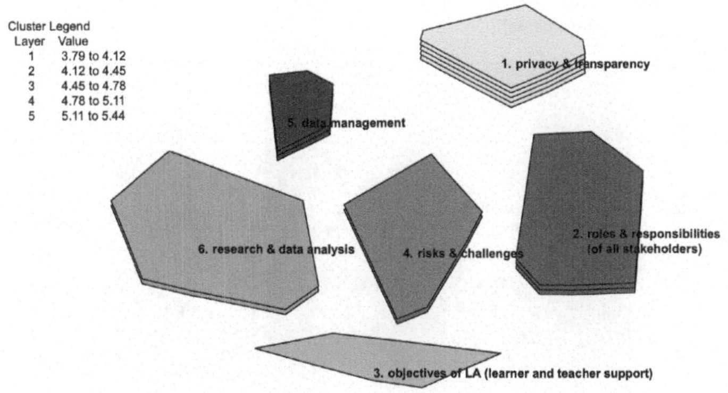

Fig. 3. Rating map on *ease of implementation* (legend shows average ratings of layers)

objectives of LA (0.28). In the middle with similar coherence values were Cluster 4, *risks & challenges* (0.41), and Cluster 2, *roles & responsibilities* (0.45). The last two clusters, also with similar values of coherence, were Cluster 6, *research & data analysis* (0.60), and Cluster 5, *data management* (0.64).

With the clusters identified and labelled, the experts' ratings of the features according to their *importance* and *ease of implementation* in LA policy were taken into account as well. The GCM tool automatically applied the experts' ratings to the cluster map and indicated the levels of *importance* and *ease of implementation* by layering the clusters. The GCM tool always bases its calculations on a maximum of five layers. The actual number of layers per cluster is then based on the average ratings provided by the experts for the features in that cluster. The anchors for the map legend are based on the high and low average ratings across all participating experts. One layer indicates an overall low rating, while five layers indicate an overall high rating for a given cluster (see Figs. 2 and 3).

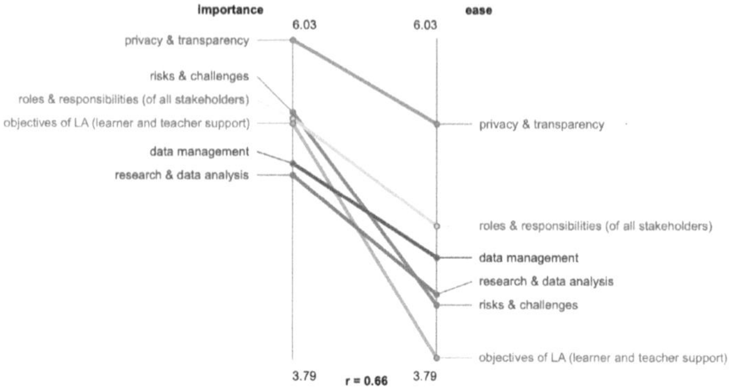

Fig. 4. Ladder graph of the *importance* and *ease of implementation* rating values for the six clusters

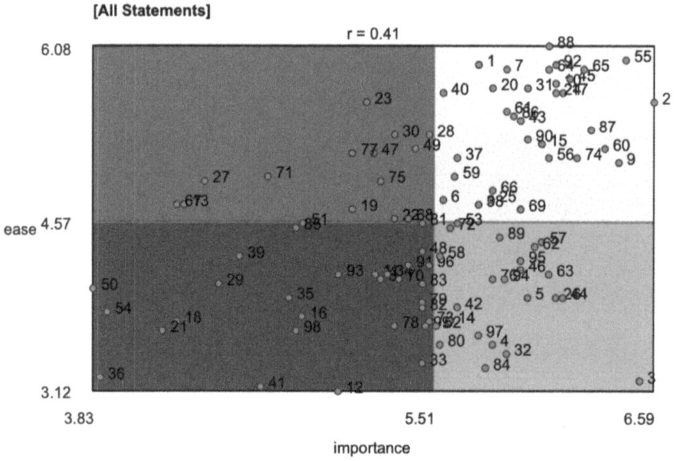

Fig. 5. Go-zone graph of all 99 features mapped on the two axes of *importance* and *ease of implementation* according to their average rating

A visualisation well-suited for the comparison of clusters' ratings is a ladder graph. Figure 4 shows such a graph for the results of our study. The rating values are based on a cluster's average rating. A Pearson product-moment correlation coefficient of $r = 0.66$ indicates an intermediate positive relation between the two aspects of *importance* and *ease of implementation*. For both aspects, the *privacy & transparency* cluster by far received the highest value. As was already observable from the two rating maps, the order of the other clusters differs between the two rating aspects. What the ladder graph shows very clearly, however, is that the experts' *importance* ratings were considerably higher than those for *ease of implementation*. All cluster average ratings for *importance* were higher than those for *ease of implementation* except for the *ease* cluster on *privacy & transparency* which was at a similar value as the *importance* clusters.

A third visualisation for the rating data offered by the GCM tool are go-zone graphs. These graphs allow us to explore the features in relation to their ratings more deeply. In a go-zone graph each point, i.e. each feature, is mapped onto a space between x- and y-axis based on the mean values of the two ratings *importance* and *ease of implementation.* Go-zone graphs were created for individual clusters or for all features together. Figure 5 shows the go-zone graph for all 99 features in our study. These types of graphs made it easy to identify features that are particularly important or particularly easy to implement in a LA policy. They also allow the identification of features with a good balance of *importance* and *ease* and are thus are very useful in the selection of features suitable for a LA policy. For example, the results of the GCM have been adopted to update the first version of the SHEILA framework [43].

5 Discussion and Conclusion

The clustering results (see Fig. 1) show that a wide range of topics were considered essential to a LA policy in higher education. In particular, the cluster on *objectives of LA* forms the basis of our cluster landscape. Formulating an aim for the use of LA can thus be seen as an entry point. This is in line with Ferguson et al. [13] who propose to identify the overarching policy objectives as the first step of the ROMA model when it is being used in the LA context. As can be seen from the ratings (see Fig. 4), features in this cluster were not deemed overly important by LA experts and not easy (i.e., they are rather difficult) to implement. This finding seems to suggest that defining objectives of LA in a HEI's LA policy is not a straightforward process. It is unclear whether this is due to a data-driven (rather than question-driven) approach to LA as an observed issue in the literature [17], or due to insufficient empirical evidence proving that LA has reached its ultimate goals to enhance learning and teaching [12,42,45]. However, as the set goals for LA would inevitably affect approaches to LA [13], and hence all the issues represented through these clustered themes, an LA policy in HEIs must explicitly state the objectives of LA, despite their low ease of implementation.

Above this quite coherent base layer, a group of clusters forms the intermediate body. At the centre of the map and thus connecting all other clusters with one another, was the one about *risks & challenges.* The cluster was flanked by two more technical clusters (*data management* and *research & data analysis*) in the West and one stakeholder-related cluster (*roles & responsibilities*) in the East. This latter cluster is seen by the experts as fairly important and also quite easy to implement (Fig. 4). As also exemplified by Jisc's code of practice [39,40], LA requires collective efforts from a wide range of stakeholders, and it is therefore crucial to clarify roles and responsibilities for stakeholders ranging from managers to students which the LA field has clearly identified as a need [18,41]. A policy can be seen as something rather prescriptive that is imposed by an institution's management, but LA adoption needs both top-down and bottom-up approaches, i.e. all stakeholders need to be involved. It has, however, also been identified that current LA policies have paid relatively low attention to skill development of key users and two-way communication channels [18,42]. We thus suggest that policy makers should address these areas when considering roles and responsibilities of stakeholders.

At the very top of the map, i.e. in the North, sits the cluster on *privacy & transparency*. While the bottom cluster about objectives can be seen as a base, this cluster can be seen as the pinnacle or the lid that rounds out a LA policy. Without it, a policy would thus not be complete. Aspects about transparency and privacy are considered the most important ones but also the easiest to implement in LA policy by far according to the GCM participants. Another interesting result with regards to the statements of the *privacy & transparency* cluster was the overall positive rating on the *ease of implementation*. This raised our attention as privacy and ethics have been considered as difficult issues in the literature so far. Looking closer at the ratings of this cluster reveals a discrepancy between more theoretical and practical privacy-related statements. For instance, the most highly rated statement with regards to *importance* '2. transparency, i.e. clearly informing students of how their data is collected, used and protected' as well as the most highly rated statement with regards to *ease* '88. a clear description of data protection measures taken' can both be considered as theoretical statements that can be easily safeguarded by university policy. A more privacy practical item like '96. an agreement between learners, teachers and policy makers on regulating a proper use of data' on the other hand, is rated less easy to be implemented in LA policy as it pinpoints to the difficult situation of establishing privacy protection in daily practice.

This finding thus warrants future research considering that the challenges identified in the literature related to transparency and privacy are never straightforward [31,36]. That is to say, while data policies tend to highlight transparency and privacy procedures, the implementation of them in the real world tend to meet complex challenges [42] that derive from the conflicts of interests among different actors in a social network and the increasing focus on the 'ownership of data', control of data for students and issues with informed consent [32,33]. Therefore, it is important that the development of LA policy involves inputs from all relevant stakeholders, and that communication channels are clearly indicated in the policy to invite feedback on the implementation of the written policy in the real world, so as to ensure its relevance to the institutional practices.

The clustered themes shown in this study coincide with the argument made by Siemens et al. [41] that the main challenges in the deployment of LA are not technical but social. We could also see from the decline of average values in the ratings of *ease of implementation* compared to the ratings of *importance* that each of the identified themes are potential challenges to address in practice. This study has highlighted important aspects to address in LA policy. However, it is not our intention to suggest that policy makers should prioritise one aspect more than the other given the experts' ratings of the *importance* and *ease of implementation*. Instead, the study reflects the current emphasis on privacy and legal compliance in the deployment of LA, and the views presented in this study are based on a particular stakeholder group only, i.e., LA experts. All the aspects should receive equal attention, as suggested in the literature, though one aspect might be easier to define than another. Involving all the relevant stakeholders in a co-creation process [9] of LA policy could help clarify the 'foggy areas' of these identified aspects and ensure their relevance to the experiences of different stakeholders in the institution.

References

1. Arnold, K.E., Lonn, S., Pistilli, M.D.: An exercise in institutional reflection: the learning analytics readiness instrument (LARI). In: Proceedings of the 4th International Conference on Learning Analytics & Knowledge, pp. 163–167. ACM (2014)
2. Arnold, K.E., Lynch, G., Huston, D., Wong, L., Jorn, L., Olsen, C.W.: Building institutional capacities and competencies for systemic learning analytics initiatives. In: Proceedings of the 4th International Conference on Learning Analytics & Knowledge, pp. 257–260. ACM (2014)
3. Arroway, P., Morgan, G., O'Keefe, M., Yanosky, R.: Learning analytics in higher education. Technical report, EDUCAUSE Center for Analysis and Research (2016)
4. Bodily, R., Verbert, K.: Review of research on student-facing learning analytics dashboards and educational recommender systems. IEEE Trans. Learn. Technol. **10**(4), 405–418 (2017)
5. Clow, D.: The learning analytics cycle: closing the loop effectively. In: Proceedings of the 2nd International Conference on Learning Analytics & Knowledge, pp. 134–138. ACM (2012)
6. Colvin, C., et al.: Student retention and learning analytics: a snapshot of Australian practices and a framework for advancement. Australian Government Office for Learning and Teaching, Canberra, ACT (2016)
7. Cormack, A.N.: Downstream consent: a better legal framework for big data. J. Inf. Rights Policy Pract. **1**(1) (2016). https://jirpp.winchesteruniversitypress.org/articles/abstract/10.21039/irpandp.v1i1.9/
8. Dawson, S., Joksimovic, S., Poquet, O., Siemens, G.: Increasing the impact of learning analytics. In: Proceedings of the 9th International Conference on Learning Analytics & Knowledge, pp. 446–455. ACM (2019)
9. Dollinger, M., Lodge, J.M.: Co-creation strategies for learning analytics. In: Proceedings of the 8th International Conference on Learning Analytics & Knowledge, pp. 97–101. ACM (2018)
10. Drachsler, H., Greller, W.: Privacy and analytics: it's a DELICATE issue - a checklist for trusted learning analytics. In: Proceedings of the 6th International Conference on Learning Analytics & Knowledge, pp. 89–98. ACM (2016)
11. Drachsler, H., Stoyanov, S., Specht, M.: The impact of learning analytics on the Dutch education system. In: Proceedings of the 4th International Conference on Learning Analytics & Knowledge, pp. 158–162. ACM (2014)
12. Ferguson, R., Clow, D.: Where is the evidence? A call to action for learning analytics. In: Proceedings of the 7th International Conference on Learning Analytics & Knowledge, pp. 56–65. ACM (2017)
13. Ferguson, R., Macfadyen, L.P., Clow, D., Tynan, B., Alexander, S., Dawson, S.: Setting learning analytics in context: overcoming the barriers to large-scale adoption. J. Learn. Analytics **1**(3), 120–144 (2015)

14. Fincham, E., Whitelock-Wainwright, A., Kovanović, V., Joksimović, S., van Staalduinen, J.P., Gašević, D.: Counting clicks is not enough: validating a theorized model of engagement in learning analytics. In: Proceedings of the 9th International Conference on Learning Analytics & Knowledge, pp. 501–510. ACM (2019)
15. Gašević, D., Dawson, S., Siemens, G.: Let's not forget: learning analytics are about learning. TechTrends **59**(1), 64–71 (2015)
16. Gašević, D., Kovanović, V., Joksimović, S.: Piecing the learning analytics puzzle: a consolidated model of a field of research and practice. Learn. Res. Pract. **3**(1), 63–78 (2017)
17. Gašević, D., Tsai, Y.S., Dawson, S., Pardo, A.: How do we start? An approach to learning analytics adoption in higher education. Int. J. Inf. Learn. Technol. (in press)
18. Greller, W., Drachsler, H.: Translating learning into numbers: a generic framework for learning analytics. Educ. Technol. Soc. **15**(3), 42–57 (2012)
19. Howell, J.A., Roberts, L.D., Seaman, K., Gibson, D.C.: Are we on our way to becoming a "helicopter university"? Academics' views on learning analytics. Technol. Knowl. Learn. **23**(1), 1–20 (2018)
20. Jivet, I., Scheffel, M., Drachsler, H., Specht, M.: Awareness is not enough: pitfalls of learning analytics dashboards in the educational practice. In: Lavoué, É., Drachsler, H., Verbert, K., Broisin, J., Pérez-Sanagustín, M. (eds.) EC-TEL 2017. LNCS, vol. 10474, pp. 82–96. Springer, Cham (2017). https://doi.org/10.1007/978-3-319-66610-5_7
21. Jivet, I., Scheffel, M., Specht, M., Drachsler, H.: License to evaluate: preparing learning analytics dashboards for educational practice. In: Proceedings of the 8th International Conference on Learning Analytics & Knowledge, pp. 31–40. ACM (2018)
22. Joksimović, S., Manataki, A., Gašević, D., Dawson, S., Kovanović, V., De Kereki, I.F.: Translating network position into performance: importance of centrality in different network configurations. In: Proceedings of the 6th International Conference on Learning Analytics & Knowledge, pp. 314–323. ACM (2016)
23. Kane, M., Trochim, W.M.K.: Concept Mapping for Planning and Evaluation. Sage Publication, Thousand Oaks (2007)
24. Kitto, K., Shum, S.B., Gibson, A.: Embracing imperfection in learning analytics. In: Proceedings of the 8th International Conference on Learning Analytics & Knowledge, pp. 451–460. ACM (2018)
25. Knox, J.: Data power in education: exploring critical awareness with the "learning analytics report card". Telev. New Media **18**(8), 734–752 (2017)
26. Macfadyen, L.P., Dawson, S., Pardo, A., Gašević, D.: Embracing big data in complex educational systems: the learning analytics imperative and the policy challenge. Res. Pract. Assess. **9**, 17–28 (2014)
27. Mangaroska, K., Giannakos, M.: Learning analytics for learning design: towards evidence-driven decisions to enhance learning. In: Lavoué, É., Drachsler, H., Verbert, K., Broisin, J., Pérez-Sanagustín, M. (eds.) EC-TEL 2017. LNCS, vol. 10474, pp. 428–433. Springer, Cham (2017). https://doi.org/10.1007/978-3-319-66610-5_38
28. Mustafina, J., Galiullin, L., Al-Jumeily, D., Petrov, E., Alloghani, M., Kaky, A.: Application of learning analytics in higher educational institutions. In: Proceedings of the 11th International Conference on Developments in eSystems Engineering (DeSE), pp. 163–168. IEEE (2018)

29. Oster, M., Lonn, S., Pistilli, M.D., Brown, M.G.: The learning analytics readiness instrument. In: Proceedings of the 6th International Conference on Learning Analytics & Knowledge, pp. 173–182. ACM (2016)
30. Pardo, A., Jovanovic, J., Dawson, S., Gašević, D., Mirriahi, N.: Using learning analytics to scale the provision of personalised feedback. Br. J. Educ. Technol. **50**(1), 128–138 (2019)
31. Pardo, A., Siemens, G.: Ethical and privacy principles for learning analytics. Br. J. Educ. Technol. **45**(3), 438–450 (2014)
32. Prinsloo, P., Slade, S.: Student privacy self-management: implications for learning analytics. In: Proceedings of the 5th International Conference on Learning Analytics & Knowledge, pp. 83–92. ACM (2015)
33. Prinsloo, P., Slade, S.: Student vulnerability, agency, and learning analytics: an exploration. J. Learn. Analytics **3**(1), 159–182 (2016)
34. Roberts, L.D., Howell, J.A., Seaman, K., Gibson, D.C.: Student attitudes toward learning analytics in higher education: "the fitbit version of the learning world". Front. Psychol, **7** (2016). https://www.frontiersin.org/articles/10.3389/fpsyg.2016.01959/full. Article No. 1959
35. Rogers, T.: Critical realism and learning analytics research: epistemological implications of an ontological foundation. In: Proceedings of the 5th International Conference on Learning Analytics & Knowledge, pp. 223–230. ACM (2015)
36. Rubel, A., Jones, K.M.: Student privacy in learning analytics: an information ethics perspective. Inf. Soc. **32**(2), 143–159 (2016)
37. Scheffel, M., Drachsler, H., Stoyanov, S., Specht, M.: Quality indicators for learning analytics. Educ. Technol. Soc. **17**(4), 117–132 (2014)
38. Sclater, N.: Learning analytics: the current state of play in UK higher and further education (2014). http://repository.jisc.ac.uk/5657/1/Learning_analytics_report.pdf
39. Sclater, N.: Developing a code of practice for learning analytics. J. Learn. Analytics **3**(1), 16–42 (2016)
40. Sclater, N., Bailey, P.: Code of practice for learning analytics (2015). https://www.jisc.ac.uk/guides/code-of-practice-for-learning-analytics
41. Siemens, G., Dawson, S., Lynch, G.: Improving the Quality and Productivity of the Higher Education Sector. Policy and Strategy for Systems-Level Deployment of Learning Analytics. Society for Learning Analytics Research for the Australian Office for Learning and Teaching, Canberra, Australia (2013)
42. Tsai, Y.S., Gašević, D.: Learning analytics in higher education - challenges and policies: a review of eight learning analytics policies. In: Proceedings of the 7th International Conference on Learning Analytics & Knowledge, pp. 233–242. ACM (2017)
43. Tsai, Y.S., et al.: The SHEILA framework: informing institutional strategies and policy processes of learning analytics. J. Learn. Analytics **5**(3), 5–20 (2018)
44. Tsai, Y.S., Perrotta, C., Gašević, D.: Empowering learners with personalised learning approaches? Agency, equity and transparency in the context of learning analytics. Assess. Eval. High. Educ. (in press)
45. Viberg, O., Hatakka, M., Bälter, O., Mavroudi, A.: The current landscape of learning analytics in higher education. Comput. Hum. Behav. **89**, 98–110 (2018)

46. Wolff, A., Moore, J., Zdrahal, Z., Hlosta, M., Kuzilek, J.: Data literacy for learning analytics. In: Proceedings of the 6th International Conference on Learning Analytics & Knowledge, pp. 500–501. ACM (2016)
47. Young, J., Mendizabel, E.: Helping researchers become policy entrepreneurs - how to develop engagement strategies for evidence-based policy-making. Overseas Development Institute London (2009)

Detection of Learning Strategies: A Comparison of Process, Sequence and Network Analytic Approaches

Wannisa Matcha[1(✉)], Dragan Gašević[1,2(✉)], Nora'ayu Ahmad Uzir[1,3(✉)], Jelena Jovanović[4(✉)], Abelardo Pardo[5(✉)], Jorge Maldonado-Mahauad[6,7(✉)], and Mar Pérez-Sanagustín[6,8(✉)]

[1] University of Edinburgh, Edinburgh EH8 9AB, UK
{w.matcha,n.uzir}@ed.ac.uk
[2] Monash University, Clayton, VIC 3800, Australia
dragan.gasevic@monash.edu
[3] Universiti Teknologi MARA, 40150 Shah Alam, Malaysia
[4] University of Belgrade, 11000 Belgrade, Serbia
jelena.jovanovic@fon.bg.ac.rs
[5] University of South Australia, Adelaide, SA 5000, Australia
abelardo.pardo@unisa.edu.au
[6] Pontificia Universidad Católica de Chile, Santiago, Chile
jjmaldonado@uc.cl, mar.perez@ing.puc.cl
[7] Universidad de Cuenca, Cuenca, Ecuador
[8] Institute de Recherche en Informatique de Toulouse (IRIT), Université Paul Sabatier Toulouse III, 31062 Toulouse Cedex 9, France

Abstract. Research in learning analytics proposed different computational techniques to detect learning tactics and strategies adopted by learners in digital environments through the analysis of students' trace data. While many promising insights have been produced, there has been much less understanding about how and to what extent different data analytic approaches influence results. This paper presents a comparison of three analytic approaches including process, sequence, and network approaches for detection of learning tactics and strategies. The analysis was performed on a dataset collected in a massive open online course on software programming. All three approaches produced four tactics and three strategy groups. The tactics detected by using the sequence analysis approach differed from those identified by the other two methods. The process and network analytic approaches had more than 66% of similarity in the detected tactics. Learning strategies detected by the three approaches proved to be highly similar.

Keywords: Learning strategy · Learning analytics · Data analytics

1 Introduction

The objective of massive open online courses (MOOCs) is to offer learning opportunities to a wide range of learners. However, MOOCs have been associated with high dropout and failure rates [1, 2]. Research identified several factors associated with such

M. Scheffel et al. (Eds.): EC-TEL 2019, LNCS 11722, pp. 525–540, 2019.
https://doi.org/10.1007/978-3-030-29736-7_39

course outcomes including motivation, intention, time management, and learning experiences, to name a few [3, 4]. Learning tactics and strategies adopted by MOOC participants have been identified as key factors of success prediction [5–7]. Much research in traditional learning environments explored students' learning strategies [6, 8]. However, students' learning strategies in MOOCs are much less understood. MOOC platforms allow for recording trace data of the actual learners' behavior. However, such data are large, diverse, and complex to analyze. As a consequence, researchers have proposed a variety of methods that go beyond traditional statistics methods to unveil students' learning strategies [9, 10]. While the applied data analytic methods led to useful findings, the diversity of the adopted methods hindered the replication and generalization of the results. Little work has been done to compare how the applied approaches differ in terms of the tactics and strategies that they identify. This study explored how three analytic approaches – drawing from sequence, process, and network analytic techniques – could influence the detection of learning tactics and strategies.

2 Background

Research has emphasised the importance of using effective learning strategies as one of the key factors of successful learning. Learning strategy can be defined as *"any thoughts, behaviors, beliefs or emotions that facilitate the acquisition, understanding, or later transfer of new knowledge and skills"* [12, p. 727]. A closely related construct is the one of learning tactic, which can be defined as a sequence of actions that a student performs in relation to a given task within a learning session [12]. Defined in terms of tactics, learning strategies can be considered the regularity in the application of learning tactics or a pattern of how each student uses certain tactics [13]. Such patterns of tactic application evolve and become the characteristics of one's learning, which may be considered as aptitudes that could further predict the future behaviors [14].

Thanks to the large dataset of trace data on students' behavior, contemporary research aims to leverage these datasets to explore learning tactics and strategies by considering how these dynamic constructs unfold. In *network analytic approaches*, learning tactics and strategies are identified from networks built based on the co-occurrence of learning states or actions. These approaches were originally proposed for studying learning strategies as learning sequences [15]. The application of graph multiplicity measures, as commonly used in network science, has been then suggested to analyze the importance of individual events that contribute to student learning. For example, Siadaty et al. [16] applied this methodology to identify how technological interventions activated different processes of self-regulated learning. More recently, approaches suggest the use of *sequence analysis* techniques combined with unsupervised learning to detect learning tactics and strategies from trace data [9]. Similarly, learning tactics and strategies can be identified by analyzing the distribution of learning sequences [17].

Process-oriented data analysis approach emphasise the timing of the events. Malmberg et al. explored self-regulated learning strategies in a collaborative learning context by using a process mining technique [18]. Similarly, Matcha et al. [10] detected learning tactics and strategies from trace data by combining temporal analysis of the trace data (first-order Markov models) and clustering (Expectation-Maximization) [10]. Maldonado-Mahauad et al. [19] used a combination of process mining and clustering techniques to identify self-regulated learning strategies that different group of learners employed when interacting with the course contents (video-lectures and assessments).

Despite the interesting insights produced by these individual approaches, there has been limited research that explored how these three analytic approaches might have influenced the results. Hence, this paper aims to answer the following research question: *How do different data analytics techniques proposed in the literature for the detection of learning tactics and strategies apply to the same dataset?* That is, the paper compares approaches that emphasize sequence, network and process dimensions.

3 Methods

3.1 Data

The data used in this study was collected from the Introduction to Python course offered by the Pontificia Universidad católica de Chile on the Coursera MOOC platform in its two different editions. A total of 4,217 students registered their interest in the course. The course was in Spanish and was offered on demand (i.e. self-pace). In 8 weeks, the course covered six programming topics with 2–3 subtopics each. For each topic, the course offered a set of short video lectures with embedded questions (to provoke a simple recall of the concepts) and a set of reading materials. The students also had several theoretical exercises (11 quizzes) and practical exercises (13 exams). Among the quizzes and exams, 22 items were graded and accumulated to calculate students final mark. At least 80% of these items had to be answered correctly to pass the course. The students were also offered the discussion board to discuss course topics. In this study, we considered only the trace data of those students who completed at least one assignment during the official course schedule between September 17th and November 4th 2018. As a result, 368 students were considered for the study. We coded the different learning actions captured in the trace data as described in Table 1.

The resulting dataset for the analysis study contained the following items for each learning actions: the anonymous user ID, timestamp, type of learning action, and reference to course items. Each two consecutive learning sessions were separated by at least 30 min of inactive time [20]. Due to the requirements of analytic methods to be applied, the outliers were excluded: extremely short sessions (one action in a session) and extremely long sessions (>95th percentile of actions per session).

3.2 Methods

Figure 1 illustrates the pipeline of the analytic methods used to extract learning tactics and strategies from the trace data following the three analytic approaches discussed in Sect. 2. The data were pre-processed based on the requirement of each analytic approach.

Table 1. Coding of learning actions from the data trace

Events	Coded events	Description
Video lecture	lecture_start	Start the video lecture
	lecture_complete	Complete the video lecture
	in_video_quiz	Answer a quiz embedded in the video
	In_video_quiz_correct	Correctly answer a quiz embedded in the video lecture
	In_video_quiz_incorrect	Incorrectly answer a quiz embedded in the video lecture
Reading	Supplement_complete	View the supplementary documents
Theoretical exercises	Quiz_start	Start a theoretical exercise
	Quiz_complete	Complete a theoretical exercise
	Quiz	Theoretical exercise progress
Practical exercise	Exam_start	Start a practical exercise
	Exam_complete	Complete a practical exercise
	Exam	Practical exercise progress
	Exam_correct	Correctly solved a practical exercise
	Exam_inccorect	Incorrectly solved a practical exercise
	Code_execute	Command to execute the code
Discussion	Discussion_question	Post a question to the discussion board
	Discussion_answer	Post an answer to a question in a discussion board
	Discussion_question_vote	Vote for a question
	Discussion_answer_vote	Vote for an answer to a question
	Discussion_answer_del_vote	Deleted a vote for an answer
	Discussion_follow	Flag to follow a discussion
	Discussion_unfollow	Flag to unfollow a discussion

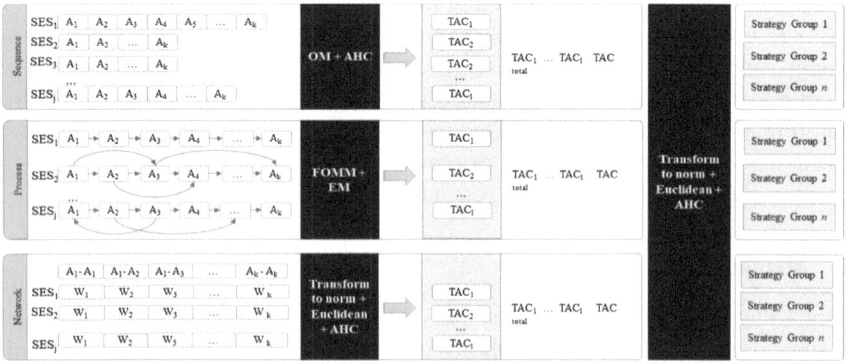

(*SES: Learning Session; A : Learning Action; W : Weight of co-occurrence between two actions; FOMM: First Order Markov Model; EM: Expectation-Maximization; OM: Optimal Matching Score; AHC: Agglomerative Hierarchical Clustering; TAC: Learning Tactic)

Fig. 1. The pipeline of the analytic methods used in the study

Sequential Dimension. Following the work in [9], the TraMineR R package [21] was used to explore the sequential data. Learning actions were arranged chronologically and split into learning sessions. Sessions were encoded as learning sequences using a TraMineR's sequence representation format [21]. The optimal matching technique, with substitution costs based on transition rates, was used to compute the (dis)similarity of the sequences. Agglomerative hierarchical clustering based on Ward's algorithm was used to group learning sequences based on shared patterns of learning actions.

Process Dimension. The process dimension was explored by replicating the steps proposed in [10]. The pMineR R package was used to generate a process model of learning and compute the probability of state transitions by using the first-order Markov model (FOMM) [22]. The process model was formulated using timestamped learning events in each learning session. The Expectation-Maximization (EM) algorithm was used for clustering of learning sequences as it works well with the FOMM.

Network Dimension. The rENA R package for Epistemic Network Analysis (ENA) was used to compute the co-occurrence of learning actions in each learning session [23]. By generating a network using ENA, a matrix of co-occurrences of learning actions was created. The co-occurrence values in the matrix were normalized and subsequently used as an input to the agglomerative hierarchical clustering, based on Ward's algorithm. The Euclidean method was used to calculate the (dis)similarity.

The clusters of sequences (i.e., tactics) detected by each of the three data analytic approaches were then explored in terms of sequence length and event distributions. The similarities between the three approaches were also calculated as proportions of learning sessions shared across the tactics detected by the three approaches.

To compute learning strategies, we used the results of cluster assignments of each of the three above approaches. Specifically, for each student, we computed the counts of each of the detected tactics and the total count of tactics. These counts were then normalized (i.e., reduced to the range of 0 to 1) and used as input to the agglomerative hierarchical clustering method. The computation of the (dis)similarity of students' tactic use was based on the Euclidean metric. The identified clusters were considered manifestations of the students' learning strategies (i.e., patterns of learning tactics). This was done for each of the three examined approaches. The identified learning strategies were explored based on how students applied the tactics according to the course topics. Furthermore, the association of the identified strategies and the final course marks was examined using Kruskal Wallis tests followed by pairwise Mann Whitney U tests.

4 Results

4.1 Learning Tactics

The results revealed that the three detection approaches identified four similar learning tactics. Figure 2 presents the counts of learning actions in each tactic as identified with the three analytics approaches. Further details of the tactic characteristics are provided in the supplementary document (Tables 1, 2 and 3)[1].

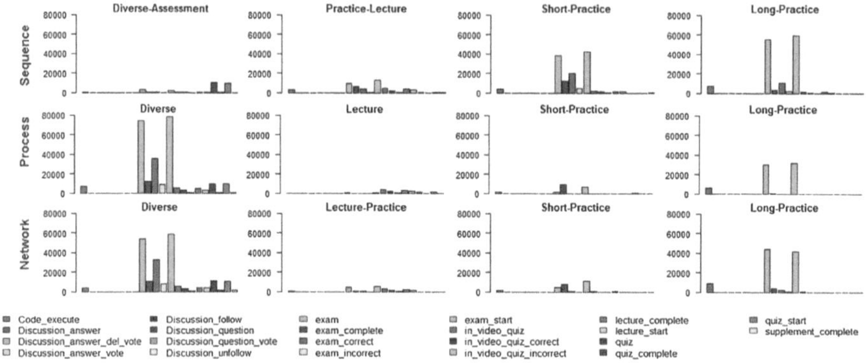

Fig. 2. The distribution of learning action counts across the tactics detected by the three analytic approaches

Sequence Approach. The dendrogram suggested four clusters as the best result. The *Practice and Lecture-oriented* cluster (N = 3134 sessions, 59.34%) was the largest and contained the shortest sequences (Mdn = 10 actions). The most dominant actions included those related to the exam activities, interaction with the video lecture, and quizzes embedded in the video. The *Diverse Assessment-oriented* (N = 208 sessions, 3.94%) cluster was very small and contained long sessions ranging from 54 to 355 actions. This tactic often began by interacting with the video lectures, followed by doing the exam and ended by interacting with the quiz items. The *Short Practice-oriented* (N = 1292 session, 24.47%) cluster included practical exams and code as the most dominant actions. Access to the video lectures was also prominent. The length of the sequences was moderate as compared to the other three tactics (Mdn = 93 actions). The *Long Practice-oriented* cluster (N = 647 sessions, 12.25%) was relatively small exhibiting a pattern similar to the previous one (Short Practice-oriented). However, learning sequences were longer, ranging from 103 to 359 events (Mdn = 214).

Process Approach. Four tactics were identified with the process analytic approach as optimal. The *Diverse* cluster (N = 2000 sessions, 37.87%) varied in the number of actions in each session in the [3–359] range (Mdn = 105). The main learning actions were related to exam activities, followed by quizzes, code execution, and interaction with lecture videos. The *Lecture-oriented* cluster (N = 1391 sessions, 26.34%) contained short sessions (Mdn = 7 actions). The most dominant actions included interaction with the video lectures and the quizzes embedded in the videos, followed by interaction with the quizzes that were part of the theoretical questionnaires. The *Short Practice-oriented* cluster (N = 772 sessions, 14.62%) consisted mostly of short

[1] Supplementary Document can be found at: https://bit.ly/2E4pFCu

sessions (Mdn = 8 actions) that were generally of two types: (i) short sessions of code executions and (ii) longer sessions of completing an exam. The *Long Practice-oriented* cluster (N = 1118 sessions, 21.17%) mostly included actions related to the exam or code execution. Unlike the *Short-practice-oriented* tactic, completed exams were rarely observed in this tactic.

Network Approach. The dendrogram inspection suggested four clusters as optimal. *Diverse-oriented* (N = 1892 sessions, 35.83%) was similar to the Diverse tactic detected by the other two approaches; this tactic included a variety of actions, dominated by those related to exam and quiz related activities. However, the number of actions within a session was much higher compared to the Diverse tactic detected by the other two methods (Mdn = 93 actions). *Lecture and Practice-oriented* (N = 929 sessions, 17.59%) was the most dominant with exam-related actions and a small proportion of actions related to the lecture videos. However, when inspecting all the sequences, this cluster contained multiple short sessions of video lecture related actions often followed by long sequences of exam related actions. Unlike the Lecture and Exam-oriented tactic detected by the process analytic approach, the frequency of interactions with exam items outnumbered lecture-related actions, while quizzes-related actions were almost invisible. *Short Practice-oriented* (N = 1776 sessions, 33.63%) was similar to the Short Practice-oriented tactic detected with the process approach. This tactic consisted of short learning sessions (Mdn = 7 actions). It was dominated by two types of sequences: (i) short session of code executes, and (ii) longer sessions of initiating and completing an exam. *Long Practice-oriented* (N = 684 sessions, 12.95%) contained longer sequences of action (Mdn = 126 actions). The most dominant learning actions were related to the exam or code execution. The proportion of initiated but not necessarily completed exams and continuing doing the exam was relatively high.

4.2 Comparison of Detected Tactics

The *Diverse* tactic detected by the process and network approaches showed similar patterns; that is, it was composed of several different learning actions and diverse length of sequences. The most frequent action was interaction with the exam, followed by the interaction with quizzes. *Diverse-assessment-oriented*, as detected by the sequence approach, showed that the interactions with the quizzes were more frequent than the exams. *Lecture and practice*-oriented included events about actions related to video lectures and exams as the most dominant. Opposite to the other two approaches, the lecture related events outnumbered the exam focused events in the case of the process approach. *Short Practice-oriented* was defined by intense interaction with the exam items and code implementation. The median length of sequences of this tactic was smaller than of that of the *Long Practice-oriented* tactic. This tactic, as identified by the sequence approach, had the highest mean length of sequences and higher frequency of video lecture interactions than the same tactic detected by the other two approaches.

The sequence approach proved to be the best in distinguishing *Long Practice-oriented* as the one characterized by long sessions of exam interaction and code execution. The process and network approaches showed inconsistency in categorising based on the length of the sequences.

Table 2. The similarity of tactics detection based on three analytic approaches

Similarity: 1861 Sessions (35.24%)		Process Analytic Approach (100%)			
		Diverse - Practice	Lecture	Long-Practice	Short-Practice
Sequence Analytic Approach	Diverse-Assessment	9.25	1.65	0	0
	Lecture and Exam	22.4	98.35	58.94	85.36
	Long-Practice	21.6	0	18.34	1.3
	Short-Practice	46.75	0	22.72	13.34
Similarity: 1500 Sessions (28.40 %)		**Network Analytic Approach (100%)**			
		Diverse – Practice	Lecture and Practice	Long-Practice	Short-Practice
Sequence Analytic Approach	Diverse-Assessment	10.84	0.32	0	0
	Lecture and Exam	29.49	89.56	14.62	92.57
	Long-Practice	14.64	2.26	49.71	0.51
	Short-Practice	45.03	7.86	35.67	6.93
Similarity: 3526 Sessions (66.77%)		**Network Analytic Approach (100%)**			
		Diverse – Practice	Lecture and Practice	Long-Practice	Short-Practice
Process Analytic Approach	Diverse	85.68	17.33	25.44	2.48
	Lecture	10.94	78.26	0	25.73
	Long-Practice	2.11	3.34	69.44	32.21
	Short-Practice	1.27	1.08	5.12	39.58

Table 2 compares the results of the three analytic approaches based on cluster assignments of study sessions. The similarity was computed by calculating the proportion of learning sequences that were categorized as the same tactic. The sequence approach had 35% of overlap in session assignment with that of the process analytic approach, and 28% with that of the network approach. Almost 67% of sessions were categorized as representing the same tactics by the process and network analytic approaches. The *Lecture-oriented* tactic showed a high consistency among the three methods. About 98% of sessions labelled as the lecture-oriented tactic detected with the process analytic approach were also categorised as the same tactic in the sequence analytic approach. This high consistency might be a result of the high number of short learning sessions that coincide with interaction with lecture videos. The highest inconsistency among the approaches was for the *Short Practice-oriented* tactic.

The process and network analytic approaches categorised 3,526 (out of 5,281) sessions as the same tactics. We further explored the sequences that were grouped differently to examine how the approaches differ in grouping the sequences. One of the examples is SequenceID13745 that consisted of actions shifting between practical exam_start and exam_progress. Execution of code was also observed during the exam progress, as shown in Fig. 3. This session consisted of 29 actions, which were inferred as representative of the *Long Practice-oriented* tactic by the process analytic approach. However, in case of the network analytic approach, the *Long-practice oriented* tactic had a higher median session length (Mdn = 126), so that the considered sequence (SequenceID13745) was not qualified as an instance of the *Long Practice-oriented* tactic, but rather fitted in the *Short-Practice-oriented* tactic.

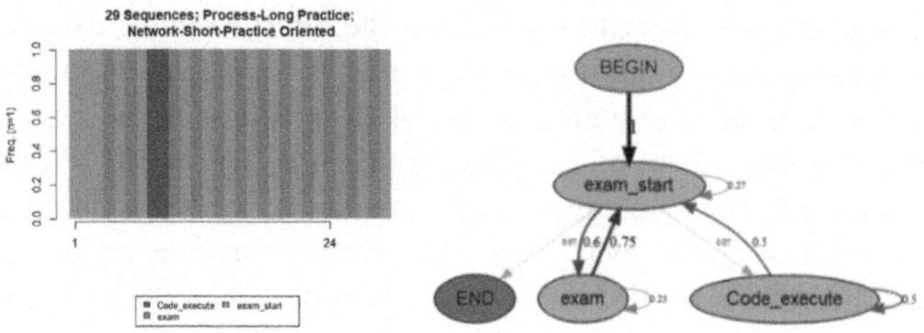

Fig. 3. The visualisation of sequenceID13745 and its first order Markov model

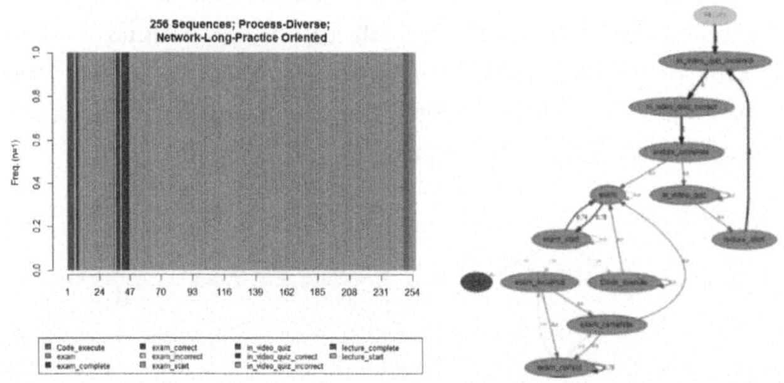

Fig. 4. The visualisation of sequenceID21601 and its process model

Another example of differences in the tactic detection is SequenceID21601 which contained 256 events. The sequence began by interacting with a quiz in a lecture video, followed by transitions between exam_start, exam progress, a correct/incorrect exam answer, and exam complete; the command to execute the code was observed towards the end of the session, as presented in Fig. 4. The sequence and network analytic approaches associated this session with the *Long Practice-oriented* tactic. This is reasonable, since this sequence was relatively long, and the events showed dynamic transitions between the exam related actions. Meanwhile, the process analytic considered this sequence as an instance of the *Diverse* tactic. This is presumably because the sequence began by interacting with the video lecture. The Diverse tactic exhibited events about a variety of learning activities in a session.

4.3 Learning Strategy Groups

Learning strategies were identified as patterns of how students regulated the tactics according to the study topic. Detail characteristics of each strategy group are provided in the supplementary document (see footnote 1).

Sequence Approach. Three strategy groups were extracted based on how the students employed the tactics identified with the Sequence approach. Figure 5 presents the mean number of tactics employed according to the studied topic. ***Strategy Group 1*** (N = 151 students, 41.03%) exhibited a low level of engagement. The dominant tactic was *Lecture-oriented* with short sessions. The mean number of sessions declined as the course topic progressed for all tactics except for the *Short Practice-oriented* tactic. The students who employed this strategy pattern had a high rate of failing the course (77.48%); their median course grade was 36.14 over 100, and the median number of passed graded items was 9 (out of 22). ***Strategy Group 2*** (N = 151 students, 41.03%) exhibited a high level of engagement when interacting with the first two topics by utilising the *Lecture-oriented* tactic. The *Short* and *Long practice-oriented* tactics increased when the course reached the second topic. However, the level of engagement dropped remarkably after completing the third topic. This strategy group had the highest failure rate (88.74%). The median of the completed graded items was four, and the median course grade was 18.04. ***Strategy Group 3*** (N = 66 students, 17.94%) had the highest course grade (Mdn = 82.86/100), highest number of passed graded items (Mdn = 20 items), and the smallest failure rate (54.55%). Similar to the other strategy groups, the students frequently used the *Lecture-oriented* and *Short practice-oriented* tactics. Unlike the first two strategy groups, the mean number of sessions increased as the students moved to more difficult topics.

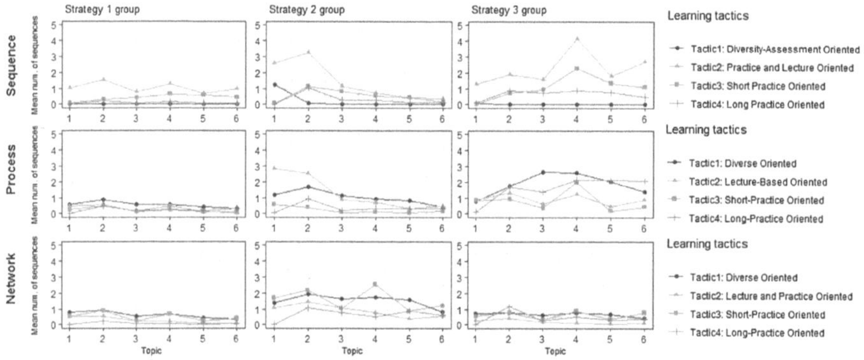

Fig. 5. Frequency of tactics used for each topic and for each strategy group as detected by the three analytic approaches

Process Approach. The mean number of employed tactics detected based on the process analytics approach according to the studied topic is presented in Fig. 5. ***Strategy Group 1*** (N = 215 students, 58.42%) exhibited a low engagement level. The mean number of sessions was consistently below one per study topic. The students who adopted this strategy had a high failing rate (82.79%); their median course grade was 29.33 over 100, and the number of passed graded item was 7 out of 22 items. ***Strategy Group 2*** (N = 89 students, 24.18%) included the students who were quite selective. The *Lecture-oriented* and *Diverse* tactics were dominant at the beginning of the course. The level of engagement dropped constantly from Topic 3 onwards. Despite putting a higher level of effort than *strategy group 1*, the students in this group passed less graded items (Mdn = 5), and had lower course grade (Mdn = 20.41). *Strategy Group 3* (N = 64 students; 17.39%) showed the highest passing rate (43.75%) and grades (Mdn = 82.71/100). Unlike the other strategy groups, the students in this group were consistently increasing their engagement with the course topics. As the MOOC progressed and the topics became more challenging, this group put more effort and used diverse learning tactics, as shown by the high use of the *Practice-oriented* and *Diverse* tactics.

Network Approach. Figure 5 shows three strategy groups with similar tactic enactment patterns. ***Strategy Group 1*** (N = 188 students, 51.09%) used multiple tactics but with a low frequency, and the frequency decreased as the course progressed. The group had a high failure rate (83.51%) with the median score of 27.29 (over 100), and passed, on average, 7 (out of 22) graded items. ***Strategy Group 2*** (N = 94 students, 25.54%) included the students who were the most active. They employed a variety of tactics to study each topic. The use of the *Diverse* and *Lecture-oriented* tactics slightly declined as the course progressed. There was some fluctuation in the use of the *Short Practice-oriented* tactic, especially during the fourth topic. The students with this strategy had the highest course score (Mdn = 56.95), and passed more graded items (Mdn = 15 items) than those following the other two strategies. ***Strategy Group 3*** (N = 86 students, 23.37%) had a similar pattern as the first one. Yet, the rate of students who failed was lower (74.42%), and the median grade was higher (Mdn = 37.04) than for strategy 1.

Association with Performance. The strategy groups detected by using the sequence approach showed no significant association with the course grade, nor with the number of item passed (Table 3). However, we detected a significant association of the strategy and the potential of failing/passing the course. The pairwise comparison (Table 3) showed statistically significant associations among all the strategy groups and the potential of failing/passing the course. The effect sizes ranged from small to medium.

Table 3. Kruskal-Wallis (above) and pairwise comparison (below) of strategy groups with respect to performance

	Sequence	Process	Network
Course Grade	p = 0.125	p = 0.067	p = 0.14
Passed Graded Items	p = 0.082	p = 0.0004*	p = 0.01*
Passed Course	p = 0.046*	p = 0.0004*	p = 0.025*

Approach	Item	Strategy	Strategy	Z	p	r
Sequence	Passed Course	S1	S2	2.607	0.014*	0.150
		S1	S3	-3.401	<0.001*	0.231
		S2	S3	-5.613	<0.001*	0.381
Process	Passed Course	S1	S2	-0.160	0.88	0.009
		S1	S3	-4.401	<0.001*	0.263
		S2	S3	-3.463	<0.001*	0.28
	Passed Graded Items	S1	S2	0.102	0.87	0.006
		S1	S3	-7.206	<0.001*	0.431
		S2	S3	-6.359	<0.001*	0.514
Network	Passed Course	S1	S2	-2.440	0.05	0.146
		S1	S3	-1.765	0.18	0.107
		S2	S3	0.516	0.57	0.039
	Passed Graded Items	S1	S2	-4.323	<0.001*	0.258
		S1	S3	-2.762	0.05	0.167
		S2	S3	1.613	0.059	0.121

Note: * marks statistically significant differences

The strategy groups detected with the process analytic approach had no significant differences in course grades. A significant association was present between the strategy groups and the number of passed graded items and the potential of failing/passing the course. Pairwise comparisons of strategy groups with respect to the completed performance items showed significant differences between strategy group 1 and 3 and groups 2 and 3. The effect sizes were medium except for the passed graded items between strategy groups 2 and 3 where the effect size was large ($r = 0.514$).

The strategy groups identified with the network analytic approach had no significant difference on course grades. The strategy groups proved to differ significantly with respect to the number of items passed and the potential of failing/passing the course. Pairwise comparisons showed significant differences between strategy groups 1 and 2 on the number of passed graded items with the small effect sizes.

4.4 Comparison of Detected Strategy Groups

Table 4 summarises the detected strategy groups along several dimensions related to the students' pattern of course engagement and academic achievement.

Table 4. Comparison of the strategy groups as detected by the three analytic approaches

	Sequence	Process	Network
Highly active and multiple tactics used	Strategy3	Strategy3	Strategy 2
Highly active at the beginning	Strategy2	Strategy2	–
Surface engagement	Strategy1	Strategy1	Strategy1, Strategy3

Highly Active and Multiple Tactics Used. These strategy groups reflect the deep learning approach as defined by Biggs (1987). The deep approach is characterised by high efforts, a variety of learning tactics used [7, 10], and associated with the high academic performance [4]. The students employed a variety of tactics when interacting with each topic. Based on the sequence approach, the most dominant tactic used was *Lecture-oriented.* Based on the process and network approaches, the dominant tactics were *Diverse* and *Practice-oriented.* Regardless of the tactic detection method, a similar pattern of interaction with the fourth course topic was observed – high enactment of the *Short Practice-oriented* tactic. This suggested that students might have been facing some challenges with the fourth topic that the instructor should consider when designing the next course iteration.

Highly Active at the Beginning. The sequence and process analytic approaches detected this similar pattern of tactic use, but not the network approach. The students were actively engaged during the first two topics, and then the effort significantly declined. The tactics employed during the first three topics showed that students were strategic in choosing tactics. The dominant tactics were *Lecture-oriented* and *Diverse.* This reflects the *Strategic* approach to learning [24], characterized by the aim of achieving high performance with the strategic choice of tactics [8, 24]. As the students faced more difficulty, their learning strategy shifted from strategic to the surface approach to learning. This suggested that some interventions are needed to maintain the level of students' engagement with the third topic. This group showed high engagement as compared to the Surface group, but the group missed to complete a few graded items.

Surface Engagement. This group represented the surface approach to learning. As defined by Biggs (1987), students who follow this approach to learning employ surface effort and have low academic performance [8, 24]. In our study, the students who followed this strategy group exhibited a low level of engagement and high failure rate.

None of the analytic approaches identified strategy groups that were predictive of performance. A significant association was found between the strategy group and the passed graded items for all cases. The process analytic approach proved the best in detecting strategy groups predictive of the passed graded items.

5 Conclusions

Summary. The findings in this study showed that sequence, process, and network analytic approaches can be used to detect meaningful learning tactics from MOOC trace data. The three approaches resulted in tactics that were similar to some extent (Table 2). The highest similarity (67% of detected tactics) was found between the process and network approaches. As for strategy detection, the results of the network analytic approach differed from the other two approaches. The sequence and process analytic approaches resulted in similar strategy groups.

In general, we observed that sequences with similar learning actions were grouped in the same cluster. The length of the sequences affected the clustering in the sequence analytic approach. For example, short learning sessions were grouped into a single cluster (i.e. short diverse oriented) and this was the key distinguishing characteristic of this tactic group. In contrast, the process and network analytics were less based on the length of the sequences. Therefore, in the tactics detected using these two approaches the number of actions per learning sessions varied, ranging from two to hundred or more.

The proportion of learning sessions that belonged to each of the detected tactics impacted the learning strategy detection. The sequence approach detected one large tactic, i.e. *Short Practice-Lecture oriented*, showed that all strategy groups were dominated by this tactic. Furthermore, we found that all of the strategy groups exhibited a high frequency of using the *Short Practice and Lecture-oriented* tactics. This is unsurprising considering the course design that emphasized the use of video lectures and practice exercises.

Implications. The key finding of the study is that the choice of the data analytic approach for detection of learning tactics and strategies affects the results. Specifically, the three approaches emphasize different dimensions of learning tactics – sequential, process, and network. The differences in the underlying modelling of the three analytic approaches produced different data representations that are then fed to an unsupervised (i.e., clustering) machine learning algorithm. The properties of these underlying representations – sequence, process, and network – had direct implications on the computation of the similarities between individual sessions, and thus, the way how clusters were formed to detect learning tactics. Moreover, the choice of the underlying modelling approaches for tactics had a direct impact on the choice of clustering algorithm. For example, the process approach produced the data structure (i.e., adjacency matrix) that was not suitable for analysis with AHC; EM was used instead as also used in the literature [10]. AHC was more suited for the other two approaches, as commonly applied in the literature on similar tasks [9].

Based on the results of our findings, we cannot indicate which of the approaches is 'best'. Instead, the (dis)similarities in the results the three approaches produced and interpretations of the (dis)similarities in this study can inform decisions of researchers and practitioners who work on the detection of learning tactics and strategies. Given that each of the three approaches used unsupervised machine learning at its core, it is also important that the interpretation of results should be done by considering a well-grounded educational learning theory and the learning context the data originate from. In our case, we offered examples that grounded in the theory of approaches to learning and the design of the MOOC used in the study. The use of these two sources demonstrated that all three approaches produced practically and theoretically meaningful learning tactics and strategies.

The differences in the learning strategies detected by the three approaches can directly be attributed to the differences in the modelling approaches used for the detection of learning tactics. This is due to the use of the identical methodology applied in the second step of the three detection approaches (see Fig. 1). Future research should investigate the extent to which changes in the modeling approaches in the second step will influence the results in the detection of learning strategies.

Limitations. Some limitations of this research must be highlighted. First, the detection of learning tactics and strategies relied primarily on trace data. Although limitations of self-reports are well document [12, 25], self-reports could add to the understanding of students' conditions, intention and motivation. Moreover, using multimodal techniques to capture the data could offer a fine-grained dataset. Second, some degree of subjectivity was evident in the selection of the number of clusters identified, even though the selection was informed by the information generated with the clustering technique (e.g., dendrogram in agglomerative hierarchical clustering) and further informed by the interpretability of the cluster solutions. Future research should explore approaches that can be used to produce a 'stable' number of clusters across different contexts.

Acknowledgements. This work was funded by the LALA project (grant no. 586120-EPP-1-2017-1-ES-EPPKA2-CBHE-JP). This project has been funded with support from the European Commission. This publication reflects the views only of the author, and the Commission and the Agency cannot be held responsible for any use which may be made of the information contained therein.

References

1. Zurita, G., Hasbun, B., Baloian, N., Jerez, O.: A blended learning environment for enhancing meaningful learning using 21st century skills. In: Chen, G., Kumar, V., Kinshuk, Huang, R., Kong, S.C. (eds.) Emerging Issues in Smart Learning. LNET, pp. 1–8. Springer, Heidelberg (2015). https://doi.org/10.1007/978-3-662-44188-6_1
2. Drachsler, H., Kalz, M.: The MOOC and learning analytics innovation cycle (MOLAC): a reflective summary of ongoing research and its challenges. J. Comput. Assist. Learn. **32**, 281–290 (2016)
3. Kizilcec, R.F., Pérez-Sanagustín, M., Maldonado, J.J.: Self-regulated learning strategies predict learner behavior and goal attainment in massive open online courses. Comput. Educ. **104**, 18–33 (2017)
4. Broadbent, J., Poon, W.L.: Self-regulated learning strategies & academic achievement in online higher education learning environments: a systematic review. Internet High. Educ. **27**, 1–13 (2015)
5. Winne, P.H.: How software technologies can improve research on learning and bolster school reform. Educ. Psychol. **41**, 5–17 (2006). https://doi.org/10.1207/s15326985ep4101
6. Yip, M.C.W.: Differences in learning and study strategies between high and low achieving university students: a Hong Kong study. Educ. Psychol. **27**, 597–606 (2007)
7. Maldonado-Mahauad, J., Pérez-Sanagustín, M., Moreno-Marcos, P.M., Alario-Hoyos, C., Muñoz-Merino, P.J., Delgado-Kloos, C.: Predicting learners' success in a self-paced MOOC through sequence patterns of self-regulated learning. In: Pammer-Schindler, V., Pérez-Sanagustín, M., Drachsler, H., Elferink, R., Scheffel, M. (eds.) EC-TEL 2018. LNCS, vol. 11082, pp. 355–369. Springer, Cham (2018). https://doi.org/10.1007/978-3-319-98572-5_27
8. Chonkar, S.P., et al.: The predominant learning approaches of medical students. BMC Med. Educ. **18**, 1–8 (2018)
9. Jovanovic, J., Gasevic, D., Dawson, S., Pardo, A., Mirriahi, N.: Learning analytics to unveil learning strategies in a flipped classroom. Internet High. Educ. **33**, 74–85 (2017)
10. Matcha, W., Gašević, D., Uzir, N.A., Jovanović, J., Pardo, A.: Analytics of learning strategies: associations with academic performance and feedback. In: Proceedings of the 9th International Conference on Learning Analytics and Knowledge, pp. 461–470 (2019)
11. Weinstein, C.E., Husman, J., Dierking, D.R.: Self-regulation interventions with a focus on learning strategies. Handb. Self-Regulation. **22**, 727–747 (2000)
12. Hadwin, A.F., Nesbit, J.C., Jamieson-Noel, D., Code, J., Winne, P.H.: Examining trace data to explore self-regulated learning. Metacogn. Learn. **2**, 107–124 (2007)
13. Derry, S.J.: Putting learning strategies to work. Educ. Leadersh. **47**, 4–10 (1989)
14. Winne, P.H., Jamieson-Noel, D., Muis, K.: Methodological issues and advances in researching tactics, strategies, and self-regulated learning (2002)
15. Winne, P.H., Gupta, L., Nesbit, J.C.: Exploring individual differences in studying strategies using graph theoretic statistics. Alberta J. Educ. Res. **40**, 177–193 (1994)
16. Siadaty, M., Gašević, D., Hatala, M.: Associations between technological scaffolding and micro-level processes of self-regulated learning: a workplace study. Comput. Human Behav. **55**, 1007–1019 (2016). Part B
17. Boroujeni, M.S., Dillenbourg, P.: Discovery and temporal analysis of latent study patterns in MOOC interaction sequences. In: Proceedings of the 8th International Conference on Learning Analytics and Knowledge, pp. 206–215. ACM, New York (2018)
18. Sobocinski, M., Malmberg, J., Järvelä, S.: Exploring temporal sequences of regulatory phases and associated interactions in low- and high-challenge collaborative learning sessions. Metacogn. Learn. **12**, 275–294 (2017)

19. Maldonado-Mahauad, J., Pérez-Sanagustín, M., Kizilcec, R.F., Morales, N., Munoz-Gama, J.: Mining theory-based patterns from big data: identifying self-regulated learning strategies in massive open online courses. Comput. Human Behav. **80**, 179–196 (2018)
20. Kovanović, V., Gašević, D., Dawson, S., Joksimović, S., Baker, R.S., Hatala, M.: Penetrating the black box of time-on-task estimation. In: the Fifth International Conference on Learning Analytics And Knowledge, pp. 184–193 (2015)
21. Gabadinho, A., Ritschard, G., Studer, M., Muller, N.S.: Mining sequence data in R with the TraMineR package: a user's guide, vol. 1, pp. 1–124. Department of. Economic Labor and Demographic, University of Geneva, Switzerland (2008)
22. Gatta, R., Lenkowicz, J., Vallati, M., Stefanini, A.: pMineR: processes mining in medicine (2017). https://cran.r-project.org/package=pMineR
23. Shaffer, D.W., Collier, W., Ruis, A.R.: A tutorial on epistemic network analysis: analyzing the structure of connections in cognitive, social, and interaction data. J. Learn. Anal. **3**, 9–45 (2016)
24. Biggs: Student Approaches to Learning and Studying (1987)
25. Zhou, M., Winne, P.H.: Modeling academic achievement by self-reported versus traced goal orientation. Learn. Instr. **22**, 413–419 (2012)

Concept-Level Design Analytics for Blended Courses

Laia Albó[1(✉)], Jordan Barria-Pineda[2], Peter Brusilovsky[2], and Davinia Hernández-Leo[1]

[1] Universitat Pompeu Fabra, Barcelona, Spain
{laia.albo, davinia.hernandez-leo}@upf.edu
[2] University of Pittsburgh, Pittsburgh, PA, USA
{jab464, peterb}@pitt.edu

Abstract. Although many efforts are being made to provide educators with dashboards and tools to understand student behaviors within specific technological environments (learning analytics), there is a lack of work in supporting educators in making data-informed design decisions when designing a blended course and planning learning activities. In this paper, we introduce concept-level design analytics, a knowledge-based visualization, which uncovers facets of the learning activities that are being authored. The visualization is integrated into a (blended) learning design authoring tool, edCrumble. This new approach is explored in the context of a higher education programming course, where teaching assistants design labs and home practice sessions with online smart learning content on a weekly basis. We performed a within-subjects user study to compare the use of the design tool both with and without the visualization. We studied the differences in terms of cognitive load, design outcomes and user actions within the system to compare both conditions to the objective of evaluating the impact of using design analytics during the decision-making phase of course design.

Keywords: Design analytics · Blended learning · Concept-level visualization · Authoring tool · Learning design · Smart learning content

1 Introduction

Learning analytics (LA) has attracted a lot of attention of e-learning researchers and practitioners over the last 10 years. Learning analytics allows instructors to evaluate how students are learning within a learning context, providing them with data-based evidence to improve the overall quality of the learning experience [1]. As the field broadened, it has become customary to recognize different categories of learning analytics and to distinguish each category by its targeted group of users or tasks. This paper focuses on *design analytics*, one of the least explored areas within this broad research field.

We adopt the definition of the term "design analytics" as the "metrics of design decisions and related aspects that characterize learning designs" [2]. A learning design (LD) is an explicit representation of a lesson plan created by a teacher [3]. Authoring

M. Scheffel et al. (Eds.): EC-TEL 2019, LNCS 11722, pp. 541–554, 2019.
https://doi.org/10.1007/978-3-030-29736-7_40

tools can assist teachers in the creation of learning designs, which can lead to computational representations of the elements within a learning design that can be automatically analyzed. Some representations are generic or neutral, which enable only some options for structural analysis of a course (e.g. the number of tasks, time planned for a set of tasks, etc.). Other representations are specific to pedagogical approaches or subject matter concepts and enables a more detailed level of analysis. Analytics of these representations can support teachers' awareness and reflection about the accumulated decisions taken along the learning process to inform pending decisions toward completion of the course designs [2].

This paper explores some approaches for fine-grained design analytics focused on visualizing critical metadata associated with learning content. Our proposed visualization covers various metadata aspects, such as the type of learning content, the nature of knowledge supported, and a list of specific knowledge concepts that a specific fragment of learning content seeks to reinforce. After a brief review of related work (Sect. 2), we explain what we mean by concept-level design analytics (Sect. 3) and introduce its implementation in a design tool that supports teachers in selecting the learning content. The design and results of an experimental study as a first exploration of the value of concept-level design analytics are reported in Sects. 4 and 5.

2 Related Work

2.1 Design Analytics in Learning Design Environments

The term design analytics, in the cross-road of LD and LA, was coined and defined in the framework proposed by [2]. The framework is built on existing learning design tooling that included features that align with the concept of design analytics. An example of design analytics is provided by Web Collage, which analyzes the accumulated design aspects specified by the teacher when completing a template that is based on a collaborative learning flow pattern [4]. With this analysis, the tool computes and visualizes alerts that point teachers to pending actions needed to complete the design, as required by the design guidelines underpinning the pattern [4].

The idea of learning design analytics can be also observed in the *Activity or Pedagogy Profile* tool, which enables the creation of a bar chart representation to help teachers describe the distribution of tutorials and directed study modules [5]. The profile represents tasks across six activity types of a detailed unit-by-unit or week-by-week analysis. The tool was created to be helpful at different times in the design process, from first ideas to evaluation and review. Moreover, the analytics bar charts can be shared with learners and other stakeholders to express how learners are expected to spend their time, in terms of balance and shape of the expected learning activity.

Another example is the *Learning Design Support Environment* (LDSE or the Learning Designer). The LDSE provides an analysis of the properties of the designs being created by the teacher with the environment as a learning design tool [6]. In particular, it generates charts that visualize the proportion of time that students are expected to spend on the diverse types of tasks that are planned in the design, from "acquisition" to more active forms of "inquiry, discussion, production and practice".

This information serves as feedback to teachers about the nature of the learning experience that the learning design proposes.

The *Educational Design Studio* [7] is a physical environment for multiple designers working in teams that is equipped with wall projectors, whiteboards, a digital tabletop, and other tools. The various displays allow for several representations of the designs being created. The environment collects data from the designs and generates various charts; for example, the proportion of learning tasks distributed in the learning spaces (e.g. tasks occurring at the lecture room, at the lab, or online). This information enhances awareness of the broad view and the progress of their designs while building and editing individual tasks, as well as facilitating comparison between designs.

The concept of design analytics has been more extensively exploited in the edCrumble learning design tool. edCrumble is a pedagogical planner that provides a visual representation of the learning designs, strongly characterized by data analytics, that can facilitate the planning, visualization, understanding and reuse of complex blended learning designs [8]. Specifically, the decision-making that occurs during the design process is supported by design analytics that result from the design of the activities sequenced in a timeline. The design analytics provided include several categories: in-class/out-of-class time analytics, tasks' cognitive process, type of student work, teacher presence, and task evaluation mode. In each category, it is possible to have different visualizations: global time analytics, analytics that depend on the activities' type (in or out-of-class), and analytics that depend on the learning objectives.

In this paper, we present our attempt to further expand the design analytics component of edCrumble in order to support teachers at an extremely fine-grained design level. The new design analytics proposals will account for the metadata from the new integration of smart learning content into the resources' panel.

2.2 Open Learner Modelling and Navigation Support for Smart Learning Content

Blended learning approaches usually attempt to focus each of their different learning contexts on the activities that could be performed most efficiently in this context. For example, lecture classroom time could focus on the explanation of complicated topics and discussions and a lab session could focus on solving sample problems where the help of a human teaching assistant might be necessary, while online learning might be devoted to self-study, self-assessment, and practice. As the complexity of learning tools increases, the online component of blended learning is increasingly focused on practicing with so-called *smart learning content* [9]. Each element of this smart content is a relatively complex interactive activity, which engages students in exploration and provides real-time performance feedback. For example, in the area of computer science education, some previously explored types of smart content included interactive animations, worked examples, parameterized semantics questions, Parson's puzzles, and programming problems. As each smart learning content item is relatively complex and advanced, it usually allows a student to practice a number of different course concepts or skills, which could be introduced in different lectures or course units. This complex nature of smart learning content makes it hard for the student to accurately track progress and to select the most relevant learning content item for further practice.

To improve student knowledge-tracking ability in their work with smart learning content, several researchers suggested concept-level *open learner models (OLM)* [10]. A concept-level OLM recognizes the presence of multiple domain knowledge components (KC), such as concepts and skills, and visualizes student knowledge progress separately for each of these skills. Made popular by the field of intelligent tutoring systems as *skillometers* [11], concept-level OLM has become popular in other types of e-learning systems. A brief review of different concept-level OLM visualizations can be found in [12].

In our own work, we have explored visual interfaces, which combine topic-level open learner modeling with navigation support in order to help learners in selecting most relevant learning content [13]. Most recently, we explored student-focused concept-level knowledge visualization to help students in tracking their knowledge and selecting relevant smart content [14]. In this paper, we attempt to further expand the application area of concept-level knowledge visualization by exploring its value in a different context—helping instructors select learning content in a blended learning context.

3 Concept-Level Design Analytics for Blended Learning

The key idea of concept-level design analytics is to visualize the concept coverage of individual learning activities as well as learning sessions (such as a lecture, a lab, or a home practice) to help instructors in creating balanced learning designs. A learning activity is usually associated with metadata, which describes its type, engaged concepts or learning objectives, expected time to complete, and other aspects. This metadata is critical to create balanced learning designs. For example, learning practice prepared for a specific lecture should offer a balance of examples and problems, rather than over-focus on just one of these types of activities, and should cover all critical concepts introduced during the lecture, rather than over-focusing on some of them. Such a balance is usually hard to achieve without supporting the instructors with appropriate design analytics.

In this section, we present the design of a concept-level *design visualization* component, which extends the design analytics offered to the users of edCrumble. To demonstrate the power of the concept-based approach, we apply it to a relatively challenging design context: developing lab and practice sessions for an introductory programming course that uses several kinds of smart learning content. This context is challenging, since these kinds of smart content are of a different nature (examples vs. problems) and cover different kinds of programming knowledge (program comprehension vs. program construction). Moreover, each content item engages students in practicing a number of different programming concepts.

To support teachers in adapting this complex context, our designed visualization offered a concept-level visualization of a learning session being constructed and allowed teachers to compare different aspects of the constructed session on the concept-level by using a mirrored bar chart visualization (i.e., balance of concepts between problems and examples). Firstly, the bar chart approach for showing the distribution of concepts in a programming domain was defined after a series of user studies described in [14]. Secondly, the mirrored layout was grounded by findings in information visualization research, which show that correlation tasks (i.e. easily detecting if two data distributions were similar or not) are better supported when presented through graphs with a mirrored layout [15], and that the visual system's capability for detecting differences between two regions is more efficient when they are shown as mirror images of each other, as compared to repeated translations of each other [16].

We explain the behavior of this visualization with the following scenario. The process of adding a new activity to a learning session starts with selecting a type of learning activity to add. To support the programming context, six types of smart learning content for introductory programming (Table 1) have been integrated into the resources panel of the design tool (Fig. 1A).

Table 1. Smart learning content integrated into the learning design tool, distinguishing between examples and problems and construction and comprehension types.

ID	Title	Type	Description
WebEx	Annotated examples	Example Compr.	Annotated program examples. Students can click each line of code to see the related explanation for that line [17]
AnimEx	Animated examples	Example Compr.	Animated program execution examples, which visualize line-by-line execution of a piece of code [18]
PCEX	Program construction examples	Example Constr.	Interactive program construction examples. Each example provides a goal that specifies the given example's functionality. User can click on each line of code for getting explanations [19]
PCEXch	Program construction challenges	Problem Constr.	Small problems to help students developing program construction skills. Each challenge is a code example with 1–3 removed lines. Students need to drag-drop candidate lines to complete a program to achieve the provided goal [19]
Quizjet	Parameterized problems	Problem Compr.	Parameterized problems for self-assessment of student knowledge of programming semantics. Students are asked to predict the final value of a program output [20]
PCRS	Programming exercises	Problem Constr.	Coding exercises with automatic assessment. The system asks user to complete a partial code skeleton and then, it checks the submitted answer using a set of tests [21]

By clicking on each resource tab, the system shows a list of the corresponding activities available for this content type. Users can select the preview button to open and try each activity and make an informed decision when selecting the activities for a new session. When an activity is judged as suitable to be used in the design, users can drag and drop the activity's icon to the open session (lecture, lab or practice) in the

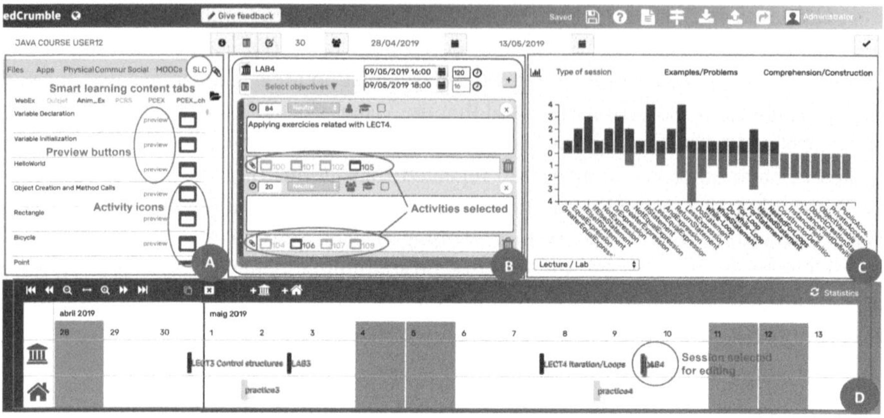

Fig. 1. Screenshot of the learning design tool's editor. (A) Resources panel with the 6 categories of smart learning content; (B) Editor for the selected session in the timeline; (C) Design analytics' visualizations; (D) Timeline with the in-class and out-of-class sessions.

editor (Fig. 1B). Once an activity has been aggregated into the design, the design analytics panel (Fig. 1C) offers a short animation that allows the user to visualize the activity's contribution in terms of concept-level knowledge coverage (knowledge gained upon its completion).

Each bar on the concept-level knowledge visualization chart (Fig. 1C) represents a domain concept, and its length represents how frequently the concept will be practiced by the learner when working with the selected session content (which could be also considered to be an estimation of knowledge gained after completing the session). The name of concepts that the instructor should target when designing for a specific lecture (e.g. lecture 4, with its subsequent lab-4 and practice-4 sessions) are highlighted in yellow for facilitating their coverage (see the seven concepts highlighted in Figs. 1 and 2). The concepts shown to the left of the highlighted ones are those targeted by the previous lecture, whereas those placed to the right are the ones which has not yet been introduced past lectures. The system also offers the possibility of previewing the contribution of a candidate activity to the overall design by situating the mouse over it, before dragging and dropping it into the selected session. The system then shows the preview of its contribution to learning different concepts by adding striped-bars to the visualization, as a short animation is shown when bars are added (Fig. 2 left).

In the analytics panel, we can find three tabs that offer different types of concept-level comparisons, depending on the sessions and the activities' types and knowledge. This comparisons help to balance the concept coverage of selected content by content type, session type, or covered knowledge. The first tab 'Type of session' (Fig. 2 left) allows a user to compare the concept-contribution of the activities selected, depending in which type of session they have been placed. It also offers the possibility of switching between three comparisons (Lecture/Lab, Lecture/Practice and Lab/Practice sessions). The second tab 'Examples/Problems' (Fig. 2 right) offers a unique comparison between these two types of activities but gives the option of filtering the results by visualizing only Lab, Practice, or both. The same applies for the third tab 'Comprehension/Construction'.

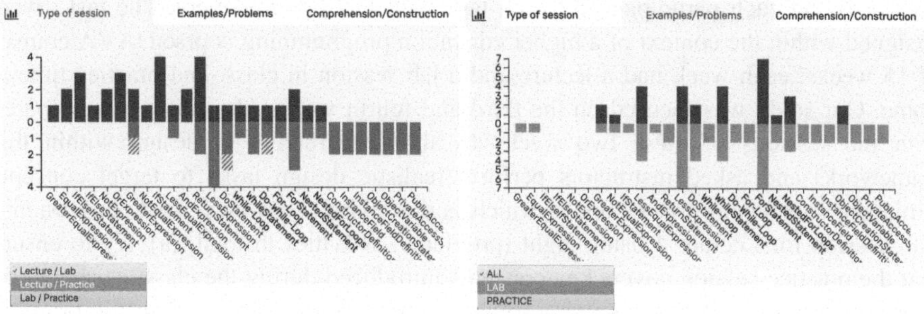

Fig. 2. Design analytics provided in concept-level visualizations. Left: activity contribution split by the type of session (i.e., lecture on top, lab on the bottom). Right: activity contribution split by content type (i.e., examples on top, problems on the bottom. Striped bars (left) indicate the preview of the contribution of a possible addition of a new resource.

4 Exploring the Value of Concept-Level Design Analytics

4.1 Participants and Sample

Evaluating a system focused on instructors as users is a known challenge, due to the limited availability of qualified participants. For our study, we recruited a total of 10 domain experts (six female) who were sufficiently qualified as introductory programming instructors. All of the instructors were computer or information science PhD students in a public university. Eligibility criteria required individuals to have knowledge in programming languages and experience as instructors or teaching assistants. Their ages ranged from 24 to 32 (M = 28, SE = 0.90) and they had between one and 13 years of teaching experience (M = 3.50, SE = 1.15). The scores (on a six-point scale) of how often their teaching tasks had implied selecting what activities and what type of teaching resources would be used during a course were (M = 3.70, SE = 0.42; M = 3.60, SE = 0.48), respectively. The scores (on a five-point scale) related to the instructors' background knowledge of programming in general, in Java, and interpreting graphs were (M = 4.50, SE = 0.17; M = 4.20, SE = 0.20; M = 4.20, SE = 0.20) respectively. In addition to the 10 instructors, two teaching assistants were recruited as pilot users to test and refine the procedure; however, their work has not been considered in the analysis. All 12 subjects were compensated for their participation in the study.

4.2 Design and Procedure

To assess the value of the design analytics that were provided, we compared the interface without the visualizations (baseline interface) to the one with the visualizations (visualizations interface). Due to the size of our sample, we used a within-subjects design. Instructors were asked to perform two different tasks with the system, and all of them experienced both treatments. The order of treatments was randomized to control for the effect of ordering (half of the instructors started the study using the baseline interface) and each participant did each task with just one treatment. The tasks were designed within the context of a higher education programming course (JAVA course) of 15 weeks: each week had a lecture and a lab session in class, and practice time at home. Our study was focused on the third and fourth weeks (the editor was prepared with the sessions of these two weeks to allow instructors to design within this framework) and asked instructors perform realistic design tasks to target concepts explained specifically in Lecture 4, which is described as follows. **Task 1:** Design a Lab session for Lecture 4 using eight (problems) activities in total. (a) Try to ensure that the practice session covers key concepts introduced during the class (as shown by lecture examples). (b) Try to strike a balance between problems that focus on program comprehension and program construction. **Task 2:** Design a Practice session for the Lecture 4 using 20 (examples and problems) activities in total. (a) Try to ensure that the practice covers key concepts introduced at the class (as shown by lecture examples). (b) Try to ensure a balance of examples and problems. (c) Make sure that the student will have a chance to practice both program comprehension and program construction skills. The order of the tasks was not randomized, since we considered the second task to be an extension of the first (albeit with a higher difficulty). Instructors received two training sessions, one about the use of the design tool itself and the other about the use of the visualization. The group that started the study with the baseline interface received the tool training before the first task and the visualization training before the second task, while the group that started with the visualization got both trainings before the first task. During the tasks, instructors had access to help files on the six types of activities with a short description of each one (indicating the categories to which they belonged: examples/problems and construction/comprehension). After each task, we asked instructors to complete a post-task questionnaire. At the end of the study, instructors filled out a final questionnaire.

4.3 Data Collection and Analysis

We collected the action logs of the instructors while they interacted with the system. Above all, we focused on the actions that took place within the resources panel and the visualizations tabs. Moreover, we also gathered the learning design outcomes generated during the study to assess the instructors' performance of the tasks. After each task, we used the NASA_TLX questionnaire [22] which aimed to measure the instructors' cognitive load of the tasks' performances. We used a paper version of the questionnaire that included both known parts (rating and weights). The final questionnaire asked instructors to provide their feedback about the use of visualizations and the design tool. It had two open questions to ask instructors about their preferences between the two treatments, as well as which interface they found to be more efficient in performing the given tasks and why. The third question asked instructors to order the three type of visualizations by their level of usefulness. Next, 14 + 5 items were presented to instructors for gathering their feedback about the visualizations and the design tool (all of them were seven-point Likert scale: strongly disagree: 1, strongly agree: 7). The final open question gave instructors the opportunity to provide general suggestions or comments.

5 Results and Discussion

5.1 Cognitive Load

The first result of the NASA_TLX questionnaire indicates that the second task (TLX index of 56.2) presented more difficulties to the instructors than the first task (TLX index of 37.1). This is an expected result that validates the design of the study, which ordered the tasks by its level of difficulty (not randomized). Global TLX indexes indicate that, in both tasks, the perceived workload was higher when instructors do not use visualizations. The perceived mental demand (MD) is always higher when without visualization, and this difference is significant when comparing all tasks' performances together (using the visualization: M = 169, SE = 36.2; without visualization: M = 253, SE = 35; $p < 0.05$). Significant results were also found for the temporal demand (TD) ($p = 0.043$) and frustration (FR) ($p = 0.015$) values when performing the first task. Instructors using the visualization felt that more time was needed to perform the task (time was also slightly higher in the second task when using visualizations), whereas those using the baseline interface felt more frustrated.

5.2 Action Analysis

The click data collected when instructors worked on the tasks provided an objective measure of how the two conditions (with and without the visualization) affect the way subjects use the system. Results of the action analysis (Table 2) reveal significant difference between the number of clicks performed for previewing the activities (the number of clicks being significantly higher in the case of not using the visualizations).

The fact of introducing the visualizations seems to change the behavior of the instructors in selecting the activities. When visual analytics were available, instructors previewed the activities much less frequently (4.2 and 6.2 times on average in tasks 1 and 2, compared with 21.4 and 23.4 in the baseline case). In other words, they decided whether or not to add the activity to the session by previewing the activity's contribution to the concept-level visualization, rather than previewing the activity itself. We can also observe that the time needed to perform the tasks was slightly higher on average in the condition with visualizations; however, this difference was not significant. Thus, the introduction of the visualization did not significantly influence the design time. Actions related to the addition and deletion of activities indicated similar results for both treatments.

5.3 Learning Design Outcomes

The learning designs collected after instructors completed the tasks provide an objective measure of how the two treatments affect the way subjects designed the two sessions (the lab and practice sessions required in the two tasks, respectively). As shown in Table 3, the presence of visualization slightly increased the instructors' ability to focus on the concepts of the target and immediate previous lectures when selecting activities (*onTopicCurrent* and *OnTopicPrevious*). However, the most impressive difference between the conditions was the almost complete disappearance of

Table 2. User actions with the system while performing each task during the two treatments.

Task	Action	With visualization	Without visualization	P
		M (SE)	M (SE)	
T 1	Total actions	119.4 (18.16)	136.6 (23.0)	
	Click preview activity	4.2 (2.8)	21.4 (3.04)	
	Add activity	10.2 (0.73)	11.2 (1.69)	
	Delete activity selected	2.2 (0.73)	3.4 (1.75)	
	Time spent (min)	13.78	11.88	
T 2	Total actions	236.4 (26.28)	211.4 (17.4)	
	Click preview activity	**1.6 (1.03)***	**23.4 (5.3)***	*p = 0.03 T-test between-subjects
	Add activity	26.4 (2.79)	23.4 (1.8)	
	Delete activity selected	6.2 (2.96)	4 (1.9)	
	Time spent (min)	19.14	17.72	

concepts that had not yet been introduced during the lectures (*outTopic*). The presence of these "future" concepts in practice and lab sessions is undesirable, since the students have not yet been introduced to them; yet instructors frequently miss these unwanted concepts when selecting learning content. As our data shows, the concept-level design analytics helped designers to avoid these future concepts in their design. When instructors used the baseline interface, they introduced, on average, a significantly higher number of future concepts (M = 5.6, SE = 2.61 in the first task; M = 8.2, SE = 5.3 in the second task). When using the visualization, the cases of introducing future concepts practically disappeared (0 in task 1; M = 1, SE = .63 in task 2).

Table 3. Learning designs' outcomes. *(p = 0.011; $p < 0.05$) T-test between subjects.

Task	Selected concepts	With visualization	Without visualization	P
		M (SE)	M (SE)	
T 1	OnTopicCurrent	13 (.84)	10.6 (.60)	
	OnTopicPrevious	10.2 (1.59)	8.2 (1.28)	
	OutTopic (future)	0	5.6 (2.61)	*
T 2	OnTopicCurrent	29.2 (1.39)	28.8 (1.90)	
	OnTopicPrevious	28 (5.06)	21 (2.12)	
	OutTopic (future)	1 (.63)	8.2 (5.3)	

Consider the distribution of the concepts' coverage from the learning design outcomes. Figure 3 shows how many times concepts have been practiced in the designed sessions, on average, depending on the tasks and the treatments. Results show that using the visualization approach may have a positive impact on concept-level balance when it is necessary to select just a few activities (task 1), as the educator needs to be more precise when selecting the best ones for their class. However, when the instructor can select a higher number of activities (task 2), the probability of covering the necessary concepts by chance is higher and the presence of visualizations has a lower impact on improving the concept-level balance. However, the selection of a higher number of activities in the second task without using the visualizations led users to introduce a higher number of future concepts. When using the visualizations, in both cases, the number of future concepts selected was reduced drastically.

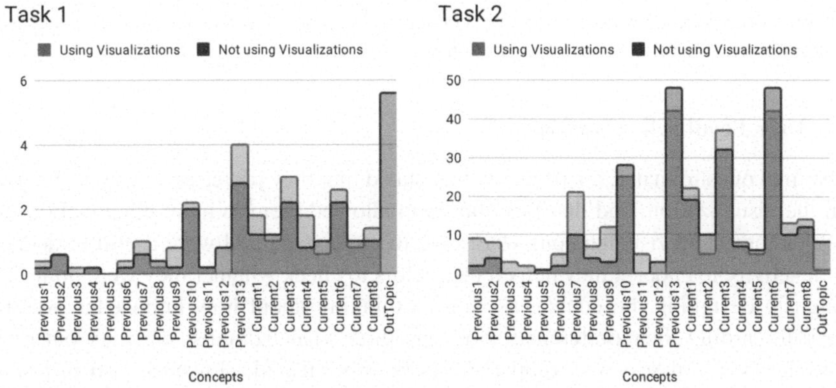

Fig. 3. Mean of the number of times that a concept is practiced during Task 1 (left) and Task 2 (right) (extracted from the learning designs outcomes) depending on the learning designs' conditions (either using or not using the visualizations). Activities can practice a concept more than once, and more than one concept at the same time. Note that there are 13 previous concepts, 8 current concepts, and a counter for future concepts.

Figure 4 presents the balance of concepts from the design outcomes, depending on the characteristics of the smart learning content. Contrary to expectations, the difference for the balance of example versus problem activities between using or not using visualizations is very low; and this balance is also very low in the case of balancing comprehension versus construction activities. We can observe only a moderate improvement of the balance and coverage of the previous concepts in both graphs when using visualizations, as well as a reduction of future concepts, as we discussed above. These results are not entirely surprising. Being domain experts, the instructors were able to understand the type and the most essential concepts of each activity by carefully reviewing its content and were sufficiently successful in balancing the number of activities added to the design (as tasks were requiring). As the log data shows, by previewing the activities, the instructors were able to achieve a reasonably balance, however, for the price of higher load. With the visualization, however, the instructors were able to reach a slightly better balance by using visual previews rather than content previews and with lower load.

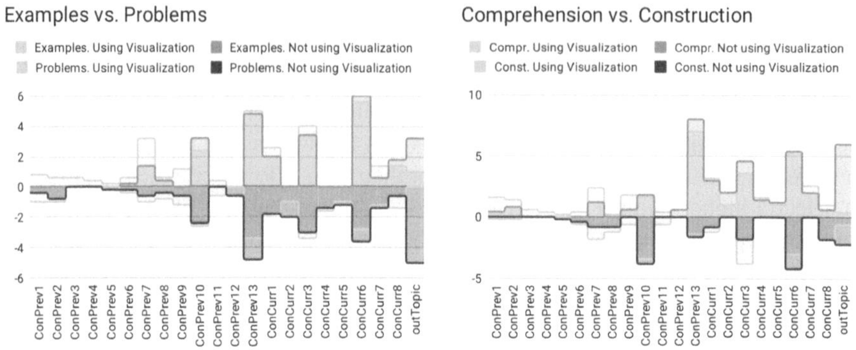

Fig. 4. Mean of the number of times that a concept is practiced during Task 2 (extracted from the learning designs' outcomes), depending on the learning designs' conditions (using or not using the visualizations). Comparison between example activities versus problem activities (left), and comprehension versus construction (right).

5.4 User Feedback Analysis

In the final questionnaire, all 10 instructors stated that they preferred to use the interface with the visualization, and that this condition allowed them to more effectively design their sessions. The visualizations were easy to understand and were useful in deciding which activity to choose; they helped instructors to check whether they were doing well enough in designing the course, as well as thinking about how knowledge was balanced. Regarding their preference about the three visualizations' tabs, six out of ten found the 'Type of session' comparison to be more useful. However, two instructors indicated the 'Examples vs. Problems' comparison as their preferred option, and two other instructors selected the 'Construction vs. Comprehension' comparison as their favorite. We can conclude that all three comparisons were meaningful for the instructors in order to create their course designs.

6 Conclusions

This paper explores some approaches for fine-grained level design analytics focused in visualizing critical metadata associated with smart learning content. Among metadata aspects covered by our visualization are the type of learning content, the nature of knowledge supported by it, and the list of specific knowledge concepts that a specific fragment of learning content allows students to practice. The visualization has been integrated into a (blended) learning design authoring tool. We expected that the concept-level design analytics would help instructors in selecting the most appropriate learning content and would result in designing more balanced learning sessions. We performed a within-subjects user study contrasting conditions both with and without the visualization. Our results indicate that the use of concept-level design analytics may reduce the cognitive load of design tasks, especially in terms of mental demand. We also demonstrated that the use of design analytics has facilitated the selection of the most suitable activities without significantly affecting the overall design time. Interestingly, the presence of the visualizations has changed the behavior of instructors in the process of selecting the activities, by just previewing their contribution to the visualization without looking deeper within their content. When examining the learning outcomes, the most impressive result was an almost complete disappearance of future concepts from sessions designed with the help of visualization. Selecting content that requires future concepts is usually a design error, and the presence of the concept-level design analytics helped users to avoid these errors. Beyond that, the differences in concept balance between the conditions were small. In addition, our results hint that the visualization may have a higher impact on the concept-level balance when it is necessary to select just a few activities, as the instructor needs to be more precise selecting the best ones. On the contrary, when the instructor can select a higher number of activities, the probability of covering the concepts by chance is higher and the visualizations have a smaller impact on improving the overall balance among concept levels.

Although our results indicate that the use of design analytics improves the overall learning design quality, our study has some limitations. Most importantly, the number of subjects was too small to draw a general conclusion, which is, however, typical for studies focused on instructor-level users. Future research will be necessary to explore and evaluate the use of concept-level design analytics with a larger sample in other educational contexts and in comparing different types of visualizations. Moreover, further research may explore the connection of design analytics with learning analytics extracted from the existing smart learning content.

Acknowledgements. The authors would like to thank all the instructors who participated in the study. This work is a result of a collaboration within a mobility grant for research funded by the SEBAP, *Societat Econòmica Barcelonesa d'Amics del País*. This work has also been partially funded by NSF DRL 1740775, "la Caixa Foundation" (CoT project, 100010434) and FEDER, the National Research Agency of the Spanish Ministry of Science, Innovations and Universities MDM-2015-0502, TIN2014-53199-C3-3-R, TIN2017-85179-C3-3-R. DHL is a Serra Húnter Fellow.

References

1. Lockyer, L., Dawson, S.: Learning designs and learning analytics. In: Proceedings of the 1st International Conference on Learning Analytics and Knowledge, LAK 2011, p. 153 (2011)
2. Hernández-Leo, D., Martinez-Maldonado, R., Pardo, A., Muñoz-Cristóbal, J.A., Rodríguez-Triana, M.J.: Analytics for learning design: a layered framework and tools. Br. J. Edu. Technol. **51**(1), 139–152 (2019)
3. Persico, D., et al.: Learning design Rashomon I – supporting the design of one lesson through different approaches. J. Res. Learn. Technol. **21** (2013)
4. Villasclaras-Fernández, E.D., Hernández-Leo, D., Asensio-Pérez, J.I., Dimitriadis, Y.: Web collage: an implementation of support for assessment design in CSCL macro-scripts. Comput. Educ. **67**, 79–97 (2013)
5. Cross, S., Galley, R., Brasher, A., Weller, M.: OULDI-JISC project evaluation report: the impact of new curriculum design tools and approaches on institutional process and design cultures. OULDI Project (2012). http://oro.open.ac.uk/34140/

6. Laurillard, D., et al.: A constructionist learning environment for teachers to model learning designs. J. Comput. Assist. Learn. **29**(1), 15–30 (2013)
7. Martinez-Maldonado, R., et al.: Supporting collaborative design activity in a multi-user digital design ecology. Comput. Hum. Behav. **71**, 327–342 (2017)
8. Albó, L., Hernández-Leo, D.: edCrumble: designing for learning with data analytics. In: Pammer-Schindler, V., Pérez-Sanagustín, M., Drachsler, H., Elferink, R., Scheffel, M. (eds.) EC-TEL 2018. LNCS, vol. 11082, pp. 605–608. Springer, Cham (2018). https://doi.org/10.1007/978-3-319-98572-5_55
9. Brusilovsky, P., et al.: Increasing adoption of smart learning content for computer science education. Working Group Reports of the 2014 on Innovation and Technology in Computer Science Education Conference. ACM, Uppsala (2014)
10. Bull, S., Kay, J.: Student models that invite the learner in: the SMILI: open learner modelling framework. Int. J. Artif. Intell. Educ. **17**(2), 89–120 (2007)
11. Corbett, A., McLaughlin, M., Scarpinatto, C.: Modeling student knowledge: cognitive tutors in high school and college. User Model. User-Adap. Inter. **10**(2–3), 81–108 (2000)
12. Bull, S., Brusilovsky, P., Guerra, J.: Which learning visualisations to offer students? In: Pammer-Schindler, V., Pérez-Sanagustín, M., Drachsler, H., Elferink, R., Scheffel, M. (eds.) EC-TEL 2018. LNCS, vol. 11082, pp. 524–530. Springer, Cham (2018). https://doi.org/10.1007/978-3-319-98572-5_40
13. Sosnovsky, S., Brusilovsky, P.: Evaluation of topic-based adaptation and student modeling in QuizGuide. User Model. User-Adap. Inter. **25**(4), 371–424 (2015)
14. Guerra, J., Schunn, C., Bull, S., Barria-Pineda, J., Brusilovsky, P.: Navigation support in complex open learner models: assessing visual design alternatives. New Rev. Hypermed. Multimed. **24**(3), 160–192 (2018)
15. Ondov, B.D., Jardine, N., Elmqvist, N., Franconeri, S.L.: Face to face: evaluating visual comparison. IEEE TVCG **25**(2), 861–871 (2018)
16. Treder, M.S.: Behind the looking-glass: A review on human symmetry perception. Symmetry **2**(3), 1510–1543 (2010)
17. Brusilovsky, P.: WebEx: learning from examples in a programming course. In: WebNet, no. 1, pp. 124–129 (2001)
18. Hosseini, R., Sirkiä, T., Guerra, J., Brusilovsky, P., Malmi, L.: Animated examples as practice content in a java programming course. In: Proceedings of the 47th ACM Technical Symposium on Computing Science Education - SIGCSE 2016, pp. 540–545 (2016)
19. Hosseini, R., Akhuseyinoglu, K., Petersen, A., Schunn, C.D., Brusilovsky, P.: PCEX: interactive program construction examples for learning programming. In: Proceedings of the 18th Koli Calling International Conference on Computing Education Research. ACM, Koli (2018)
20. Hsiao, I.-H., Sosnovsky, S., Brusilovsky, P.: Guiding students to the right questions: adaptive navigation support in an e-learning system for Java programming. J. Comput. Assist. Learn. **26**(4), 270–283 (2010)
21. Zingaro, D., Cherenkova, Y., Karpova, O., Petersen, A.: Facilitating code-writing in PI classes. In: The 44th ACM Technical Symposium on Computer Science Education, SIGCSE 2013, Denver, CO, USA, 6–9 March, pp. 585–590 (2013)
22. Hart, S.G.: Nasa-task load index (NASA-TLX): 20 years later. In: Proceedings of the Human Factors and Ergonomics Society Annual Meeting, vol. 50, no. 9, pp. 904–908 (2012)

Discovering Time Management Strategies in Learning Processes Using Process Mining Techniques

Nora'ayu Ahmad Uzir[1,2], Dragan Gašević[1,3(✉)], Wannisa Matcha[1(✉)], Jelena Jovanović[4(✉)], Abelardo Pardo[5(✉)], Lisa-Angelique Lim[5(✉)], and Sheridan Gentili[5(✉)]

[1] University of Edinburgh, Edinburgh EH8 9AB, UK
{n.uzir, w.matcha}@ed.ac.uk
[2] Universiti Teknologi MARA, 40150 Shah Alam, Malaysia
[3] Monash University, Clayton, VIC 3800, Australia
dragan.gasevic@monash.edu
[4] University of Belgrade, 11000 Belgrade, Serbia
jelena.jovanovic@fon.bg.ac.rs
[5] University of South Australia, Adelaide, SA 5000, Australia
{abelardo.pardo, lisa.lim, sheridan.gentili}@unisa.edu.au

Abstract. This paper reports the findings of a study that proposed a novel learning analytic methodology that combines process mining with cluster analysis to study time management in the context of blended and online learning. The study was conducted with first-year students (N = 241) who were enrolled in blended learning of a health science course. The study identified four distinct time management tactics and three strategies. The tactics and strategies were interpreted according to the established theoretical framework of self-regulated learning in terms of student decisions about what to study, how long to study, and how to study. The study also identified significant differences in academic performance among students who followed different time management strategies.

Keywords: Blended learning · Learning analytics · Self-Regulated Learning · Time management strategies

1 Introduction

In higher education, blended learning is a well-recognized learning mode that combines online and face-to-face interaction among teachers and learners. It offers learners flexibility to control their own learning experiences and opportunity to extend their learning time from in-class instruction to out-of-class study time. However, flexibility comes with a great responsibility for learners to define learning tasks and set goals; plan and manage resources, time, and environment; and apply effective learning tactics and strategies with the aim of achieving desired academic outcomes [1].

M. Scheffel et al. (Eds.): EC-TEL 2019, LNCS 11722, pp. 555–569, 2019.
https://doi.org/10.1007/978-3-030-29736-7_41

It has been well-established that self-regulation is linked to a significant improvement in learners' time management, which, in turn, can contribute to learners' success in blended learning [2]. However, only a few empirical studies have examined the link between self-regulated learning (SRL) and actual time management practices in blended learning settings. To bridge this gap, the current study aims to provide evidence and solid understanding of how learners enact specific time management tactics and strategies while progressing in a blended course.

The paper proposes a learning analytic methodology to analyse time management within blended and online learning. The application of the proposed methodology identified four distinct tactics and three strategies of time management in a blended course in health sciences; the use of different strategies was associated with achievement. The results were interrogated against an established theoretical model of SRL to understand how student make decisions about what to study, how long to study, and how to study.

2 Background

2.1 Time Management Strategies and Self-regulated Learning

Time management is commonly linked to self-regulated learning, since it is closely related to learners' decision about what to study, how long to study, and how to study [3–5] with instructors' minimal intervention. In line with the self-regulation viewpoint, time management has been recognized as learners' effort to effectively use their time while progressing toward set learning goals. To define time management tactics and strategies, we borrow from the literature on study tactics and study strategies. In the literature, study tactics are described as cognitive routines that include several actions done in a sequence for performing specified tasks, while study strategies are made-up from a set of enacted tactics by means of selecting, combining, or redesigning these cognitive routines, directed by a learning goal [6–8]. Time management tactics and strategies refer to how timely students manage their study tactics and strategies.

Most models of SRL emphasize three kinds of strategies focused on planning, monitoring, and regulating [9]. In the context of this study, planning involves preparation at the cognitive level; for instance, learners decide to access certain course material in advance, before it was scheduled (*ahead*) or complete a learning task just in time before the relevant face-to-face session (*preparing*) rather than delay task engagement till later in the course (*catching-up*). Meanwhile, monitoring allows learners to evaluate the differences between their current condition (e.g., learning progress) and standards (e.g., predefined learning goals), which, in turn, activates control processes to reduce discrepancies (e.g., engaging more intensively in a certain topic) [10]. Finally, regulation strategies refer to deliberate acts of learners evaluating their comprehension in a specific learning context, such as re-studying learning materials after they have completed it as a part of preparation (*revisiting*). Obviously, all kinds of SRL strategies are inextricably associated with time management, as all include a temporal aspect and a need to plan and manage one's time to put the strategies in practice.

Students' decisions about learning are not random choices; they are driven by learning goals [4]. The current study builds on the work presented in [5] to unveil the students' decision made on their time management strategies, what tactics to use (e.g., how to modify their tactics to support their learning goal), frequency of tactics use (e.g., deciding how long to persist to master a concept) and timing of tactic use (e.g., how to space their learning).

2.2 Temporal Analysis of SRL

Research on SRL has emphasized the use of trace data as artifacts of students' learning [4] recorded over a given period of time in an authentic educational setting. Trace data captures fine-grained learning events and dynamics of learning sessions [11]. As such, trace data are used to unveil latent behavior of learners, indicative of how learners regulate their effort to achieve their learning goals. The SRL literature also stressed the importance of temporal and sequential dimensions of learning [12–16] with the objective of uncovering how patterns and processes of SRL unfold over time [14]. According to Chen et al. [17], the temporal dimension relates to the passage of time (e.g., how long and how often learners engage), whereas the sequential relates to the order in which learning tasks take place. Both dimensions are closely related to the research on time management. Thus, a combined temporal and sequential analysis promises to provide new perspectives into time management and ways to improve SRL as a whole.

Process mining has been used by several scholars in the field of learning sciences to investigate regulatory patterns of groups and individual learners [22]. For instance, Sonnenberg and Bannert [18] used process mining techniques to analyze coded think aloud data about SRL processes of students who studied with hypermedia. Similarly, Bannert et al. [16] employed process mining to detect differences in frequencies of SRL events between most and least successful groups of students with respect to post-test scores. Process mining models of the two groups detected a substantial temporal difference between the groups and more regulation activities in the group of high performing students. A novel approach that combines process mining and clustering to detect learning tactics and strategies from trace data has recently been proposed [19]. This approach was applied for the analysis of trace data about students' online activities in a flipped classroom. The findings showed five learning tactics that were combined in three different learning strategies. The identified learning strategies could explain (a) how the students enacted the learning tactics over course timeline and (b) academic performance in the course. The learning strategies were well aligned with approaches to learning [20], with high engagement students following a deep learning approach and having high academic performance, while low engagement students employed a surface approach to learning and had relatively low performance.

In line with the previous works, the current study aimed to explore meaningful time management tactics and strategies by combining process mining and clustering techniques to shed some light on this notable resource of learning within online spaces. Specifically, the study addressed the following three research questions:

(1) What time management tactics and strategies can be detected from the students' interactions with online learning activities within a blended learning course?
(2) How do students in different strategy groups enact time management tactics throughout the course timeline?
(3) To what extent do the way students enact the tactics improve their self-regulated learning and course performance?

3 Methodology

3.1 Study Context

This study was conducted in a first year undergraduate course at an Australian university. The trace data were collected from 241 students enrolled in a Health Science course that ran for 13 weeks (1 semester). The course adopted a blended learning model which required students to complete online learning exercises provided via the university's LMS (Moodle) prior to face-to-face classroom activities. Two components of the online learning task were available to the students to prepare for the class in each week: tutorials and pre-laboratory exercises. Although the tutorials and pre-laboratory exercises were not mandatory to complete during the preparatory stage, they were beneficial for developing a strong foundation in the topics taught in the course. In the face-to-face setting, students were required to attend two weekly sessions: a 3 h lecture and a 1 h tutorial. The students were also required to attend 7 practical sessions (3 h each) and 3 laboratory sessions (2 h each).

3.2 Data Sources

Digital Traces. This study relied on digital traces from students' interactions with the online course activities in the period from February to June 2017, covering 13 weeks of the course. In total, there were 5,993 online learning sessions performed by the students throughout the entire course. The data were derived from LMS records which comprised every event's timestamp, unique user ID, event context, event name, IP address, and a description of the learning action. Time management was analysed by looking at times when the students performed online activities (out-of-class study), as evidenced in the trace data (timestamps) and validated against the course schedule provided by the course instructor. Note that the students were recommended to study one topic per week and complete pre-laboratory exercises during the assigned week. Each learning action was labelled with an appropriate ***mode of study*** based on its timing with respect to the week's topic as: (i) *preparing* - if the learning action was related to the topic the students were supposed to study in the given week, (ii) *ahead* - if the learning action was advance of the schedule, (iii) *revisiting* - if the learning action was related to a behind-the-schedule topic that the student had already studied at some earlier point in time, and (iv) *catching-up* – if the student had never accessed activities related to the behind-the-schedule topic. Successive learning actions between any two consecutive events that were within 30 min of one another were grouped into a learning session [21]. Learning sessions served as the unit of analysis when identifying patterns indicative of students' time management tactics.

Academic Performance. The second data source was derived from the overall course score in the 0–100 range. The assessments contributing to the final course mark included 2 quizzes (contributing 20%), practical marks (25%), and the final exam (55%). Quiz 1 and Quiz 2 were administered in Week 7 and Week 13, respectively. Both quizzes were conducted in a conventional setting.

3.3 Data Analysis

Time Management Tactics. Initially, time management tactics were detected from sequences of study modes. In particular, First Order Markov Model (FOMM), implemented in the pMineR R package [22], was used to compute and visualize the process model from learning sessions. By inspecting the overall process model, potential time management tactics were inferred based on the density of connections among events (i.e., modes of study). To move from observations to automated detection of tactics, we used the matrix of transition probabilities between events, produced by the FOMM, as the input to the Expectation Maximization (EM) algorithm [19] to identify clusters of sequences. The identified clusters reflect patterns in the sequences of study modes and can be considered manifestation of students' time management tactics.

Time Management Strategy Groups. Time management strategies were inferred from the way a student employed time management tactics; i.e., strategies were characterized by one or more tactics [23]. Agglomerative Hierarchical Clustering based on Ward's algorithm [24] was used to identify time management strategies by grouping students with similar usage patterns of time management tactics. To identify such student groups, we represented each student as a vector of the following variables: (a) counts of instances of the identified time management tactics followed by the student (one variable per time management tactic); and (b) the total number of instances of time management tactics. The distance between students, required for the Ward algorithm, was computed as the Euclidean distance of the corresponding vectors. The optimal number of clusters was determined by inspecting dendrograms.

Time Management Tactics Use Across Strategy Group. To further explore the temporal data, we used another process mining technique implemented in the bupaR R-package [25]. The unique features introduced in bupaR assure that the time frame is relevant enough to bring insight into the learning process and has a great potential to inform and enhance understanding of how students make complex learning decisions. In our analysis, we considered event logs that recorded each student's active learning process from the beginning (Week 1) to the end (Week 13) of the course. Each event belonged to a case. A case, in general, is an instance of the process; in this study, a case is an individual student enrolled in the course. In addition, each event relates to a coarser concept of activity. In this study, activities are the tactics adopted by a student while progressing in their learning. For this analysis, we combined the identified time management tactics with online learning resources (e.g., tutorials and pre-lab exercise) to provide meaningful representations of time management (e.g., *ahead_tutorial* and *prepare_tutorial*). When an activity is performed, an activity instance (occurrence) is recorded. For a given case (user_id), we would obtain, from the event logs, a set of execution traces. We denote the traces as a sequence of activities ordered by their time of occurrences in the course timeline (see Table 1).

Table 1. An example of a sequence of activities (trace) for each student obtained from event logs

user_id	trace_length	start_timestamp	complete_timestamp	trace
8	1	2017-06-08 09:56:00	2017-06-08 09:56:00	Prepare_Tutorial
14	2	2017-03-28 08:21:00	2017-04-28 15:37:00	Prepare_Tutorial,Catch.up_Prelab
212	2	2017-03-08 09:09:00	2017-04-06 22:55:00	Ahead_Tutorial,Prepare_Tutorial
12	3	2017-02-28 08:41:00	2017-03-17 08:19:00	Ahead_Tutorial,Mixed_Tutorial,Prepare_Tutorial
19	3	2017-03-06 22:07:00	2017-03-27 22:39:00	Prepare_Tutorial,Mixed_Tutorial,Prepare_Tutorial
35	3	2017-03-22 01:26:00	2017-04-27 12:20:00	Catch.up_Tutorial,Catch.up_Tutorial,Ahead_Tutorial
41	3	2017-03-15 15:01:00	2017-06-08 11:39:00	Catch.up_Tutorial,Prepare_Tutorial,Prepare_Tutorial
52	4	2017-03-15 19:57:00	2017-06-10 07:15:00	Catch.up_Tutorial,Catch.up_Tutorial,Catch.up_Tutorial,Prepare_Tutorial
77	4	2017-03-14 09:16:00	2017-03-19 21:31:00	Prepare_Tutorial,Prepare_Tutorial,Catch.up_Tutorial,Prepare_Tutorial

Process models were then generated based on the identified traces. A process model consisted of a set of nodes and a set of arcs, where the nodes were the process activities and the arcs were the order of the activities. The discovered models were often "spaghetti-like" showing all details of a process. To make the models usable for interpretation, 80% of the most frequent activities were kept for each time management strategy group. This allowed us to study temporal characteristics of different strategy groups.

Association Between Strategy Group and Academic Performance. To examine if there was a significant difference between the identified strategy groups on academic performance, we used Kruskal Wallis tests followed by pairwise Mann Whitney U tests.

4 Results

4.1 Time Management Tactics

By examining density of connections among events of the overall process model resulting from FOMM, a solution of four clusters was identified. Figure 1 illustrates a temporal distribution plot of study modes in each cluster indicative of time management tactics. Each point on the X-axis corresponds to one event (mode of study), whereas the position on the Y-axis represents the probability of study modes.

The characteristics of the identified clusters could be described as follows: (i) Tactic 1 – *Mixed* (N = 1511, 25.21% of all sequences). This tactic was comprised of ahead, preparing, and revisiting modes of study. Sequences in this tactic were focused on revisiting learning materials in a future week after they has been completed in advance or during the week when those activities were scheduled, (ii) Tactic 2 – *Catching-up* (N = 128, 2.14%). It was the least used tactic and consisted predominantly of the catching-up behavior apart from revisiting and preparing modes, (iii) Tactic 3 – *Preparing* (N = 2441, 40.73%). This is the most widely applied tactic and had the highest frequency of preparation activities compared to the other tactics, and (iv) Tactic 4 – *Ahead* (N = 1913, 31.92%) consisted predominantly of ahead activities.

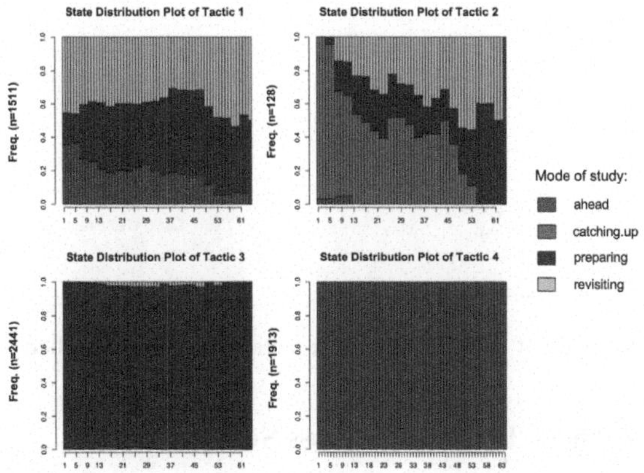

Fig. 1. Temporal distribution of study modes within the detected clusters (manifestations of the students' time management tactics).

4.2 Time Management Strategy Groups

By inspecting the dendrogram resulting from the applied agglomerative hierarchical clustering, a three cluster solution was chosen as the optimal one. To better understand the identified clusters as manifestations of the students' time management strategies, we examined, for each cluster (strategy), how the use of time management tactics changed throughout the course. Figure 2 shows, for each detected strategy, median number of different tactics applied in each week of the course.

Strategy 1 – Active (N = 74, 30.71% of all students) was the most active and dynamic group. This group was consistent in the use of the *Preparing* tactic throughout the course, but also applied different tactics (ahead, preparing and mixed) interchangeably along the course timeline. *Strategy 2 – Passive* (N = 101, 41.91%) had the highest number of students who adopted it. The students were averse towards spending time for studying online with low use of all tactics. Their activity level declined rapidly right after Week 2; in Week 4 they were back on track by adopting the *Preparing* tactic, but failed to maintain the momentum for the rest of the course. *Strategy 3 – Selective* (N = 66, 27.39%) included the students who were highly focused on the

Preparing tactic beginning from Week 3. Their effort dropped in Week 7, but they were able to get back on track and maintained the *Preparing* tactic until the end of the course.

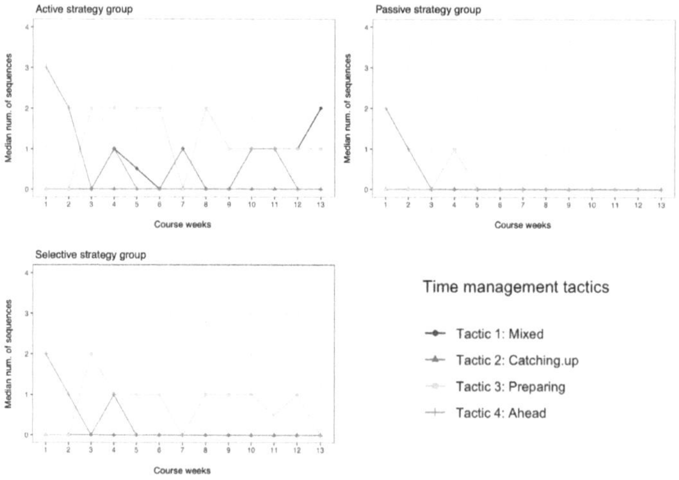

Fig. 2. The dynamics of time management tactics for each identified strategy group

4.3 Time Management Tactic Use Across Strategy Groups

Three process models were created to represent each identified strategy. Figure 3 illustrates the learning processes performed by the students (by enacting several tactics) in each strategy group. The course design permitted the students to decide which tactic to start with and they could change the tactics at any time. Clear differences in the temporal pattern can be identified between the groups, as explained below.

The total duration of time spent to complete the course (in days) was Mdn = 99.62, Q1 = 97.82, Q3 = 101.81 for the *Active* strategy group (Fig. 3(a)) had. This group was characterized by *Ahead_Tutorial* → *Prepare_Tutorial* → *Mixed_Tutorial* as a common activities sequence; that is, a path of transitions with high certainty in activity instances. The frequency of activity instances was relatively equally distributed among the tactics; i.e., all tactics are equally important. The students in this group tended to stay long in the same mode of study (loops around ahead, preparing, and revisiting). The transition often occurred between two tactics (based on the high frequency of activity instances); i.e., *prepare_tutorial* to *mixed_tutorial* (191 instances) and *mixed_tutorial* to *prepare_tutorial* (164 instances). The students in this group showed careful choices between cognitive, metacognitive, and regulation activities while progressing in their learning. This is evidenced by repeated efforts in preparing and reviewing course materials and the regularity in applying various tactics.

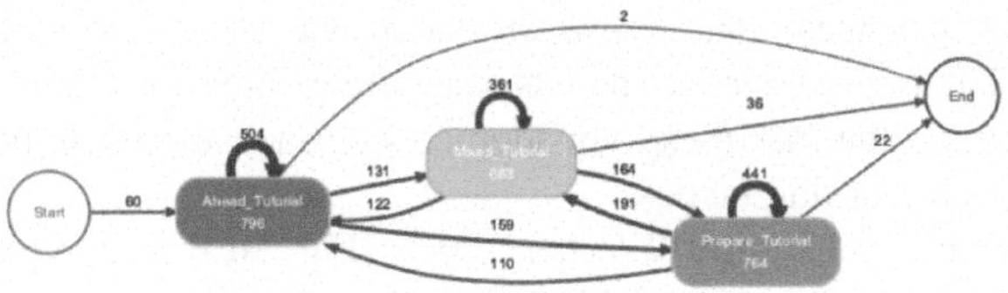

(a) Active Strategy Group

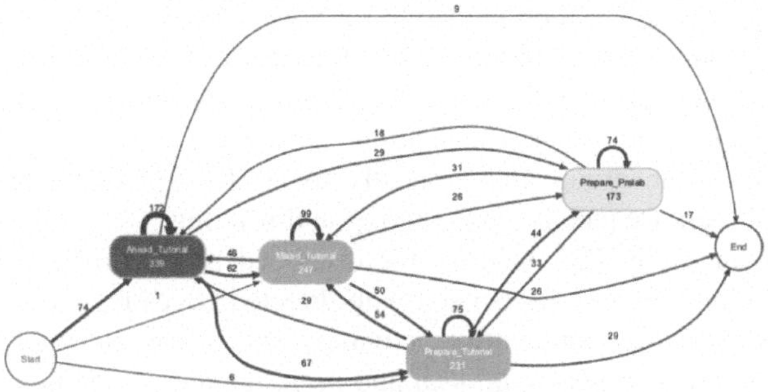

(b) Passive Strategy Group

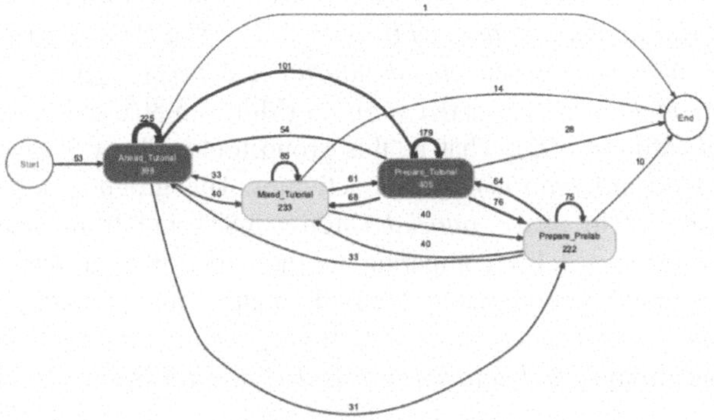

(c) Selective Strategy Group

Fig. 3. Process models for the learning processes of the three identified strategy groups. The number in the box represents the absolute frequency of occurrences of events (activity instances), while the numbers associated with edges represent absolute frequency of transitions between consecutive activities. Darker node colour represents higher frequency of activities. (Color figure online)

The median time spent by the *Passive* group (Fig. 3(b)) to complete the course (in days) was 86.68 days (Q1 = 70.06, Q3 = 97.89). The most common path of transition displayed by this group was *Ahead_Tutorial* → *Mixed_Tutorial* → *Prepare_Tutorial* → *Prepare_Prelab*. In contrast to the *Active* group, this group demonstrated high transitions from *ahead_tutorial* to *prepare_tutorial* (67 instances) and *ahead_tutorial* to *mixed_tutorial* (62 instances), while, *prepare_tutorial* showed low connection with *mixed_tutorial* (54 instances). The *Preparing* tactic was connected with both tutorial materials and pre-laboratory exercises and its usage frequency was relatively low. These results seem to suggest the *Passive* group adopted a surface approach to learning, with low frequencies in all learning tactics.

The median time spent by the *Selective* group (Fig. 3(c)) to complete the course was 98.04 days (Q1 = 92.48, Q3 = 99.90). *Prepare_Tutorial* → *Ahead_Tutorial* → *Mixed_Tutorial* → *Prepare_Prelab* was the most common sequence. Like the *Passive* group, this group was focused on preparing for both tutorials and laboratory exercises. Similarly, both groups showed relatively low frequency of re-studying (*mixed tactics*). In comparison to other groups, this group had frequent transitions from *ahead_tutorial* to *prepare_tutorial* (101 instances) and from *prepare_tutorial* to *prepare_prelab* (76 instances). That is, the group predominantly focused on planning (e.g., ahead and preparing), while less frequently on preparing and revising.

The graphs shown in Fig. 4 depict the discussed process models from the time perspective. The time periods associated with directed edges represent idle time; i.e., time period between two consecutive activities. The *Active* strategy group had the longest idle time between *ahead_tutorial* and *prepare_tutorial* (Mdn = 4.20 days). In comparison with other group, students in this group took less than 2 days to prepare and revisit the topics; i.e., from *prepare_tutorial* to *mixed_tutorial* (Mdn = 1.90) and from *mixed_tutorial* to *prepare_tutorial* (Mdn = 1.21). The *Passive* strategy group had the longest idle time is between *ahead_tutorial* and *prepare_prelab* (Mdn = 7.34) followed by *ahead_tutorial* to *mixed_tutorial* (Mdn = 5.80) and *ahead_tutorial* to *prepare_tutorial* (Mdn = 5.95). That is, this group took at least 5 days to shift from their first activity (*ahead_tutorial*) to other activities. This group took the longest time from *prepare_tutorial* to *mixed_tutorial* (Mdn = 5.83) and from *mixed_tutorial* to *prepare_tutorial* (Mdn = 4.40) comparing to the other two groups. Although the *Selective* strategy group predominantly focused on ahead and preparing tactics, it took them a long time (almost a week) to shift from *prepare_tutorial* to *ahead_tutorial* (Mdn = 6.14) and from *ahead_tutorial* to *prepare_tutorial* (Mdn = 6.11).

4.4 Association Between Strategy Groups and Academic Performance

The results of the Kruskal Wallis test showed a significant association between the identified strategy groups and the students' course performance (p-value < 0.001 for total score). The pairwise tests showed significant difference with effect sizes (r) ranging from small to medium (Table 2).

The *Active* group (Mdn = 78.01, Q1 = 72.57, Q3 = 84.05) was highest performing. The *Passive* group (Mdn = 74.29, Q1 = 59.57, Q3 = 81.28) was lowest performing. The *Selective* group (Mdn = 76.46, Q1 = 73.65, Q3 = 82.66) was mid-performing.

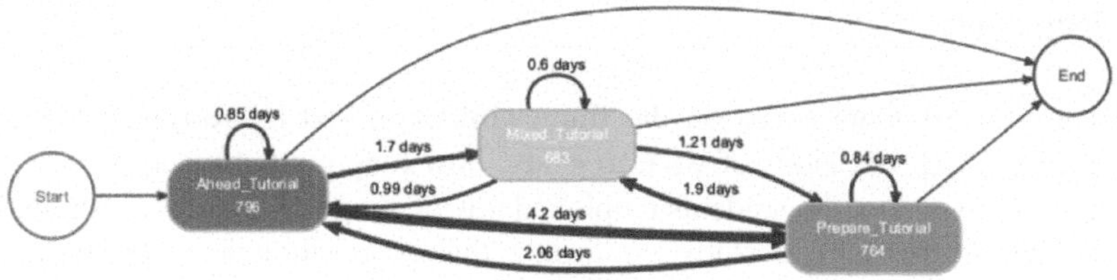

(a) Active Strategy Group

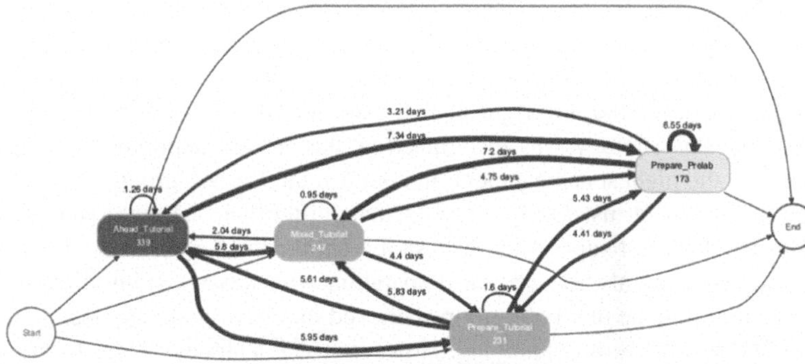

(b) Passive Strategy Group

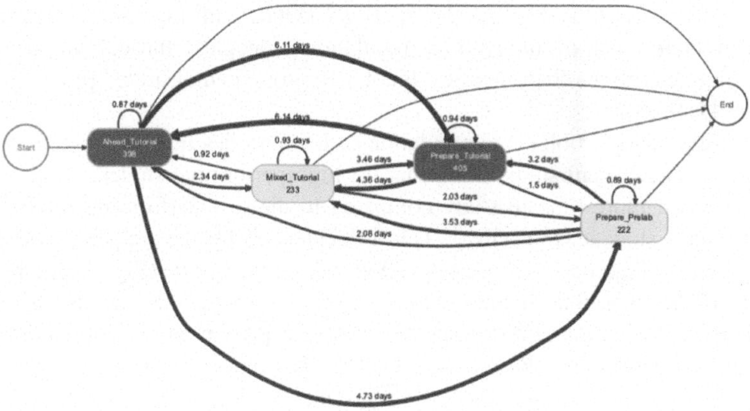

(c) Selective Strategy Group

Fig. 4. Idle time (in days) between the end of the from-activity and the start of the to-activity across three identified strategy groups. Darker line color represents longer idle time. (Color figure online)

Table 2. Pairwise comparison of strategy groups with respect to the total course score.

Cluster 1	Cluster 2	Z	p	r
Passive	Selective	1.0226	<0.001	0.198
Active	Passive	–0.2921	<0.001	0.203
Selective	Active	–0.6678	<0.001	0.020

5 Discussion

We discuss the findings based on the framework proposed by Kornell and his colleagues [5] on SRL decisions of what to study, how long to study, and how to study. The results showed that the students employed a wide range of tactics and strategies to manage their learning. The study confirmed this proposition by identifying three strategy groups – *Active, Passive,* and *Selective.* The profiles of these groups reflect their time management strategies and academic achievement in the course. The *Active* group was the most active and dynamic; the students in it adopted diverse tactics and used them throughout the course. Due to the careful alignment of diverse tactics such as study in advance (*ahead tactics*), prepare learning prior to a face-to-face session (*preparing tactics*), re-studying right after a class and revision during the test weeks (*mixed tactics*), this strategy was recognized as the one of autonomous learners and associated with the highest achievement. In contrast, the *Passive* group, associated with the lowest achievement, used only a few tactics during their learning, and sometimes used tactics in a way not supporting their study. Unlike the *Active* group, the *Selective* and *Passive* groups highly focused on preparation with less revisiting efforts. A possible explanation may be that both groups believed that having already learned a topic, little would be gained from re-studying. However, such a strategy is far from optimal. To sum up, our results indicate that students who were identified as high performing – the *Active* group – put efforts to plan their study (cognitive), modified their learning accordingly (metacognitive), aligned their study tactics with the course structure and maintained their level of motivation (regulation strategies) throughout the course timeline. In line with the SRL theories, the *Active* group demonstrated productive self-regulation [4, 9, 26].

One of the major problems in regulation of learning lies in how much time to put into practice. The current study found that the high performing students (*Active*) were willing to invest more time to study compared to the low performing (*Passive*) and mid-performing students (*Selective*). This is evidenced by the frequency of activity instances that the high performing group allocated for each tactic (Fig. 3(a)) which was two times higher than that of the lowest performing group. The students in the high performing (*Active*) group also devoted to course completion on average 13 days more than the lowest performing (*Passive*) group. This may reflect the *perseverance of effort* exhibited by high performing students to sustain the time and efforts necessary for completing long-term tasks [27]. Furthermore, on average, the *Active* group spent more time revisiting (*mixed_tutorial*) weekly topics ($M = 5.45$, $SD = 10.42$) minutes. The *Passive* and *Selective* groups spent longer time on preparing for pre-laboratory exercises (*prepare_prelab*) ($M = 9.74$, $SD = 13.57$ and $M = 11.81$, $SD = 18.61$ min, respectively). This may be attributed to the students' *judgement of rate of learning* (jROL). Maybe the two groups perceived pre-laboratory exercises as a difficult task and, thus, maintained a high learning rate. Commonly, the students in all three strategy groups spent more time revisiting learning materials (*mixed_tutorial*) after the week to which the materials were assigned. This was almost twice the time they spent using those materials to prepare (*prepare_tutorial*) for the class. These findings suggest that, all students used regulatory processes to some degree, but self-regulated learners were distinguished by their awareness of active decisions between regulatory processes and learning outcomes and their use of these strategies to achieve academic goals [28].

Furthermore, the use of time in learning is often linked to the *spacing effect* [29]. Spacing—defined as separating successive study sessions rather than massing such sessions—has positive effects on long-term memory [30]. The finding of this study indicated that, after preparatory work, the *Active* group took 2 days on average before immediately returning to the course material to review it, whereas the *Passive* and *Selective* groups waited approximately 6 and 4 days, respectively, before returning to the materials to re-study. A possible explanation may be that the *Active* groups established optimal metacognitive judgments that they could forget some items they had previously studied, so they kept coming back to the items immediately as a priority [26] thereby promoting better recall. In contrast, the *Passive* and *Selective* groups were less sensitive to change as they allowed for maladaptive delay between two tactics. Undoubtedly, long idle time did not benefit recall. Students could forget what they have learned before. In summary, the students in the highest performing group (*Active*) showed a clear endorsement of massing over spacing for predicted learning outcomes [31] contrary to consistent findings in the literature of a benefit for spacing [32].

6 Conclusions and Implications

The purpose of this study was to explore the differences in time management tactics and strategies from the perspective of self-regulated learning theories. We present the time management aspects based on study decisions students make on what to study (what tactic to use), how long to study (frequency of tactics used) and how to study (timing of tactic use). From a methodological point of view, we demonstrated how quantitative temporal data about students' online learning activities can be analysed by methods of process mining. Although used in SRL research, the application of this method, as done in the current study, for exploring students' time management tactics and strategies in the context of online and blended learning activities is original.

This study contributes to the literature on time management and SRL by providing empirical evidence on what, how, and how long students enacted their tactics across different strategy groups and academic achievement. Our research reinforced the importance of time management tactics in students' learning that improve their SRL and performance. From an instructor viewpoint, this study has a potential to inform instructors about what tactics students applied to learn, how students spaced out their learning, and how regularly students engaged in online preparatory work. This allows instructors to understand different characteristics of students to make necessary adjustment in their learning approach and feedback to the students. From a student viewpoint, this study can provide awareness and useful guidelines for the students to inform them about the effective tactics and strategies they could employ while studying online and the opportunities to improve their time-management skills as well as their academic success.

This study highly relied on the trace data of students' interactions with online preparatory learning activities. Although this data allowed for examining actual behavior in an authentic online settings, we could not capture activities that occurred offline (e.g., downloading the learning material) nor in-class activities; such activities which take place in a physical context could influence students' decision in learning.

References

1. Zhu, Y., Au, W., Yates, G.: University students' self-control and self-regulated learning in a blended course. Internet High. Educ. **30**, 54–62 (2016). https://doi.org/10.1016/j.iheduc.2016.04.001
2. Broadbent, J.: Comparing online and blended learner's self-regulated learning strategies and academic performance. Internet High. Educ. **33**, 24–32 (2017). https://doi.org/10.1016/j.iheduc.2017.01.004
3. Winne, P.H.: Learning analytics for self-regulated learning. Handb. Learn. Anal. 241–249 (2017)
4. Winne, P.H.: Self-Regulated Learning. Elsevier (2015). https://doi.org/10.1016/B978-0-08-097086-8.25091-5
5. Kornell, N., Bjork, R.A.: The promise and perils of self-regulated study. Psychon. Bull. Rev. **14**, 219–224 (2007). https://doi.org/10.3758/BF03194055
6. Fincham, O.E., Gasevic, D.V., Jovanovic, J.M., Pardo, A.: From study tactics to learning strategies: an analytical method for extracting interpretable representations. IEEE Trans. Learn. Technol. 1 (2018). https://doi.org/10.1109/TLT.2018.2823317
7. Winne, P.H.: Self-regulated learning viewed from models of information processing. Self-Regulated Learn. Acad. Achiev. Theor. Perspect. **2**, 153–189 (2001)
8. Zimmerman, B.J.: Academic studing and the development of personal skill: a self-regulatory perspective. Educ. Psychol. **33**, 73–86 (1998). https://doi.org/10.1207/s15326985ep3302&3_3
9. Cicchinelli, A., et al.: Finding traces of self-regulated learning in activity streams, pp. 191–200 (2018). https://doi.org/10.1145/3170358.3170381
10. Winne, P.H., Hadwin, A.F.: The weave of motivation and self-regulated learning. Motiv. Self-Regulated Learn. Theory, Res. Appl. **2**, 297–314 (2008)
11. Hadwin, A.F., Nesbit, J.C., Jamieson-Noel, D., Code, J., Winne, P.H.: Examining trace data to explore self-regulated learning. Metacognition Learn. **2**, 107–124 (2007). https://doi.org/10.1007/s11409-007-9016-7
12. Bennett, A., Burke, P.J.: Re/conceptualising time and temporality: an exploration of time in higher education. Discourse. **6306**, 1–13 (2017). https://doi.org/10.1080/01596306.2017.1312285
13. Papamitsiou, Z., Economides, A.A.: Exhibiting achievement behavior during computer-based testing: what temporal trace data and personality traits tell us? Comput. Hum. Behav. **75**, 423–438 (2017). https://doi.org/10.1016/j.chb.2017.05.036
14. Malmberg, J., Järvelä, S., Järvenoja, H.: Capturing temporal and sequential patterns of self-, co-, and socially shared regulation in the context of collaborative learning. Contemp. Educ. Psychol. **49**, 160–174 (2017). https://doi.org/10.1016/j.cedpsych.2017.01.009
15. Sobocinski, M., Malmberg, J., Järvelä, S.: Exploring temporal sequences of regulatory phases and associated interactions in low- and high-challenge collaborative learning sessions. Metacognition Learn. **12**, 275–294 (2017). https://doi.org/10.1007/s11409-016-9167-5

16. Bannert, M., Reimann, P., Sonnenberg, C.: Process mining techniques for analysing patterns and strategies in students' self-regulated learning. Metacognition Learn. **9**, 161–185 (2014). https://doi.org/10.1007/s11409-013-9107-6
17. Chen, B., Knight, S., Wise, A.: Critical issues in designing and implementing temporal analytics. J. Learn. Anal. **5**, 1–9 (2018). https://doi.org/10.18608/jla.2018.51.1
18. Sonnenberg, C., Bannert, M.: Discovering the effects of metacognitive prompts on the sequential structure of SRL-processes using process mining techniques. J. Learn. Anal. **2**, 72–100 (2015)
19. Matcha, W., Gašević, D., Uzir, N.A., Jovanović, J., Pardo, A.: Analytics of learning strategies: associations with academic performance and feedback. In: Proceedings of the 9th International Conference on Learning Analytics & Knowledge, pp. 461–470. ACM (2019)
20. Biggs, J., Kember, D., Leung, D.Y.P.: The revised two factor study process questionnaire: R-SPQ-2F. Br. J. Educ. Psychol. **71**, 133–149 (2001). https://doi.org/10.1348/000709901158433
21. Jovanović, J., Gašević, D., Dawson, S., Pardo, A., Mirriahi, N.: Learning analytics to unveil learning strategies in a flipped classroom. Internet High. Educ. **33**, 74–85 (2017). https://doi.org/10.1016/j.iheduc.2017.02.001
22. Gatta, R., et al.: pMineR: an innovative R library for performing process mining in medicine. In: ten Teije, A., Popow, C., Holmes, J.H., Sacchi, L. (eds.) AIME 2017. LNCS (LNAI), vol. 10259, pp. 351–355. Springer, Cham (2017). https://doi.org/10.1007/978-3-319-59758-4_42
23. Derry, S.J.: Putting learning strategies to work. Educ. Leadersh. **46**, 4 (1988)
24. Hastie, T., Tibshirani, R., Friedman, J.: The Elements of Statistical Learning. SSS. Springer, New York (2009). https://doi.org/10.1007/978-0-387-84858-7
25. Janssenswillen, G., Depaire, B., Swennen, M., Jans, M., Vanhoof, K.: bupaR: enabling reproducible business process analysis. Knowl.-Based Syst. **163**, 927–930 (2019)
26. Zimmerman, B.J.: Investigating self-regulation and motivation: historical background, methodological developments, and future prospects. Am. Educ. Res. J. **45**, 166–183 (2008). https://doi.org/10.3102/0002831207312909
27. Wolters, C.A., Hussain, M.: Investigating grit and its relations with college students' self-regulated learning and academic achievement. Metacognition Learn. **10**, 293–311 (2015). https://doi.org/10.1007/s11409-014-9128-9
28. Zimmerman, B.J.: Theories of self-regulated learning and academic achievement: an overview and analysis. In: Zimmerman, B.J., Schunk, D.H. (eds.) self-Regulated Learning and Academic Achievement, 2nd edn, pp. 1–37. Lawrence Erlbaum Associates, Mahwah (2001)
29. Benjamin, A.S., Bird, R.D.: Metacognitive control of the spacing of study repetitions. J. Mem. Lang. **55**, 126–137 (2006). https://doi.org/10.1016/j.jml.2006.02.003
30. Crowder, R.G.: Principles of Learning and Memory: Classic edn. Psychology Press (2014)
31. Glenberg, A.M.: Influences of retrieval processes on the spacing effect in free recall. J. Exp. Psychol. Hum. Learn. Mem. **3**, 282 (1977)
32. Kornell, N., Bjork, R.A.: Learning concepts and categories. Psychol. Sci. **19**, 585–592 (2008). https://doi.org/10.1111/j.1467-9280.2008.02127.x

Poster and Demo Papers

Computational Thinking in Problem Based Learning – Exploring the Reciprocal Potential

Sandra Burri Gram-Hansen(✉) and Tanja Svarre Jonasen

Department of Communication and Psychology,
Aalborg University, Aalborg, Denmark
{Burri, tanjasj}@hum.aau.dk

Abstract. This paper presents the initial insights from a study in which we explored the relation between computational thinking (CT) and problem-based learning in higher education. CT skills are increasingly recognized as a necessity to all lines of study, as they not only facilitate digital proficiency, but potentially also a sense of computational empowerment and an ability to take a critical and constructive approach to applying computers when solving complex problems. The distinct focus on higher education is routed in theoretical as well as empirically based challenges, as this particular group of learners for the vast majority have started their education in a mainly analogue learning setting, yet now face employments with a much stronger demand for digital competences. The discussions presented in this paper takes its point of departure in the Aalborg PBL-model.

Keywords: Problem based learning · Computational Thinking · Learning process recognition · Digital skills · Digital empowerment

1 Introduction

The vast majority of research in CT in educational settings focuses on K12 learners and on STEM oriented educations [1]. While recognizing the value of these studies, we find it necessary to focus equally on the possibilities and limitations of CT in higher education. Firstly, in consideration of the rapidly developing need for digital literacy in the labour market, and the responsibility of higher educations to also consider employability of students once their education is complete. Secondly in recognition of the development in K12 educations, where the focus on CT and digital proficiency at an earlier age will greatly influence the demands of higher education in the future.

Most often, CT is associated with learning designs, which focus particularly on product development, where different learning material and tools are applied in practice with the aim of establishing CT competences [2, 3]. However, if learners are to gain a deeper understanding of CT, exploring and identifying pedagogical frameworks with particular potential to this subject is of equal importance. Steps towards investigating best practices in learning designs for CT have been made in relation to e.g. game based learning [4]. Contributing to this ongoing research, we argue that if CT is to influence

M. Scheffel et al. (Eds.): EC-TEL 2019, LNCS 11722, pp. 573–576, 2019.
https://doi.org/10.1007/978-3-030-29736-7_42

educational practices at all levels of education, and be of value to learners who do not have a distinct study focus on technical subjects, it is reasonable to also investigate the relation between CT and more generic pedagogical frameworks such as problem based learning (PBL).

2 Computational Thinking in a PBL Context

In essence, CT represents the notion that concepts and perspectives from computer science may be applied in areas such as problem solving and in exploring and describing complex systems. By approaching complex problems with a computational mind-set, complex problems may be reduced into smaller and more manageable problems [5] and as such be solved more efficiently [6]. As such, CT is argued to hold potential in different levels of education and across a broad variety of subjects.

Problem Based Learning (PBL) on the other hand is generally recognized as an exploratory approach to learning, which based on real world problems, enable students to learn through practical experience. Contrary to traditional approaches to higher education with lectures and independent studies, PBL is widely understood as providing an engaging learning environment where different study activities are planned in a manner, which facilitates and inspires the students work as they explore and respond to identified problems [7].

While PBL is internationally recognized and applied, we place a particular focus on the AAU PBL approach. This approach maintains that optimal learning conditions require that the students acquire new skills and insights by actively exploring and testing theories and methods in practice. Moreover, the approach distinguished itself by focusing on prolonged learning processes allowing the students to immerse themselves into their problem solving process [8].

In spite of the recognized potential of the PBL approach and in recognition that the PBL practice is often identified as one of the factors which motivate both Danish and International students to apply to Aalborg university, the approach is not without its challenges. Supervisors and lecturers across different faculties indicate that students often find it challenging to maintain and articulate the value of the project process in comparison to the results of an exam. Experiences show that students at both bachelor and master level have a tendency to refer to their project reports as "the project" leading the PBL process to be recognized as secondary to the documentation process and the grade of the semester [9]. It is with this challenge in mind, that our study aimed at exploring the reciprocal benefits of considering CT in a PBL context in higher education.

2.1 Exploring Theory in Practice

Having explored the relation between CT and PBL from a theoretical perspective, a pilot study which aimed to combine these two fields in practice was conducted at Master level programs in communication and information technology under the faculty of humanities. 20 students from Master.it programs were included in the study. Students were distinctly introduced to CT at two different occasions. First as part of the semester introduction and secondly at the end of the first semester. As such the study enabled us to benchmark the students' CT skills at the beginning of their studies and again after having completed a PBL process. The data collected at the start of the study revealed that while all students were able to briefly explain what they had done in their bachelor project, few students at the beginning of the semester were able to reflect upon or even consider the individual CT skills. In direct contrast, the data collected at the end of the students first PBL based semester revealed that the students had acquired a much deeper understanding of their problem solving process during their first PBL semester. Distinct competences were richly expressed with reference to CT skills. E.g. specific methods were related to the process of decomposition.

3 Preliminary Findings

3.1 CT Provides a Vocabulary for Problem Analysis and Problem Solving

While CT has the potential to enable students to acquire not only diverse digital competences but also an ability to critically asses the implications of technology both in professional and private settings, the PBL approach to learning has benefit of ensuring that these skills are acquired with direct relation to actual real world problems. It is however crucial that students not only become able to assess, apply and construct new solutions with technologies, but also that they acquire competences which qualify them to articulate their process and discuss which parts can be generalized and transferred to other problems and which steps are related distinctly to the individual problem. One of the distinct benefits of bringing a CT perspective into the PBL practice was identified in the students' development of a much richer vocabulary and ability to articulate their problem solving process.

3.2 CT in Humanities Calls for a Stronger Focus on Problem Analysis Rather than Simply Problem Solving

The conducted studies, both theoretical and empirical, prompts us to further consider the PBL process itself and where in this process the CT perspective might comprise a contribution. CT must be implemented and assessed in consideration of the research field in which it is applied. The PBL approach is comprised by three phases where problem solving is central, however it is particularly in humanities a case that the problem analysis is the essential part of a study. Consequently, it may be necessary to clarify that PBL activities such as group work, lectures and literature studies are of as much value to the problem solving process and that CT skills may also serve a distinct purpose in the problem analysis phase. When considering CT in humanities, future research should include investigating if for instance a conceptual understanding of decomposition can contribute to a more structured identification of a problem, or if the PBL process benefits more from a more spontaneous curiosity amongst project group members.

3.3 CT Calls for Prolonged Learning Designs and Practical Experience

In line with the argument that CT comprises an ability to not only apply technologies but also critically and constructively reflect upon their possibilities and limitations in a given context, we argue that the acquiring of CT competences calls for prolonged use of technologies in educational settings, rather than brief introductions. While other technology related perspectives such as usability may be assessed in shorter periods, the ability to critically assess the potential of a technology calls for a contextual understanding as well as practical experience with the technology. Problems do not magically appear, but rather they are identified as a result of a deeper understanding of a given context. By this, we argue that actual experience is fundamental to acquiring CT skills at is through experience that we become able to not only see the potential of a technology but also identify its limitations.

Based on the above points, we recommend that future studies emphasises prolonged use of technologies in educational settings, in order to ensure that students reach a level of reflections which goes beyond usability and leads to a more critical assessment of technologies. We recommend that CT in educational settings include a particular attention towards the problem analysis phase, partly to ensure that students recognize how and where problems emerge and partly to explore further what role CT skills may play in this part of the process. Finally, we recommend that the relation between CT and PBL is explored further both in theory and in practice, with a particular focus on ensuring that CT skills are made relevant not only in an academic context but also related to real world problems.

References

1. Kalelioglu, F., Gülbahar, Y., Kukul, V.: A framework for computational thinking based on a systematic research review. Baltic J. Mod. Comput. **4**, 583–596 (2016)
2. Grover, S., Pea, R.: Computational thinking in K–12: a review of the state of the field. Educ. Res. **42**, 38–43 (2013)
3. Repenning, A., Basawapatna, A.R., Escherle, N.A.: Principles of computational thinking tools. In: Rich, P., Hodges, C. (eds.) Emerging Research, Practice, and Policy on Computational Thinking, pp. 291–305. Springer, Heidelberg (2017). https://doi.org/10.1007/978-3-319-52691-1_18
4. Czerkawski, B.C., Lyman, E.W.: Exploring issues about computational thinking in higher education. Techtr. Tech Trends **59**, 57–65 (2015). https://doi.org/10.1007/s11528-015-0840-3
5. Wing, J.M.: Computational thinking. Commun. ACM **49**, 33–35 (2006)
6. Shute, V.J., Sun, C., Asbell-Clarke, J.: Demystifying computational thinking. Educ. Res. Rev. **22**, 142–158 (2017). https://doi.org/10.1016/j.edurev.2017.09.003
7. Kwan, A.: Problem based learning. In: The Routledge International Handbook of Higher Education. Routledge, London (2012)
8. Kolmos, A., Fink, F.K., Krogh, L.: The Aalborg model: problem-based and project-organized learning. In: The Aalborg Model : Progress, Diversity and Challenges, pp. 9–18. Aalborg Universitetsforlag, Aalborg (2004)
9. Huttel, H., Gnaur, D.: If PBL is the answer, then what is the problem? J. Probl. Based Learn. High. Educ. **5**, 1–21 (2017)

Don't Wait Until it Is Too Late: The Effect of Timing of Automated Feedback on Revision in ESL Writing

Rianne Conijn[1,2(✉)], Menno van Zaanen[1], and Luuk van Waes[2]

[1] Department of Cognitive Science and Artificial Intelligence, Tilburg University, Tilburg, The Netherlands
{m.a.conijn,mvzaanen}@uvt.nl

[2] Department of Management, University of Antwerp, Antwerp, Belgium
luuk.vanwaes@uantwerpen.be

Abstract. Automated writing evaluation tools have been shown to improve writing quality. However, the impact of automated feedback, and especially the timing of the feedback, on students' writing process is still unknown. Hence, we analyzed how feedback timing influences the revision process. Three experimental conditions were implemented into the writing tool CyWrite: no feedback, immediate feedback during the drafting and revision stage, and feedback during the revision stage only. Keystroke data were collected from 60 ESL students while conducting a source-based argumentative writing task. The revisions made during the writing process and the students' satisfaction with the system were analyzed. The results showed little differences in the amount, size, and duration of revisions between the three conditions. However, students reported they felt more disrupted when feedback was provided during the full writing process rather than in the revision stage only.

Keywords: Feedback · Writing analytics · Keystroke analysis · Revision · Automated writing evaluation

1 Introduction

Receiving timely and personalized feedback on writing is very useful for (learner) writers, but providing it is a time-intensive task for teachers. Therefore, a wide variety of writing tools have been developed to assist teachers by providing automated grading and feedback on students' writing. They can be classified as follows: automated essay scoring (AES), automated writing evaluation (AWE), and intelligent tutoring systems (ITS) [1]. AES are mostly used for summative feedback [4], AWE for formative feedback [3], and ITS include instructional elements and interactivity next to the feedback [10]. Several researchers started to evaluate these systems both on the accuracy of the automated feedback provided (e.g., [6]) as well as on the effectiveness of the tools used in classroom settings

M. Scheffel et al. (Eds.): EC-TEL 2019, LNCS 11722, pp. 577–581, 2019.
https://doi.org/10.1007/978-3-030-29736-7_43

(e.g., [13]). Overall, the automated feedback components have fairly high accuracies [1]. In addition, most of these tools have been shown to improve writing quality and enhance student motivation and autonomy [3].

Most of these evaluations, however, evaluate the impact on the writing product, rather than the impact on the writing process [3,14]. Hence, we cannot determine *how* the tool is used, for example, whether the automated feedback leads to more revisions. Some studies did indicate an effect of feedback on the revision of errors, but these are mostly descriptive case studies, e.g., [5]. In addition, it has been argued that for (automated) feedback to be effective it needs to be timely and frequently [1,3,7]. However, little is known about the impact of the timing of automated feedback on the writing process. Therefore, in the current study we aim to identify how the timing of automated feedback during English as a Second Language (ESL) writing impacts the frequency, level, and duration of revisions.

2 Method

In this study, participants were asked to write an argumentative text on global warming of 250–350 words, by using two short sources of text (250 words each). The participants were allowed 20 min to read the sources and write the text (drafting stage). Thereafter, the participants received unlimited time to revise their text (revision stage). In total, 60 ESL undergraduate students participated in this study. The writing task was conducted using the web-based AWE tool CyWrite [12]. CyWrite uses both statistical and rule-based natural language processing to provide formative feedback on spelling, grammar, style, and discourse patterns [2,6]. This feedback is generated during the writing process, by underlining errors and providing feedback in the margin. A screenshot of CyWrite with two examples of feedback (spelling in red, grammar in green) is shown in Fig. 1. The participants were randomly divided into three conditions (each N = 20) regarding the timing of the feedback: (1) no feedback; (2) feedback during the revision stage only; (3) immediate feedback during the full writing process (both drafting and revision stages).

During the writing task, keystroke data were collected using CyWrite. After the writing task, a questionnaire collected students' demographics, writing style [8], and satisfaction with the feedback [15]. For the current study, only the keystroke data and satisfaction data were analyzed. The number of revisions, size of the revision, and duration of the revisions were extracted using R. The size of the revision was calculated by the number of word-level (as opposed to sub-word level) revisions [11]. ANOVAs were used to analyze the differences in the frequency and size of the revisions and the duration of the revision stage between the three conditions. In addition, ANOVAs were used to determine the differences in satisfaction between the two feedback conditions.

3 Results

On average, the participants typed 1999 (SD = 517) characters, resulting in a final text of 258 (SD = 64) words. All students, except for six students in the no feedback condition, revised during the revision stage. The descriptive statistics for the revision behavior per condition are shown in Table 1. Little differences were found in the number of revisions, especially in the drafting stage. The number of revisions in the revision stage was higher when feedback was provided, compared to no feedback, but this difference was not significant ($F(2, 57) = 1.86$, $p = .17$, $\eta^2 = .06$). In addition, the revision stage was longer when feedback was provided in the revision stage, compared to no feedback, and even longer when feedback was immediately provided. However, this difference was also not significant ($F(2, 57) = 1.99$, $p = .15$, $\eta^2 = .07$). No differences were found between satisfaction with the feedback in the two feedback conditions ($F(1, 38) = 0.57$, $p = .46$, $\eta^2 = .01$). Interestingly, when immediate feedback was provided, students felt more disrupted ($F(1, 38) = 25.25$, $p < .001$, $\eta^2 = .40$).

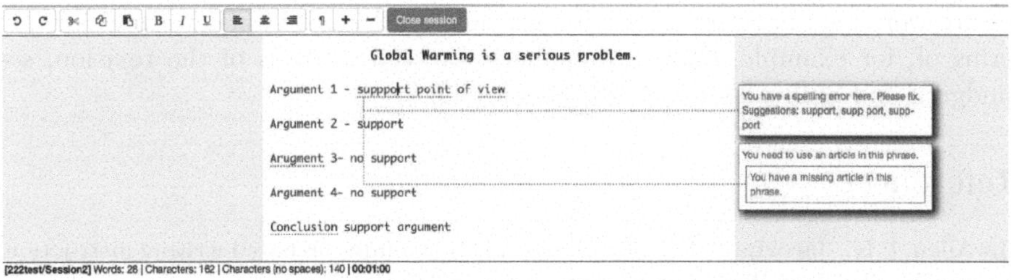

Fig. 1. Screenshot of CyWrite with formative feedback.

Table 1. Descriptive statistics for the three conditions and the full dataset (N = 60).

Feedback	No feedback	Revision stage	Immediate	All data
	Mean (SD)	Mean (SD)	Mean (SD)	Mean (SD)
#Revisions drafting stage	88.5 (53.9)	102 (50.0)	92.8 (40.8)	94.5 (48.0)
#Revisions revision stage	17.0 (19.7)	29.7 (26.9)	28.2 (21.2)	25.0 (23.1)
#Word-level revisions drafting	29.9 (15.1)	32.6 (14.4)	27.8 (12.6)	30.1 (14.0)
#Word-level revisions revision	7.90 (9.89)	7.45 (8.80)	11.1 (8.61)	8.80 (9.11)
Duration revision stage (sec)	247 (233)	347 (233)	403 (284)	333 (255)

4 Discussion and Conclusion

In the current study we aimed to identify the effect of timing of automated feedback on how ESL students revise. A trend was found that students revised more when automated feedback was provided, compared to no feedback. In addition, students took more time to revise when immediate feedback was provided during the full writing process, compared to when students received no feedback or only feedback during the revision stage. However, these differences were not found significant. In addition, feedback during the full writing process did not result in higher satisfaction, but was considered significantly more disruptive compared to feedback during the revision stage only. Thus, although timely feedback has been argued to be most useful [1], this is not clearly reflected in the revision patterns nor the users' satisfaction. These results can be explained by the high variance in the revisions made between the students. This is in line with previous work that also indicated that nature and size of the effect of automated feedback on revision differs across ESL students [5]. Hence, larger sample sizes or more insight into individual differences might be necessary to determine the effect of (the timing of) feedback on revisions.

This study showed a first step into analyzing the effect of automated writing feedback on the writing process, and specifically on how ESL students revise. The current results are inherently bound by the content and format of the feedback as provided in the CyWrite system. Future work should investigate the effect of the content or format of the feedback on the revision process. Current writing tools are often criticized based on the low-level of the feedback they provide. Future work should investigate whether this also leads to low-level revisions, in terms of, for example, depth, immediacy, or recursiveness of the revision, see Lindgren and Sullivan's revision taxonomy [9].

References

1. Allen, L.K., Jacovina, M.E., McNamara, D.S.: Computer-based writing instruction. In: Handbook of Writing Research, pp. 316–329 (2015)
2. Chukharev-Hudilainen, E., Saricaoglu, A.: Causal discourse analyzer: improving automated feedback on academic ESL writing. Comput. Assist. Lang. Learn. **29**(3), 494–516 (2016)
3. Cotos, E.: Automated writing analysis for writing pedagogy: from healthy tension to tangible prospects. Writ. Pedag. **7**(2–3), 197–231 (2015)
4. Dikli, S.: An overview of automated scoring of essays. J. Technol. Learn. Assess. **5**(1) (2006)
5. El Ebyary, K., Windeatt, S.: The impact of computer-based feedback on students' written work. Int. J. Engl. Stud. **10**(2), 121–142 (2010)
6. Feng, H.H., Saricaoglu, A., Chukharev-Hudilainen, E.: Automated error detection for developing grammar proficiency of ESL learners. Calico J. **33**(1), 49–70 (2016)
7. Ferguson, P.: Student perceptions of quality feedback in teacher education. Assess. Eval. High. Educ. **36**(1), 51–62 (2011)
8. Kieft, M., Rijlaarsdam, G., van den Bergh, H.: An aptitude—treatment interaction approach to writing-to-learn. Learn. Instr. **18**(4), 379–390 (2008)
9. Lindgren, E., Sullivan, K.: Analysing online revision, pp. 157–188. Elsevier (2006)
10. Ma, W., Adesope, O., Nesbit, J., Liu, Q.: Intelligent tutoring systems and learning outcomes: a meta-analysis. J. Educ. Psychol. **106**(4), 901–918 (2014)
11. Monahan, B.D.: Revision strategies of basic and competent writers as they write for different audiences. Res. Teach. Engl. **18**(3), 288–304 (1984)
12. Ranalli, J.R., Feng, H.H., Chukharev-Khudilaynen, E.: The affordances of process-tracing technologies for supporting L2 writing instruction. Lang. Learn. Technol. **23**(2), 1–11 (2018)

13. Roscoe, R.D., Allen, L.K., Weston, J.L., Crossley, S.A., McNamara, D.S.: The writing pal intelligent tutoring system: usability testing and development. Comput. Compos. **34**, 39–59 (2014)
14. Stevenson, M., Phakiti, A.: The effects of computer-generated feedback on the quality of writing. Assess. Writ. **19**, 51–65 (2014)
15. Wang, Y.S.: Assessment of learner satisfaction with asynchronous electronic learning systems. Inform. Manage. **41**(1), 75–86 (2003)

Talk2Learn: A Framework for Chatbot Learning

Mohammed Bahja[1(✉)], Rawad Hammad[2(✉)], and Mohammed Hassouna[3]

[1] Birmingham University, Birmingham, UK
M.Bahja@bham.ac.uk
[2] King's College London, London, UK
Rawad.Hammad@kcl.ac.uk
[3] University of Greenwich, London, UK
M.hassouna@ieee.org

Abstract. The rapid expansion of technologies in the education sector has led to the development of innovative pedagogical approaches being integrated with new technologies for enhancing the learning experience. Virtual assistants or chatbot technologies have been one of the primary focus in streamlining and enhancing learning processes by integrating pedagogic approaches with innovative technologies. This paper focuses on analyzing the recent developments in educational chatbots, as well as the identified issues in the design, development, and application of chatbots in e-Learning. Accordingly, a framework that reflects the various factors that need to be considered in chatbot design and developments in e-Learning is proposed and discussed in this paper.

Keywords: Chatbot Learning · Virtual assistants · E-learning · M-learning · Technology enhanced learning · Conversational agent

1 Introduction and Background

The effective use of e-learning technologies enhanced the learner's experience in various ways [1]. For instance, Game-enhanced learning [2] and mobile learning [3] use a spectrum of tools and approaches to improve the e-learner experience based on contexts. However, lessons learnt from current e-learning practices proved that most of the above-mentioned approaches are combined to achieve the overall learning objectives. Such multimodal e-learning approach reflects the multi-faceted nature of e-learning. Embedding virtual assistance in e-learning should provide value to students while they are creating, sharing and participating in various learning activities. The recent developments in Artificial Intelligence (AI), Machine Learning (ML) along with robust linguistic processing tools, has leveraged the applicability of chatbots or virtual assistants across various commercial applications [4]. However, this needs to be applied into educational contexts to allow students to personalise their learning and use more inclusive pedagogical approaches, e.g., socially oriented. Despite the growth in

M. Scheffel et al. (Eds.): EC-TEL 2019, LNCS 11722, pp. 582–586, 2019.
https://doi.org/10.1007/978-3-030-29736-7_44

Chatbots implementation, a substantive research gap in methods and frameworks that may help in developing chatbots applications is noticed. Hence, a framework for developing chatbots for e-learning is proposed in the next section.

2 Talk2Learn Chatbot Learning Framework

Given the above-mentioned drawbacks, Talk2Learn Chatbot Learning framework, shown in Fig. 1, is proposed. It is composed of the following twelve elements:

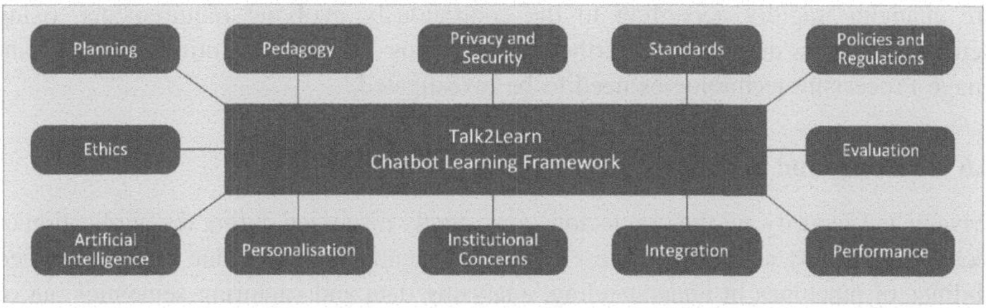

Fig. 1. Talk2Learn Chatbot Learning framework.

2.1 Planning

Rigorous planning is inevitable in technological innovations and it becomes more important in chatbot platforms. Planning includes requirement elicitation, and requirements management associated with processes and policies to apply evolving changes in educational contexts during design, development and transition phases.

2.2 Pedagogy

Effective chatbot platforms should be able to accommodate relevant pedagogies and learning approaches adopted in educational contexts. Learning is a complex process that includes various dimensions such as: assessment, learning, reflections, self-regulation, collaborative-based or connectivism-oriented learning approaches.

2.3 Policies and Regulations

The demand on chatbot technology is rising across various industries. However, the success of such innovations is not restricted to their capabilities. It includes processes that govern who is doing what and how. This can be formalised in policies and regulations. Responding to this gap is intrinsic because mistaken responses given by chatbot might lead to learner's misconceptions, student failure and further consequences.

2.4 Ethics

Chatbots are seamlessly connected with various data repositories which process enormous amount of data. This highlights the importance of the ownership of the information shared by chatbots and the ethics of collecting, sharing, processing, and other use cases associated with information manipulation.

2.5 Artificial Intelligence

Artificial Intelligence, Machine Learning, Language processors and Semantics Analysers are few technologies related chatbot development. However, such technologies are changing rapidly according to the continuously evolving requirements, rising demands, process automation. Furthermore, various Voice Recognition, Natural Language Processing technologies need to be investigated.

2.6 Privacy and Security

Privacy and security are the two factors consistently discussed during the application of technology in any setting [8]. These concerns recently increased due to the amplified abilities of machines in understanding, analysing data and capturing semantics out of thee. The rising concerns over these two issues can be attributed to the loopholes in the technology applications. Privacy and security need to be considered in chatbot development as they are developed to directly interact with humans.

2.7 Personalisation

Personalisation is one of the most important functionalities of chatbot applications in relation to learning [3]. The intelligent conversational agents must be able to recognise the user behaviors, needs, expectations and abilities. Accordingly, they need to adopt various personalised pedagogic approaches for individual users in order to enhance and improve their learning processes [5].

2.8 Performance

The performance factor can be analysed in two folds. First, the ability of chatbot applications to provide prompt responses that have quality information and services. Second, learners' performance improvement when using these applications for educational purposes, based on indicators such as user satisfaction, learners' marks, etc.

2.9 Evaluation

There is a limitation of available evaluation studies for chatbot applications. Therefore, there is a need to develop sufficient methods and processes for evaluating these applications from various perspectives. These concerns include those users-oriented, developers-oriented, technological-oriented, etc. Such evaluation needs to consider realness or naturalness in the conversation as well as the quality of conversation.

2.10 Standards

Despite chatbots development having gained popularity, few studies focused on identifying the standards for the development of such a platform and its applications. Hence, there is a need to develop universally-recognised standards and to use these when developing chatbot platforms.

2.11 Institutional

This institutional aspect acts as an umbrella for all related institutional concerns such as resources, support, and so on. Generally, these concerns belong to the following clusters. First, academic concerns where academic knowledge and supportive information are represented to chatbot applications. Second, administrative concerns where resources, support, terms and conditions, service quality can be addressed.

2.12 Integration

One great challenge of a chatbot application is its ability to efficiently co-exist with other educational systems and services. Currently, most of the universities have a various e-learning services including virtual learning environments, students record systems, etc. Effective chatbot applications should be able to co-exist with other systems, exchange and process data, etc. Current e-learning standards such as LTI are not sufficient to be extended to include chatbot applications.

3 Conclusion and Future Work

The paper has discussed various aspects relating to e-learning, virtual assistance and the development of chatbot applications in the field of e-learning. Various issues have been identified in the context of chatbot applications development, their usage and management in e-learning context. It has been shown how chatbots have a huge potential for revolutionising learning through effective human computer interaction in a natural setting. Talk2Learn framework for chatbot learning has been presented in this paper to guide the process of educational chatbot design and development. Currently, researchers are in the process of implementing Talk2Learn framework to develop different educational chatbots prototypes using various technologies. The extended version of this work will be based on real use cases from authentic learning experiences to measure the actual impact of such technologies on learning and teaching.

References

1. Hammad, R., Odeh, M., Khan, Z.: eLEM: a novel e-learner experience model. Int. Arab J. Inform. Technol. **14**(4A), 586–597 (2017). ISSN 1683-3198
2. Hammad, R.: Game-enhanced and process-based e-learning framework. In: Tian, F., Gatzidis, C., El Rhalibi, A., Tang, W., Charles, F. (eds.) Edutainment 2017. LNCS, vol. 10345, pp. 279–284. Springer, Cham (2017). https://doi.org/10.1007/978-3-319-65849-0_30

3. Bahja, M., Hammad, R.: A user-centric design and pedagogical-based approach for mobile learning. In: Proceedings of the tenth International Conference on Mobile, Hybrid and Online Learning, IARIA, Rome, Italy, pp. 100–105 (2018). ISBN 978-1-61208-619-4
4. Hussain, S., Ameri Sianaki, O., Ababneh, N.: A survey on conversational agents/chatbots classification and design techniques. In: Barolli, L., Takizawa, M., Xhafa, F., Enokido, T. (eds.) WAINA 2019. AISC, vol. 927, pp. 946–956. Springer, Cham (2019). https://doi.org/10.1007/978-3-030-15035-8_93
5. Winkler, R., Söllner, M.: Unleashing the potential of chatbots in education: a state-of-the-art analysis (2018)
6. Shum, H.-Y., He, X., Li, D.: From Eliza to XiaoIce: challenges and opportunities with social chatbots. Front. Inform. Technol. Electron. Eng. **19**(1), 10–26 (2018)

Analysing Student VLE Behaviour Intensity and Performance

Jakub Kuzilek[1(✉)], Jonas Vaclavek[1], Zdenek Zdrahal[1,2], and Viktor Fuglik[1,3]

[1] CIIRC, CTU in Prague, Jugoslavskych partyzanu 1580/3, 160 00 Prague, Czech Republic
jakub.kuzilek@cvut.cz

[2] KMi, Open University, Walton Hall, Milton Keynes MK7 6AA, UK

[3] Faculty of Education, Charles University, Magdaleny Rettigove 4, 116 39 Prague 1, Czech Republic

Abstract. Almost all higher educational institutions use Virtual Learning Environments (VLE) for the delivery of educational content to the students. Those systems collect information about student behaviour, and university can take advantage of analysing such data to model and predict student outcomes. Our work aims at discovering whether there exists a direct connection between the intensity of VLE behaviour represented as recorded student activities and their study outcomes and analyse how intense this connection is. For that purpose, we employed the clustering method to divide students into so-called VLE intensity groups and compared formed groups (clusters) with the student outcomes in the course. Our analysis has been performed using Open University Learning Analytics dataset (OULAD).

Keywords: Clustering · Virtual Learning Environment · Student performance · Predictive modeling

1 Introduction

At present, many higher education institutions already introduced ICT based online education systems in their portfolio. These Virtual Learning Environment systems such as Moodle platform [1] deliver educational content directly to students anytime and anywhere. This trend is further boosted by the introduction of Massive Open Online Courses (MOOCs) platforms.

Online educational platforms collect data about their users. VLEs together with other data sources commonly used by higher education institutions make it possible to analyse student data. Various methods of using data for education improvement have been investigated in more than 200 studies in recent years [2].

M. Scheffel et al. (Eds.): EC-TEL 2019, LNCS 11722, pp. 587–590, 2019.
https://doi.org/10.1007/978-3-030-29736-7_45

2 Research Question

The research aims at answering the question: *Is it possible to uncover natural grouping of students based on their VLE activities without prior knowledge of their results?* To answer this question, we employed expectation maximisation clustering[1] on VLE behaviour data available in Open University Learning Analytics dataset (OULAD) [3] and compare the created activity groups with the student assessments results. The reported results are part of the larger outgoing project at CTU in Prague.

3 Data

The OULAD [3] contains data of about 32,593 students studying 22 OU courses in years 2013 and 2014. The OU is the largest British distance learning university with approximately 170,000 students. The typical OU course has one or more assignments, final exam and has a length of about 35 weeks. OU uses the Moodle platform to provide learning materials to students. In addition, the system provides the framework for submitting assignments and their evaluation. For more details see the original paper [3]. The dataset includes data about both students and courses. We analyse data of the FFF course and the 2014 J presentation, which is one of the STEM subjects offered by the university. More than 1/3 of the students have withdrawn during the presentation.

4 Methods

To compare the student's VLE behaviour with their performance in assessments, it is necessary to transform VLE logs and to adjust "performance classes" based on student scores in assessments.

4.1 VLE Behaviour Intensity and Assessment Performance

At first, all VLE log entries from the time prior to the start of the course have been filtered out. Those represent outliers, and their added value in this task is minimal. Next, we transformed daily VLE logs into the weekly aggregates. Keeping the information about how many times the student clicked into the VLE system every week makes data less sparse and more robust against spikes of activities. The summary number of weekly clicks is considered as a measure of VLE behaviour intensity.

For the analysis, we need to adjust the student assessment scores and create performance groups. For that purpose, the scores ranging from 0 to 100 are divided into six possible performance classes: **Not submit** (the student did not submit the assessment); **Submitted and failed** (student failed with score less than 40 points); **Lowest**

[1] L. Scrucca, M. Fop, T. B. Murphy and A. E. Raftery, "mclust 5: clustering, classification and density estimation using Gaussian finite mixture models," *The R Journal*, 2016.

passing score (student scored 41–55 points); **Low passing score** (student scored 56–70 points); **Medium passing score** (student scored 71–85 points); **High passing score** (student scored more than 86 points). We assigned numbers 1 (Not submit) – 6 (High passing score) to student performance classes.

4.2 Clustering Student VLE Behaviour Data

Student VLE behaviour intensity forms the dataset for unsupervised learning. For that purpose, we employed Gaussian finite mixture models fitted via the EM algorithm. The resulting model then produced a set of labels which can be further compared with the assessment performance classes to explore whether the student behaviour intensity relates to the assessment performance classes. In our research, we set the number of clusters to 6 to keep the comparison simple.

4.3 Comparing Clusters and Assessment Performance

We are interested in "overlaps" between the clusters created by Gaussian finite mixture models and assessment performance classes. Thus the type of contingency can be created, which element x_{ij} represents the proportion of students from cluster i belonging to assessment performance class j.

Table 1. Comparison of VLE behaviour intensity based clusters and assessment performance

	Class	1	2	3	4	5	6	1	2	3	4	5	6
		Assessment 1						Assessment 2					
Cluster	1	1	0	3	22	43	31	5	4	7	20	37	28
	2	0	0	1	16	43	39	0	1	3	14	33	49
	3	34	3	6	23	25	9	86	4	4	5	2	0
	4	6	0	5	30	40	20	35	7	8	23	17	10
	5	0	1	2	11	40	47	0	1	4	11	25	60
	6	90	0	1	4	5	1	91	0	1	5	2	0
		Assessment 3						Assessment 4					
Cluster	1	11	8	10	18	37	16	22	7	13	19	28	11
	2	1	3	5	18	45	28	2	4	8	16	41	29
	3	100	0	0	0	0	0	100	0	0	0	0	0
	4	85	6	1	5	2	1	95	2	2	1	0	0
	5	2	2	5	10	43	39	4	2	6	12	32	44
	6	96	0	0	3	0	1	99	1	0	1	0	0
		Assessment 5											
Cluster	1	43	9	6	14	16	11						
	2	9	4	5	14	32	37						
	3	100	0	0	0	0	0						
	4	100	0	0	0	0	0						
	5	9	3	2	9	24	53						
	6	99	0	1	0	0	0						

5 Results and Discussion

Table 1 contains the results of a comparison of student VLE behavioural clusters with the assessment performance classes for all assessments in the course *FFF*.

One can observe that clusters can be divided into those with high assessment performance and those with low assessment performance. From the very first assessment, one can find that the majority of students in cluster 6 are not going to submit any assessment and this cluster can be viewed as the lowest performing cluster. Cluster 3 is the cluster with second lowest performance, and these students tend to give up after submitting their first assessment. Cluster 4 is formed by students who tend to give up after the second assessment. On the other hand, clusters 2 and 5 consists of students who have the highest performance in the assessments. Cluster 5 is containing the best students, which can be viewed especially in the second and fifth assessment. The "average" students fall into cluster 1. These students are uniformly distributed at the beginning, and when time progresses, they perform slightly worse.

6 Conclusion

In this paper, we analysed VLE data of one OU course with the expectation maximization algorithm to answer the question whether the student activities form "performance" groups. The formed clusters of students based on behavioural intensity were compared with student's performance in their assessments. The comparison shows that even if data does not contain the information about the outcomes, one can still efficiently analyse and detect groups of students at risk of failure. For example, there exists clear group of students who failing from the very beginning of the course. In overall, one can observe that the results of students same as students VLE activity drops. We plan to further extend this research by a deeper analysis of formed clusters to better understand the phenomena lying behind the formed behavioural groups. For example, the comparison of average VLE intensity and assessment scores will give us insight to the relationship between activities in VLE and assessments.

Acknowledgement. This work was supported by junior research project no. GJ18-04150Y and student research grant no. SGS19/209/OHK3/3T/37.

References

1. Moodle HQ: Moodle statistics. Moodle HQ (2018). https://moodle.org/stats/. Accessed 25 Apr 2018
2. Papamitsiou, Z., Economides, A.A.: Learning analytics and educational data mining in practice: a systematic literature review of empirical evidence. Educ. Technol. Soc. **17**, 49–64 (2014)
3. Kuzilek, J., Hlosta, M., Zdrahal, Z.: Open university learning analytics dataset. Sci. Data **4** (2017)

Adaptive Orchestration of Scripted Collaborative Learning in MOOCs

Ishari Amarasinghe(✉) and Davinia Hernández-Leo

ICT Department, Universitat Pompeu Fabra, Barcelona, Spain
{ishari.amarasinghe,davinia.hernandez}@upf.edu

Abstract. This study presents the design, implementation and evaluation of several intervention strategies to address orchestration challenges associated with scripted collaborative learning activities in Massive Open Online Courses (MOOCs). The interventions are based on artificially simulated students and teachers. Findings of pilot studies conducted in real-world contexts revealed that the proposed interventions facilitate collaboration orchestration in MOOCs and help to trigger beneficial collaboration interactions among students.

Keywords: CSCL · Scripts · MOOCs · Orchestration · Adaptive systems

1 Introduction

In the domain of Computer Supported Collaborative Learning (CSCL), carefully designed scripts facilitate to structure group processes while triggering beneficial social interactions that may be rare in free collaboration [1]. In CSCL, Collaborative Learning Flow Patterns (CLFPs) formulate the essence of script structures and represent best practices to structure the flows of collaboration [2]. However, the achievement of success within scripted collaboration depends on the continuous activity participation of the learners as scripts constitute successive phases [2]. On the other hand, orchestration or the real-time management of scripted collaborative learning sessions deployed within Massive Open Online Courses (MOOCs) were seen challenging due to learner's activity distribution in time and level of involvement [3]. Implementation of carefully designed adaptive and intelligent techniques that facilitate to maintain pedagogical method structures proposed by scripts was seen beneficial in such spaces [3]. This study presents several adaptive intervention strategies based on the use of artificial simulated students and teachers to achieve orchestration of the scripted collaboration within MOOCs in presence of diverse individual learner behaviors.

2 Proposed Approach

In this study, a tool called PyramidApp [4] inspired by the pyramid collaborative learning flow pattern was used to design and deploy scripted CSCL activities. The collaboration flow within the tool initiates as individual students provide answers to a

M. Scheffel et al. (Eds.): EC-TEL 2019, LNCS 11722, pp. 591–594, 2019.
https://doi.org/10.1007/978-3-030-29736-7_46

given task. In the next levels of the script, students are allocated into increasingly larger groups to discuss and rate the individual answers to reach a consensus at the group level and finally at the class level as the flow advances. The interventions to facilitate the orchestration of Pyramid activities in MOOCs are categorized into two categories namely (a) a Simulated Teacher (ST) and (b) a Simulated Student (SS) intervention, for the sake of clarity in representation. A ST is a software functionality that detects lack of rating and discussion engagement within collaborative groups and performs appropriate interventions (Table 1). A SS is also a software functionality which is pre-configured by the real-teacher during the activity design stage by assigning a pre-configured email and an answer to the given task (the answers are independent of real-students' answers). Whenever the minimum number of real-students required to create a Pyramid flow is not presented the SS's were automatically logged into the PyramidApp to initiate collaboration. The design requirements for the implementation of the proposed intervention strategies are described in detail in previous work [3].

Table 1. Adaptive intervention strategies proposed to orchestrate Pyramid based collaboration.

Pyramid level and problems identified in MOOC contexts	Proposed intervention
Pyramid instantiation phase: A Pyramid will be generated only when the minimum number of students stated in the activity design is satisfied. If the number of students logged into the system is less than the minimum count system keeps waiting until the minimum count is reached	As soon as the time limit mentioned in the activity design is reached SS are logged into the system with pre-configured email
Initial Option Submission Phase: Each student requires to submit an individual answer. A problem is students do not write answers, generating groups without answers to discuss	SS's answers are shown to the students, eliminating groups that do not have options to discuss
Small and large group collaboration Phases: Lack of rating participation	ST chooses a random answer to be populated at the next level
Small and large group collaboration Phases: Lack of discussion participation	ST sends a greeting in the chat. e.g., *Hello* ST sends a reminder in the chat. e.g., *Shall we start rating?* ST asks students for self-explanation. e.g., *Hi Jane, I'm not clear about your answer. Can you elaborate a bit on it?* ST motivates students for collaboration. e.g. *It's been a nice collaborative learning experience!*

3 Pilot Study

The proposed interventions have been implemented to the PyramidApp tool [4] and deployed within the first and second weeks of a MOOC course. The collaborative learning task within the first week was to discuss the importance of Responsible Research and Innovation (RRI). The two tasks within the second week were to discuss which RRI key issues are easier and harder to implement. According to the PyramidApp mechanism a pyramid can be instantiated when the minimum number of students required to generate a pyramid is logged into the system. In the pilot studies the minimum size of a Pyramid was set to 15. Each pyramid was configured to have two rating levels (small group and large group levels) and the small group size within a Pyramid was set to 5. Students were automatically allocated to Pyramids and subsequently to small groups randomly. Small groups were later combined into larger groups within each Pyramid. In pilot studies, the number of participants logged into the PyramidApp varied across weeks. e.g., 62, 51 and 43 participants. 3 Pyramids were generated for activity in the first week, 3 Pyramids were generated for activity 1 and 3 pyramids were generated for activity 2 in the second week. Log data collected from the tool was analyzed to report results. Based on the log data analysis it was seen that the SS and ST interventions became important at different stages of Pyramids for meaningful flow orchestration. For instance, there were not enough participants to generate pyramids hence the addition of SS was required (marked as x number of SS required in Table 2). Further, lack of rating participation was detected (marked as "Yes" in Table 2) which required the ST interventions. However, in the large group phase, no ST interventions were required as students displayed satisfactory rating participation.

Table 2. Simulated Student and Simulated Teacher intervention in pyramids.

Problem	Week 1 – Pyramid 3			Week 2- Activity1 Pyramid 3			Week 2- Activity 2 Pyramid 3		
	Small Groups			Small Groups			Small Groups		
	A	B	C	D	E	F	G	H	I
Lack of students	X1	X1		X1	X1	X1	X3	X3	X2
Lack of rating participation		Y	Y		Y	Y	Y	Y	Y
Lack of discussion participation	Y	Y	Y	Y	Y	Y	Y	Y	Y
No. of prompts sent by ST before receiving replies	1	N/A	N/A	1	N/A	N/A	7	N/A	N/A
No. of students responded	1	0	0	2	0	0	2	0	0
No. of responses	2	0	0	4	0	0	7	0	0
	Large Groups			Large Groups			Large Groups		
Lack of rating or discussion									

* Gray colored cells show where no interventions are performed

MOOC participants also responded to the timed ST prompts in the chat, although the number of participants who responded and after which timed ST prompt they submitted a response varied. In group A and Group D (see Table 2) students responded 2 min after receiving a greeting message from the ST. In group G one student responded 2 min after receiving a greeting and the other student after 4 min receiving the self-explanation request from the ST. Further, students who responded to the timed interventions performed by the ST in the small group collaboration phases were seen to build collaborative conversations in the large group phase of the Pyramid activity.

4 Conclusions and Future Work

The results of the log data analysis showed that the proposed interventions became important in the CSCL activities that were generated at the end of each week of the MOOC. This shows that the proposed interventions could facilitate to orchestrate collaboration in such time-frames automatically where lack of engagement is detected. Hence this study contributes by proposing adaptive intervention strategies to orchestrate CSCL activities deployed in MOOC spaces. However, a limitation of the study is that we did not vary learning design configurations (e.g., the number of rating levels per Pyramids, small group size) during pilot studies. In future studies we are planning to experiment further the adaptiveness of the proposed strategies when enacting different learning designs. Further, we still believe that the role of the teacher managing the behavior of these adaptive aids in the orchestration is very important. We are currently working on an actionable orchestration dashboard that enables teachers to monitor PyramidApp activities and intervene with a set of actions when needed. The activation and deactivation of simulated students and a simulated teacher are part of these actions.

Acknowledgments. This work has been partially funded by FEDER, the National Research Agency of the Spanish Ministry of Science, Innovations and Universities MDM-2015-0502, TIN2014-53199-C3-3-R, TIN2017-85179-C3-3-R and "la Caixa Foundation" (CoT project, 100010434). DHL is a Serra Húnter Fellow.

References

1. Dillenbourg, P., Tchounikine, P.: Flexibility in macro-scripts for computer-supported collaborative learning. J. Comput. Assist. Learn. **23**, 1–13 (2007)
2. Hernández-Leo, D., et al.: COLLAGE: a collaborative learning design editor based on patterns. Educ. Technol. Soc. **9**(1), 58–71 (2006)
3. Amarasinghe, I., Hernández Leo, D., Manathunga, K., Jonsson, A.: Sustaining continuous collaborative learning flows in MOOCs: orchestration agent approach. J. Univ. Comput. Sci. **24**(8), 1034–1051 (2018)
4. Manathunga, K., Hernández-Leo, D.: Authoring and enactment of mobile pyramid-based collaborative learning activities. Br. J. Edu. Technol. **49**(2), 262–275 (2018)

Investigating In-Service Teachers' Concerns About Adopting Technology-Enhanced Embodied Learning

Yiannis Georgiou[1,2](✉) and Andri Ioannou[1,2]

[1] Research Center on Interactive Media, Smart Systems and Emerging Technologies (RISE), Nicosia, Cyprus
[2] Cyprus Interaction Lab, Cyprus University of Technology, Limassol, Cyprus
{Ioannis.Georgiou, andri.i.ioannou}@cut.ac.cy

Abstract. Despite the affordances of technology-enhanced embodied learning, its integration in mainstream education is currently at slow pace given that in-service teachers are reluctant to adopt this innovation. This exploratory study investigated the concerns of 31 in-service primary education teachers, who took part in a Professional Development (PD) programme, using a questionnaire grounded in the Concerns Based Adoption Model (CBAM) about the adoption of technology-enhanced embodied learning. The findings of this study indicated that, at the outset of the PD programme, the participating teachers had relatively few personal and management concerns; in contrast, they were highly concerned about obtaining more information, collaborating with other colleagues as well as about expanding the innovation further. Teachers' participation in the PD programme had a significant impact on the mitigation of these concerns. By the end of the PD programme teachers retained only some high-level concerns, which are essential for the sustainability of technology-enhanced embodied learning.

Keywords: Technology-enhanced embodied learning · Concerns-based adoption model · Teacher attitudes · Teacher professional development

1 Introduction and Theoretical Background

Technology-enhanced embodied learning constitutes a contemporary pedagogy of learning, which emphasizes the use of the body in the educational practice. This novel pedagogy is supported by the widespread population of affordable motion-based technologies in combination with the emergence of immersive interfaces, which have opened the doors for the design of embodied digital learning apps [1]. Despite the tremendous educational affordances of technology-enhanced embodied learning, its integration in mainstream education is currently at very slow pace [2], given that in-service teachers are reluctant to adopt such educational innovations, as they lack appropriate training [3]. However, little are yet known about teachers' concerns towards the adoption of technology-enhanced embodied learning, while there is also a lack of Professional Development (PD) programmes supporting teachers on the topic.

M. Scheffel et al. (Eds.): EC-TEL 2019, LNCS 11722, pp. 595–599, 2019.
https://doi.org/10.1007/978-3-030-29736-7_47

This study was based on the Concerns Based Adoption Model (CBAM) [4] to investigate the concerns of 31 in-service primary education teachers towards the adoption of technology-enhanced embodied learning as well as the impact of a PD programme on their concerns. This study addressed the following research questions: (a) Which are the main teachers' concerns about the adoption of technology-enhanced embodied learning prior the PD programme? and (b) How did participation in the PD programme affect teachers' concerns about the adoption of technology-enhanced embodied learning?

2 Methods

2.1 Participants and Professional Development (PD) Programme

Thirty-one in-service teachers in primary education were the total sample of this study from which twenty-five were female (81%). Our PD programme, which was enacted in the context of the INTELed European project (https://inteled.org/), adopted a cyclical framework, which was based on a prior PD model suggested by Kyza and Georgiou [5]. The framework was organized in two sequential phases: a Training and a Practical phase. As part of the Training phase, teachers assumed the roles of "Learners" via experiencing a variety of embodied digital learning apps and the role of "Designers" by designing a lesson plan for integrating technology-enhanced learning in their classrooms. As part of the Practical phase teachers were involved in school pilots, assuming the roles of "*Innovators*" and "*Reflective practitioners*" to transfer in praxis the knowledge gained during the previous phase.

2.2 Instrumentation and Data Collection

In order to explore the concerns of the teachers as innovation adopters, a revised version of the Stages of Concern (SoC) questionnaire was employed, adapted from de Vocht, Laherto and Parchmann [4]. The SoC questionnaire consisted of 30 items and used a 5-point Likert scale for capturing teachers' concerns as they moved through a developmental series of 6 stages about technology-enhanced embodied learning: (a) Information, (b) Personal, (c) Management, (d) Consequence, (e) Collaboration and (f) Refocusing. Agreeing with most items, presents a high concern in each concern stage. An open-ended question was also appended to the questionnaire focusing on teachers' needs in relation to adopting technology-enhanced embodied learning, to shed more light in the quantitative data collected. The questionnaire was administered in 3 different timepoints to capture the trajectory of teachers' concerns during the PD programme: (a) at the outset of the PD programme (Pre-test), (b) after the completion of the Training phase (Post-test) and (c) after the completion of the Practical phase (Pospost-test).

2.3 Data Analysis

Descriptive statistics were used to investigate the pre-test concerns stage intensities collectively. Subsequently, for the comparison of teachers' concerns at the different timepoints of the PD programme (pre-test, post-test, postpost-test) the Friedman test was employed. The Wilcoxon signed-rank test was also employed on the different combinations of the related timepoints, to investigate when the differences actually occurred. Finally, the data collected by the participating teachers at the open-ended question were analyzed using a top-down thematic analysis approach. That is, our thematic analysis was theoretically driven by Concerns Based Adoption Model (CBAM) and it was guided by our research focus in classifying teachers' self-reported needs according to the stages of concern.

3 Findings and Discussion

3.1 Teachers' Initial Concerns and Concerns' Profiles

Overall, according to our findings the stages of collaboration and interest had the highest intensity. In contrast, the personal, management and consequence stages had the lowest intensity. Going a step further, when identifying the SoC individual profiles for the participating teachers by comparing the relative intensities of teachers concern stages, the participating teachers approached the "Co-operator" profile. This finding was encouraging, as according to de Vocht et al. [4] "Having many Co-operators at the beginning of the adoption process is productive for an innovation, as these individuals seek information and possess a willingness to collaborate yet have relatively few personal and management concerns" (p. 333).

3.2 Comparison of Teachers' Concerns Across Time

The Friedman test indicated that across time, there were not statistically significant difference in the Personal stage $\chi2(2) = 1.298$, $p = 0.593$, in the Management stage $\chi2(2) = 0.689$, $p = 0.709$ as well as in the Consequence stage $\chi2(2) = 2.469$, $p = 0.291$. However, the Friedman test indicated that there was statistically significant difference on the Information stage $\chi2(2) = 12.094$, $p = 0.002$, on the Collaboration stage $\chi2(2) = 8.760$, $p = 0.013$ as well as on the Refocusing stage $\chi2(2) = 7.309$, $p = 0.026$ across time. Post hoc analysis with Wilcoxon signed-rank tests with a Bonferroni correction applied ($p < 0.017$) indicated that there was a statistically significant decrease in concern intensities in the stages of Information, Collaboration and Refocusing only between the outset (Pre-Test) and the end of the PD programme (Postpost-test). This finding expands research-based conclusions from previous PD projects all pointing to the need to engage teachers in extended PD experiences, which combine not only a training part but also a practical part, allowing teachers to implement educational innovations in their classrooms [5].

3.3 Teachers' Needs

According to the teachers' responses it seems that, during the PD programme, the participating teachers moved through the developmental series of the six concern stages. In particular, while at the outset of the PD programme teachers' needs were mostly related to low-level concern at the Information and Personal stages (e.g., receiving more information about embodied pedagogy or improving their ICT skills), by the end of the PD programme their needs had mostly to do with high-level concerns at the Collaboration and Refocusing stages (e.g., have access to additional embodied digital learning apps or additional opportunities for continuous PD). This finding also warrants the success of our PD programme. According to de Vocth et al. [4], while the low-level stages are considered less valuable for an educational innovation, the high-level concerns are essential for the sustainability of an innovation.

4 Conclusions and Implications

The present study provides some initial empirical evidence of teachers' concerns when adopting technology-enhanced embodied learning. At the same time, it contributes to the identification and tracking the mitigation of teachers' concerns during a PD programme using the CBAM model.

Acknowledgements. This work is part of the project that has received funding from the European Union's Horizon 2020 research and innovation programme under grant agreement No 739578 (RISE-Call:H2020-WIDESPREAD-01-2016-2017-TeamingPhase2) and the government of the Republic of Cyprus through the Directorate General for European Programmes, Coordination and Development.

References

1. Georgiou, Y., Ioannou, A.: Embodied learning in a digital world: a systematic review of empirical research in K-12 education. In: Díaz, P., Ioannou, A., Spector, M., Bhagat, K.-K. (eds.) Learning in a Digital World: A Multidisciplinary Perspective on Interactive Technologies for Formal and Informal Education. Smart Computing and Intelligence, pp. 155–177. Springer, Singapore (2019)
2. Ioannou, M., Georgiou, Y., Ioannou, A., Johnson-Glenberg, M.: On the understanding of students' learning and perceptions of technology integration in low- and high-embodied group learning. In: Proceedings of the 13th International Conference on Computer Supported Collaborative Learning (2019)
3. Karakostas, A., Palaigeorgiou, G., Kompatsiaris, Y.: WeMake: a framework for letting students create tangible, embedded and embodied environments for their own STEAM learning. In: Kompatsiaris, I., et al. (eds.) INSCI 2017. LNCS, vol. 10673, pp. 3–18. Springer, Cham (2017). https://doi.org/10.1007/978-3-319-70284-1_1

4. de Vocht, M., Laherto, A., Parchmann, I.: Exploring teachers' concerns about bringing responsible research and innovation to European science classrooms. J. Sci. Teach. Educ. **28**, 326–346 (2017). https://doi.org/10.1080/1046560X.2017.1343602
5. Kyza, E.A., Georgiou, Y.: Developing in-service science teachers' ownership of the PROFILES pedagogical framework through a technology-supported participatory design approach to professional development. Sci. Educ. Int. **25**, 55–77 (2014)

What Do Educational Data, Generated by an Online Platform, Tell Us About Reciprocal Web-Based Peer Assessment?

Olia Tsivitanidou[1(✉)] and Andri Ioannou[1,2(✉)]

[1] Research Center on Interactive Media, Smart Systems and Emerging Technologies (RISE), Nicosia, Cyprus
o.tsivitanidou@rise.org.cy

[2] Cyprus Interaction Lab, Cyprus University of Technology, Limassol, Cyprus
andri.i.ioannou@cut.ac.cy

Abstract. Peer Assessment (PA) is a promising evaluation strategy in the educational context, not only due to its effectiveness to reduce instructor's evaluation loading, but mainly due to its benefit towards student development e.g., teamwork, in-depth thinking. In this exploratory study we sought to explore how do educational data, as generated by an online platform (i.e., Peergrade) and displayed in teacher's and students' Learning Analytics Dashboard (LAD), can potentially inform us of the PA process and the peer interactions, as they take place. Participants in the study were 21 undergraduate teacher-students who attended a science course (electrical circuits topic) following the inquiry-based approach. Students were asked to reciprocally and individually assess the responses of a peer in a given task. The findings of this study have implications towards the establishment of new theoretical frameworks and developments for bridging educational theory, design process and data science, in the field of assessment.

Keywords: Web-based peer assessment · Peer feedback · Online assessment · Science education · Science learning

1 Introduction

Peer Assessment (PA) constitutes an educational activity in which students judge the performance of their peers by offering oral and/or written peer feedback. It is often integrated in the wider context of formative assessment and it endorses many benefits in terms of students' learning especially when it is reciprocally implemented [4]. When employed formatively, PA can improve students' learning accomplishments [2] and their overall performance (e.g., specific skills and practices) in various domains including science education [3, 4]. PA has received attention in participative inquiry-oriented science learning environments, especially computer-supported learning environments and in recent years in Massive Online Open Courses (MOOCs) [1]. Yet, research on how educational data, as generated by online platforms and communicated via a Learning Analytics Dashboard (LAD) to teachers and students, can potentially inform us of the PA process and the interactions that take place among peers, is still

M. Scheffel et al. (Eds.): EC-TEL 2019, LNCS 11722, pp. 600–603, 2019.
https://doi.org/10.1007/978-3-030-29736-7_48

scarce. The analysis and interpretation of such data can provide some insights into the emerging field of Learning Analytics (LA), which has become a must in education, with the critical goal to use them for understanding and supporting learning. Among the challenges that still exist in this research area, is how to ensure the quality, timing, and form of feedback, which is critical to effective learning.

2 Rationale and Research Questions

We sought to explore how educational data, generated by an online platform and communicated via a LAD to teachers and students, can potentially inform us of the PA process and the interactions that take place among peers. We focused on data connected to both the role of the assessor and the assessee, so as to explore both segments of reciprocal peer assessment. Overall, we aimed to examine how LA data conjecturing peer feedback validity are presented via LAD and whether it can be interpreted in a meaningful manner. In view of the above, the following Research Questions (RQs) were sought to be addressed in this study: **RQ1:** How does the 'submission score' generated by the online platform used in this study, associate with the quality and validity of students' assessed artifacts (submissions)? **RQ2:** How is the median time spent per review per peer assessor, associated with the length of the qualitative peer feedback? **RQ3:** Did students, as assessees, proceed with revising their initial responses after the completion of PA? (If yes, did those revisions contribute towards improving the validity of their initial responses?) **RQ4:** How do students, as assessees, react to the peer feedback received? (Do reaction 'likes' relate to the reaction comments that follow and how?).

3 Methodology

The sample was consisted by 21 undergraduate teacher students (19 females and 2 males), who worked in groups of two while studying the learning material on the topic of Electric Circuits in the module of Electromagnetism of the Physics by Inquiry material following the inquiry-based approach. In a carefully chosen check point of the learning material, the students were asked to complete, on an individual basis, a diagnostic task comprised by three distinct questions e.g., *"List the light bulbs numbered as 1, 2 and 3 in the given circuit (figure provided), in a decreasing order of brightness. Explain your reasoning"*. Upon completing the task and having submitted their responses in the Peergrade online platform (https://app.peergrade.io/), they implemented reciprocal web-based PA. The platform automatically assigned students' responses to their peers for peer evaluation. Students were asked to provide feedback to two peer submissions, via the 'review' tab of the platform, with the assistance of a given rubric, that was comprised by 3-point Likert scaled 10 assessment criteria. Students, as assessors, rated their peers' responses on 10 criteria e.g., *"The order in which the bulbs are classified in order of decreasing brightness is justified"*, in accordance with a 3-point Likert scale and also provided written comments for justifying their ratings. Each student individually assessed the responses of two other students which were automatically assigned to her/him. This review task lasted on average 20 min per evaluation, with a quite substantial standard deviation in time (M = 20.3 min, SD = 7.8 min). After the implementation of the PA, students, as peer-assessees, were allowed to revise their responses, after studying the peer feedback comments that they received from two other peers, via the 'react' tab of the platform. This tab allows to students to react to peer feedback in the following manner: (a) like a feedback comment, (b) comment on a feedback comment, (c) flag an issue (merely teachers get informed about flags). At the end of the 'react' phase, students were asked to evaluate the peer feedback, by rating a 4-point Likert scale question (mandatory) and provide a comment (optional).

Data were collected from four sources; namely: (a) pre-instructional questionnaire; (b) data displayed in the LAD of the Peergrade online platform, i.e., the median time spent per review, per student, measured in minutes; the average word count of peer feedback comments per student; submission score generated upon completion of the peer review phase (the submission score was generated based on the scores that peers provided to the assessment criteria, while peer reviewing); feedback score generated for every student for each assignment (the feedback score for a reviewer is based on the feedback reactions s/he receives); assessees' reaction to peer feedback (likes and reaction comments); (c) students' initial and revised responses to a given diagnostic task; (d) audio recordings data resulted from Think Aloud Protocols (TAP), which were used during the provision and review of peer feedback by students, for triangulation purposes. A mixed-method approach was used that involved both qualitative and quantitative data.

4 Results

With respect to RQ1 we ran linear Pearson's r correlation to check the existence of potential correlation between submission scores (M = 0.64, SD = 0.10) that the Peergrade tool generates and the quality of initial responses (M = 2.80, SD = 2.27) to the given task, which resulted through open coding by the authors. The results indicate that there is no correlation between the two aforementioned variables $r = 0.160$, $p => .05$, $n = 21$. We further explored how the median time spent per review per student (assessor) is associated with the length of the qualitative peer feedback (measured via word counts) for addressing RQ2. A positive correlation was found to exist between median time spent (M = 20.32 min, SD = 7.84) and the average word count of peer feed-back comments per student (M = 341.8, SD = 147.4), Pearson's $r = 0.560$, $p = < .001$, $n = 21$. Think aloud protocols data shed light into the reasons behindhand difference in time spent for giving feedback among peer assessors (e.g., students, who spent more time while giving feedback, where those who were cross-checking their own responses, before providing feedback, and this additional activity implied more time needed).

In relation to the peer assessee role, findings of RQ3 revealed that out of the 21 students who received peer feedback in this study, 12 students (in the assessee role), proceeded with revising their responses. Wilcoxon Signed-Ranks Test outcomes indicated that the median post-test ranks were statistically significantly higher than the median pre-test ranks $Z = -2.132$, $p < 0.033$. With respect to 'reaction' data generated by the Peergrade tool (RQ4), a total of 403 valid entries for reaction likes and reaction comments (as resulted from peer feedback data from all students) were provided. A negative correlation between reaction likes ($M = 0.35$, $SD = 0.48$) and reaction comments ($M = 0.17$, $SD = 0.38$), $r = -0.248$, $p = < .001$, $n = 403$ was found to exist. The qualitative analysis of the reaction comments, has shown that whenever students offered comments, instead of likes, that was mostly due to disagreements they had with their peers' feedback comments. This finding indicates that reaction likes can be interpreted in a meaningful manner, as they can provide signs to teachers on whether assessors and assessees agree or disagree on the peer feedback exchanged. Nevertheless, such a trend should be treated with caution, since disagreements in reaction comments offered by the assessees were identified in two different cases: (a) assessees disagreed with the content of the critical peer feedback received and insisted on the validity of their own initial response; (b) assessees disagreed with the content of the embracing peer feedback received and scrutinized the validity of their own initial response.

An in-depth analysis of the data is being conducted to answer the research questions of the study; we hope to present some of this further analysis during the conference. Overall, the proposed work is expected to have immediate implications in science teaching and learning but is also expected to inform formative assessment research and practice in different domains and contexts, namely in peer-assessment in blended, online learning and MOOC courses. Designers of web-based learning platforms and technological tools for education could utilize this piece of information in several manners already explicated above, e.g., framing and interpreting educational data for learning analytics derived from peer-assessment activities; developing appropriate tools for peer assessment.

Acknowledgements. This project has received funding for the European Union's Horizon 2020 research and innovation programme under grant agreement No 739578 and the Government of the Republic of Cyprus through the Directorate General for European Programmes, Coordination and Development.

References

1. Alcarria, R., Bordel, B., de Andrs, D.M., Robles, T.: Enhanced peer assessment in MOOC evaluation through assignment and review analysis. Int. J. Emerg. Technol. Learn. (iJET) **13**(1), 206–219 (2018)
2. Falchikov, N.: Involving students in assessment. Psychol. Learn. Teach. **3**, 102–108 (2003)
3. Tsivitanidou, O., Constantinou, C.: A study of students' heuristics and strategy patterns in web-based reciprocal peer assessment for science learning. Internet High. Educ. **12**, 12–22 (2016)
4. Tsivitanidou, O.E., Constantinou, C.P., Labudde, P., Rönnebeck, S., Ropohl, M.: Reciprocal peer assessment as a learning tool for secondary school students in modeling-based learning. Eur. J. Psychol. Educ. **33**(1), 51–73 (2018)

Motion Capture as an Instrument in Multimodal Collaborative Learning Analytics

Milica Vujovic(✉), Simone Tassani, and Davinia Hernández-Leo

Universitat Pompeu Fabra, Barcelona, Spain
{milica.vujovic, simone.tassani, davinia.hernandez-leo}@upf.edu

Abstract. In this paper, we describe an exploratory study where we investigate the possibilities of motion capture system as an instrument to consider in multimodal analyses of face-to-face collaborative learning scenarios. The goal is to understand to what extent motion capture can facilitate certain measurements leading to collaborative learning indicators that are currently time-consuming to achieve with other instruments. We focus on the simultaneous measurement of known physical collaboration indicators such as gaze direction, the distance between learners and the speed of movement/reactions. The study considers a lab setting simulating a classroom scenario based on the Jigsaw collaborative learning flow pattern, which proposes a sequence of activities with changes in group size and formation. Preliminary results indicate a high degree of applicability of the system in measuring these indicators, with certain limitations for gaze direction measurements. With appropriate marker position on the participants, the system is able to automatically provide desired measurements with satisfactory precision. Additionally, with a small number of additional markers, we were able to determine the way students used working surfaces (shared desks).

Keywords: Motion Capture System · Multimodal Learning Analytics · CSCL

1 Introduction

Despite there is accumulated evidence about the benefits of collaborative learning, there are still many research questions about what happens in the collaboration process and what makes it more effective. In face-to-face settings, there is emerging research that uses multimodal learning analytics (MMLA) to identify indicators of fruitful collaboration. Some indicators have been already identified, such as collaborative will [1], equality and mutuality [2], symmetry [3], synchrony of groups' actions and gaze [4], the reaction time of participants to the actions of members of the group [5] or the distance between learners (DBL) [6] etc. Multimodal measures leading to these indicators are diverse (video, audio, physiological data, …) and generate large amount of data, which require significant time-consuming analysis. In this paper, we select concrete physical collaboration indicators such as gaze direction (GD), the distance

M. Scheffel et al. (Eds.): EC-TEL 2019, LNCS 11722, pp. 604–608, 2019.
https://doi.org/10.1007/978-3-030-29736-7_49

between learners (DBL) and the movement speed/reaction (MS), and propose and evaluate the application of a motion capture system (MCS) with the objective to simultaneously measure these indicators and accelerate the analysis process (Fig. 1).

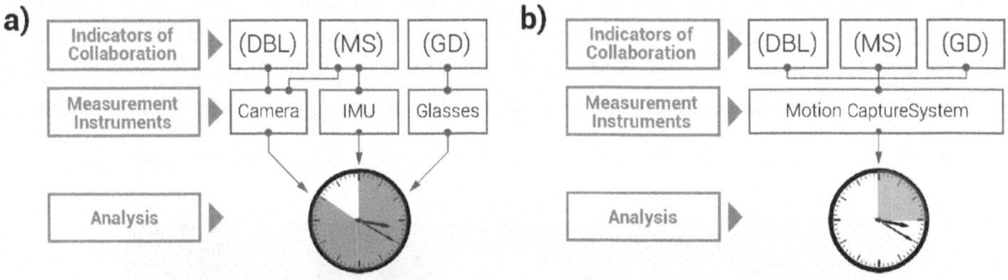

Fig. 1. Substituting various instruments with Motion Capture to accelerate the analysis.

2 Motion Capture in Collaborative Learning Analytics

To illustrate and evaluate the possibilities of MCS for collaborative learning analytics, we use a scenario based on the Jigsaw pattern [7] where students are grouped into small independent groups and where each student is assigned with a specific role. Students are then regrouped on the basis of their roles in order to gain expertise and share that expertise with other members of the group. Such a context is a complex environment where there are constant interactions of participants and group size and formation transformations. The monitoring of participant behaviour and factors that influence the collaboration process is a demanding task. As aforementioned, by selecting three indicators (DBL, MS, GD) we propose to substitute different sensors, like cameras, Inertial Measurement Units, eye-tracking glasses etc. with MCS. In comparison to other technologies that address the issue of movement detection (such as possibility of detecting pose using web camera, or deep learning algorithms for depth perception), we found that they face problems such as tracking bigger group of people or having nor so high accuracy rate. Regarding ethical issues, we have informed participants on details of the experiment and collected a consent form.

Application of motion capture systems is wide and cross-disciplinary [8]. The system applied in this study uses reflective markers and infrared cameras, where markers are placed on objects whose movement we want to detect. Because of the reflective surface, the cameras recognize them as points in space, based on which we get the desired physical parameters. The main advantage of the system is that it is possible to develop a marker protocol fully adapted to the needs of the research.

3 Evaluation of the Motion Capture System

We studied to what extend MCS represents a useful MMLA tool in the analysis of collaborative learning indicators in a Motion Caption Laboratory (left-down, Fig. 2), where we run an experimental protocol for a pair of three member groups that participated in one Jigsaw session. Movement analysis was performed using eight cameras BTS Smart-DX 700, 1.5 MP 125 fps (BTS S.p.A., Milan, Italy). A custom marker protocol was developed to follow the movement of the subjects analyzed using headbands with 5 non-aligned markers for each of the participants. Two lateral markers were placed at the level of the ears, the other two were at the back of the head at different levels and one marker on the top of the head (Head Motion Marker Protocol). Middle points between the rear and lateral markers were identified, together with the vector passing through these points. A calibration process was performed to identify the GD.

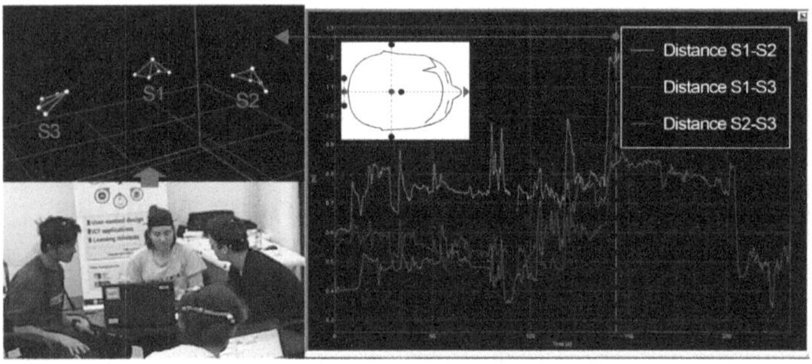

Fig. 2. Reconstruction of markers and presentation of the DBL in specific point in time (Color figure online)

Nine measurements of five minutes each were performed to cover the three phases of the collaborative Jigsaw activity. The analysis tool enabled us to calculate the DBL and the MS within a few minutes based on the marker positioned at the top of the head and by selecting two operators (distance and derivatives). The GD calculation required additional operators, which took more time.

The Fig. 2 shows the reconstruction of the markers (left-top, Fig. 2), capture from a video recording (left-down, Fig. 2), position of markers (middle, Fig. 2), and a graph that displays the DBL (left-down, Fig. 2) during one recording (300 s). One of the moments during the activity was randomly selected (red dashed line) to show that the tool can display the values at any given moment and various indicators at the same time.

The scope of this study is efficiency and comprehensiveness, which we analyzed through the speed of analysis and obtaining the desired indicators. The most time consuming phase is the reconstruction of markers. Calculation of results in the case of two indicators (DBL and MS) takes several minutes, while the calculation of the GD takes 20–30 min. Video recordings are included and used to control the obtained results.

4 Discussion and Conclusion

The use of MCS as an instrument for multimodal analysis of collaborative learning has proved to be effective in the context of this study. The results of the study indicate the advantage of ease of detection of DBL and MS, due to the use of only one marker and the rapid analysis of data. With these indicators, the number of participants in the study does not affect the quality of the recording and analysis. Identifying the GD is done based on the position of the head and ignoring the movement of the eyes, which represents a limitation that is difficult to overcome without the use of additional resources. With all indicators, a comprehensive display of data is possible and clearly visible, which is an additional quality of the system. The constraints that occur, in addition to the precise detection of GD, are the connection of the system to the physical environment, which possible to overcome with different interventions, such as displacing system outside the laboratory or using mobile motion capture systems. All these interventions have disadvantages in terms of time or price, but they can be justified by beneficial contributions in the field of multimodal analysis. Future work should focus on additional features useful to analyze collaboration processes (sitting arrangement, use of the desk surface) and that can be easily labeled, recorded and analyzed.

Acknowledgements. This project has received funding from the European Union's Horizon 2020 research and innovation programme under the Marie Skłodowska-Curie grant agreement No. 713673. Milica Vujovic has received financial support through the "la Caixa" INPhINIT Fellowship Grant for Doctoral studies at Spanish Research Centres of Excellence, "la Caixa" Banking Foundation, Barcelona, Spain. This work has been partially supported by the National Research Agency of the Spanish Ministry of Science, Innovations and Universities MDM-2015-0502, TIN2014-53199-C3-3-R, TIN2017-85179-C3-3-R.

References

1. Pijeira-Díaz, H.J., Drachsler, H., Järvelä, S., Kirschner, P.A.: Investigating collaborative learning success with physiological coupling indices based on electrodermal activity. In: ACM Proceedings of the Sixth International Conference on Learning Analytics & Knowledge, pp. 64–73 (2016)
2. Damon, W., Phelps, E.: Critical distinctions among three approaches to peer education. Int. J. Educ. Res. **13**(1), 9–19 (1989)
3. Dillenbourg, P.: Collaborative Learning. Pergamon, Amsterdam (1999)
4. Schneider, B., Blikstein, P.: Unraveling students' interaction around a tangible interface using multimodal learning analytics. J. Educ. Data Min. **7**(3), 89–116 (2015)
5. Raca, M., Tormey, R., Dillenbourg, P.: Sleepers' lag-study on motion and attention. In: ACM Proceedings of the Fourth International Conference on Learning Analytics and Knowledge, pp. 36–43 (2014)
6. Spikol, D., Ruffaldi, E., Cukurova, M.: Using multimodal learning analytics to identify aspects of collaboration in project-based learning. In: 12th International Conference on Computer Supported Collaborative Learning (CSCL), pp. 263–270 (2017)

7. Aronson, E., Patnoe, S.: Cooperation in the Classroom: The Jigsaw Method, 3rd edn. Pinter & Martin Ltd., London (2011)
8. Park, S.W., Park, H.S., Kim, J.H., Adeli, H.: 3D displacement measurement model for health monitoring of structures using a motion capture system. Measurement **59**, 352–362 (2015)

Constructing an Open Learning Analytics Architecture for an Open University

Jun Xiao[1(✉)], Tore Hoel[2], and XueJiao Li[3]

[1] Shanghai Open University, 288 Guoshun Road, Shanghai, China
xiaoj@sou.edu.cn

[2] Oslo Metropolitan University, Pilestredet 46, 0167 Oslo, Norway
tore.hoel@oslomet.no

[3] East China University of Science and Technology, 130 Meilong Road, Shanghai, China
lixuejiao9405@163.com

Abstract. Open learning analytics (OLA) aims to meet diversified needs for insights into different stakeholders' efforts to improve learning and learning contexts integrating heterogeneous learning analytics techniques. From an abstract point of view, OLA aligns well with the ideas of open and distance education institutions, of which Shanghai Open University (SOU) is a learning Chinese representative. The paper reports on the design of an OLA framework for SOU, based on different users' service demands and the diverse sources of data and multiple platforms in use at the university. The proposed architecture is based on a discussion of the general characteristics of OLA architecture. The final model is achieved through an iterative development method.

Keywords: Online learning · Open Learning Analytics · Open University

1 Introduction

Application of learning analytics can help learners achieve better learning results and improve the quality of online education However, open universities face a complex environment with a wide range of data collected from different learning environments, heterogeneous learning contexts, as well as diverse needs and analytical objectives from stakeholders. The technical infrastructure (learning analytics platforms, etc.) should ideally accommodate a number of learning analytics methods [1]. These diverse elements lead to a new concept of learning analytics [3], open learning analytics (OLA). It deals with learning data collected from multiple environments and contexts, analyzed with a wide range of analytics methods to address the requirements of different stakeholders [3]. As the guiding framework of open learning analysis, there are many typical architectures in the world (eg. Integrated learning analytics system/Open Learning Analytics Diamond/Open learning analytics architecture) [1, 2, 4]. The paper has carried out an extensive literature review, and extract the following characteristics from the literature review of international open LA architectures: (1) the architecture should be goal oriented; (2) based on open standards; (3) consist of modules that can be interchanged.

M. Scheffel et al. (Eds.): EC-TEL 2019, LNCS 11722, pp. 609–612, 2019.
https://doi.org/10.1007/978-3-030-29736-7_50

SOU has used learning analytics to provide personalized learning services for learners by monitoring their learning process. However, SOU faces the same challenges as other open universities that is to integrate multi-platform learning data and better understand the learning status of learners. In order to solve the challenge faced by SOU, this paper based on the analysis of the general characteristics of open learning architecture and the requirements of SOU, an iterative approach is used to propose an Open Learning Analytics Architecture for SOU (SOU_OA4LA).

2 Methodology

This research studied SOU_OA4LA with research methodology of iterative design science and interview. In the design of open learning analytics framework, initially evaluates SOU_OA4LA1 Open Learning Analytics architecture's three aspects, including the intelligibility, integrity and openness. The survey is in the form of questionnaire and interviews, which contains 11 questions, including 10 multiple choice questions, with answer range from 0 to 5 grades; and 1 open question which allows the subjects to give their own suggestions on this open learning analytics architecture. The subjects of the survey are teachers, managers and technical personnel, such as data base administrator, architecture engineer, software engineer and project manager. According to the survey results of this questionnaire, this study improved SOU_OA4LA1 Open Learning Analytics architecture and obtained SOU_OA4LA2 Open Learning Analytics architecture. Focus group interviews are a method for collecting qualitative data. Then, experts are invited again to evaluate the architecture through focus group interviews, and we updated the SOU_OA4LA2 based on the results of the interview and finally gained SOU_OA4LA3-the final version.

3 Results

3.1 Process of SOU_OA4LA Formation

SOU_OA4LA1 (Fig. 1) is the first generation of open learning analytics architecture we designed. The statistical results from 27 valid respondenses to the questionnaire showed that SOU_OA4LA1 architecture scores below 4.2 on average in terms of completeness and clarity, and the evaluation results in the target module (only 21 people think that the architecture reflects the openness of the target), the analysis module (mean = 4.148) and the visualization part (mean = 4.037) are not ideal.

So the research improved the architecture and got SOU_OA4LA2 (Fig. 2): (1) learning system is added to access data; (2) stakeholders are added to the architecture; (3) learning models are added to the module section; (4) open services replace analysis output. 'Service-orientation architecture' from Information Technology domain is introduced to the SOU_OA4LA2.

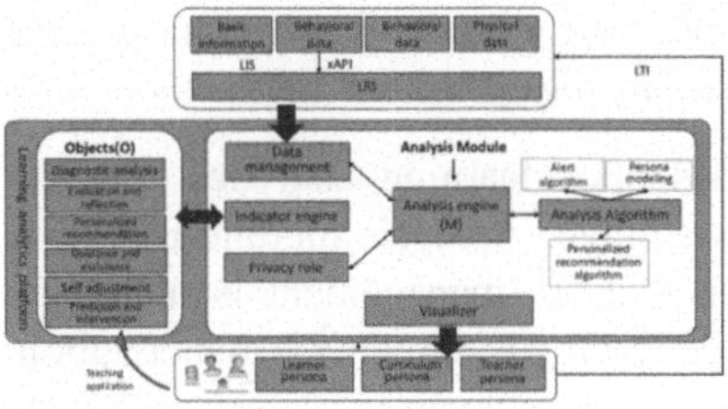

Fig. 1. SOU_OA4LA1

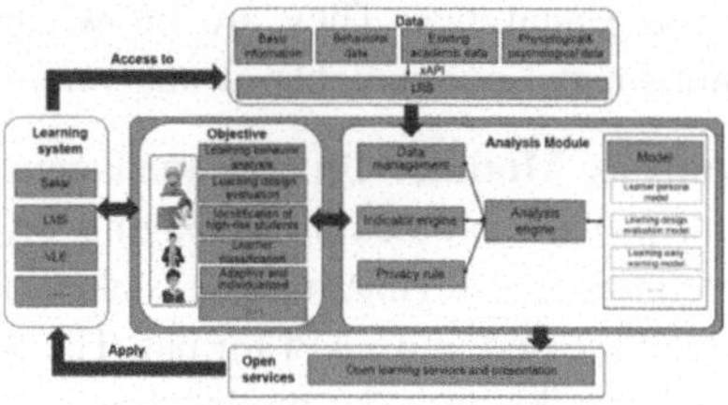

Fig. 2. SOU_OA4LA2

To polish the architecture, experts of educational technology are interviewed to evaluate for SOU_OA4LA2. They are approval of the overall structure design of architecture, which assist with teaching and learning activities. More importantly, experts also pointed out a problem that part of the four types of data does not belong to the same dimension. And, the architecture did not reflect the "ecological" well.

3.2 The Description of SOU_OA4LA3

According to the evaluation results, the revision is made again and the latest version of architecture SOU_OA4LA3 is shown in the Fig. 3. This architecture is an objective-oriented ecological system, accessible to different learning system. More importantly, its analysis result output is also available to different learning system. The procedure of analysis and format of analysis output are both determined by the analysis objectives. Therefore, the final application performance should be evaluated by whether achieve a preset analysis objective. This architecture consists of four modules, which are objective, data, analysis, as well as open service.

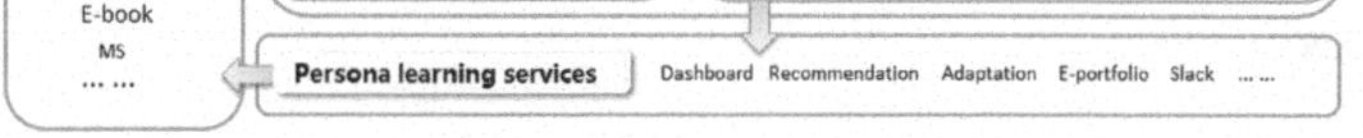

Fig. 3. SOU_OA4LA3

Objective Module: Objective is determined by the demands from different stakeholders, eg teachers, students, researchers, management personnel.

Data Module: There three categories of data access to the learning platform of open learning analytics. They are knowledge, behaviour and attitude. These data are the fundamental components of analysis, in xAPI format storage within LRS.

Analysis Module: Privacy management provides open learning analytics platform with privacy protection, managing privacy rules storage. Analysis module runs in a precondition of guaranteeing stakeholders' privacy. Data management is managing data processed into xAPI format. The indicators are acquired from data polymerization, providing the basis for model construction. Indicator management is to form indicators according to analysis objectives, then undertake management, for instance, indicator storage management. Model management is to preset corresponding model or to add new models according to analysis objectives, for example, alert model. Analysis engine takes advantage of the other four parts, adopting certain of data analysis methods, and algorithm, receives the analysis result relating to analysis objectives.

Open Service Module: Open service is the output of analysis procedure. It could be demonstrated as a teaching service accessible to learning system, also could be a visualized report. For example, an alerting service based on alert objective, is an open learning service applied to learning system, an evaluation report generated according to 'Learning Design Evaluation' objectives is one form of visualization.

4 Conclusion and Future Work

In conclusion, SOU_OA4LA can help stakeholders to conduct better open learning analytics, moreover, has great potential to be expanded to a wider environment. This architecture is highly feasible on various platforms, learning objectives and data flows. The SOU_OA4LA compensates for the lack of operational open learning analytics architecture, and integrates the existing open learning analytics architecture type, which is conceptual. It is also developable and can serve technicians for different purposes. More case study are needed to feedback the application effect in the future to evaluate the effectiveness of SOU_OA4LA.

Acknowledgements. This paper is supported by China's National General Project granted by China National Office for Education Sciences Planning (Grant No. BCA160053). The Construction and Application of Online Learners' Persona based on Big Data Analysis.

References

1. Chatti, M.A., Muslim, A., Schroeder, U.: Toward an open learning analytics ecosystem. In: Kei Daniel, B. (ed.) Big Data and Learning Analytics in Higher Education, pp. 195–219. Springer, Cham (2017). https://doi.org/10.1007/978-3-319-06520-5_12
2. Greller, W., Drachsler, H.: Translating learning into numbers: a generic framework for learning analytics (2012)
3. Muslim, A., Chatti, M.A., Bashir, M.B., Varela, O.E.B., Schroeder, U.: A modular and extensible framework for open learning analytics. J. Learn. Anal. **5**(1), 92–100 (2018)
4. Siemens, G., et al.: Open learning analytics: an integrated & modularized platform, Doctoral dissertation, Open University Press (2011)

Gamifire - A Cloud-Based Infrastructure for Deep Gamification of MOOC

Roland Klemke[1,2(✉)], Alessandra Antonaci[1], and Bibeg Limbu[1]

[1] Open University of the Netherlands, Heerlen, The Netherlands
{roland.klemke,alessandra.antonaci,bibeg.limbu}@ou.nl
[2] Cologne Game Lab, TH Köln, Cologne, Germany

Abstract. Gamification aims at addressing problems of MOOC (high dropouts, low success rates, lack of engagement, isolation, lack of individualization). We define our understanding of deep gamification and present the Gamifire infrastructure. We also point out planned development activities on this platform.

Keywords: Gamifire · Gamification · Architecture · Scalability · MOOC · Platform Independence · Infrastructure

1 Introduction

The success of MOOCs comes with downsides: high-drop out rates [3] and low engagement [5]. Gamification was initially introduced to improve situations of motivational gaps by applying elements of gaming into otherwise boring activities [4]. Relying mostly on game elements fostering extrinsic motivational factors (such as points, badges, and levels), mainly in a way that is not even challenging for those who need to be extrinsically motivated, gamification as seen so far does not exploit the true potential of human motivation and passion for learning [6]. Also, many approaches towards gamification fail due to the lack of a clear design methodology [8]. However, *deep gamification* as the thoughtful integration of gamification with the learning processes can be beneficial to learners [7]. We have developed a methodology for the gamification of MOOCs [2] backed up by a technological solution that aims to reliably support the process. In this article, we highlight the technical side of this research. The following research questions (Q) are investigated in this work: (q1) Can we develop a platform-independent, scalable deep gamification platform for the gamification of MOOC? (q2) Can we resolve the conflict between platform-independence and the required platform integration for deep gamification?

To answer the research questions and to base Gamifire on solid methodological grounds, our methodology comprises three main perspectives: (1) A *design perspective*, combining game design with problem-based selection of theories into an evaluation-based continuous improvement cycle. (2) A *user-experience and usability perspective*, taking the interplay of learning environment and gamification into account. (3) A *software-engineering perspective*, transforming outcomes

M. Scheffel et al. (Eds.): EC-TEL 2019, LNCS 11722, pp. 613–616, 2019.
https://doi.org/10.1007/978-3-030-29736-7_51

of the other two perspectives into implementable requirements and architectural specifications. Approaches towards gamification design frameworks have been extensively discussed in [8]. Our own approaches towards a methodologically sound gamification design and towards user-experience evaluation have been reported in [1,2], respectively. This article takes the software-engineering perspective and reports the corresponding process steps and results.

2 Gamifire - Architecture and Implementation

Gamifire is implemented on top of the Google App Engine (GAE) cloud platform. Gamifire uses a three-tier architecture, with database back-end (cloud data-store), an application server, and front-end user-interface (UI) components. The back-end stores logging information collecting data about user interactions, time-stamps, and progress related data. Each game element/widget can also store widget specific data. The application server handles user related sessions, tracks user interactions, manages logging operations and generates feedback and UI-related content. To generate the UI, Gamifire relies on a library of game

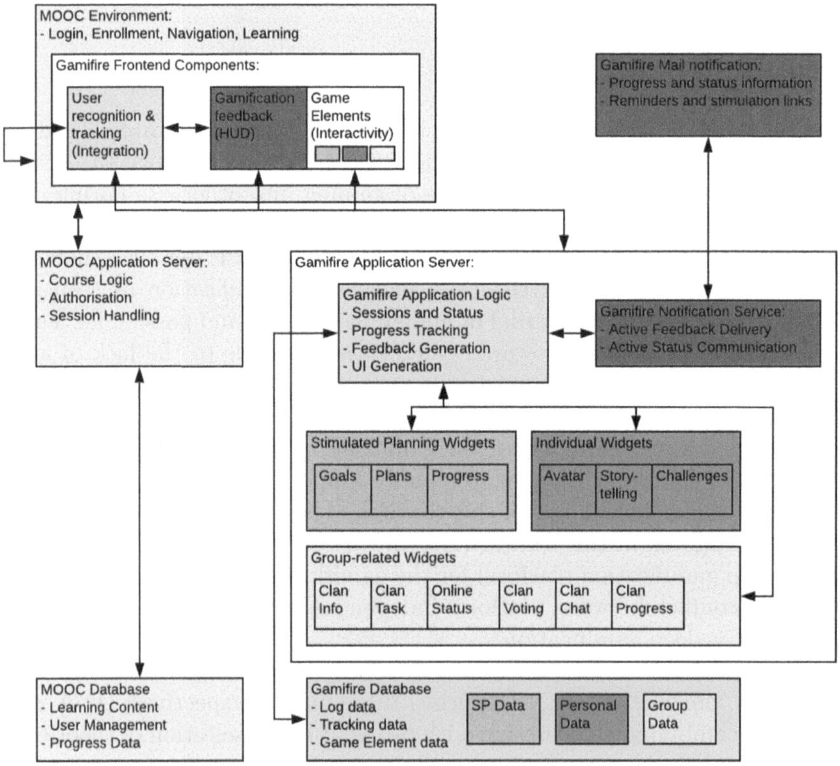

Fig. 1. Architecture of the Gamifire platform

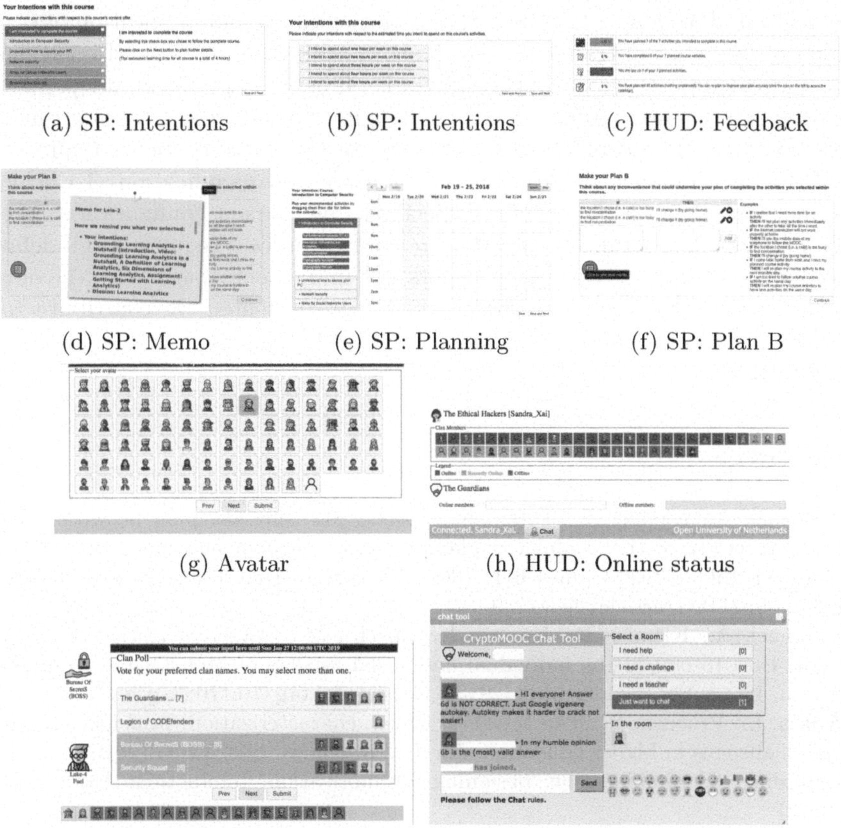

(a) SP: Intentions (b) SP: Intentions (c) HUD: Feedback

(d) SP: Memo (e) SP: Planning (f) SP: Plan B

(g) Avatar (h) HUD: Online status

(i) Clan voting (j) Clan chat

Fig. 2. Screen-shots of Gamifire UI components.

element widgets, which are triggered by the main application logic and which provide the individualized view on the game elements with respect to the user status. These UI elements are embedded into the MOOC platform by front-end integration, which means, they are added to the web-based front-end of the MOOC platform as partial HTML components. Through JavaScript introspection, these front-end elements gather user information from the MOOC platform and can thus synchronize user sessions and data between MOOC and Gamifire. Figure 1 shows the general Gamifire component architecture and its integration into an (abstract) MOOC platform. Figure 2 shows the user interface components displaying different game elements and components.

3 Conclusions and Future Work

With the implementation of Gamifire, we were able to show that it is possible to deliver a "scalable, platform-independent, cloud-based Infrastructure for deep gamification of MOOC". However, the implementation and application of Gamifire faces a number of trade-offs, which show, that some conceptual issues have to be addressed in future work: (1) The trade-off between platform-independence and deep gamification requires to be re-thought, in order to get rid of erroneous extra work. (2) The conflicts between some of the game elements requires us to offer more guidance to designers of MOOCs and gamification. To achieve this, more research on the effects of specific game element configurations needs to be performed. Overall, gamification remains a process requiring well-defined procedures and thought through concepts and implementations. With the development of Gamifire based on the methodology presented we contribute to a better understanding and applicability of deep gamification in the context of online learning.

References

1. Antonaci, A., Klemke, R., Dirkx, K., Specht, M.: May the plan be with you! A usability study of the stimulated planning game element embedded in a MOOC platform. Int. J. Ser. Games **6**(1) (2019). http://journal.seriousgamessociety.org/index.php/IJSG/article/view/239
2. Antonaci, A., Klemke, R., Kreijns, K., Specht, M.: Get Gamification of MOOC right! How to embed the individual and social aspects of MOOCs in gamification design. Int. J. Ser. Games **5**(3) (2018). https://doi.org/10.17083/ijsg.v5i3.255
3. Atiaja, L., Proenza, R.: The MOOCs: origin, characterization, principal problems and challenges in higher education. J. e-Learn. Knowl. Soc. **12**(1) (2016)
4. Deterding, S.: Gamification: designing for motivation. Interactions **19**(4), 14–17 (2012)
5. Dillon, J., et al.: Student emotion, co-occurrence, and dropout in a MOOC context. Educ. Data Min. (2016)
6. Hamari, J., Koivisto, J., Sarsa, H.: Does gamification work?-A literature review of empirical studies on gamification. HICSS **14**, 3025–3034 (2014)
7. de Marcos, L., Garcia-Lopez, E., Garcia-Cabot, A.: On the effectiveness of game-like and social approaches in learning: comparing educational gaming, gamification & social networking. Comput. Educ. **95**, 99–113 (2016)
8. Mora, A., Riera, D., Gonzalez, C., Arnedo-Moreno, J.: A literature review of gamification design frameworks. In: VS-Games 2015–7th International Conference on Games and Virtual Worlds for Serious Applications. IEEE (2015)

Increasing STEM Engagement Through the Mediation of Textile Materials Combined with Physical Computing

Ali Hamidi[1(✉)] and Marcelo Milrad[2(✉)]

[1] Department of Informatics, Linnaeus University, Växjö, Sweden
ali.hamidi@lnu.se

[2] Department of Media Technology, Linnaeus University, Växjö, Sweden
marcelo.milrad@lnu.se

Abstract. Recent trends indicate an increasing global demand for skilled IT and Engineering professionals. At the same, it has been acknowledged that there is a decline in the number of graduates in the disciplines of Science, Technology, Engineering and Mathematics (STEM). The lack of interest in these subjects, which has been addressed by many scholars, has triggered recent efforts in order to investigate novel ways to attract and engage more young students in STEM related subjects. In this paper, we describe an exploratory qualitative research study that has been carried out by combining the subjects of technology and programming in a series of workshops hosting sixty pupils 12–13 years old. Children have used the Makey-Makey kit and the Scratch programming language together with textiles to explore how the combination of these different forms of expression can influence their engagement and interest with STEM related topics. The theoretical ideas used for the design and implementation of this study were guided by *flow theory*. Data was collected through observations, video recordings, and semi-structured interviews. The initial results of this study indicate that the attributes of attention, motivation, and empowerment shape the levels of engagement to retain and reinforce the flow state by using all these materials.

Keywords: STEM subjects · Fabric/textiles · Physical computing · Flow theory

1 Introduction

Although there is a decline in the number of graduates in STEM related subjects, it is agreed that knowledge and skills in these areas become essential for preparing *"twenty-first-century" citizens* not only for professionals but also for all people. Therefore, more students should be actively involved and engaged in STEM related fields of study. Many scholars have addressed that the lack of interest in these subjects has triggered recent efforts to investigate alternative ways for increasing students' engagement [1]. To our knowledge, there are few studies to target the issue of *engagement* by the application of *flow theory* in Maker inspired related activities that combine textile and physical computing. In this article, we describe an exploratory study in which elementary school

M. Scheffel et al. (Eds.): EC-TEL 2019, LNCS 11722, pp. 617–621, 2019.
https://doi.org/10.1007/978-3-030-29736-7_52

children have used self-made textile elements as soft materials combined with *Maker* technologies and a visual programming environment to explore how the combination of these different forms of expression can influence children's engagement and interest with STEM topics. In the next section we present the theoretical ideas that guided our work and the settings in which the study took place. We then proceed by analyzing the outcomes and discussing those. We end this paper by presenting our initial conclusions and possible lines of future research.

2 Theoretical Ideas and the Exploratory Study

2.1 Flow Theory and STEM

In order to promote new opportunities to develop K-12 education activities that integrate novel STEM practices, a wide variety of digital tools and platforms are used by hobbyists, tinkerers, engineers, and artists to design and build playful projects in innovative ways. Looking at children's engagement with this kind of activities, *flow* can be defined as an optimal psychological state when a student deeply engages in a task that prevent other disruptions to interfere with it [2]. The *flow experience* has different characteristics such as high concentration, feeling of control, and on-hold perception of time. The theoretical ideas used for the design and implementation of this study were guided by *flow theory*. One of our goals has been to increase the levels of *behavioral* (both individual and social), *emotional*, and *cognitive* engagement that are three dimensions of students' engagement with an activity [3]. Due to the nature of this study, an interpretivist approach has been used to answer the main research question that guided our work; "*How the combination of physical computing and programming with soft materials impact students' engagement with STEM subjects in a Maker movement activity*?" In the next sub-section, we describe the settings and the participants of the study.

2.2 Setting and Participants

In total, 60 children of age 12–13 from a school located in the south of Sweden together with four teachers participated in four workshops carried out over a two weeks period during the spring 2018. Each workshop lasted for 3 hours hosting 15 students who worked in groups of 3 members including both genders each. While students work together, shared and collective experiences shift them from individual *flow* to group *flow* where they carried out the different tasks. We used the *Makey Makey* toolkit, the *Scratch* programming language, and also colorful fabrics with the *AngryBird* (AB) theme as a mediator (see Fig. 1).

In order to approach the *flow* state, a *stimulating* activity was designed and presented at the beginning of workshop. We used a carrot as a conductive material that *screamed* when cutting it with a steel knife. The latest stirred up participants' interest and curiosity as a dimension of the *flow* experience [4]. The overall aim was lighting up the LEDs and playing a song when touching the AB through the connections established between the textiles, the *Makey Makey* kit and Scratch. Children were supposed

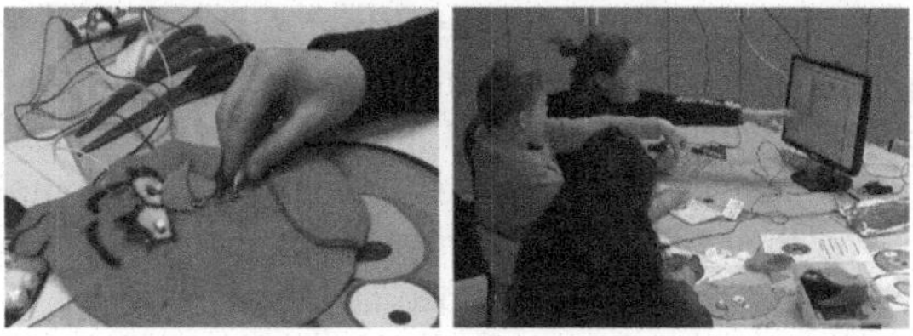

Fig. 1. Workshop themes and settings

to tailor the AB fabrics and decorate them with LEDs. Afterwards, they were asked to create a circuit with the *Makey Makey* parts and the LEDs connected to the AB. A Scratch piece of code was the final step to generate the sound.

The methods used for data collection included observations, video recordings, and semi-structured interviews. One camera was set up to record the activities of one group in each one of the workshops. Since each group of children provided one common response to the questions, in total we collected 17 group responses while 3 groups did not reply. The senior teacher who was the main coordinator and responsible from the school also took part in the interview. We initially observed students' behaviors, emotions, actions and reactions, collaboration and communication patterns during the workshops. We analyzed those in more details later in the videos. Then, data from the observations and videotapes were analyzed through thematic analysis. In the next section, we elaborate on these results and present our initial findings.

3 Elaboration of Results, Findings and Discussion

Children's engagement in the workshops illustrated different behavioral and phenomenological characteristics such as *concentration, happiness, boredom, excitement, and teamwork*. While some features such as concentration and excitement were central to the flow experience, others like as boredom and anxiety were out of the flow state [2]. By considering that, we also connect them to behavioral, emotional, and cognitive engagement levels [3] which are experienced in the *flow condition* such as following rules, interest, emotions, motivation, effort, and sequence of activities. After that, we have identified four categories of engagement that are labeled as *the levels of engagement* including attention, motivation, empowerment, and social interaction (Fig. 2).

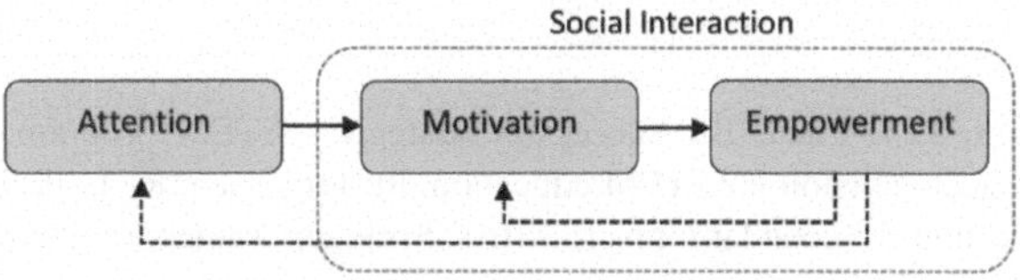

Fig. 2. Levels of engagement

Each level embraced its specific features. *Attention* encompassed the knowledge gained, toolkit/equipment recognition, activity planning, and thinking about the questions to be solved. *Motivation* included interest, lust, enjoyment and satisfaction. *Empowerment* settled in the practical phases included task accomplishment, owning and having control over the challenge, solving a problem, experiencing new challenges related to STEM. *Social interaction* developed and evolved in the group working and sharing the different experiences. Figure 2 illustrates that the *Levels of Engagement* do not follow just a one-way direction. *Empowerment* may augment *Motivation* and *Attention* in an iterative progress. The data collected from the interviews illustrated that programming activities showed maximum attention and motivation with no negative responses. Conversely, working with textiles took less interest, so that four groups of students responded that they were not interested in that part at all. Nevertheless, the use of the soft materials in combination with other components gathered mostly positive reflections. The similarities of the different engagement phases with the main concepts of *flow theory* enabled us to look at the engagement levels from a *flow perspective*. As perceived from these findings, blending technology with programming and soft materials and a proper pedagogical design may help students to reach the *flow state*. Where attention and motivation were primary steps to engage in the STEM activity, motivation plays an important role to shift the level of attention towards empowerment. Accordingly, the presence of soft materials can be considered to influence the balance in the *flow state* as it seems to *soften* the STEM engagement and make it smoother.

4 Conclusion

We conducted an exploratory study that combined the subjects of technology and programming with textiles to explore how it influences students' engagement with STEM topics. Our initial results indicate that while a *flow state* is reached in the activity, the mentioned above combination provides four attributes of *Attention, Motivation, Empowerment, and Social Interaction* as levels of engagement. The soft and colorful fabrics made the activity softer, friendly, and pleasant and at the same time they have enriched the *flow experience*. This study was the first step towards the formulation of an *Engagement Model* by mediating soft materials and physical computing combined with the ideas of flow theory. Since we instructed children to follow a pre-designed task, it could be possible in future studies to redesign the activity workflow in order to develop more creative scenarios combining these materials.

References

1. Hobbs, L., Clark, J.C., Plant, B.: Successful students – STEM program: teacher learning through a multifaceted vision for STEM education. In: Jorgensen, R., Larkin, K. (eds.) STEM Education in the Junior Secondary, pp. 133–168. Springer, Singapore (2018). https://doi.org/10.1007/978-981-10-5448-8_8

2. Sahid, D.S.S., Nugroho, L.E., Santosa, P.I.: Modeling the flow experience for personalized context aware e-learning. In: 8th International Conference on Information Technology and Electrical Engineering, pp. 1–6. IEEE (2016)
3. Fredricks, J.A., Blumenfeld, P.C., Paris, A.H.: School engagement: potential of the concept, state of the evidence. Rev. Educ. Res. **74**(1), 59–109 (2004)
4. Shernoff, D.J., Csikszentmihalyi, M., Schneider, B., Shernoff, E.S.: Student engagement in high school classrooms from the perspective of flow theory. Applications of Flow in Human Development and Education, pp. 475–494. Springer, Dordrecht (2014). https://doi.org/10.1007/978-94-017-9094-9_24

StudyGotchi: Tamagotchi-Like Game-Mechanics to Motivate Students During a Programming Course

Jan Hellings(✉), Pieter Leek, and Bert Bredeweg

Amsterdam University of Applied Science, Post box 1025, 1000BA Amsterdam, The Netherlands
{j.f.hellings,p.d.Leek,b.bredeweg}@hva.nl

Abstract. Motivating students to actively engage in their studying efforts is an ongoing challenge, because motivation is a key factor in study success. In the work presented here, we investigate whether the use of a mobile app with a teacher-like avatar (StudyGotchi), based on the successful digital pet Tamagotchi, can be deployed to motivate and engage computer science university students in their blended learning programming course. A randomized controlled study was performed which showed mixed results. Lessons learned include (*i*) better understanding of how to effectively implement the game-mechanics, and (*ii*) ways to circumvent technical limitations in usage.

Keywords: Gamification · Learning analytics · Motivation

1 Introduction

In education, motivation is an important factor in the student's learning performance [7]. Motivated students perform better and drop out less quickly [5]. Motivation and thereby learning can be influenced by gaming in two ways, namely by changing cognitive processes and by affecting intrinsic motivation [11]. Self-determination theory (SDT) [4] describes three basic psychological needs that promote (intrinsic) motivation. These are autonomy, social solidarity and competence. Games can have a positive influence on these three basic psychological needs and therefore may have a positive effect on motivation [2]. Games connect well to the interests and the world of the student. However, there are mixed results on the effectiveness of gamification [6]. In addition, there is some consensus in the literature on the positive effect of games on motivation [11]. Hence, more research is needed to learn about the effect of gamification on motivation.

For the research presented in this paper, StudyGotchi game-mechanics were developed inspired by the popular Tamagotchi game in the nineties [1]. The perceived usefulness of an app for learning is studied by [3] by use of the Technology Acceptance Model (TAM). In our situation, the way students believed learning with the mobile phone can save time was expected to be a factor in the acceptance of the app. Tamagotchi-like game-mechanics motivate players to keep the avatar happy because the mechanics promote a sense of reality to the users. This emotional bonding is

M. Scheffel et al. (Eds.): EC-TEL 2019, LNCS 11722, pp. 622–625, 2019.
https://doi.org/10.1007/978-3-030-29736-7_53

accomplished by the natural interactive communication with the avatar and personalisation of the avatar [9]. According to [10] it is important in an app for changing behaviour of adolescents to give immediate and meaningful feedback with rewards.

The research presented here was done in the context of a first-year Java programming course at the Amsterdam University of Applied Sciences (AUAS). The StudyGotchi app tries to motivate students to complete their assignments in the Learning Management System (LMS) (Moodle[1]), which are positively related to the course results [8]. The study addresses the following research questions: What is the effect of the StudyGotchi on the online activities of students and their presence in the classroom? What is the effect of the StudyGotchi on the passing rate and obtained grades of the students participating in the Java programming course? What lessons can be learned from deploying the StudyGotchi app?

2 Interventions and Results

The research was performed with 880 freshman computer science students following a blended learning Java programming course. The experiment was set up as a randomized controlled trial with A/B testing using two variants of the StudyGotchi app. The A-version included only the ‘presence in the classroom’ registration function and was assigned to the control group. The B-version included this registration function, but also had the game function with the avatar like ‘virtual lecturer’. The B-version was assigned to the treatment group. 374 students downloaded the app and 180 students received the A-version and 194 received the B-version of the app. During the course the students had to keep the virtual teacher cheerful and happy by carrying out (online) assignments for the course and by attending the classroom lectures.

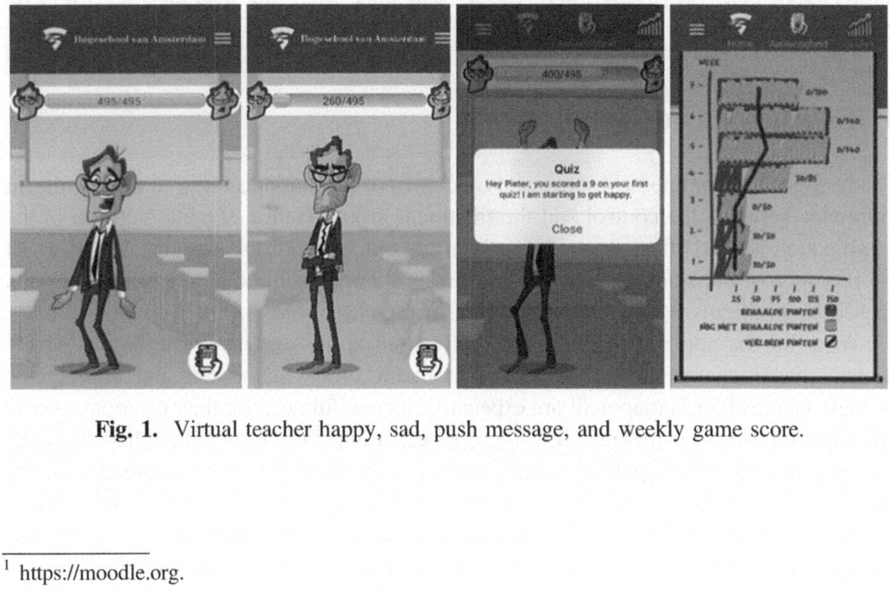

Fig. 1. Virtual teacher happy, sad, push message, and weekly game score.

[1] https://moodle.org.

The StudyGotchi system consists of four parts: (*i*) Moodle LMS for the quizzes and practical assignment, (*ii*) QR scanning for classroom presence, (*iii*) backend program where all the data is collected, the game score calculated, the message generated and pushed to the app, and (*iv*) mobile app where the 'virtual lecturer' lives and the game score is depicted based on the game score received from the backend (Fig. 1).

Analysing the distribution of features such as age, gender and pre-education showed no significant difference between the control and treatment, so randomization was successful on the observed variables. The data was collected during September – November 2018. The quiz, practical assignment and exam results were stored in the Moodle LMS and send to the backend server for processing.

The online behaviour was analysed by a t-test on the total score of the quizzes and the total score of the practical assignment and showed no significant difference between the treatment and control group. There was too little data available to analyse the presence data, only 15% of all possible presences was recorded, because the QR-code scanning had some practical shortcomings. A t-test was carried out to analyse the grades of the students in the course. The course was assessed by a first exam and a retake. There are were no significant differences in grades for the exam (and the retake) between the treatment group and the control group. The results of the succeeding course were analysed by a chi-square test. There was again no significant difference in succeeding the exams between the control and treatment group.

A questionnaire was held among students consisting of five questions with values ranging from 1 (strongly disagree) to 7 (strongly agree), to measure perception of usefulness and the ease of use of the StudyGotchi app. One question about rating the app used a 5-pointscale: 1 to 5. The question: 'Did you use the app during the classes of programming?' was answered by 240 students, 93 answered yes (39%). The question: 'Why didn't you downloaded the app?' was answered by 140 students, 63 answered that they had no interest in the app (45%). The question: 'Give a rating for the StudyGotchi app' was answered by 92 students with an average rate of 2.66 ($SD = 1.11$).

3 Conclusions and Implications

The results of the online behaviour and outcomes of the students showed no significant difference between the control and the treatment group. Hence, the intervention of the gamification had no effect on the behaviour and outcomes of the students. Analyses of the presence of the students in the classroom was not possible due to insufficient data, caused by problems with the QR scanning in the classrooms.

Why did the app not increase the motivation of the students? The results of the student questionnaire showed that the fun factor of the game was not appreciated enough. Games like Tamagotchi are especially successful because they promote a sense of reality for users by making the avatar appear alive. This is accomplished by interactivity with the avatar and personal attachment towards the avatar. Apparently, the StudyGotchi app had insufficient interaction and means for personalizing the avatar.

The perceived usefulness of the app (can the app save me study time), was unclear for students. Only 374 of the 880 (43%) students downloaded the app. In the questionnaire 45% of the 140 students said that they didn't download the app because they were not interested in it. Probably because the advantages of using the app were not obvious to them. This was also reflected in the answers to the question whether the app helped with the course.

The next version of the StudyGotchi app may be accompanied by a help function explaining the purpose of the app and explaining the game score. Important features of an app for changing behaviour of adolescents is immediate and meaningful feedback and rewards. Apparently, the feedback in the StudyGotchi lacked this. The game score was not immediately changed when the students performed some action in the LMS, such as making a quiz. This should be changed in the next version. Maybe rewards can be given in the form of batches or accessories to customize the appearance of the avatar.

References

1. Besser, H.: Tamagotchi effect. N. Y. U. (1997). http://besser.tsoa.nyu.edu/impact/s97/Focus/Identity/FINAL/ov.htm. Accessed 5 Mar 2019
2. Birk, M.V., Atkins, C., Bowey, J.T., Mandryk, R.L.: Fostering intrinsic motivation through avatar identification in digital games, pp. 2982–2995 (2016). https://doi.org/10.1145/2858036.2858062
3. Chung, H.-H., Chen, S.-C., Kuo, M.-H.: A study of EFL college students' acceptance of mobile learning. Proc. Soc. Behav. Sci. **176**, 333–339 (2015). https://doi.org/10.1016/j.sbspro.2015.01.479
4. Deci, E.L., Ryan, R.M.: The "what" and "why" of goal pursuits: human needs and the self-determination of behavior. Psychol. Inq. **11**(4), 227–268 (2000)
5. Garris, R., Ahlers, R., Driskell, J.E.: Games, motivation, and learning: a research and practice model. Simul. Gaming **33**(4), 441–467 (2002). https://doi.org/10.1177/1046878102238607
6. Hamari, J., Koivisto, J., Sarsa, H.: Does gamification work? - A literature review of empirical studies on gamification. In: Proceedings of the Annual Hawaii International Conference on System Sciences, pp. 3025–3034 (2014). https://doi.org/10.1109/HICSS.2014.377
7. Hattie, J., Yates, G.C.R.: Visible Learning and the Science of How We Learn. Routledge, Abingdon (2013)
8. Hellings, J.: Learning analytics dashboard for improving the course passing rate in a randomized controlled experiment. In: 6th International Learning Analytics and Knowledge Conference (LAK16): Practitioner Track, pp. 24–27 (2016). HvA H.-I. http://oro.open.ac.uk/46142/
9. Kusahara, M.: The art of creating subjective reality: an analysis of japanese digital pets. Leonardo **34**(4), 299–302 (2001). https://doi.org/10.1162/00240940152549203
10. Nour, M.M., Rouf, A.S., Allman-Farinelli, M.: Exploring young adult perspectives on the use of gamification and social media in a smartphone platform for improving vegetable intake. Appetite **120**, 547–556 (2018)
11. Wouters, P., van Nimwegen, C., van Oostendorp, H., van Der Spek, E.D.: A meta-analysis of the cognitive and motivational effects of serious games. J. Educ. Psychol. **105**(2), 249–265 (2013). https://doi.org/10.1037/a0031311

To Gamify or Not to Gamify: Towards Developing Design Guidelines for Mobile Language Learning Applications to Support User Experience

Joshua Schiefelbein(✉), Irene-Angelica Chounta, and Emanuele Bardone

University of Tartu, Tartu, Estonia
{joshua.michael.schiefelbein, chounta, bardone}@ut.ee

Abstract. This paper explores the design and development of two mobile applications that can be used to study a foreign language. Each application is designed with a different approach to learning. One immerses the learner into a traditional environment with the ability to review grammar, track personal statistics, and complete tasks. The other employs gamification as the primary method to engage learners. After the prototypes for both applications were created, we carried out extensive, in-depth interviews to assess the applications' user experience and learning experience. The findings suggest that gamification can support long-term student retention, but "gamified" applications should provide some degree of language instruction to help guide users towards proficiency.

Keywords: Gamification · Mobile learning · ESL · Design · Language learning

1 Introduction

The popularity of games has caused many industries to shift from their traditional offerings to products that are gamified, including the foreign language industry. The top language learning applications, such as DuoLingo, use gamification to retain users and enhance the user experience. Gamification is the usage of game-play mechanics in a non-game context by involving *gamefulness, gameful interaction,* and *gameful design* [3]. The integration of gamification in education has been extensively studied in several settings, such as to support location-based educational activities [2] and language learning [6]. However, few studies explore the effects of gamification on second language learning. Furthermore, it is unclear which gamification elements or design guidelines effectively support aspects of learning unique to language learning [4].

This paper aims to develop design guidelines for mobile language learning applications and whether gamification is advised and to what extent. We focus on mobile applications as they are relatively easier to build and test while having generic and scalable features, and language learning applications are currently popular. To that end, we designed two applications - LearnIT ASAP and Starfighter - for learning English as

M. Scheffel et al. (Eds.): EC-TEL 2019, LNCS 11722, pp. 626–630, 2019.
https://doi.org/10.1007/978-3-030-29736-7_54

a second language using two different design approaches: LearnIT ASAP uses a traditional approach to language learning while Starfighter uses gamification. Then, we conducted user interviews to evaluate the design prototypes in terms of user experience and to gain insight with respect to designing guidelines [1]. The research question we aimed to study was how gamification can be integrated into language learning applications and which mechanics are the most effective.

2 Methodology

In this work, we present two applications - LearnIT ASAP and Starfighter (see Fig. 1) - that were designed in order to facilitate language learning following two different pedagogical and design approaches. LearnIT ASAP was designed as a website paradigm to facilitate traditional language learning using content and feedback to support learners and, at the same time, minimizing the amount of text and other distractions for the interface. Learners complete tasks by filling in the missing words. Based on the learner's response, the application provides feedback by coloring buttons green for correct responses and red for incorrect. Should all buttons be green, the advance button appears, allowing the user to move to the next task. LearnIT ASAP provides feedback in a summative manner and records statistics to allow users to track their progress. Starfighter employs a gaming interface with buttons positioned in the center or at the bottom. Implemented gamification mechanics seek to increase engagement. The game mechanics used were selected from a list of the most common mechanics [5]. The learner practices vocabulary and grammar by steering through an asteroid field. The app also maintains a Leaderboard to track the user's score and competitive game-play mechanics for practicing with peers.

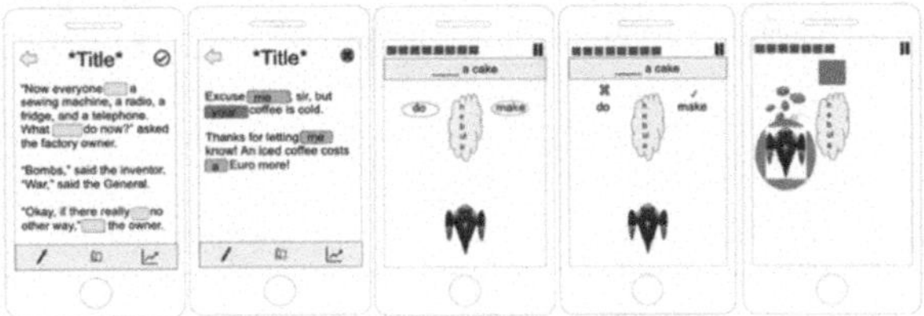

Fig. 1. LearnIT ASAP and Starfighter prototypes: The first two screens show LearnIT ASAP. The last three screens show Starfighter.

To evaluate both design prototypes, we carried out user interviews following a tested interview protocol. The interviews focused on user experience and usability aspects. Eleven individuals participated in the interviews. Participants aged between 20 and 50 years old with seven participants in the 18–29 demographic. One was a native English speaker, while the other ten had an English level of at least B2. Participants came from Europe, North America, South America, Asia, and Africa, and all were enrolled in or had completed some level of university education. Seven reported using a language learning application before, and eight believed such applications could be effective. Data was collected in video and written form. Prior to the interview, participants were provided a brief description of each application, its purpose, and user scenarios. Then, they were instructed to interact with the application and navigate to specific sections or to complete certain tasks without assistance, voicing their thought processes as they did so. After the interaction sequence, the participants critiqued each application. The final questions asked if they perceived the applications as useful and what changes are needed to enhance the effectiveness.

3 Results

Figure 2 displays the results of the user interviews according to five user experience criteria and three learning criteria. For user experience, gamification indicates how users felt while using the application. Interaction refers to if users considered the interactions natural. Navigation measures if users could logically reach the target screen. Aesthetics is if the application has a visually appealing style, and Usability is how usable the users found the application. In Learning, Gamification defines whether the users perceived the application as effective at helping them learn. Content was divided into two categories: informative and engaging. Informative indicates the users perceive the application as providing valuable educational information, while engaging encouraged the user to continue out of interest. Each criterion is graded according to a five-point Likert scale, which was then mapped to a positive-neutral-negative spectrum.

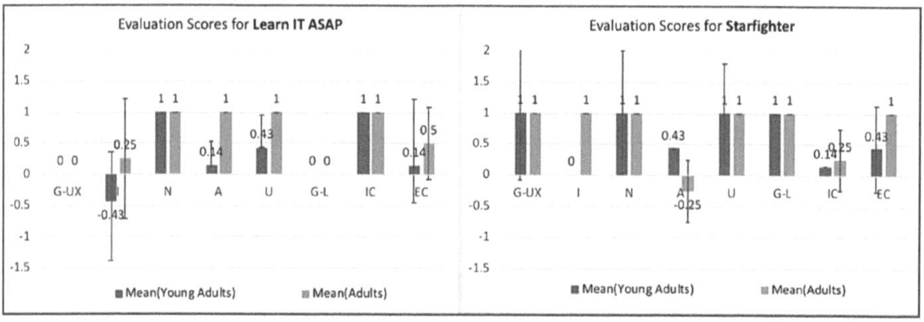

Fig. 2. User Interview Scores for LearnIT ASAP and Starfighter by age group. The evaluation criteria for User Experience were: Gamification (G-UX), Interaction (I), Navigability (N), Aesthetics (A) and Usability (U). The evaluation criteria for learning were: Gamification (G-L), Informative Content (IC) and Engaging Content (EC).

LearnIT ASAP was considered more educational than Starfighter. One user said, "*For a student of the level it is intended for, it would be useful. It practices one of the main tasks students do in school...*" The usage of dropdown menus over writing or swiping was contended. One user in favor stated that dropdowns were perfect because of the size of the standard smartphone screen. Adults had a positive impression of the interaction patterns, aesthetics, and usability, likening them to a comfortable webpage, while young adults possessed a lower opinion, stating that a webpage style does not fit a mobile app. Starfighter was preferred because of the gamification and aesthetics. One user said, "*It was good for me to have this concept like I'm in space… I keep answering and going forward so that my ship doesn't crash into the nebula.*" Similar to LearnIT ASAP, young adults disliked tapping, while adults accepted the interaction, yet were more likely to be ambivalent to the space and gaming aesthetics. Young adults wanted to swipe, with one saying, "*I wish I could have controlled the ship.*" Leaderboards were an interesting point of contention. Participants who considered themselves averse to competition or games disliked the function, but those who loved games enjoyed the communal and motivational aspect.

4 Discussion

The primary objective of both applications is to scaffold the user's skills in the target foreign language. The main difference between the two applications is the usage of gamification, which means the debate centers on whether gamification is a necessary and effective method for use in a language learning application. The results seem to confirm existing literature on the effects of gamification and the balancing of short-term and long-term educational goals [5]. While the pedagogical approach of LearnIT ASAP is perceived as having greater instructional value and being more effective in the long term by exposing the user to a greater amount of vocabulary and grammar in potential real-life situations with more challenging tasks, the non-existence of a clear incentives-based system may render the application unable to retain users. At the same time, Starfighter may be incapable of scaffolding a user to proficiency due to limited content, short prompts, and no real-life context, but the game mechanics were indicated as the reason for content being engaging and motivating for users. The lack of grammar could be appealing to casual learners who do not want to stress over grammar lessons. Comparing the demographic groupings of young adults aged 18–29 and adults aged 30–50, while there was no major difference in the perception of the applications' contents, young adults preferred swiping whereas adults indicated tapping was better.

For future work, we aim to test these applications using functioning apps with animations and timing to accurately evaluate user experience. We also plan to integrate further functionalities (Learning Analytics mechanisms) to provide personalized and adaptive, user-specific learning experiences and multiplayer game modes to facilitate group and classroom play.

Acknowledgements. This work is supported by the Estonian Research Council grant PSG286.

References

1. Avouris, N., Sintoris, C., Yiannoutsou, N.: Design guidelines for location-based mobile games for learning. In: Proceedings of the 17th ACM Conference on Interaction Design and Children, pp. 741–744. ACM (2018)

2. Chounta, I-A., Sintoris, C., Masoura, M., Yiannoutsou, N., Avouris, N.M.: The good, the bad and the neutral: an analysis of team-gaming activity. In: Proceedings of ECTEL Meets ECSCW 2013, pp. 10–14 (2013)
3. Deterding, S., Björk, S.L., Nacke, L.E., Dixon, D., Lawley, E.: Designing gamification: creating gameful and playful experiences. In: CHI 2013 Extended Abstracts on Human Factors in Computing Systems, pp. 3263–3266. ACM (2013)
4. Flores, J.F.: Using gamification to enhance second language learning. Digit. Educ. Rev. **27**, 32–54 (2015)
5. Hamari, J., Koivisto, J., Sarsa, H.: Does gamification work?-a literature review of empirical studies on gamification. In: HICSS, pp. 3025–3034 (2014)
6. Perry, B.: Gamifying French language learning: a case study examining a quest-based, augmented reality mobile learning-tool. Procedia-Soc. Behav. Sci. **174**, 2308–2315 (2015)

The Influence of Self-regulation, Self-efficacy and Motivation as Predictors of Barriers to Satisfaction in MOOCs

Eyal Rabin[1,2(✉)], Maartje Henderikx[3], Yoram M. Kalman[4], and Marco Kalz[2,5]

[1] Education and Psychology, The Open University of Israel, 1 University Road, Ra'anana, Israel
eyalra@openu.ac.il

[2] UNESCO Chair of Open Education, Faculty Management, Science and Technologies, Open University of the Netherlands, Valkenburgerweg 177, 6419 AT Heerlen, The Netherlands

[3] Welten Institute, Open University of the Netherlands, Valkenburgerweg 177, 6419 AT Heerlen, The Netherlands
Maartje.Henderikx@ou.nl

[4] The Department of Management and Economics, The Open University of Israel, 1 University Road, Ra'anana, Israel
yoramka@openu.ac.il

[5] Institute for Arts, Music and Media, Heidelberg University of Education, Im Neuenheimer Feld 561, 69120 Heidelberg, Germany
kalz@ph-heidelberg.de

Abstract. This study focuses on identifying the barriers to satisfaction of MOOC participants, and the predictors of these barriers. Five hundred and forty-two English as a Second Language MOOC participants responded to pre- and post-questionnaires. Using exploratory factor analysis three kinds of barriers were identified, namely: 'Lack of interestingness/relevance', 'Lack of time/bad planning' and 'Lack of knowledge/technical problem'. The effects of the participant's age, gender and level of self-efficacy, motivation, self-regulation learning skills and the intention to complete the course were analyzed as predictors of those barriers. Theoretical and practical implications regarding online learner satisfaction are discussed.

Keywords: MOOCs · Self-efficacy · Self-regulated learning · Motivation · Barriers

1 Introduction

Participants may enroll in massive open online courses (MOOCs) for a variety of reasons [1–3], and may have a variety of expected learning outcomes. Learning outcomes in MOOCs, as a non-formal format of education, should be evaluated through learner-centered measures such as learner satisfaction [4, 5]. Learner satisfaction reflects students' perception of their learning experience [1, 6, 7] and is defined as the

M. Scheffel et al. (Eds.): EC-TEL 2019, LNCS 11722, pp. 631–635, 2019.
https://doi.org/10.1007/978-3-030-29736-7_55

student's overall positive assessment of his or her learning experience [8]. The unstructured, self-paced nature of the MOOC learning environment creates unique types of barriers in the learning process, and these barriers, in turn, can affect the level of satisfaction of the students [9]. In the current study, we define barriers to satisfaction as issues that harm participant satisfaction. This research focuses on those barriers to satisfaction and the antecedes to these barriers. Recent studies identify several variables associated with MOOC participant learning, course outcomes, and barriers to learning. These variables include: age [10], pre-course intentions [3, 5, 11, 12], self-regulated learning [4, 13], levels of motivation and commitment to learning [1, 14] and the level of self-efficacy of the learner [15]. This study focuses on the associations between these variables and barriers to satisfaction in MOOCs. It focuses on two research questions: 1. What types of barriers to satisfaction do MOOC participants experience while studying in a MOOC? 2. How do age, gender, learner intentions, level of self-efficacy, level of motivation and level of self-regulation affect the different barriers to satisfaction that MOOC participants experience?

2 Method

2.1 Participants

Five hundred and forty-two ESL (English as a Second Language) MOOC participants participated in this study. The participants responded to a pre- and a post-questionnaire. Data were collected between July 2016 and February 2018. The course was free of charge, had no prerequisites, and no official start and end dates. The mean age of the sample was 32.4 years (St.d. 11.70; age range: 18–81 years; 71% females, 29% males).

2.2 Instruments and Procedure

Dependent Variable. *Barriers* – In the post-questionnaire MOOC participants were asked to rate 12 barriers to satisfaction that they have faced during the course. The list of barriers was adapted from Henderikx *et al.* [16, 17] and the items were rated on a 7-point Likert scale ranging from 1 ('not at all') to 7 ('fully'). An exploratory factor analysis with Varimax rotation was used in order to answer the first research question. The exploratory factor analysis (EFA) revealed three factors that accounted for 65.73% of the overall variance. The factors that were identified are: (1) "Lack of interestingness/relevance", (2) "Lack of time/bad planning", (3) "Lack of knowledge/technical problem". Factor scores were calculated for each of the factors.

Independent Variables. An online pre-course questionnaire was administered at the beginning of the course. The questionnaire consisted of: *Demographics* (Participants reported gender and age), *Intentions to complete the course activities* (single item), *Self-efficacy for learning and performance* and *motivation* (MSLQ) [18] and *Online self-regulated learning skills (OLSQ)* [19].

3 Results

For the second research question, three prediction models for the three indices of barriers to satisfaction were created, using stepwise linear regression models. Statistically significant findings are reported. Factor 1, "Lack of interestingness/relevance" was negatively predicted by the SRL indices *self-evaluation* and *study strategy*, and positively by the SRL index *help-seeking*. Factor 2, "Lack of time/bad planning" was negatively predicted by the two SRL indices *goal setting*, and *study strategy* and the *age* of the respondent, and positively by the SRL index *time management*. Factor 3, "Lack of knowledge/technical problem" was predicted significantly negatively by the level of the participant's *self-efficacy* and positively by the level of his or her *extrinsic motivation* toward the participation and by the SRL index *time management*. Interestingly the pre-course *behavioral intentions* of the participants, *gender*, and the SRL index *environmental setting* did not predict any type of barriers.

4 Discussion

The goal of this study was to identify barriers to learner satisfaction in MOOCs, and the predictors of those barriers. Three kinds of barriers to satisfaction were identified. Results suggest that the antecedes of the barriers vary. The three predictors of the **first factor** that dealt with barriers regarding interest and relevance of the course materials were indices of self-regulation. The predictors help-seeking, self-evaluation and study strategy suggested that we can lower the impact of this barrier by improving the learning skills of the participants. In order to help learners to overcome the **second factor** that deals with barriers regarding lack of time or bad planning, they should be encouraged to set educational goals or sub-goals at the beginning of the MOOC and to improve their study strategy. Yet, it is important to note that learners who try to manage their time too strictly might also face the lack of time or bad planning barriers. The findings also show that younger participants are more likely to experience the second barrier. This finding is complementary to the findings of Henderikx *et al.* [10], who argue that specific barriers predominantly appear at specific life phases. Course designers and instructors should pay more attention to younger learners, who are more likely to face this type of barrier. **The third factor**, "lack of knowledge or a technical problem", was negatively associated with the SRL dimension of time management, the level of self-efficacy and the level of the external motivation of the participant. Participants who scored low on self-efficacy and had a high level of *external* motivation were more likely to face those barriers. Apparently, participants with low self efficacy and high external motivation were likely to label the difficulties they experienced as technical and/or a result of lack of knowledge. Interestingly, although studies found that the pre-course intention to complete the course predicts the fulfilling of the course obligations and the earning of a certificate [20], in our study it did not predict subjective barriers to satisfaction. Furthermore, the gender of the participant did not play a role in determining the barriers to satisfaction. The gender results are in line with the findings of Rabin *et al.* [4] that showed no differences between females and males regarding learner satisfaction while studying in a MOOC. Future research will explore how participants' intentions and gender affected their actual learning behavior and their learning outcomes.

References

1. Littlejohn, A., Hood, N., Milligan, C., Mustain, P.: Learning in MOOCs: motivations and self-regulated learning in MOOCs. Internet High. Educ. **29**, 40–48 (2016)
2. Onah, D., Sinclair, J., Boyatt, R.: Dropout rates of massive open online courses: behavioural patterns. In: 6th International conference on Education and New Learning, Barcelona, Spain, pp. 5825–5834 (2014)
3. Wang, Y., Baker, R.: Grit and Intention: why do learners complete MOOCs? Int. Rev. Res. Open Distrib. Learn. **19** (2018)
4. Rabin, E., Kalman, Y.M., Kalz, M.: Predicting learner-centered MOOC outcomes: satisfaction and intention-fulfillment. Int. J. Educ. Technol. High. Educ. **16**, Article number: 14 (2019). https://doi.org/10.1186/s41239-019-0144-3
5. Reich: MOOC Completion and Retention in the Context of Student Intent. www.educause.edu/ero/article/mooc-completion-and-retention-context-student-intent
6. Kuo, Y.C., Walker, A.E., Schroder, K.E.E., Belland, B.R.: Interaction, internet self-efficacy, and self-regulated learning as predictors of student satisfaction in online education courses. Internet High. Educ. **20**, 35–50 (2014)
7. Alqurashi, E.: Predicting student satisfaction and perceived learning within online learning environments. Dist. Educ. **40**, 133–148 (2019)
8. Keller, J.: Motivational design of instruction. In: Reigeluth, C. (ed.) Instructional Design Theories and Models: An Overview, pp. 386–434. Erlbaum, Hillsdale, NJ (1983)
9. Gutiérrez-Santiuste, E., Gámiz-Sánchez, V.-M., Gutiérrez-Pérez, J.: MOOC & B-learning: students' barriers and satisfaction in formal and non-formal learning environments. J. Interact. Online Learn. **13** (2015)
10. Henderikx, M., Kreijns, K., Kalz, M.: What hinders learners in pursuing goals in MOOCs? An empirical study on factors influencing barriers to learning. Dist. Educ. **40**, 187–204 (2019)
11. Koller, D., Ng, A., Do, C., Chen, Z.: Retention and intention in massive open online courses: in depth. Educ. Rev. **48**, 62–63 (2013)
12. Wang, Y., Baker, R.: MOOC research initiative-final report. Project MOOC Learner Motivation and Course Completion Rates (2014)
13. Kizilcec, R.F., Perez-Sanagustín, M., Maldonado, J.J.: Self-regulated learning strategies predict learner behavior and goal attainment in massive open online courses. Comput. Educ. **104**, 18–33 (2017)
14. Margaryan, A., Bianco, M., Littlejohn, A.: Instructional quality of massive open online courses (MOOCs). Comput. Educ. **80**, 77–83 (2015)
15. Alqurashi, E.: Self-efficacy in online learning environments: a literature review. Contemp. Issues Educ. Res. Quart. **9**, 45 (2016)
16. Henderikx, M., Kreijns, K., Kalz, M.: To change or not to change? That's the question… on MOOC-success, barriers and their implications. In: Delgado Kloos, C., Jermann, P., Pérez-Sanagustín, M., Seaton, D.T., White, S. (eds.) EMOOCs 2017. LNCS, vol. 10254, pp. 210–216. Springer, Cham (2017). https://doi.org/10.1007/978-3-319-59044-8_25

17. Henderikx, M., Kreijns, K., Kalz, M.: A classification of barriers that influence intention achievement in MOOCs. In: Pammer-Schindler, V., Pérez-Sanagustín, M., Drachsler, H., Elferink, R., Scheffel, M. (eds.) EC-TEL 2018. LNCS, vol. 11082, pp. 3–15. Springer, Cham (2018). https://doi.org/10.1007/978-3-319-98572-5_1
18. Pintrich, P.: A manual for the use of the Motivated Strategies for Learning Questionnaire (MSLQ) (1991)
19. Barnard, L., Lan, W.Y., To, Y.M., Paton, V.O., Lai, S.-L.: Measuring self-regulation in online and blended learning environments. Internet High. Educ. **12**, 1–6 (2009)
20. Ho, A.D., et al.: HarvardX and MITx: two years of open online courses fall 2012-summer 2014 (2015)

"Error 404- Struggling Learners Not Found" Exploring the Behavior of MOOC Learners

Paraskevi Topali(✉), Alejandro Ortega-Arranz, Yannis Dimitriadis, Alejandra Martínez-Monés, Sara L. Villagrá-Sobrino, and Juan I. Asensio-Pérez

GSIC-EMIC Research Group, Universidad de Valladolid, Valladolid, Spain
evi.topali@gsic.uva.es

Abstract. Lack of timely instructors' support when the learners are struggling with the course contents and activities is one frequent problem of MOOC learners. The early identification of these learners could help instructors spend part of their limited time assisting them and avoid potential dropouts. This paper presents a MOOC case study that explores the behavior of learners who reported problems in private messages and discussion forums. The study aimed at the identification of parameters that might allow the detection of learners struggling with different course aspects. As the results suggested, the comparison of the learners' activity traces reveals some common sequences that in the future could facilitate the identification of learners facing problems, even without reporting them. On the other hand, statistical analyses on learners' behavior showed non-significant differences between the learners reporting putting their maximum effort to overcome a problem before asking for help and the ones who did not.

Keywords: MOOCs · Learner's problems · Learner's behavior

1 Introduction

Despite the learning opportunities that Massive Open Online Courses (MOOCs) offer, usually MOOC learners face problems during course runtime [1]. While some of these learners are reluctant to share their problems with course peers and instructors, others prefer to post their questions in course forums, eventually without receiving timely the expected support [2]. In both cases, some of these learners that initially showed an interest in the course, disengage due to the experienced problems and drop out.

The large learners' population and the instructors' high workload in MOOCs make unmanageable the timely awareness and assistance of every learner facing problems [3]. The early identification of learners who face difficulties could help instructors spend part of their limited time assisting them and trying to prevent them from dropping out. Among the different forms of detecting these students, the identification of indicators of learners' behavior could help to understand whether the learner is experiencing a concrete problem without reporting it [4]. Additionally, the learners' effort to overcome their problems could be considered as a parameter to prioritize the instructors' limited time (i.e., assist first those students who have already tried to solve

M. Scheffel et al. (Eds.): EC-TEL 2019, LNCS 11722, pp. 636–639, 2019.
https://doi.org/10.1007/978-3-030-29736-7_56

the problems). Previous studies have focused on identifying the problems of MOOC learners [1, 2] and on creating predictive models for detecting critical cohorts of learners at risk of dropout [5]. However, to the best of our knowledge, none of the previous works has explicitly studied activity traces of learners reporting problems nor conducted comparative analysis between different cohorts of learners based on their experiences towards solving MOOC problems.

This paper presents a MOOC case study that explores the learners' behavioral activity traces to provide useful information for the identification of learners who face problems during a MOOC. Two research questions (RQ) guided this study: (RQ·1) ***"To what extent is it possible to identify learners who face problems by looking at their effort before asking for help?"*** and (RQ·2) ***"Is there any kind of common behavior among the MOOC learners who reported problems before asking for help?".***

2 Methodology of the Study

The study was conducted in a MOOC about English-Spanish translation in the financial and business fields, launched in the Canvas Network platform by the University of Valladolid. The course consisted of seven weekly modules including video lectures, readings, extra material/resources, discussion forums and several compulsory and optional activities. A total number of 866 learners enrolled in the course, out of whom 169 obtained the certificate (19.52% completion rate). The certificate was issued to those participants completing all the compulsory activities.

In order to answer the two RQs, three data sources were used: (a) self-reported data from discussion forums (N = 156) and private messages (N = 38); (b) learners' trace data (number of forum posts, assignments' submissions, pageviews and the total time spent in the course); and (c) the answers to a post-course questionnaire (N = 172).

3 Results

RQ·1: In the post-course questionnaire the subjects were asked about the effort they put before asking for help. Many learners (N = 44) reported that they could have solved their problem by putting some personal extra effort, but more learners (N = 54) claimed that they turned for assistance after putting their maximum effort to overcome their challenge. The early identification of the latter learners could help the instructor assist first the ones who need help and have put their maximum effort. For that reason, the behavioral activity of these two cohorts of learners was explored regarding the pageviews, tasks submissions, time spent in the course and their general participation (see Table 1). Results show non-significant differences between the two groups for the four variables measuring behavioral activity. Z-tests (two-tailed, alpha = .05) were performed to analyze the mean differences of the previous variables between cohorts due to the large sample sizes (>30 answers).

RQ·2: The previous analysis was complemented with an analysis of the activity traces of the learners who reported problems in private messages and discussion forums. For the analysis, the activity of the learners previous to the communication of the problem

Table 1. Statistical analysis of the two different learners' cohorts

	Pageviews	Submissions	Posts	Activity time
"Min. effort" mean	639.36	12.5	3.24	1676.21
"Max. effort" mean	595.93	12.13	3.68	1743.25
Z-test p-value	0.463	0.2396	0.6751	0.8377

and two days after the communication of the problem was considered. Common activity sequences were detected among 13 (out of N = 14) learners mentioning collaboration problems in discussion forums; 9 learners stated that only a few group members were active, and 4 learners reported that their group members were totally absent. The sequences of the learners' trace activity were: (1) visiting many times the communication threads (general discussion and group discussion forums[1]) (N = 12) and (2) reporting the problem in both threads, first in the group forum making it visible to group peers (N = 13), and then to the general forum to make it visible to the rest of the students and to the course team. Additionally, two learners (out of the 4 who did not find other group members) tended to (3) revisit several times the private message page probably waiting a message from the instructors. Figure 1 illustrates the activity traces of two representative learners' cases. In Case 1 the learner was not able to find any active member of his group. According to his traces, he visited many times both the general discussion and group discussion forums, and he also posted in group discussion forums to communicate with his peers. Without receiving answer, he continued visiting both communication threads and finally he posted his problem in general discussion forums as well. In Case 2, the learner was experiencing the same problem as the student before behaving similar. However, instead of only visiting the two discussion forums (group and general), she was visiting many times the private messages' page, suggesting that she was waiting for the instructor's answer to her message.

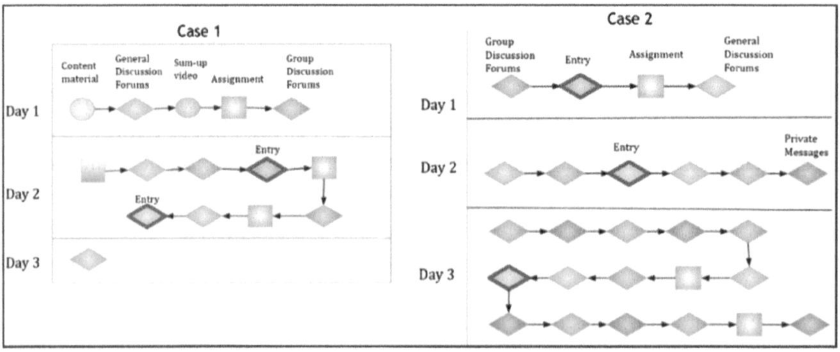

Fig. 1. Representation of two learners' activity traces

[1] Learners were expected to discuss and complete the group activities by communicating in private group forums. Groups were composed by 5 or 6 learners.

4 Discussion and Conclusions

This study attempted to shed light on the behavior of MOOC learners' tracking their activity traces to explore indicators for the identification of learners who face problems during a MOOC. The evidence gathered from RQ·1 showed non-significant differences between the learners reporting putting their maximum effort to overcome a problem before asking for help and the ones who did not. Whilst the indicators of posts in discussion forums, time spent, pageviews and assignments' submission applied in our study are commonly used in the literature analyzing activity traces, probably they did not provide fruitful information regarding our question. This finding points out the need of collecting richer data, from different sources, to help instructors understand better who needs help and what kind of help. Regarding RQ·2 we identified two patterns of behavior that could help instructors or, eventually systems, to spot learners that are not finding the needed support to continue with their tasks even without communicating their problems. These patterns are the recurring visits to the forums/private messages after posting in them, and the broadcasting of help-seeking messages in all possible channels. Our findings may not be generalized but they contribute to a better understanding of learners' course activity and open new lines of future work.

Acknowledgements. This research has been partially funded by the European Regional Development Fund and the National Research Agency of the Spanish Ministry of Science, Innovations and Universities under project grants TIN2017-85179-C3-2-R and TIN2014-53199-C3-2R, by the European Regional Development Fund (Operational program of Castile and León) and the Regional Government of Castile and León by the Regional Ministry of Education under the grant BOCYL-D-07062018-6 and the project grant VA257P18, and by the European Commission under project grant 588438-EPP-1-2017-1-EL-EPPKA2-KA.

References

1. Henderikx, M., Kreijns, K., Kalz, M.: A classification of barriers that influence intention achievement in MOOCs. In: Pammer-Schindler, V., Pérez-Sanagustín, M., Drachsler, H., Elferink, R., Scheffel, M. (eds.) EC-TEL 2018. LNCS, vol. 11082, pp. 3–15. Springer, Cham (2018). https://doi.org/10.1007/978-3-319-98572-5_1
2. Almatrafi, O., Johri, A., Rangwala, H.: Needle in a haystack: identifying learner posts that require urgent response in MOOC discussion forums. Comput. Educ. **118**, 1–9 (2018)
3. Hew, K.F., Cheung, W.S.: Students' and instructors' use of massive open online courses (MOOCs): motivations and challenges. Educ. Res. Rev. **12**, 45–58 (2014)
4. Teusner, R., Hille, T., Staubitz, T.: Effects of automated interventions in programming assignments : evidence from a field experiment. In: Proceedings of the Fifth ACM Conference on Learning @ Scale - L@S 2018, London, United Kingdom (2018)
5. He, J., Bailey, J., Rubinstein, B.I., Zhang, R.: Identifying at-risk students in massive open online courses. In: Proceedings of the Twenty Ninth AAAI Conference on Artificial Intelligence, pp. 1749–1755 (2015)

Orchestration of Robotic Activities in Classrooms: Challenges and Opportunities

Sina Shahmoradi[1(✉)], Jennifer K. Olsen[1], Stian Haklev[1], Wafa Johal[1,2], Utku Norman[1], Jauwairia Nasir[1], and Pierre Dillenbourg[1]

[1] Computer-Human Interaction in Learning and Instruction (CHILI) Laboratory, EPFL, Lausanne, Switzerland
sina.shahmoradi@epfl.ch

[2] Biorobotics Laboratory (BioRob), EPFL, Lausanne, Switzerland
http://chili.epfl.ch/, http://biorob.epfl.ch/

Abstract. Bringing robots into classrooms presents a new set of challenges for classroom management and teacher support compared to traditional technology-enhanced learning and has been left almost unexplored by the research community. In this paper, we present the opportunities and challenges of orchestrating Educational Robotics (ER) activities in classrooms. To support our discussion, we present a case study of 25 students working in pairs using handheld robots to engage in a computational thinking activity. While performing the activity, students' behavioral information was sent from the robots to an orchestration dashboard that was used in a debriefing activity. Although this work is in its preliminary stages, it contributes to framing the challenges that need to be addressed to realistically scale-up usage of ER in classrooms.

Keywords: Classroom orchestration · Educational Robotics

1 Introduction

The main pedagogical advantage of learning activities with Educational Robotics (ER) is to facilitate constructivism activities, which gives the active role to students [1]. An open question in ER research is whether robots would be viable options for supporting learning in ecologically valid classroom environments [1]. To answer this question, we must consider what role the teacher plays with the use of robots in the classroom and the impact it has on classroom orchestration [3]. Classroom management, even in traditional classes, is a complex problem and adding multiple robots to learning activities creates new management challenges for teachers. There have been a few studies that presented awareness tools for ER activities, for instance by classifying students' progress in an ER activity [4]. In this work, the main challenge addressed is to face the unpredictable nature of ER learning activities, which makes it hard for teachers

M. Scheffel et al. (Eds.): EC-TEL 2019, LNCS 11722, pp. 640–644, 2019.
https://doi.org/10.1007/978-3-030-29736-7_57

to follow students' work and may make teachers' interventions harder than in other TEL classrooms. Furthermore, the added complexity of robots increases the frequency of interventions for technical failures. However, these studies have not been mainly conducted around the core idea of orchestration, which is minimalist, teacher-centric deign [3]. Additionally, there is no concrete study in the literature that investigates ER classrooms from an orchestrational perspective, which is an essential step to design orchestration technologies. As the preliminary step of our work, in this paper, we present the findings around observations from a case study of running an ER session with two main goals: (1) what problems would teachers encounter in conducting ER activities? and (2) what do teachers need in terms of technology for conducting such activities? These finding pave the way through designing orchestration technologies for ER classrooms.

2 Study Context

We conducted a preliminary study with 25 students, 11–12 years old and novice users with our robot, working in pairs (do to the quantity of available robots), on a computational thinking task in an hour long session. For the primary learning activity, which lasted thirty minutes, the students were asked to use a handheld, low-cost, tangible robot, *Cellulo* [5] to explore different paths on a paper map to find the optimal path, see Fig. 1a. Before the main activity, they had enough time to experience using the robots. During the activity, the students received feedback from the robot through LED lights that indicated the level of pretend battery, which depleted as the robot is moved on a route. During this activity, we collected the position of the robot on the map and remaining battery level to measure the exploration behavior of the students. More details about the experimental settings is available online[1].

After the path-finding activity, the students were given two short quizzes to assess their knowledge, one individual and one collaborative, before participating in a whole class debriefing activity. For the debriefing activity, a preliminary version of a dashboard was used that displayed the number of exploration trials (that robot is moved from home to target) that each team completed and battery level at target. During the debriefing, a member of the research team led a whole class session with the students to discuss these results and explained how the path-finding activity was tied to the concepts they were trying to learn, see Fig. 1b. Throughout the study, four experimenters conducted the activity and took field notes pertaining to the classroom orchestration. After the experiment, the research team discussed their observations to find common themes.

3 Challenges and Opportunities

We begin this section by evaluating the preliminary version of the dashboard used in the debriefing activity. Based on experimenters' observations, students

[1] https://github.com/chili-epfl/robot-analytics.

(a) Cellulo robot and a paper map (b) Debriefing activity

Fig. 1. An overview of the ER activity: (a) Children working on the path-finding activity with a Cellulo robot in pairs (b) Using an orchestration dashboard monitoring robot sensory data in a debriefing activity to explain learning goals and discuss children's performance

were very engaged in observing their own behaviours and the review helped them to understand the learning goal of the activity. Experimenters suggested that using data from an ER activity in a subsequent debriefing activity and functionalities of making data flow between ER activities and other activities in the classroom can be very useful for teachers. For example, a teacher can use students' activity data as an example to prove a point in his/her lecture or show the classroom performance on a central screen during an ER activity to increase competition between groups. In the continue of this section, the experimenters' notes and discussions around them are summarized as four points:

(1) Managing robot technical failures: All the experimenters insisted the emergence for monitoring the technical status of robots. In our case study, although the technical system had an overall acceptable performance, three robots failed during the activity and required intervention. In a classroom with one teacher rather than four experimenters, it could take some time for the teacher to be notified about the problem, which is not efficient time management. This case happened for us since the robot technical failures were hard to diagnose for experimenters during the session.

(2) Teacher control over robotic activities: Experimenters mentioned their interests to be able to control robots for fostering the meta-cognitive skills of the students, such as through changing the difficulty level of an activity or inhibiting the running of robots to regulate learners' reflection and stopping them from playing too much with the robot, which is one of the challenges with open-ended ER activities [2]. The latter could be achieved by providing simple orchestration commands over robots, like pausing them.

(3) Managing collaboration in ER group activities: Due to the cost of educational robots, in the group activities, one robot is shared between group members,

which could lead to social loafing as we also observed in our case study. Although this problem is not specific to ER classes, the interaction patterns that students have during the activity are different than traditional collaborative activities and the awareness and interventions need to be designed differently. An open question that arose from the experimenters' notes was: how can students' activity data with robots be used to raise teachers' awareness about social loafing and how can teachers intervene using control over robots to solve the problem?

(4) Improving teachers' distributed awareness: Experimenters mentioned several features of robots that can enhance teacher awareness: (1) in contrast to tablets or laptop screens, robots materialize learners' activity and collaboration patterns in groups on tables, giving the activity more visibility. (2) In learning tasks that require student interactions with both tablets and robots, like programming a robot, working with a robot reifies what is happening in the screen for teachers to see. In other words, instead of going to each group's desk and checking whether they finished the activity or cluttering the teacher dashboard with more information, teachers can easily understand the class performance by having a glance at all robots in the classroom, which is not possible with laptops/tablets.

4 Conclusion and Future Works

Taking into account the findings from observing our case study in the third section, we propose the following features in orchestrating tools for ER classrooms: The teacher dashboard should aware teachers about (1) robot technical status to notify teachers about technical problems and (2) students' interaction patterns with robots to represent students' progress and collaboration behaviour. Also, orchestrating tools should provide (1) teacher control over robots for interventions like meta-cognitive support for encouraging reflection and (2) aggregating students' activity data with robots in teachers' lectures and debriefing activities regarding our observation of implementing such a system. In the way of designing orchestration tools with the mentioned functionalities for ER classrooms, there are still important open questions such as: what type of information from students' activities with robots is useful for teachers, and considering the mentioned potentials of robots in providing awareness in classroom, can they be utilized as distributed orchestration tools instead of orchestral tools? We believe that answering these questions will create new insights to research on both educational robotics and orchestrating technology-enhanced learning.

References

1. Alimisis, D.: Educational robotics: open questions and new challenges. Themes Sci. Technol. Educ. **6**(1), 63–71 (2013)
2. Benitti, F.B.V.: Exploring the educational potential of robotics in schools: a systematic review. Comput. Educ. **58**(3), 978–988 (2012)

3. Dillenbourg, P.: Design for classroom orchestration. Comput. Educ. **69**, 485–492 (2013)
4. Jormanainen, I.: Supporting teachers in unpredictable robotics learning environments. Ph.D. thesis, University of Eastern Finland (2013)
5. Özgür, A., et al.: Cellulo: versatile handheld robots for education. In: 2017 12th ACM/IEEE International Conference on Human-Robot Interaction (HRI), pp. 119–127. IEEE (2017)

A Methodological Approach for Cross-Cultural Comparisons of Multimodal Emotional Expressions in Online Collaborative Learning Environments

Matthias Heintz[1](✉), Effie Law[1], Nigel Bannister[1], and Marlia Puteh[2]

[1] University of Leicester, Leicester LE1 7RH, UK
{mmh21,lcl9,nbl01}@le.ac.uk
[2] Universiti Teknologi Malaysia, 81310 Johor Bahru, Malaysia
marlia.kl@utm.my

Abstract. Online collaborative learning environments (OCLEs) can elicit from students different emotions, which affect their learning experience. Our work aimed to study whether emotions expressed by students with different cultural backgrounds when working in an OCLE were similar. In our empirical study, students from a UK university and a Malaysian university were grouped to solve tasks in an OCLE. We proposed a methodological approach for analysing the multimodal data (text, voice, image) captured, outlining a process for evaluating cross-cultural differences in emotional expressions in OCLEs.

Keywords: Emotions · Cross-cultural · Online collaborative learning environment

1 Introduction and Related Work

Research on emotions experienced by students in physical classrooms and factors influencing them can be dated back to a time long before the introduction of virtual classrooms [1]. One reason for this long-standing research interest is the influence of emotions on cognitive processes and learning outcomes. Students in a positive emotional state can achieve better results. However, inconsistent research findings show positive emotions can also distract students whereas negative ones can motivate them [2].

In online collaborative learning environments (OCLEs), students may experience emotions different from face-to-face settings, given the influence of technology, as evident by previous computer-mediated communication research. For our cross-cultural comparisons of emotions expressed by students, we utilized an OCLE to bring students from the UK and Malaysia together for collaborative learning experience. By analysing the emotions captured in the recordings of these sessions, differences, if any, between students with different cultural backgrounds can be identified.

For improving the accuracy of recognizing emotions, multimodal data analysis approaches have shown to be much more effective than uni-modal ones. Instead of relying on one channel from the learning environment, we analyse and cross-compare several (at least two) communication channels.

M. Scheffel et al. (Eds.): EC-TEL 2019, LNCS 11722, pp. 645–649, 2019.
https://doi.org/10.1007/978-3-030-29736-7_58

Shen et al. [4] developed a system to recognize emotions and adapt the learning environment accordingly. However, they used intrusive and motion-sensitive sensors for skin conductance, blood volume pressure, heart rate, and brain waves (EEG) to capture emotion signals, as opposed to the non-intrusive data collection through chat protocols, microphones, and webcams applied in our data collection process.

Vuorela and Nummenmaa [3] studied the emotional responses of students to an online learning environment. But their environment for collaborative group work only supported asynchronous comments and discussions. In addition, they interrupted the learning process by asking the learners to fill in a short questionnaire during their interaction with the system. To address these weaknesses, our OCLE enabled synchronous communications with different modalities – text, audio and video, which were recorded to capture the students' emotions without interrupting their learning process.

Our ultimate research goal is to verify empirically that augmenting data modality with images in addition to speech (text, audio) can further improve the accuracy of emotion recognition. The foremost and critical step is to develop a methodological approach for data collection and analysis.

2 Empirical Study

To address our research goal, we conducted two empirical studies with 14 (9 male, 5 female) and 15 (4 male, 11 female) undergraduates from a UK and a Malaysian university, respectively. All of them majored in physics or physics-related (e.g. engineering) subjects. In the two-hour sessions, they were grouped into five groups with five to six students each and worked on tasks pertaining to specific astronomy online laboratories (https://www.golabz.eu). The UK and Malaysian students attended the sessions physically in their respective computer labs (single-country local teams) and collaborated with their overseas counterparts (mixed-country remote teams).

In preparation of the first session the participants filled in consent forms and a questionnaire collecting general information. The respective sessions were kicked off with a short introduction by the lead of the Malaysian team, followed by the description of the learning content and tasks given by a UK physicist. After that, the students were split into pre-assigned groups, working collaboratively with their local as well as remote peers on the tasks set out by the research team. The OCLE platform we selected to use was BigBlueButton (https://bigbluebutton.org), because it is open source, making it flexible to be adapted for different users and contexts and allowing full control of data access. It was at the individual student's discretion which modality, text or audio, to communicate with their remote peers. Some students used webcam to share diagrams drawn. They could solicit help from the research team when needed.

To not interrupt the learning process, we did not apply traditional emotion sampling methods to collect self-reported data in real-time during the sessions. Instead, all three communication channels available to the students during the OCLE sessions were recorded for retrospective analysis. The resulting three datasets for each student allowed multimodal analysis of emotions expressed verbally (text chat or audio) and non-verbally (voices and facial expressions). While the pedagogical aspect of the online collaborative learning is relevant, due to the space constraint in this paper we focus on the technical and emotional aspect.

3 Methodological Approach

To facilitate adoption, our methodological approach has been built upon existing software solutions. With the webcam video data recording continuously the group work as part of the OCLE session, it was used to validate the emotions detected in one or both of the other channels. Note that text and audio data were only available when students wrote or said something; they were thus discontinuous. Figure 1 illustrates the methodological approach, which comprises four major steps.

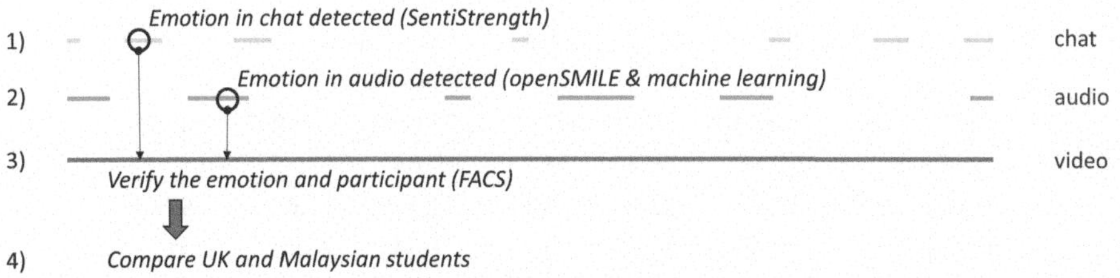

Fig. 1. Visualization of the methodological approach.

In the first step, the application *SentiStrength,* which has been proven to be accurate for the detection of emotions in small texts [5], is used for the analysis of the text chat data. For each negative or positive emotional expression, the timestamp is determined for the subsequent cross-check with the video image.

In the second step, *openSMILE* is used for acoustic feature extraction from the audio data. Emotion analysis is then performed with the extracted features and emotional corpora such as IEMOCAP [6], utilizing the ever-increasing sophisticated machine learning approaches such as Support Vector Machines (SVMs) and Deep Learning (see e.g. [7, 8]). Timestamps are extracted for the cross-check with the video.

In the third step, each identified emotion is cross-checked by at least two different researchers independently looking at the video recording at this timestamp. The Facial Action Coding System (FACS) [9] is used to code each emotion expressed by the participants. A subsequent comparison of the emotion identified in text or audio with the emotion coded from the video will be used to verify the emotion initially detected. In case an emotional expression from the same participant is available in all three channels, all will be compared to accurately determine the participant's emotion.

In the fourth step, the previous results are analysed to determine differences and similarities in emotions based on cultural background. To get a general first impression, the number of positive and negative emotions expressed by the UK and Malaysian students will be counted and the totals compared. Based on the timestamps a more detailed analysis will then be performed by looking at experiences that happened in parallel or close proximity to each other to determine if and how the emotions of students with different cultural backgrounds differ in the same situations and contexts.

4 Preliminary Results and Conclusion

While the multimodal analysis of the data collected during the empirical studies as described in Sect. 3 is ongoing, here we present some preliminary text chat analysis results in Table 1. In total the two cultural groups show differences, though not statistically significant (χ^2 (2) = 0.29, $p > .05$). Next steps will be the analysis of the remaining chat data, analysis of the audio data, and the cross-reference with the video data.

Table 1. Preliminary SentiStrength text chat analysis results of first session (in %).

Group number	Emotions by UK students			Emotions by Malaysian students		
	Negative	Neutral	Positive	Negative	Neutral	Positive
Group 1	9.80	76.47	13.73	9.64	73.49	16.87
Group 2	12.50	82.14	5.36	22.39	71.64	5.97
Group 3	9.52	80.95	9.52	1.54	86.15	12.31
Group 4	5.17	75.00	19.83	5.19	90.37	4.44
Group 5	9.09	81.82	9.09	7.45	73.40	19.15
Total	8.57	78.96	12.47	8.56	80.18	11.26

Identifying cultural differences and commonalities in participants' emotional responses when working in an OCLE, based on the methodological approach outlined above, will enable us to gain insights into design ideas for enhancing such a learning environment. This can then lead to design guidelines for cross-cultural OCLEs.

References

1. Ripple, R.E.: Affective factors influence classroom learning. Educ. Leadersh. **22**(7), 476–491 (1965)
2. Knörzer, L., Brünken, R., Park, B.: Facilitators or suppressors: effects of experimentally induced emotions on multimedia learning. Learn. Instr. **44**, 97–107 (2016)
3. Vuorela, M., Nummenmaa, L.: Experienced emotions, emotion regulation and student activity in a web-based learning environment. Eur. J. Psychol. Educ. **19**(4), 423–436 (2004)
4. Shen, L., Wang, M., Shen, R.: Affective e-learning: using "emotional" data to improve learning in pervasive learning environment. J. Educ. Technol. Soc. **12**(2), 176–189 (2009)
5. Thelwall, M., Buckley, K., Paltoglou, G., Cai, D., Kappas, A.: Sentiment strength detection in short informal text. JASIST **61**(12), 2544–2558 (2010)
6. Busso, C., et al.: IEMOCAP: interactive emotional dyadic motion capture database. Lang. Resour. Eval. **42**(4), 335 (2008)

7. Soleimani, S., Law, E.L.C.: What can self-reports and acoustic data analyses on emotions tell us? In: Proceedings ACM DIS, pp. 489–501 (2017)
8. Schuller, B.W.: Speech emotion recognition: two decades in a nut-shell, benchmarks, and ongoing trends. Commun. ACM **61**(5), 90–99 (2018)
9. Ekman, R.: What the Face Reveals: Basic and Applied Studies of Spontaneous Expression Using the Facial Action Coding System (FACS). Oxford University Press, Oxford (1997)

Auditing the Accessibility of MOOCs: A Four-Component Approach

Francisco Iniesto[1(✉)], Patrick McAndrew[1], Shailey Minocha[2], and Tim Coughlan[1]

[1] Institute of Educational Technology, The Open University, Milton Keynes, UK
{francisco.iniesto, patrick.mcandrew, tim.coughlan}@open.ac.uk
[2] School of Computing and Communications, The Open University, Milton Keynes, UK
shailey.minocha@open.ac.uk

Abstract. This paper reports the design of a four-component audit to evaluate the accessibility of Massive Open Online Courses (MOOCs). The MOOC accessibility audit was designed as part of a research programme at The Open University (UK) that aimed to assess the current state of accessibility of MOOC platforms and resources, to uncover accessibility barriers, and to derive recommendations on how the barriers could be addressed. The audit is composed of four evaluation components: technical accessibility, user experience (UX), quality and learning design. The audit consists of four processes supported by checklists corresponding to each of the four components implemented via a heuristic evaluation approach, an evaluation technique from Human-Computer Interaction literature.

Keywords: MOOCs · Accessibility audit · Heuristic evaluation · Human-Computer Interaction · Usability · User experience · Quality · Learning design

1 Introduction

The pedagogical and visual design of MOOCs, their information architecture, usability and interaction design can have a negative impact on learners' engagement [1]. In particular for disabled learners there are accessibility barriers that can affect the learners' experience; these barriers are not only in access to the technology, but the way educational resources are pedagogically designed.

A study from Blackboard [2] assessing the overall accessibility of content in online courses over a 5-year period from 2012 to 2017 identified that the progress in making accessible educational resources has been slow, describing such materials as having become *"only slightly more accessible"*. The study showed the value of an automated process to help quantify the issues that need to be addressed and supports the need to provide processes for making MOOCs accessible for disabled learners.

Rodrigo and Iniesto [3] also argue the need to provide a holistic vision for creating accessible MOOCs. As part of a research programme at The Open University

M. Scheffel et al. (Eds.): EC-TEL 2019, LNCS 11722, pp. 650–654, 2019.
https://doi.org/10.1007/978-3-030-29736-7_59

(UK) interviews were carried out with MOOC providers and learners [4] which showed that issues extended beyond the technical considerations that are typically considered in accessibility testing and compliance. In this paper several accessibility evaluation methods are brought together into an accessibility audit to evaluate MOOCs, to provide indicators of the accessibility barriers and to propose processes to address them.

2 MOOC Accessibility Audit

The methodology in the audit combines existing or adapted methods from four main evaluation areas to provide four checklists that can be applied in a heuristic evaluation approach. The selection of these components combines different aspects of accessibility to provide a holistic approach, evaluating not only technical aspects related to accessibility but also the experience of learners [5], the quality of the educational resources produced and its pedagogical design, the four components are:

1. **Technical Accessibility evaluation.** Conformance to guidelines and standards through WCAG[1], with additional analysis of the text-based files [6].
2. **User experience (UX) evaluation.** Evaluation of usability and user experience characteristics of the user interface design and pedagogical design with cognitive and UX walkthroughs [7].
3. **Quality evaluation.** Assessing the properties of MOOCs, the quality of the design, platform and support for learners adapting an approach from OpenupEd [8].
4. **Learning design evaluation.** Evaluation of the learning design characteristics within MOOCs through Universal Design for Learning (UDL) [9].

2.1 Technical Accessibility Evaluation

WCAG-EM[2] methodology was designed for experts to follow a common approach for evaluating the conformance of websites to WCAG. The use of WCAG is a standardised and commonly used instrument for accessibility evaluation in MOOCs [5]. WCAG-EM has been designed with a heuristic evaluation approach in mind and based on previous methodologies such as Unified Web Evaluation Methodology (UWEM). Due to its extensive use, WCAG was the selected standard for the accessibility evaluation of the audit applying AAA conformance level (the most restrictive) adding evaluation of text-based files commonly used in MOOCs such as PDFs.

2.2 User Experience Evaluation

UX evaluation takes the approach of usability inspections following cognitive walkthroughs that include two separate activities: the use of personas and scenarios [7]. This component required new development as an established reference set for accessibility is not available. A set of engaging personas perspective was developed, which incorporate

[1] WCAG https://www.w3.org/WAI/standards-guidelines/wcag/.

[2] WCAG-EM https://www.w3.org/TR/WCAG-EM/.

goal-directed personas [10]. Engaging personas take a realistic description of people to draw evaluators into the lives of the personas, and so avoid stereotypical stories that focus only on behaviours rather than considering the whole person. To gain a focus on accessibility, these personas were abstracted from self-description of disabled learners interviewed in related research in MOOCs [4].

The narrative scenarios were developed from the scenarios used in a major European project (EU4ALL) reviewed to be reused in MOOCs [11]. The set of cognitive walkthroughs is complemented with UX walkthroughs oriented to the learning design as used in the Fluid project[3]. UX walkthrough is a synthesis of methods that enables the evaluator to make assessments both from the learner's point of view and of a design expert. In this case, the aim is to check if the designed tasks within the MOOC are feasible to be achieved by the personas.

2.3 Quality Evaluation

Quality evaluation was adapted from the OpenupEd quality label influenced by the Quality Code at the Quality Assurance Agency (QAA) and based on the E-xcellence[4] approach of using a benchmark for quality assessment in MOOCs [8]. The label has been used to evaluate the quality in MOOC platforms such as FutureLearn and UNED Abierta [12]. There have been several projects about quality in MOOCs within OpenupEd: Score2020 and BizMOOC. The tested version of the checklists produced and available under creative commons (CC) licence was adapted to provide an evaluative perspective for this audit component.

2.4 Learning Design Evaluation

MOOCs by definition aim for *"massiveness"*, which leads to difficulties in taking a personalised approach, though makes them suitable for a universal design approach to evaluate the learning design. Universal design considers how to meet the needs of all learners through design. The approach selected for this audit component to evaluate the learning design has been UDL, due to its greater development and its widespread use [13]. The UDL approach is to present the information in ways that fit learners' needs, rather than requiring learners to adapt to the information [9]. This approach is relevant to understand learners who may like to adjust the curriculum to their needs rather than them to the curriculum. This component required new development to apply UDL in the context of MOOCs.

[3] Fluid Project https://wiki.fluidproject.org/display/fluid/Design+Handbook.

[4] E-xcellence https://e-xcellencelabel.eadtu.eu/.

3 Conclusions and Future Work

A four-component audit has been designed for improving the accessibility in MOOCs for disabled learners from an expert evaluation perspective. The components for standards compliance, quality and learning design were developed by adapting existing tools after extensive research on the available options. User experience personas have also been built from interviews with learners. At this stage:

- The audit has been validated by ten experts through inter-rater reliability evaluations to establish usefulness as a tool to identify and address accessibility barriers.
- The audit has been trialled by application to MOOCs from four providers to help to understand the current state of accessibility in MOOCs: FutureLearn, Coursera, edX and Canvas.

The validation and implementations suggest the audit is a robust tool with the following advantages: visualisation of the results; overlap between components and the strength of the criteria; and complementarity in the checklists. The aim of the audit is to derive recommendations to address accessibility barriers. The processes of validation and implementation allow barriers to be identified and also facilitate discussions to address them in the MOOC design stages. Future work with the audit includes: evaluating further platforms; evaluating several MOOCs per platform; refinement of the audit itself; and involvement of stakeholders in the evaluation process.

References

1. Liyanagunawardena, T.R., Parslow, P., Williams, S.: Dropout: MOOC participants' perspective (2014)
2. Straumsheim, C.: Glacial Progress' on Digital Accessibility. Inside Higher Ed. https://www.insidehighered.com/news/2017/05/18/data-show-small-improvements-accessibility-course-materials. Accessed 13 May 2019
3. Rodrigo, C., Iniesto, F.: Holistic vision for creating accessible services based on MOOCs. In: Open Education Global Conference 2015. Innovation and Entrepreneurship, Banff, Alberta, Canada (2015)
4. Iniesto, F., McAndrew, P., Minocha, S., Coughlan, T.: An investigation into the perspectives of providers and learners on MOOC accessibility. In: TEEM 2017: International Conference Technological Ecosystems for Enhancing Multiculturality, Cadiz, Spain, 18–20 October 2017 (2017)
5. Iniesto, F., McAndrew, P., Minocha, S., Coughlan, T.: Auditing the accessibility of massive open online courses (MOOCs). In: 14th AAATE Congress 2017, Sheffield, 13–14 September 2017 (2017)
6. Sanchez-Gordon, S., Luján-Mora, S.: Research challenges in accessible MOOCs: a systematic literature review 2008–2016. Univ. Access Inf. Soc. **17**, 775–789 (2017)
7. Rieman, J., Franzke, M., Redmiles, D.: Usability evaluation with the cognitive walkthrough. In: CHI 1995 Conference Companion, pp. 387–388 (1995)
8. Kear, K., et al.: Quality assessment for e-learning: a benchmarking approach. European Association of Distance Teaching Universities (2016)

9. Meyer, A., Rose, D.H., Gordon, D.T.: Universal Design for Learning: Theory and Practice. CAST Professional Publishing, Wakefield (2014)
10. Floyd, I.R., Cameron Jones, M., Twidale, M.B.: Resolving incommensurable debates: a preliminary identification of persona kinds, attributes, and characteristics. Artifact **2**(1), 12–26 (2008)
11. Rodríguez-Ascaso, A., Boticario, J.G.: Accessibility and MOOC: towards a holistic perspective. RIED: Revista Iberoamericana de Educación a Distancia **18**, 61–85 (2015)
12. Jansen, D., Rosewell, J., Kear, K.: Quality frameworks for MOOCs. In: Jemni, M., Kinshuk, Khribi, M. (eds.) Open Education: from OERs to MOOCs. Lecture Notes in Educational Technology, pp. 261–281. Springer, Heidelberg (2017). https://doi.org/10.1007/978-3-662-52925-6_14
13. Gronseth, S., Dalton, E., Khanna, R., Alvarez, B., Iglesias, I., Vergara, P.: Inclusive instructional design and UDL around the world. In: Society for Information Technology & Teacher Education International Conference, pp. 2357–2359 (2019)

Metacognitive Processes and Self-regulation in the Use of Automated Writing Evaluation Programs

Ana Isabel Hibert(✉)

University of Edinburgh, Edinburgh EH8 8AJ, UK
ana.hibert@ed.ac.uk

Abstract. Automated writing evaluation (AWE) programs are increasingly being used to offer formative evaluation to English as a second language (ESL) students. Some critics are concerned that the use of AWE programs may encourage students to uncritically accept their often-flawed feedback and that this will impede the development of their writing skills. This paper details the results of a pilot study conducted on 11 ESL postgraduate students who used an AWE program to revise their dissertations. The pilot study found evidence to suggest that, far from uncritically accepting the AWE-generated feedback, students employed metacognitive strategies to engage with feedback they received and their knowledge of their own writing skills. These strategies include reflecting on how the feedback fits within the genre of academic writing, noticing of common trends in the feedback received, reflecting on advice received by supervisors and previous schooling, and the reasons they chose a particular writing form. The paper concludes by reflecting on how research into AWE tools might help us understand the development of metacognitive monitoring skills in students and how these technologies can be implemented in classrooms to promote the development of writing skills.

Keywords: Self-regulated learning · Automated Writing Evaluation · Technology-enhanced learning · Metacognitive monitoring

1 Metacognition and AWE Technologies

Metacognition, as one of the key processes used by learners in the self-regulation of their learning [1], has been thought to play an integral part in the successful adoption of new technologies as learning tools [2]. Evidence suggests that metacognition influences the quality of student interaction with tools, as the ability to use them strategically can be considered a metacognitive ability [3]. Students need to be aware of their own learning problems and regulate their learning to effectively use tools.

Most research on metacognition and the use of learning technologies has focused on structured learning management systems (LMS) and digital environments that provide learning content and activities, but little attention has been paid to unstructured learning opportunities such as those afforded by Automated Writing Evaluation (AWE).

AWE programs were originally designed to automatically provide summative feedback and evaluate written texts, although they have increasingly been used to

M. Scheffel et al. (Eds.): EC-TEL 2019, LNCS 11722, pp. 655–658, 2019.
https://doi.org/10.1007/978-3-030-29736-7_60

provide formative evaluation in English as second language (ESL) and English as foreign language (EFL) classrooms in response to the increasing number of students [4, 5]. However, research on the effectiveness of AWE programs as formative feedback tools is both scarce and methodologically fragmented [6, 7], making it difficult to draw any strong conclusions.

Some researchers have voiced concerns about the use of AWE technologies to provide feedback because of the formulaic nature of the feedback, the mistakes a computer makes when trying to interpret natural language and the fear that students will uncritically accept it's feedback [8]. Therefore, if we want to address these issues in the use of AWE technologies to give students formative feedback, it is not enough that it corrects student texts, but that it gives them the tools they need to reflect on their writing and develop the metacognitive abilities to construct and regulate their learning.

The present pilot study was designed to look into whether students employed any metacognitive strategies while using an AWE program to revise their written texts.

2 Methodology

The pilot study was conducted during the summer of 2018. Eleven postgraduate students were recruited from a research-intensive university in the United Kingdom. The participants self-selected after an invitation e-mail was sent to students who had enrolled in writing workshops in the previous academic year.

The ProWritingAid program was selected for this study as it is very typical of AWE programs in that it not only provides feedback on grammar and spelling, but also on style, composition and sentence structure, among other categories, as well as containing additional tools like a thesaurus and resources explaining English grammar.

A think-aloud protocol was the main tool for collecting data. During four sessions of half an hour each, the students revised sections of their dissertation using ProWritingAid while describing their actions and talking about their impressions of the program. At the end of the fourth session, a brief interview was conducted with them to gain more insight into their strategies for using the feedback provided.

The think-aloud transcripts were analysed and coded for five metacognitive processes adapted from Sonnenberg and Bannert [9]: goal setting, planning, judging information, monitoring and feeling of knowing. These codes were used to analyse how the students used these metacognitive strategies to engage with the feedback, monitor their English writing skills and reflect on their texts as belonging to the broader genre of academic writing.

3 Results

Analysing the transcripts revealed that the students employed metacognitive strategies to make sense of the feedback they received in different ways, which are summarised in Table 1.

By engaging with the feedback through the different metacognitive processes, participants reflected on their own knowledge of English writing. Most of the

Table 1. Employment of metacognitive strategies by the participants

Metacognitive process	Usage
Goal setting	Making notes of concepts to look up in the future Signal out parts of the text that need more comprehensive revision in the future
Planning	Using feedback previously offered by the program to plan a writing session
Judging information	Reflecting on how AWE feedback fits within the genre of academic writing Comparing AWE feedback to previous feedback received by supervisors
Monitoring	Judging the perceived distance between their writing and standard English grammar Monitoring the quality of their writing as compared to other academic texts

participants used their metacognitive skills to put the AWE-generated feedback within the context of their previous knowledge of academic English writing or feedback they had received from other sources, and they were able to identify patterns within the feedback they received. Fears that automated feedback would result in the loss of individual voices and formulaic writing therefore were unsupported by the results of the current study.

Out of the 11 students in the sample, at least 10 used some metacognitive strategy to engage with the feedback they received from the AWE program. While the sample was limited, there is evidence to believe that students did not just blindly accept feedback. This seems to align with the findings from Cotos [10], who found that learners who received AWE feedback engaged in "focus on discourse form, noticing of negative evidence, improved rhetorical quality, and increased learning gains" (p. 444). Preliminary evidence, therefore, suggests that AWE feedback could be useful for students not only in revising their texts, but in promoting metacognitive skills needed to reflect on their use of English and the steps they need to improve their writing in that language.

4 Conclusions

Evidence from this pilot study suggests students use metacognitive skills to engage with the feedback they receive from AWE programs. However, many of these skills rely on having previous knowledge of English grammar, knowledge of the genre and on having received previous feedback from teachers or supervisors regarding writing skills. Therefore, while AWE feedback can be used as a scaffold to help students reflect about their writing skills, for it to be effective it needs to be accompanied by previous knowledge on which metacognition will act upon. For these programs to be effective as a formative learning tool, they need to be paired up with teacher instruction that gives the students the knowledge they need to reflect on the feedback received from the AWE program. Future research into AWE programs, therefore, also needs to focus on how they can be used as a tool to promote reflection on the skills learned in the classroom and apply and develop their metacognitive skills.

The current study was limited by the small number of participants and the short amount of time the intervention lasted, as well as by the experimental conditions. Prompting the students to reflect and speak about their activity may make them engage in metacognitive activities when they otherwise would not have. A larger-scale study is being conducted over a period of 5 weeks to research self-regulation and learner engagement with their texts as a result of receiving AWE-generated feedback in non-experimental conditions, by allowing the students to engage with the program naturally. This study will delve into how their texts evolve as a response to the feedback by comparing different versions and retrieving timestamps on the software to analyse their engagement.

References

1. Butler, D.L., Winne, P.H.: Feedback and self-regulated learning: a theoretical synthesis. Rev. Educ. Res. **65**(3), 245–281 (1995)
2. Gašević, D., Mirriahi, N., Dawson, S., Joksimović, S.: Effects of instructional conditions and experience on the adoption of a learning tool. Comput. Hum. Behav. **67**, 207–220 (2017)
3. Clarebout, G., Elen, J., Collazo, N.A.J., Lust, G., Jiang, L.: Metacognition and the use of tools. In: Azevedo, R., Aleven, V. (eds.) International Handbook of Metacognition and Learning Technologies. SIHE, vol. 28, pp. 187–195. Springer, New York (2013). https://doi.org/10.1007/978-1-4419-5546-3_13
4. Stevenson, M.: A critical interpretative synthesis: the integration of automated writing evaluation into classroom writing instruction. Comput. Compos. **42**, 1–16 (2016)
5. Ranalli, J., Link, S., Chukharev-hudilainen, E.: Automated writing evaluation for formative assessment of second language writing: investigating the accuracy and usefulness of feedback as part of argument-based validation. Educ. Psychol. **37**(1), 8–25 (2017)
6. Stevenson, M., Phakiti, A.: The effects of computer-generated feedback on the quality of writing. Assess. Writ. **19**, 51–65 (2014)
7. Wang, P.: Can automated writing evaluation programs help students improve their english writing? Int. J. Appl. Linguist. English Lit. **2**(1), 6–12 (2013)
8. Chen, C.-F., Cheng, W.-Y.E.: Beyond the design of automated writing evaluation: pedagogical practices and perceived learning effectiveness in EFL writing classes. Lang. Learn. Technol. **12**(2), 94–112 (2008)
9. Sonnenberg, C., Bannert, M.: Discovering the effects of metacognitive prompts on the sequential structure of SRL-processes using process mining techniques. J. Learn. Anal. **2**(1), 72–100 (2015)
10. Cotos, E.: Potential of automated writing evaluation feedback. CALICO J. **28**(2), 420–459 (2011)
11. Van Beuningen, C.: Corrective feedback in L2 writing: theoretical perspectives, empirical insights and future directions. Int. J. English Stud. **10**(2), 1–27 (2010)

Automated Scoring of Self-explanations Using Recurrent Neural Networks

Marilena Panaite[1], Stefan Ruseti[1], Mihai Dascalu[1,2(✉)], Renu Balyan[3], Danielle S. McNamara[3], and Stefan Trausan-Matu[1,2]

[1] Faculty of Automatic Control and Computers, University "Politehnica" of Bucharest, 313 Splaiul Independenței, 60042 Bucharest, Romania
marilena.panaite@gmail.com, {stefan.ruseti, mihai.dascalu, stefan.trausan}@cs.pub.ro

[2] Academy of Romanian Scientists, Splaiul Independenței 54, 050094 Bucharest, Romania

[3] Institute for the Science of Teaching and Learning, Arizona State University, PO Box 872111, Tempe, AZ 85287, USA
{renu.balyan, dsmcnama}@asu.edu

Abstract. Intelligent Tutoring Systems (ITSs) focus on promoting knowledge acquisition, while providing relevant feedback during students' practice. Self-explanation practice is an effective method used to help students understand complex texts by leveraging comprehension. Our aim is to introduce a deep learning neural model for automatically scoring student self-explanations that are targeted at specific sentences. The first stage of the processing pipeline performs an initial text cleaning and applies a set of predefined rules established by human experts in order to identify specific cases (e.g., students who do not understand the text, or students who simply copy and paste their self-explanations from the given input text). The second step uses a Recurrent Neural Network with pre-trained Glove word embeddings to predict self-explanation scores on a scale of 1 to 3. In contrast to previous SVM models trained on the same dataset of 4109 self-explanations, we obtain a significant increase of accuracy from 59% to 73%. Moreover, the new pipeline can be integrated in learning scenarios requiring near real-time responses from the ITS, thus addressing a major limitation in terms of processing speed exhibited by the previous approach.

Keywords: Natural Language Processing · Comprehensive tutoring system · Self-explanations · Recurrent Neural Network

1 Introduction

Learning involves integration of new information into prior knowledge [1]. In this case, reading a text is not a guaranty that students have acknowledged new presented terms and that they have made connections with prior learned terms. Self-explanation facilitates this process and improves comprehension by encouraging students to engage in both metacognition and inference generation [1]. However, providing individual

M. Scheffel et al. (Eds.): EC-TEL 2019, LNCS 11722, pp. 659–663, 2019.
https://doi.org/10.1007/978-3-030-29736-7_61

feedback to each student self-explanation is cumbersome and cannot be easily scaled by tutors without the help of Intelligent Tutoring Systems. In this regard, automated systems that provide help for scoring students' self-explanations can speed up the process.

The aim of this study is to train a Recurrent Neural Network (RNN) [2] to improve the automated score prediction of the student's self-explanations. The trained RNN model is then integrated into the new workflow in the state-of-the-art tutoring system - Interactive Strategy Training for Active Reading and Thinking (iSTART) [3] which is a web-based ITS created to improve adolescent students' comprehension of complex scientific texts. In order to help them, iSTART utilizes non-game and game-based generative practice, in which learners produce their own self-explanations, and game-based identification practice, in which learners attempt to identify which strategy is being used in certain self-explanations.

With the help of the iSTART practice, the full pipeline of the Intelligent Tutoring System uses advanced Natural Language Processing (NLP) techniques for extracting the main features of the automatically scored explanations. In this regard, the ReaderBench framework [4] offers a variety of NLP techniques, all grounded in Cohesion Network Analysis. Our updated pipeline computes textual complexity indices for the input target texts and corresponding explanations that are further used in the rule system, whereas an RNN model is used to automatically assess the quality of a student's explanation in term of metacognition and capacity to infer new knowledge.

2 Integrated Workflow with RNN Model

The corpus used to train the model contains 4,109 self-explanations from 277 high-school students on two science texts, namely "Heart Diseases" ($\sim$300 words) and "Red Blood Cell" ($\sim$280 words). Each text contains nine target sentences. To assess the performance of students, two experts evaluated the student's self-explanations, assigning scores from 0 (poor) to 3 (great). The human experts performed two rounds of scoring 60% of the entire dataset and achieved a high interrater reliability (Kappa = .81).

Our approach provides an integrated workflow that can compute an automated score for each self-explanation with relevant feedback. The first step performs cleaning the input data using a spell-check algorithm and the NLP processing pipeline from ReaderBench [4]. The second step of the pipeline consists of predefined rules that identify poorly written self-explanations. For example, a rule checks whether a self-explanation contains more than 75% frozen expressions by comparing the text with a predefined set of regular expressions. Moreover, copy and paste from the target sentence is also checked. We also identify the new concepts introduced by the student in the response, by checking words that are neither synonyms nor identical lemmas of the words present in the target sentence. If there are no new concepts introduced, students receive a score of 1 (fair) with corresponding feedback (e.g., "Can you add more information to explain what the text means?"). After making specific inferences using the rule-based system, the remaining self-explanations are assessed using an automated scoring system.

For the current approach we rely on an RNN model [2] wherein (a) Gated Recurrent Units (GRUs) [5] are used to represent the target sentences, and (b) Bidirectional Gated Recurrent Units (BiGRU) represent self-explanation obtained from student responses. After the encoding phase, each output matrix is reduced to a fixed size by retaining only the most meaningful features using an attention mechanism. The network uses max-pooling for obtaining the maximum of each sentence encoding matrix. Further, the outputs are concatenated, and a dropout regularization mechanism is used in order to avoid overfitting. A hidden layer of size 50 with sigmoid activation function is then added. The last step uses a softmax layer and computes the probabilities to classify the self-explanations into one of the three classes that reflect the quality of the self-explanation (Fig. 1).

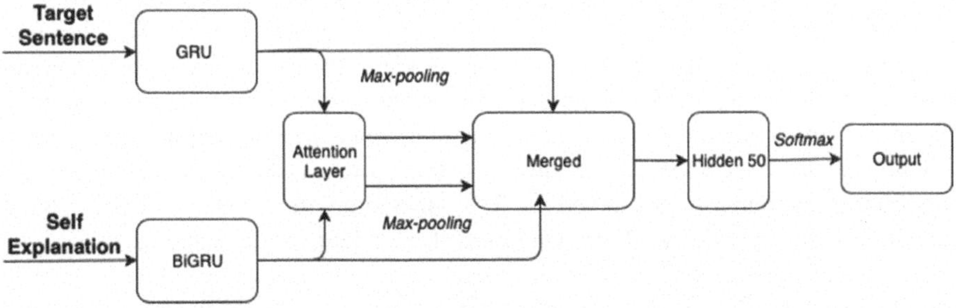

Fig. 1. Architecture of RNN model used for automated scoring.

In the final version of the model, sentences (target and self-explanations) were encoded using Glove-300d word embeddings [6] which provided the best overall results, but we experimented with other embeddings (e.g., Glove-100d, FastText) and obtained an accuracy that was 1–2% lower.

3 Results and Discussion

The current paper introduces major improvements to the automated scoring system for self-explanations by considering deep learning models in place of SVMs. The rule system for predicting poor (0) and fair (1) scores was retained from the previous version of the automated pipeline, while the SVM model trained with the textual complexity indices from ReaderBench was replaced with the RNN trained using Glove-300 for encoding the target sentences and the self-explanations of the students. In the initial SVM experiments, the best accuracy obtained was 59%. Using the same pre-checked rule-based system, the pre-trained RNN model was used to score the self-explanations; the best accuracy obtained in this case was 73.6%.

Another indication of the accuracy of a model is adjacent accuracy, which is assessed by calculating the proportion of automated scores that differ by no more than 1 from the expert scores. The best adjacent accuracy was 97% for the SVM [7] indicating that, although the accuracy was 59%, the automated scoring model was close to the expert scores. The same metric was computed for the updated pipeline that uses the RNN trained model; the model achieved an adjacent accuracy of 93.87%, which was slightly lower than the previous SVM model.

Moreover, the new approach eliminated the need for computing linguistic features and introduced the RNN model which only needs to encode the input data using Glove-300-word embeddings. Our results indicate that the use of deep learning models with specific NLP techniques can improve the performance of the overall system and perform better in terms of time and accuracy than classic machine learning models [8].

The current study is principally limited by the dataset, which includes only two target texts. Hence, one consideration concerns generalization of the model to other texts and populations. Our limitation stems from the resources necessary to have self-explanations (reliably) scored by experts. We will continue to explore more affordable options such as crowdsourcing for both explanation and their respective scores.

Another cautionary note stems from low accuracy achieved for self-explanations that received a score of 3 by experts. The model performance is higher than that reported by the previous SVM model, but the new model still struggles to make inferences similar to those generated by humans when judging explanations that go well beyond the text. One way to improve the score would be to include specific features for detecting scores noted as 3 by including the scores and the relevant embeddings from previous self-explanations of a student for the same text.

Acknowledgments. This work was supported by a grant of the Romanian National Authority for Scientific Research and Innovation, CNCS – UEFISCDI, project number PN-III 72PCCDI/2018, ROBIN – "Roboții și Societatea: Sisteme Cognitive pentru Roboți Personali și Vehicule Autonome", the Department of Education, Institute of Education Sciences - Grant R305A130124 and R305A190063, and the Department of Defense, Office of Naval Research - Grants N00014140343 and N000141712300.

References

1. Chi, M.T., De Leeuw, N., Chiu, M.-H., LaVancher, C.: Eliciting self-explanations improves understanding. Cogn. Sci. **18**(3), 439–477 (1994)
2. Sundermeyer, M., Ney, H., Schlüter, R.: From feedforward to recurrent LSTM neural networks for language modeling. IEEE Trans. Audio Speech Lang. Process. **23**(3), 517–529 (2015)
3. McNamara, D.S., O'Reilly, T.P., Rowe, M., Boonthum, C., Levinstein, I.B.: iSTART: a web-based tutor that teaches self-explanation and metacognitive reading strategies. In: McNamara, D.S. (ed.) Reading comprehension strategies: Theories, interventions, and technologies, pp. 397–420. Erlbaum, Mahwah, NJ (2007)
4. Dascalu, M., McNamara, D.S., Trausan-Matu, S., Allen, L.K.: Cohesion network analysis of CSCL participation. Behav. Res. Methods, 1–16 (2017)
5. Chung, J., Gulcehre, C., Cho, K., Bengio, Y.: Empirical evaluation of gated recurrent neural networks on sequence modeling. arXiv preprint arXiv:1412.3555 (2014)
6. Pennington, J., Socher, R., Manning, C.: Glove: Global vectors for word representation. In: Empirical Methods in Natural Language Processing (EMNLP), pp. 1532–1543 (2014)

7. Panaite, M., et al.: Bring it on! challenges encountered while building a comprehensive tutoring system using ReaderBench. In: International Conference on AI in Ed., pp. 409–419. Springer (2018)
8. Balyan, R., McCarthy, K.S., McNamara, D.S.: Comparing machine learning classification approaches for predicting expository text difficulty. In: The Thirty-First International Flairs Conference (FLAIRS 31), pp. 421–426. AAAI, Melbourne, FL (2018)

Exploring the Triangulation of Dimensionality Reduction When Interpreting Multimodal Learning Data from Authentic Settings

Pankaj Chejara[1(✉)], Luis P. Prieto[1], Adolfo Ruiz-Calleja[2], María Jesús Rodríguez-Triana[1], and Shashi Kant Shankar[1]

[1] Tallinn University, Tallinn, Estonia
{pankajch,lprisan,mjrt,shashik}@tlu.ee
[2] GSIC-EMIC Group, University of Valladolid, Valladolid, Spain
adolfo@gsic.uva.es

Abstract. Multimodal Learning Analytics (MMLA) has sparked researcher interest in investigating learning in real-world settings by capturing learning traces from multiple sources of data. Though multimodal data offers a more holistic picture of learning, its inherent complexity makes it difficult to understand and interpret. This paper illustrates the use of dimensionality reduction (DR) to find a simple representation of multimodal learning data collected from co-located collaboration in authentic settings. We employed multiple DR methods and used triangulation to interpret their result which in turn provided a more simplistic representation. Additionally, we also show how unexpected events in authentic settings (e.g., missing data) can affect the analysis results.

Keywords: Co-located collaboration · Multimodal Learning Analytics · Dimensionality reduction method · Computer-supported collaborative learning

1 Introduction

Learning Analytics (LA) approaches are often based on digital traces, which offer only a partial picture of learning [1]. MMLA has the potential to address this issue by providing a more holistic picture of learning taking place across (physical and digital) spaces [2]. Due to the challenges associated with the deployment of MMLA (e.g., complex setups and interference in the learning activity), most MMLA studies are conducted in laboratory settings [3]. Using MMLA in authentic settings usually requires technical support, and the absence of such support (or unexpected events) can affect the data quality and, consequently, the reliability of their analysis. To address these issues in real classroom practices, we explore the use of Dimensionality Reduction (DR) methods to extract a simpler representation of MMLA data which can eventually help different stakeholders

M. Scheffel et al. (Eds.): EC-TEL 2019, LNCS 11722, pp. 664–667, 2019.
https://doi.org/10.1007/978-3-030-29736-7_62

(e.g., teachers and researchers) in understanding teaching and learning practices. Particularly, we explore DR-based analysis on the data gathered across spaces from two authentic learning settings to extract information regarding learner group's engagement in co-located collaboration (CC).

2 Proposed DR-Based Method

Our proposed DR-based process includes following steps:

1. **Data preprocessing.** It preprocesses the collected multimodal data which involves extracting features from raw digital traces, e.g., counting the number of log entries of a particular kind in a certain time window.
2. **Data aggregation.** It performs a feature-level fusion of data from different sources.
3. **Data scaling.** It transforms the value of the features into the same data range to avoid the effect of uneven data range on analysis.
4. **Dimensionality reduction.** It uses well-known DR methods to map high-dimensional data into a lower number of dimensions (while preserving most of the variance in the dataset).
5. **Correlation computation.** This step computes the correlation between original features and DR dimensions (obtained after applying DR).
6. **Interpretation.** This step interprets the DR dimensions on the basis of correlation and uses triangulation to support it.

3 Two Case Studies

We collected multimodal data (logs and observations) from two collaboration activities conducted in authentic classroom conditions. These activities involved the use of Graasp[1] – a digital environment for inquiry learning. Aside from the logs from student activities on Graasp, structured observations were also gathered every 5 min by human observers, on six binary variables at the individual level: disengaged (i.e., the student is totally disengaged from the task), talking (the student is talking about the task), looking (the student is looking at others doing the task), intTech (the student is interacting with technology to solve the task), intExt (the student is interacting with teachers and other actors outside the group), and intRes (the student is interacting with learning resources such as paper notebooks, to solve the task). Table 1 shows the details of the two cases. In case-1, there were no data missing. However, in case-2, three logs attributes were missing and only one was available.

As part of the first step (see previous section), we pre-processed the Graasp logs and extracted simple log-based features, by counting the log entries of various kinds (e.g., access, update, delete, create) in each observation window. We thus unified the data sources to an uniform sample rate of one data point every 5 min.

[1] https://graasp.eu/.

Table 1. Characteristics of learning scenarios.

Case	Dataset (no. of records)	Students	Groups	Group size	Total duration
Case-1	77 observations + 77 logs	22	10	2–3	3 h 19 m
Case-2	167 observations + 167 logs	22	5	4–5	3 h 28 m

In the second step, observations were aggregated at the group level by averaging the individual observation. Later on, these group-level observation features were combined with the aforementioned log features. In the third step, we normalized the data using the standard scaling method. In the fourth step, we employed Principal Component Analysis (PCA), Multiple Factor analysis (MFA), t-distributed Stochastic Neighbor Embedding (t-SNE) and Isomap, to transform our high-dimension data (i.e., 10 features per data point) into different lower-dimension spaces. In the fifth step, we computed Pearson's correlation between the original features and the new DR-based dimensions. Figure 1 shows the correlation matrix for each case study[2].

3.1 Results

In this section, we present our interpretation of DR dimensions found in each case.

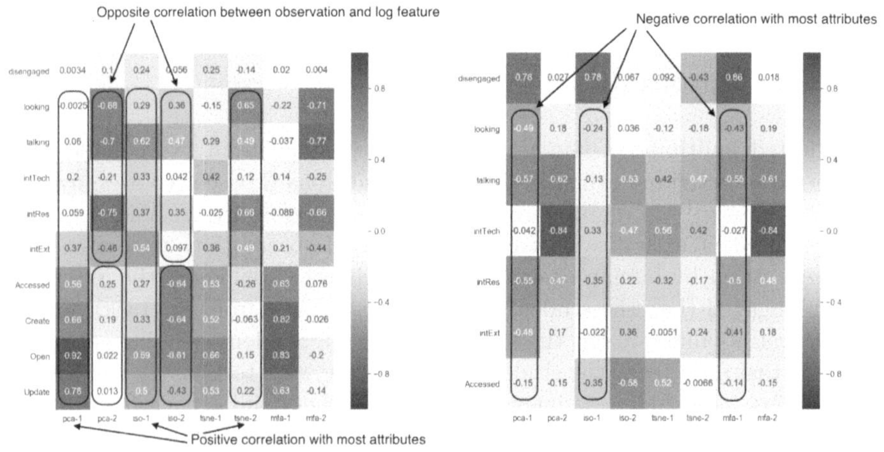

(a) Case-1 (b) Case-2

Fig. 1. Correlation between features and dimensions

In the first case (Fig. 1a), the first PCA dimension (pca-1) showed a positive correlation with most attributes. A similar correlation can be noticed for

[2] Further details on source code of the analysis can be found at: https://bit.ly/2Iwb59z.

iso-1 and tsne-2, as well. This correlation trend among multiple DR dimensions provided a basis of our interpretation of it as the group's overall engagement. Another pattern found was the opposite correlations between certain DR dimensions with observation and log features, respectively. For instance, pca-2 showed a positive correlation with all log features (e.g., accessed, update, etc.) and negative correlation with all observations except 'disengaged'. As similar correlation trend (but in reverse) emerged for iso-2. We interpreted this second pattern as a "digital versus physical" engagement attribute. In the second case (Fig. 1(b)), the teachers used Graasp in an unexpected way: only to provide activity instructions to students, but not to submit the student work (done on paper to save time). This lead to certain columns in our dataset (e.g., update, delete, create) to be completely empty. Despite these important qualitative variations in the data, the first correlation pattern was similar to the previous case (with a flipped sign). This can be observed in pca-1, iso-1, and mfa-1. Thus, we interpreted these DR dimensions as overall (dis-)engagement. The second pattern was not visible in this case study, showing that substantially different classroom variations (in terms of technology use), even with a similar MMLA setup, can endanger the conclusions of automated analyses.

4 Discussion and Conclusion

In this paper, we presented our exploration of how DR could be used to find simpler representations of multimodal learning data. Analyzing multimodal data collected about engagement in co-located collaboration, we showed the potential usefulness of these techniques within the constraints of authentic settings (e.g., lack of human-labeled data, preserving privacy or avoiding obtrusive data collection) where access to ground-truth data is limited. Our study also shows that how an unexpected use of classroom technologies can affect the data quality and analysis results even with similar data collection procedures.

Acknowledgements. This research has been partially funded by the European Union via the European Regional Development Fund, in the context of CEITER and Next-Lab (Horizon 2020 Research and Innovation Programme, grant no. 669074 and 731685).

References

1. Pardo, A., Delgado Kloos, C.: Stepping out of the box: towards analytics outside the learning management system. In: 1st International Conference on Learning Analytics and Knowledge (LAK 2011), pp. 163–167. ACM, New York (2011)
2. Ochoa, X.: Multimodal Learning Analytics. In: Lang, C., Siemens, G., Wise, A.F., Gaevic, D. (eds.) The Handbook of Learning Analytics, Alberta, Canada, pp. 129–141. Society for Learning Analytics Research (SoLAR). https://doi.org/10.18608/hla17.011
3. Chua, Y.H.V., Dauwels, J., Tan, S.C.: Technologies for automated analysis of co-located, real-life, physical learning spaces. In: Proceedings of the 9th International Conference on Learning Analytics and Knowledge (LAK 2019), pp. 11–20. ACM, New York (2019)

Observing Learner Engagement on Mind Mapping Activities Using Learning Analytics

Rubiela Carrillo[1(✉)], Yannick Prié[2], and Élise Lavoué[3]

[1] Université de Lyon, Université Lyon 1, LIRIS, CNRS5205, Lyon, France
rubiela.carrillo-rozo@liris.cnrs.fr
[2] Université de Nantes, LS2N - UMR 6004, CNRS, Nantes, France
yannick.prie@univ-nantes.fr
[3] University of Lyon, University Jean Moulin Lyon 3,
IAE Lyon School of Management, CNRS, LIRIS, Lyon, France
elise.lavoue@univ-lyon3.fr

Abstract. Research on learner engagement has increased in recent years arguing that it favors academic success. Teachers want their learners to engage in meaningful learning activities, like mind mapping, but they lack clues for observing their engagement along the activity. In this paper, we propose indicators of behavioural and cognitive dimensions of learner engagement for mind mapping activities based on interaction traces. Our indicators have been defined from final mind maps as well as from the mind mapping processes. We discuss implications for the observation of learner engagement in learning activities similar to mind mapping.

Keywords: Engagement · Indicators · Mind map · Learning Analytics

1 Introduction

Mind maps are graphic representations composed of nodes and links, in which the nodes represent ideas and the links represent their connections. Their first educational uses were mainly to support instruction and reading, while latest uses support the mapping processes inspired by constructivist theories [6] and the active learning benefits. Researchers in educational psychology have defined several dimensions of learner engagement (e.g. behavioural, cognitive) [2] to facilitate its observation. *Behavioural engagement* refers to observable actions to carry out a learning task. *Cognitive engagement* relates to strategies for accomplishing a learning task. We consider that learners' actions to elaborate mind maps may describe their behaviour, and that mapping activity may expose their cognitive processes and strategies.

Indicators could highlight learner engagement in mind mapping activities and help teachers to adapt their pedagogical strategies. However, existing indicators mainly target the assessment of the final mind maps [1], and those that are

M. Scheffel et al. (Eds.): EC-TEL 2019, LNCS 11722, pp. 668–672, 2019.
https://doi.org/10.1007/978-3-030-29736-7_63

obtained from the mapping processes lack representations of such processes [8]. [4] propose indicators from learners' traces and represent mind mapping processes but only for strictly hierarchical graphs. We think that mind mapping activities should allow learners to express freely their ideas, without imposing structures. In this paper, we propose behavioural and cognitive indicators of learner engagement to assist teachers in monitoring and assessing mind mapping activities. Methods from Learning Analytics can be used to collect and analyse learners' interaction traces during mind mapping in order to obtain such indicators.

2 Theoretical Model and Data Sources to Define Indicators

We propose a model of behavioural and cognitive engagement with four characteristics (i.e. *participation*, *effort*, *meta-cognitive* and *cognitive strategies*) that could be observed along mind mapping activities. Participation [5] is associated with the behavioural dimension. Effort is present in both dimensions, as behavioural effort (i.e. quantity) and cognitive effort (i.e. quality) [3]. Meta-cognitive and cognitive strategies [7] are related to the cognitive dimension of engagement. We associate each of these characteristics with indicators obtained from the final mind maps and the sequences of actions carried out to construct them. Final maps refer to their elements (i.e. nodes and links), and to their properties (e.g. title, description, URL, position X, position Y). Sequences of actions are defined by the *creation*, *deletion*, *modification* and *displacement* actions, applied to the mind map elements. Each action is associated with its time stamp, which allows to reconstruct the activity.

3 Behavioural and Cognitive Engagement Indicators

3.1 Indicators of Participation

- **Number of elements:** different trends can be found according to the type of elements created: definition of ideas (a greater number of nodes than links), or association of ideas (a greater number of links than nodes).
- **Duration of the construction:** period of time between the first and the last action to build the mind map.
- **Time between two consecutive actions:** a learner who interrupts his/her actions for a significant amount of time (determined by the teacher) may be in difficulty or poorly engaged behaviourally.

3.2 Indicators of Behavioural Effort

- **Ratio between the number of elements and the minimum expected number:** a mind map with a very poor proportion of expected elements may suggest a difficulty not overcome because of lack of knowledge or effort.

- **Number of elements with expected minimum properties:** when learners do not define the properties of an element, considered crucial for interpreting the final map, they may have difficulties and lack effort.
- **Number of consecutive sequences of creation-deletion of a element:** the creation of the last element that is not removed may be interpreted as a possible solution to a difficulty, and to show the learner's effort.
- **Number of displacements on the set of nodes:** too high values may indicate difficulties with the subject of the map, or possible problems with the mapping tool interface.
- **Number of displacements of each node on the mind map:** may identify concepts that require more structuring effort.
- **Number of modifications on the set of elements:** may provide clues on the difficulties in defining the elements and the efforts made to solve them; or a lack of control over the mapping tool.
- **Number of modifications in the properties of each element:** a very high value of the number of title modifications may indicate the difficulty in defining it.

3.3 Indicators of Cognitive Effort

- **Pertinence of the element properties:** inadequate values of the properties may be the result of a weak cognitive engagement to overcome a difficulty.
- **Pertinence of a created (and not deleted) element following consecutive sequences of creation-deletion:** the last created element may be evaluated to judge if it brings quality to the map. It may reflect the learner's cognitive effort in face of a difficulty.
- **Pertinence of displacements of the same node:** when the learner move repeatedly a node to a place that does not add meaning to the close and connected elements, the idea represented by the node may require more cognitive effort from the learner to be articulated.
- **Pertinence of modifications made to the set of elements:** modifications improving the mind map quality may reflect cognitive effort.
- **Pertinence of modifications to the properties of a element:** modifications not considered relevant may reflect a low cognitive effort of the learner.

3.4 Indicators of Meta-cognitive Strategies

- **Construction approach:** may be (1) based on a logical order (creating links between two nodes when these nodes are created, or creating links at the end once all the nodes have been created), or (2) based on a strong trial and error. A trial and error approach does not show the follow-up of a meta-cognitive planning strategy because of difficulties to understand the subject and to use the mapping tool, or because of a low cognitive engagement in the activity.
- **Pertinence of the actions on the elements following a help request:** learners self-regulate when they monitor their own activity, identify their needs, seek for help, and adapt their map according to the answers.

- **Pertinence of the actions on the elements following a search for information:** learners self-regulate when they identify their information needs to build the map, search the information in a tool, and adapt their map according to the results obtained.

3.5 Indicators of Cognitive Strategies

- **Ratio between the number of titled elements and the total number of elements:** calculated from the final mind map, it focuses on the elaboration strategies used.
- **Length of the node titles:** length of the node titles in the final map.
- **Pertinence of the links:** refers to the pertinence of the links between the nodes in the final map, and to the pertinence of the titles of these links.
- **Pertinence of the topological structure:** pertinence of the spatial distribution of the nodes in the final graph.
- **Pertinence of all actions on the elements over time:** can be evaluated from the sequences of actions identified over time.

4 Discussion and Future Works

The next step will be to implement and evaluate our indicators on a dashboard. The visualization of indicators over time on a dashboard could favor the monitoring of learner engagement during mind mapping processes. Our main concern is to evaluate the relevance of the proposed indicators for teachers. Our future works will be directed toward the evaluation of our model of engagement for monitoring other learning activities that rely on the construction of resources such as text writing. We may consider the paragraphs as nodes, and the ideas that articulate them as links.

References

1. Cañas, A.J., Bunch, L., Novak, J.D., Reiska, P.: Cmapanalysis: an extensible concept map analysis tool. J. Educ. Teac. Trainers **4**(1), 36–46 (2013)
2. Fredricks, J.A., Blumenfeld, P.C., Paris, A.H.: School engagement: potential of the concept, state of the evidence. Rev. Educ. Res. **74**(1), 59–109 (2004)
3. Fredricks, J.A., McColskey, W.: The measurement of student engagement: a comparative analysis of various methods and student self-report instruments. In: Christenson, S.L., Reschly, A.L., Wylie, C. (eds.) Handbook of Research on Student Engagement, pp. 763–782. Springer, US (2012)
4. Miller, N.L., Cañas, A.J., Novak, J.D.: Use of the Cmaptools Recorder to explore acquisition of skill in concept mapping, p. 8. Tallinn, Estonia & Helsinki, Finland (2008)
5. Newmann, F.M.: Student Engagement and Achievement in American Secondary Schools. Teachers College Press, 1234 Amsterdam Avenue, New York, NY 10027 (1992)

6. Novak, J.D.: Learning, creating, and using knowledge: concept maps as facilitative tools in schools and corporations. J. e-Learning Knowl. Soc. **6**(3), 21–30 (2010)
7. Pintrich, P.R.: The role of motivation in promoting and sustaining self-regulated learning. Int. J. Educ. Res. **31**(6), 459–470 (1999)
8. Yin, Y., Vanides, J., Ruiz-Primo, M.A., Ayala, C.C., Shavelson, R.J.: Comparison of two concept-mapping techniques: Implications for scoring, interpretation, and use. J. Res. Sci. Teach. **42**(2), 166–184 (2005)

The Quality Reference Framework for MOOC Design

Christian M. Stracke(✉)

Open University of the Netherlands, Heerlen, The Netherlands
christian.stracke@ou.nl

Abstract. This paper introduces "The Quality Reference Framework (QRF) for the Quality of MOOCs". It was developed by the European Alliance for the Quality of Massive Open Online Courses (MOOCs), called MOOQ that could involve in the QRF finalization more than 10,000 MOOC learners, designers, facilitators and providers. The QRF consists of three dimensions: Phases, Perspectives and Roles. It includes two quality instruments: the QRF Key Quality Criteria for MOOC experts and QRF Quality Checklist for MOOC beginners.

Keywords: Quality Reference Framework · Massive Open Online Courses · MOOC design · MOOC quality · QRF Key Quality Criteria · QRF Quality Checklist

1 The QRF - Based on Truly International Collaboration

"The Quality Reference Framework (QRF) for the Quality of MOOCs" [13] was developed by the European Alliance for the Quality of Massive Open Online Courses (MOOCs), called MOOQ. MOOQ was started due to the huge demand for improving the quality of MOOCs from research [7–10, 16, 17] and from practice [4, 6, 10, 11]. Overall, MOOQ could address and reach out to more than 100,000 MOOC learners, designers, facilitators and providers through dissemination and exploitation activities. The main objective of MOOQ was the development of the QRF that was finalized and published in the year 2018 after more than three years of revisions and refinements [13]. In close cooperation with leading European and international institutions and associations, MOOQ could involve in the QRF finalization more than 10,000 MOOC learners, designers, facilitators and providers through divers means including the Mixed Methods research with the Global MOOC Quality Survey (GMQS), MOOQ presentations and workshops at regional and international conferences and communication and collaboration in traditional and social media [12, 14].

2 The Three Dimensions of the QRF

The QRF consists of three dimensions: 1. Phases, 2. Perspectives and 3. Roles (see below). These three dimensions were carefully selected, discussed and agreed with all MOOC stakeholder groups to cover the different views, requirements and responsibilities during the lifetime of a MOOC. They are mainly based on the results from the

M. Scheffel et al. (Eds.): EC-TEL 2019, LNCS 11722, pp. 673–677, 2019.
https://doi.org/10.1007/978-3-030-29736-7_64

Mixed Methods research by MOOQ [12, 14, 15]: That included the realization and evaluation of the first Global MOOC Quality Surveys (for MOOC learners, designers and facilitators), the 27 semi-structured interviews conducted with MOOC experts (designers, facilitators and providers) and the MOOQ Workshops at eight international conferences (ICDE 2015 in Sun City, South Africa, OE Global 2016 in Krakow, Poland, EC-TEL 2016 in Lyon, France, OE Global 2017 in Cape Town, South Africa, IEEE EDUCON 2017 in Athens, Greece, ICALT 2017 in Timisoara, Romania, EARLI 2017 in Tampere, Finland and EC-TEL 2017 in Tallinn, Estonia). Furthermore, the QRF has adapted the International learning quality standard ISO/IEC 40180 (former ISO/IEC 19796-1) to the specific requirements and needs for MOOCs.

The first dimension of the QRF is called "Phases" and consists of five phases that normally overlap and can be repeated in iterative cycles:

Analysis (A): identify and describe requirements, demands and constraints
Design (D): conceptualise and design the MOOC
Implementation (I): implement a MOOC draft and finalize it through testing
Realization (R): realise and perform the MOOC including support and assessment
Evaluation (E): define, run and analyse the evaluation and improve the MOOC

The second dimension of the QRF is called "Perspectives" and distinguishes three perspectives that have to be addressed and focused during the different phases:

Pedagogical (P): how has **the** MOOC to be designed and developed?
Technological (T): how **has** the MOOC to be implemented and realized?
Strategic (S): how has the MOOC to be managed and offered?

The third dimension of the QRF is called "Roles" and covers three roles and indicates their involvement and responsibilities in relation to the phases and perspectives:

Designer: Designer includes content experts, content authors, instructional designers, experts for MOOC platforms, technology-enhanced learning and digital media as well as any others who may contribute to the design of a MOOC.

Facilitator: Facilitator includes the pedagogical facilitators and experts with content knowledge (such as moderators, tutors, teaching assistants) who manage forum, provide feedback and monitor learning progress, the technical facilitators (such as technical support for learners) as well as others who may contribute to support participants in their learning process in a MOOC.

Provider: Provider includes the (internal and external) MOOC providers, the technical providers (such as technology providers, programmers, software designers and developers), managers, communication and marketing staff as well as others who are involved in the decision-making processes leading to the delivery of a MOOC.

3 The Structure of the QRF and Its Usage and Benefits

The QRF presents the quality framework as general template to be adapted together with two applications: the QRF Key Quality Criteria and the QRF Checklist. The general framework of the QRF is a table that has to be adapted and completed. It integrates the three dimensions into a holistic quality framework that can be used for different purposes and by different user groups answering the needs identified by current research [1–3, 5]. To demonstrate the opportunities and to provide an easier start for its usage, the QRF offers and presents two instruments for two user groups: the QRF Key Quality Criteria for MOOC experts and the QRF Checklist for MOOC beginners.

The QRF Key Quality Criteria are provided in a table for experienced MOOC designers, facilitators and providers. They are intended as support for analysing, designing, implementing, realizing and evaluating a MOOC. The QRF Key Quality Criteria are defined as action items for potential activities in the different processes.

The QRF Quality Checklist presents leading questions for all three QRF dimensions. They are intended for both, beginners and experts in the MOOC design and development. Therefore, the QRF Quality Checklist serves as a starting point and a reminder on critical issues to be addressed. It complements the QRF Key Quality Criteria that defines the phases and processes of the MOOC design and development.

To use the QRF, it is most important to adapt it to own specific needs. MOOC designers, facilitators and providers have to select and define the relevant phases including their perspectives and roles according to their own situation, learning objectives, target groups, context and further conditions. Such adaptations should be documented to inform all involved stakeholders as well as to allow their review in the evaluation and further improvement of the MOOCs.

There are four core benefits of the QRF: First, the QRF provides a generic framework that can be adapted to each specific context. Second, the QRF identifies key quality criteria for better orientation on the MOOC design. Third, the QRF presents a checklist for the quality development and evaluation of MOOCs. And fourth, the QRF enables a continuous improvement cycle for MOOC design and provision.

4 Innovative Impact and Conclusions

The QRF has already achieved direct short-term innovative impact: It was used for the design and implementation for the development of two MOOCs as pilot implementations. They were following different pedagogical approaches (one xMOOC as traditional online course and one cMOOC for collaborative online learning). In both cases, the usage of the QRF was considered as very helpful by the MOOC designers and leading to reduced efforts due to the design support provided by the QRF.

Thus, the QRF will achieve long term innovative impact for the development of MOOCs, too. In addition, the QRF will also help MOOC providers and MOOC facilitators to improve the provision and facilitation of future MOOCs: The QRF Key Quality Criteria and the QRF Quality Checklist are addressing all stakeholder groups offering support for beginners as well as experts.

The QRF can be downloaded for free with an open Creative Commons license CC-BY from: www.MOOC-quality.eu/QRF. It is the first and unique guideline for the quality of MOOCs based on Mixed Methods research and involvement of the global MOOC community. The QRF Quality Checklist offers MOOC beginners an easy tool for the design and implementation of a first MOOC. And the QRF Key Quality Criteria support MOOC experts to continuously evaluate and improve their MOOC designs. Thus, the QRF will improve the future MOOCs and online learning in general.

References

1. Alario-Hoyos, C., Estévez-Ayres, I., Pérez-Sanagustín, M., Delgado Kloos, C., Fernández-Panadero, C.: Understanding learners' motivation and learning strategies in MOOCs. IRRODL **18**(3), 119–137 (2017). https://doi.org/10.19173/irrodl.v18i3.2996
2. Bayeck, R.Y.: Exploratory study of MOOC learners' demographics and motivation: the case of students involved in groups. Open Praxis **8**(3), 223–233 (2016). https://doi.org/10.5944/openpraxis.8.3.282
3. Brooker, A., Corrin, L., de Barba, P., Lodge, J., Kennedy, G.: A tale of two MOOCs: how student motivation and participation predict learning outcomes in different MOOCs. AJET **34**(1), 73–87 (2018). https://doi.org/10.14742/ajet.3237
4. Conole, G.: Designing effective MOOCs. Educ. Media Int. **52**(4), 239–252 (2015). https://doi.org/10.1080/09523987.2015.1125989
5. Glass, C.R., Shiokawa-Baklan, M.S., Saltarelli, A.J.: Who takes MOOCs? New Dir. Inst. Res. **2015**(167), 41–55 (2016). https://doi.org/10.1002/ir.20153
6. Lowenthal, P., Hodges, C.: In search of quality: using quality matters to analyze the quality of massive, open, online courses (MOOCs). IRRODL **16**(5), 83–101 (2015). https://doi.org/10.19173/irrodl.v16i5.2348
7. Margaryan, A., Bianco, M., Littlejohn, A.: Instructional quality of massive open online courses (MOOCs). CAE **80**, 77–83 (2015). https://doi.org/10.1016/j.compedu.2014.08.005
8. Reich, J.: Rebooting MOOC research. Science **347**(6217), 34–35 (2015). https://doi.org/10.1126/science.1261627
9. Stracke, C.M.: Quality frameworks and learning design for open education. IRRODL **20**(2), 180–203 (2019). https://doi.org/10.19173/irrodl.v20i2.4213
10. Stracke, C.M.: The quality of MOOCs: how to improve the design of open education and online courses for learners? In: Zaphiris, P., Ioannou, A. (eds.) LCT 2017. LNCS, Part I, vol. 10295, pp. 285–293. Springer, Cham (2017). https://doi.org/10.1007/978-3-319-58509-3_23
11. Stracke, C.M.: Open education and learning quality. In: Proceedings of the 2017 IEEE EDUCON, pp. 1044–1048 (2017b). https://doi.org/10.1109/educon.2017.7942977
12. Stracke, C.M., Tan, E.: The quality of open online learning and education. In: Kay, J., Luckin, R. (eds.) Proceedings of the ICLS 2018, pp. 1029–1032 (2018). http://hdl.handle.net/1820/9909
13. Stracke, C.M., et al.: Quality Reference Framework (QRF) for the Quality of Massive Open Online Courses (MOOCs) (2018). www.mooc-quality.eu/QRF
14. Stracke, C.M., et al.: Gap between MOOC designers' and MOOC learners' perspectives on interaction and experiences in MOOCs. In: Chang, M., Chen, N.-S., Huang, R., Kinshuk, K.M., Murthy, S., Sampson, D.G. (eds.) Proceedings of the 18th IEEE ICALT, pp. 1–5 (2018). https://doi.org/10.1109/icalt.2018.00007

15. Stracke, C.M., et al.: The quality of open online education. In: Proceedings of the 2017 IEEE EDUCON, pp. 1712–1715 (2017). https://doi.org/10.1109/educon.2017.7943080
16. Veletsianos, G., Shepherdson, P.: A systematic analysis and synthesis of the empirical MOOC literature published in 2013-2015. IRRODL **17**(2), 198–221 (2016). https://doi.org/10.19173/irrodl.v17i2.2448
17. Zawacki-Richter, O., Bozkurt, A., Alturki, U., Aldraiweesh, A.: What research says about MOOCs. IRRODL **19**(1), 242–259 (2018). https://doi.org/10.19173/irrodl.v19i1.3356

Perception of Industry 4.0 Competency Challenges and Workplace TEL in the Estonian Manufacturing Industry

Kadri-Liis Kusmin(✉), Triinu Künnapas, Tobias Ley, and Peeter Normak

Tallinn University, Narva mnt. 25, Tallinn, Estonia
kadri-liis@kusmin.eu

Abstract. Industry 4.0 is triggering substantial changes in the core competency profiles of manufacturing professions which may lead the industries to recruitment challenges and talent shortage. While policy makers are emphasizing the importance of lifelong learning and digital learning tools, TEL in the workplace is an under-researched area currently not aligned with the needs of the industry, especially SMEs. The study suggests that the competency-issues and perceptions regarding TEL in industry differ from the current assumptions of academia. The article aims to contribute to closing the gap between industry requirements and what research currently delivers by outlining the current needs and challenges of the Estonian manufacturing industry regarding competencies and TEL solutions.

Keywords: Industry 4.0 · Technology-enhanced workplace learning · Continuous competency development · Digital learning tools

1 Introduction

Recent technological advancements known as Industry 4.0 [1] cause profound shifts in many aspects of the manufacturing workplace [2–5]. Increasing levels of automation allow the workforce to migrate to less repetitive and more interesting tasks, but they will also require entirely new competency sets of shorter shelf-life [2, 3, 6]. This increases the need for lifelong continuous workplace learning, training, and education [6, 7]. European Union member states are already reporting skilled workforce shortages [8]. Thus, it is important to insure the relevance of lifelong learning [2, 9] and capitalize on the potential of ICT in workplace learning [10]. TEL systems have great capacity for supporting workplace competency development. However, the adoption of TEL solutions in the industry, especially in SMEs remains low due to several reasons, including a mismatch between what is offered by research and its suitability for the industry context [11, 12]. One cause is the scarcity of TEL research in the workplace as the focal point of research has been on technology usage in academic institutions [11]. The article aims to contribute to filling this gap by providing insight into the competency challenges as well as the perception towards TEL solutions in Estonian manufacturing SMEs.

M. Scheffel et al. (Eds.): EC-TEL 2019, LNCS 11722, pp. 678–682, 2019.
https://doi.org/10.1007/978-3-030-29736-7_65

2 Study Design

The objectives of the study were to map the perceived competency-related challenges of Estonian manufacturing industry enterprises, and determine the attitudes towards different TEL solutions. The study comprised of two phases: an exploratory case study in a single enterprise, and a validation study with six manufacturing companies in Estonia. Both phases consisted of an interview study ($N_{P1} = 9$; $N_{P2} = 7$) and a survey ($N_{P1} = 42$; $N_{P2} = 51$). The interview instrument used was developed by researchers at Know-Center Graz [13] who sought insight into similar questions in German-speaking countries. They had identified five competency-related challenges of Industry 4.0 (Table 1), and five possible technological solutions: mobile learning technologies, assistance systems with language input or gesture control, augmented reality systems (AR), virtual reality systems (VR) and data-driven reflective learning systems (LA). In the second phase of the study, data-driven recommendation systems (DDR) were added as potential solution based on findings from the first phase. Interview participants described the relevance of each challenge, provided examples, and suggested potential solutions and implications. For each proposed TEL solution they provided their insight regarding their opportunities and challenges, and assessed the overall potential of each technology. Survey participants were asked to assess the importance and perceptibility of the challenges on 5-point Likert scales, and TEL solutions potential on a 3-point Likert scale.

3 Results

The challenges identified by Thalmann et al. [13] were highly relevant for respondents: at the managerial level the most perceptible challenges were C1 and C3, for blue-collars C3 and C4, and C4 for white-collars (Table 1).

Table 1. Relevance of competency-related challenges in the context of Industry 4.0. (M–managers, W–white-collars, B–blue-collars), N = 51.

#	Challenge description	M	W	B
C1	New knowledge must be attained at ever shorter intervals	87.5%	76.9%	76.5%
C2	Learning must happen flexibly in the current working context	62.5%	73.1%	64.7%
C3	A broader range of complex knowledge must be learned	87.5%	69.2%	82.4%
C4	Quality and requirements compliance must be demonstrable	75.0%	84.6%	82.4%
C5	The company culture needs to become more adaptive in terms of learning and knowledge	75.0%	76.9%	70.6%

From the more specific competency-related aspects, A11 (see Table 2) was found to be the most important with the average assessed importance of 4.92/5 and 4.61/5 perceptibility in participants' organizations. The smallest perceived gap between the importance and perceptibility was attributed to A1 (4.78/5 of importance and 4.75/5 perceptibility). The largest perceived gap with statistically significant difference between the assessed importance and perceptibility was A10: importance 4.75/5 and perception 4.00/5. The importance of A2 was 4.75/5, but the perceptibility only at 4.31/5. 4.63/5 importance was attributed to A7, but the average assessed situation in organizations was 4.08/5.

Table 2. Perceived importance and perceptibility of competency-related aspects in daily work life (I–importance, P–perceptibility), N = 51.

#	Aspect	I	P	t	p
A1	A great part of learning takes place in the practical working context	4.78	4.75	0.6	0.56
A2	The key to individual and organizational success is intrinsic motivation	4.75	4.31	3.1	<0.01
A3	Recruitment is becoming more attitude-oriented than skill-based	4.43	4.61	−0.9	0.38
A4	Modern mentors are younger with greater aptitude for problem solving in novel situations	4.14	4.59	−1.8	0.09
A5	Organization should allow employees to err within reasonable limits	3.86	3.59	1.4	0.16
A6	Leader's role is not finding the solution but creating the premises for it	4.35	4.02	1.7	0.1
A7	Organization should support adapting to change with both value-based and physical environments	4.63	4.08	2.4	0.02
A8	The benefits of new technologies have to be communicated to employees	4.55	4.04	2.1	0.04
A9	New technological tools must have a low learning curve	4.71	4.39	1.2	0.25
A10	Organizations need to understand that everything is in constant change and employees have to regularly adapt	4.75	4.00	3.3	<0.01
A11	Flexibility and openness are essential for employees and organizations	4.92	4.61	1.5	0.13

From the technological viewpoint, mobile learning technologies were attributed with the highest applicability potential (2.49/3) due to the lowest resource cost. LA systems (2.57/3) were considered the most tangible option for integrating worker learning into real work while increasing production efficiency. AR solutions (2.47/3) were seen as tools to prevent unnecessary time expenditure for trivial tasks. DDR (2.51/3) systems were seen useful for motivating employees to learn and facilitating horizontal reallocation. Voice or gesture based systems (2.1/3) and VR systems (2.33/3) were not considered to have enough positive impact compared to potential issues, but this might be due to low awareness of what can already be offered by research (Fig. 1).

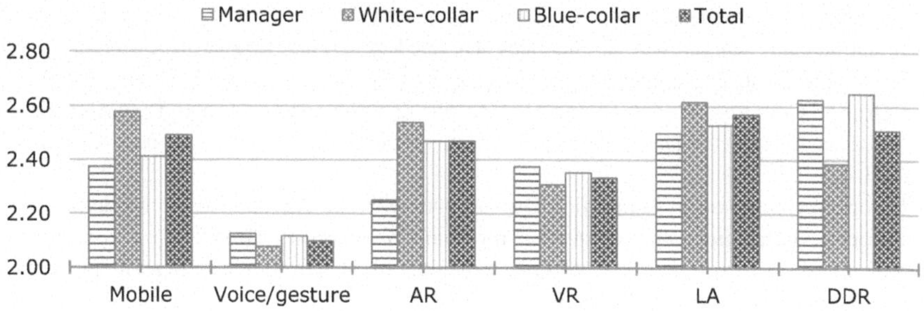

Fig. 1. Average assessments of TEL tools across organization levels and in total (N = 51).

4 Conclusion

The adoption of workplace TEL solutions in industry is low, partly caused by a mismatch between the views of industry and research regarding TEL. For effectively closing this gap, TEL communities must understand the perceived competency-related challenges of industry enterprises and their attitudes towards the opportunities and challenges of different TEL solutions. The study confirms that the challenges identified by Thalmann et al. [13] are highly relevant in the Estonian manufacturing industry, and highlights the importance and perceptibility of several further aspects. The results suggest that organizations see higher potential in more traditional technologies, such as mobile technologies, learning analytics and data-driven recommendation systems. Less potential was attributed to tools that employ more novel technologies: language and gesture input systems, virtual reality, and augmented reality. This indicates towards a need for closer and more practical cooperation between stakeholders to increase awareness of how such tools could be developed and sustainably implemented.

References

1. Kinzel, H.: Industry 4.0–where does this leave the Human Factor? J. Urban Cult. Res. **15**, 70 (2017)
2. Smit, J., Kreutzer, S., Moeller, C., Carlberg, M.: Industry 4.0. Report. European Parliament (2016)
3. World Economic Forum: The future of jobs: employment, skills and workforce strategy for the fourth industrial revolution. World Economic Forum, Geneva, Switzerland (2016)
4. Romero, D., et al.: Towards an operator 4.0 typology: a human-centric perspective on the fourth industrial revolution technologies. In: International Conference on Computers and Industrial Engineering (CIE46) Proceedings (2016)
5. Kagermann, H., Helbig, J., Hellinger, A., Wahlster, W.: Recommendations for implementing the strategic initiative INDUSTRIE 4.0: securing the future of German manufacturing industry; final report of the Industrie 4.0 Working Group. Forschungsunion (2013)
6. World Bank: World Development Report 2019: The Changing Nature of Work (2018). https://doi.org/10.1596/978-1-4648-1328-3
7. Bonekamp, L., Sure, M.: Consequences of Industry 4.0 on human labour and work organisation. J. Bus. Media Psychol. 6(1), 33–40 (2015)

8. Caprile, M., Palmén, R., Sanz, P., Dente, G.: Encouraging STEM Studies: Labour Market Situation and Comparison of Practices Targeted at Young People in Different Member States. European Parliament's Committee on Employment and Social Affairs (2015)
9. European Commission: Advancing Manufacturing – Advancing Europe. Report of the Task Force on Advanced Manufacturing for Clean Production. Brussels: European Commission (2014)
10. European Commission: Supporting Growth and Jobs: An Agenda for the Modernisation of Europe's Higher Education Systems. European Commission (2011)
11. Attwell, G.: E-Learning at the Workplace. Handbook of Vocational Education and Training (2019). https://doi.org/10.1007/978-3-319-49789-1_110-1
12. Guiney, P.: E-learning in the workplace: An annotated bibliography. Tertiary Sector Performance Analysis, Tertiary, International and System Performance (2015)
13. Thalmann, S., Pammer-Schindler, V.: Die Rolle des Mitarbeiters in der Smart Factory. wissensmanagement: Das Magazin für Führungskräfte (2017)

APACHES: Human-Centered and Project-Based Methods in Higher Education

Mathieu Vermeulen[1(✉)], Abir Karami[2], Anthony Fleury[1], François Bouchet[3], Nadine Mandran[4], Jannik Laval[5], and Jean-Marc Labat[3]

[1] IMT Lille Douai, Université de Lille, Lille, France
{mathieu.vermeulen,anthony.fleury}@imt-lille-douai.fr
[2] FGES-Université Catholique de Lille, Lille, France
abir.karami@imt-lille-douai.fr
[3] Sorbonne Université, CNRS, LIP6, 75005 Paris, France
{francois.bouchet,jean-Marc.labat}@lip6.fr
[4] Université Grenoble ALPES, Grenoble, France
nadine.mandran@imag.fr
[5] DISP, Université Lyon 2, Lyon, France
jannik.laval@univ-lyon2.fr

Abstract. Human-centered project-based teaching methods have proved their efficiency and popularity in the last decade. Such practice emphasizes the existence of interdisciplinary skills that students manipulate and incrementally learn to master throughout their higher education curriculum. This paper addresses some questions around the integration and evaluation of interdisciplinary skills. The first question focuses on the establishment of a skill-based approach to keep track of the students' competencies over human-centered computing skills all along their curriculum. To this end, we discuss the advantages and disadvantages of existing approaches in the context of agile practices and interdisciplinary skills in human-centered project-based teaching methods. The second question deals with the tools that can accompany such approach and how they can affect the teaching courses, the university instructors' habits and the motivation of the students. A semi-structured interviews were conducted with five instructors regarding these two questions. One main conclusion is the need to keep track of the students progress during the courses to help an efficient follow up. For this end, we propose to co-design a framework named APACHES.

Keywords: Human centered computer sciences · Agile project · Traceability · Skill based approach · Learning analytic

1 Context

Today, we notice a lack of awareness regarding human-centered project-based teaching methods in higher education, partly caused by the deficiency in existing tools to help university instructors integrate such approaches to their courses.

M. Scheffel et al. (Eds.): EC-TEL 2019, LNCS 11722, pp. 683–687, 2019.
https://doi.org/10.1007/978-3-030-29736-7_66

Consequently, students lack knowledge of such methods and skills such as agile project management skills in concrete contexts. Furthermore, when used, the focus in project-based teaching approaches tends to be from a project management point of view and rarely on the Human and Social Sciences aspects.

An existing agile project based method is formalized by ALPES (agile based learning in higher education) [5]. The objective is to give to the students the concepts of project management using agile approaches. These are integrated in various disciplinary courses all along the curriculum. ALPES is inspired from social constructivism, promoting the co-construction of knowledge and skills rather than the transmission of knowledge. Thus, it insists on the human interactions.

Another existing approach, THEDRE [3] (Traceable Human Experiment Design) provides a method for conducting Research in Human-Centered Computer Sciences (RHCCS). The purpose of RHCCS is the construction and evaluation of instruments by and for humans. Such research requires an experimental approach to produce and analyze field data by integrating the human in both design and evaluation. To be complete, this experimental approach must also take into account the context in which humans evolve. RHCCS requires proceeding in successive steps to build and evaluate instruments. The objective of THEDRE is to propose the RHCCS process that accompanies the researcher and the conceptual and technical tools to ensure the traceability of such process.

In this paper, we present the motivation behind the APACHES[1] project, which goal is to provide both a theoretical framework and tools to train undergraduate, graduate, PhD students, university instructors and supervisors on human-centered project management and human-centered research methods. The project is part of an ambitious skill-based approach throughout the higher education curriculum. APACHES will rely on the two aforementioned methods (ALPES and THEDRE), not to replace the human in project-based courses, but to support the different actors in the education process. APACHES is therefore concerned by the mastery of the method in order to reuse it in other contexts.

2 WAAT: Web Application for APACHES Tools

To define the different features to integrate into the APACHES framework, we have chosen to apply a participatory design approach [4] by identifying the practices and needs of university instructors. We interviewed five of them who apply, in a way or another, principles of the ALPES method during their courses. The interviews were based on qualitative questions to evaluate the current state of use of the human-centered project-based approaches in undergraduate courses and to identify how to improve and reinforce such practices (this collect was recommended by tools offered by THEDRE). First, university instructors shared with us a number of ALPES method concepts and tools that they use in their courses. The most commonly used one (used by all the interviewees) is the decomposition of the project into a number of independent user stories. Each user story is divided into tasks. A user story should answer to a need or intention from the

[1] Funded by the I-Site ULNE (University of Lille, North Europe) foundation.

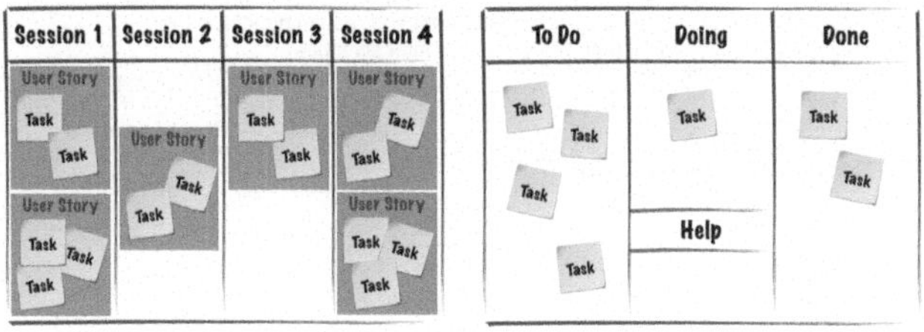

Fig. 1. Planning Board (left) and Task Board (right)

user point of view and an education objective from a pedagogical point of view. Other commonly used tools are the planning board and task board Fig. 1 and the tweetback board (a tool for the students to give feedback). These boards allow to visualize the overall project organization and furthermore permit to trace the student progress in the project and courses. These boards are materialized by papers and post-it notes (representing user stories or tasks). According to 3 "The boards are efficient for the visibility over what we should expect from the course and what we are heading for. This is reassuring for the students and therefore for their university instructor".

According to the interviews, the APACHES tool should allow to (1) dematerialize the boards in order to collect the students' traces to understand and optimize the learning and the environments in which it occurs [1]); (2) design a learning dashboard that helps the university instructor to have a global vision of progress of all the students in the class [6].

Some instructors are particularly interested by the idea of possible assistance issued from trace-based analysis. Through progress estimation from trace analysis, WAAT will be able to provide skill based personalized assistance [2] to them and their students. However, others are more reluctant to that idea, and were concerned that such a feature would tend to make instructors too dependent on the tools; number 5 said "It should be an aid tool to trace their work and detect indicators. It should not stop or replace the communication with the students".

3 Summary

The project will implement human-centered, iterative, incremental and adaptive methodology, thus respecting the concepts that we wish to transmit and recommend [3]. The designed approach, tools and concepts will be based on and inspired from ALPES, THEDRE methods, agile approaches and research methods for human-centered computer sciences (Fig. 2). It will be integrated into undergraduate courses or addressed in dedicated courses on agile approaches in graduate level courses in engineer schools and university. Based on a model domain and the participatory design involving instructors, the APACHES method allows to design and develop WAAT, a tool that will include an instructor dashboard and allow to keep track of students' progresses during courses.

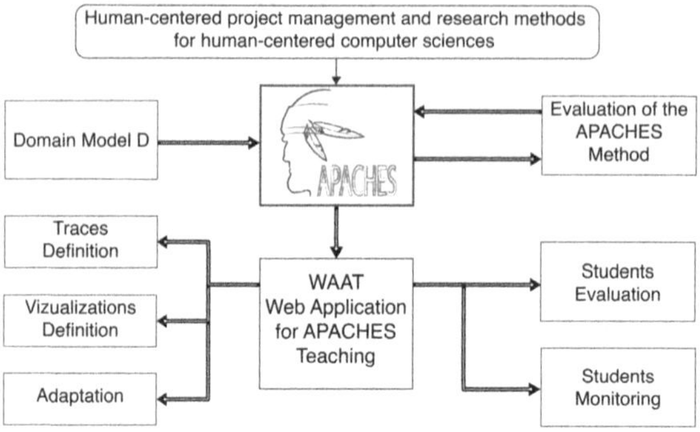

Fig. 2. The APACHES project

This will be evaluated throughout its starting in September 2019. A first iteration of experiments on the first version of WAAT tool will be done by volunteer university instructors. In addition to this group, we will select a panel of representative students to identify their needs and propositions to refine the tools and the method. The second iteration will concern the modalities of transmitting the method to other instructors and how the tool can accompany them in transforming their courses. During the training, we will do regular interviews with them to understand their appropriation and the diffusion of the method. WAAT will allow to collect student activity traces, allowing an a posteriori analysis. In the long term, such data can help in developing student monitoring indicators. To build and evaluate the different indicators, we will use a user-centered approach as prescribed by THEDRE. Thus, we will involve the instructors in the three steps of this process: exploring their needs, co-constructing the indicators and evaluating them. To ensure the follow-up of this work, we will use confirmed protocols[2] for each step. APACHES involves more than 2000 students in three french institutions, more than 15 PhD students and 13 instructors in order to transform the teaching of human-centered computer sciences.

References

1. Ferguson, R.: Learning analytics: drivers, developments and challenges. Int. J. Technol. Enhanced Learn. **4**(5–6), 304–317 (2012)
2. Heller, J., Steiner, C., Hockemeyer, C., Albert, D.: Competence-based knowledge structures for personalised learning. Int. J. E-learning **5**(1), 75–88 (2006)
3. Mandran, N., Dupuy-Chessa, S.: THEDRE: a traceable process for high quality in human centred computer science research. In: Paspallis, N. et al. (eds.) Information Systems Development: Advances in Methods, Tools and Management (ISD2017 Proceedings), Lanarca, Cyprus (2017)
4. Muller, M.J., Kuhn, S.: Participatory design. Commun. ACM **36**(6), 24–28 (1993)

[2] The digital notebook for collabor-active learning https://labnbook.fr/.

5. Vermeulen, M., Fleury, A., Fronton, K., Laval, J.: LES ALPES: Approches agiles pour l'enseignement supérieur. In: QPES 2015 Conference (2015)
6. Xhakaj, F., Aleven, V., McLaren, B.M.: Effects of a teacher dashboard for an intelligent tutoring system on teacher knowledge, lesson planning, lessons and student learning. In: Lavoué, É., Drachsler, H., Verbert, K., Broisin, J., Pérez-Sanagustín, M. (eds.) EC-TEL 2017. LNCS, vol. 10474, pp. 315–329. Springer, Cham (2017). https://doi.org/10.1007/978-3-319-66610-5_23

Media Literacy Training Against Fake News in Online Media

Christian Scheibenzuber[1(✉)] and Nicolae Nistor[1,2]

[1] Faculty of Psychology and Educational Sciences, Ludwig-Maximilians-Universität, Leopoldstr. 13, 80802 Munich, Germany
christian.scheibenzuber@t-online.de, nic.nistor@uni-muenchen.de

[2] Richard W. Riley College of Education and Leadership, Walden University, 100 Washington Avenue South, Suite 900, Minneapolis, MN 55401, USA

Abstract. Fake news undermine democratic processes by misinforming citizens and discrediting official institutions as well as established media platforms. While many theories and approaches to combat fake news have been proposed within the last couple of years, there has been a lack of implementation and evaluation of media literacy trainings to oppose widespread online misinformation. To fill the void, this research combines digital game-based learning and classic theories of competency acquisition in order to provide an evaluation method for future media literacy trainings. To achieve this, the web based digital game "Bad News" has been evaluated in comparison to a classic text-based form of information transfer. While there have been no significant results supporting a higher efficiency of the digital game-based approach, positive effects on subjective learning success and motivation could be shown. This piece of research can act as a stepping stone for further research as well as grant first insights into the effectiveness of interactive digital game-based learning on the perception of fake news in online media.

Keywords: Fake news · Media literacy · Digital game-based learning

1 Introduction

With the amount of attention fake news have been getting since the 2016 US presidential election, the subject matter has only grown over the last few years. Fake News impact not only politics, but also journalism [1] by misinforming citizens and lowering the trust in established media organizations and news in general [2]. This paper combines approaches from media and communication science, psychology and educational science to propose one way of dealing with this issue: digital game-based learning as a means of inoculating the public against fake news in online media. Said approach has been evaluated in form of an online media literacy training and provides insights into the effectiveness of learning through digital games when dealing with fake news.

M. Scheffel et al. (Eds.): EC-TEL 2019, LNCS 11722, pp. 688–691, 2019.
https://doi.org/10.1007/978-3-030-29736-7_67

2 Theoretical Background

Fake News have been defined and classified in various ways over the last few years depending on their form or function. They can be defined as news articles which are intentionally and verifiably false and aim to mislead media recipients [1]. Fake News can be characterised by an assortment of commonly used strategies to appeal to recipients in order to spread them as efficiently as possible. A report issued by NATO StratCOM [3] described some of those tactics: Polarising language which follows the goal of splitting societal groups, like the political left and right. Language that appeals to recipients' emotions in order to get media users to share content more quickly and efficiently. Spreading of conspiracy theories and discrediting established institutions to undermine governments and mainstream media systems. Impersonation of public figures through fake profiles on social media to harm the reputation of said figures or use their wide range of followers to spread a message.

Users' **media literacy** can offer one way of dealing with the rising problem of fake news. Media literacy can be defined as a "set of perspectives that we actively use to expose ourselves to the mass media to interpret the meaning of the messages we encounter" [4, p. 19]. By properly analysing and evaluating these perspectives deception within media messages can be detected and therefore avoided. Some ways of doing this include checking the sources of news articles, looking for missing pieces of information or analysing the tone of an article.

Digital Game-Based Learning (DGBL). One way of furthering media literacy can be DGBL. Digital learning games can be described as entertainment media aiming at cognitive changes within the player [5]. One goal of this study was evaluating the efficacy of DGBL in the context of fake news detection.

3 Methodology

Setting. The "Bad News" game, developed by the Netherlands based group DROG, (aboutbadnews.com), aims at showing players the strategies used by fake news creators. Players take on the role of a professional fake news monger themselves and are tasked with creating a growingly successful fake news website. They are guided throughout the game by an unnamed moderator who provides them with choices for further action, e.g. posting certain headlines. Fictional tweets provide the players with feedback on their actions.
The "Bad News" game evaluation comprises the following main hypothesis:

H1: The digital game "Bad News" improves the detection of fake news headlines more than an informational text with similar contents.

Research Design. In order to test this hypothesis, a pre-post design with an experimental and a control group was chosen. The experimental group was trained using "Bad News", while the control group learned the same from a text. Both participant groups were given the same performance test before and after learning inputs.

Participants. . A total of N = 71 German and Swiss adults participated in the study. The average age was 29 years (SD = 10, 16) with a range of 17 to 59 years. Of this sample, 60% were female. Descriptive statistics showed that the degree of education was very homogenous with 45% of participants' having completed a bachelor or master program and 42% having achieved a higher education entrance qualification. From the participant group, n_1 = 38 learned with the game, and n_2 = 33 with the text. The participants were randomly assigned to the two groups, between which no significant differences in terms of demographic data could be found.

Measures. To measure the ability of detecting fake news in online media a performance test with a seven-point Likert scale was created ad hoc. Participants were asked to estimate the credibility of 14 news headlines – seven of which were actual fake news. To ensure pre-existing knowledge was taken into account, each headline had the possibility to be labelled as previously known which would disqualify it for further measurements.

In addition, the participants were also asked to rate how far the credibility was impacted by the factors defined in the StratCOM [3] report.

The measure of the ability to detect fake news was calculated as the difference between participants' estimates and an expert solution. The smaller the difference between solutions, the better the result hinting at a higher media literacy. Participants' knowledge gain was calculated as the difference post- minus pre-treatment performance scores. A positive value indicated learning success in detecting deception.

In addition to the performance test, the effects of the fake news game were assessed by self-report. Participants could state whether they thought they had learned something throughout the study in general or more specifically about the different strategies used by fake news creators. The self-report learning effect scale proved reliable with Cronbach's alpha .97.

Data Collection Procedure. The experiment was conducted online, running for three weeks. Invitations were advertised within several student groups as well as through word of mouth and sent to 120 interested parties by email. At the end of the experiment, the data were downloaded from the online questionnaire platform and processed using IBM SPSS Statistics version 24.

4 Findings

Examining H1 by the performance test, the knowledge gain of the experimental group was slightly lower than the knowledge gain of the control group, but the difference was not significant (M *(Treatment)* = −0.36, SE = 0.65 vs. M *(Control)* = −0.23, SE = 0.66, $t(69) = -0.83$, $p = 0.58$). Within the different dimensions portraying the used tactics and strategies (usage of polarizing or emotional language etc.) to spread fake news, no significant differences between the groups could be found either.

The subjective learning success resulted in members of the treatment group estimating their knowledge gain as higher than their counterparts with the information text (M *(Treatment)* = 4.84, SE = 1.44 vs. M *(Control)* = 4.09, SE = 1.65; $t(69) = 2.05$, $p = 0.12$).

5 Discussion

In terms of objectively measured knowledge gain, our participants' performance was roughly similar while learning with the digital game and using the text. However the differences between participants' and experts' solutions in the pretest were within 1.5 points. This means, the sample as a whole was rather proficient at accurately detecting fake news headlines. The fact that the game did not improve knowledge gain significantly may be attributed to participants becoming more wary of fake news after learning more about them and hence seeing even real news more cautiously. This can support claims by Barthel et al. [2] that fake news spike confusion within society. As an alternative interpretation, the cognitive changes may have occurred in participants' news reception skills, which may require consolidation before the news can be mentally processed with similar self-confidence and speed as before.

Although the game did not improve participants' knowledge gain more than the comparable informational text, the subjectively perceived learning effect was greater for the treatment group. A perceived positive learning outcome can increase participants' self-efficacy perceptions which can furthermore improve motivation for additional learning activities [6].

6 Conclusion

The study provides a bridge between several research fields to offer a way of tackling the rising issue of fake news in modern society. With children and young adults spending a significant amount of their free time playing video-games [7] educators can use this interest in the medium to implement media literacy trainings as a way of providing knowledge and maybe even more so motivation for further learning activities.

References

1. Allcott, H., Gentzkow, M.: Social media and fake news in the 2016 election. J. Econ. Persp. **31**(2), 211–236 (2017)
2. Barthel, B.Y.M., Mitchell, A., Holcomb, J.: Many Americans believe fake news is sowing confusion. Pew Research Center, pp. 1–15 (2016)
3. NATO StratCOM Website: Digital Hydra: Security Implications of False Information. https://www.stratcomcoe.org/digital-hydra-security-implications-false-information-online. Accessed 18 Jan 2019
4. Potter, W.J.: Introduction to Media Literacy. SAGE, Thousand Oaks (2016)
5. Erhel, S., Jamet, E.: Digital game-based learning: impact of instructions and feedback on motivation and learning effectiveness. Comput. Educ. **67**, 156–167 (2013)
6. Shen, D., Cho, M.H., Tsai, C.L., Marra, R.: Unpacking online learning experiences: online learning self-efficacy and learning satisfaction. Internet High. Educ. **19**, 10–17 (2013)
7. Papastergiou, M.: Digital game-based learning in high school computer science education: impact on educational effectiveness and student motivation. Comput. Educ. **52**(1), 1–12 (2009)

Usage Simulation and Testing with xAPI for Adaptive E-Learning

Alexander Streicher(✉), Lukas Bach, and Wolfgang Roller

Fraunhofer IOSB, Karlsruhe, Germany
{alexander.streicher,lukas.bach,wolfgang.roller}@iosb.fraunhofer.de

Abstract. The systematic development of adaptive e-learning systems benefits from the principles of test-driven development, i.e., pre-defined software test cases help to improve the systems to meet the expected (adaptive) behavior. However, the inherent variability of adaptive systems can make test case development tedious and inflexible to maintain. This paper presents a concept for an interoperable, flexible testing tool for adaptive e-learning system development and systematic testing of xAPI compliant e-learning systems. It provides visual inspection and editing functionalities, xAPI simulation, and checks for adaptivity responses. This enables the systematic testing of adaptive systems and an improved development process. An xAPI recording functionality combined with a visualization of the usage flow helps in the test case development. A prototype implementation in a serious game for image interpretation verifies the concept. The concept is domain independent and valid for any xAPI compliant system.

Keywords: Adaptivity · Testing · Interoperability · Modeling · xAPI

1 Introduction

Adaptive learning systems (ALS) can help the users to better achieve their learning goals [5]. In this context, Intelligent Tutoring Systems (ITS) try to personalize the learning experience and adapt learning environments to the needs of the users. However, the development of verified adaptive learning engines (ALE) can be hard because just a verification of single software units does typically not reflect how the whole ALE responds to varying interactions of real users. Here, the systematic development of adaptive learning systems can benefit from established testing principles in software development, e.g., test-driven development or data-driven testing [3]. To this end a black-box and data-driven testing approach can be applied not only to software units but at a higher-level to the whole system. This is done in our solution approach. In this paper we present the concept for a usage simulator and adaptivity testing tool which is compatible with the Experience API (xAPI) to achieve interoperability with other learning systems. It offers xAPI recording functionalities to live capture activity streams to generate test cases. This can help in the systematic development or parametrization of adaptive systems. ALS pose additional challenges to the testing methodology

M. Scheffel et al. (Eds.): EC-TEL 2019, LNCS 11722, pp. 692–695, 2019.
https://doi.org/10.1007/978-3-030-29736-7_68

because of their often high complexity and deliberate variability. As the human factor introduces further non-deterministic aspects it makes the high-level testing of all usage combinations a non trivial task. In contrast to typical unit-testing of smaller software components, the high-level testing addresses test cases for the overall system, i.e., collections of xAPI usage interaction sequences are used as input and the responses of adaptive systems are checked as output. An analogy from software development would be regression tests with invariance classes.

Our field of application is adaptive learning for image interpretation [6]. The research questions concern systematic development of ALS, interoperability, analysis of behavioral usage data, and visualization of adaptivity.

Similar work has been presented by [1,4,7]. We target adaptive computer simulations and serious games. In this context, user and behavioral modeling for serious games is done by [4]. The automatic generation of user models in adaptive serious games has been shown by [1]. Standardization and interoperability for e-learning systems is an active and evolving research topic [2].

2 AdapSimTester - Simulation and Testing Tool Concept

From the necessity to systematize the higher-level systems tests during software development, the desire arose for a tool in which behavior patterns can be edited, visualized and simulated in a deterministic yet realistic way.

Questions. Based on interviews with adaptive technology developers various challenges have been identified:

- How to realize black-box testing and generalizability?
- What standards exist for modeling and handling behavioral usage data?
- How to simulate realistic usage data? How to synthesize that data?
- How to achieve variability and realism in the simulated data?
- How to visualize adaptivity? How to visualize the responses of an adaptive system, e.g., for visual inspection and analysis?
- How to simulate realistic bad or wrong behavior? How to simulate unsure or nonconstructive behavior?

Requirements. The req. specifications for the targeted assistance tool include:

- Record usages (scenarios) from attached learning environments via xAPI.
- Visualize scenarios and provide graphical editing capabilities.
- Scenarios can be sent as xAPI statements to other systems.
- Dynamic modifications and randomization of scenarios.
- Visualization and verification of adaptivity responses.

Test Cases. Information about the context is crucial for adaptivity; a single data point does typically not contain enough information as a set of observed usage actions (context). Therefore our concept makes use of usage sequences to form test cases or scenarios, i.e., the collection of serial user interaction data points which are basically the sequence of xAPI input statements. The context and the sequence of actions define a scenario $S = (A, T)$, where $A = a_i | i \in \mathbb{N}, a_i \in X$ is a set of actions, $T : A \rightarrow \mathbb{N}_0$ is a time function, and $X = \mathcal{A} \times \mathcal{V} \times \mathcal{O}$ is the set of all possible actions X consisting of all actors $\mathcal{A}$, all verbs $\mathcal{V}$, and all objects $\mathcal{O}$.

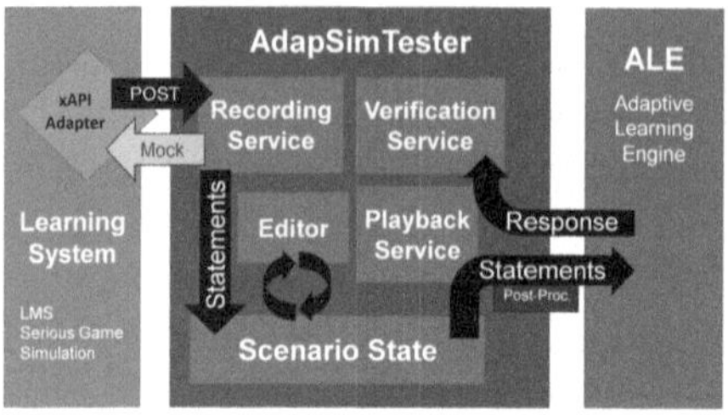

Fig. 1. Software architecture

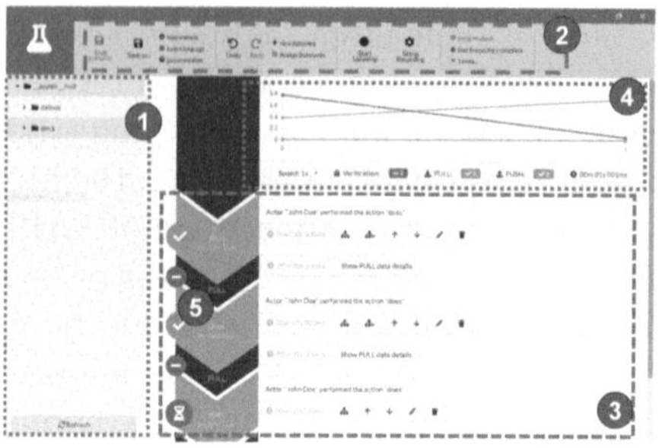

Fig. 2. Web user interface

Functionalities. The tool "*AdapSimTester*" basically consists of four main parts (Fig. 2): (1) scenario repository; (2) management, recording and playback functionalities; (3) editing, visualization and control of usage sequence elements; and (4) visualization and verification (5) of adaptivity responses. The scenario repository (1) lists stored usage sequences which can be loaded for editing and simulation. The loaded or edited scenario can then be simulated (2) by sending the underlying xAPI statements to attached xAPI compliant systems. The central UI element (3) displays the usage sequence. Each xAPI statement is represented as one element. Variability of the statements is addresses by different coloring, i.e., statements with identical classes are identically colored. Each statement box can be edited, i.e., in an edit dialog the xAPI values for actor, verb, object, etc. can be edited, and randomization can be applied to increase variability. Elements can be manually added or removed. To ease the development of complex usage sequences, AdapSimTester offers a recording mode where it listens to the xAPI statements of an attached system. The author uses the attached system in a prototypical way according to a (adaptive) user story. In simulation or playback mode AdapSimTester "plays" the xAPI statements to the adaptive engine. The engine's responses are displayed (4) for visual inspection and verification (5).

Visualization. The objective of adaptivity is to dynamically adjust (adapt) the learning environment to the needs of the users [5], typically based on an interpretation of the perceived interaction data input. The result of the interpretation process is used to control the adaptivity, e.g., dynamic difficulty adjustment, content modification, or learning path changes. One implementation possibility is to value each action with a normalized performance score $S \in [0;1]$ [6]. This can also be found in the xAPI specification in the optional attribute *result*. Although this score encodes no further information on the quality of an action itself, it can however be used in an application invariant, generic way. Further scores can enrich the quality of the adaptation [6], e.g., outputs like a $skillLevel \in [0;1]$ or a $helpingLevel \in [0;1]$. These scores can be checked and visualized, and they can be used to evaluate the users' actions, i.e., constructive/progressing, neutral/stagnating, or nonconstructive/declining.

3 Realization and Application

We implemented our usage simulator concept as a Web application using NodeJs and ReactJs (Figs. 1 and 2). It has been applied to an adaptive learning engine [6] for educational serious games in image interpretation. A preliminary study on helpfulness and applicability by a small software team have shown positive results. Two serious game have been attached to AdapSimTester via xAPI and the recorded activity streams have been used as test scenarios. The tool has been used to successfully verify an already implemented adaptivity logic [6].

4 Conclusion and Outlook

We present the concept for a simulation and testing tool "AdapSimTester" which can help in the development of adaptive learning systems. Our concept makes use of the xAPI to achieve interoperability and easy applicability to other systems and domains. The black-box approach as well as the recording and playback functionalities support generalizability and ease of use.

The usage simulator is going to mature in the ongoing development of our next adaptive systems for educational serious games. An evaluation is going to test hypothesis on usefulness, applicability and usability.

Acknowledgements. The underlying project to this article is funded by the Federal Office of Bundeswehr Equipment, Information Technology and In-Service Support under promotional references. The authors are responsible for the content of this article.

References

1. Arnold, S., Fujima, J., Karsten, A., Simeit, H.: Adaptive behavior with user modeling and storyboarding in serious games. In: SITIS 2013, pp. 345–350 (2013)
2. Bakhouyi, A., Dehbi, R., Lti, M.T., Hajoui, O.: Evolution of standardization and interoperability on e-learning systems: an overview. In: ITHET 2017 (2017)
3. Beck, K.: Test-Driven Development By Example. Rivers (2003)
4. Berdun, F.D., Armentano, M.G.: Modeling users collaborative behavior with a serious game. IEEE Trans. Games **11**(2), 121–128 (2018). https://doi.org/10.1109/TG.2018.2794419
5. Streicher, A., Leidig, S., Roller, W.: Eye-tracking for user attention evaluation in adaptive serious games. In: Pammer-Schindler, V., Pérez-Sanagustín, M., Drachsler, H., Elferink, R., Scheffel, M. (eds.) EC-TEL 2018. LNCS, vol. 11082, pp. 583–586. Springer, Cham (2018). https://doi.org/10.1007/978-3-319-98572-5_50
6. Streicher, A., Smeddinck, J.D.: Personalized and adaptive serious games. In: Dörner, R., Göbel, S., Kickmeier-Rust, M., Masuch, M., Zweig, K. (eds.) Entertainment Computing and Serious Games. LNCS, vol. 9970, pp. 332–377. Springer, Cham (2016). https://doi.org/10.1007/978-3-319-46152-6_14
7. Xie, T., Zheng, Q., Zhang, W., Qu, H.: Modeling and predicting the active video-viewing time in a large-scale e-learning system. IEEE Access **5**, 11490–11504 (2017)

Modeling and Evaluating of Human 3d+t Activities in Virtual Environment

Djadja Jean Delest Djadja(✉), Ludovic Hamon(✉), and Sébastien George(✉)

LIUM - EA 4023, Le Mans Université, 72085 Le Mans, Cedex 9, France
{djddja,ludovic.hamon,sebastien.george}@univ-lemans.fr

Abstract. This paper studies the problem of evaluation of human 3d+t activities in Virtual Environments (VE) for Learning (VEL). Current evaluation methods focus mostly on: (i) the automatic identification of an ordered sequence of actions and/or (ii), an empirical analysis made by experts through the VE. In many cases, the learner's activity can be represented by some specific time series made of geometrical data of 3D artefacts. For the extraction and analysis of such Motions Of Interest (MOI), one can manually segment them among the traces, and/or use automatic approaches requiring a database of annotated examples. Both cases usually require too many resources to design such environments. Consequently, this work presents a method allowing teachers to quickly build, compare and evaluate a 3d+t learning activity in VE. This method is based on a semi-automatic approach combining the Dynamic Time Warping algorithm, with 3D reference shapes and few expert's demonstrations of the task to learn.

Keywords: Virtual reality · Activity evaluation · Motion · Human learning

1 Human 3d+t Activity in Virtual Environment

Virtual Environments (VE) for learning (VEL) offer advanced interaction possibilities such as human movements and gestures for 3D objects selection, manipulation and navigation [2,6]. Regarding the human activity, most of the time, it is evaluated after the activity execution in VEL [4], according to an empirical evaluation and/or the use of task-dependant metrics characterizing the activity at the action level (done or not), and/or considering the search of an ordered sequence of actions. However, in many cases, it is crucial to characterize and evaluate each human action in terms of interactions and 3d+t features to provide an appropriate and real-time feedback in VEL [5]. Although there are a lot of 3d+t metrics [3] to characterize a motion (velocity, jerk, curvature, etc.). They can have a pedagogical value only if they are related to a domain and a task-dependent analysis of the learning situation with some experts [7]. VEL based on this approach, require a heavy re-engineering process if the task or the application domain change. Usually, the re-engineering process cannot be made

M. Scheffel et al. (Eds.): EC-TEL 2019, LNCS 11722, pp. 696–700, 2019.
https://doi.org/10.1007/978-3-030-29736-7_69

by the expert or the teacher [1]. Furthermore, the identification of the Motions Of Interest (MOI) that would be analyzed, is a difficult task if we consider a VE where the user can start, pause and resume the learning scenario at anytime. Therefore, given a predefined task to learn, our method consists in automatically capturing, segmenting and evaluating targeted MOIs during the learning activity in VE. These MOIs represents the evolution in time and space (3d+t) of some monitored virtual artefacts resulting from the learner's activity in VE. Our approach relies on the comparison between the expert performing the task and the learner thanks to some reference shapes considered as checkpoints, the Dynamic Time Warping (DTW) algorithm and some kinematic metrics [5]. The details of our method and the implemented system are presented in the next section.

2 Activity Modeling and Evaluation: System Functioning and Use Cases

Suppose a toy problem like a navigation task, where the learner has to walk according to two specific paths for reeducation purposes (Fig. 1, left). To set up the system, the expert (*i.e.* the expert of the task to learn) has to firstly select the virtual element to monitor (*e.g.* the learner's body). Next, the expert places three kinds of 3D reference shapes, acting as CheckPoints (CP) with which the artefact must collide with: a unique Starting and a unique Ending CP (SCP and ECP) for the task beginning and ending, and some optional Intermediate CPs (ICP). The ICPs represent sub-sequences of the task to learn. In case of several intermediate ICPs, the artefact must collide with them according to a sequential order. For the navigation example, boxes are used as CPs and the expert makes several demonstrations of a walking made of a curving path followed by a turning path. The SCP acts as an oriented local landmark from which, the positions and orientations of the artefact are computed and recorded until the ECP is reached. Finally, the teacher chooses one demonstration as a task to imitate.

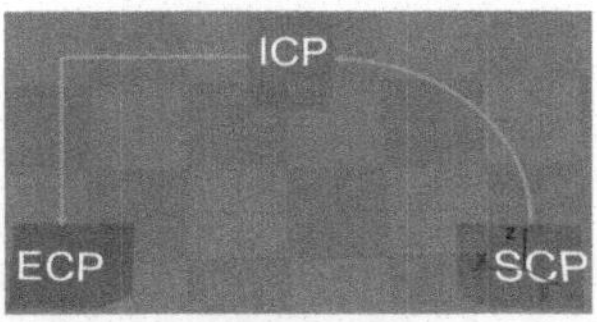

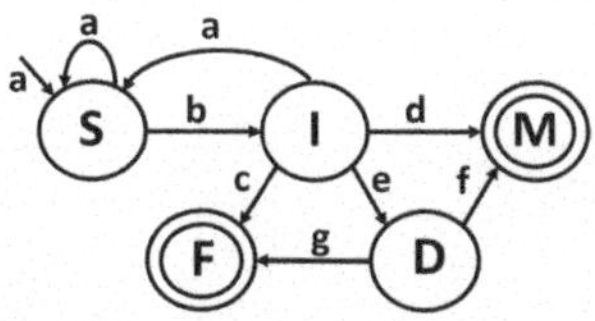

Fig. 1. (Left) Navigation task (Bird's eye); (Right) State machine for the expert's demonstration and learner evaluation with one ICP

The learner tries to reproduce the task. The system will then record the learner's MOI from the SCP to the ECP. The shape of the learner's path will not necessarily match with the expert's demonstration. Therefore, the system compares the learner's MOI to the expert one by using DTW that gives a value indicating the similarity of two signals in terms of shape regardless of the duration (the lower the value is, the closer the two signals are, [5]). If the value is acceptable (under a threshold), the learner can compare the performance to the expert's one thanks to a visual feedback, on a wall within the VE, that can display: the value of the DTW, the values of two kinematic metrics (for this example) the velocity and the jerk *i.e.* the rate of change of the movement acceleration. The lower the value is, the smoother the motion is [3] (Fig. 2, right). A replay of the learner's performance and/or the expert's demonstration is also available. Finally, the system functioning, with one ICP, is represented by the finite-state machine with the following transitions (Fig. 1, right):

- a: SCP collision, go to state S *i.e.* the artefact evolution is monitored and recorded, the previous recording is deleted if existing
- b: ICP collision, go to state I *i.e.* the ICP collides
- c: ICP collision, go to state F, *i.e.* the expert's demonstration or the learner task fails
- d (for the expert's demonstration): ECP collision, go to the ending state M, *i.e.* the recording stops, the metrics are computed and displayed within the VE.
- e (for the learner evaluation): ECP collision, go to state D, *i.e.* the recording stops, the learner's performance is compared to the expert's one thanks to DTW
- f: the DTW value is under or equal to the threshold, go to the ending state M
- g: the DTW value is above the threshold go to the ending state F

Two other simple toy problems related to (a) a throwing task of a ball and a manipulation task of a glass has been implemented (Fig. 2, demonstrations video can be found by following the link below[1]). The task (a) was built to address, in the future, an example of a throwing task. The monitored artefact is the ball that must be thrown in a bin according to a basketball launch (hand close to the head on start and elbow down, Fig. 2, left).

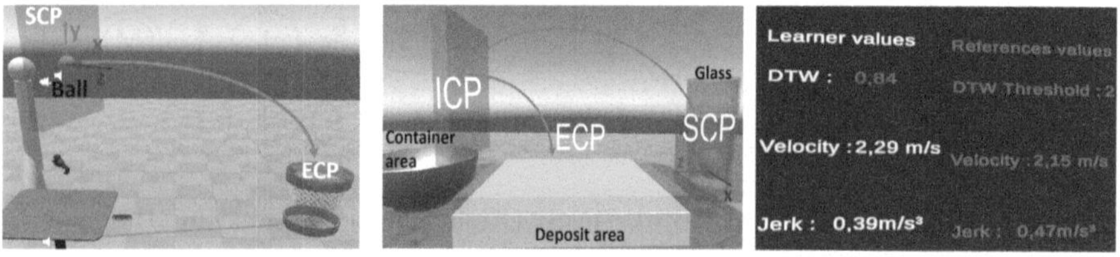

Fig. 2. Left: throwing task (Side view); Middle: manipulation task of glass (front view); Right: Metrics display within the VE

[1] https://www.dropbox.com/s/5t6e80j3oe85eiy/EC_TEL_2019_Activity_3dt.zip?dl=1.

The SCP is placed close to the user's head on her/his right (if right-handed) and attached to her/him to allow the launch of the ball around the bin. The task (b) illustrates the manipulation of object such a beaker in chemistry. This use case consists in monitoring a glass with a ball inside. The user must take the glass and put the ball into another container. The user must finish the task by turning over the glass and put it on the deposit area (Fig. 2, middle). In both tasks, the motions of the object are compared to the demonstration, thanks to DTW.

3 Conclusion and Future Work

With the proposed method, we hope that experts and teachers will be able to easily build a learning situation in VE and evaluate the learner's 3d+t activities. Once the checkpoints are placed in the scene and the demonstration is performed, the system can automatically record and analyse every learner's MOI, colliding an ordered sequence of virtual checkpoints and fitting the expert's demonstration. The future works will focus on the evolution of this prototype with the implementation of an appropriate interaction paradigm to allow teachers to build their own learning situations in VE. The limits and advantages of our method will also be studied by conducting an experiment to evaluate the authoring aspects of the proposed solution. The dart game and some simple chemistry exercises will be simulated to allow experts to put in place learning situations. The goal is to study the operationalization capacity of our system regarding the proposed learning scenarios. The learner evaluation process based on DTW and some kinematic metrics must be improved on three main points: (a) an inclusion of temporal aspects as the DTW algorithm works regardless of the signal duration, (b) a contextual and application-domain-dependent model to choose a minimal set of appropriate metrics to display within the VE and (c) visual feedbacks with affordance properties.

References

1. Buche, C., Querrec, R., De Loor, P., Chevaillier, P.: MASCARET: a pedagogical multi-agent system for virtual environment for training. Int. J. Distance Educ. Technol. **2**, 41–61 (2004)
2. Emma-Ogbangwo, C., Cope, N., Behringer, R., Fabri, M.: Enhancing user immersion and virtual presence in interactive multiuser virtual environments through the development and integration of a gesture-centric natural user interface developed from existing virtual reality technologies. In: Stephanidis, C. (ed.) HCI 2014. CCIS, vol. 434, pp. 410–414. Springer, Cham (2014). https://doi.org/10.1007/978-3-319-07857-1_72
3. Larboulette, C., Gibet, S.: A review of computable expressive descriptors of human motion. In: 2nd International Workshop on Movement and Computing, pp. 21–28 (2015)

4. Lee, G.I., Lee, M.R.: Can a virtual reality surgical simulation training provide a self-driven and mentor-free skills learning? Investigation of the practical influence of the performance metrics from the virtual reality robotic surgery simulator on the skill learning and associated cognitive workloads. Surg. Endosc. **32**(1), 62–72 (2018)
5. Morel, M., Kulpa, R., Sorel, A., Achard, C., Dubuisson, S.: Automatic and generic evaluation of spatial and temporal errors in sport motions. In: 11th International Conference on Computer Vision Theory and Applications, pp. 542–551 (2016)
6. Penichet, V.M.R., Peñalver, A., Gallud, J.A.: New Trends in Interaction, Virtual Title Reality and Modeling. Human-Computer Interaction Series. Springer, London (2013). https://doi.org/10.1007/978-1-4471-5445-7
7. Toussaint, B.M., Luengo, V., Tonetti, J.: Towards using similarity measure for automatic detection of significant behaviors from continuous data. In: Proceedings of the 7th International Conference on Educational Data Mining, pp. 427–428 (2014)

The Means to a Blend: A Practical Model for the Redesign of Face-to-Face Education to Blended Learning

Maren Scheffel[1](✉), Evelien van Limbeek[2], Didi Joppe[2], Judith van Hooijdonk[2], Chris Kockelkoren[2], Marcel Schmitz[2], Peter Ebus[1], Peter Sloep[1], and Hendrik Drachsler[1,3,4]

[1] Open Universiteit, Valkenburgerweg 177, 6419AT Heerlen, The Netherlands
{maren.scheffel,peter.ebus,peter.sloep,hendrik.drachsler}@ou.nl

[2] Zuyd Hogeschool, Nieuw Eyckholt 300, 6419DJ Heerlen, The Netherlands
{evelien.vanlimbeek,didi.joppe,judith.vanhooijdonk, chris.kockelkoren,marcel.schmitz}@zuyd.nl

[3] DIPF, Schloßstr. 29, 60486 Frankfurt am Main, Germany

[4] Goethe Universität, Robert-Mayer-Str. 11-15, 60629 Frankfurt am Main, Germany

Abstract. Learning design models provide guidelines and guidance for educators and course designers in the production and delivery of educational products. It is seen as beneficial to base learning designs on general learning theories, but these must be operationalised into concrete learning design solutions. We therefore present one such educational design model: the Design Cycle for Education (DC4E). The model has primarily been created to support the shift from traditional face-to-face education to blended learning scenarios. The cycle describes eight steps that can be used iteratively in the (re)design of educational products and provides educators and course designers with a flexible but clearly structured design model that enables them to reinvent traditional course content for blended learning with appropriate learning design tools.

Keywords: Blended learning · Learning design · Design model

1 Introduction

Many higher education institutions aim at enticing their learners to get the best out of themselves and to realise their ambitions. One of the ways to achieve this is to develop and offer flexible and attractive blended learning, i.e. the combination of traditional face-to-face and IT-based education. Turning existing educational products such as courses and modules created for face-to-face settings into more flexible and blended ones, however, is not an easy process and does not only require substantive content knowledge for a given course, module or program, but also educational, didactic and technological knowledge [6].

There is a range of existing models in the field of learning design and instructional design, of which the most commonly known ones are the Principles of

M. Scheffel et al. (Eds.): EC-TEL 2019, LNCS 11722, pp. 701–704, 2019.
https://doi.org/10.1007/978-3-030-29736-7_70

Instructional Design by Gagne and Briggs [3], the ARCS Model [5], the ADDIE Model [8], the 4C-ID Model [10], the Curricular Spider Web Model [9] and the Systems Approach Model [2]. Models differ in nature and can be categorised in different ways [4], which makes it hard for educators to select an appropriate design model. A recent systematic review of 21 TEL-models concluded that most existing models were conceptual in nature rather than procedural [1]. They also differed in pedagogical flexibility, i.e. the degree in which models adopt a pedagogical underpinning or do not mention any pedagogical orientation at all. Many models did not consider context or did not specify the level of design the model was intended for. There is very limited attention for student-teacher interaction, selection of appropriate technologies and evaluation in most models and examples of the application of the model are lacking as Bower and Vlachopoulos conclude [1]. This makes it hard for educators to asses which model to adopt and practical design support is overall limited in these models.

Therefore, as we have been in the need to extend a traditional face-to-face university with a part-time higher education programme for professionals in the work context with blended learning scenarios, we opted for the creation of our own design cycle, i.e. a procedural model, enriched with templates, tools, information and design examples for educators to specifically support and facilitate the redesign of blended learning. By creating the Design Cycle for Education (DC4E) we aim to retain the strong characteristics of the autonomous design of education, while at the same time exercising a normative function on the development process. Within the DC4E, sufficient space is provided for the unique culture of education, but at the same time we are also able to offer guidance. Finally, the development of such a broadly supported design cycle also provides the framework for a common language within which (re)design of education can be shared and communicated. We hope to contribute to the longstanding ambition of the learning design field to help educators create, describe and share teaching ideas.

2 The Design Cycle for Education

The DC4E was developed in close collaboration with different stakeholders, such as educators, instructional designers, researchers from the technology-enhanced learning field and members of the educational support service within our institutions. The model was developed, edited and adapted iteratively by members of Zuyd Hogeschool and Open Universiteit based on existing literature and in close collaboration with researchers, the support experts and associate professors from the Research Centre for Educational Innovation and CPD and the Research Centre for Professional Assessment at Zuyd University of Applied Sciences. Although the model is developed as pedagogically flexible, it includes elements of different design approaches such as backward design, rapid prototyping and multimodal design, which are recognisable within the model.

We developed the DC4E to support the transition through (re)design of face-to-face education to blended learning. The model was thus enriched with

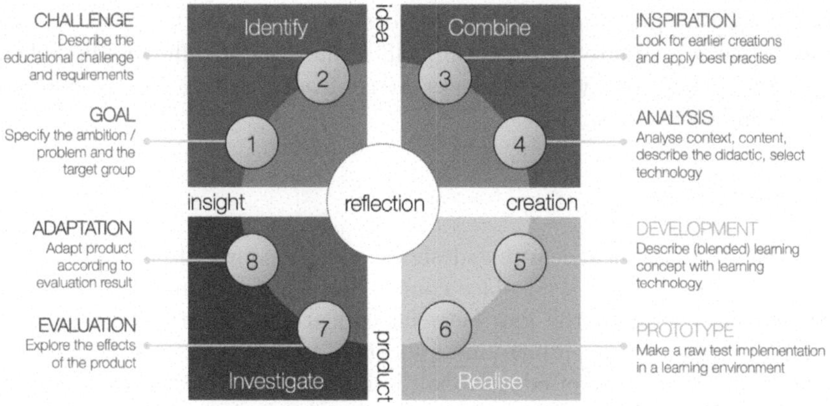

Fig. 1. Visualisation of the eight steps of the DC4E

a number of elements that can enhance the transition, defining a number of tasks in the various steps and referencing tools and templates that can be used. When designing blended education, one can make use of a wide range of educational technologies to support learners and teachers in their learning and teaching processes. The visualisation of our model, inspired by the work from Mor and Mogilevsky [7], is depicted in Fig. 1. There are four phases with two steps each: phase *Identify* – from insight to idea – with the steps *Goal* and *Challenge*; phase *Combine* – from idea to creation – with the steps *Inspiration* and *Analysis*; phase *Realise* – from creation to product – with the steps *Development* and *Prototype*; and phase *Investigate* – from product to insight – with the steps *Evaluation* and *Adaptation*.

The concept of reflection is central to the model. This means that the DC4E is not only based on a cyclical, iterative structure in general, but that the designing educator is forced to critically look at and reflect on the result of each of the eight steps and to properly document any design choices made. In addition to the design cycle and its eight steps we provide ready-made tools and templates for each of the steps that can be applied by the educator to gain evidenced-based insights or technical solutions for the (re)design of the course and its stakeholder group (https://onderwijsontwikkeling.zuyd.nl/tag/dc4e/).

At many educational institutions LMSs are used in a rather basic way, i.e. learning material is provided, assignments are handed in, or announcements are made. From a didactic perspective, such use of an LMS adds little if any value. With the DC4E we aim at enriching the didactic side of blended learning by offering a structure that makes the design of blended learning activities communicable and mutually comparable and thus inspires educators with examples of blended learning designs. Our ambition is to create a culture within an institution where the potential of blended learning is known. An essential part of such a culture is a very user-friendly and powerful LMS that is able to support various designs for blended learning. The DC4E very strongly supports the use of the

LMS not only by providing a structured design process but also various examples as well as a template for the local LMS. Educators are offered a flexible and design-appropriate tool, while students are confronted with a clearly-structured set of learning activities.

3 Conclusion

We presented a practical learning design cycle for course designers that need to (re)design traditional face-to-face courses to blended learning scenarios. The DC4E therefore bridges the gap between educational theory and educational practise; at the same time, it introduces a form of standardisation of courses while upholding the autonomy of educational designers. The experiences so far show that the DC4E enables communication of course design from different disciplines very well. The DC4E therefore contributes towards an institutional culture of (blended) course design. This leads to higher awareness of good design decisions as well as a common knowledge on good blended learning design. Finally, a model alone is not enough to drive this change: for the final realisation of successful blended learning, templates and examples as well as a community of practitioners within the university are needed to sustainably implement new learning offers. Within the close future, we will explore whether the DC4E can also be applied for the design of other learning scenarios. Additionally, we will look into how learning analytics indicators can be considered and suggested in the design process of new course modules and learning activities.

References

1. Bower, M., Vlachopoulos, P.: A critical analysis of technology-enhanced learning design frameworks. BJET **49**(6), 981–997 (2018)
2. Dick, W., Carey, L., Carey, J.O.: The systematic Design of Instruction, 8th edn. Pearson, Boston (2015)
3. Gagne, R., Briggs, L.: Principles of Instructional Design. Holt, Rinehart and Winston, New York (1979)
4. Göksu, I., Özcan, K.V., Çakir, R., Göktas, Y.: Content analysis of research trends in instructional design models: 1999–2014. J. Learn. Des. **10**(2), 85–109 (2017)
5. Keller, J.M.: Motivational Design for Learning and Performance: The ARCS Model Approach. Springer, New York (2010)
6. Mishra, P., Koehler, M.: Technological pedagogical content knowledge: a framework for teacher knowledge. Teach. Coll. Rec. **108**(6), 1017–1054 (2006)
7. Mor, Y., Mogilevsky, O.: The learning design studio: collaborative design inquiry as teachers' professional development. Res. Learn. Technol. **21**, 22054 (2013)
8. Peterson, C.: Bringing addie to life: instructional design at its best. J. Educ. Multimedia Hypermedia **12**(3), 227–241 (2003)
9. Van den Akker, J.: Curriculum perspectives: an introduction. In: van den Akker, J., Kuiper, W., Hameyer, U. (eds.) Curriculum Landscapes and Trends, pp. 1–10. Springer, Dordrecht (2003). https://doi.org/10.1007/978-94-017-1205-7_1
10. Van Merriënboer, J., Kirschner, P.: Ten Steps to Complex Learning: A Systematic Approach to Four-Component Instructional Design. Routledge, New York (2007)

Agile Development of Learning Analytics Tools in a Rigid Environment like a University: Benefits, Challenges and Strategies

Henrique Chevreux(✉), Valeria Henríquez, Julio Guerra, and Eliana Scheihing

Instituto de Informática, Facultad Ciencias de la Ingeniería, Universidad Austral de Chile, Valdivia, Chile
{henrique.chevreux,valeria.henriquez,jguerra,escheihi}@inf.uach.cl

Abstract. Because academic and learning analytics tools aim to inform and improve the teaching and learning process, users have a fundamental role in their conception and design. The early involvement of end-users helps to ensure the delivery of a valuable and understandable tool. Consequently this eases adoption by an educational institution. In this regard, the development of learning analytics tools has many reasons to benefit from agile practices but paradoxically they are usually inserted in traditionally rigid environments such as higher education institutions. This inherent rigidity poses challenges in conflict with the usual agile software development lifecycle (SDLC) practices and principles (eg. increased discomfort with late requirement changes). This work presents, through the experience of the Austral University of Chile with the SDLC of the TrAC and VERA tools, how to reconcile the necessary agile practices to overcome these challenges to create useful analytics tools and incorporate them into a higher education institution. Both tools are in pilot phase in the university and the partial findings show that it is possible to reconcile agile development in a rigid environment with appropriate strategies.

Keywords: Learning analytics · Agile methodologies · User modelling

1 Introduction and Related Work

Academics and Learning Analytics provides a model for university leaders to improve teaching, learning, organizational efficiency and decision making [4]. Nonetheless learning analytics (LA) initiatives often have difficulty to move out of their prototype setting into the real educational practice. It has proven to be challenging to create scalable implementations of LA in authentic contexts that go beyond a particular course or setting [1,2]. According to [6], the involvement of the relevant stakeholders (e.g., learners, instructors, instructional designers, information technology support, and institutional administrators) is necessary in all stages of the development, implementation, and evaluation of LA and the culture that the extensive use of data in education carries.

M. Scheffel et al. (Eds.): EC-TEL 2019, LNCS 11722, pp. 705–708, 2019.
https://doi.org/10.1007/978-3-030-29736-7_71

Agile methodologies are largely used in the software industry. According to [7], 52% of companies stated that more than half of the teams in their organizations are using agile practices, in 97% of them at least one team practiced agile. The most cited reasons for adopting agile are: Accelerate software delivery (75%), Enhance ability to manage changing priorities (64%), Increase productivity (55%), Improve business/IT alignment (49%), Enhance software quality (46%), Enhance delivery predictability (46%) and Improve project visibility (42%).

Therefore, LA tools software development lifecycle (SDLC) has many reasons to benefit from agile approach but paradoxically they are usually inserted in traditionally rigid environments such as a university. This inherent rigidity poses challenges in conflict with the usual agile SDLC values and practices.

This work describes the agile approach employed in the development and adoption of TrAC and VERA tools in the context of the LALA project (Building Capacity to Use Learning Analytics to Improve Higher Education in Latin America - https://www.lalaproject.org).

2 Materials and Methods

Fig. 1. Screenshots of VERA (a) and TrAC (b) dashboards

2.1 TrAC and VERA in the LALA Context

TrAC (Curricular Academic Trajectory) and VERA (Surveys Display for Academic Reflection) are tools developed in the context of the LALA project. Figure 1 shows a screenshot of each platform. Both tools were implemented and are being piloted mainly in Austral University of Chile (UACh). The pilot phase of TrAC started the first semester of 2019 and the VERA pilot starts its second semester. TrAC will be adopted too by another Chilean University: Catholic University of the Most Holy Conception. Detailed information about design is available at https://bit.ly/2WHPZtx

2.2 Agile Collides with the Academic Rigidity: How to Succeed

Despite the benefits of agile, it is not possible to apply directly every practice of any specific methodology. It happens because the academic environment

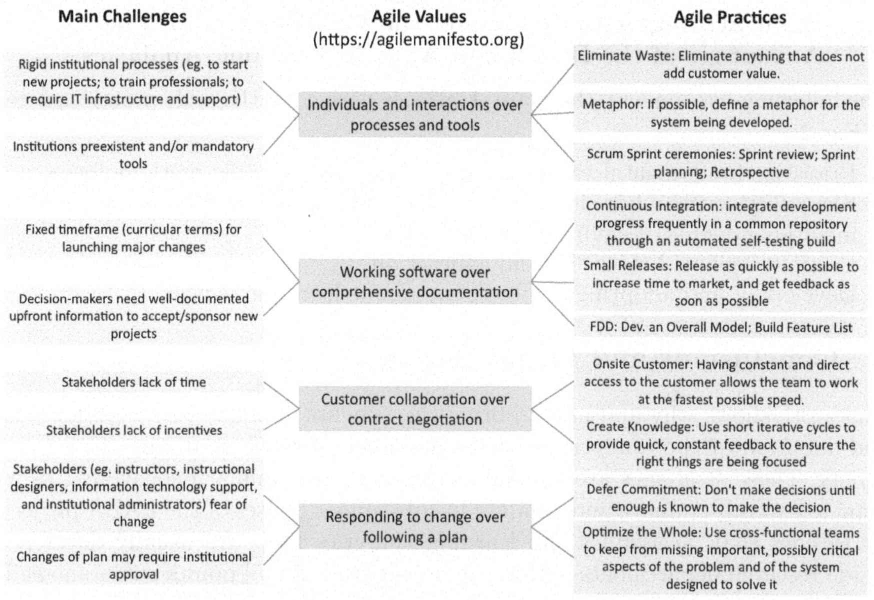

Fig. 2. Agile in a rigid educational environment: a practical guide

imposes some inherent rigidity. As noted by [3], even points relatively trivial, as the fact that the academic year revolves around semesters, requires special awareness, because major platform launches or changes are generally viable just prior the beginning of a particular semester. The left column of Fig. 2 lists the main challenges gathered from literature [3,6] and discussion sessions among our development team members, mainly in the first sprint planning meetings and continuous validation in retrospective sessions. Therefore we decided to revisit the fundamental agile values, as transcribed in the center column of Fig. 2, and look for specific practices from different methodologies (right column) that could be applied together to overcome these challenges.

3 Results

3.1 Main Benefits of Agile in Learning Analytics

Preliminary results show that the easy-of-use achieved was so high that the required training sessions were almost regarded as redundant as the end-users can learn to use the tools by themselves. Then early adopters become ambassadors driving the expansion and continuity of use of the platforms in the university.

3.2 Main Challenges of Agile in Learning Analytics

Even if the list shown in Fig. 2 may not be exhaustive of every challenge faced in this kind of environment, we seem to have prioritized and tested the most relevant challenges found in the literature and analyzed by ourselves towards the sustainable adoption of LA.

3.3 Main Strategies to Overcome the Challenges and Take Advantage of the Benefits of Agile in Learning Analytics

The following list sums up the main strategies derived of the agile practices listed in Fig. 2:

- Prioritize fundamental values and principles over specific methodologies.
- Flexibility even when it paradoxically means to compromise with some inevitable degree of environmental rigidity.
- Partially agile is better than no agile at all.
- Developing and adopting LA tools are about learning as well.

4 Conclusions and Future Steps

This work shows why and how to bring the benefits of agile to the development and adoption of two analytics tools in the inherent rigid environment of a university. These strategies are general enough to guide similar endeavours, as we hope to extend, evaluate and validate in subsequent phases of the LALA project.

Besides that, academics and learning analytics tools are usually developed inside research departments within the universities. As [5] points out, some agile practices are most learned in the industry or are self-taught (i.e., not pervasive yet to the research environment). Future work can assess if it is related to the abundance of failed or abandoned LA projects. Either way, we hope the model emerged in this work can be a simple yet powerful guide to help the agile world meets smoothly with the environment of LA tools.

Acknowledgments. The underlying project to this article is funded by the LALA project (grant no. 586120-EPP-1-2017-1-ES-EPPKA2-CBHE-JP) of the European Comission. The authors are responsible for the content of this article.

References

1. De Laet, T., et al.: Involving stakeholders in learning analytics: opportunity or threat for learning analytics at scale. In: Proceedings 8th International Conference on Learning Analytics & Knowledge, pp. 602–606 (2018)
2. Ferguson, R., Clow, D., Macfadyen, L., Essa, A., Dawson, S., Alexander, S.: Setting learning analytics in context. In: Proceedings of the Fourth International Conference on Learning Analytics And Knowledge - LAK 2014, pp. 251–253 (2014)
3. Doherty, I.: Agile project management for e-learning developments. J. Distance Educ. **24**(1), 91–106 (2010)
4. Howlin, C., Lynch, D.: Learning and academic analytics in the realizeit system. In: E-Learn: World Conference on E-Learning in Corporate, Government, Healthcare, and Higher Education, pp. 862–872 (2014)
5. Vargas, T., Chevreux, H., Henriquez, V., Lima, H.: Continuous integration in Chile: knowledge, perception, and interest. In: Jornadas Iberoamericanas de Ingenieria de Software e Ingenieria del Conocimiento - JIISIC 2018, pp. 247–259 (2018)
6. Gašević, D., Dawson, S., Siemens, G.: Let's not forget: learning analytics are about learning. TechTrends **59**(1), 64–71 (2015)
7. One, V.: 12th Annual State of Agile Survey Report (2018). http://stateofagile.versionone.com

Synergy: A Web-Based Tool to Facilitate Dialogic Peer Feedback

Erkan Er[1(✉)], Yannis Dimitriadis[1], and Dragan Gašević[2]

[1] GSIC-EMIC Research Group, Universidad de Valladolid, Valladolid, Spain
erkan@gsic.uva.es, yannis@tel.uva.es
[2] Monash University, Clayton, Australia
dragan.gasevic@monash.edu

Abstract. The goal of this demonstration session is to introduce Synergy, a platform to help design and implement dialogic feedback practices. Synergy is grounded in a theoretical framework of dialogic feedback, which suggests an ongoing dialogue among the peers (providing feedback) and the target student (receiving feedback). Synergy allows instructors to create multiple review sessions with specific tasks depending on the role as feedback receiver or provider. Peer review activities are organized around three phases, in accordance with theoretical framework. Using Synergy, peers in the first phase assess student work, discuss together to align their perspectives toward the quality of the work. Then, the peers create feedback tasks (to identify who gives which feedback). In the second phase, Synergy enables peers to provide the intended feedback (based on the feedback tasks) and to build dialogue with the target student. During dialogue, in collaboration with peers, Synergy allows students to identify learning actions to translate the feedback received into concrete progress. In the last phase, when students perform the planned actions, Synergy tracks student engagement and progress per each action and also allows the students to set their progress manually. Synergy is enhanced with Learning Analytics tools to support the feedback processes During the demo, we will show interactively the use case of how Synergy can help design and facilitate dialogic peer feedback.

Keywords: Dialogic feedback · Peer feedback · Peer learning · Learning analytics

1 Pedagogical Background

In early 2000, Askew and Lodge (2000), criticizing the dominant stance in the literature that feedback is a gift given to students, proposed that feedback is a process in which students as active learners co-construct knowledge through dialogue (i.e., two-way 'ping-pong' interaction). This re-conceptualization of feedback within the socio-constructivist theory of learning has guided the research in the last years [2, 3]. Accordingly, the recent literature views feedback as a dialogic process that aims to develop students' capacity to monitor, evaluate, and regulate their learning through continuous and refined interactions with others [2, 4]. In dialogic feedback, students are considered active learners who construct meaning and regulate their learning by engaging in fruitful social interactions with others [5].

M. Scheffel et al. (Eds.): EC-TEL 2019, LNCS 11722, pp. 709–713, 2019.
https://doi.org/10.1007/978-3-030-29736-7_72

Adhering to this change in the paradigm of feedback, the most recent theoretical models and frameworks have investigated dialogue as part of the feedback practice [5, 6]. The fast advancing knowledge on enhancing and sustaining feedback dialogue is fairly promising. However, so far, the literature focuses on scenarios where the instructors are assumed to actively engage in dialogue with student. The practice of dialogic feedback that increases the workload for instructors needs to be reconsidered in large-scale learning contexts. Initiating and continuing dialogue with every student and addressing their distinct learning needs is infeasible for instructors who teach large enrolment classes. There is a need for new theoretical models of dialogic feedback that can scale to large learning populations in today's digitalized higher education context.

We present a theoretical framework of dialogic peer feedback in Fig. 1, targeting large scale online or blended learning environments. This model conceptualizes three interconnected phases. First phase involves planning and coordination of feedback activities. In the second phase, students and peers together discuss the provided feedback in an attempt to make meaning out of it correctly. The third phase refers to the translation of the feedback into task progress by the recipient student. Each of these phases involves different levels of regulated learning: socially shared regulation of learning (SSRL), co-regulation of learning (CoRL), and self-regulation of their learning (SRL).

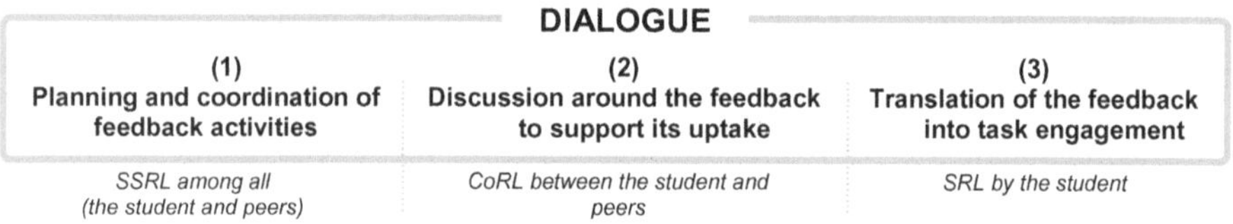

Fig. 1. Theoretical framework of dialogic peer feedback

2 Technological Background

Informed by the presented theoretical framework, the Synergy platform was designed and developed to facilitate dialogic feedback among peers. Synergy is a web application developed using React and ASP.NET. Synergy can be seamlessly integrated into learning management systems (LMS). Instructors can import assignments from their courses to Synergy or create course assessments directly within Synergy. Students can upload their submissions in Synergy to receive peers' reviews. Once users are signed in their LMS, they also become authenticated users in Synergy.

Synergy offers distinct features for instructors and students (who have two roles as feedback provider and feedback recipient) and these features comprise over 15 user interfaces in total. That is, it goes far beyond classic features offered by existing systems (e.g., Canvas) to enable uploading the work and sending the feedback. For a peer-review round to take place, Synergy requires the instructors to set up the activity first. Synergy provides instructors with interfaces to create (or import) an assignment, rubric, review round, and peer groups. Once set up, students can upload their work and start to collaborative with their peers to complete the review round assigned. Two of the critical user interfaces are shared in Figs. 2 and 3.

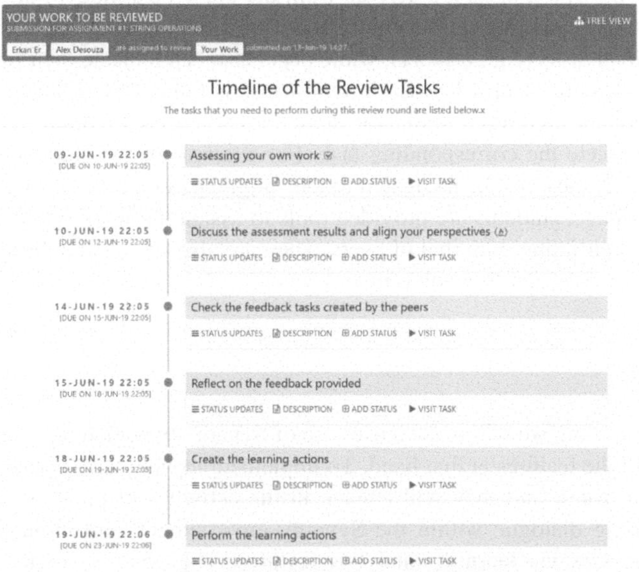

Fig. 2. Peer-review round main page (student interface)

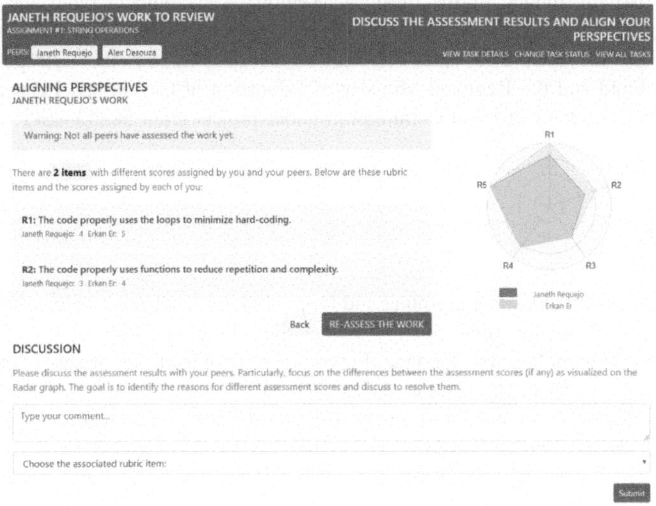

Fig. 3. Aligning the perspectives (student interface)

The interfaces provided in Fig. 2 serves as the home page of the current review round. In this page, students can view information about the current review round (e.g., description, dates), access their submission (if any), and locate their peers to work with during the reviews. More importantly, in this page students can track their progress on the review tasks. These tasks are derived from the theoretical model but can be edited by the instructor depending on the contextual needs. Students can mark their progress on the individual tasks (e.g., task #1), while peers also can indicate their opinion on the collaborative tasks (e.g., task #2). Each review task is linked to a different page, where Synergy offers the necessary tools for students (or peers) to perform the required actions to complete the corresponding task. For example, when students click on the task #2 in Fig. 2, they will be navigated to the "aligning perspective" page as shown in Fig. 3. In this page, students are provided tools to assign the work based on the rubric and compare their rating with that of peers. They are also provided a discussion tool to discuss the discrepancies to resolve them.

3 Use Case

In the demonstration, we will make a use case of Synergy by which the participants will use and test all the features at first hand. To implement the use case, participants will be given different roles, and they will engage in the activities of planning the feedback activity, building dialogue within the Synergy environment, and monitoring various feedback processes via learning analytics features. The opinions of the participants about the possible uses of Synergy in different learning scenarios will be solicited.

Acknowledgements. This research has been fully funded by the European Union's Horizon 2020 research and innovation programme under the Marie Sklodowska-Curie grant agreement 793317, and partially funded by the European Regional Development Fund and the National Research Agency of the Spanish Ministry of Science, Innovations and Universities under project grants TIN2017-85179-C3-2-R and TIN2014-53199-C3-2-R, by the European Regional Development Fund and the Regional Ministry of Education of Castile and Leon under project grant VA257P18, by the European Commission under project grant 588438-EPP-1-2017-1-EL-EPPKA2-KA.

References

1. Askew, S., Lodge, C.: Gifts, ping-pong and loops -linking feedback and learning. In: Askew, S. (ed.) Feedback for Learning, pp. 1–17. Routledge, London (2000)
2. Nicol, D.: From monologue to dialogue: Improving written feedback processes in mass higher education. Assess. Eval. High. Educ. **35**(5), 501–517 (2010)
3. Carless, D., Salter, D., Yang, M., Lam, J.: Developing sustainable feedback practices. Stud. High. Educ. **36**(4), 395–407 (2011)

4. Carless, D.: Feedback as dialogue. In: Peters, M. (ed.) Encyclopedia of Educational Philosophy and Theory, pp. 1–6. Springer, Singapore (2016)
5. Orsmond, P., Maw, S.J., Park, J.R., Crook, A.C.: Moving feedback forward: theory to practice. Assess. Eval. High. Educ. **38**(2), 240–252 (2013)
6. O'Donovan, B.O., Rust, C., Price, M.: A scholarly approach to solving the feedback dilemma in practice. Assess. Eval. High. Educ. **41**(6), 938–949 (2015)

ADA: A System for Automating the Learning Data Analytics Processing Life Cycle

Dilek Celik(✉), Alexander Mikroyannidis, Martin Hlosta, Allan Third, and John Domingue

Knowledge Media Institute, The Open University, Milton Keynes, UK
dilek@dcs.bbk.ac.uk, {alexander.mikroyannidis,martin.hlosta,allan.third,john.domingue}@open.ac.uk

Abstract. Learning analytics is an emerging field focusing on tracing, collecting, and analysing data through learners' interactions with educational content. The standardisation of the data collected to supporting interoperability and reuse is one of the key open issues in this field. One of the most promising routes to data standardisation is through the xAPI: a framework for developing standard 'statements' as representations of learning activity. This paper presents work conducted within the context of the Institute of Coding (https://instituteofcoding.org/). Additionally, we have developed a system called ADA for automating the learning analytics data processing life cycle. To our knowledge, ADA is the only system aiming to automate the turning data into xAPI statements for standardisation, sending data to and extracting data from a learning record store or mongoDB, and providing learning analytics. The Open University Learning Analytics Dataset is used in the test case. The test case study has led to the extension of the xAPI with five new methods: (1) persona attributes, (2) register, (3) unregister, (4) submit, and (5) a number of views information.

Keywords: Learning analytics · Data standardisation · xAPI

1 Introduction

There exists a rising interest in learning analytics (LA). LA focuses on collecting learners' data and analysing them using advanced technologies including Machine Learning (ML) to improve educational outcomes [1]. One of the key open issues in LA is the standardisation of the data collected to support interoperability and reuse [1].

Open University Analyse (OU Analyse)[1] also encountered with the data standardisation problem in LA. OU Analyse aims to provide early prediction of at-risk students building on their demographic data and interactions extracted from virtual learning environment (VLE) with the clicks of students to increase the retention rate at the OU and improve the quality of education [2]. To support research in this field, OU Analyse developed the Open University Learning Analytics Dataset (OULAD)[2] based on the courses presented at the OU [3]. The dataset contains demographic data of

[1] https://analyse.kmi.open.ac.uk/open_dataset.

M. Scheffel et al. (Eds.): EC-TEL 2019, LNCS 11722, pp. 714–718, 2019.
https://doi.org/10.1007/978-3-030-29736-7_73

students and clickstream data of students' interactions in the VLE. Based on the demographic data and selected activity types of this legacy dataset, OU Analyse constructed four ML-based predictive models. To run these predictive models over other institutions learning dataset, data standardisation is required as they have various underlying data structure.

Unfortunately, there are yet no established standards of LA data usage on how to monitor, feedback and improve students' educational performances. Currently, the enormous amount of data generated through LA is processed in ad hoc and task specific ways that prevent interoperability and reuse.

In this paper, we introduce Automated Data Analytics (ADA) as the first attempt to address the above-mentioned challenge which is neglected in LA. ADA is a system that automates end-to-end execution of learning data analytics building upon the outcomes of the OU Analyse as part of the Institute of Coding (IoC). IoC is a UK Government's £40 m + initiative aims to transform the digital skills required by the 21st by innovative and industry-focused education in HE across the UK.

2 Pedagogical Background

ADA contributes to enhancing teaching and improving educational outcomes in HE through LA. LA is seen as an innovative pedagogy in the 21st century [4]. [4] highlighted that "our LA is our pedagogy" arguing that the ways followed for gathering data, interpreting them, and acting on them connect, enshrine, and show a role in pedagogy in action. LA's relationship with established pedagogic approaches is conceptualised in the literature [5]. Specifically, our proposed system provides analytical dashboards to the HE lecturers and course team about their students' progress. Since each student's interactions with VLE is recorded, it is easy to find the learning material that the student has missed. When a student identified as at-risk, the system recommends the resources that will be him/her back to track. Predictions of at-risk students and providing them right-support also promotes the personalised learning.

3 Technological Background

ADA is a system designed to automate end-to-end execution of learning data analytics. The flow of the ADA is presented in Fig. 1.

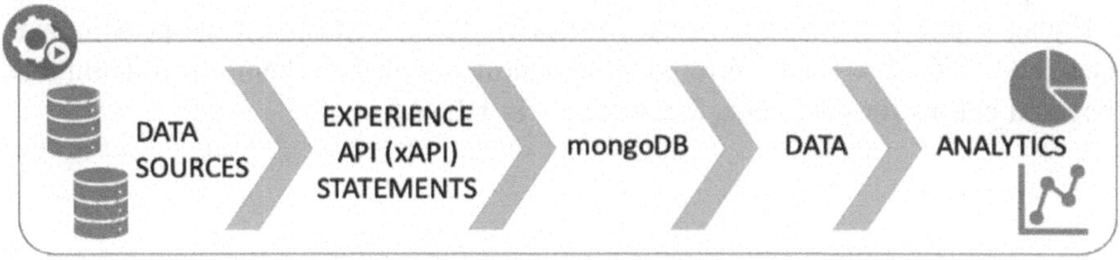

Fig. 1. The flow of the ADA System

The system comprised of four main features: (1) turning data into xAPI statements; (2) storing data in mongoDB; (3) extracting data from mongoDB and preparing for analytics; and (4) providing learning analytics. ADA's main features are explained in the following paragraphs with details.

3.1 The System Features

Turning Data into xAPI Statements. ADA allows users to insert mass data in .csv file format or directly connecting to VLE and then turns the data into xAPI Statements. xAPI is a technical specification to standardise data about a learner or group's activities from various sources in a consistent manner. Creating or extending xAPI verbs are needed when there are not appropriate built-in properties of xAPI verbs.

Storing Data in mongoDB. Another feature of ADA is sending the data that is in the form of xAPI statements into mongoDB. It is possible to send the data into mongo DB directly using xAPI verbs or using learning record store (LRS).

Data Extracting and Preparation for the Analysis. ADA extracts data from mongoDB and prepares it for the predictive analysis.

Analytics. ADA provides predictive analytics to the teachers using predictive models of OU Analyse with the available data. The analytical dashboard of ADA informs lecturers and course team about their students' progress to provide them right-support.

4 Test Case and Results

The OULAD is used in our test case. OULAD consists of information about 32,593 students, 22 courses, students' assessment results, logs of students' interactions with the VLE (10,655,280 entries). Our test case shows how the ADA system standardises data, processes data, and provides useful learning analytics. The test case led to the extension of xAPI verbs, which are presented in the following sub-sections.

4.1 XAPI Persona Attributes

The general form of xAPI statements is "[actor] [verb] [object]". In xAPI, each person's profile is named as a persona. A Persona describes an actual person with a compound of zero or more identifiers and attributes.

We proposed a schema for students' persona data according to data standardisation of Higher Education Statistics Agency (HESA). Table 1 illustrates the persona attributes used in OULAD and corresponding data items of the schema with definitions. The valid entries for data items are available in HESA[2].

[2] https://www.hesa.ac.uk/collection/c18051/index.

Table 1. OULAD persona attributes and their corresponding data items of HESA

OULAD attribute	HESA data item	Definition
gender	SEXID	Gender of the learner.
age_band	BIRTHDATE	Date of birth of the student.
highest_education	QUALENT3	The highest qualification a student holds on entry.
region	TTPCODE	Postcode for the student's term-time address.
	TTACCOM	Student's living place during the current year.
imd-band	IMD	The official measure of relative deprivation.
disability	DISABLE	Type of disability that a student has.
final_result	OUTGRADE	The examination grade awarded to the student.

4.2 OULAD XAPI Verbs

To define OULAD, the following verbs are extended or created, as there are no corresponding built-in properties of xAPI verbs: register, unregister, submit with banked and unbanked, and view.

For register and unregister verbs, an object which was the name of the course at the OULAD needed to be specified. However, existing xAPI does not provide objects for this. Therefore, we created an object to define a course with its type as follows.

```
"object":{"id": "http:\/\/kmi.open.ac.uk\/xapi\/verb\/course",
"definition":{
"type":"http:\/\/kmi.open.ac.uk\/xapi\/verb\/course\/"CourseName",
"name":{"en": "CourseName"}}}
```

"Submit" verb is extended with an object to make it specific for the assessment types of OULAD as presented in the example below. The object is also extended in two ways: isBanked and belongs to.

```
"object":{"id":"http:\/\/http://adlnet.gov/expapi/activities/assessment,
"definition":{ "type": "http:\/\/kmi.open.ac.uk\/xapi\/verb\/assess-
menttype\/"NameofAssessment", "name": {"en": "NameofAssessment"}
"extensions":{"http:\/\/kmi.open.ac.uk\/xapi\/verb\/isBanked":true,
"http:\/\/kmi.open.ac.uk\/xapi\/verb\/belongsto": "ModuleName"}}}
```

"Viewed" is a new verb created in OULAD case. This verb helps to define the number of clicks that are made on specific assessments at the VLE.

```
"verb": {"id": "http:\/\/kmi.open.ac.uk\/xapi\/verb\/viewed",
"display":{"en": "viewed"}}
```

References

1. Siemens, G.: Learning analytics: the emergence of a discipline. Am. Behav. Sci. **57**, 1380–1400 (2013)
2. Kuzilek, J., Hlosta, M., Herrmannova, D., Zdrahal, Z., Wolff, A.: OU Analyse : analysing at - risk students at the open university. Learn. Anal. Rev. LAK15–1. 1–16 (2015)

3. Kuzilek, J., Hlosta, M., Zdrahal, Z.: Open university learning analytics dataset. Sci. Data **4**, 170171 (2017)
4. Shum, S.B.: Our learning analytics are our pedagogy. In: Expanding Horizons 2012 Conference. Macquarie University (2012)
5. Knight, S., Buckingham Shum, S., Littleton, K.: Epistemology, pedagogy, assessment and learning analytics. In: Learning Analytics and Knowledge (LAK), pp. 75–84 (2013)

Learning with the Dancing Coach

Gianluca Romano[1(✉)], Jan Schneider[2(✉)], and Hendrik Drachsler[2(✉)]

[1] Goethe University Frankfurt, Frankfurt on the Main, 60323 Frankfurt, Germany
romanogianluca@stud.uni-frankfurt.de

[2] DIPF Leibniz Institute, Frankfurt on the Main, 60323 Frankfurt, Germany
{schneider.jan,drachsler}@dipf.de

Abstract. Dancing is a discipline that makes enhances the mood in people and is challenging to learn because it requires good coordination and feeling of the rhythm. In this paper we present and describe the Dancing Coach (DC), a tutoring system designed to help users to learn and practice dancing steps. The current implementation of the DC provides guidance and practice options for basic salsa dancing steps. However, its design allows the addition of different steps and dancing styles for future implementations.

Keywords: Multimodal · Kinect · Dancing · Salsa · Human computer interaction

1 Introduction

Dancing is a discipline that makes people feel good. It consists of moving the body rhythmically to music. Learning how to dance can be challenging. It requires physical coordination and feeling the rhythm. You can learn dancing by attending dancing courses imparted by human teachers. Other alternatives are online courses, where one can imitate the exercises suggested by the tutors, and videogames like Just Dance where one can imitate predefined choreographies performed by an avatar. Unlike Just Dance or similar video games the DC prioritizes to support more the learning of dancing rather than having fun and aiming for the highest scores with the leas amount of effort possible. Online courses have the advantage of a structured program to teach people how to dance. But, they do not provide students with any type of feedback. Videogames, on the other hand, provide the user with simple verification feedback. However, they do not provide a structured program e.g. like (online) dancing courses. Lately, some dancing tutoring systems [1–4] emerged to support the teaching of one specific dancing style. They follow a similar feedback approach as the videogames, where learners have to mimic an avatar. The performance evaluation uses similarity measurements or machine learning (SVM, NN). On the contrary, SalsaAsst [5] supports users with salsa dancing beat assistance through vibration or voice prompts over headphones. To contribute to the state-of-the-art of dancing tutoring systems, we developed the Dancing Coach (DC). The current implementation provides learners with instructional feedback for basic Salsa steps. However, its design allows the addition of different dancing steps and styles.

M. Scheffel et al. (Eds.): EC-TEL 2019, LNCS 11722, pp. 719–722, 2019.
https://doi.org/10.1007/978-3-030-29736-7_74

2 Dancing Coach

The DC is designed to help people to learn and practice dancing steps. It uses the Kinect V2 to track the learner performing the dancing steps. It has been designed as a generic dancing tutoring system that can be used to practice different types of dancing styles and skill levels. Users can select a music genre, load a song and start practicing the steps. But currently the DC supports only basic Salsa dancing steps. The DC has two execution modes: tutorial and practice. The tutorial mode helps learners to memorize the steps at their own pace. It guides the learner through the sequence of the 8 basic salsa steps (see Fig. 1), that start with both feet aligned. The DC always suggests the next step and waits until the user performs it correctly.

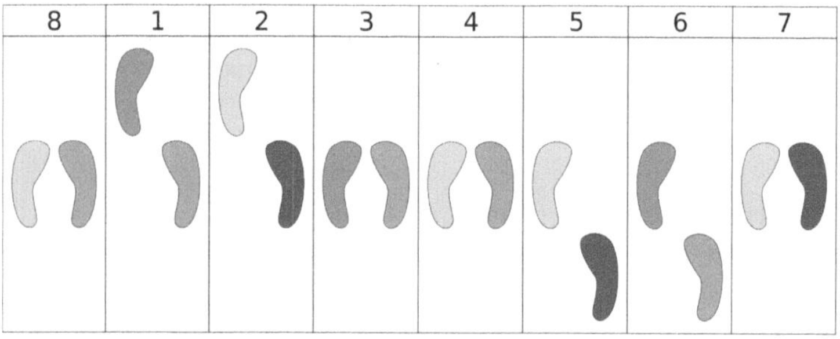

Fig. 1. UI guide for the basic forth and back Salsa dancing steps. The solid color indicates the foot that needs to be moved. (Color figure online)

The practice mode can be entered after the learner has memorized the basic steps. Now, the learner has to pay attention to the beat and the receiving feedback. The feedback can be *Online Feedback* and *Offline Feedback. Online Feedback* is the feedback displayed in real-time. It is displayed one at a time [6] to not overwhelm the learner [7]. The feedback consists of icons supported by instructions to facilitate the understanding of it (see Fig. 3). To come up with correct feedback, we interviewed a Salsa dancing teacher who pointed out some common mistakes performed by beginners. Based on this, we implemented the following feedback instructions: Reset Dancing, Look Straight, Move Body, and Smile (see Fig. 2).

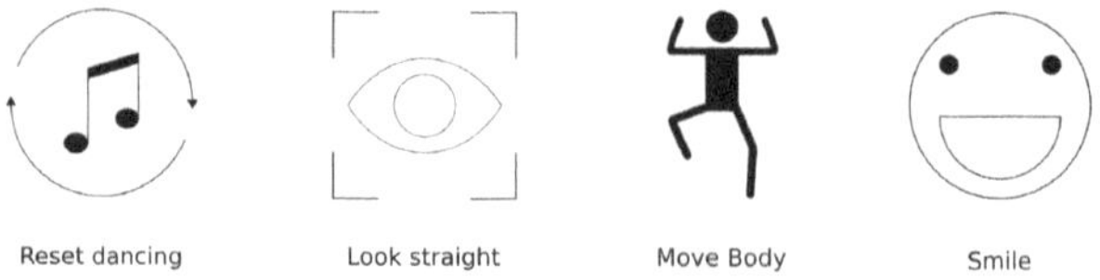

Fig. 2. Feedback instructions presented by the *Online Feedback*

Offline Feedback can be reviewed after a dancing session. It can cover up the missing detail of the *Online Feedback* because users can spend more time reviewing it. The DC provides the user with two timelines. One timeline summarizes all *Online Feedback* and highlights when the feedback starts, when it is displayed and when it ends. The other timeline shows a plot of the suggested steps (orange) and the Salsa steps recognized from the user (green) (See Fig. 3).

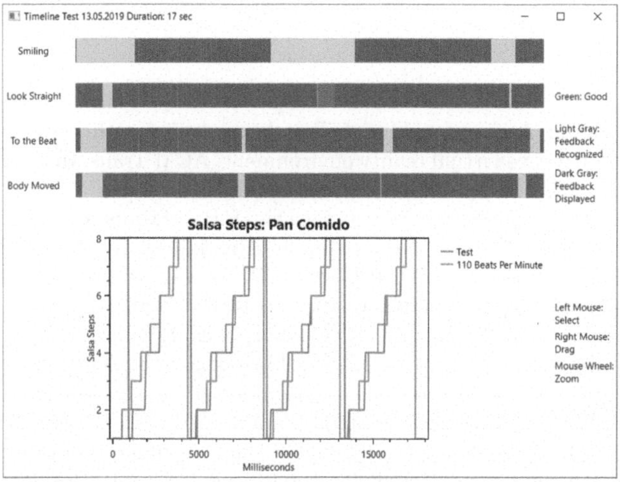

Fig. 3. An example of the *Offline Feedback*. Top: Summary of the *Online Feedback* that distinguishes between good (green), recognized (light gray) and displayed (dark gray). Down. Plot of ms and Salsa steps between the suggested (orange, 110 BPM) and the recognized steps (green, Test). (Color figure online)

3 Gesture and Beat Recognition

To guide the learners through the dancing steps and give feedback, the DC has to track the learner and recognize his movements. The DC uses the Kinect V2 sensor to track the learner performing the dancing steps. We used Kinect Studio and Kinect Visual Gesture Builder to build the recognition of the Salsa dancing steps. We recorded clips of a professional salsa dancing teacher with Kinect Studio, and tagged them with Kinect Visual Gesture Builder to create gesture detectors.

Following the beat is important in dancing and the aim of the DC is to be used for different songs and music styles. Hence, it is important to identify the beat of the songs. To achieve this, we manually denoted the beats per minute (BPM) of a song and started to build a beat annotated music library (BAML). In the current version of the DC the BPM are not aligned with the true onsets of each song. Nonetheless, we consider this good enough to indicate the learner to move with the rhythm.

4 Conclusion and Future Work

This is a demo paper where we present the DC a dancing tutoring system that helps users to learn and practice basic salsa dancing steps, and that can be expanded to support the practice of different dancing styles. Our plan is to follow a designed-based research approach to iteratively improve the DC and hence enhance current practices aimed to teach people how to dance.

References

1. Kyan, M., et al.: An approach to ballet dance training through ms kinect and visualization in a cave virtual reality environment. ACM Trans. Intell. Syst. Technol. (TIST) **6**, 23 (2015). https://doi.org/10.1145/2735951
2. Aich, A., Mallick, T., Bhuyan, H.B.G.S., Das, P.P., Majumdar, A.K.: *NrityaGuru*: a dance tutoring system for *Bharatanatyam* using kinect. In: Rameshan, R., Arora, C., Dutta Roy, S. (eds.) NCVPRIPG 2017. CCIS, vol. 841, pp. 481–493. Springer, Singapore (2018). https://doi.org/10.1007/978-981-13-0020-2_42
3. Alexiadis, D.S., Kelly, P., Daras, P., O'Connor, N.E., Boubekeur, T., Moussa, M.B.: Evaluating a dancer's performance using kinect-based skeleton tracking. In: Proceedings of the 19th ACM International Conference on Multimedia, MM 2011, pp. 659–662, ACM, New York (2011). https://doi.org/10.1145/2072298.2072412
4. Muangmoon, O., Sureephong, P., Tabia, K.: Dance training tool using kinect-based skeleton tracking and evaluating dancer's performance. In: Benferhat, S., Tabia, K., Ali, M. (eds.) IEA/AIE 2017. LNCS (LNAI), vol. 10351, pp. 27–32. Springer, Cham (2017). https://doi.org/10.1007/978-3-319-60045-1_4
5. Dong, Y., Liu, J., Chen, Y., Lee, W.Y.: Salsaasst: Beat counting system empowered by mobile devices to assist salsa dancers. In: 2017 IEEE 14th International Conference on Mobile Ad Hoc and Sensor Systems (MASS), pp. 81–89, October 2017. https://doi.org/10.1109/MASS.2017.25
6. Schneider, J., Boerner, D., van Rosmalen, P., Specht, M.: Can you help me with my pitch? studying a tool for real-time automated feedback. IEEE Trans. Learn. Technol. **9**(4), 318–327 (2016)
7. Schneider, J., Börner, D., van Rosmalen, P., Specht, M.: Stand tall and raise your voice! a study on the presentation trainer. In: Conole, G., Klobučar, T., Rensing, C., Konert, J., Lavoué, É. (eds.) EC-TEL 2015. LNCS, vol. 9307, pp. 311–324. Springer, Cham (2015). https://doi.org/10.1007/978-3-319-24258-3_23

ClassMood App: A Classroom Orchestration Tool for Identifying and Influencing Student Moods

Marc Beardsley[1(✉)], Milica Vujovic[1], Marta Portero-Tresserra[2], and Davinia Hernández-Leo[1]

[1] Universitat Pompeu Fabra, Barcelona, Spain
marc.beardsley@upf.edu
[2] Universitat Autònoma de Barcelona, Barcelona, Spain

Abstract. Certain affective states are less conducive to learning than others. Moreover, results from studies suggest that a classroom's social-emotional climate affects student motivation and performance; and that moods can be automatically transferred among individuals in a group. The ClassMood App is an online classroom orchestration tool for social emotional learning that identifies the aggregate mood of a class and suggests classroom activities for educators to help shift the class mood to one that is more conducive to learning. Suggested activities are categorized based on how they aim to impact students' internal state of arousal. The application aims to facilitate learner and educator development of self-awareness and self-management competencies consistent with the CASEL framework for systemic social and emotional learning. Preliminary results, conducted as part of an iterative designed-based research process, suggest that the tool is perceived as being easy-to-use for both educators and undergraduate students.

Keywords: Learning design · Learning analytics · Orchestration tool · Social Emotional Learning · Self-regulated learning · Mindfulness

1 Pedagogical Background

Studies about the relationship between affective states and student performance suggest that certain physiological states or moods are less conducive to learning than others [1, 2]. Study results also suggest that the emotional climate of a class affects student motivation, conduct, and performance [3, 4]; and that moods can be automatically transferred among individuals in a group [5]. A classroom emotional climate can be described as "the extent to which teachers promote positive emotions and make students feel comfortable" [3]. Further, investigations have found that immediate interventions such as mindful breathing are able to induce a change in the affective state of individuals, specifically in reducing test anxiety and in increasing positive automatic thoughts [6]. Arguments to better support student social-emotional learning (SEL) in formal education have been put forth [7, 8] and interventions supporting the social-emotional learning of students have been found to positively impact student wellbeing

M. Scheffel et al. (Eds.): EC-TEL 2019, LNCS 11722, pp. 723–726, 2019.
https://doi.org/10.1007/978-3-030-29736-7_75

and their academic outcomes [9, 10]. Weissberg et al., 2015 propose a framework, the CASEL framework for systemic social and emotional learning, to help educators identify the core SEL competencies to prioritize. The ClassMood App has been conceptualized to facilitate learner and educator development of two of the prioritized competencies: self-awareness and self-management.

Therefore, it is important for teachers to consider the classroom emotional climate when orchestrating the activities proposed to their students, both to reach the best possible emotional conditions for their students to learn and to facilitate the development of the related competencies. The concept of classroom orchestration refers to "how a teacher manages, in real time, multi-layered activities in a multi-constraints context" [11]. Several orchestrations tools have been proposed in the literature to support teachers in classroom real-time management considering the specific needs and constraints of a given context. However, these tools have focused on cognitive and social aspects [12] and there is a lack in addressing the emotional facet. The ClassMood App aims to fill this gap.

2 Technological Background

The ClassMood App is a standalone, web-based, social and emotional learning orchestration tool that provides teachers with real-time data that identifies the aggregate mood of a class and suggests classroom activities to help teachers guide learners to moods that are more conducive to learning. The application is compatible with mobile, tablet and laptop devices.

Students insert a unique code and are prompted to select their current mood from a graphical interface that plots a selection of moods. The U-shaped graphical interface is based on an interpretation of the affective circumplex model [13, 14] (see Fig. 1). After selecting their current state, students have the opportunity to submit a comment to notify the teacher of the cause of their mood. Student data and comments are collected anonymously.

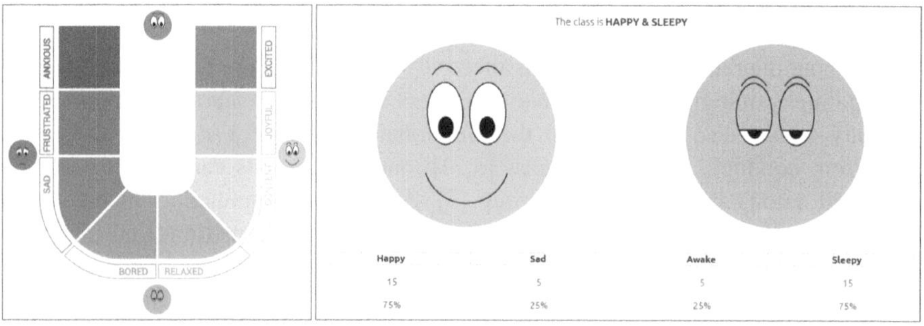

Fig. 1. Screenshots of the ClassMood App (https://classmood.upf.edu/). (a) Student mood selection interface & (b) Teacher dashboard displaying an aggregate class mood.

Teachers start by creating a mood measuring event. The creation of the event results in teachers receiving a code to share with their students. As students enter their mood selections, teachers can monitor the submissions in the teacher's dashboard. The learning analytics are displayed with differing levels of granularity (see Fig. 1). The first level categorizes the mood of the class based on aggregated categories of valence (e.g. happy or sad) and arousal (e.g. awake or sleepy). The second level presents a count of students per mood – to provide a more detailed mood mapping of the class. The final level displays the individual comments entered by students to explain their moods. The dashboard data is updated every 8 s. When ready, teachers can generate an activity suggestion from the dashboard.

Suggested activities are categorized based on how they aim to impact students' internal state of arousal (see Table 1). The aggregate mood is calculated based on the ratio of awake-to-sleepy ratings with greater weight given to low arousal ratings. Activities are evidence-based or have been contributed by collaborating educators.

Table 1. Categories of suggested activities to impact student moods.

Category	Arousal	Sample activity names
Energize	Increase	Mindful walking
Calm	Decrease	Progressive muscular relaxation [15]

3 Use Case, Preliminary Results and Future Work

As part of an iterative designed-based research process, the ClassMood App was presented to individual educators to elicit feedback and was tested in an undergraduate university class. In the class, the application was used to gauge the mood of the class and suggest an activity for the teacher to run for students as a warm-up activity prior to a regular lesson. Preliminary results suggest that the tool is perceived as being useful and easy-to-use for educators and undergraduate students. Future work is needed to validate and expand the offering of suggested activities, to refine the interface for younger students, to integrate historical data into the teacher dashboard, and to facilitate teacher-adoption of the tool with formative training.

Acknowledgements. This work has been co-funded by the European Union, Project Number 2018-1-ES01-KA201-050646 (Spotlighters) under the Erasmus + programme; and partially supported by FEDER, the National Research Agency of the Spanish Ministry of Science MDM-2015-0502, TIN2014-53199-C3-3-R, TIN2017-85179-C3-3-R. DHL is a Serra Húnter Fellow. Note: The material in this paper reflects only the authors' views and the European Commission cannot be held responsible for any use that may be made of the information it contains. The authors want to thank Pablo Abenia for the technical implementation of the application, and Minna Huotilainen for her advice regarding the student graphical interface.

References

1. Mega, C., Ronconi, L., De Beni, R.: What makes a good student? How emotions, self-regulated learning, and motivation contribute to academic achievement. J. Educ. Psychol. **106**(1), 121 (2014)
2. Pardos, Z.A., Baker, R.S., San Pedro, M.O., Gowda, S.M., Gowda, S.M.: Affective states and state tests: investigating how affect and engagement during the school year predict end-of-year learning outcomes. J. Learn. Anal. **1**(1), 107–128 (2014)
3. Brackett, M.A., Reyes, M.R., Rivers, S.E., Elbertson, N.A., Salovey, P.: Classroom emotional climate, teacher affiliation, and student conduct. J. Classr. Interact. **46**, 27–36 (2011)
4. Reyes, M.R., Brackett, M.A., Rivers, S.E., White, M., Salovey, P.: Classroom emotional climate, student engagement, and academic achievement. J. Educ. Psychol. **104**(3), 700 (2012)
5. Barsade, S.G.: The ripple effect: emotional contagion and its influence on group behavior. Adm. Sci. Q. **47**(4), 644–675 (2002)
6. Cho, H., Ryu, S., Noh, J., Lee, J.: The effectiveness of daily mindful breathing practices on test anxiety of students. PLoS One **11**(10), e0164822 (2016)
7. Zins, J.E., Bloodworth, M.R., Weissberg, R.P., Walberg, H.J.: The scientific base linking social and emotional learning to school success. J. Educ. Psychol. Consult. **17**(2–3), 191–210 (2007)
8. Weissberg, R.P., Durlak, J.A., Domitrovich, C.E., Gullotta, T.P.: Social and emotional learning: past, present, and future. In: Durlak, J.A., Domitrovich, C.E., Weissberg, R.P., Gullotta, T.P. (eds.) Handbook of Social and Emotional Learning: Research and Practice, pp. 3–19. Guilford Press, New York (2015)
9. Durlak, J.A., Weissberg, R.P., Dymnicki, A.B., Taylor, R.D., Schellinger, K.B.: The impact of enhancing students' social and emotional learning: a meta-analysis of school-based universal interventions. Child Dev. **82**(1), 405–432 (2011)
10. Nathanson, L., Rivers, S.E., Flynn, L.M., Brackett, M.A.: Creating emotionally intelligent schools with RULER. Emot. Rev. **8**(4), 305–310 (2016)
11. Dillenbourg, P.: Design for classroom orchestration. Comput. Educ. **69**, 485–492 (2013)
12. van Leeuwen, A., Rummel, N.: Orchestration tools to support the teacher during student collaboration: a review. Unterrichtswissenschaft **47**, 143–158 (2019). https://doi.org/10.1007/s42010-019-00052-9
13. Russell, J.A., Peterson, B.S.: The circumplex model of affect: an integrative approach to affective neuroscience, cognitive development, and psychopathology. Dev. Psychopathol. **17**(3), 715–734 (2005)
14. Plutchik, R.: The nature of emotions: human emotions have deep evolutionary roots, a fact that may explain their complexity and provide tools for clinical practice. Am. Sci. **89**(4), 344–350 (2001)
15. Jacobson, E.: Progressive Relaxation. University of Chicago Press, Chicago (1938)

BloomGraph: Graph-Based Exploration of Bouquet Designs for Florist Apprentices

Kevin Gonyop Kim(✉), Catharine Oertel, and Pierre Dillenbourg

Computer-Human Interaction for Learning and Instruction (CHILI) Laboratory, École Polytechnique Fédérale de Lausanne (EPFL), Lausanne, Switzerland
{kevin.kim,catharine.oertel,pierre.dillenbourg}@epfl.ch

Abstract. Exploring design space is an important process in finding solutions to a design task. In this paper, we present BloomGraph, an online application developed for florist apprentices to explore the space of bouquet designs. BloomGraph provides a graph-based interface that allows users to explore design variations as they follow the nodes in a graph. This paper presents the preliminary result from an experimental study with florist apprentices in vocational education in Switzerland. Based on the early findings, we discuss the potential of the application as a learning tool and address the next steps to be followed.

Keywords: Vocational education and training · Design exploration

1 Introduction

A common structure of the vocational education and training (VET) system in Switzerland is dual-track – students learn in schools for one or two days per week while they do apprenticeship at workplaces for the remaining days. The idea behind the dual-track system is based on the concept of learning through experience which has been explored with various theoretical models such as experiential learning and situated learning [2,5]. Although the dual VET is considered as an effective system for developing professional competence, one of the main challenges is on the richness of the experience. The practical experience gained from a workplace is often limited to the specific situations the apprentices are exposed to and it does not usually cover the whole spectrum of the practical experience related to the profession.

Given the situation, our interest is on how we can "expand the experience" of the learners in vocational education. We consider digital technologies as a means to approach the problem. In addition to the school-workplace setup, we create a digital space between the two where the learners can gain some additional experience in their learning journey. The concept of the shared digital space between school and workplace is based on the "Erfarraum" model proposed by Schwendimann et al. in [6]. It is a pedagogical model for designing educational technologies for dual vocational systems.

M. Scheffel et al. (Eds.): EC-TEL 2019, LNCS 11722, pp. 727–731, 2019.
https://doi.org/10.1007/978-3-030-29736-7_76

What kind of activities can be designed in the expanded digital space? The idea that motivated this study is to expand the experience by exploring digital variations of designs. In most design-related vocations, exposure to examples and design variations is an important part of learning. Exploring design variations can help the learners in acquiring better understanding of the design space [3,4,7]. Although it is not a direct experience from real-world situations, we believe that it is an additional experience that could supplement the real experience and enrich the practical side of their learning.

We have chosen florist as the target profession to explore the idea. We implemented a web application called "BloomGraph" that allows florist apprentices to explore the variations of a bouquet design. BloomGraph proposes variations of the bouquet design and allows learners to systematically navigate through them.

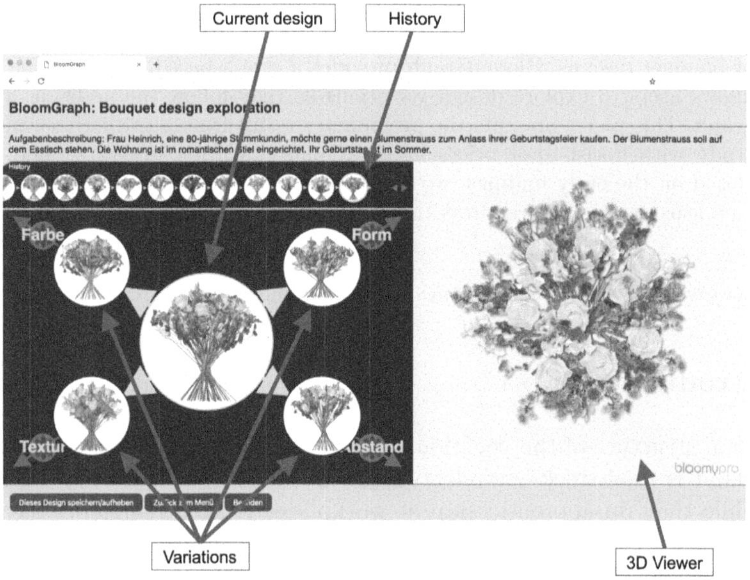

Fig. 1. BloomGraph application.

2 System Description

The development of the BloomGraph application is based on the curiosity about the florist apprentices' understanding of the design space and the choices they make in the exploration. Can florist apprentices think of a bouquet designing task as a combinatorial problem of different attributes? Will they navigate the design space in a systematic way or just randomly? If we provide a structure in their exploration, will it be helpful?

We came up with a graph-based interface that allows users to explore design variations as they follow the nodes in a graph. In the graph, each axis leads to transforming the design in terms of one particular attribute of the bouquet. By clicking the nodes in different axes, users can vary the design systematically in terms of the important attributes, thus providing a structured way of exploring the design variations.

The interface of the BloomGraph application is shown in Fig. 1. The graph interface is shown on the left where the centre node shows the current design and the four variations of the current design in the surrounding nodes. After discussions with florist teachers, we have chosen four important attributes of a bouquet design to be the four axes (color, form, texture and spacing). In each axis, a variation of the current bouquet in terms of the specific attribute is proposed. When you click one of the four variations, it comes to the centre and the new variations of that design are proposed. Above the graph, there is a history bar that shows all the designs the user went through. Using the history bar, the user can backtrack to previous designs. On the right side, there is the interactive 3D viewer. User can rotate and zoom in/out the design. The viewer also shows the names of flowers if the user hovers the mouse pointer over them.

The application is written in JavaScript and built using *Meteor* framework. We used *React* and *D3.js* libraries for the front-end rendering. The 3d viewer is provided by BloomyPro [1].

3 Preliminary Findings and Future Work

We have conducted an experimental study using BloomGraph. The goal of the experiment is to investigate how florist apprentices would explore the space of design variations given the graph-based interface of BloomGraph. Forty-four florist apprentices from 3 vocational schools in Switzerland were randomly assigned to experimental and control groups. The experimental group was given the graph-based interface of the BloomGraph application. The control group was given the linear interface. In the linear interface, four random variations are proposed in a linear formation. It resembles the way people go through a catalog or a search result. The task for the participants was to select a bouquet design that is most appropriate for a virtual customer. Each participant was asked to do two trials on two different scenarios.

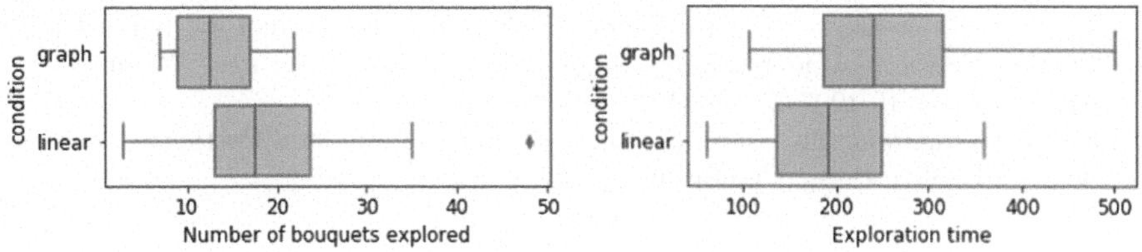

Fig. 2. Comparison between graph and linear conditions: number of bouquets explored (*left*) and total exploration time (*right*).

From the preliminary look at the result, we observe some interesting differences in their exploration behaviour. We first observe that the number of bouquets participants explored for a task is significantly different in the two conditions ($Stat = 8.60$, $p < 0.01$). In the graph condition, they explored fewer bouquets ($mean = 13.2$, $SD = 4.46$) before making their choices compared to the linear condition ($mean = 18.5$, $SD = 9.42$). It is logical since the graph allows more direct navigation than the linear presentation, but what it shows is that the apprentices were able to navigate using the graph. The large standard deviation in the linear condition shows that the number of explored bouquets is quite divergent among the participants when using the linear interface. In terms of the exploration time, we observe that it was significantly longer in the graph condition ($Stat = 8.60$, $p < 0.01$). Therefore, in the graph condition, participants spent more time on fewer bouquets. The results are shown in Fig. 2. We also looked at the diversity of bouquets explored and we observe that it is higher in the experimental condition. The difference is significant between the two conditions ($Stat = 5.71$, $p < 0.05$). We interpret these observations as the evidence of some strategy-driven behaviour in the exploration.

The early findings from the experiment suggest research directions and questions to be addressed using the BloomGraph application. What is the effect of the structured navigation in design space exploration? What are the strategies adopted in the graph exploration and how do they affect the learning gain? Can we predict the next choice of a learner or can we guide them to explore undiscovered designs? The future work will address these questions by analyzing the following topics: (i) classification of the learners based on the exploration strategies, (ii) how the learners' understanding of design space changes from the exploration activity, and (iii) how it can be integrated in the learning journey of an apprentice in VET.

References

1. BloomyPro: 3D Floral Platform (2019). https://bloomypro.com/
2. Kolb, A., Kolb, D.: Experiential learning theory: a dynamic, holistic approach to management learning, education and development. In: Steven, J.A., Cynthia, V.F. (eds.) The SAGE Handbook of Management Learning, Education and Development, pp. 42–68. SAGE Publications, Thousand Oaks (2009)
3. Kolodner, J., Wills, L.: Case-based creative design. AISB Q. **85**, 1–8 (1993)
4. Kulkarni, C., Dow, S.P., Klemmer, S.R.: Early and repeated exposure to examples improves creative work. In: Leifer, L., Plattner, H., Meinel, C. (eds.) Design Thinking Research. Understanding Innovation, pp. 49–62. Springer, Cham (2014). https://doi.org/10.1007/978-3-319-01303-9_4
5. Lave, J., Wenger, E.: Situated Learning: Legitimate Peripheral Participation. Cambridge University Press, Cambridge (1991)

6. Schwendimann, B., Cattaneo, A., Dehler-Zufferey, J., Gurtner, J., Bétrancourt, M., Dillenbourg, P.: The 'Erfahrraum': a pedagogical model for designing educational technologies in dual vocational systems. J. Vocat. Educ. Train. **67**(3), 367–396 (2015)
7. Tohidi, M., Buxton, W., Baecker, R., Sellen, A.: Getting the right design and the design right. In: Proceedings of the SIGCHI Conference on Human Factors in Computing Systems, pp. 1243–1252. ACM (2006)

Group Coach for Co-located Collaboration

Sambit Praharaj[1(✉)], Maren Scheffel[1], Hendrik Drachsler[1,2,3], and Marcus Specht[1]

[1] Open Universiteit, Valkenburgerweg 177, 6419AT Heerlen, The Netherlands
{sambit.praharaj,maren.scheffel,hendrik.drachsler,marcus.specht}@ou.nl
[2] DIPF, Schloßstr. 29, 60486 Frankfurt am Main, Germany
[3] Goethe Universität, Robert-Mayer-Str. 11-15, 60629 Frankfurt am Main, Germany

Abstract. Collaboration is an important 21st century skill; it can take place in a remote or co-located setting. Co-located collaboration (CC) gives rise to subtle human interactions that can be described with multimodal indicators like gaze, speech and social skills. In this demo paper, we first give a brief overview of related work that has identified indicators during CC. Then, we look briefly at the feedback mechanisms that have been designed based on these indicators to facilitate CC. Using these theoretical insights, we design a prototype to give automated real-time feedback to facilitate CC taking the help of the most abundant modality during CC i.e., audio cues.

Keywords: Co-located collaboration · Real-time feedback · CSCL · Collaboration indicators · Multimodal learning analytics

1 Introduction

Collaboration is an important skill in the 21st century. It can take place in different settings and for different purposes: collaborative meetings [5,8,11], collaborative project work [3], collaborative programming [4] and collaborative brainstorming [10]. Collaboration can be either co-located (or face-to-face) or in a remote setting. "The requirement of successful collaboration is *complex, multimodal, subtle,* and learned over a lifetime. It involves *discourse, gesture, gaze, cognition, social skills, tacit practices,* etc." [9, p. 1–2, emphasis added]. Furthermore, in each context, the indicators of collaboration vary. For example, in collaborative programming pointing to the screen, grabbing the mouse from the partner and synchrony in body posture are relevant indicators for good collaboration [4]; whereas in collaborative meetings gaze direction, body posture, speaking time of group members are relevant indicators for good collaboration quality [5,11]. Different feedback mechanisms are designed based on these indicators of CC to facilitate CC [1,5]. Most of these feedback mechanisms are designed by analyzing the indicators of collaboration in a post-hoc manner instead of a real-time operational design [3]. Some studies which have used real-time feedback

M. Scheffel et al. (Eds.): EC-TEL 2019, LNCS 11722, pp. 732–736, 2019.
https://doi.org/10.1007/978-3-030-29736-7_77

suffer from the limitation of employing human observers to drive those feedback mechanisms and others have used simplistic automated feedback mechanisms [7]. For instance, Tausch et al. [10] used human observers to drive the real-time feedback system and Bachour et al. [1] used the total speaking time of each group member to drive a real-time feedback LED table-top display which displayed the amount of total speaking time of each group member by glowing different colour LED lights assigned to each member. So, to address this problem, we seek answer to the following research question:

RQ: How can we design an automated *real-time feedback* system using *audio cues* to facilitate co-located collaboration *in-the-wild*?

2 Related Work

In this section, we will first analyze related work according to the different indicators obtained from audio-based cues during CC; and secondly, we review some of the feedback mechanisms designed using these indicators.

2.1 Audio-Based Indicators During Co-located Collaboration

Different types of verbal and non-verbal indicators have been used in the past to measure collaboration quality ranging from tangible interaction, audio-based cues, gesture, posture to gaze and eye interaction [3]. For the scope of this paper, we focus on the most abundantly occurring modality during CC, i.e., audio cues. Lubold and Pon-Barry [6] found that *proximity, convergence* and *synchrony* are different types of coordination (or rapport) cues obtained from the audio features (like intensity, pitch and jitter) of the collaborating dyads.

Bassiou et al. [2] assessed collaboration among students using *non-lexical speech* features. Types of collaboration levels marked are: Good (all 3 members are working together and contributing to the discussion), Cold (only two members are working together), Follow (one leader is not integrating the whole group) and Not (everyone is working independently). This coding was based on two types of engagement: simple (i.e., talking and paying attention) and intellectual (i.e., actively engaged in the conversation). Combination of both the speech-activity features (i.e., *solo duration*, *overlap duration of two persons*, *overlap duration of all three persons*) and speaker-based features (i.e., *spectral*, *temporal*, *prosodic* and *tonal* features of speech) were good predictors of collaboration. Speaking time of each member can also be a good indicator of collaboration [1].

2.2 Feedback Based on Audio Cues During Co-located Collaboration

Simpler versions of feedback which leverage the audio cues (like speaking time) during collaboration have proved effective in the past. For instance, Bachour et al. [1] reflected back the speaking time of each group member using a real-time feedback during CC by glowing different coloured LED lights on a smart table. According to this study, the real-time feedback helped to maintain the equity of participation. Similarly, Praharaj et al. [8] reflected back the speaking time of each member on the fly by a multicoloured line chart. Tausch et al. [10] used an intuitive metaphorical feedback moderated by human observers during *collaborative brainstorming*. The group members brainstormed on a certain topic and their collaboration was measured by the number of ideas generated from the audio. Then the human observers controlled the public shared display which showed a *metaphorical garden*. This garden comprised of flower plants symbolizing the individual state of a group member and a tree symbolizing the state of the group which was well grown with fruits and flowers when a group had balanced participation.

In summary, most of these studies were in controlled conditions using specialized furniture and devices. Some real-time feedback mechanisms employed human observers (i.e., the non-automated ones), were simplistic (i.e., the automated ones) and acted as a mere reflection for the group to self-regulate instead of an actionable feedback; while others used a post-hoc analysis for the teachers (or facilitators) to reflect on the group activity.

3 Group Coach

Our technological infrastructure[1] is mostly driven by the need to analyze the audio input not disregarding the need for accommodating the input from other modalities in future. So, we looked at different solutions for automated audio analysis in real-time and the possibility of using different real-time feedback mechanisms to our maximum advantage. Finally we decided to use Unity over Audacity, Supercollider and Praat because of the readily-available real-time audio input analysis and game design interface support making it easy to design the automated real-time feedback. For the feedback in unity, we represent each group member as a tree which is nothing but a game object. For the audio input, we use one microphone for each group member and connect this to a single laptop which displayed the feedback using the Unity interface. We use different audio cues such as the speaking time, number of turns and change in loudness and map it to growth of different parts of the tree such as tree trunk, branches, leaves and flowers. Figures 1 and 2 show the growth of the tree at initial and late-mid stages respectively. Inspired from previous works [10], we chose metaphorical feedback which is easier for group members to understand and act as they can associate it with their day-to-day life or surroundings.

4 Use-Case for the Group Coach

We tested this prototype design in different types of meetings and continued refining the design further based on the feedback of the stakeholders. We will expand this prototype in future work using video modality in other collaboration

[1] https://github.com/sambit2/GroupCoachCC.

Fig. 1. Initial tree

Fig. 2. Late-mid tree

settings such as collaborative programming and engineering design in order to test its usability. We will test it further in future meetings with varying numbers of participant ranging between 2 and 6 members for large scale adoption.

5 Conclusions

We succeeded in designing an automated real-time feedback prototype. Its design will be further refined in follow-up studies based on the requirements of the different stakeholders that will be using the system.

References

1. Bachour, K., Kaplan, F., Dillenbourg, P.: An interactive table for supporting participation balance in face-to-face collaborative learning. IEEE Trans. Learn. Technol. **3**(3), 203–213 (2010)
2. Bassiou, N., et al.: Privacy-preserving speech analytics for automatic assessment of student collaboration. In: INTERSPEECH, pp. 888–892 (2016)
3. Cukurova, M., Luckin, R., Mavrikis, M., Millán, E.: Machine and human observable differences in groups' collaborative problem-solving behaviours. In: Lavoué, É., Drachsler, H., Verbert, K., Broisin, J., Pérez-Sanagustín, M. (eds.) EC-TEL 2017. LNCS, vol. 10474, pp. 17–29. Springer, Cham (2017). https://doi.org/10.1007/978-3-319-66610-5_2
4. Grover, S., Bienkowski, M., Tamrakar, A., Siddiquie, B., Salter, D., Divakaran, A.: Multimodal analytics to study collaborative problem solving in pair programming. In: Proceedings of the 6th International Conference on LAK, pp. 516–517. ACM (2016)
5. Kim, T., Chang, A., Holland, L., Pentland, A.S.: Meeting mediator: enhancing group collaboration using sociometric feedback. In: Proceedings of the 2008 ACM Conference on CSCW, pp. 457–466. ACM (2008)
6. Lubold, N., Pon-Barry, H.: Acoustic-prosodic entrainment and rapport in collaborative learning dialogues. In: Proceedings of the 2014 ACM WS on Multimodal Learning Analytics Workshop and Grand Challenge, pp. 5–12. ACM (2014)
7. Praharaj, S., Scheffel, M., Drachsler, H., Specht, M.: MULTIFOCUS: MULTImodal learning analytics for co-located collaboration understanding and support. In: EC-TEL (Doctoral Consortium) (2018)

8. Praharaj, S., Scheffel, M., Drachsler, H., Specht, M.: Multimodal analytics for real-time feedback in co-located collaboration. In: Pammer-Schindler, V., Pérez-Sanagustín, M., Drachsler, H., Elferink, R., Scheffel, M. (eds.) EC-TEL 2018. LNCS, vol. 11082, pp. 187–201. Springer, Cham (2018). https://doi.org/10.1007/978-3-319-98572-5_15
9. Stahl, G., Law, N., Hesse, F.: Reigniting CSCL flash themes. Int. J. CSCL **8**(4), 369–374 (2013)
10. Tausch, S., Hausen, D., Kosan, I., Raltchev, A., Hussmann, H.: Groupgarden: supporting brainstorming through a metaphorical group mirror on table or wall. In: Proceedings of the 8th Nordic Conference on HCI, pp. 541–550. ACM (2014)
11. Terken, J., Sturm, J.: Multimodal support for social dynamics in co-located meetings. Pers. Ubiquit. Comput. **14**(8), 703–714 (2010)

Visual Learning Analytics of Multidimensional Student Behavior in Self-regulated Learning

Rafael M. Martins[1](✉), Elias Berge[2], Marcelo Milrad[1], and Italo Masiello[3]

[1] Department of Computer Science and Media Technology, Linnaeus University, 351 95 Växjö, Sweden
{rafael.martins,marcelo.milrad}@lnu.se

[2] Hypocampus AB, 412 92 Gothenburg, Sweden
elias@hypocampus.se

[3] Department of Pedagogy and Learning, Linnaeus University, 351 95 Växjö, Sweden
italo.masiello@lnu.se

Abstract. In Self-Regulated Learning (SLR), the lack of a predefined, formal learning trajectory makes it more challenging to assess students' progress (e.g. by comparing it to specific baselines) and to offer relevant feedback and scaffolding when appropriate. In this paper we describe a Visual Learning Analytics (VLA) solution for exploring students' datasets collected in a Web-Based Learning Environment (WBLE). We employ mining techniques for the analysis of multidimensional data, such as t-SNE and clustering, in an exploratory study for identifying patterns of students with similar study behavior and interests. An example use case is presented as evidence of the effectiveness of our proposed method, with a dataset of learning behaviors of 6423 students who used an online study tool during 18 months.

Keywords: Visual Learning Analytics · Self-Regulated Learning · Exploratory data analysis · Multidimensional data · t-SNE

1 Pedagogical Background

Directing one's own learning experience, e.g. through the practice of Self-Regulated Learning (SLR), may bring benefits to the individual's learning processes [1]. SLR-related concepts and ideas are very common in massive online learning environments such as MOOCs [2] or other learning platforms [3], where the student's independence is a requirement of the underlying pedagogical design and practices. In such systems, students are usually offered several options of educational materials to choose from upfront, and can follow their own learning

This work was financially supported by the Linnaeus University Centre for Data Intensive Sciences and Applications (DISA).

M. Scheffel et al. (Eds.): EC-TEL 2019, LNCS 11722, pp. 737–741, 2019.
https://doi.org/10.1007/978-3-030-29736-7_78

paths through the material as they see fit for their self-regulated learning goals. While this flexibility is important for such online learning environments to exist and thrive among students with radically different backgrounds and learning goals, this approach also introduces new challenges: the apparent lack of structure in the students' activities makes it harder for the teacher to understand and assess their progress, or to organize students into meaningful groups (e.g. for adaptive learning).

In this paper we describe an interactive Visual Learning Analytics (VLA) [7] system designed to provide insights, through exploratory data analysis, about the behaviors of groups of students in an SLR-based WBLE. The research question that drives this work is: *How can VLA techniques support teachers/instructors in detecting and understanding emergent SLR behaviors in large groups of students?* The outcomes might lead, among other possibilities, to the construction of custom representations for different groups of learners in different contexts, the emergence of communities, and the introduction of effective gamification concepts tailored towards the deliberate cognitive efforts on skills needed for enhanced SRL-performance in specific subjects.

2 Technical Background

A simplified version of the architecture of our proposed system is illustrated in Fig. 1. We first model students as *learning vectors* based on their free choice of study material (mined from their actual behavior in the system). A student's learning vector indicates, for every topic available in the system, how active that student is within that topic. In Fig. 1, the collection of all learning vectors is referred to as M. In order to make sure the data is as representative and meaningful as possible, and inspired by techniques from Natural Language Processing (NLP) [8], we apply a TF-IDF (*Term Frequency* $\times$ *Inverse Document Frequency*) transformation to M, diminishing the effect of general and non-discriminative topics. The result is a preprocessed "bag-of-topics" we refer to as M_p (Fig. 1).

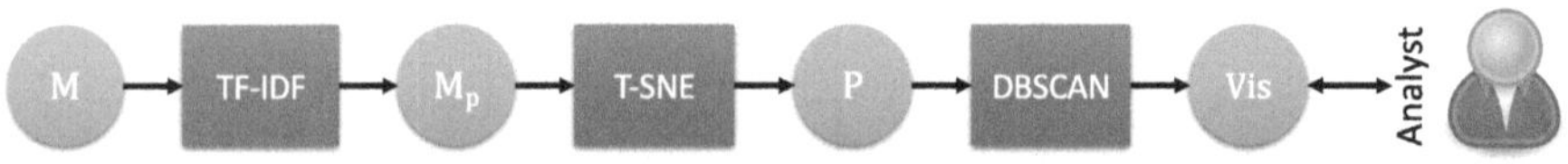

Fig. 1. Overview of the architecture of our proposed VLA system.

The next step is to generate the overview visualization using t-Distributed Stochastic Neighbor Embedding (t-SNE) [6], a very popular dimensionality reduction technique. Through an involved process of statistical modeling and optimization, t-SNE generates a $2D$ representation (P) of a multidimensional dataset such that points are positioned close to their nearest neighbors. The outcome is visualized as a scatterplot (cf. Fig. 2), where each point is a student, and tight groups of points represent students that have similar learning

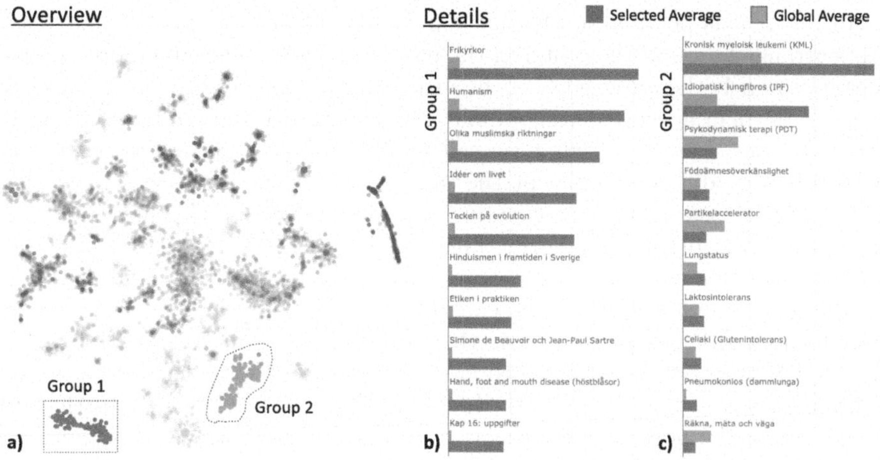

Fig. 2. Overview of case study with Hypocampus students. (Color figure online)

vectors and, thus, are interested/active in similar topics. As an extra step in order to make it easier to navigate the overview and identify relevant groups, the clustering technique DBSCAN [4] is applied to P, highlighting clusters with different colors and removing outliers and noise in the final visualization (Vis). The teacher can then interact with Vis and select specific clusters to investigate details. The details view consists on vertical bar charts containing the average level of interest of the students of the selected group in their 10 most-active topics (blue bars), compared to the average level of interest of the entire population of students in the same topics (orange bars). This allows the teacher to not only explore *which* are the topics of interest for each cluster, but also to compare *how* they differ from the rest of the students.

3 Use Case

Our approach is demonstrated in a use case with data extracted from the behaviors of students that used the online study app Hypocampus[1] from September 2017 to March 2019. In Hypocampus, the students choose their own path through the material, which is arranged in *books* and *chapters*, and are frequently faced with free text and multiple choice questions to test what they learned so far, following a method of spaced repetitions [5]. We aggregated all students' answers according to (a) their related topics (in this case, book chapters), and (b) the students who answered them, resulting in 6423 learning vectors (one per student), each with 1445 topics. Thus, the activity of a student in a topic reflects how many questions she answered that are related to that topic, and groups are formed by students who are active in similar combinations of topics.

[1] https://www.hypocampus.se/.

In Fig. 2, it is possible to identify many small clusters of closely-related students arranged around the center of the plot, and a few larger and more isolated clusters towards the outer edge of the visualization. As an example, we investigate two of them in more details (annotated as Group 1 and Group 2 in Fig. 2). Group 1 is an example of what we call *prolific* groups: students who are very active in many different topics at the same time. In this case, we can see that they are interested mostly in topics such as "Humanism", "Free church", "Muslim rights", and others. The large difference between the blue and the orange bars indicate that they are much more active than the average in these topics. On the other hand, Group 2 is an example of a group of students with a much more focused and specific approach: they are very active in a handful of topics, but are not very interested in much else. In this case, the topics of interest are "Chronic Myeloid Leukemia" and "Idiopatic Pulmonary Fibrosis". In the rest of the topics (the bottom 8 bar charts from Fig. 2c) their activity is either very close to, or below, the average.

4 Results and Outcomes

In this paper we have described our interactive VLA system for exploring the multidimensional SLR behaviors (or *learning vectors*) of students in a WBLE. For the initial results shown here, we consider "SLR behavior" as the students' choice of material and their level of activity in the selected topics. The same techniques and methods could be adapted, however, to include a broader view on SLR, i.e., with self-evaluation, self-reflection, and the students' planning of activities to reach their goals, or to include different types of learning resources. A possible implication is that a better understanding of the learning activities by the clusters/communities may support the teacher in directing the communities of learners towards subjects which may be neglected by the students but judged as of greater importance for the learning progress.

References

1. Broadbent, J., Poon, W.: Self-regulated learning strategies & academic achievement in online higher education learning environments: a systematic review. Internet High. Educ. **27**, 1–13 (2015)
2. Maldonado-Mahauad, J., Pérez-Sanagustín, M., Kizilcec, R.F., Morales, N., Munoz-Gama, J.: Mining theory-based patterns from big data: identifying self-regulated learning strategies in massive open online courses. Comput. Hum. Behav. **80**, 179–196 (2018)
3. Markant, D.B., Settles, B., Gureckis, T.M.: Self-directed learning favors local, rather than global, uncertainty. Cogn. Sci. **40**(1), 100–120 (2016)
4. Schubert, E., Sander, J., Ester, M., Kriegel, H.P., Xu, X.: DBSCAN revisited, revisited: why and how you should (still) use DBSCAN. ACM Trans. Database Syst. **42**(3), 19:1–19:21 (2017)
5. Settles, B., Meeder, B.: A trainable spaced repetition model for language learning. In: Proceedings of the 54th Annual Meeting of the Association for Computational Linguistics (Volume 1: Long Papers), vol. 1, pp. 1848–1858 (2016)

6. Van Der Maaten, L., Hinton, G.: Visualizing data using t-SNE. J. Mach. Learn. Res. **9**, 2579–2605 (2008)
7. Vieira, C., Parsons, P., Byrd, V.: Visual learning analytics of educational data: a systematic literature review and research agenda. Comput. Educ. **122**, 119–135 (2018)
8. Zhang, Y., Jin, R., Zhou, Z.H.: Understanding bag-of-words model: a statistical framework. Int. J. Mach. Learn. Cybern. **1**(1–4), 43–52 (2010)

ATest – An Online Tool to Solve Arithmetic Constructions

Šárka Gergelitsová and Tomáš Holan(✉)

Faculty of Mathematics and Physics, Charles University, Prague, Czech Republic
Tomas.Holan@mff.cuni.cz

Abstract. During school arithmetic classes, it often happens that some pupils are not confident enough in performing a particular type of operations in the time before the teacher moves to another topic. Therefore, we are looking for help for the case when the pupil needs to practice, but the topic is already felt as boring. For this purpose, we suggest tasks of arithmetic constructions where a pupil constructs the required value from given numbers and operations.

ATest application is designed to give pupils such tasks and to allow pupils to solve them. It works on a browser, so it can be run on computers as well as mobile devices. The application itself evaluates the pupils' answers and thus provides immediate feedback. The answers are saved to the database, so the teacher can follow the pupils' progress.

After a short period of free ATest operation, we performed a controlled experiment with a group of 30 pupils aged 11. Then they filled in a questionnaire. The results are promising.

Keywords: Counting · Arithmetics · Construction · Online application

1 Pedagogical Background

In the early years of school, children learn to do operations with integers: addition, subtraction, multiplication, division. As long as they acquire the necessary algorithms and until these operations are automated, they examine them from different sides, looking for missing values at different positions in the operation: result, first operand, second operand (similarly to TIMSS tasks). At this time, it is still a search for them.

Then counting and performing the operations are learned (for some well, others are still making mistakes) and the teacher moves to another topic, where it is assumed the ability has been acquired. A recent adventure becomes a routine, a rather uninteresting skill to use, the last step in solving another, more interesting problems. In this last step a lot of mistakes are made, some caused by inattention, because pupils are thinking of another problem, others caused by the fact that pupils have not learned to count quickly and reliably.

1.1 The Problem

If we run too fast from counting, some kids will not learn to count quickly and correctly (see e.g. [1, 2]). Therefore, we return to basic operations with ATest. We want children

M. Scheffel et al. (Eds.): EC-TEL 2019, LNCS 11722, pp. 742–745, 2019.
https://doi.org/10.1007/978-3-030-29736-7_79

to learn to count reliably, want them to "see" the result of an operation and keep the result in mind for further calculation. Thus, we suggest a new kind of task described below.

1.2 Arithmetic Constructions

ATest is an online application for performing arithmetic constructions.

The arithmetic construction is such connection of given building blocks whose final result is the required number. The building blocks are numbers and arithmetic operations; every operation has two inputs and one output. A building block can be used at most once, but the value from its output can be used multiple times.

A task can be for example "Construct the value of 40 from numbers 3 and 5 using addition and multiplication operations", expressed to pupil graphically as can be seen in Fig. 1 (left). There can be more different constructions for a task. However, the task mentioned has only one solution which can be seen in Fig. 1 (right). Operation results can be hidden or displayed depending on the task variant.

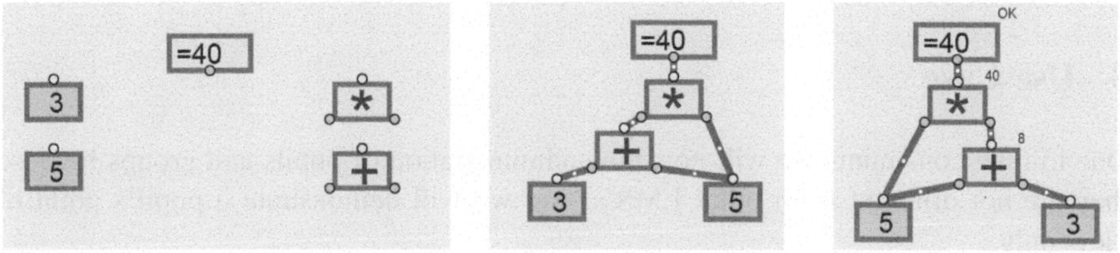

Fig. 1. Example of a task (left) and correct answers in two task versions (right)

1.3 Constructivist Pedagogy

The characteristics of constructivist pedagogy can be found in e.g. [3]. In [4] authors try to sort out some of the different meanings of constructivism relative to math education and characterize "moderate constructivism", which meets the following views:

- People construct their own knowledge.
- This is done via mental processes, including reflection (perhaps on actions).
- This allows them to adapt to their environment.
- People's old knowledge is used in constructing their new knowledge.

All these processes and principles have a very broad meaning, but, except for the third of the above mentioned, which applies more to the application of scientific knowledge in the real world, arithmetic constructions meet the mentioned views.

It is disputable to claim that ATest is a typical application for constructivist learning and teaching. But, in fact, in ATest pupils have to "classify", "analyze", "create" and derive their own strategies while solving the tasks. What pupils are looking for, is the way how to construct the target, and they are not equipped with any general, unambiguous guidance or algorithm to achieve this.

2 Technological Background

ATest is an online application working on a browser.

Teacher creates and manages pupils' accounts, creates groups (i.e. "containers" for tasks) with given deadlines and selects tasks from the list of available tasks (actually hundreds of tasks).

After logging in, the pupil chooses a group (homework, test…) and then its particular task to solve. The task-solving process involves moving building blocks and connecting their inputs with outputs of other blocks.

When a pupil decides to submit his/her solution, the construction is sent to the server, where it is evaluated and stored and the pupil is given a message whether the solution was correct. In the case of an error the pupil can continue and try to fix the solution or try to find a completely new different way how to solve it.

Backend of the ATest application uses PHP and MySQL, frontend uses HTML and JavaScript. Except for the JavaScript construction of the editing part, the application reuses the source code of GeoTest application [5].

Tasks were verified and mostly even generated using a Python program.

3 Use Case

Due to time constraints we will not show administration of pupils and groups because they are not different from other LMS's, and we will demonstrate a pupil's point of view only.

We will use the GUEST-login that is publicly accessible, so participants will have a possibility to try it later themselves using their own devices. The address is http://atest.geometry.cz/EN. Demonstrated use shows the individual steps the pupil makes while solving and submitting a solution and correcting a wrong answer.

4 Results and Outcomes Achieved

After putting ATest into operation, 100 pupils aged 11–14 and 50 older pupils were using it. Then, we did a one-hour test lesson in one class with 30 pupils aged 11 years.

Pupils were assigned 13 tasks two of which have already been solved before and 11 were completely new. We have included these two "well-known" tasks in the test tasks to prevent the loss of motivation for the less successful pupils.

ATest allows pupils to solve the tasks in any order. From the records, we can estimate how much time pupils have spent on solving a particular task, and which tasks were solved first (by all or most of pupils).

The pupils completed the job gradually, they had 35 min to deal with the tasks, but the fastest pupil finished the test in 13 min and 10 pupils needed less than 30 min to work. There were 18 out of 30 pupils who successfully finished all the tasks (13), 5 pupils resolved 12 tasks, the lowest number of successfully resolved tasks was 9.

The data obtained from the test during the solution process show:

- Pupils learn, they discover new ways to get the desired value
  - To solve task *K* (required *90*; given *10, 5,* + + *), they needed much less time than to deal with task *D* (required *37*; given *10, 5, 2,* + + *). But, they resolved it later, task *K* was lower than *D* in the task list (the tasks were numbered *A–K*).
  - To solve *C* task (required *48*; given *11, 4,* + + +), they needed significantly less time than solving task *A* (required *44*; given *11, 9, 4,* + +), though the values of outputs of the blocks were displayed in *A* and not in *C* (a teacher can enable or disable it while assigning the task) – the absence of displayed results doesn't matter in case of easy counting.
- The most difficult task proved to be task *J* (required *108*; given *11, 4,* + * *).

The pupils were asked to fill in a survey after solving the tasks. Assessment was in the form of a multiple choice where a selection of more options was allowed. In three questions the pupils were asked to formulate their own answer.

It shows that for most of the pupils (19) solving tasks was fun till the end, they were not tired at all (16) and displayed results were helpful if the results were large numbers (15).

5 Conclusion

We designed a new kind of tasks to motivate pupils to practice operations with numbers. It is supported by an online application that provides pupils with immediate feedback and stores results for a teacher. Its applicability was tested during a one-hour lesson with 30 pupils and it was evaluated using the data stored and a survey. The results look promising, but more data and more detailed analysis are needed to get a reliable conclusion. There are many applications with the similar goal (e.g. Math Garden, Prodigy Math Game) but we have found none with such kind of task.

References

1. Ashman, G.: Why students make silly mistakes in class (and what can be done), The Conversation (2015). http://theconversation.com/why-students-make-silly-mistakes-in-class-and-what-can-be-done-48826. Accessed 23 Jun 2019
2. Rushton, N.: Common Errors in Mathematics. Research Matters: A Cambridge Assessment publication, vol. 17, pp. 8–17 (2014)
3. Hanley, S.: On constructivism. Maryland collaborative for teacher preparation (1994). http://www.inform.umd.edu/UMS+State/UMD-projects/MCTP/Essays/Constructivism.txt. Accessed 23 Jun 2019
4. Selden, J., Selden, A.: Constructivism in mathematics education – what does it mean? In: Research Conference in Collegiate Mathematics Education (1996)
5. Gergelitsová, Š., Holan, T.: GeoTest – a system for the automatic evaluation of geometry-based problem. Comput. Appl. Eng. Educ. **24**(2), 297–304 (2016)

YourMOOC4all: A Recommender System for MOOCs Based on Collaborative Filtering Implementing UDL

Francisco Iniesto[1(✉)] and Covadonga Rodrigo[2]

[1] Institute of Educational Technology, The Open University, Milton Keynes, UK
francisco.iniesto@open.ac.uk

[2] School of Computer Science, UNED, Madrid, Spain
covadonga@lsi.uned.es

Abstract. YourMOOC4all is a pilot research project to collect feedback requests regarding accessible design for Massive Open Online Courses (MOOCs). In this online application, a specific website offers the possibility for any learner to freely judge if a particular MOOC complies Universal Design for Learning (UDL) principles. User feedback is of great value for the future development of MOOC platforms and MOOC educational resources, as it will help to follow Design for All guidelines. YourMOOC4all is a recommender system which gathers valuable information directly from learners to improve aspects such as the quality, accessibility and usability of this online learning environment. The final objective of collecting user's feedback is to advice MOOC providers about the missing means for meeting learner needs. This paper describes the pedagogical and technological background of YourMOOC4all and its use cases.

Keywords: Accessibility · MOOCs · Recommender system · UDL · Collaborative filtering · Design for All

1 YourMOOC4all Recommender System

Massive Open Online Courses (MOOCs) are attracting a wide range of disabled learners, but there is still a gap in providing accessible platforms and educational resources to them [1]. Choosing which MOOC to enrol in, among many options, is one influential decision learners must undertake during online lifelong learning. The ambiguity of the factors to be considered may lead learners to miss chances or make wrong decisions that could affect their professional development.

Recommender systems have recently been used in the educational context advising learners to enrol in specific courses depending on learners' performance in previous courses [2]. The recommendations can be applied to particular parts of MOOCs, such as the forums where discussions can be difficult to track [3] or using external sources like opinions in social media [4]. The curriculum recommendation mechanism has not gone unnoticed by the big MOOC providers, edX or Coursera, for whom trying to offer courses of interest for their learners is a priority in their sustainable development and business model [5].

M. Scheffel et al. (Eds.): EC-TEL 2019, LNCS 11722, pp. 746–750, 2019.
https://doi.org/10.1007/978-3-030-29736-7_80

The objective of the recommender systems is to show learners elements according to their interests in a personalised way, but recommendation based on content has the disadvantage of not recommending elements that have never previously been sought by the learner. The add-on of collaborative filtering helps to recommend new elements based on learner's preferences and also on the ratings of other learners on those appreciations [6, 7]; that is, the system makes automatic predictions about the interests of a user after accumulating opinions of many users [8] in a *"person-person correlation"* [9]. Applying the memory-based method, also called neighbourhood-based filtering algorithms, the recommendations made to a user are based on other users with similar ideas to that target user [10], building what is known as a neighbourhood.

Due to the high amount of MOOC offerings in the world, over 800 universities globally have launched at least one MOOC, existing more than 9 K MOOCs [11], the need for specific recommender sites is indisputable. The work presented here, called YourMOOC4all[1], is a recommender system influenced by other systems that use learners' feedback. There exist several MOOC aggregator sites, such as CourseTalk[2], where learners can add feedback about the MOOCs they are participating in and receive recommendations based on their feedback. It is also possible to review different pedagogical aspects of the MOOCs, for instance by rating them or adding free text comments, which includes giving an opinion about the content of the MOOC, the provider, or the instructor.

There is a critical point ignored in the MOOC recommender systems while dealing with inclusive design and it is the lack of detailed information regarding the accessibility level to ensure that all learners can access the platform and the educational resources. Universal Design for Learning (UDL) offers a framework to evaluate MOOC design and determine possible improvements to make at an early stage of development [12]. Therefore, YourMOOC4all targets the accessibility in MOOCs for all learners aiming to get recommendations directly from user needs.

2 YourMOOC4all Prototype

In this work, collaborative filtering is used and learner feedback is organised from a wide range of participants into a coherent and actionable structure. Among the advantages of the recommender systems based on collaborative filtering is the ability to represent elements based on the opinions of the community of participating learners. Learners are the best to provide compliments and criticisms of course designs, especially those with diverse needs [13]. YourMOOC4all is a programmed prototype in a testing stage [14]. The current version of the prototype includes the evaluation framework using UDL; the next version will link the questionnaire information into the recommender system through the learner's profile.

The evaluation process is created following the framework proposed by UDL principles. These indicators have been developed by the authors based on the last

[1] YourMOOC4all, http://yourmooc4all.lsi.uned.es.

[2] Course Talk, https://www.coursetalk.com/.

guidelines version from 2018 implementing its three principles: (1) provide multiple means of engagement, (2) provide multiple means of representation and (3) provide multiple means for action and expression [12]. Table 1 shows the selected search criteria, the information harvested from the MOOC providers and the UDL indicators for managing user's evaluation.

The technologies used throughout the project have been all open source, and are listed below:

- **Web server.** Ubuntu Server operating system version 17.4, with Apache to serve the static pages and Passenger to serve as an application server.
- **Harvesting.** To obtain information from MOOC providers, a gateway has been implemented using the Open Archives Initiative Protocol for Metadata Harvesting (OAI-PMH) standard that defines the XML (e.g., format, labels) of the content that can be collected.
- **Programming language and framework.** The language used for business logic is Ruby version 2.3.6. Ruby On Rails has been used in version 4.2.10, for the Framework used in the back-end of the web application. HTML5 and CSS have been used as layout languages.
- **Database.** The web hosting database server is PostgreSQL.

Table 1. Search criteria, harvested information and UDL evaluation

Search criteria	Harvested information	UDL evaluation
1. Course title 2. Theme 3. General information	1. Name 2. MOOC platform 3. Provider institution 4. General information 5. Learning objectives 6. Previous knowledge required 7. Target group 8. Accessibility information	1. UDL 31 indicators (Likert scale) a. Means of engagement (10) b. Means of representation (12) c. Means for action and expression (9) 2. Free text evaluations

Table 2. YourMOOC4all use cases

Use cases	
1. Search a course in the system 2. Change system language 3. Register\Login the system 4. Recover\Change password	5. Evaluating a MOOC 6. Select a course as interesting 7. Harvest information from platforms and MOOCs 8. Manage the courses, institutions, platforms, languages, previous edition and users

Eight use cases have been included, as shown in Table 2. The use case to evaluate a MOOC is formed by the following components and scenario (Table 3): **Main actor**: Registered user; **Preconditions**: User must have an active account in the system;

Table 3. Evaluating the use case success scenario

The action of the registered user	The system's response
1. The user enters the home page (home)	2. The system displays the homepage for unidentified users
3. User clicks on the link "Login"	4. The system shows the login
5. User fills in the email and password and clicks on the button "Login"	6. System checks that it is a valid user and shows the home page
7. User does a search of the MOOC in which he is interested	8. The system shows the results
9. User clicks the evaluating icon	10. The system displays a UDL form
11. User completes the questionnaire and clicks on the button "Create evaluation"	12. The system records the evaluation and shows the new evaluation

Post-conditions: User logins and evaluates a MOOC; **Alternative flow:** User clicks on the cancel button (11). The system returns to show the detail of the course that was being evaluated and discards the scores marked for this course (12).

3 Outcomes

In this work, learners' experiences on MOOC platforms are used to fulfil other learners' interests and diverse needs following UDL principles through a recommender system based on collaborative filtering. The aim of the project is to provide information to MOOC providers to integrate accessibility features into the platforms and educational resources, and to the learners who are in search of relevant and accessible MOOCs.

References

1. Iniesto, F., McAndrew, P., Minocha, S., Coughlan, T.: An investigation into the perspectives of providers and learners on MOOC accessibility. In: Proceedings of the 5th International Conference on Technological Ecosystems for Enhancing Multiculturality, p. 95. ACM (2017)
2. Lu, J., Wu, D., Mao, M., Wang, W., Zhang, G.: Recommender system application developments: a survey. Decis. Support Syst. **74**, 12–32 (2015)
3. Mi, F., Faltings, B.: Adaptive sequential recommendation for discussion forums on MOOCs using context trees. Educational Data Mining, pp. 24–31 (2017)
4. Wang, Y., Maruyama, N., Yasui, G., Kawai, Y., Akiyama, T.: A Twitter-based recommendation system for MOOCs based on spatiotemporal event detection. In: iConference 2017 Proceedings, vol. 2 (2017)
5. Tan, M., Wu, M.: An association rule model of course recommendation in MOOCs: based on edX platform. Europ. Sci. J., ESJ **14**(25), 284 (2018)
6. Adomavicius, G., Zhang, J.: Impact of data characteristics on recommender systems performance. ACM Trans. Manage. Inform. Syst. **3**(1), 3 (2012)
7. Ekstrand, M.D., Riedl, J.T., Konstan, J.A.: Collaborative filtering recommender systems. Found. Trends Hum.-Comput. Interact. **4**(2), 81–173 (2011)

8. Puntheeranurak, S., Chaiwitooanukool, T.: An item-based collaborative filtering method using item based hybrid similarity. In: Software Engineering and Service Science (2011)
9. Schafer, J.B., Frankowski, D., Herlocker, J., Sen, S.: Collaborative filtering recommender systems. In: Brusilovsky, P., Kobsa, A., Nejdl, W. (eds.) The Adaptive Web. LNCS, vol. 4321, pp. 291–324. Springer, Heidelberg (2007). https://doi.org/10.1007/978-3-540-72079-9_9
10. Herlocker, L., Konstan, J.A., Terveen, L.G., Riedl, J.T.: Evaluating collaborative filtering recommender systems. ACM Trans. Inf. Syst. **22**(1), 5–53 (2004)
11. Shah D.: Class Central Report. https://www.class-central.com/report/mooc-stats-2017/. Accessed 13 May 2019
12. Meyer, A., Rose, D.H., Gordon, D.T.: Universal Design for Learning: Theory and Practice. CAST Professional Publishing, Wakefield (2014)
13. Järkestig Berggren, U., Rowan, D., Bergbäck, E., Blomberg, B.: Disabled students' experiences of higher education in Sweden, the Czech Republic, and the United States–a comparative institutional analysis. Disabil. Soc. **31**(3), 339–356 (2016)
14. Iniesto, F., Rodrigo, C.: YourMOOC4all: a MOOCs inclusive design and useful feedback research project. In: Learning with MOOCs 2018: MOOCs for All – A Social and International Approach, Madrid, pp. 26–28, September 2018

ReadME – Your Personal Writing Assistant

Irina Toma[1], Teodor-Mihai Cotet[1,2], Mihai Dascalu[1,2,3(✉)], and Stefan Trausan-Matu[1,2,3]

[1] University Politehnica of Bucharest, 313 Splaiul Independentei, 060042 Bucharest, Romania
irina_toma@rocketmail.com, teodor.cotet@gmail.com, {mihai.dascalu, stefan.trausan}@cs.pub.ro
[2] Academy of Romanian Scientists, 54 Splaiul Independenţei, 050094 Bucharest, Romania
[3] Cognos Business Consulting S.R.L., 32 Bd. Regina Maria, Bucharest, Romania

Abstract. Essay writing is a difficult cognitive task for both students striving to express their ideas, as well as for tutors investing time to perform evaluations. Besides the validity of the presented ideas, students should verify that their writing is correct and coherent before submitting their essay. ReadME provides an automated method for students to evaluate and improve their writing style based on personalized suggestions. The system is also beneficial for tutors who receive a substantial number of essays for grading and require support. ReadME provides feedback at different granularity levels based on advanced Natural Language Processing techniques used to analyze the submitted texts in terms of lexicon, morphology, syntax, semantics, discourse, with emphasis on text cohesion. The prototype system is available for Romanian and English languages.

Keywords: Essay writing · Natural Language Processing · Automated evaluation · Personalized feedback

1 Introduction

Writing is a mandatory skill in the digital era. Either when referring to essays, discourses, newsletters, or even software code, writing needs to be correct, coherent, and consistent. In Romanian schools and universities, writing essays has yet to become a mandatory subject. With the implementation of the education system based on the Bologna Declaration of 2002, the education system is transitioning from the traditional final examination grading system to a more research-oriented one [1]. The new curricula encourage students to write research papers and argumentative essays, on which teachers provide personalized feedback. This sets high expectations; thus, students experience writing anxiety, which leads to a low writing motivation, and eventually to poor performance on writing exams [2]. Moreover, teachers are overwhelmed by the amount of papers they must provide feedback on. A statistical report conducted by EUROSTAT in 2014 [3] declared that an average of 15 students is assigned to each teacher.

M. Scheffel et al. (Eds.): EC-TEL 2019, LNCS 11722, pp. 751–755, 2019.
https://doi.org/10.1007/978-3-030-29736-7_81

Several online applications are available to help students write essays and proofread texts. One application is Grammarly (https://www.grammarly.com/), which offers checks of grammar, spelling punctuation, context and sentence structure, vocabulary enhancement suggestions, as well as plagiarism checks. The second application, EduBirdie (https://edubirdie.com/), provides, besides grammar checks, different automated text writing tools (such as conclusion and topic generator) and a paraphrasing tool for finding word synonyms. Both applications are available only for the English language.

ReadME is an interactive application designed to automatically evaluate written texts and provide personalized feedback and scoring. The application helps users strengthen their essay writing skills in terms of presentation, structure and text cohesion. The system is available for both Romanian and English languages.

2 Feedback Pipeline and User Experience

ReadME is an application that suits both teachers (mentors) and students (trainees). Mentors can propose essay topics as homeworks and provide feedback on the uploaded essays, while trainees introduce essays and go through the essay feedback pipeline in a wizard-style graphical interface. This paper focuses only on the trainee workflow centered on providing essay feedback.

The first step of the wizard consists of the file upload and automated language detection (see Fig. 1). The system accepts typed input texts and various file formats for import, namely PDFs and text files. Depending on the language, the number of wizard steps is modified, as Romanian language contains an additional processing step, diacritics restauration.

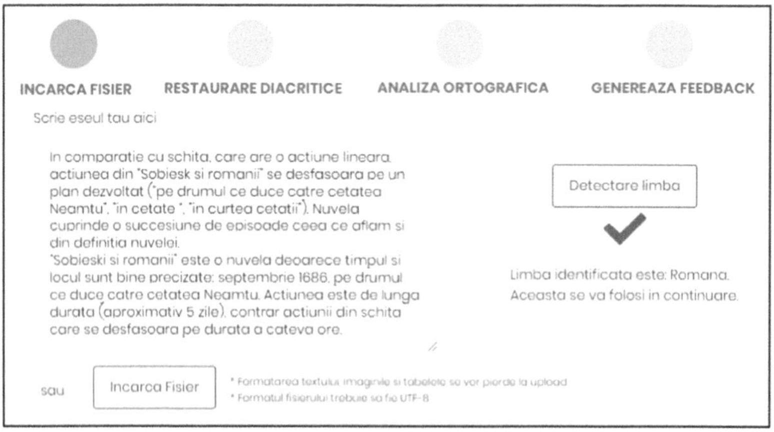

Fig. 1. Processing pipeline for Romanian language

The second step of the wizard is diacritics restauration. Romanian language extensively uses diacritics and approximately 26% of all words contain at least one character with diacritics (i.e. "ă", "â", "î", "ţ", "ş") [4]; thus, any subsequent NLP process requires the correct form of the words. Our solution consists of a neural network model, trained on an artificially constructed corpus containing well-written Romanian texts with diacritics, which were stripped off in order to construct the input for the model. The prediction is performed separately for each character which may accept diacritics. The architecture consists of 3 branches. Each branch has a separate input, the outputs of the branches being concatenated and connected with a final dense layer. The first branch consists a window of characters around the letter for which the prediction is performed. The window of characters is passed through a Bidirectional Long Short Term Memory (BiLSTM) [5]. The second branch consists of the word embedding of the word containing the letter in case. The third one is also a BiLSTM through the word embeddings of the entire sentence. We used FastText as pre-trained word embeddings [6].

Once the diacritics are restored, the user can go to the next step, the orthographic analysis. Feedback is generated for the following categories: dissonances, repetitions and punctuation errors. For the Romanian language, the corpus consisted of reports from the National Audiovisual Council of Romania containing the most frequently orthographic mistakes encountered in different media channels [7].

Further, the text is analyzed based on the complexity indices generated by the ReaderBench framework, which were properly calibrated for Romanian language [8]. Some examples of indices include: surface indices (e.g., average length of characters, average number of commas per paragraph/sentence), syntax indices (e.g., number of adjectives, verbs, etc. per paragraph/sentence), semantic indices computed using semantic similarity measures (Wu-Palmer) on ontologies and semantic models, as well as discourse structure indices. Based on these indices, a rule-based system is implemented for providing personalized feedback. The system is composed of simple rules, having a minimum and a maximum value threshold for each index. If the respective index reports a value outside the defined range, then the rule is triggered and feedback is generated. The maximum and minimum value thresholds are chosen statistically by running the indices on several well-written texts, namely popular books, generally endorsed by critics. Based on the distribution of each index, the threshold values were chosen to be 3 or 4 standard deviations from the mean.

In the user interface, the feedback is structured on four granularity levels: document, paragraph, phrase, and word. Figure 2 represents the phrase-level feedback for a text written in Romanian. The interface is divided in two parts. The left part highlights the sentences with identified issues, and, on hover, the issues are displayed on the righthand side of the screen (e.g., the number of prepositions and of nouns is too high and the phrase should be split).

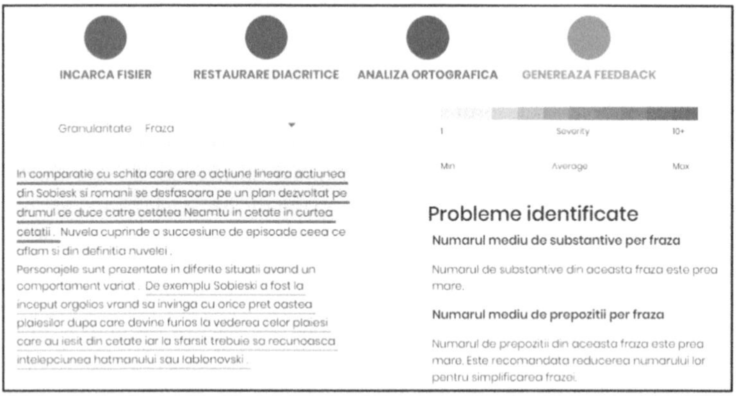

Fig. 2. Feedback at phrase level for Romanian language.

3 Conclusions and Future Development

ReadME is an interactive application that automatically evaluates written texts. Unlike other applications available on the market, it is designed to benefit two categories of users, both students (trainees) and teachers (mentors). Trainees upload an essay and go through all the feedback generation pipeline: diacritics restauration (for Romanian language), orthographic, syntactic, semantic and discourse analyses. The pipeline is not pre-imposed, as trainees can modify the text and go through the steps multiple times, until the results are adequate. In addition, mentors have access to their trainees' final essay version together with the system results, including an automated essay scoring component, which greatly reduces the required time to manually assess each essay.

The next development step is to enhance the connections between mentors and trainees, as well as to include additional visualizations for providing personalized feedback (e.g., concept heatmaps, conceptual networks, etc.). Afterwards, the system needs to undergo extensive evaluations in classroom environments to ensure that the learners' expectations match the system capabilities.

Acknowledgments. This research was supported by the ReadME project "Interactive and Innovative application for evaluating the readability of texts in Romanian Language and for improving users' writing styles", contract no. 114/15.09.2017, MySMIS 2014 code 119286.

References

1. Dascălu, C.-E.: The Knowledge Society and the Reform of Creative Writing. Annals of "Stefan cel Mare" University of Suceava, 23 (2011)
2. Martinez, C.T., Kock, N., Cass, J.: Pain and pleasure in short essay writing: Factors predicting university students' writing anxiety and writing self-efficacy. J. Adolesc. Adult Literacy **54** (5), 351–360 (2011)

3. Apostu, O., et al.: Analiza sistemului de învăţământ preuniversitar din România din perspectiva unor indicatori statistici. Universitara Publishing House, Politici educaţionale bazate pe date. Bucureşti (2015)
4. Ruseti, S., Cotet, T.-M., Dascalu, M.: Romanian diactrics restoration using recurrent neural networks. In: ConsILR 2018, Iasi, Romania, pp. 61–68 (2018)
5. Graves, A., Schmidhuber, J.: Framewise phoneme classification with bidirectional LSTM and other neural network architectures. Neural Netw. **18**(5–6), 602–610 (2005)
6. Bojanowski, P., Grave, E., Joulin, A., Mikolov, T.: Enriching word vectors with subword information. Trans. Assoc. Comput. Linguist. **5**, 135–146 (2017)
7. Florea, A.-M., Dascalu, M., Sirbu, M.-D., Trausan-Matu, S.: Improving writing for Romanian language. In: 4th International Conference on Smart Learning Ecosystems and Regional Development (SLERD 2019), Rome, Italy. Springer (2019)
8. Sirbu, M.-D., Dascalu, M., Gifu, D., Cotet, T.-M., Tosca, A., Trausan-Matu, S.: ReadME – improving writing skills in romanian language. In: ConsILR 2018, Iasi, Romania, pp. 135–145 (2018)

Towards an Editor for VR-Oriented Educational Scenarios

Oussema Mahdi(✉), Lahcen Oubahssi(✉), Claudine Piau-Toffolon(✉), and Sebastien Iksal(✉)

LIUM Laboratory, EA 4023, UBL, Le Mans University, 72085 Le Mans, France
{oussema.mahdi, lahcen.oubahssi, claudine.piau-toffolon, sebastien.iksal}@univ-lemans.fr

Abstract. VRLE (Virtual Reality Learning Environment) has long been used as an education tool. Our research work aims to propose solutions for assisting teachers to design, reuse and deploy their pedagogical scenarios in VRLE. In this demonstration paper, we present a VR-oriented pedagogical scenario editor that embeds our model allowing teachers to design and adapt their situations (in scenario form) and generate their own VRLE.

Keywords: VRLE · TEL · Pedagogical activity · Pedagogical scenario

1 Introduction

For many years, teachers have been customizing their own virtual environments to promote learning. This is known as VRLE (Virtual Reality Learning Environment). However, the design and integration of VRLE into training is a complex and costly process. The production of a VRLE is an activity that involves new technical difficulties, which are caused by the interdisciplinary intrinsic to VR or cognitive, inherited from the TEL [1, 2]. We aim to offer technical and methodological solutions for assisting teachers to produce VRLE adapted to their needs. As reflection in teachers' design practice occurred before, during, and after pedagogical situation implementation [4], we propose an iterative and participatory teacher-centered design approach.

A study of the literature on VRLE design and development models, learning scenario models, functional and technical architecture [3] permit us to identify some limits in the propositions but give us some strong basis for our proposal. Main limitations are related to (1) the difficulty of implementing design models, the inadequacy of defining adaptable and reusable models by non-computer-scientists teachers in different contexts (2) the lack of solutions for assisting the teachers in their design process (3) the model of scenario that must be defined since the design of the environment without all the pedagogical situations being necessarily known (4) the functional and technical architectures for producing a VRLE that have been developed for specific domains. In particular, the problems of design (adaptation or reuse) and operationalization of scenario models directly by teachers according to their pedagogical situations are not sufficiently addressed.

M. Scheffel et al. (Eds.): EC-TEL 2019, LNCS 11722, pp. 756–760, 2019.
https://doi.org/10.1007/978-3-030-29736-7_82

These findings revealed the following research question: how do to help teachers and design, reuse and deploy their virtual reality oriented pedagogical scenarios?

2 Theoretical Proposal

In order to help teachers in producing VRLE, we propose a methodological solution based on a design process that includes several steps from the definition of the learning situation to its operationalization (see the design process in detail in [3]). As part of this research work, we propose a VR-oriented pedagogical scenario model. That model has been designed from the theoretical analysis of the different existing scenario models (in TEL and VRLE) and the design of three examples of different pedagogical situations in different fields (chemistry, physics and biology). Our approach aims at creating a model that links the description of the pedagogical activity to the learner's activity in the virtual environment. Each activity can be divided into a sequence of actions to ensure the learner's interaction. These actions can be divided into some basic behaviors named "Virtual Behavioral Primitive" (VBP) [5] grouped into four categories: (1) Observe the virtual world; (2) Move around in the virtual world; (3) Interact in the virtual world; (4) Communicate with others or with the application. In order to carry out these activities, we notice the importance of a VR-oriented pedagogical object. We define a VR-oriented pedagogical object as a raw object (3D object) with educational and technical properties. Properties are used to store values associated with these objects. Some technical properties are common to all objects (such as those that govern the position, shape or color of objects), while others are specific to the object or the learning domain. For example, a cube (raw object) should have the technical properties "weight" as well as "position" and if it is released, it will fall and become deformed. It can be associated with educational properties related to gravitation to be used in a pedagogical context such as a physics course.

3 Technical Proposal

To provide the necessary elements for modeling such pedagogical situation, a prototype of a VR-oriented scenario editor has been developed (using Unity[1]). This editor is the concretization of our theoretical proposals. It is intended for any teacher looking to design a pedagogical content and it allows the editing and visual modeling of scenarios. To illustrate, we define a pedagogical situation in biology field. This use case shows how the editor can support teachers to design, reuse and deploy their virtual reality oriented pedagogical scenarios. The demo scenario is a learner who must first anesthetize the animal (rat or frog) intraperitoneally injected after fixing it in dorsal decubitus on a plate. Then, he intervenes on the animal by cutting, opening the skin, opening the flesh and lifting the trachea (Table 1). Finally, he places the catheter in a canal (tracheotomy).

[1] https://unity.com

Table 1. The pedagogical activity example (intervening on an anesthetized animal)

VR pedagogical situation	Placing a catheter in a canal in an anesthetized animal
Virtual environment	Virtual biology laboratory
VR activity	Intervening on an anesthetized animal
VR actions (VBP)	Cut
	Open the skin
	Open the flesh
	Lift trachea with a rope

The Fig. 1 illustrates how the teacher can script this activity via the proposed editor and presents its interfaces. First, once the teacher is logged in (Fig. 1.1), he may create a new scenario or modify an existing one (Fig. 1.2). Then, he chooses a virtual environment adapted to his pedagogical situation (Fig. 1.2A). In the following steps, objects are selected from the inventory and placed in the chosen environment (Fig. 1.4). Each pedagogical object has a list of properties; the teacher then defines the expected values. We note that the adaptation of virtual environments and VR-oriented pedagogical objects will be realized on a virtual pedagogical object's platform. This environment includes rules that describe the dynamic behavior of raw objects and their educational properties. The objective of this platform of VR-oriented pedagogical objects is to ensure their reuse in various situations regardless of the learning context. It is related to a *VR data loader module*. It embeds a VR environment loader, which defines virtual environments, and a VR objects loader which defines the graphic elements as well as their behavior and translates them into objects interpretable by the editor.

Thereafter, the step dedicated to the definition of the scenario begins. In this step the teacher identifies the pedagogical activities related to the pedagogical objectives (Fig. 1.3 and Fig. 1.3A). For each activity, a description of the expected actions is done using the bar containing the list of possible actions (Fig. 1.3, 3B and 3C). Actions represent all the operations done by the learner (for example: moving, pouring, cutting, etc.). To adapt the learning content, the prototype allows the teacher to control and orchestrate the pedagogical activities (as well as all VR actions). This ensures that the learner always solves the current activity.

The editor mainly consists of a *scenario manager* which allows teachers to manage their own scenarios (creation, reuse and modification). More particularly, it allows them to define their pedagogical activities and lead the sequencing of these activities in the scenario through a *pedagogical activity manager*. The actions of each pedagogical activity are also defined through an *action manager*. The editor uses a *data context module* which provides a concise way to translate the elements of our scenario-model in data and exchange with the *scenario database*. The following link illustrates the global architecture of the editor by presenting its modules and their interactions: https://umbox.univ-lemans.fr/index.php/apps/gallery/s/0pDf0Yg40gvnlV3.

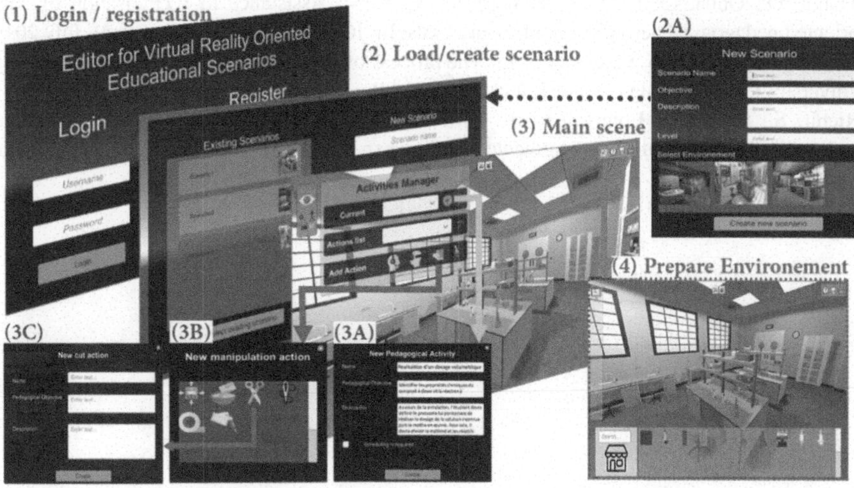

Fig. 1. Definition of VR actions to be realized in the pedagogical activity.

4 Evaluation and Conclusion

Our approach aims at proposing both technical and methodological solutions to assist teachers in describing, adapting or reusing their pedagogical scenarios. In this paper we are interested in the first part of our design process, dedicated to the design of VR-oriented pedagogical situations. We first sought to provide solutions to structure pedagogical situations in the form of reusable scenario models. In that way, we developed a VR-oriented pedagogical scenario editor. We explain the experimental objectives and discuss the different characteristics of our editor. We studied the impact of our editor on teacher-designers via an evaluation phase. The teachers were led to freely manipulate the tool in order to test its functionalities. They could propose the activities that seemed most appropriate to their pedagogical situation. The results revealed overall positive and constructive feedback on the usability and usefulness of the editor. However, the tool in its current version has some gaps therefore we aim to develop additional functionalities for our editor in order to further facilitate the design task of teachers and allow them to reuse and adapt existing situations.

References

1. Carpentier, K., Lourdeaux, D.: Generation of learning situations according to the learner's profile within a virtual environment. In: Filipe, J., Fred, A. (eds.) ICAART 2013. CCIS, vol. 449, pp. 245–260. Springer, Heidelberg (2014). https://doi.org/10.1007/978-3-662-44440-5_15
2. Marion, N., Querrec, R., Chevaillier, P.: Integrating knowledge from virtual reality environments to learning scenario models-a meta-modeling approach. In: International Conference of Computer Supported Education, pp. 254–259 (2009)

3. Mahdi, O., Oubahssi, L., Piau-Toffolon, C., Iksal, S.: Assistance to scenarisation of VR-oriented pedagogical activities: models and tools. In: ICALT 2019, Maceio, Brazil, July 2019
4. Bennett, S., Agostinho, S., Lockyer, L.: The process of designing for learning: understanding university teachers design work. Education Tech. Research Dev. **65**(11), 125–145 (2017)
5. Richir, S., Fuchs, P., Lourdeaux, D., Millet, D., Buche, C., Querrec, R.: How to design compelling virtual reality or augmented reality experience. Int. J. Virtual Reality **15**(11), 35–47 (2015)

Soéle: A Tool for Teachers to Evaluate Social Awareness in Their Learning Designs

Emily Theophilou, Anna Guxens, Dimitar Karageorgiev, Marc Beardsley(✉), Patricia Santos, and Davinia Hernández-Leo

Universitat Pompeu Fabra, Barcelona, Spain
{emily.theophilou, anna.guxens, dimitar.karageorgiev, marc.beardsley, patricia.santos, davinia.hernandez-leo}@upf.edu

Abstract. Social and Emotional Learning (SEL) has been found to positively affect academic performance and student behaviour. Nevertheless, the consideration of SEL is regularly omitted from teachers' learning design processes. Soéle is a web-based application aiming to facilitate teacher inclusion of SEL-oriented components to their lessons – with an initial focus on fostering student social awareness competencies. Soéle functions as an interactive evaluation form that allows educators to quickly and easily evaluate their learning designs and, with the help of data analytics, receive suggestions on how to improve their learning designs from a SEL perspective. Further, Soéle offers a feedback form through which students can share their impressions of the SEL tasks. This student-teacher feedback loop encourages teacher reflection and aims to establish a habit of keeping SEL skills in mind when developing new learning designs.

Keywords: Social and Emotional Learning · Learning design · Social awareness · Analytics

1 Pedagogical Background

Studies indicate that many students in the United States and Europe struggle to adjust to school environments [1], leave school early or become chronically disengaged from it [2, 3] and are in danger of developing social-emotional and mental health problems that warrant treatment [4]. Fortunately, Social and Emotional Learning (SEL), aims to foster abilities to recognize and manage emotions, solve problems effectively, and establish positive relationships with others [5].

The CASEL framework for systemic social and emotional learning identifies five core SEL competencies: self-awareness, social awareness, responsible decision making, self-management, and relationship skills [5]. Social Awareness, defined as the ability to take others' perspectives, understand their feelings and empathize with them, is a competence linked to improved academic success [6]. Yet, social awareness has been negatively impacted by technology [7] and studies in the United States show that college students' "empathic concern" and "perspective taking" scores have been plummeting in recent decades [7]. Despite teachers acknowledging the benefits of

M. Scheffel et al. (Eds.): EC-TEL 2019, LNCS 11722, pp. 761–764, 2019.
https://doi.org/10.1007/978-3-030-29736-7_83

incorporating SEL in the classroom, they also report a lack of support for implementing it [8]. Soéle is a web-based application aiming to facilitate teacher inclusion of SEL-oriented tasks to the design of their lessons – with an initial focus on fostering student social awareness competencies.

2 Technological Background

Soéle is a responsive, web-based application that functions as an interactive evaluation form allowing educators to quickly and easily evaluate their learning designs and, with the help of data analytics, receive suggestions on how to improve their learning designs from a SEL perspective. Further, Soéle offers a feedback form through which students can share their impressions of the implemented SEL tasks. This student-teacher feedback loop encourages teacher reflection and aims to establish a habit of keeping SEL skills in mind when developing new learning designs.

In using Soéle's interactive evaluation form, teachers are able to check which social awareness aspects their learning design is encompassing and which have been left out (Fig. 1C). The evaluation form contains questions covering the four categories of social awareness; empathy, perspective taking, appreciating diversity, and respect for others [5]. The questions for each category have been extracted from research studies that have successfully implemented social awareness activities in classrooms [9, 10]. Labels

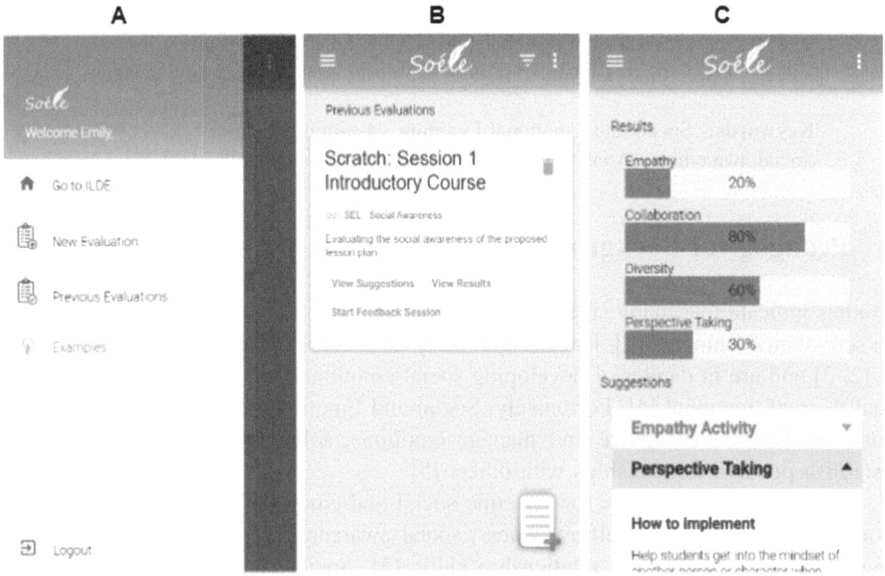

Fig. 1. Screenshots of the application: (A) Soéle menu. (B) Previous evaluations page: here, the teacher can access the results and suggestions from their previous evaluations. (C) Results page: this page is generated after a new evaluation has been completed. The teacher can see how well each SEL social awareness competency has been accounted for in their learning design and receive suggestions on how to make improvements.

related to the social awareness categories have been associated to each of the questions used in the evaluation. To tailor feedback to the teacher, the application calculates the percentage of implementation of each social awareness category using the aforementioned labels. If the percentage of implementation for a category in the evaluated learning design falls below a threshold, Soéle generates category-specific suggestions that can be used to improve the learning design. Finally, teachers can generate a feedback form to be filled in by students at the conclusion of the lesson that can be used to confirm whether students felt the lesson accomplished its objectives.

Soéle has been developed to complement the Integrated Learning Design Environment (ILDE). ILDE is an online environment that integrates tools to support teachers throughout their design process, from conceptualization to implementation [11]. While ILDE's learning design templates and tools are broad enough to encompass both SEL and cognitive learning, it lacks guidelines on how to effectively integrate SEL aspects into learning designs. Thus, Soéle complements the ILDE environment by supporting teachers in evaluating social awareness in their learning designs (Fig. 2).

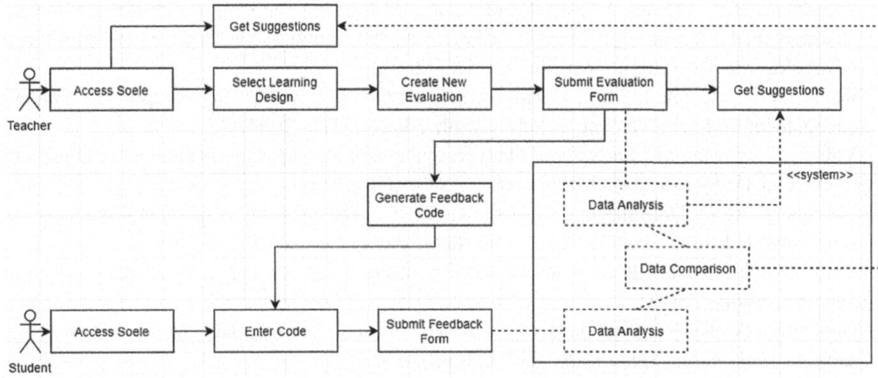

Fig. 2. Flowchart of Soéle's functionality.

3 Use Case

An elementary school teacher wants to better support the SEL competency of social awareness in her lessons. First, the teacher navigates to the Soéle website (Fig. 1A) to see examples of methods and activities to support student social awareness in classroom lessons. She then creates or amends an existing learning design in ILDE and proceeds to the Soéle evaluation form. In it, she selects her SEL competency goals, and Soéle prompts her with a series of yes or no questions. Each question is linked to one or more related SEL labels, that Soéle then uses to assess which aspects of social awareness she has effectively supported and which are lacking support (Fig. 1C). Once the evaluation form has been completed, the tool suggests different methods and activities that can be used to improve the aspects of social awareness that could be better supported. The teacher is then able to update her design and generate a feedback code (Fig. 1B) which links her Soéle evaluation with a feedback form to be completed by her students. The students' feedback form is a mirrored set of questions that Soéle then compares to the teacher's answers, to determine how well she has implemented her design. Analytics based on students' feedback allows the teacher to see how the various aspects of social awareness have been implemented. The data collected by the tool enables the teacher to reflect on her learning design and improve it for the future. Future iterations of the tool aim to support additional SEL competencies and provide teachers with data to determine how well each competency has been supported over time.

Acknowledgments. This work has been partially supported by FEDER, the National Research Agency of the Spanish Ministry of Science MDM-2015-0502, TIN2014-53199-C3-3-R, TIN2017-85179-C3-3-R. DHL is a Serra Húnter Fellow.

References

1. Weissberg, R.P., Durlak, J.: Social and emotional learning for school and life success. In: Distinguished Contribution Award Address at the Annual Meeting of the American Psychological Association, Washington, DC (2005)
2. Klem, A.M., Connell, J.P.: Relationships matter: linking teacher support to student engagement and achievement. J. Sch. Health **74**, 262–273 (2004)
3. Vallejo, C., Dooly, M.: Early school leavers and social disadvantage in spain: from books to bricks and vice-versa. Eur. J. Educ. **48**(3), 390–404 (2013)
4. Greenberg, M.T., Domitrovich, C., Bumbarger, B.: The prevention of mental disorders in school-aged children: current state of the field. Prevent. Treat. **4**, 1a (2001)
5. 2015 CASEL Guide: Effective Social and Emotional Learning Programs-Middle and High School Edition (2015)
6. Denham, S.A., Brown, C.: "Plays nice with others": social–emotional learning and academic success. Early Educ. Dev. **21**(5), 652–680 (2010)
7. Konrath, S.H., O'brien, E.H., Hsing, C.: Changes in dispositional empathy in american college students over time: a meta-analysis. Pers. Soc. Psychol. Rev. **15**(2), 180–198 (2011). https://doi.org/10.1177/1088868310377395
8. Bridgeland, J., Bruce, M., Hariharan, A.: The missing piece: a national survey on how social and emotional learning can empower children and transform schools. Civic Enterprises, Washington (2013)
9. Velsor, P.V.: Task groups in the school setting: promoting children's social and emotional learning. J. Spec. Group Work **34**(3), 276–292 (2009)
10. UNESCO: Teaching Respect for All (2014)
11. Hernández-Leo, D., et al.: An integrated environment for learning design. Front. ICT **5**, 9 (2018). https://doi.org/10.3389/fict.2018.00009

TrAC: Visualizing Students Academic Trajectories

Julio Guerra[(✉)], Eliana Scheihing, Valeria Henríquez, Cristian Olivares-Rodríguez, and Henrique Chevreux

Instituto de Informática, Universidad Austral de Chile, Valdivia, Chile
jguerra@inf.uach.cl

Abstract. TrAC is a one-shot visualisation application designed to help program directors to create an informed opinion of the academic situation of students. TrAC overlays academic data on top of the (fixed) curricular structure that the programs in our University have, and includes features to track the evolution of the academic situation term by term. The design of TrAC actively involved program directors, and the software architecture was designed to facilitate deployment in a complex institution. An ongoing pilot study with directors of diverse programs shows how TrAC effectively helps not only to inspect the academic situation of students, but also allows to discover issues of the structure of the programs, and spot difficult courses and special situations.

Keywords: Learning analytics · Curricula · Academic trajectories

1 Academic Background

At our university, as in most of the Chilean Universities, career programs offered have a fixed structure: the study progression is pre-defined. Programs have a number semesters (or years), and a fixed set of courses that are located in specific semesters, with few electives courses. A strong structure of (pre) requisite relations between courses tighten the program plan. A student who could follow the study plan as it is, is considered as an "on-time" student, and is a rare case. The usual situation is that students "get delayed" as they fail courses and end the program in more time than what is estimated by the program plan. A study of the Education Ministry of Chile [3] shows that the over-duration of university careers reached 31.3% in 2017, without any relevant variation in the last ten years. The over-duration represents a high direct cost for the students who have to finance their studies.

This situation motivates *flexibilities* offered depending on the situation of each student, such as registering a course and not meeting all the (pre) requisites. Program directors, who make decisions about exceptions, receive a many special requests for course registration and dropout each term. Student situations are very diverse, and even when the majority of cases are solved online through the

M. Scheffel et al. (Eds.): EC-TEL 2019, LNCS 11722, pp. 765–768, 2019.
https://doi.org/10.1007/978-3-030-29736-7_84

university system, some cases need face to face sessions. For each request (online or face to face) a program director has to quickly picture the overall situation of the student before making a decision. Currently, directors need to access snippets of information about the program structure and the student academic information from different parts of the university information system. We surveyed 24 program directors at our University, from different schools and three campuses, to know their perceptions of the amount of work and time these special requests means each term. The results show that 60.9% of the interviewees consider that the magnitude of the work related these special requests is greater than other tasks of the school management. All surveyed directors reported solving more than 50 requests, and in some cases reaching 200 and 300. Each request takes between 5 to 10 min online, and more than 10 min when face to face. With the goal of supporting program directors in their work, we designed and developed a visual tool that is presented in the next section.

2 Technological Background

TrAC (from Spanish *Trayectoria Académica y Curricular*) is a visualization tool that shows the curricula structure of university career programs and overlays the academic information of a given student, i.e. courses pass and failed. Figure 1 shows the different visual elements of TrAC. (A) Shows the average grade of the student in each term. (B) Shows the student program structure, with courses organized in columns representing the semesters of the plan, and the trajectory and the performance of a particular student on top of it, with different colors for passed (green) and failed (red) courses. Small circles represent previous tries of the course (failed and repeated courses). By clicking in axis button of the chart in (A), a snapshot of the student's situation of the specific semester/year is shown in (B). User can click on a course box to see more detail about it including two histograms, one of grades of the class and another with historical grades of the course (C). This also shows requisite courses ("Req") and courses that have the clicked course as a requisite ("Fluj").

TrAC was designed as an adaptation of LISSA [1], a tool that presents curricular trajectories of individual students and it is used to support face-to-face counseling. Adaptation according to our institution's needs followed an iterative process with early and continuous involvement of users [2]: (1) LISSA was presented to program directors and academic administrators to collect first adaptation requirements. (2) We had weekly meetings with one program director discussing visualization options and refining and validating semi-functional prototypes. (3) A final prototype was evaluated with other three program directors. From this process we learned that the visualization should be based on the fixed curricular structure of the program, and we based the layout in the catalogs that the university provides. The academic information should be overlaid. Design decisions were made to enable easy grasp of the academic information displayed: color represent academic results and other color features of the original catalog such as *type* of each course (e.g. foundational, general, professional, etc) was discarded to avoid color interference.

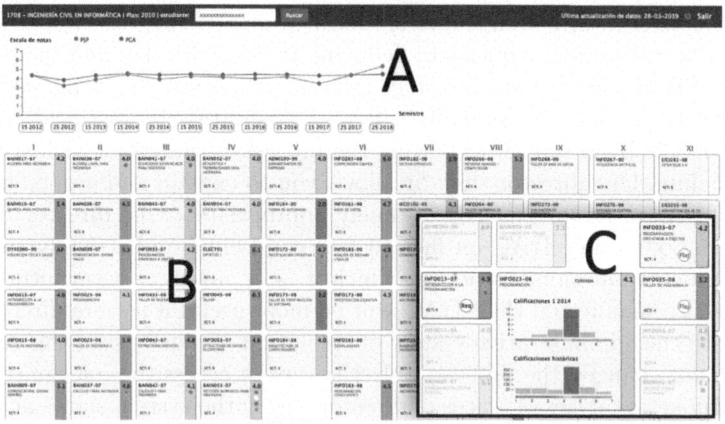

Fig. 1. Screenshot of TrAC dashboard (Color figure online)

TrAC was built using a 3-Tier Architecture [4] allowing each layer to expand, configure and deploy independently. This is very important in our context because the sources of academic data used by TrAC are diverse and the system should guarantee protection and anonymity of the data. Figure 2 presents the components of the TrAC architecture. (A) User interface accessible through a web browser (ReactJS). (B) Manage requests made by A (Angular JS). (C) contains the functional business logic and manage the connection with the database (Angular JS). (D) Database/data storage system (PostgreSQL). (E) Contains the functional business logic to perform the ETL (Extract-Transform-Load) process from *csv* files (Python). (F) Institutional data storage system. (G) Institutional API, it receives a student ID and returns a token allowing data to be anonymous.

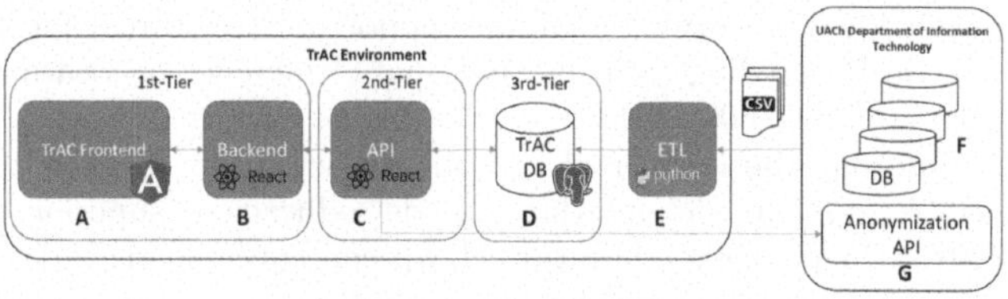

Fig. 2. Architecture of TrAC

3 Results and Outcomes Achieved

TrAC has been deployed in a pilot (currently ongoing) starting in March 2019 with 16 program directors of three campuses of our University. Alongside using the tool, the pilot has included three sessions of socialization in the different campuses, two training workshops, and a half-time meeting for feedback of the experience. Overall directors shows enthusiasm about using the tool and agree that it facilitates solving requests by reducing the time it takes and the potential errors: "it [TrAC] gives you a sense of reliability because you don't need to do computations or analysis manually". It also facilitates the justification of the decisions made, by graphically showing the progress situation of each student in his curriculum. One director said "it allows you to explain and argue about the decision because the information is timely appropriate". One director reported positively about using TrAC on face to face counseling and strongly suggested to give students autonomous access, which it is in our short-term future plans. Directors also manifested that TrAC will be more useful if it were directly integrated with the administrative system of resolution of requests. In this sense the tool "has not changed the process, only the way to access the information".

Preliminary analyses of traces of directors using the system shows active and diverse patterns of use: some users only need an overall view (and few actions requesting details of courses and requisite structure), while others go deep in each case. These preliminary observations open interesting opportunities for research that we plan to address later as more data is collected.

Acknowledgement. Work funded by the LALA project (grant no. 586120-EPP-1-2017-1-ES-EPPKA2-CBHE-JP). This project has been funded with support from the European Commission. This publication reflects only the views of the authors, and the Commission cannot be held responsible for any use which may be made of the information contained therein.

References

1. Charleer, S., Moere, A.V., Klerkx, J., Verbert, K., De Laet, T.: Learning analytics dashboards to support adviser-student dialogue. IEEE Trans. Learn. Technol. **11**(3), 389–399 (2018). https://doi.org/10.1109/TLT.2017.2720670
2. De Laet, T., Broos, T., Verbert, K., Van Staalduinen, J.P., Ebner, M., Leitner, P.: Involving stakeholders in learning analytics: opportunity or threat for learning analytics at scale. In: Proceedings 8th International Conference on Learning Analytics and Knowledge, pp. 602–606 (2018)
3. MINEDUC: Informe duración real y sobreduración de las carreras de educación superior. servicio de información de educación superior (2013–2017) (Spanish) (2018). https://www.mifuturo.cl/wp-content/uploads/2019/03/informe_duracion_real_de_las_carreras_sies_2018_editado.pdf
4. Schuldt, H.: Multi-tier Architecture, pp. 1862–1865. Springer, Boston (2009). https://doi.org/10.1007/978-0-387-39940-9_652

Demonstration of an Innovative Reading Comprehension Diagnostic Tool

Sarah E. Carlson[1(✉)], Ben Seipel[2], Gina Biancarosa[3], Mark L. Davison[4], and Virginia Clinton[5]

[1] Georgia State University, Atlanta, GA 30303, USA
scarlson@gsu.edu
[2] California State University, Chico, CA 95929, USA
bseipel@cuchico.edu
[3] University of Oregon, Eugene, OR 97403, USA
ginab@uoregon.edu
[4] University of Minnesota, Minneapolis, MN 55455, USA
mld@umn.edu
[5] University of North Dakota, Grand Forks, ND 58202, USA
virginia.clinton@UND.edu

Abstract. This demonstration introduces and presents an innovative online cognitive diagnostic assessment, developed to identify the types of cognitive processes that readers use during comprehension; specifically, processes that distinguish between subtypes of struggling comprehenders. Cognitive diagnostic assessments are designed to provide valuable information by measuring specific processes emphasized during learning, and can provide instructionally relevant results aligned with curriculum that other large-scale, standardized assessments cannot provide (e.g., [1]). This hands-on session includes information behind how the technology of MOCCA™ ([2]) was developed, as well as how a reader would experience taking this assessment, how a teacher/educator would find the results of a user's assessment, and which instructional techniques to then use. Interpretation of assessment results and instructional recommendations are obtainable online. Future directions for the continued development of online digital learning regarding how to generate appropriate cognitive processes (e.g., inferences) during reading are ongoing and discussed.

Keywords: Cognitive diagnostic assessment · Reading comprehension · Cognitive processing · Online instructional recommendations

1 Pedagogical Background

Reading is a complex process comprised of many components, and students have been shown to struggle with reading for various reasons (e.g., decoding, fluency, comprehension [3]). Therefore, knowing the specific reasons why some students struggle with such components would provide valuable information for intervention development. The following assessment (i.e., MOCCA™) is a classroom-based cognitive diagnostic assessment designed to identify *WHY* students struggle specifically with the cognitive processing of reading comprehension [1, 2].

M. Scheffel et al. (Eds.): EC-TEL 2019, LNCS 11722, pp. 769–772, 2019.
https://doi.org/10.1007/978-3-030-29736-7_85

Previous research has established two types of struggling readers: Those who struggle with lower-level (e.g., decoding) and those who struggle with higher-level (e.g., comprehension) reading skills [2–4]. The latter group is commonly termed *poor comprehenders*: Readers who exhibit poor comprehension compared to peers with similar word-reading and vocabulary skills (e.g., [4]). Moreover, research has revealed that poor comprehenders exhibit difficulty with causally coherent inferences (e.g., [4]).

Causally coherent inferences require synthesis of why an event occurs based on relevant goals and subgoals previously identified in the text *and* generate missing information from background knowledge consistent with this synthesis. Although poor comprehenders *do* make these inferences, they do not make them as *consistently* as good comprehenders. Instead, they often use other types of comprehension processes that are strategic and useful, but fail to fill the causal gap in the text. These are either paraphrases (i.e., rephrasing of prior text but do not generate missing information) or lateral connections (i.e., elaborations or personal associations, which use background knowledge but may *not be causally coherent* with the text). These trends have been found repeatedly with intermediate grade readers (i.e., Grades 3-5; e.g., [4]); however, have been found with less efficient methods (i.e., think alouds). Researchers have, thus, been prompted to develop more practical measures of the comprehension process. To date, some measures target specific populations (e.g., adult readers; [5]). Others look at inferences in the presence or absence of supportive illustrations [6]. Some use texts that are a series of logical, relational statements rather than more common narrative and expository forms [5]. Critically, none offer diagnostic information about what poor comprehenders *are doing* when they read, just what they are *not doing successfully*. Thus, an efficient assessment that distinguishes which processes poor comprehenders rely on would help deliver more targeted instruction.

2 Technological Background

MOCCA™ is such an assessment as described above. There are currently three versions available to educators at different levels: An original, a Lite, and a college version. Both the original and Lite versions are designed and validated to be used with students in Grades 3–5. The Lite version can also be used for benchmarking. All three versions include narrative texts, and the college version also includes expository texts. All versions are administered online. Each item is a discourse-level maze task where students complete a missing sentence with one of three choices to best complete a 7-sentence text. Examinees choose among three multiple-choice responses to complete the text: (1) causally-coherent inference, (2) paraphrase, and (3) elaborative inference. Causally-coherent inferences are the best response to complete the text in a comprehensible manner. Paraphrases are an incorrect response and involve reiteration of the main goal or a summary of the main idea, mimicking what one group of poor comprehenders does while reading [4]. Elaborative inferences are also an incorrect response and involve connections based on background knowledge that may be tangential, mimicking what another group of poor comprehenders does during reading [4]. There are 40 items on the original and Lite versions, and 50 items on the college version per form.

MOCCA™ uses innovative scoring of response types to guide the propensity of the types of comprehension processes readers use during reading. Response type patterns of not only the correct responses are calculated, but the incorrect sentences chosen are also calculated based on the number of times a reader chooses a particular response type. An item response type model consistent with a three-response type structure of items is used for the propensity of error patterns [1].

The assessment, scoring system, and session reports are built into the system that is delivered online with a state-of-the-art encryption and security. The web-based application is built on four Microsoft technologies: ASP.Net, C#.Net, SQL Server/Access database, and ADO; and works with Firefox, Chrome, and Safari browsers. Examples of an online item are displayed below (see Figs. 1 and 2).

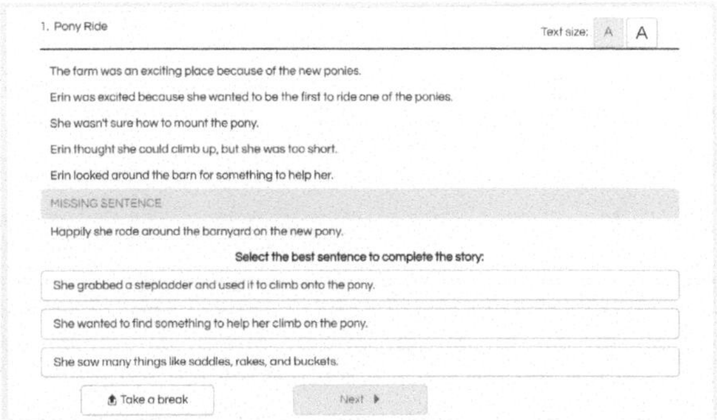

Fig. 1. Item 1. Pony Ride demonstrates how an item is displayed to a student before choosing a response type. The sixth sentence is still missing as shown.

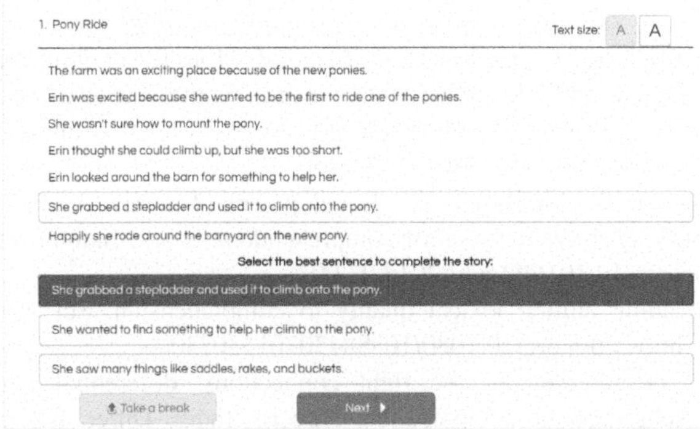

Fig. 2. Item 1. Pony Ride demonstrates how an item is displayed to a student after choosing a response type. The sixth sentence is now chosen with the first response type and is inserted into the text.

3 Use Case

Demonstration of MOCCA^{TM} is interactive where participants can play an active role as a student, teacher, administrator, and/or researcher to work with session reports and interpretation guides. Error propensity scores, number correct, percentage attempt correct, minutes per correct item, and comprehension efficiency scores are reported. Participants are able to access the session reports and the interpretation guide to learn about the classroom interventions recommended based on assessment results. Interventions and related professional development are being further developed to be digitally available to educators. The report and interpretation guide are currently accessible for teachers, administrators, and researchers who use the assessment. An example of the online session report that participants are able to access is displayed below (see Fig. 3).

Student Name	Grade (Assessment Grade)	Form	Number Correct	Percentage Attempted Correct	Error Propensity	Minutes per Correct Item	Comprehension Efficiency
Child, Julia	4(4)	4.1	7	50%	Indeterminate	11:00	Slow and inaccurate
Derry, Tiffany	4(4)	4.2	21	58%	Paraphraser	06:04	Slow and inaccurate
Garten, Ina	5(5)	5.1	15	38%	Elaborator	02:56	Slow and inaccurate
Gump, Forest	3(3)	3.1	28	70%	Paraphraser	02:00	Slow and inaccurate
Puck, Wolfgang	5(5)	5.2	36	90%	Not applicable	00:23	Fast and accurate
Ramsey, Gordon	3(3)	3.2	19	48%	Elaborator	03:40	Slow and inaccurate
Woody, Knute	3(3)	3.3	13	50%	Elaborator	15:06	Slow and inaccurate
Yamaguchi, Roy	4(4)	4.3	3	100%	Indeterminate	12:29	Slow but accurate

Fig. 3. The session report shows the performance for each student based on the type and speed of the response types chosen.

References

1. Davison, M.L., Biancarosa, G., Carlson, S.E., Seipel, B., Liu, B.: Preliminary findings on the computer administered multiple-choice online causal comprehension assessment (MOCCA^{TM}), a diagnostic reading comprehension test. Assess. Effective Interv. **43**(4), 169–181 (2018). https://doi.org/10.1177/1534508417728685
2. Carlson, S.E., Seipel, B., McMaster, K.: Development of a new reading comprehension assessment: identifying different types of comprehenders. Learn. Individ. Differ. **32**, 40–53 (2014). https://doi.org/10.1016/j.lindif.2014.03.003
3. Perfetti, C.A.: Reading ability: lexical quality to comprehension. Sci. Stud. Reading **11**, 357–383 (2007). https://doi.org/10.1080/10888430701530730
4. McMaster, K.L., et al.: Making the right connections: differential effects of reading intervention for subgroups of comprehenders. Learn. Indiv. Differ. **22**, 100–111 (2012). https://doi.org/10.1016/j.lindif.2011.11.017
5. Hannon, B., Daneman, M.: A new tool for measuring and understanding individual differences in the component processes of reading comprehension. J. Educ. Psychol. **93**, 103–128 (2001). https://doi.org/10.1037/0022-0663.93.1.103
6. Pike, M.M., Barnes, M.A., Barron, R.W.: The role of illustrations in children's inferential comprehension. J. Exp. Child Psychol. **105**, 243–255 (2010). https://doi.org/10.1016/j.jecp.2009.10.006

A Novel Approach to Monitor Loco-Motor Skills in Children: A Pilot Study

Benoit Bossavit(✉) and Inmaculada Arnedillo-Sánchez(✉)

School of Computer Science and Statistics, Trinity College, Dublin, Ireland
{bossavib, Macu.Arnedillo}@scss.tcd.ie

Abstract. As children grow, they undergo loco-motor and cognitive development and acquire skills and abilities matched to their developmental stage. Correlations between gross-motor and cognitive development, for instance walking and language learning, have been reported. This insunateS loco-motor development echoes on cognitive development and delays on the first, may impact on a child's potential to learn. Concerns regarding loco-motor development are commonly raised by parents or diagnosed by healthcare professionals. Motion gesture detection gaming technologies, may be used to screen and monitor gross-motor skills in developing children. However, challenges concerning: the accuracy of these sensors to detect the gestures of young children and, the design of activities that provide clear instructions and virtual environments that adapt to the real-world remain. This paper presents activities designed to guide children (2–7 years old) to perform loco-motor skills: jump, hop and run, matched to their developmental stage. It also provides results from pilot studies informing the design choices and the scaffolds children require to engage with the activities.

Keywords: Motor skills · Active Video Game · Motion-based technology · Game design · Children

1 Introduction

As normally developing children grow, they develop the same motor and cognitive skills and abilities at approximatively the same age. Theories mapping the acquisition of skills to developmental stages exists. For instance, Piaget's cognitive development theory defines skills according to stages which are associated to age [1] and, indicates correlation between cognitive and motor skills development. The study of this correlation suggests the development of motor skills may also affect the ability to learn [2]. Thus, delays in children's motor development may impact their potential to learn.

Gross-motor skills involve the use of large muscles and include, *stability skills:* involved in gaining and maintaining body balance; *loco-motor skills*: required to move the body from one location to another; and *manipulative skills:* involved in exchanges of forces with external objects [3]. The assessment of motor functioning is typically conducted on one-to-one sessions with professionals who observe the motor performance of children, as they do activities, to judge incremental improvement. They use standardised analysis tools such as the Peabody Developmental Motor Scales (PDMS-2), a screening

M. Scheffel et al. (Eds.): EC-TEL 2019, LNCS 11722, pp. 773–776, 2019.
https://doi.org/10.1007/978-3-030-29736-7_86

test providing observable criteria of fine and gross motor abilities for children from birth to age 5 [4]. However, the use of technology to screen and monitor gross-motor skills in developing children remains unexplored.

Active Video Games (AVG) or Exergames are video-games that enable users to control and play games using gestures without the need to use a game controller. They use motion detection technology such as the Microsoft Kinect, a camera that detects the 3D position of the players' joints, to recognise gestures involving gross-motor skills. AVG are popular entertainment activities and their regular use may have a positive impact on players when used as physical education tools in schools [5], or as therapeutic tools to improve gross-motor skills, particularly balance, in non-typically developing children [6].

A challenge in the design of AVGs for children, specially very young children still undergoing cognitive development and with no reading skills, is to provide clear, intuitive, flexible but controlled scaffolds and instructions to make them interact with the AVGs in the ways intended by the designers. To this end, Höysniemi et al. [7] used the "Wizard of Oz" technique and observe the gestures used by children between 7–9 years old, to control an avatar swimming, diving, running and jumping. Similarly, Connell et al. [8] collected data from children between 3–8 years old to find common gestures for object manipulation, navigation and selection. While these studies are insightful and offer techniques to study young children interactions, their approach to the design of gesture controlled AVGs is bottom-up. Thus, they observe child behaviour and arising from the observation develop design guidelines for interaction. However, in instances when AVGs are intended to guide users to perform specific predetermined motor-skills tasks mapped to standardised motor functioning tests, a top-down iterative design process with in-built pilot studies on each iteration to inform design may be more appropriate.

This paper presents five activities designed to make children (2–7 years old) perform loco-motor skills: jog on the spot, jump forward, jump high, jump sideway and hop; matched to their developmental stage. Although the ultimate aim of the activities is to screen and monitor gross-motor skills in developing children, this work focuses on challenges regarding: 1. the accuracy of these sensors to detect the gestures of young children and; 2. the design of activity-like tasks which provide clear instructions and flexible virtual environments that adapt to the real-world remain and guide the children to perform specific motor-skill tasks. It also provides results from pilot studies aimed at informing the design of the activity-like tasks and the scaffolds children require to engage with the activities.

2 Design of the Activities

The final goal of our research is to use motion-based technology to design and develop activities to screen and monitor gross-motor skills in developing children 2–7 years-old. To this end, it is paramount to design intuitive and engaging activities that scaffold and guide children to perform specific predetermined loco-motor tasks in front of the Microsoft Kinect. Informed by literature in motor development in children [3], standardised assessment for motor functioning [4], and design principles for child computer interaction [9], we designed and developed a framework with five prototype activities: jog on the spot, jump forward, jump high, jump sideway and hop. Our top-down iterative designed process underwent four iterations each followed by a pilot study. In total we conducted five pilot studies with children of different ages starting from older: >7 years-old; to younger: 20 month-old. From the results of these studies, we present a series of design decisions to promote autonomy and stimulation.

Autonomy. In order to complete the activities players need to understand what they have to do. However, our audience (2–7 years old children) may not have yet reading skills and even if they have, they are unlikely to follow the activities' narrative text [10]. Hence, the activities should be self-explanatory and implement *visual and auditory feedback* designed to instruct the players on what to do, as well as on what not to do.

To endow children with agency and control of the activities, an avatar that mirrors the player's movements was implemented. However, the use of an avatar to bridge the virtual and real worlds, poses two main design challenges: *virtual discrepancy*, due to the difference of depth perception or degrees of freedom between these two worlds; and *time discrepancy,* due to the fact that the avatar moves at the same time as the player but the interpretation of the gesture only takes place after the performance of the player.

Stimulation. Goal-oriented activities may be motivating and help children persist in performing a task until they master it. To this end, the design of the activities should address matters related to *challenges* and *progression of difficulty*. In terms of gross-motor development while children acquire skills by certain stages, they improve and master their ability to perform the skills as they develop. For instance, while two year old children can jump forward, as they develop, they improve their ability to perform the skill by increasing the distance to be jumped and coordinating body and balance to avoid falling. Thus, while the skill jump forward has been acquired, the degree and ability of execution of the skill is still developing and hence a two year old should not be able to perform a proficient jump forward. As a result, a child may experience frustration completing a motor task over his/her capacities or boredom if it is below. As a consequence, it is paramount to provide different levels of difficulties which map children's developmental stages.

3 Challenges Ahead

Our pilot studies with young children indicate that relying solely on virtual activities may not be always feasible because virtual propositions do not cater for the cognitive development of the children [1]. For instance, toddlers (up to 36 months) focus and interact only with their immediate environment. Then, in the pre-operational stage (between 2 and 7 years), children start developing the concepts of symbols and time. It is only in the concrete-operational stage (between 7 and 12 years) when children acquire logical and concrete reasoning. Therefore, a degree of real world and human input is necessary to provide instructions and maintain children focused on the task. For instance, we realised that at age 4–5 years the use of physical feedback was important to support a good execution of the tasks. At age 2, the toddler hardly paid attention to the screen and needed the constant assistance of the parent. Therefore, it is crucial to take the cognitive developmental stage into account in the design of motor skill activities.

Acknowledgment. Benoît Bossavit receives funding from the EU H2020 under the Marie Skłodowska-Curie Career-FIT fellowship (Co-fund grant No. 713654). A special thanks to all the children and parents who participated and spent their time on our study.

References

1. Piaget, J.: Development and learning. In: Riple, R.E., Rockcastle, V.N. (eds.) Piaget Rediscovered. Cornell University Press, Ithaca (1974)
2. Heineman, K.R., Schendelaar, P., Van den Heuvel, E.R., Hadders-Algra, M.: Motor development in infancy is related to cognitive function at 4 years of age. Dev. Med. Child Neurol. **60**, 1149–1155 (2018). https://doi.org/10.1111/dmcn.13761
3. Gallahue, D.L., Ozmun, J.C., Goodway, J.D.: Understanding Motor Development. McGraw-Hill, Boston (2012)
4. Folio, M.R., Fewell, R.R.: Peabody Developmental Motor Scales, 2nd edn. Pro-Ed, Austin (2000)
5. Norris, E., Hamer, M., Stamatakis, E.: Active video games in schools and effects on physical activity and health: a systematic review. J. Pediatr. **172**, 40–46e5 (2016). https://doi.org/10.1016/j.jpeds.2016.02.001
6. Page, Z.E., Barrington, S., Edwards, J., Barnett, L.M.: Do active video games benefit the motor skill development of non-typically developing children and adolescents: a systematic review. J. Sci. Med. Sport **20**(12), 1087–1100 (2017)
7. Höysniemi, J., Hämäläinen, P., Turkki, L.: Wizard of Oz prototyping of computer vision based action games for children. In: Proceedings of Interaction Design Children: (IDC 2004), pp. 27–34 (2004)
8. Connell, S., Kuo, P.Y., Liu, L., Piper, A.M.: Wizard-of-Oz elicitation study examining child-defined gestures with a whole-body interface. In: Proceedings of Interaction Design Children: (IDC 2013), pp. 277–280 (2013)
9. Lieberman, D.A., Fisk, M.C., Biely, E.: Digital games for young children ages three to six: from research to design. Comput. Sch. **26**(4), 299–313 (2009)
10. Caro, K., Tentori, M., Martinez-Garcia, A.I., Zavala-Ibarra, I.: FroggyBobby: an exergame to support children with motor problems practicing motor coordination exercises during therapeutic interventions. Comput. Hum. Behav. **71**, 479–498 (2017)

Author Index

The manufacturer's authorised representative in the EU is Springer Nature Customer Service Centre GmbH, Europaplatz 3, 69115 Heidelberg, Germany. If you have any concerns regarding our products, please contact ProductSafety@springernature.com

Printed and bound by CPI Group (UK) Ltd, Croydon, CR0 4YY
30/09/2026
02225660-0020